ISBN 978-1-5279-9258-0
PIBN 10978389

VI. AMERICAN EQUITY DIGEST.
Equity Cases, decided in the Co...
States, from ...
C...

Standard Law Books,

PUBLISHED AND SOLD BY

G. & C. MERRIAM, SPRINGFIELD, MASS.

AND SOLD ALSO BY

Gould, Banks & Co., Halsted & Voorhies, Collins, Keese & Co., New York; Nicklin & Johnson, Grigg & Elliott, Desilver, Thomas & Co., Philadelphia; Wm. & Jos. Neal, Baltimore; Hilliard, Gray & Co., Boston, and other principal Law Booksellers throughout the United States.

I. CHITTY'S PLEADINGS. A Treatise on Pleading: with a collection of practical Precedents, and Notes thereon. In three volumes. By JOSEPH CHITTY, Esq. of the Middle Temple, Barrister at Law. Seventh American, from the sixth London edition. Corrected and enlarged; with *Notes and* Additions, by JOHN A. DUNLAP, Esq. and additional Notes and References to later decisions, by E. D. INGRAHAM, Esq.

"It is to a writer of our own day that the honor is due, of having first thrown effectual light upon the science of Pleading, by an elaborate work, in which all its different rules are collected, arranged in convenient divisions, and illustrated by explanation and example. The work here mentioned, is the well known treatise on Pleading by Mr. Chitty, which no person competent to appreciate the difficulty of the task performed, can ever peruse without high admiration of the learning, talent, and industry of the author."—*Mr. Serjeant Stephen.*

II. CHITTY ON BILLS. A Practical Treatise on Bills of Exchange, Checks on Bankers, Promissory Notes, Bankers' Cash Notes, and Bank Notes. By JOSEPH CHITTY, Esq. of the Middle Temple, Barrister at Law. Eighth American from the eighth London edition, newly modelled, and greatly enlarged and improved; and with References to the Law of Scotland, France, and America; and new chapters on Agents, Partners, Consideration, Stamps, Requisites, Loss, Times of Presentment, Non-payment, Protest and Notice, Evidence, Bankruptcy, Forgery, Larceny, Embezzlement, and False Pretences; and an Appendix of Precedents. Containing the American Notes of former editions, by Judge STORY, E. D. INGRAHAM, and THOMAS HUNTINGTON, Esqs. To which are now added, the Cases decided in the Courts of the United States, and of the several States, to the present time, and the decisions of all the English Courts in 1833 and '34. By PIERRE OGILVIE BEEBEE, Attorney at Law.

☞A new edition just published, from a new English edition, "newly modelled and greatly enlarged and improved" by the author. The present American edition contains the Notes of former editions, by Judge Story, E. D. Ingraham, and Thos. Huntington, Esquires, with *more than eighty pages* of new Notes, closely printed, the whole work comprising over 1000 pages.

Mr. Warren, in his "Popular Introduction to the Study of Law," giving directions to the student for selecting a Library, mentions on Bills of Exchange, the Treatises of Joseph Chitty, Sen., Joseph Chitty, Jun., Bayley, and Roscoe, and then adds, "The *first* of these, and the edition of 1833, [from which the last American edition is taken] WILL BE FOUND INCOMPARABLY THE MOST USEFUL FOR THE PRACTITIONER."

In another place he says—" a ... Exchange, Promissory Notes, &c.] and one w ... almost daily. * * Mr. Chitty's Treatise, which is a very ... contains every thing relating to the subject very conveniently arranged, and with ... cellent Analytical Index."

III. CHITTY'S CRIMINAL LAW. A Practical Treatise on the Criminal Law, comprising the Practice, Pleadings, and Evidence, which occur in the course of Criminal Prosecutions, whether by Indictment or Information: with a copious collection of Precedents of Indictments, Informations, Presentments, and every description of practical Forms, with comprehensive Notes upon each offence, the Process, Indictment, Plea, Defence, Evidence, Trial, Verdict, Judgment, and Punishment. In three volumes. By Joseph Chitty, Esq. of the Middle Temple, Barrister at Law. Third American from the second and last London edition, corrected and enlarged by the Author. With Notes and Corrections, by Richard Peters, and Thomas Huntington, Esquires. To which are now added, Notes and References to the cases decided in the Courts of the United States and of the several States, to the present time, as well as to the late English decisions. By J. C. Perkins, Esq. Counsellor at Law.

☞ A new edition just published, thoroughly edited, nearly 2000 cases cited by the American editor, and all the American Reports, as well of the Courts of the several States, as of the United States, are referred to.

"We regard this as the most comprehensive manual that exists on the subject of the Criminal Law, and one of the most valuable among the many contributions made by its distinguished author to the cause of jurisprudence. * * The notes and references by Mr. Perkins, to the present edition. deserve especial mention. They place the author, among American annotators, by the side of Story and Metcalf. * * Mr. Perkins' notes are acute, thorough and learned, and, what is very important, appended with critical accuracy, to their natural places in the text. The student will always be rewarded by the interruption which they cause, and the practitioner will find in them great facilities in any research. Reference has been made to nearly two thousand cases, in addition to the former editions. All the American Reports have been sifted, and every case, which bears upon any part of the Criminal Law, correctly cited. We do not hesitate to say, that Mr. Perkins' labors have essentially enhanced the value of Mr. Chitty's work."—*American Jurist.*

IV. COLLYER ON PARTNERSHIP. A Practical Treatise on the Law of Partnership. By John Collyer, of Lincoln's Inn, Esq. Barrister at Law. With Notes of American Cases. By Willard Phillips and Edward Pickering, Esqrs. First American from the London edition.

The above work, recently published, has been introduced into the Law School at Cambridge, by Judge Story, and is believed to be the best Treatise extant on the Law of Partnership.

"Of the four treatises above mentioned, [Watson, Montague, Gow, and Collyer,] the chief are Gow's and Collyer's,—the former published in 1830, the latter in 1833. * * *Mr. Collyer is, perhaps, upon the whole to be preferred,* on account of his fuller statement of the cases, whereby the reader will be better able to understand and appreciate," &c.—*Warren's Popular Introduction to the Study of Law.*

V. CHITTY Jr. ON BILLS. A Practical Treatise on Bills of Exchange, Promissory Notes, and Bankers' Checks: containing Forms of Affidavits of Debt in actions thereon; and of Declarations and Pleas in such actions, adapted to the new Rules of Pleading. By Joseph Chitty, Jun., Esq., of the Middle Temple. To which are added American Notes. By Erastus Smith, Counsellor at Law.

VI. AMERICAN EQUITY DIGEST. An Analytical Digest of the Equity Cases, decided in the Courts of the Several States, and of the United States, from the earliest period: and of the Decisions in Equity, in the Courts of Chancery and Exchequer in England and Ireland, and the Privy Council and House of Lords, from Hilary Term, 1822: and forming with the third edition of Bridgman's Digest, a complete Abstract of all the American, English and Irish Equity Reports, down to 1836. By O. L. BARBOUR, Counsellor at Law, and E. B. HARRINGTON. 3 Vols.

The following Recommendations of this work have been received by the Publishers, from gentlemen whose names are familiar to every member of the American bar.

From CHANCELLOR WALWORTH.

Saratoga Springs, June 14, 1836.

The EQUITY DIGEST of Messrs. Barbour and Harrington, of which the first volume is now published, and the residue is ready for the press, has been compiled from the books in my Library, and embraces all the American Equity Reports, and all the English and Irish Equity Reports, subsequent to those contained in the American edition of Bridgman's Digest. I have had occasion frequently to refer to the work in manuscript, and have also examined very fully the volume which is published. I have no hesitation, therefore, in recommending it to the Profession as a valuable Digest of Equity Cases, which will be found very useful to those whose Libraries are furnished with the Reports, and indispensable to other members of the Profession, who wish to become acquainted with the decisions of the various Equity Courts in this country and in England in a condensed form.

R. HYDE WALWORTH.

From JUDGE COWEN.

I have bestowed considerable attention on Mr. Barbour's plan of his Chancery Digest. It is the carrying out, by supplemental Cases, of the long tried and highly approved Index of Mr. Bridgman, with the addition, where necessary, of new heads. I know Mr. Barbour's means of research, his ability and industry; and do not hesitate to say, that the plan cannot be better executed than it has been by him. I speak with the more confidence, because I have used several of his heads in the course of judicial research, and found them of very great assistance. The book is essentially necessary to the Chancery practitioner. Our undigested Chancery Reports are numerous, and the publication of a work of the kind has already been too long delayed.

E. COWEN.

August 11, 1836.

From CHIEF JUSTICE SAVAGE.

O. L. BARBOUR, ESQ. *Albany, May* 18, 1836.

Dear Sir,—Please accept my thanks for the first number of your Digest of Equity Decisions. From the pressure of official duties, my examination of the Digest has necessarily been rather superficial. It has been sufficient, however, to satisfy me of the great usefulness of such a work to the Profession, and of the ability and industry with which, thus far, it has been executed. With the abundant resources at your command, it is but reasonable to expect a very perfect work of its kind.

I am, Sir, very respectfully,
Your obedient servant,
JOHN SAVAGE.

From DAVID HOFFMAN, LL. D., *Professor of Law in the University of Maryland.*

Baltimore, Sept. 2, 1836.

I have examined with some care the first volume, now published, of the EQUITY DIGEST, By O. L. Barbour, and E. B. Harrington, Esquires. The great utility of such

Digests, when faithfully executed, cannot be questioned—they greatly facilitate research, and to those engaged in extensive practice, are almost *essential*. This Digest is analytically arranged, and with all requisite clearness, in its cardinal and minor divisions, and embraces an extensive series of British and American Chancery cases. Such labor-saving auxiliaries are eminently useful to practitioners, and can never mislead the inquiring and philosophical student, who will be sure to regard them in no other light than as faithful and well arranged indexes, for a further and more laborious research.

DAVID HOFFMAN.

A

TREATISE

ON

THE PARTIES TO ACTIONS,

AND ON

PLEADING,

WITH

SECOND AND THIRD VOLUMES,

CONTAINING

PRECEDENTS OF PLEADINGS,

AND

COPIOUS DIRECTORY NOTES.

IN THREE VOLUMES.

VOL. I.

BY JOSEPH CHITTY, ESQ.

OF THE MIDDLE TEMPLE, BARRISTER AT LAW.

AND

THOMAS CHITTY, ESQ.

OF THE INNER TEMPLE.

Seventh American Edition,

FROM THE SIXTH LONDON EDITION, CORRECTED AND ENLARGED.

CONTAINING

ALL THE RECENT IMPROVEMENTS, AND AN APPENDIX OF RECENT STATUTES AND RULES.

WITH NOTES AND ADDITIONS,

BY JOHN A. DUNLAP, ESQ.

AND

ADDITIONAL NOTES, AND REFERENCES TO LATER DECISIONS,

BY E. D. INGRAHAM, ESQ.

SPRINGFIELD, MASS.

PUBLISHED BY G. AND C. MERRIAM.

1837.

THE

AMERICAN EDITOR'S PREFACE

TO THE

SEVENTH AMERICAN EDITION.

At the time when the call of the profession induced the Publishers of the present and former editions of Mr. Chitty's work on Pleading, to make arrangements to put it again to press, the first volume of the Sixth London edition had been received from England. The second volume has since been received, but the third is yet unpublished. An attentive examination induced the editor to prepare the first volume only of that edition, containing the principles and rules upon which Pleadings should be framed, for republication. The second and third volumes of the Sixth American Edition, with additional notes, have been reprinted, and contain the Precedents of the Seventh American Edition. He was induced to adopt this course, because, in addition to the great delay which waiting for the completion of the work in England would have caused, sufficient reason appears to him to exist for not presenting to the Profession in the United States a set of Precedents, which, in the numerous jurisdictions of the Union, would not be considered as having the stamp of authority. The Precedents under the New Rules are very concise and convenient; but it would be presumption in the Editor, upon his own view of their superior utility, to offer them instead of those which, from long adoption and use, have the weight of judicial decision.

An Appendix of Forms in Assumpsit, adapted to the New Rules, from the second volume of the new London edition, is inserted at the end of the third volume of this edition. If when the third English volume is received the wishes of the Profession in this country shall seem to require it, the publishers will issue a supplement of forms prescribed by the New Rules, and some others which have been prepared by eminent pleaders, who have deemed a more succinct mode of declaring in all cases to be authorized by the spirit of one of those Rules.* The adoption generally of those forms in practice in this country will be the sanction of the Publishers for their insertion in a future edition.

PHILADELPHIA, April 17th, 1837.

---

* Reg. Gen. Trin. T. 1 W. 4.

PREFACE

TO THIS SIXTH [ENGLISH] EDITION.

The subjects of this work are, 1st, who are to be the *Parties* to an action; 2dly, the proper *Forms of Action*, and which must now be accurately stated, even in the *writ;* and 3dly, the *Pleadings* therein. And as a mistake in either of these would in general be fatal to the action or the defence, it is obvious that a very accurate knowledge of these subjects is essential not only to the *professed Special Pleader* and *Barrister*, but also to every *Attorney*, who is responsible to his client for the sufficiency of the proceedings, and who, if generally informed on the subjects of this volume, and duly attentive, would frequently discover errors which have been overlooked by the Pleader, or Barrister, and by a timely suggestion might prevent a disastrous defeat, which would be as injurious to his own as his client's interest, and discreditable to the administration of justice. Since the recent enactments and rules, these subjects have greatly risen in practical importance, and a new edition of the work has become essential. The Editors have spared no exertions to render the work more worthy of the flattering reception the prior editions have received.

The principal modern alterations in Pleadings have been the prohibition of more than one count upon each cause of action, and the exercise of more care in preparing that single count than heretofore, and the abolition or rendering less frequent the use of a plea of general issue, and requiring almost every ground of defence to be pleaded specially. The great increase in the number of pleas has rendered it necessary to prepare *an entirely new Third Volume of Pleas and Replications, and subsequent Pleadings*, most of which have occurred in actual practice, and been decided to be sufficient, and all have been carefully examined, adapted to the new rules, and annotated.

The modern *Statutes* and *Rules* relating to *Practice* and *Pleading* are so peculiarly important, that it has been deemed advisable to print the same in the *Appendix* concluding this Volume; and Students and Practitioners will find it essential to read them attentively, so as to be well informed upon their general inport, and not merely to refer to them occasionally.

The practitioner who will resolve to make himself master of these confessedly dry but essential subjects of legal knowledge, will soon find himself on the vantage ground, and in many collateral circumstances, especially as regards *Evidence*, would be enabled to anticipate advantages or difficulties which others could not perceive; at all events, he cannot safely even *commence* an action without being well informed upon all subjects relating to the *parties* to an action, which constitute the basis of the subsequent proceedings.

12th May,
A. D. 1836.

PREFACE

TO THE FIRST EDITION.

In submitting this treatise to the public, it may not be improper to prefix a short prospectus or analytical view of its contents, by which the reader may be enabled to judge, how far the subject proposed to be considered may be worthy of his attention.

Upon the *Practice* of the courts of common law, there are already before the public several very able treatises; but there is no work of any magnitude which points out, the *Parties* to Actions, or the *Forms of Action*, or the *Pleadings therein;* and the very frequent defects in actions and defences, occasioned by mistakes in these points, sufficiently evince the utility of a practical work upon the subject; I have therefore been induced to submit the following pages to the profession.

In the *first* chapter, which relates to *The Parties* to an Action, I have endeavored to point out who should be made the plaintiffs and who the defendants, as well in actions on contracts as for torts, and not only with reference to the interest and liability of the original parties, and the number of them, and whether standing in the situation of agents, joint-tenants, tenants in common, or partners, and who are to join or be joined; but also where there has been an assignment of interest, or change of credit, or survivorship between several, or death of all the contracting parties, or bankruptcy, insolvency or marriage. The consequences of mistakes in the proper parties, and how they are to be taken advantage of, and when they are aided, are also pointed out.

In the *second chapter* are considered the *Form and the particular Applicability of each Action;* the pleadings, judgment, and costs therein in general; the consequences of mistake; the *Joinder* of different *Forms* and of different *rights* of action; the consequences of *Misjoinder;* and the *Election* of the best remedy, where the plaintiff has the choice of several. In considering each personal action, viz. assumpsit, debt, covenant, detinue, case, trover, replevin, trespass, and ejectment, I have endeavored to confine my observations to the cases where the action is sustainable, or when it is preferable to another remedy, without inquiring into the nature of rights or of injuries, which would have been foreign to the object of this treatise (*a*). I have, however, in one instance, thought it advisable to depart from this plan, in order the better to explain the distinction between the action of *trespass* and that of *trespass on the case*; and for this purpose I have endeavored to state the distinctions between torts committed in fact, or in legal consideration, with and without force, and between torts immediate and consequential, and how far the legality of the original act, or the defendant's intention, may affect the form of action, and the difference arising from the circumstance of the defendant's having acted under color of process. The consequences of mistake in the form of action are also stated.

The *Joinder* of different *Forms*, and of different *Rights* of action, and the consequences of mistake, are of the greatest importance to the success of a cause, and I have, therefore, with some minuteness, pointed out the particular instances of *joinder*, which may be most likely to arise in practice.

In various cases the plaintiff has an *Election* of several different forms of action for the same injury, and a judicious choice is so material, that it may frequently enable the plaintiff to enforce his claim, which would be defeated or delayed by the adoption of a different course; I have therefore stated several leading points, which may direct the Pleader in his choice of the various remedies.

In the *third chapter*, a few *General Rules relating to Pleading* are collected, and pursuing the definition of pleading (viz. a statement in a *logical and legal form* of the *facts* of which

---

(*a*) In many works, under the title of a particular action, we find the nature of *rights* considered; as, for instance under the head "Assumpsit," after stating that it lies on a bill of exchange, we find the whole law upon bills of exchange is collected. This is not a convenient mode of arranging the subject in a *pleading* point of view, where the object of inquiry is merely the application of the *form* of action, and not the *right*.

the Courts are not bound, *ex officio*, to take notice,) I have first pointed out *what facts* are necessary to be stated, distinguishing those of which the Court will, *ex officio*, take notice, without their being shown in pleading ; and secondly, *the mode* of stating those facts with reference to certainty, and other particulars; and thirdly, I have considered the *rules of construction*, concluding the chapter with the division of the parts of pleading.

The *fourth* chapter relates to the form and requisites of *the Præcipe*, when the plaintiff proceeds by special original, and of *the Declaration* in personal actions; and with respect to the latter, are stated, first, *the general requisites*, and secondly, the *different parts*, and *more particular requisites*, whether in actions founded on contracts or for torts. In *assumpsit*, the appropriate special and common counts are fully examined, and the structure of declarations in *debt* and *covenant* is separately and distinctly considered.

Actions in form *ex delicto* are so multifarious, that I have thought it better to refer the reader to the Precedents and Notes in the Second Volume, than to attempt, in the First, to point out the structure of the declaration in *each particular* case; I have, however, considered the *general rules* to be observed in framing declarations in actions for torts, and which will be found to relate to the statement of, 1st, the matter or *thing* affected; 2dly, the plaintiff's *right* or interest; 3dly, the *injury;* and, 4thly, the resulting *damages*.

The utility of *Several Counts* in the same declaration, and the forms thereof, are also treated of in this chapter, which concludes with a summary of the instances in which different defects in a declaration will be aided.

The *Claim of Conusance*, statement of the defendant's *Appearance* and *Defence*, the *Demand* of *Oyer*, and statement of a Deed upon it, and the different descriptions of *Imparlances*, being connected with Pleading, are examined in the fifth Chapter.

In the remaining chapters are considered in their natural order—*Pleas to the Jurisdiction and in Abatement*, and the proceedings thereon; pleas in *Bar* to the action, and *Avowries*, and *Cognizances* in replevin, and pleas and notices of *Set-off;*

Replications and *New Assignments*, and pleas in bar to avowries and cognizances in replevin; *Rejoinders*, and the *subsequent Pleadings; Issues, Repleaders, Pleas Puis Darrein Continuance; Demurrers*, and *Joinders in Demurrer*; and this Volume concludes with a copious Index of the Contents.

As the principal object of the *First* Volume is directed to the statement of the *General Rules* affecting the Pleading, I have thought it advisable in a Second Volume to give *Precedents of the Pleadings* most likely to occur in practice, with notes. The contents of this Second Volume will appear from the *Analytical Table prefixed*, and from the *Index* at the end of the Third Volume.

The form of Courts, (being the commencements and conclusions of declarations in each Court, and in particular actions,) are incorporated in the present edition; but as the Precedents of Declarations on Bills of Exchange, Checks, and Promissory Notes, are printed in the appendix of my workon Bills of Exchange, they are not given at length in the Second Volume. The counts for common debts, in all the cases which ordinarily occur in practice, are given, on account of their great utility; the statement of the subject-matter of the debt in these Precedents, not only serving in declarations in assumpsit, but also in debt on simple contract, pleas and notices of set-off, and in affidavits to hold to bail.

In stating different *titles* to real property, and the *conveyances* and other means by which such titles have been acquired, the pleader frequently has very considerable difficulty; I have therefore given a great variety of Precedents under this head. With respect to other special counts, and to pleas, replications, rejoinders, &c. I have endeavored to give one or more of the most usual Precedents under each head, and have in general, in the notes, referred to the Precedents which may be found in print. It was impracticable to give a Precedent for every case which might occur, but those contained in this Volume may be readily applied to the particular circumstances of each case, or at least may assist in the structure of other pleadings; and though the student may derive some assistance from this collection, yet he must not be thereby induced to refrain from taking, or at least analysing other Pleadings, according to the course which his own judgment, or that of a friend more experienced, may suggest.

The utility of a work of this description must depend on the mode in which the subject is arranged, the correctness of the positions supported by legal decisions, for selection of the best authorities, and the facility of access by means of a full and accurate Index. To these points, therefore, I have endeavored to pay attention, and, besides the Reports which I have consulted, the reader is frequently referred to the Digests and Elementary writers. Indeed, it was impracticable to write on the subject upon which the authors alluded to had touched, without occasionally finding some parts pre-occupied, and the matter so ably treated of as to leave it open to me to do little more than enlarge upon, and arrange such parts of the subject according to my own plan. When this has occurred, I have considered that it would be the most candid mode of acknowledging the assistance I have derived from these works, and at the same time most useful to the profession, if, in the notes, I referred to those authors, in addition to the reported decisions, sanctioning my own view of the subject by the weight of their authority.

The kindness of my friends has so engaged me in professional avocations, that I have with difficulty prepared this work for publication, and the various interruptions which I have experienced, must, I fear, have occasioned some inaccuracies, for which, however, I hope the candour of the reader will make allowance.

J. CHITTY.

Temple, 7th November,
A. D. 1808.

TABLE OF CONTENTS.

[*The figures refer to the original paging, of the fifth English Edition as numbered in the margin; as they also do in the Analytical Table, and in the Indexes to the several volumes.*]

CHAPTER I.

CHAPTER II.

CHAP. II.—OF THE FORMS OF ACTION—(*continued.*)

CHAPTER III.

Of Pleading in general.

CHAPTER IV.

Of the Declaration, 276 to 454

CHAP. IV.—OF THE DECLARATION—(*continued.*)

CHAP. IV.—OF THE DECLARATION—(*continued.*)

CHAPTER V.

OF THE CLAIM OF CONUSANCE, APPEARANCE AND DEFENCE, OYER AND IMPARLANCES, 455 to 473

CHAPTER VI.

CHAPTER VII.

Of Pleas in Bar, 502 to 503

CHAPTER VIII.

OF REPLICATIONS.

CHAPTER IX.

CHAPTER X.

Defects in Pleading, when and how aided.

APPENDIX.

Statutes and Rules affecting Pleadings.

A

PRACTICAL TREATISE

ON

PLEADING.

CHAPTER I.

Of the Parties to Actions.

There are no rules connected with the science and practice of pleading so important as those which relate to the *persons* who should be *the parties to the action*; for if there be any mistake in this respect, the plaintiff is, in general, compelled to abandon his suit, and to proceed *de novo*, after having incurred great expense; whilst, with respect to most other objections, they do not thus affect the proceeding *ab initio*, and occasion comparatively but small expense. An attorney, special pleader, or barrister, before he can safely advise his client what is his remedy, must, before he can venture to issue a writ, be *certain* who ought to be the *plaintiff* or *plaintiffs*, and also the *defendant* or *defendants*, and unquestionably an extensive knowledge of the law regarding the *parties to an action* is of *paramount importance*. *The general rule is, that the action should be brought in the name of the party whose legal right has been affected* (*a*), *against the party who committed or caused the injury* (*b*), *or by or against his personal representative*; and therefore a correct knowledge of *legal* rights, and of *wrongs* remediable at *law*, will, in general, direct by and against whom an action should be brought. But as in the *application* of this rule, difficulties frequently occur, and as there are many particular rules relating to the *joinder* of persons in actions, whether as plaintiffs or defendants, and to the *mode* in which, and the *time* when, a mistake of parties should be objected to or be rectified, it is advisable, before we consider the *form of the action*, and the *pleadings* therein, to take a concise view of these rules, which we will examine under two general heads. *First*, when the action is in *form ex* *contractu (1), [*2]

(*a*) In general, Courts of *law* do not *directly* recognize *mere equitable* rights, but leave them to the protection of courts of *equity*. That rule, however, prevails more strictly as regards *real property* than with respect to injuries to the *person* or *personal property*. See fully, and the reasons, 1 Chitty's Gen. Prac. 6, 7; Bridlen *v.* Perrott, 2 Cromp. & M. 602; Foreman *v.* Jervis, 5 Bar. & Adol. 836; see qualification, and when a Court of *law* will restrain the proceedings of a plaintiff contrary to justice and equity, Jones *v.* Bramwell, 3 Dowl. 488; 3 Chitty's Gen. Prac. 626 to 629, 632 to 634.

(*b*) 1 Maule & Sel. 722; 1 Marsh. 260; 8 T. R. 332; 1 East, 499.

(1) The following note was inserted, by Mr. Chitty, at this place, in the first edition of his work: "A plaintiff frequently has an election to proceed, even for a breach of an express contract, either in *assumpsit* or in case; and where the latter form of action is adopted, many of the rules as to the parties to the action do not apply. See Govett *v.*

and *secondly*, when it is in *form ex delicto*; and under each of those heads, we will examine, *first*, who are to be the *plaintiffs*, and, *secondly*, who are to be the *defendants*.

1. IN ACTIONS IN FORM *EX CONTRACTU.*

The rules which direct *who are to be the parties* to an action in form *ex contractu*, whether as plaintiffs or defendants, are to be considered, *first*, as between the *original* parties to the contract; and, *secondly*, where there has been a *change* of parties, interest, or liability. Under the *first* head, the rules may be considered with reference to the interest or liability of the parties, as whether *legally*, or *only beneficially interested*, or acting merely as agents, or standing in the situation of joint-tenants, tenants in common, partners, &c.; and in the case of several contracting parties, who must or may join, or be joined. Under the *second* head, the subject will be examined with relation to the instances of an assignment of interest or a change of credit; of survivorship of one of several; death of all; bankruptcy; insolvency; and marriage of one of the contracting parties. We will consider these rules, *first*, as they relate to the *plaintiffs* in an action.

---

1. PLAINTIFFS.

1st. As between the *original* parties, and with reference to the *interest* of the plaintiff in the contract.

In general the action on a *contract*, whether express or implied, or whether by parol, or under seal, or of record, *must be brought in the name of the party in whom the legal interest* in such contract was vested (*c*) (2); and in general *with his knowledge and concurrence*, or, at least, a sufficient indemnity must be tendered before his name can properly be used by the party beneficially interested (*d*). The Courts of *law* will not in general notice mere *equitable* rights, as contradistinguished from the strict *legal* title and interest, so as to

(*c*) 1 East, 497; 8 T. R. 332; 1 Saund. 153, n. 1; 7 Mod. 116; 2 Sanders on Uses and Trusts, 222; 2 T. R. 696; 7 T. R. 667; and see 2 Bing. 20.

(*d*) Spicer *v.* Todd, 2 Tyr. Rep. 172; 3 Chitty's Gen. Prac. 127.

Radnidge, 3 East, 70. Buddle *v.* Willson, 6 T. R. 373. Samuel *v.* Judin, 6 East, 333. 335, and therefore I have considered the following rules, in their relation to the form of the action, rather than to the subject matter of it." In a note to the second American edition, Mr. Day observes, that, "The decision in Govett *v.* Radnidge, has been overruled by two subsequent cases in the Common Pleas, Powel *v.* Layton, 2 New Rep. 365, and Max *v.* Roberts, et al., 2 New Rep. 454, and by a very recent case in the King's Bench, Weall *v.* King, et al., 12 East, 452. {3 Conn. Rep. 198.} In Connecticut, declarations in tort, stating the injury to have been effected by means of a contract, have been sustained. Stoyell *v.* Wescott, 2 Day, 418. Bulkley *v.* Storer, 2 Day, 531." {Wolcott *v.* Canfield, 3 Conn. Rep. 194.} Vide 2 Esp. Dig. 129.

(2) A parent is entitled to the earnings of his *child*, being a minor, where there is no agreement, either express or implied, that payment may be made to the child; and an action for the work, labor and services of such child, in such case must be brought in the name of the parent. Shute *v.* Dorr, 5 Wend. R. 204. But a special contract with a third person, authorizing him to employ and pay the child, will be a defence to an action brought by the father. The intention of the parent may also be inferred from circumstances; and where the circumstances of any particular case warrant the conclusion that it was understood that the child might receive his earnings, payment to such child will be good. Ib. 3 Cowen, 92. 2 Mass. R. 115. 8 Cowen, 84. Although the father is entitled to the services of his children till the age of 21, yet he may waive that right. He may emancipate his child; or the child may, by the father's consent, be entitled to his own services. Ib.

invest the equitable or merely beneficial claimant with the ability to adopt legal proceedings in his own name; although the equitable right embrace the most extensive, or even the exclusive interest in the *benefit* to be derived from the contract or subject-matter of litigation. This rule could not be disregarded without destroying the fundamental distinction between Courts of *law* and Courts of *equity*, with regard to the remedy peculiar to each jurisdiction; if the *cestui que trust* were permitted *to sue at law in his own name, the benefits and protection intended to result from the intervention of a trustee, clothed with a legal title, might be lost, and the advantages arising from giving Courts of equity exclusive control over matters of trust would be defeated (*e*). Besides, it would be impossible, consistently with the common principles of jurisprudence, to exclude the power of the trustee to sue in respect of his legal right; and it would be highly mischievous and unjust to permit the defendant to be harassed by two actions upon the same contract or transaction. The *right of action at law* has therefore been wisely vested solely in the party having the strict *legal* title and interest, in exclusion of the mere equitable claim.

1. PLAINTIFFS. In general party in whom legal interest is vested must be the plaintiff. [*3]

If a bond be given to A. conditioned for the payment of money to him for the use or *benefit* of B., or conditioned to pay the money to B., the action must be brought in the name of A. (3), and B. cannot sue for or release the demand (*f*). In such case, A. is evidently a trustee, and the obligatory part of the instrument, and the acknowledgment of legal responsibility, are to him (*f*).

On Bonds.

It is an inflexible rule, that if a *deed* be *inter partes*, that is, on the face of it expressly describe and denote who are the parties to it, (as "between A. of the first part, and B. of the second part,") C., if not expressly named as a party, cannot sue thereon, although the contract purport to have been made for his sole advantage, and contain an express covenant *with him* to perform an act for his benefit (*g*) (4); in such a case, C. is a stranger to the deed, and violence

On deeds *inter partes*.

(*e*) See the observations of Lord Kenyon, as to the legal title alone being recognized in an action of ejectment, in Goodtitle *v.* Jones, 7 T. R. 50; and his observations as to the necessity of preserving inviolate the distinction between *legal* and *equitable* rights, in Bauerman *v.* Radenius, 7 T. R. 667.

(*f*) 2 Inst. 673; 1 Lev. 235; 3 Id. 139, 140; 3 B. & P. 149, n. (*a*); 7 East, 148; 1 M. & S. 575; 6 Vin. Abr. Covenant, 374; 1 East, 501.

(*g*) Per Tindall, C. J. in Bushell *v.* Beavan, 1 Bing. N. C. 120; 2 Inst. 673; 2 Rol. Abr. *Faits*, F. 1; 3 M. & S. 308, 322; 5 Moore, 23; 2 B. & B. 333; S. C. 5 B. & C. 355. See 2 Preston on Conveyancing, 184; Platt on Covenants, 7, 8. This rule does not interfere with the *liability* of a party who executes the deed as a covenantor, although he is not described as one of the parties to the deed in the introductory part of it; see Carth. 76; Holt, R. 210, S. C.; Platt on Cov. 7, 8.

(3) Vide Sanford *v.* Sanford, 2 Day, 559. In the case in 20 Johns. Rep. 74, the bond was given to the "people of Niagara county," and the suit was brought in a justice's court, in the name of the party aggrieved, who there recovered. The judgment was reversed in the Supreme Court, on the ground that there was no evidence of any breach of the condition. The court also say that the bond is not in the form contemplated by the statute; that it should have been given to the people of the State of New York, and not to the people of Niagara county. In the subsequent case of Lawton *v.* Erwin, 9 Wend. R. 233, the question was distinctly presented, whether a party interested in the condition of a constable's bond can maintain *debt* upon it *in his own name*, where the bond is given to the people; *Held*, that the action should be *covenant* on the condition, in the name of the party, or *debt* in the name of the people.

(4) { Strohecker *v.* Grant, 16 Serg. & Rawle, 237. } Vide Hornbeck *v.* Westbrook, 9 Johns. Rep. 73. Hornbeck *v.* Sleght, 12 Johns. Rep. 199.

The general principle is, that no other person than the obligee in the bond can be the nominal plaintiff. In the case of a security required to be given by a constable before

1 PLAINTIFFS. would be done to the expressed intention of the parties, were he to be allowed to sustain an action in his own name( ); the form of the instrument, and the [*4] *reciprocity of obligation between the parties to it, created by the express terms of the deed, negative and destroy any presumption that the contract was with him; and in such case, the right of suit is constituted, and must be governed, by the deed; and this rule applies, although the covenant be with the third party, C., (whose benefit is the declared object of the deed), and a person who is a party to the deed *jointly* (g). Even in such case, C. cannot join with the other covenantee (h). And where a deed of composition was made between a debtor of the first part, his surety of the second part, and "the several other persons whose hands and seals are set and subscribed hereto, being creditors, &c. of the third part," and A. one of the members of a firm to which the debtor owed money, set *his own seal only* to the deed; it was held, that A. only, and not the firm, should sue on the covenant to pay the composition, although A. subscribed the deed as for himself and partners: for the partners did not become parties and privies to the deed, as their seals were not affixed thereto (i).

On Deeds-Poll. If a deed-poll, *not* being a deed *inter partes*, contain a covenant *with A.* to pay B. a sum of money, it may be doubtful whether B. could sue in his own name; the covenant being *with A.* though for the benefit of another, and the contract being under seal, it would appear that in such case A. should be the plaintiff; for the terms of the express covenant seem to invest him with the legal interest (k) (5); and it is clear, that upon a covenant with two persons to pay a sum of money to one of them, they take a joint legal interest, and must jointly sue upon the covenant (l).

If, however, the covenant in a deed-poll be *generally* "to pay B.," or be expressly *with him* to pay the money *to him*, there appears to be no difficulty

(g) See ante, n. (g).
(h) 6 B. & C. 718.
(i) 6 M. & S. 75.
(k) 1 East, 497, 501. See Platt on Covenants, 513.
(l) 1 East, 496; 3 B. & C. 256.

entering upon the duties of his office in form of a *penal bond* to the people, *debt* may be maintained on such bond, by any person to whom the constable has become liable. *Covenant* may also be maintained on the condition of such bond in his own name. The People v. Holmes, et al. 5 Wend. R. 191.

(5) Chaplin v. Canada, 8 Conn. R. 286. 4 Wend. R. 419. It must undoubtedly appear that the covenant which is alleged to have been broken was made *for the benefit* of the person bringing the action. He must in some manner be pointed out and designated in the instrument; but it is not necessary that his *name* should in terms be used. A familiar illustration of this is to be found in the case of a covenant with a man and his heirs or his executors. There the names of his heirs or the executors do not appear in the deed; but still they can sue upon the covenant, if broken. So, where the defendants covenanted to pay to each and every person, such sum or sums of money as the constable should become liable for on account of any execution which might be delivered to him; *Held*, that covenant may be sustained by a plaintiff in an execution delivered to such constable for collection, and for the payment of which the constable had become liable; he may claim the benefit of such covenant by proper averments in his declaration, although he is not named in the instrument. Fellows v. Gilman, et al. 4 Wend. R. 414.

Where A. covenanted with the rector, wardens and vestry, to pay rent to the rector or wardens; *Held*, that neither separately; nor could both the rector and wardens jointly maintain a suit for the rent; but the vestry should also be joined with the rector and wardens. The principle is, that the action should be sued in the name of the parties with whom the covenant was made. Montagaue et al. v. Smith, 13 Mass. R. 405.

Where all the members of a corporation entered into a covenant for themselves and heirs, that the corporation should do certain acts; *Held*, that all were holden in their individual capacities, and parties to the covenant. Tileston et al. v. Newell et al., 13 Mass. R. 406.

in his maintaining an action in his own name, although he did not execute the deed, and were in all other respects a stranger to it (*m*). 1. PLAINTIFFS.

The rule upon this subject appears to be materially influenced or affected by the nature of the instrument upon which the contract arises. If the instrument be *not under seal*, it seems to be a general principle, that the party, for *whose sole benefit it is evidently made, may sue thereon in his own name, although the engagement be not directly to or with him (6). Thus, if A. give goods to B. of the value of £80, on condition that he pay £20 to C., if B. do not pay the money, C. may have an action against him, and declare that he was indebted to him in £20, for goods of the value of £80, given to him by A. on condition that he should pay £20 to C.; for when the goods were delivered to B. upon this condition, the £20 became a debt to C. (*n*). An express privity of contract between A. and C. seems to be created by the stipulations of the parties, in a case of this nature. A father was seised in fee of lands, and was about to cut timber therefrom to raise a portion for his daughter; the defendant, being his son and heir, verbally promised *the father*, in consideration that he would forbear to fell the timber, to pay the daughter this portion; the Court of King's Bench held, that the daughter might sue the son for the recovery of the money, although the consideration moved from the father to the son; the contract having been made for her benefit, the object being to secure a portion for her (*o*) (7). This decision was affirmed upon a writ of error in the Exchequer Chamber. This appears to be a strong authority to support the general rule, that the party to be benefited by a contract, *not* under seal, may sue thereon, although the promise be not made to him. The Court attached some weight to the nearness of relationship between the father and the daughter; but this does not appear to be a circumstance which can render the case of less utility and importance, as affording a general rule upon this sub-

On simple Contracts.

[*5]

(*m*) See 2 Lev. 74; 3 Keb. 94, 115, S. C.; Lutw. 305; Com. Dig. *Covenant*, A. (1); 2 Inst. 673. See *post*, 11.

(*n*) Mich. Term, 1651, Starkey *v.* Mylne, 1 Rol. Abr. *Action sur Case*, 32, pl. 13.

(*o*) Dutton *v.* Poole, Mich. 29 Car. 2; 1 Ventr. 318, 332, S. C. in 2 Lev. 210; Sir T. Raym. 302, and Sir T. Jones, 102, recognized by Lord Mansfield in Cowp. 443, and Mr. J. Burrough in 5 Moore, 31, 32; 2 B. & B. 337, S. C. See Bul. N. P. 133 a.

(6) See the principle stated, Potter *v.* Yale College, 8 Conn. R. 60. Where an agreement is made with an agent for the sole and exclusive benefit of his principal, the latter has the legal interest and the right of action; but if the agent have a special property and personal interest in an agreement made with him, his is the legal interest and right of action.

(7) The case of Schermerhorn *v.* Van Aerheyden, 1 J. R. 139, was much like Dutton *v.* Pool, upon the authority of which it was decided. The defendant in the court below, Schermerhorn, applied to his father for an assignment of his property, which the father gave the son, the defendant promising to purchase for his sister, the plaintiff's wife, a cherry desk. The court said, where one person makes a promise to another for the benefit of a third, that third person may maintain an action on such promise. This case has ever since been considered as correctly decided, and the principle a sound one. It was accordingly decided, where a collector of the customs put certain property seized by him into the hands of a third person, and took a promise for its delivery on demand to the marshal of the district, or to the deputy of such marshal, that the marshal having no interest in the property, and the collector having an interest in it, being the contracting party and furnishing the consideration, the suit on the contract must be brought in the name of the collector. Sailly *v.* Cleaveland et al., 10 Wend. R. 156. In all the cases where a third person has been permitted to sue on such a promise, such person had the legal interest. In M'Menomy *v.* Ferrers, 3 J. R. 71, it was held that an order to pay to Roosevelt was an assignment of the amount due on the securities mentioned, and therefore the drawers of the order had no interest and could not prosecute.

I. PLAINTIFFS. ject; and Mr. Justice Buller is reported to have remarked (p), that if one person make a promise to another for the benefit of a third, the latter may maintain an action upon it. And in a subsequent case (d), Eyre, C. J. said, "as to the case of a promise to A. for the benefit of B. and an action brought by B., there the promise must be laid as having been made to B., and the promise actually made to A. may be given in evidence to support the declaration."
[*6] In *Martin* v. **Hind*(r), the defendant, the rector of a parish, by a written certificate addressed to the bishop, appointed the plaintiff his curate, and signified that he promised to pay the plaintiff a yearly stipend; it was held, that the plaintiff might sue for the salary (r). This case proceeded, however, upon the ground that the contract was entirely with the curate, that there was no promise to the bishop, and that the certificate was a mere assurance or information to him of a matter of fact, and the consideration was entirely between the plaintiff and defendant. The case of *Carnegie* v. *Waugh* (s), strongly shows, that a written or verbal promise to A. for the benefit of B. will support an action in the name of the latter; and the Chief Justice appeared to have been of opinion in that case, that the rule that a third person cannot take advantage of a deed *inter partes*, could not be extended to contracts not under seal. And an action may be maintained by the several partners of a firm upon a guarantee addressed and apparently given to one of them, if there be evidence that it was given for the benefit of all (t). There is, in the case of bills of exchange and promissory notes, an *option* of plaintiff, that might be considered an *exception* to the general peremptory rule, that the right of suing can only be in *one* person, or set of persons, *viz.* that a party to a bill may, by arrangement between the parties, be the plaintiff, although the bill at the time be in the rightful possession of another party to the bill (u).

Exception in case of bills of exchange.

Against carriers.

The action against a carrier for loss of goods sent by a vendor to a vendee, must in general be brought in the name of the latter, and not of the consignor; because the law implies that by the delivery to the carrier, the goods became the property of the consignee, and at his risk, (subject, of course, to the unpaid vendor's right of stoppage in transitu) (x). As the delivery to the carrier by the consignor presumptively vests the property in the goods in the consignee, it is an inference of law, that the contract for the safe carriage is between the carrier and the consignee, and consequently the latter has the legal right of action; and this rule obtains, although the consignor paid the carrier for the conveyance of the goods, and the consignee gave no express directions
[*7] that the goods should be sent by the particular carrier selected *by the ven-

(p) Marchington v. Vernon, N. P. mentioned in 1 B. & P. 101, n.

(q) 1 B. & P. 102.

(r) Dougl. 142, S. C.; Cowp. 437.

(s) 2 D. & R. 277. See 4 B. & C. 664; 3 B. & A. 280, 281. The decision in Crow v. Rogers, 1 Stra. 592, is perhaps hardly to be reconciled with this doctrine. The plaintiff declared, that Hardy, being indebted to the plaintiff in 70*l*., it was agreed between Hardy and the defendant, that the defendant should pay the money to the plaintiff, and that Hardy should make the defendant a title to a house,—that Hardy was ready to do so, and, in consideration thereof, the defendant promised to pay the plaintiff. "And without much debate, the Court held the plaintiff was a stranger to the consideration, and gave judgment for the defendant."

(t) 4 B. & C. 664.

(u) Stone v. Butt, 2 Crom. & M. 416; 2 Dowl. 335, S. C.; Chitty on Bills, 8th ed. 566; and exceptions, *id. ibid.*

(x) 8 T. R. 330; 2 Campb. 36; 3 Id. 255; 2 Saund. 47 h.

dee (y). In these cases it is, however, only an assumption of law that the goods vested in the vendee and were at his risk upon the delivery to the carrier; and if by virtue of an agreement between the vendor and vendee, the goods did not become the property of the latter, and he was not at any risk with regard to the goods until they actually reached him, the consignor should be the plaintiff. But in general the property vests in the consignee by the mere delivery to the carrier, and the consignee ought to sue, although he ordered the goods to be sent to him, "on an insurance being effected, and on the terms of three months' credit from the time of arrival," for in such case the actual arrival of the goods is not a condition precedent to the vendee's liability to pay for them, and the vendor having complied with the stipulation as to insurance, had provided the vendee with a remedy over (z).

I. PLAINTIFFS.

If goods by a *bill of lading* are consigned "to A." he is *prima facie* the owner, and must bring the action against the master of the ship if they be lost; but if the bill be special to deliver to A. *for the use of B.*, the latter should bring the action (a) (8). And where by a bill of lading the captain was to deliver the goods, *for the consignor and in his name*, to the consignee, and the latter, at the time of the shipment, had no property in the goods, it was decided that the consignor should be the plaintiff in an action for an injury to the goods, although the consignee had at his own expense previously insured the goods (b). And it seems that an agent in this country, who ships goods to the foreign principal and pays the freight, may maintain an action in his own name on the bill of lading, if it express that the goods were shipped by the agent, and that the freight was paid here; for in such case a privity of contract is established between the parties by means of a bill of lading (c).

In general a mere *servant* or agent, with whom a contract is expressed to be made on behalf of another, and who has no direct beneficial interest in the transaction, cannot support an action thereon (d) (9). As where lands were

When an Agent may sue.

(y) 3 B. & P. 584.
(z) 4 B. & C. 219.
(a) 1 Ld. Raym. 271; 3 B. & A. 283.
(b) 3 B. & Ald. 277.
(c) 3 Campb. 320.
(d) Evans *v.* Evans, 1 Harr. & Wo. 239.

(8) Vide Potter *v.* Lansing, 1 Johns. Rep. 215. M'Intyre, 1 Johns. Rep. 221. Ludlow *v.* Browne, 1 Johns. Rep. 1. {Sanderson *v.* Lambetton, 6 Binn. 129. A. of Liverpool shipped goods which by the bill of lading were to be delivered to B. or his assigns in Philadelphia. The goods belonged to A. and the freight was payable in Liverpool. *Held*, that the bill of lading vested the property in the consignee, who might maintain an action in his own name against the ship-owner for the negligent carriage of the goods. Griffith *v.* Ingledew, 6 Serg. & Rawle, 429. Gibson, C. J. dissenting.}

A cargo was consigned to merchants in New York, and the master put into Norfolk in distress; and was obliged to sell part of the cargo to pay expenses, and transferred the residue of the cargo to another vessel, obtaining a bill of lading for the delivery of the cargo to himself; and on the arrival of the latter vessel in New York, ordered the same to be delivered to persons other than the original consignees. In *trover* sued by the owner against the persons thus receiving the cargo, held, that they were liable to pay the value of the goods. Everett *v.* Coffin, et al., 6 Wend. R. 603.

(9) Vide Medway Cotton Manufactory *v.* Adams and another, 10 Mass. Rep. 362. Bogert *v.* De Bussy, 6 Johns. Rep. 94. Gunn *v.* Cantine, 10 Johns. Rep. 387. Jones *v.* Hart's Exrs. 1 Hen. & Mun. 470. Gilmore *v.* Pope, 5 Mass. Rep. 491. Bainbridge *v.* Downie, 6 Mass. R. 253. Kinsey *v.* Hollingshead, 1 Penn. 380. So, the trustees or committee, for conducting the affairs of an unincorporated company, cannot maintain an action in their own name. Niven *v.* Spickerman, 12 Johns. Rep. 401. It is different in the case of a note or check payable to bearer; in the latter case the opposite party cannot raise the objection of the plaintiff's want of interest. Mauran *v.* Lamb, 7 Cow. R. 174. A mere agent, holding such a note or check, may sue on it in his own name.

If one effects an insurance for whom it may concern; and in his declaration he avers

I. PLAINTIFFS. let by auction, and there was an agreement between the intended lessee and the *auctioneer*, stating the terms, and subscribed by the intended lessor; it was held, that the auctioneer could not sue the intended lessee for use and occupation, or for breach of the agreement (*d*). And where A. by a memorandum in writing, signed by himself only, agreed in writing to pay the rent of certain tolls which he had hired, to the treasurer of certain commissioners (*e*), it was decided that no [*8] *action for the rent could be supported in the name of the treasurer, the contract being in legal contemplation with the commissioners, and to pay them (*f*). And where several persons took a lease of premises, to be used as a Jewish synagogue, and the seats therein were let by an officer annually appointed, whose duty it was to let them and receive the rents, and apply them partly in payment of the rent secured by the lease, and partly for general purposes connected with the establishment; it was held, that the lessees were properly made the plaintiffs in an action to recover the rent due from an occupier of one of the seats (*g*). Upon the same principle, the captain of a ship cannot maintain an action in his own name upon an *implied* promise to pay demurrage, although he may on an express contract with him to pay it (*h*). And it has been determined that the mayor of a corporation, who, on the sale of certain lands by auction, of which the corporation were the vendors, signed a contract on behalf of himself and the corporation with the purchaser, for the due performance of the conditions of sale, could not, in his individual capacity, maintain an action against such purchaser for the breach of his contract (*i*).

But when an *agent* has any *beneficial interest* in the performance of the contract, as for commission, &c., or a special property or interest in the subject-matter of the agreement, he may support an action in his own name upon the contract; as in the case of a factor, or a broker (*k*), or a warehouseman, or carrier (*l*), an auctioneer (*m*), a policy broker whose name is on the policy (*n*), (10) or the captain of a ship for freight (*o*). So where a contract is in terms

(*d*) Evans *v.* Evans, 1 Harr. & Wo. 239.

(*e*) The instances in which treasurers and trustees are by statute allowed to be made plaintiffs, and the decisions on enactments of this nature, will be noticed hereafter, *post*, 14.

(*f*) 3 B. & P. 147. See Sir J. Mansfield's observation, 2 Taunt. 381.

(*g*) 2 Stark. Rep. 356.

(*h*) 4 Taunt. 1, 52. See 3 Chit. Com. Law, 430.

(*i*) 2 Taunt. 374, 387. See 5 Moore, 277.

(*k*) 1 T. R. 112; 2 Esp. Rep. 493; 1 H. Bl. 82; 7 T. R. 359; 11 East, 180; 4 Camp. 195; 1 M. & S. 581.

(*l*) See *per* Lord Ellenborough, 1 M. & S. 147.

(*m*) 1 H. Bl. 81; 2 Marsh. 497, 501; 7 Taunt. 237, S. C. See 5 B. & Ald. 333.

(*n*) Park on Ins. 403; 1 T. R. 114; 2 M. & S. 485, 486; 4 B. & C. 666, but not otherwise; 1 M. & S. 497; 15 East, 4. In Cosack *v.* Wells, A. D. 1813, the plaintiff effected the policy thus: "I. C. agent;" and though he was jointly interested with another person, he recovered in a separate action in his own name, the declaration averring that he was jointly interested with another person.

(*o*) 6 Taunt. 65; 4 Taunt. 189.

---

that the policy was made for himself and another; yet, he is entitled to maintain the action in his own name. Ward *v.* Wood, 13 Mass. R. 539. It is otherwise, however, where his own interest was fully insured in a prior policy; in the latter case, if he sue, he must state the interest of the others concerned, and bring the action expressly as agent. Gardner *v.* Bedford Ins. Co., 17 Mass. R. 615.

(10) De Vignier *v.* Swanson, 1 Bos. & Pul. 346, n. b.

Two persons by name insured; and in the policy was added *or whom it may concern*, with a clause also in the policy that the loss should be paid to the two persons named, *held*, that they might recover the whole sum insured, although it appeared they were in

made with an agent personally, *he may sue thereon (11); and if a servant personally carry on a business for his principal, and appear to be the proprietor, and sell goods in the trade as such apparent owner, he may, it seems, sustain an action in his own name for the price (p). Where the supposed principal repudiates the contract, the agent may sue after notice of the facts to the defendant; as to recover back a deposit paid on the sale of an estate (q). 1. PLAINTIFFS.

Where a person assumes, on the face of the contract, the character, not of a principal, but of an agent to another named person, he cannot retract that assumed capacity and sue as a principal, without previously undeceiving the defendant, and giving him notice of the real nature and extent of his, the plaintiff's, claim and interest (r). And it should be observed that in these cases the right of the agent to sue on a contract made by him for his principal, whether it be expressed that the agent contracts personally or on the behalf of another, is subservient to the right of the principal to interfere, and to bring the action in his own name upon the unperformed agreement, in exclusion of the agent's right, and although the agent has not expressly disclaimed (s). There is an exception in the case of a contract *under seal* entered into with the agent personally in a matter within the scope of his authority; in this instance the implied right of action of the principal merges in the higher security taken, by his authority, by the agent, and the remedy is in the name of the latter only (t)(12).

(p) 2 C. & P. 49; 3 Campb. 320; 3 Stark. R. 147; 4 B. & C. 666; 4 Bing. 2.
(q) 3 Stark. Rep. 145.
(r) 5 M. & Sel. 383.
(s) Stra. 1182; 1 Campb. 337; 1 M. & S. 579, 580; 5 M. & S. 385, 386, 390; see 7 Taunt. 237.
(t) 1 M. & S. 575; 5 B. & C. 355; 4 Bingh. 2.

fact owners of but one half; the other half belonging to a person not joined as plaintiff in the action. Jefferson Ins. Co. *v.* Cothral, 7 Wend. R. 72.

(11) { Potter *v.* Yale College, 8 Conn. Rep. 60. } An action on a promissory note given to the agent of a company, lies in the name of the agent, and his styling himself agent, &c. in his writ and declaration, was held to be merely *descriptio personæ.* Buffum *v.* Chadwick, 8 Mass. Rep. 103. So, where A. for his own account and risk, carries on trade in the name of B., an action for goods sold, in the course of such trade, is properly brought in the name of B. Alsop and others *v.* Caines, 10 Johns. Rep. 396. But where goods are purchased from a factor, *scienter*, with intent by the purchaser, to set off against the purchase, a demand which he may have against the factor, the principal may, in such case, as on a sale made immediately by himself, have a suit against the purchaser, any time before payment to the factor. Brown & others *v.* Robinson & Hartshorne, 2 Caines' Cas. 341.

Although a *simple contract* may be enforced in the name of the promisee when made for the benefit of a third person, if the promisee has an interest in the subject matter; but if the contract is *under seal* and *inter partes*, the action must be sued by a party to the instrument. Spencer *v.* Field, 10 Wend. R. 87. The person having the legal interest and also furnishing the consideration, is the proper person to sue on a promise made to him, Sailly *v.* Cleveland, 10 Wend. R. 156.

(12) Where money has been deposited by an agent, on the account of an unknown principal, an action to recover back the deposit, lies in the name of the principal. The Duke of Norfolk *v.* Worthy, 1 Campb. 337. Vescher *v.* Yates, 11 Johns. Rep. 23. Yates *v.* Foot, 12 Johns. Rep. 1. So, where a factor sells his principal's goods, the principal may, on notice to the buyer, before payment, not to pay the factor, sue the buyer in his own name. Kelly *v.* Munson, 7 Mass. Rep. 324. Railton *v.* Hodgson, 15 East's Rep. 67. A factor selling goods in his own name, and being alone known to the purchaser, may maintain an action for the price although he receives no *del credere* commission; but if there has been a communication between the principal and factor, by which the former agrees to consider the purchaser as his debtor, and takes steps for recovering the debt directly from him, the factor's right to sue is gone. Sadler *v.* Leigh and another, 4 Campb. 195. An action to recover back a wager in the event of a horse race (under the acts of the State of New York to prevent horse racing and gaming) is properly brought by the person who made the bet, although he acted as the agent or depository of other persons,

I. PLAINTIFFS.

If a principal allow his agent to appear to be the principal, and to contract in the latter character, and the defendant has thereby been induced to give credit to the agent, the principal's right of action in his own name is subject to the set-off which the defendant has against the agent, and which would be available if the latter were the plaintiff (*u*) (13).

Qualified right to use the name of a trustee, &c.

If a trustee or husband object to his name being used in an action for the benefit of the *cestui que trust* or wife, the latter may, after tendering a sufficient indemnity, use his name, or may file a bill in equity for that purpose (*x*).

[*10]

2dly. With reference to the *number* of plaintiffs; and when they should join or sever.

When the contract was made with *several* persons, whether it were under seal, or in writing but not under seal, or by parol, if their *legal interest* were *joint*, they *must all, if living, join in an action in form *ex contractu*, for the breach of it, though the covenant or contract with them was in terms joint and several (*y*) (14). And if it appear on the record that there was another cove-

(*u*) 7 T. R. 359; 1 Camp. 85; 5 B. & C. 354; 4 Camp. 60; 1 East, 335; Holt, N. P. R. 124; 6 Geo. 4, c. 94, s. 6; 4 B. & C. 547.

(*x*) Doe *d.* Prosser *v.* King, 2 Dowl. 58; 3 Chit. Gen Prac. 127, &c.

(*y*) Eccleston *v.* Clipsham, 1 Saund. 153, and note 1; 1 East, 497, 501; 1 Taunt. 7. 2 Campb. 190; 5 Price, 529; and see an explicit case, Hatsall *v.* Griffith, 4 Tyr. 487. One of such parties may lawfully use the name of the other in the proceedings without his consent, 1 Ld. Raym. 380; 9 East, 471; at least after tendering an indemnity, 1 Chit. Rep. 390. See fully and how to proceed as regards the indemnity, 3 Chit. Gen. Prac. 127 to 129. So a covenant with two and every of them is joint, 3 Taunt. 87.

Haywood *v.* Sheldon, 13 Johns. Rep. 88. Et vide Vischer *v.* Yates, and Yates *v.* Foot' ubi sup. Bell et al. *v.* Gilson, 1 Bos. & Pull 351.

If an agent employ a broker to effect an insurance for his principal, the broker, who knew his employer was acting as agent, cannot retain the money he receives from the insurer for a debt due from such agent to himself. Foster *v.* Hoyt, 2 Johns. Cas. 327.

The sale by a factor of several lots of goods, belonging to several persons, to one purchaser; taking the promissory note of the latter to himself; held, that this did not prejudice the rights of the several principals, who were, notwithstanding, entitled to sue severally the purchaser. Corlies *v.* Cumming, 6 Cowen, 181.

(13) A mere receiptor of goods taken by the sheriff upon an execution, while such goods remain constructively in the custody of the law, has not such a general or special property in the goods as will enable him to recover in *trover* or *replevin*, in which actions the property in the goods is drawn in question. In trover or replevin, it is a good defence to the action, that the plaintiff has neither the general or special property in the goods; but in an action of trespass, a bare possession is sufficient to enable the plaintiff to recover against a wrong-doer, who takes the property out of his possession without authority. Cook *v.* Howard, 13 Johns. Rep. 276. Demick *v.* Chapman, 11 ib. 132. Schermerhorn *v.* Van Valkenburgh, ib. 529. Aikin *v.* Buck, 2 Wend. Rep. 466 Butts *v.* Collins, 13 ib. 139.

Where the agent of a defendant in an execution became the receiptor to the sheriff of the property of his principal, levied upon by virtue of such execution, and agreed with the sheriff and the plaintiff in the execution, that he would cause such property, consisting of yarn and other materials found in a factory, to be manufactured into flannels, and would furnish such materials as should be necessary for that purpose, the avails to be applied on the execution after satisfying his advances—and the agent accordingly made the necessary advances, caused the materials to be manufactured into flannels, and put them into the hands of a manufacturer to be dressed, it was *held*, that the agent was not entitled to *set off* the value of such flannels, in an action brought by the manufacturer against the agent for work done, although the manufacturer, after the flannels were dressed, had refused to surrender them to him. Butts *v.* Collins, 13 Wend. Rep. 139. It is only where the agent has a lien upon the property sold by him, or has a commission *del credere*, that he has a right to sue in his own name on a contract made for his principal, or to set off a demand due to his principal against his own private debt. Ib.

(14) Where a bond is joint in *form* only, but several *ratione subjectæ materiæ*, an action may be maintained in the name of one of several obligees. But, *it seems*, if he can maintain such an action on the bond, he must set forth the bond truly, and then by proper averments, show a cause of action to himself alone, clearly embraced within the condition of the bond. Ehly *v.* Purdy, 6 Wend. Rep. 629. In that case, it was *held*, that one of two

I. PLAINTIFFS.

Joint interest.

nantee who ought to have joined, the judgment will be arrested (*z*). So if one of several bankers lend money to a third person, all the members of the firm may join in an action to recover the amount (*a*). And where a broker was employed to sell a ship belonging to three part-owners, two of whom communicated with him on the subject, and to them he paid their shares of the proceeds of the sale, but, after admitting the amount of the third part-owner's share to be in his hands, refused to pay it to him without the consent of the other two, and he alone brought an action for his share, it was held, that he could not sue alone, but should have joined the other part-owners (*b*). The contradictions in the decisions and difference in the opinions of particular judges are attributable to doubts upon *facts* whether the contract were only joint or several (*c*). The reason assigned why all should join is, that when the interest is joint, if several were permitted to bring several actions for one and the same cause, the Court would be in doubt for which of them to give judgment (*d*). If a third person collude with one partner of a firm to injure the other partners, the latter may (omitting such colluding partner) maintain an action against such third person so colluding (*e*).

There may, however, be cases where the employment of an agent may be *several* as well as joint, or cases of *a subsequent severance*, so as to entitle one partner to sue for his share (*f*).

The avowant and party making conusance in replevin, may join in an action on a replevin bond (*g*).

When several.

Thus, if A. convey an estate to several persons, and covenant with them, "and to and with each and every of them," that he is lawfully seised, the action upon the covenant must be brought by all the covenantees, and the words of severalty shall not prevail (*h*). So, if a party covenant to and with A. and B. to pay an annuity to A., this vests a joint legal interest in A. and B., although the former is to derive the sole benefit; for only one duty or act was to be performed, and there could not be a separate legal interest therein (*i*). And where A. declared upon an account stated with him of monies due to him and a third person, after verdict judgment was arrested, on the ground that the

(*z*) Lane *v.* Drinkwater, 3 Dowl. 223.
(*a*) Alexander *v.* Barker, 2 Tyr. Rep. 140.
(*b*) Hatsall *v.* Griffith, 4 Tyr. 487, qualifying the cases there cited.
(*c*) *Semble*, see Break *v.* Douglas, cited 4 Tyr. 489.
(*d*) Per Lord Kenyon, 1 East, 501.
(*e*) Longman and others *v.* Pole, 1 Moo. & M. 223; but note, it was an action *on the case* not *ex contractu*.
(*f*) *Semble*, see cases cited in Hatsall *v.* Griffiths, 4 Tyr. 488, notes *a*, *b*, *c*; and Break *v.* Douglas, id. 489.
(*g*) 1 B. & P. 381; 3 M. & Sel. 180.
(*h*) 5 Co. 18 b; 3 Lev. 160; Dyer, 337.
(*i*) 1 East, 469; 3 B. & C. 256.

obligee cannot have an action on a bond in his own name, without averring the death of his co-obligee. If the *oyer* varies from the instrument declared on, the defendant may set it forth in his plea and *demur*, or he may, without setting it forth, plead *non est factum*, and avail himself of the variance on the trial.

If the promise is made jointly to two or more persons, they must all join, if living, in the action, or they will be nonsuited on the trial. Thus, in Wright et al. *v.* Post, 3 Conn. Rep. 142, where twenty persons, feeling interested in a public right of fishery, entered into an agreement with each other that if any of them were sued for exercising the right, each of the others would pay to those who were sued their proportion of what might be recovered against them; and three of them were sued jointly, and after a joint recovery, each of those defendants paid his share of the judgment; in a suit brought against one of the associates to recover the amount he had agreed to contribute, it was held that the promise to indemnify was a *joint promise to the three* who were sued jointly for exercising the right, and that they must therefore bring a joint suit of indemnity, although they paid the judgment in several proportions, and out of their separate property.

1. PLAINTIFFS. — When several.

promise, whether express or implied, must, in point of law, be considered as made to all the persons whose debt it was, and therefore they all ought to have joined in the action (k). And where A. and B. brought an action of assumpsit, and declared that their several cattle had been distrained, and that the defendant, in consideration of £10 paid him by the plaintiffs, promised to procure the cattle to be re-delivered to them by such a time, and that he had not done so; after verdict for the plaintiffs, it was objected, in arrest of judgment, that the plaintiffs ought to have brought several actions, because the promise was not an entire, but a several promise made to each of the plaintiffs; but it was adjudged by Rolle, C. J. and two other judges against one, that the action was well brought jointly by A. and B.; for though the cattle which belonged to A. ought to be restored to him, and the other cattle to be restored to B., and
[*11] so the thing to be *performed was several, and not joint; yet as the *contract and consideration were joint*, and it was not known how much the one gave, and how much the other, the action was well brought jointly (l) (15). And if bail call together upon an attorney, and employ him to surrender their principal, one of them cannot afterwards maintain a separate action against the attorney, for neglecting to effect the render, for their situations and interests were identified (m).

Several Interests.

But when the *legal interest* and cause of action of the covenantees are *several*, each *may* and *should* sue *separately* for the particular damage resulting to him individually, although the covenant be, in its terms, joint (n) (16). And it is improper, as well in *equity* as at *law*, for a party to be joined in a suit who has neither legal nor beneficial interest in its subject-matter (o).

Thus if A. by indenture demise Blackacre to B. and Whiteacre to C., and covenant with them and each of them (or it seems if he covenant with them in express terms jointly) that he is owner of the closes, each should sue separately in respect of his distinct interest, and they cannot jointly sue, for they have no joint or entire interest in the same subject-matter (p). So, if a party covenant with A. and B. to pay them £10 *each*, or an annuity to *each*, there, although the covenant be in its terms joint, yet the distinct interest of each in a separate subject-matter shall attract to each covenantee an exclusive right of action in regard to his own particular damage; and they cannot maintain a joint action, although the deed contain covenants and stipulations for securities which are joint (p). So, where A., B. and C. were appointed assignees under a commission of bankrupt, and A. and B. each paid half of the solicitor's bill, it was decided that A. and B. could not maintain a *joint* action against C. for his pro-

(k) 7 Mod. 116; Yelv. 177.
(l) 1 Rol. Abr. 31, pl. 9; Styles, 156, 157, 203; 2 Saund. 116 a, note.
(m) 1 Taunt. 7.
(n) 5 Co. 186; 1 Saund. 153, n. 1; 8 Taunt. 245; 2 Moore, 195, S. C.; 5 Price, 529, S. C.
(o) See the excellent arguments in The King of Spain v. Machado, 4 Russ. Rep. 231.
(p) *Supra* note (n); 3 B. & C. 254.

(15) { See Shearman v. Akins, 4 Pick. Rep. 283. }
(16) Vide Dunham v. Gillis, 8 Mass. Rep. 462. { Withers v. Bircham, 5 Dow. & Ryl. 106. } Vide Phillips v. Bonsall, 2 Binn. 138. 143. Vide Austin v. Walsh, 2 Mass. Rep. 401. Baker v. Jewell, 6 Mass. Rep. 465. Where several persons are engaged in a joint transaction, the proceeds of which are received by a third person, who promises to pay each partner his respective proportion, in an action against him by one of the partners for his proportion, he cannot object that there are others jointly concerned. Bunn v. Morris and Wisner, 3 Caines' Rep. 54. Vide etiam Austin v. Walsh, ubi supra. Hall v. Leigh et al., 8 Cranch, 50. Gould v. Gould, 6 Wend. Rep. 263.

I. PLAINTIFFS. When several.

portion of the money paid, but must each bring a separate action, and A. and B. having sued jointly, were nonsuited (q) (17). But if A. and B. had borrowed the money, which they paid on their *joint* credit, or their attorney had paid it for them on their joint account, they might have joined in the action against C (r) (18).

Agreement that one should sue.

It is competent to *a corporation*, in making a by-law, to provide that a fine shall be paid to, and recoverable by, the *head of the corporation*, for the use of the corporation; and in such case the action may be brought in the name of the *officer to whom the penalty is so reserved (s). [*12] And a corporation aggregate may maintain assumpsit for the by-gone use and occupation of *tolls*, although they did not grant the tolls to the occupier by any instrument under their common seal (t). So the members of a company, or partnership firm, may stipulate that in certain events one of the members shall incur a fine, and that the action for the recovery of it shall be brought by a particular person interested in the concern, for the use of the rest, excepting the defendant, and the law will give effect to such arrangement by upholding the action (u). But if by a deed constituting a company, certain trustees are to sue a member for goods he may purchase of the company, no subsequent regulation, made without the consent of the defendant (an original member), that another party should be competent to sue, can enable the latter to maintain the action (x); for in this instance there is no original undertaking by the defendant not to object to the non-joinder of the parties who ought otherwise to have been joined in the action (x).

A covenantee not executing.

Where a covenant is made with two or more parties, to pay them money for themselves, or for the use of another, it is not correct to use the name of one only of the covenantees, although the others have omitted to execute the deed (y). Where joint covenantees *may* join, they *must* do so (z). The mere

(q) 3 B. & P. 235; see 2 T. R. 282.
(r) 5 East, 225.
(s) 1 B & P. 98; 3 Bingh. 470.
(t) The Mayor and Burgesses of Carmarthen v. Lewis, 6 Car. & P. 608.
(u) 3 Bingh. 463.
(x) 3 M. & S. 488; 3 Bingh. 470.
(y) 3 B. & C. 353.
(z) Id.

(17) Vide Yates v. Foot, 12 Johns. Rep. 1. Hatch & Clap v. Brooks, 2 Mass. Rep. 293. { Doremus v. Selden, 19 Johns. Rep. 213. Gould v. Gould, 8 Cow. Rep. 168. } In the case last cited, W. Gould and D. Banks, Jr. were, as between themselves, equitably bound to contribute equally to the payment of a certain sum of money. W. Gould was holden for Stephen Gould as his surety in two several bonds; and for the payment of the same debts the ancestor of D. Banks, Jr. was also security, and the property descended to him was therefore holden, W. Gould and D. Banks thus being liable; and being also in partnership, they paid the amount out of their partnership funds. They sued a joint action for the money paid, and were nonsuited, on the ground that they could not maintain a *joint* action, the original responsibility of the bail being several. Although they happened to be partners at the time of the payment, they could not, without some agreement or request from S. Gould, so shape their payment as to raise a joint promise by implication to both. If each had been liable as a surety on a distinct demand against the defendant, although the amounts were the same, they could not have raised a joint promise as against him. If the payment was made out of a fund in which they were equally interested, then each did in fact pay one half, and the law raised a corresponding promise from the defendant to each for so much money paid for him and at his request; which request was the original agreement to indemnify each of his sureties. Gould v. Gould, 6 Wend. Rep. 263. In Graham v. Green, 4 Hayw. Rep. 188, the supreme court of appeals in Tennessee say: "It is certain that by the rules of the common law, two sureties cannot join in an action to recover the money which they have been compelled to pay for the principal."

(18) { 9 Johns. Rep. 217. } Where two join in the purchase of lottery tickets, and also agree to share in the prizes, each may sue his action against the managers for his moiety of the prize drawn. Homer v. Whitman, et al., 15 Mass. Rep. 132.

1. PLAINTIFFS. — When several.

non-execution of the deed by one of them, does not, even in the case of trustees, render it invalid (a), or afford a legal excuse for not joining him as a plaintiff, for his assent is to be presumed (a); but an express disclaimer, renunciation, or refusal by him, would probably justify the omission to make him a party to the action (b).

By Partners.

It is a general rule, that in the case of partners, all the members of the firm should be the plaintiffs in an action upon a contract made with the firm; nor can any private arrangement by the firm, that one only of the partners shall bring the action, give him a right to sue alone (c). So, although a guarantee has been given nominally to one of several partners, all may sue upon the same, if there be evidence that it was intended for the benefit of all (d). Whether or not one member may sue alone, where he is solely interested in the concern, and the other *ostensible* partner is a mere nominal party, without any interest in the business, *was* a question of some difficulty. It appears that in such case the partner having the exclusive interest might sue alone (e), and in a recent case, where an attorney carried on [*13] *business under the firm of A. and Son, and the son was not in fact a partner, but acted as clerk to his father, and received a salary, it was held, that A. might maintain an action in his own name, to recover from a client the amount of a bill for business done (f). But in these instances the plaintiff must adduce clear evidence, disproving that his ostensible partner, though a minor, had any interest whatever in the business, or right to participate in the profits (g).

In the case of *dormant* partners, not privy to the contract, it seems that the other members of the firm *may omit* their names in an action (h) (19); and it has been decided (i), that the joint owners of a vessel engaged in the whale fishery may sue a purchaser for the price of whale oil, although the contract of purchase was made with one of the part-owners, and the purchaser did not know that other persons had any interest in the transaction, the joinder of the other parties making no difference to the defendant, and not affecting any right of set-off (i) (20). But where a contract was made by one of several partners in his individual capacity, who at the time declared that the subject-matter of the contract was his property alone; it was held, that his declaration was evidence against all the partners, and consequently that they could not sue jointly upon such a contract (k). And where a farm was demised to A. and B. jointly, and A. by written agreement between himself and C., underlet part of it to C., and gave receipts for payment of rent, and a notice to quit in his own name

(a) 9 B. & C. 300; 2 Bar. & Adol. 822.
(b) 3 B. & C. 355; 9 Id. 308
(c) See ante, 8, 9, 10; and see Alexander v. Barker, 2 Tyr. Rep. 140.
(d) 4 Bar. & Cres. 664.
(e) 5 Esp. Rep. 199; 1 Stark. 25; 1 C. & P. 69; 7 Moore, 31, 32; sed vide 2 Campb. 302.
(f) Kell v. Nainby, 10 B. & C. 20.
(g) 14 East, 210.
(h) 1 Esp. Rep. 463; 2 Taunt. 324; 1 Montag. on Part. 182; see 6 Ves. 438; 2 Bingh. 177.
(i) 4 B. & A. 437; 7 Moore, 31, 32.
(k) 1 M. & Sel. 249; 2 Bar. & Adol. 303, S. P.

(19) { Clark v. Miller, et al., 4 Wend. Rep. 628. 8 Serg. & Raw'e, 55. 6 Pick. Rep. 352. Mitchell v. Dall, 2 Har. & Gill, 159. Clarkson v. Carter, 3 Cow. Rep. 85. }

(20) { But in an action on a contract of *mateship*, (in regard to which, see Baxter v. Rodman, 3 Pick. Rep. 435,) entered into by the masters of two whaling vessels, the officers and crew of one of the ships cannot be joined as co-plaintiffs with the owner. Grozier v. Atwood, 4 Pick. Rep. 234. }

I. PLAINTIFFS.

only; it was decided, that A. and B. could not maintain a joint action against C. for pulling down a shed which stood on part of the premises demised (*l*) (21).

When several. By Tenants in Common.

If *tenants in common* (who hold by distinct titles) *jointly* demise premises reserving an entire rent, they may, and perhaps should, join in an *action* to recover it (*m*). If the rent be reserved to them separately in distinct parts, they must sue separately; for in such case, as well their estates or interests, as the terms of the contract, are distinct and divisible (*n*). And where, in fact, there have been *separate* demises by tenants in common of their interests, or where tenants in common, by conveyance or purchase, become landlords, they *must* sever in an action for rent or double value (*o*); though where they have actually *joined* in a demise they might join (*o*), and it seems that tenants in common must sever in an *avowry* for rent (*p*).

[*14] *Joint-tenants and Parceners.*

**Joint-tenants* (unlike tenants in common) have a unity of title and interest, in respect of which they *must jointly sue* upon a contract relating to the estate which is made by, or enures to, the benefit of all (*q*). And for the same reason *Parceners* must jôin in an action *ex contractu*, which relates to their tenements (*r*); and accordingly it has been recently determined that an action will not lie at the suit of one of three coparceners to recover her proportion of rents of the estate received by an agent (*s*).

Consequences of mistake.

The *consequences of a mistake*, in *omitting* to join a party who ought to have been made a plaintiff in an action *ex contractu*, or in *adding* a party improperly in such an action, are extremely serious.

In all cases of contracts, if it appear upon the face of the pleadings that there are other obligees, covenantees, or parties to the contract, who ought to be, but are not joined as plaintiffs in the action, it is fatal on demurrer, or on motion in arrest of judgment, or on error (*t*) (22); and though the objection

(*l*) 7 Moore, 29.

(*m*) 1 Ld. Raym. 340; Lit. sect. 315, 316; 5 T. R. 249; 5 B. & A. 851; and see 1 Bingh. N. C. 713; 1 Hodges, 170, S. C.

(*n*) Id; Bac. Abr. Joint-tenants, K.; Lit. sect. 315; Kirkman *v.* Newstead, 1 Esp. N. P. Dig. 145, 4th ed.; 5 T. R. 249.

(*o*) Wilkinson *v.* Hall, 1 Bingh. N. C. 713; 1 Hodges' Rep. 170, S. C.

(*p*) Ante, n. (*m*), p. 12; 5 T. R. 249. As to the mode of avowing or declaring for rent in such case, id.; post, vols. ii. & iii.; 4 B. & C. 157.

(*q*) 2 Bla. Com 182; Co. Lit. 180 b; Bac. Abr. Joint-tenants, K.; 1 B. & P. 67.

(*r*) 2 Bla. Com. 187, 188; Vin. Ab. Parceners, T.; Rep. temp. Hardw. 398.

(*s*) Decharms *v.* Harwood, 4 Moore & Sc. 400; 10 Bingh. 526, S. C.

(*t*) 2 Stra 1146; 1 East, 497; 1 Saund. 153, n. 1, 291 f.

(21) { See Barstow *v* Gray, 3 Greenleaf's Rep. 409. }
Where two persons, who were joint partners in business, were subjected to the payment of a debt of a third person, the one as surety, and the other as the heir of a *co-surety*, which debt was paid from the partnership funds; *Held*, that each might sue the principal for his moiety of the money paid. Gould *v.* Gould, 6 Wend. Rep. 263.

(22) The general rule is, that the omission of proper parties, as plaintiff in cases of contract, may be taken advantage of at the trial under the general issue; and if it appear on the face of the pleadings, it is fatal on demurrer, or on motion in arrest of judgment, or in error. Accordingly where it appeared on the face of the declaration that the plaintiffs were not overseers of the poor when the suit was brought, and of course that the right of action was not in them, but had passed to their successors, the judgment rendered in the court below for the plaintiffs was reversed. Armine et al. Overseers of the Poor, &c. *v.* Spencer, 4 Wend. Rep. 406. It is settled by repeated decisions in New York, that overseers of the poor are a *quasi* corporation, and as such can sue and be sued. Pittstown *v.* Plattsburgh, 18 Johns. Rep. 418. Norwich *v.* New Berlin, ib. 382. It has also been decided that the acting overseers of the poor are responsible for the *official contracts* of their predecessors in office; (Todd et al., Overseers *v.* Birdsall, 1 Cowen, 260, and 5 Cowen, 309;) and in Jansen *v.* Ostrander, (1 Cowen, 670,) it was held that the rights and liabili-

I. PLAINTIFFS. — When several.

may not appear on the face of the pleadings, the defendant may avail himself of it, either by *plea in abatement* (u), or as a ground of nonsuit on the trial, as a variance upon *non est factum*, if the action be upon a specialty, or if it be upon any other contract, upon the plea of the general issue (x) (23). When the [*15] *objection appears on the face of the pleadings, it is sometimes advisable to demur, in order to obtain costs, as each party pays his own costs when the judgment is arrested (y) (24).

Where the action is upon a deed, and only one of the covenantees improperly sues, the defendant may also avail himself of the nonjoinder, by praying oyer of the deed, and setting it out, and then demurring generally to the declaration (z).

If there be a legal ground for omitting to use the name of one of several covenantees as a plaintiff, as his death, &c., it is necessary to show such excuse for the nonjoinder in the declaration, and to declare as surviving partner (a).

Trustees, &c. by Statute.

There are various acts of parliament which, without incorporating certain bodies of individuals, &c., enable them to sue, and entitle others to sue them, in the names of their clerks, treasurers, &c. for the time being. Thus, by the General *Turnpike* Act (b), the trustees and commissioners of any turnpike road may sue and be sued in the name of one of the trustees, or of their clerk or clerks *for the time being*, that is, at the time the action is brought (c). the

(u) Com. Dig. "Abatement," E. 12. See forms of plea and replication and points, Davies v. Evans, 6 Car. & P. 619.

(x) 1 Saund. 154, n. 1, 291 f. g.; 2 Stra. 820; 2 Stark. 424. The good sense of this rule, (which, as we shall see hereafter, does not prevail in the case of plaintiffs in *torts*, or of several *defendants*), has been questioned; but it is admitted to prevail. See 1 Saund. 291 f. g.; 1 B. & P. 73; 6 T. R. 770; 2 Stark. 424. In the case of *co-executors*, the objection can only be taken advantage of by a plea in abatement, 1 Saund. 291 g.; 3 T. R. 558; 1 Chit. Rep. 71. As the *omission* of a party is said to be no ground of nonsuit in an action in form *ex delicto*, (see 6 T. R. 770; 3 East, 62, *acc. sed quære*, see 2 New Rep. 365, 454; 12 East, 94, 454), it appears to be advisable where there is a doubt as to the number of persons to be made plaintiffs, and when the declaration may be *in case*, to adopt that form of action. So many instances occur in which a cause is defeated by the accidental nonjoinder or misjoinder of the plaintiff, that it is perhaps to be regretted that no legislative provision has been made upon the subject, analogous to the enactment in the 7 Geo. 4, c. 64, s. 14, respecting *indictments*, see *post*, 14, note (g). However, in modern practice, the *doctrine of amendment* has been, in some instances, usefully applied to remedy or mitigate the evil, as orders have been made to strike out the name of one of the plaintiffs in a late stage of the proceedings, where otherwise, the statute of limitation would bar a fresh action; and in Fox v. Clifton and others, C. P. Nov. 1829, an order was made just before the trial, that *some of the defendants' names be struck out*. The action was in *assumpsit*. See the present practice as to amendments of writ, 3 Chitty's Gen. Prac. 173, 174.

(y) Cowp. 407.

(z) 1 Saund. 154 a, note.

(a) 4 B. & Ald. 374: 2 Saund. 121, n. 1, {2 Johns. Rep. 34.}

(b) 3 Geo. 4, c. 126, s. 74.

(c) 1 R. & M. 214. Whitmore v. Wilks, 1 M. & Malk. 222, 223.

---

ties of these *quasi* corporations, whether they arise from torts or contracts, and whether the latter be simple or by specialty, pass to their successors in office. In Jansen v. Ostrander, the action was brought by Janson as supervisor of Ringston, in *his own name*, upon a collector's bond given to Gaasbeck, his predecessor in office, and the action was sustained: and this upon the principle that all the rights of his predecessor have devolved by law upon him. The decision in that case was considered sound. Armine v. Spencer, 4 Wend. Rep. 408.

(23) Baker v. Jewell, 6 Mass. Rep 460 Converse v. Symmes, 10 ib. 379. Ziele et al. v. Campbell's Ex'rs, 2 J. C. 384. Brown v. Belches, 1 Wash. Rep. 9. 15 Johns. Rep. 482. Dob et al. v. Halsey, 16 Johns. Rep. 34. Robertson v. Smith et al., 10 Johns. Rep. 459. Wilson v. Wallace, 8 S. & R. 53.

(24) Pangburn v. Ramsey, 11 Johns. Rep. 141.

I. PLAINTIFFS.

When several.

West India *Dock* (*d*), the London Dock (*e*), and some *Insurance* companies (*f*) may sue or be sued in the names of their treasurers or clerks (*g*). The 7 & 8 Geo. 4, c. 36, s. 9, enables co-partners, *as bankers*, carrying on business as such under the provisions of that act, to sue and adopt proceedings at law and in equity, and in bankruptcy, in the name of any one of their *public officers*, nominated as therein mentioned, for the time being (*h*).

[*16] *It should be observed, that where trustees, clerks, or treasurers, &c. sue or are sued in their official characters by virtue of an act of parliament, the cause of action should, in the pleadings, be stated to have accrued to or against the *principals or company of individuals* whom they, for this purpose, represent (*i*). If, however, the statute provide not only that these parties shall be the nominal plaintiffs, but also that the cause of action shall be vested *in them in trust*, they should then declare accordingly.

3dly. When the *interest* in the contract has been *assigned*.

Where a party with whom a bond, simple contract, or other mere *personal* contract was made, has assigned his interest therein to a third person, the latter cannot, in general, sue in his own name, the interest in, and remedy upon, *personal* contracts being *choses in action*, which are not, in general, assignable at law (25), so as to give the assignee a right of action in his own name, but

(*d*) 39 Geo. 3, c. lxix. s. 184.

(*e*) 39 & 40 Geo. 3, c. xlvii. s. 150.

(*f*) 53 Geo. 3, c. cxxvi.; 3 B. & C. 178; and see 4 B. & C. 962; 7 D. & R. 376, S. C.

(*g*) As to actions by *Friendly Societies*, see 10 Geo. 4, c. 56, s. 21. And by the statute 57 Geo. 3, c. 130, s. 8, actions by and against the trustees of Savings' Banks are permitted, in matters relating to such banks. *Overseers* of the poor for the time being may, by that description, sue on *Bastardy Bonds*, and other securities of that nature, 54 Geo. 3, c. 170, s. 8; see also 59 Geo. 3, c. 12, s. 17, as to actions, &c. by churchwardens and overseers, with regard to parish lands and buildings, and the assistant overseer's bond; see 2 D. & R. 708. As to suits by societies or partnerships in *Ireland*, see 5 Geo. 4, c. 73; 6 G. 4, c. 42, s. 10; and *Scotland*, 6 G. 4, c. 131. Where goods *stolen* are the property of *partners or joint owners*, they may be described, in an *indictment or information for a felony or misdemeanor*, as the goods and chattels of any *one or more* of the *partners or joint owners*, and *another or other*, as the case may be, and this provision extends to all joint-stock *companies* and *trustees*, 7 Geo. 4, c. 64, s. 14. The same statute, s. 15, also provides that property, whether real or personal, belonging to any *county*, riding, or division, may, in such indictment, be stated to belong to the inhabitants of such county, riding or division, without specifying the names of such inhabitants; and by s. 16, that property belonging to any *parish*, township, or hamlet, may be stated to belong to the overseers of the poor for the time being of such parish, township, or hamlet, without specifying the names of all or any of such overseers; and by s. 17, that property under *turnpike* trusts may be stated to belong to the trustees, or commissioners of the road, without specifying their names; and by s. 18, that property under the commissioners of *sewers* may be stated to belong to the commissioners having the management of it, without specifying their names. But it is observable, that these provisions in the 7 Geo. 4, do not extend to the pleadings in a *civil* proceeding.

(*h*) See the statute and decisions, Chit. on Bills, 8 ed. 72 to 77.

(25) {In Pennsylvania, by the act of 28th May, 1715, (1 Sm. Laws, 90,) all bonds, specialties, and notes in writing, made or to be made, and signed by any person or persons, whereby such person or persons is or are obliged or doth or shall promise to pay to any other person or persons, his, her or their order, or assigns, (See Aldricks *v.* Higgins, 16 Serg. & Rawle, 212,) any sum or sums of money mentioned in such bonds, specialties, note or notes, may, by the person or persons to whom the same is or are made payable, be assigned, indorsed and made over to such person or persons as shall think fit to accept thereof. The person or persons to whom such bonds, specialties or notes are or shall be assigned, indorsed, or made over, their factors, agents, executors, or assigns, may at his, her or their pleasure again assign, indorse, and make over the same, and so *toties quoties*. The assignees of bonds, specialties and notes, are authorized to sue in their own names; and it is provided, that it shall not be in the power of the assignors after assignment, to

I. PLAINTIFFS. — 3. When interest assigned.

he must proceed in that of the assignor (26), or if he be dead, in the name of his personal representative (*k*) (27). Upon this principle it was held, that although the Scotch Bankrupt Act (*l*) vests in the trustee for behoof of the creditors the estate and effects of the bankrupt, so far as may be consistent with the laws of other countries, when the effects are out of Scotland, yet the trustee [*17] cannot sue in his own name for a *chose in action* *which was vested in the bankrupt, the statute containing no words giving to the plaintiff a right of suit (*m*). And in the common case of a composition deed, the trustees can only sue in the name of the original creditor in whom the legal interest in the contract still remains. Where the assignor of the *chose in action* has become bankrupt, the action must be in his own name, and not in the name of the assignee of such bankrupt, because the assignee of a bankrupt can only sue upon contracts in which the bankrupt was beneficially interested (*n*); and if after a charter-party the owner assigns, and then become bankrupt, he should sue (*o*). If, however, an express promise or contract to pay the debt, or perform the contract, be made to the assignee of the *chose in action*, in consideration of forbearance, or in respect of any other *new* consideration, such assignee may proceed in his own name, declaring upon such promise and new consideration (*p*) (28).

By Successor, &c. by statute.

There are many instances, in which, by express legislative provision, the assignee of a *chose in action* may sue in his own name to enforce the recovery

(*k*) 10 East, 281; 4 T. R. 340; 1 East, 104; 3 Wils. 27; 1 Saund. 210, 153, 154; 2 Moore, 185; 13 East, 73; 16 East, 36; 8 B. & C. 395. But a revived corporation may sue on a bond given to the old corporation, 3 Bur. 1872, 1873; 3 Lev. 273. As to a churchwarden suing, see 2 Hen. Bla. 559. A *chose in action* may be assigned by parol, 4 T. R. 690; 4 Taunt. 326.

(*l*) 54 Geo. 3, c. 137.

(*m*) 6 M. & S. 126; 4 D. & R. 669.

(*n*) 3 B & P. 40; 1 T. R. 619; 3 B. & A. 697. The *executor* of the assignor must sue if the assignor be dead, 2 Moore, 784.

(*o*) 10 East, 279; 2 Taunt. 407; 1 Marsh. 248.

(*p*) 1 Saund. 210, n. 1; 8 T. R. 595; 4 Bar. & Cres. 525.

---

release, &c. The assignment of bonds or specialties must be "under hand and seal before two or more credible witnesses." See a precedent of a declaration in debt on a bond by the assignee, Read's Plead. Ass. 251. }

(26) } See 10 Serg. & Rawle, 320, 321. But the case there put, of the bond informally assigned, is entirely inconsistent with the principle stated in the text, and seems to be founded upon Fenner *v.* Meares. } Vide Crocker et ux. *v.* Whitney, 10 Mass. Rep. 319. Where a person receives securities from A. to dispose of the money to be received thereon, to certain specified purposes, and to hold the balance subject to the order of A. and the trust is accepted, the assignee of the balance may maintain an action, for money had and received, against the trustee, the acceptance of the trust being equivalent to an express promise to the person, to whom A. should direct the money, when received, to be paid. Weston *v.* Barker, 12 Johns. Rep. 276. Et vide Neilson *v.* Blight, 1 Johns. Cas. 235. Crocker *v.* Whitney, *ubi sup.*

(27) The indorsee of a promissory note given in Connecticut; where promissory notes are not negotiable, may, in the state of New York, maintain an action in his own name against the maker; for the *lex loci contractus* does not govern as to the mode of enforcing the contract. Lodge *v.* Phelps, 1 Johns. Cas. 139. 2 Caines' Cas. *in error*, 321.

(28) In Boggs *v.* Ingraham, 3 Dall. 505, 2 Yeates, 487, it was held that the assignee of a stock contract in the following words, "On the 18th of April, 1792, I promise to receive from Joseph Boggs, or order, ten thousand dollars, six per cent., and pay him for the same, at the rate of twenty-three shillings and seven pence three fourths per pound," could maintain an action in his own name, without any new consideration or promise made to the assignee. The court founded their opinion upon Fenner *v.* Meares, 2 W. Bl. 1269. (2 Yeates, 492); but that case has often been doubted, both in England and in this country; (1 East, 104. 432; 14 East, 587 n. (a); 12 East, 582; 5 Wend. R. 203.) and the only ground upon which either Fenner *v.* Meares, or Boggs *v.* Ingraham, can be sustained at all is, that the determination having been made according to equity and good conscience, the court would not, upon a motion for a new trial, disturb the verdict.

of the demand. The operation of the bankrupt and insolvent acts is to this effect (q); and by various statutes the assignee of a bail bond (r), replevin bond (s), an India bond (t), or a judgment by confession in Ireland (u), or a promissory note(v)(29), may sue in his own name; and the avowant may join with a party making cognizance in an action on the replevin bond (x). The remedy upon a *bastardy bond*, or other security given to a parish or district, as an indemnity against the expenses to be incurred by reason of the birth or support of a bastard child, is vested "in the overseers of the poor for the time being," and in their names only can the action be brought (y). And a voluntary bond conditioned for the payment of a weekly sum for the support of a bastard child, though not strictly a bastardy bond, may yet be sued upon by a succeeding overseer (z). The acts for the encouragement and protection of Friendly Societies, enable them to sue in the names of their "treasurers or trustees for the time being;" and as the right or cause of action is vested by the statutes in such treasurers *or trustees, (for the use and benefit of the society), they must necessarily be the plaintiffs (a). [*18]

I. PLAINTIFFS.

3. When interest assigned.

By the custom of merchants, the assignee or transferee of a bill of exchange or cheque on a banker, may sue thereon in his own name (30).

(q) *Post*, 22, 26.
(r) 4 Ann. c. 16, s. 20.
(s) 11 Geo. 2, c. 19, s. 23; 1 B. & P. 381, n. (a); 3 Mau. & Sel. 180.
(t) 51 Geo. 3, c. 64, s. 4; see 13 East, 509. But not the assignee of an India certificate, 16 Ves. 443.
(u) 3 Taunt. 82.
(v) 3 & 4 Ann. c. 9, s. 1.
(x) *Ante*, 9, note (g).
(y) 54 Geo. 3, c. 170, s. 8; 3 Moore, 21; 8 Taunt. 691. S. C.
(z) 7 Bingh. 477.
(a) 10 Geo. 4, c. 56, s. 21.

(29) The defendant cannot defeat the suit by showing a want of interest in the nominal plaintiff. Alsop v. Caines, 10 J. R. 400. Raymond v. Johnson, 10 ib. 488. Where three adjoining towns on a river are by statute authorized to regulate the times of taking fish, and also to sell the right within such towns; and two of the towns having sold their interest to the third; *held*, that the latter might sue an action to recover the purchase money, she having transferred her interest in the fishery. Watertown v. White, 13 Mass. R. 477.

(30) Where a banking corporation accepts a check of a third person for part of the amount of a note falling due, and also takes a new note for the balance, at the same time delivering up the old note; *held*, that in case the check is dishonored, an action would lie on the old note against the maker. Olcott v. Rathbone, 5 Wend. R. 490. So when a creditor receives a note or check for his debt, and gives a receipt in full, he is not concluded by his receipt, ib. 1 Cowen, 290. 9 J. R. 310. Nothing is considered as an actual payment which is not in truth such, unless there be an express agreement that something short of a payment shall be taken in lieu of it. The case of Kean v. Dufresne, 3 S. & R. 233, was thus. Dufresne held a note against Kean and Foster, who were partners. Subsequent to the dissolution of the partnership, Kean gave his own note for one of the firm. Dufresne got Kean's note discounted, and applied the avails to the company's note. *Held*, that Dufresne might maintain action on the note of the firm; the note of Kean being dishonored. In that case, however, it did not appear that the old note had been given up. And Chancellor Loughborough, in ex parte Backley, 7 Vesey, jun. 597, seems to consider that an important circumstance. But this circumstance is not decisive. It is but matter of evidence to show the nature of the transaction and the intention of the parties. Olcott v. Rathbone, 5 Wend. R. 490.

Where, however, the action was sued in the name of the *cashier*, and there was no evidence that the note had been transferred to him, or that the suit was instituted in his name by the direction of the bank, it was decided that he was not entitled to recover. The owner of a promissory note indorsed in blank can make whom he pleases the holder of it without divesting himself of all interest in it, and a suit may be sustained in the name of such holder; but the bare using of a person's name as plaintiff does not make him a holder or assignee. The cashier had the custody, but the bank had the legal possession. Ib.

The holder of a note payable to bearer, or of a note payable to order, and indorsed by the payee to him or in blank, may sustain a count for money had and received by proof of such note, 12 J. R. 90; 4 Pick. 421; but if a plaintiff cannot recover on the note as *bear-*

I. PLAINTIFFS. — 3. When interest assigned.

An exception to the rule, that a debt or *chose in action* cannot be assigned at law, arises in the following case, put by Buller, J., in *Tatlock* v. *Harris* (b): "Suppose A. owes B. £100, and B. owes C. £100, and the three

(b) 3 T. R. 180; Israel v. Douglas, Hen. Bla. 239; see also 3 B. & C. 855; 4 Id. 166; 8 Id. 395; see Chitty, jun. on contracts. 184.

ee or *holder* for the want of title or authority to sue in his own name, he cannot recover on the common counts. Olcott v. Rathbone, 5 Wend. R. 490.

A note was made payable at a bank for the purpose of being discounted to pay a specific debt, and the debtor procures a person to sign said note as surety; and he signs "A. B. surety;" and the bank not discounting the note, the creditor for whose benefit the note was made, may maintain an action upon such in the name of the bank—the latter assenting to such use being made of the note. Utica Bank v. Granson, 10 Wend. R. 314. The maker of the note thus signing, by operation of the law merchant, engages to pay the note, without any restriction as to the design or object for which it is made. Ib. In such case, the holder need not show such a consideration as is required where the note is wrongfully put in circulation. Where the object of the making fails, and it is sent into the world by fraud, the holder in such a case must show not only a valuable consideration, but that he took the paper in the usual course of business. 3 Kent's Com. 84. 20 J. R. 637. A consideration which would be valid between him and the person from whom he received it, might not be sufficient in such a case against the maker. These cases turn upon commercial principles, peculiar to negotiable paper, and are to be governed by the somewhat analogous doctrine relating to the liability of sureties and guarantors simply as such. Utica Bank v. Granson, 10 Wend. Rep. 314.

An action on a note, payable to bearer, or indorsed in blank, may be maintained in the name of any person, without being required to show that he has an interest in it, unless he gains the possession of the note under suspicious circumstances. Ogilby v. Wallace, 2 Hall's R. 553. Thus, where the note was payable to order, and the plaintiff of record was a fictitious person who was non-suited at the trial; the note being the property of a real party whose name was disclosed. The court, however, directed the non-suit to be set aside, that the questions of fact in respect to the possession and prosecution of the note, might be submitted to a jury.

Where the defendant was the payee of a promissory note, and indorsed it to the plaintiff, who indorsed it to a bank. The note being protested, the defendant paid a part, and promised to pay the balance; but not paying, he was sued as indorser and recovered a judgment for the balance due. Afterwards the defendant paid 380 dollars, and they held the note which had not been fully paid. The plaintiff sued the defendant as indorser in the usual form; and also for money paid, &c. It was decided that the plaintiff was not entitled to maintain his action as it had not been fully paid, and was the property of the bank; but that he might recover the 380 dollars as money paid for the defendant. Butler v. Wright, 20 Johns. Rep. 367.

Where a note was indorsed by the defendant for the accommodation of the makers, who before the note was negotiated become insolvent, and the defendant requested them not to part with the note, and they promised not to negotiate it. Afterwards, it was passed to the plaintiff, who had notice of all facts. In an action on the note against the indorser, *held*, that the plaintiffs were not entitled to maintain their action. Skelding v. Warren, 15 Johns. Rep. 270.

An indorsee of a promissory note, which is made payable to bearer, may maintain an action against the heirs, &c. of the maker, though the note was indorsed after the death of the maker, under the act 1 R. L. 316. Parsons v. Parsons, 5 Cowen, 476.

A. was the holder of a note and passed it to B. as collateral security for the payment of a debt due to the latter; and the note being deposited in a bank for collection, the latter having neglected to give notice of the non-payment to the indorsers, *held*, that A. might maintain an action against the bank, although it appeared he had assigned his interest in the note to third persons. The plaintiff was the party injured, and he is entitled to the remedy which the law affords. M'Kinster v. Bank of Utica, 9 Wend. Rep. 46.

Where a note has effected the substantial purpose for which it was designed by the parties, an accommodation indorser cannot object that it was not effected in the precise manner contemplated at the time of its creation. Upon that principle, the cases of Powell v. Waters, 17 Johns. Rep. 176, The Bank of Chenango v. Hyde et al., 4 Cowen, 567, and The Bank of Rutland v. Buck, 4 Wend. Rep. 66, were decided. See also 2 Gall. 233; Payson v. Coolidge, 2 Wheat. 66. But where a note has been diverted from its original destination, and fraudulently put in circulation by the maker or his agent, the holder cannot recover upon it against an accommodation indorser, whithout showing that he received it in good faith, in the ordinary course of trade, and paid for it a valuable consideration. Woodhull v. Holmes, 10 Johns. Rep. 231. Skelding et al. v. Warren, 15 Johns. Rep. 270. Brown v. Taber, 5 Wend. Rep. 566. Vallett v. Parker, 6 ib. 615. In

meet, and it is agreed between them that A. shall pay C. the £100, B.'s debt is extinguished, and C. may recover that sum against A." In such case an express agreement between all the parties that A. should become C.'s debtor instead of B. must be proved (c); and it must appear that A.'s debt to B. was ascertained and fixed (d).

I. PLAINTIFFS.

3. When interest assigned.

The common law confers on the *grantee* of the *reversion* of an estate, an action in his own name upon such *implied* covenants, or covenants *in law*, as are annexed to, and which run with, the reversion: as upon the *reddendum*, or word "demise," contained in the lease (e) (31). But at common law none but parties or privies to *express* covenants, as the parties or their heirs or devisees (f), could sue thereon, the privity of contract being in such case wanting; and the grantee of the reversion being therefore considered as a mere stranger (g). This defect was remedied by the statute, 32 Hen. 8. c. 34. s. 1, which transfers the remedy and right of action to the grantee, against the lessee or his assigns: although the grantee be not named in the lease (h). The

Real property.

(c) 4 B. & C. 163; see 8 B. & C. 402.
(d) 8 B. & C. 395.
(e) 2 Lev. 206; 1 B. & C. 410; 2 D. & R. 670, S. C.
(f) As to action by *heirs* and *devisees*, post, 19 to 22.
(g) See 3 T. R. 401; Platt on Cov. 527, 531; Bac. Ab. Covenant, E. Debt, C.; Com. Dig. Covenant, B. 3.
(h) T. Raym. 80; Platt on Cov. 534. Where there is a further reversion, the second reversioner may also sue for the diminution in the value of his interest which may arise from the breach of covenant. See 3 Lev. 130, 209; 4 Bur. 2141; Platt on Cov. 537. Each reversioner will recover damages commensurate with his particular interest; Holt, Ni. Pri. Rep. 543; 1 Taunt. 194. But the grantee of the reversion of part of the premises cannot maintain *ejectment* upon a condition broken, 5 Co 55 b.; 2 B. & A. 109; The reason is, that a condition is entire and indivisible.

Coddington v. Bay, 20 Johns. Rep. 637, the English cases upon this branch of the law are very fully and ably reviewed. In that case judge Spencer says, "I understand by the usual course of trade, not that the holder shall receive the bills or notes thus obtained as securities for antecedent debts, but that he shall take them in his business, and as payment of a debt contracted at the time." Again, "all the cases cited have been decided on the ground that the notes or bills were taken in the usual course of trade, and for a present consideration paid. Not one of the cases is like the present, where notes or bills thus passed were received in security of an antecedent debt." Judge Woodworth says, "in every case it appears that the holder gave credit to the paper, received it in the way of business, and gave money or property in exchange."—"Something must be paid in money or property, or some subsisting debt satisfied, or some new responsibility incurred, in consequence of the transfer of the paper." Viele, Senator, says, "though an indemnity for prior responsibilities may be a sufficient consideration for some purposes, and between parties, &c. yet it cannot be taken as sufficient in principle to bar the owner of his title by a fraudulent transfer."

(31) The doctrine that a covenant of warranty runs with the land, and enures to the benefit of the assignee of the covenantee, who may bring an action in his own name against the original covenantor for the breach thereof, is not questioned or denied. The only doubt upon this point was, whether, when a covenantee conveys with warrantee, his grantee, upon eviction, could sue the original warrantor, or whether his remedy was confined to his immediate covenant of indemnity. The latter opinion was expressed in Kane v. Sanger, 14 Johns. Rep. 89; but the whole subject was fully reviewed and considered in Withy v. Mumford, 5 Cowen, 137, where the broad doctrine that the assignee may maintain an action against the original covenantor, whether the immediate conveyance was with or without warranty, was, upon a consideration and a review of all the cases, fully established. Coke Litt. 384, b, 385, a. 4 Cruise's Dig. 452, 3. Cro. Eliz. 503. Shep. Touch. 198, tit. Warranty. 2 Mass. Rep. 460. Booth v. Starr, 1 Conn. Rep. 244.

The assignee of such a covenant is not affected by any equities existing between the original parties; thus, where premises were conveyed subject to a mortgage, and it was agreed at the time of the conveyance that the grantee should assume the payment of the mortgage, and pay to the grantor only the difference between the amount thereof and the sum agreed on as the consideration of the conveyance, and that the covenants of warranty and of quiet enjoyment should not be considered to extend to the mortgage, it was *held*, that such agreement could not be set up in bar to an action brought by the assignee of the covenantee who was evicted under the mortgage. Suydam v. Jones, 10 Wend. Rep. 180.

I. PLAINTIFFS. — 3. When interest assigned.

statute extends *to the grantee or surrenderee of the reversion of a copyhold tenement (*i*); and to the grantee of the reversion of part of the premises, as well as to the grantee of part of the estate of reversion (*k*). And it applies to the grantee of a reversion of a lease for life as well as for years (*l*); and where a tenant for life makes a lease in pursuance of a leasing power, the remainder-man is considered to be an assignee of the reversion within the statute (*m*). But it does not relate to covenants entered into in a conveyance in fee or gift in tail (*n*); and where J. B. being seised in fee conveyed to the defendant and T. J. their heirs and assigns, to the use that J. B. his heirs and assigns, might have and take to his use a rent certain, to be issuing out of the premises, and subject to the said rent to the use of the defendant, his heirs and assigns; and the defendant covenanted with J. B. his heirs and assigns, to pay to him, his heirs and assigns, the said rent, and to build a house to secure it; and J. B. demised the rent to the plaintiff for a long term; it was held that the latter could not sue upon the covenants, for they were personal to J. B. and the rent was reserved out of the original estate, and there was neither privity of contract nor privity of estate (*o*). In general, in order to enable a person to sue as *an assignee*, he ought to come in of *the same estate*, as that in respect of which the covenant was made, and not by title paramount (*p*). And if a person, having only the equitable fee in freehold or copyhold, grant a lease and then devise the equitable fee to A., and A., after the death of testator, acquire the legal estate from the person in whom it was vested at the time of the lease and devise, and then sell and convey the legal estate to B., the latter could not sue the lessee or his assignees, because he takes not any legal estate from the lessor (*q*).

It is to be remembered that the statute has no effect on covenants which are *collateral* to and do not *run with the land*. Upon such covenants the grantee of the reversion cannot maintain an action in his own name (*r*).

After the grant of the reversion, the grantor cannot sue for breaches of covenant subsequently committed by the lessee or his assigns (*s*), but his remedy

[*20] for prior breaches *is not (like the remedy by *distress*) destroyed (*t*). And as a *chose in action* is not transferable at law, the remedy for breaches of covenant, which occurred before the grant of the reversion, must necessarily be *enforced* in the name of the grantor (*u*) (32). And rent accrued due before a

(*i*) Glover *v.* Cope, 3 Lev. 326; Carth. 205; 3 M. & Sel. 386; 1 Saund. 241, note (*a*); Platt on Cov. 537.

(*k*) 2 B. & Ald. 105; 4 B. & C. 157, 158.

(*l*) Co. Lit. 215; Platt, 535.

(*m*) 3 M. & Sel. 382.

(*n*) Co. Lit. 215; Cro. Eliz. 863; Platt. 535.

(*o*) 5 M. & Sel. 411.

(*p*) See Webb *v.* Russel, 3 T. R. 393; Platt on Cov. 341; Co. Lit. 215.

(*q*) Seymour *v.* Franco, 7 Law Journal, part 2, K. B., page 18. Whitton *v.* Peacock, special case, June, 1835, in C. P. argued by Mr. Coote and Wightman. Sherman, Attorney. Author's MS.

(*r*) 5 Co. 17, *Spencer's Case*; Co. Lit. 215 b.; 1 Saund. 241 a. note 9, 5th edit.; 1 B. & C. 417; 2 D. & R. 670, S. C. The assignee of a mere *rent-charge* is not within the statute, 5 M. & Sel. 411. A covenant to insure a house within the weekly bills of mortality runs with the land, 5 B. & Ald. 1. See the judgment of the Court in that case as to what covenants run with the land, 1 B. & C. 410; 9 Id. 505; 1 Cromp. & J. 105.

(*s*) 3 Lev. 154; 3 T. R. 394, *arg.*

(*t*) Skin. 367; Carth. 289; 12 Mod. 45; 2 Show. 133.

(*u*) Cro. Eliz. 863; 4 M. & Sel. 56; 8 Taunt. 227; 2 Moore, 164, S. C. But for so much of the breach as continues after the assignment the grantee may sue, *Mascal's case*, Mo. 242; 1 Leon. 62, S. C.

(32) Greenby & Kellogg *v.* Wilcocks, 2 Johns. Rep. 1. Bickford *v.* Page, 2 Mass. Rep. 455. Marston *v.* Hobbs, 2 Mass. Rep. 439. {Chapman *v.* Holmes, 5 Halst. Rep. 20.

I. PLAINTIFFS.

conveyance of the reversion, will not pass to the grantee, but is at law as well as in equity severed from the inheritance (*x*).

3. When interest assigned.

The statute 32 Hen. 8, refers only to the remedies for and against the assignees and grantees of *reversions*. The *common law* gives a remedy by action upon a covenant real annexed to the estate, and running with it, to the assignee of the assignee of such estate, against the original assignor, who conveyed his whole interest in the property (33). As if a party grant an estate in fee with a covenant for further assurance, and his grantee grant it over to A., the latter may maintain covenant against the original grantor, on the ground that a privity of estate subsists between them (*y*). So the assignee of the original grantee may sue the original assignor upon his covenant for quiet enjoyment, whether the interest assigned be an estate of inheritance or a chattel real only; and whether any estate remain in the covenantor or not (*z*). And if A. demise to B. rendering rent, and then A. assign the rent, the counterpart of the lease, and the benefit of the covenant to C. for the remainder of the term, the latter may maintain debt for the rent against B. (*a*).

Attornment by the tenant to the grantee of the reversion is not necessary in any of these cases to perfect the remedy of the latter, but the tenant shall not be prejudiced by any payment of rent to the grantor before he had notice of the grantee's title (*b*).

In the case of a lunatic, the action upon a contract made with *him* should be brought in his name, not in the name of his committee (*c*).

[*21]

4thly. When one of several obligees, &c. is dead.

*When one or more of several obligees, covenantees, partners, or others, having a *joint legal* interest in the contract, dies, the action must be brought *in the name* of the survivor, (34) and the executor or administrator of the deceased must not be joined, nor can he sue separately, though the deceased alone might be entitled to the *beneficial* interest in the contract; and the executor must resort to a court of equity to obtain from the survivor the testator's share of the sum recovered (*d*)(35): but if the interest of the covenantees

(*x*) Flight *v.* Bently, Vice Chancellor's Court, 13 May, 1835.

(*y*) Cro. Car. 503, 3 B. & Ald. 396.

(*z*) Id.; Cro Eliz. 373; Lewis *v.* Campbell, 8 Taunt. 715; 3 Moore, 35, S. C.; affirmed in error, 3 B. & Ald. 392. See further, Platt on Cov. 522, *et subs.*

(*a*) 5 B. & C. 512.

(*b*) 4 & 5 Ann. c. 16, s. 9, 10; 16 East, 99.

(*c*) 2 Sid. 124, 125. Ejectment must be brought in the name of the lunatic, for his committee is but a bailiff, and has no interest, Adams, Ej. 2d ed. 81, cites Hutton, 16; Hob. 215; 2 Wils. 130. But the committee may, by order of the Court of Chancery, grant leases, see 43 Geo. 3, c. 75, s. 14, and in such case the remedy would be by the committee. See further 6 Geo. 4, c. 74; 9 Geo. 4, c. 78.

(*d*) 1 East, 497; Salk. 444; Ld Raym. 340; Com. Dig. Merchants, D.; Vin. Ab. Partner, D.; 2 M. & S. 225.

Garrison *v.* Sandford, 7 Halst. Rep. 261. Demarest *v.* Willard, 8 Cow. Rep. 206.} So as assignee of part may maintain an action *pro tanto;* and if the assignee has warranted the title, or covenanted for the quiet enjoyment of his assignee, he may support an action for a breach, after the assignment, of covenants of warranty and quiet enjoyment, contained in the deed to himself. Kane *v.* Sanger, 14 Johns. Rep. 89. Bickford *v.* Page, 2 Mass. Rep. 460. {See as to the authority of Kane *v.* Sanger, and Bickford *v.* Page, the case of Withy *v.* Mumford, 5 Cow. Rep. 137; and Garlock *v.* Closs, 5 Cow. Rep. 143.} Demarest *v.* Willard, 8 Cow. Rep. 206.}

(33) Withy *v.* Mumford, 5 Cow. Rep. 137. Demarest *v.* Willard, 8 ib. 206.

(34) Vide Bernard *v.* Wilcox, 2 Johns. Cas. 374. 1 Dall. 250; Penn *v.* Butler, 4 ib. 354. Nixon *v.* M'Carty, 2 ib. 65, 66, note, 5. S. & R. 86.

(35) 5 S. & R. 86. The administrator of a deceased partner cannot maintain an action

I. PLAINTIFFS.

When one of several obligees, &c. is dead.

were *several*, the executor of one of them may sue, though the other be living (*e*). In an action at the suit of a surviving partner, he may include a debt due to him in his own separate right (*f*). In the case of a deed, we have seen that it is necessary to declare as surviving obligee, &c. (*g*); and in other actions on contracts, it is necessary to declare as surviving partner, noticing the deceased and his death (*h*) (36). However, in the case of a bill of exchange indorsed in blank, and not specially, to a firm, it is competent to the surviving members to sue, without noticing the death of a partner, who was in the firm when the bill was received (*i*).

5thly, In the case of executors, or administrators, heirs, &c.

In the case of a mere *personal* contract, or of *a covenant not running with the land*, if it were made only with *one* person, and he be dead, the action for the breach of it must be brought in the name of his executor or administrator, in whom the legal interest in such contract is vested (*k*). But on a covenant relating to the *realty*, as for good title, on a deed of conveyance, an *executor* cannot sue even for a breach in the life-time of his testator, [*22] *without showing some special damage to the *personal estate of the latter*, but the action must be brought in the name of the *heir or devisee* (*l*). But the executors and not the *heir* of a purchaser must sue for breach of contract on sale of an estate in fee simple, and the consequent loss of interest and expense (*m*). For the breach of the implied promise of an attorney to investigate the title to a freehold estate, the executor of the purchaser cannot sue, without stating that the testator sustained some actual damage (*n*); and an executor cannot sue for the breach of a promise which impliedly occasions only a personal suffering to the testator, and is not shown to have occasioned a special damage to his estate; as a breach of promise of marriage (*o*) (37). And the 3 & 4 W. 4, c. 42, sect. 2, which only enables an executor or administrator to sue for a *tort* affecting the *personal* or *real estate* of the deceased, does not appear to alter the law in that respect. Where a personal contract was made jointly with *several* persons, then during the life of the survivor of them the action must be brought in his name, (*p*) and upon his death *his* executor or administrator alone can sue, and the personal representatives of the partner who first died cannot be joined (*q*). If there be *several* executors or administrators, they ought all to

(*e*) 1 Saund. 153, n. 1; Burr. 1197; Cro. Eliz. 729.

(*f*) 3 T. R. 433; 5 T. R. 493; 6 T. R. 582; 4 B. & Ald. 374.

(*g*) *Ante*, 15; 1 B. & P. 74.

(*h*) 4 B. & Ald. 374; 2 Stark. 356; 2 Saund. 121, n. 1; *vide* 5 Esp. Rep. 32; 2 T. R. 477; Vin. Ab. Partners, D.; 7 Moore, 583, 584. See 1 Crom. M. & Ros. 900; 5 Tyr. 392; 3 Dowl. 495, S. C.

(*i*) 7 Moore, 579. As to the effect of the death of one of the plaintiffs during the suit, see 8 & 9 W. 3, c. 11, s. 7; Tidd, 9th ed. 934.

(*k*) 2 Hen. Bla. 310; 3 T. R. 393, 401; Com. Dig. Covenant, 1.

(*l*) 2 Lev. 26; 1 Vent. 176, S. C.; 1 M. & Sel. 355; 1 Marsh. 107; 5 Taunt. 418; 4 M. & Sel. 53, 188.

(*m*) 4 M. & Scott, 417; 10 Bing. 51, S. C.

(*n*) 4 Moore, 532; 2 B. & B. 102, S. C. *Sed quære*, whether damage, *viz.* deterioration in value of saleable interest, would not be inferred.

(*o*) 2 M. & Sel. 408.

(*p*) *Ante*, 19.

(*q*) *Id.*

for a partnership demand, notwithstanding an adjustment of all the partnership demands between him and the survivor, by which it was agreed that the proceeds of such demand should be equally divided between them. Peters *v.* Davis, 7 Mass. Rep. 257.

(36) See Holmes *v.* D'Camp, 1 Johns. Rep. 34. Moore *v.* Fenwick, Gilm. R. 214. Pickens *v.* Garnett, 2 Bay's S. C. R. 543.

(37) Lattimore *v.* Simmons, 13 S. & R. 183.

join, though some be under the age of seventeen years, *or have not proved the will* (r); for the grant of a probate to one enures to the benefit of all (s). And it seems, that even the refusal of one of the executors before the ordinary to accept the trust, does not render it necessary to join him as a plaintiff (t). But his formal disclaimer and renunciation in the Ecclesiastical Court, on citation, would probably entitle the other executors to sue without him (u)(38).

1. PLAINTIFFS.

5. Executors, heirs, &c.

If, however, only one of several executors or administrators bring an action either of debt or assumpsit, or in tort, it is settled that the defendant can only take advantage of the nonjoinder of the co-executor or co-administrator, by pleading in abatement, after *oyer* of the probate or letters of administration, that the other executor or administrator therein mentioned is alive and not joined in the action (x) (39). This, it is observable, is a material distinction between the effect of the nonjoinder of a party when he sues in *autre droit*, and when in his own right; in the latter case we have seen that the omission would be a ground of non-suit (y). An executor may sue as such upon a contract made with him in *that character, as for goods sold by him *as* executor, or for money lent as such, and in other cases when the sum to be recovered would be assets (z); and in these cases the cause of action should be stated to have accrued, and the promise to have been made to them "*as* executors" (a). And a party may sue as executor for money had and received to his use in that character, although he was guilty of a *devastavit*, in paying the money sued for to the defendant (b). But executors who contract for the sale of their testator's [*23]

(r) Bro. Executors, 83; Yelv. 130; 1 Salk. 3; 1 Saund. 291 h. n. 4; 4 T. R. 565; 2 Bing. 178; Laking v. Watson, 2 Dowl. 633; 4 Tyr. 839, S. C.; 2 You. & Jer. 75. Effect of the rule in equity, *id.* In Davies v. Williams, 1 Simons' Rep. 5, it was said that the rule at law as well as in equity was, if only one executor has proved he may sue alone, though the others have not renounced.

(s) *Per* Bayley, J., 3 B. & Ald. 363.

(t) 9 Rep. 37 a.; 1 Saund. 291 h. n. 4; 2 You. & Jer. 75.

(u) 4 T. R. 565, *per* Buller, J. See 2 You. & Jer. 77. See as to trustees, *ante*, 12. If a debtor make his creditor and another his executors, and the creditor neither prove the will nor act as executor, he may sue the other for the debt, although he has not renounced, 3 T. R. 557.

(x) 1 Saund. 291 i, k. *Aliter* in the case of assignees of a bankrupt, *post*, 22, 23.

(y) *Ante*, 14.

(z) 6 East, 405; 3 B. & Ald. 360; 2 Chit. Rep. 325; 6 Taunt. 453.

(a) *Id.*

(b) 2 B. & C. 149.

(38) Bodlie v. Hulise, 5 Wend. Rep. 313. The proper practice, where one renounces, is to prosecute in the name of all the executors named in the will, if living, and on summons to those who will not join, there will be judgment of severance; and then the others may proceed and recover in their own names. Ib.

{ (39) In Pennsylvania, it is provided by the 7th section of the Act of 28th March, 1818, (Purd. Dig. 27.) "that no suit, &c. by executors, administrators, trustees, or assignees, shall abate, or the judgment be reversed or set aside, for or by reason of all or any of such executors, administrators, trustees, or assignees, being dead, either at the time of the suit brought, or during the pendency thereof; or by reason of all or any of them being superseded or removed; or the letters testamentary, or of administration being repealed or annulled; but the same may be proceeded in to final judgment, by their legal representatives, upon making the proper suggestions upon the record which the case may require: nor shall any suit or action abate, or the judgment thereon be reversed or set aside, by omission to name on the record any one of the party or parties; but in such case, the names of the parties so omitted may, upon application to the court, be added to the record; and the cause shall thereupon be proceeded in to trial and final judgment, with the same effect, as if such name had been originally inserted in the record." The construction given to this section confines the substitution of parties to the cases of suits by executors, administrators, trustees or assignees; and therefore, where goods were sold to a defendant by a house in England, trading under the name of Thomas Wilson, but consisting of Thomas Wilson, W. Rowlett, and G. Shaw, and an action was brought in the name of Wilson alone, to recover the price, the court refused an application to add the names of Rowlett and Shaw upon the record. Wilson v. Wallace, 8 Serg. & Rawle, 53. }

1. PLAINTIFFS. 6. Executors, heirs, &c.

effects, or make any other agreement in their representative character, are not bound to declare in that capacity, but may sue in their individual right; and in such case it is sufficient to join as plaintiffs such only of the executors as interfered, and were actual parties to the contract with the defendant (c). An executor cannot sue as such upon a penal statute (d). In the case of an aggregate corporation the successors may sue on a contract with, or cause of action vested in, their predecessors (e).

Before the 3 & 4 W. 4, c. 42, sect. 31, executors and administrators who sued at law unsuccessfully for the breach of a supposed contract with the deceased, were *not liable to pay costs, de bonis propriis*, which immunity encouraged many indiscreet and hasty actions; but now executors and administrators are as much liable to pay costs as other unsuccessful plaintiffs, unless the judge who tries the cause certifies so as to *protect them from costs.* So that now a personal representative must fully inquire into the sustainability of an action before it is commenced (*f*).

The right of the *grantee* of a reversion to sue upon a *covenant relating to and running with the estate*, has been already noticed (*g*). In the case of the death of the covenantee seised in fee, the executor may sue at common law upon such covenants, though they affected the realty, as were broken in the *testator's life-time* and actually diminished his personal estate (*h*). But it is only by virtue of the statute 32 Hen. 8, c. 32 (40), that an executor can sue for arrears of rent which accrued to his testator, who was seised in fee or for life (*i*). With regard to such breaches of real covenants as occurred in the [*24] life-time of the ancestor, but *occasioned him no actual damage, or after his death, the action should be brought in the name of his *heir*, or his *devisee*, who, in this respect, is invested with the same rights as would have devolved on the heir (*k*) (41). The heir or devisee need not be expressly named in the cove-

(c) 2 Bing. 177; 9 Moore, 340, S. C.; See *ante*, 13.

(d) Carth. 361; Cro. Eliz. 766; Com. Dig. Administration, B. 15; 2 Hen. Bla. 311.

(e) Com. Dig. Biens, C.; Bac. Ab. Corporations, E. 4; 2 Bla. Com. 430; 3 Burr. 1886.

(*f*) 2 Dowl. Rep. 807; 3 Dowl. 465; 1 Gale, 57.

(*g*) *Ante*, 18, 19.

(*h*) *Ante*, 21. Except in the case of joint-tenancy of the testator with a person who survives. Bac. Ab. Debt, C. Heir, E.; Vin. Ab. Covenant, K. 2 pl. 5; *ante*, 21.

(*i*) The 11 Geo. 2, c. 19, s. 15, gives an executor of a tenant for life the right to sue for a proportion of the rent to the death of the testator, where he dies before the rent was actually due, unless the tenant held under a lease granted pursuant to a leasing power, in which case the whole rent goes to the remainder-man. 1 Chit. Col. Stat. 673 note (*i*); *Ex parte Smyth*, 1 Swanst. 337; 8 Ves. 311; 2 Ves. & B. 334; 1 P. Wms. 177.

(*k*) 1 M. & Sel. 365; 4 *Id.* 53; 5 Taunt. 418; 4 M. & Sel. 188, S. C.; 1 B. & C. 410; see 12 East, 461; Platt on Cov. 513, 519.

---

(40) In force in Pennsylvania, except the 2d section. Roberts' Dig. 254. 3 Binn. 620. By Laws of New York, sess. 36. c. 63. s. 18. 1 R. L. 439, executors or administrators are authorized to sue an action of debt, or to distrain, for arrearages of rent in the life-time of their testator or intestate. (1 R. S. 747.) Independent of these provisions, an executor or administrator may have an action of covenant, on an express covenant in the lease, for the payment of rent in arrear at the death of the testator or intestate. Van Rensselaer's Executors v. Platner's Executors, 2 J. Cas. 17. As to the general rule that the personal representative only shall have an action on a covenant broken in the life-time of his testator or intestate, see *Com. Dig. Administration* (B. 13), *Covenant*, (B. 1.) Hamilton et al. v. Wilson, 4 J. R. 72.

(41) 12 S. & R. 139. But in Pennsylvania an action for the non-performance of an agreement under seal for the conveyance of land, is to be brought by the personal representative of the covenantor, and not by his heir. Watson v. Blaine, 12 S. & R. 131.

I. PLAINTIFFS.

nant in order to entitle him to sue: the slightest indication of an intention that the covenant should not determine with the death of the testator would leave the remedy to the representative of his realty (m). The executor of a termor (although he has demised for a longer term than his own) may support an action on the covenant for the stipulated rent, due since the death of his testator, on the *privity of contract*, though not on any supposed privity of *estate* (n).

5. Executors, heirs, &c.

If an executrix or administratrix marry, she and her husband should join for the breach of any *personal* contract made with the deceased (o); but if she sue alone, the defendant cannot avail himself of the nonjoinder except by a plea in abatement (p); and when a bond or other contract is made to husband and wife as executrix, he may sue alone (q).

When an executor dies after he has proved the will, his executor, or the executor of such executor, is the party to sue on the contract made with the original testator, provided the money to be recovered would be the assets of the representatives of the original testator himself; and the same rule applies in the case of the death of an administrator of the intestate (r). If the money to be recovered would be assets of the original testator, then, in case of the death of his first representative, administration *de bonis non* must be obtained, and the defendant sued accordingly; and, therefore, where A. died intestate, and B. took out administration, and died before the effects were fully administered, and C. took out administration *de bonis non*, and sued D. as acceptor of the bill of exchange indorsed to the administratrix in payment of a debt due to the intestate; it was held that the action was well brought by the administrator *de bonis non* (s). And if a promise be made to the personal *representative of an intestate, the administrator *de bonis non* may sue on it in his character of administrator, and may join such a cause of action with counts upon promises made to the intestate (t). Where an infant is a sole executor, probate is not to be granted to him till he attain the age of twenty-one years, and in the interim administration with the will annexed is to be granted to another person (u). [* 25]

6thly. In the case of Bankruptcy.

In the case of bankruptcy the *legal* rights of the bankrupt arising from contracts made with him, and in the performance whereof the bankrupt is beneficially interested, are, by the express provisions of the Bankrupt Act, transferred to and vested in his assignees (42), which enacts, that the commissioners shall assign all debts due or to be due to the bankrupt, and such assignment

(m) 2 Lev. 92; 2 Saund. 367 a, 371; Platt. on Cov. 517, 518. It is well observed by Mr Platt, that perhaps the best way of putting it is, that the covenant will in all these cases run with the land in favor of the heir, unless an evident intention be manifested to confine it to the covenantee. As to warranty, see Co. Lit. 384 b.

(n) Baker v. Gosling, 1 Bing. N. C. 19, 284; 2 Chitty's Rep. 461; 2 Chit. Pl. 665 a, 5 ed.

(o) Com. Dig. Baron and Feme, V.

(p) 3 T. R. 631; 1 Saund. 291 g.

(q) 4 T. R. 616; 1 Salk. 117.

(r) See Toller, 1st edit. 41, 26. What are such assets, and when representatives of first representative should sue, 1 Vern. 473; Yelv. 33; Cro. Jac. 4; Moore, 680, S. C.

(s) 2 D. & R. 271; 1 B. & C. 150, S. C.; 1 B. & B. 310; Toller, 84.

(t) 7 T. R. 182.

(u) 38 Geo. 3, c. 87; see Toller, 367; Wood's Inst. 14; 3 Burr. 1802.

(42) In the case of assignees appointed under the bankrupt law of a foreign country, the suit must be in the name of the bankrupt, and not of the foreign assignees. Bird et al. v. Caritat, 2 Johns. Rep. 342. So the assignees under the insolvent law of another state must, in the state of New York, sue in the name of the insolvent. Raymond v. Johnson, 11 Johns. Rep. 48.

shall vest the property, right and interest in such debts, in such assignees as fully as if the assurance whereby they are secured had been made to such assignees; and after such assignment, neither the bankrupt, nor any person claiming through or under him, shall have power to recover the same, nor to make any release or discharge thereof, neither shall the same be attached as the debt of the bankrupt by any person, according to the custom of the city of London or otherwise, but such assignees shall have like remedy to recover the same, *in their own names*, as the bankrupt himself might have had if he had not been adjudged bankrupt (v). There are cases, however, in which the bankrupt may sue as trustee for his creditors (w).

The right of action is vested in *all* the assignees jointly, and the nonjoinder of one of them as a plaintiff in an action was considered a ground of nonsuit (x). But in the case deciding that point, the contract declared on was exclusively made with the *assignees*, and therefore they did not altogether sue in *autre droit*; and, in general, when assignees sue on a contract with the bankrupt, there seems no reason why, if two out of three be plaintiffs, the defendant should not be required (if he will set up the objection) to plead the nonjoinder of the third in abatement (y).

Where an action has been commenced by the bankrupt before the bankruptcy, the defendant may defeat the action by specially pleading the bankruptcy and assignment, and the assignees will be compelled to proceed *de novo* in their own names (z).

[*26] *Where one of several assignees has been removed by order of the Chancellor, such order, unless it has been followed up by a re-assignment or release from the removed assignee to the remaining assignees, or by a new assignment by the Commissioners, does not operate to divest the legal interest of the removed assignee, and he is therefore still a necessary party to an action (a) (43). When a fresh assignment to new assignees has been ordered, it is enacted by the 6 Geo. 4, (b) that the debts and personal estate of the bankrupt shall be thereby vested in the new assignees, and that it shall be lawful for them to sue for the same, and to discharge any action or suit and release debts as effectually as the former assignees might have done, and that the new conveyance shall be valid without any conveyance from any former assignee. A new assignee may sue upon a judgment recovered by a former assignee where such judgment was recovered, as well for damages sustained by reason

(v) 6 Geo. 4, c. 16, s. 63. The consent of the creditors to the assignees suing at *law* is not necessary, *vide* sect. 88; 2 Y. & J. 475. As to right of assignees to sue for unliquidated damages, see 2 Bar. & Adol. 727; 9 Bing. 33; and for injury to bankrupt's personal property, 8 Bing. 358.

(w) 1 Bar. & Adol. 459.

(x) Snelgrove v. Hunt, 2 Stark. R. 424; 1 Chit. R. 71; but the contract declared on was made exclusively with the *assignees*, and therefore they did not sue merely in a representative character, see observations in Alivon v. Furnival, 1 Cr. M. & R. 285. 296.

(y) *Quære*, if it ought not to be pleaded in abatement, as in case of nonjoinder of a co-executor; see argument and judgment in Alivon v. Furnival, 1 Cr. M. & Ros. 290. 296.

(z) 15 East, 622; 4 B. & C. 920. That this defence, if it arise after the commencement of the action, must be specially pleaded, and cannot be given in evidence under the general issue, see 4 B. & Ald. 345; 4 B. & C. 390. Where the bankruptcy of the plaintiff occurs after judgment, the action does not abate, and the assignees may proceed therewith to execution, &c. See Tidd, 9th edit. 1115, 1116.

(a) 5 East, 407; 6 Moore, 599; 1 Chit. Rep. 71.

(b) Section 66.

(43) Vide Van Valkenburg v. Elmendorf, 13 J. R. 314.

of injuries committed by the defendant against the bankrupt before his bankruptcy, as against the assignee *as such* after the bankruptcy (c). By the 67th sect. of the 6 Geo. 4, it is provided that "whenever an assignee shall die, or a new assignee or assignees shall be chosen, no action at law or suit in equity shall be thereby abated; but the Court in which any action or suit is depending may, upon the suggestion of such death or removal and new choice allow the name of the surviving or new assignee to be substituted in the place of the former, and such action or suit shall be prosecuted in the name or names of the said surviving or new assignee or assignees, in the same manner as if he or they had originally commenced the same." And under the 6 G. 4, c. 16, s. 67, it has been decided, that a second assignee, who continues by suggestion on the record, a suit commenced by his predecessor, may recover a *penalty* as well as his assignee (d).

1. PLAINTIFFS.

6. Bankruptcy.

Before assignees have been appointed, the provisional assignee (e) may sue; and when assumpsit was brought in the name of the provisional assignee, it was held, that the fact of the bankrupt's estate having been assigned by the provisional assignee to the new assignees, between the time of issuing the latitat and the delivery of the declaration, was no ground of nonsuit upon a plea of non assumpsit (f).

When one of several partners becomes bankrupt, the action must be in the name of the solvent partner and the *assignees of the bankrupt (g) (44); but the Bankrupt Act (h) provides "that the Chancellor, upon petition, may authorize the assignees to use the name of the solvent partner without his consent, provided that such partner, if no benefit be claimed by him by virtue of the proceedings, shall be indemnified against costs, and upon petition the Chancellor may order that he shall receive his share of the proceeds of the action." [*27]

The assignees of two partners, under *separate* commissions against each, may jointly sue for and recover a debt which was due to both the partners; but they cannot recover in the same action a joint debt due to both, and separate debts due to each of the partners (i). When there are several sets of assignees under separate commissions against partners, they may join in suing for a debt due to all the partners, but in such case the declaration should state what the several titles and interests of the plaintiffs are; and if they sue, describing themselves generally as assignees of the bankrupts, it will be a fatal variance (k); but where the plaintiffs sued "as assignees of A. and B. and also as assignees of C." for a joint demand due to the three bankrupts, the declaration was held sufficient, on a motion in arrest of judgment after verdict, since there was nothing upon the record to show that the plaintiffs did not claim under a joint commission against all, or under separate commissions against each of the bankrupts, in either of which cases the action is maintainable (l).

Where there is a *joint* commission against two partners, the assignees may

(c) 10 East, 61.
(d) Bates v. Sturgess, 7 Bing. 585.
(e) 6 Geo. 4, c. 16, s. 47.
(f) 4 B. & Ald. 345. *Quære*, if it had been specially pleaded. It has been doubted whether assignees can sue for a tort committed against the estate of the provisional assignee, 6 Taunt. 358; Eden, 2d edit. 337.
(g) 10 East, 418; 8 T. R. 140; 12 Mod. 446.
(h) 6 Geo. 4, c. 16, s. 89.
(i) 3 T. R. 433.
(k) 8 Taunt. 134; 2 Moore, 3, S. C.
(l) 3 T. R. 779.

(44) Per Kent, Murray v. Murray, 5 J. Ch. R. 703.

1. PLAINTIFFS. 6. Bankruptcy. recover in the same action debts due to the partners jointly, and also debts due to them separately (m); but when the plaintiffs sued as assignees under a joint commission against two partners, and it appeared that only one had in fact committed an act of bankruptcy, it was held, the plaintiffs were not entitled to recover in respect of the interest of the partner who had become a bankrupt (n). The assignees under a joint commission against two partners in an action brought to recover a debt due to one of them, may, and indeed ought, to describe themselves in the declaration as assignees of such partner alone (o).

[*28] *When a contract is made with the assignees after the bankruptcy, it is *not necessary* that they should sue thereon in the character of assignees (p); though, where the sum to be recovered would belong to the estate, they *may* sue as assignees, as where they have lent or paid money in that character (q); but they cannot proceed in the same action both in their own right and as assignees (r) (45).

There are some cases in which, notwithstanding the bankruptcy, an action may be brought in the name of the *bankrupt* himself. Thus, where the bankrupt, prior to his bankruptcy, has assigned over the beneficial interest in a *chose in action* to a third person, the action must be brought in the name of the bankrupt, and not of the assignees (s); for mere trust estates and interests do not pass by the assignment, but only property in which the bankrupt has an equitable or beneficial as well as legal title, and which may be made available towards the payment of his debts (t); but if the bankrupt retained *any* beneficial interest, though he had parted with the rest, it seems the assignees should sue (u).

The bankrupt is also, in several instances, allowed to sue in his own name in respect of property acquired and contracts made by him after the bankruptcy and before he has obtained his certificate; for although the assignment gives to the assignees all property which may accrue in any way to the bankrupt before he obtains his certificate (x), it has been determined in many cases that such property does not vest *absolutely* in the assignees, although they have a right to claim it; but if they forbear from making any claim, the bankrupt has a right against all other persons, and may maintain actions accordingly (y). It has also been held, that where a third person has held out the bankrupt to the world as a party capable of doing a particular act which would confer a right of action upon another, as where he has made a promissory *note payable [*29] to the bankrupt or his order after the bankruptcy, he will be estopped from set-

(m) 4 Bing. 115.
(n) 8 Taunt. 200; 2 Moore, 123, S. C.
(o) 2 Stark. R. 17; 3 Campb. 399; 15 East, 435.
(p) Cowp. 569; 1 Esp. N. P. C. 342.
(q) 2 Chit. Rep. 325; 5 M. & Sel. 294. So as to executor, 3 B. & Ald. 360.
(r) 5 M. & Sel. 297.
(s) 1 T. R. 619; 3 B. & P. 40; 3 B. & Ald. 697; *ante*, 18.
(t) *Ibid.*; and see Eden's B. L. 244, 2d edit.; 7 East, 53.
(u) *Id.*
(x) 6 Geo. 4, c. 16, s. 63, 64.
(y) 2 B. & C. 293; 2 Stra. 1207; 7 T. R. 391; 2 B. & P. 44. *Semble*, the interference and claim of the assignees *after* action brought by the bankrupt would be sufficient to afford a defence, see 3 Moore, 612; and it seems a bankrupt cannot sue as to property acquired *before* the bankruptcy, though the assignees do not interfere, 1 C. & P. 147.

(45) Upon the death of a sole assignee under the late bankrupt law of the United States, the right of action, for a debt due to the bankrupt, vested in the executor of the assignee. Richards and others v. The Maryland Insurance Company, 8 Cranch, 84.

I. PLAINTIFFS. 6. Bankruptcy.

ting up the bankruptcy as an answer to an action brought by a party claiming under the bankrupt (z). But it appears to be fully settled that a bankrupt is incapable of retaining property against his assignees (a); and that, when the dispute is between the bankrupt and a third party, their intervention will at once annihilate all right on the part of the former, such right being entirely conditional upon the non-interference of the assignees (b). It has even been held (c), that if the assignees enter into an express contract with the bankrupt to remunerate him for his work and labor performed in their behalf, he may maintain an action against them upon such contract, but the soundness of this doctrine may reasonably be doubted (d).

When all the creditors of the bankrupt, who have proved under the commission, have been paid in full, the bankrupt is entitled to sue for and recover the remainder of the debts due to him (e).

7thly, In the case of an insolvent debtor.

In the case of *insolvency*, the Insolvent Debtors' Act directs that the prisoner shall, at the time of petitioning for relief, assign all the estate and effects he is then possessed of, and all future effects which may come to him, before he shall become entitled to his discharge, to the provisional assignee of the Court (f). And it is enacted (g), "That it shall be lawful for the provisional assignee to sue in his own name (46). *if the Court shall so order*, for the recovering, obtaining, and enforcing, of any estate, debts, effects, or rights, of any such prisoner: and that all the real and personal estate, money, and effects, vested in or possessed by such provisional assignee, by virtue of such conveyances and assignments so to be made by such prisoners shall not remain in him, if he shall resign or be removed from his office, nor in his heirs, executors, or administrators, in case of his death, but shall go and be vested in his successor in office." It has been held on the provisions of former insolvent acts, the enactments of which were in this respect of nearly a similar *description [*30] to those above noticed, that the provisional assignee may proceed in ejectment for the recovery of property assigned to him, without applying for the leave of the Insolvent Debtors' Court; that it was not necessary to prove upon the trial that such Court had authorized the proceedings (h); and that the Court in which the action was brought would not, at the instance of a *defendant*, interfere to stay the proceedings in such an action, on the ground of no such authority having been obtained (i). By a subsequent section (k), the Insolvent Court is empowered at any time, after the filing of the prisoner's petition, to appoint assignees for the purposes of the act, and, immediately upon

(z) 2 B. & C. 293; 2 B. & P. 48.
(a) Cowp. 570; 3 B. & Ald. 235; 3 B. & P. 565.
(b) 7 East, 53; 1 B. & B. 282.
(c) 4 Taunt. 754.
(d) See 3 B. & Ald. 232; 4 Taunt. 759.
(e) 6 Geo. 4, c. 16, s. 132.
(f) 7 Geo. 4, c. 57, s. 11, continued and amended by 1 Wm. 4, c. 38.
(g) 7 Geo. 4, c. 57, s. 16.
(h) 3 Bing. 203; 10 Moore, 7, S. C.
(i) 3 Bing. 370; S. P. Casborne v. Barsham, in Vice Chancellor's Court, 2d July, 1835.
(k) Sect. 19.

{(46) In Pennsylvania, by the 4th sect. of the act of 26th March, 1814, (Purd. Dig. 278.) the trustee or trustees of an insolvent debtor "shall be capable in his or their own names to sue for and recover any property or debts belonging to such debtor at the time of his or their appointment." See Cooper v. Henderson, 6 Binn. 189. Kennedy v. Ferris, 5 Serg. & Rawle, 394. Testor v. Robinson, 7 Serg. & Rawle, 188. Stoever v. Stoever, 9 Serg. & Rawle, 434. See Winchester v. The Union Bank of Maryland, 2 Harr. & Gill, 73. 79.}

1. PLAINTIFFS.

7. Insolvency.

such assignee accepting the office, the estate and effects of the prisoner vested in the provisional assignee, are to be assigned by the provisional assignee to the assignees so appointed. And it is declared, that, after such assignment, "All the estate and effects of the prisoner shall be, to all intents and purposes, as effectually and legally vested in such assignee or assignees as if the said conveyance and assignment had been made by such prisoner to him or them: Provided nevertheless, that no act done under or by virtue of such first conveyance and assignment shall be thereby rendered void or defeated, but shall remain as valid as if no such relation had taken place." And it is afterwards enacted (l), "That it shall be lawful for the assignee or assignees of such prisoner, and such assignee or assignees is and are thereby empowered to sue from time to time, as there may be occasion, in his or their own name or names, for the recovering, obtaining, and enforcing of any estate, effects, or rights of such prisoner." It is also provided (m), that upon the death or removal of assignees, or the appointment of new assignees, no action or suit shall be thereby abated, but that the Court in which such action or suit is depending, may, upon the suggestion of such death or removal and new appointment, allow the names of the new assignees to be substituted in the place of the former; and that such action or suit shall be prosecuted in the names of the surviving or new assignees in the same manner as if it had been originally commenced by them. There is no clause rendering it necessary for the assignees to apply to the creditors, or to the Insolvent Court, for authority to commence an action at law.

[*31] *From the above provisions it will be seen, that many of the decisions relative to actions by the assignees of a bankrupt (n), will be applicable to the case of actions by the assignees of an insolvent debtor.

It has been determined, upon the 11th and 19th sections of the above-mentioned act, that the death of an insolvent, after the assignment to the provisional assignee, but before the assignment to the assignee in chief, does not affect the validity of the latter assignment, but that all the rights of the provisional assignee pass to the assignee in chief (o).

When an action was brought by a person who had assigned his property under an insolvent act, for a debt due to him before his assignment, the assignee refusing to sue, the Court have refused to interfere in a summary manner to stay the proceedings (p). And it appears to be considered that an insolvent debtor, in the absence of any claim by his assignees, possesses a similar right to that possessed by a bankrupt against third persons, in respect to property and contracts which his assignees might claim the benefit of, if they chose to interfere (q).

The assignees of a person discharged under the *Lords' Act* are also authorized to sue for the recovery of the estate and effects of the party discharged (r).

8thly. In the case of *marriage*.

The effect of *marriage*, at least in Courts of *law*, is to deprive the wife of all separate legal existence, her husband and herself being in law but one per-

(l) Sect. 24.
(m) Sect. 26.
(n) See *ante*, 24 to 29.
(o) 4 Bing. 392.
(p) 6 Taunt. 123; 1 Marsh. 477, S. C. See 3 Campb. 13. 236.
(q) 4 B. & C. 419, 420; 1 C. & P. 146, 147.
(r) 32 Geo. 2, c. 28, s. 12, s. 17, and other statutes. See Tidd, 9th edit. 375.

son(*s*) (47), though in the Ecclesiastical Courts a wife may sue alone for a legacy, &c. (*t*). It is therefore a general rule, that she cannot, during the marriage, maintain an action without her husband; either upon contracts made by her before or after the marriage (*u*), although they may be living apart under the provisions of a formal deed of separation (*x*); or by virtue of a divorce *à mensa et thoro*, for adultery (*y*); or he may have left the country and deserted her (*z*). The exceptions are in the instances of a divorce *à vinculo matrimonii* (*a*), or where the *husband is dead in law (48) by reason of his transportation under a judicial sentence (*b*) (49). Where the husband has been abroad, and not heard of for seven years, his death will be presumed (*c*).

I. PLAINTIFFS.

8. Marriage.

[*32]

All *chattels* personal of the wife, in possession, are by marriage absolutely given to the husband, and for the recovery of them he may sue alone (*d*); and in a late case, where a bill of exchange was payable to a feme sole, who intermarried *before the same was due*, it was held, that the husband might sue in his own name without joining the wife, although the latter had not indorsed the bill, such a bill or a note not being a mere *chose in action* (*e*). And it is a general principle, "that that which the husband may discharge alone, and of which he may make disposition to his own use, for the recovery of this he may sue without his wife" (*f*).

As mere *choses in action* of the wife do not by the marriage vest absolutely in the husband until he reduce them in possession, and if not reduced into

(*s*) Lit. sect. 28; Bac. Abr. Baron and Feme, M.

(*t*) Norris *v.* Hemingway, 1 Hagg. R. 4; 2 Add. R 151. Capel *v.* Roberts, 3 Hagg. Ecc. Rep. 161, in note; 2 Chitty's Gen. Prac. 467.

(*u*) *Supra*, note (*s*); 4 T. R. 361; 2 B. & P. 93.

(*x*) 8 T. R. 545; 2 New Rep. 148; 2 B. & C. 555. A deed providing for *future* separation was considered void, 6 B. & C. 200; but see 3 Chit. Gen. Prac. 129.

(*y*) 3 B. & C. 291.

(*z*) 11 East, 301.

(*a*) 3 B. & C. 297.

(*b*) 2 Bla. Rep. 1197; 1 T. R. 7; 2 B. & P. 231; 4 Esp. Rep. 27; 3 B. & C. 297.

(*c*) 2 Camp. 113, 273; 1 Jac. 1, c. 11, s. 2; 1 Bla. Rep. 404; 6 East, 80.

(*d*) 3 T. R. 631; Co. Lit. 351 b; Com. Dig. Bar. & Feme, E. 3.

(*e*) 1 B. & Ald. 218. He alone may petition for a commission of bankruptcy, upon a note given to his wife *dum sola*, 1 G. & J. 1.

(*f*) Per Doddridge, J. in 3 Bulst. 164, recognized in 1 B. & Ald. 224.

(47) The legality of a marriage may be tried in a personal action in Pennsylvania (not brought for crim. con.). Hantz *v.* Sealy, 6 Binn. 405. Vide Fenton *v.* Reed, 4 J. R. 52; Newburyport *v.* Boothbay, 9 Mass. R. 414.

(48) A person sentenced to imprisonment in the state prison, for life, is *civiliter mortuus*. Deming's Case, 10 Johns. Rep. 232. { Deming's Case does not decide, that a person sentenced to imprisonment for life in the state prison is *civiliter mortuus* by the common law—the *civil death*, referred to in that case, was the consequence of the provisions of the act of 29th March, 1799. Chancellor KENT has recently decided, that such a sentence prior to the 29th March, 1799, was not productive of *civil death*. Platner *v.* Sherwood, 6 Johns. Cha. Rep. 118. See 2 Rev. Stat. 701, sect. 19. } A divorce *à vinculo matrimonii* restores the woman to the condition of a *feme sole*. Bac. Abr. Marriage and Divorce (E) 3. In the state of New York a divorce *à vinculo matrimonii* may be obtained on account of adultery in either of the parties. and if granted on the application of the wife, she is secured in the enjoyment of lands which she may be the owner of; or goods, chattels, or choses in action, in her possession; (which were left with her by her husband, which she may have acquired by her own industry, or which may have been given her by devise or otherwise, or may have come to her, or to which she may have been entitled by the decease of any relative intestate;) at the time of pronouncing the decree; for which she may sue the defendant (the husband) in her own name. Sess. 36. c. 102. s. 6. 2 R. L. 199. { For the several Acts of Assembly in Pennsylvania, see Purdon's Digest, p. 128. and notes. }

{ (49) Wright *v.* Wright's Ex. 2 Desaus. Cha. Rep. 244 See Rhea *v.* Rhenner, 1 Peters' Sup. Ct. Rep. 105. So where the husband abjures the realm, Cornwall *v.* Hoyt, 7 Conn. Rep. 420,) or deserts her in a foreign country, Gregory *v.* Paul, 15 Mass. Rep. 31. }

I. PLAINTIFFS.

3. Marriage.

possession, she would take them by survivorship, in general he cannot sue alone (50), but must join his wife in all actions upon bonds, and other personal contracts, made with the wife *before* the marriage, whether the breach were before or during the coverture; and also for rent or any other cause of action accruing before the marriage, in respect of the real estate of the wife(*g*)(51). There are, indeed, decisions and opinions which appear to militate against this rule (*h*); but the current of authorities seems fully to establish it, and it is observable that it prevails also in equity and in cases of bankruptcy (*i*); and that the rule is the [*33] same when the action is brought on a contract *made by a feme whilst sole, in which case the husband cannot be sued alone (*k*). And when the wife is executrix or administratrix, as her interest is in *autre droit* (52), they must in general join in the action (*l*). But if in respect of a contract made to the wife whilst sole, the party thereto, after the marriage, give a bond to the husband and wife, or in respect to some new consideration, as forbearance, &c., make a written or parol promise to the husband and wife, they may join, or the husband may sue alone upon such new contract (*m*). If such bond or fresh promise were made to the husband alone, he alone can sue thereon, the wife not being privy to the new contract (*n*); but they may jointly sue on the original contract in cases where it is not merged by a higher security. If a bond be given to a husband and wife administratrix, he may declare on it as a bond made to himself (*o*).

In general, the wife cannot join in an action upon a contract made during the marriage, as for her work and labor, goods sold, or money lent by her during that time (*p*); for the husband is entitled to her earnings, and they shall not survive to her, but go to the personal representatives of the husband, and she could have no property in the money lent or the goods sold (*q*). But when the wife can be considered as the *meritorious* cause of action, as if a bond or

(*g*) 3 T. R. 631; 1 M. & Sel. 180, 181; Com. Dig. Bar. & Feme, V.; Bac. Abr. Bar. & Feme, K.; 1 Roll. Ab. 347, R. pl. 3; 2 Ves. 676, 677; Bul. N. P. 179; 10 Ves. 578; 3 Mod. 186; 2 Wils. 423; 1 Hen. Bla. 109; 1 B. & Ald. 222, 223.

(*h*) 3 Lev. 403; Selw. N. P. 295, 5th edit.; Co. Lit. 351 a, 396, n. 2; 7 T. R. 319; 1 Vern. 396.

(*i*) 1 M. & Sel. 176; 2 Freem. 160; Bac. Abr. Baron & Feme, K.; 15 Ves. 495; 1 B. & Ald. 222, 223.

(*k*) 7 T. R. 348.

(*l*) Vin. Ab. Bar. & Feme, Q. 22; Com. Dig. Bar. & Feme, V.

(*m*) 1 M. & Sel. 180; 4 T. R. 616; 1 Salk. 117; Ld. Raym. 368.

(*n*) See *id.*; Cro. Jac. 110; Yelv. 89; 1 Saund. 210.

(*o*) 4 T. R. 616.

(*p*) 2 Bla. Rep. 1239; 1 Salk. 114; Com. Dig. Bar. & Feme, W.; 2 Wils. 424; 9 East, 472. Where the wife is separated from her husband, she may in some cases, without his concurrence, sue in his name, 9 East, 471.

(*q*) *Id. ibid.*; Cro. Jac. 644; 2 Wils. 424; 2 Bl. Rep. 1237; Carth. 251. *Semble*, that although by the laws of a foreign country, husband and wife, natives of that country, and resident there, may be partners in trade, they cannot jointly sue here for a debt due to the firm, R. & M. Rep. 102.

(50) See, however, Cornwall *v.* Hoyt, 7 Conn. R. 420. In all actions for choses in action due to the wife before marriage, the husband and wife must join. The true rule is, that in all cases where the cause of action by law survives to the wife, the husband cannot sue alone. Clapp *v.* Inhabitants of Stoughton, 10 Pick. R. 463.

(51) Morse *v.* Earle et al., 13 Wend. R 271. It is well settled that the husband cannot be sued alone, upon a contract of the wife when sole and before marriage. 15 J. R. 403, 402, 8 ib. 150. Neither should he be permitted to prosecute alone upon such a contract. Reeve Dom. Rel. ch. 10, p. 126. As a husband cannot maintain a suit in his own name, to recover a demand which accrued to his wife before marriage under a contract made with her, the wife *must* be joined in the action. So also where a husband performs the stipulations of a contract entered into by his wife before marriage, which if performed by her whilst sole would have given her a right of action, the action for the recovery of a demand thus arising must be brought in the joint names of husband and wife. Morse *v.* Earle et al., 13 Wend R. 271.

(52) So, where the wife is guardian in socage. Byrne *v.* Van Hoesen, 5 J. R. 66.

other contract under seal, or a promissory note, be made to her separately, or with her husband (r), or if she bestow her personal labor and skill in curing a wound, &c. (s), she may join with the husband, or he may sue alone (53). 8. Marriage.

Where the wife is joined in the action, in these cases the *declaration must distinctly disclose her interest, and show in what respect she is the meritorious cause of action, and there is no intendment to this effect (t). [*34] In the case of a bond or note payable to her or to her husband and herself, it would sufficiently appear from the instrument itself, as set out in the declaration, without further averment, that she had a peculiar interest, justifying the use of her name as a plaintiff (u). But care should be taken that the declaration does not embrace a cause of action which affords the husband only a right to sue. Therefore where husband and wife declared for a debt due for a cure effected by the wife during their marriage, and the declaration also contained a charge for medicines supplied, "upon general demurrer it was objected that the wife could not join, for that she was not the sole cause of action, because the medicines were the husband's own property, and the damages could not be severed, and of that opinion was the Court." (x)

A feme covert *executrix* must join in an action upon an implied promise in respect of the estate of the deceased; as if money, part of the assets of the testator, be received by a party after the coverture, the husband cannot, it seems, sue alone in assumpsit, as for money had and received to his use, but he and his wife should join, and declare in the character of executrix (y).

For rent, or other cause of action accruing during the marriage, on a lease or demise, or other contract relating to the land or other real property of the wife, whether such contract were made before or during the coverture, the husband and wife *may join*, or *he may sue alone* (z). When a lease for years has been granted to husband and wife, and the lessor evicts them, they may join, or the husband may sue alone (a); and in all actions for a profit, &c.

(r) 3 Lev. 403; Stra. 230; 4 T. R. 616; Co. Lit. 351 a, note 1, 120; 2 M. & Sel. 393. 395.

(s) 2 Sid. 128; Cro. Jac. 77; 2 Wils. 424. See Bac. Abr. Bar. & Feme, K.

(t) 2 Bla. Rep. 1236; 2 M. & Sel. 396. In *replevin* by husband and wife for taking their goods, it may perhaps be presumed *after verdict*, though it would not be so on demurrer, (2 New Rep. 405), that the taking was before coverture, and that they then were jointly possessed, or that she was entitled as executrix, &c. in either of which cases she might be joined, *post*.

(u) 2 M. & Sel. 393, 396.

(x) Holmes and wife *v.* Wood, cited in 2 Wils. 424, noticed by Lord Ellenborough in 3 M. & Sel. 396.

(y) 1 Salk. 282; Com. Dig. Bar. & Feme, V.

(z) Stra. 229; 1 Wils. 224; Com. Dig. Bar. & Feme, X. Y.

(a) Bro. Abr. Bar. & Feme, pl. 25; 2 Mod. 217; Cro. Jac. 399; Bulst. 163.

(53) A gift or bequest to the wife is in effect a gift or bequest to the husband, and he cannot be deprived of it, without an unequivocal intention manifested by the donor or the testator, that he is to have no interest or part in it. Evans *v.* Knorr, 4 S. & R. R. 66. Marriage is an absolute gift to the husband of the wife's personal chattels in possession; and so it is also of choses in action, if he reduce them into possession by receiving or recovering them at law. Commonwealth *v.* Manly et al., 12 Pick. R. 173. 8 ib. 218. But a legacy given to the wife, and to be paid to her when she is divorced from her husband or voluntarily withdraws from him; *held*, that she became entitled to the legacy for her sole and separate use, without the intervention, and beyond the control of her husband. Perry *v.* Boileau, 10 S. & R. R. 208. If a bond or obligation be made to husband and wife, the wife would have it by survivorship. Thus, where the plaintiff's intestate joined in a conveyance of the wife's land, and the grantee executed a promissory note to the husband and wife together with a mortgage as collateral security. Upon the death of the husband and marriage of the wife with the defendant, who was sued in trover for a conversion of the note; but the court decided that the plaintiff was not entitled to recover; because the wife had it by survivorship. Draper's Adm'x *v.* Jackson and wife, 16 Mass. R. 480.

I. PLAINTIFFS. — 8. Marriage.

accruing *during coverture* in right of the *real* estate of the wife, they *may join, or the husband may sue alone, as in debt, for not setting out tithes payable to the wife (*b*).

The effect of joining the wife in an action when the husband might sue alone is, that if the husband die whilst it is pending, or after judgment, and before it is satisfied, the interest in the cause of action will survive to the wife, and not to the executors of the husband, though if he sued alone she would have had no interest (*c*). A feme covert, being a sole trader, according to the custom of London, can only sue and be sued in the city courts, and even there the husband must be joined for conformity (*d*) (54). If a right accrue or injury be committed to a feme covert whilst living separate from her husband, an indemnity should be tendered to the husband against costs, after which, even without his consent, an action may be brought in his name, either separately or jointly with his wife, according to the then circumstances of the case (*e*); but the indemnity should be previously tendered, or the court might stay proceedings (*f*).

If the *husband survive* (*g*), there is a material distinction between chattels real and *choses in action*. The husband is entitled to the chattel real by survivorship, and to all rent, &c. accruing during the coverture; he is also entitled to all chattels given to the wife during the coverture in her own right (*h*), though not to her rights in *autre droit* (*i*). But mere *choses in action*, or contracts made with the wife before coverture, do not survive to the husband, and he must, to recover the same, sue as administrator of his wife (*k*)(55). So, the administrator of a husband, who survived his wife, and died without taking

(*b*) Com. Dig. Bar. & Feme, X.; 2 Wils. 423, 424; Cro. Jac. 399; Cro. Eliz. 608.

(*c*) Co. Lit. 351 a, n. 1; Cro. Jac. 77. 205; 2 Bl. Rep. 1236.

(*d*) 2 B. & P. 93; 4 T. R. 361.

(*e*) Chambers *v.* Donaldson, 9 East, 471; 4 Bar. & Ald. 419, *post*.

(*f*) Morgan and wife *v.* Thomas, 2 C. & M. 388.

(*g*) As to the effect of survivorship in general between baron and feme, see Bac. Abr. Executors and Administrators, H. 4; 2 Bla. Com. 433 to 436; Co. Lit. 351, n. 1; Com. Dig. Bar. & Feme, F. 1, E. 2, 3, Z. (2 A.); 1 M. & Sel. 180.

(*h*) Com. Dig. Bar. & Feme, E. 2, 3, Z.; 2 Bla. Com. 424; Co. Lit. 351 a, note 1.

(*i*) *Id. Ibid.*; 4 T. R. 616; 1 Roll. Ab. 889, pl. 10; Dyer, 331 a.

(*k*) Com. Dig. Bar. & Feme, E. 3; 2 Bla. Com. 435; 3 Mod. 186; 2 Ves. sen. 676; Rep. temp. Talb. 173; Co. Lit. 351, n.

{(54) *Aliter* in Pennsylvania. Act of 22d Feb. 1718, sect. 1. Purd. Dig. 298. 1 Sm. Laws, 99.}

A husband cannot convey an estate by deed to his wife. Martin *v.* Martin, 1 Greenl. R. 398. Post-nuptial contracts are sanctioned upon the principle that the convenience and interest of families require such exchanges. Thus, it was held that a conveyance made in trust for the wife, after marriage upon the transfer to him by the wife, of an equivalent out of her property, will be established both at law and in equity. But such contracts must be honest; not feigned or pretended. Bullard *v.* Briggs, 7 Pick. R. 533.

(55) Although the husband cannot sue for a debt due his wife, *dum sola*, after her death, without obtaining letters of administration, yet the necessity of doing this has relation merely to the *mode*, and not the *right* of reducing her *choses in action* into possession; the right to them resides in no other person; if he gain possession of them without suit, his title is as perfect as though he had taken out letters of administration; if he die without reducing them into possession, the right to them survives to his, and not the wife's representatives, and if any other person obtain the possession, he can hold only as trustee for the husband or his representatives. Whitaker *v.* Whitaker, 6 Johns. Rep. 112. Co. Litt. 351. a. n. 1. {See, however, Cornwall *v.* Hoyt, 7 Conn Rep. 420. Beach *v.* Norton, 8 Conn. Rep. 71. Griswold *v.* Penniman, 2 Conn. Rep. 564.}

Where a legacy had been left to the wife, and the husband had been absent, so that the wife obtained a divorce dissolving the ties of matrimony; *held*, that the wife was entitled to the legacy. Wintercast *v.* Smith, 4 Rawle's R. 177.

out administration to her effects, cannot recover her *choses in action*, and for the latter purpose administration must be taken out to the wife (*l*). And he may sue as administrator on a bond to his wife during coverture (*m*). And if pending an action by husband and wife for such *chose in action*, the wife die, the suit abates (*n*); but if they obtain judgment, he may, notwithstanding her subsequent death, issue execution, or support an action of debt on such judgment (*o*). He is entitled to sue or distrain for arrears of rent which became due in the life-time of his wife, from persons who were tenants of her freehold property (*p*). But the husband cannot sue for arrears of rent accruing after the death of his wife, on a lease of her land by himself and wife under seal during coverture, in which the lessee *covenanted with the husband and wife and the *heirs* of the *wife* (*q*). [*36]

If the *wife survive*, she is entitled to all chattels real which her husband had in her right, and which he did not dispose of in his life-time, and to arrears of rent, &c. which became due during the coverture, upon her antecedent demise, or upon their joint demise (*r*) during the coverture, to which she assents after his death; and to all arrears of rent and other *choses in action* to which she was entitled before the coverture, and which the husband did not reduce into actual possession (*s*). She also takes by survivorship a debt due upon a judgment recovered by husband and wife (56), whether obtained for a debt due to the wife whilst sole (*t*), or upon a contract made with the wife during coverture, where she is the meritorious cause of action (*u*); and she is entitled to a bond given to her and her husband (*x*), or to her alone (*y*); she is also entitled to all rights of action in *autre droit* as executrix or administratrix (*z*). And where, during coverture of an administratrix, her husband joined with two sureties in a note for money lent to the husband, out of the estate vested in the wife as administratrix, it was held, that *after the death of her husband* she might sue the other two parties to the note (*a*). In all these cases where the wife is joined in the action, if the husband die pending the suit, it will not abate, and the wife may proceed to judgment and execution, the death of the husband being suggested upon the record (*b*)(57). And when a feme executrix marries a debtor to the testator, the right of action is only suspended during the coverture, and if she survive, she may, in her character of executrix, sue the executors of the husband (*c*). But if the husband made a separate demise of the wife's land, his executor will

(*l*) Betts *v.* Kempton, 2 B. & Adol. 273.
(*m*) 2 M. & Sel. 396, 397.
(*n*) 6 B. & C 253.
(*o*) 3 Mod. 189, notes (*g*) (*h*).
(*p*) 32 Hen. 8, c. 37, s. 3.
(*q*) 2 Bingh. 112; 4 B. & C. 529, S. C. in error.
(*r*) Not if the husband demise alone. *Dict.* Sir J. Mansfield, 2 Taunt. 181; 1 Roll. Ab. 350 d.
(*s*) 1 Roll. Ab. 350; Co. Lit. 351 a; Com. Dig. Bar. & Feme, F. 1.
(*t*) Com. Dig. Bar. & Feme, F. 1; 2 Bla. Com. 434; 2 Ves. sen. 676; 1 Vern. 396.
(*u*) 2 Bla. Rep. 1239; Cro. Jac. 77. 205; Co. Lit. 351 a, n. 1; 1 Vern. 396.
(*x*) 2 P. W. 496.
(*y*) 2 M. & Sel. 396, 397, n. b.
(*z*) 4 T. R. 616; Com. Dig. Bar. & Feme, F. 1.
(*a*) Richards *v.* Richards, 2 Bar. & Adol. 447.
(*b*) 8 & 9 W. 3, c. 11, s. 7; Rep. temp. Hardw. 397 to 399.
(*c*) Cro. Eliz. 114; 3 Atk. 726.

(56) Gibson *v.* Todd, adm., 1 Rawle, 452. Hammick *v.* Bronson, 5 Day's R. 290.
(57) Vide Schoonmaker's Ex'rs *v.* Elmendorf, 10 J. R. 49. Vaughan *v.* Wilson, 4 Hen. & Munf. 452.

I. PLAINTIFFS. — 8. Marriage.

be entitled to the rent which became due before his death, and not his surviving wife (*d*).

The *consequences of a mistake* in the proper parties, in the case of baron and feme, are, that when a married woman might be joined in the action with her husband, but sues alone, the objection can only be pleaded in abate-
[*37] ment (58), and not in bar, though the husband might sustain a writ of *error (*e*), and if she marry after writ, and before plea, her coverture must be pleaded in abatement, and cannot be given in evidence under the general issue (*f*). But when a feme improperly sues alone, having no legal right of action, she will be nonsuited (*g*); and if she improperly join in an action with her husband, who ought to sue alone, the defendant may demur (*h*), or the judgment will be arrested (*i*), or reversed on a writ of error (*k*). And if the husband sue alone, when the wife ought to be joined, either in her own right, or in *autre droit*, he will be nonsuited (*l*); or if the objection appear on the record, it will be fatal in arrest of judgment or on error (*m*).

II. WHO TO BE DEFENDANTS.

II. DEFENDANTS. — 1st. As between the *original* parties, and with reference to the *liability* of the party.

The action upon an *express* contract, whether it be by deed, or merely in writing, or by parol, must in general be brought against the party who made it, either in person or by agent (*n*). And although in the case of a deed *inter partes*, an individual not named as a party cannot sue thereon, although it contain a covenant with him, and for his benefit (*o*), yet this rule does not protect from liability a party who executes such a deed containing a covenant by him, although he is not described as a party thereto (*p*).

And a party who expressly contracts, and permits credit to be given to him, is liable, although he were not the strict *legal owner* of the property in respect of which the contract is made, nor *beneficially* interested. Thus the owner of a ship is *prima facie* liable for repairs necessarily done to it (*q*); but where the legal title to a vessel remained for some time after the sale in the vendor, and during that time the captain, by the direction of the purchaser,
[*38] ordered repairs, it was decided that the vendor was *not liable for the amount (*r*)(60). So the mortgagee of a ship is not liable for wages or repairs

(*d*) 2 Taunt. 181.
(*e*) 3 T. R. 631.
(*f*) 6 T. R. 265; Bac. Abr. Abatement, G. It would be pleadable *puis darrein continuance* in abatement, if it occurred after the defendant had pleaded in chief to the declaration. See Tidd, 9th edit. 849 (59).
(*g*) 4 T. R. 361.
(*h*) 1 Salk. 114; 1 Hen. Bla. 108; 2 Wils. 424.
(*i*) Cro. Jac. 644.
(*k*) 2 Bla. Rep. 1236.
(*l*) 1 Salk. 282; Bac. Abr. Bar. & Feme, K.; 1 M. & Sel. 180, 181.
(*m*) 1 Stra. 229; Cro. Jac. 424.
(*n*) 8 East, 12; 3 Esp. R. 27; 3 Campb. 354. 356.
(*o*) *Ante*, 3.
(*p*) Carth. 76; Holt, R. 210, S. C.; Platt on Cov. 7, 8.
(*q*) 2 Campb. 339. 517; 4 B. & A. 352; Cowp. 636. See also 8 East, 10; 11 Id. 435; 13 Id. 238.
(*r*) 8 East, 10. See 13 East, 238; 16 Id. 169; 2 Campb. 517.

(58) Vide Newton *v.* Robinson, Tayl. 72.
(59) Wilson *v.* Hamilton, 4 S. & R. 238.
(60) Vide Wendover et al. *v.* Hogeboom et al., 7 J. R. 308. Hussey *v.* Allen et al., 6 Mass. R. 163. In the case last cited, neither the plaintiff nor the master had notice of the previous transfer.

where the party claiming the debt was employed by the mortgagor (*s*), or expressly gave him credit (*t*). So if an executor trustee carry on trade as trustee for the benefit of the children of the testator, he will be personally liable to pay the debts, and may even be made a bankrupt in respect of them (*u*).

II. DEFENDANTS.

1. Who legally liable.

In the case of an *express* contract, the agreement itself will, therefore, in general, remove all difficulty with regard to the person who should be sued upon it.

In cases where a contract can only be implied.

But difficulties frequently occur in deciding who should be made the defendant in an action upon a promise created or *implied by law* from a particular state of facts. In this case it must be ascertained who is the party subject to the *legal liability*; for he is the person who should be sued (*x*). A mere *equitable* or *moral* obligation to pay a demand is, in the absence of an express promise, insufficient to support an action (*y*) (61). And there are some instances in which even an express promise will give no additional force to mere equitable liability, as in the case of a promise, without any new consideration, to pay a legacy (*z*), or the share of an intestate's effects to which the plaintiff is entitled under the Statute of Distributions (*a*). In these cases, the subject-matter is more peculiarly within the province of the Courts of Equity, and a Court of Common Law cannot so effectually do justice between all parties; and therefore will not recognize even an express promise so as to allow an action to be brought thereon.

When or not against a trustee.

The general rule is, that a *cestui que trust* cannot sue his trustee at law (*b*). But if a trustee state an account, and admit a balance due from him to the *cestui que trust*, he may be sued at law (*c*).

Against Agents, &c.

A contract made by an *agent*, as such, is in law the contract of the principal; *Qui facit per alium facit per se*. The assent of the agent is the assent of the principal; the former is the mere conduit or medium by which the contract is effected, and is not clothed with any legal or beneficial interest in it which can render him responsible upon the agreement (*d*), although in some instances he may sue thereon (*e*). The general rule therefore is, that when a person has contracted, in the capacity of an *agent*, and that circumstance *is [*39] known at the time to the person with whom he contracts, such agent is not liable to an action for non-performance of the contract (*f*), even for a deceit-

(*s*) 3 Campb. 354.

(*t*) 7 B. & C. 30; Ry. & M. N. P. C. 199; 2 Bingh. 179; 9 Moore, 344, S. C.

(*u*) Viner *v.* Cadell, 3 Esp. Rep. 88.

(*x*) 2 Hen. Bla. 563; 1 Hen. Bla. 93.

(*y*) See Chit. jun. on Con. 10.

(*z*) 5 T. R. 690; 7 B. & C. 544.

(*a*) 7 B. & C. 542.

(*b*) 1 Holt. N. P. C. 641. See 2 Moore, 240; 8 Taunt. 263, S. C.; Sand. on Uses, 222; 2 Bro. C. C. 265. See further and qualification of that rule, 1 Chitty's Gen. Prac. 6, 7, 8.

(*c*) 1 Harr. & Wol. 167.

(*d*) 3 Chit. Com. Law, 194. 211; Paley, Prin. & Agent, 251. Who may be an agent, Co. Lit. 52 a.

(*e*) *Ante*, 7, 8.

(*f*) See rule and principle, 12 Ves. 352; 15 East, 62. 66; Paley, Prin. and Agent, 246; 3 Campb. 317; 2 M. & Sel. 438; 2 Taunt. 387.

(61) A moral obligation is available as a consideration for an *express* promise, in those cases only, where a prior legal obligation has existed, which, by reason of some statute, or stubborn rule of law, cannot now be enforced. Cook *v.* Bradley, 7 Conn. R. 57.

II. DEFENDANTS.

1. Who legally liable.

ful warranty (*g*), if he had authority (62) from his principal to make the contract (*h*). For the same reasons, if an attorney "for and on the behalf of his client, and as his agent," promise to pay money, he is not personally liable if he had authority from his client (*i*) (63). And where a trader, after an act of bankruptcy, employed an auctioneer to sell goods, who sent him the proceeds by the hands of the defendant, it was decided that the assignees could not sue the latter for the money (*j*). So where A., an auctioneer, being employed to sell an estate belonging to B., entered into and signed an agreement with C. for the purchase, in his own name, as agent of B., and B. shortly afterwards signed it, and added, "I hereby sanction this agreement, and approve of A.'s having signed the same on my behalf," it was held A. was not personally liable (*k*).

But if an agent covenant under seal for the act of another, though he describe himself in the deed as contracting for and on the part and behalf of such other person (*l*) (64); or if he accept or draw a bill of exchange generally and not as agent, he is personally liable, (*m*) unless in the case of an agent on behalf of government (*n*) (65). So where the defendant by a written agreement, expressed to be made "by himself on behalf of A. B. of the one part, and the plaintiff of the other part," stipulated that he the defendant would execute to the plaintiff a lease of certain premises, which, as it was proved, belonged to A. B., Best, C. J., held, that the defendant was personally liable; and he added, that there was no distinction between deeds and parol agree-

(*g*) 3 P. Wms. 278, 279; 1 Bla. Rep. 670; 2 Ld. Raym. 1210; Cowp. 565; Burr. 1986; 1 T. R. 181. 674; 4 T. R. 553; Peake, C. N. P. 120; Bac. Abr. Action on the Case, B.; Abbott, 1st ed. 229; 1 East, 507.

(*h*) 3 P. Wms. 279.

(*i*) 3 P. Wms. 277; 2 M. & Sel. 439.

(*j*) 4 Taunt. 198; 3 Campb. 183; 9 Bingh. 378; but see 4 M. & Sel. 259.

(*k*) 5 Moore, 270; 2 B. & B. 452, S. C.; and see 2 Taunt. 374, 387.

(*l*) 5 East, 148.

(*m*) Stra. 995; 1 B. & P. 368; Sowerby v. Butcher, 2 Crom. & Mees. 368.

(*n*) 1 T. R. 674; Gow's Cas. N. P. 117; 3 Brod. & Bing. 275 to 286; 7 Moore, 91, 110, S. C.

(62) Hopkins v. Mehaffy, 11 S. & R. 128. Vide Carew v. Otis, 1 J. R. 418. 6 ib. 255, n. i. Passmore v. Mott, 2 Binn. 201. Bethune v. Neilson, 2 Cai. R. 139. Mann v. Chandler, 9. Mass. R. 335. Dusenbury v. Ellis, 3 J. Cas. 70.

Doty v. Wilson, 14 J. R. 378. Smith v. Ware, 13 J. R. 257. In Frear v. Hardenburgh, 5 J. R. 272, it was held that, there was neither a legal nor moral obligation on the owner of land to pay for work done on it by one who entered, without his consent, or any consent, or color of right. See 20 J. R. 28. Such a consideration will not support an assumpsit, ib.

Dubois v. The Delaware and Hudson Canal Company, 4 Wend. R. 285. An agent renders himself personally liable when he makes a contract upon terms which he knows he has no authority to agree to, although the contract be made in the line of his business as agent. Meech v. Smith, 7 Wend. R. 315. Cunningham v. Soules, 7 Wend. R. 106.

(63) An attorney is personally liable to a sheriff, and so, it would seem, to any other officer of the court, for his fees, as it is to be presumed that the credit was given to the attorney. Adams v. Hopkins, 5 J. R. 252. Ousterhout v. Day, 9. J. R. 114.

(64) Vide White and others v. Skinner, 13 Johns. Rep. 307. Tippets v. Walker and others, 4 Mass. Rep. 595. Cutter v. Whittemore, 10 Mass. Rep. 447. Meyer and another v. Barker, 6 Binn. 228. Sumner v. Williams, 8 Mass. Rep. 362. } Mitchell v. Hazen, 4 Conn. Rep. 495. Belden v. Seymour, 8 Conn. Rep. 24. Duvall v. Craig, 2 Wheat. Rep. 45. }

(65) { Or draw a bill of exchange generally, without stating any qualification of his responsibility as drawer, though the payees knew that he was but an agent. Mayhew v. Prince, 11 Mass. Rep. 54. } The drawer of a note *as guardian* of another, was held personally liable. Thatcher v. Dinsmore, 5 Mass. Rep. 299. Foster v. Fuller, 6 Mass. Rep. 58. A covenant by an executor, as executor, and *not otherwise*, was held not to bind him personally. Thayer v. Wendell, Rep. C. C. U. S. First Circ't, 37. { Gallis. Rep. 37. }

ments in this respect (o). And where the solicitors of the assignees of a bankrupt, upon whose lands a distress had been made by the landlord, gave a written undertaking, stating that "they, *as* solicitors to the assignees, undertook to pay the rent, &c." they were held *personally liable (p); and in general, where an agent enters into a written agreement as if he were the principal, and the credit is given to him, he is personally liable (q); but this liability must be collected from the instrument upon a reasonable exposition of the whole of its terms (r) (66). So, if a person being an agent act as a principal, and do not disclose his principal, or declare that he acts as agent at the time of making a verbal contract, and the credit be given expressly to him, he will be personally responsible (s) (67). The master of a ship is in general liable for necessaries furnished abroad (t), or in this country, unless they were furnished upon the credit of the owners (u); and he or the owners may be sued upon the bill of lading, or generally, for the loss of goods, unless there has been an express contract with the owners (x) (68); and it seems that a policy broker alone can be sued for the premiums of insurance (y).

II. DEFENDANTS.

1. Who legally liable.

Agents, &c.

[*40]

Where an agent does not pursue in any degree the principal's authority (z); or so far exceeds it as to discharge the principal from responsibility for his acts (a); or where he acts under an authority, which he knows the principal has no right to give, as an agent selling property under a notice that it does not belong to his principal; he is personally responsible (b).

(o) 1 Ry. & Moo. 229; see 5 Moore, 278.

(p) 3 B. & Ald. 47; see also 2 D. & R. 307; 1 B. & C. 160, S. C.; 1 Gow, 117; 1 Stark. 14.

(q) 2 East, 142; 6 T. R. 176; 1 T. R. 675; 15 East, 62; 6 Taunt. 147; 1 Marsh 500.

(r) 5 Moore, 270; 2 Taunt. 374, 387.

(s) 3 Campb. 317; 15 East, 63, 66; 12 Ves. 352; Payl. 246; Peake, C. N. P. 120; 1 T. R. 181; 7 T. R. 359; Burr. 1921.

(t) Cowp. 639; 7 T. R. 312.

(u) Abbott on Shipping, 1st edit. 95.

(x) Carth. 58; Bac. Ab. Actions, B.

(y) 1 Marsh. on Ins. 204.

(z) 1 Eq. Ab. 308.

(a) 3 T. R. 761; 1 Esp. N. P. C. 112; 3 P. Wms. 279; 5 B. & Ald. 34; 2 Taunt. 386; 10 Ves. 400.

(b) Cowp. 565, 566; 4 Burr. 1984; Bul. N. P. 133; Ld. Raym. 1210; 4 T. R. 558; Stra. 480; 1 Taunt. 359; 2 *Id.* 386.

(66) An agent contracting on behalf of government is not personally liable. Vide Bainbridge v. Downie, 6 Mass. Rep. 257. Jones v. Le Tombe, 3 Dall. 384. So, the Secretary at War, taking a lease of a building, in Washington, for the use of the war office, was held not to be liable under a covenant contained in the lease. Hodgson v. Dexter, 1 Cranch, 345. { So, the president of a corporation sealing a covenant, as president, and on behalf of the corporation. Hopkins v. Mehaffy, 11 Serg. & Rawle, 126. Randall v. Van Vechten, 19 Johns. Rep. 60. } But a public officer may render himself liable by his express promise. Gill v. Brown, 12 Johns. Rep. 385. The Supreme Court of the State of New York have decided, that an agent of government, known as such, is personally liable on a contract made by him on account of government, unless it appear, as well that he contracted in his official capacity, and on account of government, as that the other party gave the credit, and intended to look to government for compensation Sheffield v. Watson, 3 Caines' Rep. 69. Sed Vide Walker v. Swartwout, 12 Johns. Rep. 444. Swift v. Hopkins, 13 Johns. Rep. 313.

(67) { Allen v. Rostain, 11 Serg. & Rawle, 375. } If the seller of goods, knowing at the time that the buyer, though dealing with him in his own name, is in truth the agent of another, elect to give the credit to such agent, he cannot afterwards recover the value against the known principal; but if the principal be not known at the time of the purchase made by the agent it seems that when discovered, the principal or the agent may be sued at the election of the seller; unless where by the usage of trade, the credit is understood to be confined to the agent so dealing; as particularly in the case of principals residing abroad. Patterson and another v. Guadasequi, 15 East's Rep. 62. Et vide Mauri v. Heffernan, 13 Johns. Rep. 59 Jaques v. Todd, 3 Wend. R. 83. Lincoln v. Battelle, 6 ib. 475. Pentz v. Stanton, 10 ib. 271. Tradesman's Bank v. Astor, 11 Wend. R. 87. Jeffrey v. Bigelow, 13 ib. 518.

(68) The plaintiff has his election to sue either the one or the other, unless there were a special promise from either, in which case the other is discharged. Garnham v. Bennet, Str. 816. Farmer and another v. Davies, 1 Term Rep. 108.

II. DEFENDANTS.

1. Who legally liable.

Agents, &c.

There is a material distinction between an action against an agent for the recovery of damages for the non-performance of the contract, and an action to recover back a specific sum of money received by him; for when a contract has been rescinded, or a person has received money as agent of another who had no right thereto, and has not paid it over, an action may be sustained against the agent to recover the money (69); and the mere passing of such mo- [*41] ney in account with his principal, *or making a rest, without any new credit given to him, fresh bills accepted, or further sums advanced to the principal in consequence of it, is not equivalent to a payment of the money to the principal (*c*). But, in general, if the money be paid over before notice to retain it, the agent is not liable (*d*) (70), unless his receipt of the money was obviously illegal, or his authority was wholly void (*e*) (71).

Where persons received money for the express purpose of taking up a bill of exchange two days after it became due, and upon tendering it to the holders, and demanding the bill, find that they have sent it back, protested for non-acceptance, to the person who indorsed it to them, it was held, that such persons, having received fresh orders not to pay the bill, were not liable to an action by the holders for money had and received, when, upon the bill being procured and tendered to them, they refused to pay the money (*f*). A person, who, as a banker or agent, receives money from A. to be paid to B., and to other different persons, cannot in general be sued by B. for his share, unless he has expressly agreed to appropriate the money to the purpose for which it was sent (*g*). Nor can an action for money had and received be maintained against a mere bearer of money from one person to another (*h*); or a mere collector or receiver who has *bonâ fide* paid it over (*i*); or against a churchwarden to recover back dues which, before the commencement of the action, had been paid over to the trustee of a chapel, for whom it was received (*k*); or against an arbitrator to recover money deposited with him by a bankrupt, subject to an award, and which money the arbitrator *bonâ fide* paid over to the person whom he thought entitled to receive it, before the issuing of the commission, and without notice of an act of bankruptcy (*l*). But auctioneers and stakeholders are considered in the light of trustees for both parties, and are [*42] *bound to retain the money deposited with them, until it be ascertained which of the parties is entitled to receive it (*m*).

(*c*) 3 M. & Sel. 344; Cowp. 565; Stra. 480; 5 Taunt. 815.

(*d*) Cowp. 565; Burr. 1986; Ld. Raym. 1210; 4 T. R. 553; Stra. 480; Bul. N. P. 133; 10 Mod. 23; 2 Esp. Rep. 507; 5 Moore, 105; 8 Taunt. 737.

(*e*) 1 Campb. 396, 564; 3 Esp. Rep. 153; 1 Stra. 480; Cowp. 69; 1 Taunt. 359.

(*f*) 1 Moore, 74; see 14 East, 582, 590; 2 Bing. 7; 9 Moore, 31, S. C.

(*g*) 14 East, 582; 7 Taunt. 339; 1 R. & M. 68; 3 Cromp. & J. 83; 1 Marsh. Rep. 132.

(*h*) 4 Taunt. 198.

(*i*) 4 Burr. 1985; 4 T. R. 554, 555.

(*k*) 8 Taunt. 136.

(*l*) 7 B. & C. 101.

(*m*) 5 Burr. 2639; 7 Moore, 465. As to deposits on legal or illegal wagers, see Chit. jun. Con. 193; 7 Price, 540; 8 B. & C. 227.

(69) Vide Campbell *v.* Hall, Cowp. 204. Hardacre *v.* Stewart, 5 Esp. Rep. 103. Hearsey *v.* Pruyn, 7 Johns. Rep. 179. Whitbread *v.* Brooksbank, Cowp. 69.

(70) Vide Carew *v.* Otis, 1 J. R. 418.

(71) Or the payment was compulsory, and not made expressly for the use of the principal. Ripley et al. *v.* Gelston, 9 J. R. 201. Mowatt *v.* M'Clellan, 1 Wend. R. 173. Mitchell *v.* Bristol, 10 ib. 492.

II. DEFENDANTS.

1. Who legally liable.

Agents, &c.

The *agents of government* are not in general liable upon contracts avowedly entered into by them in their official capacity. Thus, neither the governor of a fort or colony (n), nor a military commissary (o), nor the captain of a regiment (p), or ship (q), is liable for goods ordered by him for the public service, in cases where he does not expressly pledge his individual credit and responsibility. Nor is the secretary at war liable to a retired clerk of the war-office for his retired allowance, although such allowance was included in certain funds received by the defendant in his official character (r). Nor are justices of the peace, contracting on behalf of the public for rebuilding a public bridge, under the provisions of an act of parliament which provides a fund for the payment, liable to the contractor (s); and it seems that where a servant of the crown expressly contracts on account of government, he is not responsible, although the agreement be under seal (t).

In *Horsley* v. *Bell* (u), a bill having been filed by the plaintiff, the undertaker of a navigation, against the commissioners named in the act for carrying it on, who had signed the several orders, it was contended, first, that the defendants were not personally liable, because they were exercising a public trust, and the credit was given to the undertaking itself, and not personally to them, and the remedy was therefore *in rem;* secondly, that those who had been present at the meetings, and had signed some, but not all the orders, were liable only to those which they had respectively signed. But Lord Chancellor Thurlow, assisted by Ashhurst and Gould, Justices, held, first, that the commissioners were personally liable; and, secondly, they were all liable in respect of all the orders. Lord Thurlow said, "Who would make a contract on the credit of toll, which it is in the power *of the commissioners to raise, [*43] or not, at their pleasure? Then, upon whose credit must the contract be? Certainly that of the commissioners who act. It is their fault if they enter into contracts when they have no money to answer them. They have made themselves liable by their own acts." And this doctrine was confirmed in the recent case of *Eaton* v. *Bell* (x). It appeared that an inclosure act empowered the commissioners to make a rate to defray the expenses of passing and executing the act; and enacted, that persons advancing money should be repaid out of the first money raised by the commissioners. Expenses were incurred in the execution of the act before any rate was made. To defray these expenses, the commissioners drew drafts upon their bankers, requiring them to pay the sums therein mentioned, on account of the public drainage, and to place the same to their account as commissioners. The bankers, during a period of six years, continued to advance considerable sums, by paying these drafts; and it was held, that the commissioners were personally responsible to the bankers for the drafts so made. And a churchwarden, who employs a person to make a plan of the church, in order that the plan may be laid before certain commissioners for building new churches, is personally liable to such person (y). These cases appear to have been decided upon the

(n) 1 T. R. 172; 2 Moore, 627.
(o) 1 T. R. 180.
(p) 1 East, 135, 579.
(q) 1 T. R. 674.
(r) 7 Moore, 91; 3 B. & B. 275, S. C.
(s) 2 Moore, 621.
(t) 1 T. R. 674; 2 Moore, 621.
(u) 1 Bro. C. C. 101; Ambl. 770; Paley, 251.
(x) 5 B. & Ald. 34.
(y) *Brook* v. *Guest*, N. P. Stafford Summer Assizes, 1825, cited 3 Bing. 481.

II. DEFENDANTS. 1. Who legally liable. Agents, &c.

ground that the several parties sued had within their reach the means of indemnifying themselves by making rates, or out of funds in their hands or power (z). And it has been decided that vestrymen, who at a vestry meeting sign a resolution ordering the parish surveyor to take steps for defending an indictment for not repairing a road, are not liable to the attorney employed by the surveyor; because the conduct of the business relative to the road was more peculiarly the province of the surveyor, who could have afterwards charged the parish in his account, and been reimbursed by a regular parish rate (a). The surveyor of a turnpike road employed by and acting by order of commissioners, appears not to be liable to persons who perform work in repairing the road; for in such case the surveyor is to be viewed in the light of a mere servant of the commissioners (b).

[*44] *Where the agent does not, at the time the contract is made, disclose that he is acting merely as an agent, and the principal is unknown, the latter may, when discovered, be sued upon the agreement (c). And the principal is also responsible for the price of goods ordered by his agent, who disclosed that he was acting merely as such, but did not express who his principal was, although the vendor had actually debited the agent without inquiring the name of his employer; for in such case the vendor cannot be considered to have had the means of electing finally to give credit to the agent only (d).

But the principal is not liable upon the contract of his agent, if the other party to the agreement, with full knowledge of the facts, and the power and means of deciding to whom he will give credit, elect to give credit to the agent only, in his individual character (e).

Partners, tenants in common, &c. suing each other.

At law, one *partner* or *tenant in common* cannot in general sue his co-partner (72) or co-tenant, in any action in *form ex contractu* (f); but must proceed by action of account (g), or by bill in equity (73). This rule is founded on the nature of the situation of the parties, the difficulty at law of adjusting complicated accounts between them, and the propriety, arising from the supposed confidence reposed by the parties in each other, of their being examined upon oath, which can only be effected in a Court of equity. Therefore, in the case of a partnership, whether it be a general or particular partnership, one partner cannot at law recover his share of monies received by the other on

(z) See 3 Bing. 483.

(a) 3 Bing. 478.

(b) 1 Bla. Rep. 670. As to liability of trustees of a turnpike road, 10 Bing. 283. The subscribers who attend a committee of a hospital are liable to the creditors of such hospital, 7 Bing. 705.

(c) 15 East, 67; 4 Taunt. 576, note. *Per* Lord Tenterden, 9 B. & C. 8. See *ante*, 38, 39, 40.

(d) 9 B. & C. 78.

(e) 15 East, 62; 4 Taunt. 574; 9 B. & C. 89, 90.

(f) 2 T. R. 478; 2 B. & P. 124; 4 East, 144; 4 Esp. R. 182; 2 Marsh. 319, 324; 1 B. & C. 74; 8 *Id.* 345; 2 Crom. & Mees. 361; 2 Bing. N. C. 108. But a partnership must have been actually formed, 3 B. & C. 814.

(g) Bac. Ab. Account, Willes, 208.

{ (72) Murray *v.* Bogert, 14 Johns. Rep. 318. Beach *v.* Hotchkiss, 2 Conn. 425. Walker *v.* Long, 2 P. A. Browne's Rep. 125. Ozeas *v.* Johnson, 4 Dall. 434. 1 Binn. 191. Young *v.* Brick, 2 Penn. Rep. 663. Course *v.* Prince, 1 Rep. Const. Ct. 413. Kennedy *v.* M'Fadon et al., 3 Har. & Johns. 194. *Aliter* in Massachusetts, Brigham *v.* Eveleth, Jones *v.* Harraden, 9 Mass. Rep. 538, 540. Bond *v.* Hays, 12 Mass. Rep. 34. Wilbey *v.* Phinney, 15 Mass. Rep. 112. Fanning *v.* Chadwick, 3 Pick. Rep. 420. Brinley *v.* Kupfer, 6 Pick. Rep. 179. } Westerlo *v.* Evertson, 1 Wend. R. 532. Farr *v.* Smith, 9 Wend. R. 338.

(73) Vide Niven *v.* Spickerman and Stever, 12 Johns. Rep. 401. Ozeas *v.* Johnson, 1 Binn. 191.

II. DEFENDANTS.

1. Who legally liable. Partners, &c. suing each other.

account of the firm, unless on a final balance of all accounts a particular sum be found due to one partner, which the other expressly promises to pay (*h*)(74); or unless there be an express covenant to account, &c. (*i*).

It has been held, that assumpsit for money had and received may be maintained against one who had been a member of a benefit club, for money entrusted to his keeping by the rest of the society, in the name of the officers properly *appointed for managing their affairs, under the articles (*k*) (75). [* 45] So one joint contractor who pays money for another, the whole of which, or a particular part of which, the latter had engaged to pay, may recover it from the other as money paid to his use (*l*); and if one of two joint contractors refer the claim of a third person to damages upon the contract to arbitration, and he pay over the sum awarded to the claimant, he may sue his co-contractor for money paid (*m*). In the case, however, of a general unsettled account between partners, one who has been compelled to pay the whole of a creditor's demand cannot sue his co-partner at law (*n*).

In the case of a personal chattel, or of trees severed from the land, if one of two or more joint tenants, or tenants in common, by the sale thereof, convert the thing into money, the joint interest is determined, and each hath a separate interest for a sum certain, and may support money had and received against the other (*o*)(76); and one partner may maintain an action for money had and received, against the other partner for money received to the separate use of the former, and wrongfully carried to the partnership account (*p*); and a partner may recover money paid to his co-partner for the purpose of being paid over, as the plaintiff's liquidated share of a debt to their joint creditor, if it be not so applied, and the plaintiff be obliged to pay such joint creditor (*q*)(77). So, one of several co-sureties in a bond, &c. who has been

(*h*) 2 T. R. 478; 2 Bing. 170; 3 Bing. 55, 56; 6 B. & C. 149. See 1 Holt, 368.

(*i*) 2 T. R. 482; 7 Mod. 116; 13 East. 8, 53b; 2 Crom. & Mees. 361; 1 Bing. N. C. 399; 2 Bing. N. C. 108.

(*k*) 6 Price, 131.

(*l*) 6 Taunt. 289; 1 Marsh. 603; 1 East, 29; 8 T. R. 614; Rol. Abr. Action sur le Case, 24, pl. 31; 3 Campb. 168.

(*m*) 4 Moore, 340.

(*n*) 1 Stark. 78, 79.

(*o*) Willes, 209; 8 T. R. 146.

(*p*) 2 T. R. 476.

(*q*) 1 East, 20; 13 East, 7; 6 Taunt. 289.

(74) Vide Casey *v.* Brush, 2 Caines' Rep. 293. {Halstead *v.* Schenelzel, 17 Johns. Rep. 80. Westerlo *v.* Evertson, 1 Wend. Rep. 532. Course *v.* Prince, 1 Rep Const. 416. There need not be an express promise in Pennsylvania. The action may be maintained if the accounts have been settled, and a balance struck, which must be the act of both parties. Ozeas *v.* Johnson, 1 Binn 191. Lamalire *v.* Caze, 1 Wash. C. C. Rep. 431.} So if one partner covenant to pay all debts due from the partnership, he is liable for a debt due from the partnership to one of the other co-partners. Hobart *v.* Howard, 7 Mass. Rep. 304. Clough *v.* Hoffman, 5 Wend. R. 499.

(75) {The decision in this case (Sharpe *v.* Warren, 6 Price, 131) can only be sustained on the ground, that the Act of Parliament vested the right to sue in the officers of the society.}

When a board of directors consists of sixteen, a joint action against four of the number cannot be maintained. Franklin Fire Ins. Co. *v.* Jenkins, 3 Wend. R. 130. And no action lies by one partner against another, except there has been a settlement of accounts, and a promise to pay the balance. Niven *v.* Spickerman, 12 J. R. 401.

(76) Vide Selden *v.* Hickock, 2 Caines' Rep. 166. One tenant in common cannot maintain assumpsit against his co-tenant, or the guardian of his co-tenant, or the agent of such guardian, for a portion of the rent received by either. The only remedy is by action of account, or bill in equity. Sherman *v* Ballou, 8 Cowen, 304. One tenant in common cannot, like a partner, sell the whole interest of his co-tenant. If he do so, trover lies by the other. Hyde *v.* Stone, 9 Cowen, 230. A tenant in common cannot recover for repairs to the land, without a previous request to join in making the repairs. Mumford *v.* Brown, 6 Cowen, 475.

(77) Where one partner gives a promissory note to another partner, for the use of the

II. DEFENDANTS. — 1. Who legally liable. Partners, &c. suing each other.

obliged to pay more than his proportion, may recover against any one of the others his proportion of the money paid under the bond, &c. (r)(78). And an action at law is sustainable to recover a contribution in the nature of general average by one shipper of goods against another (s)(79). And if there be not an actual partnership, one of several parties [*46] *interested in profits may in general proceed at law against a person who has received his share; thus, if a sailor engage on a whaling voyage, and is to receive a certain proportion of the profits of the voyage in lieu of wages, when the cargo is sold he may maintain an action for his wages against the captain, and shall not be considered as a partner (t) (80). And when the agreement between two does not constitute a partnership as between themselves, but only an agreement in favor of one, as a compensation for trouble and credit, he may sue the other, though, as between third persons, both might be liable as partners (u) (81).

It is an answer to an action that a party is *legally interested in each side of the question*. A party cannot be both plaintiff and defendant in an action (x). If, therefore, one of the plaintiffs be also a member of the firm against which the action is brought, upon a contract entered into by the firm, the action shall fail, although the other partners only be sued (y). And where the agent, employed in endeavoring to carry through Parliament a bill for making a railway, sued the chairman of a committee of subscribers to the undertaking for his work and labor, and expenses incurred as such agent, and it appeared that he himself was a subscriber to the undertaking, it was held the action would not lie (z). And in assumpsit by A., B. and C. against D. as one of the indorsers of a promissory note, drawn by E. in favor of himself and of the said C. and D. then in partnership, and by them indorsed to the plaintiffs, a plea in bar that C., one of the plaintiffs, is liable as an indorser, together with the defendant, was held good on special demurrer (a); and in an action by several as executors, a plea in bar that the promises were made by the defendants jointly with one of the plaintiffs, is sufficient (b). So if A. an attorney, and B. and C. were members of a trading company, and after the dissolution of that company, B. and C. be sued by creditors of the company and retain A.

(r) 2 B. & P. 268, 270; 8 T. R. 310, 614; 2 T. R. 100; 6 B. & C. 689; 1 Moore, 2. See the distinction in cases of tort, 8 T. R. 186; 1 Campb. 343, 355; 2 *Id.* 452. But no part of the costs paid or incurred by the one surety, in an action against him on the bond, &c. given for the principal, is recoverable against the co-surety by way of contribution, 3 C. & P. 467.

(s) 3 Campb. 180; 1 East, 220; 4 Taunt. 123.

(t) 4 Esp. Rep. 182; and see 3 B. & C. 814.

(u) 4 East, 144.

(x) 2 B. & P. 124; 5 Chit. Rep. 539, S. C.; 2 Marsh. 319; 6 Taunt. 597; see 9 B. & C. 356. This may be given in evidence under the general issue, 6 Bing. 197.

(y) *Id.*

(z) 1 B. & C. 74; 2 D. & R. 196, S. C.

(a) 2 B. & P. 120; 2 Marsh. 329; see 8 B. & C. 345.

(b) 2 B. & P. 124, note (c); 6 Moore, 332; 1 Went. 17, 18.

firm, the payee may maintain an action in his own name. Van Ness v. Forest, 8 Cranch, 30. But if one partner pays the debt of his firm, it is not competent to the creditor to keep the debt alive, and authorize such partner to enforce it against his co-partner. Le Page v. M'Crea, 1 Wend. R. 164.

(78) Vide The People v. Duncan, 1 J. R. 311.

(79) As in the case of persons running a line of stages, where each has his separate portion of the road, and provides horses and carriages at his own expense and risk. Wetmore v. Cheeseborough, and Baker v. Swan, 9 J. R. 307.

(80) See 17 Mass. R. 206.

(81) Vide Muzzy v. Whitney et al., 10 J. R. 228. Dry v. Boswell, 1 Camp. 329.

to defend the action, the latter being, as a member of the company, *jointly liable to contribute to the expense of defending those actions, cannot sue B. and C. for his bill of costs (c).

II. DEFENDANTS.

1. Who legally liable. Partners, &c. suing each other.

A *lunatic* is liable for goods suitable to his rank supplied to him upon a contract, which a person, not aware of his infirmity, *bona fide* enters into with him (d).

2dly. With reference to the number of the defendants, and who must be sued.

A contract, whether it be by specialty or not, is either joint, or it is several; or parties may bind themselves jointly and severally. It would be a pursuit foreign to the object of this Treatise, to detail the various instances in which contracts shall be considered to entail upon the parties a joint or separate responsibility (e). The rule is, that several persons contracting together with the same party, for one and the same act, shall be regarded as jointly and not individually or separately liable, in the absence of any express words to show that a distinct as well as entire liability was intended to fasten upon the promisers (f). This rule is more particularly obvious in the case of promises *implied* by law. But in the case of parties demising or granting the separate interest of each in an estate, it seems that the covenant implied by law from the word "demise," or even an express covenant by the two, without express words of severalty, shall be considered co-extensive with the interest granted, and therefore shall be several where a several interest is granted, and joint, if a joint estate be granted (g).

Joint contract.

First, Where there are several parties, if their contract be *joint* they must all be made defendants (h); although they subsequently arrange amongst themselves that one only of them shall perform the contract (i). And a partner who retires *from a firm is liable for the old debt, although the debt be carried by the consent of the creditor to the account of the remaining partners, and he take their bill of exchange; there being no actual satisfaction or release of the responsibility of the retiring partner (k). When an insurance has been made for the benefit of several, a jury may infer a joint contract to pay the broker (l). Where it appears from an instrument, that a promise by two contractors is intended to be *joint*, it may be treated as such, although the promise be in terms several only (m).

[*48]

A contract made by two partners to pay a sum of money to a third person equally, out of their own private funds, is a joint contract, and they should be

(c) 7 B. & C. 419.
(d) 5 B. & C. 170.
(e) See Bac. Ab. Obligations; 1 B. & C. 682; Platt on Cov. 115. Persons may be *jointly* liable, as *partners*, either as having expressly contracted, or by holding themselves out to the world as such, or by a participation in the loss or profit, 16 East, 174; Dougl. 373; 2 H. Bl. 246, 247. If several persons dine together at a tavern, they are *prima facie* jointly liable for the whole bill, and not merely each for his own share; but each of the officers of a regimental mess is only separately liable for his own share, 3 Campb. 51, 53, 168; 2 Campb. 640. As to who are partners in general, see 3 Chit. Com. Law, 231. As to joint stock companies, 10 B. & C. 128, 288.
(f) Freem. 218; 7 Mod. 154; S. C. in 1 Salk. 393; see Platt on Cov. 117, 118.
(g) See 1 Show. 79; S. C. in Carth. 97; 1 Salk. 137; Comb. 163; Noy, 86; 6 Bing. 656.
(h) 1 Saund. 153, n. 1; 291 b. note 4.
(i) 3 B. & Ald. 611; 1 H. Bla. 236; 2 B. & B. 38; see 9 Bing. 297.
(k) 5 B. & C. 196.
(l) 2 Bing. 156; and as to where two overseers are jointly liable, 1 Adol. & El. 691.
(m) Lee v. Nixon, 3 Nev. & Man. 441.

II. DEFENDANTS. — 1. Who legally liable. Partners, &c. suing each other.

jointly sued upon it (n)(82); but if A. lease for years to B. and C., rendering rent, and C. assign his moiety to D., A. may sue B. and D. jointly or severally, at his election, for rent in arrear (o). And where two several tenants of a farm agreed with a succeeding tenant to refer certain matters in difference respecting the farm to arbitration, and jointly and severally promised to perform the award, and the arbitrators awarded that each of the two should pay a certain sum of money to the third, it was decided that they were liable to be sued jointly for the sums awarded to be paid by each; because, by the terms of the agreement they had promised jointly as well as severally, which made each of them liable for the act of the other (p). Parceners should, before partition, be jointly sued, though they be entitled to the estate by different descents (q).

Joint contractors must all be sued, although one has become bankrupt, and obtained his certificate, for if not sued, the others may plead in abatement (r). In the case of a joint contract, if one of the parties cannot be arrested or served with process, and a plea in abatement be apprehended, the only safe course is to proceed to outlawry against him (83); and even then, if after outlawry and interlocutory judgment against the defendant who was served with process, he die, no proceedings at law against his executors are sustainable, the debt still continuing to be joint (s).

[*49] It seems that mere dormant partners (t), and nominal partners *having no interest (u) need not necessarily be joined as defendants; more especially if the right or interest of the plaintiff might otherwise be varied or affected. And in the case of infants, or married women (x), contracting jointly with other persons competent to enter into agreements, it is a ground of nonsuit to sue them with the persons who are legally responsible. Their names should be omitted, and if the defendant plead the nonjoinder in abatement, the plaintiff may reply the infancy or coverture (y). If one or more of several

(n) 1 Hen. Bla. 236.
(o) Palm. 263; 2 Vin. Ab. 66, 67; 2 Saund. 182, note 1; Cro. Jac. 411.
(p) 7 T. R. 352; 2 Saund. 61 h. note 2.
(q) Vin. Ab. Actions, Joinder, D. d, Parceners, Rep. temp. Hardw. 398, 399.
(r) 2 M. & Sel. 23, 444; 6 Taunt. 178; 4 Taunt. 326; *post*, 59.
(s) 1 M. & Sel. 242, *sed quære*.
(t) 3 Price, 538; 1 Stark. R. 272, 338; 3 *Id.* 8; Holt, N. P. C. 253; 4 M. & Sel. 475; 1 M. & M. 88; 1 D. & R. 584; 4 *Id.* 240, 243; 10 B. & C. 128, 288; Demantort *v.* Saunders, 1 Bar. & Adol. 398, overrules 5 Taunt. 609. As to a dormant partner suing, see *ante*, 13, 14; and 10 B. & C. 20.
(u) 2 Campb. 302; 14 East, 210; 1 Stark. 25; 1 Marsh. 246. See as to plaintiffs, 10 B. & C. 20, and *ante*, 13.
(x) 3 Esp. Rep. 76; 5 *Id.* 47; 4 Taunt. 468; 1 Wils. 89.
(y) *Id.*; but see 3 Taunt. 307.

(82) A covenant in a lease to two persons, as tenants in common, that the lessees shall pay the rent, is a joint covenant, notwithstanding their several interests. Phillips *v.* Bonsall, *survivor*, *&c.*, 2 Binn. 138. If a partner purchase goods for the partnership account, but on his individual credit, he may be sued alone. Sylvester and another *v.* Smith, 9 Mass. Rep. 119. And if a partner raise money by way of discount, on a bill drawn by himself individually, the lender cannot resort to the partnership neither in an action on the bill, or on an implied assumpsit, although the proceeds of the bill were carried to the partnership account. Emly and others *v.* Lye, 15 East's Rep. 7. But where a partner raises money for the use of the partnership by drawing bills of exchange upon the firm, although the partners are not jointly liable upon an unaccepted bill, yet they are jointly liable as for money lent, or money had and received. Denton and others *v.* Rodie and another, 3 Campb. 493. If one partner make a warranty in a sale, an action may be sustained against him, without joining his co-partner. Clark *v.* Holmes, 3 Johns. Rep. 148.

(83) { In Pennsylvania, there is no *outlawry* in civil cases—the return of *non est inventus* has, in pleading, the same effect. Dilman *v.* Shultz, 5 Serg. & Rawle, 35. }

II. DEFENDANTS. — 2. Who should be joined or omitted.

partners originally jointly liable has taken the case out of the statute of limitations as to himself only, by promising or acknowledging the debt, then the action should be only against *him*, and not against him and his co-partner, who has been discharged from liability (*z*).

In the case of *defendants*, if one of the parties originally bound be dead, it is not necessary to notice him in the declaration, and the survivors need not be declared against as such, but may be sued as if they alone were the parties primarily liable (*a*).

Several contract.

Secondly, Where the covenant or promise is so framed that it does not confer upon the plaintiff a remedy against the contractors jointly, but each is only *separately* responsible for his own act, it is essential to sue them distinctly; but where it appears upon an instrument that a promise by two contractors was *intended* to be *joint*, it may be treated as such, although the promise be *in terms* several only (*b*).

Joint and several contract.

Thirdly, When the contract is several as well as joint, the plaintiff is at liberty to proceed against the parties jointly, or each separately, though their interest be joint (*c*). But if there be more than two parties to a joint and several contract, as where three obligors are jointly and severally bound, the plaintiff must either sue them all jointly or each of them separately (*d*) (84); though if two only be improperly sued, the objection should be taken by plea in abatement, or by writ of error if the defect appear on the record, and it is not a ground of nonsuit (*e*). Where parties are sued separately, on a joint and several engagement to do a certain act, the *breach may be assigned in [*50]

(*z*) See 9 Geo. 4, c. 14. s. 2.

(*a*) 1 B. & Ald. 29; 3 B. & B. 302.

(*b*) Lee *v.* Nixon and another, 3 Nev. & Mann. 441.

(*c*) Bac. Ab. Obligation, D. 4; 1 Saund. 153, note 1; 2 Burr. 1190; Poph. 161. In what cases the court will restrain a party from proceeding in several actions on bail bond, 2 B. & A. 598. And as to the consolidation of actions, see Tidd, 9th edit. 614. *Semble*, that a creditor cannot sue jointly and separately at the same time, 1 Ves. & B. 65. And where separate actions were brought against several persons for the same debt, who (if at all) were jointly liable, the defendant in one action having paid the debt and costs in that action, the Court stayed the proceedings in the others without costs, 6 B. & C. 124.

(*d*) 3 T. R. 782; Bac. Ab. Obligation, D. 4; 1 Saund. 291 e.; 2 Vin. Ab. 68, pl. 7; Platt on Cov. 134.

(*e*) 1 Saund. 291 e.; 2 Taunt. 254.

(84) Vide Cutter *v.* Whittemore, 16 Mass. R. 446. Carter *v.* Carter, 2 Day, 442. On a note given by several for a sum to be paid in the following proportions, viz. half by A., one sixth by B., one sixth by E., &c. *several* actions must be brought against each, and not a *joint* action against all. M'Bean *v.* Todd, 2 Bibb's R. 320. And if a joint and several promissory note is made by one of the members of a firm in the partnership name, and by another in his individual character, a suit may be maintained against the firm, without joining the other maker of the note; it being the note of the firm, and not of the individuals composing it, so far as the remedy to enforce payment was concerned. Partners cannot be individually sued for a partnership debt. Each partner is bound for the whole until the debt is paid; but payment can be enforced only by a joint action against all. Their responsibilities are joint only, and not joint and several, so as to subject each to a separate action. Robertson *v.* Smith, 18 J. R. 459. Henry Van Tine *v.* Crane et al., 1 Wend. R. 524.

A contract under seal, purporting by its terms to be between two *firms* in their partnership names, and the partnership name of one firm is subscribed to the contract, and that of the other firm is subscribed to a counterpart thereof, *held* that an action could be maintained against the member of the firm *individually*, who subscribed the name of his firm, unless he shows his authority to bind his co-partners in that manner. And such action may be sued in the joint names of the partners with whom the contract is made, although but one of the firm signed the counterpart, in the name of the firm; and although no authority be shown authorizing him to sign the name of his firm to a sealed contract. Gates *v.* Graham et al., 12 Wend. R. 53.

II. DEFENDANTS. — 2. Who should be joined or omitted.

both (*f*); and a recovery (85), and execution against the body of one, producing no actual satisfaction, will be no bar to an action against the other (*k*). And when the contract is joint and several, and the debt or demand considerable, it is most advisable to proceed separately, for if all the parties be joined, and one of them die after judgment, and before execution, the remedy at law against the personal estate or assets of the deceased is determined (*l*) (86); and in the case of the death of a surety, even a court of equity will not in all cases relieve (*m*); whereas, if the plaintiff proceed separately, the executor of the deceased, as well as the survivor, continue severally liable at law (*n*). In general, when a contract was joint and several, if the debt be considerable, it is most advisable to proceed separately, so that the creditor may thereby retain his legal remedies against each in case of death of one or more of the parties.

Mis-joinder.—It has been already observed, that at law, as well as in equity, the courts will not take cognizance of distinct and separate claims or liabilities of different persons in one suit, though standing in the same relative situations (*o*). And, therefore, in an action *ex contractu* against several, it

(*f*) 1 Stra. 553; 2 Burr. 1197.

(*k*) Cro. Jac. 74; 5 Co. 86; 3 Mod. 87; 2 Show. 494.

(*l*) Com. Dig. Pleader, 3 L. 3, Action, K. 4; Bac. Abr. Obligation, D. 4, vol. v. and vol. vii. Obligation, B.; 2 Saund. 50 a. 51, (4); Tidd, 9th edit. 1121; 1 Bing. 138.

(*m*) *Id. Ibid.*; 3 Ves. 399; 2 Ves. sen. 106, 171.

(*n*) 2 Burr. 1190.

(*o*) *Ante*, 9 to 16; 1 East, 226, 227; 1 Mad. 88, 89.

---

(85) Minor v. Mech. Bank, 1 Peters' Sup. Ct. Rep. 46. Vide Meredith's Administratrix v. Duval 1 Mun. 79. Leftwich and others v. Berkeley, 1 Hen. & Mun. 61. But by the New York statute for the amendment of the law, sess. 36, c. 56. s. 14. 1 R. L. 521, it is enacted that all or any part of the obligors in a joint and several or several bond or recognizance may be joined in one action, and if the whole amount due shall not be levied in such suit, a further action may be brought against the residue of the obligors jointly or severally; but no more than the debt and damages due, with costs of suit, can be levied: the plaintiff may at any stage consolidate the suits; and where more than one suit is depending at the same time, on one bond, recognizance, promissory note or bill of exchange, he can recover costs in only one suit, except the costs of writs issued into several counties, against defendants residing in different counties. { See as to actions against joint debtors, 2 Rev. Laws, 277. In Pennsylvania, by the provisions of the Act of April 6th, 1830, entitled "an Act for the furtherance of justice between obligors and obligees, and other creditors and debtors," it is provided, "that in all suits now pending, or hereafter brought in any court of record in this commonwealth, against joint and several obligors, co-partners, promissors or the indorsers of promissory notes, in which the writ or process has not been, or may not be served on all the defendants, and judgment may be obtained against those served with process, such writ, process, or judgment shall not be a bar to recovery in another suit against the defendant or defendants not served with process, and that from and after the passing of this act, in all cases of amicable confession of judgment by one or more of several obligors, co-partners, or promissors, or the indorsers of promissory notes, such judgment shall not be a bar to recovery in such suit or suits as may have to be brought against those who refuse to confess judgment." Purd. Dig. 481. }

(86) { Comm. v. Miller's Adm., 8 Serg. & Rawle, 452. } Vide Foster v. Hooper, 2 Mass. Rep. 572. But by a statute passed 26th February, 1800, his assets are rendered liable in the hands of his executors or administrators. 3 Laws Mass. 69. And see the statute of the State of New York, cited above, note (85,) which authorizes the plaintiff to prosecute the action against all or any of the obligors to judgment and execution against the defendants, *and against their joint or separate property*, and in an action against the residue of the obligors, to prosecute the same to judgment and execution against the said residue, *and against their joint or separate property*. Judgment was recovered against A., one of two joint makers of a promissory note: the plaintiff brought an action afterwards against A. and B. the other maker, on the same note, and B. pleaded separately the recovery against A.; the plea was held bad. Sheehy v. Mandeville and Jameson, 6 Cranch, 253. { See, however, the remarks of Ch. Justice SPENCER upon the case of Sheehy v. Mandeville, 18 Johns. Rep. 482. }

II. DEFENDANTS. 2. Who should be joined or omitted.

must appear on the face of the pleadings that their contract was joint (87), and that fact must also be proved on the trial. If *too many* persons be made defendants, and the objection appear on the pleadings, either of the defendants may demur, move in arrest of judgment, or support a writ of error (p); and even if the objection do not appear upon the pleadings, the plaintiff may be nonsuited upon the trial, if he fail in proving a joint contract (q) (88). Although in actions for *torts* one defendant may be found guilty, and the other acquitted, yet in actions for the breach of a *contract*, whether it be framed in assumpsit, covenant, debt, or case, a verdict or judgment cannot in general be given in a joint action against one defendant without the other (r). In an action of assumpsit *against three persons, two only of whom were liable [*51] to be sued, the party not liable, together with one of those who was liable, suffered judgment by default, and the other party pleaded the general issue, and a verdict was found for the defendant who pleaded, on the ground that the plaintiff having declared as upon a promise by three defendants, to entitle himself to recover, he should have proved a promise, either express or implied, binding upon all the three (s); and where the plaintiff declared on a joint and several promissory note, against all the makers jointly, and one of them, by his plea, admitted his hand-writing to the note, but the other defendants pleaded non-assumpsit, the plaintiff was nonsuited, for not proving the hand-writing of the defendant, who by his plea had so admitted it (t). And though a contract be proved to have been in *fact* made by all the defendants, yet if in point of *law* it was not obligatory on one of the defendants, either on the ground of infancy or coverture, at the time it was entered into, the plaintiff will be nonsuited, and in this instance he cannot avoid the objection by entering a *nolle prosequi* as to the infant or feme covert (u) (89); but must discontinue and commence a fresh action, omitting such parties; in

(p) 7 T. R. 352.

(q) 1 East, 52; 1 Lev. 63; 1 Esp. Rep. 363; Bul. N. P. 129; 1 H. Bla. 37; 2 N. R. 365, 454; 12 East, 94, 454; 2 Taunt. 49; 2 Campb. 308; 6 Car. & P. 545, and the Court will not permit the striking out the names of one or more defendants to cure the defect, *id. ibid.* The same rule prevails under a joint commission of bankruptcy. Cooke's Bank. Law, 6, 7.

(r) 1 Lev. 63; 2 New Rep. 365, 454; 12 East, 93, 454; *aliter* in case against a carrier; and as to parties to actions *ex delicto*, see *post*.

(s) 1 East, 52; 3 T. R. 662; 1 Lev. 63.

(t) 1 Esp. Rep. 135.

(u) *Ante*, 50.

(87) Walcott v. Canfield, 3 Conn. Rep. 198.

(88) Masahan v. Gibbons et al., 19 Johns. Rep. 109. Vide Jackson d. Haines and others v. Woods and others, 5 Johns. Rep. 280, 281. Tom v. Goodrich, 2 Johns. Rep. 213. Livingston's Ex'rs v. Tremper and others, 11 Johns. Rep. 101. Elmendorph v. Tappan and others, 5 Johns. Rep. 176. Burnham v. Webster, 5 Mass. Rep. 270.

(89) Vide contra Hartness and another v. Thompson and others, 5 Johns. Rep. 160. Woodward v. Newhall, 1 Pick. Rep. 500. See 20 Johns. 160, 161. A plea in abatement that the defendant made the promise jointly with another, is supported by evidence that the promise was made by the defendant jointly with an infant. Gibbs v. Merrill, 3 Taunt. 307. Burgess v. Merrill, 4 Taunt. 468, 469. {In an action in a joint and several bond, some of the parties' sureties severed in their pleadings from their principal, and a trial and verdict were had against them; afterwards the principal was called upon to plead, and did so—judgment was then entered up against the sureties, and a *nolle prosequi* as to the principal—to this judgment, or the proceedings, no exception was taken in the court below, nor was a new trial asked by the sureties, but a writ of error was taken. The Supreme Court of the United States affirmed the judgment; holding that there was no decision exactly in point to such a case; that there was no distinction between the entry of a *nolle prosequi* before and after judgment as applicable to such a case; and that the decisions of the Courts of the United States upon this proceeding, have been on the ground that the question is matter of practice and convenience. Minor v. Mech. Bank, 1 Peters, Sup. Ct. Rep. 46.}

II. DEFENDANTS. 2. Who should be joined or omitted.

which case, should the defendants plead the non-joinder of the infant or feme covert in abatement, the plaintiff may reply the infancy or coverture (x). But when one of the defendants is discharged from liability by matter *subsequent* to the making of the contract, and which operates only to protect him individually, leaving the contract in other respects in full force, as by bankruptcy and certificate, or by the order of the Insolvent Court, the failure on the trial as to him on that ground does not preclude the plaintiff from recovering against the other parties, or a *nolle prosequi* as to him may be entered, upon his plea of his personal discharge (y). And by virtue of the late statute (z), the success of one defendant upon the Statute of limitations [*52] *shall not defeat the action against another defendant who has admitted the claim within six years. In debt on a penal statute at the suit of a common informer, or of the party aggrieved, for an offence which may be committed by several jointly, the plaintiff will succeed if he prove either of the defendants to be liable; for in this case the action, though in form *ex contractu*, is founded upon a *tort* (a) (91). So against executors, though the plaintiff may fail as to one, on the plea of *plene administravit*, he may recover against the other, and the defendant who is acquitted is not even entitled to costs (b).

As the consequences of the joinder of *too many* defendants, in an action founded on a *contract* (c), are in general so important, it is advisable, in cases where it is doubtful how many parties are liable, to proceed only against those defendants who are certainly liable, in which case we shall see the non-joinder can only be taken advantage of by a plea in abatement (d) (92).

Non-Joinder.—With respect to the mode of taking advantage of the *omission* of a party who ought to be made a co-defendant, there is a material distinction between this case, and that of co-plaintiffs. We have seen that if a person who ought to join as *plaintiff* be omitted, and the objection appear upon the pleadings, the defendant may demur, move in arrest of judgment, or bring a writ of error; or if the objection do not appear on the pleadings, the plaintiff, except in the case of co-executors or co-administrators, will be nonsuited (e). But in the case of *defendants*, if a party be omitted,

(x) 4 Taunt. 468, 470; 3 *Id.* 307; 14 East, 214; 3 Esp. Rep. 76; Vin. Ab. Actions, Joinder, D. d. pl. 8; 5 Esp. Rep. 47.

(y) 1 Wils. 89; 1 Saund. 207 a. n. 2; 3 Esp. Rep. 77; 2 M. & Sel. 23, 444. If the general issue also be pleaded by the defendant, who sets up his bankruptcy or insolvency, a *nolle prosequi* cannot be entered. For the entry of a *nolle prosequi* against one defendant, who pleads the general issue in an action *ex contractu* against several, discharges all, see Tidd, 9th edit. 682, 896.

(z) 9 Geo. 4, c. 14, s. 1.

(a) Carth. 361; 2 East, 569; 1 New Rep. 245; 3 East, 62.

(b) Tidd's Prac. 9th edit. 986; 1 Saund. 207 a, b. note.

(c) According to the case of Govett v. Radnidge, 3 East, 62, when the plaintiff declares in *case* for the breach of a contract, the defendant cannot plead in abatement that another person was liable, nor is it a ground of nonsuit that *too many* defendants were joined in the action; but since the cases in 2 New Rep. 365, 454, and 12 East, 95, 454; 3 B. & B. 54, 171; 6 Moore, 141, 154, 158; 2 Chit. Rep. 1, it should seem that the form of action cannot vary the right of defence; and that therefore in an action on the case founded merely on contract, the joinder of too many would be as fatal as in assumpsit. In an action upon the case against public carriers for negligence, the non-joinder of a party cannot be pleaded in abatement, *id.*; 2 Chit. Rep. 1; see *post.*

(d) *Infra*, 52.

(e) *Ante*, 9, 10, 14.

(91) { Whitbeck v. Cook et ux., 15 Johns. Rep. 483. Beibman v. Vandenlia, 2 Rawle, 334. }

(92) Vide Burnham v. Webster, 5 Mass. Rep. 270.

whether liable to be jointly sued upon a personal contract or as pernor of the profits of a real estate, as in *debt for a rent charge (*f*), or on one of the assignees of a term (*g*), the objection can only be taken by plea in abatement, verified by affidavit (*h*); and the statute 3 & 4 W. 4, ch. 42, sect. 8, requires the affidavit to state the residence in England of the omitted defendant, and if this be omitted, the defendant will be chargeable with the whole debt, and it cannot be objected at the trial upon the general issue as a variance, that a bill or note stated in the declaration to have been made by the defendant, was in fact made by him and others (*i*). If, however, it expressly appear on the face of the declaration, or some other pleading of the plaintiff, that the party omitted is *still living*, as well as that he jointly contracted; in that case the defendant may demur (93) or move in arrest of judgment, or sustain a writ of error (*k*). There may, however, be this objection in the case of a joint contract, to the non-joinder of one or more of the several parties liable, that if judgment be obtained against one, and in a separate action against him on such contract, the plaintiff may have difficulty in afterwards proceeding against the parties omitted (*l*). If the defendant plead in abatement the non-joinder of a party, and it turns out there are other joint-contractors not named in the plea, the defendant will not succeed thereon (*m*).

II. DEFENDANTS.

2. Who should be joined or omitted.

(*f*) 1 Saund. 284, n. 4.

(*g*) 5 B. & C. 479.

(*h*) Whelpdale's case, 5 Co. 119 a; 2 Taunt. 254; 1 Saund. 154, n. 1, 291 b. n. 4, &c.; 5 T. R. 651; 1 East, 20; 4 T. R. 725; 2 Bla. Rep. 947; 3 Camp. 50.

(*i*) 1 B. & Ald. 224; Gow, R. 161.

(*k*) 1 Saund. 291 b. &c. n. 4, 154, n. 1; 1 B. & P. 73; 7 T. R. 596, 597; 2 Taunt. 254. Suing only two of the inhabitants of the hundred under the black act is fatal in arrest of judgment, 2 D. & R. 439. In general a person is presumed to be living, until it be proved that he is dead, unless seven years have elapsed since he was heard of, 2 East, 313; 6 East, 85; 1 Saund. 235 a, n. 8; but this seems an exception, *sed quære*. See 2 Taunt. 256; 2 Anstr 448; 3 Anstr. 811, from which it should seem that if it appear in a declaration or in a *scire facias* at the suit of the king, on a bond, that there were other joint contractors, though it be not averred that they be living, the declaration and *scire facias* will be deemed insufficient.

(*l*) Com. Dig. Action, K. 4, L. 4; 6 Co. 45 a. 46 a.; Cro. Jac. 73, 74; Yelv. 67.

(*m*) 6 Taunt. 587; 2 Marsh. 302; 2 Bla. Rep. 951.

---

(93) { Whitaker *v.* Young, 2 Cowen's Reports, 572. } In the second edition, the passage in the text stands thus: "There is, however, this objection in the case of a joint contract to the non-joinder of one or more of the several parties liable, that if judgment be obtained against one, in a separate action against him on such contract, the plaintiff cannot afterwards proceed against the parties omitted, and consequently loses their security;"—upon which it has been well remarked, by Chief Justice SPENCER, (18 Johns. Rep. 478.) "that by reference to the cases cited by Chitty, it will be found, that they were actions in *tort;* and even in those actions which are, in their nature, joint and several, it has been held, that where the plaintiff proceeded to judgment against one, the others might plead this in bar. (Cro. Jac. 73. Yelv. 67. Com. Dig. Action, K. 4, 6 Co. Rep. 75.) These cases come under the review of this court in Livingston *v.* Bishop, (1 Johns. Rep. 291.) and it was decided, that a judgment alone would be no bar, without satisfaction. In Wilkes *v.* Jackson, (2 Hen. & Munf. 358, 361.) it was decided that a judgment for damages, in a separate action against one of several joint trespasses, is a bar to an action against the rest. There is, however, a wide difference between a judgment against one of several *tort feasors*, and one of several *joint debtors*. In the latter case whatever extinguishes the debt as to one, merges it as to all." See Robertson *v.* Smith, 18 Johns. Rep. 459. Willings et al. *v.* Consequa, 1 Peters' Rep. 301. Penny *v.* Martin, 4 Johns. Cha. Rep. 566. Smith *v.* Black, 9 Serg. & Rawle, 143. Downey *v.* Farmers' Bank, 13 Serg. & Rawle, 288. Ward *v.* Johnson, 13 Mass. Rep. 148. See also Williams *v.* M'Fall, 2 Serg. & Rawle, 280. Reed *v.* Garvin's Ex'rs, 7 Serg. & Rawle, 354. The supreme court of Massachusetts, however, have recently decided, (two judges of the five composing the court, *dissenting*,) that after a judgment in trespass *de bonis asportatis* against a deputy sheriff, and an execution levied on his body, *but not satisfied*, no action lies against the sheriff. Campbell *v.* Phelps, 1 Pick. Rep. 62.

II. DEFENDANTS.

3dly. In the case of assignment of interest or change of credit, and of covenants running with the land, &c.

In general, in the case of a mere *personal* contract, the action for the breach of it cannot be brought against a person to whom the contracting party has assigned his interest, and the original party alone can be sued: thus if one demise cattle *or goods, and the lessee covenant for himself and his assigns, at the end of the term to deliver such cattle or goods, and the lessee assign the cattle, &c., this covenant will not bind the assignee, for it is merely a thing in action in the personalty, and wants such privity as exists between the lessor and lessee of *real* property in respect of the reversion (n); and if two parties dissolve their partnership, and one of them covenant with the other that he will pay all the debts, a creditor must nevertheless sue both (o).

[*54] There may, however, in some cases, be a *change of credit*, by agreement between the parties, so as to transfer the liability from the original contracting party to another, or to one only of the original parties (p): thus where the plaintiffs were creditors of T. and the defendants were debtors to T., and by the express consent of all parties an arrangement was made, that the defendant should pay to plaintiffs the debt due from them to T.; it was held, that the plaintiffs were entitled to recover (q). But unless it was agreed that T. should be discharged from all liability, it seems that no such action could be supported (r). The general rule of the law is, that a debt cannot be assigned. The exception to that rule is, that where there is a defined and ascertained debt due from A. to B. and a debt to the same or a larger amount due from C. to A., and the three agree that C. shall be B.'s debtor instead of A., and C. promises to pay B., the latter may maintain an action against C. But in such action it is incumbent on the plaintiff to show, that at the time when C. promised to pay B. there was an ascertained debt due from A. to B. (s). So in the case of a tenancy from year to year, if the landlord accept another person as tenant, in the room of the former tenant, without any surrender in writing, such acceptance will be a dispensation of any notice to quit, and the original tenant will be

[*55] discharged (t). So if one take the security of the agent of the *principal, with whom he dealt, unknown to the principal, and give the agent a receipt as for the money due from the principal, in consequence of which the principal deals differently with his agent on the faith of such receipt, the principal is discharged, although the security fail; but if the principal were not prejudiced he would not be discharged (u). Where one of three joint covenantors gave a bill of exchange as a collateral security, not expressly accepted in satisfaction of the debt, the judgment recovered on the bill was decided to be no bar to an action of covenant against the three (x); and the creditor of a firm does not

(n) 3 Wils. 27; 4 T. R. 730, 726; *chose in action* not assignable at law, see *ante*, 17, 18.

(o) See *ante*, 12, 13.

(p) 1 New Rep. 124, 131; 4 Esp. Rep. 91, 92; 5 Esp. Rep. 122; 8 T. R. 451; 3 East, 147; 2 Campb. 99; 12 East, 421; 2 Taunt. 49; 13 East, 7; 4 Taunt. 58. See instances of a new firm adopting a debt of an old firm, and thereby becoming liable; 1 Mont. Bank. Law, 619, 620; 4 Taunt. 673; 3 B. & Ald. 39; 2 B. & C. 72.

(q) 5 B. & Ald. 228; 1 Hen. Bla. 239; *ante*, 18.

(r) 3 B. & C. 855; 4 B. & C. 166; 5 B. & Ald. 228; 8 B. & C. 395, 396.

(s) 8 B. & C. 396.

(t) 2 Esp. Rep. 505; 1 Campb. 318; 2 B. & Ald. 119; but see 2 Campb. 103; 5 Taunt. 518. See cases as to this point 2 Stark. Rep. 236; 4 Bar. & Cres. 922, 933; 3 Bing. 462.

(u) 3 East, 147; 8 T. R. 451; 9 B. & C. 449; see observations of Lord Hardwick, Ambl. 271, 272.

(x) 3 East, 251; 8 T. R. 451; 2 B. & A. 210; 3 B. & A. 611.

II. DEFENDANTS.

3. When interest, &c. assigned.

discharge a retiring partner by agreeing to carry the debt to the account of the remaining partners, and by taking their bill, which is afterwards dishonored (y) (94); or unless it clearly appear that the creditor has accepted the substituted credit of a new partnership instead of the liability of the old firm, and not merely as a continuing or additional security (z). But taking a new security from continuing partner may discharge the retiring one if so agreed (a). The consignor of goods may be primarily liable for the freight, but the consignee or purchaser, if he accept the goods in pursuance of the usual bill of lading, may be sued for the same, unless it be known to the master of the ship that he acted only as agent for the consignor (b). And the indorsee of a bill of lading requiring the delivery to order, on payment of freight, is liable, though he only acted as broker for the consignee (c). But where there is a charter-party under seal providing for payment of freight by the freighter, and the goods are received under an indorsed bill of lading, by which they are deliverable to the freighter or order, he or they paying freight as per charter-party, there is no implied contract on the part of the indorsee of the bill of lading to pay freight to the owner of the ship (d).

In case of covenants running with real property.

Upon a covenant running with the *land*, which must concern real property or the estate therein (e), the assignee of the *lessee* is liable to an action for a breach of covenant after the assignment of the estate to him (h) (95), and although he afterwards re-assign or assign to a third party, he continues liable for all breaches accruing *whilst the term was legally vested in him* (i), and though he have not taken possession (k). And executors or administrators of a lessee may be sued as *assignees* of the term if they accept the term, though if one of two executors of a lessee enter, such entry does not enure as the entry of both so as to make them *jointly* liable to an action for use and occupation (l). But his liability ceases when he assigns his interest, though even purposely, to

(y) 5 B. & C. 196.

(z) Kirwan v. Kirwan, 2 Cr. & M. 617, 627; 4 Tyr. 491, S. C.

(a) Thompson v. Percival, 3 Nev. & Man. 167, citing Kirwan v. Kirwan, *supra*.

(b) Abott, 1st edit. 229; 1 East, 507; 1 Marsh. 248; 13 East, 399; M. & S. 157; 2 M. & S. 303, 320.

(c) 1 Marsh. 146, 250; 1 M. & S. 157.

(d) 2 M. & S. 303; but see 3 M. & S. 218; 3 Campb. 545.

(e) 3 Wils. 29; 2 H. Bla. 133; 10 East, 138, 139; 2 Marsh. 1, 4. As to what is a covenant running with the land, see 5 B. & A. 1; 4 B. & A. 266; 1 B. & C. 410; 3 Moore, 45; 2 Chit. Rep. 482, 608; *ante*, 13.

(h) 32 H. 8, c. 34; Bac. Ab. Covenant, E. 34; 3 Wils. 25; 2 Saund. 304, n. 12; Platt on Cov. 489. As to the liability of the assignee of *part* of the premises, 5 B. & C. 479, 484; 8 D. & R. 264, S. C. The leading principle, as to the construction of covenants of this description, in which an assignee has or has not a right to sue, are laid down in 5 Rep. 16. An assignee of a lease under covenant to repair, without qualification, must repair the premises if destroyed by fire, 2 Chit. Rep. 608. The assignee of the lessee is bound to protect the latter from liability, although the assignment contain no covenant so to do. 5 B. & C. 589; 8 D. & R. 368, S. C., and see Flight v. Glossopp, 2 Bing. N. C. 125.

(i) Harley v. King, 1 Gale R. 100; 2 Cr. M. & Ross. 18.

(k) Woodfall, L. & T. 7th edit. 113; 7 T. R. 312; 2 Saund. 182; 1 Salk. 196; 1 Lord Raym. 322; 1 B. & B. 238; 3 Moore, 500, S. C. *acc.*; Dougl. 438, *cont.*

(l) Nation v. Tozer and another, 1 Crom. M. & Ros. 172.

(94) See Smith et al. v. Rogers et al., 17 Johns. Rep. 340. But the bond, or obligation under seal, of one of the partners is an extinguishment of a simple contract debt from the partnership to the obligee. Clement v. Brush, 3 Johns. Cas. 180. Tom v. Goodrich and others, 2 Johns. Rep. 213. The principle of law is, that a security of a higher nature extinguishes inferior securities, but not securities of an equal degree. Andrews v. Smith, 9 Wend. R. 53.

(95) Vide Polland v. Shaeffer, 1 Dall. 210.

II. DEFENDANTS.

3 When interest, &c. assigned.

a married woman, or an insolvent person (*m*); and although the lease contain a covenant not to assign; for the assignment destroys the privity of estate (*n*). The same rule prevails in equity (*o*). If the covenant be merely *collateral* and *personal*, an assignee is not in any case liable, and the lessee alone can be sued (*p*). Upon a covenant running with the land, the lessee, or the assignee of the lessee, may sue the *reversioner* for a breach of it (*q*), as well in case of freehold as copyhold (*r*). An assignee of a lease, to whom an assignment has been made by way of mortgage security, is liable for the [*56] rent, although he has never entered, or taken *actual possession (*s*)(96). *Debt* cannot be supported against the assignee of *part* of the land demised by a lease, but only against the assignee of the whole (*t*), though *covenant* is sustainable (*u*).

When there is an *express* covenant in a lease to pay rent or perform any other act, the original lessee, and his personal representatives, having assets, are liable to an action of *covenant* during the lease for non-performance of covenants; notwithstanding, before the breach complained of, the interest in the lease has been assigned, and rent has been accepted from the assignee (*v*)(97). But an action cannot, it seems, be supported against the lessee, or his personal representatives, for a breach of a covenant merely *implied* by law, committed after acceptance of rent from the assignee (*a*); nor can the lessor, after such acceptance of the assignee, maintain an action of *debt* against the lessee or his representatives, even upon an express covenant (*w*).

[*57] An *under-lessee* (98), not having the *whole* of the lessee's interest *assigned to him, cannot be sued by the original lessor for any breach of covenant contained in the original lease (*x*); though for voluntary and not mere permissive waste he would be liable to an action on the case (*y*).

4thly. When one of several obligors, &c. is dead.

In the case of a *joint* contract, if one of the parties die, his executor or administrator is *at law* discharged from liability, and the survivor alone can be

(*m*) 1 B. & P. 21; Bac. Ab. Covenant, E. 4; 2 Stra. 1221; Platt on Cov. 503.
(*n*) 8 B. & C. 486.
(*o*) Onslow *v.* Currie, 2 Mad. 330; 2 Atk. 546; 1 Bro. P. C. 516.
(*p*) Bac. Ab. Covenant, E. 3, 4; 3 Wils. 25; 2 Saund. 304, n. 12.
(*q*) 4 B. & A. 266.
(*r*) 1 Saund. 241 a; ante, 20, 21.
(*s*) 3 Moore, 500; 1 B. & P. 238, S. C.
(*t*) Curtis *v.* Spitty, 1 Bing N. C. 756.
(*u*) Conghart *v.* King, Cro. Car. 221.
(*v*) 1 Saund. 241, *note* 5; 1 T. R. 92; 7 T. R. 305; 1 Hen. Bla. 443; 4 T. R. 94, 100; Bac. Ab. Covenant, E. 4; 8 East, 311; Platt on Cov. 539. See 6 Geo. 4, c. 16, s. 75, as to bankrupt lessees, &c.
(*a*) 1 Saund. 241 b; 4 T. R. 98; 1 Sid. 447; Sir W. Jones, 223; Cro. Jac. 583. See Platt on Cov. Index, "Implied Covenants." 6 Bing 656.
(*w*) 1 T. R. 92; 1 Saund. 241, n. 5, see *post*; 5 Taunt. 452.
(*x*) Dougl. 183.
(*y*) 2 Bl. Rep. 1111; 1 Moore, 100; 6 Taunt. 301; 1 New Rep. 290; *post*.

---

(96) { In Pennsylvania one who owns the *equitable* interest in land, and who as the owner of such interest is in the *constructive* possession, and may receive the income of it, is liable in covenant, as assignee, for a ground rent charged thereon, although the legal title is in another, and no trust appears by the deed. Berry *v.* M'Mullen, 17 Serg. & Rawle, 84. }

(97) Vide Kunckle *v.* Wynick, 1 Dall. 305.

(98) A declaration in covenant for rent, against the assignee of a lessee, averring that the rent accrued subsequent to the assignment to the defendant, was due and owing to the plaintiff's testator, and still remains wholly in arrear, and unpaid to the defendant, states a breach in sufficient terms; and it is unnecessary to go further and say that the lessee had not paid it, for that was already implied in the averment that the defendant owed it. Dubois's Executors *v.* Van Orden, 6 Johns. Rep. 105.

sued (*z*)(99); and if the executor be sued, he may either plead the survivorship in bar, or give it in evidence under the general issue (*a*) (100); but in equity the executor of the deceased party is liable, unless in some instances of a surety (*b*) (101). If the contract were *several* (102) or joint and several, the executor of the deceased may be sued at law in a separate action (*c*); but he cannot be sued jointly with the survivor, because one is to be charged *de bonis testatoris*, and the other *de bonis propriis* (*d*). When the surviving party dies, his executor or administrator is to be made defendant (*e*). It is not unusual to declare, at least in one count, against the survivor as such, noticing the death of his co-obligee or co-partner (*f*); but the survivor or his executor may be declared against, without noticing the first deceased party (*g*) (103); and in an action against such survivor, a debt which became due from himself separately, before or after the death of his partner, may be included (*h*); and when the survivor is sued for his own separate debt, he may set off a demand due to him as surviving partner (*i*) (104).

II. DEFENDANTS.

4thly. When an obligor is dead.

*When the contracting party is dead, his *executor or administrator*, or, in case of a joint contract, the executor or administrator of the survivor, is the party to be made defendant (*j*) and is liable though not expressly named in the covenant (105) or contract. But no action lies against executors upon a

[*58]

5thly. In the case of executors or administrators, heirs and devisees.

(*z*) 2 Marsh. Rep. 302; 6 Taunt. 587; Bac. Ab. Obligation, vol. v. D. 4; Vin. Ab. Obligation, P. 20; 2 Burr. 1196; 1 Meriv. 563, 566; 2 Meriv. 30. The rule is so (upon a judgment against several) as to the personalty, but not as to the realty, 2 Saund. 51, n. 4; Tidd, 9th edit. 1121; 1 B. & A. 31; see 47 Geo. 3, sess. 2, c. 74.

(*a*) 5 East, 261.

(*b*) Bac. Ab. Obligation, vol. vii. Addenda, Obligation, 506; 2 Vern. 277, 292; 3 Ves. 399. 2 Ves. J. 106, 244, 265; Lane *v.* Williams, 2 Vern. 277, 292; Chitty on Bills, 8th edit. 50; Daniel *v.* Cross, 3 Ves. 277; Anderson *v.* Maltby, Bro. C. C. 423; 2 Ves. J. 244, S. C.; Jacomb *v.* Harwood, 2 Ves. 265; Devaynes *v.* Noble, 1 Mer. 568. *Quære*, whether equity would give relief against the executor, if the creditor could obtain payment from the surviving partner.

(*c*) 2 Burr. 1190.

(*d*) Carth. 171; 2 Lev. 228; 2 Vin. Ab. 67, 70.

(*e*) 3 B. & B. 302; 9 Co. 89 a; 1 B. & A. 31.

(*f*) *Per* Le Blanc, J. 2 M. & Sel. 25; 6 T. R. 363; Vin. Ab. Obligation, P. 20; *ante*, 52.

(*g*) 1 B. & Ald. 29; 3 B. & B. 302; 7 Moore, 158; *ante*, 50.

(*h*) 2 T. R. 476; 6 T. R. 582. See, as to joinder of actions, *post*.

(*i*) 5 T. R. 493; 1 Esp. R. 47.

(*j*) 9 Co. 89 a.; 3 Bla. Com. 302; 1 Com. on Contr. 258.

(99) Vide Foster *v.* Hooper, 2 Mass. Rep. 572. ante, 31, n. 67. Atwell's Administrators *v.* Milton, 4 Hen. & Mun. 253. Chandler's Executors *v.* Neale's Executors, 2 Hen. & Mun. 124. Braxton's Adm'x *v.* Hilyard, 2 Mun. 49. Simonds *v.* Center, 6 Mass. Rep. 18.

(100) { Burgwin *v.* Hosteler's Adm., Tayl. Rep. 124, S. C. 2 Hayw. Rep. 104. nom. Burgwin *v.* ——. }

(101) Vide Jenkins *v.* De Groot, 1 Caines' Cas. in Err. 122. Lang and Whitaker *v.* Keppele. 1 Binn. 123.

(102) Vide Harrison *v.* Field, 2 Wash. 136. { Weaver *v.* Shryock's Executors, 6 Serg. & Rawle, 262. } In the case of a joint contract, if one of the parties die, his executor is at law discharged from liability, and the survivor alone can be sued; he may plead the survivorship or give it in evidence under the general issue. Grout *v.* Shurter, 1 Wend. R. 148. The doctrine which allows an action against the executor, is applicable to cases where the contract, by the express assent of the parties, is made joint and several. It does not authorize a creditor to sue the executor or administrator of a deceased partner, ib.

(103) Raborg *v.* The Bank of Columbia, 1 Harr. & Gill, 231. Thus, in an action of assumpsit for goods, which were sold to two partners, against the survivor, it is unnecessary to notice the survivorship. Goelet *v.* M'Kinstry, 1 Johns. Cas. 405.

(104) Vide Hogg's Executors *v.* Ashe, 1 Hayw. 477.

(105) Harrison's Ex. *v.* Sampson, 2 Wash. Rep. 156. Lee, Ex. of Daniel, *v.* Cooke, 1 Wash. Rep. 306.

II. DEFENDANTS.

5. Executors, heirs, &c.

covenant to be performed by the testator in person, and which consequently the executor cannot perform (*k*); or for the breach of a personal contract where the breach can occasion no injury to the personal estate of the testator, or intestate, and where therefore the remedy dies with the person, as a breach of a promise of marriage (*l*) (106). The executor of a lessee is liable as such upon a breach of covenant committed after the testator's death, by the assignee of the lease (*m*) (107). In a recent case, the Court of Common Pleas held, that the executors of a lessor, who was tenant for life, are not liable to the lessee to whom a term of years was granted, for the breach of the *implied* covenant, or covenant in law, for quiet enjoyment resulting from, and created by, the word *demise*, the lessee having been evicted by the remainder-man (*n*).

If a person intermeddle *as* executor with the estate of the deceased, he may in general be sued as executor *de son tort*, although there be a lawful executor (*o*); and in such case he is uniformly declared against as if he were a lawful executor, though the party died intestate, and he may be joined in the same action with the lawful executor (108), though not with the lawful administrator (*p*); and if the husband of an executrix after her death detain part of the goods of the testator, he may be sued as executor *de son tort* (*q*). So if a stranger take away the goods of the deceased, and there be no lawful executor, he also is liable to be sued as executor *de son tort* (109), though he claim them as his *own* (*r*); but in this case if there be a lawful executor or administrator, the stranger cannot be sued as executor *de son tort* (*s*). And no person can ever be sued as *administrator de son tort* (110), nor can an executor *de son tort* of an executor *de son tort* be sued *as such* at law (*t*). The 3 & 4 W. 4, c. 42, s. 14, gives an action of debt on simple contract against an executor or administrator in any Court of law.

[*59] *If there be several executors, they should all be sued, in case they have all

(*k*) 3 Wils. 29; Cro. Eliz. 553; 1 Rol. Rep. 359.
(*l*) 2 M. & Sel. 408; 1 Com. on Contr. 528; *ante*, 21.
(*m*) 10 East, 313.
(*n*) Adams *v.* Gibney, 6 Bing. 656.
(*o*) 5 Co. 34 a.
(*p*) 1 Saund. 265, n. 2; Com. Dig. *Administrator*, C. 3; Toller, 369, 340.
(*q*) 5 Cro. Eliz. 472.
(*r*) 5 Co. 33 b.
(*s*) 5 Co. 34 a.
(*t*) 2 Mod. 293, 294; Andr. Rep. 252.

(106) Lattimore *v.* Rogers, 13 Serg. & Rawle, 183.

(107) Where there is an express covenant in a lease in fee for the payment of rent, the executors of the lessee are liable for the rent accruing subsequent to the testator's death, as far as they have assets, although the land has gone into the hands of the heir. Executors of Van Rensselaer *v.* Executors of Platner, 2 Johns. Cas. 17. But covenant does not in such case lie against them by the devisees of the grantor. Devisees of Van Rensselaer *v.* Executors of Platner, Id. 24.

(108) Though a person who is sued as executor *de son tort*, shall not defeat the suit by taking out letters of administration pending the suit, because the suit was well commenced; yet such an administration will legitimate all intermediate acts *ab initio*; and justify a retainer. Vaughan *v.* Brown, Str. 1106, S. C. Andr. 328. Curtis *v.* Vernon, 3 Term Rep. 587. Rattoon and another *v.* Overacker, 8 Johns. Rep. 126.

(109) Glenn *v.* Smith, 2 Gill & Johns. Rep. 494. Campbell *v.* Tousey, 7 Cowen, 64. And may be sued as executor generally. *Ib.*

(110) At common law an action of account did not lie against an executor for want of privity, but such action is now given by statute 4 and 5 Ann. c. 16. The first thirteen sections of which are in force in Pennsylvania, and the 20th and 27th sections. Roberts' Dig. 43. Griffith *v.* Willing, 3 Binn. 317. Laws N. Y. sess. 36, c. 75. s. 5. 1 R. L. 311. against the executors or administrators of every guardian, bailiff, or receiver. Litt. § 125. Co. Litt. 90 b. F. N. B. 117. E. Com. Dig. Accompt, D.

3. Executors, heirs, &c.

administered and have assets, or the defendant may plead the non-joinder in abatement; but if one hath not proved, nor administered, he may be omitted (*u*). A plaintiff who sues several persons as executors, shall not be defeated *in toto* upon causes of action stated in the declaration to have accrued to the deceased, merely on the ground that one of the defendants was not an executor, and succeeded on his plea to that effect; but in such case the plaintiff cannot recover on counts laying promises by the defendants as executors (*v*). So if several executors plead *plene administravit*, the plaintiff may succeed as to one of them only (111). If a married woman be executrix, the husband must be joined in the action (*w*); and an infant cannot be an executor till he be of full age (*x*); nor can an executor be sued as such for money lent to (*y*), or had and received by him (*z*), or upon a penal statute (*zz*). By the Statute against Frauds the representatives of a deceased person are not personally liable without a written promise, and even such promise is not available in this respect, unless there be an adequate consideration (*a*) (112); but in some cases executors will render themselves personally liable, if they contract as principals, and on their own personal liability (*b*). If a creditor appoint his debtor to be his *executor*, *such voluntary* act is deemed a *release at law*; but when a debtor becomes *administrator*, *such* appointment being only by an act of Court, and not of the creditor himself, it merely suspends the right (*c*).

If the contract be under seal, (or of record), the *heir* of the party contracting is liable to an action for the breach of an *express* covenant therein; provided the ancestor expressly bound himself "and his *heirs*" by the deed or obligation; and provided the heir have *legal* assets by descent from the obligor (*d*) (113). And if there be a *devisee*, (otherwise than for the payment of debts, or in pursuance of a marriage contract *entered into before marriage,) [*60] he may be sued in an action of debt for the breach of a contract of the testator under seal, or of record; but the heir must be joined in the action; and an action of *covenant* cannot in any case be supported upon a *personal* contract

(*u*) Toller, 367; 1 Moo. & P. 663; 4 T. R. 565. Several executors, though of different things, and though not jointly appointed, &c. may be joined in an action. 1 Vin. Ab. 139; Cro. Car. 293. As to *plaintiffs* executors, see *ante*, 21, 22.

(*v*) 1 M. & M. 146; 1 Saund. 207 a.

(*w*) Cro. Car. 145, 519; Toller, 367; *post*.

(*x*) 38 Geo. 3. c. 87, s. 6; Toller, 367.

(*y*) 1 Hen. Bla. 109; 2 Saund. 117 d.; 4 T. R. 347. As to suing him as such, for funeral expenses, see 3 Campb. 298; or money paid, see 7 B. & C. 444, 449; 1 Man. & R. 169, S. C.; account stated, 7 Taunt. 580; 1 Moore, 305, S. C.

(*z*) 7 B. & C. 444; 1 Man. & R. 180, S. C.

(*zz*) Carth. 361; Cro. Eliz. 766; Com. Dig. *Administrator*, B. 15.

(*a*) See 7 T. R. 350; 3 B. & B. 460.

(*b*) 2 B. & B. 460; 5 Moore, 282, S. C.

(*c*) See Went. Off. Ex. chap. 2, p. 76, 14 ed.; Needham's case, 8 Coke R. 136; Wankford v. Wankford, 1 Salk. 306; Crosman's case, 1 Leonard, 328.

(*d*) Bac. Ab. *Heir and Ancestor*, F.; 2 Saund. 136, 137, n. 4; Plowd. 439, 441; Willes, 585; 2 Bla. Com. 243; Platt on Cov. 41, 449.

(111) App v. Dreisbach, 2 Rawle, 287.

(112) { Such as giving up securities against the testator's estate. Stebbins v. Smith, 4 Pick. Rep. 97. See Clark v. Herring, 5 Binn. 33. }

(113) So, the heir of the heir is liable as far as he has assets by descent from the original obligor. Walker's Executors v. Ellis and others, 2 Mun. 88. In the State of New York heirs are liable on a simple contract or specialty, whether mentioned therein or not, in case the debtor died intestate seised of lands, &c. and the heirs of devisees in case he made a will. Laws of N. Y. sess. 36. c. 93. s. 1. 1 R. L. 316. { 2 Rev. Stat. 452. s. 32. } Eting and others v. Vanderlyn, 4 Johns. Rep. 234.

II. DEFENDANTS. 5. Executors, heirs, &c.

against a devisee, the statute 3 & 4 W. & M. only giving an action of *debt* (e). Though the devisee be an infant, he cannot pray the parol to demur by reason of his non-age (114), such privilege being confined to an infant heir (f). But an equity of redemption is not assets at law, in respect of which an heir or devisee is chargeable, and the creditor must proceed in a Court of Equity (g). An heir or devisee having a *legal* estate, is liable to an action for the breach of a covenant running with the land committed in his own time (h). If there be several heirs, as in the case of gavel-kind, or of parceners, they should all be joined, or the defendant may plead in abatement (i); and a devisee must be sued with the heir jointly at law as well as in equity (k). And though an executor cannot in any case be sued jointly with the heir (l), yet the executor may be sued at the same time as the heir, and if the heir be also executor, separate actions may be sustained against him in both capacities (m). If assets by descent vest in the heir, it appears that the charge will continue to run against *his* heir taking the same assets (n).

6thly. In the case of bankruptcy.

When the contracting party has become bankrupt and has obtained his certificate, he is in general no longer liable to be sued in respect of any debt due from him when he became bankrupt, or of any claim or demand which the creditor might have proved under the commission (o)(115). The present Bankrupt Act enables creditors to prove under the commission in respect to *contingent* debts, although the contingency had not happened at the time of the proof (p); consequently such debts will now be barred by the certificate as effectually as other debts. In cases where the plaintiff has an election to sue either in form *ex contractu* or *in tort* (116), [*61] *though the bankruptcy will be no answer to the latter mode of proceeding (q), it will be a bar to any action founded on contract if the amount of the plaintiff's demand was capable of being ascertained at the time of the bankruptcy (r), and might have been proved under the commission (117).

There are also some demands which are barred by the certificate though they were not provable under the commission. Thus where an action upon a contract has been brought against a party, and he becomes bankrupt *before* verdict, the *costs* in such actions, for want of a previous verdict, are not prov-

(e) 3 & 4 W. & M. c. 14; Bac. Ab. *Heir and Ancestor*, F.; 1 P. Wms. 99; 7 East, 128.

(f) 4 East, 485.

(g) 2 Saund. 7, n. 4, 8 d. 5th ed.

(h) If only *equitable* estate *descend*, the heir cannot be sued at *law*, per Lord Hardwicke, Plunkett v. Pearson, 2 Atk. 294.

(i) 2 Vin. Ab. 67; Com. Dig. *Abatement*, F. 9.

(k) 2 Saund. 7, n. 4; Bac. Ab. *Heir*; Vin. Ab. *Heir*, Z. d. See 2 Atk. 125, 433, why preferable to proceed in equity.

(l) 18 Edw. 3, 4; Com. Dig. *Abatement*, F. 10; Vin. Ab *Actions*, c. d. pl. 8.

(m) Com. Dig. *Pleader*, 2 E. 3.

(n) Dyer, 368 a. pl. 46; Cro. Car. 151; 2 Ch. Cas. 175; Plowd. 441.

(o) 6 Geo. 4, c. 16, s. 121.

(p) *Id.* s. 56.

(q) Doug. 583; 6 T. R. 695; 5 Bing. 63.

(r) Doug. 767; 6 T. R. 699, 701; and see 3 Madd. 51; Buck, 153.

(114) In the State of New York, in a personal action against either heirs or devisees, the parol shall not demur; but no execution shall issue within a year after rendition of judgment, sess. 36. c. 93. s. 6. 1 R. L. 318. {2 Rev. Stat. 454. s. 42. 455. s 56.}

(115) So, the discharge of an insolvent is no bar to an action, on an express covenant, brought to recover rent accruing subsequent to the insolvent's discharge. Lansing v. Prendergast, 9 Johns. Rep. 127. See Murray v. De Rottenham, 6 Johns. Cha. Rep. 63. Hamilton v. Atherton, 1 Ashm. Rep. 67.

(116) Denied by Livingston, J., Hutton v. Speyer, 1 Johns. Rep. 41, 42.

(117) See Dufar v. Murgatroyd, 1 Wash. C. C. Rep. 15.

able under the commission, but they are notwithstanding considered as accessorial to the original debt and barred together with such debt by the certificate (s) (118). II. DEFENDANTS. — 6. Bankruptcy.

But in certain cases the bankrupt may still remain liable to an action in respect of contracts made before his bankruptcy. Leasehold property belonging to the bankrupt does not pass to the assignees unless they elect to take it. By the 6 Geo. 4, c. 16, s. 75, the bankrupt is enabled to free himself from future liability upon the lease by delivering it up to the lessor within fourteen days after he shall have had notice that the assignees have declined to accept the same; but unless he avail himself of this privilege, he will still continue subject to such liability.

The bankrupt may also *revive* his liability upon a contract made before his bankruptcy, by a subsequent promise to pay the debt (119); which promise, it appears, will in general be equally available to the creditor, whether made before (120) or after (121) the allowance of the certificate (t). But it should be observed, that promises and contracts made with a creditor expressly in consideration of his signing the certificate; and also promises made before the signing of the certificate to a creditor who was one of the commissioners, and who subsequently signed the certificate, would be void in the former case, under the express provisions of the Bankrupt Act (u), and in the latter, as being against public policy (x) (122). In order that the pre-existing obligation should be revived by a subsequent *promise, the promise should be express, distinct, and unequivocal (y); and by the provisions of the present Bankrupt Act, such promise must be in writing, signed by the bankrupt, or by some person thereto lawfully authorized in writing by him (z). When the subsequent promise is effectual, it is sufficient to declare upon the original consideration (a) (123); unless the promise be conditional, in which case it seems to be necessary for the creditor to declare specially (b). [*62]

In cases where a party becomes bankrupt after a former bankruptcy, a prior discharge under an insolvent act, or after a composition with his creditors, the

(s) 3 M. & Sel. 326; 2 B. & B. 8; see also 3 B. & A. 13; Eden, 2d edit. 136; 7 B. & C. 436, 706; 1 Man. & R. 330, S. C.

(t) Cowp. 544; 1 T. R. 715; 1 Bing. 281.

(u) 6 Geo. 4, c. 16, s. 125.

(x) 5 B. & A. 753; 1 D. & R. 411, S. C.

(y) 1 Stark. 370; 5 Esp. 198.

(z) 6 Geo 4, c. 16, s 131.

(a) Peak, R. 68; 2 Stark. 68; 2 Hen. Bla. 116; 4 Campb. 205.

(b) 4 Campb. 205.

(118) Costs on a judgment obtained before the discharge of an insolvent, although not taxed, are barred by the discharge. Warne v. Constant, 5 Johns. Rep. 135. Sed vide cases cited in n. b. Ibid. See the cases cited, Ingraham's Insolvent Laws of Pennsylvania, 171, note, 2d edit.

(119) Shippey v. Henderson, 14 Johns. Rep. 178. An action cannot be maintained by the assignee of a note payable to bearer directly on the note, when the negotiability of such note has been destroyed by an insolvent discharge granted the maker. Moore v. Viele, 4 Wend. R. 420. Nor can such assignee avail himself of a new promise subsequent to that discharge, if made neither to himself or his agent. *Ib.*

(120) { Kingston v. Wharton, 2 Serg. & Rawle, 208. }

(121) Maxim v. Morse, 8 Mass. Rep. 127. A promise by a debtor, after the execution of a voluntary release under seal by the creditor, at the debtor's request, to pay the balance of the debt, is founded on a sufficient consideration, and is binding Willing v. Peters, 12 Serg. & Rawle, 177. The promise must, however, be *express*, and be distinctly proved. Reff v. Reff, 2 Penn. N. T. Rep. 418. }

(122) { See Baker v. Matlack, 1 Ashm. Rep. 68. Tuxbury v. Miller, 19 Johns. Rep. 311. Wiggin v. Bush, 12 Johns. Rep. 306, and the American cases there cited. }

(123) { Shippey v. Henderson, 14 Johns. Rep. 178. }

II. DEFENDANTS. certificate only extends to protect his *person*, and his future *effects* are liable to the claims of his creditors, unless he pays 15*s*. in the pound. And before the late Bankrupt Act, the bankrupt was still liable to be sued in respect of his subsequently acquired effects (*c*); but by the provisions of that Act, the future estate and effects of the bankrupt are declared to vest in the assignees under the second commission (*d*)

6. Bankruptcy.

Where there are several contracting parties, and one has been bankrupt, the action should be brought jointly against the solvent partner or partners and the bankrupt, and if the latter should have obtained his certificate, and should plead it, a *nolle prosequi* may be entered as against him (*e*).

The following points, relative to the liability of the *assignees* of a bankrupt to actions in form *ex contractu*, may be here noticed. No action can be brought by any creditor against the assignees for the recovery of any dividend (124), the only remedy being by petition to the Lord Chancellor (*f*). Nor are the assignees liable to an action at the suit of the bankrupt, for his allowance in respect of the amount of dividends paid under his estate (*g*), unless he shall have obtained his certificate before the declaration and payment of the dividend, so as to enable the assignees to take such allowance into account, and to retain for the same before the assets are exhausted (*h*). It has been previously noticed, that assignees of a bankrupt lessee will not be liable to be sued in respect of the rent and covenant, unless they elect to take [*63] *to the premises comprised in the lease (*i*). And when they have elected to take possession, they may nevertheless discharge themselves from future liability, by assigning their interest in the premises even to a pauper (*k*). The assignees are not liable to be sued by the messenger under the commission, for fees due to him before the choice of assignees, the petitioning creditor being the party answerable for these expenses (*l*). And though assignees cannot contract debts in their political capacity, and be sued therein as such (*m*); yet when they personally contract, or when they receive money to the use of another (*n*), they are liable to be sued in their individual capacities. An assignee who has been removed, and has assigned his interest to his co-assignee, may be sued by them (*o*).

A certificate of discharge obtained in a foreign country, is a bar to an action upon a contract made in such country before the certificate (*p*) (125), but not to an action by a creditor, a subject of this country, for a debt contracted here (*q*). And it has been decided, that a certificate under an Irish Commission of bankuptcy, though it be since the Union, is no discharge of a debt con-

(*c*) 7 East, 154.
(*d*) 6 Geo. 4, c. 16, s. 127.
(*e*) 2 M. & Sel. 23. 444; 1 Wils. 89; *ante*, 48.
(*f*) 6 Geo. 4, c. 16, s. 111.
(*g*) *Id.* s. 128.
(*h*) 1 Atk. 207; 6 T. R. 545; *ante*, 29.
(*i*) *Ante*, 62. And see Peake, N. P. C. 238; 7 East, 335; 1 B. & A. 593. The *provisional assignee* of a bankrupt is not responsible for the fraud of an agent appointed with due care, 9 Bing. 96.
(*k*) 1 B. & P. 21; *ante*, 55, 56.
(*l*) 3 B. & C. 43; 4 D. & R. 621, S. C.; 6 Geo. 4, c. 16, s. 14; 2 M. & Sel. 438.
(*m*) Cowp. 134, 135.
(*n*) 1 M. & Sel. 714.
(*o*) Peake, N. P. 213.
(*p*) 5 East, 124.
(*q*) 1 East, 6.

(124) Vide Peck *v*. Trustees of Randall, 1 Johns. Rep. 165.
(125) Vide Hicks *v*. Brown, 12 Johns. Rep. 286. n. b. {Smith *v*. Brown, 3 Binn. 201. Walsh *v*. Farrand, 13 Mass. Rep. 19.}

tracted in England (r); but it has been held, that a debt contracted in this country, by a trader resident in Scotland, is barred by a discharge under a Scottish sequestration, issued in conformity to the Statute 54 Geo. 3, c. 137 (s). II. DEFENDANTS.

7thly. In the case of an insolvent debtor.

By the *Insolvent Act* (t), an insolvent complying with the requisitions of the Act is to be discharged by the Court, "as to the several *debts* and sums of money due, or claimed to be due, at the time of filing his petition from such prisoner, to the several *persons named* in his or her schedule as creditors, or claiming to be creditors for the same, respectively, or for which such persons shall have given credit to such prisoner, before the time of filing such petition, and which were not then payable, and as to the claims of all other persons not known to such prisoner at *the time of such adjudication, who may be indorsers or holders of any negotiable security set forth in such schedule." (u) [*64]

And by section 50 it is provided, that the discharge shall extend to all process for contempt of any Court for non-payment of money (126), and to all costs relative thereto; also to all costs incurred in any actions brought against the insolvent before the filing of his schedule for any debt or damages; and the persons bringing actions are to be deemed creditors for the amount of such costs subject to taxation. The discharge is also declared to extend to sums payable by way of annuity (x).

*It has been decided upon the 1 Geo. 4, c. 119, that the effect of the discharge is only to liberate the insolvent to the extent of the specific debts described in the schedule; and where less than the full amount due is speci- [*65]

(r) 4 B. & Ald. 654; and see 2 H. Bla. 553.

(s) 3 B. & C. 12; 4 D. & R. 658, S. C.; see 1 Rose, 462; Buck, 57; 3 Moore, 623.

(t) 7 Geo. 4, c. 57, s. 40 and 46; continued and amended by 1 Wm. 4, c. 38. A discharge under this act must be pleaded specially, 10 Bing. 11.

(u) See, as to holders of negotiable securities, and what a sufficient description of the debt, &c. in the schedule, 4 B. & C. 15; 6 D. & R. 75, S. C.; 4 B. & C. 214; Ry. & Mo. 322; 2 Car. & P. 122; 1 Mo. & Mal. 202; 3 Stark. R. 54; 3 Moore, 231. Under the 37 Geo. 3, c. 90, s. 30, it was held, that a person is only discharged as to those creditors to whom he has given notice of his intention to apply for his discharge, 1 Chitty's Rep. 222; but such notice is no longer essential. The 53 Geo. 3, c. 102, s. 10, directed that the order of discharge should name the creditors as to whose claim the prisoner should be discharged, 7 Taunt. 179; but this is no longer necessary, and it suffices, if the schedule name the creditor or the debt as distinctly as the debtor can do, which is still necessary. With respect to the necessity of naming the creditor in the schedule, it is observable that the 40th and 46th sections require that the name of the creditor be named if possible, but suppose the difficulty of stating such creditor in the case of negotiable security. Under the 1 Geo. 4, c. 119, s. 50, (nearly corresponding in terms with the above), where an insolvent contracted for goods with A. the agent for a company, and after giving him two promissory notes for the debt, amounting to £82 2s. 6d. took the benefit of the Act, without describing the company as his creditors, and stating the debt to be only £52: it was held, that his discharge was an answer to the action by the company upon the promissory notes, 6 D. & R. 75; 4 B. & C. 15, S. C. So where an insolvent in his schedule stated that A. held his acceptance, and A. had in fact indorsed it to B. but unknown to the insolvent: it was held, that the description was sufficient, 4 B & C. 214; 2 C. & P. 120; 1 R. & M. 322, S. C.

And if an insolvent state a bill in his schedule, as drawn by himself on M. whereas it was drawn by M. on him, if the jury are satisfied that the same bill was meant, and the description was by mistake, it is a good discharge, 2 C. & P. 120; 1 R. & M. 322, S. C. Where a creditor authorizes his debtor to omit any statement of his debt in the schedule, he cannot take advantage of such omission, and the discharge will be a bar to any action, 3 Moore, 231. See further 4 Adol. & Ell. 887; 4 Tyr. 160.

(x) Sect. 51. See, as to the construction of the former Insolvent Acts, 5 B. & C. 381; 1 M. & P. 91. As to bastardy bonds, 3 Bing. 154.

(126) Maag's Case, 1 Ashm. Rep. 97.

II. DEFENDANTS. 7. Insolvency.

fied, the balance in favor of the creditor still remains as a debt for which the insolvent is liable (y). But by the 7 Geo. 4, c. 57, s. 63, it is provided, that the discharge shall protect the insolvent, although there has been an error in the amount of the debt specified in the schedule, where there has been no culpable negligence, fraud, or evil intention on the part of such prisoner (z). Formerly an insolvent was only considered to be discharged as to his person, and he remained liable to be sued as to his subsequently acquired effects by the creditors named in the schedule; but it is now provided, that no future execution shall issue against the goods of a prisoner discharged, upon any judgment for any debt in respect of which such prisoner shall have become entitled to the benefit of the Act; nor in any action upon any new contract or security for payment thereof, except upon the judgment entered up against such prisoner, in the name of the assignee, or provisional assignee, according to the provisions of the Insolvent Act in that behalf (a).

A married woman may, under the 72d section of the Insolvent Act, petition and obtain her discharge from debts the same as a feme sole, on assigning her separate property, but so as not to prejudice any rights of her husbnnd to her property (b). The discharge of the husband under the Insolvent Act does not preclude a creditor from taking the wife in execution for her debt contracted *dum sola*, unless she has no separate property (c).

When a prisoner has been discharged under the *Lords' Act*, the judgment obtained against the prisoner remains in force, and execution may at any time be taken out thereon against the property and effects of the prisoner, except his wearing apparel, bedding, and tools of trade, to the value of £10, but no action of debt can be supported upon such judgment (d)(127).

[*66] 8thly. In the case of marriage.

*In general a feme-covert cannot be sued alone at law (e); and when a feme sole, who has entered into a contract, marries (f), the husband and wife

(y) 4 B. & C. 419; 6 D. & R. 491, S. C.

(z) See *ante*, 63, note (u).

(a) Sect. 61. See 6 Bing. 293. As to warrant of attorney to be given to provisional assignee, s. 57; 1 Wm. 4, c. 37, s. 3.

(b) 7 Geo. 4, c. 57, s. 72. That clause was introduced in consequence of the decision in *Ex parte Deacon*, 5 B. & Ald. 759.

(c) 8 B. & C. 1; 2 Man. & R. 124, S. C. But see 5 Bar. & Adol. 303.

(d) 32 Geo. 2, c. 28, s. 20.

(e) 2 B. & P. 105; 2 T. R. 363; Com. Dig. Plead. 2 A. 1; 3 Campb. 123.

(f) A marriage in fact, though not strictly legal, is sufficient for this purpose, Andr. 227, 228; 1 Campb. 245; 2 Esp. 637.

(127) In the fourth edition the passage in the text was followed by this remark—"If, however, in either of these cases, the debtor, after his discharge, expressly and indefinitely promise to pay the debt, he may be sued and taken in execution upon such new contract, as in the case of a bankrupt," and referring to the following authorities—3 M. & S. 395.—2 Stra 1233.—2 Bl. 1217.—2 Campb. 443.—3 B. & P. 394; acc. sed vide 6 Taunt. 563. to which the following note was added by the Editor,—"But see Couch v. Ash, and Herbert v. Williams, 5 Cow. Rep. 265, 537, contra. See also the views taken of the text, the authorities referred to by Mr. Chitty in support of it, and the reasons for a different doctrine. Ingraham's Insolvent Laws of Pennsylvania, 202 to 214, 2d edit.

The Supreme Court in New York decided that an action could not be maintained against the maker of a promissory note payable to bearer, by a person to whom the same has been transferred, where the maker has obtained a discharge from all his debts as an insolvent debtor, previous to the transfer; although after the discharge, but before the transfer, the maker makes a *new promise* to the payee to pay the debt, and such new promise is set up by way of replication to the plea of discharge. Depuy v. Swart, 3 Wend. R. 135. Insolvent discharges reach to the contract itself and impair its obligation. Sturges v. Crowningshield, 4 Wheat. R. 122. The note is *functus officio*, and can have no negotiable qualities, because it has no legal existence. Baker v. Wheaton, 5 Mass. R. 509. Although the insolvent is legally exonerated from the payment of his antecedent debts, the moral obligation remains; and this obligation is a sufficient consideration for a new promise. M'Nair v. Gilbert, 3 Wend. R. 344.

must in general be jointly sued (128), though the husband state an account, and expressly promise to pay the debt or perform the contract (*g*); and where the wife was a yearly tenant before marriage, at a rent payable quarterly, and she married before a quarter's rent became payable, it was held, that in an action to recover such quarter's rent, the wife should be joined (*h*). But if the husband, in respect of some new consideration, as for forbearance, &c. expressly undertake in writing to pay the debt, or perform the contract of the feme, he may be sued alone on such undertaking (*i*). II. DEFENDANTS. — 8. Marriage.

When rent becomes due after the marriage, upon a lease to the feme whilst sole, or any other breach of the covenants contained in such lease is committed during the coverture (129), the action may be against both, or against the husband alone (*k*). But the feme can in no case be sued upon a mere *personal* contract made during coverture (*l*), although she live apart from her husband, and have a separate maintenance secured to her by deed (*m*), or be separated under a sentence of divorce *a mensa et thoro* (*n*). But it seems that she is liable upon such a contract, if, being under a moral obligation in regard to the nature of the contract, she, after the death of the husband, expressly promise to perform it (*o*). And an action on the assumpsit of husband and wife, against both, is bad, for *quoad* the wife the promise is void (*p*). But an action of covenant on the warranty in a fine, or on a covenant *running [*67] with the land of the wife demised by her, pursuant to the statute, during the coverture, may be supported against her (*q*); and it is said that upon a lease to the husband and wife for her benefit, the action may be against both (*r*). If the husband be *civiliter mortuus*, or even transported for a term of years, or has been abroad seven years and not heard of (*s*), though he voluntarily left the kingdom (*t*) (130), the wife may be sued alone upon a contract made by

(*g*) 7 T. R. 348; Alleyn, 72; 1 Keb. 281; 2 T. R. 480; 3 Mod. 186; Bac. Ab. *Bar. and Feme*, L.; 1 Taunt. 217, 245; Com. Dig. *Pleader*, 2 A. 1.

(*h*) 3 Moore, 307; 1 B. & B. 50, S. C.

(*i*) Alleyn, 73; 7 T. R. 349.

(*k*) 6 Mod. 239; 1 Roll. Ab. 348, pl. 45, 50; Thomp. Ent. 117; Com. Dig. *Bar. and Feme*, Y.; 6 T. R. 176; 1 New R. 174.

(*l*) 8 T. R. 545; 2 B. & P. 105; Palm. 312; 1 Taunt. 217; 4 Price, 48.

(*m*) 8 T. R. 545; 2 New R. 143. How and when liable in equity on a bill or note, 3 Mad. 387.

(*n*) 6 M. & Sel. 73; 3 B. & C. 291. *Aliter* as to a divorce *à vinculo matrimonii*, 1 Gow R. 10.

(*o*) See 5 Taunt. 36; 1 Stra. 94.

(*p*) Palm. 313; 1 Taunt. 217. See 7 Taunt. 432; 1 Moore, 126.

(*q*) 2 Saund. 180, n. 9.

(*r*) 1 Roll. Ab. 348, 350; Bac. Ab. *Bar. and Feme*, L.

(*s*) 2 Campb. 113, 273.

(*t*) Id.

(128) Vide Angel *v.* Felton, 8 J. R. 149. But if a feme sole marries pending a suit against her, the marriage need not be noticed in the subsequent proceedings. It does not affect the form of the proceedings. The suit goes on as if no marriage had taken place. Roosevelt *v.* Dale, 2 Cowen, 581. The husband, however, though not a party on the record, is, so far as his interest is concerned, a party with his wife; and he is to be received to make an affidavit of merits under the rule which requires this to be done by the party. He is substantially a party; and on recovering judgment against her he may be made an actual party by a *scire facias*, and in this manner be subjected to execution. Ib.

(129) Vide Grasser and wife *v.* Eckart and wife, 1 Binn. 575. { Robinson *v.* Reynolds, 1 Aiken's (Vermont) Rep. 125. Or where the husband being an alien, and never within the United States, has deserted his wife. Gregory *v.* Paul, 15 Mass. Rep. 31. }

{ (130) See Rhea *v.* Rhenner, 1 Peters' Sup. Ct. Rep. 105. In Pennsylvania if a husband desert his wife, and ceases to perform his marital duties, the acquisitions of property made by the wife during such desertion are her separate estate, and she may dispose of them by will or otherwise. Starrett *v.* Wynn, 17 Serg. & Rawle, 130. So, if a husband, by deed of separation without trustees, relinquish to his wife all his right to her land, reserving the payment of an annual sum, the land is not liable to the execution of a credi-

II. DEFENDANTS.

8. Marriage.

her during that time (u); but a woman by birth an alien, and the wife of an alien, cannot be sued as a feme sole, if her husband has lived with her in this country, although he has left her here, and entered into the service of a foreign state (x). In the case of a feme covert executrix or administratrix, she must be joined with the husband in an action on any personal contract of the deceased (y); and if a man marry an administratrix to her former husband, who had wasted the assets during her widowhood, they may be jointly sued for such *devastavit* (z); but for rent due during the coverture on a lease which the wife has as executrix, the husband may be sued alone (a).

Where husband survives.

When the *husband survives*, he is not liable to be sued in that character for any contract of the feme made before the coverture, unless judgment had been obtained against him and his wife before her death (131); and if she die before judgment the suit will abate (b). But if the husband neglect, during her life, to reduce her *choses in action* into possession, the creditor may sue the person who administers thereto, for debts due before her marriage (c); and for rent accruing during the coverture, or for money due upon a judgment obtained against husband and wife, he may be sued alone as the survivor (d).

Where wife survives.

[*68]

In case the *wife survive*, she may be sued upon all her unsatisfied contracts made before coverture (e). But the bankruptcy and certificate of the husband will discharge her from *all liability to satisfy debts which could have been proved under his commission; and if the husband and wife be sued jointly, his bankruptcy may be pleaded in bar (f) (132).

However, we have seen that the discharge of her husband under the Insolvent Act does not preclude a creditor from taking a married woman, having separate property, in execution for a debt contracted by her *dum sola* (g).

Consequences of mistakes.

If the husband be sued alone upon the contract of his wife before coverture, and the objection appear upon the face of the declaration, the defendant may demur, move in arrest of judgment, or bring a writ of error (h). If the contract were misdescribed as being that of the husband, the plaintiff would be nonsuited under the general issue at the trial, upon the ground of a variance

(u) 1 B. & P. 358, n. (f); Co. Lit. 133 a.; 2 B. & P. 105; 4 Esp. Rep. 27, 28.

(x) 3 Campb. 123.

(y) Cro. Car. 145, 519; *ante*, 59.

(z) Cro. Car. 603.

(a) Com. Dig. *Bar. and Feme*, Y.; Thomp. Ent. 117.

(b) 7 T. R. 350; Com. Dig. *Bar. and Feme*, 2 C.; Rep. temp. Talb. 173; 3 P. W. 410.

(c) 3 P. W. 409; Rep. temp. Talb. 173.

(d) 3 Mod. 189, n. (k); 6 Mod. 239; Com. Dig. *Bar. and Feme*, 2 B.

(e) 7 T. R. 350; 1 Campb 189.

(f) 1 P. W. 249; 2 Ves. 181; Cullen, 392.

(g) *Ante*, 65; 8 B. & C. 1; 2 Man. & R. 124, S. C.

(h) 7 T. R. 348; 2 Chit. Rep. 697.

tor of the husband, who obtains judgment against him, after he and his wife have been notoriously separated for nine years. Bouslaugh v. Bouslaugh, 13 Serg. & Rawle, 361. } A father placed the proceeds of lands under the control of a son, for the benefit of a daughter who was a feme covert; held, that no action could be maintained at law in the name of the husband and wife; the remedy being in equity. Duval and wife v. Covenhoven, 4 Wend. Rep. 561.

(131) Buckner v. Smith, 4 Desau. Ch. R. 371. Beach v. Lee, 2 Dall. 257.

(132) In an action against husband and wife for the debt of the wife, contracted by her while sole, a plea that the husband is an infant is no bar to a recovery. Roach et al. v. Quick and wife, 9 Wend. Rep. 238. Prior to her marriage, the wife was responsible for such debts, and unless the liability to pay them attached to the husband, her creditors would be remediless, as she cannot be sued alone separate from her husband; and if she could, a judgment against her would be fruitless, as all her estate is absolutely or qualifiedly vested in her husband. Reeve's Dom. Rel. 234. Barnes, 95.

between the contract stated in the declaration and that proved. But if the wife be sued alone upon her contract before marriage, she must plead her coverture in abatement, or a writ of *error coram nobis* must be brought; and the coverture in such case cannot be pleaded in bar, or given in evidence upon the trial as a ground of nonsuit (*i*); and if she marry pending an action against her, it will not abate, but the plaintiff may proceed to execution without noticing the husband (*k*). But if a feme covert be sued upon her supposed contract made during coverture, she may in general plead the coverture in bar, or give it in evidence under the general issue, or under *non est factum*, in the case of a deed (*l*). And if the husband and wife be improperly sued jointly on a contract after marriage, the action will fail as to both (*m*) (133).

II. DEFENDANTS. 8. Marriage.

II IN ACTIONS IN FORM *EX DELICTO*.

GENERAL RULES.

The rules which direct who are to be the parties to an action in form *ex delicto*, whether as plaintiffs or defendants, may, as in actions in form *ex contractu*, be considered with reference, 1st, to the *interest* of the plaintiff in the matter affected, and the liability of the defendant; 2dly, the *number* *of the parties, and who must or may sue or be sued; 3dly, where there has been an *assignment* of interest, &c.; 4thly in the case of *survivorship*; 5thly, where the party injured, or committing the injury, is *dead*; 6thly, in the case of *bankruptcy*; 7thly, *insolvency*; and, 8thly, in that of *marriage*. [*69]

I. PLAINTIFFS. 1st. Who to sue, with reference to the *interest* of the plaintiff.

The action for a tort must in general be brought in the name of the person whose *legal* right has been affected, and who was *legally* interested in the property at the time the injury thereto was committed (*n*); for he is impliedly the party injured by the tort, and whoever has sustained the loss is the proper person to call for compensation from the wrong doer. A *cestui que trust* or other person having only an *equitable* interest, cannot in general sue in the Courts of common law against his trustee (134), or even a third per-

(*i*) 3 T. R. 631; 2 Roll. Rep. 53; Sty. 280; Bac. Ab. *Bar. and Feme*, L.
(*k*) 2 Stra. 811; 4 East, 521; Cro. Jac. 323; Bac. Ab. *Abatement*, G.
(*l*) 12 Mod. 101; 1 Salk. 7; 3 Keb. 228; Bul. N. P. 172; 2 Stra. 1104.
(*m*) Palm. 312; *ante*, 66.
(*n*) *Per* Lord Kenyon, 8 T. R. 332; 3 Campb. 417.

(133) A count charging man and wife upon a joint assumption in consideration of money had and received by them to the plaintiff's use is bad. Grasser and wife *v.* Eckart and wife, 1 Binn. 575.

(134) {It is otherwise in Pennsylvania, for the reason stated in the next note. Reese *v.* Roth, 13 Serg. & Rawle, 434. But since the passage of the act of 29th March, 1823, entitled "A supplement to the act to compel assignees to settle their accounts," &c. (Purd. Dig. 64.) complete relief may be had in the mode of proceedings provided by the act, which is nearly as effectual as the proceedings in a regular Court of Equity; and it is questionable whether an action at law would now be sustained by the courts. See Rush *v.* Good, 14 Serg. & Rawle, 226.} It is now the settled law of the state of New York, that a mortgagor has the legal estate and seisin of the land until foreclosure, or entry by the mortgagee. Sedgwick *v.* Hollenbach, 7 Johns. Rep. 380. {Stanard *v.* Eldridge, 16 Johns.

I. PLAINTIFFS.

1. Who to sue, &c.

son (o) (135); unless in cases where the action is against a mere wrong doer, and for an injury to the actual possession of the *cestui que trust* (p). Many of the rules and instances which have been stated in respect to the person to be made the plaintiff in actions in form *ex contractu*, here also govern and are applicable (q).

Actions in form *ex delicto* are for injuries to the *absolute* or *relative* rights of *persons* or to *personal* or *real property*.

For injuries to the *person*.

The action for an injury to the *absolute* rights of *persons*, as for assaults, batteries, wounding, injuries to the health, liberty, and reputation, can only be brought in the name of the party immediately injured, and if he die, the remedy determines. With respect to injuries to the *relative* rights of persons, the instances in which a *husband* may sue alone, or should join his wife in an action for injuries to the person of his wife, will be hereafter noticed (r). In the case of *master and servant*, the master may sue alone for the battery of (136), or for debauching his servant, although they are not related, when there is evidence to prove a consequent loss of service (s); and a father may sue for the seduction of his daughter, although she was married, provided some loss of [*70] service can be *proved (t). But if there be no evidence of such loss, an action cannot be supported in the name of the master (u). A parent cannot, it should seem, sue in that character, even for taking away his child, unless it be his son and heir, or unless a loss of service be sustained (x); clearly he cannot support an action for debauching his daughter, or beating his child, unless there be evidence to support the allegation *per quod servitium amisit* (y) (137).

(o) 1 Sanders on Uses and Trusts, 222, 223; 7 T. R. 47. See Holt C. N. P. 641; 8 Taunt. 263, S. C.; 2 Moore, 240, S. C.

(p) 1 East, 244; 2 Saund. 47 d.

(q) *Ante*, 2 to 9.

(r) *Post*, 83.

(s) Peake, C. N. P. 55, 233; 5 East, 45, 47; 3 Bla. Com. 142; 11 East, 23; 9 Co. 113; 10 Co. 330; 2 New Rep. 476.

(t) 7 B. & C. 387; 1 Man. & R. 166, S. C.

(u) Id.; 3 Bla. Com. 142; 9 Co. 113; 10 Co. 330.

(x) Cro. Eliz. 55, 770; 3 Bla. Com. 141. Per Holroyd, J., 4 B. & C. 662; 7 D. & R. 138, S. C.

(y) 5 East, 45. See Holt, C. N. P. 453. Very slight evidence of service is sufficient, 2 T. R. 168; 5 T. R. 360; Peake, C. N. P. 55, 233; Sir T. Raym. 259. A. with intent to seduce B.'s servant, hires her as his servant, and then seduces her. B. may sue A. for the seduction, 2 Stark. Rep. 493.

Rep. 254. See also, for the doctrine in Pennsylvania, Sehuylkill Nav. Co. v. Thoburn, 7 Serg. & Rawle, 411 } And his wife may support a writ of dower to be endowed of the equity of redemption. Hitchcock and wife v. Harrington, 6 Johns. Rep. 235. Collins v. Torry, 7 Johns. Rep. 278. { Tabele v. Tabele, 1 Johns. Cha. Rep. 45. So also in Massachusetts, Snow v. Stevens, 15 Mass. Rep. 279. } And although the mortgage is a sufficient title to enable the mortgagee to recover in ejectment, Jackson d. Ferris v. Fuller, 4 Johns. Rep. 215. { Lessee of Simpson v. Ammons, 1 Binn. 175 } yet the mortgagor may maintain trespass against the mortgagee, and to a plea of liberum tenementum by the latter may reply that the freehold was in himself. Runyan v. Mersereau, 11 Johns. Rep. 534.

(135) { It is otherwise in Pennsylvania, there being no courts of equity in that state. Kennedy v Fury, 1 Dall. 72. Lessee of Simpson v. Ammons, 1 Binn. 177. }

(136) This was law at the time of Bracton. 7 Reeve's Hist. E. L. 45.

(137) Contra Martin v. Payne, 9 Johns. Rep. 387. } Hornketh v. Barr, 8 Serg. & Rawle, 36. Vanhorn v Freeman, 1 Halst. Rep. 322. } where it was held that the right of the parent to the services of his daughter, *under the age of twenty-one*, was sufficient to maintain the action without proof of an actual service. But where the daughter is above that age, she must be in her father's service, so as to constitute in law and in fact, the relation of master and servant, in order to entitle her father to a suit for seducing her. Nickleson v. Stryker, 10 Johns. Rep. 115. { Mercer v. Walmesley, 5 Har. & Johns. 27. 6 Serg. & Rawle, 177, acc. In Pennsylvania an action cannot be maintained by a mother for debauching her daughter, *per quod servitum amisit* where the seduction was during the life of the father, with whom the daughter resided at the time; although after the father's death

And if, from its extreme youth, no services could be rendered by the child, the parent cannot sue for a personal injury inflicted upon the child; the father not having necessarily incurred any expense upon the occasion (z). In cases of the battery of the wife or servant, if there be any evidence sufficient to support an action in the name of the husband or master, it is frequently most advisable to proceed accordingly, because in such action, if the plaintiff recover less than 40s. damages, he will be entitled to full costs (a). The wife, the child, and the servant, having no legal interest in the person or property of the husband, the parent, or master, cannot support an action for any injury to them (b) (138).

1. PLAINTIFFS. 1. Who to sue, &c.

In treating of the action of *trover*, it is proposed to consider the nature and extent of the property in or right to *personal* property, necessary to support an action against a wrong doer, but it may be expedient to notice in this place some of the general rules upon the subject.

The *absolute* or *general* owner of *personal* property, having also the right of immediate possession, may in general support an action for any injury thereto, although he never had the actual possession (c) (139).

For ries to personalty.

An action for an injury to personalty may also be brought in the name of the person having only a *special* property or interest of a limited or temporary nature therein (d). But in *this case the general rule seems to be, that the party should have had the actual possession (e). [*71]

There are cases in which a party having the *bare possession* of goods, which is *prima facie* evidence of property, may sue a mere wrong doer who takes or injures them, although it should appear that the plaintiff has not the strict legal title (140); there being no claim by the real owner, and the defendant *having no* right or authority from him (f).

Although in the above instances the action may be brought by the general or special owner of goods, against a stranger (141), yet a judgment obtained

(z) 4 B. & C. 660; 7 D. & R. 133, S. C.
(a) 3 Wils. 319; 1 Salk. 206; 2 Ld. Raym. 831.
(b) 3 Bla. Com. 143; 1 Salk. 119.
(c) 2 Saund. 47 a., note 1.
(d) 2 Saund. 47 b, c, d.
(e) 1 B. & P. 47; 2 Saund. 47 d.
(f) 2 Saund. 47 c, d.

she remained with the mother, who was at the expense of her lying-in, and who supported her and her child, Logan v. Murray, 6 Serg. & Rawle, 175. *Aliter* in New Jersey, Coon v. Moffet, 2 Penn. Rep. 583. | The slightest acts of service are sufficient. Moran v. Dawes, 4 Cowen, 412. Thus, where a bound apprentice was seduced; the indentures being subsequently cancelled when she returned and was delivered at her widowed mother's house Sargent v. ——, 5 ib. 106. A female under age is presumed to be so under the control of the parent as to entitle the latter to maintain the action. Thompson v. Millar, 1 Wend. R. 447. Although the daughter be a servant *de facto* of another, and the father has relinquished all claim to her services, still the latter may maintain the action, he being liable for the expenses of her lying in. Clark v. Fitch, 2 ib. But if the daughter be twenty-one years of age, it is different. In such case, there must be actual service. Stewart v. Kip, 1 ib. 376.

(138) Vide 2 Reeve's Hist. E. L. 45, 46.

(139) Vide Thorp v. Burling. 11 Johns. Rep. 285. Smith v. Plomer and another, 15 East's Rep. 607. Bird v. Clarke, 3 Day, 272. Williams v. Lewis, ibid. 498.

(140) So, possession of a ship under a transfer, void for non-compliance with the register acts, is a sufficient title against a stranger. Sutton v. Buck, 3 Taunt. 302. An officer who has seized goods under an execution may bring trespass or trover against a stranger for taking them away. Barker and Knapp v. Miller, 6 Johns. Rep. 195. Gibbs v. Chase, 10 Mass. Rep. 125. 7 Cow. Rep. 297 Taylor v. Manderson, 1 Ashm. Rep. 129; but a mere servant, having only the custody of goods, and not responsible over, cannot in general sue. Dillenback v. Jerome, 7 Cow. Rep. 294. See Ludden v. Leavitt, 9 Mass. Rep. 104.

(141) Vide Putnam v. Wylie, 8 Johns. Rep. 432. 7 Conn. Rep. 235.

I. PLAINTIFFS.

by one in an action against a stranger for a conversion, is a bar to an action by the other (*g*).

1. Who to sue, &c.

When the general owner has not the right of immediate possession, as where he has demised the goods, or let them to hire for a term unexpired, he cannot maintain trespass or trover, which are forms of action founded on possession, even against a stranger (*h*); although if the injury were sufficient to affect his reversionary interest, he may support a special action on the case to recover damages to the extent of the injury he has sustained (*i*); and a recovery in an action by a party having the possessory title for the damage he has sustained, would be no bar to an action for an injury to the reversionary interest (*k*).

For injuries to *real property*.

The person in possession of *real property corporeal*, whether lawfully or not, may sue for an injury committed by a stranger, or by any person who cannot establish a better title (*l*) (142); and in trespass to land, the person actually in possession, though he be only a *cestui que trust*, should be the plaintiff, and not the trustee. But the rule is otherwise in ejectment, which is an action to try the right; and the fictitious demise must be in the name of the party legally entitled to the possession, although the beneficial interest may be in another (*m*) (143), and according to the strict nature of the right; thus tenants in common *cannot join*, but must *sever*, in separate demises in a declaration in ejectment (*n*). Nor should tenants in common join in debt for double rent (*o*). The party, however, must be in the *actual possession*, or he must [*72] have the general property, *in respect of which possession *immediately* follows, (as in the instance of the possession of his mere servant) (*p*), or he cannot maintain an action of trespass; a mere *right* to enter is not sufficient (*q*)(144). In the case of *real* property, there is not that constructive possession which may exist in the case of personalty, and the party entitled to possession cannot maintain trespass, unless he has had actual possession by himself or his servant, though he have the freehold in law (*r*); and after a feoffment with livery

(*g*) 2 Saund. 47 e.; 1 Bulst. 68; 2 Vin. Ab. 49, pl 6.

(*h*) 7 T. R. 9; 3 Campb. 417; 1 R. & M. 99; 1 Price, 53; *post*. See an illustrative case, Bloxam v. Sanders, 4 Bar. & Cres. 941; 7 D. & R. 396, S. C.

(*i*) 7 T. R. 9; 3 Lev. 209; 1 Taunt. 190, 191.

(*k*) 3 Lev. 209; 1 Taunt. 190, 191, 194; 2 Cruise, 458.

(*l*) 1 East, 244; Willes, 221; 3 Burr. 1563; 2 Stra. 123; Cro. Car. 586; Peake, 67; 1 Taunt. 83, 190, 191, 194; 8 East, 394; 5 B. & Ald. 600; 1 D. & R. 225, S. C.

(*m*) 7 T. R. 47, 50.

(*n*) Doe v. Errington, 3 Nev. & Man. 616.

(*o*) Wilkinson v. Hall, 1 Bing. N. C. 713.

(*p*) 6 B. & C. 703.

(*q*) 5 B. & Ald. 600; 1 D. & R. 225, S. C.; 2 Moore, 666. Commissioners of sewers cannot maintain an action against the commissioners of a harbor, for breaking down a dam erected by the former as such commissioners, across a navigable river, as the authority to be exercised by them on behalf of the public does not vest in them such a property or possessory interest as will enable them to maintain such action. 3 Moore, 666. But the contractors for making a navigable canal having, with the permission of the owner of the soil, erected a dam of earth and wood upon his close across a stream there, for the purpose of completing their work, have a possession sufficient to entitle them to maintain trespass against a wrong doer. 5 B. & Ald. 600; 1 D. & R. 225, S. C. See other cases in Burn, J. tit. *Poor*, as to the ratability of mines, &c.

(*r*) Com. Dig. *Trespass*, B. 3.

(142) A guardian in socage may maintain trespass for an injury to the land of the ward. Byrne and wife v. Van Hoesen, 5 Johns. Rep. 66. But a person occupying land merely as a servant of the owner, and not as a tenant, cannot maintain an action. Bertie v. Beaumont, 16 East's Rep. 33.

(143) See ante, p. 69.

(144) See, however, Bulkley v. Dolybeare, 7 Conn. Rep. 232.

of seisin, the feoffee may maintain trespass, notwithstanding a tenant at will was in possession at the time of such feoffment, and did not assent to the same (*s*). These rules will be more fully considered in the next chapter, when considering the cases in which an action of trespass is sustainable (*t*). A person having the *immediate* reversion or remainder in fee or in tail, or for a less estate, may support an action on the *case* for waste (145), or any nuisance of a permanent nature, or which affects, litigates, and injures the *right*, and which is injurious to his reversionary interest (*u*); but he cannot sue in *trespass* when the possession is lawfully in his tenant or other person (*x*) (146). The *tenant* may support *trespass* against a stranger for an injury to his possession; and the *immediate reversioner* may, at the same time, support an action on the *case*, if the injury were sufficient to prejudice his right and interest; and a recovery by one will be no bar to an action by the other (*y*). But the reversioner, when he sues, must allege and prove such a permanent *injury as necessarily affects his interest (*z*). When trees are excepted in a lease, the lessee has no interest therein, and cannot sue even a stranger for cutting them down, though he might for the trespass to the land; and in such case the lessor may support trespass against the lessee or a stranger, if he either fell or damage them; but if there be no exception of the trees in the lease, the lessee has a particular interest therein, and may support trespass against the lessor or a stranger for an injury to them during the term; but the interest in the body of the trees remains in the lessor as part of his inheritance, and he may support an action on the case against a lessee or a stranger for an injury thereto, or even trover, if they be cut down and carried away (*a*) (147). But to sustain a count for an injury to an alleged *reversionary* interest subject to a demise, the written lease or agreement must be proved (*b*). After a recovery in an action of ejectment, trespass for mesne

I. PLAINTIFFS.

1. Who to sue, &c.

[*73]

(*s*) Ball *v.* Cullimore and another, 1 Gale, 96.

(*t*) *Post.*

(*u*) 1 Saund. 323 b.; 2 Saund. 252 b.; 3 Lev. 209, 360; 4 Burr. 2141; Com. Dig. *Action, Case, Nuisance;* 1 Taunt 183, 190, 191, 194; 1 M. & Sel. 234; Ancient Lights, 4 Burr. 2141; 3 Car. & Pay. 617. The remedy for *waste* is fully considered under the head of *Case, post.*

(*x*) *Id. Ibid.*; 1 Taunt. 190; 7 T. R 9.

(*y*) 4 Burr. 2141; 3 Lev. 209, 359, 360; Com. Dig. *Action, Case, Nuisance,* B.; 1 Taunt. 183, 190, 191, 194. As to remedy by reversioner, also by tenant, on 9 Geo. 1, c. 22, against the hundred in case of a malicious fire, 9 B. & C. 134, 142; 4 Man. & Ry. 130, S. C.

(*z*) 1 M. & Sel. 234; 1 Taunt. 202.

(*a*) 1 Saund. 322, note 5; 7 T. R. 13; Com. Dig. Biens; 1 Taunt. 190, 191, 194; 2 M. & Sel. 498, 499; *ante*, 71.

(*b*) Cotterill *v.* Hobby, 4 Bar. & Cres. 465.

(145) Vide Provost and Scholars of Queen's College *v.* Hallet, 14 East's Rep. 489. Attersol *v.* Stevens, 1 Taunt. 190, 194, 195, 202, 203, ante, 36. n. 78.

(146) Vide Campbell *v.* Arnold, 1 Johns. Rep. 511. So, the lessor cannot maintain trespass against the sub-tenant at will of his lessee. Tobey *v.* Webster, 3 Johns. Rep. 468. At common law an action of waste could not be maintained against a tenant for life, except by him who had the immediate estate of inheritance expectant on the determination of the estate for life; but a statute of the state of New York gives an action of waste for trespass to any person seised in remainder or reversion, for an injury to the inheritance, notwithstanding any intervening estate for life or for years. Ses. 36, c. 56, s. 33. 1 R. L. 527. {1 Rev. Stat. 750, s. 8.} As to the construction of this section of the *act for the amendment of the law*, vide Livingston *v.* Haywood, 11 Johns. Rep. 429. Wickham *v.* Freeman, 12 Johns. Rep. 183. A reversioner cannot maintain trespass for an injury to the inheritance, committed by a person who acts under the authority or by the permission of the tenant for life; such person not being a stranger within the meaning of the statute authorizing actions by reversioners. Livingston *v.* Mott, 2 Wend. Rep. 605.

(147) See Bulkley *v.* Dolybeare, 7 Conn. Rep. 232.

I. PLAINTIFFS.

1. Who to sue, &c.

profits may be brought in the name of the lessor of plaintiff or of the nominal plaintiff (c), and after an escape in the latter action, the sheriff may be sued for it in the name of the nominal plaintiff (d).

Many of these rules prevail also in the case of an injury to real property *incorporeal*, and if there be any injury to such right, an action may be supported, however small the damage; and therefore a commoner may maintain an action on the case for an injury done to the common, though his proportion of the damage be found to amount only to a farthing (e).

2dly. Who to join or sever with reference to the number of plaintiffs.

When two or more persons are *jointly entitled*, or have a *joint legal interest* in the property affected, they must in general join in the action, or the defendant may plead *in abatement* (f)(148); and though the interest be several, yet if the wrong complained of caused an entire joint damage, the parties may join or sever in the action (149); but as the Courts will not in one suit take cognizance of distinct and separate claims of different persons, where the damage as well as the interest is several, each party injured must, in that case, sue separately (g). If a third person collude with one partner in a firm to injure the other partners, the latter may separately maintain an action on the case against the third person so colluding (h).

[*74] *Therefore, several parties cannot, in general, sue jointly for injuries to the *person*, as for slander, battery, or false imprisonment of both, and each must bring a separate action (i)(150). In these cases the wrong done to one person cannot in law be to the prejudice of the other; nor is there any criterion by which an entire sum can be awarded to them for damages. But partners in trade may join in an action for slanderous words spoken, or a libel published concerning them in the way of their joint business, without showing the proportion of their respective shares (k)(151). So joint-tenants or coparceners may join in an action for slander of their title to the estate (l)(152). A

(c) 2 M. & Sel. 423; Adams on Eject. 333. See 5 M. & Sel. 64; 2 Chit. Rep. 410. See *post*, as to the action for mesne profits.

(d) 2 M. & Sel. 473.

(e) 2 East, 154.

(f) Post, 74, 75.

(g) *Ante*, 10; 1 Saund, 291 g.; 2 Saund. 116, n. 2; Bac. Ab. Action, C.; 2 Wils. 423.

(h) Longman *v.* Pole, 1 Mood. & Mal. 223.

(i) 2 Saund. 117 a.; 10 Moore, 446, 451.

(k) 3 B. & P. 150; 2 East, 426; and see fully Foster *v.* Lawson, 3 Bing. 452; 11 Moore, 360, S. C.

(l) 2 Saund. 117 a.

(148) Russell *v.* Stocking, 8 Conn. Rep. 237. Sweigart *v.* Berk, 8 Serg. & Rawle, 308. Two incorporated companies may unite in an action of assumpsit to recover a sum of money deposited in a bank in their joint names. The N. Y. and Sharon Canal Company et al. *v.* The Fulton Bank, 7 Wend. Rep. 412.

(149) In an action of ejectment against one defendant for an entire lot of land, it was held that separate demises from several lessors, might be laid in the declaration, who might give in evidence their titles to distinct parts of the premises, in severalty, and recover accordingly. Jackson d. Roman and others *v.* Sidney, 12 Johns. Rep. 185.

(150) But in favor of liberty the law permits two to join in suing the writ *de homine replegiando*. F. N. B. 66. F.

(151) So, an action lies for co-partners in trade against two or more, also co-partners, for falsely and fraudulently recommending an insolvent person as worthy of credit, whereby the plaintiffs were induced to trust him with goods. Patten et al. *v.* Gurney et al., 17 Mass. Rep. 182.

(152) Two purchasers of an estate cannot maintain a joint action for a false and fraudulent affirmation by the seller. Baker *v.* Jewell, 6 Mass. Rep. 460. Co-partners, however, may join in a suit against other co-partners, for falsely and fraudulently recommending an insolvent person as worthy of credit, whereby the plaintiffs incurred a loss by trusting him with goods. Patten et al. *v.* Gurney et al., 17 Mass. Rep. 182.

husband and wife may sue jointly for a malicious prosecution and imprisonment of both, or the husband may sue alone (m). And two persons may jointly sue for a malicious arrest of both, in an action brought without reasonable cause, if it be laid as special damage that they jointly incurred an expense in procuring their liberation (n). For in these instances there is an entirety of interest, or a joint damage resulting from the tort. Where an action was brought, and a verdict obtained by two plaintiffs against a defendant for a malicious arrest, and the declaration alleged as a special damage, not only a joint expense incurred, but also the false imprisonment of both; the Court ordered the judgment to be arrested, but as the verdict confined the damages to the *joint expense* incurred by the plaintiffs in obtaining their liberation, an amendment of the postea was allowed (o).

I. PLAINTIFFS.

2. Who to join or sever, &c.

In actions for injuries to *personal property*, joint-tenants and tenants in common must join, or the defendant may plead in abatement (p) (153): but parties having several and distinct interests, cannot in general join. Thus, if goods of A. and B., the separate property of each, be unlawfully distrained, they cannot join in the replevin (q); and an *audita querela* in the joint names of the conusors of a statute staple, for levying several executions on their lands respectively, cannot be supported (r); nor could persons robbed on the highway join *in an action against the hundred, unless they were jointly interested in the property (s). [*75]

But though the interests of the parties be distinct, yet if the injury occasion an entire joint damage to them, they may in some cases join (t); as where two persons were severally seised of two ancient mills, at one or the other of which the defendant ought to have ground his corn, but neglected to grind at either, it was decided that both might join (u); and on the same principle it was holden, that the dippers at Tunbridge Wells might join in an action against a person who exercised the business of a dipper, not being duly appointed (x). And where goods are bailed to two, and only one has the possession in fact, and a stranger carries them away, both may have detinue or trespass, or the one who had actual possession may sue alone (y).

For injuries to *real* property.

In actions for injuries to *real* property, joint-tenants (z), and parceners (a) (154), must join in real as well as personal actions, or the non-joinder

(m) Cro. Car. 553. See *ante*, 69.
(n) 10 Moore, 446.
(o) 10 Moore, 446.
(p) Bac. Ab. Joint-tenants, K. 7 T. R. 279; 5 East, 407; Co. Lit. 198 a.
(q) Co. Lit. 145 b.
(r) Cro. Eliz. 473; Noy, 1.
(s) Dyer, 370; 2 Saund. 116 a. 377 a.
(t) 2 Saund. 115.
(u) 2 Saund. 115, 116.
(x) 2 Wils. 423; 2 Saund. 116, note 2.
(y) 2 Vin. Ab. 59; Com. Dig. Abatement, E. 12.
(z) 2 Vin. Ab 59; Bac. Ab. Joint-tenants, K; Moore, 466. But see 12 East, 61, 221. See 7 Moore, 29.
(a) Vin. Ab. Parceners; Moore, 466; 12 East, 61, 221.

(153) Vide Bradish v. Schenck, 8 Johns. Rep. 151. {But where the sheriff seized on execution and sold a chattel owned by the judgment debtor and another in common, and paid the whole proceeds over to the judgment creditor, it was holden, that although he might lawfully seize the whole, he should have sold but the share of the judgment debtor; and that the abuse of his authority made him a trespasser *ab initio*, and he was liable to the other part owner of the chattel, in trover or trespass at his election. Melville v. Brown, 15 Mass. Rep. 82.}

(154) Vide Contra Doe d. Raper v. Lonsdale, 12 East's Rep. 39, and in Connecticut one, or any number of them may bring an action against a person who has no title. Bush and others v. Bradley, 4 Day, 298. Sanford and others v. Button, 4 Day, 310. Vide Litt. sec. 313.

I. PLAINTIFFS. — 2. Who to join or sever, &c.

may be pleaded in abatement (155); and if one of several joint-tenants die pending a real action, it will abate, as the survivor is entitled to a different estate; but it is otherwise in personal and mixed actions (b) (156). Tenants in common must in general sever in real actions, unless in a *quare impedit*, and in ejectment a joint demise would be improper (157); but in personal actions, as for a trespass or nuisance to their land, they may join (158), because in these actions, though their estates are several, yet the damages survive to all, and it would be unreasonable when the damage is thus entire to bring several actions for a single trespass (c) (159). A tenant in common may however in general sue separately; as in ejectment for his undivided share, or in trespass for the *mesne* profits, or in debt for double value against a person who has held over after the expiration of his tenancy (d). But a joint action for [*76] *mesne* profits may be supported by several lessors *of the plaintiff in ejectment after recovery therein, although there were only separate demises by each (e).

Consequences of non-joinder.

In actions in form *ex delicto*, and which are not for the breach of a contract, if a party who ought to join be omitted, the objection can only be taken by plea in abatement, or by way of apportionment of the damages on the trial; and the defendant cannot, as in actions in form *ex contractu*, give in evidence the non-joinder, as a ground of nonsuit on the plea of the general issue; or demur; or move in arrest of judgment (160); or support a writ of error; although it appear upon the face of the declaration, or other pleading of the plaintiff, that there is another party who ought to have joined (f) (161). And

(b) Rep. temp. Hardw. 398; Co. Lit. 188, 197.

(c) Bac. Ab. Joint-tenants, K; 2 Bla. Rep. 1077; 5 T. R. 247; Yelv. 161; Cro. Jac. 231; 2 H. Bla. 386; 5 Mod. 151.

(d) 5 T. R. 248; 2 Bl. Rep. 1077. In some cases he may sue in ejectment for the whole premises, 3 Moore, 229.

(e) 5 M. & Sel. 64; 2 Chit. Rep. 410.

(f) 1 Saund. 291 g.; 6 T. R. 766; 7 T. R. 279; 2 Saund. 117, 47 g.; 1 B. & P. 75; 2 Id. 123; 5 East, 407, 420.

(155) If four joint-tenants jointly demise from year to year, such of them as give notice to quit may recover their several shares in ejectment on their several demises. Doe d. Whayman v. Chaplin, 3 Taunt. 120.

(156) Vide Litt. sec. 311, 312, 313. { Carter v. Carr, Gilm. Rep. 145. Drago v. Stead, 2 Rand. Rep. 454. }

(157) It has been held by the Supreme Court of the State of New York, that tenants in common might declare on a joint demise. Jackson d. Van Denbergh and others v. Bradt, 2 Caines' Rep. 169. The law is the same in Vermont. Hicks et al. v. Rogers, 4 Cranch, 165.

(158) { Where five were seised of a mill as tenants in common, and the mill was burned through the negligence of one of them, it was held the other four might maintain an action on the case against him. Chelsey v. Thompson, 3 New Hamp. Rep. 1. See Daniels et al v. Daniels, 7 Mass. Rep. 135. }

(159) Tenants in common shall join in *detinue* of charters. Co. Lit. 197 b. post, 54. And in *case* for the destruction of their charters or title deeds. Daniels v. Daniels, 7 Mass. Rep. 135. Vide Litt sec. 315, 316. Bradish v. Schenck, 8 Johns. Rep. 151. That tenants in common must join in trespass *quare clausum fregit*, see Austin and others v. Hall, 13 Johns. Rep. 286. { See, however 14 Serg. & Rawle, 370. }

(160) But in an action of replevin brought by one part owner of a chattel, after verdict for the plaintiff, the judgment was arrested: and the court took a distinction between this case, in which the judgment would be for a chattel, not capable in law of severance, as well as for damages, and those actions in which damages only can be recovered. Hart v. Fitzgerald, 2 Mass. Rep. 509.

(161) Vide Wheelwright v. Depeyster, 1 Johns. Rep. 471. Brotherson and others v. Hodges et al., 6 Johns. Rep. 108. Bradish v. Schenck, 8 Johns. Rep. 151. If the husband distrains and avows for rent arising from the wife's land, without joining her, he must show affirmatively, that the rent accrued after the marriage, for such fact cannot be intended; and if it is not shown, the objection may be taken at the trial. Decker v. Livingston, 15 Johns. Rep. 479.

if one of several part-owners of a chattel sue alone for a tort, and the defendant do not plead in abatement, the other part-owners may afterwards sue alone for the injury to their undivided shares, and the defendant cannot plead in abatement of such action (g).

I. PLAINTIFFS.

2. Who to join or sever, &c.

Consequences of mis-joinder.

If however *too many* persons be made co-plaintiffs, the objection, if it appear on the record, may be taken advantage of either by demurrer, in arrest of judgment (h), or by writ of error (i); or if the objection do not appear on the face of the pleadings, it would be a ground of nonsuit on the trial (k); though if two tenants in common join in detinue of charters, it is said if one be nonsuit the other shall recover (l) (162).

3dly. When the interest in the property has been assigned.

We have already seen that *choses in action ex contractu* are not in general assignable at law, so as to enable the assignee to sue in his own name (m); the same rule also prevails in the case of injuries *ex delicto* either to the person, or to personal (163) or real property. Therefore an heir cannot maintain an action for waste committed in the time of his ancestor; nor the grantee of a reversion for waste committed before the grant (n); though we have already seen that if a person have the immediate reversion or remainder in fee, in tail, or for life, or years, vested in him at the time of the waste committed, *he may maintain an action on the case for such injury to his estate (o). And a devisee may support an action for the continuance of a nuisance erected in the life-time of the testator, for every continuance of a nuisance makes it a fresh one (p). So a remainder-man may support an action for undermining a wall during the tenancy for life, if the excavation should be continued, and the wall fall down during his own time (q). And if the owner of an estate deliver the title-deeds to a bailee, and afterwards convey away the estate, the new proprietor must be the plaintiff if the bailee wrongfully detain the deeds after the purchase (r). And the assignee of a copyright, or the purchaser of any personal chattel, may sue for an injury after he became the proprietor (s). So it seems that a wrongful seizure of goods by a sheriff, under a *fi. fa.* against B., does not preclude C. the real owner, from afterwards, and whilst the goods remain in the possession of the sheriff, selling and assigning his property in the goods to D., and if the sheriff afterwards sell the goods, D. may support trover against him (t).

[*77]

(g) 7 T. R. 279; 3 Keb. 244; 5 East, 407.
(h) 10 Moore, 446.
(i) 3 B. & P. 150; 2 Saund. 116 a.; Cro. Eliz. 473.
(k) Cro. Eliz. 143.
(l) Co. Lit. 197 b.; 3 East, 62; 12 East, 452; 2 New Rep. 454, 365.
(m) *Ante*, 16.
(n) 2 Saund. 252 a. note 7; 2 Inst. 305.
(o) *Ante*, 72; 2 Saund. 252 b.
(p) Cro. Jac. 231.
(q) 1 R. & Moo. C. N. P. 162; 5 B. & C. 263, 268; 2 Dow. & R. 14, S. C.
(r) 4 Bing. 106.
(s) See 5 M. & Sel. 105.
(t) Friday *v.* Hart, tried at Maidstone and afterwards decided in K. B. on motion for a new trial, N. B. Osbaldeston and Murray attorneys. MS.

(162) If the defendant, in an action for a tort, settle with one of the plaintiffs, he is still answerable to the others. Baker *v.* Jewell, 6 Mass. Rep. 460. That the rule is the same in actions ex contractu, vide ante, 8. But if one of the co-plaintiffs release the defendant, it is a complete bar to the action. Austin and others *v.* Hall, 13 Johns. Rep. 286.

(163) But it has been held, that the assignee of a bond might maintain trover for it in his own name, against the obligor, who had got it into his possession, and converted it. Clowes *v.* Hawley, 12 Johns. Rep. 484. The grantee of demised premises cannot sue in

I. PLAINTIFFS.

4thly. When one of several parties interested is dead.

When one or more of several parties jointly interested in the property at the time the injury was committed is dead, the action should be in the name of the survivor, and the executor or administrator of the deceased cannot be joined, nor can he sue separately; and therefore to an action of trover brought by the survivor of three partners in trade, it cannot be objected that the two deceased partners and the plaintiff were joint merchants, and that in respect of the *lex mercatoria* the right of survivorship did not exist, for the *legal* right of action survives, though the beneficial interest may not (w). But if the parties had separate interests, in respect of which they might have served in suing, the personal representative of the deceased may maintain a separate action, provided the *tort* was not of such a nature that it died with the person. At common law, when an action had been commenced in the name of two or [*78] more persons, and one of them died pending the suit, it abated; but *by the 8 & 9 W. 3, c. 11, s. 7 (x), it was enacted, "that if there be two or more plaintiffs or defendants, and one or more of them should die, if the cause of such action shall survive to the surviving plaintiff or plaintiffs, or against the surviving defendant or defendants, the writ or action shall not be thereby abated, but such death being suggested upon the record, the action shall proceed at the suit of the surviving plaintiff or plaintiffs against the surviving defendant or defendants (164);" and consequently, since that statute, if one of several plaintiffs die pending a suit, and the cause of action would survive to the survivor, he may proceed in the action. But if the cause of action do not survive, then the action would abate; as if the husband and wife sue for the slander of the wife, if she die pending the suit, the husband cannot proceed further (y).

5thly. In case of the *death* of the party injured.

We have seen that the right of action for the breach of a *contract* upon the *death* of either party, in general survives to and against the executor or administrator of each (z); but in the case of *torts*, when the action must be in form *ex delicto*, for the recovery of damages, and the plea not guilty, the rule at common law was otherwise; it being a maxim that *actio personalis moritur cum persona* (a); and we shall find that the statute 4 Ed. 3, c. 7 (165), has altered this rule only in its relation to *personal property*, and in favor of the personal representative of the *party injured*; but if the action can be framed in form *ex contractu*, this rule does not apply (b). We will now consider the rule as it affects actions for injuries to the *person*, and to *personal* and *real* property.

(w) 1 Show. 188; Carth. 170; 2 M. & S. 225; *ante*, 21.

(x) See the cases 2 Saund. 72 i.; Rep. temp. Hardw. 395; Bac. Ab. Joint-tenants, K.

(y) 4 Taunt. 884.

(z) *Ante*, 21.

(a) See the observations on this rule in general, 3 Bla. Com. 302; 1 Saund. 216, 217, n. 1; Cowp. 371 to 377; 3 Woodes. Lect. 73; Vin. Ab. Executors, 123; Com. Dig. Administrator, B. 13.

(b) See 3 Woodes. Lect. 78, 79; Marsh. 14.

his own name, upon a guaranty as to the rent reserved in the lease, given by a third person to his grantor; the action, notwithstanding the Revised Statutes, must be sued in the name of the grantor. Harbeck v. Sylvester, 13 Wend. Rep. 608.

(164) Vide Laws of New York. Act for amendment of the law, s. 9, 1 R. L. 519. 2 Rev. Stat. 386. 1. See also 3 Smith's Laws of Pennsylvania, p. 30.

(165) {In force in Pennsylvania, Robert's Dig. 248. *Report of the Judges*. 3 Binn. 610.}

I. PLAINTIFFS. 5. Death of party injured. Injuries to the *person*.

In the case of injuries to the *person*, whether by assault, battery (166), false imprisonment, slander, or otherwise, if either the party who received or committed the injury die, no action can be supported either by or against the executors or other personal representatives (*c*); for the statute 4 Ed. 3, c. 7, has made no alteration in the common law in that respect (*d*); and the statute 3 & 4 W. 4, c. 42, s. 3, only gives executors and administrators an action for *torts* to the *personal* or *real estate* of the party injured, and not for mere injuries to the *person*; and a promise to *marry* is considered of so *personal* a nature, that although the action for its breach is in form *ex contractu*, yet the executor of the party to whom the promise was made cannot sue (*e*).

[*79] *At *common law*, in case of injuries to *personal property*, if either party died, in general no action could be supported, either by or against the personal representatives of the parties, where the action must have been in *form ex delicto* and the plea not guilty (*f*); but if any *contract* could be implied, as if the wrong-doer converted the property into money, or if the goods remained in specie in the hands of the executor of the wrong-doer, assumpsit for money had and received might be supported at common law by or against the executors in the former case, and trover against the executors in the latter (*g*). By the statute 3 Ed. 3, c. 7, intituled "Executors shall have an action of *trespass* for a *wrong* done to the testator," and reciting "that in times past executors have not had actions for a *trespass* done to their testators, *as* of the goods and chattels of the same testators carried away in their life, and so such trespassers have hitherto remained unpunished," it is enacted, "that the executors in such cases shall have an action against the trespassers, and recover their damages in like manner as they, whose executors they be, should have had if they were in life (167);" and this remedy is further extended to executors of executors (*h*), and to administrators (*i*). It has been observed, that the taking of goods and chattels was put in the statute merely as an instance, and not as restrictive to such injuries only, and that the term "trespass" must, with reference to the language of the times when the statute was passed, signify *any wrong* (*k*); and accordingly the statute has been construed to extend to every description of injury to *personal* property, by which it has been rendered *less beneficial* to the executor, whatever the form of action may be (*l*); so that an executor may support trespass or trover (*m*)(168), case for a false return to final process (*n*), and case or debt for an escape (169), &c. on final pro-

(*c*) 3 Bla. Com 302; 2 M. & Sel. 408.
(*d*) 1 Saund. 217, n. 1; Sir W. Jones, 174.
(*e*) *Ante*, 21.
(*f*) Cowp. 371 to 377.
(*g*) Cowp. 374; Latch. 168; 2 M. & Sel. 415, 416.
(*h*) 25 Edw. 3, c. 5.
(*i*) 31 Edw. 3, c. 11.
(*k*) Owen, 99; 7 East, 134, 136; 11 Vin. Ab. 125; Latch. 167.
(*l*) 2 M. & Sel. 416.
(*m*) Latch. 168; 5 Co. 27 a; Sir W. Jones, 174.
(*n*) 4 Mod. 403; 12 Mod. 71.

(166) {Miller v. Umbehower, 10 Serg. & Rawle, 31.}
(167) Vide *Laws of New York*, sess. 36, c. 71, s. 6, 7. 1 R. L. 311, 312.
(168) Or replevin, Reist, adm. v. Heilbrenner, 11 Serg. & Rawle, 131. And an executor need not describe himself as such, in an action of trover to recover property of the testator, wrongfully converted by a stranger. Trash v. Donoghue, Aiken's (Vermont) Rep. 370. Vide Toule v. Lovet, 6 Mass. Rep. 394. Snider and Van Vechten v. Croy, 2 Johns. Rep. 227.
(169) The executor of a sheriff cannot maintain an action on the case against the gaoler, for the escape of a prisoner committed to his custody by the testator. Kain and others v. Ostrander, 8 Johns. Rep. 207.

1. PLAINTIFFS. — 5. Death of party injured. [*80]

cess (o)(170). And although it has been doubted whether an executor could sue for an escape on *mesne process* in the life-time of his testator (p), it seems that on principle *he might (q); and he may support debt for not setting out tithes (r); or against a tenant for double value for holding over (s); or against an attorney for negligence (t); or debt against an executor, suggesting a *devastavit* in the life-time of the plaintiff's testator (u); or case against the sheriff for removing goods taken in execution, without paying the testator a year's rent (x): or an action of ejectment or *quare impedit*, for the disturbance of the testator (y). We will presently state the extension of remedy by 3 & 4 W. 4, c. 42, s. 2.

Injuries to *real* property.

With respect to injuries to *real* property, if either party die, no action in form *ex delicto* could be supported either by or against his personal representatives before the 3 & 4 W. 4, c. 42, s. 2; and although the statute 4 Ed. 3, c. 7, *might* bear a more liberal construction, the decisions confined its operation to injuries to *personal* property (z); and therefore an executor could not support an action of trespass *quare clausum fregit* (171), or merely for cutting down trees or other waste in the life-time of his testator (a)(172): and though in *Emerson* v. *Emerson* (b), it was holden that a declaration by an executor for mowing, cutting down, taking and carrying away corn, might be supported, the allegation of the cutting down being considered merely as a description of the manner of taking away the corn, for which an action is sustainable by virtue of the statute; yet it was decided that if the declaration had been *quare clausum fregit, et blada asportavit*, it would have been insufficient; and that if the defendant had merely cut the corn and let it lie, or if the grass of the testator had been cut and carried away at the same time, no action could have been supported by the executor. We have seen, however, that an action may be supported by a devisee for the continuance of a nuisance erected in the life-time of the testator (c)(173). And a bill in equity, for an account of

(o) Lord Raym. 973.
(p) 1 Ventr. 31; 1 Rol. Ab. 912; Latch. 168; Sir W. Jones, 173; 4 Mod. 404; Cro. Car. 297; Vin. Ab. Executors, P. pl. 2, *acc.*; Ld. Raym. 973; 12 Mod. 72; 1 Salk. 12, *contr.*
(q) Owen, 99; 7 East, 134, 136.
(r) 1 Sid. 88, 407, 181; 1 Eagle & Young on Tithes, 437, 440, 480; 2 Eagle on Tithes, 307, 308.
(s) 4 Geo. 2. c. 28.
(t) 2 B. & B. 103.
(u) 1 Salk. 314.
(x) 1 Stra. 212.
(y) Vin. Ab. Executors, P. pl. 7; Latch. 168, 169; Sir W. Jones, 175; Poph. 190; 1 Vent. 30.
(z) 1 Saund. 207, n. 1; Sir W. Jones, 174; Latch. 169; Vin. Ab. Executors, P. 22, &c.; Toller, 168; 1 Vent. 187.
(a) Sir W. Jones, 174; 1 B. & P. 330, n. a.
(b) 1 Vent. 187; 2 Keb. 874; Sir W. Jones, 177, 174; 1 B. & P. 329.
(c) *Ante*, 76.

(170) So, case against a sheriff for the default of his deputy in not returning an execution. Paine v Ulmer, 7 Mass. Rep. 317. And an executor may maintain an action for an injury done to goods of his testator, before Probate or seizure; and in his individual right without declaring *as executor*. So an administrator may sue trover in his own name for the goods of his intestate converted before the granting of administration, and need not declare in his representative character. Valentine v. Jackson, 9 Wend. 302. The right of the former commences upon the death of the testator; the latter accrues upon the grant of letter of administration and exists when the wrong is done only by relation, ib.

(171) Vide contra Griswold v. Brown, 1 Day, 180.

(172) Nor can an action on the case, for overflowing and drowning the land of the testator in his life-time, be supported by an executor. Laughlin v. Dorsey, 1 Harr. & M'Hen. 224.

(173) But in an action for a nuisance to land all the co-tenants must join as plaintiffs. Low v. Mumford, 14 J. R. 426.

equitable waste committed by a tenant for life, may be maintained against his *personal* representat ve (*d*). 1. PLAINTIFFS.

5. Death of party injured.

Alterations, by 3 & 4 W. 4, c. 42, in the ru'e *actio personalis*, &c. and actions for injuries to personal and real property, by and against executors and administrators, are now sustainable.

The 3 & 4 W. 4, c. 42, s. 2, has introduced a material alteration in the common law doctrine, *actio personalis moritur cum persona*, as well *in favor* of executors and administrators of the party injured, as *against* the personal representative of the party injured, but respects only injuries to *personal* and *real property*, and subject to certain *restrictions* as regards the commencement of an action for such injury within *a short time after the death*, and declaring that the damages to be recovered from an executor or administrator shall be ranked or classed with *simple contract debts*. The act *recites*, that there is no remedy provided by law for injuries to the real estate of any person deceased committed in his life-time, nor for certain wrongs done by a person deceased in his life-time to another, in respect of his *property, real or personal*: for remedy thereof it enacts, that an action of trespass or trespass on the case, as the case may be, may be maintained by the executors or administrators of any person deceased, for any injury to the real estate of such person, committed in his life-time, for which an action might have been maintained by such person; so as such injury shall have been committed within six calendar months before the death of such deceased person, and provided such action shall be brought within one year after the death of such person, and the damages, when recovered, shall be part of the personal estate of such person; and further, that an action of trespass, or trespass on the case, as the case may be, may be maintained against the executors or administrators of any person deceased, for any wrong committed by him in his life-time to another, in respect of his property real or personal, so as such injury shall have been committed within six calendar months before such person's death, and so as such action shall be brought within six calendar months after such executors or administrators shall have taken upon themselves the administration of the estate and effects of such person; and the damages to be recovered in such action shall be payable in like order of administration as the simple contract debts of such persons.

6thly. In case of bankruptcy.

We have before considered what rights of action pass to the assignees of a bankrupt, where the cause of action is *founded on the *contract* of the bankrupt (*e*). When the cause of action is founded on a *tort*, the question whether a right to sue will pass to the assignees will depend upon the nature of the [*81] right that has been injured. All the bankrupt's *property, real* and *personal*, passes to the assignees, and all powers to turn such property to profit (*f*), and consequently when the injury complained of consists in the unlawful detention of any part of *such* property, the assignees may bring actions for the purpose of recovering the possession or value thereof. Thus they may bring a real action to recover any part of the bankrupt's estate (*g*), or an action of ejectment; they may sue in trover for any of his goods upon a conversion either before or after the bankruptcy (*h*); or in debt to recover from

(*d*) Lansdown *v.* Lansdown, 1 Madd. 116; 1 Chit. Eq. Dig. 395.

(*e*) *Ante*, 25

(*f*) See 8 Taunt. 751.

(*g*) 2 Hen. Bla. 444.

(*h*) Cullen, 418, 419; 5 East, 407; Holt, N. P. C. 172.

I. PLAINTIFFS.

6. In case of bankruptcy.

the winner money lost at play by the bankrupt before his bankruptcy (i). But for mere *personal torts* to the *bankrupt*, such as assault or slander (174), it seems no right of action passes to the assignees (k); such rights are not considered in law as the subject of property, and there are no expressions in the bankrupt laws which direct that they shall pass by the assignment. It has been made a subject of some discussion among writers on the bankrupt laws, whether any right of action passes to the assignees in respect of mere *torts*, not consisting in the detention or conversion of any property legally belonging to the bankrupt, but which have only had the effect of *deteriorating* the value of some part of the bankrupt's estate before the title of the assignees accrued (l). It does not appear that there has been any express determination of the Courts on this subject, but it seems reasonable, and consistent with the spirit of the bankrupt laws, that the assignees should be entitled to recover satisfaction for injuries of this description.

When the right of action does not pass to the assignees, the bankrupt may, it should seem, sue, notwithstanding his bankruptcy (m); and even where the assignees are entitled to sue in respect of injuries to property acquired by the bankrupt after his bankruptcy, and before certificate, it follows, from the principle before noticed (n), (viz. that the bankrupt [*62] *has a right against all other persons when his assignees do not interpose,) that the bankrupt will, on the non-intervention of his assignees, be entitled to maintain actions of *tort* for all such injuries. Thus he may sue in trover against a stranger for goods acquired by him *after* his bankruptcy (o), (though not for goods acquired *before*) (p); and an action of trespass is maintainable by a tenant from year to year, who had become bankrupt after the committing the trespass, and before the commencement of the suit; and the right of such action does not pass to the assignees by the assignment, unless they interfere, as the bankrupt may sue as a trustee for, and has a good title against all persons but them (q). But an uncertificated bankrupt cannot maintain an action of trespass against subsequent creditors for breaking open his house, and seizing his after-acquired property, his assignees having assented to the seizure; though they were unknown to the defendants until after the commencement of the action (r). A party may support trover or trespass against his assignees if he were not liable to the commission (s).

7thly. In case of insolvency.

The general provisions of the Insolvent Act (t), with regard to the transfer

(i) 2 Hen. Bla. 308, and see 10 East, 418.

(k) Sir W. Jones, 215; Cullen, 177; Eden's B. L. 2d edit. 235.

(l) See 4 Evans's Stat. 329, 2d edit.; see *per Cur.* 8 Taunt. 751, 752; Cullen, 418; Eden. 235, 2d edit.

(m) *Id.*

(n) *Ante*, 28.

(o) 7 T. R. 391; Cullen, 414.

(p) 1 Car. & P. 147; 4 B. & C. 419; 6 Dow. & Ry. 491, S. C.; 3 Moore, 612; *infra*, "Insolvency."

(q) 3 Moore, 96, 8 Taunt. 742, S. C. See *ante*, 28. 29; but see 1 Car. & P. 147.

(r) 3 Moore, 612; 3 B. & Ald. 225,

(s) 2 Wils. 382; 1 Atk. 102; Cullen, 412. When not, see 9 East, 21; 1 M. & Sel. 123; 2 New Rep. 352. This action lies, though the commission be not superseded, 2 Wils. 333, 384. *Sed quære vide* 7 Taunt. 400.

(t) 7 Geo. 4, c. 57.

(174) {Deceit in the sale of goods, (Shoemaker v. Keelty 2 Dall. 213. 1 Yeates 245,) malicious abuse of legal process, (Sommer v. Wilt, 4 Serg. & Rawle, 19.) libel, (Strong v. White, 9 Johns. Rep. 161.) carelessness or unskilfulness of the master of a vessel, by which goods are damaged, (Dusac v. Mugatroyd, 1 Wash. C. C. Rep. 13.) are cases not affected by the discharge of a party as an insolvent debtor or bankrupt.}

to the assignees of the insolvent's rights and property, have been already mentioned (*u*). Certain articles are to be excepted from the assignment, namely, "wearing apparel, bedding, and other such necessaries (*x*) of the insolvent and his family, and his working tools and implements, not exceeding in the whole the value of £20." As to the excepted articles, the insolvent retains his rights and remedies (175). It seems that an insolvent may maintain an action for injury to, or conversion of, chattels which he acquires after the petition, though before his discharge, and which are in his possession; provided the assignees do not interfere (*y*). But with regard to property acquired *before the petition, and which passes by the assignment, it appears that the insolvent cannot sue, although the assignees do not interpose (*z*). The rules upon this subject appear to be analogous to those which prevail in the case of bankruptcy (*a*). With regard to remedies for personal *torts*, as they do not appear to pass to the insolvent's assignee, it would seem he retains the right of action. [*83]

I. PLAINTIFFS. 7. In case of insolvency.

8thly. In case of marriage.

The wife having no legal interest in the person or property of her husband, cannot in general join with him in any action for an injury to them (*b*), except in an action for a joint malicious prosecution of both, in which they may join in respect of the injury to both, or the husband may sue alone for the injury to himself and expenses of defence (*c*).

As regards injuries to *the person*.

For injuries to the person, or to the personal or real property of the wife, committed *before* the marriage, when the cause of action would survive to the wife, she *must* join in the action, and if she die before judgment therein it will abate (*d*) (176). But in detinue to recover personal chattels of the wife, in the possession of the defendant before the marriage, perhaps the husband must sue alone, because the law transfers the property to him, and the wife has no interest (*e*). In detinue for charters of the wife's inheritance, they may join, on account of the continuing interest of the wife in the estate to which they relate (*f*).

When an injury is committed to the *person* of the wife *during coverture*, by battery, slander, &c., the wife cannot sue alone in any case (*g*); and the hus-

(*u*) *Ante*, 29.

(*x*) That is, *ejusdem generis*, and it seems these words would not comprehend plate, 1 C. & P. 147.

(*y*) 1 C. & P. 146, 147; 4 B. & C. 419; 6 Dow. & R. 491, S. C. Interference by assignees *after* action brought, *semble* sufficient, 3 Moore, 612.

(*z*) 1 C. & P. 147.

(*a*) See *id.* and *ante*, 29.

(*b*) 3 Bla. Com. 143; Lord Raym. 1208; 2 Wils. 424; 1 Lev. 140; 1 Salk. 119, n. h.; Sir W. Jones, 440.

(*c*) Cro. Jac. 553; Com. Dig. Bar. & Feme, X.; *ante*, 74. Where wife may make use of husband's name against his will, see 9 East, 471.

(*d*) 3 T. R. 627, 631; 7 T. R. 348, 349; Com. Dig. Bar. & Feme, V.; Rol. Ab. 347, R. pl. 3; *ante*, 31, 32; 4 Taunt. 884.

(*e*) Bac. Ab. Detinue, A.; Bul. N. P. 50; 1 Salk. 114. *Sed vide* R. temp. Hardw. 120.

(*f*) 1 Rol. Ab. 347, R. pl. 1; Bac. Ab. Detinue, B.

(*g*) 11 East, 301; 9 East, 471. A marriage *de facto* is sufficient, unless it be void *ab initio*, as in the case of polygamy, 1 Stra. 79, 480; Andr. 227, 228; Dougl. 174; *ante*, 65.

(175) { Although the assignment of an insolvent debtor passes the legal estate in his lands, yet a trust results by operation of law, which, as soon as the debts are satisfied, entitles him to the possession against his assignees, *et a multo fortiori* against a stranger, against whom he may maintain ejectment in his own name. Ross *v.* M'Junkin, 14 Serg. & Rawle, 365. }

(176) Stroop et ux. *v.* Swartz, 12 Serg. & Rawle, 76.

1. PLAINTIFFS.

8. In case of marriage.

[*84]

band and wife *must* join, if the action be brought for the personal suffering or injury to the wife, and in such case the declaration ought to conclude to their damage, and not to that of the husband alone; *for the damages will survive to the wife if the husband die before they are recovered (*h*) (177). Care must be taken not to include in the declaration by the husband and wife any statement of a cause of action for which the husband alone ought to sue (178); therefore, after stating the injury to the wife, the declaration ought not to proceed to state any loss of assistance, or expenses sustained in curing her (*i*). If the battery, imprisonment, or malicious prosecution of the wife, deprive the husband for any time of her company or assistance, or occasion him expense, he may and ought to sue separately for such consequential injuries (*k*); and he may in the same action proceed for a battery or other injury to himself (*l*). Of course the husband must sue alone for criminal conversation with his wife. For words spoken of the wife not actionable of themselves, but which occasion some special damage to the husband, he must sue alone (*m*).

As to personal property.

With respect to *personal property*, when the cause of action had only its inception before the marriage but its completion afterwards: as in the case of trover before marriage, and conversion during it, or of rent due before marriage, and a rescue afterwards, the husband and wife may join, or they may sever in trover or trespass (*n*). It seems that in detinue the husband should sue alone (*o*). When the cause of action has its inception as well as completion after the marriage, the husband must sue alone, the legal interest in personalty being vested by the marriage in him (*p*); and therefore a declaration in trover at the suit of husband and wife, should state that the wife was possessed before the marriage, or held the goods with him in her character of executrix; and if it be merely stated that the *husband and wife were possessed*, the defendant may demur: for the possession of the wife is in law the possession

[*85]

of the husband, and the *property vests in him exclusively (*q*). The same rule prevails in replevin; but if the husband and wife join as plaintiffs in that action, although the declaration is bad on demurrer, if no special cause for joining her be specifically shown therein (*r*); yet, if the defendant, instead of demurring, avow the taking, it will, *after verdict*, be intended, (if the declaration show nothing to the contrary,) that the taking was before the coverture, and that the plaintiffs then had a joint property; or that the wife held the goods as executrix; in either of which cases she might be joined (*s*). Though the

(*h*) 1 Sid. 346, 386; Ld. Raym. 1208; Com. Dig. Bar. & Feme, V.; Pleader, 2 A. 9; 3 Bla. Com. 140; 1 Salk. 111; Yelv. 89; 2 Keb. 387, pl. 63; Freem. 224.

(*i*) 1 Salk. 119; Com. Dig. Pleader, 2 A. 1.

(*k*) 3 Bla. Com. 140; Cro. Jac. 538; 1 Stra. 61; 2 Stra. 977; Com. Dig. Bar. & Feme, W.

(*l*) Cro. Jac. 501; 1 Salk. 119; Selw. N. P. 286, 5th edit.; Year Book, 9 Edw. 4, 51.

(*m*) 1 Sid. 346; 2 Keb. 387, pl. 63; 1 Lev. 140; 3 Mod. 120; 1 Salk. 119.

(*n*) 2 Saund. 47 h.; Salk. 114; 2 Lev. 107; Com. Dig. Bar. & Feme, X.; Bac. Ab. Bar. & Feme, K.

(*o*) *Ante*, 83; Bac. Ab. Detinue; Bul. N. P. 53.

(*p*) 2 Saund. 47 h. i.; Salk. 114, 119; 2 Bla. Rep. 1236; 2 C. & P. 34.

(*q*) 2 Saund. 47 i.; 1 Salk. 114; Com. Dig. Pleader, 2 A. 1.

(*r*) 2 New Rep. 405; see 7 Taunt. 72, replevin by the wife only.

(*s*) Bourn and Wife *v.* Mattaire, Bul. N. P. 53; Selw. N. P. Bar. & Feme, III. 6th edit. 298; Com. Dig. Pleader, 3 K. 10; see 2 New Rep. 407.

(177) But if the wife die after judgment, the judgment survives to the husband. Stroop et ux. *v.* Swarts, 12 Serg. & Rawle, 76.

(178) Lewis et ux. *v.* Babcock, 18 Johns. Rep. 443.

8. In case of marriage.

wife may join in trespass for cutting down corn upon her land, yet she cannot for carrying it away (*t*). However, a feme covert executrix may and ought to join with her husband; the declaration stating her interest, and showing that she sues in *autre droit* (*u*). And there are some cases in which, though the produce of the wife's labor be the property of the husband, yet in respect of her being the meritorious cause of action, she may be joined, as in the case of the dippers at Tunbridge Wells (*x*).

With respect to real property.

In *real* actions for the recovery of the land of the wife, and in a writ of waste thereto, the husband and wife must join (*y*). But where the action is merely for the recovery of damages to the land or other real property of the wife during the coverture; or for a *tort*, which prejudices a remedy by husband and wife, as in the case of *quare impedit*, a rescue, &c. the husband may sue alone (*z*), or the wife may be joined (*a*); her interest in the land being stated in the declaration. But a demand for removal of personal property, as corn or grass when severed from the land, ought not, in the latter case, to be included, because, as we have seen, the entire interest in personalty is vested in the husband (*b*) (179).

[*86]

*If the *husband survive*, he may maintain an action of trespass, &c. for any injury in regard to the person or property of the wife, for which he might have sued alone during the coverture. Thus, he might maintain an action after his wife's death for any battery or personal *tort* to her, which occasioned him particular injury; as the loss of her society and assistance in his domestic affairs; or a pecuniary expense (*c*); or for any injury to the land of the wife when living (*d*). If the wife die pending an action by her husband and herself for any *tort* committed either before or during coverture, and to which action she is a necessary party, the suit will abate (*e*).

If the *wife survive*, any action for a *tort* committed to her personally, or to her goods or real property before marriage, or to her personal or real property during coverture, will survive to her (*f*); and she may include in the declaration in such action counts for wrongs committed after her husband's death (*g*).

Consequences of mis-joinder or non-joinder.

The *consequences of a mistake* in the proper parties in the case of husband and wife, may be collected from the preceding observations, and seem to be nearly the same in actions in form *ex delicto* as in those *ex contractu* (*h*). If the wife be improperly joined in the action, and the objection appear from the declaration, the defendant may in general demur, move in arrest of judgment,

(*t*) 2 Wils. 424; Cro. Eliz. 133; Salk. 119.

(*u*) Salk. 114; Wentw. Exec. 207; Bro. Bar. & Feme, pl. 85. Bourn *v.* Mattaire, *ante*, note (*s*).

(*x*) 2 Wils. 414, 424; Com. Dig. Bar. & Feme, X.; *ante*, 75.

(*y*) 1 Bulst. 21; 7 H. 4, 15 a.; 3 H. 6, 53; Com. Dig. Bar. & Feme, V. Wife must join in an *ejectione firmæ*, though ejection after marriage, Plowd. 418.

(*z*) Bro. Bar. & Feme, pl. 16, 28, 41; Selw. N. P. 291, 5th ed.; 295, 6th ed.; Com. Dig. Bar. & Feme, X.

(*a*) Com. Dig. Bar. & Feme, X.; 2 Wils. 423, 424; 2 Bla. Rep. 1236; Cro. Car. 418, 437; Com. Dig. Bar. & Feme, V. X.; Pleader, 2 A. 1.

(*b*) *Ante*, 82, 83; 1 Salk. 119, note (*b*).

(*c*) *Ante*, 83.

(*d*) Com. Dig. Bar. & Feme, Z.

(*e*) Freem. 225; Yelv. 89; 4 Taunt. 884.

(*f*) Rep. temp. Hardw. 398, 399; Freem. 224; Palm. 313.

(*g*) Palm. 313; Com. Dig. Bar. & Feme, 2 A.

(*h*) *Ante*, 37, 68; 3 T. R. 631.

(179) Husband and wife cannot maintain a joint action for a penalty given by statute. (*Semble.*) Hill and wife *v.* Davis, 4 Mass. Rep. 137.

I. PLAINTIFFS. — 7. In case of marriage.

or support a writ of error (*i*); though we have seen that after verdict the mistake may sometimes be aided by intendment (*k*)(180). If the husband sue alone when the wife ought to be joined either in her own right or in *autre droit*, he will be nonsuited; for though in general the non-joinder of a party as a co-plaintiff in an action for a *tort* can only be pleaded in abatement; yet that rule only applies in those cases in which the party suing had some legal interest in his own right in the property affected. A husband has, *independently of his wife*, *no* legal interest or cause of action whatever for injuries to her, or her property, in those instances in which it is necessary to join her as a plaintiff in an action.

[*87]

*II. DEFENDANTS.

II. DEFENDANTS. — 1st. As between the original parties, and with reference to their liability.

In *personal* or *mixed* actions, in form *ex delicto*, the person committing the injury, either by himself or his agent, is in general to be made the defendant; but *real* actions can only be supported against the claimant of the freehold (*l*). The general rule is, that all persons are liable to be sued for their own *tortious* acts, unconnected with, or in disaffirmance of, a contract. Therefore, although an *infant* cannot in general be sued in an action in form *ex contractu*, except for necessaries, he is liable for all *torts* committed by him, as for slander, assaults, and batteries, &c. (*m*); and also in detinue for goods delivered

Infants.

to him for a purpose which he has failed to perform, and which goods he refuses to return (*n*)(181). But a plaintiff cannot in general, by changing his *form* of action, charge an infant for a breach of contract; as for the negligent or immoderate use of a horse, &c. (*o*)(182); nor can he be a trespasser by

Married women.

prior or subsequent assent, but only by his own act (*p*). A *married woman* is liable for *torts* actually committed by her, though she cannot be a trespasser

(*i*) 1 Salk. 114, 119; 2 Bla. Rep. 1236. 2 Chit. Rep. 697.
(*k*) *Ante*, 37, 68; Ashton's Entr. 61.
(*l*) Booth, 3, 28, 29; 3 Lev. 330.
(*m*) 8 T. R. 336, 337; Bac. Abr. Infancy, H.
(*n*) 1 New Rep. 140.
(*o*) 8 T. R. 335.
(*p*) Co. Lit. 180 b. n. 4.

(180) Lewis et ux. *v.* Babcock, 18 Johns. Rep. 443.

(181) Per curiam, 3 Pick. Rep. 494. So an infant is liable in trover. Vasse *v.* Smith, 6 Cranch, 231. But by electing to bring trover, the plaintiff cannot convert a case founded on contract, and upon which an infant would not be liable, into a tort so as to charge him. Curtin *v.* Patton, 11 Serg. & Rawle, 310. See Schenck *v.* Strong, 1 South. Rep. 87.

(182) But an infant who hires a horse to go to a place agreed on, but goes to another place in a different direction, is liable in trover for an unlawful conversion of the horse. Homer *v.* Thwing, 3 Pick. Rep. 492. Contra Schenck *v.* Strong, 1 South. Rep. 87. The court of errors in New York decided, that if an infant having an horse on hire, does a wilful and positive act, amounting to an election, on his part, to disaffirm the contract of hiring, the owner was entitled to the immediate possession. And where an infant drove a mare, which he had on hire, with such violence, as that she died of his cruel treatment; *held*, that though case would not lie, *trespass* might be maintained against him. Campbell *v.* Stakes, 2 Wend. R. 137. Independent of the contract of hiring, trespass would be the proper remedy. If the plaintiff orders in case, he affirms the contract of hiring, and the plea of infancy is a good defence to such an action; for he cannot affirm the contract, and at the same time, by alleging a tortious breach thereof, deprive the defendant of his plea of infancy, ib.

II. DEFENDANTS.

1. Who liable.

Lunatics.

by prior or subsequent assent (*q*). And although a *lunatic* is not punishable criminally, he is liable to a civil action for any *tort* he may commit (*r*)(183).

Corporations.

With regard to the liability of *corporations*, it is a clear general rule that they are liable to be sued as such in case or trover for any *torts* they may cause to be committed (*s*)(184). It has been laid down that a corporation cannot be sued in its corporate capacity in trespass (*t*); but this position appears to be incorrect, for although a corporation cannot, as a corporate body, actually commit a trespass, yet they may order it to be done, and ought therefore to be responsible for the consequences (*u*). In these cases it is often very material to fix the corporation with liability, and to be entitled to redress from the corporate funds, rather than to be driven to a remedy against servants of the corporation. It seems that a corporation may be sued for a false return (*x*).

[*88] *The *inhabitants of a county* are not a corporation, and therefore cannot be sued by that description for an injury occasioned by the neglect to build a public bridge, or for any other injury arising from the neglect of the county at large (*y*).

Companies.

It is a general rule that corporations and incorporated companies may be sued in that character, for damages arising from the breach by them of a duty imposed upon them by law (185). An individual who has suffered loss in consequence of the decay of sea walls, which a corporation is directed to repair, under the terms of a grant from the crown, conveying a borough, and pier or quay, with tolls, to the corporation, may sue the corporation for the recovery of damages (*z*)(186). The Bank of England are liable to an action if they improperly refuse to transfer stock (*a*); or are guilty of unreasonable delay in the passing of a power of attorney to transfer it (*b*); but they are not liable for refusing to pay dividends due upon stock if they have not received the dividends from government (*c*).

(*q*) *Id.*; *post*, 91, n. (*p*).

(*r*) Hob. 134; 2 East, 104; Bac. Abr. Trespass, G., Idiot, E.; 2 Rol. Ab. 547, pl. 4, E.

(*s*) 16 East, 6; Smith *v.* Birmingham Gas Light Company, 1 Adol. & El. 526.

(*t*) Bro. Corporation, pl. 43; Bac. Ab. Trespass, E. 2; 8 East, 230.

(*u*) See 16 East, 7, &c. *per* Lord Ellenborough.

(*x*) *Id.*

(*y*) 2 T. R. 667; see 11 East, 347, 355.

(*z*) 5 Bing. 91.

(*a*) 5 Bing. 108.

(*b*) 1 Car. & P. 193.

(*c*) 5 B. & C. 185; 7 D. & R. 828, S. C.; See S. C. 2 Bing. 393.

(183) Ex parte Leighton, 14 Mass. R. 207. The institution of a suit against a lunatic, pending a proceeding in chancery and after lunacy found is improper. 5 Paige Ch. R. 489.

(184) {Trespass on the case lies against a corporate aggregate for a *tort*. Chesnut Hill Turnp. Co. *v.* Rutter, 4 Serg. & Rawle, 6. See the early English cases cited by Ch. Justice TILGHMAN, in his opinion. See also Gray *v.* The Portland Bank, 3 Mass. Rep. 364.}

(185) An action on the case will lie against a corporation for the neglect of a corporate duty, as, for not repairing a creek as from time immemorial they had been used. Mayor of Lynn *v.* Turner, Cowp. 86. Riddle *v.* Proprietors, &c, 7 Mass. Rep. 169. Townsend *v.* Susquehannah Turnpike Company, 6 Johns. Rep. 90. Steele *v.* W. Lock Company, 2 Johns. Rep. 283. So, it will lie against them for the negligence of their subordinate agents, although not immediately employed by them. Matthews *v.* West London Water Works Company, 3 Campb. 403. {Corporations created for their own benefit stand on the same ground in this respect as individuals, but *quasi* corporations created by the legislature for purposes of public policy, are subject, by the common law, to an indictment for the neglect of duties enjoined on them, but are not liable to an action for any neglect unless the action be given by some statute. Mower *v.* Inhab. of Leicester, 9 Mass. Rep. 247.}

(186) {Goshen T. Co. *v.* Sears, 7 Conn. Rep. 87.}

II. DEFENDANTS.

1. Who liable.

The London Dock Company is liable in case for the carelessness of their servants in unloading goods, although the Company derive no profit from the labor (*d*); and an action lies against an incorporated water-works company, if workmen employed by the persons contracting with the company to lay down pipes for conducting water through a public street, are guilty of negligence in performing the work, in consequence of which a passenger is injured (*e*).

Commissioners or trustees under a statute.

But trustees and commissioners acting gratuitously in the execution of acts of parliament for the benefit of the public, and entrusted with the conduct of public works, are not liable in damages for an injury occasioned by the negligence or unskilfulness of workmen and contractors necessarily employed by them in the execution of the works (*f*). Upon this principle, where the defendant, as a trustee under a turnpike act, being authorized to cut a drain, had ordered it to be cut in an improper manner, it was decided that he was not liable for a resulting injury, as it appeared that he acted *bona fide* according to
[*89] the best of his judgment, and under *the best advice he could obtain (*g*). And in another case (*h*), the clerk to commissioners for making a road under an act which contained a clause directing actions to be brought against such clerk for acts done by the trustees, was holden not to be liable to an action for an injury sustained in consequence of heaps of dirt being left by the laborers employed by the side of the road, and no lights being placed to enable persons to avoid such heaps. And if a statute enable trustees to do an act, and do not give compensation, they are not liable for a consequential injury resulting to an individual from the act done in pursuance of the statute (*i*).

But if commissioners or trustees under an act of parliament order something to be done which is not within the scope of their authority (*k*); or are themselves guilty of negligence in doing that which they are empowered to do; or are guilty of arbitrary, wanton, or oppressive conduct (*l*); they render themselves liable to an action, although they are not answerable for the misconduct of perons they are obliged to employ in the execution of orders properly given (*m*). Therefore, an action was held to be maintainable against commissioners of the lottery, who were compensated for their services, for their negligence, &c. in not adjudging a prize to the holder of a ticket entitled to receive it (*n*). And persons who negligently or unskilfully perform work, or omit proper precautions in the course of the necessary repair of a sewer, under the authority of the *commissioners of sewers*, are liable to an action for the consequential injury sustained by an individual (*o*).

Judicial and other public officers, &c.

An action cannot be maintained against a civil or ecclesiastical judge or justice of the peace, acting *judicially* in a matter within the scope of his jurisdiction, although he may decide erroneously in the particular case (*p*) (187).

(*d*) 4 Campb. 72.
(*e*) 3 Campb. 403. See *post*.
(*f*) 2 Bing. 156.
(*g*) 1 Marsh. 489; 6 Taunt. 29, S. C. See 2 Bing. 162.
(*h*) 4 M. & Sel. 27. See 2 Bing. 162.
(*i*) 2 B. & C. 703; 4 D. & R. 195, S. C.
(*k*) 3 Wils. 461; 2 Bla. Rep. 924; 2 B. & C. 710; 4 D. & R. 195, S. C.
(*l*) 2 B. & C. 707, *id.* &c.
(*m*) 2 Bing. 159, *per* Best, C. J.; 2 B. & C. 707, &c.
(*n*) 6 T. R. 646; 2 Bing. 161.
(*o*) 5 B. & A. 837; 1 D. & R. 497, S. C.; 2 B. & C. 710, 711; 4 D. & R. 201, 202, S. C.
(*p*) 1 Salk. 306; Vaugh. 138; 12 Co. 24; Ld. Raym. 466; 5 T. R. 186; 6 *Id.* 449; 3 M. & Sel. 411. As to *justices* in general, *post*, "Trespass."

(187) Vide Yates *v.* Lansing, 5 Johns. Rep. 282. S. C. 9 Johns. Rep. 395. Briggs *v.* Wardwell, 10 Mass. Rep. 356. Phelps *v.* Sill, 1 Day, 315. The following additional

II. DEFENDANTS.

1. Who liable.

Nor can an action be maintained against a juryman (*q*), or the attorney-general (*r*), or a superior military or naval officer (*s*), for an act *done in the execution of his office, and within the purview of his general authority. And commissioners of bankrupts are not liable to an action of *trespass* for committing a person who does not answer *to their satisfaction* when examined before them touching the bankrupt's estate and effects (*t*).

But if a public officer have no jurisdiction whatever over the subject-matter, and his proceedings are altogether *coram non judice*, he is responsible (*u*). And it was held, that if a justice of the peace acting ministerially, refuse an examination upon the Statute of Hue and Cry, he is liable to an action (*x*). And it has been observed with regard to the liability of ministerial officers not acting gratuitously, that "if a man take a reward, whatever may be the nature of that reward, for the discharge of a public duty, that instant he becomes a public officer; and if by an act of negligence, or any abuse of his office, any individual sustain an injury, that individual is entitled to redress in a civil action." (*y*) But magistrates cannot be affected as trespassers, if facts stated to them on oath by a complainant were such whereof they had jurisdiction to inquire, and nothing appeared in answer to contradict the first statement (*z*). And before any action can be brought against a magistrate for any thing done in the discharge of his duty, it must appear that his attention was drawn to all the facts necessary to enable him to form a judgment as to the course he ought to have pursued (*a*).

Tenants in common.

With regard to *joint-tenants* and *tenants in common* of *realty*, the general rule appears to be, that ejectment will lie by one against the other only in the case of an *actual* ouster (*b*) (188); and after a recovery in such action, trespass for mesne profits may be brought (*c*). So trespass will lie where there has been a total destruction of the subject-matter of the tenancy in common; as if one tenant in common destroy the whole flight of a dove cote, or all the deer in their park (*d*); or if one grub up a hedge (*e*), or destroy a wall (*f*), holden in common. But if the wall, being old, be pulled down by one *tenant in common with the intention of rebuilding it, and a new wall be accordingly erected, this is not such a total destruction of the wall as will enable his [*91]

(*q*) 1 T. R. 513, 514, 535.

(*r*) 1 T. R. 514, 535.

(*s*) 1 T. R. 493, 550, 784; 4 Taunt. 67; 2 C. & P. 146.

(*t*) 1 B. & C. 163; 2 D. & R. 353, S. C. See Eden, 2d edit. 97, 98.

(*u*) 3 M. & Sel. 425; 1 B. & C. 163; 2 D. & R. 350, S. C.

(*x*) 1 Leon. 323. The Statute of Hue and Cry was repealed by 7 & 8 Geo. 4, c. 27, and other provisions substituted by chap. 31.

(*y*) *Per* Best, C. J., 5 Bing. 108.

(*z*) 8 East, 113.

(*a*) 3 Bing. 78.

(*b*) See Salk. 285; 1 East, 568; Adams on Ejectment, 2d edit. 52, 53, 81, 89.

(*c*) 3 Wils. 118.

(*d*) Com. Dig. Estates, K. 8; 8 B. & C. 268; 2 Man. & Ry. 272, S. C.

(*e*) Gow, 201. As to the property in trees growing in a hedge dividing two estates, 1 M. & M. 112.

(*f*) 5 Taunt. 20; 8 B. & C. 257; 2 Man. & Ry. 267, S. C.

cases were here cited by Day in the former edition; Book of Assize, 27 Ed. 3. pl. 18. 21 Ed. 3. Hil. pl. 16. 9 Hen. 6. 60 pl. 9. 9 Ed. 4. 3. pl. 10. 21 Ed. 4. 67. pl. 49. Standf. P. C. 173. Aire *v.* Sedgwick, 2 Ro. Rep. 199. Hammond *v.* Howell, 1 Mod. 184. S. C. 2 Mod. 218. Miller *v.* Searle *et al.*, 2 Bla. Rep. 1145. Mostyn *v.* Fabrigas, Cowp. 172. Vide Brodie *v.* Rutledge, 2 Bay, 69.

(188) { Erwin *v.* Olmstead, 7 Cow. Rep. 229. So he may though there has been *no actual ouster* proved. Per Spencer, C. J., Shepherd *v.* Ryers, 15 Johns. Rep. 501. See the cases cited in note (*a*) by the Reporter. }

II. DEFENDANTS.

1. Who liable.

co-tenant to maintain trespass (*g*). And in other cases where there has not been a total destruction of the subject-matter of the tenancy in common, but only a partial injury to it, waste, or an action upon the case, will lie by one tenant in common against the other; as if one tenant in common of a wood or piscary does waste against the will of the other, he shall have waste; or if one corrupt the water, the other shall have an action upon the case. There are other cases where the only remedy is to retake the property (*h*).

With respect to a tenancy in common of a *chattel*, the rule is, that one tenant in common cannot sue his co-tenant if he merely take the chattel away; for in law the possession of one is the possession of both, and each has equally a right to take and retain such possession (*i*) (189). But if one of the tenants in common destroy (190), misuse, or spoil the chattel, the other may maintain an action at law (*k*) (191).

Against a partner or third person colluding with him.

If a *third* person collude with one partner in a firm to injure the other partners in their joint trade, the latter may maintain a joint action against the person so colluding (*l*).

Who are liable as *principals*.

All persons who direct or order the commission of a trespass, or the conversion of personal property, or assist upon the occasion, are in general liable as principals, though not benefited by the act (*m*) (192); and therefore trover may be supported against a person who illegally makes a distress or seizes goods, though the same were taken by him in the character of bailiff for another, or as a custom-house officer, &c. (*n*)(193). And where several are concerned, they may be jointly sued(194), whether they assented to the act before or after it was committed (*o*), unless the party be an infant or a feme covert, who, we have seen, cannot be sued in respect of a subsequent assent (*p*); and no person can be guilty of a forcible entry by such assent (*q*). And it may ap-

(*g*) 8 B. & C. 257; 2 M. & R. 267, S. C.

(*h*) *Per* Littledale, J. 8 B. & C. 268; 2 M. & R. 272, S. C.; 4 East, 117, 121; Co. Lit. 200 a; 8 T. R. 145; 2 Saund. 47 h; 1 T. R. 658.

(*i*) *Id. ibid.*

(*k*) *Id. ibid.*

(*l*) Longman and others *v.* Pole and others, 1 Mood. & Mal. 223.

(*m*) 2 Saund. 47 i; Bul. N. P. 41; 6 T. R. 300; 1 B. & P. 369; 2 Esp. R. 553; 1 Campb. 187.

(*n*) *Ante*, 91, n. (*m*); 1 Campb. 343; *post*, 96.

(*o*) 2 Bla. Rep. 1055; 1 Salk. 409; 2 Rol. 1, 7, 555; Com. Dig. Trespass, C. 1; Co. Lit. 180 b. n. 4; Cowp. 478; 3 Wils. 377; Lane, 90.

(*p*) Co. Lit. 180 b. note 4; *ante*, 87.

(*q*) *Id. ibid.*

(189) { Cowan et al. *v.* Buyers, Cooke's Rep. 53. 2 Caines' Rep. 167. Oviatt *v.* Sage, 7 Conn. Rep. 95. }

(190) { 2 Caines' Rep. 167. See Lowthorp *v.* Smith, 1 Hayw. Rep. 255. } Vide Webb *v.* Danforth, 1 Day, 301. Litt. sec. 323.

(191) Vide St. John *v.* Standring, 2 Johns. Rep. 468. So, if one co-tenant sell the thing holden in common, the other may bring trover against him. Wilson and Gibbs *v.* Reed, 3 Johns. Rep. 175. { Thompson *v.* Cook, 2 South. Rep. 580. } Heath *v.* Hubbard, 4 East, 110. *Semble contra.* One tenant in common may convert the chattel to its general and profitable use, although it change the form of the substance, as wheat into flour, a whale into oil, &c. without subjecting himself to an action by the other. Fennings *v.* Lord Grenville, 1 Taunt. 241. One tenant in common of real property cannot sue the other to recover possession of the documents relative to their joint estate. Clowes *v.* Hawley, 12 Johns. Rep. 484. { But he may sustain an action on the case against him for destroying them. Daniels *v.* Daniels, 7 Mass. Rep. 10; and for negligence, in consequence of which a mill of which they were seised in common was burned. Chelsey *v.* Thompson, 3 New Hampshire Rep. 1. }

(192) Vide Thorp *v.* Burling, 11 Johns. Rep. 285.

(193) Vide Hoyt *v.* Gelston and Schenck, 13 Johns. Rep. 141.

(194) Vide Bishop *v.* Ely, 9 Johns. Rep. 294. Thorp *v.* Burling, 11 Johns. Rep. 285.

II. DEFENDANTS. — 1. Who liable.

pear unnecessary to say, that if a person does not assist in a trespass either in word or deed he is not liable, though it may have been done by a person assuming to act on his behalf (r). Nor can a pound-keeper be sued merely for receiving in the pound a distress illegally taken (s). If, however, a person sue out execution, and give a *bond of indemnity to the sheriff to induce [*92] him to sell the goods of another, this is a sufficient interference to subject him to an action (t); so if he be in company with the sheriff's officer at the time of the execution (u); or he adopt his acts by receiving the goods or money (x); but the mere act of making an inventory or drawing a notice of distress by a stranger, is not such an interference as will subject him to an action (y). Although trespass may be supported against a sheriff for the act of his bailiff in taking the goods of A. under an execution against B. (z), it cannot be brought against the plaintiff in the action, unless he actually interfered or assented to the levy (a). And in general where goods are sold under the authority of a sheriff in the exercise of his official duty, he is the proper party to be made defendant in an action by the owner for selling his goods, and a *bona fide* purchaser without notice at the sale cannot be sued (b); but the purchaser of the goods of B. illegally taken by the sheriff under an execution against C. is liable to be sued in trover by B.; because in that case the seizure and sale are wholly unauthorized by the writ (c).

In some cases a party may be liable to be sued for a *tort*, though in fact he neither committed the act, nor assented to the commission of it. Thus a *master* or *principal* is liable to be sued for injuries occasioned by the *negligence* or *unskilfulness* of his servant or agent whilst in the course of his employ (195), though the act was obviously *tortious* (196); as if he laid lime in the *street* without any direction for that purpose from the principal (d); so for the negligent driving of a carriage (197) or navigating a ship (e) (198),

(r) Timothy v. Simpson, 6 Car. & P. 499.

(s) Cowp. 476; 1 T. R. 60, 62; Sir T. Jones, 214. *Sed vide* 3 Campb. 35.

(t) Bul. N. P. 41.

(u) 1 B. & P. 369.

(x) 1 M. & Sel. 583, 599; Stra. 996.

(y) 2 Esp. Rep. 553.

(z) 3 Wils. 309.

(a) *Id. Ibid.* See a *quære* whether receipt of the money is an interference, 1 Mont. B. L. 476; 1 M. & Sel. 583, 599.

(b) 2 Rol. Ab. 556, pl. 50; Bro. Ab. Trespass, pl. 48; 1 M. & Sel. 425; 8 Co. Rep. 191; Yelv 179; 1 Ld. Raym. 724. But landlord may sue purchaser of fixtures from tenant, *id.*; 2 D. & R. 1.

(c) 3 Stark. 130; 2 D. & R. 1.

(d) 1 East, 106; 2 Hen. Bla. 442; 3 Wils. 317; 1 Bos. & Pul. 404; 1 Bla. Com. 431; 2 Lev. 172; Ld. Raym. 739; Dyer, 238; 3 Mod 323.

(e) 1 East, 105; *ante*, 92, n. (c). But the *owner of a ship* is not liable for the neglect of a pilot he was obliged to take on board. 6 B. & C. 657; 7 D. & R. 738, S. C.; 2 Bing. 219.

(195) And although the master derive no advantage from the labor of the servant. Gibson v Ingles, 4 Campb. 72.

(196) Therefore where the defendant was possessed of a loaded gun, and sent a young girl to fetch it, with directions to another person to take the priming out, which was accordingly done, and a damage occurred to the plaintiff's son, in consequence of the girl's presenting the gun at him, and drawing the trigger, by which the gun went off, it was held that the defendant was liable to damage in an action upon the case. Dixon v. Bell, 5 Man. & Selw. 198. So, if a man's servant, in the ordinary course of his business, obstruct the highway, from which a traveller receives an injury, the master is liable. Harlow v. Humiston, 6 Cowen, 189.

(197) { So if one of three joint proprietors of a stage coach be driving when an accident happens in consequence of his negligence, the others, though not present, are liable in an action on the case, although trespass might perhaps be maintained against the one who was driving, in which latter form of action all could not be joined. Moreton v. Harding, 6 Dowl. & Ryl. 275. }

(198) But an action will not lie against the master of a ship for negligence of the pilot;

II. DEFENDANTS.

1. Who liable.

[*93]

(even whilst the servant was driving out of the direct road, and for his own purpose) (*f*); or for a libel inserted in a newspaper of which the defendant was the proprietor (*g*); and the party in a cause is liable for any irregularity in the *proceedings of his attorney (*h*), or his attorney's agent (*i*). The principal is also liable not only for the acts of those immediately employed by him and by his steward or general agent, but even for the act of a sub-agent, however remote, if committed in the course of his service (*k*); and a corporate company, acting for its own benefit, are liable to be sued for the negligence of their servants (*l*). But a party is not liable for the act of another, unless the latter acted as his servant at the time when *the injury was committed* (*m*); and therefore a person who hires a post-chaise is not liable for the negligence of the driver, but the action must, it seems, be against the driver or the owner of the chaise and horses (*n*) (199). Where the owner of a carriage hired of a stable-keeper a pair of horses, to draw it for a day, and the owner of the horses provided a driver, through whose negligent driving an injury was done to a horse belonging to a third person, the Court were equally divided in opinion upon the question, whether the owner of the carriage was liable to be sued for such injury (*o*) (200). If a servant or agent *wilfully* commit an injury to another, though he be at the time engaged in the business of the principal, yet the principal is not in general liable; as if a servant *wilfully* drive his master's carriage against another's, or ride or beat a distress taken *damage feasant* (*p*). The rule was thus explained in a recent case: "if a servant driving a carriage, in order to effect some purpose of his own, wantonly strikes the horses of another person, and produce the accident, his master will not be liable. But if in order to perform his master's orders, he strikes, but injudiciously, and in order to extricate himself from a supposed difficulty, that will

(*f*) Joel *v.* Morison, 6 Car. & P. 501.
(*g*) 1 B. & P. 409.
(*h*) 2 Bls. Rep. 845; 3 Wils. 341, 368; *ante*, 92.
(*i*) 6 B. & C. 38; 9 D. & R. 44, S. C.
(*k*) 1 B. & P. 404; 6 T. R. 411; 4 M. & Sel. 27.
(*l*) 3 Campb. 403. When not, see 4 M. & Sel. 27; *ante*, 88.
(*m*) 1 East, 106; Rep. temp. Hardw. 87.
(*n*) 5 Esp. Rep. 35; 1 B. & P. 409, *semble contra*; and it would perhaps be otherwise if the party hired a carriage, but furnished the coachman and horses. 4 B. & Ald. 590.
(*o*) 5 B. & C. 547; 8 D. & R. 556, S. C.
(*p*) 1 East, 106; Rep. temp. Hardw. 87; 3 Wils 217; 1 Salk. 282; 2 Rol. Ab. 553; 1 Bla. Com. 431.

even, as it would seem, if the master were on board at the time of the accident, for the pilot is master *pro hac vice*. Snell and others *v.* Rich, 1 Johns. Rep. 305. But the owner of a ship is in such case liable, although the pilot be appointed by public authority. Bussy *v.* Donaldson, 4 Dall. 206. Fletcher *v.* Braddick, 2 New Rep. 182. The captain of a public vessel is not liable for the act of one of his inferior officers, done at a time when he was not engaged in the direction and management of the vessel, as such inferior officer is not the servant of the captain. Nicholson and another *v.* Mounsey and Symes, 15 East's Rep. 384.

(199) Bishop *v.* Ely and others, 9 Johns. Rep. 294.

(200) { Reported also, 8 Dowl. & Ryl. 556. The defendant was held not liable by ABBOT, C. J. and LITTLEDALE; *aliter per* BAYLEY and HOLROYD, Justices. } In Bostwick *v.* Champion, Bissell, Ewers and Dodge, 11 Wend. R. 571, where the defendants run a line of stages from Utica to Rochester, the route being divided into sections; one section being by Dodge; another by Ewers and others; and the remainder of the route by Champion and Bissell. The occupant of each section furnishing his own carriages and horses, hiring drivers and paying the expenses of his own section; and the money received as the fare of passengers being divided among the parties in proportion to the number of miles of the route run by each; and an injury happening through the negligence of a driver on one of the sections; it was *held*, that all the defendants were jointly liable in an action on the case at the suit of the party injured.

II. DEFENDANTS. — 1. Who liable.

be negligent and careless conduct, for which the master will be liable, being an act done in pursuance of the servant's employment" (*q*). So if a servant take out his master's cart at a time when it is not wanted for the purposes of his master's business, and drive it about for his own purposes, the master will not be responsible for any injury arising whilst so doing (*r*). Though if a servant, driving his master's cart on his master's business, make a detour from the direct road for some purpose of his own, his master will be answerable in damages for any injury occasioned by his careless driving whilst so out of his road (*r*).

Liability of the sheriff and his officers.

On principles of public policy a *sheriff* is liable civilly for the tortious act, default, extortion, or other misconduct, *whether it be wilful or inadvertent, of his under-sheriff or bailiff, in the course of the execution of their duties (*s*) (201). But if the wrong complained of be neither expressly sanctioned by the sheriff, or impliedly committed by his authority; if it be an act not within the scope of the authority given; the sheriff is not responsible (*t*). And if the plaintiff in an action, or an execution creditor, induce the bailiff to depart from the ordinary course of his duty without the sheriff's knowledge, it is not competent to such plaintiff or execution creditor to fix the sheriff for the consequences (*u*).

[*94]

Liability of owners of animals.

The distinctions with regard to the liabilities of the owners of *animals* are important, particularly as they affect the form of the action. The owner of domestic or other animals not naturally inclined to commit mischief, as dogs, horses, and oxen, is not liable for any injury committed by them to the person or personal property; unless it can be shown that he previously had notice of the animal's mischievous propensity (202), or that the injury was attributable to some other neglect on his part; it being in general necessary in an action for an injury committed by *such* animals to allege and prove the *scienter*; and though notice can be proved, yet the action must be *case*, and not *trespass* (*v*)(203). But if the owner himself acted illegally, he may be liable even as a trespasser; as where a person in company with his dog trespassed in a close through which there was no footpath, and the dog, without his concurrence, killed the plaintiff's deer (*x*): and if a person let loose or permit a dangerous

(*q*) 4 B. & Ald. 590; see 9 B. & C. 591; 4 M. & R. 506, S. C.

(*r*) Joel *v.* Morison, 6 Car. & P. 501.

(*s*) 2 T. R. 151, 712; 7 Id. 267; Dougl. 40; 11 East, 25; 8 B. & C. 602; 3 M. & R. 20, S. C.

(*t*) 6 B. & C. 739; 9 D. & R. 723, S. C.; 8 B. & C. 598; 3 M. & R. 7, S. C.; and see *further infra*, 96, 97; 9 Price, 237; 5 Moore, 183; 1 R. & M. 310.

(*u*) 6 B. & C. 739; 9 D. & R. 723, S. C.; 8 B. & C. 598; 3 M. & R. 7, S. C. and see *further infra*, 96, 97.

(*v*) 12 Mod. 333; Salk. 662; Ld. Raym. 608, 609; Dyer, 25, pl. 162; Cro. Car. 254; 2 Salk. 662; Bac. Ab. Action Case, F.; Lutw. 90; Peake's Law of Evid. 291, 292. Evidence of *scienter*, 2 Esp. 482; 4 Campb. 198. The omission of the averment in the declaration renders it bad in arrest of judgment, Salk. 662; 2 M. & Sel. 238.

(*x*) Burr. 2092; 2 Lev. 172; 1 Car. & P. 119, S. P.

(201) Grinnell *v.* Phillips, 1 Mass. Rep. 530. Campbell *v.* Phelps, 17 Mass. Rep. 245. Vide Hazard *v.* Israel, 1 Binn. 240. M'Intyre *v.* Trumbull, 7 Johns. Rep. 35. Blake *v.* Shaw, 7 Mass. Rep. 505. Parrot *v.* Mumford, 2 Esp. Rep. 585. White *v.* Johnson, 1 Wash. 159. Moore's Adm'rs *v.* Downey and another, 3 Hen. and Mun. 127. Gorham *v.* Gale, 7 Cowen, 739.

(202) Vide Vrooman *v.* Lawyer, 13 Johns. Rep. 339.

(203) What is sufficient notice to the owner of a dog accustomed to bite. See Smith *v.* Pelah, Str. 1264. Peck *v.* Dyson, 4 Campb. 198.

II. DEFENDANTS.

1. Who liable.

animal to go at large, and mischief ensue, he is liable as a trespasser; the law in such cases presuming notice to the defendant of the mischievous propensity of such animal (y). With respect to animals *mansuetæ naturæ*, as cows and sheep, as their propensity to rove is notorious, the owner is bound at all events to confine them on his own [*95] *land; and if they escape, and commit a trespass on the land of another, unless through the defect of fences which the latter ought to repair (204), the owner is liable to an action of trespass (205), though he had notice in fact of such propensity (z). But for damage by animals, &c., *feræ naturæ*, escaping from the land of one person to that of another, as by rabbits, pigeons, &c. no action can in general be supported; because the instant they escaped from the land of the owner his property in them was determined (a). And a person cannot be liable for the act of cattle, unless he were the general owner, or he actually put them into the place where the injury was committed (b); nor is he liable for trespass committed by his dog (c); and if a servant or a stranger, without the concurrence of the owner, chase or put his cattle into another's land, such owner is not liable; but the action must be against the servant or stranger, who, as it has been said, gains a special property in the cattle for the time (d).

Injuries to land.

The liability to an action in respect of *real* property may be for *misfeasance* or *malfeasance*, as for obstructing ancient lights; or for *nonfeasance*, as for not taking care of premises, so as to prevent the consequence of a public nuisance, as for leaving open an area door, or coal plate (e); or for not repairing fences (f), private ways (g), or water-courses, &c. (h). In these cases the action should in general be against the party who did the act complained of, or against the occupier (i)(206); and not against the owner, if the premises were in the possession of his tenant, unless he covenanted to repair (k)(207). But if the owner of land, having erected a nuisance thereon, demise the land, an action may be supported against him, though out of possession, for the continuance of it; for by the demise he affirmed such continuance (l); and

(y) 3 East, 595, 596; 12 Mod. 333; Lord Raym. 1583; Bac. Ab. Action, Case, F.

(z) 12 Mod. 335; Lord Raym. 606, 1583; Dyer, 25, pl. 162; Vin. Ab. Fences, Trespass, B. vol. xx. MS. 424; Poph. 161; Sir W. Jones, 131; Latch. 119; Salk. 662.

(a) 5 Co. 104 b.; Cro. Car. 387; 1 Burr. 259; Bac. Ab. Game; Cro. Eliz. 547.

(b) 1 Saund. 27; 1 Car. & P. 119.

(c) 1 Car. & P. 119.

(d) Bro. Ab. Trespass, pl. 435; 2 Rol. Ab. 553; 1 East, 107.

(e) 3 Camp. 389, 403. When not, see 4 M. & Sel. 27.

(f) 4 T. R. 318.

(g) 3 T. R. 766.

(h) 6 Taunt. 44.

(i) 4 T. R. 318.

(k) 1 Hen. Bla. 350.

(l) 1 Salk. 460; 4 T. R. 320; 1 B. & P. 409.

---

(204) Vide Shepherd v. Hees, 12 Johns. Rep. 433.

(205) 10 Serg. and Rawle, 395.

(206) Vide Compton v. Richards, 1 Price's Ex. Rep. 27. An action does not lie for carelessly leaving a maple syrup in one's unenclosed wood, whereby the plaintiff's cow being suffered to run at large, and having strayed there, is killed by drinking it. Bush v. Brainard, 1 Cowen, 78. So, where A. sets fire to his own fallow ground, as he may lawfully do, which communicates to and fires the wood land of his neighbor, no action lies against A. unless there be some negligence or misconduct in him or his servants. Clark v. Foot, 8 J. R. 421.

(207) The defendant was lessor of a house which the lessee had ceased to inhabit, for the purpose of having it thoroughly repaired, which was done at the expense of the lessee, but under the superintendence of the defendant's lessor; it was held that an action on the case was properly brought against the lessor, for the negligence of his workmen, in leaving open the cellar door, whereby the plaintiff in the night fell in and hurt himself. Leslie v. Pounds, 4 Taunt. 649.

II. DEFENDANTS. 1. Who liable.

every occupier is liable for the continuance of the nuisance on his land, &c. though erected by another, if he refuse to remove the same after notice (*m*). When there are several owners or persons chargeable as joint-tenants or tenants in *common in respect of their real property, though the action be in form *ex delicto*, they should all be made defendants, or the party who is sued alone may plead in abatement (*n*). [*96]

Liability of agents, servants, and attornies.

An agent or servant, though acting *bona fide* under the directions and for the benefit of his employer, is personally liable to third persons for any tort or trespass he may commit in the execution of the orders he has received (*o*). If the master has not the right or power to do the act complained of, he cannot delegate an authority to the servant, which will protect the latter from responsibility. Therefore a servant may be charged in trover, although the act of conversion be done by him for his master's benefit (*p*)(208). And a bailiff who distrains is liable, if the principal has no right of distress (*q*). And a custom-house officer may be sued for a wrongful seizure made by him in that character (*r*)(209). There is no injustice in this doctrine as regards the servant; for if the act were not manifestly illegal, the indemnity of the principal to the servant against the consequences is not illegal, and will, in many instances, be implied (*s*). And where a servant received a bill of exchange, which he promised to the deliverer that his master should discount, but which the latter refused to do, and insisted on retaining the same as a security for a previous debt from the deliverer, it was held that such deliverer might support trover against the servant (*t*).

But in order to sue a servant in trover, an actual, not a constructive, conversion should be shown; and the servant's reasonable and qualified refusal to deliver up the goods until he had consulted his master, and obtained his sanction, does not amount to a conversion (*u*). And in cases in which a *contract*, express or implied, with the master, is the ground of action, the servant seems not to be liable for any mere neglect or nonfeazance, which, as such servant, he is guilty of in the execution of, or with relation to, the contract (*x*). If a coachman lose a parcel, the master, not the coachman, should be sued; and it seems that a servant is not liable for his false warranty, or deceit, on the sale of goods by his master's orders (*y*).

An attorney acting *bona fide*, and professionally, may not be personally liable in cases where he does not exceed *the line of his duty. Thus, it seems, that he is not liable in case for a malicious and unfounded arrest (regular in form), which may be considered the tort of his client only (*z*). But if an attorney, [*9

(*m*) Com. Dig. Action Case, Nuisance, B.
(*n*) 1 Saund. 291; 5 T. R. 651; *post*, 99.
(*o*) 4 M. & Sel. 259. What is considered an interference, which will subject the party to an action, *ante*, 91, 92.
(*p*) *Id.*
(*q*) 2 Rol. Ab. 431.
(*r*) 5 Burr. 2687; 7 Price, 300; 3 Wils. 146.
(*s*) 8 T. R. 186; Bul. N. P. 146.
(*t*) Cranch *v.* White, 1 Hodges' Rep. 61; 1 Bing. N. C. 414, S. C.
(*u*) 5 B. & A. 247; 1 Hodges, 61; 1 Bing. N. C. 414.
(*x*) See *ante*, 38, 39; 12 Mod. 488; Say. 41; Bac. Ab. Action on the Case, B.
(*y*) *Id.*; Rol. Abr. 95, T.; Com. Dig. Action upon the Case for Deceit, B.; 3 P. Wms. 379.
(*z*) 1 Mod. 209, cited *per cur.*, 3 Wils. 378, 379. It was there said the attorney was not liable, although he knew the demand was unfounded. *Sed quære.*

(208) { See, however, Berry *v.* Vantries, 12 Serg. & Rawle, 89, where Mires *v.* Solebay, 2 Mod. Rep. 242, was held to be law. }
(209) Vide Hoyt *v.* Gilston, 13 Johns. Rep. 141.

II. DEFENDANTS. by himself or his agent, issue any illegal or irregular process or execution in a cause, he, equally with the client, is liable as a trespasser (*a*).

1. Who liable. Sheriffs. In general, an action for the breach of a duty in execution of the office of sheriff must be brought against the high sheriff (210), although the under-sheriff or the bailiff of the sheriff were the party actually in default (*b*). The under-sheriff, or bailiff, cannot in general be sued; but there are some instances of *misfeazance* and *malfeazance* in which they may be liable to the party aggrieved; as if they *voluntarily* permit an escape, or are personally guilty of extortion, or any act of trespass in executing process, for in such cases the under-sheriff or officer becomes an active personal wrong-doer (*c*). So a sheriff is liable in trover if he seize and sell goods after an act of bankruptcy, although unknown to him and before fiat (*d*). But an action is not sustainable against the *sheriff* for the act of a bailiff in taking the goods of a party under an execution of the County Court against a third person, because there the sheriff as *judge* of that Court acted judicially (*e*), and a steward of a Court Baron has the same privilege and protection (*f*).

Intermediate agents. It is a general rule that an action does not lie against a steward, manager, or agent, for damage done by the negligence of those employed by him in the service of his principal, but the principal, or those actually employed, alone can be sued. This was decided in *Stone* v. *Cartwright* (*g*), and Lord Kenyon observed, "that the action must, in these cases, be brought against the hand committing the injury, or against the owner, for whom the act was done." The first principal is liable on the ground that the original authority flows from him, and the tort occurs in the course of the execution of work done for his benefit (*h*). But in these cases, if the intermediate agent personally interfere, and particularly order those acts to be done from whence the damage ensues, he is responsible (*i*); and it was therefore held, in an action on the case for obstructing the plaintiff's lights, that a clerk who superintended the erection of the building by which they were darkened, and who alone directed the *workmen, might be joined as a co-defendant with the original contractor, by whom he was employed (*j*). [*98]

The liability of *government* and other public officers has been before adverted to (*k*).

2. With reference to the *number* of the defendants. There are some torts which in legal consideration *may* be committed by several, and for which a *joint* action may be supported against all the parties.

(*a*) 3 Wils. 368; 6 B. & C. 38. In 3 Esp. 202, 203, Lord Kenyon is stated to have been of opinion, that an attorney acting *bona fide*, and professionally, is not liable in trespass for causing a suspected party to be taken on a warrant.

(*b*) *Ante*, 92, 93, Cowp. 403.

(*c*) See 12 Mod. 488; 1 Mod. 209; 1 Salk. 18; 1 Lord Raym. 655. The statutes against extortion expressly render liable the bailiff or officer committing it.

(*d*) Garland *v.* Carlisle, 2 Cr. & M. 31.

(*e*) Tinsley *v.* Nassau, 1 Mood. & Malk. 52; and see 1 Bar. & Cress. 256; 2 D. & R. 407, S. C.; and Holroyd *v.* Breare, 2 Bar. & Ald. 473.

(*f*) Holroyde *v.* Breare, 2 B. & Ald. 473.

(*g*) 6 T. R. 411.

(*h*) 1 B. & P. 404; 3 Campb. 403.

(*i*) *Per* Lawrence, J. 6 T. R. 413.

(*j*) 6 Moore, 47; 2 D. & R. 33.

(*k*) *Ante*, 42, 48.

(210) Vide White *v* Johnson, 1 Wash. Rep. 160, 161. Armistead *v.* Marks, 1 Wash. Rep. 325. For an injury done by a deputy or under-sheriff to the person or property of another, the action must be the same, whether brought against the deputy or the sheriff. Campbell *v.* Phelps, 17 Mass. R. 246.

II. DEFENDANTS.

2. Who to be joined or omitted.

Thus a *joint* action may be brought against several for a malicious prosecution, or an assault and battery; or for composing, publishing or singing a libel (*k*)(211); or for not setting out tithe (*l*); or for keeping a dog to kill game, not being qualified (*m*). But if in legal consideration the act complained of *could not have been committed by several persons*, and can only be considered the tort of the actual aggressor, or the distinct tort of each, a separate action against the actual wrong-doer only, or against each, must be brought. Therefore a joint action cannot be supported against two for verbal slander (*n*)(212); nor will debt on a penal statute lie against several for what in law is a separate offence in each; as against two proctors for not obtaining and entering their certificates (*o*)(213); or against several persons for bribery (*p*). In an action of debt to recover money lost at play, the defendant cannot plead a non-joinder in abatement (*q*). And if a joint action of trespass be brought against several persons, the plaintiff cannot declare for an assault and battery by one, and for the taking away of goods by the others, because these trespasses are of several natures (*r*). And in trover against several defendants, all cannot be found guilty on the same count, without proof of a *joint* conversion by all (*s*). These rules, however, do not prevail in *criminal* proceedings, so as necessarily to defeat an indictment against several for distinct offences in separate counts, *though the Court have a discretionary power to quash the indictment, where inconvenience might arise from the joinder of many persons for different offences (*t*). [*99]

Consequences of misjoinder or nonjoinder.

If several persons be made defendants jointly, where the tort *could not* in point of law be joint, they may demur, and if a verdict be taken against all, the *judgment* may be arrested or reversed on a writ of error (*u*); but the objection may be aided by the plaintiff's taking a verdict against only one (*x*); or if several damages be assessed against each, by entering a *nolle prosequi* as to one after the verdict and before judgment (*y*). In other cases (214), where in point of fact and of law several persons *might have been jointly guilty of the same offence*, the joinder of more persons than were liable in a personal or mixed action in *form ex delicto*, constitutes no objection to a par-

(*k*) 2 Saund. 117 a; Latch. 262; 2 Burr. 985; Bac. Ab. Actions in General, C.
(*l*) Carth. 361; 2 Vin. Ab. 70, pl 21.
(*m*) 2 East, 573.
(*n*) *Id. ibid.*; 2 Wils. 227; Dyer, 19 a; Palm. 313; Cro. Jac. 647; 1 Bulst. 15; 1 Rol. Ab. 781; 2 Vin. Ab. 64, pl. 27.
(*o*) 1 New Rep. 245; 2 East, 574.
(*p*) Griffiths *v.* Stratton and others, judgment in error in the House of Lords from the Exchequer in Ireland, 17th April, A. D. 1806.
(*q*) 28 MSS. Ashhurst Paper Books, 233. *Sed vide* 7 T. R. 257.
(*r*) 2 Saund. 117 a; Sty. 153, 154; 3 Esp. Rep. 202, 204.
(*s*) 1 M. & Sel. 588.
(*t*) 8 East, 46, 47; 1 Chitty on Crim. Law, 270, 271, 1st edit.
(*u*) 1 New Rep. 245; 1 Saund. 117, b. n.; Bac. Ab. Actions in General, C.; 1 Rol. Ab. 781; Sty. 349.
(*x*) *Id. ibid.*
(*y*) 1 Saund. 207 a.

(211) Vide Thomas *v.* Rumsey, 6 Johns. Rep. 26.
(212) Vide Thomas *v.* Rumsey, 6 Johns. Rep. 32. {17 Mass. Rep. 186.}
(213) If debt *qui tam* be sued against several, demanding a joint forfeiture, on a plea of *nil debet*, all the defendants ought to be found indebted, because the form of the action and plea is on a joint contract, although the debt arises from a tort. Burnham *v.* Webster, 5 Mass. Rep. 270.
(214) An action of ejectment was brought against five defendants, who entered into the consent rule jointly, and pleaded jointly. They severally possessed the premises in separate parts; and the jury having found each defendant separately guilty as to the part in his possession, and not guilty as to the residue, judgment was rendered accordingly. Jackson d. Haines and others *v.* Woods and others, 5 Johns. Rep. 278.

II. DEFENDANTS.

2. Who to be joined or omitted.

tial recovery, and one of them may be acquitted, and a verdict taken against the others (z)(215). On the other hand, if several persons jointly commit a tort, the plaintiff in general has his election to sue all or some of the parties jointly, or one of them separately (216), because a tort is in its nature a separate act of each individual (a). Therefore in actions in *form ex delicto*, as trespass, trover, or case for malfeasance, against one only for a tort committed by several, he cannot plead the non-joinder of the others in abatement or in bar, or give it in evidence under the general issue; for a plea in abatement can only be adopted in those cases where regularly all the parties *must* be joined, and not where the plaintiff *may* join them all, or not, at his election (b). And even if it appear from the declaration or other pleadings that the tort was jointly committed by the defendant and another person, no objection can be taken (c) (217). This rule applies only in actions for torts strictly unconnected with contract; for where an action on the case is brought merely for the nonfeasance of a contract, and in order to support the action a contract must be proved, and is the basis of the suit, (as in case for a breach of a warranty on a sale, &c.) the joinder of too many defendants will be a ground of nonsuit; [*100] *and it should seem, that if a joint contractor be not included, the defendant may plead his non-joinder in abatement; for it is not competent to the plaintiff in such an instance to alter or obviate the rules of law with regard to the parties to be sued upon the contract, merely by varying the *form* of his action, where in substance it is founded on the agreement (d). But it must appear from the declaration, that the gist of the action is for a breach of contract (e). And with regard to carriers and inn-keepers, as their liability is founded on the breach of an *implied* common-law *duty* in respect of their particular capacities, if they be sued in case for negligence, no valid objection can be made in respect to the non-joinder of a party; although they may be sued in assumpsit, in which event the objection would be tenable (f). There is a settled distinction in this respect between mere personal actions of tort, and such as concern *real* property; for if only one tenant in common of *realty* be sued in trespass, trover, or case, for any thing respecting the land held in common, as for not setting out tithe, &c., he may plead the tenancy in common in abatement (g) (218). And in an action of debt for money lost at play, the defendant

(z) 3 East, 62; 1 M. & Sel. 589. Cannot after judgment, Tidd's Prac. 9th ed. 895; 2 East, 574; 1 M. & Sel. 588; Bac. Ab. Action of *Qui Tam*, D.; 2 Rol. Ab. 707; Lane, 19, 59; Cowp. 610.

(a) 6 Taunt. 29, 35, 42.

(b) *Id. ibid*; 1 Saund. 291 d. e; 5 T. R. 649; 6 Taunt. 29, 35, 42.

(c) 1 Saund. 291.

(d) 12 East, 454; 2 New Rep. 454; 12 East, 89, S. C. and see 2 New Rep. 365; 1 Wils. 281; 6 Moore, 141; 3 B. & B. 54; 9 Price, 408, S. C.; 1 Saund. 291 e, and note (e).

(e) *Id. ibid.*; 2 New Rep. 369; 6 Moore, 158.

(f) 3 East, 62; 2 Chit. R. 1; 3 B. & B. 54, 171; 6 Moore, 141, 154, 159; 9 Price, 408, S. C. But the declaration must be framed accordingly, 6 Moore, 154; 2 Chit. Rep. 1; 9 Price, 408, S. C.

(g) 1 Saund. 291 e; 5 T. R. 651; 7 T. R. 257; Bac. Ab. Joint-tenants, K.; 2 East, 574.

(215) Vide Lansing *v.* Montgomery, 2 Johns. Rep. 382. Cooper and another *v.* South and others, 4 Taunt. 802. Jackson d. Haines and others *v.* Woods and others, 5 Johns. Rep. 280, 281.

(216) Vide Thomas *v.* Rumsey, 6 Johns. Rep. 31. Burnham *v.* Webster, 5 Mass. Rep. 269, 270. Johnson *v.* Brown, 1 Wash. Rep. 187.

(217) Vide Rose *v.* Oliver, 2 Johns. Rep. 365.

(218) { *Per curiam*, 4 Pick. Rep. 308. But in case against three for erecting a dam by means whereof plaintiff's mills were obstructed, two of the defendants pleaded in

may plead in abatement, that the money was due from others as well as from himself; such action, though given by statute, being founded on contract (h) (219). These distinctions between the effect of too many or too few persons being made defendants in actions in form *ex contractu* and in those *ex delicto*, may in some cases render it advisable to adopt, if practicable, the latter form of action, when it is doubtful who should be made the defendants.

II. DEFENDANTS. 2. Who to be joined or omitted.

In an action on the *case*, and in *trover*, or *replevin*, if one of the defendants was acquitted, he was not entitled to costs (i), but in *trespass* it was otherwise, unless the judge certified that there was reasonable cause for making the acquitted person a defendant (j) (220). And *now*, by 3 & 4 W. 4, c. 42, s. 32, one of several defendants acquitted in an action on the *case*, or for a tort, may recover his costs (k); and this constitutes a very important consideration in commencing an action; and although it might be desirable to include a party as a defendant in order to exclude his evidence, yet unless it be certain that a verdict will be obtained against him, it will be imprudent to join him; because, if acquitted, he would probably recover his costs, and they may be set off or deducted from the damages and costs recovered by the plaintiff against another defendant or defendants, and may be nearly equal to, if not exceed, the sum payable to the plaintiff (l). And it is now the course, in an action on the case or trover against several persons, at the close of the *plaintiff's case and evidence*, if there be no proof against one of the defendants, immediately to acquit him, so that he may thereupon instantly be enabled to give evidence for the remaining defendants (m). And as well before as since the 3 & 4 W. 4, c. 42, s. 32, it was and is considered improper to join all the parties present at the time of an irregular distress or other tort, with a view merely to exclude evidence (n); and the fair way is to bring the action against the landlord, or at most against the landlord and broker, and not to include the appraisers or the man in possession (o); and where a police-man joined as a defendant with others, obtained a verdict, it was held that he was abso-

Costs now payable in general to an acquitted defendant, unless, &c.

(h) 7 T. R. 257. *Sed quære*, see 28 Ashhurst, J.'s MSS. Paper Books, 233.

(i) 2 Stra. 1005; Tidd, 9th ed. 986.

(j) 8 & 9 W. 3, c 11; Tidd's Prac. 9th edit. 986. If, however, all the defendants joined in pleading, the acquitted defendant was only entitled to forty shillings costs. *Id. ibid.*; 2 M. & Sel. 172; 4 B. & Ald. 43, 709.

(k) The 3 & 4 W. 4, c. 42, s. 32, enacts, that where several persons shall be made defendants *in any personal action*, and any one or more of them shall have a *nolle prosequi* entered as to him or them, or upon the trial of such action shall have a verdict pass for him or them, every such person shall have judgment for and recover his reasonable costs, unless in the case of a trial *the judge* before whom such cause shall be tried *shall certify upon the record* under his hand, that there was a reasonable cause for making such person a defendant in such action.

(l) George v. Elston and others, 1 Bing. N. C. 513; 1 Hodges, 63; 3 Dowl. 419, S. C. Where in an action against three for an irregular distress, plaintiff recovered damages and costs £15 against one, but the other two defendants obtained verdicts, and their costs were £37, and were set off against the plaintiff's claim.

(m) Child v. Chamberlain, 6 Car. & P. 215; 1 Mood. & R. 318, S. C.; 3 Chitty's Gen. Prac. 902.

(n) Child v. Chamberlain, 6 Car. & P. 213.

(o) Per Parke, J., *Id. ibid.*

abatement the death of the third, pending the suit; but upon demurrer the plea was held ill, for that it did not appear by the pleadings that the defendants were charged by reason of their holding real estate as joint-tenants or tenants in common. Sumner v. Tilcoton, 4 Pick. Rep. 308. }

(219) Vide Hill and wife v. Davis and others, 4 Mass. Rep. 137. Burnham v. Webster, 5 Mass. Rep. 270.

(220) Acc. Laws N. Y. sess. 36. c. 96. s. 10. 1 R. L. 345. { 2 Rev. Stat. 616. s. 19 }

II. DEFENDANTS.

lutely entitled to costs under 10 Geo. 4, c. 44, independently of the enactment in 3 & 4 W. 4, c. 42, s. 32 (*p*).

2. Who to be joined or omitted.

[*101] *Where separate actions have been brought against several defendants for the same act of trespass committed by them concurrently, the party against whom the last action was commenced may plead the pendency of the first in abatement (*q*) (221). A recovery against one of several parties who jointly committed a tort, precludes the plaintiff from proceeding against any other party not included in such action (*r*) (222). Thus in an action against one for a battery, or for taking away the plaintiff's posts, or destroying grass in a field where several persons are concerned, the recovery against one will be a bar to an action against the others (*s*); and where the plaintiff had previously recovered in an action against his servant for quitting his service, it was decided that he could not also support an action against the person for seducing away such servant (*t*). In these cases the Court will in general on a summary application stay the proceedings in the second action, where it is manifest that the entire damages have been recovered in the first (*u*). But where the evidence and the damages in the two actions might be different, as where two persons on different occasions have published the same libel, separate actions may be supported against each (*x*) (223). So the recovery against one party in an action for criminal conversation, is no bar to an action against another party for a similar injury (*y*).

3dly. Where the interest has been *assigned*, &c.

3. As in the case of a breach of covenant, so in that of torts, the assignee of an estate is not liable for an injury resulting from any nuisance, or wrongful act, committed thereon before he came to the estate; but if he *continues* the nuisance he may be sued for such continuance (*z*). In some cases it is necessary, and in all cases it is judicious, prior to the commencement of the action, to require the defendant to abate the nuisance (*a*). If a tenant for

(*p*) Humphrey *v.* Wodehouse and others, 1 Bing. N. C. 506.

(*q*) 1 Campb. 60, 61.

(*r*) Cro. Jac. 74; Com. Dig. Action, K. 4. L.; 2 B. & P. 70, 71; 1 Saund. 207 a; 4 Taunt. 88.

(*s*) Yelv. 68; 2 B. & P. 71; Bul. N. P. 20.

(*t*) 3 Burr. 1345; 1 Bla. Rep. 387, 373, S. C.

(*u*) 2 P. & P. 71.

(*x*) 2 B. & P. 69.

(*y*) 1 Campb. 415.

(*z*) Com. Dig. Action on the Case, Nuisance, B.; Dyer, 320; 2 Salk. 460; 1 B. & P. 409; *ante*, 54, 55.

(*a*) Willes, 583; Cro. Jac. 555; 5 Co. 100, 101.

(221) Contra Livingston *v* Bishop, 1 Johns. Rep. 290.

(222) Vide Warden *v.* Bailey, 4 Taunt 87, 88. acc. Where Lawrence, J., says, that two several actions could not be sustained against several for the same act of imprisonment. { And see Campbell *v.* Phelps, 1 Pick. Rep. 290. } But in Livingston *v.* Bishop and others, 1 Johns. Rep. 290, it was held that separate actions might be brought against several joint trespassers, in each of which the plaintiff might proceed to judgment, and then should elect *de melioribus damnis*, and issue his execution against one of the defendants, which was a determination of his election, and precluded him from proceeding against the others, except for the costs in their respective suits. It seems, if a plaintiff discharge the action against one *tort feazor* on receiving satisfaction, that it is a discharge of the others. Dufresne *v* Hutchinson, 3 Taunt. 117. { See Knox *v.* Work, 1 P. A. Browne's Rep. 101. }

(223) Where B. and C., printers in partnership, publish jointly a libel, and separate suits are brought against each, and a judgment is first obtained in the suit against C. which is satisfied, that judgment and satisfaction may be pleaded in bar of the suit against B. Thomas *v.* Rumsey, 6 Johns. Rep. 26. In this case the doctrine in Livingston *v.* Bishop and others, 1 Johns. Rep. 290, was confirmed, and applied to actions for libels.

years erect a nuisance, and *make an underlease to B., an action lies against either (b); and if A. take the goods of C., and B. take them from A., C. may have his action against A. or B. at his election (c). II. DEFENDANTS.

4. At *common law*, upon the *death* of the wrong-doer, the remedy for torts unconnected with contract in general determines; and as the statute 4 Edw. 3, c. 7, (d) before referred to (e), does not give any remedy *against* personal representatives, we shall find that few actions in form *ex delicto*, and in which the plea would be not guilty, could, before the 3 & 4 W. 4, c. 42, s. 2, be supported against the executor or administrator of the party who committed the injury (f) (224). Many of the preceding observations on the rule *actio personalis moritur cum persona*, in its relation to the death of *plaintiffs*, are equally applicable to the case of the death of the wrong-doer (g). 4thly. In case of the *death of* the wrong-doer.

For injuries to the *person*, if the wrong-doer die before judgment, the remedy determines, and there is no instance of an action having been supported for such injuries against his personal representatives (h); and certainly neither of the statutes afford any remedy.

In general also no action in form *ex delicto*, as trover (225), case (226), or trespass (227), could, before the 3 & 4 W. 4, c. 42, s. 2, be supported against an executor for an injury to *personal property*, committed by his testator (k) (228). If, however, the testator converted the property into money, assumpsit was sustainable against his executor; or if the property came in specie to the possession of the latter, trover would be sustainable against him; but then he was not to be sued in the character of executor, but as for his own tortious conversion (l). It is said that an action is sustainable against the executor of a carrier for the loss of goods, but then the action should be *framed in assumpsit* (m). And an action of assumpsit might at common law be maintained against the executor of an attorney for unskilfulness or carelessness in the conduct of a cause, or other professional business in which the testator was employed, being a breach of an express or *implied contract* (n). We have seen that debt may be supported *by* an executor for an escape on final process, but it could not be maintained *against* the executor of a sheriff or gaoler; for though the action is not in form *ex delicto*, it was considered founded on a tort, namely, the *negligence and breach of duty of the deceas- [*103]

(b) 2 Salk. 460; 1 B. & P. 409.
(c) Bac. Ab. Actions, B.
(d) 4 Edw. 3, c. 7.
(e) *Ante*, 78.
(f) Cowp. 374, 377; 1 Saund. 216, note 1.
(g) See *ante*, 78, 79.
(h) Cowp. 375; 1 Saund. 216, n.; Com. Dig. Administration, B. 15; 2 M. & S. 408.
(k) Cowp. 371; 1 Saund. 216 a; Com. Dig. Administration, B. 15.
(l) Cowp. 371, 374; 1 Saund. 216 a.
(m) 2 New Rep. 370.
(n) 3 Stark R. 154.

(224) Vide Franklin v Low and Swartwout, 1 Johns. Rep. 396. In Virginia, trespass for the mesne profits of land recovered in ejectment against A. lies against his executor. The 64 sect. ch. 104, Rev. Code, is an extension of the 4th Edw. III. ch. 7, de bonis asportatis. Lee v. Cooke's Ex., Gilm. Rep. 331.

(225) Hench v. Metzer's Ex., 6 Serg. & Rawle, 272. 15 Mass. Rep. 398.

(226) An action for breach of promise of marriage is within the rule. Lattimore v. Simmons, 13 Serg. & Rawle, 183. Stebbins v. Palmer, 1 Pick. Rep. 71.

(227) Nicholson v. Elton, 13 Serg. & Rawle, 415.

(228) Sed vide Powell v. Layton, 2 New Rep. 370, where Mansfield, C. J., seems to be of opinion that case would lie against the executor of a carrier, the foundation of the action being essentially contract.

II. DEFENDANTS.

4thly. Death of wrong-doer.

ed sheriff or gaoler (o) (229); but where a sheriff had levied money under an execution, and died before he had paid it over, his executors might be sued either in debt or *scire facias*, upon his return of *fieri feci*, or by action of assumpsit, as for money had and received (p). It was held, that an action cannot be supported against an executor for a penalty forfeited by the testator under a penal statute (q); and that debt is not sustainable against an executor for treble the value of tithes which his testator ought to have set out (r). At common law no executor was answerable for a devastavit by his testator, on the principle that it is a personal tort, which dies with the person; but by the statute 30 Car. 2, c. 7, (explained and made perpetual by 4 & 5 W. & M. c. 24, s. 12,) "the executors or administrators of any executor or administrator, whether rightful or of his own wrong, who shall waste or convert to his own use the estate of his testator or intestate, shall be liable and chargeable in the same manner as their testator or intestate would have been if they had been living." (230) So that since these statutes, if a judgment be obtained against an executor who afterwards dies, an action may be brought against *his* executor or administrator upon the judgment, suggesting a devastavit by the first executor (s). But it would seem that an executor *de son tort* of an executor *de son tort* cannot be declared against *as such* upon the statutes (t).

For injuries to *real* property no action in form *ex delicto* could in general be supported against the personal representatives of the wrong-doer (u). If, however, trees, &c. were taken away and sold by the testator, assumpsit for money had and received lies against his executor (x); and the latter is personally liable in trover if the trees, &c. remain in specie, and the executor refuse to restore them (y) (231). A Court of equity will frequently afford relief against

[*104] the executor of the *wrong-doer, though at law the action *moritur cum persona* (z); and, therefore, where a tenant for life cut down timber and died, relief was decreed against his executors in favor of the remainder-man (a).

(o) *Ante*, 78, 79; Dyer, 322 a; Lord Raym. 973; Com. Dig. Administration, B. 15; Vin. Ab. Executor, H. a. pl. 1, 7, 20.

(p) Cro. Car. 539; 2 Show. 79, 281; Gilb. Executor, 25; 2 Saund. 343.

(q) Com. Dig. Administration B. 15.

(r) 1 Sid. 88, 181, 407; 2 Keb. 502; 1 E. & Y. 437, 440, 480; 2 Eagle on Tithes, 308.

(s) 1 Saund. 219 d.

(t) Andr. 252, 254; 2 Vent. 360; see 10 East, 315.

(u) 7 T. R. 732; 1 Saund. 216, n. 1; 2 Saund. 252 a. n. 7.

(x) 3 T. R. 549; Cowp. 373, 374.

(y) Cowp. 373, 374; 7 T. R. 13; 1 Saund 216 a.

(z) 3 Atk. 757; 2 Ves. 560; 2 Vent. 360; Landsdown v. Landsdown, 1 Madd. 146; 5 Madd 369.

(a) 7 T. R. 732; Landsdown v. Landsdown, 1 Jac. & W. 522; Chit. Eq. Dig. Waste.

(229) Vide Martin v. Bradley, 1 Caines' Rep 124. So an action will not lie against the executors of a sheriff for the default of his deputy in returning process, for the omission to return which an action is given by statute. The People v. Gibbs et al., 9 Wend. R. 29. Cravath v. Plympton, 13 Mass. R. 454.

(230) Vide Laws of N. Y. sess. 36 c. 75. s 8. 1 R. L. 312. 2 Rev. Stat. 447, 448, s. 1, 2. The English statute is in force in Pennsylvania, Roberts' Dig. 258. 3 Binn. 624.

(231) In Cravath v. Plympton, 13 Mass. Rep. 454, the principle was stated to be, that where the deceased by a tortious act acquired the property of the plaintiff, as by cutting his trees and converting them to his own use, although trover does not lie, yet the plaintiff may recover the value of his trees in some other form of action; but where by the act complained of, the deceased acquired no gain, although the plaintiff may have suffered great loss, then the rule applies, *actio personalis moritur cum persona*. The case of Cutler and Hay v. Brown's Ex'rs, 2 Haywood, 182, and Ex'rs of Crane v. Crane, 4 Halsted, 173, do not establish a different doctrine, nor are they at all at variance with the other cases referred to.

There is an exception to the common law rule in the case of the executors of a deceased rector or vicar, &c., against whom, upon the custom of the realm, the successor may support an action on the case for waste and dilapidations permitted or committed by the deceased (*b*).

II. DEFENDANTS. 4thly. Death of wrong-doer.

In many cases of injury to *personal* or *real* property, in the event of the death of the *wrong-doer*, it will be essential well to consider whether the 3 & 4 W. 4, c. 42, s. 2, does not afford redress against *his personal representative* (*c*).

5thly. In the case of *Bankruptcy*.

The Bankrupt Act (*d*) does not contain any provision, enabling a person injured by any personal tort, committed by the bankrupt before his bankruptcy; as an assault or battery (*e*), false imprisonment, slander (*f*), libel, seduction, criminal conversation, and the like; or by any trespass or wrong to real (*g*) or personal property (*h*)(232), of which the bankrupt may be guilty; to obtain remuneration from the funds of the bankrupt, which become vested in the assignees for the benefit of the creditors. As a party thus injured cannot prove the damages he has sustained against the estate of the bankrupt, the only redress which is left to him is an action against the bankrupt; and this remedy is not therefore affected by the certificate of the latter (*i*).

There are many instances in which the law reserves to a party the election to sue upon a contract, or in tort, for some wrong having relation to a contract express or implied between the parties (*k*). It is evident that by selecting the latter form of proceeding, the advantage which the defendant might otherwise derive from his certificate may be obviated. Thus, if the plaintiff has an election to sue for money had and received, or in trover, he may maintain the latter, notwithstanding the bankruptcy of the debtor after the debt accrued (*l*). And bankruptcy and certificate are no *bar to an action in tort against a broker for selling out stock contrary to orders (*m*). [*105]

6thly. Insolvency.

The same rules hold in the case of an insolvent as in the instance of a bankrupt, with regard to a claim to *damages* for a *tort* committed by the insolvent. The Insolvent Act (*n*), as before observed (*o*), only discharges the party as against those who are *creditors*, and who are described as such in his schedule. He remains liable for torts; and the discharge has no operation even against a claim for mesne profits accruing before, if unliquidated at the time of, the discharge (*p*). And even where there has been, prior to the petition, a judgment in an action for damages, the Court may remand the insolvent for a period not exceeding two years in the whole, at the suit of the plaintiff in such action, provided the damages were recovered for criminal conversation, seduction, breach of promise of marriage, malicious prosecution, libel or slander, or

(*b*) 4 M. & Sel. 183; Willes, 421. But the reasons given in Willes are not satisfactory. See 1 Saund. 216 a. note (*a*), 5th ed.
(*c*) See the enactment verbatim, *ante*, 60.
(*d*) 6 Geo. 4, c. 16.
(*e*) 3 Wils. 272.
(*f*) 1 Hen. Bla. 29.
(*g*) Dougl. 562; 2 T. R. 261.
(*h*) 4 T. R. 695; Dougl. 167; 5 Bing 63.
(*i*) As to proof of *damages* in general, Eden, 2d ed. 129. As to proof of damages where there has been a verdict or judgment, *id.* 131, 132, 135, 136; 7 B. & C. 436, 705.
(*k*) See *ante*, 60; *post*.
(*l*) 6 T. R. 695.
(*m*) 5 Bing. 63; see Eden, 2d ed.t. 130.
(*n*) 7 Geo. 4, c. 57.
(*o*) *Ante*, 63.
(*p*) 3 B. & A. 407; 2 Chit. Rep. 222.

(232) {See Bird *v.* Clark, 3 Day's Rep. 272. Shoemaker *v.* Keely, 2 Dall. 213. Sommer *v.* Wilt, 4 Serg. & Rawle, 28. Kennedy *v.* Strong, 10 Johns. Rep. 289.} Dusar *v.* Murgatroyd, 1 Wash. C. C. Rep. 13.

II. DEFENDANTS.

6thly. Insolvency.

for *any malicious* injury, or "in any action of trespass or tort to the person or property of the plaintiff therein, where it shall appear to the satisfaction of the said Court that the injury complained of was *malicious*."(q)

7thly. In the case of Marriage.

Actions for torts committed by a woman *before* her marriage, must be brought against the husband and wife jointly (r) (233). For torts committed by the wife *during* coverture, as for slander, assault, &c., or for any forfeiture under a penal statute, they must also be jointly sued (s) (234); and the plaintiff cannot in the same action proceed also for slander, assault, or other tort committed by the husband alone (t); nor can the husband and wife be sued jointly for slander by both (u). For assaults or trespasses, which may in legal contemplation be committed by two persons conjointly, and for which several persons may be jointly sued (x), the husband and wife may be sued
[*106] jointly for the joint act of both (y). Detinue, it seems, *can only be supported against the husband, if the detention be of goods delivered to the husband and wife during the coverture (z). If a woman convert goods before her marriage, or during it, without her husband, trover may be supported against her and her husband (a). For a conversion by husband and wife jointly, during coverture, the action of trover should perhaps in strictness be against him alone: but a declaration in trover against husband and wife, charging that "they converted the property to *their own* use" is at all events good after verdict (b). A feme covert can only be sued for her own actual wrong or trespass, and cannot become a trespasser merely by her previous or subsequent assent during coverture (c); but she may be jointly sued with her husband for her enticing away or harboring the servant of another (d). A person may sue husband and wife jointly for her libel or slander, though she have committed adultery, and they live separate, but have not been divorced *a vinculo matrimonii* (e). In an action of trespass against husband and wife for her tort before coverture, or a wrong committed by her alone during the coverture, if she die before judgment, the suit will abate; but if the husband die or become bankrupt, her liability will continue (f).

Consequence of mistake.

If the wife be sued alone for her tort before or after marriage, she must plead her coverture in abatement, and cannot otherwise take advantage of it (g); but if the husband and wife be sued jointly for torts of which they could not in law be jointly guilty, as for slander by both, if the objection appear on the face of the declaration the defendant may demur, move in arrest of judgment, or support a writ of error (h).

(q) 7 Geo. 4, c 57, s. 49.

(r) Bac. Ab. Bar. & Feme, L.; Co. Lit. 351 b.; Com. Dig. Bar. & Feme, Y.

(s) *Id. ibid*; 1 Hawk. P. C. 3, 4, Bac. Ab. Bar. & Feme, L.

(t) 2 Wils. 227; Dyer, 19 a. pl. 112; Com. Dig. Bar. & Feme, Y.

(u) *Id. ibid.*; Bac. Ab. Bar. & Feme, L.

(x) See *ante*, 98.

(y) 1 Vent. 93; 3 B. & Ald. 685, 687; Com. Dig. Pleader, 2 A. 2.

(z) 1 Leon. 312; Bac. Ab. Detinue; 2 Bulst. 308; 3 B. & Ald. 689; Com. Dig. Bar. & Feme, Y.

(a) 1 Leon. 312; Yelv. 165; Selw. N. P. Bar. & Feme.

(b) 3 B. & Ald. 685; see Com Dig. Bar. & Feme, Y.; and Pleader, 2 A. 2.

(c) 2 Wils. 227; Co. Lit. 180 b. n. 4; 357 b.

(d) 2 Lev. 63.

(e) Head *v.* Briscoe and Wife, C. P. Monday, 11th February, 1833, before Tindal, C. J. and special jury.

(f) Rep. temp. Hard. 399; Cullen, 392.

(g) *Ante*, 68.

(h) 2 Wils. 227; Dyer, 19 a.

(233) So an action for slander by the wife *dum sola* will lie against husband and wife. Hauk and wife *v.* Harman and wife, 5 Binn. 43.

(234) { The husband was sued alone in Hasbrouck *v.* Weaver, 10 Johns. Rep. 247, and the judgment was affirmed by the Supreme Court. }

*CHAPTER II.

Of the Forms of Actions.

IN GENERAL.

It *was* a general rule or maxim of law, that the sanction of the king's *original* writ, issued out of Chancery, was an essential preliminary form to the institution of a suit in the Common Law Courts. *Non potest quis sine brevi agere* (a); this was the prevailing doctrine. The practice of proceeding by *bill* without the original writ from Chancery, in personal actions and in ejectment, formed an exception to the rule. The practice of commencing an action by bill only obtained in each of the superior Courts in the case of certain persons, privileged in regard to their official characters, or as officers of the Courts, to be sued as being already present in Court. And in the King's Bench and Exchequer the proceedings by bill in other cases was introduced by fictions, and afterwards sanctioned and legalized by usage. But the great variety of writs and bills led to so much intricacy and confusion, that, as regards *personal* actions, the former writs, bills, and proceeding were abolished, and the present writs of summons, capias, and detainer were introduced by 2 W. 4, c. 39, and which writs now do not, as formerly, set out the *whole form* and cause of action, but are only adopted as *modes* of bringing the defendant into Court, and then, and not before, the *declaration*, stating the *full* form and cause of action, is delivered.

But although it is no longer necessary, as formerly, to state the *whole* cause of action and form of complaint in the writ, yet it is still necessary for the practitioner, before he issues any process under the Uniformity of Process Act, 2 W. 4, c. 39, to decide on the *proper form of action* to be adopted, and to state it, though very concisely, in the writ, as by requiring the defendant to answer, "*in an action upon promises*," or, "*in an action of debt*," or "*in an action of covenant*," or "*in an action of trespass on the case*," &c., and which form of action must afterwards be adhered to in the declaration, or the latter may be set aside for irregularity. Hence it is necessary for every practitioner to have *a competent knowledge of every form of action*, and its application, before he even commences the action. In this chapter we will give the forms of action full consideration.

Origin of the different *forms* of action.

In considering the *forms of action*, it was always important to advert to the general principle that the original writ, issued from the Chancery, was the foundation of the suit, and essential to give the Court of Common Law authority to entertain it. The writ, whether actually or presumptively issued, had a double purpose and object. It gave the Court in which the defendant was directed to appear cognizance of the suit, and it enjoined or enforced his

(a) Bract. 413 b; 3 Bl. Com. 273; Gilb. Hist. C. P. 2; Steph. on Pl. 2d ed. 5, 6. As to the origin of the issuing of writs as the foundation of a suit, see Stephen, 2d ed. Appendix, ii. n. (2).

IN GENERAL.

appearance. With these views, the form and nature of the intended suit, and the ground of complaint, were formerly *fully* or *specifically* shown in the *writ*. The original writ, from the most ancient times, *defined and determined concisely the form of the action* (b). At a very early period, specific forms of action were provided for such injuries as had then most usually occurred; and
[*108] Bracton *observing on the original writs on which our actions were founded, declared them to be fixed and immutable, unless by authority of parliament (c). These ancient forms, which had from time to time been collected and preserved in Chancery, in a book called *The Register of Writs*, were, in the reign of Henry the eighth, first printed and published in the book termed *Registrum Brevium* (d).

Enactments of Stat. West. 2, that as new injuries arise, new writs to be framed.

At common law also, though no form could be found in the Register, adapted to the nature of the plaintiff's case, yet he was at liberty to bring *a special action on his own case*, and writs were framed accordingly, which were termed *magistralia* (e); but as the officers of the Court of Chancery, whose duty it was to frame the writs for the solicitor, were found reluctant in new cases to frame the proper remedy, or doubted their authority to do so (f), the legislature thought fit to *enforce* the duty to issue a proper writ; and it was enacted by Statute Westminster 2d (g), "that if it shall fortune in the Chancery, that in one case a writ is found, and *in like case* (*consimili casu*) falling under like law, (*i. e.* principle), and requiring like remedy, is found none, the clerks of the Chancery *shall* agree in making the writ, or adjourn the plaintiffs until the next Parliament, and that the cases be written in which they cannot agree, and that they shall refer such cases (h), (or complaint) until the next Parliament; and by consent of men learned in the law, a writ shall be made, lest it might happen after that the Court should long time fail to minister justice unto complainants." (235) To this statute the copious production of new forms of writs, and the great encouragement and frequency of actions *on the case so infinitely various* is to be attributed (i).

The circumstance of a remedy being new *in form* not conclusive as to its inadmissibility.

Notwithstanding these provisions, it was once thought that the circumstance of an action being of the first impression, *and unprecedented, constituted a conclusive objection against it; and it is observable, that the Statute Westminster 2d, does not recognize or confer any right to frame writs in cases *entirely new* (k); it merely gives or enforces the power to frame new writs

[*109]

(b) It may also be observed of the bill actually filed or exhibited, or presumed to be so, instead of the proceeding by original, that it always disclosed and gave fully the form and nature of the action, and in that respect was parallel with the declaration upon the original writ, and which declaration was confined to the form of action prescribed by the writ.

(c) 3 Bla. Com. 117.

(d) 4 Reeves, 426, 432; 3 Bla. Com. 183; Gilb. C. P. 4; Fitzherbert's Natura Brevium is a comment upon these ancient forms, which were called *brevia formata*.

(e) 8 Co 47 b, 48 a; 2 Bla. Rep. 1113; 3 Woodd. 168. It has been observed, that there are many writs in the Register not accordant to law, R. 103, as trespass *per* baron and feme, for assaulting the wife, and taking the goods of the husband, 2 Salk. 637.

(f) 2 Reeves, 203; 2 Bla. Com. 50.

(g) 13 Edw. I. stat. 1, c. 24. See observations on this statute, 3 Bla. Com. 123, 183, 184; 3 Woodd. 168; and Webb's case, 8 Co. 45 b to 49 b; 4 Reeves, 430.

(h) There appears a mistake in the Statute Book in the translation, which is here corrected.

(i) 4 Reeves, 430; 3 Bla. Com. 51; 3 Woodd. 168.

(k) Stephen on Plead. 2d edit. 7, 8.

(235) As to the origin and history of the action on the case, see further, 3 Reeves' Hist. E. L. 89. 93. 243, 244, 391, 397.

by analogy to and upon the principle of such as had previously existed, (i. e. *in consimili casu*). It has, however, been observed, that it by no means follows, that because in cases unprovided for by the Register, the statute directs an action upon the case to be framed, that the action upon the case or a remedy for every new injury in general did not subsist at common law (*l*). There is also the authority of Lord Kenyon for the doctrine, that whenever the common law recognizes or creates a legal right, it will also confer a remedy by action (*m*)(236); and Lord Chief Justice Pratt, in answer to the objection of novelty, said, that he wished never to hear it urged again, for torts are infinitely various, not limited or confined, and there is nothing in nature that may not be an instrument of mischief, and the special action on the case was introduced, because the law will not suffer an injury without affording a remedy, and there must be new facts in every special action on the case (*n*). In the case of *Pasley* v. *Freeman*(*o*), Mr. J. Ashhurst observed, that where cases are new in their *principle*, it is necessary to have recourse to legislative interposition in order to remedy the grievance; but where the case is only new in the *instance*, and the only question is upon the application of a principle recognized by law to such new case, it will be just as competent to Courts of justice to apply the acknowledged principle to any case which may arise two centuries hence as it was two centuries ago. However, the novelty of an action may frequently be fairly urged as a strong *presumptive* argument against it (*p*).

Ancient prescribed forms not to be departed from.

When the prescribed form of action is to be found in the Register, the proceeding should not materially vary from it (*q*), unless in those cases where *another form* of action has long been sanctioned by usage (*r*); and the Courts *will not* permit parties, even by agreement, to depart from the appropriate *remedy (*s*); for it has been considered to be of the greatest importance to observe the boundaries of the different actions (237), not only in respect of their being most logically framed, and best adapted to the nature of each particular case, but also in order that causes may not be brought into Court confusedly and immethodically, and that the record may at once clearly ascertain the matter in dispute; a regulation which, since the different legislative provisions respecting costs, (the right to which varies in different forms of action), has become of still greater importance (*t*). Hence we find that even the slightest [*110]

(*l*) *Per* Blackstone, J., 2 Bla. Rep. 1113; and *per* Dallas, C. J., 3 B. & B. 62, 63.

(*m*) 1 East, 226.

(*n*) Willes, 581; Bul. N. P. 79.

(*o*) 3 T. R. 63.

(*p*) Co. Lit. 81 b; 2 T. R. 673; 1 T. R. 517; Dougl. 602; Cro. Eliz. 770; 1 Bing. 343; 8 Taunt. 620, 621; 3 Bing. 256.

(*q*) Bac. Ab. Abatement, H.; and this because *nihil simul inventum est et perfectum*, and the long adoption and use of a form is a strong argument in its favor.

(*r*) *Id. ibid.*; 4 Co. 94 b; 3 Woodd. 169; 4 Reeves, 432.

(*s*) 9 East, 381; 15 East, 309; 1 Ld. Raym. 188; Peake, 128.

(*t*) 1 Ld. Raym. 188. Thus, in 6 T. R. 129, 130, Lord Kenyon, C. J., said, "It is of importance *that the boundaries between the different actions should be preserved*, and particularly in cases of this kind; for if in an action of trespass the plaintiff recover less than 40*s*., he is entitled to no more costs than damages, whereas a verdict with nominal damages only, in an action on the case, carries full costs." And in 1 Hen. Bla. 243,

(236) Vide Yates *v.* Joyce, 11 Johns. Rep. 140.

(237) Vide Vail *v.* Lewis and Livingston, 4 Johns. Rep. 457, 458.

If a party has a remedy at common law, and a remedy is given in the affirmative by statute, without a negative express or implied of the action at common law, he may avail himself of either. Almy *v.* Harris, 5 J. R. 175 Farmers' Turnpike Co. *v.* Coventry, 10 J. R. 390.

IN GENERAL.

alterations in the form of action or of plea are usually introduced by *express enactment*, and not by mere rule of Court, as in 3 & 4 W. 4, c. 42, s. 14, which declares, that an action of *debt on simple contract* shall be maintainable in any Court of Common Law against an executor or administrator.

Actions are *real*, *personal* or *mixed*.

Actions are, from their subject-matter, distinguished into *real*, *personal*, and *mixed*. *Real* actions are for the specific recovery of real property only, and in which the plaintiff, then called the demandant, claims title to lands, tenements, or hereditaments, in fee-simple, fee-tail, or for term of life, such as writs of right, formedon, dower, &c. *Personal* actions are for the recovery of a debt or damages for the breach of a contract, or a specific personal chattel, or a satisfaction in damages for some injury to the person, personal, or real property. In *Mixed* actions, which partake of the nature of the other two, the plaintiff proceeds for the specific recovery of some real property, and also for damages for an injury thereto, as in the instance of an action of ejectment or of waste, or *quare impedit* (u). We will confine our observations [*111] *to such *personal* and *mixed* actions as most frequently occur in practice.

Actions are in form *ex contractu* or *ex delicto*.

Personal actions are in form *ex contractu* or *ex delicto*, or, in other words, are for breach of *contract*, or for *wrongs* unconnected with contract. Those upon *contracts* are principally assumpsit, debt, covenant, and detinue (x); and those for *wrongs* are case, trover, replevin, and trespass *vi et armis*. We will take a concise view of the nature and particular applicability of each of these respective remedies, and of the action of ejectment, and of that of trespass for mesne profit; in effect a branch of trespass *quare clausum fregit*.

Suggestions on the mode of considering and arranging the subject.

In arranging the law upon the *forms of action*, and their applicability, care must be observed only to notice such decisions as elucidate the rules or create exceptions or distinctions *upon this particular subject*, and to avoid crowding the context with an accumulation of *instances*. Thus, after stating that *assumpsit* is the proper form of action on all simple contracts, and consequently on a bill of exchange or promissory note, it would be improper to introduce numerous decisions on the *requisites* of bills of exchange or promissory notes, which would throw no light on the *application* of the *form of action*, but extend the inquiry to the whole law respecting bills of exchange. So

Mr. J. Wilson said, "It is highly necessary that *the forms of action should be kept distinct*." And in 1 B. & B. 476, Eyre, C. J., observed, that "undoubtedly *we ought to endeavor to preserve the distinction of actions*; and if it appear upon the pleadings that actions of a different nature have been mixed, that is a sufficient ground for arresting the judgment." And in 1 Stra. 635, the Chief Justice observed, "We must keep up the *boundaries* of actions, otherwise we shall introduce the utmost confusion." So in 5 B. & A. 654; 1 D. & R. 286, S. C., Abbott, C. J., observes, "The law has provided certain *specific forms* of action for particular cases, and *it is of importance that they should be preserved*." See also 11 Mod. 180; 2 Burr. 1114; 2 Saund. 47 b; 2 Inst. 434; Fitzg. 85; and see the observations of Park, J., in Deane v. Clayton, 1 J. B. Moore Rep. 298.

(u) Bract. 101 b; 3 Bla. Com. 117; Stephen on Pl. 2d ed. 3. As to the various *real* actions, see Co. Lit. 239, n. 1.; 1 Bla. Com. ch. 10; Bac. Ab. Actions in General, A. Now in general abolished by 3 & 4 W. 4, c. 27, s. 36. Mr. Serjeant Stephen considers that ejectment should be ranked as a personal rather than a mixed action, Stephen, 2d edit. 23, Appendix, viii. 56, n. (y). But the statutes relative to writs of error, and the Uniformity of Process Act, 2 W. 4, c. 39, seem to import that ejectment is not a *personal* but a *mixed* action.

(x) Detinue may in some respects be considered an action *ex delicto*. As, however, it may be joined with debt, I have classed it with actions *ex contractu*; see *post*. The actions of account and annuity, though sometimes adopted, do not often occur in practice, and therefore I have not observed upon them.

after stating that *covenant* is the proper remedy on a lease, cases respecting the construction of particular covenants ought not to be introduced. It will be found, that notwithstanding the very extensive alterations of late introduced respecting *writs* or *process* to bring a defendant into Court, in *personal* actions, by the Uniformity of Process Act, 2 W. 4, c. 39, and generally throughout the *practical* mode of conducting an action by numerous modern rules, and in the *pleadings* in an action by Reg. Gen. Hilary Term, 4 W. 4, yet there have been very few alterations respecting the *forms of action*, and which will principally be found in 3 & 4 W. 4, c. 42, such as the enactments authorizing actions of debt on simple contract against executors or administrators, and allowing actions for torts to *personal or real property* to be sustained by and against executors. IN GENERAL.

I. ASSUMPSIT.

This action is so called from the word *assumpsit*, which, when the pleadings were in Latin, was always inserted in the declaration, as descriptive of the defendant's undertaking (*y*). It may be *defined* to be an action for the recovery of *damages* for the non-performance of a *parol* or *simple* contract, or, in other words, a contract not under seal nor of record (*z*), circumstances which distinguish this remedy from others; for the action of *debt* is, in legal consideration, for the recovery of a *debt eo nomine*, and *in numero*, and is most frequently brought upon a deed (*a*); and the action of *covenant*, although in form for the recovery of *damages*, can only be supported upon a contract under *seal*. Assumpsit, *however, is not sustainable, unless there have been an [*112] *express contract*, or unless the law will *imply* a contract. Though founded upon *contract*, this action, as distinguishable from the *brevia formata*, and falling within the provision of the Statute of Westminster, may be termed an action on the case (*b*). It is now, however, called an action of assumpsit, and when the term "*case*" is adopted in a statute, or otherwise, an action for a *tort* and in form *ex delicto*, is usually intended, and not an action in form *ex contractu* (*c*). I. ASSUMPSIT.

A minute inquiry into the *history* of this action would at this time be matter of curiosity, rather than of practical utility. The origin and progress of it may be collected from the reports and works referred to in the note (*d*); and from which it appears, that till *Slade's case* (*e*), a notion prevailed, that on a

(*y*) The word "*undertook*" was *always* considered proper to be inserted in the declaration, though the promise be founded on a legal liability, and though in evidence it would be implied, Bac. Ab. Assumpsit, F. But it is sufficient to aver that the defendant *promised*. And the forms of declaration prescribed by Reg. Gen. Trin. Term, 1 W. 4, adopt only the word "*promise*," and are in other respects more concise than heretofore.

(*z*) Contracts are, 1. of *Record*; 2. by *Specialty*; or 3. by *Parol*. The term *Parol*, or *simple* contract, signifies every contract not under seal nor of record, whether verbal or written, 7 T. R. 351.

(*a*) 1 Hen. Bla. 551, 554, 555; Bul. N. P. 167.

(*b*) Bac. Ab. Assumpsit; Gilb. C. P. 6; 2 Bla. Rep. 850.

(*c*) 7 T. R. 36. The declaration in assumpsit describes the plea to be "trespass on the case upon promises."

(*d*) Rudder *v.* Price, 1 Hen. Bla. 550 to 555; Doug. 6, 7; Slade's Case, 4 Co. 91 to 95; 3 Woodd. 168, 169, n. (*c*); Reeves, vols. iii. & iv.; 1 Vin. Ab. 276; Bro. Ab. Action sur le Case, pl. 7, 69, 72; Fitz. N. B. 94, A. n. (*a*), 145, G.; 1 New Rep. 295; 2 Bla. Rep. 850.

(*e*) 4 Co. 91 to 95, 44 Eliz.

I. ASSUMPSIT. simple contract for a sum certain, or for any money demand, the action must be in debt; but it was holden in that case, that the plaintiff had his election either to bring assumpsit or debt. From the penning of the statute 3 Jac. 1. (*f*) it is probable the action of assumpsit was not then much in use; but afterwards it became very general (*g*), and it is now more frequently adopted for the recovery of money due on a simple contract, than the action of debt. From these cases it also appears (*h*), that though before *Slade's case* an action on the case might be supported, as well for the non-feasance of a contract, as for misfeasance or malfeasance in the performance of it, yet from the form of the writ in Fitzherbert (*i*), it may be collected that the remedy was not similar to our present action of assumpsit, but rather resembled the present form of a declaration in case for a *tort* (*k*).

The breach of all *parol* or *simple* contracts, whether verbal or written, or [*113] express or implied (*l*), or for the payment of *money, or for the performance or omission of any other act, is remediable by action of assumpsit. Thus it lies to recover *money* lent by the plaintiff to the defendant, or paid by the plaintiff on the account of the defendant at his request, or had and received by the defendant to the use of the plaintiff. In some cases, though money may have been received by the defendant tortiously, or by duress of the person or goods, it may be recovered in this form of action (238), the law implying a contract in favor of the party entitled (*m*) (239) as against a person who has usurped an office, and received the known and accustomed fees of office, but mere gratuitous donations cannot be recovered in assumpsit (*n*). So assumpsit lies for the value of goods which the defendant by fraud induced the plaintiff to sell to an insolvent person, and afterwards obtained for his own benefit (*o*). And where the goods of a trader, after his act of bankruptcy, are taken in execution, or otherwise tortiously disposed of without the concurrence of the assignees, they may waive the tort, and declare in assumpsit for money had and received, if the goods have been sold (*p*), but they *must* adopt the latter form of action if they have affirmed and recognized the wrongful sale and

(*f*) 3 James 1, c. 8.
(*g*) *Per* Buller, J., Dougl. 6.
(*h*) Bro. Ab. Actions sur le Case, pl. 7, 69, 72; Fitz. N. B. 94, A. 145, G.; Bac. Ab. Assumpsit, C.
(*i*) N. B. 94, A.; 3 Woodd. 165; 2 Bla. Rep. 850.
(*k*) 1 Hen. Bla. 550, 551.
(*l*) 4 M. & Sel. 275; 3 M. & Sel. 191; 1 Taunt. 112.
(*m*) 3 Wils. 304; 2 T. R. 144; Cowp. 419; Bul. N. P. 131; 5 Moore, 525; 1 B. & C. 418; 2 D. & R. 568, S. C.; 2 Bar. & Cres 729; 4 D. & R. 283, S. C.
(*n*) 6 T. R. 681; 8 Taunt. 264; 1 Camp. 124.
(*o*) 3 Taunt. 274; 5 Moore, 98; 1 B. & C. 418; 2 D. & R. 568, S. C.
(*p*) *Supra*, note (*m*).

(238) So, an action for money had and received lies against a collector, for money unlawfully demanded, and paid by the plaintiff to obtain a clearance for his vessel, which was refused until the money was paid. Ripley *v.* Gelston, 9 Johns. Rep. 201. So, it lies against a clerk of the District Court to recover money exacted *colore officii* from the plaintiff, as a condition of the re-delivery of property which had been liberated from seizure. Clinton *v.* Strong, 9 Johns. Rep. 370. So, it has been held to lie against a deputy postmaster, to recover the excess of postage on a letter, beyond what was allowed by law. Williams *v.* Dodd, Superior Court of Connecticut, cited 2 Day's Esp. Rep. 154. n. 1. Against a magistrate to recover fees illegally taken. Prior *v.* Craig, 5 Serg. & Rawle, 48. But in the case of a voluntary payment of money which the party could not have been compelled to pay, no action will lie to recover it back. Hall *v.* Schultz, 4 Johns. Rep. 240. and n. a. 2d ed. Ibid. 1 Esp. Dig. 119.

(239) Vide Dumond's Adm'r *v.* Carpenter, 3 Johns. Rep. 183. Sturtevant *v.* Waterbury, 2 Hall's N. Y. R. 453.

waived the original tort (*q*). Assumpsit also lies to recover money paid or goods delivered by a bankrupt by way of fraudulent preference (*r*); and there are many other instances in which a party may waive the tort, and sue for money had and received (*s*). But in these cases it is sometimes most advisable to declare in case or trover, in order to avoid a set-off, or the effect of the law of mutual credit (240), in the case of bankruptcy (*t*). So a master may sue a person who has enticed away or harbored his apprentice in assumpsit, for the work and labor of such apprentice (*u*)(241); and it lies to recover back rents tortiously received (*x*). In some cases also where money has been *extorted by duress of goods, it may be recovered back in assumpsit (*y*). But the proprietor of cattle wrongfully distrained *damage feasant*, who has paid money for the purpose of having them re-delivered to him, cannot recover back that money in this action, because such mode of proceeding would impose great difficulties on the defendant, by not apprizing him of what he was to defend; and the law has provided specific remedies for trying the legality of a distress (242), viz. replevin, trespass, or trover (*z*). Again, this action lies to recover interest (243); money due on an account stated (244); or for services and works of different descriptions, and for poundage due to the sheriff (*a*); or for the sale, use, or hire of goods or of land, or other personal or real property; and upon bills of exchange, whether foreign or inland; checks on bankers; promissory notes; policies of insurance on ships, or on lives, or against fire; or on charter-parties, when not under seal; and upon the implied contract to contribute towards the general average (*b*).

I. ASSUMPSIT.

[*114]

(*q*) 7 B. & C. 310; 1 M. & R. 2, S. C.

(*r*) See 4 T. R. 211; 2 D. & R. 568; 1 B. & C. 418, S. C.

(*s*) 4 Bar. & Cres. 211; 6 D. & R. 265, S. C.; Pratt *v.* Vizard and another, 5 B. & Adol. 808.

(*t*) 4 T. R. 211; see 10 East, 378, 418; 16 East, 130. Where the ground of action is assumpsit, declaring in tort will not render a person liable who would not have been so on his promise, 2 Marsh. 485; 3 B & B. 62; 1 B. & C. 94; 2 D. & R. 198, S. C.; nor will it in general avoid the consequences of non-joinder of a party, *ante*, 99, 100.

(*u*) 3 M. & Sel. 191; 1 Taunt. 112; When not, 4 Taunt. 876.

(*x*) 6 T. R. 683; Bul. N. P. 133; Cowp. 414.

(*y*) Pratt *v.* Vizard and another, 5 Bar. & Adol. 808; 2 Stra. 915; 4 T. R. 485; Bul. N. P. 132; 5 Bing. 37; 7 B. & C. 73; 9 D. & R. 889, S. C.; 1 Wightw. 22.

(*z*) Cowp. 414; 6 T. R. 298; 15 East, 309.

(*a*) Cro. Eliz. 654.

(*b*) 3 Campb. 480; 1 East, 220; 4 Taunt. 123.

(240) Vide Billon *v.* Hyde, 1 Ves. 329. S. C. 1 Atk. 126. Hussey *v.* Fidell, 12 Mod. 324. S. C. Holt, 95. Philips *v.* Thompson, 3 Lev. 191. Authorities limiting the right of set-off to cases of mutual debts, and excluding the right to set off torts, and damages upon a special agreement. M'Donald *v.* Neilson, 2 Cowen, 139.

(241) If a slave deserts his master and goes into the service of another, the master can recover for services performed by the slave before he gives notice of his claim. Trongott *v.* Byrea, 5 Cowen, 480. Case of James Le Roy, 6 J. R. 274. But this principle is not to be applied to a case where the master never had possession of the slave, and was chargeable with concealing his claim from the defendant while the slave was performing the services. Demyer *v.* Souzer, 6 Wend. R. 436.

(242) By recovering a judgment in trespass for carrying away the plaintiff's goods, his property in the goods is divested; and such judgment is a bar to an action of indebitatus assumpsit against any one for the proceeds of the sale of the goods which were the subject of the trespass. Floyd *v.* Browne, 1 Rawle, 121.

The owner of property in possession of a tenant of demised premises, may buy it on a sale of the same as a distress for rent, and bring his action for money paid against the tenant. Wells *v.* Porter et al., 7 Wend. R. 119.

(243) Vide Tucker *v.* Randall, 2 Mass. Rep. 284. Greenleaf *v.* Kellog, 2 Mass. Rep. 568. But after acceptance of the principal, an action will not lie for the interest. Tillotson *v.* Preston, 3 Johns. Rep. 229. Johnston and Brannan, 5 Johns. Rep. 268.

(244) But not on a running account. Scott *v.* M'Intosh, 2 Camp. 238.

I. ASSUMPSIT.

Assumpsit is also sustainable specially upon wagers (245) and feigned issues; and upon awards, where the submission was not by deed (246); also, to recover money due on an award made by virtue of an order of Nisi Prius (c); on by-laws (d); on an Irish (e), or foreign judgment (f); or for legacies charged on land (g) (247), though debt is more usual in the last three instances. But neither assumpsit nor any other form of action at law, is sustainable for a pecuniary legacy payable out of the general assets of the testator (h) (248); or for a distributive share of an intestate's property, to which the plaintiff is entitled (i), although the personal representative has promised payment; unless there be evidence showing that he holds the money, not as executor or administrator, but in his individual character upon a new contract [*115] for a loan of it to him (k). It may *also be supported for money due for tithes, where there has been an agreement for a composition (l): but unless there have been such a composition, the only remedy is in a Court of Equity or in the Ecclesiastical Courts; or in debt upon the statute (m), to recover the treble value of the tithe omitted to be set out, and which act extends only to prædial tithe that are capable of being set out in kind (n). This form of action is also maintainable for money due for *tolls*, or to recover the value of

(c) 5 East, 139.
(d) 1 B. & P. 98.
(e) 4 B. & C. 411; 6 D. & R. 471, S. C.; see 5 East, 474.
(f) Dougl. 1; 4 T. R. 493; 3 East, 221; 11 East, 124; 3 Taunt. 85.
(g) 2 Salk. 415; 6 Mod. 27; Lord Raym. 937; 4 M. & Sel. 114.
(h) 5 T. R. 690; 7 B. & C. 544; 1 M. & R. 420, S. C.
(i) 7 B. & C. 542; 1 M. & R. 420, S. C.
(k) 1 M. & P. 209.
(l) *Post*, vol. ii.; Bac. Ab. Tithe, Y. D. d.; Bul. N. P. 488 to 191.
(m) 2 & 3 Edw. 6, c. 13.
(n) Bul. N. P. 188; Eagle on Tithes, 150.

(245) Philips v. Ives, 1 Rawle, 36.

(246) { Mitchell v. Bush, 7 Cow. Rep. 185. And a revocation of a submission to arbitration not under seal, before an award made, is in effect a breach of an agreement to stand to, obey, perform, &c. an award, for which assumpsit will lie. Brown v. Tanner, 2 M'Clell. & Young's Rep. 464. }

Vide Hubbell v. Coudrey, 5 Johns. Rep. 132. and n. a. ibid. { But *debt* will not lie against an administrator in *Pennsylvania* on a judgment obtained in a foreign court against a foreign administrator of the same intestate. Brodie v. Bickley, Adm., 2 Rawle, 431. }

(247) Vide Beecker v. Beecker, 7 Johns. Rep. 99, which was an action of *assumpsit* against a devisee of land charged with a legacy; the devisee having entered on the land, and the executors assented to the legacy, it was held that he was liable on his express promise to pay the legatee: the court avoided giving an opinion, whether he would have been liable on an implied promise. There are circumstances, however, which may amount to an express promise; as where an annuity is charged by the will of the devisor upon the land devised, if the devisee has entered and actually paid part of the annuity, the legatee may maintain *assumpsit* for the residue. Van Orden v. Van Orden, 10 Johns. Rep. 30. See Deaks v. Strutt, 5 Term Rep. 690, *contra*, and the observations of the court upon that case in 10 Johns. Rep. 31. { That the action cannot be maintained without an *express* promise, see Brown v. Furer, 4 Serg. & Rawle, 213. The proper mode of proceeding in such a case in *Pennsylvania*, is, to bring the action against the *executor* and *terre tenants*, and to enter the judgment so as to charge the *land*, and not the *persons* of the defendants. Brown v. Furer, Gauze v. Wiley, 4 Serg. & Rawle, 504. And in such action it is improper to join, as a defendant, the executor of the devisee. Moore v. Rees, 13 Serg. & Rawle, 436. }

(248) *Assumpsit* lies against an executor for a pecuniary legacy on his express promise in consideration of assets. Atkins and ux. v. Hill, and Hawkes and ux. v. Saunders, Cowp. 284. 289. Beecker v. Beecker, 7 Johns. Rep. 103, 104. Opinion of KENT, C. J., Clark and others v. Herring, 5 Binn. 33. Van Orden v. Van Orden, 10 Johns. Rep. 31. And, in the states of New York and Pennsylvania, actions at law against executors for legacies, are given by statute. Laws N. Y. sess. 36. c. 75. s. 19. 1 R. L. 314. { 2 Rev. Stat. 114. s. 9. } Dewitt and wife v. Schoonmaker and others, 2 Johns. Rep. 243. Wilson v. Wilson, 3 Binn. 559.

goods which should have been rendered in specie for toll; but in such case the declaration must state that the goods were of some certain value (o). Assumpsit also lies for money due for port duties, and for *stallage*, where there is a legal liability to pay, although there has not been any express contract (p), and this although trespass might be sustainable, because the owner may waive the tort (p). So it lies for contributions to party-walls (q) (249); or canal calls (r); or on promises to pay money in consideration of forbearance to sue the defendant, or a third person (250); or in consideration of services or work done; or goods sold to the defendant, or a third person at the defendant's request; and upon contracts to guarantee (s); indemnify (t); to serve and employ (u); or perform works (x); and against attorneys and solicitors, wharfingers (y), surgeons (z), inn-keepers (a), carriers and other bailees, for neglect or other breach of duty. Assumpsit is also the proper remedy for a breach of a promise to marry; and against a vendor for not delivering goods bought; or against the vendee for not accepting goods sold; or for not delivering a bill of exchange in payment for the same (b); or upon an express warranty of the goodness or quality of any personal chattel, either on the sale or exchange thereof, or upon an express or implied warranty as to the property therein (c); and by and against vendors and purchasers for not completing a contract of sale, and for not rendering a just account of monies or goods (d). So where there has been an express *agreement not under seal between landlord and tenant; or where the law implies a contract on the part of the latter to manage the farm in a husbandlike manner; this action may be sustained for the breach of such contract (e). But where the tenant has been guilty of voluntary waste, it is usual to declare in case, unless there be also a money demand, which might be included in a declaration in assumpsit (f). And by the statute (g) (251), the executor of a tenant for life may, in assumpsit, recover a proportion of rent up to the day of his testator's death, where the tenancy determined on such death; though when the tenant held under a lease granted in pursuance of a leasing power, the remainder-man must sue for the whole rent on such lease (h). The difficulty of investigating a disputed account before a jury seems also to constitute no legal objection to this action (i). [*116]

I. ASSUMPSIT.

When the peculiar remedy.

The action of assumpsit is in general the only remedy against an executor or administrator, for the breach by the testator of a contract not under seal,

(o) 4 B. & A. 268; 6 B. & C. 385; 9 D. & R. 452, S. C.
(p) The Mayor of Newport v. Saunders, 3 Bar. & Adol. 411.
(q) 14 Geo. 3, c. 78; 5 T. R. 130; 8 T. R. 314; 1 B. & P. 303.
(r) 7 T. R. 36.
(s) 1 Saund. 211 a; 5 East, 10.
(t) 3 Wils. 362; 3 East, 169; 2 T. R. 105; 2 B. & P. 98, 268.
(u) 2 East, 145; 4 Esp. Rep. 77; Cowp. 437.
(x) 5 T. R. 143.
(y) 7 T. R. 171; *post*, vol. ii.
(z) 1 Saund. 312, n. 2.; Wils. 359.
(a) 8 Co. 32; 5 T. R. 273.
(b) 4 East, 147; 3 B. & P. 582.
(c) *Post*, vol. ii.; 2 Bla. Com. 451; 3 *id.* 160; Cro. Jac. 474; 1 Rol. Abr. 90.
(d) 1 Marsh. 115; 1 Taunt. 572; *post*, vol. ii.
(e) 5 T. R. 373; 4 East, 154; 1 Hen. Bla. 99.
(f) *Id. ibid.*; 3 East, 70.
(g) 11 Geo. 2, c. 19, s. 15.
(h) 1 Swanst. 337; 2 Saund. 282, e. n. 2; 8 Ves. 311; 2 Ves. & B. 334; 1 P. W. 117; 2 Bro. C. C. 659.
(i) 5 Taunt. 431; 1 Marsh. 115.

(249) Ingles v. Bringhurst, 1 Dall. 341. See Hart v. Rucher, 5 Serg. & Rawle, 1.
(250) Sidwell v. Evans, 1 Penn. Rep. 383.
(251) {The 14th and 15th sections of this statute, are in force in *Pennsylvania.*} Roberts' Dig. 236. 3 Binn. 626.

I. ASSUMPSIT. which was made with him (k); for (unless in the Court of Exchequer, in which wager of law is not allowed,) (l) *debt* is not sustainable against an executor, as such, upon the simple contract of his testator; although it lies against an executor on a simple contract made with *him* in that character (m). And in general assumpsit is the only remedy for the recovery of an instalment (252) due on a simple contract, in respect of an entire sum payable by instalments, the whole of which have not accrued due; as debt is not sustainable in such case (n). Where a simple contract creates a collateral liability, as for the payment of the debt of a third person, debt not being sustainable, assumpsit is the only form of action (o). For the same reason, assumpsit is the only remedy at the suit of the payee or indorsee of a bill of exchange against the acceptor, or of the indorsee of a promissory note against

[*117] the maker (p). And on an award to *perform any act, except to pay money, assumpsit is the only remedy, unless the submission were by bond (q). Formerly it was thought, that in an action of debt on simple contract, the precise sum stated to be due in the declaration must be recovered, or that the plaintiff would be nonsuited (r); and therefore at that time it was usual, when the amount of the debt was uncertain, to declare in assumpsit; but as this notion no longer prevails, and the plaintiff will recover, if he prove any sum to be due to him, though less than that stated in the declaration, it is no longer material in this respect whether the plaintiff declare in assumpsit or debt (s).

Of assumpsit where there are several securities, &c.

When a party has different securities of different descriptions for the same debt or demand, and from the same person, he must found his action on that security which is in law of the higher nature and efficacy. The law has prescribed different forms of action on different securities. Thus assumpsit cannot in general be supported when there has been an express contract under seal (253) or of record (254), which relates to the same subject matter, and is still in force; but the party must proceed in debt or covenant where the contract is under seal (255), or in debt or *scire facias* if it be of record, even though the debtor, after such contract were made, expressly promised (256) to perform it (t). And if there be a charter-party under seal between the mas-

(k) 1 New Rep. 293; 9 Co. 86 b.
(l) 3 Bla. Com. 347; 9 Co. 88 a.
(m) 5 Bing. 200.
(n) 1 Hen. Bla. 547; Cro. Jac. 504; 2 Saund. 303, n. 6, 337, 350, 374; Fitzg. 302; Com. Dig. Action, F.; 3 Co. 22 a; *post.*
(o) Hardr. 486; Com. Dig. Debt, B.; 2 Lord Raym. 1040.
(p) 2 B. & P. 78; 1 Taunt. 540, and Chitty on Bills, 7th ed. 428; *post.*
(q) 2 Saund. 62 b. n. 5.
(r) 3 Bla. Com. 155.
(s) 1 Hen. Bla. 249, 550; Dougl. 6, 732.
(t) 1 Roll. Abr. 11, 517; 1 Leon. 293; 2 Leon. 110; Cro. Jac. 506, 598; 2 Stra. 1027; 2 T. R. 100, 105; 1 New Rep. 108. See the observation of Bayley, J., on this

(252) Vide Tucker v. Randall, 2 Mass. Rep. 283. Assumpsit lies on a promissory note by which the interest is payable annually, although the principal is not yet payable. Greenleaf v. Kellogg, 2 Mass. Rep. 568, 284. Cooley v. Rose, 3 Mass. Rep. 221.

(253) Vide Young v. Preston, 4 Cranch, 239. {Codman v Jenkins, 14 Mass. Rep. 93.} In some cases where a party has covenanted to do an act, and failed in the performance, the covenantee has been allowed to recover back the consideration paid, in *assumpsit*. Weaver v. Bentley, 1 Caines' Rep. 47. D'Utricht v. Melchor, 1 Dall. 428. Howes v. Barker, 3 Johns. Rep. 509.

(254) {Andrews v. Montgomery et al., 19 Johns. Rep. 162.}

(255) Vide Richards v. Killam, 10 Mass. Rep. 243. 247.

(256) {Landis v. Urie, 10 Serg. and Rawle, 321. 14 Mass. 99. Miller v. Watson, 5 Cow. Rep. 195.} But it has been held that where there is a covenant to pay money, and part has been paid, assumpsit will lie on a promise to pay the balance. Danforth v. Schoharie Turnp. Co., 12 Johns. Rep. 227.

ter and freighter, assumpsit will not lie by the owners for freight, which the defendant by the deed covenanted with the master to pay (*u*). But if the owners of a ship be not charged directly on the contract of charter-party, but upon their general liability, they may be sued in case for negligence in conveying the goods, notwithstanding the charter-party be under seal, entered into by the master, and whereby he covenanted to convey the cargo: the action not being inconsistent with the provisions of the deed, and the master, contracting as such, not as part-owner (*x*). If the deed be only executed by the plaintiff and not by the defendant, the action *must be in assumpsit (*y*) (257); and if there be an agreement by deed to let a house, by words not amounting to an actual demise, the party may maintain assumpsit for use and occupation (*z*). So assumpsit lies for the use and occupation of a water-course (*a*). Where on the separation of a husband and wife, he covenanted by deed with a trustee to pay an allowance for her separate maintenance, but made default, and the trustee provided the wife with necessaries, it was decided that he might support assumpsit on the common law obligation (*b*). So if the contract under seal be invalid (258) and there be any evidence upon which an implied contract can be raised, assumpsit may in some cases be supported, as where an annuity deed has been set aside, or objected to for some defect (259) in the memorial, &c. (*c*); and the taking a security by deed on usurious terms, for money previously lent and not affected by usury, would not bar an action of assumpsit for money lent (*d*). And where a feme covert, without authority from her husband, contracted with a servant by deed, the service having been performed, it was decided, that the servant might maintain assumpsit against the husband (*e*). If in respect of a *new consideration*, there has been a *new simple* contract to pay a debt, or perform a contract under seal, assumpsit may be supported (*f*) (260); as on a promise to an assignee of a bond, to

I. ASSUMPSIT.

[*118]

case in 4 Bar. & Cres. 968; 7 D. & R. 361, S. C.; 10 East, 378; 3 C. & P. 358. A *foreign* judgment does not merge a simple contract debt, 11 East, 118, 126.

(*u*) 1 M. & Sel. 573; 3 Campb. 549, n. a. Where it does not lie for interest secured by deed, 1 M. & Sel. 575.

(*x*) 6 Moore, 415; 3 B. & B. 171, S. C.

(*y*) 3 Esp. Rep. 42.

(*z*) 4 Esp. Rep. 59, When not, 2 Taunt. 145; 5 B. & A. 322.

(*a*) 4 Bar. & Cres. 8; 6 D. & R. 42, S. C.

(*b*) 2 New Rep. 148.

(*c*) 6 East, 241; 3 Taunt. 56. See exception, 8 East, 331.

(*d*) 1 Saund. 295, note 1.

(*e*) 6 T. R. 176.

(*f*) 12 East, 578.

(257) Where land is conveyed by deed poll, and the grantee enters under the deed, certain duties being reserved to be performed, as no action lies against the grantee on the deed, the grantor may maintain assumpsit for the non-performance of the duties reserved. Goodwin and another *v.* Gilbert and another, 9 Mass. Rep. 510.

(258) Or be rescinded. Hill *v.* Green, 4 Pick. Rep. 114.

(259) Vide Shore *v.* Webb, 1 Term Rep. 732. Beauchamp *v.* Borrett, Peake's Cas. 109. Richards *v.* Borrett, 3 Esp. Rep. 102.

(260) Miller *v.* Watson, 7 Cow. Rep. 39. A promise to pay a specialty debt, which has been discharged by a certificate of Bankruptcy, does not revive the original debt as a debt by specialty. The original debt is merely a consideration, which renders the new promise available. Case of Field's Estate, 2 Rawle, 351. Where a tenant has held by lease with the usual covenants, and the lease expires, and the tenant still continues to hold the land with the consent and permission of the landlord, he shall hold subject to all the covenants contained in the expired lease, for the breach of any of which he may be sued in assumpsit; for the law raises the implied assumpsit of his continuing to hold on the same terms as he did by the lease. 1 Esp. Dig. 7.

I. ASSUMPSIT. pay him in consideration of forbearance (g) (261); or on a promise by an heir, having assets by descent, to pay the debt of his ancestor for the same consideration (h); or on a promise to the husband to pay the arrears of a rent-charge due to the wife in her life-time, although the rent was secured by deed (i); or by the debtor himself, in respect of any new consideration (k). And though it has been decided that assumpsit cannot be supported against a party, on his undertaking to pay the debt and costs recovered against himself, in consideration that the plaintiff would stay execution (l); it is clear that such
[*119] action might be supported *on a similar undertaking made by a third person (m) (262). So between partners, who have by deed covenanted to account with each other, and to pay over what shall appear to be due; if they state an account, and one expressly promise to pay the balance, assumpsit may be supported (263), notwithstanding the deed (n). And where a contract under seal has afterwards been varied in the terms of it by a distinct simple contract, made upon a sufficient consideration, such substituted or new agreement must be the subject of an action of assumpsit, and not of an action of covenant (o) (264); and where several things unconnected with a deed, are, with other stipulations in a deed, afterwards made the subject of a parol contract, assumpsit may be sustained for the breach of it (p); and when freight is recoverable *pro rata itineris*, assumpsit is the proper remedy, and not covenant on the charter-party (q).

It is also a rule, that when a bond or other security, under seal or of record, has been accepted in *satisfaction* of a simple contract, the latter is *merged* in such higher security, and assumpsit is not sustainable (r); unless such new security be void on account of usury (s) or under the annuity act, &c. in

(g) 2 Bla. R. 1269; 1 Saund. 210, n. 1; 8 T. R. 595.
(h) 2 Saund. 137 b; Com. Dig. Action Assumpsit, B. 1.
(i) 1 Leon. 293; 2 M. & Sel. 309.
(k) Cro. Car. 343; Cro. Eliz. 67; 12 Mod. 511; 1 Vin. Ab. 272; 1 Rol. Ab. 8, pl. 6; Bac. Ab. Assumpsit, A.
(l) Cowp. 128, 129; see Hutton, 77; Cro. Car 8. *Semble* that a party discharged out of custody on a *ca. sa.* on his promise to pay at a future period, is liable in assumpsit upon such new agreement, 4 Burr. 2483.
(m) Cowp. 129; Hardr. 71; 1 Lev. 188.
(n) 2 T. R. 483, 478. When partners may sue each other, see *ante*, 44.
(o) 1 East, 630; 3 T. R. 596; 4 Taunt. 748.
(p) 1 M. & Sel. 575; 2 T. R. 479.
(q) 10 East, 295; 1 New Rep. 240.
(r) Cro. Car. 415; Bac. Ab. Debt, G. Obligation, A. note; 3 East, 259.
(s) 1 Saund. 295, note 1.

(261) 10 Serg. & Rawle, 321. In Dubois v. Doubleday, 9 Wend. R. 317, it was *held*, that assumpsit would not lie by the assignee of a bond, except on an express promise, although his right to the money has been recognized, a partial payment made to him, and a negotiation had for the payment of the balance.

(262) Duncan v. Kirkpatrick, 13 S. & R. 293.

(263) In an action on an arbitration bond, on the back of which the parties had indorsed an agreement under seal, enlarging the time for making the award, and it was made within such time. The court said that by the decision in Brown v. Goodman, (3 T. R. 592.) an action would not lie on the bond; the party has another remedy upon the submission implied in the agreement to enlarge the time. Freeman v. Adams, 9 J. R. 110. They say, that if a contract be subsequently changed, you must declare otherwise than on the contract itself; and they distinguish between cases where actions are brought upon such agreements, and those cases where the enlargement of time is presented by way of defence, as in Fleming v. Gilbert, 3 J. R 528.

(264) Vide Casey and Lawrence v. Brush, 2 Caines' Rep. 296. See also Baits v. Peters and Stebbins, 9 Wheat. Rep. 556. A parol enlargement of the time set in a sealed instrument for the performance of covenants is good; but where there is such enlargement of a condition precedent, the plaintiff loses his remedy upon the covenant itself, and must seek it upon the agreement enlarging the time of performance. Langworthy v. Smith, 2 Wend. Rep. 587. 6 Hals. Rep. 327.

which cases the party may proceed on the original simple contract if valid (*t*) (265). So if an infant give a bond (266) in a penalty for necessaries, the bond being inoperative, the creditor may proceed in assumpsit (*u*); (267) and if after a secret act of bankruptcy, the bankrupt give a bond in satisfaction of a simple contract debt, it will not so far extinguish the simple contract as to preclude the creditor from petitioning thereon for a commission (*x*). And the acceptance by a landlord of a bond for rent is no extinguishment of the rent, because the rent, issuing out of the realty, is a debt of as high a nature as a specialty claim (*y*). But a judgment obtained on a bond [*120] *would extinguish the demand on the bond (*z*). The taking a *collateral security* of an higher nature, whether from the principal or a surety, does not preclude the creditor from suing the original debtor in assumpsit on the first contract (*a*); though judgment may have been obtained upon such collateral security (*b*) (268).

I. ASSUMPSIT.

For rent, &c.

It was also a branch of this rule, that assumpsit could not be supported for rent, &c. *issuing out of real property*, though not reserved by deed, unless an express promise to pay could be proved (269); the demand, in the technical phrase, *savoring of the realty*, and being recoverable by higher remedies, as by debt or distress (*c*). The statute 11 Geo. 2, c. 19 (270), was passed to remedy the common law in this respect; since which, rent due on a demise not under seal may be recovered by action of assumpsit as well as debt (*d*). And indeed, the notion that assumpsit does not lie for a duty, merely because the plaintiff claims an inheritance, in respect whereof *the duty is payable, appears no longer to exist* (*e*) (271). And if a party hold over, after the expiration of a demise by deed, he may be sued in assumpsit for use and occupation, to recover rent accruing due after the end of the term (*f*). A corpora-

(*t*) 6 East, 241.

(*u*) Bul. N. P. 182; Co. Lit. 172; Cro. Eliz. 920.

(*x*) Bul. N. P. 182; Stra. 1042; 1 Hen. Bla. 462.

(*y*) Buller's N. P. 182 a. cites 3 Danv. Abr. 507, A. 1. That rent, whether due on a lease or a parol demise, is of equal degree with a specialty, at least in the administration of assets, see Com. Dig. Administration, C. 2; Toller, 278.

(*z*) Bul. N. P. 182 a; 6 Co. 44.

(*a*) 2 Leon. 110; 6 T. R. 176, 177; 18 Ves. 20; 5 Dow, 234.

(*b*) 3 East, 251.

(*c*) 1 Rol. Ab. 7, Action sur Case, O.; Cro. Jac. 598, 414; Cro. Eliz. 242; 3 Lev. 150, 261; 3 Woodes. 152, 153; Freem. 234.

(*d*) See as to the count for Use and Occupation, *post.*

(*e*) Willes, 111, 118.

(*f*) 4 B. & C. 8; 6 S. & R. 42, S. C.

(265) Or promissory note, M'Crillis v. How, 3 New Hampshire Rep. 348. Hammond v. Hopping, 13 Wend. Rep. 505. But where a note, given at the time when the liability of the defendant to the plaintiff occurs, is usurious, there can be no recovery in the same action on the money counts. Rice v. Welling, 5 Wend. Rep. 595.

(266) As to promise by the debtor after usurious securities have been destroyed, to repay principal and interest, vide Barnes and others v. Hedley and another, 2 Taunt. 184.

(267) Vide 1 Campb. 553, n. See the doctrine stated, Roof v. Stafford, 7 Cow. Rep. 179, and the cases there cited.

(268) Vide Norris v. Aylett, 3 Campb. 330. A mortgage of lands as security for a simple contract debt, though it contain a stipulation against personal liability on the mortgage, does not operate as payment of the debt; nor discharge the mortgagor from personal liability for it. Ainslee v. Wilson, 7 Cowen, 662.

(269) Vide Smith v. Stewart, 6 Johns. Rep. 48.

(270) { The xiv. and xv. sections of this statute are in force in *Pennsylvania*, Roberts' Dig. 236. 3 Binn. 626. }

(271) Vide Eppe's Ex'rs v. Cole and wife, 4 Hen. and Mun. 161. Hayes v. Acre, Cam. & Norw. Rep. 19. Smith v. Sheriff of Charleston, 1 Bay, 444. See also Cummings v. Noyes, 10 Mass. Rep. 433, where, after reversal of a judgment in favor of the demandant, who had entered into possession, it was held, that the tenant might maintain assumpsit for the *mesne* profits.

1. ASSUMPSIT. tion aggregate may maintain *assumpsit for the use and occupation* of buildings, or land, *or tolls*, though they did not grant the tolls to the occupier by any instrument under their common seal (*g*).

On a statute. Though a *statute* may in some respects be considered as a specialty (*h*), yet assumpsit may be supported for money, &c. accruing due to the plaintiff under the provisions thereof (272), he not being thereby restricted to any other particular remedy (*i*). The order of an inferior Court of justice may be the subject of this action, if there be an express agreement to observe the same (*k*).

On a judgment. This action is also sustainable upon the *judgment* of a *foreign* Court (273), which is not considered as a debt of record in this country (*l*); and it lies upon an Irish judgment (*m*) (274), and upon a Scotch decree (*n*). But neither assumpsit nor debt [*121] *can be sustained on the decree of the Court of Chancery for a specific sum of money, founded on equitable considerations

(*g*) Mayor of Stafford *v.* Till, 12 Moore, 260; The Mayor and Burgesses of Carmarthen *v* Lewis, 6 Car. & P. 608.

(*h*) 1 Saund. 37, 38.

(*i*) Bul. N. P. 129; Cowp. 474; Doug. 10, n. 2, 402, 407; 5 T. R. 130; Com. Dig. Action upon the Statute. See *post*, 128.

(*k*) 2 B. & P. 464.

(*l*) 1 Dougl. 4; 11 East, 124. When not, 1 Campb. 63, 253.

(*m*) 4 B. & C. 411; 6 D. & R. 471, S. C.

(*n*) 4 Bing. 686; 1 M. & P. 663, S. C.

---

(272) *Assumpsit* will not lie to recover back money won at play. Billon *v.* Hyde, 1 Ves. 330, S. C. 1 Atk. 128. {It should be *debt*, if the party sue under the stat. 9 Ann, c. 14. Turner *v.* Warner, Andr. Rep. 70. Bristow *v.* James, 7 Term Rep 257. In *Pennsylvania* the action may be *debt* or *case*. Act of 22d April, 1794. 3 Sm. Laws, 182. *Aliter* in *Massachusetts*, if the action be brought within three months from the losing of the money. Babcock *v.* Thompson, 3 Pick. Rep. 446.}

(273) Vide Phil. Ev. 242, 243. Buttrick and wife *v.* Allen, 8 Mass. Rep. 273. Bissel *v.* Bridges, 9 Mass. Rep. 464. Hubbell *v.* Coudrey, 5 Johns. Rep. 132.

(274) As to the effect of a judgment obtained in one of the United States, when made the subject of an action in another, (respecting which the courts in this country have varied essentially from one another, some, as the Supreme Court of *New York*, regarding it merely as a foreign judgment, and others allowing it greater weight,) see Armstrong *v.* Carson's Ex'rs, 2 Dall. 302. Bartlett *v.* Knight, 1 Mass. Rep. 401. Bissell *v* Briggs, 9 Mass. Rep. 462. Hitchcock and Fitch *v.* Aicken, 1 Caines' Rep 460. Taylor *v.* Bryden, 8 Johns. Rep. 173. Hubbell *v.* Coudrey, 5 Johns. Rep. 132. Phillips' Ev. Dunl. Ed. 254. n. Pauling and wife *v.* Wilson and Smith, 13 Johns. Rep. 192. But in Mills *v.* Duryee, in the Supreme Court of the U. S., 7 Cranch, 481, it was held that *nil debet* was not a good plea to an action of debt founded on the judgment of another State; because such judgment was conclusive between the parties, such being the effect to which it was entitled in the State where rendered, and therefore it could only be denied by the plea of *nul tiel record*. {The same point was decided in Hampton *v.* M'Connel, 3 Wheat. Rep. 234. See Jones's Adm. *v.* Hoar's Adm., 2 Rand. Rep. 303. The decision in Mills *v.* Duryee has been acquiesced in by the courts of New York, (Andrews *v.* Montgomery, 19 Johns. Rep. 160,) subject to these qualifications, that the party against whom judgment was rendered is not to be precluded from showing, that such judgment was fraudulently obtained, or that the State court had not jurisdiction of the person of the defendant. Borden *v.* Fitch, 15 Johns. Rep. 121. *Nil debet*, however, is a proper plea in an action of debt on a judgment recovered before a justice of the peace of another State. Warren *v.* Flagg, 2 Pick. Rep. 448.} In the case of Aldrich *v.* Kinney, 4 Conn. Rep. 380, Ch. J. Hosmer reviews all the decisions, and comes to the conclusion, that the records of the courts of other States are conclusive in cases only where they had jurisdiction of the cause, and of the person of the defendant. In Hall *v.* Williams et al., 6 Pick. 237, Ch. J. Parker has expressed the opinion that in all instances the jurisdiction of the court rendering the judgment may be inquired into. The court were further of opinion, with the Supreme Court of Connecticut, that if it appeared that the court rendering the judgment had jurisdiction, the record is conclusive evidence of the debt. The case of Starbuck *v.* Murray, 5 Wend. Rep. 148, is to the same effect. In Shumway *v.* Stillman, 6 Wend. Rep. 447, in an action on a judgment of a court of a sister State, it was held, that the record being only *prima facie* evidence of the defendant's appearance by attorney, that fact might be contested.

only (o)(275), or on a mere interlocutory order of a Court of Law (p). But an action may be maintained on the decree of a Colonial Court for payment of a balance due on a partnership account (q). We have already noticed the instances in which an action is sustainable by a party against his *co-partner* (r)(276).

I. ASSUMPSIT.

Assumpsit cannot be supported against a *corporation* (277), because a corporation cannot contract by parol (s); except in the case of promissory notes (t) and bills of exchange, where the power of drawing and accepting them is recognized by statute (u), and other contracts sanctioned by particular legislative provisions (v)(278). But a corporation may be plaintiffs in this form of action; at least upon an executed consideration, as for use and occupation of buildings or land, or even tolls, where the tenant has held the premises under them, and paid rent (w). And the London Gas Company may sue in assumpsit for gas supplied, although there was no contract by deed under their seal (x).

By and against corporations.

Where there has been an express contract, the party injured may sustain an action of assumpsit, though the breach amount to a trespass (y); but unless there have been such contract, or the law will, under the circumstances, imply a contract, the plaintiff must resort to another form of action (z). Therefore, assumpsit for use and occupation cannot be supported where the possession is adverse (279), and the relation of landlord and tenant has never subsisted

In general there must be a contract.

(o) 3 B. & Ald. 52; 8 B. & C. 20; 2 M. & R. 165, S. C.

(p) 2 Hen. Bla. 248; 4 Taunt. 705; 3 B. & Ald. 56.

(q) 8 B. & C. 16; 2 M. & R. 153, S. C.; 1 Camph. 253.

(r) *Ante*, 44.

(s) 1 Rol. R. 82; see 5 Taunt. 792; 4 Bing. 77.

(t) 3 & 4 Ann. c. 9.

(u) 5 B. & Ald. 204; 3 B. & Ald. 1; 2 Burr. 1216.

(v) 6 Vin. Ab. 317, pl. 49; 5 East, 239, 242; see 16 East, 6.

(w) 2 Lev. 252; 1 Campb. 466; 4 Bing. 75, 287; when not, *id.* 283; Mayor of Stafford v. Till, 1 Moore, 260; Mayor of Carmarthen v. Lewis, 6 Car. & P. 608; 4 Bar. & Cres. 962, 968; 7 D. & R. 376, 381, S.C.

(x) 2 C. & P. 395.

(y) 2 Wils. 321; 3 Wils. 354.

(z) 1 Campb. 360; 1 T. R. 386.

(275) { *Aliter*, in Pennsylvania, Evans v. Tatem, 9 Serg. & Rawle, 252. See Dubois v. Dubois, 6 Cow. Rep. 494. }

(276) { See also Atwater v. Fowler, 1 Hall's Rep. 181. }

(277) But it has been decided in some late cases in this country, that assumpsit would lie against a corporation, even on an implied promise. Danforth v. Schoharie Turnp. Co., 12 Johns. Rep. 227. Bank of Columbia v Patterson's Adm'r. in Sup. Court of U. S. 5 Hall's L. J. 489, cited 12 Johns. Rep. 231, S. C. 7 Cranch, 299. Hayden and another v. Middlesex Turnp. Corporation, 10 Mass. Rep. 397. Dunn v. Rector, &c. of St. Andrew's Church, 14 Johns. Rep. 118. } Overseers of N. Whitehall v. Overseers of S. Whitehall, 3 Serg. & Rawle, 117. Ellis v. Merrimack Bridge, 2 Pick. Rep 243. Poultney v. Wells, 1 Aiken's (Vermont) Rep. 180. Savings Bank v. Davis, 8 Conn. Rep. 202, and the cases there cited. } A special action of assumpsit will lie against a bank for refusing to transfer stock. The King v. Bank of England, 2 Doug. 524. Shipley and others v. Mechanics' Bank, 10 Johns. Rep. 484. See also Gray v. Portland Bank, 3 Mass. Rep. 364. An insurance company may make a valid promissory note, which will be held good until the contrary be shown. Barker v. Mechanics' Fire Ins. Co., 3 Wend. R. 94. But a note by which J. F., as president of an insurance company, promises to pay a sum certain, is not the note of the company, but of the maker alone. *ib.*

(278) An action of assumpsit will lie against a corporation upon simple contracts of its authorized agents, when acting within the scope of the legitimate purposes of such corporations. Mott v. Hicks, 1 Cowen, 513.

(279) See 3 Serg. & Rawle, 501. Wharton v. Fitzgerald. 3 Dall. 503. Polt v. Lesher, 1 Yeates, 576. Stockett v. Watkins' Adm., 2 Gilb. & Johns. Rep. 327. Featherstonhaugh v. Bradshaw, 1 Wend. Rep. 134. Nor can it be supported against a person who has entered under a contract to purchase, which he has refused to perform, but he should be sued for the mesne profits. Smith v. Stewart, 7 Johns. Rep. 46. Nor to recover the value of sand taken from a sand-bar in another State, to which both parties claimed title, and sold by the defendant. Baker v. Howell, 6 Serg. & Rawle, 476.

I. ASSUMPSIT. between the parties; but the plaintiff must declare in ejectment or trespass (a)(280). Nor is assumpsit the proper remedy in the case of a deceitful representation, not embodied in, or noticed on the face of, a written contract between the parties; but the [*122] *remedy should be case for the fraud (b). But where the defendant in selling a horse refused to warrant it, and yet said that it was "sound, as far as he knew," it was held, that he was liable in assumpsit, on proof negativing the soundness, and showing that the defendant knew the horse was unsound, and that it was not necessary to declare in case for the deceitful representation (c). The cases in which the plaintiff may waive a tort or trespass and declare in assumpsit, have been already adverted to (d). It is not judicious to adopt this form of action where the plaintiff may declare in tort in cases where, by suing *ex contractu*, the right of set-off may attach (e). And if goods be obtained under a fraudulent contract, giving the purchaser a specified credit, although the vendor may disaffirm the contract, and maintain trover before the expiration of the credit, yet he cannot, during the prescribed period, maintain assumpsit for goods sold (f)(281). And where the debt is small, and it is important to avoid the expense and delay of executing a writ of inquiry, it is judicious to declare in debt.

Declaration, &c. The *Declaration* in this action must, except in the instances of bills of exchange, promissory notes, and checks, disclose the consideration upon which the contract was founded, the contract itself, whether express or implied, and the breach thereof (g); and damages should be laid sufficient to cover the real amount; and Reg. Gen. H. T. 4 W. 4, prohibits more than *one count* upon the same transaction. The most general *plea* was non assumpsit, that the defendant did not undertake and promise as alleged by the plaintiff, and under which the defendant might formerly give in evidence most matters of defence. But now the Reg. Gen. H. T. 4 W. 4, wholly abolishes the plea of non assumpsit in some actions, and greatly narrows its utility in others, as will be fully shown in the chapter on pleas, where the rules with regard to the *form* and application of pleas in this action will be fully noticed.

The *judgment* in favor of the plaintiff is, that he recover a specified sum, assessed by a jury, or on reference to the master, for his damages which he hath sustained by reason of the defendant's non-performance of his promises and undertakings; and for full *costs* of suit, to which the plaintiff is in all cases entitled in this action, though the damages recovered be under 40s., unless the judge certify to take away costs under the statute (h); or unless the plaintiff ought to have proceeded for the recovery of the debt in some inferior [*123] Court established by virtue of an act *of parliament, which deprives a party suing elsewhere of the right to costs. In some cases the superior Courts will stay the proceedings where the debt sued for is under 40s., and the plaintiff may recover it in an inferior Court (i).

(a) 1 T. R. 378, 386, 387; Lord Raym. 1216; Bac. Ab. Assumpsit, A.; 2 Stra. 1239; 1 Campb. 360.
(b) 4 Campb. 22, 144, 169; 12 East, 11.
(c) 4 C. & P. 45.
(d) *Ante*, 113, 114.
(e) *Ibid.*
(f) 9 B. & C. 59.
(g) Bac. Ab. Assumpsit, F.
(h) 43 Eliz. c. 6.
(i) Tidd, 9th edit. 516.

(280) Vide Cummings and wife v. Noyes, 10 Mass. Rep. 435, 436.
(281) Vide Bailey and Bogert v. Freeman, 4 Johns. Rep. 283. See Edgerton v. Edgerton, 8 Conn. Rep. 6.

II. DEBT.

This action is so called because it is in legal consideration for the recovery of a *debt* (282) *eo nomine* and *in numero;* and though *damages* are in general awarded for the detention of the debt, yet in most instances they are merely nominal, and are not, as in assumpsit and covenant, the principal object of the suit, and though this distinction may now be considered as merely technical, where the contract on which the action is founded is for the payment of money, yet in many instances we shall find it material to be attended to (*k*). II. DEBT.

Debt is, in some respects, a more extensive remedy for the recovery of money than assumpsit or covenant; for *assumpsit* is not sustainable upon a specialty, and *covenant* does not lie upon a contract not under seal; whereas *debt* lies to recover money due upon legal liabilities (*l*); or upon simple contracts, express or implied (*m*), whether verbal or written; and upon contracts under seal (*n*); or of record (*o*)(283); and on statutes by a party grieved, or by a common informer; whenever the demand is for a sum certain, or is capable of being readily reduced to a certainty (*p*)(284). It may be supported on a contract to pay so much per load for wood, the quantity of which was not then ascertained; or on a *quantum meruit* (*q*) for work; or to pay a proportion of the costs of a suit expected to be incurred (*r*); or to recover the treble value of tithes not set out according to the statute (*s*). But it is not sustainable when the demand is rather for unliquidated *damages than for money (*t*); unless the performance of the contract were secured by a penalty, in which case debt may be supported for the penalty, and the real demand is to be ascertained according to the provisions of the 8 & 9 W. 3, c. 11. Debt also lies in the *detinet* for goods, as upon a contract to deliver a quantity of malt; which action differs from that of detinue in respect of the property in any specific goods, not being necessarily vested in the plaintiff at the time the action is brought, which is essential in detinue (*u*). IN GENERAL. [*124]

On *simple contracts* and *legal liabilities* (*x*) debt lies to recover money lent, paid, had and received, and due on an account stated (*y*); for interest due on ON SIMPLE CONTRACTS.

(*k*) 1 H. Bl. 550; Bul. N. P. 167; Cowp. 588.

(*l*) Hob. 206; Com. Dig. Debt, A. 1.

(*m*) Hob. 206; Bul. N. P. 167; Com. Dig. Debt, A. 9.

(*n*) *Id. ibid.*

(*o*) *Id. ibid.*

(*p*) Bul. N. P. 167; 3 Lev. 429; Sir T. Jones, 104; Ld. Raym. 814; 2 Stra. 1089; Dougl. 6; 2 T. R. 29.

(*q*) It has been doubted whether debt lies upon a *quantum meruit;* and of late it has been usual to omit the *quantum meruit* count in debt.

(*r*) 3 Lev. 429.

(*s*) Lord Raym. 682; 1 Rol. Ab. 598, pl. 19.

(*t*) *Ante*, 123, n. (*p*); Ld. Raym. 1040; 2 Saund. 62 b.

(*u*) Dyer, 24 b; Com. Dig. Debt, A. 5; Bac. Ab. Debt, F.; 3 Woodd. 103, 104.

(*x*) *Ante*, 123.

(*y*) Com. Dig. Debt, A.; 1 Rol. Ab. 593, pl. 25; Hob. 207.

(282) For the ancient law respecting this action, vide 1 Reeve's Hist. E. L. 158, 159. 2 Reeve's Hist. E. L. 252, 262, 329, 333. 3 Reeve's Hist. E. L. 58, 65. 5 Pet. S.C. R. 150.

(283) See Republica *v.* Lacaze et al, 2 Dall. 123.

(284) U. States *v.* Colt, 1 Peters' Rep. 147. So, where the plaintiff's land has been taken by a turnpike company in order to make their road, and the damages have been assessed according to the provisions of the act, debt will lie for the sum assessed, if no other specific remedy were provided by the act. Bigelow *v.* Cambridge Turn. Co., 7 Mass. Rep. 202. Gedney *v.* Inhabitants of Tewksbury, 3 Mass. Rep. 309, 310.

II. DEBT. the loan or forbearance of money (*z*); for work and labor (*a*); for fees (*b*); for goods sold (*c*); and for use and occupation (*d*) (285). It is sustainable for any debt or duty created by common law or custom (*e*), as on a bill of exchange (286), by the payee against the drawer, on the default of the acceptor, or by the drawer against the acceptor of a bill of exchange, expressed to be for value received (*f*); and by first indorsee against first indorser, who was also the drawer of a bill payable to his own order (*g*) (287); and on a promissory note by the payee against the maker, when shown to have been drawn for value received (*h*); but not by or against any other collateral party (*i*); and for tolls, port duties, and copyhold fines (*k*); and for quit rent (*l*). And it lies on an award to pay money (288), but not if it were to perform any other act, unless there were an arbitration bond, in which case the action must be brought thereon (*m*). It lies also on by-laws (*n*), for fines and amerciaments (*o*) (289), on English judgments not of record (*p*) (290), as well as on [*125] such as are of record, on an *Irish judgment (*q*), and on foreign judgments (*r*) (291), and upon the decree of a Colonial Court for payment of a balance due on a partnership account (*s*) (292). Debt clearly lies against a corporation for the recovery of a debt in those cases in which assumpsit may be maintained against them (*t*), and in all those instances in which they contract by deed to pay money. And even assuming that a corporation cannot in

(*z*) 5 T. R. 553.

(*a*) Com. Dig. Debt, B.

(*b*) Bac. Ab. Debt, A; 1 Rol. Ab. 598; Com. Dig. Pleader, 2 W. 11.

(*c*) 2 T. R. 28.

(*d*) 5 Taunt. 25; 6 T. R. 62; 6 East, 348.

(*e*) Com. Dig. Debt, A. 9; Hob. 206.

(*f*) 3 D. & R. 165; 1 B. & C. 674, S. C.

(*g*) 3 Price, 253.

(*h*) Creswell *v.* Crisp, 2 Dowl. 635; Lyons *v.* Cohen, 3 Dowl. 243; Priddy *v.* Henbrey, 1 Barn. & Cres. 674; 3 Dowl. & Ryl. 165; and *post*, 2 vol. 6th ed. 251, 252.

(*i*) 1 Taunt. 540; 2 B. & P. 78; Chitty on Bills, 7th edit. 428; 2 Campb. 187, n. (*a*); *ante*, 116, 117.

(*k*) Com. Dig. Debt, A. 9.

(*l*) 5 Wentw. 152, 153.

(*m*) 2 Saund. 62, n. 5; Burr. 278; Salk. 72; Lord Raym. 715; Str. 923.

(*n*) 1 B. & P. 98.

(*o*) Cro. Eliz. 581; Bul. N. P. 167; 1 Hen. Bla. 162; Rep. temp. Hard. 116; Hob. 206.

(*p*) 1 Saund. 92. n. 2.

(*q*) 3 Taunt. 85. Assumpsit is also maintainable, 4 B. & C. 411; 6 D. & R. 471, S. C.

(*r*) 3 East, 221; Doug. 1; 4 Bing. 686; *ante*, 120.

(*s*) 8 B. & C. 16; 2 M. & R. 153, S. C.

(*t*) *Ante*, 121.

(285) { Davis *v.* Shoemaker, 1 Rawle, 135. } Vide 3 Reeve's Hist. E. L. 64.

(286) Vide 1 Cranch, Appendix, 462, 465.

(287) It is said that, in Maryland, such an action cannot be sustained. Lindo *v.* Gardner, 1 Cranch, 343. Since the statute making promissory notes negotiable, the legal operation and effect of the transfer is, that the money due upon the note to the original payee is due from the maker to the assignee or holder, and that in judgment of law there is privity of contract between the maker and indorsee or holder by the terms of the note and the operation of the statute. Accordingly, an action of debt on a promissory note may be maintained by an indorsee against the maker. Wilmarth *v.* Crawford, 10 Wend. R. 340.

(288) Stanley *v.* Chappel, 8 Cowen R. 235. And debt on an award of money will lie, without regard to the penalty of the bond. Ex parte Wallis, 7 Cowen, 522.

(289) { But debt will not lie on a judgment for damages obtained under the act of the 6th of April, 1802, (Purd. Dig. 621,) "to enable purchasers at sheriffs' and coroners' sales to obtain possession." The remedy prescribed by the act can alone be pursued. Moyer *v.* Kirby, 14 Serg. & Rawle, 162. }

(290) Pease *v.* Howard, 14 J. R. 479. Bennet *v.* Moody, 2 Hall's N. Y. R. 471.

(291) Hubbell *v.* Cowdrey, 5 J. R. 132. Andrews *v.* Montgomery, 19 ib. 162. Mills *v.* Duryee, 7 Cranch, 481.

(292) Debt lies on the decree of a court of chancery, in another State, for the payment, by the defendant, of money only, without any acts to be done by the plaintiff. Post and La Rue *v.* Neafie, 3 Caines' Rep. 22. { Evans *v.* Tatem, 9 Serg. & Rawle, 252. }

general contract but by deed, the Court will presume on general demurrer that there was a deed, in order to support a count in debt that the corporation was "indebted," &c. (*u*). And it is laid down as a general rule, that debt lies upon every contract in deed or in law (*x*). And now by express enactment, debt on simple contract is sustainable against an executor in any court of law (*y*). II. DEBT.

ON SPECIALTIES.

Debt lies also to recover money due on any *specialty*, or contract under seal to pay money (*z*), as on single bonds (*a*), on charter-parties (*b*), on policies of insurance under seal (*c*) (293), and on bonds conditioned for the payment of money, or for the performance of any other act, by or against the parties thereto and their personal representatives (*d*), and against the heir of the obligor, if he be expressly named in the deed, or against a devisee having legal assets (*e*), and by the sheriff or his assignee on bail bonds (*f*)(294), and replevin bonds (*g*), on eases for rent or penalties, as for ploughing up meadow, &c. (*h*), on annuity deeds, and on mortgage deeds. An action of debt is not sustainable against the assignee of *part* of land demised (*i*). Debt is the remedy given by the statute (*k*) to the executor of a tenant in fee or for life, to recover rent which accrued due to the testator, and to husbands to recover rent which became due to them and their wives, for rents of the wives' freeholds during the life of the wives. Debt is also sustainable for a rent-charge or annuity granted for years, or by the executors of a tenant for life of a rent-charge, or of a tenant *pur autre vie* after the death of **cestui qui vie* (*l*). [*126] But it should seem that no action can be supported at law for the arrears of an annuity, unless it be granted by deed, and there must be an express grant in such deed (*m*). And debt is not sustainable for the arrears of an annuity or yearly rent devised, payably out of lands to A. during the life of B., to whom the lands are devised for life, B. paying the same thereout, so long as the estate of freehold continues (*n*); and this although it is not stated in the declaration that the grantor had a freehold in the premises out of which it was payable, as it must be inferred that he had such an interest, where nothing appears to the contrary (*o*). The reason assigned is, that the law will not *suffer a real injury* to be remedied by an action merely personal; neither does the action lie by the statute 8 Anne (*p*), for that statute applies only to cases of

(*u*) 4 B. & C. 962; 7 D. & R. 376.
(*x*) Com. Dig. Debt, A. 1; 1 M'Clel. & Y. 457.
(*y*) 3 & 4 W. 4, c. 42, s. 14.
(*z*) 2 Stra. 1089; 12 East, 583.
(*a*) Com. Dig. Debt, A. 4; Stra. 1089; 1 T. R. 40.
(*b*) Stra. 1089; 1 New Rep. 104.
(*c*) Marsh. on Ins. 596; 6 G. 1, c. 18, s. 4.
(*d*) Com. Dig. Debt, A. 4; *post*, vol. ii.
(*e*) Bac. Ab. Heir; 7 East, 128.
(*f*) 4 Ann. c. 16, s. 20.
(*g*) 11 Geo. 2, c. 19.
(*h*) Com. Dig. Debt, A. 5, B.; 3 Bla. Com. 231; 1 New Rep. 104, 109.
(*i*) Curtis *v*. Spitley, 1 Bing. N. C. 759; but the landlord must proceed by distress, *id. ibid.*; or by action of covenant, *id.*; Longham *v*. King, Cro. Car. 221.
(*k*) 32 Hen. 8, c. 36.
(*l*) 1 Saund. 282, note 1, 276.
(*m*) 2 D & R. 603; 14 Ves. 491.
(*n*) 4 M. & Sel. 113; 2 Saund. 304, note 8.
(*o*) 6 Moore, 335; 3 B. & B. 30, S. C.
(*p*) 8 Ann. c. 14.

(293) Judgment reversed where an action of *assumpsit* had been brought against an Insurance Company on a policy sealed with their corporate seal. Marine Insurance Company of Alexandria *v*. Young, 1 Cranch, 332.

(294) {It seems to be doubtful whether *debt* will lie on a bail bond in Massachusetts. See Lane *v*. Smith, 2 Pick. Rep. 231.}

II. DEBT. demises from landlord to tenant (q). The assignee of a rent reserved upon a lease, may maintain debt for the arrears (r).

ON RECORDS. This action also lies on *records*, as upon the *judgment* of a superior or inferior Court of record (s), either generally, or against an executor or administrator, suggesting a devastavit (t). Although the judgment was erroneous, debt lies until it has been reversed (u); and the mere circumstance of the defendant having been rendered, will not bar the action. Where, however, the defendant has been charged in execution on the judgment, no action can be supported on the judgment; although he was discharged out of custody upon a promise to pay the sum recovered by instalments, and which he neglects to do (x). And where the defendant has been discharged out of custody under the Lord's Act, debt is not sustainable (y); and an action upon a judgment has become less frequent since the statute (z) which precludes the plaintiff from recovering costs in an action on a judgment, unless the Court or one of the judges thereof shall otherwise direct (a). It appears that debt lies upon [*127] *the judgment or decree of a colonial or foreign Court, &c. (b) in those instances in which assumpsit is maintainable upon them, and which have been already alluded to (c). Debt is often brought upon a recognizance of bail (d), and the remedy by *scire facias* is also frequently adopted. Upon the proceeding by *scire facias*, the bail are not liable to the costs of the *scire facias*, unless they appear and plead thereto (e); nor are damages for detaining the debt recoverable (f). And it appears therefore judicious to proceed by action upon the recognizance in ordinary cases (g). So debt lies upon a *statute merchant*, though not upon a statute staple, because the seal of the party is not affixed to the latter; but it lies on a recognizance in the *nature* of a *statute staple*, to which the seal of the conusor is affixed (h). It lies also on a *sheriff's return* of *fieri feci*, which is in the nature of a record, to recover the money which he has received (i).

ON STATUTES. Debt is frequently the remedy on *statutes* either at the suit of the party grieved, or of a common informer (k). In some cases it is given to the *party grieved*, by the express words of a statute, as for an *escape out* of execution (l); though not for an escape out of custody under an attachment for non-payment of costs under a decree in equity (m) (295); or against a tenant for double value for not quitting in pursuance of a notice to quit given by his

(q) 4 M. & Sel. 113.
(r) 5 B. & C. 512.
(s) Gilb. Debt, 391, 392; Salk. 209; Com. Dig. Debt, A. 2.
(t) 1 Saund. 216, 218, 219, n. 7, 8; 6 Mod. 306; 3 East, 2.
(u) 2 Lev. 161; 1 Marsh. 284; 5 Taunt. 667.
(x) 4 Burr. 2482; 5 M. & Sel. 103. *Qu.* if the defendant died in execution, *id.* 104.
(y) 32 Geo. 2, c. 28, s. 20.
(z) 43 Geo. 3, c. 46, s. 4.
(a) When such costs will be allowed, see Tidd Prac, 9th ed. 969.
(b) See 4 B. & Cres. 418; 6 D. & R. 474, S. C.; 3 Taunt. 85; 9 Price, 1.
(c) *Ante*, 121.
(d) *Post*, vol. ii.; Gilb. Debt, 395.
(e) See 8 & 9 W. 3, c. 11, s. 3; 3 B. & P. 14.
(f) 3 Burr. 1791.
(g) See Tidd, 9th edit. 1100.
(h) 2 Saund. 60, 70, in notis; Com. Dig. Debt, A. 3.
(i) 2 Saund. 343, 344, note 2; 2 Show. 79; Hob. 206.
(k) Com. Dig. Action on Statute, E.; Bac. Ab. Debt, A.
(l) 1 Ric 2, c. 12; 1 Saund. 34, 35, 39, 218; Com. Dig. Debt, A.
(m) Blower v. Hollis, Cromp. & M. 93.

(295) { Koones v. Maddox, 2 Harr. & Gill, 106. }

landlord (n). And if a statute prohibit the doing an act under a penalty or forfeiture to be paid to a party grieved, and do not prescribe any mode of recovery, it may be recovered in this form of action (o)(296); as treble the value of tithes not duly set forth (p), or treble the amount of damages incurred by extortion (q). Where a statute, incorporating a gas company, provided that the expenses of obtaining the act should be first paid out of the subscriptions, it was held, that the attornies who obtained the act might recover their costs in an action of debt founded upon the statute (r). On the other hand, upon a new statute, which prescribes a particular remedy, no remedy *can be taken but that particular remedy given by the act. Therefore no action of debt will lie for a poor's rate (s); and surveyors of highways cannot maintain debt to recover composition money duly assessed in lieu of statute-duty, the remedy by distress being prescribed by the Acts of Parliament (t). Where a *penal* statute expressly gives the whole or a part of a penalty to a *common informer*, and enables him generally to sue for the same, debt is sustainable (u); and he need not declare *qui tam* unless where a penalty is given for a contempt (x); but if there be no express provision enabling an informer to sue, debt cannot be supported in his name for the recovery of the penalty (y). [*128]

When the peculiar remedy.

In some cases this action is the *peculiar* remedy, as against a lessee for an apportionment of rent, where he has been evicted from part of the premises by a third person; though covenant is in such case sustainable against the assignee of the lessee (z). It is also the only remedy against a devisee of land, for a breach of covenant by the devisor (a).

When not sustainable.

Debt, however, is not in any case sustainable, unless the demand be for a sum certain, or for a pecuniary demand which can readily be reduced to a certainty, as in the instances before enumerated (b); nor could it be supported against an executor, on a simple contract made with the testator, unless in the Court of Exchequer (c), or in those cases in which the testator, if living, could not have waged his law (d), though if the executor pleaded, and did not demur, he could not afterwards object to the form of action (e); and an executor might be sued in debt upon a simple contract which he had entered into in his representative capacity (f); and now by 3 & 4 W. 4, c. 42, s. 14,

(n) 4 Geo. 2, c. 28, s. 1; 1 New Rep. 174.
(o) 1 Rol. Ab. 598, pl. 18, 19; 1 M. & Y. 457.
(p) *Id. ibid.*; 1 Ld. Raym. 682; *post*, vol. ii.
(q) 2 Bla. Rep. 1101.
(r) 4 B. & C. 962; 7 D. & R. 376, S. C.
(s) *Per* Dennison, J., 2 Burr. 1157.
(t) 1 M'Clel. & Y. 450.
(u) Com. Dig. Action, Debt, E. 1, 2.
(x) *Id. ibid.*; 2 Saund. 374, n. 1, 2; 1 Saund. 136, n. 1.
(y) 5 East, 313, 315; Stra. 828; Bac. Ab. Action, Qui *tam*, A.
(z) 2 East, 579, 580.
(a) 7 East, 12.
(b) *Ante*, 123, 124.
(c) 1 New Rep. 293; Plowd. 182; 9 Co. 86 b.; 1 Saund. 63, 216, 286; 2 Saund. 74, n. 2; *ante*, 116, 117. But no third person can object; 1 Marsh. 280; 5 Taunt. 665; 3 B. & C. 317.
(d) 1 Saund. 216 a, note 4; 9 Co. 87 b.
(e) Plowd. 182; 1 Marsh. 72; 5 Taunt. 335, 665, S. C.; 3 B. & C. 317.
(f) 5 Bing. 200.

(296) { But *one* penalty can be recovered against a justice of the peace under the "supplement to the act for preventing clandestine marriages," passed the 14th day of February, 1729-30. (Purd. Dig. 540.) Hill *v.* Williams, 14 Serg. & Rawle, 287. } Under a penal statute only one penalty is recoverable for one offence or entire transaction. Corporation of New York *v.* Ordrenan, 12 Johns. Rep. 122. If the partyhas no other right than what is derived from the statute, his remedy also must be under the statute. Almy *v.* Harris, 5 Johns. Rep. 175.

II. DEBT. it is enacted, "that an action of debt on simple contract shall be maintainable in any Court of common law against any executor or administrator. Debt cannot be supported for a debt payable by instalments till the whole of [*129] them be due (*g*); though for rent payable quarterly, or otherwise, or *for an annuity, or on a stipulation to pay £10 on one day, and £10 on another, debt lies on each default (*h*); and even where one sum is payable by instalments, if the payment be secured by a penalty, debt is sustainable for such penalty (*i*)(297). When the landlord has accepted rent from the assignee of a lessee, he cannot sustain debt against the lessee or his personal representative, but must proceed by action of covenant on the express contract (*k*); and debt is not sustainable on a *collateral contract*, as on a promise to pay the debt of another in consideration of forbearance, &c. (*l*), nor against the indorser of a bill or note, or by an indorsee against the acceptor (*m*); and it seems questionable whether it is sustainable in any case upon a note or bill, unless on the face of it it appears that it was given for value received (*n*). But it may be supported by the drawer against the acceptor of a bill of exchange, payable to the drawer or his order, for value received in goods (*o*).

Of wager of law and other difficulties and advantages.

Formerly, when the trial by wager of law was in practice, the action of assumpsit was preferable to that of debt on simple contract (*p*). That mode of defence and trial was in general in force when the debt was due on a simple verbal contract (*q*)(298), and it might have been adopted (except in the Exchequer, or when the creditor had become so by legal necessity, as in the case of a debt to a gaoler, or innkeeper, &c. for fees)(*r*); but of late it was so much disused and discountenanced (*s*)(299), that debt had become very frequent, and was preferable in some respects to the action of assumpsit, the judgment therein being final in the first instance, and not interlocutory as in assumpsit. And at length the 3 & 4 W. 4, c. 42, sect. 13, enacts "that no wager of law shall hereafter be allowed." It was once considered that in an action of debt

(*g*) 1 Hen. Bla. 554; 2 Saund. 303, n. 6; 3 Co 22 a.; Selw. N. P. 531, n.; *ante*, 116, 117; Bac. Ab 669.

(*h*) *Id. ibid.*

(*i*) 8 & 9 Wm. 3, c. 11; Bac. Ab. Debt, B.; 1 Wils. 80; Com. Dig. Action, F.

(*k*) *Ante*, 55; 1 Saund. 241. 242, n 5; 2 Saund. 181, 182, 297, n. 1, 303. n. 5, 306; Bac. Ab. Debt, D.; Com. Dig. Debt; 4 Taunt. 642.

(*l*) Hardr. 486; Com. Dig D.bt, B; 2 B. & P. 83; Cro. Car. 107, 193; 1 Salk. 23.

(*m*) 2 B. & P. 78.

(*n*) Creswell *v.* Crisp, 2 Dowl. 635; Lyons *v.* Cohen, 3 Dowl. 243; *ante*, 124.

(*o*) 1 B. & C. 674; 3 D. & R. 165, S. C.

(*p*) 3 Bla. Com. 347.

(*q*) 3 Bla. Com 347; Barry *v.* Robinson, 1 New Rep. 293; 4 D. & R. 207; King *v.* Williams, 3 Bar. & Cres. 538.

(*r*) 3 Bla Com. 345, 346; 1 Saund. 216 a. n. 1; 9 Co. 87 b.

(*s*) 4 D. & R. 206.

(297) It has been held that where the condition of a bond was for the payment of interest annually, and the principal at a distant day, the interest might be recovered before the principal was due, by an action of debt on the bond. Sparks *v.* Garrigues, 1 Binn. 152.

(298) By the *act for the amendment of the law*, wager of law is abolished in every case except that of non summons in real actions. Laws N. Y. sess. 36. c. 56. s. 24.—1 R. L. 524. {It still exists as part of the law of Pennsylvania, 1 Binn. 543; and there are other recognitions of its existence to be found in various Acts of Assembly, which provide that in certain actions it shall not be admitted. See 8th sec. of the Act of 18th Feb. 1785, [*habeas corpus*] 2 Sm. Laws, 275; and sect. 9 of the Act of 22d April, 1794, [*vice*, &c.] 3 Sm. Laws, 182.—10 Serg & Rawle, 321, 322.—See, however, Childress *v.* Emory, 8 Wheat. Rep. 612, denying the doctrine of Barry *v.* Robinson, 1 New Rep. 293.}

(299) {In a recent instance, however, a defendant succeeded in forcing the plaintiff to abandon his action, by having recourse to it. King *v.* Williams, 2 Barn. & Cressw. 538.}

the plaintiff could not in any case recover less than the sum demanded (*t*); and that if the plaintiff could not, upon the *indebitatus* or *quantum meruit* count, prove that he was entitled to recover the precise sum alleged to be due, he must be nonsuited. It is, however, now completely settled, that the plaintiff may, in debt on simple *contract, prove and recover less than the sum stated to be due in his declaration (*u*)(300); for the difference is, that where debt is brought upon a covenant to pay a sum certain, a variance in the statement of the sum mentioned in the deed will vitiate; but where the deed relates to the matter of fact, there, though the plaintiff demand more than is due, he may enter a *remittitur* (*x*).

II. DEBT. [*130]

Declarations, pleadings, &c.

The *declaration* in this action, if on *simple* contract, must show the consideration on which the contract was founded, precisely as in assumpsit; and should state either a legal liability, or an express *agreement;* but it must be alleged that the defendant *agreed*, not that he *promised*, to pay the debt, &c. (*y*). But on *specialties*, or *records*, no consideration need be shown, unless where the performance of the consideration constitutes a condition precedent, when performance of such consideration must be averred; and where the action is founded on a deed, it must be declared upon, except in the instance of debt for rent (*z*). If the declaration go for damages for detention of the sum *expressly* agreed to be paid, as for interest, *the damages at the conclusion* must be proportionably increased and not as usual be merely nominal (*a*). The plea of the general issue to debt on simple contracts, or on statutes, or where the deed was only matter of inducement, was formerly *nil debet.* But now, by reg. gen. Hil. T. 4 W. 4, the plea of *nil debet* is abolished, and it is ordered that in actions of debt on simple contract, other than on bills of exchange and promissory notes, the defendant may plead "that he *never was* indebted in manner and form as in the declaration alleged," &c. (*b*). In debt on specialty, the plea denying the execution of the deed set out in the declaration, is *non est factum* (*c*); and to debt on record, *nul tiel record;* and as those pleas merely deny the existence of the deed, or record, most matters or grounds of defence must *now* in debt on a deed be specially pleaded. The pleadings in debt will be fully noticed in subsequent parts of the work. The *judgment* in the plaintiff's favor, which at common law is final, in all cases is, that the plaintiff recover his debt, and, in general, nominal damages for the detention thereof; and in cases under the 8 & 9 W. 3, c. 11, it may also be awarded, that the plaintiff have execution for the damages sustained by the breach of a bond, conditioned for the performance of covenants; and the plaintiff, unless in some penal and other particular actions, is in general entitled to full *costs* of suit, although the damages recovered be under 40*s*. (*d*); unless the judge certify under the statute (*e*).

(*t*) 3 Bla. Com. 155; 2 Sir W. Bla. 1221; 2 T. R. 28; Bul. N. P. 171; Stra. 1089.

(*u*) 1 Hen. Bla. 249, 550; Dougl. 6; 11 East, 62.

(*x*) *Per* Holt, C. J., 2 Lord Raym. 816.

(*y*) 2 T. R. 28, 30; 12 Mod. 511; 3 B. & A. 208; 2 Smith, 618; 2 B. & P. 78; *post.*

(*z*) 1 New Rep 104.

(*a*) Watkins *v.* Morgan, 6 Car. & P. 661.

(*b*) *Post*, chapter on Pleas.

(*c*) 2 Lord Raym. 1500.

(*d*) Tidd's Prac. 9th ed. 945, 963, 984.

(*e*) 43 Eliz. c. 6.

(300) {Newlin *v.* Palmer, 11 Serg. & Rawle, 100. United States *v.* Colt, Peters' Rep. 145.} Where a penalty of double the value of a specific article, was given by statute to a common informer, it was held that the plaintiff might recover in debt less than the sum stated in the declaration. Perrin *v.* Sikes, 1 Day's Rep. 19.

*III. COVENANT.

III. COVENANT. — In general. The rules respecting this action are few and simple. It is a remedy provided by law for the recovery of *damages* for the breach of a *covenant* or contract under seal (*g*). It cannot be maintained except against a person who, by himself, or some other person acting on his behalf, has executed a deed under seal, or who, under some very peculiar circumstances, which will be noticed hereafter (*h*), has agreed by deed to do a certain thing (*i*). In the case of a covenant under seal, action of covenant may be supported, whether such covenant be contained in a deed-poll or indenture (*k*); or be *express or implied by law from the terms of the deed* (*l*) (301); or be for the performance of something *in futuro*, or that something has been done (*m*). In some cases it is sustainable, although the covenant relate to matter *in presenti*, as that the covenantor is seised and *hath* good title (*n*): though it is said, that in general covenant will not lie on a contract *in presenti*, as on a covenant to stand seised; or that a certain horse is yours; or shall henceforth be the property of another (*o*). It is not essential that the word "covenant" should be in the instrument, in order to render the defendant liable in covenant (*p*); nor is it material that the covenantee has not executed the deed (*q*). It would be foreign to the present inquiry, relating merely to the application of the remedy, to examine into the nature and description of the different covenants, which are to be found in the works referred to in the note (*r*).

Implied for title, 6 Bing. 656.

[*132] On what particular deeds and covenants it lies. *Covenant is the usual remedy upon indentures of apprenticeship, against the master for not instructing his apprentice, or against the party who covenanted for the due service of such apprentice, but it will not lie against an infant apprentice (*s*) (302). It lies also on articles of agreement under seal (*t*), or deeds of separate maintenance (*u*); and on covenants in deeds of conveyance, &c. for good title, &c. (*x*); on charter-parties of affreightment (*y*); on

(*g*) 2 Lord Raym. 1536; F. N. B. 145; Cro. Jac. 508; Com. Dig. Pleader, 2 V. 2, Covenant, A. 1.
(*h*) *Post*, 134.
(*i*) 5 B. & C. 602.
(*k*) 1 Rol. Ab. 517, pl. 40; Com. Dig. Covenant, A 1.
(*l*) Com. Dig. Covenant, A. 2; 6 Moore, 199, 202, note a.; 1 Bing. 433; 9 B & C. 505; 1 C. & J. 105, S. C.
(*m*) Com. Dig. Covenant, A. 1; Bac. Ab. Covenant, A.; Plowd. 308; 6 Bing. 666. What is considered an *implied* covenant, so as to render this the proper remedy, see 12 East, 179, 182; 13 East, 63, 71, 74; Platt on Cov. 46, &c.; Index, *Id.* Implied Covenant. Covenant on the word "demise" in a lease, 5 B. & Cres. 609; 4 Taunt. 329; 6 Bing. 666; *ante*, 58.
(*n*) 3 Woodd. 85, 86; 2 B. & P. 13; 2 Saund. 181 b.; 4 M. & Sel. 53; 6 Bing. 656.
(*o*) Plowd. 308; Finch, 49 b.; Com. Dig. Covenant, A. 1; Vin. Ab. Covenant, A. pl. 6, G. 3; Platt on Cov. 3.
(*p*) 6 Moore, 203.
(*q*) *Post*, 135.
(*r*) Selw. N. P. Covenant; Com. Dig. Covenant, A. 2, 3, 4; Bac. Ab. Covenant; Platt on Cov.
(*s*) Cro. Car. 179.
(*t*) 3 Swanst. 647.
(*u*) 2 New Rep. 148.
(*x*) 2 Saund. 175, 178, 181; 2 B. & P. 13; 3 East, 491.
(*y*) 3 East, 233; 1 New Rep. 104; 12 East, 179, 578, 583; see 6 Moore, 415.

(301) As to implied covenants of title or warranty, see Frost and others *v.* Raymond, 2 Caines' Rep. 83. Kent *v.* Welch, 7 Johns. Rep. 258. Dorsey *v.* Jackman, 1 Serg. & Rawle, 42.
(302) Aliter in Pennsylvania, where the remedy is given by statute, and where an infant cannot be bound apprentice unless by an instrument under seal. Comm. *v.* Wiltbank, 10 Serg. & Rawle, 416.

policies of insurance under seal against fire, &c. (z); and on annuity and mortgage deeds; though debt in the last instances is in general preferable when the demand is for money; and it seems that covenant lies on a bond, for it proves an agreement (a). III. COVENANT.

An action of covenant is also the usual remedy on leases at the suit of the lessee, his executor or assignee, against the lessor, &c. for the breach of a covenant for quiet enjoyment, &c., and by the lessor, &c. against the lessee, &c. for non-payment of rent, not repairing, &c. ON LEASES.

At common law, upon the death of a lessor seised in fee, his heir might sue for a subsequent breach of a covenant running with the land, although not named in the lease (b); and the action of *debt* lay for the assignee of the reversion for *rent*, at common law (c); but no persons could formerly support an action of *covenant*, or take advantage of any covenant or condition, except such as were parties or privies thereto; and of course no grantee or assignee of any reversion or rent could maintain this form of action. To remedy this the statute 32 Hen. 8, c. 34 (303), gives the assignee of a reversion the same remedies against the lessee, or his assignee, or their personal representatives, upon covenants running with the land, as the lessor or his heir, or their successor, had at common law; and on the other hand, such assignee is liable by the statute to an action for a breach of covenant *running with the land, [*133] as the lessor, &c. was at common law (d). An assignee of *part* of the reversion (e), and a remainder-man (f), are within the statute. We have already observed, that *debt* is the remedy given by the 32 Hen. 8, c. 37, to executors of persons who were seised in fee, or for life, of property, to recover arrears of rent which accrued due to the testators; and to husbands, who survive their wives, to recover rents which became due in the life-time of the latter, in respect of their freehold property (304).

Where the demand is for rent or any other liquidated sum, the lessor has an election to proceed in debt, or covenant, against the *lessee*, unless he has accepted the assignee as his tenant, or the lessee has become bankrupt, in which case the action of debt is not in general sustainable; and the lessor can only sue the lessee, after such assignment, in covenant, and then only upon an *express* covenant, and not upon a covenant in law (g). On the other hand, as a personal contract cannot be apportioned, where there has been an eviction from a part of the land, even by a stranger, the *lessee* cannot be sued in

(z) 6 T. R. 710; 2 Marsh. 601, n. a, and 6 Geo. 1, c. 18; 6 Moore, 199 202. When the directors of an insurance company are not personally liable, 6 Moore, 199, 202, note.

(a) 1 Ch. Ca. 294; 3 Swanst. 618; 3 Lev. 119; Hard. 178; Com. Dig. Covenant, A. 2.

(b) 2 Lev. 92, and see the concluding words of the statute 32 H. 8, c. 34, s. 1.

(c) 1 Saund. 241 c.

(d) 8 Bla. Com. 158. See the observations on the Statute, Bac. Abr. Covenant, E. 5; Vin. Abr. Covenant, K. 3. As to the parties to sue and be sued, *ante*, 17, 55.

(e) 2 B. & Ald. 105; 4 B. & C. 157.

(f) 3 M. & Sel. 382.

(g) *Ante*, 55; 1 Saund. 241, n. 5; 1 T. R. 92; Cro. Jac. 523; Cullen, 392, 393.

(303) Vide Laws N. Y. sess. 36. c. 31. R. L. 363. { The *English* statute is in force in Pennsylvania, except such parts as relate to the king of England and his grantees. Roberts' Dig. 226. 3 Binn. 620. }

(304) { A warranty of lands, in a deed in fee, is the subject of a personal action of covenant against the executors of the warrantor, in New York and New Jersey. Townsend v. Morris et al., 6 Cow. Rep. 123. Chapman v. Holmes' Ex., 5 Halst. Rep. 20. }

III. COVENANT.

covenant, but only in debt; though a distress may be supported (*h*). With respect to the *assignee* of the lessee, the lessor may support debt (305), or covenant, at common law (*i*); and an assignee of a part of the premises may be sued in *covenant* (*k*), though not in *debt* (*l*), and it lies for an apportionment against the assignee of the lessee, in case of a partial eviction by a stranger, though we have seen that it is not in such case sustainable against the lessee (*m*).

It is a general rule, as before observed (*n*), that covenant lies upon an implied covenant, or a covenant in law; as on the word "demise," which amounts, in general, in the absence of an express covenant, to a stipulation for quiet enjoyment during the term; but we may remember that such implied covenant ceases with the estate of the covenantor, and will not furnish the
[*134] lessee with a remedy against the *executors of his lessor, if the latter were only tenant for life, and the remainder-man evict the lessee (*o*).

From the preceding observations, it appears that the action of covenant, being for the recovery of *damages* for the non-performance of a contract *under seal*, differs very materially from the actions of assumpsit and debt. Assumpsit, though for the recovery of damages, is not in general sustainable where the contract was originally under seal, or where a deed has been taken in satisfaction (*p*); and though debt is sustainable upon a simple contract, a specialty, a record, or a statute, yet it lies only for the recovery of a sum of money *in numero*, and not where the damages are unliquidated and incapable of being reduced by averment to a certainty (*q*); and though, where the object of the action of covenant is the recovery of a money demand, the distinction between the terms "damages" and "money *in numero*," may not on first view appear substantial, yet we shall find it material to be attended to (*r*). Covenant and debt are concurrent remedies for the recovery of any *money* demand, where there is an express or implied contract in an instrument under seal to pay it; but in general debt is the preferable remedy, as in that form of action the judgment is final in the first instance, if the defendant do not plead.

When the peculiar or best remedy.

Covenant is the *peculiar* remedy for the non-performance of a contract under seal, where the damages are unliquidated, and depend in amount on the opinion of a jury, in which case we have seen that neither debt or assumpsit can be supported (*s*). It is the proper remedy where an entire sum is by deed stipulated to be paid by instalments, and the whole is not due, nor the payment secured by a penalty (*t*)(306). And it is frequently more advisable to proceed in covenant on a lease, &c. for general damages than to declare in debt

(*h*) 2 East, 575; 2 M. & Sel. 277.
(*i*) 1 Saund. 241 c.; 3 Co. 22 b.; 2 East, 580.
(*k*) Congham *v.* King, Cro. Car. 221, cited 1 Bing. N. C. 758; Sir W. Jo. 245; 2 East, 580.
(*l*) Curtis *v.* Spitty, 1 Bing. N. C. 756.
(*m*) 2 East, 575; 2 M. & Sel. 277.
(*n*) *Ante*, 131.
(*o*) 6 Bing. 656; *ante*, 58.
(*p*) *Ante*, 111, 112.
(*q*) 3 Lev. 129; Bul. N. P. 167.
(*r*) *Rien in arrere* is a good plea in *debt* for rent, but not in *covenant*, because the latter action is for damages, Cowp. 588, 589.
(*s*) *Ante*, 111, 128, 129.
(*t*) Com. Dig. Action, F.; 2 Saund. 303, n. b.

(305) { Norton *v.* Vultee, 1 Hall's Rep. 384. }
(306) Vide Co. Litt. 292. Bac. Abr. Debt, B.

for a penalty, securing the performance of a covenant; because, if the party elect to proceed for the penalty, he is precluded from afterwards suing for general damages; and he cannot, in case of further breaches, recover more than the amount of the penalty, and in many cases before he can issue execution, he must proceed under the statute 8 & 9 *W. 3, c. 11; whereas if he proceed in covenant for every repeated breach, he may ultimately recover beyond the amount of the penalty (u). And where rent is due upon a lease, and there has also been another breach, as for not repairing, for which the plaintiff claims unliquidated damages, covenant is preferable to debt; because in the former, both the breaches of covenant may be included in one action, and damages for the whole demand may be recovered.

When not sustainable.

On the other hand, covenant *cannot* in general be supported unless the contract were under *seal*, and when it is by parol the plaintiff must proceed by action of assumpsit, &c. (x). But by special custom in London (y) and Bristol (z), covenant lies, although the contract be not under seal. So against the lessee or patentee of the crown, covenant may be supported, although he did not seal the lease or any counterpart of the lease, it being matter of record, and the lessee's acceptance of the demise being in such case as obligatory as an express covenant (d). A peculiar case is put in Co. Lit. (e); viz. that if a lease be made to A. and B. by indenture between the landlord of the one part, and A. and B. of the other part, and A. only execute it, but B. agree thereto, and enjoy the premises by virtue of the demise, "an action" may be maintained against A. and B. jointly, upon a covenant therein running with the land, and purporting to be made by them. This has been supposed to be an authority for the position, that in the above instance an action of *covenant* may be maintained against A. and B. (f). But the authorities cited in Co. Lit. (g) do not support that position; and it has been disputed, with much appearance of reason, in a recent valuable publication (h). And it would seem that if a lessee by deed-poll assign the term, although in express terms, "*subject* to the covenants in the lease," the proper *remedy by the *lessee* against the assignee for not performing the covenants, whereby the lessee was damnified, is an action of assumpsit, not an action of covenant; the assignee not having executed any deed covenanting to perform the covenants in the lease (i).

Covenant may be supported, although the covenantee did not sign the indenture (k); and we have seen that in the case of a deed-poll, a stranger to it may sue on a covenant therein to pay him a sum of money, though it is otherwise in the case of a deed *inter partes* (l)(307). The right of suit is consti-

(u) Burr. 1087, 1351; Lord Raym. 814; Dougl. 97; 13 East, 347, 348.

(x) *Ante*, 111, 112.

(y) 22 E. 4, 2 a.; Priv. Lond. 149; F. N. B. 146, A.; Com. Dig. London, N. 1.

(z) 1 Leon. 2.

(d) Cro. Jac. 240, 399, 521; Com. Dig. Covenant, A. 1; Vin. Ab. Covenant, B. pl. 1; Platt on Cov. 9, 10.

(e) 231 a.

(f) See 4 Cru. Dig. 393, 3d ed.; Com. Dig. Covenant, A. 1; Vin. Ab. Condition, I. a. 2; Dyer, 13 b. pl. 66; 2 Rol. R. 63, 159; 3 Bulst. 164; Co. Lit. 230 b, n. 1, by Butler; Co. Lit. by Thomas, vol. ii. 229, n. *Per* Lord Tenterden, 5 B. & C. 602.

(g) Namely, 38 Edw. 3, 8 a.; 3 Hen. 6, 26 b.; 45 Edw. 3, 11, 12.

(h) Platt on Cov. 10 to 18.

(i) 5 B. & C. 589, 602; 8 D. & R. 368, S. C. *Case* lies, *id.* *Sed vide* 3 C. & P. 462.

(k) 2 Roll. Ab. 22, Faits, F. pl. 2; Lutw. 305; Com. Dig. Covenant, A. 1; 3 B. & C. 353.

(l) Com. Dig. Covenant, A. 1; *ante*, 2, 3.

(307) {Berkley *v.* Hardy, 8 Dowl. & Ryl. 102. Smith *v.* Emery, 7 Halst. Rep. 53.}

III. COVENANT.

tuted by the covenantor's execution of the deed; and in these cases the acceptance of the deed by the covenantee, and his production of it at the trial, sufficiently testify his assent to the contract, if necessary, to render it binding (*m*). But it appears to be essential that the party claiming the benefit of the covenant should be named therein as the covenantee (*n*). Where a contract under seal has afterwards been varied in the terms of it by a subsequent parol contract, made on a new consideration, such substituted agreement must be the subject of an action of assumpsit, and not of covenant (*o*)(308); and it has been holden, that covenant cannot be supported against the assignee of the grantor of a rent-charge, though debt is sustainable against the pernor of the profits (*p*). In some cases where the breach of a covenant is misfeasance, the party has an election to proceed by action of covenant, or by action on the case for the tort, as against a lessee, either during his term or afterwards, for waste (*q*).

Declarations and pleadings.

The rules which affect the *form* of the pleadings in covenant will be fully considered hereafter. We may here observe generally, that the *declaration* in this action must state that the contract was under seal (*r*)(309); and should usually make a profert thereof, or show some excuse for the omission (*s*)(310).
[*137] It is not necessary to state the consideration of the defendant's *covenant, unless the performance of it constituted a condition precedent, when such performance must be averred; or unless a consideration be by law necessary; and even in that case an averment that the defendant, "for the consideration mentioned in the deed," thereby covenanted, &c. will be sufficient on general demurrer, the defendant not craving oyer of, and setting out, a deed showing no consideration, &c. (*t*). Only so much of the deed and covenant should be set forth as is essential to the cause of action; and each may be stated according to the legal effect, though it is more usual to declare in the words of the deed. The *breach* also may be assigned in the negative of the covenant generally, or according to the legal effect. Several breaches may be assigned at common law (*u*); and as the recovery of damages is the object of the suit, a sum sufficient to cover the real amount should be laid at the end of the declaration, as the amount of the damage sustained.

In covenant there is strictly no *plea* which can be termed a general issue, for *non est factum* only puts in issue the fact of sealing the deed; and *non infregit conventionem* and *nil debet*, are insufficient pleas (*x*); and therefore

(*m*) 4 Cruise Dig. 393, 3d ed.; Shep. Touch. 162.
(*n*) 1 Salk. 197; Comb. 219, S. C. *Sed vide* 1 Ld. Raym. 28; 1 Salk. 214, S. C. See 14 Ves. 187; 16 *id.* 454; Platt on Cov. 5.
(*o*) *Ante*, 117; 1 East, 630; 3 T. R. 596.
(*p*) 1 Salk. 198; 1 Ld. Raym. 322.
(*q*) 2 Bla. Rep. 848, 1111. *Sed quære*, see *post.*
(*r*) *Ante*, 134; 2 Ld. Raym. 1536; Com. Dig. Pleader, 2 V. 2; see Platt on Cov. 6.
(*s*) 3 T. R. 151.
(*t*) 3 Bing. 322.
(*u*) Com. Dig. Pleader, 2 V. 2, 3; Com. Rep. 146.
(*x*) Com. Dig. Pleader, 2 V. 4, &c.; 8 T. R. 283; 1 Lev. 183.

(308) {If a person enters into a bond for the performance of certain matters, and afterwards a parol agreement is made between the parties varying the time of performance, an action cannot be maintained upon the bond for the penalty, but the plaintiff must seek his remedy upon the agreement enlarging the time of performance. Ford *v.* Campfield, 6 Halst. Rep. 327.}
(309) {Smith *v.* Emery.} Vide Van Santwood *v.* Sandford, 12 Johns. Rep. 197.
(310) {Cutts *v.* United States, 1 Gallis. Rep. 69 Smith *v.* Emery.}

most matters of defence must be pleaded specially (*y*). These rules will be fully explained hereafter. The *judgment* in this action is, that the plaintiff recover a named sum for his *damages* which he hath sustained by reason of the breach or breaches of covenant; together with full costs of suit, to which the plaintiff is in general entitled, although the damages recovered be under 40s. (*z*) unless the judge certify under the statute of Eliz. (*a*). III. COVENANT.

IV. DETINUE.

The action of *detinue* is the only remedy by suit at law for the recovery of a personal chattel *in specie*, except in those instances where the party can obtain possession by replevying the same, and by action of replevin (*b*). In trespass, or trover, for taking or *detaining goods, or in assumpsit for not delivering them, *damages* only can be recovered. IV. DETINUE. [*138]

This is an action somewhat peculiar in its nature, and it may be difficult to decide whether it should be classed amongst forms of action *ex contractu*, or should be ranked with actions *ex delicto*. The right to join detinue with debt (*c*), and to sue in detinue for not delivering goods in pursuance of the terms of a bailment to the defendant (*d*), seem to afford ground for considering it rather as an action *ex contractu* (311) than an action of tort. On the other hand, it seems that detinue lies although the defendant wrongfully became the possessor thereof in the first instance, without relation to any contract (*e*). And it has recently been considered as an action for *tort*, the gist of the action not being the breach of a contract, but the *wrongful detainer;* for which reason, although a declaration in detinue has stated a bailment to the defendant, and his engagement to *re-deliver on request*, and the defendant has pleaded that the bailment was as a security for a loan, the plaintiff may, without being guilty of a departure, reply that he tendered the debt, and that the defendant afterwards wrongfully withheld the goods (*f*). Since the 3 & 4 W. 4, c. 42, s. 13, abolished wager of law, this action has become more frequent (*g*).

This action may be considered, 1st, with reference to the nature of the thing to be recovered; 2dly, the plaintiff's interest therein; 3dly, the injury; 4thly, the pleadings; and 5thly, the judgment.

(*y*) Com. Dig. Pleader, V. 4, &c.
(*z*) Tidd, 9th ed. 945, 963, 977, 978.
(*a*) 43 Eliz. c. 6; Tidd, 9th ed. 952, 953, 954.
(*b*) 3 Bla. Com. 146, 152; Willes, 120; Co. Lit. 286 b; Com. Dig. Detinue, A.
(*c*) 2 Saund. 117 b.
(*d*) *Post*, 141.
(*e*) *Post*, 139. It is also clear, that a set-off is not available in this form of action, Bul. N. P. 181. But this may be on the ground that in detinue the value of the goods is unliquidated, and the claim is not reduced to a sufficiently liquidated amount to render the application of the law of set-off possible.
(*f*) Gledstone *v.* Hewitt, 1 Cromp. & Jerv. 565; 1 Tyr. 450, S. C.
(*g*) See *before*, Barry *v.* Robinson, 1 New Rep. 295; King *v.* Williams, 3 Bar. & Cres. 538.

(311) This is certainly confirmed by the history of the action, from which it will appear that detinue was originally no other than an action of debt in the detinet, instead of the debt. As to which, as well as the ancient law respecting this action, vide 2 Reeve's Hist. E. L. 261, 333, 336. 3 Reeve's Hist. E. L. 66, 74.

IV. DETINUE.

1st. For what property it lies.

This action is only sustainable for the recovery of a specific *chattel*, and not for real property (*h*). The goods for which it is brought must be distinguishable from other property, and their identity ascertainable by some certain means, so that if the plaintiff recover, the sheriff may be able to deliver the goods to him; thus it lies for a horse, a cow, or money in a bag; but for money or corn, &c. not in a bag or chest, or otherwise distinguishable from property of the same description, detinue cannot be supported (*i*). It lies for the recovery of charters and title-deeds, the property in which generally accompanies the title to the land to which they relate (*k*). And it is sustainable upon a contract for not delivering a specific chattel in pursuance of a bailment or other contract (*l*); but to support this action, the property in some particular chattel must be vested in the plaintiff; and therefore assumpsit, or
[*139] debt in the detinet, is the only remedy *for the non-delivery of corn, &c. sold, where no specific corn was contracted for (*m*).

2dly. The plaintiff's interest.

A person who has the absolute or general property in certain specific goods, and the right to the immediate possession thereof, may support this action, although he has never had the actual possession; therefore an heir may maintain detinue for an heir-loom; and if goods be delivered to A. to deliver to B., the latter may support this action, the property being vested in him by the delivery to his use (*n*). But if the plaintiff have not the right to the immediate possession of the goods, and his interest be in reversion, he cannot support detinue, trover, or trespass (*o*). And it seems to be a general rule, that the plaintiff must have a general or special property in the goods, *at the time the action was commenced*, in order to maintain detinue (*p*). A person who has only a special property, as a bailee, &c. may also support this action, where he delivered the goods to the defendant, or they were taken out of such bailee's custody (*q*). It is said, that if a person detain the goods of a woman, which came to his hands before her marriage, the husband alone must bring this action, because the property is in him alone at the time of the action brought (*r*). And an heir who is entitled to an estate *per autre vie*, as special occupant, may in this action recover the title-deeds relating to the estate (*s*). If the owner of an estate deliver the title-deeds to a bailee, and then convey away the estate, the action for the detention of the deeds should be brought in the name of the new proprietor of the property (*t*).

3dly. The injury.

The gist of this action is the wrongful *detainer*, and not the original taking (*u*). It lies against any person who has the actual possession of the chattel, and who acquired it by lawful means, as either by bailment, delivery, or

(*h*) Cro. Jac. 39.
(*i*) Com. Dig. Detinue, B. C.; Co. Lit. 286 b; 3 Bla. Com. 152; 2 Bulst. 308; Moore, 394.
(*k*) 4 T. R. 229, 231.
(*l*) Fitz. N. B. 138; Willes, 120; 3 Bla. Com. 152.
(*m*) 3 Woodd. 104; 1 Dyer, 24 b.
(*n*) 2 Saund. 47 a. note; 1 Bro. Ab. Detinue, pl. 30, 45; 1 Rol. Ab. 606; Com. Dig. Detinue, A.; 4 Bing. 111.
(*o*) 7 T. R. 9.
(*p*) 4 Bing. 106.
(*q*) Bro. Ab. Detinue; 1 Saund. 47 b, c, d; 4 Bing. 111.
(*r*) Bul. N. P. 50; *ante*, 83. *Sed vide* Rep. temp. Hardw. 120.
(*s*) 4 T. R. 229, 231.
(*t*) See 4 Bing. 106.
(*u*) 3 Bla. Com. 152; Co. Lit. 286 b; 2 Bulst. 308; Gledstone *v.* Hewitt, 1 Cromp. & Jerv. 565; 1 Tyr. 450, S. C.

finding (x). It is a common doctrine in the books, that this action cannot *be supported, if the defendant *took* the goods *tortiously* (y); an opinion which appears to be founded on the judgment of Brian, C. J., who held (z) that detinue could not in such case be supported; on this fallacious reasoning, that by the trespass the property of the plaintiff was divested, and consequently that the property in the chattel was not vested in the plaintiff at the time of the commencement of his action (a). But it is observable, that Vavasor, J., in the same case, was of a different opinion; and the notion that the property can be changed by the trespass appears unfounded, for though a trespasser die possessed, the property is not thereby altered (b); and it is a principle of law, that no person can avail himself of his own wrong. It has been decided, that if goods, &c. taken away continue in specie in the hands of the executor of the wrong-doer, replevin or detinue may be supported against the executor (c). In pleading it is usual to state that the defendant acquired the goods by *finding*, (except where he is declared against as a bailee); yet that allegation is not traversable (d); and, as observed in *Kettle* v. *Broomsell* (e), if detinue could not be supported because the original taking was tortious, a person might be greatly injured, and have no adequate remedy; for in trover damages only can be recovered, and the thing detained may be of such a description, that a judgment merely for damages would be an inadequate satisfaction (f). Detinue cannot be supported against a person who never had the possession of the goods; as against an executor on a bailment to the testator, unless the goods came to the possession of the executor (g); nor does it lie against a bailee, if before demand *he lose them by accident (h); though if he wrongfully deliver [*141] *the goods to* another, he will continue liable (i). And it seems that if the defendant represent that he has the goods, and thereby induce the owner to bring the action against him, he is liable, although it does not appear that he had the general controlling power over the goods (k). If goods be delivered to a feme before her marriage, and afterwards detained, the action may be brought against husband and wife (l); but if the bailment were to the husband and wife after marriage, it is said that the husband must be sued alone (m). If an infant have bought goods, and on application for payment he refuse to pay on the ground of his infancy, and any of the goods remain in specie, they should be demanded, and afterwards the prudent course will be to declare in detinue for the goods, with a count in debt for goods sold and delivered, and at least

(x) Willes, 118; Co. Lit. 286 b.; Fitz. N. B. 138, E.; Bac. Ab. Detinue.

(y) 6 H. 7, 9; 3 Bla. Com. 152; Bro. Ab. Detinue, pl. 36, 53; Com. Dig. Detinue, D.; Vin. Ab Detinue, B. 2, pl. 5, Trespass, Y. pl. 12; Cro. Eliz. 824; Selw. N. P. Detinue, 2d edit. 697, note 3; but see 4th edit. 635, note 3; 7th edit. 668, note 3. In equity, see 10 Ves. 163.

(z) 6 H. 7, 9.

(a) 6 H. 7, 9. Lord Kenyon, C. J., in 1 East, 107, 108, observed upon this doctrine of the property being altered by a trespass.

(b) Com. Dig. Bien, E.; Selw. Detinue; *ante*, 101, 102.

(c) Bro. Ab. Detinue, pl. 19. For a conversion by a testator, *trover* would be the remedy against his executor, to whose hands the goods did not come, see 1 Saund. 216, 217, n.

(d) Doc. Plac. 124; Bro. Ab. Detinue, pl. 50; 1 New Rep. 140; Jenk. 2 Cent. p. 78.

(e) Willes, 120.

(f) See also Cro. Eliz. 824; Com. Dig. Action, M. 6; 27 H. 8, 22; Vin. Ab. Detinue, D. 5, pl. 62.

(g) Bro. Detinue, 19; 2 Bulst. 303; *supra*, note (c).

(h) Bro. Detinue, pl. 1, 33, 40.

(i) *Id.* and pl. 2, 34; 2 B. & Ald. 703; Peake, C. N. P. 42.

(k) 3 B. & C. 136.

(l) Co. Lit. 351 b.

(m) 3 Bulst. 308; 38 Ed. 3, fo. 1; see *ante*, 105, 106.

IV. DETINUE. on the former the plaintiff would recover, should the defendant plead infancy to the latter (n).

The pleadings, &c. With respect to the *Pleadings* in this action, more certainty is necessary in the description of the chattels than in an action of trover or replevin (o); but it is not necessary to state the date of a deed (p); and if the action be brought for several articles, the value of each need not be stated separately in the declaration, though the jury should sever the value of each by their verdict (q). In the case of a special bailment it is proper to declare, at least in one count, on the bailment (r); and to lay a special request (s); but in other cases it is sufficient to declare upon the supposed finding, which we have seen is not traversable (t). And the plaintiff may declare on a bailment to re-deliver on request, and yet in his replication rely on a different bailment (u).

The Reg. Gen. Hil. Term, 4 W. 4, r. III., orders that in detinue the plea of non detinet shall operate as a denial of the detention of the goods by the defendant, but not of the plaintiff's property therein, and that no other defence than such denial shall be admissible under that plea, consequently the defendant must plead specially almost every ground of defence, as that the goods were pawned to him for money remaining unpaid (y); and he must also plead specially any other description of lien (z).

The nature of this action requires that the *verdict* and judgment be such, that a specific remedy may be had for recovery of the goods detained, or a satisfaction in value for each several parcel, in case they, or either of them, cannot be returned; and therefore, where the action is for several chattels [*142] *the jury ought by their verdict to assess the value of each separately (a); and if the jury neglect to find the value, the omission cannot be supplied by writ of inquiry (b). The *judgment* is in the alternative, that the plaintiff do recover the goods, or the value thereof, if he cannot have the goods themselves, and his damages for the detention and his full costs of suit (c). This action, before the 3 & 4 W. 4, c. 42, s. 13, abolishing wager of law in all cases, was in most cases subject to wager of law, on which account it was not much in use; but now it is frequently adopted; and it is a very advantageous remedy, especially where it is material to embrace in the same action a count in debt for a money demand as due upon a contract.

OF ACTIONS IN FORM *EX DELICTO*.

NATURE OF INJURIES EX DELICTO. Personal actions in form *ex delicto*, and which are principally for the redress of wrongs unconnected with contract, are case, trover (d), replevin, and

(n) *Supra*, n. (c).
(o) 2 Saund. 74 b.; Co. Lit. 286 b.
(p) Bac. Ab. Detinue, B.; 1 Wils. 116.
(q) 2 Bla. Rep. 853; Jenk. 2 Cent. 112; Bul. N. P. 51 a.
(r) 1 New Rep. 146.
(s) Willes, 120.
(t) 1 New Rep. 140; 4 T. R. 229; Willes, 120.
(u) Gledstone v. Hewitt, 1 Tyr. 445; 1 Crom. & J. 565, S. C.
(y) Co. Lit. 283.
(z) Alexander v. M'Gowan, Sittings after M. T. 3 Geo. 4. *Per* Abbott, C. J., and *per* Gaselee, J., 4 Bing. 112, and *post*, Chapter on Pleas.
(a) 2 Bla. Rep. 854; 3 H. 6, 43 a.; Jenk. 2 cent. 112.
(b) 10 Co. 119 b.; Salk. 206.
(c) Cro. Jac. 682, 683; Tidd's Forms, 388; Townshend's Judgment, 1 Book, 344, 2 Book, 82, 83, 84, 85; Aston's Ent. 202; 2 Keilw. 64.
(d) *Trover* is only a *branch* of actions upon the case. *Detinue* has been already noticed as an action *ex contractu*, *ante*, 137, 138; but see *id.* note.

trespass *vi et armis*. *Mixed* actions are ejectment, waste, &c. Before we consider the application of these remedies, it is advisable to take a concise view of the *nature* of the different *injuries ex delicto*, because they in general govern the form of the action. Thus if the injury be *forcible*, and occasioned *immediately* by the act of the defendant, *trespass vi et armis* is the proper remedy; but if the injury be not in legal contemplation *forcible*, or *not direct* and *immediate* on the act done, but only *consequential*, then the remedy is by *action on the case* (*e*); and there are other points relating to the nature of injuries, which, as they affect the form of the action, it is material to ascertain. NATURE OF INJURIES EX DELICTO.

Injuries *ex delicto* are in legal consideration committed *with force*, as assaults and batteries, &c., or *without force*, as slander, &c. (*f*). They are also either *immediate and direct*, or *mediate and consequential*. It is frequently difficult to determine when the injury is to be considered forcible or not, *and [*143] when immediate or consequential, and therefore whether trespass or case is the proper remedy.

Force is, in legal consideration, of two descriptions, either *implied* by law, or *actual*; force is *implied* in every trespass *quare clausum fregit* (*g*). The distinction is material, and is thus put in Salkeld: "If one enter into my ground, I must request him to depart, before I can lay hands on him to turn him out; for every *impositio manuum* is an assault and battery, which cannot be justified upon the account of breaking the close *in law*, without a previous request to depart; the other is an *actual* force, as in burglary, or breaking open a door or gate, and in that case it is lawful to oppose force to force; *or if* one break down the gate, or come into my close *vi et armis*, I *need not* request him to be gone, but may lay hands on him immediately; so if one come forcibly and take away my goods, I may immediately oppose him, for there is no time to make a request." (*h*) (312) In the case of false imprisonment also force is implied (*i*). And the law implies force where a wife, daughter, or servant, has been enticed away or debauched, though in fact they consented, the law considering them incapable of consenting; and therefore in such case trespass may be supported, though case for the consequence of the wrong has, till of late, been the more usual form of declaration (*k*)(313). The *degree* of violence with which the act is done, is not material as far as regards the *form* of action, for if a log were put down in the most quiet way upon a man's foot, the action would be trespass; but if thrown into the road When forcible or not.

(*e*) 3 East, 593; 2 New Rep. 117, 446.
(*f*) 3 Bla. Com. 118, 398, 399.
(*g*) 2 Salk. 641; Co. Lit. 257 b. 161 b. 162 a; 1 Saund. 81, 140, n. 4; 8 T. R. 78; Bac. Ab. Trespass.
(*h*) 2 Salk. 641; 8 T. R. 78, 357.
(*i*) But an imprisonment does not impliedly and necessarily include a battery, 1 New Rep. 255.
(*k*) 3 Wils. 18; Fitz. N. B. 89, O.; 5 T. R. 361; 6 East, 387; 3 Bla. Com. 140. According to 2 New Rep. 476, trespass seems now to be the proper form, see 2 Stark. R. 495.

(312) The plea of non detinet by an executor is a bad plea to a declaration on a judgment against his testator; and being shown to be false, will, on motion, be struck out with costs. Ames et al. *v.* Webber's Ex'rs, 10 Wend. R. 624.

(313) In trespass *de bonis asportatis*, no actual force is necessary to be proved.—Gibbs *v.* Chase, 10 Mass. Rep. 125. It lies for levying upon the property of the plaintiff under an execution against another, and requiring the engagement of a receiptor that the property shall be forthcoming, or the amount of the execution paid, although there has been no removal of the property, and the receiptor permits the party to remain in possession, and to dispose of it as his own. Phillips *v.* Hall, 8 Wend. R. 610.

NATURE OF INJURIES EX DELICTO. with whatever violence, and one *afterwards* fell over it, it would be case and not trespass (*l*). And trespass is the remedy where rubbish is laid so *near* my wall that the *natural* consequence is, that some of it rolls against and comes in contact therewith (*m*). With respect to injuries to rights or property not *tangible*, such as reputation and health, and real property incorporeal, as a
[*144] right *of way, common, &c.; as the matter or property injured cannot be affected immediately by any substance, the injuries thereto, however malevolent and however contrived, cannot be considered as committed with force (*n*).

In general a mere *nonfeasance* cannot be considered as forcible, for where there has been no act, there cannot be force, as in the case of a neglect to take away tithes (*o*), or a mere detention of goods without an unlawful taking (*p*), or the neglect to repair the banks of a river whereby the plaintiff's land was overflowed (*q*), or neglect to re-deliver a beast distrained damage feasant, when sufficient amends were tendered before the beast was impounded (*r*).

When it is material to rely upon *actual* force in *pleading*, as in the case of a forcible entry, the words "*manu forti*," or "with strong hand," should be adopted (*s*); but in other cases the words "*vi et armis*," or with force and arms, are sufficient (*t*).

When immediate or consequential. An injury is considered as *immediate* when the act complained of *itself*, and not merely a *consequence* of that act, occasions the injury. Thus if a blow be given by one to another (314), or he drive a carriage and horses against him or his property (*u*)(315), or if he pour water on another person or his land (*x*), or do any act thereon (*y*), or if a wild beast or other dangerous thing be turned out or put in motion, and mischief immediately ensue (*z*), or if a log be thrown into a highway, and in the act of throwing or falling, hit another, or if a party, as just observed, lay rubbish so *near* the plaintiff's wall that the necessary or natural consequence is, that some of it will roll, and it accordingly comes against the wall (*a*), the injury is immediate, and trespass is the remedy (*b*). And where a lighted squib was thrown in a market-place, and afterwards thrown about by others in self defence, and ultimately hurt the plaintiff, the injury was considered as the immediate act of the first thrower (316),

(*l*) *Per* Le Blanc, J., 3 East, 602; 1 Stra. 636; 5 T. R. 649.
(*m*) 9 B. & C. 591.
(*n*) 3 Bla. Com. 122, 123.
(*o*) 1 B. & P. 476; Ld. Raym. 188.
(*p*) 2 Saund. 47 k, l.
(*q*) Bro. Ab. Action sur le Case, pl. 36; Fitz. N. B. 93; Bac. Ab. Trespass.
(*r*) 8 Co. 146.
(*s*) 8 T. R. 357, 378.
(*t*) *Id. ibid.* But the omission of the words *vi et armis*, is not objectionable on general demurrer, and is aided by verdict. 1 Saund. 81, n. 1.
(*u*) 3 East, 593; 1 Campb. 497; 2 Campb. 465.
(*x*) 2 Ld. Raym. 1403.
(*y*) 1 Ld. Raym. 183.
(*z*) 3 East, 596.
(*a*) 9 B. & C. 591.
(*b*) 1 Stra. 636; 5 T. R. 609.

(314) Ream *v.* Rank, 3 Serg. & Rawle, 215. Parker *v.* Elliotte, Gilm. Rep. 33. Martin *v.* Payne, 9. Johns. Rep. 387. Lyon *v.* Hamilton, Spear *v.* Patterson, Zurtman *v.* Miller, cited 3 Serg. & Rawle, 216. Mercer *v.* Walmsley, 5 Harr. & Johns. Rep. 27. Vaughan *v.* Rhodes, 2 M'Cord's Rep. 227. Case, and not trespass, is the proper form of debauching his daughter, where the injury was done in the house of another. Clough *v.* Tenney, 5 Greenl. Rep. 446.

(315) Vide Taylor *v.* Rainbow, 2 Hen. & Mun. 423. { Rappelyea *v.* Hulse, 7 Halst. Rep. 257. }

(316) { So where the defendant by discharging a gun frightened the plaintiff's horse, who ran away and broke his carriage, trespass was held to be the proper remedy. Cole *v.* Fisher, 11 Mass. Rep. 137. }

*and a trespass; the new direction and new force given to it by the other persons not being a new trespass, but merely a continuation of the original force (c). It is a direct trespass to injure the person of another by driving a carriage against the carriage wherein such person is sitting, although the last-mentioned carriage be not the property of, nor in the possession of the person injured; and where the defendant drove his gig against another chaise, whereby the plaintiff's wife was much hurt and injured, it was held, that an action at the suit of the husband and wife was properly brought in trespass (d). And where the defendant driving his carriage on the wrong side of a road, when it was dark, by accident drove against the plaintiff's curricle, it was holden that the injury which the plaintiff had sustained, having been immediate, from the act of driving by the defendant, trespass might be maintained (e)(317). Case must be adopted where the defendant's servant, and not the defendant personally, caused the injury by his carelessness, &c. (f). NATURE OF INJURIES EX DELICTO.

But where the damage or injury ensued not directly from the act complained of, it is termed *consequential* or mediate, and cannot amount to a *trespass*. Thus, in the instance just stated, if a log, in the act of being thrown into the highway, hit another, the injury is immediate; but if *after* it has reached the highway, a person fall over it and be hurt, the injury is only consequential, and the remedy should be case (318), for wrongfully or carelessly throwing and leaving the timber in the road (g). So if a person pour water on my land, the injury is immediate; but if he stop up a water-course on his own land, whereby it is prevented from flowing to mine as usual, or if he place a spout on his own building, in consequence of which water afterwards runs therefrom into my land, the injury is consequential; because the flowing of the water, which was the immediate injury, was not the wrong-doer's immediate act, but only the consequence thereof, *and which will not render the act itself a trespass or immediate wrong (h)(319). [*146]

(c) 3 Wils. 403; 2 Bl. R. 892; 8 T. R. 190.

(d) 1 Moore, 407; 7 Taunt. 698, S. C.

(e) 3 East, 593; 1 Campb. 497; 2 Id. 465; 5 T. R. 648; see 2 New Rep. 117, 446; 3 Campb. 188, in which it is questioned whether the plaintiff may not, in this instance, waive the force or trespass, and declare in case for the negligence, if provable; and see 4 B. & C. 227, *per* Bayley, J.

(f) *Post.*

(g) 3 East, 602; 1 Stra. 636; 5 T. R. 649.

(h) Stra. 634, 635; Ld. Raym. 1399; 2 Burr. 1114.

---

(317) { For the criterion of trespass, see Smith *v.* Rutherforth et al., 2 Serg. and Rawle, 358, and when the action should be trespass, and when case. Cotteral *v.* Cummins, 6 Serg. & Rawle, 343. } The invasion of a franchise or mere incorporeal right, is to be redressed by an *action on the case;* but when visible, tangible, corporal property is injured, if the injury be direct, immediate and wilful, trespass is the proper form of action, although that property be connected with, or be the means by which an incorporeal right is enjoyed. Thus, where a party was authorized by an act of the legislature to erect a dam in a river previously declared a public highway, and after its erection it was *wilfully* and *intentionally* cut away by third persons, and an immediate and direct injury ensued; *held*, that the remedy was by action of trespass, and not case. Wilson *v.* Smith et al., 10 Wend. R. 324. Where the injury is direct and immediate, proceeding from the *wilful* and *intentional* act of the defendant, the action *must be trespass;* but if the injury be attributable to *negligence* though it be *immediate*, either *case or trespass* may be brought. Ib. and Percival *v.* Hickey, 18 Johns. Rep. 257.

(318) But in such a case, if it appear that the party injured did not use ordinary care, by which the obstruction might have been avoided, he cannot maintain the action. Smith *v.* Smith, 2 Pick. Rep. 621.

(319) Vide Adams *v.* Hemmenway, 1 Mass. Rep. 145. Arnold *v.* Foot, 12 Wend. R. 330.

NATURE OF INJURIES EX DELICTO.

It is chiefly in actions for running down ships that difficulties occur, because the force which occasions the injury is not in such case necessarily the immediate act of the person steering, for the wind and waves may and generally do occasion the force, and the personal act of the party rather consists in putting the vessel in the way to be acted upon by the wind, and the injury might even have happened from the operation of the wind and tide counteracting his efforts (*i*). In the case of an injury arising from carelessness or unskilfulness in navigating a ship, if the injury were merely attributable to negligence or want of skill, and not to the *wilful* act of the defendant, with intent to injure the plaintiff, the party injured has, it seems, an election, either to treat the negligence or unskilfulness of the defendant as the cause of action, and to declare in case, or to consider the act itself as the injury, and to declare in trespass (*k*)(320). And it is probable the same doctrine would be applied to the case of an injury resulting from the careless or unskilful driving of a carriage (*l*). And it was recently held, that where through *negligent and careless* driving, one vehicle is *caused forcibly* to strike another, an *action on the case* is sustainable for the injury done, although it be immediate upon the violence, unless the act producing it was *wilful* (*m*), and if both parties were to blame and guilty of negligence, then neither can sue at law (*n*). So where there has been an illegal distress, the plaintiff has frequently the option of declaring in case or in trespass (*o*). And it is clear that trover (*p*), or it seems detinue (*q*), may be supported, although the defendant obtained the goods by an act of trespass. In *Scott* v. *Sheppard* (*r*), Mr. J. Blackstone said, that a person may bring trespass for the immediate injury, and subjoin a *per quod* for the consequential damage, or case for the consequential damage, passing over the immediate injury; and in *Pitts* v. *Gaince and another*(*s*), where the declaration was in case, and stated that the plaintiff was master of a ship laden with corn ready to sail, and that the defendant seized the ship and detained her, whereby the plaintiff was prevented from proceeding in his voyage, an exception was taken that the declaration should have been trespass, and several
[*147] cases were cited; but Lord Holt observed, that in *those cases, the plaintiff had a property in the thing taken, but here the ship was not the master's, but the owner's; the master only declared as a particular officer, and could only recover for his particular loss, yet he might have brought trespass, as a bailee of goods may, and declared upon his possession, which is sufficient to maintain trespass. Hence it appears that either trespass or case may sometimes be supported where there is *both an immediate* and also a *consequential* injury (*t*).

(*i*) 8 East, 601, 603; 8 T. R. 192; 1 B. & P. 476.

(*k*) 2 New Rep. 117; 8 T. R. 188; 3 East, 601; 1 B. & P. 472; 4 B. & C. 226 to 228; but see *ante*, 145, and note (*e*).

(*l*) *Id.*; see next case, supporting the author's suggestions.

(*m*) Williams v. Holland, 6 Car. & P. 23.

(*n*) *Id. ibid.*; but in Admiralty Courts it is otherwise, see 2 Chitty's Gen. Prac. 514, 515.

(*o*) 1 B. & C. 145; 2 D. & R. 256; 3 Stark. 171.

(*p*) 1 B. & C. 146; 4 *Id.* 228.

(*q*) *Ante*, 139, 140.

(*r*) 2 Bla. Rep. 897; 11 Mod. 180; 4 Co. 94 b, 95; Hob. 180; Str. 99; 1 B. & P. 475; 2 Burr. 1113; Salk. 110.

(*s*) 1 Salk. 10; 2 D. & R. 256.

(*t*) See the last eight notes, and Williams v. Holland, 6 Car. & P. 23.

(320) Percival v. Hickey, 18 Johns. Rep. 257. Where the cases are reviewed by C. J. Spencer. Where the injury is both direct or immediate and consequential, the party injured has an election to sue either case or trespass. M'Allister v. Hammond, 6 Cowen, 342.

Cases sometimes arise where the law considers special consequential damage as *too remote*, but case lies for not repairing the defendant's fence, *per quod* plaintiff's horses escaped into the defendant's close, and were there killed by the falling of a hay stack, the Court considering that such damage was not too remote (*x*).

NATURE OF INJURIES EX DELICTO.

When the consequential damage not too remote.

The *legality* or *illegality* of the original act is not in general the criterion whether the injury was immediate or consequential, and will not therefore be the test whether the remedy should be trespass or case (*y*). A person may become an immediate trespasser *vi et armis* (321), even in the performance of a lawful act, if in the course of such performance he be guilty of neglect; as if he hurt another by accident (*z*). And case will lie for doing an unlawful act if the damage sustained thereby be not immediate but consequential, although the defendant has no malicious intention (*a*). However, if the injury were committed through the medium of and under regular process, as in the case of a malicious arrest or prosecution, although such injury were forcible and immediate, yet the remedy must be case (*b*)(322). If, however, the act complained of amount to a *felony*, as if the house were entered, or the goods were taken burglariously or feloniously, the civil remedy is merged in the criminal offence, and no action can be maintained until the offender has been duly prosecuted, &c. (*c*).

As to the *legality* of the original act.

Nor is the *motive*, *intent*, or *design* of the wrong-doer towards the complainant the criterion as to the form of the remedy (*d*); for where the act occasioning an injury is unlawful, the intent of the wrong-doer is immaterial (*e*); and it is clear that the mind need not in general concur in the act that occasions an injury to another, and if the action occasion *an immediate injury, trespass is the proper remedy without reference to the intent (*f*). If, however, in pleading, the injury be stated to have been committed wilfully, and in other respects it be uncertain whether it be immediate or consequential, the Court will consider it as an immediate injury (*g*). There are many cases in the books, where the injury being direct and immediate, trespass has been holden to lie, though the injury were not intentional; as in *Weaver* v. *Ward* (*h*), where the defendant exercising in the trained bands, and firing his musket by accident hurt the plaintiff: and in *Underwood* v. *Hewson* (*i*), where one

Intent, when material.

[*148]

(*x*) Powell v. Salisbury, 2 Younge & Jerv. 391.

(*y*) 1 Stra. 635, n. 2; 3 East, 601; 3 Wils. 409; 2 Bla. Rep. 894.

(*z*) *Id.*; 3 Wils. 411; 1 Stra. 596; 27 H. 6, 28 a; 1 Bing. 213.

(*a*) 11 Mod. 180; 3 Wils. 111, 410; 2 Bla. Rep. 895.

(*b*) 3 T. R. 185; 2 Chit. Rep. 304; 1 D. & R. 97.

(*c*) See Sty. 346; Yelv. 90; 1 Sid. 375; 2 B. & P. 410; 5 T. R. 175; 2 C. & P. 41.

(*d*) 3 Wils. 309; 2 Bla. Rep. 832; 3 East, 599, 601. The intent, however, is considered by the jury in the damages, 2 Stark. 213.

(*e*) 6 East, 464, 473, 474; 2 East, 107; 5 Esp. Rep. 214, 215.

(*f*) *Per* Lord Kenyon, 8 T. R. 190; 3 East, 599, 601; 1 Campb. 497; 2 *id.* 465.

(*g*) 3 East, 595, 601; 8 T. R. 191; 1 East, 109; 2 Burr. 1114.

(*h*) Hob. 134; see 1 Bing. 213.

(*i*) 1 Stra. 596.

(321) { Blin v. Campbell, 14 Johns. Rep. 432. 18 Johns. Rep. 288. Cotterall v. Cummins et al., 6 Serg. & Rawle, 343. } Vide Stultz v. Dickey, 5 Binn. 288.

(322) But where a sheriff levies a *fi fa.* after the return day, the proper action is trespass and not case. Vail v. Lewis and Livingston, 4 Johns. Rep. 450. { A *fi. fa.* issued within the period of stay of execution, and after security has been given for the purpose of obtaining it, is a nullity, and trespass lies against the plaintiff or prothonotary for issuing it. Milliken v. Brown, 10 Serg. & Rawle, 188. }

NATURE OF INJURIES EX-DELICTO. uncocking a gun, it went off, and accidentally wounded a by-stander. And if one turning round suddenly were to knock another down (323), whom he did not see, without intending it, no doubt the action should be trespass (*k*); and where a person accidentally drives a carriage against that of another, the injury is immediate, and trespass or case is sustainable, though the defendant was no otherwise blamable than in driving on the wrong side of the road on a dark night (*l*). There is an exception, however, in favor of public officers, who are bound to obey the process of the Courts; thus if a sheriff, after a secret act of bankruptcy committed by A., levy his goods under an execution against him, he cannot be sued by the assignees in trespass, but only in trover, because such public officers ought not to be made trespassers by relation (*m*). And in some other cases, though the intent may not be material to the form of action, it may decide whether any action be sustainable. In some instances, words *prima facie* slanderous are not actionable, if not spoken maliciously. And it seems to be a general rule, that if a party be in the prosecution of a legal act, an action does not lie for an injury resulting from an *inevitable* or *unavoidable* accident, which occurs without *any* blame or default on his part (*n*).

In some cases of involuntary trespasses upon land, a tender of amends may
[*149] be pleaded (*o*). And in actions against public *agents, the intent may be frequently material in considering their liability (*p*).

For some *torts* which may *prima facie* appear to be forcible and immediate; as for an excessive distress (*q*); or for driving a distress out of the county in which it was taken (*r*); or for injuries to personal or real property in reversion (*s*); or against a bailee of personal property having an interest therein, and who has injured the same, but not destroyed it (*t*); an action on the case is a proper remedy. So though a master may be liable under the circumstances to compensate an immediate injury committed by his servant, in the course of his employ, with force (*u*); yet the action against the master in general must be case, though against the servant it might for the same act be trespass (*x*)(324). Where an injury arose from the careless driving of a person

(*k*) *Per* Lord Ellenborough, and Lawrence, J., 3 East, 595, 596.

(*l*) 3 East, 593; Williams *v.* Holland, 6 Car. & P. 23; see *ante*, 145.

(*m*) 1 T. R. 480; 1 Lev. 173; see 1 Burr. 20.

(*n*) 2 Chit. R. 639; 1 Bing. 213; *ante*, 88.

(*o*) 21 Jac. 1, c. 16, s. 5; Vin. Ab. Trespass, 542; 3 Lev. 37.

(*p*) *Ante*, 88; 6 Taunt. 29.

(*q*) 52 Hen. 3, c. 4; 3 Bla. Com. 12; 2 Stra. 851; 1 Burr. 590; Fitzgib. 85; 1 B. & C. 145; 2 D. & R. 256; 3 Stark. 177.

(*r*) *Id. ibid.*; 2 Inst. 106; 3 Lev. 47; 2 Stra. 1272.

(*s*) 4 T. R. 489; 7 T. R. 9; Com. Dig. Action on Case, Nuisance, B.

(*t*) Bac. Ab. Trespass, B.

(*u*) *Ante*, 92, 93.

(*x*) 1 East, 108; see 9 B. & C. 591; 4 M. & R. 500, S. C.

(323) In Taylor *v.* Rainbow, 2 Hen. & Mun. 423, the defendant had negligently, but without any design to injure, discharged a gun, and wounded the plaintiff, who brought an action on the case: it was held that trespass was the proper remedy, and that it was immaterial whether the injury were committed wilfully or not. { See also Cole *v.* Fisher, 11 Mass. Rep. 137. But see Blin *v.* Campbell, 14 Johns. Rep. 432. } In the case last cited Judge Spencer, in delivering the judgment of the court, recognizes the distinction in cases of injuries arising from driving carriages or navigating ships, &c. If the injury were immediate, and be stated in the declaration to have been wilfully committed, or appear to have been so on the trial, the remedy *must be trespass*; but if the injury arises from negligence, though immediate, the party injured has his election to bring either trespass or case. Subsequent cases in the same court also recognize the same distinction. Percival *v.* Hickey, 18 Johns. Rep. 257. Wilson *v.* Smith, 10 Wend. R. 324.

(324) Per Curiam, 17 Mass. Rep. 244. Campbell *v.* Phelps. "The principal cases

who was one of the proprietors of the coach, it was held that he and the other proprietors might be jointly sued in case (y). If the injury arise from the want of care or negligence of the servant, case is the remedy; but if it occurred as the necessary, probable, or natural consequence of the act ordered by the master, then the act is the master's, and he should be sued in trespass (if the act were forcible and immediate). Therefore where a master ordered a servant to lay some rubbish near his neighbor's wall, but that so it might not touch the same, and the servant used ordinary care, but some of the rubbish naturally ran against the wall, it was held that trespass was maintainable against the master (z). NATURE OF INJURIES EX DELICTO.

Fom this concise view of the nature of injuries *ex delicto*, as well as from the following observations on the properties of each particular action, it may be collected that there are *four* leading points to be attended to in deciding what form of action should be adopted. *First*, the nature of the *matter* or *thing* affected; *secondly*, the plaintiff's *right* thereto; *thirdly*, the *means* by which the *injury* was effected; and, *fourthly*, the situation in which the defendant stood. Summary of the principal points on which the form of action *ex delicto* may depend.

[*150] *And, *first*, the nature of the matter or thing affected; as whether it were substance or tangible, as the body, personal chattels, and real property corporeal; or not tangible, as health, reputation, and real property incorporeal. In the first instances, as the property might be affected immediately by an injury committed with force, trespass, case, replevin, trover, or detinue, may or may not be sustainable, depending on the other three points, and the particular properties of each action (a); but in the latter instances, an action on the case is in *general* the only remedy, because the property could not be injured immediately by force.

Secondly, The nature of the plaintiff's *right* to the matter or thing affected; as if the injury were to the person, whether the right were absolute or relative; in the latter instance case being sustainable, however forcible the injury; or if the damage were to personal or real property, whether the right were in severalty or joint-tenancy, or in common, or in possession or reversion; in the last instance neither trespass, trover, replevin, nor detinue could be supported, but only case (b).

Thirdly, The *means* by which the *injury* was effected; as whether it were a commission or omission; in the latter case, trespass is not in general sustainable (c); or with or without force, actual or implied, for if without force, case is in general the remedy (d); or immediate or consequential; in the latter case, trespass is not sustainable (e); or whether the injury were committed by the defendant himself, or by his agent or servant, or by his cattle or property (f), or under color of a distress for rent, &c. or of the process of a superior or inferior Court.

(y) 4 B. & C. 223; 6 D. & R. 275, S. C.
(z) 9 B. & C. 591; 4 M. & R. 500, S. C.
(a) Replevin lies only for personal property, and not for taking part of the freehold, 4 T. R. 504 (325).
(b) 7 T. R. 9.
(c) *Ante*, 143, 144.
(d) *Ante*, 143, 144; 3 Campb. 187.
(e) *Ante*, 143, 144, 145.
(f) *Ante*, 149.

which appear to have turned upon the distinction between trespass and case are collected and classed according to their characteristic circumstances, in a note to Huggett v. Montgomery, 2 New Rep. 448.—Day's edit." Note by Mr. Day.

(325) { Brown v. Caldwell, 10 Serg. & Rawle, 114. Nor trover, Mather v. Ministers

NATURE OF INJURIES EX DELICTO. *Fourthly*, The situation or character in which the defendant stood, as whether he were joint-tenant or tenant in common with the plaintiff (*g*); or whether there were any privity of contract between the plaintiff or defendant, in respect of the latter being tenant or bailee, when in general trespass cannot be [*151] supported (*h*). Keeping in view these important points, we *proceed to consider the nature and particular applicability of the several actions in form *ex delicto*.

I. ACTION ON THE CASE.

I. ON THE CASE. We have before remarked that an action upon the case was a remedy given by the common law, but that it appears to have existed only in a limited form, and to a certain prescribed extent, until the statute of Westminster 2 (*i*). In its most comprehensive signification it includes *assumpsit*, as well as an action in form *ex delicto* (*k*); but at the present time, when an action on the case is mentioned, it is usually understood to mean an action in form *ex delicto*; and therefore, where a navigation act enacted that the company might sue for calls, &c. by action of debt, or *on the case*, it was holden that an action on the case in tort lay, though the defendant might thereby be deprived of the benefit of a set-off (*l*).

Actions on the case are founded on the common law, or upon acts of parliament, and lie generally to recover *damages* for *torts* not committed with force, actual or implied; or having been occasioned by force, where the matter affected was not tangible, or the injury was not immediate, but consequential; or where the interest in the property was only in reversion; in all which cases trespass is not sustainable (*m*). Torts of this nature are, to the absolute or relative rights of *persons*, or to *personal property* in possession or reversion, or to *real* property, corporeal or incorporeal, in possession or reversion. These injuries may be either by *nonfeasance*, or the omission of some act which the defendant ought to perform; or by *misfeasance*, being the improper performance of some act which might lawfully be done; or by *malfeasance*, the doing what the defendant ought not to do; and these respective torts are commonly the performance or omission of some act contrary to the general obligation of the law, or the particular rights or duties of the parties, or of some express or implied contract between them.

To persons absolutely. Case is the proper remedy for an injury to the *absolute rights of persons* not immediate, but consequential; as for keeping mischievous animals, having [*152] notice of their propensity (*n*); *or for special damage arising from a public

(*g*) *Ante*, 90; 2 Saund. 47 g.
(*h*) *Post*; Bac. Ab. Trespass, B.
(*i*) *Ante*, 108.
(*k*) See Steph. on Pleading, 16.
(*l*) 7 T. R. 36.
(*m*) 4 T. R. 489; 7 T. R. 9.
(*n*) *Ante*, 94.

of Trinity Church, 3 Serg. & Rawle, 509. Nor money had and received for the proceeds of it, if sold by the taker. Baker *v.* Howell, 6 Serg. & Rawle, 476.}

nuisance (o) (326). But if the injury were immediate, as if the defendant incited his dog to bite another, or let loose a dangerous animal (p); or if in the act of throwing a log into a public street, it hurt the plaintiff (q); or if an injury be committed by cattle (r) to land; the action should be trespass. Also, whenever an injury to a person is occasioned by *regular process* of a Court of competent jurisdiction, though maliciously adopted, case is the proper remedy, and trespass is not sustainable (s); as for a malicious arrest; or for malicious prosecution of a criminal charge before a magistrate or otherwise (t). If the proceeding be malicious and *unfounded*, though it were instituted by a Court having no jurisdiction, case may be supported, or trespass (u). Formerly it was usual, in these instances, where several persons combined in the prosecution, to proceed by writ of conspiracy, but the action on the case is now the usual remedy (x). If, on the other hand, the proceeding complained of were *irregular* (327), the remedy in general must be trespass; and therefore, where a justice of the peace maliciously and irregularly granted a warrant against a person for felony, without any information upon oath, it was decided that the remedy against the justice should have been trespass and not case (y) (328); and though case may be supported for maliciously suing out a commission of bankruptcy (z), or now a fiat, yet an action of trespass is also sustainable for the seizure of goods under the same, because if the plaintiff were not subject to the bankrupt laws, the commissioners had no jurisdiction, in which case trespass is always sustainable, if in other respects the injury were forcible and immediate (a).' Case, we have seen, *is also the proper remedy, where the right affected was not tangible, and consequently could not be affected by force, as reputation and health, the injuries to which are always remediable by action on the case; as libels, or verbal slander. It is also the only remedy against sheriffs, justices, especially after convictions quashed (b), or other officers acting ministerially and not judicially (c), for refusing bail (d), or to receive an examination upon the statute of hue and [*153]

(o) Willes, 71 to 75; and see note to the precedent in case for laying rubbish in a street, *post*, vol. ii. and 11 East, 60. When not, see 12 East, 432. Injuries arising from keeping mischievous animals, and from public nuisances, also frequently affect *personal* property; and on the other hand, many of the wrongs hereafter enumerated as affecting personal property may also affect persons, as negligence in riding horses and driving carriages, &c.

(p) *Ante*, 94.

(q) *Ante*, 144.

(r) *Ante*, 94, 95.

(s) 3 T. R. 185; Boot *v.* Cooper, 1 T. R. 535; 3 Esp. Rep. 135; 11 East, 297; 1 Campb. 295; 2 Chit. R. 304; 1 D. & R. 97.

(t) 2 Chit. Rep. 304.

(u) 2 Wils. 302.

(x) 1 Saund. 228, 230, n. 4.

(y) 2 T. R. 225; 2 Chit. Rep. 304; 1 D. & R. 97.

(z) 2 Wils. 145.

(a) 2 Wils. 382, 381; Cullen's Bank. Law, 412, 413; see 2 D. & R. 353; 1 B. & C. 63, S. C.

(b) 43 G. 3, c 141, *post*.

(c) Com Dig. Action on the Case, Misfeasance, A. 1, &c. See *ante*, 89, 90, as to liability of public officers.

(d) 2 Saund. 61 c. d.; 3 B. & P. 551.

(326) So in case, parties may be joined as defendants, who were not present when the act complained of was done, and therefore not liable in trespass. Moreton *v.* Hardern, 6 Dowl. & Ryl. 275.

(327) {See however Moreton *v.* Hardern, 6 Dowl. and Ryl. 275, and observe the reasons upon which the form of action was sustained in that case.

(328) {Berry *v* Hamill, 12 Serg. & Rawle, 210.} Vide Beaurain *v.* Sir William Scott, 3 Campb. 388, which was an action on the case against the defendant, a judge of an ecclesiastical court, for excommunicating a party for refusing to obey an order which the court had no authority to make.

I. ON THE CASE.

cry, &c. (e); and case lies against surgeons, agents, &c. for improper treatment, or for want of skill or care; though assumpsit is also sustainable (f).

To persons relatively.

Actions for injuries to the *relative* rights of persons, as for seducing or harboring wives, enticing away or harboring apprentices or servants, are properly in case; though it is now usual, and perhaps more correct, to declare in trespass *vi et armis* and *contra pacem*, for criminal conversation, and for debauching daughters or servants (g); yet as the consequent loss of society or service is the ground of action, the plaintiff is still at liberty to declare in case (h) (329). When, however, the action is for an injury really committed with force, as by menacing, beating, or imprisoning wives, daughters, and servants, it is most proper to declare in trespass (i).

To personal property, and for breach of a duty or contract, and when it is a concurrent remedy with assumpsit.

For injuries to *personal* property not committed with force or not immediate (k), or where the plaintiff's right thereto is in reversion (l); case is the proper remedy (330). It lies against attornies or other agents *for neglect* or other breach of duty or misfeasance in the conduct of a cause, or other business (331), &c. though it has been more usual to declare against them in assumpsit (m) (332). And though we have seen that assumpsit is the usual remedy for neglect or breach of duty against bailees (n); as against carriers, wharfingers, and others having the use or care of personal property, whose liability is founded on the common law as well as on the contract; yet it is clear that they are also liable in case for an injury resulting *from their neglect or breach of duty in the course of their employ (o). For any misfeasance by a party in a trade which he professes, the law gives an action upon the case to the party grieved against him; as if a smith in shoeing my horse prick him, and other like cases (p). And it seems that although there be an express contract, still if a *common law duty* result from the facts, the party may be sued in tort for any neglect or misfeasance in the execution of the contract (q).

[*154]

(e) 1 Leon. 323, 324.
(f) 8 East, 348.
(g) 2 New Rep. 476; 2 M. & Sel 436.
(h) 5 East, 39. See the reasons, and the different precedents, *post*, vol. ii. Index, "Debauching Wife and Daughters." 2 Chit. Rep. 260, *ante*, 143.
(i) 2 M. & Sel. 436; 3 Campb. 526 n.
(k) *Ante*, 143.
(l) 7 T. R. 9; 3 Campb. 187.
(m) 6 East, 333.
(n) *Ante*, 115.
(o) See 2 B. & B. 54; 6 B. & C. 268.
(p) 1 Saund. 312 a., and n. 2.
(q) 2 Wils. 319. *Per* Bayley, J., 5 B. & C. 605; 8 D. & R. 378, S. C.; 2 Chit. Rep. 1.

---

(329) { Muse v. Heffernan, 6 Munf. 27. See 12 Serg. & Rawle, 212. Reynolds v. Orvis, 7 Cow. Rep. 269. But in such a case in Pennsylvania, no action can be maintained against a constable executing such process, unless a copy of it be previously demanded, agreeably to the 6th section of the act of 21st March, 1772, (1 Sm. Laws, 364.) Varley v Zahn, 11 Serg. & Rawle, 185. }

(330) Hornketh v. Barr, 8 Serg. & Rawle, 36. Parker v. Elliotte, Gilm. Rep. 33. Mercer v. Warmesly, 5 Harr. & Johns. 27. Lockwood v. Betts, 8 Conn. Rep. 130. Moran v. Hawes, 4 Cow. Rep. 412. Clark v. Fitch, 2 Wend. R. 459.

(331) As, if the owner of a horse hire him to another for a certain time, and while the hirer is using the horse, the defendant drives against him and kills him, the owner's remedy is by action on the case and not trespass; this being in the nature of an injury to the plaintiff's reversion. Hall v. Pickard, 3 Campb. 187. But where the owner gratuitously permits another person to use the chattel, it is still constructively in his possession, and he may maintain trespass. Lotan v. Cross, 2 Campb. 464.

(332) Dearborn v. Dearborn, 15 Mass. Rep. 316 So, if he disobey the lawful instructions of his client, and a loss ensues. Gilbert v. Williams, 8 Mass. Rep. 51. Vide Taylor, 62, 63. Church and Demilt v. Mumford, 11 Johns. Rep. 479. Stimpson v. Sprague, Adm., 6 Greenl. Rep. 470.

I. OF THE CASE.

If the contract be laid as *inducement* only, it seems that case for an act, in its nature a tort or injury, afterwards committed in breach of the contract, may often be adopted. On this ground, case for not accounting for, and for converting to the defendant's use, bills delivered to him to be discounted, or the proceeds of such bills, is probably sustainable (*r*). And in *Mast* v. *Goodson* (*s*) it was held that a count *in case*, setting out an agreement by which the plaintiff was to build a yard in defendant's close, and lay out not less than £20, and was to enjoy it for life, and averring that defendant built the yard and enjoyed it for some years as an easement, but defendant afterwards wrongfully obstructed him in the enjoyment of it, was good. In that case the action was founded on a contract; but the obstruction to the plaintiff's right for which the action was brought was *ex delicto*, although the right also arose out of the contract (*t*). And a count stating that the plaintiff being possessed of some old materials, retained the defendant to perform the carpenter's work on certain buildings of the plaintiff, and to use those old materials, but that the defendant, instead of using those, made use of new ones, thereby increasing the expense, is sustainable (*u*).

"Where there is an express promise, and a legal obligation results from it, then the plaintiff's cause of action is most accurately described in assumpsit, in which the promise is stated as the gist of the action. But where from a *given state of facts the law raises a legal obligation to do a particular act, [*155] and there is a breach of that obligation, and a consequential damage, there, although assumpsit may be maintainable upon a promise implied by law to do the act, still an action on the case founded in tort is the more proper form of action, in which the plaintiff in his declaration states the facts out of which the legal obligation arises, the obligation itself, the breach of it, and the damage resulting from that breach." (*x*) Therefore, where by *deed-poll* a lessee assigned his term to another, "subject to the rent and covenants," and in consequence of the non-performance of the covenants the lessee was damnified, it was held that he might sue the assignee in an action upon the case founded in tort; for, under the circumstances, the *law raised a duty* in the defendant to perform the covenants, and the breach of that duty had caused an injury to the plaintiff (*y*).

If there be a covenant or contract under seal between the same parties, and directly relating to the matter in dispute, the action must in general be in covenant, and founded thereon (*z*); and consequently in the instance last mentioned, if the assignee had covenanted with the lessee to perform the covenants in the lease, case could not have been maintained, though case for actual waste is sustainable, notwithstanding the defendant covenanted to keep in repair (*a*). So where there is a charter-party between the master of a ship and the freighter, case does not lie against the master for the breach of a

(*r*) 1 New Rep. 43; 6 East, 333, S. C. in error.

(*s*) 3 Wils. 349; 2 Bla. Rep. 848, S. C.

(*t*) *Per* Holroyd, J., 6 B. & C. 273; 9 D. & R. 264, S. C.; and in 1 New Rep. 46, Heath, J., observed that in Mast *v.* Goodson the Court was of opinion that a count upon a cause of action to which a contract is only inducement, may be joined with a count upon a tort.

(*u*) 5 T. Rep. 143; see 1 Esp. Rep. 75.

(*x*) *Per* Littledale, J., in 5 B. & C. 609; 8 D. & R. 381, S. C.

(*y*) 5 B. & C. 589; 8 D. & R. 368, S. C.

(*z*) *Ante*, 134. There is an exception in the case of a tenant committing waste, *post*, 160.

(*a*) 2 Bla. Rep. 1111; *post*, 181.

I. ON THE CASE. stipulation in the charter-party (b). But we have already seen, that in some cases the *owner* may be sued in case upon his general liability, if not charged directly upon the charter-party made under seal with the master (c).

With regard to *nonfeasance*, or neglect to perform the contract, not even an action of assumpsit, much less an action upon the case, can be maintained, if no consideration existed and be stated in the declaration, to give validity to the defendant's alleged obligation to do the act. Therefore a count stating that the plaintiff retained the defendant, who was a carpenter, to repair a house before a given day, and that the defendant accepted the retainer, but did not
[*156] perform *the work, *per quod* the walls were injured, cannot be supported (d). For the count shows no consideration or legal liability on the part of the defendant to proceed with the work. There are, however, some particular instances of persons exercising certain public trades or employments, who are bound by law to do what is required of them in the course of their employments, without the aid of an express contract, and are in return entitled to a recompense, and may therefore be sued in case, as for a breach of duty in refusing to exercise their callings. As where a common carrier, having convenience, refuses to carry goods, being tendered satisfaction for the carriage; or an innkeeper to receive a guest, having room for him; or a smith, having materials for the purpose, to shoe the horse of a traveller; or a ferryman to convey one over a common ferry, and the like (e). If the tort of the bailee, &c. consist in some nonfeasance or default, where the act required to be done was not imposed upon him by law, in respect of the employment, and did not impliedly result as a duty from such employment, but was created by express written contract, it would seem that case is not the proper remedy, and that the action should be in assumpsit. In an action upon the case a count charged that the plaintiff had delivered to the defendant certain pigs to be taken care of by him, "and in consideration thereof the defendant agreed to take care of the pigs, and *to re-deliver* the same on request." The Court held, that this count was to be considered in *assumpsit;* and Mr. Justice Littledale said, "Suppose a written contract had been entered into in the terms of this count, it could never have been contended that a breach of it might be laid in tort; it would be as reasonable to lay in tort a breach of an agreement to convey a house or land." (f)

Case or assumpsit may be supported for a false warranty on the sale of goods (g); but for a breach of an express or implied contract of warranty, it is usual and perhaps better to declare in assumpsit, in order that the count
[*157] for money *had and received, to recover back the consideration paid, may be included in the declaration; and where the defendant said, "the horse is sound, but mind I do not warrant him," and it was proved that he knew it was un-

(b) 6 Moore, 425.

(c) 6 Moore, 415; *ante*, 117.

(d) 5 T. R. 143.

(e) 1 Saund. 312 c. note 2; 5 T. R. 149, 150.

(f) 6 B. & C. 268, 274; 9 D & R. 265, S. C. And see 1 Saund. 312 c. note (e), 5th edit. *Sed quære* whether trover or detinue cannot be maintained against a bailee who wrongfully refuses to re-deliver the goods upon a demand, although he had expressly, verbally or in writing, agreed to restore them?

(g) Dougl. 21; 2 East, 416. Case lies for the deceitful warranty, although it was part of the contract that if the vendee disliked the goods, the vendor should exchange them for others of equal value, 2 Stark. R. 162.

sound, Lord Tenterden held that he was properly sued in assumpsit, on his promise that he was sound (*h*)(333). Case is necessarily the form of action to be adopted for (now in writing) deceitfully representing a person to be fit to be trusted (334) or other deceit, independently of and without relation to any contract between the parties (*i*)(335). And for fraudulent representations not introduced into a written contract between the parties, respecting the subject-matter of the representations, case (336) is the proper remedy, if any (*k*). In an action upon the case in tort for a breach of a *warranty* of goods, the *scienter* need not be laid in the declaration, nor if charged would it be proved (*l*). And where the plaintiff, an auctioneer, was employed by the defendant, who had goods in his possession, but was not the owner, to sell them, which the plaintiff did, and was afterwards compelled by the real owner to make satisfaction to him for the proceeds; it was held, after verdict, that a count in case for representing that the defendant was entitled to sell the goods, and thereby deceiving him, was maintainable, although the declaration did not charge that the defendant knew that he was not the owner of the goods at the time the representation was made (*m*).

If goods be obtained on credit through a fraudulent contract, the proper remedy is case or trover, at least before the expiration of the credit; for if *before* that time he sue in assumpsit for goods sold, he recognizes or affirms the contract, and may be successfully met by the objection that the credit has not expired (*n*).

We have already noticed the instances in which case or trespass should be brought against a person who causes an injury by driving his carriage against another's (*o*), or by negligence in navigating a ship (*p*); and the distinctions when the master should be sued in case, and when in trespass (337), have also been adverted to (*q*).

(*h*) Sittings at Westminster, 1830; *ante*, 122.
(*i*) 2 East, 22; 3 T. R. 51; 4 Bing. 73; 9 G. 4, c. 14.
(*k*) 4 Camph. 22; *ante*, 122.
(*l*) 2 East, 446; 4 Bing. 73.
(*m*) 4 Bing. 66.
(*n*) 9 B. & C. 59.
(*o*) *Ante*, 145. Case is the proper remedy at the suit of the owner of horses let to hire against a third person, 3 Campb. 187; 5 Esp. R. 35; but trespass should be brought if the horses were merely lent, 2 Campb. 464.
(*p*) See *ante*, 146.
(*q*) *Ante*, 149.

(333) The plaintiff is not permitted to establish deceit and fraud, when he declares in *assumpsit*, on a warranty expressed or implied. Evertson's Ex'rs *v.* Miles, 6 Johns Rep. 138. { Shepherd *v.* Worthing, 1 Aiken's (Vermont) Rep. 188. } Pickering and others *v.* Dowson and others, 4 Taunt. 786.

(334) Vide Upton *v.* Vail, 6 Johns. Rep. 181. Russell *v.* Clark's Ex'rs and others, 7 Cranch, 92.

(335) So, if on the gift of a chattel the donor affirm it to be his own, and the donee be afterwards evicted, case will lie. Barney *v.* Dewey, 13 Johns. Rep. 226. So, an action on the case lies for fraud, or a false affirmation in the sale of land, as where the land pretended to be sold has no real existence, notwithstanding any covenants in the deed. Wardell *v.* Fosdick and Davis, 13 Johns. Rep. 325. Frost and others *v* Raymond, 2 Caines' Rep. 193. Bostwick *v.* Lewis, 1 Day's Rep. 250. Monell and Weller *v.* Colden, 13 Johns. Rep. 395. In Gallagher *v.* Brunel, 6 Cowen, 346, the principles established in Pasley *v.* Freeman are fully recognized. In the later case of Benton *v.* Pratt, 2 Wend. R. 385, an action on the case was held to lie, for the assertion of falsehood with a fraudulent intent as to a present or existing fact, where a direct, positive and material injury results from such assertion. So, it was held to lie against a public officer for a false and fraudulent representation made by him in relation to property sold by him; and it is no answer that the sale was made by him in his official character. Gulver *v.* Avery, 7 Wend. R. 380.

(336) Vide Hallock *v.* Powell, 3 Cai. R. 216.

(337) Moreton *v.* Hardern, 6 Dowl. & Ryl. 275.

I. ON THE CASE.

*Where a distress has been made for rent, and there was no rent due, an action of trespass, or case on the statute (*r*), may be supported (*s*). So where a distress is made after a tender of the rent, case or trespass may be supported (*t*). If the person making the distress turn the tenant out of possession, or continue in possession an unreasonable time beyond the five days, trespass lies (*u*); and it may be supported where a party taking a distress *damage feasant* has been guilty of any irregularity (338), rendering him a trespasser *ab initio* (*x*). In the case of a distress for rent, if it were lawful in its inception, a subsequent irregularity will not render the party a trespasser *ab initio*, or subject him to an action of trespass or trover (*y*); and case is the proper remedy in these and most other instances of irregularity in the taking or sale or disposal of a distress (*z*) (339). This action also lies for the rescue or pound-breach of cattle, or goods distrained for rent or *damage feasant* (*a*); or for the rescue of a person arrested on mesne process; and for an excessive levy on a *fieri facias* (*b*); and against sheriffs, &c. for escapes, on mesne or final process; or for not arresting the debtor when he had an opportunity; or for not selling on a *fi. fa.* in a reasonable time (*c*), and for a false return of *non est inventus* to mesne process, or of *nulla bona* to a writ of *fi fa.*; or for not levying under it when he had an opportunity; or for not taking a replevin bond; or for taking insufficient pledges in replevin; or for not assigning a bail-bond (*d*) (340). For an escape on final process, it is most advisable to declare in debt, if the caption of the original defendant can

[*159] be clearly proved, because in debt the jury must give *a verdict for the entire demand (*e*)(341); but if it be doubtful whether a caption can be proved, the declaration should be in case, proceeding for the escape in one count, and in the second for not taking the defendant when the sheriff had an opportunity; and the same observation applies when it is doubtful whether a sheriff has levied under a writ of *fieri facias*, or where he has neglected to levy the whole amount. Case also lies for not delivering letters, &c. (*f*); and against a wit-

(*r*) 2 Wm. & M. c. 5.

(*s*) As to what are irregularities in a distress for which this action is maintainable, see *post*, vol. ii, and notes to the precedents.

(*t*) 2 D. & R. 256; 1 B. & C. 145; *ante*, 146.

(*u*) 1 East, 139; 11 East, 395; 2 Campb. 115. How long the landlord may remain, see 4 B. & A. 208, qualifying 1 Hen. Bla. 13.

(*x*) 8 Co. 146; Bac. Ab. Trespass, B.

(*y*) 11 Geo. 2, c. 19; 1 Hen. Bla. 13. So on any Turnpike Act, 3 Geo. 4, c. 126, s. 144.

(*z*) See the cases and precedents, *post*, vol. ii

(*a*) For law, &c. see *post*, vol. ii. But case does not lie for detaining cattle distrained *damage feasant*, where tender of sufficient amends was made after the cattle had been impounded, 1 Bing. 341; 1 Taunt. 261.

(*b*) See 9 B. & C. 840.

(*c*) Jacobs *v.* Humphrey, 4 Tyr. 272.

(*d*) See precedent and notes, *post*, vol. ii. An action on the case does not lie for not having money levied on *fieri facias* in court, where sheriff had not been ruled, 1 Stark. 388. Money had and received to recover money levied, see 3 Campb. 347; 8 B. & C. 726; 3 M. & R. 411, S. C.; 1 B. & B. 380, 370; 16 East, 274.

(*e*) 2 T. R. 129; 1 Saund. 38, n. 2; 2 Chit. R. 454.

(*f*) 3 Wils. 443.

---

(338) Vide Sackrider *v.* M'Donald, 10 Johns Rep. 252. Hopkins *v.* Hopkins, id. 369.

(339) In Pennsylvania, trespass is the proper form of action. Kerr *v.* Sharp, 14 Serg. & Rawle, 399.

(340) The 14th and 15th sections only, are in force in Pennsylvania. Roberts' Dig. 236. 3 Binn. 626. 14 Serg. & Rawle, 403.

(341) So, trespass on the case lies against an officer, for levying a warrant for a fine, in an oppressive and unreasonable manner, with intent to vex, harass, and oppress the party. Rogers *v.* Brewster, 5 Johns. Rep. 125.

ness for not obeying a writ of subpœna (*f*); and for infringing the copyright of a book, print, single sheet of music, or other work (*g*); and for the infringement of a patent (*h*); and for obstructing the proprietor of tithes from entering on land to take them away (*i*)(342). For injuries to any personal property in reversion, trespass or trover cannot be supported; and case is the only remedy (*k*). I. ON THE CASE.

In some cases, though the injury be forcible and immediate, the plaintiff may waive the trespass, and sue in trover or in case for the consequential damage, and in this respect trover is in general a concurrent remedy with trespass, for the unlawful taking and conversion of goods (*l*); and case is a good form of action for an excessive distress for rent, though the tenant has tendered the rent to his landlord before the distress was levied, and the distress was therefore void (*m*). Various other instances will be found in which trespass and case are concurrent remedies; and in many cases the owner of goods may waive the tort in taking them, and recover the proceeds in an action for money had and received (*n*).

With respect to injuries to *real property corporeal*, where the injury was immediate, and committed on land, &c. in the possession of the plaintiff, the remedy is trespass (*o*); but for nonfeasance, as for not carrying away tithes (*p*); or where the injury is not immediate but consequential, as for placing a spout To real property.

(*f*) Dougl. 556, 561; 9 East, 473; 13 East, 17, n. c.
(*g*) 11 East, 244; 1 Campb. 94, 98.
(*h*) *Post*, vol. ii.
(*i*) 2 New Rep. 466.
(*k*) 7 T. R. 9; 3 Campb. 187.
(*l*) 1 Salk. 10; 1 B. & C. 146; 2 D. & R. 256, S. C. But the converse does not so generally hold, see *post*, Trespass.
(*m*) 1 B. & C. 145; 2 D. & R. 251, S. C.
(*n*) *Ante*, 80; 1 B & C. 418; 2 D. & R. 568, S. C.
(*o*) *Ante*, 144; 1 Ld. Raym. 188.
(*p*) 1 Ld. Raym. 187; *post*, vol. ii.

(342) At common law the plaintiff had no remedy against the sheriff for an escape, whether upon mesne process, or in execution, but by special action upon the case; but now by an equitable construction of Weston, 2. c. 11, an action of debt is given against sheriffs for escapes of prisoners in execution. Bac. Abr. Escape in civil cases F. By the New York statute, sess. 36, c. 67, s. 19. 1 R. L. 425, sheriffs on an escape of a party in execution, are rendered answerable to the plaintiff for the debt and damages for which the party was arrested, and the plaintiff may recover the same with costs by action of debt. The common law remedy by action on the case is not taken away by the statute. In the action on the case, the jury may inquire what was lost by the escape, and give such damages as they suppose the party has sustained; but in the action of debt, every inquiry of that kind is improper, for the statute has fixed the extent of the sheriff's liability, that is, for the original debt and damages recovered. Rawson *v.* Dole, 2 Johns. Rep. 454. Under the statute, debt lies only for an escape, where the prisoner is in execution; and a prisoner is not in execution, until a writ of execution against the body has been issued and delivered to the sheriff, as the English practice of charging the debt in execution without the issuing of a *ca. sa.* has never been adopted in the State of New York. Debt therefore will not lie for the escape of a prisoner who has been surrendered by his bail, he not being in execution by virtue of the surrender. Van Slyck *v.* Hogeboom, 6 Johns. Rep. 270. In the action of debt for an escape, interest is not recoverable, Rawson *v.* Dole, ubi sup. {In Pennsylvania, each sheriff enters into a recognizance, and becomes bound with at least two sureties in an obligation, conditioned for the faithful performance of official conduct. It has been held in a suit upon such recognizance, against a sheriff and his sureties, for suffering a person in execution to escape, that the defendant could not give evidence of the insolvency of such person. Wolverton *v.* Comm., 8 Serge. & Rawle, 273.} In debt against sheriff for an escape of a prisoner arrested upon attachment for not paying costs, an averment in the declaration that the sheriff arrested the party and had and detained him in custody in execution, &c. is equivalent to an averment that he was committed to jail. Ames et al. *v.* Webbers, 8 Wend. R. 545. Debt for an escape against a sheriff lies only where the escape is from imprisonment on an execution issued from a court of record. It is in the nature of a penalty against the sheriff for negligence. Brown *v.* Genung, 1 Wend. R. 115.

1. ON THE CASE. near the plaintiff's land, so that water afterwards ran thereon, or for causing water to run from the defendant's *land to that of the plaintiff (q); or where the plaintiff's property is only in reversion (r), and not in possession, the action should be in case; and it has been considered that case and not trespass is the proper remedy for continuing holdfasts in the plaintiff's wall after he had recovered in trespass for the original driving (s). It appears, however, as already remarked, that the injury is sometimes considered to be immediate, if it be the natural and inevitable consequence of the act done; as if the defendant's servant by his order place rubbish so *near* the plaintiff's wall that some of it must naturally, or in all probability, roll against the wall, and it accordingly does so (t). Case is the proper remedy for obstructing light or air through ancient windows by an erection on the adjoining land; and such action may be brought in the name of the tenant in possession, or of the person entitled to the immediate reversion, though the averments in the declaration necessarily differ in the latter case. So it lies for any other nuisance to houses or lands in possession, and for injuries to water-courses where the plaintiff is not the owner of the soil, but is merely entitled to the use of the water (u).

Waste is either commissive, that is, wilful, or permissive, that is, a neglect to repair, whereby dilapidations occur. An action upon the case in the nature of waste, to the injury of the reversion, is certainly maintainable for *commissive* waste by a reversioner against his tenant (343), or a stranger (x)(344). And where the lessee even covenants not to do waste, the lessor has his election to bring either an action on the case, or of covenant, against the lessee for wilful waste done by him during the term. As where a lease was made for twenty-one years, in which the lessee covenanted to yield up the premises repaired at the end of the term, the lessee during the term committed wilful waste, and at the expiration thereof delivered up the premises to the lessor in a ruinous condition; afterwards the lessor brought an action on the case against the tenant for waste committed by him during the term, and it being [*161] objected at the trial that the *plaintiff ought to have brought an action of covenant, and not on the case, a verdict was found for the plaintiff subject to that point; but the Court of Common Pleas was clearly of opinion that an action on the case was maintainable as well as covenant; and the C. J. said "tenant for years commits waste, and delivers up the place wasted to the land-

(q) *Ante*, 145; Str. 634, 635; Lord Raym. 1399; 2 Burr. 1114; Fortesc. 212.
(r) Com. Dig. Action, Case, Nuisance, B.
(s) 1 Stark. 22.
(t) 9 B. & C. 591; 4 M. & R. 500, S. C.
(u) 2 B. & C. 910; 4 D. & R. 583, S.C.; 6 Price, 1; see 7 Moore, 345.

(x) 1 Saund. 323 b; 2 Saund. 252 b. If trees be excepted from a demise, *waste* cannot be committed in cutting them down, 8 East, 190. The injury would be a *trespass*. The *tenant's* remedy against a stranger is trespass, *id.*; 1 Taunt. 194.

(343) So an action on the case lies in favor of a landlord against any person who so wrongfully and maliciously disturbs his tenants that they abandon his premises, and the landlord thereby loses his rent. Aldridge v. Stuyvesant, 1 Hall's Rep. 210.

(344) Occupier of one of two houses built nearly at the same time, and purchased of the same proprietor, may maintain a special action on the case, against the tenant of the other, for obstructing his window lights by adding to his own building, however short the previous period of enjoyment by the plaintiff; on the principle, that where a man sells a house, he shall not afterwards be permitted to disturb the rights that appertain to it, and what the original owner could not have done, neither could his lessee do. Compton v. Richards, 1 Price's Exch. Rep. 27.

lord, had there been no deed of covenant, an action of waste, or case in the nature of waste, would have lain. Because the landlord by the special covenant acquires a new remedy, does he therefore lose his old?" (y) And a landlord may sue a tenant holding over by *sufferance*, in *case* for wilful waste (z). It was held, before the late repealing act, that a reversioner might sue the hundred on the 9 Geo. 1, c. 22, to recover damages for an injury done to premises maliciously set on fire (a).

With regard to *permissive* waste there seems to be some difficulty. It is laid down by great authority (b), that the statute of Gloucester (c), (which extended the ancient law of waste by the writ of waste) applies to *permissive* waste by a tenant from year to year. In *Gibson* v. *Wells* (d) it was held, that case for permissive waste is not sustainable against a yearly tenant; and in *Herne* v. *Bembow* (e) it was decided, that case for such waste does not lie against a tenant for a term of years holding upon a lease, which does not contain a covenant to repair. In a subsequent case, *Jones* v. *Hill* (f), it was determined that an action upon the case in the nature of waste cannot be supported against the assignee of a lease, in which the lessee had covenanted "from time to time, and at all times during the term, when need should require, sufficiently to repair the premises with all necessary reparations, and to yield up the same so well repaired at the end of the term, *in as good condition* as the same should be in when finished *under the direction of J. M.*" Upon a breach that the defendant suffered the premises to become and be in decay and ruinous during a large part of the term, and after the term wrongfully yielded them up in much worse order and condition than when the same were finished under the direction of J. M.; the Court did not decide that an action upon the case was not maintainable for permissive *waste but only that it was [*162] impossible it should be *waste* merely to omit to put the premises into such repair as A. B. had put them into (g); in other words, the peculiar terms of the covenant were such, that a breach of them could not be considered so far within the technical doctrine of *waste*, as to justify an action upon the case, and therefore covenant should have been the form of action. It has been lately decided, that if a lessee assign the term to another by *deed-poll*, "subject to the performance of the covenants in the lease," the lessee may maintain case against the assignee for a breach of covenant in the lease committed after the assignment, *per quod* the lessee was damnified (h). Assumpsit is the usual form of action against a tenant not holding by deed, upon his implied (or express) promise to cultivate a farm according to the rules of good husbandry, and to use the premises in a tenant-like manner (i).

Case may be maintained upon the custom of the realm against the personal representatives of a rector, &c. at the suit of the successor, for dilapida-

(y) 2 Bla. Rep. 1111; Kenlyside v. Thornton, 2 Saund. 252 a, b, note.

(z) Tabart v. Tipper, 1 Campb. 350.

(a) 9 B. & C. 134; 4 M. & R. 130, S. C.

(b) 1 Saund. 323 b, n. 7, cites 2 Inst. 302; Co. Lit. 54 b. See however the note in Co. Lit. 15th edit. citing Dyer, 198.

(c) 6 Edw. 1, c. 5.

(d) 1 New Rep. 290.

(e) 4 Taunt. 764.

(f) 7 Taunt. 392; 1 Moore, 100, S. C. In the latter report the marginal note seems to be too general.

(g) Per Lord Tenterden, 5 B. & C. 603; 8 D. & R. 375, S. C.

(h) 5 B. & C. 589; 8 D. & R. 368, S. C.; *ante*, 136.

(i) See the precedent and notes, *post*, vol. ii.

I. ON THE CASE.

tions (*j*); and it lies for not repairing fences, whereby the plaintiff's cattle escaped from his land, or the cattle of the defendant got into the land of the plaintiff (*k*); or whereby the cattle in the plaintiff's possession escaped and fell into a pit and were killed (*l*); or a hay-stack in the defendant's close fell on and killed plaintiff's horses (*m*). For the escape of the defendant's cattle into the plaintiff's close the plaintiff might support *trespass*, or distrain the cattle damage feasant (345).

We may remember that trespass cannot in general be supported where the matter affected is not substantial, or the estate therein is *incorporeal* (*n*). Case therefore is the proper remedy for disturbance of common of pasture, turbary, or estovers (*o*). If the plaintiff's cattle be chased off the common, trespass may be supported for such chasing; and that form of action may in some instances be advisable, in order that the right may be fully stated on the record. So case is the proper form of action for obstructing a private way (*p*), or a public way, *per quod* the plaintiff was delayed on his journey, and obliged to take a more circuitous rout (*q*), or sustained some other special damage. So case is the proper remedy for disturbing a party in the [*163] possession of a pew in *a church; but no action for such disturbance can be maintained unless the pew were annexed to a house in the parish (*r*). Perhaps trespass may be sustained if the pew to which the plaintiff is entitled as appurtenant to his messuage be *broken* (*s*)(346); and that form of action may be adopted by the erector of a tombstone against a person who wrongfully removes it from the church-yard, and erases the inscription (*t*).

Case is in general the remedy for disturbing a party in the enjoyment of an *easement* (*u*), and it may be maintained in that instance, although the right to the easement were conferred by a written agreement, which is stated in the declaration, and which stipulates for the enjoyment of the easement (*x*). It lies for disturbance, obstruction, or other injuries, to offices, franchises, ferries, markets, or tolls, or for not grinding at an ancient mill, &c. (*y*). And it may be maintained for disturbing and injuring the right to, and enjoyment of, an ancient decoy (*z*); but no action is sustainable for frightening away game from a preserve (not being a franchise), or for disturbing a rookery (*a*).

(*j*) *Ante*, 104.
(*k*) 1 Salk. 335; *post*, vol. ii.
(*l*) Rooth *v.* Wilson, 1 B. & Ald. 59; 2 Younge & Jerv. 391.
(*m*) 2 Younge & Jerv. 391.
(*n*) *Ante*, 150.
(*o*) Com. Dig. Action, Case, Disturbance, A. 1. If inclosed uninterruptedly more than twenty years *case* will not lie, and the remedy is by *assize of common*. 2 Taunt. 156, 160; see 2 B. & C. 918; 4 D. & R. 572, S. C.; 7 *id.* 346; 9 D. & R. 897, S. C.
(*p*) Com. Dig. Action, Case, Disturbance, A. 2.
(*q*) 9 Moore, 489.
(*r*) 5 B. & A. 356; 8 B. & C. 294; 2 M. & R. 332, S. C.
(*s*) See 2 Rol. R. 140; Palm. 46; *per* Best, C. J., 3 Bing. 137, 138.
(*t*) 3 Bing. 136.
(*u*) 5 B. & A. 361; 5 B. & C. 221; 7 D. & R. 783, S. C.; 8 B. & C. 288, 294, 295; 3 M. & R. 318. An easement can be granted by deed only, *id.*
(*x*) 3 Wils. 348; 6 B. & C. 273; 9 D. & R. 265, S. C.; *ante*, 144, 145.
(*y*) See Com. Dig. Action, Case, Disturbance, and Action, Case, Nuisance; 6 M. & Sel. 69. See many instances of actionable obstruction or disturbance of a party in the exercise of a right put by Holt, C. J., 11 East, 576, note.
(*z*) 11 East, 571; 2 Campb. 258.
(*a*) 4 D. & R. 518.

(345) Vide Provost, &c. of Queen's College *v.* Hallett, 14 East's Rep. 489. ante, 50, n. 106. So, it lies against the assignee of a lessee. Short *v.* Wilson and others, 13 Johns. Rep. 33. 2 Saund. 252. a. c.
(346) But not for permissive waste. Gibson *v.* Wells, 1 New Rep. 290.

An action on the case is frequently given by the express provision of some *statute* to a party aggrieved (*b*); and it has even been decided that where a navigation act empowered the company to sue for calls, &c. by action of debt or on the case, that an action on the case in tort might be supported, though the defendant were thereby deprived of the means of availing himself of a set-off (*c*). Whenever a statute prohibits an injury to an individual, or enacts that he shall recover a penalty or damages for such injury, though the statute be silent as to the form of the remedy, this action, or in some instances an action of debt (*d*), may be supported (*e*); as on the *statute (*f*) at the suit of a landlord against a sheriff, for taking goods under an execution, without paying a year's rent (*g*); and on the statute of Winton (*h*) at the suit of a party robbed against the hundred; or upon the Black Act, or the Riot Act (*i*); or on different statutes relative to irregularities in making or disposing of a distress (*k*), &c. In these and other instances case may be supported by implication; and if a statute give a remedy in the affirmative, without a negative expressed or implied, for a matter which was actionable by the common law, the party may sue at common law, as well as upon the statute (*l*) (347). But in some instances the statute prescribes a particular remedy, in conferring a new right, or creating a liability; and in that case the remedy pointed out, and no other, can be pursued (*m*). In many cases the common law remedy is altered by a statute. Thus the 43 Geo. 3, c. 141, enacts, that in all actions against any justice of the peace for any conviction, &c. which may have been quashed, or for any matter done by him for carrying it into effect, the plaintiff shall not recover more than the sum levied under the conviction, and 2*d*. damages, unless it be expressly alleged in the declaration, which shall be in an action *on the case only*, that such acts were done maliciously, and without any reasonable cause (*n*). We have seen that a common informer cannot sue unless an action be expressly given to him (*o*). [*164]

I. ON THE CASE. On a statute.

The judgment of Lord Ellenborough, C. J., in the case of *Govett* v. *Radnidge* (*p*) explains the advantages arising in many instances from the adoption of the action on the case, in preference to the action of assumpsit; viz. "there is no inconvenience in suffering the party to allege his gravamen as a breach of duty arising out of an employment for hire, and to consider that breach of duty as tortious negligence, instead of considering the same circumstances as forming a breach of promise implied from the same consideration of hire. By allowing it to be considered in either way, according as the *neglect of duty or the breach of promise is relied upon as the injury, a mul- [*165]

Of the advantages of this action, in reference to others.

(*b*) Com. Dig. Action upon Statute, A. F. and Pleader, II. s. 1 to 2, s. 30.

(*c*) 7 T. R. 36.

(*d*) *Ante*, 127.

(*e*) *Supra*, note (*q*); 10 Co. 75 b; 2 Inst. 486; 2 Salk. 451; 6 Mod. 26.

(*f*) 8 Ann c. 14.

(*g*) Dougl. 665; see 3 B. & A. 440, 645; 7 Price, 566, 690.

(*h*) 13 Edw. 1, st. 2, c. 1, 2; 2 Saund. 374, 375; Com. Dig. Pleader, 2, s. 1.

(*i*) 9 Geo. 1, c. 22, s. 7; 3 East, 400, 457. Against the parish, 11 East, 352, &c. Against the hundred, 12 East, 244; see 57 Geo. 3, c. 12; 7 & 8 Geo. 4, c. 31; 3 Geo. 4, c. 33.

(*k*) *Ante*, 158.

(*l*) Com. Dig. Action upon Statute, C.

(*m*) See *ante*, 127.

(*n*) See 12 East, 67.

(*o*) *Ante*, 127.

(*p*) 3 East, 70.

(347) Little *v*. Lathrop, 5 Greenl. Rep. 356; where the law in relation to fencing against cattle is laid down.

I. ON THE CASE. tiplicity of actions is avoided; and the plaintiff, according as the convenience of his case requires, frames his principal count in such a manner, as either to join a count in trover therewith, if he have another cause of action other than the action of assumpsit, or to join with the assumpsit the common counts, if he have another cause of action to which they are applicable." Other advantages may also sometimes ensue from the adoption of case instead of assumpsit, viz. that in the former action the defendant cannot always plead in abatement the nonjoinder of other parties as defendants (*q*); and the plaintiff in case will in general be entitled to a verdict if he prove one of several defendants to be liable, whereas a different rule prevails in an action of assumpsit (*r*). If a party has obtained goods upon a fraudulent contract, whereby credit was to be allowed, he should be sued in case, at least before the expiration of the credit, as assumpsit cannot be maintained during its currency (*s*). So if a set-off be apprehended (*t*), or the defendant's certificate would be pleadable in bar (*u*) to an action of assumpsit, it would in some cases be most advisable, if possible, to avoid it, by suing in case. And again, where there has been a fraud, and it is supposed that the statute of limitations will be set up as a defence, an action for the fraud is perhaps preferable to an action of assumpsit; as there is reason to contend that the statute only begins to run from the time the fraud is discovered (*x*); and on account of costs, case is frequently preferable to trespass, as in the former action the plaintiff is entitled to full costs though he recover less than 40*s*. damages, whereas in some actions of trespass for assault and battery, or trespass to land, if the damages be under 40*s*. the plaintiff is not entitled to full costs (*y*).

Its disadvantages. On the other hand, there were some *disadvantages* attending the action on the case, on account of the generality of the pleadings, and of the circumstance of the general issue being the usual plea, which put the plaintiff on proof of the whole of the allegations in his declaration, and left the defendant at liberty to avail himself of any matter of defence at the trial, without apprizing the [*166] plaintiff by his plea of the *circumstances on which it is founded. But this objection was removed by Reg. Gen. Hil. T. 4 W. 4, reg. 5, which now compels a defendant to plead specially almost every description of defence.†

When cattle of the defendant have trespassed in the plaintiff's land, in consequence of the defendant's neglect to repair his fences, the plaintiff had an election to proceed in case or in trespass (*z*); or to distrain, if the real damage exceed 40*s*. or the circumstances be of such a nature that a verdict for that amount may be anticipated, so as to carry full costs, an action of trespass may be advisable in preference to an action on the case, in order that the trial may be upon some particular point in issue (*a*), still narrowing the evidence more than in the action on the case. It is not advisable to distrain where the title to the *locus in quo* is doubtful, but the party should proceed by action of trespass, or on the case (*b*), and the same observations apply where a right of common is in dispute (*c*).

(*q*) *Ante*, 99.
(*r*) See *ante*, 50, 99.
(*s*) 9 B. & C. 59.
(*t*) *Ante*, 113.
(*u*) *Ante*, 61, 62, 113.
(*x*) 4 Moore, 508; 2 B. & B. 73, S. C.; 3 D. & R. 322, S. C.; see 2 B. & C. 149, 259; 3 B. & A. 626.
(*y*) 6 T. R. 129.
(*z*) 1 Salk. 335.
(*a*) 2 Saund. 284 d.
(*b*) 1 Saund. 346 e, n. 2.
(*c*) *Id.*

† See American Editor's Preface.

The *declaration* in an action on the case ought not in general to state the injury to have been committed *vi et armis*, nor should it conclude *contra pacem* (*d*); in which respects it principally differs from the declaration in trespass. In other points the form of the declaration depends on the particular circumstances on which the action is founded, and consequently there is greater variety in this than any other form of action. The leading rules will be stated when we inquire into the form of the declaration in general. It is open to this commendation that the statements are not fictitious as in trover, and that it truly and specifically discloses the grounds upon which the action is founded. The *plea* in this action until recently was principally the general issue, not guilty; and under it (except in an action for slander, and a few other instances) (*e*), any matter might be given in evidence, but the statute of limitations. But since the pleading rules, H. T. 4 W. 4,† the general issue only puts in issue the wrongful act, and not the right (*f*), and most grounds of defence must be pleaded specially. The *judgment* is, that the plaintiff do recover a sum of money ascertained by a jury, for his *damages* sustained by the committing of the grievances complained of, and full *costs* of suit; to which the plaintiff is entitled, although he recover a verdict for less than 40*s*. damages (*g*); unless the judge certify under the statute (*h*); a circumstance which we have already observed frequently renders this action preferable to that of trespass.

I. OF THE CASE.

The pleadings in general, &c.

*II. TROVER.

[*167]

II. TROVER.

General observations.

The action of *trover* or *conversion* was, in its origin, an action of trespass on the case for the recovery of damages against a person who had *found* goods, and refused to deliver them on demand to the owner, but *converted* them to his own use; from which word *finding* (*trouver*) the remedy is called an action of trover. The circumstance of the defendant not being at liberty to wage his law in this action, and the less degree of certainty requisite in describing the goods, gave it so considerable an advantage over the action of detinue, (which, before the late enactment, was subject to the defence of law wager), that by a fiction of law actions of trover were at length permitted to be brought against any person who had in his possession, by any means whatever, the personal property of another, and sold or used the same without the consent of the owner, or refused to deliver the same when demanded. The injury lies in the conversion and deprivation of the plaintiff's property, which is the gist of the action, and the statement of the *finding* or *trover* is now immaterial, and not traversable (*i*); and the fact of the conversion does not necessarily import an acquisition of property in the defendant (*k*). It is

(*d*) Com. Dig. Action on Case, C. 3, 4, A.
(*e*) 1 Saund. 130, note 1; Willes, 20.
(*f*) Frankum *v.* Earl of Falmouth, 1 Harrison, 1; 6 Car. & P. 529; Bosanquet's Rules.
(*g*) 6 T. R. 129; Tidd, 9th ed. 963.
(*h*) 43 Eliz. c. 6; Tidd, 952, 953, 9th ed. This statute deprives plaintiff of costs, notwithstanding the action be brought under the 11 Geo. 2, c. 19, s. 19, by which it is enacted, that in case plaintiff obtain a verdict, he shall be entitled to full costs, 5 B. & Ald. 796; 1 D. & R. 413, S. C.
(*i*) 3 Bla. Com. 152, 153; 1 New Rep. 140; Bul. N. P. 32; 3 Wils. 336.
(*k*) 3 B. & Ald. 687.

† See American Editor's Preface.

II. TROVER. an action for the recovery of *damages* to the extent of the value of the thing converted (*l*). The object and result of the suit are not the recovery of the thing itself, which can only be recovered by action of detinue or replevin (*m*). Lord Mansfield thus defined this action (*n*): "In *form* it (*i. e.* the trover) is a fiction; in *substance* it is a remedy to recover the value of personal chattels wrongfully converted by another to his own use; the form supposes that the defendant might have come lawfully by it, and if he did not, yet by bringing this action the plaintiff waives the trespass; no damages are recoverable for the act of taking; all must be for the act of converting. This is the tort or *maleficium*, and to entitle the plaintiff to recover, two things are necessary: 1*st*, *property in the plaintiff*; 2*dly*, *a wrongful conversion* by the defendant." We will consider this action with reference, 1st, to the *thing con-*
[*168] *verted*; 2dly, the plaintiff's *right of property* *therein; and 3dly, the nature of the *injury*, and by whom committed.

1st. The property affected.

This action is confined to the conversion of *goods or personal chattels.* It does not lie for *fixtures eo nomine*; nor for injuries to land or other real property, even by a severance of a part of what properly belongs to the freehold (348), unless there has also been an asportation; but the form of action in these cases should be trespas (*o*), (or case where the interest in the property is in reversion) (*p*). An incoming tenant, though entitled to the growing crops, cannot support trover against the outgoing tenant for taking them away, nor is that form of action proper to try a right to land (*q*). But if after the severance from the freehold, as in the case of *trees or fixtures*, or *earth*, the property severed be taken away; or if coals dug in a pit be afterwards thrown out, trover may be supported (*r*). So if a tenant, during his tenancy, remove a dung-heap, and at the time of so doing dig into and remove virgin soil that is beneath it, the landlord may maintain either trespass *de bonis asportatis* or *trover*, for the removal of the virgin soil (*s*)(349). It lies for an unstamped agree-

(*l*) See 3 Campb. 477; 1 C. & P. 626.

(*m*) 3 B. & Ald. 687; Willes, 120; 2 Stark. Rep. 288.

(*n*) 1 Burr. 31; 1 Bla. Rep. 67, 68; and see 1 M. & P. 556.

(*o*) Bac. Ab. Trover, B.; 2 B. & Ald. 167. But trover lies for salt pans, though fixed in the floor of a building; and whenever the fixed instrument, engine or utensil was an accessory to a matter of a personal nature, it is considered as personalty, 3 East, 53, 54, cites 1 Hen. Bla. 259; and see 2 B. & Ald. 165. Fixtures between landlord and tenant, 3 East, 28. A veranda, 2 Stark. 403. Lime-kilns, 2 B. & C. 608. Fixtures as between the vendor and vendee of a house, 2 B. & C. 76; 3 D. & R. 255, S C. Covenant not to move them, 1 Taunt. 19; 2 B. & C. 608; 4 D. & R. 62, S. C.

(*p*) *Ante*, 153, 159.

(*q*) 16 East, 77, 79; 1 Price, 53. But where certain parts of a machine had been put up by the tenant during his term, and were capable of being removed without either injuring the other parts of the machine or the building, and had been usually valued between the outgoing and incoming tenant, it was held, that these were the goods and chattels of the outgoing tenant, for which he might maintain trover, 2 B. & Ald. 165. As to removal after tenancy, 2 B. & C. 78, 79; 3 D. & R. 257, 258, S. C.

(*r*) Com. Dig. Biens, R.; Bac. Ab. Trover, B.; 7 T. R. 13; Bul. N. P. 44.; 4 B. & Ald. 206. When a landlord has no right to recover trees he wrongfully cuts down, 5 B. & C. 897; 8 D. & R. 651, S. C.

(*s*) Higgon *v.* Mortimer, 6 Car. & P. 616.

(348) See Gay *v.* Baker, 17 Mass. Rep. 435. It was decided in that case, that in an action of trespass for pulling down and destroying the plaintiff's pew in a town or parish meeting-house, the defendant might justify under the authority of the town or parish, which has voted to alter or pull down and rebuild the house. Gay *v.* Baker, 17 Mass. R. 435.

(349) Acc. Almy *v.* Harris, 5 Johns. Rep. 175. Farmers' Turnp. Company *v.* Coventry, 10 Johns. Rep. 389. Scidmore *v.* Smith, 13 Johns. Rep. 322; {But in Pennsylva-

1st. The property affected.

ment (*t*); and for a deed relating to land (*u*); and books of account (*x*); but in these instances detinue is the more usual, and often the preferable remedy. Where goods have been sold or money has been paid by a debtor, in contemplation of his bankruptcy, by way of fraudulent preference to his creditor, it may be safer for the assignees to proceed for the recovery thereof in trover, rather than by action of assumpsit for goods sold *by the bankrupt, or [*169] money had and received to his use; because, by adopting the latter form of action, they might enable the defendant to avail himself of his original debt as a set-off (*y*); but the set-off would not hold against a count for goods sold by the assignees as such, or money had and received to their use as assignees, after the bankruptcy (*z*). Trover is preferable to an action of assumpsit, when the defendant has converted the produce of a bill, &c. and has become bankrupt, and obtained his certificate; because to the former action the certificate could not afford a defence (*a*).

The general rule is clear, that to support trover the plaintiff must have the right to some identical or specific goods (*b*)(350). Trover does not lie for money had and received generally (*c*); but it may be maintained for so many pieces of gold or silver, though not in a bag; because damages, and not the goods or articles themselves in specie are the object of the suit (*d*); and in that case the plaintiff can only redeem himself by tendering to the plaintiff the same specific pieces (*e*). And trover lies for an undivided part of a chattel, as three-fourths of a ship (*f*). Although a contract for the sale of goods be complete and binding under the Statute against Frauds, yet the vendee acquires no property in them which can enable him to maintain trover, if any material acts remain to be done before the delivery to ascertain or distinguish the quantity or exact amount of the price to be paid by the purchaser. Thus, if a portion of an entire bulk of goods be sold, and be not in its nature ascertainable without weighing, or other act separating and distinguishing it from the rest; as in the case of the sale of ten out of twenty tons of flax, the same being in mats of an unequal size and quantity (*g*); or of so many tons of a larger quantity of oil (*h*); or of bark at so much per ton (*i*); the vendee

(*t*) 4 Taunt. 865.
(*u*) 1 Wils. 106; 2 T. R. 708; 1 Bing. 45; 7 Moore, 304, S. C.
(*x*) 2 Stark. R. 287. As to the conversion of *fixtures*, see Longstaff *v.* Meagoe, 4 Nev. & Man. 211.
(*y*) 4 T. R. 211; 2 Hen. Bla. 145; Cullen, 201, 202; see 16 East, 140; 3 M. & Sel. 199.
(*z*) See 10 East, 418; 16 East, 135.
(*a*) 6 T. R. 695; 7 Bing. 63.
(*b*) 5 B. & Ald. 654; 1 D. & R. 285, S. C.
(*c*) 5 B. & Ald. 652; 1 D. & R. 282, S. C.
(*d*) Vin. Ab. Action, Trover, K.; Bac. Ab. Trover, D. Foreign Coin, 4 Taunt. 24.
(*e*) *Per* Abbott, C. J., 5 B. & Ald. 654; 1 D. & R. 287, S. C.
(*f*) 4 Campb. 272.
(*g*) 2 M. & Sel. 397; 2 Campb. 240; 5 Taunt. 617; 4 Taunt. 644.
(*h*) 5 Taunt. 176; 13 East, 522.
(*i*) 5 B. & C. 857; 8 D. & R. 693, S. C.; 6 B. & C. 388; 9 D. & R. 293, S. C.; 8 B. & C. 277; 2 M. & R. 292, S. C.; 9 B. & C. 145.

nia, by the 13th sect. of the Act of 21st March, 1806, entitled, "An Act to regulate Arbitrations," (Purd. Dig. 2. 4 Sm. Laws, 332,) it is provided, "that in all cases where a remedy is provided, or duty enjoined, or any thing directed to be done by any Act or Acts of Assembly of this Commonwealth, the directions of the said Acts shall be strictly pursued, and no penalty shall be inflicted, or any thing done agreeably to the provisions of the common law in such cases further than shall be necessary for carrying such act into effect. Brown v. The Commonwealth, 3 Serg. & Rawle, 373. Commonwealth *v.* Evans, 13 ib. 426.

(350) As to the evidence by which a party will be estopped to say he has not the specific articles he has sold, see Chapman *v.* Searle, 3 Pick. Rep. 38.

II. TROVER. 1. The property affected.

could not maintain trover until his portion had been ascertained and set apart. The same rule holds in the case of a contract to manufacture goods, as to build a *carriage, &c. no property passes in the goods until finished, or considered and treated by both parties as finished, although the value has been paid (*k*). In these cases assumpsit upon the contract is the remedy.

In other respects, trover in general lies for the conversion of any personal property in which the plaintiff has a general or special property (*l*); but it does not lie for the conversion of a *record*, because a record is not private property; but it may be supported for the *copy* of a record, which is private property (*m*)(351).

2dly. The plaintiff's interest.

In order to support this action the plaintiff must, at the time of the conversion (*n*), have had a complete *property*, either *general* or *special* (352), in the chattel; and also the *actual possession* (353), or the *right* to the *immediate possession* of it (*o*)(354).

1st. Of an absolute property in the goods.

First. It may be premised that it is not essential to the support of this action, that the absolute ownership and special property or interest should exist in the same person: either will suffice to support this action (*p*). But we shall presently remark, that if there be an outstanding special property in another, the general owner should sue in case for the injury to his reversion, not in trover for the value of the goods (*q*).

Without an absolute or special property, this action cannot be maintained. A *right* of *immediate* possession before or at the time of the conversion is essential (*r*). Therefore, as we have seen, trover cannot be supported by a party in a suit for a record (*s*). Nor can a tenant in tail, expectant on the determination of an estate for life, without impeachment for waste, bring trover for timber which grew upon and was severed from the estate, for the tenant for

(*k*) 1 Taunt. 318; 5 Bing. 270; see 7 B. & C. 26; 9 D. & R. 791, S. C.

(*l*) For what it lies in general, see Com. Dig. Action, Case, Trover, C.; Bac. Ab. Trover, D.; Vin. Ab. Action, Trover, K.; Bul. N. P. 32 to 49.

(*m*) Hardr. 111.

(*n*) 2 T. R. 750; 4 Bing. 106.

(*o*) 2 Saund. 47 a, note 1; *ante*, 151, 139; Selw. N. P. Trover; 4 B. & C. 941; 7 D. & R. 407, S. C.

(*p*) *Per* Lawrence, J., 7 T. R. 398.

(*q*) *Post*, 174; *ante*, 150.

(*r*) Bloxam *v.* Sanders, 4 Bar. & Cres. 941; 7 D. & R. 407, S. C.

(*s*) *Supra*; Hard. 111.

---

(351) As to trover for the title deeds of an estate, bonds, bills of exchange, &c., see Yea *v.* Field, 2 Term Rep. 1708. Towle *v.* Lovett, 6 Mass. Rep. 394. Arnold *v.* Jeffrayson, 2 Salk. 654. Goggesly *v.* Cuthbert, 2 New Rep. 170. Benjamin *v.* Bank of England, 3 Campb. 417. Mercer *v.* Jones, Id. 477. Todd *v.* Crookshanks, 3 Johns. Rep. 432. Murray *v.* Burling, 10 Johns. Rep. 172. Clowes *v.* Hawley, 12 Johns. Rep. 484.

(352) { Dillenback *v.* Jerome, 7 Cow. Rep. 294. Odiorne *v.* Colley, 2 New Hamp. Rep. 66. Debow *v.* Colfax, 5 Halst. Rep. 128. }

When on a sale of goods the property vests in the purchaser so that he may maintain trover against the vendor, see Selw. N. P. 1269, 1270. 2 Esp. Dig. 40. Owenson *v.* Morse, 7 Term Rep. 60. Hanson and another *v.* Meyer, 6 East's Rep. 614. Whitehouse and others *v.* Frost and others, 12 East's Rep. 614. Austen *v.* Craven, 4 Taunt. 644. { Zwinger *v.* Samuda, 1 Moore's Rep. 12. 7 Taunt. 265. Chapman *v.* Searle, 3 Pick. Rep. 38. } Further as to the property in the plaintiff requisite to support this action, see Hunter *v.* Rice, 15 East's Rep. 100. Heyl *v.* Burling, 1 Caines' Rep. 14. Hostler's Adm'rs *v.* Skull, Taylor, 152. Floyd *v.* Day, 3 Mass. Rep. 403.

(353) Vide Smith *v.* Plomer, 15 East's Rep. 607.

(354) { In the case of a general as well as special property, the action may in most cases be brought either by the general or special owner, and judgment obtained by one is a bar to an action by the other. Smith *v.* James, 7 Cow. Rep. 328. } In this action the defendant may show title in a stranger paramount to that of the plaintiff. Kennedy *v.* Strong, 14 Johns. Rep. 132.

2. The plaintiff's interest.

life has a right to the trees immediately they are cut down (*t*). And the trustees of an estate *per autre vie* cannot maintain trover for trees felled upon the estate, for when felled the trees belonged to the owner of the inheritance (*u*). A landlord has, generally speaking, in legal consideration, even during the term, the possession of the timber growing on the estate, if it be excepted in the lease; *so that he may in such case maintain trespass even during the term, if it be cut down; and even if the timber be not excepted in the lease, the lessor has so far the possession of it when cut down by another, though cut pending the term, that if it be carried away, he may maintain trespass or trover; the interest of the lessee in the trees determining instantly they are cut down (*x*)(355). But where a landlord during the term wrongfully cut down oak pollards, unfit for timber, it was decided that, as the tenant for life or years would have been entitled to them if they had been blown down, and was entitled to the usufruct of them during the term, the lessor could not, by his own wrong, acquire a right to the pollards; and therefore could not, nor could his vendee, sue the tenant for taking them away (*y*). [*171]

The property in title-deeds generally accompanies the ownership of the estate; and therefore the person who was entitled to the estate at the time of the wrongful detention of or injury to the deeds, should be the plaintiff (*z*).

The absolute and general owner of goods may maintain trover, although he had sold or bailed them under a *void* contract, as to a married woman, because he still retains a present right (*a*). But if the owner has bailed the goods to the defendant, and before a conversion of the goods by the latter the bailor sells them, or otherwise ceases to be the owner, the action should be brought in the name of the person who was the proprietor at the time of the conversion (*b*). A party who purchases goods under a distress for rent, valid though irregular, may maintain trover (*c*); and where A. sold goods to B. which were wrongfully in C.'s possession, and B. paid for them, and on the latter demanding the goods, and informing C. of the sale, the latter said he should not deliver them to any person; whereupon A. and B. rescinded the sale, and the price was repaid, it was held that A. might sue C. in trover (*d*).

The *verbal gift* of a chattel, without actual delivery, is not sufficient to pass the property to the donee, so as to enable him to sue the donor (*e*); although it may perhaps give the donee a sufficient special interest to enable him to

(*t*) 1 T. R. 55.
(*u*) 1 New Rep. 25.
(*x*) 7 T. R. 13; 2 M. & Sel. 499, 500; 1 Saund. 322, n. 5; Vin. Ab. Trespass, S. pl. 10; 1 Taunt. 191.
(*y*) 5 B. & C. 897; 8 D. & R. 651, S. C.
(*z*) 4 T. R. 231; 4 Bing. 106.
(*a*) 15 East, 607; 2 Saund. 47 b, n. (*f*), 5th ed.
(*b*) 4 Bing. 106; *ante*, 77.
(*c*) 2 Bing. 334; see *ante*, 88.
(*d*) 5 M. & Sel. 105.
(*e*) 2 B. & Ald. 551.

(355) { Mather *v.* Ministers of Trinity Church, 3 Serg. & Rawle, 509. See Baker *v.* Howell, 6 Serg. & Rawle, 476. It has been decided in Maine, that where a tenant at will erected a dwelling house, and other buildings on the land, with the express assent of the landlord, and died, and his administrator sold them to a stranger, the purchaser might maintain *trover* for them against the owner of the land. Osgood *v.* Howard, 6 Greenl. Rep. 452. }

{ Shalt *v.* Barker, 12 Serg. & Rawle, 272. } Vide Davies *v.* Connop, 1 Price's Exch. Rep. 57. Trover lies against an outgoing tenant, for corn cut by him after the expiration of his term, though sown by him before that time, under the notion of being entitled to an away-going crop. Davies *v.* Connop, Price's Exch. Rep. 53. { Nelson *v.* Burt, 15 Mass. Rep. 204. }

II. TROVER. 2. The plaintiff's interest.

*sue a mere wrong-doer (*f*). Nor is an award that a chattel should be delivered by A. to B., on the former being paid a sum of money sufficient, *per se*, to pass the property, and entitle B. to maintain trover, although he tenders the money, it being refused by A. (*g*). And we have already observed (*h*), that in the case of a sale of goods there must be a *specific* right to some *particular* goods severed and distinguished from others; and that if there remain to be done upon the contract some act to ascertain the quantity or price, the vendee cannot maintain trover until that act be done (*i*).

Where *goods stolen* were purchased *in market overt*, and sold by the purchaser *before the felon was convicted*, it was decided that the owner prosecuting to conviction could not maintain trover against the purchaser under the statute (*k*), which gives restitution to the owner who prosecutes the felon to conviction, although he gave the purchaser notice of the robbery while they were in his possession; for the property being altered by the sale in market overt, was not revested in the owner until the conviction of the felon, but the defendant had parted with the possession before that time, and therefore could not be said to have converted the *plaintiff's* goods (*l*). But if the sale was not in market overt, then if the purchaser sell them again in market overt *before* conviction of the felon, and such purchaser had notice of the felony whilst the goods were in his possession, he will be liable to an action of trover (*m*). The statute (*n*) is confined to cases of felony; therefore where goods are obtained from a person by *false pretences*, and passed to another for a valuable consideration, the original owner is not entitled to them upon conviction of the offender; and if he has got possession of them, trover will lie at the suit of the purchaser (*o*). And if goods are obtained by false pretences under color of a purchase, the vendee or his assignee acquires no property, and after demand may be sued in trover (*p*). The action does not lie to recover the value of goods delivered by the plaintiff, under or in furtherance of an illegal contract, to which he is a party or privy (*q*).

[*173] 2dly. A special property or interest.

**Secondly*. So a person having a *special* property in the goods may support trover against a stranger who takes them out of his actual possession; as a sheriff (*r*) (356); a carrier (*s*) (357); a factor; a warehouse-man (*t*); con-

(*f*) See 2 Saund. 47 a, and note (*d*), 5th edit.; 2 C. & P. 578.

(*g*) 15 East, 100.

(*h*) *Ante*, 169.

(*i*) *Ante*, 169, 170.

(*k*) 21 Hen. 8, c. 11.

(*l*) 2 Term Rep. 750. The pawnee of stolen goods is liable, 2 Camp. 336, note. The owner must always use his best endeavors to bring the offender to justice before he can sue the purchaser, 2 C. & P. 41. As to stolen horses, 2 P. & M. c. 7; 31 Eliz. c. 12. A condemnation of goods in the Exchequer alters the property, T. Raym. 336; Carth. 327; 2 Bla. Rep. 981.

(*m*) Peer *v.* Humphrey, 1 Har. & Woll. 28.

(*n*) 21 Hen. 8, c. 11.

(*o*) 5 T. R. 175.

(*p*) 7 Taunt. 59; 9 B. & C. 60; 6 Mod. 114.

(*q*) 2 Bing. 314.

(*r*) 2 Saund. 47, provided he remain in possession, 1 M. & Sel. 711.

(*s*) 1 Rol. Ab. 4; 1 Lord Raym. 276; Bul. N. P. 33; 2 Saund. 47 b, note.

(*t*) 1 M. & Sel. 147.

(356) {7 Cow. Rep. 297.} Vide Barker and another *v.* Miller, 6 Johns. Rep. 195. Catlin *v.* Jackson, 8 Johns. Rep. 548. Hotchkiss *v.* M'Vickar, 12 Johns. Rep. 403. {But it has been held in New Jersey, that a sheriff cannot maintain trover for goods by virtue of a *fieri facias*, and a levy thereon, without he has made a particular inventory of the goods, or has taken actual possession of them. Lloyd *v.* Wyckoff, 6 Halst. Rep. 218. See as to what constitutes a good *levy*, the *American* cases cited in the opinion of Drake, J.} Yates *v.* St. John, 13 Wend. R. 74.

(357) {7 Cow. Rep. 297.}

signee (358); pawnee; or trustee; or an agister of cattle; or a gratuitous bailee (*u*); or any person who is responsible over to his principal (*x*) (359); a churchwarden (*y*); or the hirer of goods, however temporary the purpose for which they were hired may happen to be (*z*). So a person who has goods on the terms of sale and return, may sue for any damage done to them by a wrong-doer whilst in his possession (*a*). And a person who has the temporary property in goods, delivering them to the general owner for a special purpose, may, after that purpose is answered, upon a demand and refusal, maintain trover for them (*b*). Where the consignor of goods, upon the insolvency of the consignee, indorsed the bill of lading to the plaintiff without consideration, to enable him to stop the goods in transitu, it was held that the plaintiff had a sufficient property to maintain trover against the wharfingers (*c*). So an executor *de son tort*, who has not obtained probate at the time of trial, may sue for a tort committed to the property of the deceased whilst in the plaintiff's possession (*d*). And it is a general rule that the bare possession of goods, without any strict legal title, confers a right of action against a mere wrong-doer, having no right, and not clothed with any authority from the real owner (*e*). And trover lies by the owner of a ship, though not registered (*f*). The only exception which appears to exist *is in the case of a mere servant (360) acting professedly as such, and having only the custody of goods (*g*).

2. The plaintiff's interest.

[*174]

3. A right of possession.

Thirdly. In order to support this action, the plaintiff must, at the time of the conversion, have had the *actual possession*, or the *right* to *immediate possession* (*h*). Therefore, where goods leased as furniture with a house were taken in execution, and absolutely sold by the sheriff, it was decided that the *landlord* could not maintain trover against the sheriff pending the lease, but should have declared specially in an action on the case (*i*) (361). So if A. pay a Bank of England note to B. who pays it to C. who presents it at the Bank, where it is stopped, C. only can sue, and not A. (*k*). We have before observed, that a landlord has, in general, such an implied possession of timber wrongfully cut down during a lease as to enable him to support trover if it be

(*u*) 1 B. & Ald. 59.
(*x*) 2 Saund. 47 b; 11 East, 626.
(*y*) Stra. 852; 2 Saund. 47 c.
(*z*) 2 Saund. 47 b, c, d; 1 B. & Ald. 59; 4 id. 590; 5 Esp. 35.
(*a*) 2 Campb. 575.
(*b*) 2 Taunt. 268.
(*c*) 2 Bing. 260.
(*d*) Husband *v*. Smith, C. P. Hil. Term, 1823. W. C. Smith, attorney for plaintiff. It is said, that a landlord holding goods under a distress cannot maintain trover, &c. for an injury to them, or taking them wrongfully, Moneux *v*. Goreham, *per* Probyn, C. B. at Huntingdon, 29 MS. Sergeant Hill, p. 279, cited Selw. N. P. Trover; and see M'Clel. & Yo. 112, 118. But this position seems to be doubtful. It is laid down, that a party who has distrained cattle *damage feasant*, cannot maintain trover; for the cattle are in the custody of the law when impounded, 1 M'Clel. & Yo. 118.
(*e*) 2 Saund. 27 c, d; and see instances, *post*, in Trespass.
(*f*) 2 Taunt. 302; 1 East, 246.
(*g*) Owen, 52; 2 Saund. 47 a, 47 b, c, d.
(*h*) 3 Campb. 417; 4 B. & C. 941; 7 D. & R. 407, S. C.
(*i*) 7 T. R. 9; 3 Campb. 187; 1 R. & M. 99; 2 B. & P. 451; 15 East, 607.
(*k*) 3 Campb. 417; 2 T. R. 750.

(358) { Smith *v*. James, 7 Cow. Rep. 329. }
(359) { Eaton et al. *v*. Lynde, 15 Mass. Rep. 242. } Faulkner *v*. Brown, 13 Wend. R. 63. Duncan *v*. Spear, 11 ib. 54.
(360) { Dillenback *v*. Jerome, 7 Cow. Rep. 294. } Ludden *v*. Leavitt, 9 Mass. Rep. 104.
(361) { See Wheeler *v*. Train, 3 Pick. Rep. 255. }

II. TROVER. 2. The plaintiff's interest.

removed (*l*); and a remainder-man may support this action against a tenant for life, who does not hold without impeachment of waste, for taking away trees (*m*) (362). So if corn be sown by the outgoing tenant, and cut down and taken by him after the tenancy, under a mistaken claim to it as a way-going crop, the owner of the estate may support trover (*n*).

The person who has the absolute or general, and not the mere special, property in a personal chattel may support this action, although he has never had the actual possession; for it is a rule of law, that the general property of personal chattels creates a constructive possession (*o*) (363). And where the plaintiff, as executor, declared on the possession of his testator, the Court held it to be sufficient, because the property was vested in the executor, and no other person having the right of possession, the property drew after it the possession (*p*). And where a person has delivered goods to a carrier or other bailee, who has not the right to withhold the possession from the general owner, and so parted with the actual possession, yet he may maintain trover for a [*175] conversion by a (364) *stranger; for the owner has still the possession in law against the wrong-doer, and the carrier or other bailee is considered merely as his servant (*q*). This rule prevails in the case of a gratuitous loan, but not where there has been a letting to hire (*r*); and an executor or administrator is by legal construction possessed of the goods of the testator, or intestate, from the time of his death (*s*). So the trustee of goods may sue, although the goods be in the possession of the *cestui que trust* (*t*). Trover lies by a party entitled in remainder to plate, against a party to whom it was pledged by the *deceased tenant* for life, without notice of the limited title of the pawnor (*u*). And the consignee of goods, who is also the vendee, is in general the person to sue for any injury to them whilst in the hands of the carrier, although they have never reached the consignee (*x*). And where every thing has been done by the vendor of goods which he contracted to do, the property will in many cases pass to the vendee, and he may maintain trover, although the goods remain in the seller's possession (*y*). But the vendee of undelivered goods, who has not paid or tendered the price, and has not therefore acquired the right of possession, cannot maintain trover against the vendor, who wrongfully sells them (*z*).

If a person in whose possession goods are, has a lien upon them for a debt due to him from the owner, the plaintiff must pay or tender the money before the action is commenced, in order to obtain the possessory right. But if a party, on being applied to for goods, refuse to deliver them on a different ground, and do not mention his lien, he cannot afterwards set it up as a defence to the action (*a*).

(*l*) *Ante*, 170, *vide* exceptions there.
(*m*) Com. Dig. Biens, H.; 1 T. R. 55.
(*n*) 1 Price, 53.
(*o*) 2 Saund. 47 a, n. 1; Bac. Ab. Trover, C.; 3 Wils. 136; 1 B. & P. 47; 7 T. R. 12.
(*p*) Latch. 214; 3 Bac. Abr. 58.
(*q*) 1 Taunt. 391; 7 T. R. 12; 2 Saund. 47 b.
(*r*) 2 Campb. 464; 3 *id.* 187; 7 T. R. 9.
(*s*) 7 T. R. 13; Latch. 214; 2 Saund. 47 b, 47 k.
(*t*) 8 Taunt. 676.
(*u*) 2 T. R. 376.
(*x*) *Ante*, 7.
(*y*) See *ante*, 170, 171; 11 East, 210; and 5 Bing. 270.
(*z*) 4 B. & C. 941; 7 D. & R. 407, S. C.
(*a*) 1 Campb. 410, note.

(362) {Shult v. Barker, 12 Serg. & Rawle, 272}
(363) Smith v. James, 7 Cow. Rep. 329. Duncan v. Spear, 11 Wend. R. 54.
(364) Acc. Thorp. v. Burling and others, 11 Johns. Rep. 285.

It has been said, that in the case of a *special* property, it must have been accompanied with possession (365), in order to support trover (*b*); but the general rule appears to be to the contrary; and it was observed by Eyre, C. J., (*c*) "that it is not true, that in cases of special property the party must once have had possession in order to maintain trover; for a factor, to whom goods have been consigned, and who has never received them, may maintain such an action." (366) And the indorsee of a bill of lading may maintain trover against *the wharfingers, although the bill of lading was indorsed merely to enable the plaintiff to exercise the consignor's right of stopping the goods in transitu (*d*). [*176]

II. TROVER. 2. The plaintiff's interest.

With respect to the *nature of the injury*, we have already seen that a *conversion* is essential to the support of this action (*e*). It may not be altogether foreign to our present inquiry to give some general account of the different instances of conversion (*f*). They may be either, 1st, by *wrongfully taking* a personal chattel; 2dly, by some other *illegal assumption of ownership*, or by illegally *using* or *misusing* goods; or, 3dly, by a *wrongful detention*.

3. The injury.

The *wrongfully taking*, if followed by a *carrying away* of the goods of another, who has the right of immediate possession, is of itself a conversion, and so is the compelling a party to deliver up goods; and whenever trespass will lie for taking goods of the plaintiff wrongfully, trover will also lie (*g*). But it has been considered that a *mere seizure* by a stranger, who afterwards relinquishes the possession, is no conversion (*h*). Trover lies by a bankrupt against his assignees, if the plaintiff was not subject to the bankrupt laws (*i*). And if goods be wrongfully seized as a distress, though they be not removed from the place in which they were, yet trover may be supported, because the possession in point of law is changed by their being seized as a distress (*k*). A sheriff who seizes and sells goods after an act of bankruptcy committed by the defendant, against whom a *fieri facias* issued, and before the commission, is, if the *fieri facias* be void against the assignees, liable to them in trover, although the sheriff was ignorant of the act of bankruptcy (*l*). And a seizure of goods under a *fieri facias* after a party's bankruptcy, followed by a removal of them to a broker's, is a sufficient conversion (*m*). And this action may be supported after an acquittal of the defendant for the felonious taking of goods (*n*)(367). In the case of a conversion by wrongful taking, it is not necessary to prove a demand and refusal (*o*); and the intent of the party is im-

1. Wrongful taking.

(*b*) 4 East, 214.
(*c*) 1 B & P. 47; 2 Saund. 47 d. See 11 East, 626.
(*d*) 2 Bing. 260.
(*e*) *Ante*, 169; 2 Saund. 46 e.
(*f*) See 2 Saund. 47 e; Bac. Ab. Trover, B.
(*g*) 2 Saund. 47 o; Cro. Eliz. 824.
(*h*) Samuel *v.* Norris, 6 Car. & P. 620.
(*i*) 3 B. & B. 2; 6 Moore, 56, S. C.
(*k*) Willes, 56.
(*l*) 1 M. & P. 541; 4 Bing. 597; 2 Y. & J 101; Garland *v.* Carlisle, 2 Cr. & M. 31.
(*m*) 3 Campb. 396.
(*n*) 12 East, 409.
(*o*) 1 Sid. 164; 6 Mod. 212; Bul. N. P. 44; 1 Stark. 173; 3 B. & B. 2; 6 Moore, 56, S. C.

(365) Vide Hotchkiss *v.* M'Vickar, 12 Johns. Rep. 407. Thus a sheriff cannot maintain trover before he has levied on the goods; for until then they are not in his actual possession. Hotchkiss *v.* M'Vickar, 12 Johns. Rep. 403.
(336) 7 Cow. Rep. 329.
(367) See Boardman *v.* Gore, 15 Mass. Rep. 336, 337. Addington *v.* Allen, 11 Wend. R. 382.

II. TROVER. 3. The injury. material; for, although the defendant acted under a supposition that he was justified in what he did, or as a servant of, and for the benefit of, another person, he will be equally *liable to this action (*l*). But if the possession was [*177] obtained under color of a contract, trover cannot be sustained (*m*); unless a case of fraud can be proved (*n*). So if assignees affirm the act of a party who wrongfully sold the bankrupt's goods, they cannot support trover against him (*o*). And trover does not lie for an excessive levy of goods under a valid execution. And if a sheriff seize under a write of *fieri facias* more goods than was necessary, the proper remedy is *case* and not trover (*p*). A party acting under a valid, and also under an unfounded authority, may protect himself by virtue of the former (*q*).

2. Wrongful assumption of property. So the *wrongful assumption of the property* in, or right of disposing of, goods, may be a conversion in itself, and render unnecessary a demand and refusal (*r*) (368), as well as any tender of charges (*s*). It seems that the mere taking an assignment of goods from a person who has no right or authority to dispose of them, is a conversion; for this is an assumption by the assignee of a property in the goods (*t*). Thus, the sale of a ship, which was afterwards lost at sea, made by the defendant, who claimed under a defective conveyance from a trader before his bankruptcy, is a sufficient conversion to enable the assignees of the bankrupt to maintain trover, without showing a demand and refusal (*u*). So where a person entrusted with the goods of another, puts them into the hands of a third person without orders, it is a conversion (*x*). Trover may be supported against a carrier (*y*), or a wharfinger (*z*), *who by mistake* (*a*), or under a forged order (*b*), delivers goods to a wrong person; or against a person who illegally makes use of a thing found or delivered to him (*c*); or a bailee employed merely to keep or carry the goods, and having no beneficial interest, who misuses a chattel entrusted to him (*d*); or against a carrier who draws out part of the contents of a vessel, and fills it with [*178] water (*e*); or a carrier or wharfinger, &c. *who improperly breaks open a box

(*l*) 4 M. & Sel. 260; *ante*, 147.
(*m*) 3 Campb. 298, 352; 3 Taunt. 274; 2 C. & P. 266
(*n*) 7 Taunt. 59; 1 B. & C. 514; 2 D. & R. 755, S. C.
(*o*) 7 B. & C. 310; 1 M. & R. 2, S. C.
(*p*) Batchellor *v.* Vyse, 1 Mood. & Rob. 333, but *semble* the Court doubted.
(*q*) 4 B. & C. 5; 6 D. & R. 17, S. C.
(*r*) 2 East, 407; 6 *Id.* 540; 4 Taunt. 24; 3 B. & B. 2; 6 Moore, 56, S. C. Discounting a lost bill after notice is a conversion, 4 Taunt. 799.
(*s*) 1 Campb. 410; Whitaker, 75; 2 M. & S. 298; 3 Campb. 472, 473.
(*t*) Baldwin *v.* Cole, 6 Mod. 212, *per* Holt, C. J., recognized by Lord Ellenborough, in 6 East, 540. And see 2 Stark. 306; 3 C. & P. 552, 553.
(*u*) 5 East, 407, 420.
(*x*) 4 T. R. 260, 264.
(*y*) Peake, C. N. P. 68; 4 Bing. 476, 482, 483.
(*z*) 2 B. & Ald. 702.
(*a*) *Id.*; 4 Bing. 483.
(*b*) 1 Stark. 104; 4 Bing. 476.
(*c*) Cro. Eliz. 219; 2 H. Bla. 254.
(*d*) *Id. ibid.*
(*e*) 1 Stra. 576; and see 5 Bar. & Cress. 149; 7 D. & R 729, S. C., where see, as to a conversion by abuse of a trust and when the statute of limitations begins to run.

(368) Vide Bristol *v.* Burt, 7 Johns. Rep. 254. Gibbs *v.* Chase, 10 Mass. Rep. 128. An admission by the defendant that he had had the goods of the plaintiff, and that they were lost, is sufficient evidence of a conversion without showing a demand and refusal. La Place *v.* Aupoix, 1 Johns Rep. Cas. 406. Proof that the defendant promised to return the goods to the plaintiff, and that he had not returned them, is sufficient evidence of a conversion without showing a demand and refusal. Durell *v.* Mosher, 8 Johns. Rep. 445. And where a party received logs to be sawed into lumber on shares, and agreed to give the owner security for his share at a stipulated rate, payable a future day, but before doing it disposed of the property; held, that the owner was entitled to maintain trover for his share; there being no charge of property until the security was given. Rightmyer *v.* Raymond et al., 12 Wend. 51.

containing goods, or sells them (*f*)(369). And irregularity in a distress taken *damage feasant*, may amount to a conversion (*g*): but trover does not lie in the case of a distress for rent, (which is valid,) merely because a subsequent irregularity is committed (*h*). But it may be sustained by a party who pays money to redeem his goods from an illegal and unfounded distress for rent (*i*). Trover cannot in general be supported for a mere omission or nonfeasance against a party who was lawfully possessed of the goods (*k*); and therefore if a carrier, or other bailee, by negligence *lose goods* entrusted to his care, the remedy in general must be case or assumpsit (*l*). A bare non-delivery of goods by a carrier is not a conversion (*m*), unless the goods be in his possession, and he refuse to deliver them on demand (*n*). His false assertion that he had delivered the goods to the consignee is not a conversion (*o*). And the taking possession of a house and fixtures therein by the assignee of a term in the house, is not a conversion of the *fixtures* (*p*). An agent, by the act of selling at an under price, is not liable to an action of trover (*q*); and the retention of property under the decree of a court of competent jurisdiction, is no conversion (*r*). But a sub-agent may be liable in trover for his conversion (*s*). The cutting trees without removing them is not a conversion (*t*).

II. TROVER. 3. The injury.

By and against a tenant in common.

The general rule is, that *one tenant in common* of goods cannot sue his co-tenant if the goods remain in the possession of the latter, although he refuse to permit the former to participate in the use of the article (*u*). The reason is, that in law the possession of one is the possession of both. But if one tenant in common *destroy* the chattel, or commit an act which is equivalent thereto, his companion may recover the value of his share in trover (*x*). Thus, where it appeared that one tenant in common of a ship had forcibly taken it out of the possession of his companion, and secreted it from him so that he knew not where it was carried, and changed the name of it; and it afterwards got into the hands of a third person, who sent it upon a foreign voyage, where it was lost; Lord King left it to the jury, whether, under the circumstances, the *destruction was not by the means of the tenant in common (the defendant); and the jury finding in the affirmative, the Court refused to set aside the verdict (*y*). It seems to be questionable whether the mere sale by one of two joint owners of a ship is a sufficient conversion to enable his companion to [*179]

(*f*) 2 Salk. 655; 5 B. & Ald. 401.
(*g*) Cro. Jac. 148; Bac. Abr. Trover, B.
(*h*) 1 Hen. Bla. 13.
(*i*) 6 T. R. 298.
(*k*) 6 East, 540; 2 B. & Ald. 704.
(*l*) 5 Burr. 2825; 2 Saund. 47 f.
(*m*) 4 Esp. 157.
(*n*) 1 Taunt. 391.
(*o*) 1 Campb. 409.
(*p*) Longstaffe *v.* Meago, 4 Nev. & Man. 411.
(*q*) 3 Taunt. 117.
(*r*) 4 Moore, 361.
(*s*) Cranch *v.* White, 1 Bing. N. C. 414.
(*t*) 2 Mod. 244; Bul. N. P. 44; 2 Saund. 47 a.
(*u*) *Ante*, 90; 2 Saund. 47 b; 1 T. R. 658; 1 East, 363; Selw. N. P. Trover, II. 6th edit. 1347.
(*x*) 2 Saund. 47 h; 8 T. R. 146; *ante*, 79.
(*y*) Bernardiston *v.* Chapman, C. B. Hill. T. 1 Geo. 1, cited 4 East, 121; Bul. N. P. 34, 35; 2 Saund. 47 h.

(369) Trover does not lie against a carrier for not delivering goods entrusted to him to transport, if the goods are not in his possession at the time of the demand, and have either been lost or stolen; the action should be case and not trover. Packard *v.* Getman, 4 Wend. R. 613. If, however, the carrier has delivered the goods to a third person, trover will lie. *ib.* The liability of the common carrier and inn-keeper is very similar; they are both bailees, and liable for losses under similar circumstances. Therefore, it was held, that an inn-keeper was not liable for goods entrusted to him in the line of his business, unless an *actual conversion* was shown. Hallenbake *v.* Fish, 8 Wend. R. 547.

II TROVER. 2. The injury.

maintain trover against him, for such sale could not in law affect or pass more than the interest of the seller (z). Where one of two tenants in common of a whale refused to deliver a moiety of it to the other, and cut it up, and expressed the oil, it was held that this was not a destruction which would subject him to an action of trover; for it was an application of the whale to its only profitable use (a). In general if a defendant insist that he was tenant in common with the plaintiff in the chattel, he must plead that matter specially (b).

The cases in which trover is or is not the proper remedy in relation to *husband and wife* have been already mentioned (c).

3. Of a wrongful *detention*; and herein of a demand and refusal.

In most of the preceding instances, proof of the wrongful act of the defendant is sufficient to establish a conversion, without evidence of a demand of the goods, and a refusal to restore them (d). In other cases, a *demand and refusal* are essential to the support of the action; in every instance it is judicious to demand the restitution of the goods, or if they cannot be returned, a recompense equivalent to their value and the amount of the damages sustained, previously to the commencement of proceedings. The frequent occurrence of this subject in practice renders it worthy of minute attention, and it is proposed to consider it in the following order:—1st, *when* a demand and refusal are necessary; 2dly, *by* whom the demand must be made; 3dly, *upon* whom it is to be made; 4thly, the *manner* of making the demand; 5thly, the *time* of making the demand, and, 6thly, *what refusal* is sufficient.

1. When a demand is necessary. [*180]

1st. *A demand and refusal* are necessary in all cases where the defendant became, in the first instance, lawfully possessed of the goods, and the plaintiff is not prepared *to prove some distinct actual conversion (e). As where a trader, on the eve of his bankruptcy, made a collusive sale of his goods to the defendant, it was decided that the assignees could not maintain trover without proving a demand and refusal, for the parties contracting were competent at the time; and if the assignees disaffirm the contract, they should give notice by a demand (f). So where goods are delivered under a contract, as to do something with them, and return them when completed, the mere omission to perform the contract is no conversion, and a demand and refusal must be made in order to support trover (g). Where bills of exchange were delivered by a trader, in contemplation of bankruptcy, to a creditor, with a view of giving him preference, and the amount of the bills was received by the creditor after the bankruptcy, it was held, that a demand and refusal to deliver up the bills before they became due, were necessary to enable the assignees to bring an action of trover for the bills, as the receipt of the money by the creditor was not of itself a conversion (h). A demand and refusal are likewise necessary in order to maintain trover against an excise officer for the detention of goods after the payment of the penalty for which the goods were

(z) 4 East, 121; 2 Saund. 47 h, note (s), 5th edit. *Sed vide* 5 B. & Ald. 395. A *quære* is made in note (s) to 2 Saund. "as to the sale of any other chattel in market overt." A wrongful sale by one tenant in common, under circumstances which would divest his companion of his share, might be considered a destruction of the chattel.

(a) 1 Taunt. 241. And see *ante*, 91, as to tenancy in common of realty.

(b) Stancliffe v. Hardwicke, 3 Dowl. 762.

(c) *Ante*, 105, 106.

(d) See 4 Taunt. 801.

(e) 2 Saund. 47 e.

(f) 2 Hen. Bla. 135; 2 Esp. Rep. 96; see 5 East, 407; 4 Taunt. 799.

(g) 4 Esp. Rep. 156; see 2 C. & P. 266.

(h) 9 B. & C. 764; 4 M. & R. 547, S. C.

levied (*i*), or against a carrier, who, having the goods in his possession, omits to deliver them (*k*).

II. TROVER. — 3. The injury.

The demand and refusal do not necessarily amount to a conversion, but are only *prima facie evidence* of it; and therefore a finding by special verdict that the plaintiff demanded the goods, and the defendant refused them, will not warrant the Court in considering that there was a conversion (*l*); and if it be apparent that there really was no conversion, as if the party being a carrier had lost the goods (*m*), or having felled trees, had left them on the ground (*n*), the demand and refusal are inoperative.

2. Who should demand.

2dly. The demand should be made by *the person* entitled at the time to receive the goods; and it seems that if goods are bailed, and during the bailment, they are sold to, or otherwise become the property of, another, the demand on the bailee, to create a conversion, should be made by the new *owner, [*181] and the action brought in his name, if after a proper demand, the bailee improperly refuse to part with them (*o*). If goods are deposited by one person with the authority of another, and received by the bailee to keep on the joint account of the two, a demand by one alone is not sufficient without the authority of the other, so as to maintain trover against the bailee for refusing to deliver the goods. But if it appear that the bailee in such a case had no notice that he held the goods on the joint account, or had not accepted them on any such trust, the party depositing the goods may alone make the demand, although it had been previously agreed between the two parties that the bailee should receive the goods on their joint account (*p*). The demand may be made by an agent duly authorized (*q*); but such demand will not be sufficient if the defendant *bona fide* refuse to deliver the goods in consequence of his *not being* reasonably satisfied that the person who applies is properly empowered to receive them (*r*). Where the plaintiff sold goods to T., who paid for them, and was to take them away, but defendant becoming possessed of the place in which they were deposited, the plaintiff's attorney, accompanied by T., demanded them of defendant, telling him that they belonged to plaintiff, and that he had sold them to T., to which defendant replied, that he would not deliver them to any person whatsoever, and afterwards plaintiff repaid the price of the goods to T. and brought trover, it was held that this demand of the plaintiff's attorney was sufficient (*s*).

3. Upon whom the demand should be made.

3dly. The demand should of course be in general made upon the party who at the time has the possession of the goods by himself, or his servant or agent, or the general controlling power over them. If after the party has received the goods, though legally, he sell or otherwise part with them tortiously, no demand is necessary, for his subsequent act is in itself a conversion. If a party, in some way apparently concerned in the detention, be applied to for

(*i*) 6 B. & C. 464; 9 D. & R. 499, S. C.
(*k*) 1 Taunt. 391.
(*l*) 10 Co. 56 b, 57 a; 2 Saund. 47 e.
(*m*) *Ante*, 178.
(*n*) 2 Mod. 244; Bul. N. P. 44.
(*o*) 4 Bing. 106.
(*p*) 13 East, 197.
(*q*) 2 B. & P. 457. Sometimes the agent has a power of attorney, or a written authority, to demand and receive the goods; but this may not be necessary, especially if the demand be in writing, signed by the owner, and require the delivery to him or the bearer. It is usual to have a demand signed by the owner or his attorney.
(*r*) 1 Esp. Rep. 83; see also *id.* 115; 2 B. & P. 464, n. a; 5 Moore, 259, and 1 Campb. 439, were the demand appears to have been made by an agent.
(*s*) 5 M. & Sel. 105.

II. TROVER. — 3. The injury.

the restoration of *the goods, and by his answer induce the owner to believe that he, the person applied to, has the possession and power to deliver them up, and refuse to do so; and thereby the owner is induced to sue him; he cannot, it seems, defend at the trial, on the ground that he had not, when applied to, the control and disposition of the goods (t).

It is not necessary that the demand should be made upon the defendant personally. A demand in writing left at the defendant's house is sufficient (u).

4. Demand how made.

4thly. The demand in trover being only for the purpose of giving the defendant an opportunity of either restoring the goods in specie, or of making satisfaction to the party to whom they belong (x), it is not necessary to adhere to any particular form or manner of making the demand, provided it be distinctly notified to the defendant who is the claimant, and what goods are demanded. Where the plaintiff, the vendor of a house, brought trover for various articles, some of them being goods, and the remainder being fixtures, which he had left in the house on delivering it up to the defendant, the vendee, and demanded them all as *fixtures*, and the refusal was "*of the fixtures demanded*," this demand was held to be insufficient to enable the plaintiff to recover the articles which were *not fixtures;* it having been decided upon other grounds that the fixtures were not recoverable (y)(370). A demand of payment for goods of which there has been no regular sale, is a good demand to support an action of trover for them (z); so a demand of "*satisfaction*" has been adjudged to be sufficient for this purpose (a). If two *distinct* demands be made, one verbally, and the other in writing, at the same time; proof of the verbal demand alone will be sufficient, and no evidence of the written request need be given (b). A demand in writing, left at the defendant's house, may be sufficient (c).

5. Demand when made.

5thly. The demand, when necessary, must in general be made before the action is brought. Where a declaration was entitled generally of the term, whereby it had implied relation to the first day of the term, and the demand was made subsequently to that day, but before the issuing of the writ, *evidence may be received of the prior issuing, in order to show that the demand was made previously to the suing out of the writ (d). But as the refusal is

[*183]

(t) 3 C. & P. 136.

(u) 1 Esp. Rep. 22. So as to a notice to quit, 4 T. R. 464, and notice of the dishonor of a bill of exchange, Chitty on Bills, 7th ed. 220.

(x) *Per* Lord Kenyon, 1 Esp. 33.

(y) 2 B. & C. 76; 3 D. & R. 255, S. C.

(z) 1 Esp. 31.

(a) *Rockeby's case*, Clayt. 122, mentioned in 1 Esp. 31.

(b) 1 Campb. 439.

(c) 1 Esp. 22.

(d) 3 Burr. 1242. In K. B. by bill, a demand after writ issued, and before declaration, would be sufficient. In that Court the exhibiting of the bill or declaration may, at the plaintiff's election, be regarded as the commencement of the suit, see 7 T. R. 4; 4 East, 75; 11 East, 118. In C. P. see 1 B. & P. 343; 2 B. & P. 235.

(370) { Window blinds, keys, &c. and things personal in their nature, but fitted and prepared to be used with real estate, are considered as part of the real estate, though not strictly speaking fixtures, or rather as so connected with the realty as to pass with it. 6 Greenl. Rep. 223. Farrer v. Stackpole, ———. Goddard v. Bolster, 6 Greenl. Rep. 154, 427. And manure lying about a barn upon land, will pass to the grantee, upon a sale of the land, as incident to the land, unless there be a reservation of it in the deed. Kittredge v. Woods, 3 New Hamp. Rep. 503. Nor is an outgoing tenant in agriculture entitled to the manure made on the farm during his tenancy, even though lying in heaps in the farm yard when he removes, and though it were made by his own cattle and from his own fodder. Lassell v. Reed, 6 Greenl. Rep. 222. }

not *of itself* a conversion, but is merely presumptive evidence of it, it ought to be left to the jury whether a refusal upon a demand made after the action is brought, is evidence of a prior conversion (*e*). If there be evidence that the defendant received or had possession of the goods before the commencement of the action, and the plaintiff show that they then were his property, it is perhaps not an unfair *presumption* that the refusal to restore the goods, though after the action brought, was but a re-assertion of a pre-existing adverse claim to them; and therefore, until rebutted, even such refusal may be evidence that the defendant originally took or held the goods tortiously, or upon a claim of ownership, inconsistent with and opposed to the plaintiff's right.

II. TROVER. 3. The injury.

6thly. The refusal to deliver goods upon demand thereof will not *necessarily* in all cases constitute a conversion, unless the party refusing *have it in his power* to deliver up the goods detained, and the refusal be made in a distinct, unqualified manner. Where a deed was demanded from the defendant, who said he would not deliver it up, but that it was then in the hands of his attorney, who had a lien upon it, this refusal was held to be not sufficient evidence of a conversion; and Lord Ellenborough said, that the defendant would have been guilty of a conversion if it had been in his power, but the intention was not enough (*f*). So likewise a refusal upon demand is no evidence of conversion, if the party *bona fide* and reasonably refuse on the ground of his not being satisfied that the party making the demand is the real owner of the goods (*g*), or properly authorized by the real owner to receive them (*h*); nor is it sufficient evidence of a conversion by a servant of the owner of the goods demanded, that he refused to give them up until he could consult his master, and obtain his directions to deliver them (*i*). *But where the vendor of [*184] goods shipped the same on board a ship by the order of the vendee, and the captain by his bill of lading undertook to deliver them to the consignee; and the vendee having become bankrupt, the vendor demanded the goods of the captain; the refusal by the latter, who alleged that he had signed a bill of lading to deliver the goods to another, was held to be sufficient evidence of a conversion (*k*). And where tobacco was pledged by an agent who had purchased in his own name for his principal, the refusal of the pawnee to deliver the tobacco to the principal upon demand made by him, was deemed a conversion (*l*).

6. Of the refusal.

If the demand be not made upon the defendant himself, but merely left at his house during his absence, it appears that a reasonable time and opportunity to restore the goods should be suffered to elapse, before the defendant's non-compliance with the demand can be treated as a refusal, amounting to a conversion (*m*). The non-compliance with the demand after a reasonable opportunity to obey it has been afforded, is tantamount to a refusal, and is presumptive evidence of a conversion, and throws upon the defendant the burthen of rebutting the presumption, and explaining that the omission to deliver up the goods is not in law a conversion: as that being a carrier the defendant lost the goods, &c.

(*e*) *Per* Lord Mansfield, 3 Burr. 1243; 5 B. & Ald. 847; 1 D. & R. 488, S. C.
(*f*) 1 Campb. 439.
(*g*) 3 Campb. 215; 2 Bulstr. 312; 2 B. & P. 464.
(*h*) 1 Esp. 83; 5 Moore, 259.
(*i*) 5 B. & Ald. 247.
(*k*) 6 B. & C. 36; 8 D. & R. 31, S. C.
(*l*) 5 East, 538.
(*m*) See 8 B. & C. 528.

II. TROVER. When it is doubtful whether the evidence will establish a conversion so as to support a count in trover, a count in case for negligence, &c. should be added, if there be any proof to support it. If there have been a conversion, trover lies, although the goods converted be afterwards restored to the owner, for the restoration only goes in mitigation of damages (n) (371).

When optional to bring trover or trespass. We have seen, that for a wrongful taking of goods, trover is in general a concurrent remedy with trespass (o); but the converse does not hold, for trover may often be brought where trespass cannot; as where goods are lent or delivered to another to keep, and he refuse to deliver them on demand, trespass does not lie, but the proper remedy is [*185] *trover (p). So where the *taking* is lawful or excusable, trespass cannot in general be supported, but the action must be trover; as where a sheriff, after a secret act of bankruptcy, seizes and sells goods under an execution against the bankrupt (q).

Declaration, &c. The *declaration* in this action should state that the plaintiff was possessed of the goods (avoiding repetition and unnecessary description) *as of his own property*, and that they came to the defendant's possession by *finding*; but the omission of the former words is not material after verdict (r): and the finding is not traversable (s). As the *conversion* is the gist of the action, it must necessarily be stated in the declaration. It is simply averred that the defendant "converted the goods to his own use." The usual *plea* was the general issue, not guilty of the premises (t); under which any defence upon the merits, except the Statute of Limitations, might formerly be given in evidence. But the pleading rules, H. T. 4 W. 4,† now require a *special plea* in almost every case (u). The points relating to the pleadings in this action will be more fully stated hereafter. The jury may, in trover against the sheriff for a wrongful sale, allow him expenses of sale if reasonable (x). The *judgment* is for *damages* (y), *and full costs*, to which the plaintiff is entitled, though he recover less than *forty shillings* damages (z), unless the judge certify under the statute 43 Eliz ch. 6.

(n) 1 Rol. Ab. 5 L. pl. 1; 6 Mod. 212; Bul. N. P. 46; Bac. Ab. Trover, D. Accord. A.; 3 Campb. 396.

(o) *Ante*, 173, 174; Cro. Eliz. 824; 3 Wils. 33; 2 Saund. 47 o.

(p) Sir Tho. Raym. 472; 2 Saund. 47 p.

(q) 1 Burr. 20; 1 T. R. 475; 2 Saund. 47 p.; 3 Campb. 396; 4 M. & Sel. 260; 1 M. & P. 556; 4 Bing. 597.

(r) Moore, 691; Hardr. 111; Latch. 214; 2 Saund. 47 m. *Aliter* on judgment by default, Swallow v. Aycliff, B. R. Mich. Term, 2 Geo. 2, MS.; Selw. N. P. Trover, III n. (:1).

(s) *Ante*, 167; 1 New R. 140.

(t) Bul. N. P. 48.

(u) See *post*, Chapter on Pleas.

(x) Clark v. Nicholson, 6 Car. & P. 712; 1 Gale, 21, S. C.; 5 Tyr. 233.

(y) The damages to be recovered are to be equal to the value of the article converted at the time of the conversion, 3 Campb. 477; or it seems the jury may give as damages the value at any subsequent time, 1 C. & P. 626.

(z) 3 Keb. 31; 1 Salk. 208.

(371) Vide Murray v. Burling, 10 Johns. Rep. 172. Bristol v. Burt, 7 Johns. Rep. 154. Shotwell v. Wendover, 1 Johns. Rep. 65.

† See American Editor's Preface.

III. REPLEVIN (a).

By *replevin* the owner of goods unjustly taken and detained from him, may regain possession thereof through the medium of and upon application to the sheriff, upon giving him security to prosecute an action against the person who seized (372). It is principally used in cases of distress, but it seems that it may be brought in any case where the owner has goods taken from him by another (b). Replevin was formerly *commenced by writ issuing out of the Court of Chancery, directed to the sheriff. In modern practice, however, the course adopted is to make a plaint to the sheriff upon the Statute of Marlbridge, to have the goods replevied, that is, re-delivered, upon giving security to prosecute an action against the distrainer, for the purpose of trying the legality of the distress; and if the right be determined in favor of the distrainer, to return the goods; and in cases of distress for rent, also giving a bond with two sureties to the same effect (c). In the first instance, the plaint is levied in the sheriff's County Court, in pursuance of the condition of the replevin bond, but the action is usually removed into and prosecuted in one of the superior Courts. III. REPLEVIN. [*186]

The action of replevin, it is said, is of two sorts, namely, in the *detinet*, or the *detinuit*; the former, where goods are still detained by the person who took them, to recover the value thereof and damages; and the latter, as the word imports, when the goods have been delivered to the party (d). But the former is now obsolete, and according to a late case, there does not appear in any of the books any proceeding in replevin which has not commenced by writ, requiring the sheriff to cause the goods of the plaintiff to be replevied to him, or by the plaint in the sheriff's Court, the immediate process upon which, is a precept to replevy the goods of the party levying the plaint: both which modes of proceeding are *in rem*, *i. e.* to have the goods again (e). And therefore replevin is not an action within the statute (f), which protects constables, &c. acting under a magistrate's warrant, from any action, until demand made or left at their usual place of abode, &c, by the party intending to bring such action (g). In the present action in the *detinuit*, the plaintiff can only recover damages for the taking of the goods, and for the detention till the time of the replevy, and not the value of the goods themselves (h). We will consider this action with reference, 1st, to the *thing* taken; 2dly, the *property* therein; and, 3dly, the nature of the *injury*.

(a) From *re* and *plegiare*, Co. Lit. 145, 146.
(b) See *post*, 188.
(c) 3 Bla. Com. 147, 148. See generally, Wilkinson on Replevin.
(d) 1 Saund. 347 b, n. 2; Bul. N. P. 52; Com. Dig. Pleader, 3 K. 10.
(e) *Per* Ld Ellenborough, C. J., 6 East, 286.
(f) 24 Geo. 2, c. 44.
(g) 6 East, 283.
(h) 1 Saund. 347 b, note 2; Lutw. 1150, 1151.

(372) The action of replevin is grounded on a tortious taking, and it sounds in damages like an action of trespass, to which it is extremely analogous, if the sheriff has already made a return, and the plaintiff goes only for damages for the caption. Hopkins *v.* Hopkins, 10 Johns. Rep. 373. The possession of personal chattels by the plaintiff, and an actual wrongful taking by the defendant, are sufficient to support replevin; and lies where trespass *de bonis asportatis* will lie. Rogers *v.* Arnold, 12 Wend. R. 39. By the 2 R. S. 522, s. 1, it is also an appropriate remedy in any case of a wrongful detention of personal property. Ib.

III. REPLEVIN.

1st. The property affected.

Replevin can only be supported for taking personal chattels, and not for taking things attached to the freehold (373), *and which are in law considered fixtures (*i*), and cannot be delivered to the distrainer upon a writ of *retorno habendo*. Hence it does not lie for trees or timber growing (374), but it lies for removal or tenant's fixtures (*j*); and the general rule appears to be, that replevin lies for any thing that may by law be distrained (*k*). Whether it lies for personal property which cannot be distrained, (as title-deeds, money not in a bag, or a bill of exchange, &c.,) seems to depend upon the question whether the remedy by replevin extends to all unlawful takings (*l*).

2dly. The plaintiff's interest.

To support replevin, the plaintiff must, at the time of the caption, have had either the general property in the goods taken, or a special property therein (*m*)(375). Several persons having separate and distinct interests in the property distrained, as if the goods of A. together with other goods of B. be distrained, cannot join in this action (*n*); but joint tenants and tenants in common may and should join (*o*)(376). If the goods of a feme sole be taken, and afterwards she marry, the husband alone may have a replevin (*p*)(377); and if the goods be taken after marriage, and the husband and wife join in replevin, and after verdict a motion is made in arrest of judgment on the ground of their joining, it will be presumed, if nothing appear upon the record to the contrary, that the husband and wife were jointly possessed of the goods before marriage, and that the goods were taken before marriage, in which case they might join (*q*). In replevin an avowry for rent admits the property of the goods to be in the plaintiff; but if the plaintiff's plea shows property in a third person, the action cannot be supported. Therefore, if to an avowry for rent in replevin, the plaintiff pleads that she was a married woman when the rent accrued due, she cannot maintain replevin; because it must be intended that the husband continued alive until the time of the distress taken, and that [*188] therefore the goods could not be the plaintiff's, but her *husband's, and so she has no ground of action (*r*). The husband and wife may join in replevin

(*i*) 4 T. R. 584; 2 Saund. 84.
(*j*) Cowp. 414.
(*k*) Bac. Ab. Replevin and Avowry, F.; Com. Dig. Replevin, A.
(*l*) See *post*, 188.
(*m*) Co. Lit. 145 b. What is considered a general or special ownership or interest to enable a party to maintain *trover*, *ante*, 170. The same rules hold in replevin in this respect. *Quære*, whether *mere possession* is enough to support replevin, 10 Mod. 25.
(*n*) Co. Lit. 145 b.
(*o*) Bul. N. P. 53.
(*p*) F. N. B. 69.
(*q*) Bourn and Ux. *v.* Mattaire, Ca. temp. Hardw. 119; *ante*, 88.
(*r*) 7 Taunt. 72.

(373) Vausse *v* Russell, 2 M'Cord's Rep. 329. De Mott *v.* Hagerman, 8 Cowen, 220. Creason *v.* Stout, 17 Johns. Rep. 116.

(374) But if they be cut down by a stranger, who converts them into posts and rails, the action may be maintained. Snyder *v.* Vaux, 2 Rawle, 423. Cresson *v.* Stout, 17 Johns. Rep. 116.

(375) But a deposit by a person who has himself no property in the goods, does not give the depositary any right to replevy them; and it seems very questionable, whether on a mere naked bailment for safe-keeping the bailee can maintain replevin. Harrison *v.* M'Intosh, 1 Johns. Rep. 380. { A mere servant who has charge of goods, as such only, cannot maintain replevin, but if they are delivered to him by the master as bailee, he may. Harris *v.* Smith, 3 Serg. & Rawle, 20. And one joint owner of a chattel cannot maintain replevin against another. M'Elderry *v.* Flannegan's Adm., 1 Harr. & Gill, 308. }

(376) Vide Hart *v.* Fitzgerald, 2 Mass. Rep. 509, that replevin will not lie for part of a chattel. Gardner *v.* Dutch, 9 Mass. Rep. 427.

(377) { Per Curiam, Baker et al. *v.* Fales, 16 Mass. Rep. 149. }

of goods which the wife has as executrix (*s*), but in this, as in all other instances where the wife is joined, the declaration must show the wife's interest in the property as the reason for joining her in the action (*t*). Executors may have replevin of goods taken in the life-time of the testator (*u*)(378). If the plaintiff has not the immediate right of possession (379), replevin cannot be supported, but the party must proceed by action on the case (*x*). The defendant cannot, under the general issue, *non cepit*, dispute the plaintiff's property (380), which must be denied by a special plea (*y*).

3dly. The injury.

With respect to the *nature of the injury*, it has been said that replevin lies only in one instance of an unlawful taking, namely, that of a wrongful *distress* (381) of cattle damage feasant, or of chattels for rent in arrear (*z*); but, as before observed, it appears that this action is not thus limited, and that if goods be taken illegally, though not as a distress, replevin may be supported (*a*)(382); and it is often judicious to adopt it, or an action of detinue, in order to obtain possession of the goods themselves (*b*). Replevin is however now seldom brought but for distresses for rent, damage feasant, *poor's rate*, &c. (*c*). It may be brought to try the legality of a distress for rent, provided there were no sum whatever in arrear (*d*); but if any sum, however small, were due, and the distress were for a greater sum, or excessive, in regard to the quantity of goods taken, or otherwise irregular, the remedy must be by action on the case (*e*). Replevin lies also for an illegal distress taken damage feasant; and when the party in possession of the land has no title thereto

(*s*) Bro. Bar. & Feme, pl. 85.
(*t*) 2 New Rep 405; *ante*, 84, 85.
(*u*) Bro. Rep. 59; Sid. 82.
(*x*) 7 T. R. 9.
(*y*) Bul. N. P. 54 a.
(*z*) 3 Bla. Com. 146.
(*a*) 1 Scho. & Lefr. 320, 324; Vin. Ab. Replevin, B. pl. 2; Sir W. Jones, 173, 174; 6 H. 7, 8, 9; Cro. Eliz. 824; Cro. Jac. 50; Com. Dig. Replevin, A. Action, M. 6; Co. Lit. 145 b. See Wilkinson on Replevin, 2, 3.
(*b*) 2 Stark. R. 288.
(*c*) Com. Dig Action, M. 6; Lutw. 1179; see Courin *v.* Marshall, 3 Bar. & Adol. 440.
(*d*) 5 T. R. 248, n. c; 3 B. & P. 348.
(*e*) *Ante*, 170.

(378) { Reist, Adm. *v.* Heilbrenner, 11 Serg. & Rawle, 131. See Talvande *v.* Cripps, 2 M'Cord's Rep. 164. }

(379) { Wheeler *v.* Train, 3 Pick. Rep. 255. }

(380) The general issue of *non cepit*, in the case of a wrongful taking, puts in issue not only *the taking*, but the *place* where taken, if material, 2 R. S. 528, s. 29; and in case of a wrongful detention, the general issue, to wit—That the defendant does not detain the goods, &c. puts in issue not only the detention of the goods, but the *property* of the plaintiff. The distinction here made between the effect and operation of the general issue, in the cases of *non cepit* and *non detinet* is in analogy to that existing in the actions of trespass and trover. In the one the defendant cannot, under the plea of not guilty, show property out of the plaintiff, but he may in the other. 11 Johns. Rep. 132, 528. 13 ib. 284. 14 ib. 132, 353. 15 ib. 208. *Non cepit* admits property in the plaintiff, and hence the necessity of the different pleas of property in others. Nor will the court, under such issue, permit the defendant to give special matter in evidence in justification. M'Farland *v.* Barker, 1 Mass. Rep. 135.

(381) It does not seem to be settled in South Carolina whether replevin will lie in any other case than a distress for rent. Bird *v.* O'Hanlin, 1 Rep. Const. Ct. 401; but in Pennsylvania, it lies in every case on a claim of property, 11 Serg. & Rawle, 132. See also the cases cited in note 3.

(382) Acc. Pangburn *v.* Partridge, 7 Johns. Rep. 140. Isley et al. *v.* Stubbs, 5 Mass. Rep. 283, 284. Replevin is in general a co-extensive remedy with trespass *de bonis asportatis*. Pangburn *v.* Partridge, 7 Johns. Rep. 143. Thompson *v.* Button, 14 Johns. Rep. 87. See Buffington *v.* Gerish, Badger *v.* Phinney, 15 Mass. Rep. 156, 359. See also, 1 Dall. 147. 6 Binn. 3. 3 Serg. & Rawle, 562. Bruen *v.* Ogden, 6 Halst. Rep 370. Marshall *v.* Davis, 1 Wend. R. 109.

III. REPLEVIN. this action is preferable to trespass for seizing the cattle, in order to put in issue the title of the party distraining (*f*). It is also maintainable *to try the legality of a distress for poor rates (*g*); or for sewer's rate (*h*); or for a heriot, &c. (*i*). If a tenant's cattle are wrongfully distrained, and they afterwards return back to the tenant, he may still maintain replevin against the landlord (*k*). If a superior court award an execution, it seems that no replevin lies for the goods taken by the sheriff by virtue of the execution (383); and if any person should pretend to take out a replevin, the Court would commit him for a contempt of their jurisdiction (*l*). So where goods are taken by way of levy, as for a penalty on a conviction under a statute, it is generally in the nature of an execution, and unless replevin be given by the statute, this action will not lie, the conviction being conclusive, and its legality not questionable in replevin (*m*); as on a conviction for deer-stealing (*n*). So replevin does not lie for goods taken under a warrant of distress granted under the 20 Geo. 2, c. 19, s. 1, for non-payment of laborers' wages (*o*). Where however a special inferior jurisdiction is given to justices, &c. and they exceed it, in some cases replevin lies: as where a magistrate granted a warrant of distress against a person for rates, in respect of lands which the latter did not occupy (*p*). This action is maintainable for goods distrained under a warrant from commissioners, authorized by act of parliament to levy rates for specific local purposes, with power of distress (*q*).

(*f*) 1 Saund. 346 e, n. 2.

(*g*) 3 Wils. 442; 1 Salk. 20; 2 Bla. Rep. 1330; Willes, 672 b; and see 7 B. & C. 398, *id.* 338; 3 B & Adol. 440.

(*h*) 6 T. R. 522; Hardr. 478; Com. Dig. Pleader, 3 K. 26; Willes, 672, n. b.

(*i*) Cro. Jac. 50.

(*k*) F. N. B. 69.

(*l*) Gilb. Rep. 161; 2 Lutw. 1191; 3 Lev. 204.

(*m*) Bac. Ab. 5th edit. vol. vi. 58, Replevin, (C.); Com. Dig. Action, M. 6.

(*n*) 2 Stra. 1184.

(*o*) 1 B. & B. 57; 3 Moore, 294, S. C.

(*p*) Willes, 673, n b; 2 Bla. Rep. 1330.

(*q*) 1 Swanst. 304; and see 2 New Rep. 399.

(383) But it has been held, in Pennsylvania, that although replevin was prohibited by a statute of their legislature to be brought against a sheriff who has taken goods in execution, yet that after the sale, a person claiming property in the goods might maintain this action against the sheriff's vendee. Shearick *v.* Huber, 6 Binn. 2. In Massachusetts, an action of replevin is allowed, by statute, to be brought for goods taken in execution, provided the plaintiff in replevin be not the debtor; but PARSONS, C. J., observes, that this alteration of the common law has been productive of much practical inconvenience. Isley et al. *v.* Stubbs, 5 Mass. Rep. 280, 283. In a late case in the state of New York, it was held, that although the defendant in the execution could not himself maintain replevin, yet that the action might be brought by a third person against the sheriff; for, if an officer having an execution against A. undertake to execute it upon goods in the possession of B., he assumes upon himself the responsibility of showing that such goods were the property of A., and if he fail to do this, he is a trespasser by taking them. Thompson *v.* Button, 14 Johns. Rep. 84. { See Mulmholm *v.* Cheney, Addis. Rep. 301. }

So, the goods of a master or principal, taken under an execution against his servant or agent while in his possession, may be taken by a writ of replevin; the goods in such case to be deemed as taken from the actual possession of the plaintiff, (who was not the defendant in the execution) Clark *v.* Skinner, 20 J. R. 465. Replevin will lie also by the owner of goods against a sheriff for the recovery of property levied upon by him by virtue of an execution against a third person, the property at the time of the levy being in the possession of the defendant in the execution, where such property, after the levy, came peaceably into the possession of the owner, and was retaken by the sheriff. Hall *v.* Guttle, 2 Wend. Rep. 475. But replevin will not lie against a receiptor of goods taken by virtue of an execution, although the action, under the circumstances of the case, might be maintained against the sheriff, if the party becomes such receiptor at the request of the defendant in the execution. Chapman *v.* Andrews, 3 Wend. Rep. 240. A person having the property in goods, and having the right to reduce them to actual possession, may sue replevin against the officer who takes them by virtue of an execution out of the possession of the defendant in the execution. Denham *v.* Wickoff, 3 Wend. Rep. 280.

In this action both the plaintiff and defendant are considered as actors; the defendant, in respect of his having made the distress, (being a claim of right, and the avowry in the nature of a declaration) (*r*); and the plaintiff in respect of his action; on which ground principally the distinctions between the pleadings in this action and in that of trespass depend (*s*).

Declaration, &c.

The *declaration* in this action, which is local (384), requires certainty in the description of the place (385) where the distress was taken; and the description, number, and value of the *goods also must be stated with certainty, [*190] although the same strictness does not prevail as formerly (*t*). Where the distress was taken for rent, a general *avowry* is given by statute (*u*)(386); but in avowries for distresses, taken damage feasant, more certainty is necessary than in a justification in trespass, as the defendant cannot, in the former, rely on mere possession of the *locus in quo*, but must state his title (*x*)(387). The plaintiff cannot *plead in bar de injuriâ* generally (388), but must take issue upon some particular allegation in the avowry (*y*). The statute of Anne (*z*) provides that the plaintiff in replevin, in any Court of record, may, with leave of the Court, plead several pleas in bar (389); which frequently renders this action preferable to trespass or any other action, in which the plaintiff can have but one replication to each plea. The other particulars of the pleadings in this action will be stated hereafter. The *judgment* for the plaintiff is, that he recover his damages on occasion of the taking and unjustly detaining the cattle, &c.; together with *full* costs of suit, to which the plaintiff is entitled; though he recover less than 40*s*. damages, unless the judge certify under the 43 Eliz. c. 6; and under the 19th section of this act, the defendant in replevin is entitled to treble damages, with single costs also (*a*). The judgment for the avowant, or person making cognizance, varies in different cases: it may be at common law *pro retorno habendo*, or founded on the statutes (*b*)(390). If the plaintiff be nonsuited, or discontinue his action, or have judgment against him, he will be liable to double costs (*c*)(391).

(*r*) 2 Wils. 260, 261; 1 Saund. 347 e, n. 7; Willes, 221.
(*s*) 1 Saund. 347 b, n. 3.
(*t*) 2 Saund. 74 b; 7 Taunt. 613; 1 Moore, 386, S. C.
(*u*) 11 Geo. 2, c. 19, s. 22, 2 Saund. 284 e, n. 3.
(*x*) 2 B. & P. 359; 1 Saund. 347 b, n. 3.
(*y*) 1 B. & P. 76.
(*z*) 4 Anne, c. 16, s. 4.
(*a*) 4 Moore, 296; 1 Lord Raym. 19; 1 Salk. 205.
(*b*) Hen. 8. or Car. 2. See the cases in 1 Saund. 195, n. 3; 2 Saund. 286, n. 5.
(*c*) 11 Geo. 2, c. 19, s. 22; see also 1 B. & Ald. 670.

(384) Vide Robinson *v.* Mead, 7 Mass. Rep. 353.
(385) Vide Gardner *v.* Humphrey, 10 Johns. Rep. 53.
(386) The provision in the statute 11 Geo. 2 c 19. s. 22, has never been adopted in the state of New York. Harrison *v.* M'Intosh, 1 Johns. Rep. 394. {See 2 Rev. Stat. Title XII. "Replevin," p. 521. See, for the law in Pennsylvania, the act of 21st March, 1772, sect. 10. 1 Sm. Laws, 370.}
(387) Acc. Hopkins *v.* Hopkins, 10 J. R. 369. So at common law where the defendant avows for rent arrear. Harrison *v.* M'Intosh, 1 J. R. 380.
(388) Hopkins *v.* Hopkins, 10 Johns. Rep. 369. Rogers *v.* Arnold, 12 Wend. Rep. 30.
(389) See Laws N. Y., *Act for the amendment of the law*, 1 R. L. 519. 2 Rev. Stat. 528, s. 38.
(390) See Laws of N. Y. sess. 11. c. 5, s. 11. 1 R. L. 95. 2 R. S. 530 to 532, Loomis *v.* Tyler, 4 Day, 141. Easton *v.* Worthington, 5 S. & R. 132. Weidel *v.* Roseberry, 13 S. & R. 170.
(391) Acc. Act of 21st March, 1772, s. 10. Purg. Dig. 710. 1 Sm. Laws of Pennsylvania, 370.

IV. TRESPASS.

In general. The term *trespass*, in its most extensive signification, includes every description of *wrong* (d), on which account an action on the case has been usually called "trespass on the case;" but technically, it signifies an injury
[*191] committed *vi et *armis*, the meaning of which words is explained in Co. Lit. (e). The action of *trespass* (392) only lies for injuries committed with force, and generally only for such as are immediate (f). Force, we have seen, may be either actual or implied; and the distinctions between immediate and consequential injuries have already been considered (g). The words *contra pacem* should uniformly accompany the allegation of the injury, and in some cases are material to the foundation of the action. An action of trespass to land not within our king's dominions cannot be sustained (h); for the venue in trespass to realty is local, and there is not therefore any county into which the writ can in such case be issued (i). It has been doubted whether trespass for an assault committed out of the king's dominions can be supported (k); though as the fine, in strictness of law payable to the king for the violation of the public peace, is no longer regarded (l), and the words *contra pacem* are not traversable (m); and the venue is transitory; it should seem that an action for such injury, or for an injury to goods in a foreign country, might be supported. The intention of the wrong-doer is in general immaterial in this action (n); and where the defendant has been acquitted of a felonious taking he may be sued for the trespass (o).

This action cannot be sustained where the wrong complained of was a *nonfeasance*, as for not carrying away tithes, &c. (p); or where the matter affected was not tangible, and consequently could not be immediately injured by force, as reputation, health, &c. (q); or where the right affected is incorporeal, as a right of common or way, &c. (r); or where the plaintiff's interest is in reversion, and not in possession (s); or where the injury was not immediate but consequential (t). We will consider the particular applicability of this
[*192] remedy to the different injuries committed by force to the *person*, or **personal* or *real property*; and as there are material distinctions between the remedy for these injuries when committed under color of suit or process, and when not, we will consider the action of trespass under the following heads:—

(d) 7 East, 134, 135; Co Lit. 57 a.
(e) 161 b; 3 Bla. Com. 118, 398, 399.
(f) *Ante*, 142, 143.
(g) *Id.*
(h) 4 T. R. 503; 2 Bla. Rep. 1058.
(i) Stephen on Pleading, 306, 1st edit.
(k) Cowp. 176; 2 Bla. Rep. 1058; Finch's Law, 198.
(l) 3 Bla. Com. 118, 399.
(m) Com. Dig. Pleader, 3 M. 8; Vin. Ab. Trespass, Q. a.
(n) 1 Campb. 497; 2 Campb. 465; 3 East, 593; *ante*, 147.
(o) 12 East, 409; Sty. 346; 2 Rol. Ab. 557; Yelv. 90; 1 Sid. 375; 1 Bing. 401; *ante*, 148.
(p) *Ante*, 144.
(q) *Ante*, 144.
(r) *Ante*, 147, 159.
(s) 4 T. R. 489; 7 T. R. 9.
(t) *Ante*, 159. And *semble*, that after a recovery in trespass, the proper remedy for a continuance of the injury is *case*, 1 Stark. 22.

(392) As to the history of this action, vide 1 Reeve's Hist. E. L. 263, 266, 340, 347. 3 Reeve's Hist. E. L. 84, 89.

- I. When it lies for injuries not committed under color of legal proceedings.
  - 1. For the parties' own act.
    - 1. Injuries to the person.
    - 2. To personal property.
    - 3. To real property.
  - 2. For the acts of others, and of cattle, &c.
- II. When trespass lies for injuries under color of legal proceedings (u).

FIRST, FOR INJURIES NOT UNDER PROCESS.

1st. Injuries to the person.

Trespass is the only remedy for a menace to the plaintiff, attended with consequent damages (x); and for an illegal assault, battery, and wounding, or imprisonment, when not under color of process (y). It lies also when the battery, imprisonment, &c. were in the first instance lawful, but the party by an unnecessary degree of violence became a trespasser *ab initio* (z)(393); and for a wrongful imprisonment after the process is determined (a); or for an assault after an acquittal for a felonious assault and stabbing (b). So it lies for an injury to the relative rights occasioned by force, as for menacing tenants, servants, &c. and beating, wounding, and imprisoning a wife or servant (c), whereby the landlord, master, or servant, hath sustained a loss; though the injury, the loss of service, &c. were consequential, and not immediate. It lies for criminal conversation (d); seducing away a wife (e), or servant (f); or for debauching the latter (g); force being implied, and the wife and servant being considered as having no power to consent; and a count for beating the plaintiff's servant, *per quod servitium amisit*, may be joined with [*193] other counts in trespass (h); and though it has been usual to declare in case for debauching a daughter (i), it is now considered to be preferable to declare in trespass (k).

2dly. To *personal* property.

The action of trespass, in its application to injuries to *personal* property, may be considered with reference, 1st, to the nature of the *thing* affected; 2dly, the plaintiff's *right* thereto; 3dly, the nature of the *injury*; and the *situation* in which the *defendant* stood, as whether tenant in common, bailee, &c.

(u) 3 T. R. 185.
(x) 3 Bla. Com. 120.
(y) 11 Mod. 180, 181.
(z) Com. Dig. Trespass, C. 2; Bac. Ab. Trespass, B.; *post*, 198.
(a) Cro. Jac. 379.
(b) 12 East, 409.
(c) 2 M. & Sel. 436; 9 Co. 113; 10 Co. 130.
(d) 7 Mod. 81; 2 Salk. 552; 6 East, 387.
(e) Fitz. N. B. 89; 6 East, 387.
(f) 5 T. R. 361; 7 Mod. 81; 2 Salk. 552; 20 Vin. Ab. 470.
(g) Bac. Ab. Trespass, C. 1; 3 Wils. 362, 18, 19; 2 New Rep. 476; 2 M. & Sel. 436.
(h) 2 M. & Sel. 436; 2 New Rep. 476.
(i) 2 T. R. 167, 168; 20 Vin. Ab. 470; 6 East, 387.
(k) 2 New Rep. 476; 2 M. & Sel. 436.

(393) Pease *v.* Burt, 3 Day, 485. Elliott *v.* Brown, 2 Wend. R. 497. The State *v.* Wood, 1 Bay, 351. 15 Mass. R. 347, 365. In the case of an assault and battery both parties may be guilty of a breach of the peace and may be indicted; but a civil action cannot be brought by each against the other. Although the defendant may have been the aggressor, yet if the plaintiff had used not only more force than was necessary for self defence, but had unnecessarily abused the defendant, he cannot recover damages; but must pay damages. Elliott *v.* Brown, 2 Wend. R. 497.

IV. TRESPASS.

1. The nature of the *personal* property. And *first*, as to the *nature of the thing affected:* trespass lies for taking or injuring all inanimate personal property, and certain domiciled and tame animals, of which the law takes notice, as dogs, &c. (*l*), and all animals usually marketable, as parrots, monkies, &c. (394) and in which case it is not necessary to show in the pleadings that they have been reclaimed (*m*). In the case of a hawk, pheasant, hare, rabbit, fish, or other animals *feræ naturæ*, and not generally merchandizable, it should be shown in the pleadings that the same were reclaimed or dead, or at least that the plaintiff was *possessed* of them (*n*). So it lies in some cases for taking animals *feræ naturæ*, and not reclaimed; as if a hare or rabbit be *killed* on the land of another, he having a local property *ratione soli* in such hare or rabbit, may support trespass for taking it, though the wrong-doer did not enter on the land (*o*)(395); and if game be started on the land of A. and pursued and killed on the land of B., A. may support trespass for taking the hare, if *he* also pursued the same, for by the pursuit he prevented an abandonment of his local property (*p*)(396). The same rules [*194] prevail in the case of fish (*q*). In *actions of trespass for taking or killing animals *feræ naturæ* not reclaimed, it is advisable in pleading to state also an entry, if any, on the plaintiff's land (*r*); and it is said that trespass for killing rabbits, without complaining of such entry, cannot be supported (*s*).

2dly. The nature of the *interest* in the *personal* property (*t*). *Secondly*, With respect to the *plaintiff's interest in the property affected*, he must, at the time when the injury was committed, have had an *actual* or a *constructive possession* (*u*)(397), and also a general or qualified *property* therein,

(*l*) 1 Saund. 84, n. 2, 3; Com. Dig. Action, Trover, C.; Fitz. N. B. 86; Hob. 283; Cro. Eliz. 125; 3 T. R. 37, 38; see Toller's Law of Executors, 1st edit. 112, where the particulars of personal property are stated; Com. Dig. Trespass, A. 1.

(*m*) Cro. Jac. 262; 1 Saund. 84, n. 2.

(*n*) Bac. Ab. Trespass, 1, and Trover, D.; Cro. Jac. 262; 1 Ventr. 122; Dyer, 306 b.; Cro. Car. 554. As to Fish, see Bul. N. P. 79; 5 B. & C. 879. Case for disturbing a decoy, &c. *ante*, 163.

(*o*) 2 Salk. 556; 1 Ld. Raym. 251; Godb. 123; 14 East, 249.

(*p*) *Id.*

(*q*) Cro. Car. 554.

(*r*) 43 Edw. 3, p. 24, 2; 1 Ld. Raym. 250; 11 Mod. 74; 2 Salk. 556; Cro. Car. 554; Fitz. N. B. 86, 87, M. note a. A.

(*s*) 43 Edw. 3, p. 24, 2; Fitz. N. B. 87, A. c.; Cro. Car. 553, 554.

(*t*) See *ante*, 70, 149, as to who may sue in general in this action.

(*u*) 1 T. R. 480; 4 *id.* 490; 7 *id.* 9.

(394) { Trespass *vi et armis* is a proper remedy by a parent for the taking away his child. Vaughan *v.* Rhodes, 2 M'Cord's Rep. 227. }

(395) It seems that the owner of land may, in like manner, have a property *ratione soli* in bees, although they have not been hived or reclaimed by him. Gillet *v.* Mason, 7 Johns. Rep. 16. { But see Wallis *v.* Mease, 3 Binn. 546. }

(396) If A. starts a hare in the ground of B. and hunts it into the ground of C., and kills or catches it there, the property is in A., the hunter, who may maintain trespass against C. for taking away the hare. Sutton *v.* Moody, 1 Ld. Raym. 250, S. C. 2 Salk. 556. Churchward *v.* Studdy, 14 East's Rep. 249. Mere pursuit of a wild animal does not, independent of title *ratione soli*, vest any property in the pursuer: manucaption is not, however, necessary; it is sufficient if the pursuer have rendered it impossible for the animal to escape. Pierson *v.* Post, 3 Caines' Rep. 175.

(397) Vide Putnam *v.* Wiley, 8 Johns. Rep. 432. Carter *v.* Simpson, 7 Johns. Rep. 535. Hence, if a vessel has been seized by an officer of the customs as forfeited to the United States, and is afterwards acquitted, the owner cannot maintain trespass for an injury intermediate between the seizure and acquittal, since he has neither the actual possession, or the right to reduce her into possession. Van Brant *v.* Schenck, 11 Johns. Rep. 377. { But where a deputy sheriff attached goods, carried them into Rhode Island, and delivered them to a bailee, taking his receipt, and the bailee put them into the hands of another person for safe keeping, it was held that the officer might maintain trespass, and recover damages, against mere strangers who took them away from the keeper in Rhode Island. Browne *v.* Manchester, 1 Pick. Rep. 232. And in such a case, the bailee might also, it has been held in New Hampshire, maintain the action. Poole *v.* Simonds, 1 New Hamp. Rep. 289. But a different decision has taken place in Massachusetts. Ludden *v.* Leavit, Warren *v.* Leland, 9 Mass. Rep. 104, 265. }

2. Injuries to *personalty*, not under process.

which may be either, first, in the case of the *absolute* or general owner entitled to immediate possession; 2dly, the *qualified* owner coupled with an interest, and also entitled to immediate possession (*x*); 3dly, a *bailee* with a mere naked *authority*, unaccompanied with any interest, except as to remuneration for trouble, &c. but who is in actual possession; or 4thly, *actual possession*, though without the consent of the real owner, and even adverse.

These rules have been considered in detail in explaining the nature of the action of trover (*y*). It may, however, be useful to notice them here, particularly in those cases in which they have more immediate reference to the action of trespass.

In the *first* instance the person who has the absolute or general property may support this action; although he has never had the actual possession, or although he has parted with his possession to a carrier, servant, &c. giving him only a bare authority to carry or keep, &c. not coupled (398) with an interest in the thing (*z*); it being a rule of law that the general property of personal chattels *prima facie*, as to all civil purposes, draws to it the possession (*a*) (399). Therefore the owner of tithe may support trespass against the occupier of the land where it has been set out, for turning in cattle and injuring it (*b*). So the grantee of waifs, estrays, and wreck, within a *manor, [*195] or of felon's goods within a hundred, may, before seizure by him, maintain trespass against a wrong-doer (*c*); and the owner of a ship has, notwithstanding a charter-party, a sufficient possession thereof to support trespass (*d*).

This rule holds by relation; as in case of executors and administrators, &c., who may support trespass for an injury to personal property committed *after* the death of the testator, or intestate, and before the probate or administration was granted (*e*); so may a legatee, after the executor has assented to the legacy, for a trespass committed before such assent (*f*). But if the general owner part with his possession, and the bailee, at the time when the injury was committed, have a right exclusively to use the thing, the inference of possession is rebutted, and the right of possession being in reversion, the general owner cannot support trespass (400), but only an action on the case, for an injury done by a stranger while the bailee's right continued (*g*). Nor can the general owner in such case support this action even against such bailee for mere abuse; though if a bailee *destroy* the thing, trespass may be supported if the injury were forcible. If, however, the general owner merely permit another gratuitously to use the chattel, such owner may sue a stranger in trespass for an injury done to it while it was so used (*h*).

(*x*) *Ante*, 70; 1 B. & P. 44; 7 T. R. 9.

(*y*) *Ante*, 170, 171.

(*z*) 7 T. R. 12; 16 East, 33.

(*a*) 2 Saund. 47 a, b, d; see further, *ante*, 174. When not so in criminal cases, see Const's argument in Baseley's case, 2 Leach, C. L. 838 to 843, 4th edit.

(*b*) 8 T. R. 72.

(*c*) F. N. B. 91 b, 91 d, 91 F.; 1 T. R. 480.

(*d*) 3 B. & Ald. 503; 5 Moore, 211; 2 B. & B. 410, S. C.; 2 Y. & J. 310, 318.

(*e*) 1 T. R. 480; Bac. Ab. Executors, H. 1; 2 Saund. 47 a.

(*f*) Bro. Ab. Trespass, pl. 25.

(*g*) 4 T. R. 489; 7 T. R. 9; 3 Lev. 209; 3 Campb. 187; 15 East, 607; *ante*, 174.

(*h*) 2 Campb. 464; 3 *id.* 187; 16 East, 33.

(398) Vide Putnam *v.* Wiley, 8 Johns. Rep. 435. Williams *v.* Lewis, 3 Day, 498. Thorp *v.* Burling, 11 Johns. Rep. 285. East's P. C. 564, 565.

(399) Vide Bird and others *v.* Clark, 3 Day, 272. 7 Conn. Rep. 235.

(400) Vide Putnam *v.* Wiley, 8 Johns. Rep. 432. Van Brunt *v.* Schenck, 11 Johns. Rep. 385. 7 Conn. Rep. 235.

IV. TRESPASS. 2. Injuries to personalty, not under process.

In the *second* case also, that of the bailee who has an authority coupled with an interest, it should seem that trespass may be supported, though he never had actual possession, for any injury done during his interest (*i*); as in the case of a factor (401), or consignee of goods in which he has an interest in respect of his commission, &c. (*k*). The quantity or certainty of the interest is not material, and therefore a shop-keeper may maintain trespass for taking goods sent to him on sale or return (*l*). So a tenant for years has a qualified property in trees whilst growing, and may support trespass for cutting them down unless they were excepted in the lease; though he cannot support this [*196] action merely for carrying the *trees away (*m*); and if a person have a right to cut all the thorns in such a place, he may sustain trespass against any one who cuts them down, even against the grantor; but if he have only a right of estovers, and the grantor cuts the whole, the remedy is case, and not trespass (*n*); and a mere gratuitous bailee (*o*), or an executor *de son tort* (*p*), may support this action. Other instances have been before given (*q*).

In the *third* instance, that of a bailee, &c. with a mere naked authority coupled only with an interest as to remuneration, he may also support this action for an injury done while he was in the actual possession of the thing; as a carrier, factor, pawnee, a sheriff, &c. (*r*) (402); but it is otherwise in the case of a mere servant (*s*); and if a sheriff omit to continue in possession of the goods under an execution, he cannot maintain the action (*t*).

An instance of the *fourth* description is the finder of any article, who may maintain trespass or trover against any person but the real owner (*u*) (403); and even a person not having a strict legal right, but being in possession, may, it seems, support this action against any person but the legal owner (*x*). So a person in possession under an assignment fraudulent as against creditors, may support trespass against a person who cannot show that he was justified in what he did as a creditor (*y*).

Assignees of a bankrupt, though they have a constructive possession from the time of the act of bankruptcy, cannot support *trespass* against a sheriff or any other officer acting in obedience to the process of a Court of competent jurisdiction, for seizing goods after a secret act *of bankruptcy; because such

(*i*) *Ante*, 174; 1 B. & P. 45; 2 Saund. 47 d.
(*k*) 7 T. R. 359; 1 T. R. 113; 1 Hen. Bla. 81; Bul. N. P. 33; *ante*, 174, 175.
(*l*) 2 Campb. 575.
(*m*) 2 Campb. 491; 2 M. & Sel. 499. See further as to trees, *ante*, 174.
(*n*) 2 Salk. 638; 2 M. & Sel. 499; 8 East, 394.
(*o*) 1 B. & Ald. 59.
(*p*) *Ante*, 173.
(*q*) *Ante*, 72, 173.
(*r*) 2 Saund. 47 b; 1 Rol. Ab. 551; Wood's Inst. 93.
(*s*) Owen, 52; 3 Inst. 103; 2 Bla. Com. 396; 2 Saund. 47 b, c, d.
(*t*) 1 M. & Sel. 711; see 1 D. & R. 307; 2 *id.* 755.
(*u*) 2 Saund. 47 d; 4 Taunt. 547.
(*x*) 3 Wils. 332; 2 Stra. 777; 1 Salk. 290; 2 Saund. 47 c.
(*y*) 2 Marsh. 233.

(401) Vide Colwill *v.* Reeves, 2 Campb. 575.
(402) {Brown *v.* Manchester, 1 Pick. Rep. 232.} Vide Barker and Knapp *v.* Miller, 6 Johns. Rep. 195. Gibbs *v.* Chase, 10 Mass. Rep. 125. Whether a depository may maintain trespass. Harrison *v.* M'Intosh, 1 Johns. Rep. 358. {See the cases cited, ante, p. 194, n. 3.} Bare possession is in general sufficient to support this action against a wrong-doer. Hoyt *v.* Gelston and Schenck, 13 Johns. Rep. 141, 561.
(403) A bare possession is sufficient to enable the plaintiff to recover in *trespass* against a wrong-doer, who takes the property out of his possession without authority. Cook *v.* Howard, 13 Johns. Rep. 276. Demick *v.* Chapman, 11 ib. 132. Schermerhorn *v.* Van Valkenburgh, ib. 520. Aiken *v.* Buck, 2 Wend. R. 466. Butts *v.* Collins, 13 ib. 143.

officers acting *bona fide* ought not for such act to be liable as trespassers, but ought to be sued in trover, in which only the real value of the goods can be recovered (*z*).

IV. TRESPASS.

2. Injuries to *personalty*, not under process.

[*197]

3dly. The nature of the *injury* to the *personal* property, and of the person committing it.

*As to the *third* point, *the nature of the injury*, it may be either by an unlawful taking of the personal chattel, or by injuring it whilst in the possession of the general owner, or of a person having a special property in it, as a bailee.

Trespass is a concurrent remedy with trover for most illegal *takings* (*a*). Thus, even in the case of a distress for rent, where there has been an illegal taking, as for distraining when no rent was due, or taking implements of trade, or beasts of husbandry, when there was sufficiency of other property (*b*); or a horse while his rider was upon him (*c*); or if a distress be made, the outer door being shut, or if the party expel the tenant, or continue in possession, without leave, more than five days, trespass lies (*d*)(404); for the statute (*e*)(405) which enacts that a party distraining for rent shall not be a trespasser *ab initio* (*f*), only relates to irregularities after a lawful taking (*g*). There is no doubt that trespass lies for any forcible malfeasance after *legal entry* to distrain, and that the tenant's remedy is not at all affected by the statute. But the statute is clear that no subsequent irregularity shall render a legal distress a trespass *ab initio*, and confines the tenant's action to that only which is irregular (*h*). Of course case is the remedy if the subsequent irregularity be not forcible, or be of a nature which in other respects renders it matter for that form of action (*i*).

This action also in general lies though there was no wrongful intent (406) in committing the tort (*k*); as if a sheriff, or a messenger on behalf of assignees of a bankrupt, by mistake take the goods of a wrong person (*l*). If a sheriff illegally take the goods of B. under an execution against the goods of A., it seems that even the sheriff's vendee is liable; but it seems the latter is not liable if the process were only irregular, and the real defendant's goods were taken (*m*); but if a second trespasser take goods out of the custody of the first *trespasser, the owner may support trespass against such second taker, his act not being excusable (*n*). This action may be supported [*198]

(*z*) 1 Burr. 20; 1 T. R. 480; *ante*, 148, 153; 1 M. & P. 541; 4 Bing. 587, S. C.
(*a*) 3 Wils. 336; *ante*, 184.
(*b*) F. N. B. 88; 4 T. R. 565; 1 Burr. 579; *ante*, 158.
(*c*) 6 T. R. 138; 4 T. R. 569.
(*d*) 1 East, 139; 11 East, 395; 2 Campb. 115; *ante*, 158.
(*e*) 11 Geo. 2, c. 19.
(*f*) 1 Hen. Bla. 13.
(*g*) 1 Esp. N. P. 382, 383.
(*h*) See 2 Campb. 116; 11 East, 195.
(*i*) *Id.*
(*k*) *Ante*, 147; 3 Lev. 347; 1 Campb. 497; 2 *id.* 576.
(*l*) *Ante*, 147; 2 Campb. 576; Bro. Ab. Propertie, 23. It would seem that no action would lie if an injury arose from a *mere* accident, and unavoidably, without *any* default or carelessness on the defendant's part. *Ante*, 148.
(*m*) See *ante*, 92; 3 Stark. R. 130; 2 D. & R. 1.
(*n*) Sid. 438.

(404) Van Brunt and another *v.* Schenck, 13 Johns. Rep. 417. Kerr *v.* Sharp, 14 Serg. & Rawle, 399.

(405) The 19th sect. is not in force in Pennsylvania, Kerr *v.* Sharp.

(406) Vide Higginson et al. *v.* York, 5 Mass. Rep. 341. Colwill *v.* Reeves, 2 Campb. 575. But where a party becomes possessed of the property of another, for instance a wagon, and changes part of its appendages, by substituting whiffletrees and clevices for those attached to it when it came into his possession, and the owner re-possess himself of the wagon, without knowledge of the change in its appendages, *trespass* will not lie against him for the substituted articles; the remedy of the party, if any, is by action of *trover*. Parker *v.* Walrod, 13 Wend. R. 296.

IV. TRESPASS. — 2. Injuries to personalty, not under process.

against a bailee who has only a bare authority, as if a servant take goods of his master out of his shop, and convert them (*o*) (407); so it is sustainable by an outgoing tenant against the incoming tenant, for taking manure, though the latter had a right to it on paying for it (*p*). But in general trespass is not sustainable against a bailee who has the possession coupled with an interest, unless he destroy the chattel (*q*); nor against a joint-tenant or tenant in common for merely taking away and holding exclusively the property from his cotenant (*r*) because each has an interest in the whole, and a right to dispose thereof (*s*); but if the thing be *destroyed*, trespass lies (*t*), and case may be supported for injuring the thing (*u*)(408). A bailee of a chattel for a certain time, coupled with an interest, may support this action against the bailor for taking it away before the time (*x*); and it lies, though after the illegal taking the goods be restored (*y*). When the taking is unlawful, either the general owner or the bailee, if answerable over, may support trespass, but a recovery by one is a bar to an action by the other (*z*). Trespass will not lie for a refusal to deliver when the first taking was lawful; trover or detinue being in such case the only remedies (*a*).

So trespass lies for any immediate injury to personal property occasioned by actual or implied force, though the wrong-doer might not take away or dispose of the chattel; as for shooting or beating a dog or other live animal, or for hunting or chasing sheep, &c. (*b*); or for mixing water with wine (*c*); or unintentionally running down a ship or a carriage (*d*). But it is said, though without reason, that for a mere *battery* of a horse, not accompanied with special damage, no action can be supported (*e*).

[*199] *It is said, that if a bailee of a beast, &c. *kill* it, trespass cannot be supported, but only case (*f*). But this position appears to be erroneous; for although the act may not render the party a trespasser *ab initio*, yet he may be considered as a trespasser for the wrongful act itself (*g*). So case (*h*), or assumpsit, for a breach of the implied contract, may be supported (*i*); and it seems clear that if a person or bailee, though coupled with a beneficial interest, as of sheep to feed his land, or of oxen to plough it (*k*), and he kill or de-

(*o*) 1 Leon. 87; Cro. Eliz. 781; 5 Co. 13 b.
(*p*) 16 East, 116.
(*q*) *Ante*, 195.
(*r*) 1 T. R. 658; Cowp. 430; 2 Saund. 47 g; *ante*, 91.
(*s*) 1 Lev. 29; 8 T. R. 145; Co. Lit. 200 a; Cowp. 217; 4 East, 121.
(*t*) Co. Lit. 200 a; *ante*, 91.
(*u*) 8 T. R. 145; 1 Ld. Raym. 737.
(*x*) Godb. 173; F. N. B. 86, n. a.
(*y*) *Ante*, 184; Bro. Ab. Trespass, pl. 221; 2 Rol. Ab. 569, pl. 3, 6.
(*z*) 2 Saund. 47 e; Bro. Trespass, 67; 2 Rol. Ab. 569, P.
(*a*) Sir T. Raym. 472; 2 Vent. 170; 2 Saund. 47 o, p.
(*b*) Barnes, 452; 3 T. R. 37; Hob. 283; 3 Bla. Com. 153.
(*c*) F. N. B. 88.
(*d*) 1 Campb. 497; 2 *id.* 465; 3 East, 593; but see 2 New Rep. 117.
(*e*) 2 Stra. 8, 72; *quære*, Barnes, 452.
(*f*) Bac. Ab. Trespass, G. 1; Moor, 248.
(*g*) Co. Lit. 57 a; Cro. Eliz. 777, 784; 5 Co. 13 b; Bro. Trespass, pl. 295; 1 Leon. 87; 11 Co. 82 a.
(*h*) Co. Lit. 57 a, n. 4.
(*i*) Cro. Eliz. 777, 784.
(*k*) Co. Lit. 57, 58; Cro. Eliz. 784.

(407) Vide East's P. C. 564, et seq. Adkins *v.* Brewer, 3 Cowen, 206. Allen *v.* Crofoot, 5 Wend. R. 506. The distinction is, where a party enters a house by license he will not be considered a trespasser *ab initio* by reason of an unlawful act done after such entry; but where authority to enter is given by law, and the party abuses the authority thus obtained, he will be considered a trespasser *ab initio. Ib.*

(408) See Chesley *v.* Thompson, 3 New Hamp. Rep. 9. Gidney *v.* Earl, 12 Wend. R. 98.

stroy them, trespass lies, because his interest therein is thereby determined; the same as when a tenant at will cuts down trees (*l*). So one joint-tenant or tenant in common may support trespass against his co-tenant, when the chattel is *destroyed* (*m*). But for a mere misuser by one tenant in common case is the remedy (*n*); and if goods bailed be not destroyed, trespass does not, it seems, lie against a bailee, coupled with an interest, for merely abusing the chattel (*o*), provided an interest and the right of possession still continue in the bailee, and a general owner has no immediate right of possession at the time the injury was committed; nor can trespass be supported even against a stranger, unless there be an immediate right of possession (*p*). Trespass will not lie for a loss or injury occasioned by a bailee's negligence; because it does not lie for any nonfeasance (*q*).

IV. TRESPASS.

2. Injuries to personalty, not under process.

In some instances trespass may also be supported for any wrongful act or injury committed to personal property whilst in the lawful adverse possession of the wrong-doer; as where he has been guilty of an abuse which renders him a trespasser *ab initio* (*r*). This rule prevails in general whenever the person who first acted with propriety under an authority or license given by *law*, afterwards abuses it, in which case the *taking*, as well as the real tortious act, may be stated to *be illegal, as in the *Six Carpenters' case* (*s*)(409). [*200] So trespass lies for cutting nets, lawfully taken damage feasant (*t*); or for working a horse, &c. distrained (*u*). But in the case of a distress for rent, we have seen that in general a party cannot become a trespasser *ab initio* by an irregularity, when the caption was lawful (*x*)(410).

Trespass is also the proper remedy to recover damages for an illegal entry upon, or an immediate injury to, *real property corporeal, in the possession of the plaintiff* (*y*). This remedy, in its application to injuries to *real* property, may be considered with reference, 1st, to the *nature* of the property affected;

3dly. To real property.

(*l*) 7 T. R. 11; Co. Lit. 57 a; Cro. Eliz. 784; 5 Co. 13 b; 11 Co. 82 a; Dyer, 121 b, pl. 17.

(*m*) 2 Saund. 47; see further, *ante*, 91. What is a destruction for this purpose, *id.*

(*n*) 8 T. R. 146; 2 Saund. 47 h.

(*o*) 2 Saund. 47 g.

(*p*) 7 T. R. 9; 4 T. R. 489.

(*q*) 5 Co. 13 b, 14 a; *ante*, 144.

(*r*) Bac. Abr. Trespass, B. where the doctrine of a party becoming a trespasser *ab initio* is observed upon; 2 Rol. Ab. 562; see *post*, 207.

(*s*) 8 Co. 146 b.

(*t*) Cro. Car. 228.

(*u*) Cro. Jac. 147; 1 T. R. 12; 3 Wils. 20.

(*x*) *Ante*, 158.

(*y*) 3 Burr. 1114, 1556; 5 East, 485, 487; 11 East, 56; Bac. Ab. Trespass, C. 3. As to immediate and consequential injuries, see *ante*, 144.

(409) Vide Sackrider *v.* M'Donald, 10 Johns. Rep. 253. Hopkins *v.* Hopkins, 3d, 369. Hazard *v.* Israel, 1 Binn. 240. "In every case to be met with in the books, the Court, in considering who shall be deemed a trespasser *ab initio*, for the abuse of a legal trust, confine the action for such an act to those who were either the actors in the first taking, or to such as by the relation they stood in to the first takers, made themselves parties by their assent before or after the act. It would be palpably absurd to say, that a man totally unconcerned with the original caption of goods, shall, for an after act to those goods, be deemed to have originally taken them." Per SPENCER, J., Van Brunt *v.* Schenck, 11 Johns. Rep. 382. Hence it was held, that where A., a custom-house officer, having seized a vessel as forfeited, while the vessel was in his possession, permitted B. (who was also a custom-house officer, though no way engaged in the original seizure) to make use of her, B. could not be made a trespasser *ab initio*. Van Brunt and another *v.* Schenck, 11 Johns. Rep. 377.

(410) See Laws of N. Y. sess. 36. c. 63. s. 10. 1 R. L. 436. {2 Rev. Stat. 504. s. 28.}

IV. TRESPASS. 2dly, to the plaintiff's *right* thereto; and 3dly, to the nature of the *injury*, and by whom committed.

3. Injuries to *realty*, not under process.

1st. The nature of the real property affected. 1st. With respect to the *nature of the real property affected*, it must in general be something tangible and fixed, as a house, a room, out-house, or other buildings or land. Trespass may be supported for an injury to land, though not fenced from the property of others; and by the owner of the soil, &c. though it be an highway (411) or a public bridge; the term *close* being technical, and signifying the *interest* in the soil, and not merely a close or inclosure in the common acceptation of that term (*z*)(412). It lies, however temporary the plaintiff's interest, and though it be merely in the profits of the soil, as *vesturæ terræ*, or *herbagii pasturæ* (*a*), *prima tonsura*(*b*)(413), or chase, free warren, &c. (*c*) if it be in exclusion of others (*d*). So where a person contracted with the owner of a close for the purchase merely of a growing crop of grass there, it was decided that the purchaser had such an exclusive possession of the close, though for a limited purpose, that he might maintain trespass *quare clausum fregit* against any person entering the close, and taking the grass, even with the assent of the owner (*e*)(414); so it lies [*201] for a trespass *on a portion of a common field after an allotment, authorizing the feeding the same only for a certain time (*f*). So a person having an exclusive right to dig turves or coals, &c. may support trespass *quare clausum fregit* against another for digging and taking away turves, &c. therein, though others had common of pasture over the land (*g*). And if J. S. agree with the owner of the soil to plough and sow it, and to give him (the owner) half the profits, J. S. may support trespass *quare clausum fregit* against a stranger for treading down the corn (*h*)(415). But unless the plaintiff have an exclusive interest, case is the only remedy, as if he had only a profit *à prendre*, as

(*z*) Doct. & Stud. 30; 7 East, 207; 2 Stra. 1004; 6 East, 154; 1 Burr. 133.

(*a*) Co. Lit. 4 b; 5 East, 480; 6 East, 606, 609; Dyer, 285, 1, 40; Bro. Trespass, pl. 279; Moor, 302; 2 Rol. Ab. 552, pl. 8; Palm. 47; 5 T. R. 535.

(*b*) 7 East, 200.

(*c*) 2 Salk. 637.

(*d*) *Id.*; 2 Bla. Rep. 1150; 2 M. & Sel. 499.

(*e*) 6 East, 602.

(*f*) Cro. Eliz. 421; 5 T. R. 335.

(*g*) 3 Burr. 1825, 1560, 1, 2; 6 East, 606.

(*h*) Bul. N. P. 85; 4 Burr. 1827; Co. Lit. 4 b; but see Cro. Eliz. 143, and 3 Leon. 213.

(411) Acc. Cortelyon *v.* Van Brundt, 2 Johns. Rep. 357. Commonwealth *v.* Peters, 2 Mass. Rep. 127.

(412) Vide Van Rensselaer *v.* Van Rensselaer, 9 Johns. Rep. 377. For an appropriation of a road, trespass lies by the owner of the land through which the road passes. And evidence of possession of the land on each side raises a presumption of ownership in the plaintiff. *Prima facie* therefore the fee of the land over which the road passes belongs to him. The law will not presume a grant of a greater interest than is essential to the enjoyment of the easement; the rest is parcel of the close. Gidney *v.* Earl, 12 Wend. R. 98.

(413) Vide Stewart *v.* Doughty, 9 Johns. Rep. 113.

(414) So, a grantee of trees may maintain trespass quare clausum fregit against the owner of the soil for cutting them down. Clap *v.* Draper, 4 Mass. Rep. 266. So, it lies by a tenant at will, who, on the tenancy being put an end to, is entitled to the emblements. Stewart *v.* Doughty and others, 9 Johns. Rep. 108. So, by a lessee for years who, on the expiration of the tenancy, is by the custom of the country entitled to an away-going crop. Stultz *v.* Dickey, 5 Binn. 285. Van Doren *v.* Everett, 2 South. Rep. 460.

(415) Or they may maintain a joint action. Foote and Litchfield *v.* Colvin, 3 Johns. Rep. 216.

a right of common of pasture or common of piscary (*i*); and because the plaintiff hath not in law the exclusive possession of a pew, trespass cannot be supported even against a stranger for entering it (*k*); but it seems that for breaking a pew, the owner may maintain trespass (*l*); and the parson may support trespass against a person preaching in a church without his leave (*m*). It may also be brought by a person who erected a *tombstone*, against a person who wrongfully removes and defaces it (*n*). But the rule is, that case is the remedy for disturbing a party in the enjoyment of a mere *easement* (*o*).

IV. TRESPASS.

3. Injuries to *realty*, not under process.

This action also lies for an injury to plaintiff's land covered with water; but if the interest be merely in the water, case is the only remedy (*p*). When the trespass is in the plaintiff's river, pond, &c. it is to be described as an entry on the plaintiff's close or land covered with water (*q*); or it may be charged that the defendant broke and entered a pool (*r*); or that the defendant broke and entered the several fishery of the plaintiff, &c. and fished therein for fish; but it is disputed whether it lies for fishing in a free fishery (*s*).

[*202]

2dly. The nature of the plaintiff's *right*.

*2dly. With respect to the plaintiff's right or interest in the property affected, we have given it a partial consideration in the preceding pages (*t*). The *gist* of this action is the injury to the *possession;* and the general rule is, that unless at the time the injury was committed the plaintiff was in actual possession, trespass cannot be supported (*u*) (416); and though the title may come in question, yet it is not essential to the action that it should (*x*) (417). Therefore, a landlord cannot, during a subsisting lease or demise, support trespass for an injury to the land, but the action of trespass must be in the name of the tenant (418). But a feoffment with livery of seisin made on land determines the tenancy at will, though the tenant be not present nor assenting to the feoffment, and the *feoffee* may maintain *trespass* against the tenant at will who afterwards enters on his possession (*y*). The landlord can only proceed in the above instances *in case* as a reversioner; and even to support that remedy the injury must be of such a nature as to affect and prejudice his reversionary inter-

(*i*) Cro. Eliz. 421; Burr. 1827; Salk. 637; Bro. Trespass, pl. 174; 2 Rol. Ab. 552, n. pl. 8; Standing-place, 2 East, 190; 1 T. R. 430.

(*k*) 1 T. R. 430; *ante*, 163; 5 B. & Ald. 361; 8 B. & C. 294.

(*l*) *Ante*, 163; 3 Bing. 137, 138.

(*m*) 12 Mod. 420, 433.

(*n*) 3 Bing. 136.

(*o*) *Ante*, 163.

(*p*) Yelv. 143.

(*q*) Co. Lit. 4 b; Yelv. 143.

(*r*) Yelv. 143; Co. Lit. 5 b.

(*s*) 2 Salk. 637; Co. Lit. 4 b, 122 a; 2 Bla. Com. 40; 2 H. Bla. 182; Cro. Car. 554; see 5 B. & C. 897; Chitty's Game Laws, 2d edit. 283, 299.

(*t*) *Ante*, 16, 149; and see in general, Com. Dig. Trespass, B.; Vin. Ab. Entry, G. 4, Trespass, H.

(*u*) 5 East, 485, 487.

(*x*) Willes, 221; 1 East, 244; 10 East, 65, 74.

(*y*) Ball *v.* Cullimore and another, 1 Gale, 96.

(416) Acc. Stuyvesant *v.* Tompkins and Dunham, 9 Johns. Rep. 61. Wickham *v.* Freeman, 12 Johns. Rep. 183. Van Brunt and another *v.* Schenck, 11 Johns. Rep. 385. Yates *v.* Joyce, 11 Johns. Rep. 140. { Schenck *v.* Mundorf et al., 2 P. A. Browne's Rep. 107. Addleman *v.* Way, 4 Yeates, 218. 3 Serg. & Rawle, 514. Allen *v.* Thayer, 17 Mass. Rep. 299. See however Bulkely *v.* Dolbeare, 7 Conn. Rep. 232. Campbell *v.* Proctor, 6 Greenl. Rep. 12. }

(417) Vide Hyatt *v.* Wood, 4 Johns. Rep. 157. A person having a legal right of entry on land, and entering by force, is not liable to an action of trespass. Hyatt *v.* Wood, 4 Johns. Rep. 150.

(418) Acc. Campbell *v.* Arnold, 1 Johns. Rep. 511. Tobey *v.* Webster, 3 Johns. Rep. 468. { See 2 Pick. Rep. 123. 3 Pick. Rep. 255. }

IV. TRESPASS. 3. Injuries to realty, not under process.

est (z). But if trees or other property excepted in the lease be felled, or trees not excepted be felled, and afterwards carried away, the landlord may support trespass (a) (419). The mere occupation by a game-keeper or other servant of a lodge or other premises, as a hired servant, and without paying rent, is to be considered as the possession of the employer, and the latter may declare as on his own possession (b). The payment of rent by the plaintiff, his exercise of the privilege of shooting, and the taking of the grass without interruption by a third person, by the plaintiff's license, were held to be a sufficient possession to enable him to maintain trespass for breaking and entering wood land belonging to the Crown (c). But where the plaintiff who had built a chapel conveyed it to the defendant by a deed, the validity of which was questionable, and the defendant took possession, and gave the key to a gardener, who with his permission lent it to the plaintiff to preach in the chapel, and thereupon the plaintiff locked up the chapel and refused to return the key, it was held he had not sufficient possession to maintain trespass (d).

[*203] Actual and exclusive possession, without a legal title, is sufficient against a wrong-doer (420), or a person who cannot make *out a title, *prima facie* entitling him to the possession (e); or show any right or authority from the real owner (f). Therefore, a person in possession under an illegal lease from a clergyman (g); or under a *mere license* or void demise from the Crown (h); or even it should seem an intruder upon Crown land, but not treated as such (i); may maintain this action. A tenant for years (k); a lessee at will (l); and a tenant at sufferance (m); may support this action against a stranger; or even against his landlord (421) unless a right of entry be expressly or impliedly reserved to the latter (n). And the contractors for making a navigable canal having, with the permission of the owner of the soil, erected a dam of earth and wood upon his close across a stream there, for the purpose of completing their work, have a possession sufficient to entitle them to maintain trespass against a wrong-doer (o). But there must be actual possession, and a mere right to enter is not sufficient; and it has been held, that commissioners of sewers could not maintain an action against commissioners of a harbor, for breaking down a dam erected by the former, as such commis-

(z) *Ante*, 73.
(a) *Ante*, 73. When not, *ante*, 74.
(b) 16 East, 33, 36; Lit. Rep. 139.
(c) 4 B. & C. 574.
(d) 5 Bing. 7.
(e) 1 East, 244; 11 East, 65, 67; 4 Taunt. 547; and see 2 C. & P. 33. *Per* Best, C. J., 5 Bing. 9.
(f) 11 East, 65.
(g) 1 East, 244.
(h) 4 B. & C. 574.
(i) See *id. per* the Judges.
(k) 2 Rol. Ab. 551; Sid. 347.
(l) *Id.*
(m) *Id.*; 13 Co. 69; 1 East, 245, n. a; Com. Dig. Trespass, B. 1; 1 Saund. 322, n. 5.
(n) 11 Mod. 209; Com. Dig. Biens, H.; 11 Co. 48.
(o) 5 B. & Ald. 600.

(419) {See 7 Conn. Rep. 235.} So, if land be granted to A. with a reservation of all mill-seats, and the grantor permit B. to enter and erect a mill, the entry of B. and the erection of a mill, is a severance of the freehold, and renders the mill a distinct close; and B. may maintain trespass against A. for pulling down the mill. Van Rensselaer v. Van Rensselaer, 9 Johns. Rep. 377. Jackson v. Buel, Id. 299. But see Torrance v. Erwin, cited 5 Binn. 290.

(420) Van Rensselaer v. Van Rensselaer, 9 Johns. Rep. 381. {See Hall v. Davis, 2 Carr. & Payne's Rep. 33.}

(421) It has been held that a tenant at sufferance cannot maintain trespass against his landlord. Wilde v. Cantillon, 1 Johns. Cas. 123. Hyatt v. Wood, 4 Johns. Rep. 150. But see Faulkner v. Anderson, Gilm. Rep. 221.

3. Injuries to *realty*, not under process.

sioners, across a navigable river; as the authority to be exercised by them on behalf of the public does not vest in them such a property or possessory interest as would enable them to maintain such action (*p*). And the proprietors of a navigation, having by statute a mere easement or right to use land for the purposes of the navigation, do not necessarily acquire such interest in the soil of a bank adjoining to, and formed out of the earth excavated from a new channel, made for the first time under the act, as will enable them to maintain trespass (*q*).

There is a material distinction between personal and real property as to the right of the owner; in the first case we have seen that the general property draws it to the possession, sufficient to enable the owner to support trespass, though he has never been in possession (*r*)(422); but in the case of land and other real property, there is no such *constructive* *possession (423), and [*204] unless the plaintiff had the *actual possession* by himself or his servant (*s*), at the time when the injury was committed, he cannot support this action (*t*). Thus, before entry and actual possession, a person cannot maintain trespass, though he hath the freehold in law; as a parson *before* induction (*u*), or a conusee of a fine (*x*), or a purchaser by lease or release, though the statute executes the use (*y*), or an heir (*z*), or a devisee against an abator (*a*), or a lessee for years before entry (*b*). And it seems to be doubtful whether the assignees of a bankrupt can sue for a trespass before the bankruptcy; at all events it has been decided that the bankrupt may maintain such action (*c*). But if the party having the legal title to land, enter thereon, (as by going on the land, and beginning to plough, &c.,) with intent to take possession, although he does not declare that such is his intention, he may maintain trespass against a person wrongfully in possession at the time of the entry, and who, without quitting possession, desires the owner to go away, and in fact continues his wrongful possession afterwards (*d*). A party wrongfully holding possession of land, cannot treat the rightful owner who enters on the land as a trespasser (*e*). A person *after* induction may maintain this action for glebe land, though he make no actual entry, for the induction puts him in possession of part for the whole (*f*); and a disseisee may have it against a disseisor for the disseisin itself, because he was then in possession; but not for an injury

(*p*) 2 Moore, 666; 1 B. & C. 221.
(*q*) 1 B. & C. 205; 2 D. & R. 316.
(*r*) *Ante*, 71, 72; 2 Saund. 47 a; Bul. N. P. 33.
(*s*) 16 East, 33.
(*t*) 5 East, 485, 487; Bac. Ab. Trespass, C. 3.
(*u*) Vin. Ab. Entry, G. 4, and Trespass, S.; Bac. Ab. Leases, M.; Plowd. 528.
(*x*) 2 Leon. 147.
(*y*) Carter, 66; Vin. Ab. Trespass, S. pl. 13, 14; Noy, 73; Com. Dig. Trespass, B. 3.
(*z*) Plowd. 142; 2 Mod. 7.
(*a*) 2 Mod. 7.
(*b*) Bac. Ab. Leases, M.; Plowd. 142.
(*c*) 8 Taunt. 742; 3 Moore, 96, S. C.; see 3 B. & A. 225; 2 B. & C. 293.
(*d*) 7 B. & C. 399.
(*e*) 7 T. R. 431; 7 Moore, 574; 1 Bing. 158, S. C.
(*f*) 2 B. & Ald. 470.

(422) Mather *v.* Trinity Church, 3 Serg. & Rawle, 512. North *v.* Turner, 9 Serg. & Rawle, 244.

(423) Acc. Campbell *v.* Arnold, 1 Johns. Rep. 512. Stultz *v.* Dickey, 5 Binn. 290. But see Van Brunt *v.* Schenck, 11 Johns. Rep. 385, where Spencer, J., says, "We have carried the principle as to real property, further than has been done in England; and we allow the owner to maintain trespass without actual entry, on the principle that the possession follows the ownership, unless there be an adverse possession." See also Wickham *v.* Freeman, 12 Johns. Rep. 184. Bush and others *v.* Bradley, 4 Day, 306. And what is said by Duncan, J., 3 Serg. & Rawle, 513, 514.

IV. TRESPASS. — 3. Injuries to realty, not under process. [*205]

after the disseisin (g), until he hath gained possession by re-entry, and then he may support this action for the intermediate damage (424); for after the entry, the law, by a kind of *jus postliminii*, supposes the freehold to have all along continued in him (h). After recovery in ejectment, this action may be supported for mesne profits, though anterior to the *time of the demise in the declaration in ejectment (i) (425); unless where a fine has been levied, in which case trespass cannot be supported for an injury committed anterior to the entry to avoid the fine (j). So a copyholder may maintain an action of trespass for mesne profits from the time of surrender after admittance and subsequent recovery in ejectment (k).

A person having a mere incorporeal right, as a common of pasture, turbary, &c. cannot support trespass *quare clausum fregit* for treading down the grass growing upon the land upon which he has such right of common, &c.; for although a commoner has a right to take such grass by the mouths of his commonable cattle, he is not to be considered as in possession of the land (l). But whenever there is an exclusive right, trespass may be supported, if possession in corporeal property, though the party has not the absolute right to the soil, or the whole property therein (m) (426); as if a person have an exclusive right to cut turf and peat, or cut thorns, he may support trespass *quare clausum fregit*, and for cutting the turf (n); and it may be supported for a trespass in a portion of a common field after the allotment to the plaintiff (o). So the owner of the soil may support trespass, although the public or private individuals have a right of way (p), or the privilege of holding a market (q) thereon, if there be committed on the close any act not protected by the subordinate rights or easements alluded to. If the plaintiff were in possession of the lands, &c. at the time when the injury was committed, the circumstance of his having quitted possession before the commencement of the action constitutes no objection (r) (427).

(g) 2 Rol. Ab. 553; Dyer, 935; 3 Bla. Com. 210.

(h) Vin. Ab. Trespass T.; 11 Co. 51 a; 3 Bla. Com. 210; 2 Rol. Ab. 551; Bro. Trespass, pl. 35; Cro. Eliz. 540; Com. Dig. Trespass, B. 3.

(i) Run. Eject. 442; 2 Burr. 666, 667; Peake's Evid. 326; Adams' Eject. 2d ed. 333, 334; *post*.

(j) 7 T. R. 732, 733; 3 Bla. Com. 210, 211.

(k) 16 East, 210; 2 Wils. 15.

(l) Bro. Trespass, pl. 174; 2 Rol. Ab. 522, N. pl. 8; Bac. Ab. Trespass; C. 3; 3 Burr. 1825; Cro. Eliz. 421.

(m) *Ante*, 201; 2 Burr. 1563, 1824; 5 East, 485 to 487; Cro. Eliz. 421.

(n) 3 Burr. 1560, 1824; 2 Salk. 638; 2 M. & Sel. 499.

(o) Cro. Eliz. 421; 5 East, 480, 485 to 487.

(p) 1 Wils. 110.

(q) *Id.* 107.

(r) Bac. Abr. Trespass, C. 3.

(424) Vide Tobey *v.* Webster, 3 Johns. Rep. 471. But trespass will not lie against a person coming in under the disseisor. Liford's case, 11 Rep. 46. So where the defendant is put into possession under a writ of restitution, on an indictment for a forcible entry against the plaintiff, and the proceedings are afterwards quashed, and a re-restitution awarded, the plaintiff may maintain trespass against the defendant, but not against a person acting under license from him. Case *v.* De Goes, 3 Caines' Rep. 261. Wickham *v.* Freeman, 12 Johns. Rep. 184. But it was held, that if the defendant pending an action of ejectment, gives up possession to a third person, the latter will be liable for the mesne profits. Jackson *v.* Stone, 13 Johns. Rep. 447.

(425) Where the plaintiff proceeds for the *mesne profits* subsequent merely to the time of the demise laid in the declaration, the production of the judgment in ejectment, and the writ of possession executed, are sufficient to entitle him to recover; but if he go for time *before* the demise, the defendant may controvert his title. 1 Esp. Dig. 505, 506. Aslin *v.* Parkin, Burr. Rep. 668. Jackson *v.* Randall, 11 Johns. Rep. 405.

(426) Myers *v.* White, 1 Rawle, 353. Van Rensselaer *v.* Radcliff, 10 Wend. R. 639.

(427) Vide Stultz *v.* Dickey, 5 Binn. R. 285.

3. Injuries to *realty*, not under process.

3dly. The nature of the *injury* to *real* property; and of the person committing it.

With respect to the *nature* of *the injury* to *real property*, we have seen that trespass can only be supported when the injury was committed with force actual or implied, and immediate (*s*). It lies, however unintentional the trespass (*t*); and [*206] *though the *locus in quo* were uninclosed (*u*), or the door of the house were open, if the entry were not for a justifiable purpose (*x*); and even shooting at and killing game on another's land, though without an actual entry, is in law an entry (*y*); though in general when the injury was committed off the plaintiff's land, or by causing something to be suspended over it, but not touching it, the remedy must be case (*z*). Where a master ordered a servant to lay down a quantity of rubbish near his neighbor's wall, but so that it might not touch the same, and the servant used ordinary care, but some of the rubbish naturally, and as was to be expected, ran or rolled against the wall, it was held that the master was liable in trespass (*a*). A mere nonfeasance, as leaving tithe on land, we may remember, is not sufficient to support trespass (*b*); and it should seem that for the mere continuance of an injury, for the inception of which the plaintiff has already recovered damages, case, and not trespass, is the proper remedy (*c*).

As to the *person by* and *against* whom this action may be supported, it should be remembered that actual possession is necessary to support the action, and that if the right of possession be in reversion, it clearly cannot be sustained. Trespass lies against a mere tenant at will for pulling down a house, or cutting trees during the tenancy at will (428), the interest being thereby determined (*d*); but against a lessee for years, trespass for cutting down trees does not lie, and case in the nature of waste is the only remedy for the cutting (429), unless the trees were excepted in the lease (*e*). But if he afterwards take the trees away, trespass or trover lies (*f*); and if the trees be excepted in the lease, and he cut them down, trespass *quare clausum fregit* lies for such cutting (*g*). And a tenant for years cannot support trespass against a [*207] *stranger merely for carrying away trees cut down during his term (*h*).

The proper remedy by one joint-tenant or tenant in common of realty, against the other who commits a partial injury to the land or other property, as by waste, &c. is an action on the case as for misfeasance (*i*); but if one tenant in common totally destroy the subject-matter of the tenancy in com-

(*s*) *Ante*, 142, 143. As to these injuries in general, see Com. Dig. Trespass, A. 2; Bac. Ab. Trespass, F.

(*t*) *Ante*, 147; 3 Lev. 37; 1 Campb. 497; 2 *Id.* 576.

(*u*) *Ante*, 200; Doct. & Stud. 30; 7 East, 207.

(*x*) *Ante*, 143; Bac. Ab. Trespass, F.; 2 Rol. Ab. 535, l. 15.

(*y*) 11 Mod. 74, 130; 1 Stark. 58. *Quære*, if shooting *over* another's land is a trespass, 1 Stark. 58.

(*z*) 2 Burr. 1114; 11 Mod. 74, 130; 1 Stark. 59; *ante*, 144.

(*a*) 9 B. & C. 591.

(*b*) *Ante*, 144.

(*c*) 1 Stark 22.

(*d*) Cro. Eliz. 784; 5 Co. 13 b; 11 Co. 81 b, 82 a; Co. Lit. 57 a; Saville, 84.

(*e*) Alleyn, 83; 1 Saund. 332, n. 5; 4 Taunt. 316; *ante*, 160.

(*f*) *Id.*; 7 T. R. 13; 4 Co. 62; Vin. Ab. Trespass, S. pl. 10.

(*g*) Bro. Trespass, pl. 55; 1 Saund. 322, n. 5; Bac. Ab. Trespass, C. 3.

(*h*) 2 Campb. 491; 2 M. & Sel. 499. See further as to trees, *ante*, 171, 173.

(*i*) 8 T. R. 145; Com. Dig. Estate, K. 8; 8 B. & C. 268.

(428) Acc. Phillips *v.* Covert, 7 Johns. Rep. 1. Suffern *v.* Townsend, 9 Johns. Rep. 35. Tobey *v.* Webster, 3 Johns. Rep. 470.

(429) But not for cutting and carrying away the trunks of trees blown down by a tempest. Trover, it seems, is the proper remedy. Shult *v.* Barker, 12 Serg. & Rawle, 272.

IV. TRESPASS. 3. Injuries to *realty*, not under process.

mon, his companion shall have trespass (*k*). If one of two tenants in common of an old wall pull it down in order to rebuild it, and does rebuild it, this is not a destruction for which trespass lies (*l*). If two be tenants in common of a folding, and one of them by force prevent the other from erecting hurdles, trespass lies (*m*). This action does not lie against a tenant in common for taking the whole profits (430), yet if he drive out of the land any of the cattle of the other tenant in common, or hinder him from entering or occupying the land, an action of ejectment may be supported (*n*); but not it seems an action of trespass (*o*).

Though the entry were lawful, yet by a *subsequent abuse* of an authority in *law* to enter, as to distrain, &c. (except for rent or poor's rates (*p*), or under the Turnpike Act) (*q*), the party may become a trespasser *ab initio* (*r*)(431). As if an officer under an execution continue in possession longer than the law allows, his entry becomes a trespass *ab initio* (*s*). And it seems that a magistrate is a trespasser *ab initio*, if he commit a person charged with an offence for re-examination for an unreasonable time (*t*). So in the case of distress *damage feasant*, a subsequent conversion of the goods renders the original seizure illegal (*u*). But in these cases the subsequent act must, in order to render the original entry a trespass, be in itself forcible, and an act of such a nature that trespass would lie if no authority or right existed; and therefore a sheriff acting upon a *fieri facias*, is not a trespasser *ab initio*, merely because [*208] he extorts more than he was justified *in levying (*x*). In the case of a distress for *rent*, if the party remain in possession an unreasonable time more than five days (*y*); or turn the plaintiff's family out of possession (*z*); he is liable for those acts only. In the case of an authority from the complainant himself to enter, the abuse of such authority (432) will not in general render the party a trespasser *ab initio* (*a*)(433).

Against a party, for

In the next preceding pages we have considered when this action may be

(*k*) 8 B. & C. 268; Co. Lit. 200; *ante*, 91.

(*l*) 8 B. & C. 257; *ante*, 91.

(*m*) Co. Lit. 200 b.

(*n*) Co. Lit. 199 b; 3 Wils. 119; 12 Mod. 567.

(*o*) 8 B. & C. 269.

(*p*) 1 Hen. Bla. 13.

(*q*) 3 Geo. 4, c. 126, s. 144.

(*r*) Bac. Ab. Trespass, B.; Six Carpenters' case, 8 Co. 146; 2 Bla. Rep. 1218; Com. Dig. Trespass, C. 2; 3 T. R. 292; 5 B. & C. 488.

(*s*) 2 Bla. Rep. 1218; 5 Taunt. 198; see 5 B. & C. 488.

(*t*) 10 B. & C. 28.

(*u*) 3 Wils. 20.

(*x*) 5 B. & C. 485.

(*y*) 2 Stra. 717; 1 Hen. Bla. 13; 11 East, 395; 2 Campb. 115; *ante*, 158. What is a reasonable time, see 4 B. & Ald. 208, qualifying the decision in 1 Hen. Bla. 15.

(*z*) 1 East, 139.

(*a*) Lane, 90; Bac. Ab. Trespass, B; 2 T. R. 166.

(430) { *Assumpsit* lies by one tenant in common, against his co-tenant, who has sold the common property, and received all the money. Gardiner Man. Co. *v.* Heald, 5 Greenl. Rep. 381. }

(431) Vide Adams *v.* Freeman, 12 Johns. Rep. 408.

(432) Sed vide Adams *v.* Freeman, 12 Johns. Rep. 409. As to the distinction between the abuse of an authority in law and in fact, see further, Van Brunt and another *v.* Schenck, 13 Johns. Rep. 416. Allen *v.* Crofoot, 3 Cowen, 506.

(433) A person impounding cattle, taken *damage feasant*, before the damages have been ascertained by two fence viewers, under the act, sess. 36, c. 35. s. 19. 2 R. L. 134, is a trespasser *ab initio*. Pratt *v.* Petrie, 2 Johns. Rep. 191. Sackrider *v.* M'Donald, 10 Johns. Rep. 253. Hopkins *v.* Hopkins, 10 Johns. Rep. 369. { So on a distress for rent, if the goods distrained on are sold without having been appraised and advertised, agreeably to the 21st of March, 1772, the distrainer is a trespasser *ab initio*. Kerr *v.* Sharp, 14 Serg. & Rawle, 399. }

supported against a party for his own immediate act; in some cases it may be supported against a person *for the acts of another and of cattle*, &c. Thus a party may be sued in respect of his *previous* consent or request that the trespass may be committed: as if A. command or request B. to beat or impress C., or to take his goods, or to commit a trespass on his land, and B. do it, this action lies as well against A. as against B. (*b*); and trespass lies against a master where, while the servant drives his master, the horse of the latter runs away and does damage (*c*). So if A. direct the sheriff to levy particular goods, not the property of the defendant in the action, A. may be sued in trespass (*d*). It may also be supported against a person, not being an infant or feme covert, who *afterwards assents* to a trespass committed for his benefit (*e*)(434), though not so as to render him liable for a forcible entry (*f*); so for taking goods, even to subject the party to liability for the abuse of an authority in law, as a trespasser *ab initio* (*g*)(435). But without such consent, trespass does not in general lie; as if A. command his servant to do a lawful act, as to distrain the goods of B., and he wrongfully take the goods of C., A. is not liable (*h*), the liability of the sheriff being an exception (*i*)(436). And the mere acceptance of goods illegally taken by another, does not always furnish evidence of an assent (*k*); as if a pound-keeper receive goods illegally distrained (*l*). But in these cases, if the party after demand withhold the goods, trover may be supported against him. And, as we have already seen, unless there be an actual [*209] *consent to the trespass, either before or after it was committed; or unless the act was the probable result of the orders given, and the servant used due care; even a master is not liable in an action of trespass for the act of his servant; though case may be supported against him in some instances, for injuries in respect of which the servant is liable in trespass (*m*). We have before seen how far agents or partners, &c. are liable (*n*).

IV. TRESPASS.

Trespasses of *others*, or of his *cattle*, &c.

We have already partially considered the liability of a person for the *acts of his cattle* (*o*). In those cases in which the defendant is not liable, unless he had notice of the propensity of his cattle, as in the instance of a dog biting

(*b*) *Ante*, 91; 1 Campb. 187; 2 Bla. Rep. 1055; Salk. 409; 4 Inst. 317; Bac. Ab. Trespass, G.; Com. Dig. Trespass, C. 1.
(*c*) 3 Tyr. 220.
(*d*) 2 Rol. 553, l. 5, 10.
(*e*) *Ante*, 91, 92; Cowp. 478; 3 Wils. 377.
(*f*) 4 Inst. 317; Co. Lit. 180 b, n. 4.
(*g*) Lane, 90; *ante*, 92.
(*h*) 3 Wils. 312, 317; 1 East, 108; *ante*, 93.
(*i*) *Ante*, 93.
(*k*) 2 Rol. 555, l. 50.
(*l*) Cowp. 476.
(*m*) *Ante*, 93, 149; 1 East, 106; 2 Rol. 553, l. 25; 1 Taunt. 568; 4 B. & Ald. 590;
(*n*) *Ante*, 96, 98.
(*o*) *Ante*, 94, 193.

(434) Vide Smith *v.* Shaw, 12 Johns. Rep. 257. Ch. J. Spencer says: "To render one man liable for the acts of others, it must appear that they acted in concert, or that the act of the individual sought to be charged, ordinarily and naturally produced the acts of the others." Guille *v.* Swan, 19 Johns. Rep. 382. Wall *v.* Osborn, 12 Wend. R. 39. In the case last cited a party sold a mill standing upon the lot of another, and appointed a day to remove it, promising to aid the purchaser in removing it; but the mill was in fact taken down and removed by the purchaser; *held* that the vendor was liable in *trespass*, although not present, or aiding in the removal. *ib.* So where the defendant sold the plaintiff's steam engine, and requested the purchaser to take it away; and he was held liable in trespass. Morgan *v.* Varick, 8 Wend. R. 594. So a person who aids an officer in executing process, if the officer is not justified by the process, although (2 R. S. 441, s. 80.) enacts that an officer may command assistance. Elder *v.* Morrison, 10 Wend. R. 128. Oystead *v.* Shed, 12 Mass. Rep. 512.

(435) Vide Van Brunt et al. *v.* Schenck, 13 Johns. Rep. 414.

(436) Vide Hazard *v.* Israel, 1 Binn. 240.

IV. TRESPASS. — Liability for trespasses of others: or of cattle.

mankind, sheep, &c., or an unruly bull doing some injury; the remedy is in general by action on the case (*p*): and that is the proper form of action for the consequences of bringing an unruly horse, &c. into an improper place (*q*). But if the animal were naturally of the propensity to do the mischief complained of, as horses and cattle to trespass on land, though the owner had no notice in fact of their propensity, the remedy is trespass (*r*).

Trespass may also be supported for an injury committed by animals notoriously ferocious, and let loose by the owner (*s*).

SECONDLY, UNDER COLOR OF LEGAL PROCEEDINGS.

The application of the action of trespass to injuries committed under color of a legal proceeding, may be considered under the seven following heads:—

1st. For *erroneous* proceedings where jurisdiction.

First, In general no action whatever can be supported for any act, however *erroneous*, if expressly sanctioned by the judgment or direction of one of the superior Courts at Westminster; or even by an inferior magistrate, acting within the scope of his jurisdiction (*t*)(437). If the court or inferior judge has jurisdiction over the subject-matter (438), he is not liable as a trespasser,

[*210] however erroneous the conclusion at *which he arrives may be (*u*). And we have before seen that commissioners of bankrupt are not liable in trespass for committing a person who does not answer to their satisfaction, when examined before them touching the bankrupt's estate (*x*). It seems that no action will lie against a judge for what he does *judicially*, though it were done maliciously (*y*); at least he would not be liable in trespass in such case. And where the lord chancellor sitting in bankruptcy committed the solicitor to the commission for not obeying an order, it was held that he had jurisdiction to do so, and that no action was sustainable against him for so doing (*z*). But when an inferior Court is guilty of an *excess* of jurisdiction, *trespass* may be supported for any thing done under such proceeding (*a*)(439). And in the case

(*p*) *Id. ibid.*; Lutw. 90; Cro Car. 25; Ld. Raym. 608, 1533; 12 Mod. 333; Dyer, 25, pl. 162.

(*q*) Ventr. 295.

(*r*) *Ante*, 94; 2 Rol. Ab. 568, N. l. 15; 3 Bla. Com. 211; 1 Ld. Raym. 608, 1583; Bac. Ab. Trespass, G. 2.

(*s*) *Ante*, 94; Ld. Raym. 1583; 3 East, 595, 596.

(*t*) 10 Co. 76 a; 2 Wils. 384; 3 M. & Sel. 411, 425, 427, 428; 1 B. & C. 169; *ante*, 88.

(*u*) See *ante*, 210, n. (*u*); 6 Bing. 85.

(*x*) 1 B. & C. 163; *ante*, 90.

(*y*) 7 St. Tr. 412; 6 Howell, 1094; 3 M. & Sel. 425; 2 Hawk. c. 13, s. 20; see cases cited in Dicas *v.* Lord Brougham, 1 Mood. & Rob. 309; 6 Car. & P. 249, S. C. In such cases the *magistrate might* be punished by criminal information, or indictment, see *id.* and Burn, J., 26th ed. tit. "*Justices.*"

(*z*) Dicas *v.* Lord Brougham, 1 Mood. & Rob. 309; 6 Car. & P. 249, S. C.

(*a*) See *ante*, 90; 1 B. & C. 169. Note the distinction between error in the process or other proceedings where there is jurisdiction over the subject-matter, and an irregular proceeding where there is a total want of jurisdiction, 3 M. & Sel. 425, 427, 428.

(437) {See 7 Conn. Rep. 11, and the cases cited.} Vide Hecker *v.* Jarret, 3 Binn. 404. Henderson and others *v.* Brown, 1 Caines' Rep. 92.

Where a justice acts without acquiring jurisdiction, he is a trespasser; but having jurisdiction, an error in judgment does not subject him to an action. Horton *v.* Auchmoody, 7 Wend. R. 200. Brown *v.* Crowl, 5 ib. 298.

(438) {Shoemaker *v.* Nesbit, 2 Rawle, 201.}

(439) So, the trespass lies against a justice of the peace, who issues a warrant on a conviction for a forcible entry, by which the party is turned out of possession, after the service of a *certiorari*. Case *v.* Shepherd, 2 Johns. Cas. 27. The want of jurisdiction in a court

of an error by a *ministerial* officer, this action may be supported, if the injury complained of was committed with force and immediate (*b*). We have already considered how far a judicial officer or other public agent will be liable, on the ground of having exceeded his jurisdiction or authority, or acted with negligence in the exercise of his duty (*c*).

IV. TRESPASS. 1. For erroneous proceedings where jurisdiction.

Secondly, When the Court has *no jurisdiction* over the subject-matter, trespass is the proper form of action against all the parties (440) for any act, which, independently of the process, would be remediable by this action or by trover, if goods have been taken (*d*). *Trespass lies if commissioners of excise adjudge low wines to be strong waters, &c.* (*e*); or leather searchers improperly seize leather (*f*). It has been considered, that when civil proceedings in an inferior Court, having no jurisdiction over the debt, are adopted by a party with an express malicious intent, though there be a demand recoverable elsewhere, an action on the case may be supported (*g*). So where the party maliciously and unduly issues a second *fieri facias*, case may perhaps be brought (*h*); and *if a party maliciously procure a magistrate to grant an illegal warrant, it seems he is liable in case for the malice (*i*). Trespass is also the proper remedy, where an inferior Court has jurisdiction over the subject-matter, but is bound to adopt certain forms in its proceedings, from which it deviates, and whereby the proceedings are rendered *coram non judice* (*k*). But it does not lie for arresting a person privileged either *personally* or *locally*, but case is the only remedy (*l*)(441).

2dly. Where no jurisdiction.

[*211]

(*b*) 1 Ld. Raym 471; 1 Salk. 395; 2 T. R. 225. The steward of a court baron is a *judicial* and not a mere ministerial officer, 2 B. & Ald. 473.

(*c*) *Ante*, 90, 97.

(*d*) 10 Co. 76 a; 2 Wils. 385; 7 B. & C. 536.

(*e*) Hardr. 483; 2 Wils 384.

(*f*) 6 T. R. 443.

(*g*) 2 Wils. 302; 2 Chit. Rep. 304. *Sed vide* 2 T. R. 225. It would seem trespass is at least the safer remedy in such case.

(*h*) Hob. 205, 206; see 1 B. & C. 145.

(*i*) 2 Chit. Rep. 304.

(*k*) Sir W. Jones, 171; 1 East, 64; Rep. temp. Hardw. 71; Hob. 63; 2 Bulstr. 64.

(*l*) 10 Co. 76 b; 6 *Id.* 52 a; 2 Bla. Rep. 1190; Dougl. 671; 3 Wils. 378.

rendering a judgment renders the judgment *coram non judice* and void, the magistrate and all others concerned in enforcing the judgment would be trespassers. Putnam *v.* Man, 3 Wend. R. 202. Bigelow *v.* Stearns, 19 Johns. Rep. 39. 15 ib. 121. Elliott *v.* Pearsall et al., 1 Pet. U. S. R. 138. 1 Wend. R. 126.

(440) A ministerial officer is protected in the execution of process, although the court have not *in fact* jurisdiction in the case, if it appears on the face of the process that the court has jurisdiction of the *subject-matter;* and nothing appearing to apprize the officer but that the court has jurisdiction of the *person* of the party to be affected by the process. Savacool *v.* Boughton, 5 Wend. R. 170. The same principle which protects an officer who executes process of a court of *general jurisdiction* should protect him when he executes the process of a court of *limited jurisdiction*, ib. That where an inferior court has not jurisdiction of the subject-matter, or having it has not jurisdiction of the person of the defendants, all *its* proceedings are absolutely void; neither the members of the court, nor the plaintiff, if assenting, can be protected by them. ib.

Vide Wise *v.* Withers, 3 Cranch, 331. Smith *v.* Shaw, 12 Johns. Rep. 257. In the latter case, the difference between a defect of jurisdiction as to the subject-matter, and as to the person or place, is considered, by the court; in the former instance, the officer being a trespasser, but not in the latter, unless the defect of jurisdiction appear on the process. } See also Shoemaker *v.* Nesbit, 2 Rawle, 201. }

(441) But trespass has been held to lie against a justice of the peace, who { voluntarily, and without the request or authority of the plaintiff, } issued an execution against the body of a person { whom he knew to be } privileged from imprisonment. Percival *v.* Jones, 2 Johns. Cas. 49. { But see } Hess *v.* Morgan, 3 Johns. Cas. 85. So, trespass lies against a party at whose instance a { void } warrant is issued out of a justice's court against a person privileged from arrest. Curry *v.* Pringle, 11 Johns. Rep. 444. A regular process from a court having jurisdiction of the subject-matter will protect a ministerial officer of the court, but it is otherwise in respect to a party who wantonly takes an execution upon

IV. TRESPASS.

2. Injuries under color of process, &c.

Justices of the peace are liable in *trespass* in either of the following cases: —*First*, If, on their convicting or making an order on a party upon a statute, the conviction or order on the face of it does not show that any offence has been committed, and in fact discloses that they acted without jurisdiction (*m*). *Secondly*, If the conviction or order show an excess of jurisdiction by them (*n*). And in these cases trespass lies against the magistrate for any distress or imprisonment upon the conviction or order, although the conviction or order has not been quashed, and there is no imputation of malice. *Thirdly*, A justice of the peace is a trespasser, if the warrant of *commitment* do not show *an offence* over which he has jurisdiction, although there may have been a previous regular conviction which is still in force (*o*). *Fourthly*, He is liable if the warrant of *commitment* substantially vary from the conviction, so that the offence stated in the former, and that described in the latter, are in law wholly different in their nature, for in such case the commitment has no conviction to support it (*p*). And *Fifthly*, Trespass, and not case, is the proper remedy against a justice of the peace who maliciously grants a warrant against another, and causes him to be arrested thereunder, *without any information*, upon a supposed charge of felony (*q*): or who, *Sixthly*, commits a party charged with felony for re-examination for an *unreasonable time*, but without any improper motive; and it seems that a warrant of commitment for an unreasonable time is wholly void (*r*).

[*212] *Magistrates are *not* liable, *First*, If, having jurisdiction over the subject-matter, they produce a conviction drawn up in due form and remaining in force. In such case the conviction is a protection in any action against them for the act so done, and the facts therein stated cannot be controverted in such action; (there being a regular commitment or warrant) (*s*). *Secondly*, They are not liable in trespass upon such a *conviction* being *quashed*; the statute (*t*) expressly providing in such case (*u*) that the plaintiff shall not recover more than 2*d*., (without costs of suit), besides the sum levied, if any, unless it be alleged in the declaration, "and which shall be in case only," that the justice acted maliciously and without reasonable and probable cause. In such an action upon the case, it is not sufficient for the plaintiff to prove his innocence, and to call on the magistrate to show probable cause for the conviction; but the plaintiff must give such evidence of what passed on the hearing, by calling the witnesses for the prosecution, or otherwise, that it may appear there was no probable cause for the conviction (*x*). *Thirdly*, Justices are not liable for a mere error in judgment or mistake in the particular case, where they have jurisdiction over the subject-matter. The defendant, as a magistrate,

(*m*) Cowp. 640; 7 B. & C. 536; 2 Chit. Rep. 304; 1 M. & Y. 469.

(*n*) 5 M. & Sel. 314.

(*o*) 2 Bing. 483, altered in 7 & 8 G. 4, c. 29, 30; and 9 G. 4, c. 31.

(*p*) 3 B. & C. 409. A slight discrepancy is not material, 12 East, 67.

(*q*) 2 T. R. 225.

(*r*) 10 B. & C. 28.

(*s*) 16 East, 13; 3 B. & C. 649; 7 B. & C. 394; see 12 East, 67.

(*t*) 43 G. 3, c. 141, s. 1.

(*u*) See 12 East, 67; 16 *Id*. 13.

(*x*) 5 Taunt. 580.

---

a *satisfied* judgment, and sells the property of the defendant. M'Guinty *v*. Herrick, 5 Wend. R. 240. Brown *v*. Feeter, 7 Wend. R. 301. In the case last cited, it was held that an action on the case lies against a party who wrongfully and wilfully sues execution on a judgment which he knows is satisfied; and that it was not necessary to allege or prove *actual malice*.

committed to prison, as a felon, the plaintiff, against whom a charge had been made of maliciously cutting down a tree on premises in his occupation, the property of A. B.; and it was held that the defendant was not liable to an action (y). *Fourthly*, We have before observed (z), that magistrates are not liable as trespassers for what they do upon a charge or complaint in a matter over which they might have jurisdiction, unless all the facts are shown to have been laid before them, and it appear that full opportunity was afforded them of forming a correct judgment, &c.

IV. TRESPASS. 2. Injuries under color of process, &c.

The acts of a justice who has not duly qualified are not absolutely void; and therefore persons seizing goods under a warrant of distress, signed by a justice, who has not taken the oaths at the general sessions, nor delivered in the certificate required, are not trespassers (a)(442).

[*213]

***Thirdly*, When a Court *has jurisdiction*, but the proceeding is *irregular* (443), trespass against the attorney and plaintiff is in general the proper form of action (b); and where a judgment has been set aside for irregularity (444), this is the appropriate remedy for any act done under it (c). In the case of *Morgan* and *Hughes* (d), it was decided, that an action on the case could not be sustained against a magistrate, for issuing an irregular and void warrant, though maliciously, and that the action should have been trespass (e); for in general no action can be supported against a magistrate for any thing done by him in that capacity, on the gound of malice (f); and if there be an irregularity, that must be treated as such in an action of trespass (445). But with regard to a party issuing, or causing to be issued, irregular process, &c. it seems that the person prejudiced is at liberty to support an action on the case *against him* where there was no cause of action, and the proceeding was malicious as well as irregular (g). The liability of a magistrate, if a conviction be void, or be quashed, has been already observed upon (h).

3dly. Irregular proceedings.

Fourthly, When the process has been *misapplied*, as when A. or his property has been taken upon process against B., trespass is in general the only remedy (i). And trespass is the proper form of action, if there be a misnomer in the process which has not been waived, though it be executed on the person (446) or goods of the party against whom it was in fact intended to be issued (k)(447); and in these cases the sheriff and his officers are liable, as

4thly. Where process misapplied.

(y) 6 Bing. 85.
(z) *Ante*, 89.
(a) 3 B. & Ald. 266.
(b) 3 Wils. 341, 363, 376; 2 Bla. Rep. 845. Attorney and client liable for act of agents, *ante*, 93.
(c) 1 Stra. 509.
(d) 2 T. R. 225.
(e) See also 2 Stra. 710; 3 M. & Sel 425, 627; 7 State Trials, 442; 6 Howell. 1094.
(f) 1 T. R. 545; 1 Wils. 232.
(g) *Ante*, 158.
(h) *Ante*, 212.
(i) 2 Wils 309; 2 Bla. Rep. 833; 1 Bulst. 149; Moor, 457; Hardr. 322; see 7 B. & C. 486.
(k) 6 T. R. 234; 8 East, 328. When the party arresting is liable, see 2 Chit. Rep. 357; 1 B. & Ald. 647; see Tidd, 9th edit. 447; 7 B. & C. 486.

(442) } Keyser v. The Comm. of Franklin, 2 Rawle, 139. Cornish v. Young, 1 Ashm. Rep. 153. {

(443) } Green v. Morse, 5 Greenl. Rep. 291. }

(444) { Milliken v. Brown, 10 Serg. & Rawle, 183. } But if the process be erroneous or voidable only, trespass will not lie. Reynolds v. Corp and Douglas, 3 Caines' Rep. 267.

(445) { Reynolds v. Orvis, 7 Cow. Rep. 269. }

(446) } Griswold v. Sedgwick, 6 Cow. Rep. 456. Mead v. Haws, 7 Cow. Rep. 332. } So the gaoler receiving and detaining a person arrested by mistake, instead of another, is liable in trespass. Aaron v. Alexander and others, 3 Campb. 35.

(447) Acc. Wilks v. Lorck, 2 Taunt. 399. Scandover and others v. Warne, 2 Campb. 270. But if the party himself occasioned the mistake, he cannot maintain the action. Price v. Harwood, 3 Campb. 108.

IV. TRESPASS. — 2. Injuries under color of process, &c.

well as the parties who expressly directed the process to be thus irregularly executed (*l*).

5thly. When process is *abused.*

Fifthly, When the process of a superior or inferior Court has been *abused* (*m*), trespass against the sheriff and his officer, or other ministerial officer (*n*), committing the abuse, is the proper action; if the conduct of the officer was in the first instance illegal, and an immediate injury to the body, or to [*214] *personal or real property; as if the officer arrest out of the sheriff's bailiwick (*o*), or after the return day of the writ (*p*)(448); or if he break open an outer door, &c. (*q*); or seize under a *fieri facias* fixtures of the defendant, who was a freeholder (*r*). And although the conduct of the officer were in the first instance lawful, yet, if he abuse his authority and commit some act of trespass not warranted by the process; as if he detain a party on a *capias ad satisfaciendum*, after he tenders the debt and costs (*s*); he becomes a trespasser *ab initio* (*t*)(449). If the abuse be merely a nonfeasance, or any act not in itself a forcible trespass, case for such abuse or wrongful act, and not trespass, is in general the proper remedy (*u*)(450). And in general, when the act complained of consists of a mere nonfeasance; as if the sheriff, or a magistrate, &c. improperly refuse bail, or to act, when they should do so; an action upon the case, and not an action of trespass, is the form to be adopted (*x*)(451).

6thly. *Ministerial officer and party accusing.*

Sixthly, When a ministerial officer proceeds *without warrant*, on the information of another, trespass, and not case, is the proper form of action against the informer, if it turn out that no offence for which an arrest without warrant is justifiable had been committed by any person (*y*); and trespass is the remedy against the informer if there were no warrant, although it appear that some person had committed the offence, and it be one for which an arrest might legally be made without a warrant, provided there was not reasonable or probable cause for charging the plaintiff with having committed the offence. When an officer proceeds without warrant, and without foundation, upon his own apprehension, trespass is the proper form of action against him (*z*).

7thly. If proceedings *regular* in *form.*

Seventhly, But no person who acts upon a regular writ or warrant can be liable to this action, however malicious his [*215] *conduct; but case for the mali-

(*l*) *Ante*, 92, 93, 95.
(*m*) 2 T. R. 148.
(*n*) 2 B. & Ald. 473.
(*o*) Sir T. Jones, 214; 2 Bla. Rep. 834.
(*p*) 2 Esp. Rep. 585.
(*q*) Cowp. 1; 3 B. & P. 223. As to when party justified in breaking open doors, &c. see 2 Moore, 207; 8 Taunt. 250; 2 B. & Ald. 592.
(*r*) 5 B. & Ald. 625.
(*s*) *Per* Dennison, J., 1 Wils. 154.
(*t*) Bac. Ab. Trespass, B.; 2 Bla. Rep. 1218; *ante*, 207.
(*u*) *Ante*, 207; 5 B. & C. 485.
(*x*) *Ante*, 145, 153, 207; 3 B. & P. 551; 1 Leon. 323; 3 Wils. 342, 343; 3 M. & Sel. 421.
(*y*) 6 T. R. 316; 2 Bing. 523; 1 Camp. 187. The officer is not liable if he act on information of a felony, although no offence had been committed, 3 Taunt. 14; 5 Bing. 526; 1 Chit. Crim. Law, 21, 22.
(*z*) 1 Salk. 396; 1 Ld. Raym. 454; 2 Stra. 820; 3 Taunt. 14; 1 Chit. Crim. Law, 21, 22.

(448) Acc. Stoyel v. Lawrence and Adams, 3 Day, 1. Vail v. Lewis and Livingston, 4 Johns. Rep. 450. Adams v. Freeman, 9 Johns. Rep. 117. But the plaintiff or his attorney will not be liable unless the arrest were made by their direcion, and an action on the case will not lie against them for not countermanding the execution after the return day. Vail v. Lewis, Adams v. Freeman, ubi supra. Hollister v. Johnson, 4 Wend. R. 639.
(449) Melville v. Brown, 15 Mass. Rep. 82.
(450) See Humphrey v. Case, 8 Conn. Rep. 102.
(451) Vide Harne v. Constant, 4 Johns. Rep. 32.

cious motive and want of probable cause for the proceeding, is the only sustainable form of action (*a*)(452). IV. TRESPASS.

2. Injuries under color of process, &c.

Pleadings, &c.

The *declaration* in this action contains a concise statement of the injury complained of, whether to the person, or to personal or real property, and should allege that such injury was committed *vi et armis* and *contra pacem*. The pleading rules of Hilary T. 4 W. 4, ordered, that in actions of trespass *quare clausum fregit*, the close or place in which, &c. must be designated in the declaration by *name*, or *abuttals*, or *other description*, in failure whereof the defendant may demur specially. The same rules also affect the *pleas* and *other pleadings*. The stat. 3 & 4 W. 4, c. 42, s. 21, enables a defendant, in some cases of trespass for injuries to personal or real property, to pay money into Court, after obtaining leave from the Court or a judge for the purpose. The general issue is, *not guilty* of the trespasses as alleged by the plaintiff; and under it few matters of defence can be given in evidence, and consequently the pleadings in this action require much attention. In an action of trespass for assault and battery to the person, and in trespass to real property, if the damages recovered by verdict be under 40*s*. the plaintiff will *in general* recover no more *costs* than damages (*b*); but where there has been a false imprisonment, or an injury to, or asportation of, a personal chattel, it is otherwise. The verdict and judgment are for the *damages* assessed by the jury, and *costs* (453).

V. EJECTMENT (*b*).

V. EJECTMENT.

In general.

This action lies for the recovery of the possession of real property, in which the lessor of the plaintiff has the *legal interest* and a *possessory right* not barred by the statute of limitations (*c*). It is not a *real* action, nor a mere *personal* action; but it is what is termed a *mixed* action, partly for the recovery of the thing or property itself, and partly to recover damages. It is true that in general the damages recovered in an action of ejectment are merely nominal, but in some cases between landlord and tenant such damages are in effect the full amount of the mesne profits up to the time of trial (*d*). It is now brought in the name of a nominal plaintiff, whose supposed right to the possession is

(*a*) *Ante*, 152; 3 T. R. 185; Boot *v*. Cooper, 1 T. R. 535, reported also in 3 Esp. Rep. 135; 3 B. & P. 225; 6 T. R. 315; Hal. P. C. 151.

(*b*) Tidd, 9th edit. 963. There are some exceptions, *vide id*. 963 to 968.

(*b*) As to the history of this action, see 3 Bla. Com. 199; the nature of it, 3 Wils. 120; 2 Burr. 667, 668; Selwyn's Ni. Pri. Ejectment; Run. Ejectment; Tidd, ch. 45, 1189. 9th edit.; and the excellent work of Mr. Serjeant Adams, 2d edit. See the act of 1 Geo. 4, c. 87, for facilitating proceedings, &c. by landlord against tenant holding over; and 11 G. 4, and 1 W. 4, c. 70.

(*c*) 7 T. R. 47; 2 Burr. 668; 8 T. R. 2.

(*d*) Under stat. 1 G. 4, c. 87, Chitty's Sum. Prac. 227; 8 Bing 656.

(452) { Plummer *v*. Dennett, 6 Greenl. Rep. 421, and the American cases there cited. Luddington *v*. Peck, 2 Conn. Rep. 700. } Beaty *v*. Perkins, 6 Wend. R. 382. Bell *v*. Clapp, 10 Johns. R. 263.

(453) { See the effect of the recovery of a judgment in *trespass* and *trover* for carrying away the plaintiff's goods. Floyd *v*. Browne, 1 Rawle, 121. White *v*. Philbrick, 5 Greenl. Rep. 147. }

V. EJECTMENT. In general. founded on a supposed demise made to him by the party or parties really entitled to the possession of the property, or sometimes several demises. This remedy is attended with the peculiar advantage, that by introducing several [*216] counts on *the demises of different persons, all risk of defeat, on account of any doubt in whom the legal right is vested, may in general be avoided. The action cannot be commenced until the real plaintiff's *right of entry* has accrued. If that take place in term, the declaration, which is the first proceeding in the suit, may be delivered in and entitled of such term; or if the right of entry accrue in vacation, the declaration may be delivered any time before the next essoign day, entitled of the preceding term. In either case a notice accompanies the declaration, requiring the party in possession to appear in the term subsequent to that of which the declaration is entitled (e). But in ejectment by a landlord against his tenant, or other person claiming under such tenant, the practice has been very lately altered with respect to the issuable terms; in order to give landlords, whose right of entry accrues in or shortly after either of those terms, an opportunity of bringing actions of ejectment and having them tried at the ensuing assizes. The statute (f) provides, that where in such actions the tenancy expires or right of entry accrues in or after Hilary or Trinity Term, the lessor of the plaintiff may, at any time within ten days after such tenancy shall expire or right of entry accrue, serve a declaration in ejectment, entitled of the day next after the day of the demise in such declaration, whether the same shall be in term or vacation, with a notice to appear and plead within ten days; and proceedings may be had, and rules to plead given, in the same manner as if the declaration had been served before the preceding term; but no judgment can be signed against the casual ejector until default of appearance and plea within such ten days; and it is requisite to give six clear days' notice of trial before the commission day of the assizes at which the action is to be tried. That statute also provides that a judge of either of the Courts at Westminster may, upon summons, give time to plead, or stay or set aside the proceedings, or postpone the trial until the next assizes, &c.

Mere nominal damages and costs are recoverable in this action; and in order to complete the remedy for damages, when the possession has been long detained, an action of trespass for the *mesne profits* must in general be brought [*217] *after the recovery in ejectment (g) (454). This action of *ejectment* may be considered with reference, *first*, to the nature of the *property* or thing to be recovered; *secondly*, the *right* to such property; and, *thirdly*, to the nature of the *ouster* or *injury*.

1st. For what property it lies. This action is, in general, only sustainable for the recovery of the possession of real property (h), as for land, or buildings annexed to the land, upon

(e) And in certain cases between landlord and tenant to put in bail if ordered by Court, &c. 1 Geo. 4, c. 87, s. 1.

(f) 1 W. 4, c. 70, s. 36.

(g) As to the action for mesne profits, see *post*, 221.

(h) For what an ejectment lies, and the description, see Run. Eject. 121 to 136; Selwyn's Ni. Pri. Eject.; Adams on Eject. 18, &c., and Tidd, 9th edit. 1190.

(454) Vide Cummins et Ux. v. Noyes, 10 Mass. Rep. 435. Osbourn v. Osbourn, 11 Serg. & Rawle, 55.

which an *entry* might in point of *fact* be made, and of which the sheriff could deliver actual possession (455). Therefore, it is not in general sustainable for the recovery of property which in legal consideration *is not tangible;* as for an advowson, rent, common in gross or other incorporeal hereditament; or a water-course, where the land over which the water runs is not the property of the claimant, &c. (*i*). Nor is it sustainable for a *movable* chattel, such as a stall (*j*). V EJECTMENT.

But ejectment lies for common appendant or appurtenant, if demanded as such, with the land in respect of which it is claimed, for the sheriff, by giving possession of the land, gives possession of the common (*k*). *Quare impedit* is the proper remedy for the recovery of a church or rectory where the church is full; but ejectment lies for a church or rectory when demanded as such, if the lessor has been presented, instituted, and inducted; and for this purpose the church is void if the adversary was simoniacally presented (*l*). Ejectment also lies for *tithes*, by the statute of 32 Hen. 8, c. 7, s. 7 (*m*). This action is also maintainable for a coal mine (*n*); for a fishery (*o*); for the *prima tonsura* of land (*q*); for hay, grass, and after-math (*r*); and for the pasture of sheep (*s*). It is necessary to describe with some degree of certainty the nature of the property in the pleadings, and the word "tenement," except by way of reference to an antecedent specification of particular descriptions, is too general (*t*); and if a water-course (456), where the ground also *belongs to the plaintiff, is sought to be recovered, it must be described as so many acres of land *covered* with water (*u*). [*218]

With respect to the *title*, a party having a right of entry, whether his title be in fee-simple, fee-tail, in copyhold, or for life, or years, may support an action of ejectment; but the right of possession must be of some duration, and exclusive; and therefore an ejectment cannot be supported for a standing place, or where a party has merely a license to use land, &c. (*x*). 2dly. The title thereto.

The general rule governing this action is, that the lessor of the plaintiff must recover upon the *strength of his own title*, and of course he cannot in general found his claim upon the insufficiency of the defendant's (*y*) 457); for possession gives the defendant a right against every person who cannot show a sufficient and better title, and the party who would change the posses-

(*i*) 3 Bla. Com. 206; Yelv. 143; Run. Eject. 131 to 136; Adams, 18, 20.

(*j*) 1 Car. & P. 123.

(*k*) 1 Stra. 54; Rep. temp. Hardw. 127; Bul. N. P. 99.

(*l*) 8 B. & C. 25.

(*m*) 3 Bla. Com. 206; Bul. N. P. 99; 2 Saund. 304, n. 12.

(*n*) Cro. Jac. 150.

(*o*) 1 T. R. 361.

(*q*) Burr. 133, 145.

(*r*) Hardr. 330.

(*s*) 2 Dal. 95.

(*t*) 1 East, 441; 2 Stra. 834. Where, however, ejectment was brought for twenty messuages, twenty *tenements*, &c. the court of C. P., after verdict and writ of error, allowed the record to be amended by striking out "twenty tenements." 1 Moore & P. 330; and in 8 B. & C. 70, it was held, that the declaration being for a "messuage *and tenement*," was no ground of error. See in general Adams, 2 edit. 26.

(*u*) Yelv. 143; Co. Lit, 4 b.

(*x*) *Ante*, 202; 2 East, 190; 11 East, 345.

(*y*) 5 T. R. 107, n. b.; 11 East, 488; Adams, 32.

(455) Black *v.* Hepburn, 2 Yeates, 331. Vide Jackson *v.* Buel, 9 [illegible] Rep. 298.

(456) A reservation in a deed, of a right for the grantor to erect [illegible] occupy a milldam, is such a tenement as may be recovered in ejectment. Jackson *v.* Buel, 9 Johns. Rep. 298.

(457) {But a defendant cannot, in Pennsylvania, avail himself of this rule, against a party whom he has fraudulently induced to buy a bad title. Lane *v.* Reynard, 2 Serg. & Rawle, 65. Butrce Walker *v.* Coulter, Addis. Rep. 390, 393.}

V. EJECTMENT. sion must therefore first establish a legal title (z). But it seems that *prior possession*, even for a short period, is a sufficient *prima facie* title against a mere wrong-doer or intruder (a). And therefore if a stranger who has no color of title should evict a person who has been in quiet possession even short of *twenty* years, without a strict legal title, the person evicted may maintain ejectment against the intruder (b). A lessee whose tenancy is determined will not in general be permitted to insist that his lessor had no title to demise
[*219] and recover (c); nor will a third person in such case be allowed to *defend as landlord (d); and if he have entered into the consent rule, the Court will discharge the same with costs (e); but after the expiration of a notice to quit, given to him by his landlord, the tenant may show that his landlord's title is at an end (f). The lessor of the plaintiff must also have a strict *legal* right (g) (459); a mere equitable (460) and beneficial interest, without the legal title, will not suffice, and the doctrine that the legal estate cannot be set up at law by a trustee against his *cestui que trust* no longer prevails (h) (461). But where trustees *ought* to convey to the beneficial owner, it will, after a lapse of many years, and under certain circumstances, be left to the jury to presume that they have conveyed accordingly; so where the beneficial occupation of an estate by the possessor under an equitable title (i) induces a fair presumption that there has been a conveyance of the legal estate to such pos-

(z) 4 Burr. 2487; 1 East, 246; Run. Eject. 15; 2 T. R. 684; 7 *Id.* 47.

(a) 7 Bing. 346; Doe *v.* Dyball, 1 Mood. & M. 346; see fully 1 Chitty's Gen. Prac. 241, 273.

(b) *Id. ibid.*; M. & M. 246; but 2 T. R. 719, seems *contra*; see 1 East, 246; 2 East, 469; 13 Ves. 119; Adams on Eject. 32. It is clear that *trespass* would lie in such case against a stranger, 1 East, 244; 4 Taunt. 548; and according to Allen *v.* Rivington, 2 Saund. 111; 4 Taunt. 548, n. (a), priority of possession alone gives a good title to the lessor of the plaintiff against the defendant and all the world, except the person who has a better title; and this rule applies for the defendant, 8 East, 356. In the case of personal property, it is clear that a person having possession, though without any title, may support trespass, detinue, or trover, against a stranger who takes away the property, see 2 Saund. 47 c.; and it seems better policy to protect the quiet possession of land against any person but the real owner, than to encourage a struggle for the possession by a party having no color of title (458).

(c) 2 Bla. Rep. 1259; 7 T. R. 488; *sed vide* 4 T. R. 683; Peake's Law of Evid. 318; 2 Campb. 11, in notes; 3 M. & Sel. 516.

(d) 4 M. & Sel. 347, 348; Doe *v.* Mills, 1 Mood. & Rob. 385; 2 Adol. & El. 17.

(e) 2 Younge & Jervis, 88.

(f) 3 M. & Sel. 516; see 1 D. & Ry. N. P. C. 1; but see 4 M. & Sel. 347, and *ante*, 218, note (c).

(g) 8 T. R. 2; Adams, 33.

(h) 5 East, 138; 11 *Id.* 334.

(i) But no presumption that an outstanding term has been satisfied will be made in favor of a party having no merits, and not having the equitable title, &c. 6 Bing. 174.

(458) In Smith *v.* Lorillard, 10 Johns. Rep. 338, it was held that a prior possession short of twenty years under a claim or assertion of right, will prevail over a subsequent possession of less than twenty years when no other evidence of title appears on either side; but that it was to be understood that the prior possession of the plaintiff had not been voluntarily relinquished without the *animus revertendi*, (as is frequently the case with possession taken by *squatters*,) and that the subsequent possession of the defendants was acquired by mere entry without any lawful right. And see Bateman *v.* Allen, Cro. Eliz. 437. Jackson *v.* Hazen, 2 Johns. Rep. 22. Jackson *v.* Harder, 4 Johns. Rep. 202. The People *v.* Leonard, 11 Johns. Rep. 504.

(459) { See, however, Hopkins et al. *v.* Ward et al., 6 Munf. 38. }

(460) Acc. Jackson *v.* Pierce, 2 Johns. Rep. 221. Jackson *v.* Deyo, 3 Johns. Rep. 417. Jackson *v.* Sisson, 2 Johns. Cas. 321. Goodtitle *v.* Way, 1 Term Rep. 735. Doe d. Ekerall *v.* Lowe, 1 H. Rep. 447.

(461) Vide Jackson *v.* Sisson, 2 Johns. Cas. 321. Jackson *v.* Chase, 2 Johns. Rep. 84. Jackson *v.* Pierce, Id. 226. { 5 Halst. Rep. 158. But see as to what title is sufficient in Pennsylvania, Wharton's Digest, tit. Ejectment. }

sessor (*k*). But when the facts of the case preclude such presumption, the party having only the equitable interest cannot prevail in a Court of law (*l*). Where a lessor and his lessee joined in an under-lease to a third person, in which it was provided that if the under-lessee should be guilty of a breach of covenant, then the first lessor *and* his lessee might enter; it was held, that on breach of the covenant in the lease to the under-lessee, ejectment might be maintained by the first lessee alone (*m*).

The lessor of the plaintiff must also in this action have the *right of possession* at the time of the demise laid in the declaration and at the commencement of the action (*n*). Therefore, the doctrine which formerly prevailed, that a mortgagee might maintain an ejectment to get into the receipt of the rents and profits, without giving a notice to quit, though a tenant under a demise anterior to the mortgage be in possession, is now exploded (*o*); and a remainder-man, or reversioner, cannot support this action whilst the right of possession is in another (462). Nor can ejectment be sustained where the right of entry of the real owner of the estate is taken away (*p*); either by twenty years' adverse possession (*q*), or in *some cases by a descent from a person who made the ouster to his heir, when a writ of entry must be resorted to (*r*); or by a discontinuance (*s*), in which case frequently the remedy for the issue in tail is only by a writ of formedon (*t*). But the circumstances of the title of lessor of the plaintiff having expired (*u*), or of his being tenant for life and having died (*x*), since the day of the demise laid in the declaration, affords no ground of objection on the trial, and proceedings may be continued in the name of the nominal plaintiff for the recovery of mesne profits and costs. [*220]

An actual entry is not in general necessary for the support of this action (463), as it is in trespass; but to avoid a fine with proclamations, it must be made (*y*); and in many cases, though not absolutely necessary, an entry is advisable; thus an ejectment may be brought even after *twenty years'* adverse possession, if there has been an actual entry within the twenty (464) years, and the ejectment be brought within a year after such entry (*z*); and trespass will not lie for mesne profits, which accrued before an actual entry made to avoid a fine (*a*).

(*k*) 4 T. R. 683; 7 *Id.* 3, 47; 2 B. & A. 782; 8 T. R. 122; 8 East, 248, 263.

(*l*) *Id. ibid.*

(*m*) Doe d. Bedford *v.* White, 4 Bing. 276; 12 Moore, 526, S. C.

(*n*) 2 East, 257; 13 *Id.* 210; Cro. Eliz. 800; 2 M. & Sel. 446. But a copyholder may lay the day of demise between the surrender and his admittance, 16 East, 208.

(*o*) Run. Eject. 109; 3 East, 449.

(*p*) 3 Bla. Com. 171, 206; Run. Eject. 234, 43.

(*q*) 21 Jac. 1, c. 16; 7 East, 299. What is not considered adverse possession, Adams, 47, 51, 70; 3 B. & C. 757, 413; 8 *Id.* 717; see 5 B. & Ald. 232; Tidd, 9th edit. 1195.

(*r*) 3 Bla. Com. 176, 206; Run. Eject. 43; *supra*, note (*p*). When not, see 3 M. & Sel. 271.

(*s*) *Ante*, 219, n. (*p*); Selw. N. P. 652 to 657.

(*t*) 1 Saund. 312 c, 261. n. 3; Run. Eject. 42; 3 Bla. Com. 206; Bul. N. P. 99.

(*u*) 3 Campb. 447.

(*x*) 2 Stra. 1056; 3 Campb. 450.

(*y*) 1 Saund. 319, 261, n. 3; 9 East, 17.

(*z*) 1 Saund. 319 c.

(*a*) 7 T. R. 727; 1 Saund. 319 b.

---

(462) Vide Jackson *v.* Schoonmaker, 4 Johns. Rep. 390. Hall's Lessee *v.* Vandergrift and others, 3 Binn. 374.

(463) Vide Jackson *v.* Crysler, 1 Johns. Cas. 125.

(464) But such entry must be for the purpose of taking possession. Jackson *v.* Schoonmaker, 4 Johns. Rep. 390.

V. EJECTMENT.

3dly. The injury, and by whom committed.

This action is only sustainable for what in fact, or in point of law, amounted to an *ouster* or dispossession of the lessor of the plaintiff (*b*). But such *ouster* may, and usually is, by merely *holding over*; and an immediate tenant may be sued for the holding over by his under-tenant, though against his will (*c*). It is necessary that the possession should be adverse or illegal at the time of the supposed demise laid in the declaration in ejectment (*d*); for if there be no ouster, or the defendant be not in possession at the time of the bringing of the action, it will fail (*e*)(465); and in such case the plaintiff should proceed by action of trespass. An action of ejectment is sustainable against a person who occupied a house and withheld possession, though he did so merely as the servant for another (*f*). An actual ouster may be by driving cattle out of the land, or by not suffering the party to occupy it; and in such case [*221] even one tenant in common (466) may *support an ejectment against his co-tenant; but in general the mere receipt of all the profits by the latter will not amount to an ouster (*g*). If a tenant underlet, and at the end of his term his sub-tenant refuse to quit, the original lessor may support ejectment against both, and both are liable to pay mesne profits (*h*).

Pleadings, &c.

The requisites and forms of the *declaration* in this action are pointed out in the second volume. The count or counts should be on the demise of the person entitled to the *legal* estate and to the *right of possession* at the time of the supposed demise (*i*); and although the form is free from difficulty, yet great care must be observed in applying the same; thus if one or more tenants in common were stated in one count to have *jointly* demised to the nominal plaintiff, instead of inserting *separate* demises, the action would fail (*k*). On the other hand, unnecessary counts should not be inserted, because, if the plaintiff should not establish all on the trial, he would have to pay costs (*l*).

The premises must be described with certainty (*m*); and the omission of the description where the premises are situate, is *error*, though the county and vill in which the *demise* was made have been stated in the declaration and the venue in the margin (*n*).

If the defendant appear, he must, by the terms of the consent rule, *plead* only the general issue, though he may, by leave of the Court, plead to the ju-

(*b*) 3 Bla. Com. 199.
(*c*) *Post*, 224.
(*d*) 13 East, 210, 212; 2 East, 257.
(*e*) 7 T. R. 327; 1 B. & P. 573.
(*f*) Doe d. Cuff *v.* Stradling, Sittings at Westminster after Trin. Term, 1817, *coram* Mr. Justice Bayley, 1 Chit. R. 119.
(*g*) Run. Eject. 194; Co. Lit. 199 b; Cowp. 217; Adams, 52.
(*h*) Roe *v.* Wiggs, 2 New Rep. 330; but see Bourne *v.* Richards, 4 Taunt. 720.
(*i*) 7 T. R. 47; 2 M. & Sel. 447; 16 East, 208. A party's name should not be inserted as a lessor merely to exclude his evidence for the defendant, 3 Campb. 178; and if a lessor's name be inserted without his consent, the Court, on motion, will order it to be struck out of the declaration.
(*k*) Doe *v.* Errington, 3 Nev. & Man. 46.
(*l*) 1 Harr. & Wol. 10.
(*m*) As to the description of the parish, see 1 Y. & J. 492.
(*n*) Doe d. Rogers *v.* Bath, 2 Nev. & Man. 440.

(465) Acc. Jackson *v.* Hakes, 2 Caines' Rep. 335.
(466) Vide Barnitz's Lessee *v.* Casey, 7 Cranch, 456. Shaver and wife *v.* M'Graw, 12 Wend. R. 562. The revised statutes declare, that if the action of ejectment be brought by tenants in common against their co-tenants, they shall in addition to other necessary evidence, prove that the defendants ousted the plaintiffs, or did some other act amounting to a *total denial* of their right as co-tenants. Valentine *v.* Northrup, 12 Wend. R. 494.

risdiction (*o*). The *damages*, we have seen, are merely nominal, and it is usual to remit them, in order to recover a real compensation in an action of trespass for the mesne profits (467), which may be brought in the name of the nominal plaintiff or of the lessor (*p*). But by 1 Geo. 4, c. 87, s. 2, at the trial of an action of ejectment by a landlord against his tenant, the judge may permit the plaintiff, after proof of his right, to recover the whole or any part of the premises, to go into evidence of the mesne profits from the expiration of the tenancy down to the time of the verdict, or to some day specially named therein; and the jury may include damages for such mesne profits in their verdict. Full *costs* are recoverable; but when the judgment is against the casual ejector by the default of the party in possession, the only mode of recovering the costs is by an action of trespass for the mesne profits (468), which much resembles the common action of trespass, and the particular properties of which will form the next subject for our consideration. The *judgment* is, that the plaintiff do recover his term, (or terms, according to the number of demises in the declaration), of and in the tenements, and, (unless the damages be remitted, as is most *usual,) the damages assessed by a jury, with the costs of increase. The writ of possession which has hitherto followed the judgment may now be issued immediately after the trial at Nisi Prius; in cases where the verdict is given for the plaintiff, or he is nonsuited for want of the defendant's appearance to confess lease, entry and ouster, upon the judge's certificate to that effect, under the 1st Wil. 4, c. 70, s. 38.

V. EJECTMENT.

[*222]

If upon notice to quit, given to a tenant, he give notice to his under-tenants to quit at the same time, and upon the expiration of the notice he quits so much as is occupied by himself, but his under-tenants refuse to quit, an ejectment, and also an action of trespass for mesne profits, may still be maintained against him for so much as his under-tenants have not given up (*q*).

A termor who lets to an under-tenant cannot, after his term has expired, enforce the continuance of the under-tenancy by distress, if the under-tenant refuse to acknowledge him as landlord, or pay him under threat of distress, although the under-tenant still retains the possession.

VI. ON THE ACTION FOR MESNE PROFITS.

In general.

The action of ejectment, as at present conducted, though nominally a *mixed* action, being altogether a mere fiction, it being brought by a *nominal* plaintiff against a *nominal* defendant for a *supposed* ouster, merely *nominal* damages are given; and satisfaction for the injury the real plaintiff has sustained by

(*o*) Adams on Eject. 241.

(*p*) The nominal plaintiff may be made the plaintiff in an action for an escape of a defendant out of an execution in the action for mesne profits, 2 M. & Sel. 473. The lessor of the plaintiff cannot release the action of ejectment, 4 M. & Sel. 300.

(*q*) Roe *v.* Wiggs, 2 Bos. & Pul. New Rep. 330; but see Bourne *v.* Richards, 4 Taunt. 720.

(467) But the entry of the *remittitur damna* is mere form, and the want of it will not preclude the party from bringing an action for the mesne profits. Van Allen *v.* Rogers, 1 Johns. Cas. 281.

(468) Vide Baron *v.* Abeel, 3 Johns. Rep. 483.

VI. ACTION FOR MESNE PROFITS. being kept out of the mesne profits, &c. is not, in general, included in the verdict in the ejectment. The law has therefore provided a remedy for this injury; namely, by an action which is *in form* an action of trespass *vi et armis*, but *in effect* to recover the rents and profits of the estate. It is *in form* an action of trespass, because it is consequent upon, and, as it were, supplemental to, the action of ejectment, and therefore must necessarily be of the same species with it. In this action the plaintiff complains of his ejection, of the perception of the mesne profits by the defendant, and of the waste or dilapidations, if any, committed or suffered by him, and prays judgment for the damages thereby sustained. It has been said that the lessor in ejectment may, if he please, waive the trespass, and recover the mesne profits in an action for use and occupation (*r*); but this election must be limited to the profits accruing antecedently to the day of the demise in the declaration in ejectment; for the action for use and occupation is founded on a *contract*; the action of ejectment upon a *wrong*; and when applied to the same period of time, are wholly inconsistent with each other; since in the former the plaintiff treats the defendant as his tenant, and in the latter as a trespasser (*t*). When, however, a tenant holds over after the expiration of the landlord's notice to quit, the landlord, after a recovery in ejectment, may waive his action
[*223] for mesne profits, and maintain debt *upon the 4 Geo. 2, c. 28, against the tenant, for double the yearly value of the premises during the time he so holds over; for the double value is given by way of penalty, and not as rent (*u*); but it is not yet settled whether, when the ejectment is founded upon a notice to quit given by the *tenant*, the landlord is entitled to maintain debt upon the 11 Geo. 2, c. 19, for double rent: the better opinion seems to be that he is not (*x*). This action, however, is not in all cases necessary; for by the statute (*y*), in action of ejectment between landlord and tenant, the landlord may, upon such proof of his right to recover possession of the whole or any part of the premises mentioned in the declaration, give evidence of and recover in such action the mesne profits of the premises from the expiration of the tenant's interest down to the time of the verdict, or some other prior day, to be specially mentioned therein; but trespass must be resorted to for the profits accruing subsequently.

The action for mesne profits may be brought pending a writ of error in ejectment, and the plaintiff may proceed to ascertain his damages, and to sign his judgment; but the Court will stay execution until the writ of error is determined (*z*). The action is local in its nature, and must be brought in the county where the lands are situate.

By whom to be brought (*a*). The action for mesne profits may be brought *by* the lessor of the plaintiff in ejectment either in his own name, or in the name of the nominal lessee, (John Doe); but in either shape it is equally his action; for it is not in any manner affected by the fiction which prevails in the ejectment. It is, however, sometimes more advantageous to bring the action in the name of the lessor

(*r*) Doug. 584; Cowp. 243.
(*t*) 1 T. R. 378, 387.
(*u*) 9 East, 310.
(*x*) Cowp. 245; Burr. 1603; 9 East, 314; Adams on Eject. 138 and 328, 2d edit.
(*y*) 1 Geo. 4, c. 87, s. 2.
(*z*) Cas. Prac. C. P. 46; 12 Mod. 138.
(*a*) As to ejectment by church-wardens and overseers in that character, see 6 Car. & P. 525.

of the plaintiff, who is the party really concerned; as he may then recover damages for the rents and profits received by the defendant previously to the time of the demise laid in the declaration in ejectment; which cannot be done at the suit of the nominal plaintiff (*b*). And the Courts will stay the proceedings until security be given for costs, when the action for mesne profits is brought in the name of the nominal lessee (*c*). The action may be brought in the name of the nominal lessee, as well where *the judgment in ejectment is by default, as where it is upon a verdict; for there is no distinction between the judgment by default and upon verdict in this respect: in the one, the right of the plaintiff is tried and determined against the defendant, and in the other it is confessed (*d*). A tenant in common, who has recovered in ejectment, may maintain an action for mesne profits against his companion (*e*). A joint action for mesne profits may be supported by several lessors of the plaintiff in ejectment after recovery therein, although the declaration in ejectment contained only a separate demise by each (*f*). In the case of Keech *dem.* Warne *v.* Hall (*g*), where it was held, that a mortgagee might recover in ejectment, without a previous notice to quit, against a tenant claiming under a lease from the mortgagor, granted after the mortgage, without the privity of the mortgagee, it was asked by the counsel for the defendant, if such mortgagee might also maintain an action against the tenant for mesne profits, which would be a manifest hardship and injustice to the tenant, as he would then pay the rent twice. Lord Mansfield, C. J., gave no opinion on that point: but said there might be a distinction, for the mortgagor might be considered as receiving the rent in order to pay the interest, by an implied authority from the mortgagee, until he determined his will (*h*). VI. ACTION FOR MESNE PROFITS. [*224]

Against whom.

The person *against whom* the judgment in ejectment has been given, ought, in general, to be made the defendant in this action: and a recovery in ejectment against the wife cannot be admitted as evidence in an action against the husband and wife for mesne profits (*i*). It seems to have been doubted whether a tenant, whose under-tenant holds over after the expiration of his term, *is liable for mesne profits* (*k*); but in practice the former is often joined in the action with his under-tenant; and he appears to be liable, at all events, if he has expressly recognized the acts of his under-tenant, and has received rent from him for the period possession was improperly detained (*l*). And in general any person found in possession, after a recovery in ejectment, is liable to the action; and it is no defence, that he was on the premises merely as an agent, and under the license of the defendant in ejectment, *for no man can license another to do an illegal act. The defendant, however, in such case, will only be liable for the mesne profits for the time during which he actually retained possession (*m*). This action being in trespass could not be maintained by or against personal representatives for the profits accruing during [*225]

(*b*) Bul. N. P. 87; 8 B. & C. 551, note. See an additional reason there given.
(*c*) Say. Costs, 126.
(*d*) Burr. 665.
(*e*) 3 Wils. 118; Bla. Rep. 1077.
(*f*) 5 M. & Sel. 64; 2 Ch. Rep. 410.
(*g*) Doug. 21; see *ante*, 219.
(*h*) And see 4 Ann. c. 16, s. 10.
(*i*) 7 T. R. 112.
(*k*) *Per* Mansfield, C. J., 4 Taunt. 720.
(*l*) And see Roe *v.* Wiggs, 2 New Rep. 330, and 4 Taunt. 720.
(*m*) Girdlestone *v.* Porter, K. B. 39 Geo. 3; Woodf. Landl. & Ten. 7th edit. 419; Adams, 331. So a servant is liable in trover, *ante*, 147, 176.

VI. ACTION FOR MESNE PROFITS. the life-time of the testator or intestate, and received by him (n). But we have seen that the 3 & 4 W. 4, c. 42, sect. 2, altered the law in this respect (o).

The declaration, pleas, &c. The *Declaration* should state the time when the defendant ejected the plaintiff, and the length of time he was kept out of possession: and a declaration which does not contain these averments is bad on special demurrer; but the defect is aided after judgment by the statute 4 Ann. c. 16 (p). The land or other premises from which the profits arose should also be described in the declaration. It is usual to adopt the description of the premises which was given in the declaration in ejectment. It is then averred that the defendant received the mesne profits, showing their value, during the time the plaintiff was kept out of possession. If any particular waste or injury to the premises was committed by the defendant, the same should be stated specially; and as a part of the damages the costs of the action of ejectment may be claimed. And the 3 & 4 W. 4, c. 42, sect. 21, seems to enable the defendant, by leave of the Court or a judge, to pay a sum to cover damages into Court, though this was not before admissible. The plea of not guilty is the same as usual in trespass. The general rule is, that the party against whom the recovery in ejectment was had, cannot, in the action for mesne profits, dispute the right of the lessor of the plaintiff to recover mesne profits after the day of demise laid in the declaration (q). The defendant may protect himself by the statute of limitations from the mesne profits accruing more than six years before the action is brought (r). Bankruptcy is no bar to this action, because the damages are uncertain, and could not be proved under a fiat in bankruptcy (s). Nor does the discharge of the defendant under an insolvent act protect him from this action (t).

The damages recoverable. [*226] In estimating the damages the jury are not confined to the mere *rent* or annual value of the premises, but may give such *extra* damages as they may think the circumstances *of the case demand (u); and the costs of the action of ejectment are recoverable as part of the damages, not only where judgment by default was obtained in the action of ejectment, but also where the defendant appeared and pleaded in that action; nor is it material in these cases that such costs have not been taxed (x). And the plaintiff may also recover as *damages* the *costs* incurred by him in a Court of error, in reversing the judgment in ejectment erroneously obtained by the defendant, although *directly* such costs may not be recoverable (y). If the plaintiff recover less than 40s. and the judge do not certify that the title came in question, the plaintiff is entitled to no more costs than damages: and this whether the action be in the name of the lessor of the plaintiff, or in that of his nominal lessee (z).

(n) *Ante*, 80, 104.
(o) *Id. ibid.*
(p) 13 East, 407.
(q) See Adams, 333, 335; 8 B. & C. 551, note. As to the evidence, see Adams, 335.
(r) Bul. N. P. 88.
(s) Doug. 584. But where the damages are reducible to a certainty, without the intervention of a jury, it may perhaps be otherwise, *id.* n. (1). And see Adams, 333.
(t) 3 B. & Ald. 407.
(u) 3 Wils. 121.
(x) 1 Cromp. & Jerv. R. 29.
(y) 7 B. & C. 404.
(z) 2 Cromp. Prac. 225; Tidd, 9th edit. 964.

CONSEQUENCES OF A MISTAKE IN THE FORM OF ACTION.

CONSEQUENCES OF MISTAKE IN FORM OF ACTION.

We have seen that the Courts consider it of great importance that the boundaries between the different actions should be preserved (a); and the consequences of a mistake in the application of the remedy are very material.

When the objection to the *form* of the action is substantial, and appears *upon the face of the declaration*, without regard to *extrinsic facts*, it may be taken advantage of by demurrer, or by motion in arrest of judgment, or by writ of error (b). But if the objection is not now *apparent* on the face of the declaration, but may only be established by the proof of *extrinsic* facts, then the only mode of objection may be on the trial as a *varidnce* and failure in proving an injury as described in the declaration, and consequently ground of nonsuit. Thus where the plaintiff in an action in other respects on the case stated that the defendant *wilfully* drove his coach and horses *against* the plaintiff's carriage, the Court arrested the judgment, on the ground that it necessarily appeared from such allegation that the action should have been *trespass*, and not *case* (c). When the defendant demurs he is entitled to costs, but not so upon a motion in arrest of judgment (469), or writ of error (470), because he ought to have objected at an earlier stage and by demurrer; and consequently where delay is not desired by the defendant, it is preferable to demur, in order to obtain costs. The cases are contradictory upon the question, whether a substantial objection to the form of action is a ground of nonsuit (d)(471). In a case where it appeared upon the face of the declaration, that the action should have been *brought against the sheriff, and not against the under-sheriff; after verdict, upon a rule to show cause why a nonsuit should not be entered, Lord Mansfield observed, that if the Court should order a nonsuit to be entered, the plaintiff must pay the defendant his costs, but if the judgment was arrested, each party must pay his own costs; but that as it appeared upon the declaration in that case, that the defendant might have demurred, and thereby have prevented the costs of the subsequent proceedings, the Court would arrest the judgment, and not permit a nonsuit to be entered (e); but in a more recent case it was held otherwise (f). [*227]

When the objection to the form of action *does not appear on the face of the pleadings*, it can only be taken as a ground of nonsuit, in which case the defendant will be entitled to his costs (g). Thus where the action was in as-

(a) *Ante*, 109, 110, n. (t). The Courts will not decide upon a question in a wrong form of action, even though the parties agree to waive the objection, *id.*

(b) 1 B. & P. 476; 6 T. R. 125; Cowp. 407; 4 Moore, 532. Formerly it was the ground of a plea in abatement, *post*, title "Pleas in Abatement."

(c) 6 T. R. 125; 8 T. R. 188; 1 East, 109.

(d) Cowp. 407, 414; 1 Campb. 256.

(e) Cowp. 407.

(f) 1 Campb. 256.

(g) Cowp. 407, 414.

(469) Vide Paagburn *v.* Ramsay, 11 Johns. Rep. 141.

(470) In the State of New York, a late statute has given costs on the reversal of a judgment. Sess. 36. c. 96. s. 13. 1 R. L. 346. {2 Rev. Stat. 618. s. 31.}

(471) The plaintiff cannot be nonsuited on account of a defect in his declaration. Van Vechten *v.* Graves, 4 Johns. Rep. 403. {Nor can he be nonsuited without his consent, after he has given evidence in support of his cause. Irving *v.* Taggart, 1 Serg. & Rawle, 360.} And on a motion for a new trial, the defendant cannot object to the form of the action. Smith *v.* Elder, 3 Johns. Rep. 105.

CONSEQUENCES OF MISTAKE IN FORM OF ACTION.

sumpsit for money had and received, and it appeared on the trial that the plaintiff should have declared in another form of action, yet as the objection was not apparent on the face of the declaration, and consequently the defendant could not demur, or avail himself of it otherwise than on the trial, it was decided that the plaintiff was properly nonsuited (*h*). Where the plaintiff has mistaken the proper form of action, and declared in assumpsit instead of debt, *he may even* in a penal action *have leave to* amend, though not so as to charge the defendant's bail (*i*). But it seems discretionary in the Court to permit an amendment in a penal action (*k*).

If by either of these means the plaintiff fail in his action, and judgment be given against him for that reason, and not upon the merits, he is at liberty to commence a fresh action (472); and the defendant cannot plead in bar the proceedings in the first ineffectual suit (*l*). Thus, if the plaintiff by mistake bring trespass instead of trover, and judgment be given against him on that account, the defendant cannot plead it in bar to an action of trover brought afterwards against him (*m*); and if the plaintiff mistake his cause of action, and the defendant demur, the plaintiff is certainly not precluded from commencing a fresh action, and may reply to a plea in bar of the judgment on demurrer, that the same was not obtained on the merits (*n*) (473). But if the defendant plead, and the plaintiff take issue, and a verdict be found for the de- [*228] fendant *upon the merits, the plaintiff will be estopped from bringing a fresh action; provided the defendant plead the former verdict specially as an estoppel: for if he omit to do so, it is, under the general issue, merely matter of argument and inference in his favor (*o*). If the plaintiff demur to the plea in bar upon the merits, and such plea be sufficient, in that case also no second action can be commenced (*p*); but if the plea were not sufficient, and the judgment against the plaintiff was on the defect in his declaration, the former judgment against him will be no bar (*q*).

OF JOINDER OF ACTIONS (*v*).

OF JOINDER OF ACTIONS.

Where the plaintiff has two *causes of action*, which may be joined in one action, he ought to bring one action only; and if he commence two actions, he may be compelled to consolidate them, and to pay the costs of the applica-

(*h*) Cowp. 414 to 419.
(*i*) 2 Marsh. 124, 185.
(*k*) 3 Dowl. 636, 637.
(*l*) 2 Saund. 47 p; 3 Wils. 309.
(*m*) *Id. ibid.*
(*n*) 1 Mod. 207; Vin. Abr. Judgment, Q. 4; Bl. Rep. 831.
(*o*) 2 B. & Ald. 662; M'Clel. & Y. 509.
(*p*) 1 Mod. 207; Vin. Abr. Judgment, Q. 4.
(*q*) 1 Mod. 207; Vin. Abr. Judgment, Q. 4, pl. 3.
(*v*) The joinder of several *persons* in a suit has already been considered. As to joinder of actions in general, see 2 Saund. 117 a, note; Tidd, 9th ed. 10 to 14; Com. Dig. Action, G.; Bac. Ab. Actions in General, C.; 2 Vin. Ab. 38, Actions, Joinder, U. c.; Gilb. C. P. 5, &c.

(472) Vide Benton *v.* Duffy, Cam. & Norw. Rep. 98. Com. Dig. Action, L. 4. Phillips' Ev. 235. Close *v.* Stuart, 4 Wend. R. 95.

(473) A decision of the court in favor of the defendant, upon an agreed statement of facts, and a nonsuit of the plaintiff entered, and judgment thereon for the defendant for his costs, pursuant to such agreement, constitute no bar to a subsequent action for the same cause. Knox *v.* Waldborough, 5 Greenl. Rep. 185. 10 Pet. U. S. C. 298.

tion (*r*) (474). It is, therefore, material to ascertain when several demands may be included in the same action. This may be considered with reference to, *first*, the joinder of different *forms* of action; *secondly*, of different *rights* of action; and, *thirdly*, the consequences of misjoinder.

OF JOINDER OF ACTIONS.

The joinder in action often depends on the *form* (475) of the action, rather than on the *subject-matter* or *cause* of action: thus in an action against a carrier for the loss of goods, if the plaintiff declare in assumpsit he cannot join a count in trover, as he may if he declare against him in case; for the joinder depends on the *form* of the action (*s*). If a cause of action, which ought to be laid in assumpsit, be improperly laid in case, and joined with a count in trover, no objection can be taken with effect on the ground of *misjoinder*, but *only the particular defective count should be demurred to (*t*). But if the count objected to be for a nonfeasance and breach of a contract, and is substantially in *assumpsit*, though it omit the words, "undertook and faithfully promised," yet it will be considered as framed in assumpsit, and if it be joined with other counts merely for torts, the misjoinder will invalidate the whole declaration (*u*). In a declaration on the case, one count stated that the plaintiff, at the request of the defendant, had caused to be delivered to him certain swine to be taken care of for reward, and in consideration thereof defendant *agreed* with plaintiff to take care of the swine, and *re-deliver* the same on request; and the Court held, on motion in arrest of judgment, that this was a count in *assumpsit*, and could not be joined with counts in case (*x*). The result of the authorities is stated to be, that "when the *same plea* may be pleaded, and *the same judgment* given on all the counts of the declaration; *or whenever* the *counts* are of the *same nature*, and the *same judgment* is to be given on them all, though the pleas be different, as in the case of debt upon bond and on simple contract, they may be joined." (*y*) Perhaps the latter, that is, the *nature* of the causes of action, is the best test or criterion by which to decide as to the joinder of counts (*z*). By this rule we may decide in general what forms of action may be joined in the same declaration.

1st. Joinder of different *forms* of action.

[*229]

In actions in *form ex contractu*, the plaintiff may join as many different counts as he has causes of action of the same nature in *assumpsit*; so also in covenant, debt, account, annuity, or *scire facias* (*a*). So debt on bond, or other specialty, may be joined in the same action with debt on judgment, or on simple contract, or for an amerciament (476); and debt and detinue may

(*r*) 2 T. R. 639; Tidd, 9th edit. 614. *Aliter* if, at the time of bringing the first action, the other cause of action had not become perfect and complete, *id.*; 1 Chit. Rep. 709 a; 9 Price, 393.

(*s*) *Per* Buller, J., 1 T. R. 277. And see the judgment of Lord Ellenborough, C. J., in 3 East, 70; and *ante*, 153.

(*t*) 6 East, 335, 336; 1 New Rep. 45.

(*u*) Thomas *v.* Pearse, 1 Chit. Rep. 619, K. B. Easter Term, 1817. What a misjoinder of case and assumpsit, 2 Chit. Rep. 343; *ante*, 153, 155.

(*x*) 6 B. & C. 268; *ante*, 156.

(*y*) 2 Saund. 117 e, f; Bac. Ab. Actions in General; Com. Dig. Act on, G.

(*z*) Tidd, 9th ed. 12.

(*a*) Bac. Ab. Actions in General, C.; Com. Dig. Actions, G.; 2 Vin. Ab. pl. 42, 45, 64; Tidd, 9th ed. 10, 11.

(474) Vide Thompson *v.* Shepherd, 9 Johns. Rep. 262. And see Worley *v.* Glentworth, 5 Halst. Rep. 241.

(475) But see Hallock *v.* Powell, 2 Caines' Rep. 216.

(476) So, debt on simple contract and on judgment may be joined. The Union Cotton Manufactory *v.* Lobdell and another, 13 Johns. Rep. 462.

OF JOINDER OF ACTIONS. be joined together, though in all these cases the pleas are different, and in detinue the judgment also varies from the form of the judgment in debt (*b*); [*230] which *joinder has probably been allowed, because the practice is sanctioned by the entries in the *Registrum Brevium* (*c*). So several counts may be joined in one action on a penal statute for different penalties of a similar nature, as for several acts of bribery (*d*).

So, in actions in *forms ex delicto*, several distinct trespasses may be joined in the same declaration in trespass (*e*). And several causes of action in *case* may be joined with *trover* (*f*); thus case against a common carrier for losing goods; or a count for immoderately riding a horse; or for disturbing the plaintiff in his right of common; or for hindering him from landing goods upon a yard of the defendant, contrary to agreement between them (*g*); or for not returning to the plaintiff a spaniel delivered to the defendant, to be tried and returned in a reasonable time, but keeping and detaining the same from the plaintiff; may be joined in one action, with a count in trover (*h*). So a count charging defendant with having preferred a charge of felony against plaintiff before a magistrate, and having under a warrant to search the plaintiff's house for stolen goods, obtained upon such charge, entered the plaintiff's house, may be joined with counts strictly in case (*i*) (477). So in *replevin* the plaintiff may in the same declaration, count on several takings on different days, and at different places in the same county (*k*). And the plaintiff may, in a declaration in *trespass*, unite a count for the battery or seduction of his servant, *per quod servitium amisit* (*l*), with a count for battery of the plaintiff himself (*m*), or *quare clausum fregit* (*n*), or trespass and rescue (*o*) (478); and all these counts might be included in one declaration, though the loss of service, and the consequence of the rescue, might be made the subjects of an action on the case (*p*). However, if these injuries be joined with a count in *trespass*, then each should be stated to have been committed *vi et armis*.

[*231] But in order to prevent the confusion which might ensue *if different forms of actions, requiring different pleas and different judgments, and of a different nature, were allowed to be joined in one action, it is a general rule, that actions in form *ex contractu* cannot be joined with those in form *ex delicto* (*q*).

(*b*) Bro. Ab. Joinder in Action, 97; Gilb. C. P. 5; 2 Saund. 117 b; 1 Wils. 252. See the form of debt and detinue in the same declaration, *post*, vol. ii. In 5 Mod. 89, it is said by the Court, that it seems strange that debt and detinue should be joined, because these actions have different judgments. Mr. Tidd (p. 11, n. b.) observes, that "in order to join debt and detinue, it seems they must both be founded on Contract." *Sed qu.*

(*c*) Gilb. C. P. 5, 6, 7; Bac. Ab. Actions in General, C.

(*d*) 4 T. R. 229; 3 T. R. 103; 2 Vin. Ab. 44, pl. 49.

(*e*) 2 Saund. 117 b; 8 Co. 87 b; 2 Vin. Ab. 38, &c.; Heath's Max. 7.

(*f*) *Id. ibid.*; 1 T. R. 277; 3 Wils. 348.

(*g*) See *ante*, 154.

(*h*) *Supra*, note (*f*); 2 Saund. 117 b.

(*i*) Hensworth *v.* Fowkes, 1 Nev. & Man. 321.

(*k*) Fitz. N. B. 68, n. a; Bul. N. P. 54; 2 Vin. Ab. 41.

(*l*) Alleyn, 9; Bac. Ab. Actions in General, C., 3 Wils. 18; Heath's Max. 7; 2 M. & Sel. 436; 2 New Rep. 476.

(*m*) 3 Campb. 256, in notes; 2 M. & Sel. 436.

(*n*) 2 New Rep. 476; 2 M. & Sel. 436.

(*o*) 2 Lutw. 1249; Lord Raym. 83; Tidd, 9th ed. 11.

(*p*) See *ante*, 153, 158; 2 Saund. 117 e. and notes.

(*q*) The only exception seems to be debt and detinue, *ante*, 230. But it is doubtful whether detinue is to be ranked as an action *ex delicto*, *ante*, 138; and whether it can be joined with debt unless the count in detinue be founded on contract, *ante*, 229, note (*b*).

(477) { See 16 Serg. & Rawle, 375, *et seq.* }

(478) Acc. Baker *v.* Dumbolton, 10 Johns. Rep. 240.

Thus assumpsit cannot be joined with case (r) (479), or trover (s), nor trover with detinue (t), &c. OF JOINDER OF ACTIONS.

And, with the above exceptions, counts in one species of action cannot be joined with counts in another. Thus assumpsit, covenant, debt, or account, cannot be joined with each other (u); nor trespass with case (480), for they are actions of distinct natures, and the judgments are different, that in trespass being in strictness *quod capiatur*, and that in case *quod sit in misericordia* (x); and neither trespass nor case could be joined with replevin or detinue, nor can the two latter forms of action be united in a suit. In criminal proceedings, the joinder of different offences of the same degree in an indictment does not render the proceedings defective; though it is a matter of discretion in the Court on motion to quash an indictment so framed (y).

2dly. Joinder of several *rights of* action, or *liabilities.*

Where the same form of action may be adopted for several distinct injuries, the plaintiff may in general proceed for all in one action, though the several rights affected were derived from different titles; but a person cannot in the same action join a demand in *his own right*, and a demand as *representative* of another, or *in autre droit*; nor demands against a person on his *own* liability, and on his liability in his *representative* capacity (z). The points which usually occur in practice may be considered as they arise in actions, 1st, by and against *partners*; 2dly, *husband and wife*; 3dly, *the assignees of a bankrupt*; and, 4thly, *executors, &c.*

1st. Partners.

In actions *by* and *against* several persons, whether *ex contractu* or *ex delicto*, all the causes of action must be *stated to be joint (481). Thus a plaintiff cannot, in a declaration against two defendants, state that *one* of them assaulted him, and in another part that the other assaulted him, or took his [*232]

(r) 6 B. & C. 268.
(s) 2 Saund. 117 c; 6 East, 335; 2 Chit. R. 343.
(t) Willes, 118.
(u) Bac. Ab. Actions in General, C.
(x) 1 Lord Raym. 272, 273; 2 Saund. 117 e; 117 c. note (c), 5th edit.
(y) 8 East, 46, 47; 3 T. R. 103; 1 Chit. Crim. L. 252 to 255; 7 & 8 Geo. 4, c. 29, s. 48.
(z) Bac. Ab. Actions in General, C.; 2 Vin. Ab. 62; Com. Dig. Actions, G.

(479) Acc. Stoyel v. Westcott, 2 Day, 418. Wilson v. Marsh, 1 Johns. Rep. 503. Church and Demilt v. Mumford, 11 Johns. Rep. 480. But see Hallock v. Powell, 2 Caines' Rep. 216. *Contra.* Where a declaration contained several counts, in each of which the gravamen stated was a tortious breach of the defendant's duty as an attorney, as well as of the implied promise arising from an employment for hire; it was held that as each count contained allegations sufficient to support it, either in *tort or assumpsit*, they were not incompatible, and might be joined in the same declaration. Church and Demilt v. Mumford, 11 Johns. Rep. 479. { See also Jones v. Conoway et al., 4 Yeates, 109. }

(480) { Cooper v. Bissell, 16 Johns. Rep. 146, in which case trespass *vi et armis* being joined with *trover*, the misjoinder was taken advantage of by writ of error. But although *trespass* and *trover* cannot be joined, yet a complaint of an injury arising partly from a breach of contract, and partly of misfeasance, to which the plea is *not guilty*, may be joined with trover. Smith v. Rutherford, 2 Serg. & Rawle, 358. }

(481) But if two partners agree to divide an account, against a joint debtor, equally between them, and the debtor consents to it, and expressly promises to pay one of the partners his moiety of the debt, the partner to whom the promise was made may maintain an action for his half of the account. Blair v. Snover, 5 Halst. Rep. 153. See also Austin v. Walsh, 2 Mass. Rep. 401. And where three persons by bond, covenant, or note, jointly and severally contract, the creditor may treat the contract as joint or several at his election, and may join all in the same action, or sue each one severally; but he cannot after suing one alone, and recovering judgment, sue the other two jointly, having by the first action elected to treat the contract as several respecting all. Bangor Bank v. Treat, 6 Greenl. Rep. 207.

OF JOINDER OF ACTIONS. goods, for the trespasses are of several natures, and against several persons, and they cannot plead to this declaration (*a*). Neither can the plaintiff in trover recover against several defendants for several conversions of the same goods; in order to fix all the defendants, he must prove a joint conversion by all, and if the evidence show separate conversions, he must take his verdict against those defendants only who were parties to some one conversion, and all the other defendants must be found not guilty (*b*). But in the case of a survivor of several contracting parties, a demand by or against him as survivor, may be joined with a demand due to or from the party in his own right (*c*); and, subject only to a plea in abatement, counts upon a promise by the defendant, and another since become a bankrupt and certificated, may be joined in separate actions against the solvent partner alone, with counts on promises made by the defendant solely, since the other became a bankrupt (*d*).

2dly. Husband and wife. We have already fully considered the various instances in which a ***husband and wife*** ought to sue or be sued jointly or separately in an action *ex contractu* or *ex delicto* (*e*). It will be sufficient here to observe, that when the wife is co-plaintiff in an action *ex contractu*, no cause of action can be included, unless it be founded on a contract with a feme before marriage, or she be the meritorious cause of action; and her interest must expressly appear on the face of every count (*f*) 482). And in an action in form *ex delicto* for a personal injury, if the wife be joined, the declaration must proceed only for torts to her individually, and not for such wrongs as only affect the husband (*g*)(483).

3dly. Assignees of bankrupt. [*233] We have also before partially noticed what demands may be joined in an action at the suit of the *assignees of a *bankrupt* (*h*). And we remember, that counts on causes of action accruing to the assignees after the bankruptcy, may be joined with counts upon causes of action which accrued to the bankrupt before his bankruptcy, whenever the former causes of action arose upon transactions with the assignees in their representative character, and the money recovered thereon would be assets in their hands in such capacity (*k*). If there have been any promise to the assignees or cause of action since the act of bankruptcy, care must be taken to insert some count in the declaration adapted to such demand; and where two partners became bankrupts at different times, and the defendant between the two acts of bankruptcy illegally received money, and the assignees of the two partners, in their action to recover it, declared only for money had and received to the use *of the two partners*, before they became bankrupts, and in another count for money had and re-

(*a*) 2 Saund. 117 a; Sty. 153, 154; 4 T. R. 360.
(*b*) 1 M. & Sel. 588.
(*c*) 1 B. & Ald. 29; 2 Chit. Rep. 436; 3 T. R. 433; 5 *Id.* 493; 6 *Id.* 582; 1 Esp. Rep. 47.
(*d*) 6 Taunt. 179.
(*e*) As *plaintiffs ex contractu, ante,* 32; and *ex delicto, ante,* 82. As *defendants ex contractu, ante,* 65; and *ex delicto, ante,* 105.
(*f*) *Ante,* 31, 32. The declaration must not contain a count on the promise of the husband and *wife after* marriage even to pay her debt contracted *dum sola*, 1 Taunt. 212; *ante,* 65.
(*g*) *Ante,* 82, 83.
(*h*) *Ante,* 26.
(*k*) *Ante,* 28.

(482) Vide Staley *v.* Barhite, 2 Caines' Rep. 221.
(483) So, slander of husband and wife cannot be joined in the same action. Ebersol *v.* Krug, 3 Binn. 555.

ceived to the use of the *plaintiffs as assignees*, it was decided that the plaintiffs could not recover, because they should have declared in one count for money had and received to the use of the partner who last became bankrupt, and of the plaintiffs as assignees (*l*). OF JOINDER OF ACTIONS.

It is now a well settled rule, in actions by a plaintiff who is an *executor or administrator, that where the money, when recovered, would be assets, the executor may declare for it in his representative character;* and that the best line to adopt in determining whether counts may be joined, is to consider whether the sum, when recovered, would be assets (*m*). It is therefore clear, that an executor or administrator may declare *as such* for goods sold or *money* paid by him in that character, and may join such count with counts on promises to the testator or intestate (*n*). So money had and received by the defendant to the use of the plaintiff as executor (*o*), and an account stated with him as executor, for monies due and owing to the testator (*p*), or to the plaintiff as executor, or to the plaintiff and his wife as executrix (*q*), may be joined (484) *with counts on promises to the testator or intestate; and as an executor may, under circumstances, lend money, it should seem the insertion of a count for money lent by him as such would not be a misjoinder (*r*). And counts on promises made to an intestate may be joined with counts on promissory notes given to the plaintiff as administrator since the death of the intestate (*s*). And where the plaintiff declared as executor upon a bill of exchange indorsed to him in that character, it was holden sufficient (*t*). It should, however, be observed, that where the transaction takes place after the death of the testator, the executor has the option of declaring in his private character (*u*). 4thly. Executors, &c. [*234]

But an executor cannot include counts on causes of action accruing to him in his private right and individual character, with counts on causes of action which are laid to have been vested in him in his *representative* capacity (*x*), and cannot join a count upon a bond given to his testator, and a count upon a bond given to him as executor, in the same action (*y*); for the executor, by taking the bond, would extinguish the original debt, and it would not, when recovered, be assets (*z*). Where six years have elapsed since the death of the testator or intestate, or it may on any other account be material for the plaintiff to avail himself of a promise or acknowledgment since the death, counts should be introduced in the declaration, on promises to the executor in that

(*l*) 3 B. & P. 465.

(*m*) 6 East, 405; 2 Saund. 117 d, and notes, 5th edit.; 1 Taunt. 332; 2 Marsh. 147; 6 Taunt. 453, S. C.; 2 Smith's Rep. 416, *per* Le Blanc, J.; Tidd, 9th edit. 12, 13; 9 B. & C. 666.

(*n*) 3 East, 104; 6 East, 405.

(*o*) 3 T. R. 659; see 5 M. & Scl. 294; Tidd, 9th edit. 12.

(*p*) 5 East, 150; 6 East, 403, 406; 1 T. R. 487; 1 Taunt. 322; 2 Marsh. 147.

(*q*) 6 East, 405, 406; 1 Taunt. 322; 2 Marsh. 147, *ac.*; 1 Ld. Raym. 437; 2 Saund. 117 d, *semble cont.*

(*r*) 3 B. & Ald. 360.

(*s*) 5 Price, 412; 7 *Id.* 591; 1 B. & C. 150.

(*t*) 1 T. R. 487; 6 East, 410, 413; 2 Vin. Ab. 48, pl. 9.

(*u*) See 2 Bing. 177; 9 Moore, 340, S. C.

(*x*) 2 Saund. 117 c.

(*y*) 3 B & P. 7. *Sed vide* 1 T. R. 487; 6 East, 405.

(*z*) 5 Price, 412; 7 *Id.* 591; 6 Taunt. 456.

(484) {In *assumpsit* by an administrator *de bonis non*, a count alleging a promise to have been made to the first administrator, may be joined with counts alleging a promise to the plaintiff's intestate, and a promise to the plaintiff. Sullivan, Adm., *v.* Holker, 15 Mass. Rep. 374. See also, Hirst, Adm. *v.* Smith, 7 Term Rep. 182.} Fay *v.* Evans, 8 Wend. R. 530.

OF JOINDER OF ACTIONS. character (a); for otherwise such promise or acknowledgment cannot be given in evidence (b)(485). In every count stating a debt or promise to the executor or administrator in that character, the word "*as*" executor, &c. must be inserted (c). It is not enough to say that it accrued to him, "executor, or being executor, as aforesaid;" but it must be averred that it accrued to him "*as* executor." However, great care should be taken not to introduce *unnecessarily*, in a declaration by an executor, on [*235] *a cause of action accruing to the testator, counts on causes of action alleged to have accrued after the testator's death; for although an executor, *necessarily* suing *as such*, is exempt from liability to the defendant's costs, if the action fail, by reason of the wording of the statute, which gives costs to plaintiffs (d); yet, where an executor might declare in his private character, as for money had and received after the testator's death, or upon an account stated with him as such, concerning money due to him as executor, &c. (e); or even, it seems, if the account stated be alleged to relate to money due to the testator; the executor has no privilege as to costs (486).

So in an action *against* an executor, a count cannot be introduced which would charge him *personally*; for the judgment in the one case would be *de bonis testatoris*, and in the other *de bonis propriis* (f)(487). Therefore a count for money lent to, or had and received by, an executor as such, is not sustainable (g)(488). And a count in assumpsit against husband and wife, who was administratrix with the will annexed, upon promises by the testator to pay rent, cannot be joined with counts upon promises by the husband and wife as administratrix, for the use and occupation by them after the death of the testator (h). But in an action of covenant against an executor, on the deed of the testator, the plaintiff may join a breach by the testator, and a breach since his decease (i). So an account stated by the defendant *as* executor, of monies due *from the testator*, may be supported, and may be joined with counts upon promises by the testator; and this is the common mode of declaring against

(a) See the forms, *post*, vol. ii.; and the consequences as to costs, 5 Tyr. 329.

(b) 3 East, 409; Willes, 29; 2 D. & R. 363; 1 B. & C. 248, S. C.; 1 B & Ald. 93; 3 *Id.* 626; 5 Moore, 105, 508; 6 Taunt. 210.

(c) 5 East, 150; 2 Marsh. 151; 2 Saund. 117 d, e, note. But see 2 Lev. 110; 2 Vin. Ab. 47, pl. 6, 48, pl. 9; 2 B. & P. 424.

(d) See 9 B. & C. 668; Tidd, 9th ed. 978.

(e) 8 Moore, 146; 9 B. & C. 666; Tidd, 9th ed. 978.

(f) 2 Saund. 117 e. But of late, counts for funeral charges against the executor in that character have succeeded, see 3 Campb. 298, *sed quære*.

(g) 2 Saund. 117 e; 4 T. R. 347; 1 Hen. Bla. 108; 7 B. & C. 444; 1 M. & R. 102, S. C.

(h) 3 B. & Ald. 101.

(i) 10 East, 313.

(485) Acc. Jones et al. v. Moore, 5 Binn. 573.

(486) In Pennsylvania, an executor plaintiff is bound to pay costs to the defendant, in case of nonsuit, or verdict for the defendant, as well where he necessarily sues in his representative character, as where the cause of action arises after the death of the testator. Muntorf v. Muntorf, 2 Rawle, 180.

(487) See Bachelor v. Fisk et al., Ex. 17 Mass. Rep. 464. And a declaration containing a count on a promise by the defendant's testator, and a count on a promise by the defendants as executors as aforesaid, for work and labor done at their request, is bad on general demurrer. Myer and others v. Cole and Niven, 12 Johns. Rep. 349. Demott v. Field, 7 Cow. Rep. 58.

(488) Sibbit v. Lloyd, 6 Halst. Rep. 163. Myers v. Cole, 12 Johns. Rep. 349. Demott v. Field, 7 Cowen, 58. It was held that an administrator or executor may join in the same declaration counts on promises to himself, with counts on promises to the intestate or testator. Fry v. Evans, 8 Wend. R. 530.

executors and administrators, to save the statute of limitations (*k*); and a count upon an account stated by an executor as such, of monies due and owing from *him* in that character, may be joined with counts *on promises by the testator, as such account stated does not make the executor personally liable (*l*)(489). Perhaps a count for money paid for the defendant as executor may be joined with counts on promises by the testator (*m*). Whenever an executor, &c. is sued upon promises by him in that character, the words "*as* executor," &c. must be inserted in each count in stating the promise, and also in stating the debt or cause of action, if it be laid to have accrued after the testator's death (*n*).

OF JOINDER OF ACTIONS. [*236]

The *consequences* of a *misjoinder* are more important than the circumstances of a particular count being defective; for in the case of misjoinder, however perfect the counts may respectively be in themselves, the declaration will be bad on a general demurrer, or in arrest of judgment, or upon error (*o*)(490); and if on a writ of error one of several counts in a declaration in assumpsit be bad, and the defendant below suffer judgment by default, and the damages be assessed generally on the whole declaration, such judgment must be reversed (*p*). A demurrer for misjoinder must be to the whole declaration, and not merely to the defective count or breach (*q*). The plaintiff cannot, if the

3dly. Consequences of misjoinder.

(*k*) 2 Saund. 117 e; 1 Hen. Bla. 102; Forrest's Rep. Exchequer, 98. Where an actual account has not been stated by the defendant as executor, add counts, as *post*, vol. ii. Counts on promises by the defendant *as executor*, should always be inserted, *if he has* admitted the debt, or promised payment.

(*l*) 7 Taunt. 580; 1 Moore, 305, S. C.; Forrest's Rep. Exch. 98; 6 East, 405 to 412; 10 East, 313. *Sed vide* 1 Hen. Bla. 108, 114; 2 Saund. 117 d; 2 B. & P. 424.

(*m*) 7 B. & C. 444.

(*n*) 2 B. & P. 424; *ante*, 233.

(*o*) 2 Chit. R. 697; 2 B. & P. 424; 4 T. R. 347; 1 Hen. Bla. 108; 1 Taunt. 212. See in general as to the consequences of mis-joinder or non-joinder of *parties*, whether plaintiffs or defendants, *ante*, 14, 51, 76, and 99. Of husband and wife, *ante*, 36, 68, 86, and 106.

(*p*) 1 Moore, 126.

(*q*) 1 M. & Sel. 355, 366.

(489) {Collins' Adm. *v.* Weiser, 12 Serg. & Rawle, 97. Malin *v.* Bull, 13 Serg. & Rawle, 443. See the observations of Mr. Chitty in the *fourth* edition.} It has been held that a declaration stating that the defendant's testator was indebted to the plaintiff, in a certain sum for money lent and advanced, and that the testator being so indebted in his life-time, the defendant, afterwards as such executor, after the death of the testator, pro-mised, &c. was good. And SPENCER, J., in delivering the opinion of the court, says, "The counsel seemed to suppose that the judgment on this count would be *de bonis propriis*, and that the executor would, in this mode of declaring, be prevented from pleading *plene administravit*. If such would be the consequence, then I should hold the objection to be valid; but according to the cases of Secor *v.* Atkinson, (1 H. Bl. 102,) and of Executors of Hughes *v.* Hughes, (7 Bro. P. C. 550, and 2 Saund. 117, e. note 2,) the judgment will be *de bonis testatoris*, and this mode of declaring is adopted merely to save the statute of limitations; consequently the defendant is not prevented from making any defence under such a form of declaring, which he might have made, had the declaration stated the promise of the testator, and his liability only." Whitaker *v.* Whitaker, 6 Johns. Rep. 112. And promises by the defendant as executor or administrator, as well as by his testator or intestate, to pay for work and labor done for, or goods sold and delivered to the intestate, may be joined in the same declaration, and a count charging a promise by the testator or intestate in his life time, and after his death, by the defendant, his *executor, or administrator, as aforesaid*, is good. Carter *v.* Phelps' Administrator, 8 Johns. Rep. 440. A declaration by a plaintiff, *as administrator*, containing counts for goods sold, work done, and the common money counts, without stating any indebtedness to the intestate or referring to the plaintiff, in his representative character in any subsequent part of the declaration, except in a profert of letters of administration, is bad on demurrer. Christopher *v.* Stockholm, 5 Wend. R. 36. Vide 2 Leigh's R. 532.

(490) Cooper *v.* Bissell, 16 Johns. Rep. 146.

OF JOINDER OF ACTIONS. declaration be demurred to, aid the mistake by entering a *nolle prosequi*, so as to prevent the operation of the demurrer for misjoinder (r); though the Court will in general give the plaintiff leave to amend by striking out some of the counts on payment of costs (s). In some cases, however, a misjoinder may be aided by intendment after verdict (t). And by taking separate damages, or by entering a *remittitur damna*, the misjoinder may be aided (u); and though it is reported to have been decided that if assumpsit and trover be [*237] joined, and there be a verdict *for the defendant on the count in trover, that does not cure the declaration (x), such doctrine is now overruled (y).

OF THE ELECTION OF ACTIONS.

OF ELECTION OF ACTIONS. In considering the application of each particular action, we have seen that the party injured frequently has an election of several remedies for the same injury (a). As the due exercise of this election is of great importance, it may be useful concisely to state the principal points which direct the choice of several remedies. And these may be with reference to, 1st, the nature of the plaintiff's *right* or interest in the matter affected; 2dly, the security of *bail*, and the process; 3dly, the *number of the* parties to the action; 4thly, the *number* of the *causes of action*, and the *joinder* thereof in one suit; 5thly, the nature of the *defence*, and whether it be advisable to compel the defendant to plead specially; 6thly, the *venue*, or place of trial; 7thly, the *evidence* to be adduced by the plaintiff or defendant; 8thly, the *costs*; and, 9thly, the *judgment* and *execution*.

1st. Nature of the plaintiff's interest in matter affected. 1st, A strict legal title is essential to the support of some remedies, but in others the plaintiff's bare possession of the property affected is sufficient. Where the title of the plaintiff may be doubtful, it is in general advisable to adopt the latter description of remedy. Thus an action of trespass to real property may be supported against a stranger by any person in the actual possession, though he have no title; but in ejectment the lessor of the plaintiff must in general recover on the strength of his own legal title (b); and may be defeated even if an outstanding term in a trustee be shown, unless it can be presumed that such term has been satisfied, &c. Therefore, where the title of the party injured is doubtful, the action of trespass should sometimes be chosen; and as the defendant in replevin for a distress taken damage feasant, must in his avowry or cognizance state, and if denied, must prove a title to the *locus in quo*, in fee or tail, in himself, or some person from whom he derives his title, an action *of trespass is preferable to a distress, where the title

(r) 1 Hen. Bla. 110, 111, 113, 114; 4 T. R. 360; Tidd, 9th edit. 681; 1 Saund. 207 c.

(s) 4 T. R. 348.

(t) 2 Lev. 110; Com. Dig. Action, G.; 2 Vin. Ab. 47, pl. 7.

(u) 2 M. & Sel. 533; 11 Mod. 196; 2 Vin. Ab. 48, pl. 9; 3 T. R. 433.

(x) See 2 Saund. 117 c.

(y) 2 M. & Sel. 533.

(a) Com. Dig. Actions, M.; Styles, 4; Co. Lit. 145 a; 2 Bla. Rep. 1112.

(b) 1 East, 244, 246. See, however, *ante*, 218.

of the occupier of the land may be doubtful (*c*). On the other hand, where the party interested can clearly establish a title in himself or in his trustee, and yet it may be doubtful in which particular person the legal title may be vested, a distress, or an action of ejectment where there has been an ouster, may be advisable, because in replevin brought for the distress, there may be several avowries upon different titles, and in ejectment there may be several counts on demises by different parties. In some cases we have seen that where the property of a person has been taken away or withheld from him, he may waive the tort and sue in assumpsit for the value (*d*); but as bare possession is sufficient in general to sustain an action of trover or trespass against a wrongdoer (*e*); it may often be better to adopt one of those forms of action than to sue in assumpsit for money had and received, as in the latter form of action a stricter right to the goods or the proceeds might be required (*f*). So, where an injury is done to a messuage or land, it may often be better to sue in the name of the tenant than in the name of the landlord as reversioner (*g*), because in the latter form of action strict proof of the letting and reversionary interest is indispensable (*h*).

OF ELECTION OF ACTIONS.

2dly. Bail and process.

Secondly, In actions in form *ex delicto*, as in *case*, *trover*, *detinue*, and *trespass*, the defendant cannot be arrested without a special order of the Court or a judge, and it is not usual to grant such order, except where there has been an outrageous battery, or the defendant is about to quit the kingdom (*i*); and therefore in cases where it may be material to have the security of *bail*, the action should, if possible, be framed in assumpsit for money had and received, &c., adding such other special counts as may be advisable under the circumstances of each particular case (*k*). Where, however, the defendant has been already arrested, the form of action must correspond with the affidavit to hold to bail and the form of action stated in the capias, or other process; for otherwise the defendant will *be entitled to his discharge out of custody on filing common bail (*l*). But this will be the only consequence, for the Court will not on this account set aside the proceedings (491) against the defendant for irregularity (*m*). [*239]

3dly. The number of the parties.

Thirdly, In an action in form *ex contractu*, we have seen that if a person who ought to be made *co-plaintiff* be omitted, it is a ground of nonsuit, &c. (*n*) except in the case of executors or administrators (*o*), whereas in actions in form *ex delicto*, the nonjoinder of a party who should have been a co-plaintiff, can only be pleaded in abatement (*p*); and consequently the latter form of action, if it can be adopted, is in many instances preferable,

(*c*) 1 Saund. 346 e, n. 2; Willes, 221.
(*d*) *Ante*, 113.
(*e*) *Ante*, 70, 174, 176.
(*f*) 1 B. & C. 418.
(*g*) See *ante*, 159, 160.
(*h*) See 4 B. & C. 465.
(*i*) Tidd, 9th edit. 172. See Petersdorff on Bail, 40, 41, as to the expediency of adopting particular forms of action in order to obtain bail.
(*k*) 3 East, 70.
(*l*) 7 T. R. 80; 8 T. R. 27; 5 T. R. 402; 2 East, 305; 1 Hen. Bla. 310.
(*m*) 6 T. R. 363.
(*n*) *Ante*, 14.
(*o*) *Ante*, 21. The nonjoinder of an assignee of a bankrupt is no ground of nonsuit, *ante*, 25.
(*p*) *Ante*, 76.

(491) Contra Rogers *v.* Rogers, 4 Johns. Rep. 485.

OF ELECTION OF ACTIONS. where there is reason to doubt who should be joined as a plaintiff. We have also seen that a joinder of *too many defendants* in an action in form *ex contractu* is a ground of nonsuit (*q*); and that the *omission* of a person who ought to be made a defendant may be pleaded in abatement (*r*); but that in actions in form *ex delicto* the omission of a party jointly concerned in committing the injury cannot in general be pleaded in abatement, and that when the injury may in point of law have been committed by several, the joinder of too many defendants will be no ground of objection (*s*); and therefore, where it may be doubtful how many persons should be made defendants, it is advisable to declare in case, in preference to an action of assumpsit (*t*). So, a distress for a rent-charge is frequently preferable to an action, because in the latter all the pernors of the estate charged with the payment must be joined (*u*)(492).

4thly. The number of the causes of action. *Fourthly*, Where the plaintiff has several demands of a similar kind, recoverable in different forms of action, he frequently may, and then he ought to proceed for the whole in that form of action which will embrace his various claims (*x*). Thus a party may declare specially against a bailee for *neglect, [*240] either in assumpsit or in case; if he have also a money demand against the bailee, due on simple contract, he should declare for both causes of action in assumpsit; but if, instead of the money demand, he have a distinct cause of action in trover, the declaration should be in case, with a count in trover, in order to avoid the expense of two actions (*y*). So, for a money demand due on a simple contract, the plaintiff in general has an option to declare either in assumpsit or debt; if there be also another demand of an unliquidated nature, founded on a simple contract, it is then proper to declare in assumpsit for both causes of action; but if there be no unliquidated demand, or if part of the demand be due on specialty, debt may be preferable. So, in an action against the assignees of a bankrupt for rent, if it be doubtful whether they have accepted the lease, although they have taken possession, it is advisable to declare in debt on the lease, and add a count in debt for use and occupation. So debt on a life policy, with a count for money had and received, may be preferable to covenant; because, under the common count, the premium may in some cases be claimed. And as debt and detinue may be joined (*z*), the declaration should be in those forms of action, where the defendant detains the plaintiff's goods, and also owes him a debt.

5thly. The defence. *Fifthly*, By a judicious choice of the remedy, the defendant may be frequently precluded from availing himself of a defence which he might otherwise establish. Thus in assumpsit against a person, who has been a bankrupt, for

(*q*) *Ante*, 14.
(*r*) *Ante*, 53.
(*s*) *Ante*, 76. Brotherton *v.* Wood, 6 Moore, 141; 3 Brod. & Bing. 54; 9 Price, 408; 3 East, 62 to 70.
(*t*) *Id. ibid.*; 3 East, 62 to 70.
(*u*) Co. Lit. 162 b; 1 Saund. 282, n. 1, and 284, n. 3 & 4.
(*x*) *Ante*, 227 to 231.
(*y*) 3 East, 70.
(*z*) *Ante*, 228, 230.

(492) By st. 1834, c. 189, a plaintiff in an action founded on contract, brought against several defendants, might discontinue as against one who had been defaulted, and proceed against the others. Turner *v.* Bissell et al., 14 Pick. R. 192.

money had and received by him before his bankruptcy, however tortiously, his certificate would be a sufficient bar, but by declaring in case or trover, where the money was received tortiously, &c. he will be deprived of such defence (*a*). And where goods have been sold by a person in contemplation of bankruptcy by way of fraudulent preference to a creditor, the remedy by the assignees should be trover, and not assumpsit as for goods sold and delivered; because, in the latter form of action, the defendant might avail himself of the debt from the bankrupt as a set-off (*b*). And in cases of fraud, the statute of limitations *may* not begin to run *till the fraud is discovered, and therefore it would be sometimes advisable to sue for the fraud, and waive the action of assumpsit. Thus, where the defendant was guilty of a fraud in not taking a sufficient security on his investing plaintiff's money, the plaintiff might waive the fraud, and sue in assumpsit for not procuring sufficient security; but if it be apprehended that the defendant would in such action of assumpsit establish a defence under the statute of limitations, it would be better to declare in case for the fraud, as the statute might then only run from the time the fraud was discovered (*c*). The election of the form of action was also frequently material, in order to compel the defendant either to take issue upon some particular allegation in the declaration, instead of putting the plaintiff to prove the whole of his case, or to compel the defendant to state his ground of defence specially (*d*). Thus, in covenant for rent, the defendant must plead to some particular allegation, and there is no general issue; but in debt on a lease he might have pleaded *nil debit*, and thereby compelled the plaintiff to prove the whole of his declaration (*e*). So trespass was in general preferable to case, because in the latter, under the general issue, the defendant *might* not only dispute the plaintiff's statement of his cause of action, but also give in evidence most matters of defence, but which he must have pleaded specially in trespass (*f*); and detinue was in some cases preferable to trover, in order to compel the defendant to plead his lien specially (*g*). But the general pleading rules of Hil. Term, 4 W. 4, requiring a special plea, in most cases have put an end to many of the former grounds of preference.

OF ELECTION OF ACTIONS.

[*241]

Sixthly, In some cases there may be two or more actions in effect for the same injury, the one *local*, and the other *transitory*. Thus, *debt* for rent, by the assignee or devisee of the lessor against the lessee, is local, and must be laid in the county where the estate lies (*h*); but in *covenant*, at the suit of the same parties, upon an express covenant for the payment of rent, &c. the venue is transitory (*i*); and consequently the latter form of action should be adopted, where *it may be advisable to try the cause out of the county where the estate is situate.

6thly. The venue.

[*242]

Seventhly, The evidence must also be attended to in the election of actions.

7thly. The evidence.

(*a*) 6 T. R. 695; 1 Marsh. 184; *ante*, 165.

(*b*) 4 T. R. 211; 2 Hen. Bla. 135; *ante*, 165. When not, see 10 East, 378, 418.

(*c*) 4 Moore, 508; 2 B. & B. 73, S. C.; see also 3 B. & A. 288, 626; 2 B. & C. 153; 3 D. & R. 326, S. C.; *sed vide* 5 B. & C. 259; 8 D. & R. 14, S. C.

(*d*) *Post*, tit. Pleas.

(*e*) Lord Raym. 1500.

(*f*) *Ante*, 165; *post*, tit. Pleas.

(*g*) *Ante*, 141.

(*h*) 1 Saund. 238, 241; Sir W. Jones, 52.

(*i*) *Id. ibid.*

OF ELECTION OF ACTIONS. Thus, it is frequently more convenient that the action should be trespass than case, because if it be laid in trespass, no nice points can arise upon the evidence, by which the plaintiff may be defeated upon the form of the action, as there may in many instances, if case be brought (*k*). And here we may again allude to the advantage of using trespass by the tenant, rather than case by the reversioner, in the case of injury to land (*l*). And very often the form of action, by driving the defendant to plead more specially, may narrow the plaintiff's evidence (*m*).

8thly. Costs. *Eighthly*, In actions in form *ex contractu*, the plaintiff is in general entitled to full *costs*, though he recover less than 40*s*. damages, it having been decided that the 22 & 23 Car. 2, c. 9, does not extend to actions of assumpsit, debt, detinue, or covenant (*n*); and therefore it is not in general material, so far as respects the costs, which of these forms of action be adopted. But in *trespass* for injuries to the person, or to real property, if the plaintiff recovers less than 40*s*. damages, he is not entitled to more costs than damages; and therefore, for such injuries, when practicable, it is frequently advisable to declare in case or trover, in which full costs are usually recoverable (*o*). So an action on the case was frequently preferable to an action of trespass against several defendants, because in trespass, if one defendant was acquitted, he might obtain his costs, but which he was not entitled to in an action on the case (*p*). And as no fine was paid upon issuing an original writ in covenant, that action was on that account in some cases preferable to debt. The 3 & 4 W. 4, c. 42, s. 32, enabling the judge to give an acquitted defendant his costs in every form of action, and the 2 W. 4, c. 39, abolishing the use of an *original* writ in *personal* actions, have put an end to the last two grounds of preference.

9thly. Judgment and execution. *Ninthly*, The action of debt is frequently preferable to assumpsit or covenant, because the judgment in debt by *nil dicit*, &c. is in general final, and execution may be issued immediately without the expense and delay of a writ of

[*243] *inquiry, which is usually necessary in assumpsit or covenant, in the case of judgment by default (*q*); and it is better to proceed in debt on an award than on the arbitration bond, because in case of judgment by default in an action on the latter, a writ of inquiry is necessary, under the 8 and 9 W. 3, c. 11 (*r*)(493). Replevin or detinue is preferable to trover, when it is important to obtain the goods themselves (*s*).

(*k*) 3 East, 600.
(*l*) *Ante*, 238.
(*m*) *Ante*, 240.
(*n*) Tidd, 9th edit. 963.
(*o*) 6 T. R. 129, 130; Tidd, 9th edit. 963. The judge may, in the latter actions, certify to take away costs; but this power is not often exercised.
(*p*) See Tidd, 9th edit. 986.
(*q*) Tidd, 9th edit. 573. But in many cases the writ of inquiry is, it seems, necessary even in debt; as in debt for use and occupation, for not setting out tithes, or for foreign money, 5 B. & Ald. 885; Tidd, 9th edit. 573. *Sed quære*.
(*r*) *Post*, vol. ii.
(*s*) *Ante*, 142, 189; 2 Stark. 288.

(493) By the statute of the State of New York, sess. 24. c. 25. s. 2. no writ of error "brought to reverse any judgment given in any personal action," is a stay of execution, unless bail in error be put in. { 2 Rev. Stat. 595. s. 27, 28. }

OF ELECTION OF ACTIONS.

Effect of election.

The circumstance of a party having elected one of several remedies by *action*, will not in general preclude him from abandoning such suit, and after having duly discontinued it, he may adopt any other remedy. It seems that an action for rent may be supported, although a distress has been made, provided it has not produced actual satisfaction (*t*). The plaintiff cannot in general bring a fresh species of action for the same cause whilst the former is depending, or after it has been determined by a *verdict*; and it is a rule that the party applying for an information shall be understood to have made his election, and waived his remedy by action, whatever may be the fate of the motion for the information, unless the Court think fit to give him leave to bring an action (*u*).

(*t*) 1 Salk. 248; 1 Ld. Raym. 719; 2 Chit. Rep. 301; 1 B. & A. 157; 5 Moore, 542.

(*u*) 2 T. R. 198; 1 Chit. Crim. Law, 855, 856; Rex *v.* Sparrow, Tidd, 9th ed. 10, note (*c*); 1 M. & R. 278 b; see *ante*, 229.

*CHAPTER III.

Of Pleading in General (a).

DEFINITION.
I. THE FACTS NECESSARY TO BE STATED.
II. THE MODES OF STATING SUCH FACTS.
III. THE RULES OF CONSTRUING PLEADINGS.
IV. THE DIVISION OF PLEADINGS.

DEFINITION. PLEADING is the statement in a logical and *legal form* of the *facts* which constitute the plaintiff's cause of action, or the defendant's ground of defence; it is the formal mode of alleging that on the record, which would be the support of the action or the defence of the party in evidence (b). It is, as observed by Mr. Justice Buller (c), "one of the first principles of pleading, that there is only occasion to state *facts*, which must be done for the purpose of informing the Court, whose duty it is to declare the *law* arising upon those facts, and of apprizing the opposite party of what is meant to be proved, in order to give him an opportunity to answer or traverse it." The grand object contemplated by the system is the production of a certain and material issue (d) between the parties, upon some important part of the subject-matter of dispute between them. The observations of Lord Chief Justice De Grey on the structure of an indictment are very forcible, and equally applicable to the pleadings in civil actions,—"the charge must contain such a description of the injury or crime, that the *defendant* may know what injury or crime it is which he is called upon to answer, that the *jury* may appear to be warranted

(a) I forbear, in this practical treatise, to observe upon the origin, antiquity, and history of pleading, or to notice the many observations in the books upon its utility and value; upon this subject the reader may consult 3 Reeve's Hist. Com. Law, 424; Hale's Hist. Com. Law, 173; Mr. Lawes' Treatise on Pleading, 1 to 33, and a tract intituled "A Summary of Pleading," 1 to 7; See also Lord Erskine's Speeches, vol. i. 276, &c. and the valuable publication of Mr. Serjeant Stephen, p. 144, 1st edit. and p. 157, 2d edit. to the end; and *vide id.* Appendix, xiv. n. (38), and the recent third edit. (494.)

(b) *Per* Buller, J., 3 T. R. 159; Dougl. 278; and see the observations in Com. Dig. Pleader, A.; Bac. Ab. Pleas and Pleading, and the judgment of Lord Chief Justice De Grey, in Rex *v.* Horne, Cowp. 682, 683, &c. as to the general nature and object of pleading.

(c) Dougl. 159.

(d) "An *issue* is, when both the parties join upon somewhat that they refer to a trial, to make an end of the plea," (*i. e.* suit.) Finch's Law, 396.

(494) "I entertain a decided opinion, that the established principles of pleading, which compose what is called its science, are rational, concise, luminous, and admirably adapted to the investigation of truth, and ought consequently to be very carefully touched by the hand of innovation." *Per* KENT, C. J., 1 Johns. Rep. 471. As to the history of pleading, vide 2 Reeve's Hist. E. L. 264, 267, 339, 344, 349. 3 Reeve's Hist. E. L. 59, 61, 423, 443, 461, 469.

in their conclusion of 'guilty' or 'not guilty' upon the premises delivered to them, and that the *Court* may see such a definite injury or crime, that they may apply the remedy or the punishment which the law prescribes. The *certainty essential to the charge consists of two parts; the *matter* to be charged, and the *manner* of charging it." (*e*) Hence the science of special pleading may be considered under two heads; 1st, The *Facts* necessary to be stated; and, 2dly, The *Form* of the Statement; and these, together with some general rules of construction, and the division of pleadings, we will consider in the present chapter. THE DEFINITION. [*245]

I. THE FACTS NECESSARY TO BE STATED.

In general, whatever circumstances are necessary to constitute the cause of complaint or the ground of defence, must be stated in the pleadings, and all beyond is surplusage (*f*)(495); *facts* only are to be stated, and not arguments or inferences, or matter of law (*g*)(496), in which respect the pleadings at law appear to differ materially from those in equity. There are *some facts* of such a *public* or *general* nature, that the Courts *ex officio* take notice of them, and which consequently ought not to be unnecessarily stated in pleading (*h*); and therefore it is advisable to consider a few of the principal rules as to the facts of which the Courts will *ex officio* take notice. I. THE FACTS NECESSARY TO BE STATED.

The Courts will *ex officio* take notice when the *King* came to the throne (*i*), and of the king's proclamations of war, &c. (*k*), and of the articles of war, which are an emanation from the crown by virtue of acts of parliament (*l*); and consequently those matters need not be alleged in pleading. So the Courts are also bound to take notice of all the privileges of the crown (*m*). But private Orders of Council are not considered as matters of law, or of such public nature as to render it incumbent on the judges *ex officio* to take notice of them (*n*); and a pardon under the great seal will not be judicially noticed (*o*); nor will the Courts take judicial notice of an *existing war between foreign states, or a recently declared war in which this country is engaged, but the same must be proved, unless recognized by some public statute (*p*). 1st. Facts of which the Court will *ex officio* take notice, should not be stated. [*246]

(*e*) Cowp. 682, 683.
(*f*) Cowp. 683; 1 Ld. Raym. 171; 10 East, 205.
(*g*) Cowp. 683, 684; Com. Dig. Pleader, C. 78; *post*.
(*h*) 2 H. Bla. 399; See Steph. on Pleading, 351, 1st edit.; 391, 2d edit.; Co Lit. 303 b; Com. Dig. Pleader, C. 78; 4 B. & Ald. 243.
(*i*) 2 Ld. Raym. 794, 791.
(*k*) 1 Ld. Raym. 282; but see 2 Camp. 44, whence it appears that the proclamation will be required to be proved by the Gazette. See 4 M. & Sel. 532, 543. As to declaration of war, see 11 Ves. 292; Ld. Raym. 282, 283.
(*l*) 4 B. & C. 304; 6 D. & R. 424, S. C.
(*m*) Ld. Raym. 980.
(*n*) 2 Lil. Prac. Reg. 302.
(*o*) 4 Bla. Com. 402.
(*p*) 3 M. Sel. 67, 69; 11 Ves. 292; 2 Campb. 44; 3 *Id*. 61, 67.

(495) Vide Tucker *v*. Randall, 2 Mass. Rep. 283.
(496) Goshen Turnp. Co. *v*. Sears, 7 Conn. Rep. 22.

I. THE FACTS NECESSARY TO BE STATED.

The time of holding every *Parliament*, and the prorogations and sessions thereof (*q*), and also where any parliament sat, will be taken notice of judicially (*r*); and therefore neither of these facts should be stated in pleading. And if either be mis-stated, even in pleading a private act, not before the Court, the pleadings will be defective on demurrer, or in the case of a private act, on the plea of *nul tiel record*, or any other plea, putting in issue the whole of the facts stated in the declaration (*s*); but the mistake may be aided by verdict(*t*). The Courts will also take judicial notice of the course of proceedings in either house of parliament (*u*), but not of the Journals of either house (*x*), which must be stated in pleading, and proved in evidence (*y*).

Public statutes, and the facts which they recite or state, must be noticed by the Courts, without their being stated in pleading (*z*) (497); and it is only necessary to state facts, which will appear to the Court to be affected by the statute (*a*). If, however, an *offence* be created by a statute, and a penalty be inflicted, the mere statement of the facts constituting the offence will be insufficient, for there must be an express reference to the statute, as by the words "contrary to the form of the statute, &c." in order that it may appear that the plaintiff grounds his case upon and intends to bring it within the statute (*b*). In the case of a *public* statute, it is not advisable to recite or set out any part of it, for a mis-recital (498), with a conclusion "contrary to the form of the statute *aforesaid*," would be fatal even in arrest of judgment (*c*). If a statute be passed during a session extending into two years of the king's reign, yet it must be stated to have passed in that session when, by the king's assent, it became a law; and if a statute be described as passed in the 2d & 3d years of Wm. 4, it will be a fatal misdescription, and the judgment on an indictment containing such a misdescription would be arrested; though if the description had been of an act passed *in a session* holden in the second and
[*247] third years of the reign, it would be otherwise (*d*). Where a statute *has been *recently* made, it has been supposed to be necessary to allege that the facts took place after the passing of the act (*e*); but if there be a proper conclusion, *contra formam statuti*, it is not necessary to aver that the offence was after the passing of the act. The Courts will not *ex officio* take notice of *Private Acts* (499) of Parliament, and consequently such parts of them as

(*q*) 1 Ld. Raym. 343; Plowd. 77; Moor, 551; 1 Lev. 296; see Bac. Ab. Statute, L. 6. Describing an act to have passed in a reign, when, in fact, the parliament in which the act was passed was continued by prorogation to that reign, is not a misdescription, 2 Chit. Rep. 513.

(*r*) Ld. Raym. 210, 343.

(*s*) *Id.*; Cowp. 474.

(*t*) 2 Mod. 240.

(*u*) 1 Saund. 131 a.

(*x*) Ld. Raym. 15.

(*y*) Cowp. 17; Dougl. 569.

(*z*) 1 Bla. Com. 85, 86; Dougl. 97, n. 12; Bac. Ab. Statute, L.; 2 Wils. 376; Willes, 210; see the reason, *per* Lord Ellenborough, 4 M. & Sel. 542. A recital in a public statute is evidence of the fact recited, 4 M. & Sel. 532.

(*a*) 1 T. R. 145; Com. Dig. Plender, C. 76; Lane, 71; Stephen, 352.

(*b*) 3 B. & C. 186; 5 D. & R. 13, S. C.

(*c*) Ld. Raym. 382; Dougl. 97; 6 T. R. 776; Bac. Ab. Statute, L. 5.

(*d*) Rex *v.* Biers, 1 Adol. & El. 327; 3 Nev. & Man. 475.

(*e*) 1 Saund. 309 a. n. 8. *Sed quære.*

(497) Vide Dive *v.* Maningham, Plowd. 65.

(498) Vide Murray *v.* Fitzpatrick, 3 Caines' Rep. 41. A mis-recital in the title of a public statute, in a part which does not alter the sense, and when its date is truly set forth, is not a cause for arresting judgment after verdict, nor can it be assigned as error. Murray *v.* Fitzpatrick, 3 Caines' Rep. 38, 41.

(499) { Goshen Turnp. Co. *v.* Sears, 7 Conn. Rep. 92. }

may be material to the action or defence must be stated in pleading (*f*); and this in the first instance (*g*). The mis-recital of a private act can only be taken advantage of by a plea of *nul tiel record*, or in assumpsit, before the pleading rules, Hil. Term, 4 W. 4, under the general issue (*h*); though we have seen that if the time or place of holding the parliament be mis-stated, it is a ground of demurrer (*i*). By a clause in most acts that would otherwise be private, they are now declared to be public, and then the production of *any* copy without proof suffices (*j*).

I. THE FACTS NECESSARY TO BE STATED.

So the courts will *ex officio* notice the *Ecclesiastical* (*k*), *Civil*, and *Marine Laws* (*l*), without any statement of them in pleading; and if there be any mis-statement of such laws, or of facts affected by them, the pleading will be held insufficient. Thus, where an administrator *durante minore ætate*, in his declaration averred that the infant was within the age of twenty-one years, the declaration was holden bad, because the Court would take notice that by the ecclesiastical law such administration ceased at the age of seventeen, and perhaps the executor was of the age of eighteen, though not twenty-one, as alleged in the declaration (*m*); and the forest laws are not *ex officio* taken notice of (*n*) (500).

But the Courts *ex officio* will not take notice of *foreign laws*, or of the laws of our plantations; and consequently they must in general, when material, be stated in pleading (*o*).

The courts are also bound to take notice of all *Common Law Rights* and *Duties*, and of *General Customs*; and consequently these ought not to be stated in pleading (*p*). Thus if in a return to a mandamus to restore a burgess of a corporation, it be stated that the party was removed by the *corporate body at large, [*248] *it is* unnecessary to aver that the power of removal is vested in them, because by intendment of law such power exists in the body at large, unless vested by charter or otherwise in a select part of the corporation (*q*). And it has been well observed, that in an action against a common carrier or innkeeper for the

(*f*) 1 Bla. Com. 86; Ld. Raym. 381, 382; Dougl. 97; Bac. Ab. Statutes, L.

(*g*) Carth. 306.

(*h*) Bac. Ab. Statutes, L. 5; Ld. Raym. 381; Cowp. 474.

(*i*) *Ante*, 246; Cowp. 474.

(*j*) Woodward *v.* Cotton, 6 Car. & P. 491; 1 Crom. M. & Ros. 44, S. C., overruling Broomhead *v.* Beaumont, MS.; Chitty's Col. Stat. tit. Statutes.

(*k*) Bro. Quare Impedit. pl. 12; March. 205; 1 Rol. Ab. 526; Cro. Eliz. 602; 5 Co. 29; Ld. Raym. 338, 1334.

(*l*) 2 Hen. Bla. 606, n. a.

(*m*) 5 Co. 29 a; Ld. Raym. 338. But note, this was before the statute 38 Geo. 3, c. 87, which appoints twenty-one as the age at which the executor may act.

(*n*) 2 Leon. 209.

(*o*) 2 East, 273, 274; Cowp. 174, 343; Salk. 651; Burr. 1077; Rep. tem. Hardw. 85; 4 T. R. 182; 3 Esp. Rep. 164: see also 3 D. & R. 190; Cowp. 343. It should seem the Courts will not *ex officio* take notice of the law of Scotland, 4 Taunt. 40, 44; see 2 D. & R. 280. As to foreign laws in general, Harrison's Index, tit. Foreigners; Vattel L. Nat. by Chitty, per tot.

(*p*) Ld. Raym. 175, 1542; Carth. 83, 269; Co. Lit. 89 a, n. 7; see Stephen, 357, 1st edit.; 391, &c. 2d edit.

(*q*) Dougl. 149; 1 B. & P. 100; Com. Dig. Pleader, C. 78.

---

(500) The court cannot take judicial cognizance of any of the laws of our sister States at variance with the *common law*. Holmes *v.* Broughton, 10 Wend. R. 75. It was held, that a defendant who relies upon the statute of another State, must in his plea set out the statute, that the court may see whether the proceedings were warranted by the statute or not, and the general allegation that the proceedings were pursuant is not sufficient. Walker *v.* Maxwell, 1 Mass. Rep. 103. Pearsall *v.* Dwight, 2 Mass. Rep. 34. Legg *v.* Legg, 8 Mass. Rep. 99, the same court declare that they could not take judicial notice of the laws of Vermont, and upon a common law question, they must presume the laws of Vermont to be similar to their own. *ib.*

I. THE FACTS NECESSARY TO BE STATED.

loss of goods, &c. which is a liability founded on the common law or custom of the realm (501), it is not only unnecessary, but improper, to recite such custom, because it tends to confound the distinction between special customs, which ought to be pleaded, and the general customs of the realm, of which the Courts are bound to take notice without pleading (r). So it is not only unnecessary, but improper, in a declaration on a bill of exchange, to set out or recite fully the custom of merchants, because it is part of the law of the land (s). It is for the parties to confine their allegations to the *facts*, for *ex facto jus oritur*, the Court will apply for themselves the *law* arising from the facts stated; and this principle applies, although the dispute between the parties involve and directly turn upon a matter of law (t). And it is a consequence of this rule, that *mere* matters of law or legal conclusions from facts, if alleged by one party, should not be traversed by the other (u).

Such of the *Customs of Gavelkind* and *Borough English* as are of the essence of the tenure, as the course of descent, need not be stated specially in pleading, nor should be prescribed for; because the common law takes notice of them, and it is sufficient to state in the pleading that the land is of the custom of gavelkind, or of the tenure of Borough English, and subject thereto; but in regard to other customs, though incident to these tenures, they must be stated (x). And the Courts will not *ex officio* take notice of any *Particular Local Customs* (y); nor of the customs of London, except where they have been certified by the recorder to either of the courts of record (z), without which [*249] there must be either plea or an affidavit of the custom (a). *Thus, where a defendant pleaded that his debt was attached in London by one of the plaintiff's creditors, it was decided that the Court could not take notice of the custom of foreign attachment, because it was not pleaded, and consequently that the plea was bad (b); but on a writ of error from the inferior Court, the custom will be noticed (c).

The Courts take notice of the *Days of the Week*, &c. on which particular days fall, and the almanack is part of the law of the land, having been established by different statutes (d); and if there be a mis-statement, it will be fatal (e). Therefore, where a writ of inquiry was stated in pleading to have been executed on the 15th of June, which was a Sunday, the proceeding was held defective (f); and where the defendant justified an arrest under process from an inferior Court, which he stated to be held every Friday, and the process appeared by the pleading to have been dated the 7th of August, which was Saturday, upon demurrer it was held bad (g). So the Court will take notice what

(r) Co. Lit. 89 a, n. 7.
(s) Ld. Raym. 1542.
(t) Stephen, 2d edit. 392, 393.
(u) *Id.* 233.
(x) Co. Lit. 175 b, n. 4; Ld. Raym. 1025; 1 Bla. Com. 76; 2 *Id.* 82 to 84. As to tenancy by curtesy, Rob. Gav. 142.
(y) 1 Rol. Rep. 106; see 9 East, 185.
(z) Stra. 187, 1187; Dougl. 387, 380, 363; Andr. 304; 1 Bla. Com. 76.
(a) Andr. 304; Stra. 1187; 3 Atk. 44; Dougl. 363.
(b) 1 Rol. Rep. 106; Co. Ent. 139 b; 1 Saund. 67, n. 1; 5 Taunt. 228. *Sed quære*, the custom having been certified, Dougl. 378.
(c) Dougl. 380; Salk. 269.
(d) 2 & 3 Edw. 6, c. 1; 5 & 6 Edw. 6, c. 1; 1 Eliz. c. 2; but see 2 Ventr. 247.
(e) 2 Ld. Raym. 994; 6 Mod. 41, 81; Salk. 191, 626.
(f) Fortesc. 373; Stra. 387.
(g) Rep. temp. Hardw. 162; 1 T. R. 116.

(501) Which are anonymous. Co. Lit. 110 b.

I. THE FACTS NECESSARY TO BE STATED.

number of days there are in each month (*h*), and in leap year, and of the movable feasts (*i*). In pleading a *prescriptive* right of common, limited as to its exercise from a certain feast, it is sufficient to claim it, "from the feast of St. Thomas," &c. without claiming it on the pleadings from old St. Thomas's-day; for, although the alteration of the style took place within the memory of man, yet as the claim is from time immemorial, it shall be intended that the party meant the old style. But in general, "St. Thomas's-day" would signify the day appointed by the statute (*k*) for the celebration of the feast of St. Thomas (*l*). Even before the statute (*m*) which fixes the terms, the Courts took judicial notice of them as to their commencement and *conclusion, [*250] whether movable or not (*n*); and if process be stated, not under a videlicet (*o*), to have been issued on a day in vacation, and it be alleged that the Court was then sitting, the pleading will, it seems, be bad on special demurrer (*p*).

The *Division of England* into counties will also be noticed by the Court *ex officio* (*q*); and the reason of this is, that the sheriff of the county is the person to whom the Court directs its writs (*r*). But the Court will not take judicial notice of the division of England into parishes, vills, or particular liberties, which must be stated in pleading (*s*); nor will it take notice of the local situation and distances of the different places in counties in England from each other (*t*); and though the Courts will notice provinces and dioceses, they will not notice any particular place within each province or diocese, except that where the court sits (*u*). The division of Ireland, or any other country than England, into counties, or the known towns or cities of such country, will not be judicially noticed by the Courts; and the situation of such counties, towns, or cities, should be specially stated (*x*). So the Courts will take judicial notice of what towns are incorporated, and of the extent of ports, and the river Thames, &c. (*y*). And if by charter, confirmed by act of parliament, a town is exempted from the jurisdiction of the sheriff of the county, and has peculiar liberties and privileges, the Court will take judicial notice thereof (*z*).

The Courts will *ex officio* take notice of the *meaning of English words* and terms of art, according to their ordinary acceptation, however vulgar and peculiar to a particular county or place in England; and consequently the meaning of such terms need not in general be averred (*a*), unless the intendment of law be otherwise (*b*). Thus in an action on a warranty of a carroom, it

(*h*) 1 Rol. Ab. 524, C. pl. 4. In general the term *month*, in law, is to be considered as a lunar month, but this may be explained by the intention of the parties to mean a calendar month; 3 B. & B. 186; 6 T. R. 224; 1 M. & Sel. 111; 1 Stra. 652, 446.

(*i*) 6 Mod. 81; Salk. 626; Ld. Raym. 994. The calendar upon which the Courts proceed is that annexed to the Common Prayer Book, 6 Mod. 81.

(*k*) 24 Geo. 2, c. 23, s. 2.

(*l*) 3 Bingh. 401. As to a lease from or notice to quit at "Michaelmas," 11 East, 312; 2 Campb. 256.

(*m*) 1 W. 4, c. 70, s. 6.

(*n*) 1 T. R. 116; 1 Saund. 300 d, n. 7.

(*o*) It would not be bad if so stated, 5 Moore, 538; 2 B. & B. 659, S. C.

(*p*) 5 Burr. 2586; 3 T. R. 184; 1 Saund. 300 a, note 7; see 15 East, 378.

(*q*) 2 Inst. 557; March. 124; Comb. 460.

(*r*) As to the mis-spelling a county, see Hodgkinson *v.* Hodgkinson, 2 Dowl. 536.

(*s*) *Supra*, n. (*q*).

(*t*) 4 B. & Ald. 243; 1 Chit. Rep. 32.

(*u*) Ld. Raym. 854, 1379; Stra. 609; 3 T. R. 387.

(*x*) 1 Chit. Rep. 28, 32; 2 B. & A. 301, S. C.; 2 D. & R. 15; 1 B. & C. 16.

(*y*) Stra. 469; 1 Hen. Bla. 356, 357.

(*z*) See 3 Bing. 460, 461.

(*a*) 1 Rol. Ab. 86, 525.

(*b*) 4 T. R. 314.

I. THE FACTS NECESSARY TO BE STATED.

was held not necessary to aver what a carroom was, because it was a phrase then well known *in London (c). So in an action for words spoken in England, which are slanderous according to the phrase of the country in which they were uttered, though the court may not in fact know what they signify, it is not necessary to aver their signification, for the judges themselves will take judicial notice of English words in any county (d). The Courts will also take notice of the names and quantity of legal weights and measures (e); and of time according to ordinary expressions (f). But if the intendment of law be different to the statement in the pleading, the real meaning of the term in the particular instance must be alleged, and therefore it was decided that proof that the defendant agreed to sell so many bushels, according to a particular measure, will not support an allegation in a declaration to sell so many bushels generally, because "bushels," without any other explanation, signify the legal statute measure of a Winchester bushel (g). And if an instrument be described as made here for the payment of a sum of money generally, it will be intended that English money was to be paid (h).

Every Court is bound to take judicial notice of its own *course of Proceedings* (i), and of those of the other superior Courts (k); and therefore in these cases it is not necessary, in pleading, to allege any usage or prescription in support of such proceeding (l) (502). So where, upon a motion in arrest of judgment, because the declaration had not shown out of what Court a writ of latitat was issued, the Court said, that there being no writ properly called a latitat but what issues out of the King's Bench, the declaration was sufficient (m); and it is unnecessary to state matters antecedently alleged in the same record (n).

[*252] *The superior Courts will also notice the *Privileges they confer on their Officers* (o), and therefore, though in a plea of privilege it is usual to state the custom of the Court, privileging attornies, &c., such statement appears unnecessary. In *Ogle* v. *Norcliffe*, Holt, C. J., said, that the privilege claimed by the defendant was due to the clerks of the Common Pleas of common right, of which the Court of King's Bench would take notice (p). In one case where the customary privilege was mispleaded, it being urged for the defendant that the Courts would take notice of the privilege, and reject as surplusage the custom which was pleaded, the Court said, that whatever they would have done, had it stood indifferent, they could not take notice of a privilege expressly contrary to what the defendant had stated (q). But that decision

(c) 1 Rol. Ab. 525; 6 Vin. Ab. 492.

(d) 1 Rol. Ab. 86; 1 Vin. Ab. 531; 1 Saund. 242, note 1; *quære*, whether it may not be necessary to give a translation of a foreign libel or instrument, see *id.* note b. 5th edit.; 3 B. & B. 201.

(e) 1 Rol. Ab. 525.

(f) *Id.*; Ld. Raym. 794.

(g) 4 T. R. 314; see 11 East, 312; 2 Campb. 256.

(h) 2 B. & A. 301.

(i) 1 T. R. 118; 2 Lev. 176; Plowd. 145, 163; 1 Rol. Rep. 106; Burr. 811. The Court will not take judicial notice who is master of the King's Bench, 3 M. & Sel. 158.

(k) 2 Co. Rep. 18; Cro. Jac. 67, 68; 1 Rol. Rep. 106; Sir W. Jones, 417; Cro. Car. 527.

(l) 2 Co. Rep. 16 a; Year Book, 2 Rich. 3, p. 9. pl, 21.

(m) Ld. Raym. 397.

(n) Co. Lit. 303 b; Ld. Raym. 13.

(o) Ld. Raym. 869, 898.

(p) Ld. Raym. 869; 9 East, 424, 339; 12 *Id.* 544.

(q) Ld. Raym. 899.

(502) {See King v. The Bank of Gettysburg, 2 Rawle, 197.} But the practice of the court is pleadable where the very merits of the case depend upon it. Dudlow v. Watchorn and Thibault, 16 East's Rep. 39.

seems questionable (*r*). Each Court takes judicial notice that an attorney or officer of *its own Court* is its officer, without affidavit (*s*), though a plea of privilege by an attorney to be sued in *another* Court requires an affidavit of its truth to be annexed (*t*). I. THE FACTS NECESSARY TO BE STATED.

So the Courts at Westminster will notice *Courts of General Jurisdiction*, and the course of proceedings therein, as that there was a Court of Exchequer in Wales, and the course of proceedings there, and they also notice the jurisdiction of the Courts of the counties palatine (*u*). But it has been decided, that the Courts are not bound to take notice who were or are the judges of another Court at Westminster, though perhaps they ought to take notice of the judges of their own Court (*x*); and therefore where the authority of a judge may be material to the action or defence, it should be expressly stated in pleading (*y*), and in pleading a fine the names of the judges and their authority should be stated (*z*).

The superior Courts will not *ex officio* take notice of the customs, laws, or proceedings of *Inferior Courts of limited Jurisdiction* (*a*), unless when reviewing their judgments upon a writ of error, when, for the purposes of justice, they must necessarily notice them (*b*). In a return to a writ of *habeas corpus*, inferior Courts must in their return set forth the law or custom of the place by which they justify their commitment, otherwise the Court is not bound to take notice of it; but on a writ of error it is otherwise (*c*).

[*253]

2dly. Where the law presumes a fact, or it is necessarily implied, it need not be stated.

*Where the law presumes a fact, it need not be stated in pleading (*d*). Thus as it is an intendment of law, that a person is innocent of fraud, and every imputation affecting his reputation, the party insisting upon the contrary must state it in pleading (*e*). Therefore in an action for words, as for saying a man is a thief, the plaintiff has no occasion to aver that he is not a thief (*f*); and in an action on the case for maliciously suing out a commission of bankrupt, it is not necessary to state in the declaration that the plaintiff was not indebted to the defendant, or that he never committed an act of bankruptcy (*g*). It is a rule applicable in some cases to pleading, that where the law presumes the affirmative of any fact, the negative of such fact must be proved by the party averring it in pleading. Thus where any act is required to be done by a person, the omission of which would make him guilty of a criminal neglect of duty, the law presumes the affirmative, and throws the burthen of proving the negative on the party who insist on it (*h*) (503). Illegality in a transaction is never presumed; on the contrary, every thing is presumed to have been legally done till the contrary is proved (*i*). And, as observed by Lord Coke,

(*r*) 9 East, 424, 339; 12 *Id.* 544.
(*s*) Ex parte Hore, 3 Dowl. 600.
(*t*) Davidson *v.* Watkins, 3 Dowl. 129.
(*u*) 1 Ld. Raym. 154; 1 Saund. 73; 6 Mod. 74; Cro. Eliz. 502, 503; Cro. Car. 179; 1 Sid. 331.
(*x*) Andr. 74; Stra. 1226.
(*y*) *Id.*
(*z*) 2 Saund. 175, n. 2.
(*a*) 1 Rol. Rep. 105; Ld. Raym. 1334; Cro. Eliz. 502; Salk. 269.
(*b*) Cro. Car. 179; 1 Rol. Rep. 105.
(*c*) Salk. 269.
(*d*) 4 M. & S. 120; 2 Wils. 147; Stephen on Plead. 356, 1st ed.; 399, 2d ed.
(*e*) Co. Lit. 78 b; Heath's Max. 207, 212.
(*f*) 2 Wils. 147.
(*g*) *Id.* But in this case the declaration always avers that the defendant acted maliciously and without probable cause, &c.
(*h*) 3 East, 192; 2 M. & Sel. 561.
(*i*) 1 B. & Ald. 463.

(503) Vide Phillips' Ev. 151. The King *v.* Hawkins, 10 East's Rep. 216. Rex *v.* Rogers, 2 Campb. 654.

I. THE FACTS NECESSARY TO BE STATED.

necessary circumstances implied by law need not be expressed or pleaded (*g*). Thus, if a feoffment be pleaded, livery of seisin need not be alleged, for it is implied in the word "enfeoffed;" and in pleading the assignment of land for dower, it is not necessary to say, that it was by metes and bounds, for it shall be intended a lawful assignment; so in pleading a surrender, the re-entry of the lessor need not be stated, for it shall be intended; so where it is pleaded, that the sheriff made his warrant, it is unnecessary to say, that it was under his seal, for it could not be his warrant if it were not; so if a person plead that he is heir to A., he need not say either that A. is dead, or that he had no son; and in pleading an acceptance by a corporation of an assignee of the lessee as tenant, it is [*254] *not necessary to show that the acceptance was by deed, for an acceptance being pleaded, every thing that would render it a good acceptance is implied (*h*) (504). And if it be pleaded that a party to a reference "revoked the authority" of the arbitrator, it need not be alleged that the latter had notice of the revocation, for without such notice there would be no revocation (*i*). And in declaring on a contract it is sufficient if it be set forth according to its legal effect (*k*).

Great care must be taken in the application of this rule to ascertain that the *law* intends the fact proposed to be omitted. Thus, in pleading a devise of land, it must be stated to have been in writing, though in point of law it could not otherwise be a will (*l*); and it is said, that when the *defendant pleads* that another person promised to be answerable to the plaintiff for the debt, in lieu of the defendant, it must be shown to have been in writing, pursuant to the statute against frauds, so that it may appear to be such a contract as the plaintiff could enforce (*m*). But clearly in *declaring* upon a contract within the statute against frauds, it need not be alleged, or specifically shown, that the contract was in writing (*n*). And in a declaration on a bill of exchange, it need not be averred that the acceptance was in writing (*o*). The distinction is, that a will is only valid by statute, and that statute requires it to be in writing, &c.; but as to contracts and bills of exchange they were valid at common law, and the statutes merely require a certain form (*p*).

3dly. A party need not state a fact, which is more properly to be stated by the other side.

It is also a general rule of pleading, that matter which should come more properly from the other side need not be stated (*q*). In other words, it is enough for each party to make out his own case or defence (505). He suffi-

(*g*) 8 Co. Rep. 81 b; see Bac. Ab. Pleas, (I. 7); Com. Dig. Pleader, E. 9; Co. Lit. 303 b; 2 Saund. 305 a, n. (13); 2 Hen. Bla. 120; 2 B. & B. 361; 5 Moore, 74; 5 B. & Ald. 507; Steph. 2d ed. 398.

(*h*) 2 Saund. 305 a, note (13).

(*i*) 5 B. & Ald. 507; 8 Rep. 81 b, S. P.

(*k*) See *post.*

(*l*) 1 Saund. 276 d, note (2); *post.*

(*m*) *Id.;* Raym. 450; *sed qu.;* and see Steph. 2d ed. 418, 419, note.

(*n*) 1 Saund. 211, note (2); 276, note (1), (2).

(*o*) 6 Bing. 529.

(*p*) *Id.;* see Stephen, 2d ed. 417; *post.*

(*q*) Com. Dig. Pleader, C. 81; Plowd. 376; 2 Saund. 62 a, n. 4; 1 T. R. 638; 8 *Id.* 167; Steph. 1st ed. 354; 2d ed. 395.

(504) In covenant for rent due on a lease, against the assignee of the lessee, the plaintiff need not aver, that the lessee had not paid the rent: it is sufficient if he states that the rent accrued subsequent to the assignment to the defendant, and that the same was due and owing to the plaintiff, and wholly in arrear and unpaid; for it is implied in the averment, that the defendant owed it. Executors of Dubois *v.* Van Orden, 6 Johns. Rep. 105. Vide etiam, Scott *v.* Scott, 16 East's Rep. 343.

(505) Karthaus *v.* Owings, 2 Gill & Johns. 441. Goshen, &c. Turnp. Co. *v.* Sears, 7 Conn. Rep. 92, 93. Salman *v.* Bradshaw, Cro. Jac. 304. Barton *v.* Webb, 8 Term Rep.

ciently substantiates the charge or answer for the purpose of pleading, if his pleading establish a *prima facie* charge or answer. He is not bound to anticipate, and therefore is not compelled to notice and remove in his declaration or plea every *possible exception, answer, or objection, which may exist, and with which the adversary may intend to oppose him. Thus, in a declaration on a bond, it is not necessary to aver that the defendant was of full age when he executed the bond (r). In an action of debt on a bond conditioned that B. should remit all monies received for C. to C., or pay the same to him or his order, as should be directed, it is sufficient to state a non-payment to C.; and it is not necessary, in a replication to a plea of general performance, to allege any order given by C.; for if any had been given, it should be shown by the defendant (s). So in an action on a *post obit* bond, the plaintiff need not aver the death of the person on whose death the money was payable (t). So in an action on a promise made by a testator upon a good consideration, that his executor should pay it, it is not necessary to aver in the declaration that the defendant has assets (u). So in assumpsit on a contract to transfer stock to the plaintiff or his order on request, the plaintiff stated a request, and averred that the defendant had not transferred; and on an objection being taken that the plaintiff should have averred that the defendant had not paid to the plaintiff's order, it was overruled, because the averment of payment to such order ought to come from the other side (x).

1. THE FACTS NECESSARY TO BE STATED.

[*255]

If the plaintiff allege a *condition subsequent* to his estate, he need not aver performance, but the breach must be shown by the defendant; and matter in defeasance of the action need not be stated; and wherever there is a circumstance, the omission of which is to defeat the plaintiff's right of action, *prima facie* well founded, whether called by the name of a proviso or a condition subsequent, it must in its nature be a matter of defence, and ought to be shown in pleading by the opposite party (y). In pleading upon statutes, where there is an exception in the enacting clause, the plaintiff must show that the defendant is not within the exemption, but if there be an exception in a subsequent clause, that is matter of defence, and the other party must show it to exempt himself from the penalty (z)(506). And where *an act of parliament in the enacting clause creates an offence, and gives a penalty, and in the same section (a) there follows a proviso containing an exception, which is not incorporated with the enacting clause by any words of reference, it is not neces- [*256]

(r) Plowd. 564; 1 Vent. 217; Steph. 2d edit. 395, 396.

(s) 1 T. R. 485.

(t) 2 B. & C. 82; 3 D. & R. 231, S. C.

(u) 7 Taunt. 580.

(x) Ld. Raym 114, 247, 673, 989.

(y) *Per* Ashhurst, J., 1 T. R. 645, 646; Com. Dig. Pleader, C. 81.

(z) 1 T. R. 144, 145; 6 *Id.* 559; Bac. Ab. Statute, L.; 1 East, 646, 647; 2 Chit. Rep. 582.

(a) Mere placing the proviso in the same section of the printed act, does not make it necessary to notice it in pleading, unless it is also incorporated in the enacting sentence; for statutes are not divided into sections upon the rolls of parliament. *Per* Bayley, J., 3 B. & C. 189; 5 D. & R. 19, S. C.

459, 463. Shum et al. v. Farrington, 1 Bos. & Pul. 640, S. C. 8 Term Rep. 463. Postmaster General v. Cockran, 2 Johns. Rep. 415, 416. Hughes v. Smith, 5 Johns. Rep. 168. Willcocks v. Nicholls, 1 Price's Exch. Rep. 109. 9 Wend. R. 378.

(506) Acc. Jones v. Axen, 1 Ld. Raym. 120. Rex v. Ford, Str. 555. Rex v. Bryan, Id. 1101. Sheldon v. Clark, 1 Johns. Rep. 513. Bennet v. Hurd, 3 Johns. Rep. 438. Teel v. Fonda, 4 Johns. Rep. 304. Hart v. Cleis, 8 Johns. Rep. 41. Smith v. United States, Rep. C. C. U. S. First Circt., {1 Gallis. Rep.} 261. 1 Saund. 262 b. Donnelly v. Vandenburgh, 3 Johns. Rep. 41, 42.

I. THE FACTS NECESSARY TO BE STATED.

sary for the plaintiff in suing for the penalty to negative such exception (*b*)(507). The recent case of *Vavasour* v. *Ormrod* (*c*) well elucidates this doctrine. It was an action upon a lease, and the declaration described the *reddendum* as containing an *absolute* reservation of rent. In fact, the *reddendum* was "yielding and paying during the said term (*except as hereinafter mentioned*) the yearly sum, &c." In the latter part of the lease there was a covenant and proviso by which a deduction was to be made, if a certain event happened; and it was held that the declaration was bad. And Lord Tenterden said, "if an *act of parliament*, or a *private instrument*, contain in it, first, a general clause, and afterwards a separate and distinct clause, something which would otherwise be included in it, a party relying upon the general clause, in pleading may set out that clause only, without noticing the separate and distinct clause which operates as an exception. But if the exception itself be incorporated in the general clause, then the party relying upon it must in pleading state it with the exception; and if he state it as containing an absolute unconditional stipulation, without noticing the exception, it will be a variance. This is a middle case. Here the exception is not in express terms introduced into the reservation, but by *reference only* to some subsequent matter in the instrument. The words are 'except as hereinafter mentioned.' The rule here applies *verba relata inesse videntur*. And the clause thereinafter mentioned must be considered as an exception in the general clause, by which the rent is reserved; and then, according to the rule above laid down, the plaintiff [*257] *ought in his declaration to have stated the reservation and the exception. Not having done so, I am of opinion that the variance is fatal, and that there is no ground for setting aside the nonsuit."

So if the *law* raise an exception to a general right, it need not be stated in pleading (*d*). Therefore, although the holding a market on certain feasts is prohibited by statute, yet in pleading a right to hold a market, it may be alleged that the party was entitled to hold it on certain specified days in the week, without any exception as to those feasts (*e*). And it is a rule with respect to acts valid at common law, but regulated as to the mode of performance by statute, that it is sufficient to use such certainty of allegation as was sufficient before the statute (*f*).

But in acting upon the rule, that the pleading need not show and avoid distinct matter of defence or answer, which it is for the adversary to object, care should be taken to discriminate accurately whether the matter in question is not so intimately connected with the case of the party pleading, that its affirmation or denial is essential to the validity of *his* pleading, in reference to and in consequence of the prior pleadings upon the record. In case for disturbing a right of common by putting cattle thereon, the defendant pleaded a license from the lord of the manor, but did not aver that there was left a suffi-

(*b*) 1 B. & Ald. 94. Sometimes a clause apparently containing an exception is to be considered as merely explanatory of the enacting clause. See a decision upon the Wilful Trespass Act, 1 G. 4, c. 56; 4 Bing. 183, 189.

(*c*) 6 B. & C. 430; 9 D. & R. 597, S. C.; see 4 Campb. 20; 11 East, 640; 6 M. & Sel. 9. How to declare on an award, 1 Saund. 62 a, b, note.

(*d*) Cro. Eliz. 485; 9 East, 339.

(*e*) 7 B. & C. 57; 9 D. & R. 863, S. C.

(*f*) 1 Saund. 276 a and c, n. (2); 211, n. (2); Steph. 2d ed. 417; *ante*; *post*.

(507) { Smith *v.* Moore, 6 Greenl. Rep. 278, and the American cases there cited. }

cient common for the commoners; and on demurrer the Court held, that the plea was for this omission bad; for though it may be said, that the plaintiff might reply that there was not enough common left, yet as he had already alleged in his declaration that his enjoyment of the common was obstructed, the contrary of this should have been shown by the plea to render it a perfect defence (*g*).

I. THE FACTS NECESSARY TO BE STATED.

And there are certain pleas which are regarded unfavorable by the Courts; as pleadings in estoppel (*h*), and a plea of alien enemy (*i*); and as to these it is essential to their validity that they should, (contrary to the general rule,) show, not only a *prima facie* case or defence, but should mention and *affirm, or dispute, every matter which by possibility could afford the opposite party an answer to the pleading (*k*). [*258]

4thly. It is not necessary to state in pleading mere matter of evidence.

Although any particular fact may be the gist of a party's case, and the statement of it is indispensable, it is still a most important principle of the law of pleading, that in alleging the fact, it is unnecessary to state such circumstances as *merely tend to prove the truth* of it (*l*). The dry allegation of the fact, without detailing a variety of minute circumstances which constitute the evidence of it, will suffice. The object of the pleadings is to arrive at a specific issue upon a given and material fact, and this is attained, although the *evidence* of such fact, to be laid before the jury, be not specifically developed in the pleading. Therefore if the question be, whether wheat, after it had been cut, was suffered to lie on the ground "a reasonable time," it is sufficient to allege generally that such was the fact, without showing specifically how many days the corn remained on the ground, and what was the state of the weather during that period; although such matters may be material to the due consideration and decision of the question (*m*). So, under the common averment in a declaration upon a bill of exchange, that the defendant "had notice" of the dishonor, the plaintiff may show special circumstances or facts which render the notice valid, although it were given at a later period than would, in ordinary cases, have sufficed; for there is no need in pleading to state more than the legal effect of the facts (*n*). And upon this principle it is often sufficient, in setting out a custom or privilege, which is exercisable only to *reasonable* extent, or at *seasonable* times, to allege generally that such was the custom, &c., without showing specifically what was reasonable or seasonable, &c. (*o*).

This rule may indeed be difficult in its application, but it has been rightly said (*p*), that it is so elementary in its kind, and so well observed in practice as not to have become frequently the subject of illustration by decided cases, and (for that reason probably) is little, if at all noticed in the digests and treatises.

[*259] 5thly. Statements of legal fictions, &c.

*Though the general rule is, that facts only are to be stated, yet there are some instances in which the statement in the pleading is valid, though it does not accord with the real facts, the law allowing a *fiction*; as in the action of

(*g*) 2 Mod. 6; 1 Freem. 190, S. C.; Willes, 619; Steph. 2d ed. 397.
(*h*) Co. Lit. 352 b; 303 a; 2 H. Bla. 530.
(*i*) 8 T. R. 167; 8 East, 80.
(*k*) See Steph. 2d ed. 397, 398.
(*l*) 9 Rep. 9 b; Ld. Raym. 8; Carth. 491; Stephen, 1st ed. 348; 2d ed. 388.
(*m*) Willes, 131.
(*n*) 8 B. & C. 387.
(*o*) 3 Bing. 61, and cases there cited.
(*p*) Stephen on Plead. 1st ed. 351; 2d ed. 391.

I. THE FACTS NECESSARY TO BE STATED.

ejectment, in which the statement of the demise to the nominal plaintiff is fictitious (q). So in trover and detinue, the usual allegation that the defendant found the goods, rarely accords with the fact (r); and where the number, quantity, species, or value of a thing, need not be proved precisely as laid, it is usual to state a greater number than really was the case, in order to admit of greater latitude in evidence; but except in these and a few other well known instances, established and recognized in pleading for the convenience of justice, the pleading matter, known to the party to be untrue, is censurable (s). And whenever the purposes of justice require that a fiction of law with regard to time, &c. should not be attended to, and that the real facts should appear, it is competent to a party to show the truth by averment in pleading (t). Thus, a party might, before the recent enactment, show that a judgment was actually signed in vacation, although by fiction or intendment of law, all judgments were supposed to be recovered in term, whilst the Court, who were supposed to have formally pronounced it, were sitting (u). Where a bill was filed against an attorney in vacation, which by fiction of law was supposed to take place in term, it was competent to the party filing the bill to show the very day it was filed. And so in the case of writs, which, before the uniformity of process act, 2 W. 4, c. 39, were supposed to issue in term, it was competent to a party to show the time when they actually issued, if that became necessary, in order to avail himself of the statute of limitations, &c. (x).

6thly. Of duplicity.

We have before remarked that the object of the science of pleading is the production of a *single* issue upon the *same* subject-matter of dispute. The rule relating to duplicity, or doubleness, tends, more than any other, to the attainment of this object. It precludes the parties, as well the plaintiff as the defendant, in each of their pleadings, from stating or relying upon more than one *matter*, constituting a sufficient ground of action, in respect of the same demand, or a sufficient defence to the same *claim, or an adequate answer to the precedent pleading of the opponent (y). The plaintiff cannot, by the common law rule, in order to sustain a single demand, rely upon two or more distinct grounds or matters, each of which, independently of the other (508), amounts to a good cause of action in respect of such demand. Thus at common law, in a declaration upon a bond, the plaintiff could not assign two breaches of the condition, because the bond was forfeited by one breach, which was sufficient to support his action, though in covenant several breaches of different covenants might be stated (z). And the same count must not contain two promises in respect of the same subject-matter, as a promise to pay a specific sum for a horse, and also a promise to pay for the same horse so much

*260]

(q) 2 Burr. 667, 668.
(r) *Ante*, 140, 167; 1 New Rep. 140.
(s) Bac. Ab. Pleader, G. 4; 1 East, 372. See *post*, as to sham pleas.
(t) 3 B. & C. 317.
(u) *Id.*
(x) *Per* Abbott, C. J., 3 B. & C. 324.
(y) Com. Dig. Pleader, C. 33, E. 2; Bac. Ab. Pleas, K. 2, 3; Tidd, 9th edit. 661, 694, 1174; 2 Eunomus, 141; Steph. 2d ed. 292; 2 Saund. 49, 50.
(z) *Id.*; 1 Saund. 58 & 58 a, note 1. What is not duplicity in assigning a breach of the condition of a replevin bond, 3 M. & Sel. 182, 183.

(508) Vide Currie *v.* Henry, 2 Johns. Rep. 433, 437.

as it is worth (a)(509). The defendant could not, in answer to a single claim, rely on several distinct answers; nor can he now do so in one plea. Thus, in a plea of outlawry, the defendant cannot state several outlawries, because one would be sufficient to defeat the action (b); and on the same ground there cannot be a demurrer and a plea to the same part of a declaration or plea, &c. (c). The principle equally affects all pleadings; its application is, however, confined to instances in which there is, on the face of the pleading, one entire or single matter proposed to be supported or answered. Even at common law, the declaration may comprise several counts upon different distinct demands of the same nature; or distinct counts upon the same claim (d). The latter is evidently an evasion of the doctrine of duplicity, but even in this instance, the counts should *purport* to be founded on *distinct* demands (e); and at common law a distinct plea to each distinct and divisible cause of action (f), where several claims are combined in the same declaration, is admissible, although each plea differs in its nature from the others. As if there be a declaration with two counts on two bonds, the defendant might always plead *non est factum*, or other matter, to one count, and payment, *or a release, or other matter, to the other count. And it is important to remember that several distinct facts or allegations, however numerous, may be comprised in the same plea, or other pleading, without amounting to the fault of duplicity, if one fact, or some of the facts, be but dependent upon, or be mere inducement or introduction to the others, or if the different facts form together but one connected proportion, or entire matter or point (g).

1. THE FACTS NECESSARY TO BE STATED.

[*261]

With regard to *declarations*, there has been a statutable relaxation of the rule in actions upon bonds, or any penal sum for non-performance of covenants contained in any instrument. The statute (h) permits the plaintiff, in such actions, to assign as many breaches as he shall think fit, and this statute has been held to be compulsory on the plaintiff (i). And although the Reg. Gen. Hil. T. 4 W. 4, reg. 5, orders that there shall be only one count in *personal* actions on the same cause of action, yet it expressly allows several breaches of the same contract or duty to be assigned, for otherwise either the plaintiff would be precluded from recovering damages to the full extent of the injury, or the defendant would not be sufficiently apprized by the declaration of the extent of claim he would have to answer. And with respect to *pleas in bar*, the statute (k) provides that "a defendant or tenant in an action, or a plaintiff in replevin, in any court of record, may, with leave of the Court, plead as many several matters thereto as he may think necessary for his defence."

(a) 7 Mod. 143.
(b) Carth. 9.
(c) Bac. Ab. Pleas, K. 1, 3.
(d) See *post*, as to several counts.
(e) Steph. 2d edit. 318, 319; See *post*.
(f) As in the case of a libel charging that the plaintiff had been *thrice* suspended, &c. as a proctor, for misconduct, 6 Bing. 587.
(g) See 1 M. & P. 102, 123; 4 Bing. 428, S. C.; 4 B. & C. 547. And see Stephen, 2d ed. 302, 303, and the instances there given; and *post*, under the head of qualities of pleas in bar, and of replications.
(h) 8 & 9 Wm. 3, c. 11, s. 8.
(i) See 1 Saund. 58, n. 1, and *ib.* n. a.; and *post*.
(k) 4 Ann. c. 16, s. 4. The decisions upon the statute are noticed hereafter.

(509) But in Cheetham v. Tillotson, 5 Johns. Rep. 240, where two distinct causes of action were stated in what was, in form, one count, the court of Errors chose to consider them as separate counts, and reversed the judgment because entire damages had been assessed.

I. THE FACTS NECESSARY TO BE STATED.

But the common law rule still affects each plea taken separately (510); and the statute does not extend to replications or subsequent pleadings.

The doctrine of duplicity, as it more immediately affects each part of pleading, will be fully explained, and illustrated by instances, when we consider the particular properties of each division of the pleadings in a cause. It may here be remarked that in general the objection of duplicity can only be taken by special demurrer (*l*). And if a plaintiff reply to a plea bad for duplicity, he must plead to *each* distinct material matter in the plea (*m*). Where to debt on simple contract in an inferior Court, not of record, viz. the County Court, in which double pleas are not admissible, the defendant pleaded both the general issue and a set-off, and the plaintiff treated the latter as a nullity and replied only to the first, and obtained a verdict and judgment, it was held on a writ of false judgment, that as the defendant could not plead double, and the first plea was complete in itself, the second was surplusage, and that the plaintiff was justified in taking no notice of it, and the judgment was therefore affirmed (*n*).

4thly. Objections to unnecessary statements.

[*262]

The statement of immaterial or irrelevant matter or allegations, is not only censured, as creating unnecessary expense (*o*), but also frequently affords an advantage to the opposite party, either by affording him matter of objection on the ground of variance, or as rendering it incumbent on the *party pleading to adduce more evidence than would otherwise have been necessary. It is therefore of the greatest importance in pleading, to avoid any unnecessary statement of facts, as well as prolixity in the statement of those which may be necessary (*p*). If a party take upon himself to state in pleading a particular estate, where it was only required of him that he should show a general or even a less estate, title or interest, the adversary may traverse the allegation, and if it be untrue, the party will fail (511). Thus a general freehold title *liberum tenementum*, may be pleaded either in trespass or in an avowry in replevin, and under it the defendant may prove any estate of freehold, either in fee, in tail, or for life (*q*); but if he state, though unnecessarily, a seisin in fee of a particular estate or interest, and the other side traverse the allegation, it must be proved as stated (*r*). So in an action on the case against the sheriff for levying under an execution against the tenant, without paying the landlord a year's rent, if the plaintiff, though unnecessarily, profess to set out the terms of the tenancy as to the time of payment of rent, &c. and misdescribe them, the variance will be fatal (*s*)(512). These are instances of *material*

(*l*) 1 Saund. 337 a, note 3.
(*m*) 1 Ventr. 272; Stephen, 2d edit. 327.
(*n*) Chitty *v* Dendy, 1 Har. & Wol. 169.
(*o*) Cowp. 665, 727; Dougl. 668, 669.
(*p*) 1 Saund. 233, n. 2; 346, note 2; 2 *Id.* 206, n. 22; 366, note 1; Steph. 1st edit. 419; 2d edit. 467; 1 M. & Sel. 204.
(*q*) Steph. 1st ed. 335; 2d ed. 370.
(*r*) Dyer, 365; Willes, 102; 2 Saund. 206, n. 22.
(*s*) Dougl. 665; 8 East, 9.

(510) Vide King *v.* Harrison, 15 East's Rep. 615.

(511) Vide Turner *v.* Eyles, 3 Bos. & Pul. 456. Phillips' Ev. 158. Smith *v.* Casey, 3 Campb. 461. Peppin *v.* Solomons, 5 Term Rep. 497, 496.

(512) So, if in an action on a promissory note, not negotiable, but expressed to be *for value received*, (which is *prima facie* evidence of consideration,) the plaintiff unnecessarily set forth the particulars in which the value consisted, he is bound to prove them precisely as laid. Jerome *v.* Whitney, 7 Johns. Rep. 321. So, in an indictment for stopping the mail, a contract with the postmaster general to transport the mail was alleged, and it was held that the contract must be proved, although the indictment might have been good

matter being alleged with an unnecessary detail of circumstances or particularity. The *subject-matter* of the averment is material and relevant, and the evil is, that the essential and the immaterial parts are so interwoven as to expose the whole allegation to a traverse, and the consequent necessity of proof to the full extent to which it is carried by the pleading. I. THE FACTS NECESSARY TO BE STATED.

If, however, the matter unnecessarily stated be *wholly foreign* and irrelevant to the cause, so that no allegation whatever on the subject was necessary, it will be rejected as surplusage, and it need not be proved (*t*); nor will it *vitiate* (*u*)(513) *even on a special demurrer* (*x*); it being a maxim that *utile per* **inutile non vitiatur* (*y*). As observed by Lord Mansfield (*z*), "the distinction is between that which may be rejected as surplusage, which might be struck out on motion, and what cannot. Where the declaration contains impertinent matter, foreign to the cause, and which the master, on a reference to him, would strike out, (irrelevant covenants for instance,) that will be rejected by the court, and need not bo proved (514). But if the very ground of the action be mis-stated, that will be fatal, for then the case declared on is different from that which is proved, and the plaintiff must recover *secundum allegata et probata.*" (515) Thus in an action against the marshal for an escape, the declaration, after stating the original judgment, set out a judgment in *scire facias* reviving the original judgment with the usual award of execution, as appeared by the record, and then averred that "thereupon" the party was committed; it was decided that the allegation of the judgment in *scire facias* was immaterial, and need not be proved (*a*). Mr. J. Bayley observed, "a party

8thly. Superfluity and repugnancy.

[*263]

(*t*) Dukes *v.* Gostling, 1 Bing. N. C. 588.

(*u*) 1 T. R. 235; 4 East, 400; Gilb. C. P. 131, 132; Com. Dig. Pleader, C. 28; Bac. Ab. Pleas, I. 4; Co. Lit. 303 b.; 2 Saund. 306, n. 14; 5 East, 444; Heath's Maxims, 4; 4 M. & Sel. 474, 475 The terms "impertinent" and "immaterial" are synonymous. *Per* Best, J., 3 D. & R. 220. Matter immaterial, and which may be rejected as surplusage, will not make a pleading double, see Steph. 2d edit 300.

(*x*) Co. Lit. 303 b.; 11 East, 62, 65; Steph. 2d edit. 466; and 3 Bar. & Adol. 655; but see Ring *v.* Roxbrough, 2 Tyr. 468; 2 Crom. & J. 418, S. C. contra, where the declaration stated a promise to intestate on 2d of January, 1832, and yet stated that the grant of administration on 11th of January, 1831, held bad on special demurrer, *id. ibid.*; and in Hembrow *v.* Bailey, 3 Tyr. 152, it was held that *surplusage* in adding a special traverse was demurrable. So in Bishton *v.* Evans, 2 Crom. M. & Ros. 17, it was observed by Alderson, B, that the introduction of unnecessary matter into issues is forbidden, in order to prevent the parties from being embarrassed.

(*y*) Com. Dig. Pleader, C. 29; Bac. Ab. Pleas, I. 4; 3 Taunt. 139; 5 T. R. 496.

(*z*) Doug. 667. See 4 East, 100.

(*a*) 4 B. & C. 380.

without such an allegation. United States *v.* Porter, 3 Day, 283. So, in an indictment for burglary, in the house of J. D. *with intent to steal the goods of J. W.*, and it appeared in evidence that no such person had any goods in the house, but that the name of J. W. was put by mistake for J. D., the judges held that it was material to state truly the property of the goods, and on account of this variance the prisoner was acquitted. Jenks' Case, East's P. C. 514. Phillips' Ev. 160.

(513) Vide Thomas *v.* Roosa, 7 Johns. Rep. 462. Woodford *v.* Webster, 3 Day, 472. Tucker *v.* Randall, 2 Mass. Rep. 283. Chapman *v.* Smith, 13 Johns. Rep. 80. { Wilmarth et al. *v.* Mountford et al., 8 Serg. & Rawle, 124. 8 Cow. Rep. 42. }

(514) Vide Allaire *v.* Ouland, 2 Johns. Cas. 52.

(515) { The text in the fourth edition, after the quotation from Lord Mansfield's opinion, is as follows—"the distinction is between immaterial and impertinent averments, the former must be proved because relative to the point in question"—and Mr. Dunlap's note to the passage contained a reference to the following authorities: } Williamson *v.* Allison, 2 East's Rep. 451, 452. Wilson *v.* Codman's Exr., 3 Cranch, 193. Livingston et al. *v.* Swanwick, 2 Dall. 300. Peter *v.* Cocke, 1 Wash. 257. Phillips' Ev. 158, 159.

I. THE FACTS NECESSARY TO BE STATED.

is not bound to *prove* an immaterial allegation, unless he has, by his mode of pleading, so connected it with a material allegation as to make the latter depend upon it." And Mr. J. Holroyd said, "If the plaintiff state, as a cause of action, more than is necessary for the gist of the action, the jury may find so much proved, and so much not proved; and the Court would be bound to pronounce judgment for the plaintiff upon that verdict, *provided that the facts proved constituted a good cause of action.*" So in trespass for driving cattle, where the defendant justified that he was lawfully possessed of the close, and took the cattle *damage feasant* therein; and the plaintiff replied specially, title in another, and that he entered by his command, and unnecessarily gave color to the defendant; it was decided that this did not render the replication insufficient, because the introduction of unnecessary words of form will not vitiate the rest of a replication which is good (*b*).

In an action of replevin the defendants avowed the taking as a distress for rent due to one of them, (Sharr), under a demise, at £20 a year, payable quarterly, and the avowry averred that "because £10 *of the rent aforesaid* for two quarters, &c. at the time when, &c. was due from the *defendant*, (instead of plaintiff,) to the said Sharr, defendants *avow, &c. To this there was a special demurrer on account of the mistake of the word *defendant* for *plaintiff*. The court held, that the mistake was not a ground of demurrer, for the matter demurred to was superfluous and repugnant. They observed that it would have sufficed to have said that £10 of the rent aforesaid was due, without saying from whom to whom, as that was a conclusion from the previous allegation; and that surplusage is never assignable as cause of demurrer (*c*). The more recent decisions, however, establish that surplusage in tendering an *issue* or in *other part* of *pleading* tending to embarrass the opponent, may be assigned specially as cause of demurrer (*d*).

[*264]

It is a material part of the rule respecting superfluous allegations, that if the party introducing them show, on the face of his own pleading, that he has no cause of action, his pleading will be defective. Thus in an action upon the case for a disturbance of an easement, &c. it is sufficient in many

(*b*) 1 East, 212.

(*c*) Peirse *v.* Sharr and another, K. B. 7th June, 1827, before the three judges. Busby for the plaintiff, Chitty for the defendant, MS. The following are instances of untrue allegations having been rejected as surplusage, and therefore considered as not prejudicing the case, viz. an untrue description (in a plea in abatement) of the privilege of an attorney to be sued by bill in K. B., 9 East, 424; as misdescription in an action for a malicious prosecution, &c. of the record of acquittal with regard to the style of the Court, 2 Bla. Rep. 1050; 2 B. & C. 4, 5; or of the time of acquittal, 9 East, 157; or in stating the judgment of discontinuance, 13 East, 547. A variance in stating the names of the suitors of the County Court in averring in case against the sheriff, for taking insufficient sureties in a replevin bond that the tenant appeared at the next County Court held before the suitors, considered immaterial, 2 B. & C. 2 (516). The misdescription of judgment with regard to the term in which judgment was recovered is not material, and may be repudiated as surplusage, if the record be mere inducement, as in case for a false return, &c., 3 B. & C. 2. Distinction between allegations of matter of *substance*, and allegations of matter of *description*; the latter only to be literally proved, 3 B. & C. 4. Many other instances will be hereafter noticed in considering the doctrine of *variances*.

(*d*) *Ante*, 262, note (*x*). Hembrow *v.* Bailey, 3 Tyr. 152; Bishton *v.* Evans, 2 Cromp. M. & Ros. 16, 17.

(516) Aliter where it constitutes a material part of the plaintiff's case. Bevan *v.* Jones, 6 Dowl. & Ryl. 483.

cases to allege a possessory right, but if the plaintiff, instead of so doing, describe and rely upon a defective title, the declaration is bad (*e*). I. THE FACTS NECESSARY TO BE STATED.

So, though the superfluous or irrelevant allegation be *repugnant* to what was before alleged, it is void and will be rejected; and whatever is redundant, and which need not have been put into the sentence, and contradicting what was *before* alleged, will not in general vitiate the pleading (*f*). *For, *per* Holt, C. J. (*g*), "where matter is nonsense, by being contradictory, and repugnant to something precedent, there the precedent matter which is sense, shall not be defeated by the repugnancy which follows, but that which is contradictory shall be rejected." As in ejectment, where the declaration is of a demise the *second* of January, and that the defendant *postea scilicet* on the *first* of January, ejected him; here the *scilicet* may be rejected as being expressly contrary to the *postea* and the precedent matter (*h*). So where in assumpsit by executors, in a count for money paid by the testator, B. B. for the defendant's use, it was alleged that "the defendant being indebted, *he the said B. B.* promised to pay the said B. B." it was decided on special demurrer, that the words "he the said B. B." might be rejected as surplusage (*i*). But a material allegation, sensible and consistent in the place where it occurs, and not repugnant to any *antecedent* matter, cannot be rejected, merely on account of there occurring *afterwards*, in the same pleading, another allegation inconsistent with the former, and which latter allegation cannot itself be rejected (*k*); and if by the rejection of the repugnant matter, the pleading would be left without an allegation of time, or other material matter, though in some instances the pleading might be aided by verdict, yet it would be defective on special demurrer (*l*). [*265]

The *general* rule is, that a pleading inconsistent with itself, or repugnant, is objectionable (*m*). In trespass, the plaintiff declared for taking and carrying away certain timber, lying in a certain place for the completion of a house "then lately built:" this declaration was considered bad for repugnancy, for the timber could not be for the building of a house already built (*n*). So if a count in assumpsit lay a promise to pay a specific sum, if the plaintiff would provide E. with necessaries, and also a promise to pay so much as the plaintiff reasonably deserved to have on the same account, such count is bad, not only for duplicity, but also for inconsistency or uncertainty (*o*). It is only where the repugnancy is contained in an allegation capable of rejection as superfluous, *or where there is a prior averment upon the subject, which is adequate [*266] to the support of the case, that it becomes of no moment, and unobjectionable even upon demurrer. In some cases the Courts will on motion order superfluous matter to be struck out of the pleadings, and if there be any vexation, will make the party inserting it pay the costs of the application (*p*).

(*e*) 1 Salk. 363, 365; Com. Dig. Pleader, C. 22.

(*f*) Gilb. C. P. 131, 132; Co. Lit. 303 b; 10 East, 142.

(*g*) 1 Salk. 324, 325; Vin. Ab. Nonsense, A. pl. 3.

(*h*) *Id.*; 5 East, 255; and see *ante*, 263.

(*i*) 11 Moore, 552.

(*k*) 5 East, 254, 132, 133; 10 East, 142; Vin. Ab. Nonsense, A. pl. 3.

(*l*) Gilb. C. P. 131, 132.

(*m*) Steph. on Pleading, 2d edit. 420. Instance of repugnancy in stating time and place, 14 East, 291.

(*n*) 1 Salk. 213.

(*o*) 7 Mod. 148.

(*p*) See Tidd, 9th ed. 616, 617, 1132; 1 B. & B. 281; 1 Bla. Rep. 270; Stephen, 2d edit. 467.

II. THE MODES OF STATING THE FACTS.

II. MODES OF STATING FACTS.

Having considered *what facts* are to be stated in pleading, we have now to consider the *manner* in which they should be stated. The facts which constitute the cause of action, or ground of defence, should be stated logically in their natural order; as on the part of the plaintiff, his right, the injury, and the consequent damage, and these with certainty, precision, and brevity (*q*). A general statement of facts which admits of almost any proof to sustain it is objectionable (*r*). With regard to the language to be adopted, as observed by Lord C. J. De Grey (*s*), "there are cases where a direct and positive averment is necessary to be made in specific terms, as where the law has affixed and appropriated technical terms to describe a crime, as in murder, burglary, and others;" so in trespass, the words *vi et armis*, and *contra pacem* are necessary; "but except in particular cases, where precise technical expressions are required to be used, there is no rule of law that other words should be employed than such as are in ordinary use, or that in pleadings a different sense is to be put upon them than what they bear in ordinary acceptation." (*t*) Thus, though in a declaration for slander it is usual to state that the words were "maliciously" spoken, the word "falsely" has been held to be sufficiently expressive of a malicious intent (*u*). However, where there has been a long-established form of pleading, applicable to the facts of the particular case, it
[*267] should in general, for the *sake of certainty and uniformity, be adopted, and the Courts censure any unnecessary deviation from it (*x*). As observed by Lord Coke, it is safer to follow good precedents, for *nihil simul inventum est, et perfectum* (*y*); and there are cases where, although the Court have overruled a demurrer, yet they have directed the plaintiff to amend, so that no deviation from the usual form shall appear to have been sanctioned (*z*). The statute (*a*) requires, that all the pleadings and proceedings shall be in English; a regulation which, it has been observed, has occasioned the literature of the inferior part of the profession to recede (*b*).

Of the degree of certainty required.

The principal rule, as to the mode of stating the facts, is, that they must be set forth with *certainty* (*c*)(517); by which term is signified, a clear and distinct statement of the facts which constitute the cause of action or ground of

(*q*) Dougl. 666 667; Sir W. Jones, vol. iv. p. 34, 4to edit.; see Stephen on Pleading, 378 to 405.

(*r*) 1 M. & Sel. 441; 3 *Id.* 114; 1 M. & M. 218; 11 Price, 235.

(*s*) Cowp. 683.

(*t*) *Per* Lord Ellenborough, 5 East, 259, 260; 2 East, 33; 2 Bla. Rep. 843; *ante*, 251.

(*u*) 1 Saund. 242 a, note (2); 1 M. & Sel. 304.

(*x*) Co Lit. 303 a, b; 1 Hale, 1, L. 301, 302; 6 East, 351 to 353; Cro. Jac. 386; 1 M. & Sel. 439, 441; and see *ante*, 109, 110; 8 Co. 48 b; Com. Dig. Abatement, G. 7; Plowd. 123; 2 B. & P. 577; 3 B. & Ald. 453; Steph. 1st ed. 391; 2d ed. 434.

(*y*) Co. Lit. 230 a. "Precedent and practice ought to have great weight in the consideration of all points arising upon the propriety of forms, and in all legal instruments." *Per* Eldon, C., 11 Price, 193.

(*z*) 1 B. & P. 336; Barnes, 167.

(*a*) 4 Geo. 2. c. 26.

(*b*) 1 M. & Sel. 710, 711.

(*c*) Cowp. 682; Hob. 295. It was observed by Lord C. J. De Grey, in Rex *v.* Horne, Cowp. 682, that we have no precise idea of the signification of the term "certainty," which is as indefinite in itself as any word that can be used. See in general, Steph. 2d ed. 381.

(517) Vide Carpenter *v.* Alexander, 9 Johns. Rep. 291. Ward *v.* Clark, 2 Johns. Rep. 12. Jacobs Nelson, 3 Taunton, 423.

defence, so that they may be understood by the party who is to answer them, by the jury who are to ascertain the truth of the allegations, and by the Court who are to give judgment (*d*).

II. MODE OF STATING FACTS.

Of the certainty required.

In *Dovaston* v. *Payne* (*e*), Mr. Justice Buller observed, that certainty or precision in pleading has been stated by Lord Coke (*f*) to be of three sorts, *viz.* 1st, certainty to a common intent; 2dly, to a certain intent in general; 3dly, to a certain intent in every particular; and that though these distinctions had been treated by Mr. Justice Aston as a jargon of words without meaning, they had long been made, and ought not altogether to be departed from.

[*268] *By certainty to a *common intent*, is to be understood, that when words are used which will bear a natural sense, and also an artificial one, or one to be made out by argument or inference, the natural sense shall prevail; it is simply a rule of construction, and not of addition; common intent cannot add to a sentence words which are omitted (*g*). This description of certainty is sufficient in a plea in bar (*h*)(518). It is of the lowest degree, and yet we shall find, that in some instances, a statement which will suffice in a declaration will not in a plea; thus in a declaration on a contract to pay the debt of a third person, it is not necessary to show that it was in writing (519), but it is said to be otherwise in a plea (*i*); and in a plea, the statement of a deed by way of recital "*testatum existit*," instead of a direct allegation, is insufficient; though it is otherwise in a declaration (*k*).

Certainty to a *certain intent in general* is a greater degree of certainty than the last, and means what upon a fair and reasonable construction may be called certain, without recurring to *possible* facts (520) which do not appear (*521*); and is what is required in declarations (522), replications, and indictments in the charge or accusation, and in returns to writs of mandamus (*l*). The charge, we have seen, must contain such a description of the crime, &c. that without intending any thing but what appears, the defendant may know what he is to answer, and what is intended to be proved, in order that the jury may be warranted in their verdict, and the Court in the judgment they are to give (*m*).

The *third* degree of certainty, is that which precludes all argument, inference, or presumption against the party pleading (*n*); and, as it has been

(*d*) Cowp. 682; Com. Dig. Pleader, C. 17; Co. Lit. 303; 2 B. & P. 267; another reason is, that in a second action for the same cause, the defendant may be better able to plead a former recovery, &c., 13 East, 107.

(*e*) 2 Hen. Bla. 530; Dougl. 158, 159.

(*f*) Co. Lit. 303 a; 5 Co. 121.

(*g*) 2 Hen. Bla. 530; 1 Saund. 49, note 1.

(*h*) *Id.*; Cowp. 682; Dougl. 158; 5 Co. 121; Co. Lit. 303 a; Com. Dig. Pleader, C. 17; Steph. 2d ed. 423.

(*i*) 1 Saund. 276 e, note (2); Sir T. Raym. 450; *ante*, 254.

(*k*) 1 Saund. 274. n (1).

(*l*) Dougl. 159; 13 East, 107.

(*m*) Cowp. 682.

(*n*) Co. Lit. 352 b; Dougl. 159.

(518) Acc. Spencer *v.* Southwick, 9 Johns. Rep. 314.

(519) Vide ante, 228. Elting *v.* Vanderlyn, 4 Johns. Rep. 237, ibid. 339 n. a. The contract is required to be stated more precisely in a plea of usury, than in a declaration in a qui tam suit, because the facts are within the defendant's knowledge. Lawrence *v.* Kines, 10 Johns. Rep. 142.

(520) Vide Spencer *v.* Southwick, 9 Johns. Rep. 317.

(521) { Buller *v.* Hampton, 5 Conn. Rep. 423. }

(522) Sed Vide Hildreth *v.* Becker, 2 Johns. Cas. 339, where it is said, that in a declaration, certainty to a common intent is sufficient; Rex *v.* Horne, Cowp. 682, is cited, which authority, however, establishes directly the reverse. And see Coffin *v.* Coffin, 2 Mass. Rep. 363, *per* PARSONS, C. J., that certainty to a common intent is sufficient.

II. MODE OF STATING FACTS. — Of the certainty required.

well expressed, is that technical accuracy, which is not liable to the most subtle and scrupulous objection, so that it is not merely a rule of construction, but of addition: for when this certainty is necessary, the party must not only state the facts of his case, in the most precise way, but add to them such facts, as show that they are not to be controverted, and, as it were, anticipate [*269] the case of his adversary (o). It has been said, that this description of *certainty has been rejected in all cases, as partaking of too much subtlety (p); however, Buller, J., expressed a different opinion; and it appears, that it obtains in the case of estoppels (q), and in pleas which are not favored in law, such as the plea of alien enemy, in which it must be stated, not only that the plaintiff is an alien, but that he came to England without letters of safe conduct (523) from our king (r).

The application of the rules as to the necessary certainty in the various parts of pleadings, will be better considered, when the qualities of the declaration and other parts of pleading are stated. It must be confessed that it is frequently difficult in practice to apply the rules to cases which occur.

Less certainty is requisite when the law presumes that the knowledge of the facts is more *properly* or *peculiarly* in the opposite party (s). Therefore, where in an action on the case for not repairing a private road leading through the defendant's ground, the declaration stated that the defendant, by reason of his possession, ought to have repaired, &c., on general demurrer it was objected, that it did not show by what right or obligation the defendant was bound to repair, and that he was not bound of common right merely as an occupier, but the Court held that the declaration was sufficient; and Buller, J., said, the distinction is between cases where the plaintiff lays a charge upon the right of the defendant, and where the defendant himself prescribes in right of his own estate; in the former case the plaintiff is presumed to be ignorant of the defentant's title, and cannot therefore plead it, but in the latter, the defendant, knowing his own estate, in right of which he claims a privilege, must set forth such estate (t) (524). So, in a declaration against the assignee of a lease it is sufficient to aver generally that "the remainder of the term and estate of the lessee, &c. came to the defendant by assignment," as the plaintiff cannot reasonably be presumed to know the particulars of the defendant's title (u). So, less certainty is required, and general words are sufficient, where it is to be presumed that the party pleading is not acquainted with the minute [*270] circumstances (x). *Thus, where a person's house is burnt, general words are

(o) Lawes on Plead. 54, 55.
(p) Cowp. 682.
(q) 2 H. Bl. 530; Doug. 159; Com. Dig. Estoppel, E. 4; Co. Lit. 352 b; see 2 B. & Ald. 662.
(r) 8 T. R. 167.
(s) 13 East, 112; Com. Dig. Pleader, C. 26; 8 East, 85; 3 M. & Sel. 14; *ante*, 254; Steph. 413, 2d ed.
(t) 3 T. R. 766.
(u) 5 B. & C. 482.
(x) Steph. 2d edit. 411 to 413.

(523) Vide Clarke *v.* Morey, 10 Johns. Rep. 70. That this allegation is not alone sufficient, vide id. ibid. Russell *v.* Skipwith, 6 Binn. 247. {See also Bagwell *v.* Babe, 1 Rand. Rep. 270, {and Coxe *v.* Gulick, 5 Halst. Rep. 328.}

(524) In an action against the surety on an administration bond, it is sufficient for the plaintiff to state that goods, chattels, and sums of money to a large amount, to wit, the amount of, &c. had come into the hands of the administrator, which he had converted to his own use; the creditor not being presumed to know precisely what assets the administrator had, and this fact lying more properly in the knowledge of the defendant. The People *v.* Dunlap, 13 Johns. Rep. 437.

II. MODE OF STATING FACTS. — Of the certainty required.

sufficient in the description of goods thereby destroyed, because he is not presumed to be able to set forth with certainty the goods destroyed (y). So, in trespass for breaking, &c. a close with cattle and eating the plaintiff's peas there, the quantity eaten need not be stated (z). But in a declaration on the Statute of Hue and Cry the plaintiff must state the particulars of his goods taken (a).

It is also a rule of pleading, that where a subject comprehends multiplicity of matter, and a great variety of facts, there, in order to avoid prolixity, the law allows general pleading (b) (525). Thus an allegation in a declaration for necessaries supplied to a third person, at the defendant's request, or in a replication to a plea of infancy, that "necessaries" were supplied, is sufficient, without showing specially what the necessaries were (c). And in charging in a declaration, that a party has not accounted for sums he received in any particular capacity from time to time, it is sufficient to allege generally that from time to time he received divers sums, amounting to a certain sum, not stating on what particular days, or from named persons, and hath not accounted &c. (d). As there are many instances in which this rule does not apply, especially in justifications of slander, and very often in pleas of performance, we will hereafter give the rule further consideration in treating of the particular parts of pleading (e).

It will be explained in a subsequent part of the work, that much particularity is required in the statement of *special* damage.

When the facts are not really stated with sufficient certainty, the introduction of the word "*certain*" is of no avail (f). Thus a declaration in debt for a sum of money forfeited *"by virtue of a *certain* by-law," or "for money due on a *certain* bond," without stating it, is insufficient (g). So where the declaration stated that in consideration that the plaintiff had sold to the defendant a "certain" horse of the plaintiff, at and for "a certain quantity of certain oil," to be delivered within a "certain time," which had elapsed, though it was holden that the declaration was good after verdict, it was considered that it could not have been supported on demurrer (h). And a justification in trespass, "by virtue of a certain writ," &c. but not setting it forth, is insufficient (i)(526). So the words "duly," "lawfully," "sufficient," &c. without showing the matter of fact with convenient certainty, are seldom of avail in plead- [*271]

(y) Bac. Ab. Pleas, B. 5; 1 Keb. 825; Plowd. 85; *sed vide* 2 Saund. 379.

(z) Bac. Ab. Pleas, B. 5.

(a) 2 Saund. 379.

(b) 1 T. R. 753, *per* Buller, J., 2 Saund. 411, n. 4; 1 *Id.* 116, 117, n. 1; Bac. Ab. Pleas, I. 3, B. 5; Com. Dig. Pleader, C. 42, E. 26; 1 B. & P. 640; Co. Lit. 303 b, 304; Stephen, 2d ed. 400. "No greater particularity is required than the nature of the thing pleaded will conveniently admit" Stephen, 2d ed. 411: *Vide* the instances there put in illustration of this rule; and 3 Bing. 61; *ante*, 258, as to pleading a custom or right at "reasonable times, &c."

(c) 3 Bulstr. 31; Carth. 110.

(d) 1 B. & P. 640; 8 T. R. 459; 2 Burr. 772; Stephen, 2d ed. 402.

(e) *Vide* Index, "*Certainty.*"

(f) 13 East, 102. As to the word "reasonable," 3 Bing. 61, 67.

(g) 1 B. & P. 98, 102; see 2 B. & P. 120; 13 East, 116.

(h) 2 B. & P. 265.

(i) 1 Saund. 298, note 1.

(525) Vide Hughes *v.* Smith and Miller, 5 Johns. Rep. 173. So, in declaring on a policy of insurance on specified goods, it is sufficient to aver that *divers goods* were put on board. De Symons *v.* Johnston, 2 New Rep. 77.

(526) Sed vide Bennet *v.* The Executors of Pixley, 7 Johns. Rep. 249.

II. MODE OF STATING FACTS. — Of the certainty required.

ing (k) (527). So a plea justifying an imprisonment, on the ground of a suspicion of felony, should state the grounds of suspicion, and the averment, that the plaintiff "suspiciously" did such an act, is not sufficient (l). But in some cases the statement that the defendant "unlawfully" or "unjustly," &c. did the wrong complained of, without showing the particular acts, may be sufficient to designate that to be a crime or injury, which might otherwise stand indifferent; as in an action on the case for unlawfully procuring a wife to leave her husband (m). The want of certainty (n), and an ambiguous expression in a declaration (o), are cured by verdict.

To these rules affecting the *mode* of stating facts, may be added the following, which are ably collected and observed upon by Mr. Serjeant Stephen, in his valuable work on Pleading (p); viz.: that pleadings must not be insensible (q) or repugnant (r); nor ambiguous or doubtful in meaning (s); [*272] *nor argumentative (t); nor in the *alternative*. However, the recent pleading rules of Hil. T. 4 W. 4, reg. I. permit *in one case* an *alternative* allegation, as that several named persons, "*or some or one of them were, or was,*" interested in the property insured by a policy of insurance, which exception was introduced in order to avoid several counts varying the statement of the interest in the subject insured (u). The other rules are, that pleadings must not be hypothetical (v); nor by way of recital, but positive (x), and that things should be stated according to their *legal effect or operation* (y). These rules, indeed, will be more fully considered hereafter in those parts of the work which treat of the qualities of declarations and the other parts of pleadings in particular.

(k) 9 Co. 25 a; 1 Burr. 540; Dougl. 79; 7 B. & C. 468; 8 *Id.* 124. In an action on a bond conditioned to perform an award to be made under *the hands* of referees, an averment that they "duly made their award," is not sufficient. Everard *v.* Paterson, 6 Taunt. 645; 2 Marsh. 304, S. C.; see 16 East, 39; 7 B. & C. 800.

(l) 4 Taunt. 34; 2 Bing. 123; Steph. 2d ed. 386, 387.

(m) Willes, 577.

(n) 2 B. & P. 265; 3 Bing. 61.

(o) 1 B. & C. 297; Cowp. 825.

(p) 1st ed. 378 to 392; 2d ed. 420 to 434.

(q) Com. Dig. Pleader, C. 23; 1 Salk. 324; Vin. Ab. Nonsense, A. pl. 3; see, however, *ante*, 263.

(r) See *ante*, 264.

(s) Co. Lit. 303 b; Yelv. 36; 2 H. Bl. 530; 5 M. & Sel. 38; 1 Bar. & Cress. 297; 3 *Id.* 192; and also examine, Stephen, 2d edit. 421. Thus in trespass, a plea that the close was defendant's freehold, not stating "at the time of the trespass," is bad. Com. Dig. Pleader, E. 5.

(t) Bac. Ab. Pleas, &c. I. 5; Com. Dig. (E. 3); Co. Lit. 303 a; 5 B. & A. 215. In trespass *de bonis asportatis* a plea that plaintiff never had any goods is bad. Doct. pl. 41; Dyer, 43 a. Other instances, Stephen, 426, 2d ed.; 10 East, 205.

(u) Reg. Gen. Hil. Term, 4 W. 4, Pleadings in Particular Actions, reg. I.

(v) 1 B. & P. 413; 3 M. & S. 114; Steph. 430, 2d ed. If "*any*" is bad on special demurrer, Gould *v.* Lashbury, 4 Tyr. 863. Therefore a plea to assumpsit for goods sold and delivered and on an account stated, that the defendant was discharged from the causes of action in the declaration mentioned, *if any such there were*, was held bad on special demurrer, as hypothetically pleaded, and as not directly confessing and avoiding the alleged causes of action, *id. ibid.*

(x) Bac. Ab. Pleas, &c. (B.); 4 Steph. 1st ed. 388; 2d ed. 431. Mr. Serjeant Stephen states, as instances of this rule, that it is bad in trespass to charge that "whereas" the defendant assaulted, &c.: and that in a *plea*, in stating a grant by deed, it should not be stated that "it was witnessed" by the deed that the party granted.

(y) Bac. Ab. Pleas, &c. 1, 7; Com. Dig. Pleader, C. 37; 2 Saund. 97 b, n. 2; 1 *Id.* 235 b. note 9; 3 B. & A. 66; Steph. 1st ed. 389; 2d ed. 432.

(527) So, in false imprisonment, the defendant attempted to justify the arrest on a suspicion of forgery, and stated in his plea that the plaintiff was suspiciously possessed of a note, and disposed of it in a suspicious manner, and in a suspicious manner left England and went to Scotland: the plea was held too general, and that the causes of suspicion ought to have been set forth in certainty. Mure *v.* Kaye, 4 Taunt. 31. See also Van Ness *v.* Hamilton et al., 19 Johns. Rep. 349.

III. THE RULES OF CONSTRUING PLEADINGS.

III. RULES OF CONSTRUCTION.

It is a maxim in pleading, that every thing shall be taken most strongly against the party pleading (z), or rather, that if the meaning of the words be equivocal, and two meanings present themselves, that construction shall be adopted which is most unfavorable to the party pleading (a); because it is to be presumed that every person states his case as favorably to himself as possible (b)(528). But in applying this maxim, the other rules must be kept in view, and particularly those relating to the degree of certainty or precision required in pleading (c). The maxim must be received with this qualification, that the language of the pleading is to have a reasonable intendment and construction (d)(529); and where an expression is capable *of different meanings, that shall be taken which will support the declaration, &c. and not the other, which would defeat it (e). [*273] Thus, in debt on bond, conditioned to procure J. S. to surrender a copyhold "to the use of the plaintiff," a plea that J. S. surrendered and released the copyhold to the plaintiff in full Court, and that the plaintiff accepted it, without alleging that the surrender was "to the plaintiff's use," is sufficient; for this shall be intended (f). So in debt on bond, conditioned that the plaintiff shall enjoy certain land, &c. a plea, that "after the making of the bond, until the day of exhibiting the bill," the plaintiff did enjoy, is good, though it be not alleged that *continually* during that time he enjoyed; for this is intended (g).

But the matter must be *capable* of different meanings; for the Court cannot, *in order to* support the proceeding, in which the particular term occurs, arbitrarily give it a meaning against which the use, habits, and understanding of mankind would plainly revolt (530). But if it *be clearly capable* of different meanings, it does not appear to clash with any rule of construction, applied even to criminal proceedings, to construe it in that sense, in which the party framing the charge must be understood to have used it, if he intended that his

(z) 1 Saund. 259, note 8; 2 B. & P. 155; Co. Lit. 303 b; Yelv. 36; 2 Hen. Bla. 530; 5 M. & S. 38, 40; Stephen 1st ed 379; 2d edit. 421; and cases there collected.

(a) *Per* Buller, J., 2 Hen. Bla. 530; 6 B. & C. 302; Steph. 2d edit. 421. Instances of this in a plea, *id.* and *post.*

(b) Co. Lit. 303 b. *Per* Parke, B., in Pearce *v.* Champneys, 3 Dowl. 276. The same rule holds in construing *deeds*, &c.; Platt on Cov. 141.

(c) *Ante*, 267; as to rule of *reddendo singula singulis*, see 2 Campb. 139.

(d) Com. Dig. Pleader, C. 25; 1 Lev. 190; *per* Lord Ellenborough, 5 East, 259, 260; 12 *Id.* 263.

(e) 4 Taunt. 492; 1 Salk. 325; 5 East, 244, 257; 12 East, 270. As to the effect of "*prædictus*" and "*idem*," and construction of them, see 11 East, 513. So in the case of a *deed*, exposition shall be made of it so as to support rather than annul the transaction; *ut res magis valeat quam pereat*; Shep. Touch. 166; 3 Atk 136.

(f) Cro. Car. 6.

(g) *Id.* 195; Steph. 2d edit. 423.

---

(528) Fuller *v.* Hampton, 5 Conn. R. 422, 423.

(529) Vide Hastings *v.* Wood and Curtis, 13 Johns. Rep. 482.

(530) And this is the rule in regard to actions for words, either spoken or written, that the court is to understand them according to their ordinary acceptation among mankind. Backus *v.* Richardson, 5 Johns. Rep. 584. Woolmoth *v.* Meadows, 5 East's Rep. 463. Roberts *v.* Camden, 9 East's Rep. 93. Respublica *v.* De Longchamps, 1 Dall. 114. Rue *v.* Mitchell, 2 Dall. 59. Brown *v.* Lamberton, 2 Binn. 37. Pelton *v.* Ward, 3 Caines' Rep. 76. {See the subject very fully discussed, Walton *v.* Singleton, 7 Serg. & Rawle, 449.} But still the meaning of the words must be unequivocal. Harrison *v.* Stratton, 4 Esp. Rep. 218.

III. RULES OF CONSTRUCTION. charge should be consistent with itself (*h*). Every indictment, &c. ought to contain a complete description of such facts and circumstances as constitute the crime, &c. without inconsistency or repugnancy; but, except in particular cases where precise technical expressions are required to be used, there is no rule that other words shall be employed than such as are in ordinary use, or that in indictments or other pleadings a different sense is to be put upon them than what they bear in ordinary acceptation. And if, where the sense may be ambiguous, it is sufficiently marked by the context, or other means, in what sense they are intended to be used, no objection can be made on the ground of *repugnancy*, which only exists where a sense is annexed to words which is
[*274] either absolutely inconsistent therewith, or being apparently *so, is not accompanied by any thing to explain or define them. If the sense be clear, nice exceptions ought not to be regarded (*i*). It is also a rule relating to the mode of stating facts, and the form of the pleading on either side, that the Court are *ex officio* bound after verdict to give such judgment as appears upon the *whole* record to be proper, without regard to the issues found or confessed, or to any imperfection in the prayer of judgment on either side (*k*)(531); and on the same ground we shall hereafter see, that when there is a demurrer to a plea, replication, &c. if the prior pleading be defective in substance, judgment will be given against the party pleading it. After verdict, an expression must be construed in such sense as would sustain the verdict (*l*): and although in general in pleading, an equivocal expression is to be construed against the party using it, yet where the opposite party has *pleaded over*, that is an admission that the expression is to be taken in that sense which will support the previous pleading (*m*). These rules will be fully explained hereafter. Words of reference, as "*there*" and "*said*" in an indictment, will not be referred to the last antecedent where the sense requires that they should be referred to some prior antecedent (*n*).

IV. THE DIVISION OF PLEADINGS.

IV. DIVISION OF PLEADINGS. The *parts* of pleading have been considered as arrangeable under two heads; *first*, the regular, being those which occur in the ordinary course of a suit; and *secondly*, the irregular, or collateral, being those which are occasioned by mistakes in the pleadings on either side (*o*).

The *regular* parts are, 1st. The *declaration* or count.—2dly. The *plea*, which is either to the jurisdiction of the court; or in suspension of the action, as in the case of parol demurrer; or in abatement; or in bar of the action;

(*h*) *Per* Lord Ellenborough, C. J., 5 East, 257. See *id.* 463.

(*i*) *Per* Lord Ellenborough, C. J., 5 East, 259, 260; 2 East, 33.

(*k*) 4 East, 502; 5 *Id.* 270, 271; 10 *Id.* 87.

(*l*) 1 B. & C. 297; Cowp. 825; 6 B. & C. 302, 303.

(*m*) Wright *v.* The King, 3 Nev. & Man. 892.

(*n*) 6 B. & C. 295.

(*o*) Vin. Ab. Pleas, &c. C.; Bac. Ab. Pleas, &c. A.

(531) Vide Havens *v.* Bush, 2 Johns. Rep. 387. King *v.* Harrison, 15 East's Rep. 614, 615.

or in replevin, an avowry or cognizance.—3dly. The *replication*; and in case of an evasive plea, a *new assignment*; or in replevin, the *plea in bar* to the avowry or cognizance.—4thly. The *rejoinder*; or in replevin, the replication to the plea in bar.—5thly. The *surrejoinder*, being in replevin the rejoinder.—6thly. The *rebutter*.—7thly. The *surrebutter*.—And 8thly, *Pleas puis darrein continuance*, where the matter of defence arises *pending* the suit. IV. DIVISION OF PLEADINGS.

*The *irregular* or *collateral* parts of pleading are stated to be (*p*), 1st. *Demurrers* to any part of the pleadings above-mentioned.—2dly. *Demurrers to evidence* given at trials.—3dly. *Bills of Exceptions*.—4thly. *Pleas* in *scire facias*.—And 5thly. *Pleas in error*. The particular nature of each of these parts of pleading, together with the *claim of conusance*, *demand of oyer*, and *imparlances*, &c. will be considered in the following chapters. [*275]

(*p*) Vin. Ab. Pleas, &c. C.

*CHAPTER IV.

Of the Declaration (a).

I. DEFINITION AND DIVISION OF SUBJECT.
II. THE RECENT REGULATIONS AFFECTING THE FORM OF DECLARATIONS.
III. THE GENERAL REQUISITES AND QUALITIES OF DECLARATIONS.
IV. THE FORMS AND PARTICULAR PARTS AND REQUISITES OF DECLARATIONS.

I. THE DEFINITION AND DIVISION OF THE SUBJECT.

1. DEFINITION AND DIVISION OF SUBJECT.

A DECLARATION is a specification in a methodical and legal form of the circumstances which constitute the plaintiff's *cause of action* (*b*), which necessarily consists of the statement of a legal *right*, or in other words a right recognized in Courts of Law, and not merely in a Court of Equity, and of an *injury* to such right remediable at law by *action* as distinguished from the remedy by Bill in Equity. A declaration may conveniently be examined with reference to *Secondly, the Recent Alterations*, which must be observed in practice in addition to or as variations from the previously established forms; *Thirdly* to those *General Requisites* and *Qualities* which govern the *whole* declaration in general, and *Fourthly* to the *Forms* and *Parts*, and *particular Requisites*, as well in *Assumpsit*, *Debt*, *Covenant and Detinue*, as in *Case*, *Trover*, *Replevin*, *Trespass* and *Ejectment*.

[*277]

*II. THE RECENT ALTERATIONS AFFECTING DECLARATIONS IN GENERAL.

2. The recent alterations affecting declarations in general.

Before the uniformity of process act, 2 W. 4, c. 39, there were very numerous and perplexing modes of commencing *personal actions*, viz. by *original writ* issued out of Chancery and returnable in the Courts of King's Bench or Common Pleas, (but not in the Court of Exchequer); by bill of Middlesex or latitat, issued out of and returnable in K. B. by writ of *capias quare clausum fregit*, issued out of and returnable in the Court of Common Pleas, and by *quo minus* or *venire*, issued out of and returnable in the Court of Exchequer; and numerous other writs in each of those Courts by or against attornies or officers of the court and other persons. By one or other of these

(a) As to the proper *instructions* for declarations, and the *time* when the plaintiff may or must declare, and other *practical* points, see fully Chitty's General Practice, vol. iii. 429 to 497.

(b) Co. Lit. 17 a, 303 a; Bac. Ab. Pleas, B.; Com. Dig. Pleader, C. 7; Heath's Maxims, 1, 2.

process, the defendant was always actually or supposed to be brought into Court to answer the plaintiff, and after appearance, the plaintiff declared, and the *commencement* of the declaration used to state how or by what process the defendant had then been brought into Court, and consequently the commencements of declarations were infinitely various. The original writ and *capias* thereon in assumpsit, case and trespass used to state the cause of action as fully as the declaration, with the exception of time and quantity, and therefore formerly special pleaders used to frame the special original writ as requiring as much skill in pleading as the declaration itself. And except in debt and in a few other actions, the declaration used afterwards to recite the writ verbatim, and repeat it in the count with time and enumeration of all circumstances, until at length one of the first of the very recent improvements (*c*) ordered that a declaration in trespass or ejectment, on a supposed original writ, should no longer recite the writ or supposed writ, but should merely in the commencement state that the defendant was attached to answer the plaintiff "in a plea of trespass" or a "plea of trespass and ejectment," and thereupon the plaintiff by Y. Z. his attorney, complains, &c. setting out the declaration; and this more concise form is still to be observed in a declaration in *ejectment* on a supposed original in K. B. and C. P., although in *personal* actions, as the use of an original writ was abolished by 2 W. 4, c. 39, this last rule has now become of no use though it still applies in ejectment.

II. MODES OF STATING FACTS.

At length the above statute, 2 W. 4, c. 39, having abolished the use of an original writ and of all the other *mesne process* in *personal actions*, and substituted several other prescribed forms of writs in *personal* actions, printed in the *schedule to* the act, viz. the writ of summons, writ of distringas, writ of capias, *writ of* detainer, and writ of summons against an M. P. when a trader (*d*), it became desirable that the judges should, for the sake of uniformity, prescribe new forms of *commencing* a declaration according to the particular writ that had been issued, and accordingly we find such forms prescribed by Reg. Gen. Mich. Term, 3 W. 4, reg. 15, which orders, "that every declaration shall in future be entitled in the *proper Court* and of *the day of the month and year in which it is filed* or delivered, and shall commence as follows.

Reg. Gen. Mich. T. 3 W. 4, as to *Title of Court* and *Date*.

**Declaration after Summons.* [*278]

Prescribed forms of commencements (*e*).

[*Venue*].—*A. B.*, by *E. F.*, his attorney, [*or*, in his own proper person], complains of *C. D.*, who has been summoned to answer the said *A. B.*, &c.

Declaration after Arrest, where the Party is not in Custody.

[*Venue*].—*A. B.*, by *E. F.*, his attorney [*or*, in his own proper person], complains of *C. D.*, who has been arrested at the suit of the said *A. B.*, &c.

Declaration where the Party is in Custody.

[*Venue*].—*A. B.*, by *E. F.*, his attorney, [*or*, in his own proper person], complains of *C. D.* being detained at the suit of *A. B.*, in the custody of the

(*c*) Reg. Gen. Hil. Term, 2 W. 4, reg. 4.

(*d*) The statute provides that the writ of summons shall now be issued as well against ordinary persons as against attornies, officers of the Court, corporations, or hundredors, and privileged persons, excepting when sued as an M. P. being a trader, against whom the writ varies in a small respect.

(*e*) See the forms fully, *post*, vol. ii.

II. MODES OF STATING FACTS. Sheriff, [*or*, the Marshal of the *Marshalsea* of the Court of *King's Bench*, or the Warden of the *Fleet*.]

Declaration after the Arrest of one or more Defendant or Defendants, and where one or more other Defendant or Defendants shall have been served only, and not arrested.

[*Venue.*]—*A. B.*, by *E. F.*, his attorney, [*or*, in his own proper person], complains of *C. D.*, who has been arrested at the suit of the said *A. B.*, [or, "being detained at the suit of the said *A. B.*, *&c*," *as before*], and of *G. H.*, who has been served with a writ of *capias* to answer the said *A. B.*, &c.

The Reg. Gen. Hil. T. 4 W. 4, reg. 4, promulgated in consequence of the enactment in 3 & 4 W. 4. c. 42, sect. 16, prescribes a particular form of *commencing* a declaration in a second action after a plea in abatement of non-joinder in a prior action.

Prescribed *conclusion* of declaration. From the succinct form of *conclusion* of a declaration prescribed by Reg. Gen. Trin. T. 1 W. 4, it seems that in all personal actions the form should be thus, and without adding any supposed *pledges*, and the addition of which is expressly prohibited by Reg. Gen. Hil. T. 4 W. 4.

"To the plaintiff's damage of £——, and thereupon he brings suit, &c." If the action be at the suit of assignees or executors, &c., then say to the plaintiff's damage "as assignees," or as executors as aforesaid. And in an action *qui tam* omit all statement of damage.

Venue in margin but not in body. The Reg. Gen. Hil. T. 4 W. 4, reg. 8, orders that the name of a County shall in all cases be stated in the *margin* of a declaration, and shall be taken to be the *venue* intended by the plaintiff, and that *no venue* shall be stated in the *body* of the declaration or in any subsequent pleadings, provided that in cases where local description is now required the same shall be given; and a subsequent part of the rules of Hil. T. 4 W. 4, requires that in actions of trespass *quare clausum fregit*, the close or place in which, &c., must be designated in the declaration by *name* or *abuttals*, or other description, in failure whereof the defendant may demur specially.

Name or abuttals in trespass quare clausum fregit.

Conciseness in some forms prescribed and intended to be extended to all cases. In order to render pleadings in actions of assumpsit, or debt on bills of exchange, inland or foreign, and promissory notes, and for common money demands, more concise, Reg. Gen. Trin. Term, 1 W. 4, prescribes certain forms of such declaration, and punishes the plaintiff's attorney with the loss of costs in case the declaration exceed the prescribed length (*d*). These rules, introduced by Lord Tenterden, were intended not merely to be observed and adopted in the particular cases strictly within the terms of the rule, but to encourage similar conciseness *in all other cases*. It is to be observed, that the word *said*, before plaintiff or defendant, is to be omitted, and only the word "*promised*" is to be used instead of "undertook and then and there faithfully promised;" "*request*" instead of "special instance and request," and numerous other concise expressions, instead of a superfluity of words, which especially when often repeated, when there were numerous counts, considerably augmented the aggregate length of the declaration, and afterwards the issue and *nisi prius* record. This rule has introduced a practice of

(*d*) See the rule and forms, *post*, vol. ii.

conciseness, which it was intended should be extended as much as possible.

II. MODES OF STATING FACTS.

Second counts on same cause of action prohibited, but several breaches permitted.

To put an end to the vexatious practice of incumbering every declaration *with numerous varying counts* for the *same-cause of action*, the 3 & 4 W. 4, c. 42, sect. 23, gives the judge power, pending a trial, to amend a single count in cases of variance, provided the opponent will not thereby be prejudiced in his defence; and as it was considered that thereby the necessity for second counts was removed, the Reg. Gen. Hil. T. 4 W. 4, reg. 5, prohibits the use of more than one count upon each cause of action, (though several breaches are permitted), and renders it compulsory on a judge on summons to strike out any such second count, and compel the plaintiff, and ultimately his attorney, to pay the extra costs, and certain other consequences are declared to attach on a violation of this rule.

This is an outline of the principal modern improvements as they affect *declarations*; each, with its operation, will be particularly pointed out when we consider the parts and particular requisites of declarations. The *substance* of a declaration, it will be observed, is scarcely in any respect affected, and hence in general the ancient forms and the long established rules will still apply, though every pleader must at the same time take care to conform to the new regulations. And since the uniformity of process act, it would be *untechnical* in a declaration in *scire facias* or other pleading to state that an action had been commenced by *bill*, and would subject the declaration to a special demurrer, though aided by pleading over, or by a general demurrer (*e*)(532).

*III. THE GENERAL REQUISITES OR QUALITIES. [*279]

III. THE GENERAL REQUISITES, &c.

The general *requisites* or *qualities* of a declaration are, 1st, that it *correspond* with the *process* (*f*), and in bailable actions, with the *affidavit* to hold to bail; 2dly, that it contain a statement of *all the facts* necessary in point of law to sustain the action, and no more (*g*); and, 3dly, that these circumstances be set forth with certainty and truth (*h*). The pleader, before he commences drawing a declaration, should have before him a copy of the writ and affidavit to hold to bail, and very full instructions as to the facts of the case, as they can be assuredly proved by evidence already carefully ascertained.

1st. Should correspond with process.

Regularly the declaration should correspond with the process (533); but

(*e*) Darling *v.* Gurney, 2 Crom. & M. 226, 2 Dowl. 235; Peacock *v.* Day, 3 Dowl. 291. But the same cases established that this objection is not a ground of general demurrer, or arrest of judgment, or error, and is aided by pleading over; *contra*, 2 Dowl. 101.

(*f*) Com. Dig. Pleader, C. 13.

(*g*) Co. Lit. 303 a; Plowd. 84, 122.

(*h*) *Id. ibid.*

(532) Vide Reid *v.* Lord, 3 Johns. Rep. 118.
As to the form of the original writ in *assumpsit* against a corporation, see Lynch *v.* The Mechanics' Bank, 13 Johns. Rep. 127.

(533) See Gratz *v.* Phillips et al., 1 Binn. 588. Jennings *v.* Cox, ibid. Dilman *v.* Shultz, 5 Serg. & Rawle, 35.

III. THE GENERAL REQUISITES, &c.

1. Should correspond with process.

as according to the present practice of the Courts, oyer of the writ cannot be craved, a variance between the writ and declaration cannot in any case be *pleaded* in abatement (534) or otherwise; and as there are several instances in which the Court will not set aside the proceedings on account of a variance between the writ and declaration (*i*), many of the older decisions are no longer applicable in practice (535). Formerly in the King's Bench, when the proceedings were by special original, we have seen that the venue must be laid in the declaration in the county into which the original was issued, or in bailable cases the bail were discharged (*k*); but in the Common Pleas and in the King's Bench, if the proceedings are by bill, the bail were not discharged by such variance (*l*); and where an outlawry had been reversed, the plaintiff might in C. P. declare in any county (*m*). And at length Reg. Gen. Hil. T. 2 W. 4, reg. 40, ordered that a declaration laying the venue in a different county from that mentioned in the process, should not be deemed a waiver of the bail (*n*). Since the 2 W. 4, c. 39, abolishing proceedings by original, that rule has become of no practical utility. We will consider how far, according to the *present* practice of the Courts, the declaration must correspond with the process or the *affidavit* to hold to bail, with respect to, 1st, the *names* of the parties to the action; 2dly, the *number* of such parties; 3dly, the *character* or *right* in which they sue or are sued; 4thly, the *cause* and *form* of action: and under each of these heads the *consequences of a deviation* from the process will be noticed.

In what respects at present.

In names of the parties (*o*).

1st, The general rule is, that the declaration should pursue the writ in regard to the *christian and surnames of the parties.* If a person enter into a bond or deed by a wrong name, he should be sued by such name; and it will not be correct to declare against him in *his real* name, although there be an averment that he executed the instrument by the untrue description (*p*). The mis-spelling a name is not, however, material, if the two names be of the same sound (*q*). The reversing or transposing the order of christian names, as "Richard John," instead of "John Richard," was considered a misnomer, and might have been pleaded in abatement before the 3 & 4 W. 4, c. 42, sect. 11, which abolished pleas of misnomer in abatement, and gave a defendant a remedy by summons, to compel the plaintiff to state the correct name in his declaration (*r*).

When bailable process had been issued against the defendant by a wrong name, if he had put in bail above in such name, he was estopped from plead-

(*i*) 6 T. R. 364.
(*k*) 3 Lev. 235; Reg. E. 2. G. 2.
(*l*) Tidd, 9th ed. 294.
(*m*) 3 Lev. 245; Imp. C. P. 612.
(*n*) Jervis' Rules 53, note (*p*).
(*o*) As to the description of the *names* of the parties in the writ, see 3 Chitty's Gen. Prac. 3d edit. 163 to 174; *number of defendants*, 183 to 185, 466; description of by *initial*, when permitted, *id.* 164 to 169, 466; by initials or wrong name, after diligent inquiry, *id.* 165, 166.
(*p*) 3 Taunt. 504; 2 C. & P. 474; 5 B. & A. 682. That the name by which a party *signs* a deed may be adopted see 1 M. & M. 6; 2 Car. & P. 474, S. C.
(*q*) 10 East, 83; 16 *Id.* 110; 2 Taunt. 401.
(*r*) 5 T. R. 195.

(534) See, however, P——— *v.* Bogan, 2 M'Cord's Rep. 386. 1 M'Cord's Rep. 208. Duval *v.* Craig, 2 Wheat. Rep. 45. 1 Harr. & Gill, 171. Cronly *v.* Brown, 12 Wend. R. 271.
(535) See Overseers of Roxborough *v.* Bunn, 12 Serg. & Rawle, 295.

III. THE GENERAL REQUISITES, &c.

1. Should correspond with process.

ing in abatement, when misnomer was so pleadable, and the declaration might be conformable to the writ (s). And it was *held that the giving a bail bond by the wrong name, not alluding to the right name, would preclude the defendant from pleading in abatement (t)(536). It has however been recently decided that the misnomer of a defendant in bailable process renders it so invalid that the defendant might sue the sheriff for false imprisonment, and the bail bond is absolutely void, and after verdict the judgment thereon was arrested (u). If the defendant appeared or put in bail by his right name, the plaintiff might, before the recent regulations, declare against him by such name, stating that he was arrested or served with process by the other, in which case the defendant could not plead the misnomer in the writ in abatement (x); nor would the Court set aside the proceedings in such case if the plaintiff declared against the defendant by the right name, without stating that he was arrested or served with process by the other (y). If the defendant did *not appear*, it was held that the plaintiff could not rectify the mistake in the writ by appearing for him in his *right* name, according to the statute (z); or by appearing for him in the name by which he was sued, and declaring against him by his right name (a). Though the plaintiff appeared for and declared against the defendant in the wrong name, as mentioned in the writ, that would warrant him in proceeding to judgment and execution, if he omitted to object to the irregularity in due time (b). So if a defendant were served with process by a wrong christian name, and afterwards the plaintiff entered an appearance for him, and served him with notice of declaration by his *right* name, and proceeded to judgment and execution, the Court would not set aside the proceeding for irregularity, merely on the ground that the defendant had never appeared; because he ought to have objected in due time (c). As the 3 & 4 W. 4, c. 42, abolishing pleas of misnomer in abatement, merely enables a defendant to compel the plaintiff to amend his declaration by stating the real name, that now seems to be the only ill consequence in the mistake of the name in *serviceable* process, though in bailable process an arrest by the wrong name is a false impris-

(s) Willes, 461; 2 New Rep. 453; Bac. Ab. Pleas, I. 11; Tidd, 9th ed. 448.

(t) 3 Taunt. 505; Tidd, 9th ed. 448; 5 B. & A. 682; but see Willes, 461; 8 Moore, 526; 1 Bing. 424, S. C.

(u) Finch v. Cocken and others, 3 Dowl. 678.

(x) 3 T. R. 611; 1 B. & P. 645; 2 Wils. 393; 13 East, 373; Tidd, 9th ed. 449.

(y) 2 Wils. 393; 12 East, 273; Tidd, 9th ed. 449.

(z) 3 T. R. 611; 11 East, 225, 226; 2 New Rep. 132, *acc.*; 1 B. & P. 105, *contra*.

(a) 10 East, 328; 11 East, 225, 226; and see 3 M. & Sel. 450.

(b) 2 Stra. 1218; 6 T. R. 234 to 236; 6 Taunt. 115; 1 Marsh. 474, S. C.; 3 East, 167. *Sed vide* 1 Moore, 105.

(c) 3 East, 167. But it is observed in the notes, that it did not appear in what name the plaintiff *entered the appearance*. It turned on the waiver of the irregularity, 10 East, 328; 11 *Id.* 225, 226.

(536) If a person enter into a bond by a wrong christian name, and be sued on such bond, he should be sued by the name in the bond, and a declaration against him by his right name, stating that he by the wrong name executed the bond, is bad, and the defendant may avail himself of this objection under the plea of *non est factum*. Gould v. Barnes, 3 Taunt. 504. { An action for breach of promise of marriage brought by a *feme sole*, was compromised by her attorney, after her marriage to another person, by taking the defendant's promissory note, payable to her by her maiden name; the attorney and the defendant being both ignorant of the marriage. In an action by the husband alone, in his own name, upon the note, it was held that it was good, and that he was entitled to recover. Templeton v. Crane, 5 Greenl. Rep. 417. }

III. THE GENERAL REQUISITES, &c. — 1. Should correspond with process.

onment, and the bail bond is void and cannot be sued upon with effect, though a judgment obtained in the original writ may still be valid (*d*).

Where process had been issued against a defendant by a wrong name, the misnomer might, before the late act, be cured by amending the *writ, if there were any thing to amend by, and then declaring against the defendant by his right name; as where the defendant was properly named in the affidavit to [*281] hold to bail, but was mistaken in the process (*e*). So if the defendant pleaded the misnomer in abatement, the plaintiff might amend the writ and declaration even though the defendant was a prisoner (*f*), unless there had been in the interim a tender of the debt; or the plaintiff might enter a *cassetur billa* or *breve*, in which case he was not liable to pay the defendant's costs (*g*). But now it is the practice to refuse an amendment of mesne process unless in a case where otherwise the statute of limitations would be a bar (*h*). Formerly, if there was reason to doubt the defendant's name, it was advisable either to wait till the defendant has appeared, and to declare in chief, or to declare *de bene esse* with an alias; and it has been held, that a declaration against a defendant by the name of "Jonathan," otherwise "John Soans," (537) was sufficient upon *demurrer* (*i*); though not so upon a plea in abatement, for in law a party cannot have two christian names (*k*). It was considered that the defendant could never plead in abatement, if the declaration were against him by his right name only, although the process were wrong (*l*). But in such case, if the defendant had not waived the misnomer or irregularity, he might apply to the Court to set aside the proceedings; for, independently of the misnomer, there was not, under such circumstances, any writ to support the declaration.

Where there has been a misnomer in the writ, care must be taken on the part of the defendant not to waive the objection (*m*). In cases of *non-bailable* process the court would not, nor will they now, interfere on motion to set aside the proceedings, so that the defendant could not avail himself of the misnomer otherwise than by plea in abatement (*n*). And now since that plea has been abolished as regards misnomer by 3 & 4 W. 4, c. 42, sect. 11, the defendant's only course is to take out a summons returnable before a judge, to compel the plaintiff to amend the misnomer in the declaration, and insert the real name and pay the costs of the application. In no case could a misnomer, (even of one of several defendants,) in an action on a promissory note, or other written instrument, be pleaded in *bar* (*o*). If the defendant be mis-

(*d*) Finch *v.* Cocken and others, 3 Dowl. 678.

(*e*) 2 B. & P. 109; 3 Wils. 49.

(*f*) 7 T. R. 698; 3 M. & Sel. 450.

(*g*) See Tidd, 9th ed. 683.

(*h*) Horton *v.* Borough of Stamford, 2 Dowl. 96; Lakin *v.* Watson, 2 Dowl. 633; 2 Crom. & M. 685; 3 Chitty's Gen. Prac. 173, 234, 235.

(*i*) 3 East, 111. Lord Ellenborough said that "if the defendant had been sued by the name of 'Jonathan *Soans*,' otherwise 'John Soans,' it might, perhaps, have admitted of a different consideration."

(*k*) *Ante*, 280; Willes, 554; Tidd, 9th ed. 447.

(*l*) 2 Chit. Rep. 8; 3 M. & Sel. 450; Tidd, 9th ed. 449.

(*m*) See the mode of appearance and of giving the bail-bond, Tidd, 9th ed. 448, 449.

(*n*) 7 D. & R. 258; 11 Moore, 39.

(*o*) 16 East, 110.

(537) If the surname of the obligor in the body of a bond, varies by a slight mis-spelling, producing scarcely any change in the pronunciation from that in the subscription, he may be sued by the name subscribed alone, without an alias dictus. Meredith *v.* Hindsale, 2 Caines' Rep. 362.

III. THE GENERAL REQUISITES, &c.

1. Should correspond with process.

named in a *bailable* writ, he may still move the Court to set aside the proceedings *for irregularity (*p*) (538), and although he omit to do so, he may support an action of trespass for false imprisonment against the sheriff and his officers (*q*) (539); unless the Court, on setting aside the proceedings, restrain the defendant from bringing such action (*r*). And it has been recently decided that the bail bond is so void that even if judgment be recovered against the bail in an action on such bond, the judgment may be arrested (*s*).

Where the name of the *plaintiff* has been mistaken in the process, it is advisable in the commencement of the declaration, as in the case of a defendant, to state, that "A. B. (the real name) the plaintiff in this action, at whose suit, by the name of E. B., C. D. the defendant in this action, was served with process," (or "arrested") in this suit, by Y. Z. his attorney, (or in person,) complains of the said defendant being, &c." (*t*) (540); for if the plaintiff's misnomer should be continued in the declaration, the defendant might take out a summons to compel the plaintiff to amend and state the correct name, and pay the costs of the application, although he could not plead in abatement since 3 & 4 W. 4, c. 42, sect. 11. At no time, even in the case of a corporation, was misnomer of the plaintiff pleadable in bar (*u*) (541). But a mistake in the name of *a third person* in matter of description, will sometimes be fatal to the proceedings as a variance (*x*). A misnomer of the *plaintiff* could only be pleaded in abatement, and was no ground for setting aside the proceedings (*y*); or for a motion in arrest of judgment (*z*); or of nonsuit at the trial, at least if it appeared that the defendant was aware that the action was brought by the person who actually sues (*a*). It seems now to be set-

(*p*) 1 B. & P. 647; 2 Taunt. 399; Tidd, 9th ed. 447, 448; Ladbrook *v.* Phillips, 1 Har. & Wol. 109; 3 Chitty's Gen. Prac. 167, 353, 354.

(*q*) 8 East, 328; 6 T. R. 234; 2 Campb. 270; 2 Taunt. 399; 1 Marsh. 75; 6 Taunt. 623; 1 B. & Ald. 647; 7 B. & C. 486. But see 3 Campb. 108; 8 Moore, 297; 1 Bing. 314, S. C.

(*r*) 1 Chit. R. 282.

(*s*) Finch *v.* Cocken and others, 3 Dowl. 678.

(*t*) 1 B. & P. 647. As to mistakes in names once correctly stated, see 3 M. & Sel. 178; Com. Dig. Pleader, C. 18.

(*u*) 1 B. & P. 40; 3 Anstr. 935; 6 M. & Sel. 45.

(*x*) Willes, 5; 1 Stark. 100; 1 M. & M. 6; but see 1 Stark. 47.

(*y*) 4 Moore, 369; 2 B. & B. 34, S. C.

(*z*) 2 Bla. Rep. 1120.

(*a*) 3 Campb. 29; 6 Moore, 141; 3 B. & B. 54, S. C.; 7 Moore, 522; 1 Bing. 143, S. C.

(538) Vide Menzies *v.* Rodrigues and others, 1 Price's Exch. Rep. 92.

(539) { Mead *v.* Haws, 7 Cow. Rep. 322. Griswold *v.* Sedgwick, 6 Cow. Rep. 456. } But the court will not discharge the defendant on motion, unless he will undertake to bring no action. Wilks *v.* Lorch, 2 Taunt. 399. Where there is only an inaccuracy in the spelling, so that the name is still *idem sonans*, the court will not discharge the defendant. Ahitbol *v.* Beneditto, 2 Taunt. 401.

(540) { "The 1 Chitty on Pl. 251, 2, (4th edit.) is an authority for this mode of declaring: but the case to which he refers is Murray *v.* Hubbart, 1 Bos. & Pul. 645. This case does not bear him out. It is where a defendant sued by a *wrong* name, *appeared*, and was *declared against* by his right one. The case here is directly the reverse. The *capias* is at the suit of *George B. Willard*, according to which the defendant appears; *Charles Willard* then comes in and declares in his own name. The *declaration* must correspond with the *process* in the names of the parties. Tidd, 402. The case of a *defendant*, sued by a *wrong name* and appearing in his *right* one, is an exception to this rule." *Per Curiam*, Willard *v.* Missani, 1 Cow. Rep. 37. }

(541) Vide Medway Cotton Manufactory *v.* Adams and another, 10 Mass. Rep. 360, 362, 363. Where a deed is made to a corporation, by a name varying from the true name, the plaintiffs may sue in their true name, and aver in the declaration that the defendant made the deed to them, by the name mentioned in the deed. New York African Society *v.* Varick and others, 13 Johns. Rep. 38. { Inhabitants, &c. *v.* String, 5 Halst. Rep. 323. President, Managers, &c. *v.* Myers, 6 Serg. & Rawle, 12. }

III. THE GENERAL REQUISITES, &c. tled, that when the parties have been once named in the declaration, it is sufficient to describe them afterwards by the terms "*plaintiff*" and "*defendant*." (*b*) If instead of the plural *plaintiffs*, the word *plaintiff* in the singular be adopted in a material part of the *body* of a declaration, it has been supposed that the declaration will be subject to a special demurrer; but if merely in the *commencement* it would be otherwise (*c*).

1. Should correspond with process.

Number of the parties.

Number of plaintiffs.

2dly. With respect to the declaration corresponding with the process in the *number* of the parties, it has been held that if a writ be sued out in the name of *one plaintiff*, the declaration in chief must not vary, and if it be delivered in the name of *two plaintiffs*, the proceeding will be set aside for irregularity (*d*). And even in an action in *autre droit*, as by an executor, the Court will not permit an amendment by adding the name of a co-executor, unless the statute of limitations will otherwise be a bar (*e*). But in the King's [*283] Bench, where the *defendant has appeared to process at the suit of two, one of them might have declared alone by the bye, when that collateral mode of declaring was admissible, for he was considered a stranger (*f*); and though the plaintiff in the original action must have declared in chief before he could declare by the bye (*g*), yet formerly any other person might declare by the bye even before the delivery of a declaration in chief (*h*). That practice, however, seems to have been virtually abolished (*i*). Upon a writ in an action at the suit of a husband and wife, a declaration might have been delivered by the bye at the suit of the husband only: but if the writ were by the husband only, and he declared thereon, a declaration by the bye at the suit of himself and wife was irregular (*k*).

Common process in the Common Pleas might have been against four *defendants*, and the plaintiff might have declared thereon separately against each (*l*). In the King's Bench, the Reg. Easter Term, 3 G. 4, ordered, "in all actions by bill, the mesne process shall contain the name of the defendant, or if more than one, of all the defendants in that action, and shall not contain the name or names of the defendants in any other action." (*m*) (542)

In all the Courts, on *bailable* process against several, in an action on a *contract*, the declaration must always have been and still be against all jointly (543), or the declaration would be set aside for irregularity (*n*). In the

(*b*) 6 Taunt. 121; 2 Marsh. 301, S. C.; 6 Taunt. 406.

(*c*) Tyndall and another *v.* Ullesthorne, 3 Dowl. 2; but see 4 Moore & Scott, 417.

(*d*) 1 B. & P. 383.

(*e*) Lakin and another *v.* Watson, 2 Crom. & M. 685.

(*f*) Burr. 2180.

(*g*) 6 T. R. 158; 7 *Id.* 80.

(*h*) Phillips' case, 1 Cromp. 96, 3d ed.; Tidd, 9th ed. 424, 425.

(*i*) 3 Chitty's Gen. Prac. 495, 496, and authorities there cited, showing that the practice of declaring *by the bye* is now abolished, and that it ought not to be revived.

(*k*) Barnes, 337; Prac. Reg. 131, 132; 1 Sel. Prac. Ch. 6, s. 1, B. 3; Tidd, 9th ed. 425.

(*l*) 1 Bos. & Pul. 19, 49; Tidd, 9th ed. 148; 1 M. & Sel. 55; 2 New Rep. 82.

(*m*) R. E. 3 Geo. 4, 6 B. & C. 639; 2 M. & R. 367.

(*n*) Tidd, 9th ed. 149, 446; Carson *v.* Downing and another, K. B. Trin. Term,

(542) And, in the Supreme Court of the State of New York, the plaintiff may join any number of defendants in a process not liable, and declare against them severally, or against some, omitting the others. Montgomery *v.* Hasbrouck and others, 3 Johns. Rep. 530.

(543) { But the rule applies only to cases of *contract*, and it is not applicable to actions in *tort*. Wilson *v.* Edwards, 5 Dowl. & Ryl. 622. The cases referred to in Tidd, are cases of contract. } See Nelson *v.* Ayres, 7 Halst. Rep. 62, and the cases cited.

Common Pleas, however, the affidavit of debt and clause of *ac etiam* in bailable process, pointed out the person against whom the action was to proceed; therefore, where the affidavit of debt was against A., the *capias* against A. and B., and the declaration against A. only, by whom bail was put in, that Court held it to be regular (*o*); and upon a bailable *capias* against two defendants, with a clause of *ac etiam* and affidavit of debt against one, the plaintiff in that Court might have regularly declared against the latter defendant only (*p*).

III. THE GENERAL REQUISITES, &c.

1st. Should correspond with process

Recently the practice has been altered and settled for all the Courts as regards the *number of defendants*. The first general rule of Trin. Term, 3 W. 4, ordered, that every writ of summons, capias, and detainer, *shall contain* the names of *all* the *defendants* (if more than one) in the action, and shall *not contain* the name or names of any defendant or defendants *in more actions than one* (*q*). However numerous the defendants in a joint action may be, they must all be named in each and *every* writ issued against them, although they greatly exceed four; and when very numerous, if there be not room in the printed blanks for all the names and descriptions of residences, then the whole writ must be written; and if some one or more defendants be in one county, and the others in another county, then there must be at least as many *concurrent* writs precisely alike, as there are counties, (varying, of course, if writs of capias, in the direction to the sheriff of each county); and there must be as many copies of such writ as there are defendants in that county, unless there has been an attorney's written undertaking to appear for them.

Upon the affirmative or first part of this rule, it is clear that a declaration naming *more* defendants than were named in one writ would be irregular (*r*). But on the latter part of the rule, it has been held, that in process *not bailable* against several defendants, the plaintiff may regularly declare in a joint action against *some* of them, provided he has done no act showing any intention to proceed against the other defendant or defendants, and especially so when the plaintiff has entirely dropped his proceeding against such other defendant (*s*). And the same doctrine prevails even on *bailable* process, when against several persons for *a tort* (*t*). So that until the plaintiff has *declared* on his joint process, no irregularity appears that could be taken advantage of, and therefore a defendant cannot object until after declaration. But where the names of two defendants had been inserted in a writ of summons, and afterwards they were *both* declared against *separately*, the Court set aside the declaration and subsequent proceedings for irregularity, although there were two writs and the defendant had entered separate appearances, which it was insisted waived the irregularity (*u*). And where a husband and his wife had

1835, Legal Observer, 134. How to act when one of the defendants cannot be arrested or served with process, see Sell. Prac. vol. i. c. 6, s. 1, E.; Imp. Prac. K. B. 6th ed. 545, 7th ed. 599; 1 Stra. 473. But it is not always so in actions for costs, 3 Bar. & Cres. 734.

(*o*) 2 New Rep. 98; Tidd, 9th ed. 447.

(*p*) 1 Moore, 147; 7 Taunt. 458, S. C.; see 1 Bing. 48.

(*q*) See rule, Jervis's Rules.

(*r*) 1 Arch. Pr. C. P. [40].

(*s*) Tidd's Sup. 1833, p. 467; Evans *v.* Whitehead, 2 M. & R. 367; Bowles *v.* Bilton, 2 C. & P. 474; Knowles *v.* Johnson, 2 Dowl. P. C. 653, and R. E. 8 G. 4; Coldwell *v.* Blake, 3 Dowl. 656; 1 Gale, 157, S. C.

(*t*) Wilson *v.* Edwards, 3 Bar. & Cres. 734; 5 D. & R. 622, S. C.; Evans *v.* Whitehead, 2 Man. & Ry. 367; Pepper *v.* Whalley, 1 Bing. N. C. 71; 2 Dowl. 821, S. C.; Knowles *v.* Johnson, 2 Dowl. P. C. 653.

(*u*) Pepper *v.* Whalley, 1 Bing. N. C. 71; 3 Chit. Gen. Prac. 285.

III. THE GENERAL REQUISITES, &c.

1st. Should correspond with process.

been arrested on *joint process*, and the latter had been discharged out of custody upon entering a common appearance, and afterwards the plaintiff declared against the husband alone, the Court held the proceedings irregular (*x*). And in a bailable action, if the declaration should be against fewer defendants than those named in the writ, the proceeding would, although not within the terms of the rule, be irregular, and the Court would set aside the declaration (*y*).

Instances have occurred in which the name of a defendant, improperly joined with others, has been struck out upon amendment (*z*). But since the uniformity of process act, 2 W. 4, c. 39, the Courts have resolved not to permit any amendment of writs, unless the statute of limitations would be a bar (*a*); or where the parties have pleaded and joined issue, in which latter case the names of two or more defendants have on summons been struck out of the declaration and issue.

[*284]

The *character* in which plaintiff sues, or defendant is sued.

*3dly. With respect to the *character* or *right* or *liability* in which the plaintiff professed in his writ to sue, or the defendant was sued, no material alteration appears of late to have been introduced. Upon common process, not bailable, and which did not specify the *character or right* in which the plaintiff sues, it was held that he might declare specially, as *qui tam*, or as executor, or as administrator, or as assignee, or in any other special character; for this did not tend to enlarge but to narrow the demand which the defendant was called upon to answer (*b*), and it has been decided, that though the plaintiff may *style* himself executor (*c*), (not stating himself to *sue as* executor), or give himself any other superfluous description in the process, and declare otherwise, this would not be irregular, because the demand was still the same (*d*) (544). And so where the defendant was described in process generally, he might be declared against as administrator, the object of the writ being merely to bring him into Court (*e*). But where the process was to answer the plaintiff in a special character or right, as describing him as suing *qui tam* (*f*), or *as* executor (*g*), or *as* assignee of a bankrupt (*h*), the declaration could only be in the same character, and the plaintiff could not declare generally; and if he did, the Court would set aside the proceedings (*i*). Where the action was *bailable*, the Court would in the latter cases discharge the defendant out of custody on filing common bail; leaving the plaintiff, however, at liberty to proceed upon his declaration (*k*). It seems that if *bailable* process be general in the body of it, a variation between the declaration and the *ac etiam* part of the writ, (when in use, but now no longer so,) or the affidavit

(*x*) Cattarne *v.* Player, 3 Dowl. & Ry. 247.

(*y*) Carson *v.* Dowding and another, K. B. Trin. Term, 1335, Legal Observer, 134; 1 Arch. Pr. C. P. [40], citing 4 East, 589; 1 M. & Sel. 55.

(*z*) *Ante*, 14, note (*x*).

(*a*) Lakin *v.* Watson, 2 C. & M. 685.

(*b*) 2 Stra. 1232; 2 Bla. Rep. 722; 3 Wils. 141 S. C.; Burr. 2417; 1 B. & P. 383, n. b.; 1 Bar. & Adol. 19.

(*c*) Lord Tenterden so decided at chambers; but the cases do not sustain the position to the full extent; see further 1 Dowl. Rep. 97.

(*d*) 2 Bla. Rep. 722; 1 B. & P. 383, n. b.

(*e*) 6 Moore, 66; 3 B. & B. 4, S. C.

(*f*) Burr. 2417; 2 Stra. 1232, n. 1.

(*g*) 8 T. R. 416; 1 B. & P. 383; 3 Wils. 61.

(*h*) Tidd, 9th ed. 450, n. e.

(*i*) *Supra*, note (*b*).

(*k*) 8 T. R. 416; Tidd, 9th ed. 450; 3 Wils. 61.

(544) Vide Woodford *v.* Webster, 3 Day, 472.

to hold to bail, was only a ground for discharging the defendant on common bail, and not for setting aside the proceedings for irregularity (*l*). Where the plaintiffs issued a writ generally in their own names, and declared in their own right, and described themselves in the affidavit to hold to bail as surviving partners, the Court discharged the defendant on filing common bail, and ordered the bail-bond to be cancelled, and would not allow the plaintiff to amend (*m*).

III. THE GENERAL REQUISITES, &c.

1st. Should correspond with process.

The rule and decisions on this point since the uniformity of process act, 2 W. 4, c. 39(*n*).

The uniformity of process act, 2 W. 4, c. 39, as well in its enactments as in the prescribed forms in the schedule, is silent upon the necessity of inserting any description of the *character* or *right* in which the plaintiff sues or the defendant is sued; and it is probable that it was intended by that statute merely to require that the *form of action* should be stated, and the amount of the debt indorsed, which it was perhaps considered would sufficiently inform the *defendant* in all actions, and his *bail* in bailable actions, what was the nature of the claim and supposed liability. Since that act, it was considered by the Courts of K. B. and C. P., with reference to prior decisions, that upon a *general* writ, whether *serviceable* (*o*) or *bailable* (*p*), and not stating the character in which the plaintiff sued, or the defendant was sued, the plaintiff was afterwards at liberty to *declare specially* in any particular character or right, as *qui tam*, or as *executor* or administrator, or as an *assignee* of a bankrupt (*q*); or as assignee of a bail-bond (*r*); and also it was held in the Common Pleas, that on such *general process* the plaintiff may declare *against* a defendant *as* an executor or administrator (*s*). And where the *affidavit* stated the debt to be due to the intended plaintiff *as* executor, but the process was general, the Court of Exchequer refused to order the bail-bond to be cancelled (*t*). It was also held, that although the process had described the plaintiff or defendant generally *as being* executor, administrator, or assignee, without introducing any words denoting that he sued *as such*, the plaintiff might *declare* generally in his *own right*, or against the defendant on his own liability, treating the description as a mere superfluous addition, just as if the word carpenter had been idly introduced (*u*). But that by introducing into the writ any express statement that the plaintiff intended to sue in a particular character, as by using the word "*as* executor," or "*as* assignee," &c., then the plaintiff having so expressly limited his proceeding, could not declare generally, and that if he did so, then, at least in a bailable action, the defendant would be discharged out of custody, and the proceedings be set aside for irregularity (*x*).

(*l*) 6 T. R. 363; 3 Wils. 141, 161; 8 T. R. 416.

(*m*) 5 Moore, 209; see 1 B. & Ald. 29; 6 T. R. 363.

(*n*) See fully as to the necessity for correctly describing forms of action in all process, and consequences of deviation, 3 Chitty's Gen. Prac. 194 to 199, 237, 467.

(*o*) See cases, Tidd's Supp. 1833, p. 67.

(*p*) But it will be observed, that in those cases the affidavit to hold to bail correctly stated the *character* in which the plaintiff sued, the same as in the declaration. See next note.

(*q*) Ashworth *v.* Ryall, 1 Bar. & Adol. 20; Ilsley *v.* Ilsley, 2 Cromp. & Jer. 300; 2 Tyr. Rep. 214, S. C.

(*r*) Knowles *v.* Johnson, 2 Dowl. 653; and see 3 Chitty's Gen. Prac. 181 to 183, 200, 470.

(*s*) Watson *v.* Pilling, 3 Brod. & B. 446; 6 Moore, 66, S. C.

(*t*) Ilsley *v.* Ilsley, 2 Tyr. 214; 2 C. & J. 330, S. C.

(*u*) 1 Dowl. Rep. 97; Knowles *v.* Johnson, 2 Dowl. 653; and see Henshall *v.* Roberts, 5 East, 450.

(*x*) Douglas *v.* Irlam, 8 T. R. 416; Rogers *v.* Jenkins, 1 Bos. & Pul. 383; 1 Dowl. P. C. 98, 99; but see Ashworth *v.* Ryall, 1 Bar. & Adol. 20.

III. THE GENERAL REQUISITES, &c.

1st. Should correspond with process.

But it has been supposed that there is a difference in these respects in the practice of the Common Pleas (y); and it is to be collected from one reported decision, that if a *bailable* writ in C. P. be *general*, and the plaintiff declare thereon *as* executor, the bail will be entitled to have an exoneretur entered on the bail-piece, but that the defendant himself cannot avail himself of such variance (z). But in that case the affidavit to hold to bail was general, viz. for a debt due to the plaintiff in his own right, and the declaration disclosed that it was for a debt alleged to be due to the plaintiff in his representative character (a); and we have seen that in another case that Court held that a defendant may be *declared* against as administrator, though the process described him generally (b). However, it will be prudent, in a writ in the Common Pleas, when the plaintiff sues, or the defendant is sued in a particular character, to describe him accordingly in the writ; and this indeed will be the safest course in all the Courts (c).

[*285]

The form or cause of action in writ.

*4thly. *Before the uniformity of process act*, 4 W. 4, c. 39, upon common process the plaintiff might declare *in any cause of action* whatever (d). But in *bailable* actions, the declarations must have corresponded with the *cause* and the *form* of action in the *affidavit*, and the *ac etiam* part of the latitat or other process (545); for otherwise the defendant would be discharged on filing common bail (e); and the Courts would not allow the declaration to be amended in that respect (f); but that was the only consequence, for the Court would not in such case set aside the proceedings for irregularity (g)(546). And a variance in the amount of the debt between the *ac etiam* part of the latitat and the declaration was not even a ground for discharging the defendant on common bail (h); and, at least in the Common Pleas, where the sum sworn to is under £40, a variance between the form of action in the *ac etiam* and the declaration was not considered material (i). When the suit was commenced by *original*, the plaintiff was required to declare in chief for the same cause of

(y) Archbold's Prac. K. B. by T. Chitty, 4th ed. 117, 515; Arch. Prac. C. P. [19]; *Id.* [40]. In the latter it is observed, "Formerly, upon *general* process, a plaintiff might declare in autre droit as executor, &c. but *probably* that would now be deemed irregular."

(z) Manesley v. Stevens, 9 Bing. 400; 1 Dowl. P. C. 711, S. C. But note in that case the *affidavit was general*, as for a debt due to the plaintiff himself, and the declaration was for a debt due to plaintiff *as executor*, a variance which of itself discharged the bail. See Ilsley v. Ilsley, 2 Tyr. R. 215; 2 Cromp. & Jer. 331.

(a) *Id. ibid.* See observations of Court in Ilsley v. Ilsley, 2 Tyr. 215; 2 Cromp. & Jer. 331.

(b) Watson v. Pilling, 3 Brod. & B. 446; 6 Moore, 66, S. C.; 3 Chit. Gen. Prac. 182, (p).

(c) And see 1 Arch. Pr. C. P. [40], where it is observed that it is *extremely doubtful* whether the practice of issuing general process upon an affidavit in autre droit would now be allowed in any of the Courts, and refers to 1 Dowl. 97. And see 3 Wils. 61; 2 Bla. R. 722, showing that only in non-bailable actions can such a variance between process and declaration be unimportant.

(d) Cowp 455; R. E. 15 G. 2, reg. 1; Tidd, 9th ed. 450.

(e) 7 T. R. 50; 8 *id.* 27; Cowp. 455; 1 Hen. Bla. 310; 5 Moore, 483; 2 Hen. Bla. 278; 2 B. & P. 358.

(f) 5 Moore, 483.

(g) 6 T. R. 363; 2 Wils. 393; 8 Taunt. 189; 2 Moore, 89, S. C.; Tidd, 9th ed. 450.

(h) 5 T. R. 402; *sed vide* 2 East, 305.

(i) 1 Hen. Bla. 810; 2 Saund. 52 a; Tidd, 9th ed. 450, 294; and see 10 Bar. & Cres. 223.

(545) Vide Rogers v. Rogers, 4 Johns. Rep. 485.

(546) But in Rogers v. Rogers, 4 Johns. Rep. 485, where the ac etiam was in assumpsit, and the declaration in account, the proceedings were set aside for irregularity.

action as was expressed in the writ (*k*); and in bailable cases, if there were a variance between the writ and the declaration, the defendant would be discharged on a common appearance (*l*); but the proceedings were not set aside merely on account of a variance in describing the cause of action (*m*), and therefore the only consequence of the mistake was that the plaintiff lost the security of the *bail*.

III. THE GENERAL REQUISITES, &c.

1st. Should correspond with process.

The uniformity of process act, 2 W. 4, c. 39, imperatively required that the *form of action* shall be concisely stated in each of the writs thereby prescribed, whether serviceable or bailable; and if the form should be omitted or *substantially vary* from one of those enjoined, even in serviceable process, the writ would, on summons or motion, be set aside, though "promises," omitting "*on*" or "*upon*," has been holden a mere clerical mistake (*n*). The proper forms are—

In Assumpsit, "in an action on Promises."
In Debt, "in an action of Debt."
In Covenant, "in an action of Covenant."
In Detinue, "in an action of Detinue."
In a joint action of Debt and Detinue, "in an action of Debt and Detinue."
In Case or Trover, "in a plea of Trespass on the Case."
In Trespass, "in an action of Trespass."

It was the intention of the legislature that every writ, whether serviceable or bailable, should apprize the defendant of the *form of action* by which he would afterwards be declared against, and therefore it is an *indispensable requisite of every declaration that it substantially adhere to the form of action stated* in the process, *as well in serviceable as bailable process*, and if it deviate, the defendant may apply to the Court or a judge to set aside the declaration for irregularity; so that the plaintiff must abandon his first process and issue a fresh writ stating a form of action adapted to that in his declaration. But the objection is not a ground of demurrer to the declaration, but merely of a summary application to set aside the declaration for irregularity (*o*). It has been usual in the *commencement* of the declaration to state the form of action precisely as in the writ; but the forms of commencements of declarations prescribed by Reg. Gen. Mich. Term, 3 W. 4 (*p*), conclude with &c., and hence it is probable that it was not intended by the judges to state the form of action, but that the declaration should immediately proceed to state the substance of the cause of action (*q*); and according to the observations in recent cases, the form of action ought not to be stated in the commencement (*r*). If

(*k*) 5 T. R. 402; R. Hilary, 8 Car. 1.
(*l*) 6 T. R. 363; 2 Wils. 393; Tidd, 9th ed. 450, 451; but see 2 Moore, 301; 8 Taunt. 304, S. C.
(*m*) Tidd, 450, 451, 9th ed.
(*n*) Cooper *v.* Wheale, K. B. Mich. T. 1835, Legal Obs. 133, 134.
(*o*) Anderson *v.* Thomas, 9 Bing. 678; Thompson *v.* Dicas, 2 Dowl. 94; Marshall *v.* Thomas, *id.* 205; Rotton *v.* Jeffery, *id.* 637; Reynolds *v.* Welsh, 1 Crom. M. & Ros. 580; Hargreaves *v.* Holder, *id.*; and 3 Chitty's Gen. Prac. 468 to 470.
(*p*) See them, *ante*, 276.
(*q*) See 3 Chitty's Gen. Prac. 467.
(*r*) Ball *v.* Hamlett, 1 Crom. M. & Ros. 575; Reynolds *v.* Welsh, *id.* 580; Hargreaves *v.* Holder, *id.* (*s*); and see 3 Chit. Gen. Prac. 468.

III. THE GENERAL REQUISITES, &c.

the *body* of the declaration state a cause of action that is not, nor could be, properly declared for in the form of action stated in the writ, then the deviation would constitute an irregularity and ground for setting aside the declaration, but not a ground of demurrer.

1st. Should correspond with process.

The form and cause of action in declarations must correspond with the *affidavit to hold to bail.*

It has always been considered essential that the declaration should adhere to or proceed for the same *cause of action* as that expressed in the *affidavit to hold to bail,* and that if it do not, the defendant may apply by summons or motion to be discharged out of custody, or to have the bail-bond cancelled, and the bail above would be discharged from liability (*s*); and unless the plaintiff obtain a verdict for the cause of action stated in the affidavit, the bail would even at that late stage of the cause, be relieved from responsibility (*t*).

Where the affidavit to hold to bail was for goods sold and money lent, and the declaration contained no count for goods sold, it was held no ground for applying to have an exoneretur entered on the bail-piece (*u*); but that decision is doubtful, and every careful pleader should take care to insert counts in his declaration to embrace every cause of action sworn to in the affidavit.

2dly. The declaration must state all the facts essential to the support of the action.

The declaration must allege all the circumstances necessary for the support of the action, and contain a full, regular, and methodical statement of the injury which the plaintiff has sustained (547), and the time; and in trespass *quare clausum fregit,* the name or abuttals of the close (*x*); though in other actions venue is no longer to be repeated in the body, but it is to be stated only once in the margin (*y*). These, and all other circumstances essential in law to the action, must be stated with such precision, certainty, and clearness, that the defendant, knowing what he is called upon to answer (548), may *be able to plead a direct and unequivocal plea; and that the jury may be enabled to give a complete verdict upon the issue; and that the Court, consistently with the rules of law, may give a certain and distinct judgment upon the premises (*z*). The general rules as to *what facts must be stated* have been considered in the preceding chapter (*a*), as well as the inconveniences which may arise from the statement of *superfluous* or unnecessary matter (*b*). The *requisites* of the declaration in each particular case so much depend upon circumstances, that any general observations in this place upon the structure of a declaration would be but of little utility. We will presently consider the requisites in each form of action, and the precedents in the second volume must also be consulted, and, when applicable, should be followed on Lord Coke's principle, "nam nihil simul inventum est et perfectum;" *i. e.* nothing at the same instant that it is discovered or invented is perfect, but becomes so only by frequent use and perhaps correction.

[*286]

(*s*) Scrivener *v.* Wathing, 1 Harr. & Wol. 8; 3 Chitty's Gen. Prac. 337.

(*t*) 2 Taunt. Rep. 107.

(*u*) *Per* Littledale, J., in Gray *v.* Harvey, 1 Dowl. 114; 1 Arch. Prac. C. P. [40]. *Sed quære.*

(*x*) Reg. Gen. Hil. Term, 4 W. 4, r. V. In trespass, the abuttals should be *on,* not *towards,* the north, Lempriere *v.* Humphrey, 1 Harr. & Wol. 170.

(*y*) Reg. Gen. Hil. Term, 4 W. 4, r. 8.

(*z*) Cowp. 682; 6 East, 422, 423; 5 T. R. 623; Vin. Ab. Declarations.

(*a*) *Ante,* 245, 266.

(*b*) *Ante,* 262, 263.

(547) Vide Pelton *v.* Ward, 3 Caines' Rep. 77. Carpenter *v.* Alexander, 9 Johns. Rep. 291. Roget *v.* Merit and Clapp, 2 Caines' Rep. 120.

(548 Vide Coffin *v.* Coffin, 2 Mass. Rep. 363.

III. THE GENERAL REQUISITES, &c.

We have already considered the different *degrees of certainty* required in pleading, and we have seen that the certainty necessary in a declaration is to a *certain* intent in general (*d*), which should pervade the whole declaration, and is particularly required in setting forth the parties, time and other circumstances necessary to maintain the action (*e*). In *assumpsit*, the description of the contract, &c. by *whereas*, or recital, is not demurrable (*f*), though it would be otherwise in trespass *vi et armis* (*g*).

3dly. Of the certainty required in declaration (c).

Certainty of parties.

1st. It must be stated with certainty who are the *parties* to the suit (*h*); and therefore a declaration by or against "C. D. and company," not being a corporation, is insufficient (*i*)(549); so though property be vested in trustees (*k*) even by an act of parliament, yet, if they be not incorporated, they must be described by their proper names as individuals, and their character as trustees subjoined, as a description of the capacity in which the legislature authorized them to act (*l*); on the other hand, a corporation must be described in all legal proceedings by their corporate name (*m*)(550). The statute 3 & 4 W. 4, c. 42, sect. 12, authorizes the plaintiff to declare against a defendant upon a bill or note, or other *written instrument*, by the same initial or contraction of christian name used therein. But where there are several plaintiffs or defendants, whose names have been once described, it is sufficient and proper, when the names are numerous, afterwards to adopt the word "*plaintiffs*" or "*defendants*," without again enumerating all the names (*n*). But accuracy must be observed; for if in an action at the suit of several persons, the word *plaintiff* in the singular, be used in stating the *debt*, instead of plaintiffs, the defendant may demur specially (*o*), though it would be otherwise if the mistake merely occurred in the commencement. *We have seen when the declaration may vary from the process in the name of the defendant, or may describe him with the *alias dictus* (*p*). In declarations upon contracts, it should be expressly [*287]

(*c*) *Ante*, 267, 273.
(*d*) *Ante*, 268; Plowd. 84; Co. Lit. 303 a; 1 N. R. 173.
(*e*) Com. Dig. Pleader, C. 18 to C. 27; Tidd, 9th ed. 451.
(*f*) Ring *v.* Roxbrough, 2 Crom. & Jer. 418; 2 Tyr. 468.
(*g*) 2 Salk. 636; 1 Stra. 621; Com. Dig. Pleader, C.; Andr. 282. When the proceedings were by original, and the writ recited in declaration, it was otherwise, 1 Wils. 99; Barnes, 452; 2 Wils. 203.
(*h*) Com. Dig. Pleader, C. 18; see 1 Campb. 466, as to a declaration by a corporation.
(*i*) 8 T. R. 508.
(*k*) See *ante*, 15, 16.
(*l*) 1 Leach, 4th edit. 513; vol. xxii. MS. Paper Books of Mr. J. Ashhurst, 216.
(*m*) 1 Leach, 4th edit. 253.
(*n*) 1 N. R. 289; 6 Taunt. 121; 2 Marsh. 301, S. C.; 6 Taunt. 406.
(*o*) Tyndall and another *v.* Ullesthorne, 3 Dowl. 2. But see 4 Moore & Scott, 417.
(*p*) *Ante*, 280, 282.

(549) Acc. Bentley and others *v.* Smith and others, 3 Caines' Rep. 170. { And actions, to be properly brought, must be commenced and prosecuted in the proper *christian* and *surnames* of the parties, and not in the name of the company or firm. Seeley *v.* Schenck, and Denise, Crandall *v.* Fr. Denny and Co., 1 Penn. Rep. 75, 137. Tomlinson *v.* Burke et al., 5 Halst. Rep. 295. But in the case of two or more partners of the same *surname*, if the *surname* be not added to every *christian* name, it is not error. Chance *v.* Chambers, 1 Penn. Rep. 384. In Virginia, however, it has been decided, that a declaration in behalf of a mercantile company, by the name of the *firm*, without mentioning the names of the partners, is good after a verdict for the plaintiff upon the general issue. Pate *v.* Bacon et al., 6 Munf. 219. Totty's Ex. *v.* Donald and Co. 4 Munf. 430. Barnet *v.* Watson, 1 Wash. Rep. 372. And see Porter *v.* Cresson, 10 Serg. & Rawle, 257. As to whether judgment by default could be sustained *against* a mercantile company—the suit being against the *firm*—if the *names* of the partners be omitted in the writ and declaration, see Scott & Co. *v.* Dunlap & Co., 2 Munf. 349. }
(550) Taylor *v.* Green et al., 7 Halst. Rep. 124.

III. THE GENERAL REQUISITES, &c. — 3. What degree of certainty is required.

stated by and with whom the contract was made (*q*); and where there are two or more persons of the same name, they should be distinguished from each other by the insertion of some appropriate allegation, as "the now plaintiff," or "the now defendant," or "the said E. F. deceased," &c. (*r*). In general, however, the neglect thus to distinguish the parties will be aided by intendment, particularly upon a general demurrer, or after verdict (*s*). But where the plaintiff's name has by mistake been inserted instead of the defendant's, or *vice versâ*, the declaration will be bad upon special demurrer (*t*)(551); though it is aided by verdict, or upon general demurrer, by the statute of jeofails (*u*); and if the part of the declaration in which the mistake of the parties has occurred can be treated as surplusage, then no advantage can be taken even by special demurrer (*x*). But it has been decided that the statutes of jeofails do not extend to the names of *third persons* (*y*); and a plea of judgment recovered, stating that in the former suit the plaintiff impleaded the defendant in a plea, &c. to the damage of the "defendant," is bad on *general* demurrer (*z*). When the debt arose on record or specialty, it was formerly usual to state as well in the writ as declaration the defendant's description in the record or specialty under an *alias dictus*, but this is no longer the practice (*a*).

Time, certainty in statement of.

2dly. The declaration in personal actions must in general state a *time* when every material or traversable fact happened (*b*), and whenever heretofore a venue was necessary, time must also have been mentioned (*c*)(552). The statement of the real or precise time, however, is not necessary(553) even in criminal cases(*d*), unless it constitute a [*288] *material part of the contract, &c. declared upon, or unless the date, &c. of a written contract or instrument is professed to be described (*e*); and except in ejectment, in which the demise must be stated to have been made after the title of the lessor of the plaintiff (554) and his right of entry accrued (*f*). And in stating that a deed, bill, or a promissory note, &c. "*bears date*" on a certain day, or in describing an usurious

(*q*) Ld. Raym. 899; Com. Dig. Action on the Case for Assumpsit, H. 3, Pleader, C. 13, *post*.
(*r*) 2 Wils. 386; Cro. Eliz. 267; Com. Dig. Pleader, C. 18.
(*s*) *Id. ibid.*; 1 N. R. 172.
(*t*) 1 B. & P. 59; Willes, 8.
(*u*) 16 & 17 Car. 2, c. 8; 4 Anne, c. 16; Com. Dig. Action on the Case for Assumpsit, H. 3; Willes, 5.
(*x*) *Ante*, 265, 266; 4 Moore & Scott, 417.
(*y*) Willes, 8, 9.
(*z*) 7 Taunt. 271.
(*a*) 1 Saund. 14 a, n. 1.
(*b*) Ring *v.* Roxbrough, 2 Crom. & Jerv. 418; 2 Tyr. 468.
(*c*) *Per* Buller, J., 5 T. R. 620, 624, 625; Com. Dig. Pleader, C. 19; Plowd. 24; 14 East, 291; Steph. 2d edit. 343.
(*d*) *Id.*; 1 Saund. 24, n. 1; Co. Lit. 283 a; 2 Saund. 5, n. 3, 259, n. 2; Hawk. Pl. Cr. B. 2, c. 25, s. 81; 5 Taunt. 765; 2 Moore, 91.
(*e*) 4 T. R. 590; 10 Mod. 313; 2 Campb. 307, 308.
(*f*) 2 East, 257; *ante*, 216, 221.

(551) If a plaintiff have the same christian name as a defendant, and the declaration, after stating the names of each party correctly, and at full length, use the christian name only, as, "the said James being in custody," it is certain to a common intent, and good on special demurrer. Hildreth *v.* Hawes, July, 1801, M. S. Kent, C. J., cited 3 Caines' Rep. 170, note, 2d edit.

(552) Vide Denison and others *v.* Richardson, 14 East's Rep. 300, 301. Phillips' Ev. 164.

(553) Vide Phillips' Ev. 164. The United States *v.* Vigol, 2 Dall. 346. Cheetham *v.* Lewis, 3 Johns. Rep. 43. Tiffany *v.* Driggs, 13 Johns. Rep. 253. The text, in the fourth London edition, has the word "material," instead of "necessary."

(554) Vide Van Alen *v.* Rogers, 1 Johns. Cas. 283.

III. THE GENERAL REQUISITES, &c.

3dly. What degree of certainty is required.

contract where time is the very gist of the matter, the real day must be truly stated (*g*)(555). In general, the day on which a promise is laid to pay a bill of exchange is not material, unless it be expressly alleged to have been its date (*h*); and it is no objection that the day of the promise appears to have been more than six years before the commencement of the action. Thus in assumpsit upon a contract, the day upon which it is made being alleged only for form, the plaintiff is at liberty to prove that the contract, whether it be express or implied, was made at any other time (*i*). And where it is not essential that the day laid in the pleading should accord with the truth, it is not material that the time stated be so distant, that in fact the parties could not have then been alive (*k*), if in point of law there is no intrinsic impossibility that the time laid is correct (*l*). So in an action against the acceptor of a bill payable after sight, an allegation that it was accepted on the day of the date will be proved, though it appear that it was accepted on a subsequent day (*m*). And an allegation in case by a reversioner that his tenant was, "and still is," possessed of the land, is supported by proof that at the time of the *injury* the tenant occupied; and a subsequent change of tenancy is not material (*n*); so that the words "*and still is*," being immaterial, may be rejected as surplusage. [*289] *A deed also may be stated in pleading to have been made on a day different from that on which it bears date, provided in such case the words "*bearing date*," &c. be omitted (*o*), and it be merely stated that "on, &c." the deed was made. So in an action on a bill or note, though it be payable at a particular time "after date," it is not necessary to describe the instrument as "bearing date" on a given day; it suffices to state that "heretofore, to wit, on, &c." it was made, &c.; and the Court said they would intend that the date of the instrument was the day on which it was alleged to have been made (*p*). So in trespass the time is not material (*q*); and where several trespasses are stated to have been committed on divers days and times between a particular day and the commencement of the action, the plaintiff is at liberty to prove a single act of trespass anterior to the first day; though he cannot give in evidence repeated acts of trespass, unless committed during the time stated in the declaration (*r*). When in one continued sentence, or in

(*g*) Cowp. 671; 2 Stra. 806; 10 Mod. 313; 3 T. R. 531; Steph. 2d ed. 345.

(*h*) Hawkey *v.* Burwick, 1 Younge & Jerv. 376.

(*i*) 2 Stra. 806; 10 Mod. 313; 1 Younge & Jerv. 376.

(*k*) Atkins *v.* Warrington, 7th June, 1827, K. B. before the three judges, MS. Declaration in assumpsit on the common counts; 1st, stated that defendant heretofore, to wit, on the 1st day of November, A. D. *one thousand eight* (omitting *hundred*) and 26, at London, was indebted, &c. and afterwards stated "on the day and year aforesaid;" special demurrer, assigning as cause that the time mentioned was nonsensical and absurd, and no year was mentioned; and joinder. Chitty for plaintiff, and Watson for defendant, Bayley, J., held this to be no ground of demurrer, first, because the year A. D. 1826 was clearly intended, for as the year 1000 was mentioned, and then eight and 26, the word *eight* must mean *hundred*; and, 2dly, at least the word must mean 1000 eight and 26, which would be 1034, and the law does not recognize the impossibility of defendant living even since that time, and consequently there was nothing impossible in declaration. Holroyd and Littledale, Justices, concurred. Judgment for plaintiff.

(*l*) Steph. 2d edit. 344; see 2 Saund. 291 c, note 1; *Id.* 171 a, note 1.

(*m*) 1 Stark. 46.

(*n*) 3 Taunt. 137.

(*o*) 4 East, 477.

(*p*) 6 M. & Sel. 75.

(*q*) Co. Lit. 283 a.

(*r*) 1 Saund. 24, note 1; 1 Stark. R. 351.

(555) Vide Harris *v.* Hudson, 4 Esp. Rep. 152.

III. THE GENERAL REQUISITES, &c. — 3dly. What degree of certainty is required.

several sentences connected by the conjunction "and," several facts are stated, the time, though only once alleged, will apply to each fact; as in trespass, that the defendant, on, &c. at, &c. made an assault on the plaintiff, *and took* and carried away a bag (*s*). And it is said that in averring the performance of a contract, it is not necessary to state any particular day, unless time be material (*t*), and to a negative matter no time need be alleged (*u*). But there should in general be a distinct averment of time to every material fact (*x*).

In framing the declaration, care must be taken that no material part of the cause of action, or damages resulting from the injury, or other material fact, appear to have accrued after the time to which the declaration by its date at the top refers, for otherwise it will be subject to a demurrer (*y*) (556); and where it was positively and expressly averred in the declaration that the plaintiff had sustained damage from a cause subsequent (557) to the commencement of the action, or previous to the plaintiff's having any right of action, and the jury gave entire damages, [*290] *judgment will be arrested; but where the cause of action is properly laid, and the other matter either comes under a *scilicet*, or is void, insensible or impossible, and therefore it cannot be intended that the jury ever had it under their consideration, the plaintiff will be entitled to judgment (*z*) (558). And after verdict, judgment will not be stayed or reversed for a mistake of the day, month, or year, in any bill, declaration, or pleading, where the right time in any writ, plaint, roll, or record preceding, or in the same roll or record where the mistake is committed is once alleged (*a*) (559); and this provision was afterwards extended to judgment by confession, *nil dicit*, &c. in Courts of record (*b*), and to penal actions (*c*).

Moreover, the pleader must take care, in stating time, that there be no *inconsistency* in dates. Thus where a declaration at the suit of an administrator, after stating a promise to the intestate on the 2d January, A. D. 1832, afterwards stated that the letters of administration were granted to the plaintiff at a *prior date*, viz. the 2d January, 1831, this obvious inconsistency was holden fatal on special demurrer, although the latter date was preceded by an allegation that the grant was after the death, and the time was laid under a *videlicet* (*d*).

(*s*) Cro. Jac. 443, 262; Andr. 251; Com. Dig. Pleader, C. 19; 1 Ld. Raym. 576; Sir W. Jones, 56.

(*t*) Cro. Eliz. 880.

(*u*) 5 T. R. 616; Plowd. 24 a; Com. Dig. Pleader, C. 19.

(*x*) 14 East, 300; 11 Price, 400; and see note (*d*) *infra*. As to the legal import of the words "immediately," and "then and there," see Com. Rep. 480; 1 Chit. Crim. Law, 219.

(*y*) 2 Saund. 291, n. 1. c. As to this, see *post*, 291, *et subs.*; and 2 Crom. & Jer. 418, 464; 2 Tyr. 468, S. C.

(*z*) 2 Saund. 171 c; Com. Dig. Pleader, C. 19.

(*a*) 16 & 17 Car. 2, c. 8; Com. Dig. Pleader, C. 19.

(*b*) 4 Anne, c. 16.

(*c*) 4 Geo. 2, c. 26; Willes, 600.

(*d*) Ring *v.* Roxbrough, 2 Tyr. 468; 2 Crom. & Jerv. 418, S. C.

(556) Acc. Lowry *v.* Lawrence, 1 Caines' Rep. 69. Cheetham *v.* Lewis, 3 Johns. Rep. 42. Waring *v.* Yates, 10 Johns. Rep. 119. And the mistake is not cured by verdict. Ward *v.* Honeywood, Doug. 61. Cheetham *v.* Lewis, 3 Johns. Rep. 44. Contra, Bemis *v.* Faxon, 4 Mass. Rep. 263. {Crouse *v.* Miller, 10 Serg. & Rawle, 155. See Shaw *v.* Wile, 2 Rawle, 280.}

(557) {Langer *v.* Parish, 8 Serg. & Rawle, 134. See the cases cited in the opinion of the court.}

(558) {Shaw *v.* Wile, 2 Rawle, 280. 10 Serg. & Rawle, 158, 159.} Vide Buckley *v.* Kenyon, 10 East's Rep. 139.

(559) Vide Allaire *v.* Ouland, 2 Johns. Cas. 56.

Since the uniformity of process act, 2 W. 4, c. 39, all the new writs are considered the commencement of the action, and not as before mere process to bring the defendant into Court; so that now, if the writ be issued before the cause of action is complete, the plaintiff would be nonsuited, if the defendant plead so as to raise the objection (*e*); and the above expressly requires that the true day of issuing the process shall be stated therein; and Reg. Gen. Hil. Term, 4 W. 4, No. 1, requires the *issue* to state the actual date of the writ as well as of the declaration. The Reg. Gen. Mich. Term, 3 W. 4, reg. 15, and of Hil. Term, 4 W. 4, reg. 1, expressly require the declaration in all *personal* actions to be entitled of the very day of the month and year when the same is filed or delivered. But the neglect to entitle the declaration of the proper day, month, and year, is probably no ground of demurrer, but merely an irregularity to be taken advantage of by summons or motion (*f*). The declaration need not expressly notice the date of the writ (*g*), though care must be observed to state all facts to have occurred on a day before the writ issued, or at least not on a subsequent date (*h*).

III. THE GENERAL REQUISITES, &c.

3dly. What degree of certainty is required.

The present practice in declaring as to time.

It is also essential that no material fact be stated in the declaration to have happened after the *date or test of the writ*, which is now in all cases considered the commencement of the action, and cannot legally be issued until after the cause of action is complete. The Reg. Gen. Hil. Term, 4 W. 4, prescribes that the date of the first writ shall be stated in the *issue*, and consequently it will afterwards appear on the face of the nisi prius record. The pleader should therefore always ascertain the date of the first writ, and state every fact to have occurred before that day. When, however, the exact day is immaterial, as in an action for verbal slander, the statement by mistake in the declaration that the words were uttered after the writ issued, but before the title of the declaration, would be aided by verdict, and would not afterwards constitute a ground of motion in arrest of judgment or writ of error, because it will be inferred that the judge would not have suffered the plaintiff to have obtained a verdict, if the evidence had shown that the action was prematurely brought (*i*).

3dly, It was also essential that a *place* (560) should be alleged where every fact material and traversable occurred (*k*). But the pleading rules, Hil. Term, 4 W. 4, in order to abolish all unnecessary statements, now enjoin that the *venue* shall be stated only in the *margin*, and not be repeated in the body, excepting when local description is essential; and that in trespass *quare clausum fregit*, the name of the close or abuttals must be stated, or a special demurrer will be sustainable; and in a declaration in an inferior Court, or upon a judgment or proceeding of an inferior Court, every material fact must be averred to have accrued *within the jurisdiction* (*l*). We will presently consider the doctrine of *venues*. Place.

(*e*) Alston *v.* Underhill, 1 Crom. & M. 498, 768; 3 Tyr. 427; Steward *v.* Layton, 3 Dowl. 430; 3 Chitty's Gen. Prac. 159.

(*f*) Neal *v.* Richardson, 2 Dowl. 89; 3 Chitty's Gen. Prac. 463, 464.

(*g*) Dupre *v.* Langridge, 2 Dowl. 584; 3 Chitty's Gen. Prac. 464.

(*h*) *Ante*, 289.

(*i*) Steward *v.* Layton, 3 Dowl. 430.

(*k*) 5 T. R. 620; 14 East, 300, 301.

(*l*) Read v. Pope, 1 Crom. M. & Ros. 302.

(560) Vide Denison and others *v.* Richardson, 14 East's Rep. 300, 351. Gardner *v.* Humphrey, 10 Johns. Rep. 53.

III. THE GENERAL REQUISITES, &c. — 3dly. What degree of certainty is required. Of certainty in stating the cause of action.

4thly, It is still more material that certainty and accuracy be observed in the *more substantial parts* of the declaration, which state *the cause of action itself*. Thus, in assumpsit, the consideration of the contract and the contract itself must be fully stated; and therefore, in the instance before mentioned, a declaration stating that in consideration that the plaintiff had sold to the defendant a certain horse, at and for "a certain quantity of oil," not specifying the quantity, was holden insufficient (*m*). So a declaration in debt on "a certain bond," without stating the particulars, is not sufficiently certain (*n*); and a declaration in replevin for taking divers goods and chattels of the plaintiff, without naming them, is bad for uncertainty (*o*), and a declaration in trespass for taking fish, &c. or divers goods and chattels, without specifying the number or quality, is too general (*p*)(561). So is a declaration in ejectment for "a tenement," not showing of what description (*q*). On the other hand, we have seen that the declaration should contain no unnecessary statement, nor prolixity in the statement [*291] *of the facts which are alleged (*r*). The *application* of those several rules will be better considered when we examine the *particular parts* of the declaration. It may here suffice to observe that the want of sufficient certainty is generally aided by verdict at common law (*s*); or even by the defendant's pleading to the declaration (*t*); or by demurring to the whole, where only a part of the count is bad (*u*); but a judgment by default for the plaintiff does not cure the defect of uncertainty in not stating the description and quantity of goods under the statute of jeofails (*x*).

[*292] IV. ITS PARTS, &c.

*IV. THE SEVERAL PARTS AND PARTICULAR REQUISITES OF DECLARATIONS.

As explanatory of the following subdivisions and observations, it may be expedient here to give the form of a declaration in *assumpsit*, containing most of the parts to be commented upon, by way of example.

Title, Court. Title, term. Venue. Commencement. Body.

In the King's Bench, [*or* "C. P." *or* "Exchequer of Pleas."]

On the 12th day of January, A. D. 1836.

Middlesex (to wit.) John Noaks, by Y. Z. his attorney, complains of Thomas Stiles, who has been summoned to answer the plaintiff [in an action upon promises.] *For that whereas*, before and at the time of the making of the promise of the defendant hereinafter next mentioned, the defendant was an attorney, to wit, an attorney of the Court of our Lord the King, before the King himself. And thereupon heretofore, to wit, on the —

(*m*) *Ante*, 271.
(*n*) *Id.*; 13 East, 102.
(*o*) 1 Moore, 386; 7 Taunt. 642; S. C. 8 Moore, 379.
(*p*) Com. Dig. Pleader, C. 21.
(*q*) *Ante*, 273.
(*r*) *Ante*, 262, 263; Moore, 467.
(*s*) 2 B. & P. 265; 1 N. R. 172; 2 Saund. 74 b; 1 Saund. 228 a; *ante*, 271.
(*t*) 2 Saund. 74 b; 6 B. & C. 295; *ante*, 273; *post*, 295.
(*u*) Saund. 379, 380; Com. Dig. Plead. C. 32.
(*x*) 4 Anne, c. 16; 7 Taunt. 642; 1 Moore, 386, S. C.; 5 Bar. and Ald. 712. But see the late case, 8 Moore, 379, making this questionable.

(561) {In an action on the case against a Judge of Probate, for appointing, as guardian to a minor, a man who was insolvent, and neglecting to take security from him for the faithful discharge of his duty as guardian, } a declaration stating that the plaintiff was owner, and legal possessor of 2000 dollars worth of personal property, { which was spent and unaccounted for by such guardian, } was held bad, after verdict. Phelps *v.* Still, 1 Day's Rep. 315.

day of —— A. D. ——, in consideration that the plaintiff, at the request of the defendant, *would* retain and employ the defendant as such attorney, to commence and prosecute a certain action, to wit, an action at the suit of the plaintiff against one G. H., for the recovery of a certain sum of money, to wit, the sum of £——, then claimed by the plaintiff to be due to him from the defendant for fees and reward to be therefore paid to the now defendant; he, the now defendant, then promised the plaintiff to observe and perform his duty as such attorney for the plaintiff in the premises. And the plaintiff saith that he, confiding in the said promise of the defendant, did afterwards, to wit, on the day and year aforesaid, at the request of the defendant, retain and employ him as such attorney to *commence* and prosecute the said action against the said G. H. in the Court of K. B. at Westminster, for the recovery of the said sum of money, and for fees and reward to be therefore paid to the now defendant, and the defendant then accepted the said retainer and employment, and in pursuance thereof then commenced and prosecuted the said action. And although such proceedings were thereupon had in the same action, that afterwards, to wit, on, &c. a certain issue, [*or* "issues" *if several*,] before then joined between the same parties, was about to be tried, according to the course and practice of the said Court, and thereupon it then became and was the duty of the now defendant as such attorney, and in pursuance of his said retainer and employment, to cause and procure *due care* to be observed in ascertaining and adducing sufficient evidence to enable and entitle the plaintiff to obtain and recover a verdict in the said action against the then defendant therein; yet the defendant, disregarding his said duty and his promise in that behalf, did not nor would cause or procure due care to be observed in so ascertaining and adducing sufficient evidence to enable or entitle the plaintiff to obtain a verdict in the action against the said then defendant, but wholly neglected and omitted so to do. And by reason and in consequence thereof, and of the careless and improper conduct of the now defendant in and about the conduct of the said action for the plaintiff, afterwards, to wit, on, &c., the plaintiff became and was nonsuited therein. And by reason thereof the plaintiff hath been and is greatly delayed and hindered in the recovery of the said money so claimed by him as aforesaid, and the plaintiff hath incurred and paid, and hath become liable to pay, *to the said* G. H., divers sums of money amounting to a large sum, to wit, the sum of £100, as and for his costs of the defence of the said action. And thereby also the plaintiff hath incurred great trouble and expense, to wit, an expense of £100, in and about the said action, which hath been and is by means of the said negligence and improper conduct of the defendant in the premises become abortive and unproductive as aforesaid. To the damage of the plaintiff of £——, and thereupon he brings suit, &c.

Inducement. Consideration. Promise. Averments. Defendant's breach. Consequent damage. Conclusion.

We will consider the above form, and its several *parts*, and those of a declaration in general, under the following heads, viz.

Division and arrangement of parts of a declaration in assumpsit.

1. The title of the Declaration as to the *Court*.
2. The title of the Declaration as to the *Time* when it is filed or delivered.
3. The *venue* in the *margin*.
4. The *commencement*.
5. The *body*.
   - *Inducement.*
   - *Consideration.*
   - *Promise.*
   - *Averments.*
   - *Breach.*
   - *Consequent damages.*
6. The *conclusion*.
7. The *Profert* of Deeds, Probates, and Letters of Administration, &c.
8. The statement of *pledges* to be discontinued.
9. Other *miscellaneous* points.

IV. ITS PARTS, &c.

1st. Title of the Court in the former practice.

1. *Title of Court formerly.* In the King's Bench, when the proceedings were by bill, the declaration was entitled with the name of the prothonotary or chief clerk, (now "Ellenborough,") for enrolling pleas in civil causes, depending between party and party, on the plea side of the Court, and particularly so when by bill (*y*). When the proceedings were by original, the declaration was usually entitled, "In the King's Bench;" and in the Common Pleas and exchequer, the name of the Court was superscribed, as in a declaration by original in the King's Bench.

But now, and since the abolition of the previous varying writs to bring the defendant into Court in *personal* actions, by the uniformity of process act, 2 W. 4, c. 39, the Reg. Gen. Mich. T. 3 W. 4, I. reg. 15, orders that "every declaration shall in future *be entitled in the proper Court*," and if that title be omitted or be merely *indorsed*, the Court will set aside the declaration for irregularity (*z*).

2d. The title of declaration as to time.

2. *Title as to Time.* The title of the *Term*, with reference to the ancient proceedings *ore tenus*, was considered as a statement or memorandum of the time when the plaintiff and the defendant came into Court, and in form alleged his cause of complaint (*a*). This could then only be in term time, when the defendant was in Court; consequently a declaration must formerly in general be entitled in term (*b*). It was also a general rule that the declaration should be entitled of the term in which the writ was returnable, or of that of the defendant's appearance, and if it were entitled of a subsequent term it was irregular, and a judgment signed for want of a plea thereto was also irregular (*c*). A declaration by bill must regularly have been entitled of or after the day on which the bail had been filed or an appearance entered, because the bill, of which it is a copy, cannot be filed until the bail is put in, which alone in the King's Bench gives the Court jurisdiction, and when by reference to the practice of declaring *ore tenus* the defendant was in Court to hear the cause of complaint (*d*) (562); unless in the case of a declaration *de bene esse*. Therefore, if there be two defendants, and one of them could not be served or arrested on the first process, and he were brought into Court upon another writ, returnable in a subsequent term, the declaration should be entitled of the last term (*e*). So where one of several defendants had been outlawed, the declaration must be entitled after such outlawry was complete (*f*); and where a sole defendant could not be served or arrested on process returnable in one term, and an *alias* returnable in the next was issued, the declaration might and perhaps should have been entitled of the last term (*g*). In these cases, however, the plaintiff could not upon a declaration in chief give in evi-

Former practice as to Term.

(*y*) Tidd, 9th ed. 43.

(*z*) Kippling *v.* Watts, K. B. Mich. T. 1835; Legal Observer, 5 Dec. 1835, p. 86.

(*a*) 1 T. R. 116.

(*b*) The term in the midst of which the king dies, may be entitled in the first year of the succeeding king's reign, 1 Dowl. Rep. 4.

(*c*) 1 Marsh. 341; 3 T. R. 624.

(*d*) 2 Lev. 13, 176; 1 Ventr. 136; Com. Dig. Pleader, C. 6; Rep. temp. Hardw. 141; Tidd, 9th ed. 426; 1 B. & P. 367; 8 T. R. 456.

(*e*) 1 Wils. 242.

(*f*) 1 East, 133; 1 Wils. 78.

(*g*) 3 T. R. 627.

(562) Vide Sabin *v.* Wood, 10 Johns. Rep. 219.

dence a cause of action arising after the first term (*h*); though a declaration by the bye, (now not allowed,) not being founded on the original process, might have been entitled of the second term, and the plaintiff therein might give in evidence a cause of action arising after the first (*i*)(563). There were formerly many decisions as to when or not a *special title* was requisite or proper, but which now are only useful in explanation of the previous practice (*k*).

IV. ITS PARTS, &c.

2dly. Title as to time.

When on the face of the declaration, entitled generally of the term, it appeared that the cause of action accrued after the first day thereof, the defendant might demur specially (*l*). But it was holden not to be a ground of error to entitle the declaration of the term generally, although the declaration showed that the cause of action accrued after the first day of the term and during its currency (*m*). The Court would formerly in any case give leave to amend on payment of costs (*n*). And it has been holden, that if after verdict *it be made appear upon motion in arrest of judgment that the bill was filed and declaration delivered *after* the cause of action had actually accrued, the plaintiff was entitled to judgment without any amendment, for though the declaration being general, relate *prima facie* to the first day of the term, yet the bill being filed on a subsequent day, all the subsequent proceedings related thereto by the course and practice of the Court, of which, if error were brought, the Court would *ex officio* take notice (*o*); and therefore the general title was aided by reference to the time of filing bail (*p*): and in another case it was held that after verdict the only course was to allege diminution (*q*). In general it is no ground of error upon a judgment of an inferior Court, that the plaint was levied before the cause of action accrued (*r*). By an express provision (*s*) these objections are aided in the Court of Common Pleas at Lancaster. And in trespass, with a continuance after the term of which the declaration was entitled, the Court refused to arrest the judgment (*t*).

Consequences of mistake in title before 2 W. 4, c. 39, and recent rules.

[*295]

If the action were commenced before the cause of it accrued, the defendant might have pleaded that matter in abatement (*u*). Where the proceedings were entered with a general memorandum of the term, and the cause of action appeared in evidence to have arisen after the first day of the term, the plaintiff would be nonsuited, unless he produced or proved the writ, and thereby showed that it was really sued out subsequently to the cause of action (*v*). And

(*h*) *Id.* 624.
(*i*) *Id.* 627.
(*k*) See Chitty on Pleading, 5th ed. 293, 294, and 2 Crom. & Jer. 461.
(*l*) 1 T. R. 116. The demurrer should be special, 1 Stra. 21. It seems safer to demur, or the objection may be aided as a jeofail after verdict by 5 G. 1, c. 13; see Andr. 13; 2 Bing. 463; 10 Moore, 194; 1 M'Cle. & Y. 202; although not perhaps by any of the previous statutes of jeofail Cro. Eliz. 325; Cro. Car. 272, 292, 595; 1 Show. 147; Sir Wm. Jones, 304.
(*m*) 2 Bing. 463; 10 Moore, 194; 1 M'Clel. & Y. 202, S. C.
(*n*) 7 T. R. 474; 1 Wils. 78; Tidd, 9th edit. 426, 427; 2 Chit. Rep. 22. Amendment not allowed in penal actions, 6 Taunt. 19; 1 Marsh. 419, S. C.
(*o*) 2 Lev. 176; 3 Salk. 9; 1 T. R. 118; 1 Vent. 264; 1 Sid. 373, 432; Bul. N. P. 137; Tidd, 9th edit. 428; *ante*, 217, 219.
(*p*) 2 Lev. 13, 176; 1 Vent. 135; Bul. N. P. 137, 138; Carth. 114, 115; Tidd, 9th ed. 428.
(*q*) Carth. 288, 289; 2 Lev. 176; and see cases in note (*o*), *supra*.
(*r*) 3 B. & Ald. 605.
(*s*) 39 & 40 Geo. 3, c. 105.
(*t*) Andr. 250.
(*u*) Com. Dig. Abatement, G. 6.
(*v*) 2 Saund. 1, n. 1; Burr. 1241; 1 Bla. Rep. 312; Bul. Ni. Pri. 137; 5 Esp. 163; 8 B. & C. 329.

(563) { Ruston *v.* Owston, 2 M'Clell. and Young's Rep. 202. }

IV. ITS PARTS, &c. — 2dly. Title as to time.

where in a similar case the trespass complained of was admitted by the defendant's plea of *son assault demesne*, the Court held it to be well enough, for the plaintiff need not give any evidence on that plea, unless to aggravate damages, and the Court would not nonsuit him, because it was amendable by a new bill (*w*).

[*296] *The declaration might also be amended in this respect at the instance of the defendant, if necessary for his defence. Thus where the declaration was entitled of the term generally, and the defendant pleaded *plene administravit* (*x*), or a tender made before the exhibiting of the bill, upon which he would give in evidence an administration of assets, or a tender made between the first day of term and the day of suing out the writ, it was held that he should either call upon the plaintiff to entitle his declaration properly (*y*); or should plead *the fiction* of the Court specially (564), without calling upon the plaintiff to alter his declaration; or should prove or produce the writ on the trial (*z*). And where the declaration was entitled generally of the term, it was held that the defendant might give evidence at the trial of the time when it was actually filed in support of the plea, that the cause of action did not accrue within six years next before the exhibiting of the bill (*a*). But where the plaintiff improperly commenced his declaration with a special memorandum, stating that the bill was exhibited upon a certain day in vacation, the defendant's only course was to move to set aside the special memorandum (*b*).

The present practice as to the title of time.

By the *present practice* every declaration in a *personal action commenced* in either of the superior Courts, (Reg. Gen. Mich. T. 3 W. 4, reg. 15, and Hil. T. 4 W. 4, reg. 1,) is to be entitled of the day of the month and year when actually filed or delivered. The neglect so to entitle the same would in general only be an irregularity and not a ground even of special demurrer (*c*), or for a summons to compel plaintiff to state the proper title (*d*). The *date* of the *writ* need not, we have seen, be stated in the declaration, though it must in the issue (*e*). As the above rules extend only to *personal* actions *commenced* in the superior Courts, and not to *scire facias* or ejectment, a declaration in ejectment is to be entitled usually of the preceding term as heretofore (*f*), unless where the right of entry has accrued pending or after an issuable term, when the statute 1 W. 4, c. 70, sect 36, gives a new and peculiar right of declaring (*g*). When an action has been removed from an inferior Court, the title is to be of the term in which the removing process was returnable.

Repetition of time still essential.

As the Courts by Reg. Gen. Hil. T. 4 W. 4, at length ventured to promulgate that there should be no *statement or repetition* of *venue* or place in the body of a declaration when immaterial, except in trespass *quare clausum fregit*,

(*w*) 2 Stra. 1271; 1 Wils. 171.
(*x*) Rep. temp. Hardw. 141; 1 Sid. 433; Tidd, 9th ed. 427.
(*y*) 4 Esp. 72; 2 Saund. 1, n. 1; 1 Stra. 638; 1 Wils. 39, S. C. 304; Cowp. 456; Tidd, 9th ed. 427.
(*z*) 3 Burr. 1241; Tidd, 9th ed. 427; 4 Esp. Rep. 72.
(*a*) 5 B. & C. 149.
(*b*) 7 B. & C. 407.
(*c*) Neal *v.* Richardson, 2 Dowl. 89; 3 Chitty's Gen. Prac. 463.
(*d*) Wilkes *v.* Halifax, 2 Wils. 256; Thompson *v.* Marshall, 1 Wils. 304.
(*e*) Du Pre *v.* Langridge, 2 Dowl. 584.
(*f*) Doe dem. Fry *v.* Roe, 3 Moore & Scott, 370; Doe dem. Gillet *v.* Roe, *id.* 376; 1 Crom. M. & Ros. 19; 4 Tyrw. S. C.; Doe *v.* Evans, 2 Adol. & El. 11; 1 Bing. N. C. 253; 1 Dowl. 4.
(*g*) 1 W. 4, c. 70, sect. 36.

(564) Vide Dudlow *v.* Watchorn and Thibault, 16 East's Rep. 39.

or when local description is requisite; it is to be hoped that ere long there will be a similar rule, abolishing the necessity for repetition of *time*, when precise time is immaterial, but till then time must be repeated, as by the word *then*, in every distinct sentence (*h*). IV. ITS PARTS, &c. 2dly. Title as to time.

3dly. The *Venue*.

Immediately after the title of the term follows the statement in the *margin* of the *venue* or county in which the facts are alleged to have occurred, and in which the cause is to be tried. The doctrine of venues was explained and elucidated by Lord Mansfield in the case of *Fabrigas* v. *Mostyn* (*i*), and in Co. Lit. 125 a, n. 1, "There is a *substantial* and a *formal* distinction *as* to the *locality of trials*. The *substantial* distinction with regard to matters arising *within the realm* is where the proceeding is *in rem*, and where the effect of the judgment could not be had, *if it were laid in a wrong place; as in the case of ejectments, where possession is to be delivered by the sheriff of the county; and as trials in England are in particular counties, and the officers are county officers, the judgment could not have effect if the action were not laid in the proper county (*k*). So, with regard to matters that arise *out of the realm*, there is also a substantial distinction of locality, for there are some cases that arise out of the realm, which ought not to be tried any where but in the country where they arise; as if two persons fight in France, and both happening casually to be here, one should bring an action of assault against the other, it might be a doubt whether such an action could be maintained here; because, though it is not a criminal prosecution, it must be laid to be against the peace of the king, but the breach of the peace is merely local, though the trespass against the person is transitory (*l*). So if an action were brought relative to an estate in a foreign country, where the question was a matter of title only, and not of damages, there might be a solid distinction of locality." (*m*) [*297]

"The *formal* distinction arises from the *mode* of trial; for trials in England being by jury, and the kingdom being divided into counties, and each county considered as a separate district or principality, it is absolutely necessary that there should be some county where the action is brought in particular, that there may be a process to the sheriff of that county to bring a jury from thence to try it (*n*). This matter of form goes to all cases that arise abroad; but the law makes a distinction between transitory and local actions. If the matter, which is the cause of a transitory action, arise within the realm, it may be laid in any county, the place not being material; as if an imprisonment be in Middlesex, it may be laid in Surrey, and though proved to be done in Middlesex, it does not at all prevent the plaintiff from recovering damages. The place of transitory actions is never material, except where by particular acts of parliament it is made so; as in the case of churchwardens and constables, and other cases which require the action to be brought in the proper

(*h*) *Ante*, 290, note (*d*).

(*i*) Cowp. 176, 177. See 2 Camp. 274. And as to venues in general, see Com. Dig. Action, N. and Pleader, C. 20; Bac. Ab. Action, A. a; Vin. Ab. Trial, H. a. 2, &c. and Place, 7 Co. 3; Stephen, 2d edit. 328.

(*k*) 7 T. R. 587, 588; *post*, 298.

(*l*) *Sed quære*, for the *contra pacem* is not now traversable, see 2 Bla. Rep. 1058; Vin. Ab. *Contra pacem*.

(*m*) 1 Stra. 646; 4 T. R. 503. *Sed quære*, if there be no court of judicature to resort to abroad. *Id. ibid.* 6 East, 599.

(*n*) Co. Lit. 125 a, b.

IV. ITS PARTS, &c.

3dly. The *Venue.*

county. The parties, upon sufficient ground, have an opportunity of applying to the Court in time to change the venue, but if they go to trial without it, that is no objection. So all actions of a transitory nature that arise abroad may be laid as happening in an English county; but there are occasions which make
[*298] it absolutely necessary *to state in the declaration that the cause of action really happened abroad; as in the case of specialties, where the date must be set forth, if the declaration state a specialty to have been made at Westminster, in Middlesex, and upon producing the deed, it bear date at Bengal, the action is gone (*o*), because it is such a variance between the deed and the declaration as makes it appear to be a different instrument (565); but the law has in that case invented a fiction, and has said, the party shall first set out the description truly, and then give a venue only for form, and for the sake of trial by a *videlicet* in the county of Middlesex, or any other county." From these observations it appears that the points as to venues may be considered practically, with reference, 1st, To where, or in what county, the venue is to be laid; 2dly, How, and in what parts of the declaration, it is to be stated; and 3dly, The consequences of mistake and when they are aided.

1st. The venue is either *local* or *transitory;* if local, it must be laid and the cause be tried in the county in which the cause of action arose, or the injury was really committed, although even then subject to be tried by the Court or a judge in any other county or place under 3 & 4 W. 4, c. 42, sect. 22. And if the venue be transitory, it may be laid in the declaration and the cause tried in any county (*p*), subject also then to its being changed by the Court in some cases, if not laid in the county where the cause of action really arose (*q*). We will consider when the venue is local or transitory at common law, and when it is local by statute.

When the venue is local.

When the cause of action could only have arisen in a particular place or county, it is *local*, and the venue must be laid therein. As in real actions, mixed actions, waste, *quare impedit*, or ejectment, for the recovery of the seisin or possession of land, or other real property (*r*). So actions, though merely for damages, occasioned by injuries to real property, are local, as trespass, or case for nuisances (*s*), or waste, &c. to houses, lands, water-courses, right of
[*299] common, ways, or *other real property, unless there were some contract between the parties on which to ground the action (*t*)(566). And if the land, &c. be out of this kingdom, the plaintiff has no remedy in the English Courts; at least if there be a Court of justice in the country in which the land is situ-

(*o*) *Sed quære;* and *vide post*, 300 and note (*q*).

(*p*) 1 Saund. 74, note 2; Gilb. C. P. 84.

(*q*) As to changing the venue, see Tidd, 9th edit. 601. When the plaintiff may bring back the venue after it has been changed on the defendant's application, *id.* 611; and see fully 3 Chitty's Gen. Prac. 646 to 658, for the recent decisions as to *changing venue.*

(*r*) 4 T. R. 504; 2 Bla. Rep. 1070; Com. Dig. Action, N.; 7 T. R. 587, 588; Cowp. 176; 7 Co. 2 b; 3 Lev. 141; Bac. Ab. Actions, Local and Transitory, A.; 2 East, 498, 499.

(*s*) 1 Taunt. 379; 11 East, 226; 2 East, 497; 5 Taunt. 789.

(*t*) 1 Taunt. 379.

(565) Vide Alder *v.* Griner, 13 Johns. Rep. 450.

(566) { See Summer *v.* Finegan, 15 Mass. Rep. 284. } In Lewis *v.* Martin, 1 Day, 263, it was held that an action of account, for the rents and profits of land, might be brought in a different county from that in which the lands lie.

ate, to which he may resort (u). When the parties consent, with leave of the Court, to try a local action in another county, such consent should appear upon the record (x), as it does by suggestion when the Court or a judge order the trial or inquiry to take place in another county under 3 & 4 W. 4, c. 42, sect. 22. Where, however, an injury has been caused by an act done in one county to land, &c. situate in another (y); or whenever the action is founded upon two or more material facts, which took place in different counties, the venue may be laid in either (z)(567). The venue in replevin is local (a)(568).

IV. ITS PARTS, &c.

3dly. The *Venue*.

In an action of debt, or in *scire facias* on a recognizance of bail by bill, when that process, now abolished, was in force, and in an action of debt on a judgment of a Court of record, the venue must be laid in the county where the record is (569); as in Middlesex, upon the judgment or recognizance of either of the superior Courts at Westminster (b); and in *scire facias* on a recognizance of bail by *original* in K. B. the venue might be laid in Middlesex, though all the previous proceedings were in another county (c) (570). Upon a recognizance of bail in C. P. the venue might in *scire facias* be in the county where the bail piece was taken, or in Middlesex (d). But a *scire facias* on a judgment, being only a continuation of the former suit, and not an original proceeding, must be laid in the county where the venue was first laid (571), the defendants being supposed to reside in that county (e). Debt for arrears of a rent-charge against the pernor of the profits, not being the original grantor, is local, the defendant being chargeable in respect of his possession, and not *on the contract (f). And it has been decided that an action for a breach of a custom or by-law of a town is local, but that debt on a charter is not (g). [*300]

When the venue is transitory.

In all actions for injuries *ex delicto* to the *person* or to *personal* property, the venue is in general transitory, and may be laid in any county, though committed out of the jurisdiction of our Courts (h) or of the king's dominions (i)(572).

(u) 4 T. R. 503; 1 Stra. 646; Cowp. 180; 6 East, 598, 599.

(x) Co. Lit. 125 b, 126 a, n. 1; 1 Wils. 298; Tidd, 9th edit. 606.

(y) 6 Taunt. 29.

(z) 2 Taunt. 252, (which overrules 2 Campb. 266, S. C.); 7 Co. 1; 3 Leon. 141; 2 T. R. 241; 7 *Id.* 583; Com. Dig. Action, N. 3, 11. In debt *qui tam* for usury, the venue should be laid where the interest was taken, although the contract was made in another county, 3 B. & C. 700; 5 D. & R. 616, S. C.

(a) 1 Saund. 347, n. 1.

(b) Tidd, 9th edit. 1122; Vin. Ab. Trial, H. a, 2, pl. 17; Hob. 196. As to venue in an action on a recognizance taken before a commissioner at Durham, see 2 Moore, 66.

(c) 5 East, 461.

(d) 5 East, 462, n. b; Tidd, 9th edit. 1122.

(e) Tidd, 9th edit. 1122.

(f) Hob. 37; Vin. Ab. Trial, H. a, 2, pl. 16.

(g) 2 Bla. Rep. 1068.

(h) Cowp. 161; Com. Dig. Action, N. 12.

(i) *Id.*; 2 Bla. Rep. 1058; *sed quære*, Cowp. 176.

(567) Vide Bogert and Lewis *v.* Hildreth, 1 Caines' Rep. 2. Marshall *v.* Hosmer, 3 Mass. Rep. 23.

(568) {Robinson *v.* Mead, 7 Mass. Rep. 353.} Williams *v.* Welch, 5 Wend. R. 290, although brought for a cause of action for which trespass *de bonis asportatis* would lie. *ib.* Atkinson *v.* Holcomb, 4 Cowen, 45, 6.

(569) Acc. Barnes *v.* Kenyon, 2 Johns. Cas. 381.

(570) Debt on bail bond is transitory, though the action must in general be brought in the same court as the original suit. Post, vol. 2, 445, note.

(571) Acc. M'Gill *v.* Perrigo and others, 9 Johns. Rep. 259.

(572) Acc. Glen *v.* Hodges, 9 Johns. Rep. 67. So, an action will lie, here, for a trespass committed on board of a foreign vessel, on the high seas, where both parties are foreigners; but it rests in the sound discretion of the court to exercise jurisdiction or not, according to the circumstances of the case: and where an action was brought for an assault and battery committed on board of a British vessel, on the high seas, by a seaman

IV. ITS PARTS, &c. — 3dly. The *Venue.*

Thus, actions for assaults, batteries, and false imprisonment (*k*); and for words and libels (*l*); even for setting up a defamatory mark on the plaintiff's house, denoting that it was a house of ill-fame, being a personal injury to the plaintiff's character, and not considered as an injury to the building (*m*); and for taking away or injuring personal property (*n*); and for escapes (573) and false returns (*o*); and upon bail-bonds (*p*); are transitory (574). In general, also actions founded upon *contracts* are transitory, though made and even stipulated to be performed out of the kingdom, for *debitum et contractus sunt nullius loci* (*q*). Thus, account; assumpsit; and covenant between the original parties to the deed, and their executors; and debt, even for use and occupation (*r*)(575); and detinue; are in general transitory (*s*). Formerly also the necessity that in a bailable action by original in the King's Bench, the venue must not vary from the original writ, must have been kept in view (*t*), though that was altered by Reg. Gen. Hil. T. 2 W. 4, reg. 40, and now the proceeding by original writ in personal actions has been abolished by 2 W. 4, c. 39. In those transitory actions also in which the Court would change the venue on the defendant's application, and where the plaintiff might wish to bring it back again to the county where it was first laid, upon the usual undertaking to give material evidence in that county, it was necessary to lay the venue in the first instance in the county in which such material evidence could be given (*u*).

The venue in actions on leases.

In an action upon a *lease* for non-payment of rent, or other breach of covenant, when the action is founded on the *privity of contract*, it is *transitory*, and the venue may be laid in any county; but when the action is founded on [*301] the *privity of estate*, it is *local*, and the venue must be laid in the county where the estate lies (*v*). These points may be considered as they arise; 1st. Between the *original parties* to the lease; 2dly. In the case of an alienation of the estate of the *lessor*; and 3dly. Where the estate of the *lessee* has been assigned.

(*k*) Cowp. 161; Co. Lit. 282.
(*l*) 1 T. R. 571.
(*m*) 11 East, 226; 2 Campb. 3, S. C.
(*n*) Com. Dig. Action, N. 12; Salk. 670; Vin. Ab. Trial, H. a, 2, pl. 12; 1 T. R. 479.
(*o*) 1 Wils. 336; Salk. 670; 1 East, 114.
(*p*) Fort. 366; Stra. 727; Ld. Raym. 1455. See 1 Saund. 74, n. h, 5th edit.
(*q*) Com. Dig. Action, N. 12; 1 Saund. 74, 241 b; Cowp. 180; 1 Stra. 612; Ld. Raym. 1352.
(*r*) 5 Taunt. 25.
(*s*) Gilb. C. P. 84; 1 Saund. 74, n. 2.
(*t*) *Ante*, 257.
(*u*) 6 East, 433, 434; 1 Chit. R. 691 a, 377; 2 B. & A. 618.
(*v*) As to the four different descriptions of privities, and in general how far they affect the venue, see the argument in 3 T. R. 394; Walker's Case, 3 Co. 23; and 1 Saund. 237 to 242, and the notes 5 & 6; and see Tidd, 9th edit. 429; 3 Bing. 460.

---

against the master, both parties being British subjects, and intending to return to their own country at the completion of the voyage, the court refused to take cognizance of the cause, but left the injured party to seek redress in the courts of his own country. Gardner *v.* Thomas, 14 Johns. Rep. 134. { But where a foreign seaman is legally *discharged* from the vessel in this country, the action may be maintained. Johnson *v.* Dalton, 1 Cow. Rep. 543. }

(573) Vide Bogert and Lewis *v.* Hildreth, 1 Caines' Rep. 1, 3, 4.

(574) So, case against a sheriff, for refusing to assign a bail bond, is transitory.

(575) Corporation of New York *v.* Dawson, 2 Johns. Cas. 335. Low *v.* Hallett, 2 Caines' Rep. 374. Egler *v.* Marsden, 5 Taunt. 25. King *v.* Fraser, 6 East's Rep. 352, 353. Henwood *v.* Cheeseman, 3 Serg. & Rawle, 500.

3dly. The Venue.

1st. In an action of debt or covenant by the *lessor*, or his executor or administrator, against the *lessee*, or by the *lessee* against the *lessor*, the action, being founded on the mere *privity of contract*, is *transitory*, and though the land lie abroad, the action may be brought in England (*x*)(576); and debt for use and occupation in the *detinet* only, by the lessor against the executor of the lessee, is transitory (*y*); but if the action against the executor be in the *debet* and *detinet*, he being charged as assignee, the venue is local (*z*). An action of assumpsit against a party who succeeds an original tenant and impliedly engages to observe the original terms of tenancy is transitory and not local (*a*).

2dly. An action of *covenant* by the *assignee of the reversion* against the lessee, or by the lessee against the assignee of the reversion, upon an express covenant contained in the lease, and running with the estate in the land, is transitory by the operation of 32 Hen. 8, c. 34 (*b*)(577); which transfers the privity of contract with respect to such covenants, to and against the assignee of the lessor, in the same plight as the lessor had them against the lessee, or the lessee against the lessor (*c*). But in *debt* by the assignee (*d*), or devisee (*e*), of the lessor against the lessee, which is sustainable at common law, and is founded on the privity of estate, the action is local (578).

3dly. If an action of debt or covenant be brought by the lessor (*f*); or his personal representatives (*g*); or by the grantee *of the reversion (*h*); [*302] against the assignee of the lessee (579); or in an action of debt against the executor of the lessee in the *debet* and *detinet* (*i*); the venue is local, and must be laid in the county where the land lies (*k*). And in a recent case in *covenant* against the assignee of the lessee of premises, described in the declaration as situate within the liberties of *Berwick-upon-Tweed*, it was held that the venue could not be laid in Northumberland (*l*). If the land be out of England, no action on the privity of estate can in general be supported in this country (*m*). The action at the suit of the lessor against the assignee of the lessee, was given by the common law, and was local in respect of the *privity of estate*, the privity of contract being destroyed by the assignment (*n*);

(*x*) 1 Saund. 241 b, n. 6; Stra. 776; 2 East, 579.

(*y*) Gilb. Debt, 403; Gilb. C. P. 91.

(*z*) *Id.*; 2 Lev. 80; Vin. Ab. Trial, H. a, 2, pl. 22.

(*a*) Buckworth *v.* Simpson and others, 1 Crom. M. & Ros. 834.

(*b*) 1 Saund. 237, 241 b, n. 6; Carth. 183; 1 Wils. 165; 3 T. R. 394. Privies in blood, as the heir of lessor, might sue in covenant at common law, 3 T. R. 395.

(*c*) *Id. ibid.*; 1 Saund. 237, 241 b, n. 6; 3 T. R. 401, 402.

(*d*) 1 Saund. 238, 241 c, n. 6; Cro. Car. 183; 1 Wils. 165.

(*e*) Sir W. Jones, 53; Vin. Ab. Trial, H. a, 2; Latch. 271; Tidd, 9th edit. 429.

(*f*) 2 East, 579, 580; 6 Mod. 194; 7 T. R. 583.

(*g*) Latch. 197.

(*h*) 1 Saund. 241 c, note 6; 7 T. R. 583; 2 East, 580; 1 Show. 191.

(*i*) *Ante*, 301, note (*y*); 3 Keb. 375.

(*k*) 2 East, 580.

(*l*) 3 Bing. 459.

(*m*) 1 Show. 190, 199; Bac. Ab. Actions Local and Transitory, A. a. And see 4 T. R. 503; *ante*, 297, note (*m*).

(*n*) Sid. 339.

(576) See Henwood *v.* Cheeseman, 3 Serg. & Rawle, 500.

(577) { The English Statute is in force in Pennsylvania, except such parts as relate to the king of England and his grantees. Roberts' Dig. 227. 3 Binn. 620. See Henwood *v.* Cheeseman, 3 Serg. & Rawle, 502. } Vide the corresponding statute, sess. 36. c. 31. s. 12. Laws N. Y. 1 R. L. 363, and by s. 3. the provisions of the act are extended to grants in fee, reserving rent.

(578) Vide Corporation of New York *v.* Dawson, 2 Johns. Cas. 335.

(579) Vide Corporation of New York *v.* Dawson, 2 Johns. Cas. 335.

IV. ITS PARTS, &c. — 3dly. The *Venue.* and the assignee of the reversion must also sue the assignee of the term in the county where the land lies, because the statute 32 Hen. 8, transfers the privity of contract to the assignee in the *same manner* as the lessor had it (*o*). For the same reason, covenant *by* the assignee of the *lessee* against the lessor, or the grantee of the reversion, is local; for it lies at common law only in respect of the privity of *estate*, in which case the venue is always local (*p*).

Venue when local by *statute.* The statute 31 Eliz. c. 5, s. 2, enacts, "that in any declaration or information, the offence against any *penal statute* shall not be laid to be done in any other county but where the *contract* or other *matter alleged to be the offence, was in truth done* (*q*); and the statute 21 Jac. 1, c. 4, s. 2, enacts, "that in all informations, declarations, &c. for any offence against any *penal statute*, whether on the behalf of the king or any other person, the offence shall be laid and alleged to have been committed *in the county where such offence was in truth committed*, and not elsewhere; or the defendant, upon the general issue, shall be found not guilty." (580) And in a penal action for the *omission* of a *local duty*, prescribed by a statute, the venue is local (*r*). Lord Holt's opinion appears to have been, that the statute 21 Jac. 1, c. 4, s. 2, extended to *subsequent* statutes (*s*), but a contrary doctrine [*303] *was for some time entertained (*t*). It has however been recently determined, that the first-mentioned statute, 31 Eliz. c. 5, s. 2, extends as well to subsequent as to prior penal statutes, and consequently in all penal actions the venue is now local (*u*)(581). This statute also extends to offences of omission as well as commission (*v*); and a penal action for non-residence must be brought in the county in which the living is situated (*x*). But neither of the above statutes extends to actions brought by the party grieved (*y*). Upon the common law principle, where there are two material facts to constitute the offence against a penal statute, and one happened in one county, and the other in another county, it has been supposed that the venue might be laid in either (*z*). But where an usurious contract was made in one county, and the usurious interest is taken in another, in an action for the penalty, the venue must be laid in the latter county (*a*) (582); and according to the terms of 21 Jac. 1, c. 4, s. 2, it seems safer to lay the venue in the county where the *offence was committed* or *perfected.*

(*o*) 1 Saund. 241 c; 1 Show. 199.

(*p*) 5 Co. 17 a; 1 Saund. 241 d, note 6.

(*q*) As to debt for penalties against usury, see *ante*, 299, note (*z*).

(*r*) 4 East, 393.

(*s*) Lord Raym. 373.

(*t*) Parker's Rep. 186; Andr. 25; 2 Str. 1081; 1 Salk. 372, 373; Com. Dig. Action, N. 10; Bac. Ab. Action, *qui tam*, C.; 1 Saund. 312 c, in the notes; Bul. N. P. 195; Tidd, 9th ed. 430.

(*u*) 3 M. & Sel. 429; 5 Taunt. 754; 1 Marsh. 320, S. C.; 9 East, 296; Tidd, 9th edit. 430; see 3 Campb. 78.

(*v*) 5 M. & Sel. 427; 2 Chit. Rep. 490, S. C. There are several exceptions in the act, see Tidd, 9th ed. 430.

(*x*) *Id.*

(*y*) 1 Show. 354; Bul. N. P. 196; Tidd, 9th ed. 430.

(*z*) 2 Taunt. 252; 2 Campb. 266, S. C. 4 East, 385; Tidd, 9th ed. 430; *ante*, 299; *sed quære*, see the words of statute 21 Jac. 1, c. 4, *ante*, 299, and note (*a*) *infra.*

(*a*) 3 B. & C. 700; 5 D. & R. 616, S. C.

(580) And the statute of the State of New York, sess. 11. c. 9. s. 2. 1 R. L. 99, is to the same effect. See 2 Rev. Stat. 480, 481, et seq.

(581) The statute of the State of New York, cited above, speaks of actions to be commenced on any penal statute, made, or to be made, and consequently is prospective.

(582) The New York statute above referred to, expressly excepts actions concerning usury, maintenance, extortion, &c.

IV. ITS PARTS, &c.

3dly. The *Venue.*

Some actions against *particular persons*, which would otherwise be transitory, must, by different statutes, be laid in the county where the facts were committed, or the plaintiff will be nonsuited. Such are actions upon the *case* or *trespass* against *justices of the peace*, mayors, or bailiffs of cities or towns corporate, headboroughs, port-reves, *constables*, tithing-men, churchwardens, &c. or *other* persons acting in *their aid and assistance, or by their command (*b*), for any [*304] thing *done* (*c*) in their official capacity (583); and actions against any person for any thing done by him as an officer of the *Excise* (*d*), or *Customs* (*e*), or against any other person acting in his aid in execution or by reason of his office; or for any thing done in pursuance of the act for consolidating the provisions of the acts relating to the duties under the management of the commissioners for the affairs *of Taxes*, or any act for granting duties to be assessed under the regulations of that act, &c. (*f*). So, the venue is local in an action against an officer of the army, navy, or marines, for any thing done in the execution of or by reason of his office (*g*); or against any person for any thing done in pursuance of the acts relative to larceny, &c. or malicious injuries to property (*h*). And by the statute 42 Geo. 3, c. 85, s. 6, the provisions of the statute 21 Jac. 1, c. 12, with regard to the venue, &c. are extended to all persons in *any public employment*, or any office, station, or capacity, either civil or military, either in or out of the kingdom; and who, under any act of parliament, &c. have, by virtue of any such employment, &c. power to commit persons to safe custody; provided always, that when any action upon the case, trespass, battery, or false imprisonment, shall be brought against any such person in this kingdom, for or upon any act done out of the kingdom, the plaintiff may lay such act to have been done in Westminster, or any county where the defendant shall reside.

The venue in an action against a justice, constable, &c. for an act done in the execution of his office, seems to be local, if the party acted under color of his office, *intending* to act in his official character, although it did not strictly justify him; for he would want no protection, if in reality he acted in the due course of his office (*i*).

So actions against persons acting under the acts relating to *Highways* (*k*); or *Turnpikes* (*l*)(584); or the *Militia* (*m*); and various other acts; are local

(*b*) 21 Jac. 1, c. 12, s. 5. Whether a person who *desires* a constable to act, and *who assists* him, is within this provision, see Holt, N. P. R. 478; 3 Campb. 257; 2 Stark. R. 445.

(*c*) General construction of the words "for any thing *done*," see Tidd, 9th edit. 29, 19; 10 B. & C. 277. When it extends to assumpsit for money had and received, 4 B. & C. 200.

(*d*) 23 Geo. 3, c. 70, s. 34.

(*e*) 24 Geo. 3, sess. 2, c. 47, s. 35, 39; which statute is however repealed by the 6 Geo. 4, c. 105; and see 28 Geo. 3, c. 37, s. 23; 6 Geo. 4, c. 108, s. 97.

(*f*) 43 Geo. 3, c. 99, s. 70.

(*g*) 6 Geo. 4, c. 108, s. 97.

(*h*) 7 & 8 Geo. 4, c. 29, s. 75, and c. 30, s. 41.

(*i*) 2 Stark. Rep. 445, 448; 10 Moore, 63, 376; 4 T. R. 555; 5 *Id.* 1, 2; see Tidd, 9th ed. 19, 29, 31. But a constable has no protection in this respect, if he commit an assault, &c. altogether, and clearly not warranted by his office, Stra. 446.

(*k*) 13 Geo. 3, c. 78, s. 81.

(*l*) 3 Geo. 4, c. 126, s. 147. Assumpsit against a toll collector for toll improperly taken is local, 4 B. & C. 200. That was a decision on a local act, but the clause on which the decision turned contained words similar to those used in the 147th section of the 3 Geo. 4.

(*m*) 42 Geo. 3, c. 90, s. 178.

(583) Et vide Laws N. Y. sess. 24. c. 47. s. 1. 1 R. L. 155. See 2 Rev. Stat. 409. s. 3.

(584) { The venue should be laid in the county where toll is improperly collected, in

IV. ITS PARTS, &c. — 3dly. The Venue.

by express provision. *Attornies*, when plaintiffs, and suing in their own Court, have the privilege of laying and retaining the *venue in Middlesex in transitory actions, although the cause of action arose in another county (n).

The venue is thus stated in the *margin* of the declaration, "*Middlesex* to wit," or "City of Bristol and County of the same city to wit." (o) It was always a doctrine, that such venue in the margin would aid but not prejudice, and in *civil* cases, if the name of a *place only*, and no county, or a wrong county were stated in the *body* of the declaration, it would suffice, because the place was always construed to refer to the county in the margin (585), though another county also were mentioned; and on the other hand, when the proper venue was laid in the body of the declaration, the county in the margin would not vitiate and might be rejected as surplusage (p). But in *criminal* cases the rule was more strict, and though the county in the margin, when *expressly* referred to, was sufficient, yet it must then either be named in the body or be so *expressly* referred to in all cases (q).

Before the Pleading Reg. Gen. Hil. T. 4 W. 4, reg. 8, it was necessary, as well in criminal as in civil cases, to state *and repeat* the venue in the *body* of the declaration or indictment, and it was usual to name a parish, town, or hamlet, or other known place, (not being a *hundred*), as well as the county (r). In London, it was formerly considered necessary to state some parish and ward, though in other places a city or town, without naming any particular parish, was always holden sufficient (s). In *criminal* cases it is still necessary to name some parish or town as well as the county, and the statement in an indictment that a party committed perjury at Guildhall in London was insufficient (t); and though the 7 G. 4, c. 64, s. 20, aids the want of a proper venue, yet the total omission of the county in the *body* of the indictment will

[*306] be a fatal defect (u). But in *civil* actions *in the superior Courts as the jury is no longer *de vicineto*, the statement of a county alone, or that the contract was made in London, without laying a parish or ward, has long sufficed (x),

(n) 2 Salk. 668; 4 Burr. 2037; 2 Bla. Rep. 1065; 3 T. R. 573; Partington v. Woodcock, 2 Dowl. 550; but then it must appear from the declaration or proceedings that the plaintiff sues as an attorney or in person and not by another attorney, Lowless v. Tims, 3 Dowl. 707; 3 Chitty Gen. Prac. 647.

(o) Lord Hardwicke was of opinion that the "ss" in the margin of the declaration, was not originally meant to signify the county, but was only a denotation of each section or paragraph in the record, Cas. temp. Hardw. 344. In indictments the words "to wit," are generally omitted after the venue in the margin or beginning of the indictment.

(p) 1 Saund. 308, n. 1; 3 Wils. 339; 3 T. R. 387; 1 Taunt. 379; Com. Dig. Pleader, C. 20; and see 2 East, 497; 5 Taunt. 789; 1 Marsh. 363, S. C.; 2 Moore, 67; and see to this effect, Doe v. Roe, 3 Dowl. 323; and see 8 Bing. 355.

(q) 1 Saund. 301, n. 1; 1 Chit. Crim. Law, 194.

(r) Co. Lit. 125 a, n. 2.

(s) Cro. Jac. 307; Leach, Cro. Law, 930; 4 Hawk. P. C. 86, s. 83.

(t) See the authorities collected in 1 Chit. Crim. Law, 196, 197; Leach, Cro. Law, 928; Co. Lit. 125 b, n. 2. But it is not in general necessary to *prove* in evidence that there is such a parish as that named in the indictment, 1 R. & M. 433. And it seems that the indictment would be good even if it were proved negatively that there was no such parish, see *id.*

(u) Rex v. Hart, 6 Car. & P. 123.

(x) 3 M. & Sel. 148; Co. Lit. 125 b, n. 2; Vin. Ab. Trial, H. a, 6; 1 Saund. 8 a; Lutw. 337.

---

an action under a turnpike act, "providing that every such action, for any thing done in pursuance of that act, should be brought where the matter should arise." Waterhouse v. Keen, 6 Dowl. & Ryl. 257. }

(585) Vide State v. Post, 9 Johns. Rep. 81. Turberville v. Long, 3 Hen. & Mun. 312. Sharp v. Sharp, 3 Wend. R. 280.

3dly. The *Venue.*

unless where a local description is necessary, as in replevin, &c. (*y*). The same rule applied even in actions on *penal* statutes (*z*), unless part of the penalty be given to the poor of the parish in which the offence was committed, when the name of the parish is material (*a*). Where a parish is named, so much strictness does not prevail as formerly; thus in trespass *quare clausum fregit*, where the *locus in quo* is stated to be in the parish of A., it is sufficient to prove it to be a reputed parish, though strictly it be only a hamlet (*b*).

In *Inferior* Courts it continues necessary, in addition to the statement of the county as a venue, to aver that every material fact took place "within the jurisdiction of the Court," as in assumpsit, as well that the promise or contract was made, as that the goods were sold, or the money had and received, &c. *within the jurisdiction* of the Court (586); and if the allegation be omitted, the declaration will be insufficient, even after verdict (*c*). But as to such matters as are stated only in aggravation of damages, and might be omitted, it is not necessary to allege that the same arose within the jurisdiction (*d*), and it suffices to allege that an account was stated within the jurisdiction, without averring that the items of the account accrued there (*e*). It has been recently decided that even in a declaration in debt on the judgment of the inferior Court, it is necessary to show that the original cause of action accrued within its jurisdiction (*f*).

When a transitory matter has occurred *abroad*, it may in general be stated to have taken place in any English county, without noticing the place where it really happened; but if the real place abroad be stated, it should be shown under a *scilicet*, that it happened in an English county, as for instance, *"in [*307] Minorca, *to wit*, at Westminster, in the county of Middlesex."(*g*)

In *Mostyn* v. *Fabrigas* (*h*), Lord Mansfield observed, that although actions of a transitory nature that arise abroad may be laid as happening in an English county, yet in the case of a deed made abroad, it should be averred that it was made in the foreign country, laying the *venue* under a *videlicet*. But unless a deed, bond, or bill of exchange made abroad, derive from that circumstance any peculiar character unknown to the English law, or be for the

(*y*) 1 Saund. 347, n. 1.

(*z*) Co. Lit. 125 b; 24 Geo. 2, c. 18; 3 Esp. Rep. 219; 2 Saund. 376, n. 9; Willes, 99, n. a.

(*a*) 3 Esp. Rep. 219.

(*b*) 2 Campb. 5, note, and see *post*, 308, as to variance.

(*c*) 1 Saund. 74 a, n. 1; 1 T. R. 151; 8 *Id.* 127; Cro. Jac. 502; 6 T. R. 764; Read *v.* Pope, 1 Crom. M. & Ros. 302; 4 Tyr. 403, S. C.; Salter *v.* Slade, 1 Adol. & Ell. 608.

(*d*) 1 Saund. 74, n. 1; Bac. Ab. Pleas, E. 1.

(*e*) 2 Stra. 827. In assumpsit for work and labor in healing horses, *within the jurisdiction* of a County Court, and for potions, &c. administered *on those occasions*, it was held that this amounted to a sufficient allegation that the *potions* were administered within the jurisdiction of the Court, 3 B. & B. 309; 7 Moore, 137, S. C.

(*f*) Read *v.* Bope, 1 Cr. M. & R. 302; 4 Tyr. 403.

(*g*) Cowp. 177, 178; 10 Mod. 255; *ante*, 297, 298; 7 T. R. 243; Bayley on Bills, 5th edit. 172; Co. Lit. 261 b. See observations, 1 Stark. Crim. Law, 23, note (*h*); 1 Chitty Crim. Law, 178, 180. As to indictments, 7 Geo. 4, c. 64, s. 12, 13; 9 Geo. 4, c. 31.

(*h*) Cowp. 177, 178; *ante*, 296, 297, 267; 2 Ld. Raym. 1043, S. C. in Salk. 622, and 6 Mod. 228.

(586) { Thornton *v.* Smith, 1 Wash. Rep. 81, and the cases there cited. } Vide Murray *v.* Fitzpatrick, 3 Caines' Rep. 41. Wetmore and Cheeseborough *v.* Baker and Swan, 9 Johns. Rep. 307. Evans *v.* Munkley and another, 4 Taunt. 48. Shepherd *v.* Boyce, 2 Johns. Rep. 447. Briggs *v.* Nantucket Bank, 5 Mass. Rep. 95. Turberville *v.* Long, 3 Hen. & Mun. 309.

IV. ITS PARTS, &c. — 3dly. The Venue.

payment of foreign money (*i*); so that the statement that it was a foreign instrument is substantially important; there seems to be no occasion to state that it was made abroad (*k*). In stating a matter of record, no venue seems necessary, as the record must be presumed to be where the Court is (*l*); but in pleading an Irish judgment it may be otherwise (*m*).

As to *statement* and *repetition* of venue in *body* of declaration.

Before the general pleading rule, Hil. Term, 4 W. 4, reg. 8, prohibiting the repetition of venue or place in the *body* of a declaration, it was considered that the venue should be *laid* and repeated throughout every part of the declaration *distinctly to every material* traversable fact (*n*); and formerly the omission was considered fatal on the trial, though issue were taken upon another point (*o*). But even in a local action, as in case for an injury to a water-course, no precise local description of the nuisance complained of was necessary, and provided the county were properly stated, it was sufficient, except in replevin (*p*). And where there were several facts, yet if the sentences in [*308] which *they were stated were coupled with the conjunction "*and*," the venue laid in the first allegation would apply to all the facts (*q*). So the *performance* of a contract would be inferred to have been at the place where it was entered into (*r*); though it was usual to repeat the venue to each averment (*s*). No venue, however, need have been laid to matter of inducement when *not traversable*, and which consequently could not be *tried* (*t*); nor was a venue necessary in general to a negative allegation (*u*).

Where a parish was stated merely as *a venue*, it was not necessary for the plaintiff to prove that there was such a parish in the county (*x*); nor was it of any consequence that the cause of action should appear to have arisen in a different parish (*y*). That rule applied to penal actions, as in debt on the game laws (*z*); but when part of the penalty sought to be recovered was given to the poor of the parish, the name of the parish was matter of substance, and the offence must necessarily be laid and proved to have taken place therein (*a*). So, in an action, though not local, if the situation of land or other real property be described, though unnecessarily, in a material averment, to be situate in a particular parish or place, the plaintiff would fail on the trial if there were a substantial mistake (*b*). Where in debt *qui tam* the plaintiff sued

(*i*) 2 B. & Ald. 301; 2 B. & C. 16; 2 D. & R. 15, S.C. The question of stamps might perhaps also be material, if the instrument be not shown on the face of the declaration to have been made abroad. In general a contract is to be construed according to the laws of the country where it was made, &c. 7 T. R. 241; 3 Campb. 166; 3 Taunt. 82.

(*k*) See 3 Campb. 305; see Bayley on Bills; Steph. 2d edit. 342; 1 Saund. 74, note (*k*), 5th edit.

(*l*) 1 Vent. 264.

(*m*) See 5 East, 473; 4 B. & C. 411.

(*n*) Ring *v.* Roxborough, 2 Cromp. & Jerv. 418; 2 Tyr. 468, S. C.; R. T. Hardw. 288; 14 East, 291, 301; 3 M. & Sel. 149; Com. Dig. Pleader, C. 20; 5 T. R. 620; 2 Hal. P. C. 179; 10 East, 364 to 366; 13 *Id.* 142; see, however, 11 Price, 400; see the observations of Mr. Justice Le Blanc, 10 East, 365, 366; and of Lord Ellenborough, 14 East, 300, as to the words "*then and there.*"

(*o*) 2 Leon. 22.

(*p*) 2 East, 503; 1 Taunt. 380. *Sed quære*, see Co. Lit. 125 b.

(*q*) 1 Saund. 229, and note 2; Com. Dig. Pleader, C. 20; Hardr. 61; *ante*, 289; 2 Hal. P. C. 179.

(*r*) Cro. Eliz 880; Com. Dig. Pleader, C. 20.

(*s*) Com. Dig. Pleader, C. 20.

(*t*) Plowd. 191; Com. Dig Pleader, C. 20; 2 Stra. 817; Steph. 2d edit. 330.

(*u*) *Ante*, 289; 5 T. R. 616; 1 Taunt. 379.

(*x*) 1 R. & M. 433; see 3 M. & Sel. 148.

(*y*) 2 East, 497.

(*z*) 3 Esp. Rep. 218; 2 Saund. 376, n. 8.

(*a*) 3 Esp. Rep. 219; 2 Saund. 376, n. 9; Peake, Evid. 199.

(*b*) 1 Esp. Rep. 273; 2 B. & P. 281; 2 Lev. 334; Salk. 452; Bac. Ab. Trespass, K.; 6 East, 352; 11 *Id.* 226; Stra. 595.

as well for the poor of the "parish of St. James, in the county of Middlesex," as for himself, the description of the parish was held sufficient, although there were in the county the parishes of "St. James, Clerkenwell," and of "St. James, in the liberty of Westminster;" for the latter parish is sometimes called by the latter names, and sometimes St. James (c). So where, in ejectment, premises were stated to be in the "parish of St. Luke," in Middlesex, the Court held there was no variance, although *there is the parish of "St. Luke, Chelsea," in Middlesex, and there is also the parish of "St. Luke, Old Street," in that county; for the latter parish, in which the premises were, is also commonly called "St. Luke, Middlesex;" and the court recognized the principle, that it suffices to describe the parish by the name by which it is commonly known (d). It has, however, been held to be a fatal variance to describe land situate in the parish of A. as situate "in the united parishes of A. and B.;" the parishes being united by statute merely for the support of the poor (e). But if a fact be stated to have occurred "at or near" a particular place, the mistake may not be so material (f) (587). And when it is doubtful whether the place where a navigation is alleged to lie, is stated in the declaration as a venue, or as a local description, it will be referred merely to the venue, and need not be proved to be at such place (g). The mode of describing the place or venue in trespass and replevin (h), and other particular actions, is stated in the notes to the several precedents in such actions.

IV. ITS PARTS, &c. — 3dly. The *Venue.*

[*809]

At common law, if it appeared *upon the record* that the contract or cause of action arose in a county different from that in which the venue was laid, it was error (i). But by 16 & 17 Car. 2, c. 8 (588), "after verdict, judgment *shall not be* stayed or reversed, for that there is no right venue, so as the cause were tried by a jury of the proper county or place where the action is laid (589):" and this statute extends not only to those cases where there is a wrong venue in the proper county, but also to those where the cause has been improperly tried in a wrong county, and whether the objection appear on the record or not (k). And the 4 & 5 Anne (l) (590) extends this provision to a judgment by confession, *nil dicet* or *non sum informatus* (m) (591). And the same provision appears to have *been extended to penal actions by the 4 Geo. 2, c. 26, s. 4 (n). But as *inferior* Courts, not of record, are not included in these acts, a declaration in the County Court, omitting the necessary allegation as to the subject-matter of the action having arisen within the jurisdiction, will still be

Consequences of mistake in venue and when aided.

[*810]

(c) 3 Bing. 449.
(d) 1 Y. & J. 492; see also 13 East, 9.
(e) 2 Campb. 274.
(f) Peake, Evid. 4th edit. 290; 4 T. R. 558, 561; 1 B. & P. 225; 5 Taunt. 789.
(g) 2 East, 497; 11 *Id.* 226, 229; 2 Campb. 3, 5; 5 Taunt. 789.
(h) See 1 Saund. 347, n. 1.
(i) Com. Dig. Action, N. 6; 1 Saund. 74, n. 2.
(k) 1 Saund. 248, note 3; 7 T. R. 583; 2 East, 580; 2 Saund. 5 d, in notes.
(l) C. 16, s. 2.
(m) *Id.*; 2 Com. Rep. 555.
(n) Willes, 599, 601; see Tidd, 9th edit. 928. But see 4 East, 387, 388, where the *verdict* was set aside, though no objection with regard to the venue appears to have been taken at Nisi Prius. *Ante*, 290.

(587) Acc. Guest v. Caumont, 3 Campb. 235. And see further upon this subject, Phillips' Ev. 165, 166. Vowles v. Miller, 3 Taunt. 140. Williams v. Burgess, 3 Taunt. 127.
(588) { In force in Pennsylvania, Roberts' Dig. 39. 3 Binn. 624. }
(589) Vide Laws N. Y. sess. 11. c. 32. s. 6. p. 120. s. 8. p. 121. s. 11. p. 122.
(590) { The first 13 sections, and the 20th and 27th sections of this statute, are in force in Pennsylvania. Roberts' Dig. 43. 3 Binn. 625. }
(591) Vide Bowdell v. Parsons, 10 East's Rep. 359.

IV. ITS PARTS, &c. — 3dly. The Venue.

insufficient, even after verdict (*o*). Hence it follows, that even in local and penal actions in the *superior* Courts, the only modes of objecting to the venue are by demurrer (*p*), or at the trial as a ground of nonsuit (*q*). In the action of ejectment the objection could not be taken by a demurrer, but would be available on the trial; and at all events there could be no execution, because the sheriff of one county cannot deliver the possession of land in another (*r*). In a recent case it was considered that the total omission of local description in the body of a declaration in ejectment was error, although the proper county was stated in the margin, but the Court gave leave to amend, pending a writ of error (*s*). In other *local* actions, if the venue be laid in the wrong county, and the objection appear upon the record, it is clear that the defendant may *demur* (*t*); and if it do not appear on record, may, sometimes, if the declaration be upon a specialty relating to the premises, avail himself of the objection at the trial as a *ground of nonsuit* (*u*); or in trespass or ejectment, on the plea of not guilty (*x*); or in replevin, on the plea of *non cepit* (*y*); or may plead the matter in abatement (*z*). And even in transitory actions an unnecessary precise description of local situation may, if erroneous, be fatal on the trial (*a*); though where the description is rather by way of venue it will be otherwise (*b*). If *a local description or venue, when necessary, be omitted*, it is not matter of nonsuit (*c*), but now only a ground of *special demurrer* (*d*) (592); and by pleading over to the merits any formal defect in the venue is aided (*e*). In
[*311] *transitory* actions, the omission of a venue is aided at common *law by a judgment *by default*, because the defendant thereby admits that there is nothing to try (*f*); and an objection merely to the mode in which the venue is stated can be taken only by special demurrer (*g*) (593).

If no venue be laid in the margin the defendant may demur (*h*); or, it seems, may plead that matter in abatement (*i*). But even before the Reg. Gen. Hil. T. 4 W. 4, reg. 8, if a county were named in the margin it sufficed even on special demurrer (*j*).

(*o*) *Ante*, 306; when or not amendable, Salter *v.* Slade, 1 Adol. & Ell. 608.
(*p*) 1 Wils. 165.
(*q*) 7 T. R. 588; 2 East, 580; Cowp. 410; 2 Bla. Rep. 1033; Tidd, 9th edit. 427.
(*r*) 7 T. R. 587, 588; Cowp. 170; *ante*, 297.
(*s*) Doe *v.* Bath, 2 Nev. & Man. 440; but see 8 Bing. 355; and *quære*, whether after verdict it is error, for the lessor of the plaintiff must always at his peril point out the premises to the sheriff, of which he is to deliver possession, and the local description in the declaration merely of a parish is rarely any precise guide.
(*t*) 1 Saund. 241 d, note; 3 Bingh. 459; Carth. 182; 7 T. R. 588; 2 Bla. Rep. 1070; 3 T. R. 387; 1 Wils. 165; and see 10 East, 359.
(*u*) *Supra*, note (*q*); 1 Sid. 287.
(*x*) *Id.*; Stra. 595.
(*y*) 1 Saund. 347, note 1, cites Stra. 507; 2 Mod. 199; *acc.* 2 Gilb. Rep. 165; 2 Wils. 355; *semb. contra.*
(*z*) Com. Dig. Abatement, H. 17.
(*a*) *Ante*, 308, n. (*b*).
(*b*) *Ante*, 309, n. (*g*).
(*c*) 2 East, 499; 2 Wils. 354.
(*d*) Reg. Gen. Hil. T. 4 W. 4, reg. V.
(*e*) 2 Ld. Raym. 1039; Dyer, 15 a; Com. Dig. Pleader, 85; 3 T. R. 387.
(*f*) Lutw. 237; Cro. Eliz. 880.
(*g*) 3 T. R. 387.
(*h*) 1 Lutw. 235.
(*i*) Com. Dig. Abatement, H. 13.
(*j*) Duncan *v.* Passenger, 8 Bing. 355.

(592) Vide Briggs *v.* Nantucket Bank, 5 Mass. Rep. 94.
(593) Vide Briggs *v.* Nantucket Bank, 5 Mass. Rep. 94. Gilbert and another *v.* Nantucket Bank, Id. 97. Where, in a declaration on an instrument in writing, no venue is stated in the body of the declaration, but only in the margin, and no place is alleged at which the instrument was executed, it is no variance if the instrument produced in evidence bear date at a different place from that in which the venue is laid. Alder *v.* Griner, 13 Johns. Rep. 419.

The Reg. Gen. Hil. T. 4 W. 4, reg. 8, orders that "The name of a county shall in all cases be stated in the *margin* of a declaration, and shall be taken to be the venue intended by the plaintiff, and no venue shall be stated in the *body* of the declaration or *in any subsequent pleading*. Provided that in cases where local description is now required such local descriptions shall be given." †

IV. ITS PARTS, &c. — 3dly. The *Venue*.

The recent alterations as to venue and description thereof in declaration, *first* by Reg. Gen. Hil. T. 4 W. 4, reg. 8. No venue to be stated in *body* of declaration or *subsequent* pleading. Reg. Gen. Hil. T. 4 W. 4, reg. V. *In trespass*. Name of abuttals of locus in quo essential.

The same Reg. (*V. In Trespass*,) orders that "In actions of *trespass quare clausum fregit*, the close or place in which, &c. must be designated in the declaration by name or abuttals or other description, in failure whereof the defendant may demur specially."

The first of these rules has put an end to the useless statement and incessant repetition of venue in all *personal* actions, where it is in law quite immaterial in what place or what part of a county the fact or facts occurred, and has thus even rendered more concise the forms of declarations on bills of exchange, promissory notes, and common debts recoverable in assumpsit or debt under the common indebitatus counts (*k*). If venue or place be unnecessarily stated, a judge on summons may order the allegation to be struck out (*l*), but it is not a ground even of special demurrer (*m*), and if inadvertently place be incorrectly repeated only once or so, it would be more liberal practice to apply to the plaintiff's attorney to erase the useless words instead of vexatiously putting him to the trouble, loss of time, and expense of a summons or motion, which proceeding, as observed by the Court, may be even more vexatious than the useless words objected to (*n*). As to the extent of the application of the rule it would seem from its terms to apply to every declaration and pleading in which *local description* is not *clearly required*; so that even in actions where the venue is local, as in *case* for an injury to a house or land, or right of common or way, after stating the county in the margin, no subsequent statement of place is necessary; and yet it is usual in these actions to insert a local description, and this notwithstanding the terms of the rule may perhaps be applicable (*o*).

In a declaration of trespass *quare clausum fregit* the rule is express that one of three descriptions must be adopted, as *first*, a *name*; *secondly*, a description by *abuttals*; or *thirdly*, some other description; or the defendant may demur *specially*, and abutting *towards*, the frequently adopted word, is incorrect, and the proper abuttal is "*on*," so as not to admit of any intermediate property (*p*). The object of thus requiring particularity is to avoid the necessity for a new assignment, in case of a plea of liberum tenementum, which leads to a useless course of pleading (*q*). The subject of abuttals will however be more fully stated when we consider declarations in trespass more particularly (*r*).

(*k*) Reg. Gen. see the rule fully Jervis's Rules.
(*l*) Harper *v.* Chamneys, 2 Dowl. 680; 1 Crom. M. & Ros. 369; 4 Tyr. 859; Fisher *v.* Snow, 3 Dowl. 27; Townside *v.* Gurney, *id.* 168; 1 Crom. M. & Ros. 590, S. C.
(*m*) *Id. ibid.*
(*n*) *Per Cur.* in Brindley *v.* Dennett, 2 Bingh. 184; 9 Moore, 388, S. C.
(*o*) See forms, vol. ii.
(*p*) Lempriere *v.* Humphrey, 1 Harr. & Woll. 170; and as to *abuttals*, see Walford *v.* Anthony, 8 Bing. 75; and *post*, vol. ii.
(*q*) Bosanquet's Rules, 59, note 57; 3 Chitty's Gen. Prac. 471, 472.
(*r*) See references, *supra*, note (*p*).

† See American Editor's Preface.

IV. ITS PARTS, &c.

3dly. The *Venue*.

Of changing the venue in *local* actions under 3 & 4 W. 4, c. 42, sect. 22.

We have already noticed another recent improvement in the law of *venue* enabling either of the superior Courts in which any *local* action is pending, or one of the judges thereof, on the application of either party, to order the issue to be tried or writ of inquiry to be executed in any other county or place than that in which the venue is laid; and for that purpose such Court or judge may order a *suggestion* to be entered on the record that the trial may be more conveniently had or writ of inquiry executed in the county or place where the same is ordered to take place. But this regulation does not alter the form of the declaration.

4thly. The Commencement.

What is termed the *Commencement* of the declaration follows the venue in the margin, and precedes the more *circumstantial statement* of the *cause of action*. Before the recent *rules* it contained a statement, 1*st*, Of the *names* of the parties to the suit, and if they sued or were sued otherwise than in their own *right* or *liability*, or in a political capacity, (*i. e.* as executors, as assignees, or *qui tam*, &c.) of the character or right in respect of which they are parties to the suit; 2*dly*, Of the *mode* in which the defendant has been *brought into Court;* and 3*dly*, A brief recital of the *form of action* to be proceeded in.

With the exception that it is no longer necessary to refer to the form of action, the commencement in substance now contains the same requisites as formerly prescribed, and as in *mixed* actions and in actions *removed* from inferior Courts into one of those at Westminster the ancient forms still prevail, it will be advisable to state the same as in force *before* 2 W. 4, c. 39.

The ancient forms of commencement.

It is obvious that, independently of express regulation or precedent, some introduction preceding the substantial statement of the cause of action is useful; and the commencement formerly adopted was useful, as pointing out that the defendant was duly in Court to answer the complaint, and concisely intimating the character in which the parties sued or were sued, and even the nature of the action, by which the parties interested in the pleadings were enabled more readily to direct their attention to the subsequent parts of the declaration (*s*).

As to names.

The ancient rule that the declaration and the writ should in general correspond with regard to the *names of the parties;* and the consequences of a misnomer; and the mode of obviating its effect; and the instances in which the objection is waived, have been already stated (*t*). Where there was a misnomer in the process in the King's Bench, it was usual to state the fact thus, "—to wit, A. B. the plaintiff in this action, complains of C. D. the defendant in this suit, *arrested* (or if not bailable, '*served* with process,')by the name of E. F. being in the custody, &c." And in the Court of Common Pleas, the declaration was thus, "C. D. the defendant, *arrested*, (or served, &c.) by the name of E. F. was attached to answer A. B. the plaintiff in this suit, of a [*312] plea; &c. and in each *Court, in all subsequent parts of the declaration, the real name only, or the word "defendant," was to be inserted. The words *arrested* or *served with process*, were considered preferable to the word *sued* (*u*).

(*s*) 1 Saund. 318, n. 3, 111, 112; 6 T. R. 130.

(*t*) *Ante*, 276 to 291.

(*u*) 1 B. & P. 647.

If the *plaintiff's* name had been mistaken in the process, the mistake might sometimes be aided in the same manner, so as to avoid a plea in abatement (*v*). It was not necessary in any case to state in the declaration the *addition* of the defendant either of place or degree, for the statute of additions did not extend to declarations (*x*).

IV. ITS PARTS, &c. — 4thly. The Commencement. Mode in which defendant was brought into Court.

In the *King's Bench*, in actions by *bill* (the usual proceeding before 2 W. 4, c 39, which abolished it,) against a person not privileged, whether he were in the *actual* or *supposed* custody of the marshal, the declaration, (except in Middlesex, when the allegation as to the supposed custody was unnecessary,) (*y*) began by stating, "——to wit, A. B. complains of C. D. being in the custody of the marshal of the Marshalsea of our lord the king, before the king himself, of a plea of trespass on the case, (*or as the form of action might be.*) For that whereas," &c. (*z*). It was enacted by 4 & 5 W. & M. c. 21, s. 3, that "in all declarations against a *prisoner* detained in prison by virtue of any writ or process to be issued out of the *Court of King's Bench*, it shall be alleged *in custody of what sheriff*, bailiff, or steward of any franchise, such prisoner shall be at the time of such declaration, by virtue of the process of the said Court, at the suit of the plaintiffs; which allegation shall be as good and effectual as if such prisoner were in the custody of the marshal." That statute did not extend to proceedings by *original*, or in the Common Pleas, or Exchequer; and therefore that allegation was only necessary when the plaintiff proceeded upon a bill of Middlesex, or latitat, or by attachment of privilege; and if the cause of action were not bailable, the same plaintiff or a third person might in K. B. proceed against the prisoner as if he were at large (*a*). In cases within the act, if the declaration showed that the defendant was in custody of the sheriff, but not at whose *suit, the defendant might be discharged out of custody, or he might demur generally (*b*). [*313]

In the *King's Bench* by *original*, the commencement of the declaration, with the exception of the name of the Court at the top, was in general similar to that in the *Common Pleas* against persons not privileged; and which in assumpsit, case, and trover, was as follows: "—to wit, C. D. was *attached* to answer A. B. of a plea of trespass on the case, &c. (*or as the form of action might be,*) and thereupon the said A. B. by E. F. his attorney, complains, for that whereas," &c. (*c*). The defendant's addition of abode or degree ought not to be inserted (*d*); and the statement that the plaintiff complained by more than one attorney was considered improper (*e*). And in the Common Pleas, or by original in K. B. it would be incorrect to begin the declaration with a *queritur*, as in the King's Bench by bill (*f*).

With respect to the first part of this form it is observable that in actions of *assumpsit, case, trespass, ejectment*, &c. where the original was an *attachment*,

(*v*) *Ante*, 282.

(*x*) 3 B. & P. 395; Com. Dig. Pleader, C. 9; 2 Esp. Rep. 727.

(*y*) Dyer, 118 a. The action in this case was in trespass, and in such action the Court has an original jurisdiction, if the trespass were committed in Middlesex, or in any other county where the Court sits, see 3 Bla. Com. 42; Stephen, 2d ed. 4, 5.

(*z*) 3 B. & P. 399; Com. Dig. Pleader, C. 8.

(*a*) Imp. K. B. 618, 6th ed.; Tidd, 9th ed. 342, 359; 1 T. R. 192.

(*b*) 1 Wils. 119; 2 Ld. Raym. 1362; Com. Dig. Pleader, C. 8.

(*c*) 1 Saund. 317, 318, and notes; 2 Saund. 1, n. 1.

(*d*) *Ante*, 312, note (*x*).

(*e*) 4 East, 195.

(*f*) Com. Dig. Pleader, C. 11.

IV. ITS PARTS, &c. — 4thly. The Commencement.

the commencement of the declaration should state that the defendant was *attached*; and in actions of account, covenant, detinue, annuity, and replevin, where the original was a *summons*, the declaration stated that the defendant was *summoned* to answer (*g*). But formerly when the declaration stated that the defendant was *summoned* instead of *attached*, or *vice versâ*, the defendant could not demur without craving oyer of the original and setting it forth, in order to show that it did not warrant the declaration (*h*); and after it was held that the defendant could not have oyer of the writ, this technical objection was no longer available (*i*). And in general the recital or reference to the writ in the commencement of the declaration was not considered any part of the declaration, and consequently a mistake therein was no ground of demurrer (*k*).

[*314] Recital of the supposed writ.

*Anciently it was the practice in all actions founded on an *original writ* to repeat the whole writ and cause of action in the commencement of the declaration; and it was said that when the pleadings were *ore tenus*, the writ being returned, and the parties having appeared, the counter read the writ to the Court and then mentioned the time, place, and circumstances, and the particular damage accrued to the plaintiff; and if a material variance appeared between the writ and declaration, the defendant might have taken advantage of it either by motion in arrest of judgment, writ of error, plea in abatement, or demurrer (*l*). But that practice was altered in some actions by a rule of the Court of Common Pleas, A. D. 1654, by which it was ordered that in future, declarations in actions *on the case* and *on general statutes*, other than debt, should not repeat the original writ, but only the *nature of the action*, as that the defendant was attached to answer the plaintiff in a plea of trespass on the case, or in a plea of trespass and contempt, against the form of the statute (*m*). And though it was supposed that in a declaration in *trespass vi et armis* in the Common Pleas, in strictness it was necessary to set forth the supposed writ, it was not of late the practice to do more than state that the defendant was attached to answer the plaintiff "in a plea of trespass;" and which was holden sufficient on a general demurrer (*n*); and it was suggested that it would probably be held good on special demurrer, because that short recital was intended only as an intimation to the Court of the nature of the action (*n*). At length Reg. Gen. Hil. Term, 2 W. 4, reg. IV. expressly enjoined such short recital as well in trespass as in ejectment (*o*).

In the King's Bench by *bill* it was not necessary to recite or notice the *form* or nature of the action (*p*); and where in the King's Bench a declaration in assumpsit recited that the defendant was in the custody of the marshal

(*g*) Com. Dig. Pleader, C. 12; Gilb. C. P. 32.

(*h*) 1 Saund. 317, 318, and n. 3; 1 Hen. Bla. 250; Ld. Raym. 903; and no advantage could be taken of a variance between the warrants of attorney and the declaration in the names of the parties, 3 B. & B. 65.

(*i*) 1 Saund. 318, n. 3; Doug. 228; 1 B. & P. 646. *Sed vide* 2 Chit. Rep. 638.

(*k*) 2 Bla. R. 848; Ld. Raym. 903; 1 H. Bla. 250; 11 East, 62, 65; Andrew, 23, 24; see note (*q*) *infra*; *post*, 316; and 3 Chitty's Gen. Prac. 461, 462.

(*l*) 1 B. & P. 367; Gilb. C. P. 47; 2 Wils. 394; 1 Saund. 318, n. 3; Com. Dig. Pleader, C. 12.

(*m*) 1 Saund. 318, n. 3; 2 Wils. 105; 2 Saund. 376, n. 6; Com. Dig. Action on the Case, C. 2; 1 B. & P. 367; 11 East, 64, n. (*o*).

(*n*) Carth. 108; and see 1 Saund. 318, note 3; Com. Dig. Pleader, C. 9, 11, 12.

(*o*) Jervis's Rules, 73; Tidd, 433.

(*p*) 11 East, 65.

"of a plea of trespass," instead of "trespass on the case upon promises," it was held that a special demurrer for this mis-description of the plea or form of action of the declaration was not sustainable (*q*). IV. ITS PARTS, &c. — 4thly. The Commencement.

*When it was doubtful from the other parts of the declaration what was the intended form of action, the statement in the memorandum was considered decisive (*r*), and when in trespass the supposed writ was recited, it was considered to be part of the declaration, so that if it contained the words *vi et armis*, it would aid the omission in the count part (*s*). The omission in the Common Pleas of the words, "and thereupon the said A. B. by E. F. his attorney complains," &c. though untechnical, was considered not to be demurrable (*t*). Where one of several defendants had been outlawed upon an original writ in one of the Courts, the declaration should in the commencement state the outlawry in the particular suit (*u*)(594). And where one of several plaintiffs or defendants dies after the issuing of the writ and before declaration, it was always the practice in the commencement to suggest such death (*x*). [*315]

In the exchequer, the commencement, after stating the title of the Court and

(*q*) Clarke *v.* Crosby, K. B. 23d Nov. 1829, Chitty for the plaintiff. MS.
(*r*) 6 T. R. 130.
(*s*) Lutw. 1509; Com. Dig. Pleader, C. 12; 2 Stra. 1023.
(*t*) 1 B. & P. 366.
(*u*) 3 East, 144; 1 Wils. 78; 1 East, 133.
(*x*) 8 & 9 W. 3, c. 11, s. 7; 1 Burr. 363.

(594) At common law, when the plaintiff sues two or more defendants on a joint obligation, and all cannot be arrested, it is necessary to proceed to outlawry against such as cannot be brought into court; for the plaintiff cannot declare against those who have been arrested, until he has outlawed the others, which must be suggested in the declaration; and we have seen that it is not at the option of the plaintiff to bring his action against some of those who are jointly liable to him on a contract, but that all the joint obligors must be named in the process. In the state of New York these difficulties are obviated by the 13th section of the act for the amendment of the law, 1 R. L. 521, which provides, "that all persons jointly indebted to any other person upon any joint obligation, contract, or matter whatsoever, for which remedy might be had at law against such debtors, in case all were taken by process issued out of any court of this State, shall be answerable to their creditors separately for such debts, that is to say: the creditor or creditors of such debtors may issue process against them in the manner now in use; and in case any of such joint debtors be taken and brought into court, he or they so taken and brought into court shall answer to the plaintiff, and in case judgment shall pass for the plaintiff, he shall have his judgment and execution against such of them as were brought into court, and against the other joint debtors named in the process, in the same manner as if they had all been taken and brought into court by virtue of such process; but it shall not be lawful to issue or execute any such execution against the body, or against the lands or goods, the sole property of any person not brought into court." {See as to the mode of proceeding in Pennsylvania, Dillman *v.* Schultz, 5 Serg. & Rawle, 35.} This mode of proceeding does not apply to actions of trespass. Rose *v.* Oliver and others, 2 Johns. Rep. 368. Nor to actions against devisees, taking as tenants in common under a will, for a debt of their testator. Jackson d. Petan *v.* Hoag, 6 Johns. Rep. 59. The declaration in an action against joint debtors should state which of them were brought into court, and which not. Hildreth *v.* Beeker and Harvey, 2 Johns. Cas. 339. And the defendant brought into court cannot avail himself of a defence personal to the defendant not found, as infancy. Van Bramer and others *v.* Cooper and another, 2 Johns. Rep. 279. Judgment is to be entered against all the defendants in the same manner, as if all had appeared, and, such being the regular form of the judgment, if an action be brought upon it by the defendant not arrested in the original suit, he cannot plead *nul tiel record*. Dando *v.* Doll and Tremper, 2 Johns. Rep. 87. In an action on a judgment, the defendant, who had not appeared to the original action, pleaded *nul tiel record*, and that he had not been arrested in the former suit; the pleas were held bad. The court in giving their opinion say, "What defence might be made to the merits, by the defendant who was not taken in the first suit, is another question, not necessarily arising upon this record. Perhaps he might set up any defence, which he might in his distinct, individual capacity, have made in the original suit. But it is not now necessary, and therefore we do not give any definitive opinion upon the point." Bank of Columbia *v.* Newcomb, 6 Johns. Rep. 98. *Et Vide* Ballou *v.* Hurlbert, 1 Johns. Rep. 62. Hutchins and Cary *v.* Fitch, 4 Johns. Rep. 222.

IV. ITS PARTS, &c.

4thly. The Commencement.

term, ran thus:—" —— to wit, A. B. *a debtor of our lord the king*, cometh before the barons of his majesty's Exchequer, on —— the —— day of —— (*the return day of the process*) in this same term, by E. F. his attorney, and complains by bill against C. D. present here in Court the same day, of a plea of trespass on the case, &c. For that whereas," &c. (*y*).

By and against particular persons.

In suits by infants, or by or against assignees, executors, attornies, &c. the commencement always varied from the above forms. Infants were stated to sue by guardian (595) or *prochein ami* (*z*)(596). The representative character of assignees (597) and executors should be stated in the commencement, though it would suffice if it appeared in the other parts of the declaration (*a*). In actions of *debt* by or against executors or administrators, in that character, it was considered that the words "*owes to*" must be omitted (598) in the commencement (*b*); but assignees of a bankrupt may sue in the *debet and detinet* (*c*). An executor *de son tort* is stated to be "executor of the last will and testament" of the deceased, [*316] *as if he were a rightful executor (*d*) (599). In actions by or against attornies (600), peers, and members of parliament, their privilege as such was usually stated in the introduction (*e*). In actions *by surviving* partners they should be described as such either in the commencement or body of the declaration (*f*); but this is not necessary in actions *against* surviving partners (*g*). A declaration stating that the defendant was indebted to the plaintiff and E. F. his *late* partner, without adding deceased, would be untechnical, because, notwithstanding that allegation, he may be still living and then ought to join, but where the omission only occurred in a second count, a demurrer on that ground was set aside as frivolous (*h*). Where there is no

(*y*) "Debtor to the king," and "*quo minus*," are no longer to be averred in pleading, Hurst *v.* Pitt, 3 Tyr. 264, except in declarations in ejectment or on a removal from an inferior Court.

(*z*) 2 Saund. 117 f, note 1. The latter is liable for the costs. Tidd, 9th ed. 100, 101. Where an infant plaintiff was taken in execution for the costs, the Court would not discharge him on motion. 13 East, 6; 1 Hodges' Rep. 103.

(*a*) 1 Saund, 111, 112, n. 2.

(*b*) Com. Dig. Pleader, 2 D. 1, 2; W. 8; 1 Saund. 1, 112, n. 1; 3 East, 2. And this is still correctly so, but the unnecessary statement of the words "owes to" is now considered mere surplusage; those words are not now considered ground even of special demurrer, Collett *v.* Collett, 3 Dowl. 211.

(*c*) 2 T. R. 46.

(*d*) 1 Saund. 265.

(*e*) 2 Saund. 1, n. 1; 5 T. R. 323; 3 B. & P. 7.

(*f*) 4 B. & Ald. 374; 6 Moore, 332; 2 Stark. 356; 2 Marsh. 319; 6 Taunt. 597, S. C.

(*g*) 1 B. & Ald. 29; 2 Chit. Rep. 406.

(*h*) Underhill *v.* Fuller, 1 Crom. M. & Ros. 900.

---

(595) {Stewart *v* Crabbin's Guardian, 6 Munf. 280.} As to infants suing by guardian *ad litem*, and the history of suits by *prochein ami*, vide Harg. Co. Lit. 1, 2, n. 220.

(596) {8 Cow. Rep. 84. But where an infant has worked for another with the consent of his father, on a promise to pay the infant, the infant may maintain an action on the contract in his own name, Burlingame *v.* Burlingame, 7 Cow. Rep. 92.}

(597) Assignees under a joint commission against A. and B. suing for a separate debt to A., may describe themselves as assignees of A. without noticing B. Stonehouse and another *v.* De Silva, 3 Campb. 399, 400.

(598) But when the plaintiff is entitled to charge the defendant de bonis propriis as on a suggestion of a devastavit, those words "owes to" must be inserted; for if he declare in the detinet only, the judgment must be de bonis testatoris. Hope *v.* Bague and Thompson, 3 East's Rep. 6. Spotswood *v.* Price, 3 Hen. & Mun. 123, 126.

(599) Campbell *v.* Tousey, 7 Cow. Rep. 68.

(600) See Dartnal *v.* Howard, 6 Dowl. & Ryl. 443, where, in an action against the defendants for negligence as attornies, the judgment was arrested, because the declaration did not allege that the defendants were attornies, or that they were employed as such by the plaintiffs.

necessity to describe parties as suing or being sued in any special character it is advisable not to do so, and an inaccurate description of the party' interest will sometimes be fatal: as where A., B. and C., having been appointed assignees under three separate commissions of bankrupt, sued as joint assignees, not stating their several and respective interests in the declaration, it was held fatal (i). In the second volume of Precedents, the several most usual forms of declaration by and against persons suing and being sued in *particular rights or characters* will be found (k). The most salutary rule of Hil. Term, 4 W. 4, reg. 21, orders, "That in all actions by and against assignees of a bankrupt, or insolvent, or executors, or administrators, or persons authorized by act of parliament to sue or be sued as nominal parties, the character in which the plaintiff or defendant is stated on the record to sue or be sued shall not in any case be considered as in issue, unless specially denied."

IV. ITS PARTS, &c. The Commencement.

The present forms of commencements of declarations in personal actions commenced in one of the superior Courts (l).

As many of the *ancient* or *preceding* forms of *commencing* declarations were the results of the then prevalent forms of *mesne process*, it followed that when the uniformity of process act, 2 W. 4, chap. 39, abolished those processes and introduced new writs, that it became necessary or expedient to invent new forms of commencements, and accordingly the judges, after that enactment, promulgated a rule ordering that every declaration should be *entitled* at the top or head (and not by indorsement on the back) of the proper Court; secondly, that every declaration and subsequent pleading should be entitled of the *very day* when it is delivered or filed: and Reg. Gen. Mich. T. 3 W. 4, reg. 15, prescribed four forms of commencing a declaration, *first*, upon a *summons*, as thus:

No. 1.—*Declaration after Summons.*

In the ——

On the —— day of —— A. D. ——

Venue.—A. B., by E. F. his attorney, [*or*, "in his own proper person,"] complains of C. D. who has been summoned to answer the said A. B. For that, &c.

No. 2.—*Declaration after Arrest where the Party is not in Custody.*

In the ——

On the —— day of —— A. D. ——

Venue.—A. B., by E. F. his attorney, [*or*, "in his own proper person,"] complains of C. D. who has been arrested at the suit of the said A. B. For that, &c.

No. 3.—*Declaration where the Party is in Custody.*

Venue.—A. B., by E. F. his attorney, [*or*, "in his own proper person,"] complains of C. D. being detained at the suit of A. B. in the custody of the sheriff, [*or*, "the Marshal of the Marshalsea of the Court of King's Bench, or the Warden of the Fleet."]

(i) *Ante*, 27.
(k) *Post*, vol. ii.

(l) See fully as to the points of practice respecting declarations, 3 Chitty's Gen. Prac. 439 to 496.

IV. ITS PARTS, &c. — 4thly. The Commencement.

No. 4—*Declaration after the Arrest of one or more Defendant or Defendants, and where one or more other Defendant or Defendants shall have been served only and not arrested.*

Venue.—A. B., by E. F. his attorney, [or, "in his own proper person,"] complains of C. D. who has been arrested at the suit of the said A. B. [*or,* "being detained at the suit of the said A. B., &c. *as before,*"] and of G. H. who has been served with a writ of capias to answer the said A. B., &c.

No. 5.—*The Reg. Gen. Hil. T.* 4 *W.* 4, *rule* 20, *prescribes the following form of commencement of the declaration when a Plaintiff declares in a second action after a plea in abatement of non-joinder of another party liable to be sued.*

Venue.—A. B., by E. F. his attorney, [*or,* "in his own proper person,"] complains of C. D. and G. H. who have been summoned to answer the said A. B., and which said C. D. has heretofore pleaded in abatement the non-joinder of the said G. H., &c. [The same form to be used *mutatis mutandis* in cases of arrest or detainer.]

These and other forms of *commencements* of declarations since the uniformity of process act, 2 W. 4, c. 39, will be found in the second volume, [*English edition.*†] Where the action has been *removed* into one of the superior Courts from an *inferior* Court, or is in the mixed action of *ejectment,* the commencement is to continue in the same form as before the new rules, and the defendant is to be in K. B. as in custody of the Marshal, and in C. P. that the defendant had been attached or summoned, and in the Exchequer the plaintiff is then to be still described as debtor to the king; and therefore it is no ground of *special demurrer* that the declaration describes the defendant as in the custody of the marshal, but if untrue, can only be *an irregularity,* and taken advantage of as such (*m*).

Conclusion.

The Reg. Gen. Trin. T. 1 W. 4, seems to prescribe as the usual conclusion in all the Courts, the following: "to the plaintiff's damage of £——, and thereupon he brings suit, &c." But in penal actions, when no damages are recoverable, the *ad damnum* should be omitted as heretofore (*n*).

Pledges to be omitted.

The Reg. Gen. Mich. T. 3 W. 4, reg. 15, directs that the statement of *pledges to prosecute* shall be discontinued.

Consequences of deviations from such rules, viz. that they are only *irregularities,* and not grounds of *demurrer.*

In general the non-observance of either of the preceding express *rules,* although relating to and affecting the forms of *pleading, cannot* (except in the instance of the statement *of abuttals*) be taken advantage of by *demurrer* as a *defect* in *pleading;* but must, if at all, be objected to by a *summons and*

(*m*) Commencement of declaration, stating defendant to be in custody of the marshal of the Marshalsea, *good* on special demurrer, inasmuch as the uniformity of process act applies only to actions commenced in superior Courts, and not to such as are removed from inferior Courts, and the Court will presume in favor of its jurisdiction, Dod *v.* Grant, K. B., H. T. 1836, January 15th.

(*n*) Neal *v.* Richardson, 2 Dowl. 69.

† See American Editor's Preface.

order of a judge, to set aside the *proceeding for irregularity* (o). Thus, although the above rules expressly require a declaration to be entitled of the day and month when it is delivered, yet it has been decided that the omission of such date is not a ground of demurrer (p); and although the statute, 2 W. 4, c. 39, requires that the form of action shall be expressed in the writ, and it seems that the declaration should accord, yet if it vary, such variance is not a ground of *demurrer*, (partly so because a *writ* cannot now appear on the *face of the pleadings or record*); and it can only be objected to by summons or motion for irregularity to set aside the declaration on account of such deviation (q). So, if the commencement of a declaration at the suit of an executor be improperly in the debet and detinet, instead of more properly the latter only, the objection is not a ground of demurrer as part of the declaration, but may be rejected as surplusage (r). So the improper insertion or repetition of venue in the body of a declaration, contrary to the above rule, Hil. T. 4 W. 4, r. 8, is not a ground of *demurrer*, but merely of a summons to strike out the objectionable repetition (s); and although it would be absurd for any practitioner to neglect strict observance with the recent rules, yet it is obvious that it could never have been the intention of the judges that the unnecessary insertion in the *body* of a declaration of a venue should be constantly the subject of a summons to strike out those words, which would occasion much more expense, and be infinitely more vexatious than the introduction of those few words (t). The *modes* of taking advantage of informalities in the title or commencement of a declaration is perhaps matter of *practice* rather than of *pleading*, and have been fully considered as such in another work (u).

IV. ITS PARTS, &c.

4thly. The Commencement.

5thly. After the *Commencement* of the declaration, the *Body* or statement of the *cause of action* follows in natural order, and which in every description of action consists of *three principal points*, viz. the *right*, whether founded upon contract or tort independent of contract; the *injury* to such right; and the consequent *damages*. In stating such of these, all the requisites of certainty and other points before noticed must be observed.

THE REGULATIONS AFFECTING THE BODY OR SUBSTANCE OF DECLARATIONS IN GENERAL.

5thly. The body or substance of cause of action.

Keeping in view and subject to those *general requisites*, every pleader was, before the very recent pleading rules, at liberty to frame the body or substance of every declaration in such order and language as he might consider preferable. He was not however allowed vexatiously to insert any superfluous, impertinent or extraneous matter, as in an action on a mortgage deed, a long description of the mortgaged premises (x), or covenants, of which no breach

The language of description to be observed in general.

(o) And see per Tindal, C. J., in Anderson v. Thomas, 9 Bing. 678.

(p) Neal v. Richardson, 2 Dowl. 89.

(q) Thompson v. Dicas, 2 Dowl. 93; Scrivener v. Watling, 1 Harrison, 8; Ward v. Tennison, 1 Adol. & El. 619; Edwards v. Dignam, 2 Cr. & M. 346; 2 Dowl. 240, S. C.; Chit. Gen. Prac. vol. iii. 197; and see Marshall v. Thomas, 3 Moore & S. 98; and Anderson v. Thomas, 9 Bing. 678; Tidd, Supp. A. D. 1833, p. 122.

(r) Collett v. Collett, 3 Dowl. 211.

(s) Farmer v. Champneys, 1 Crom. M. & Ros. 369; 2 Dowl. 680, S. C.; Fisher v. Snow, 3 Dowl. 27; Townsend v. Gurney, id. 29.

(t) Per Cur. in Brindley v. Bennett, 2 Bing. 184; see post, "of striking out counts."

(u) 3 Chitty's Gen. Prac. 456 to 462.

(x) Cowp. 665, 727; 1 Saund. 233, n. 2; 2 Saund. 366.

IV. ITS PARTS, &c. — 5thly. The cause of action. 1. In assumpsit. 1. Inducement.

the consideration has reference. A formal inducement does not appear to be in any case necessary in pleading; it would be sufficient if the subject-matter of the inducement were alleged in any other part of the declaration; but it is useful in composition, for the purposes of perspicuity. The matter of inducement may be stated *by way of parenthesis*, as thus: "For that whereas heretofore, to wit, on, &c. in consideration that the plaintiff, at the request of the defendant, [*he then being an attorney of the Court of our lord the king before the king himself*, or *he then being a carrier of goods for hire from, &c. to, &c.*] had then retained and employed him as such attorney to, &c.; or the declaration may begin by a *formal inducement*, as in the precedent referred to in the notes (*k*). Where a variety of facts preceded the contract, and are so connected with it that the statement of them is necessary to render the count intelligible, it is obviously better to adopt a formal inducement (*l*), than in the description of the consideration or of the contract to show those facts in one continued sentence of great length. Thus, in an action on a wager on a horse-race, it is usual to begin the declaration with an *inducement* of the expected race (*m*). So, in assumpsit upon an award, the existing differences between the parties are concisely stated, as that "certain differences had existed and were depending;" (*n*) and on a contract to pay money upon a consideration of forbearance the declaration begins by stating with brevity the existence of the debt forborne, and from whom it is due (*o*). The inducement, or averment by way of introductory allegation, is peculiarly proper where a party is charged upon, or in respect of, the breach of a contract or implied duty, resulting from any particular character or capacity of the defendant. Thus, in a declaration against an attorney for negligence, or a carrier, a coach proprietor, a wharfinger, or captain of a ship, or an innkeeper, for the loss of goods, &c., it is usual and proper to show, by way of inducement, or at least by other averment in the declaration, that the defendant followed the occupation in respect of which the plaintiff employed him. If no such allegation be contained in the declaration, the defendant cannot be charged thereon for the breach of a duty which results only from the particular character which he held, and in reference to which he was retained (*p*). But where the mere statement of the consideration and promise will be sufficiently intelligible, without any prefatory allegation, they may be set forth without any inducement; as in declarations upon bills of exchange, &c. which should proceed at once to state the instrument or contract, without any preamble of the custom of merchants, which ought not to be set forth (*q*).

[*319] *It is said that as the office of an inducement is explanatory, it does not in general require exact certainty (*r*). Thus, where an agreement with a third person is stated only as inducement to the defendant's promise, which is the principal cause of the action, it was considered in general sufficient to state such agreement without certainty of name, place, or person (*s*). This rule

(*k*) See *ante*, 291, and *post*, vol. ii.
(*l*) 4 B. & C. 345; 6 D. & R. 438, S. C.
(*m*) *Post*, vol. ii.
(*n*) *Id.*
(*o*) *Id.*
(*p*) 4 B. & C. 345; 6 D. & R. 438, S. C.; see 6 Moore, 54; 2 New Rep. 345, 454; 12 East, 94.
(*q*) *Ante*, 247, 248.
(*r*) Tidd, 9th edit. 436, cites Com. Dig. Pleader, C. 31; see 13 East, 116; 3 T. R. 646, *per* Buller, J.; Stephen, 2d edit. 364, 416, cites Cro. Eliz. 715.
(*s*) Yelv. 17

IV. ITS PARTS, &c. — 5thly. The cause of action. 1. In assumpsit, 1. Inducement.

prevailed in the statement of matter which merely constituted an *executed or past consideration* (*t*); as where the declaration charged, that in consideration that the plaintiff "had, at the defendant's request, granted to him by deed the next avoidance of a certain church," the defendant promised to pay the plaintiff £100, the court held the declaration good, although it was objected, in arrest of judgment, that the time or place at which the grant was made was not stated (*u*). So, in declaring upon a promise to pay money in consideration of the forbearance of a preceding debt, though some cause of action must be alleged, it was not necessary to state the particular cause or subject-matter of the debt, or the time when or place where it was contracted (*x*); and in an action for negligence against an attorney who had been employed to sue another, it was not necessary or advisable to state in an inducement that such other person was indebted; and if it be stated though unnecessarily, it must be proved (*y*). But where the inducement disclosing a past consideration also professes to state some matter material to be ascertained with certainty, it must be stated with precision and particularity (*z*). Therefore, where in a declaration in assumpsit for not accepting a lease, the inducement charged that the plaintiff was possessed of the premises for a certain term, ending on a day named, and the proof showed that he had only a shorter term, the court held the variance fatal (*a*). It suffices if the *introductory* matter or inducement be stated according to its legal effect (*b*); and the first part of the rule, that allegations of matter of substance may *be substantially proved, but allegations [*320] of matter of description must be literally proved (*c*), applies peculiarly to *averments* in an inducement; and therefore if the inducement be not a mere *matter of* description, and it be substantially proved as alleged, a slight variance will be immaterial. Even material matter laid in an inducement need not be proved precisely as alleged when stated under a *videlicet*, if it be correct in substance. Thus, where in a declaration to recover from the defendant a debt due from a third person, which the defendant had promised to pay in consideration of forbearance, the sum due was stated in the inducement under a *videlicet* to be £26 13*s*. 6*d*., and was described as the balance of a larger sum, and the statement of the contract referred to the sum so alleged in the inducement to be due, but only £26 were due as the balance; the Court held that the variance was not material (*d*)(601). In general, however, every allegation in an inducement, which is material and not impertinent and foreign to the cause, and which consequently cannot be rejected as surplusage, must be proved as alleged, and a variance would be fatal; and consequently great attention to the facts is necessary in framing the inducement, and care

(*t*) *Id.*; 10 Co. 59 b; Com. Dig. Pleader, C. 31, 43; E. 10, 18; 13 East, 105, 116; and see 2 Chit. Rep. 311; 5 T. R. 143.
(*u*) Cro. Eliz. 715.
(*x*) Hob. 18; *post*, vol. ii.
(*y*) Peake's Rep. 119.
(*z*) 13 East, 102; *post*, vol. ii.
(*a*) 1 M. & P. 717; 4 Bingh. 653, S. C.; see 1 B. & B. 536.
(*b*) 3 Moore, 674, 695, 696.
(*c*) *Ante*, 264, note (*e*); 3 B & C. 4; 6 D. & R. 626, S. C.; see further as to this, *post*.
(*d*) 2 Moore, 114; see 1 B. & B. 536; see *post* as to the *scilicet*.

(601) In declaring in assumpsit on a collateral undertaking, the declaration must be special, setting forth the contract; but if the undertaking be original, the plaintiff may declare generally. Northrup et al. v. Jackson, 13 Wend. R. 85.

IV. ITS PARTS, &c. — 5thly. The cause of action. 1. In assumpsit. 1. Inducement.

must be taken not to insert any unnecessary allegation (*e*). Thus, in the case just mentioned against an attorney, where the declaration stated that E. F. was *indebted* to the plaintiff, and that the plaintiff employed the defendant to sue her, it being proved that E. F. was a feme covert at the time the supposed debt accrued, and consequently not in point of law indebted, the plaintiff was nonsuited; though the declaration might have been sufficient without stating that the third person was indebted (*f*). Where, however, the matter unnecessarily stated in the inducement is wholly impertinent, and might be struck out as surplusage, there are some cases in which a failure in proof of such statement would not be material (*g*).

Inducement, if not traversed, need not be proved.

The recent rules of pleading, Hilary Term, 4 W. 4, as they apply to most actions, and especially *assumpsit* and *case*, now relieve a plaintiff from the necessity for proving matter of *inducement*, or from any risk of variance in the statement thereof, unless the defendant's plea *expressly* traverse or deny the inducement; thus, in an action on the case, if the declaration state that the plaintiff *was possessed of a close and a pond full of water therein*, and then stated an injury to the water in the pond, it was held that the plea of *not guilty* did not put in issue the inducement even though connected with the description of the injury, and that therefore the defendant could not on the trial dispute the correctness of the inducement (*h*).

2dly. The *Consideration.* [*221]

In treating of the rules relative to the statement of the *Consideration* for the contract, we will consider, 1st, *What* *consideration must *appear* on the face of the declaration, and *how* it should be stated; and 2dly, the doctrine of *variances* between the statement of the *consideration* and the *evidence* in support of it.

In declaring upon a contract not under seal, it is in all cases necessary to state that it was a contract that imports and *implies* consideration, as a bill of exchange or promissory note (*i*), or *expressly* to state the particular *consideration* upon which it was founded (*k*)(602); and it is essential that the consideration stated should appear to be *legally sufficient* to support the promise, for the breach of which the action is brought. An examination of the various points of law relating to the sufficiency of consideration (*l*), would be foreign to the object of this treatise; but it may be important to make some few observations as to the *mode of stating* the consideration upon the record in such

(*e*) *Ante*, 262, 264; 4 B. & C. 380; 6 D. & R. 500, S. C.; Dougl. 667; 5 T. R. 498; 3 B. & P. 463; 2 Chit. Rep. 311; Steph. 2d edit. 285. As to what may be struck out as surplusage, see *ante*, 262.

(*f*) Peake's Rep. 119.

(*g*) *Ante*, 262; 2 Bla. R. 840; Dougl. 667; 5 T. R. 498; 3 T. R. 646.

(*h*) Dukes *v.* Gostling, 3 Dowl. 619; Prankum *v.* Earl Falmouth, 4 Nev. & Man. 330; 1 Harr. & Wol. 1; 6 Car. & P. 529, S. C.

(*i*) These instruments always *imply* a consideration, Graham *v.* Pitman, 5 Nev. & Man. 137, so that, although the statute against frauds, 29 Car. 2, c. 3, s. 4, requires an undertaking by a third person to pay the debt of another to state the consideration, yet by means of a bill or note the statute is avoided, Ridout *v.* Bristow, 1 Tyr. Rep. 84; Poplewell *v.* Wilson, 1 Stra. 264.

(*k*) Com. Dig. Action, Assumpsit, 3; Bul. N. P. 146, 147; 1 Saund. 211, n. 2.

(*l*) See, in general, 1 Saund. 211, n. 2; 3 Chit. Com. Law, 63 to 99; Chit. jun. on Contr. 6, &c.

(602) { Douglass *v.* Davie, 2 M'Cord's Rep. 218. } Vide Burnet *v.* Bisco, 4 Johns. Rep. 235. Powell *v.* Brown, 3 Johns. Rep. 100. Bailey & Bogert *v.* Freeman, 4 Johns. Rep. 280. Lansing *v.* M'Killip, 3 Caines' Rep. 288. { Beauchamp *v.* Bosworth, 3 Bibb's Rep. 115. Beverleys *v.* Holmes, 4 Munf. 95. Moseley *v.* Jones, 5 Munf. 23. }

IV. ITS PARTS, &c. — 5thly. The cause of action. 1. In assumpsit. 2. The consideration.

a manner that it may appear legally sufficient. Although no mode of pleading can enable a plaintiff to recover when the consideration is insufficient or illegal, if the defendant by his plea properly raise the question, yet it may not unfrequently occur that a sufficient consideration may exist, but that the action may be defeated in consequence of the statement upon the pleading being imperfect.

In declaring upon *bills of exchange* and *promissory notes*, and some other legal liabilities, the mere statement of the liability which constitutes the consideration is sufficient; but in other cases of simple contracts, it is necessary that the declaration should disclose a consideration, which may consist of either benefit to the defendant, or detriment to the plaintiff, or the promise will appear to be *nudum pactum*, and the declaration will consequently be insufficient (m) (603). Thus, where the plaintiff declared that a person, since deceased, was indebted to him, and that after the death, in consideration of the premises, and that the plaintiff, at the defendant's request, "would give time for the payment of the debt," the defendant promised, &c.; but did not state that there was any person in existence who was liable, in respect of assets or otherwise, to be sued by the plaintiff for the debt, and to whom he gave time; the declaration was held insufficient on demurrer; for no benefit was shown to move to the defendant, nor did it appear that any detriment had been sustained by the plaintiff, as it was not stated that any one was liable to be sued by him, or that he had suspended the enforcement of any right (n). So, where the declaration in assumpsit alleged, that in consideration *that the plaintiff would retain and employ the defendant to lay out a sum of money in the purchase of an annuity, the latter undertook to *do his duty in the premises*, and that the plaintiff accordingly did retain the defendant, but that the defendant neglected to do his duty, and took an insufficient security; it was held, on motion in arrest of judgment, that the count was bad, since it did not show that any *reward* was to be paid to the defendant, nor aver that the defendant was employed as an attorney, or in any particular character, by reason of which it became his absolute duty not to take a security of an insufficient nature (o). [*322]

Upon this subject it has been laid down as a rule, that the consideration should be co-extensive with the promise, in order to support it. Thus where the plaintiff stated that the defendant was liable in the character of *executor* to pay a certain debt, and then averred, that in consideration thereof, he per-

(m) See previous note; 4 East, 455; 1 Taunt. 522.

(n) 4 East, 455.

(o) 4 B. & C. 345; but see 2 Bingh. 464; M'Clel. & Y. 205, S. C., in which it was held that a count in *assumpsit* that the plaintiff *had retained* the defendant, at his request, to lay out £700 in purchase of an annuity; that defendant promised to lay it out securely; that plaintiff *delivered the money to him for that purpose*, and that defendant laid it out insecurely; contained a sufficient consideration for the defendant's promise, *after verdict*.

(603) {Curley v. Dean, 4 Conn. Rep. 265.} In declaring in assumpsit for the breach of a contract, it is not necessary to set forth the payment of a part of the consideration, admitted by the contract to have been received. Dox v. Dey, 3 Wend. R. 357.

Where a note is not given upon any one consideration, which whether good or not, whether it fail or not, goes to the whole note at the time it is made, but for two distinct and independent considerations, each going to a distinct portion of the note, and one is a consideration which the law deems valid and sufficient to support a contract, and the other not, there the contract shall be apportioned, and the holder shall recover to the extent of the valid consideration, and no further; and the question as to the amount, it is for the jury. Parish v. Stone, 14 Pick. R. 198.

IV. ITS PARTS, &c. — 5thly. The cause of action. 1. In assumpsit. 2. The consideration.

sonally promised to pay the debt, the declaration was held bad in arrest of judgment, no *additional* consideration being shown for the enlarged responsibility arising from the promise (*p*). And upon the same principle, a declaration against a husband alone, on his mere promise to pay the debt of his wife contracted before marriage, without showing any *new* consideration, was also considered insufficient, and the judgment was arrested (*q*)(604).

When the consideration for the defendant's contract consists of any *agreement* on the part of the plaintiff, it must appear from the declaration that such agreement was binding on the plaintiff at the time the defendant's promise was made; for if it should appear from the declaration that the obligation was all on one side, the defendant's engagement would be *nudum pactum*, and the declaration consequently bad (*r*). We have already seen, that, at least in some instances, it may be sufficient to show that the consideration moved from a third person, if the promise be made for the benefit of the plaintiff (*s*).

[*323] *When part of an entire consideration, or one of several considerations, stated in a declaration, is merely *frivolous* and void, without being illegal, and *the residue is good*, and extends to the whole of the promise, the void part will not vitiate the declaration (605), but may be rejected as surplusage; and the promise will be referred to and supported by that part of the consideration which is legally sufficient (*t*). But if part of an entire consideration, or one of several considerations stated, *be illegal*, though the residue may be good, the whole declaration will, it appears, be vitiated by the illegal part (*u*).

Another material circumstance to be attended to in the statement of the consideration is, that it should be shown with a proper degree of *certainty* and particularity. A declaration may contain enough to disclose a consideration, which is legally sufficient to support the promise, but may be liable to objection on special demurrer, on account of omitting to set out that consideration with a sufficient degree of certainty (*x*). The degree of certainty required in stating the consideration will depend, in some degree, on the particular species of consideration to be stated, and it will therefore be necessary to notice the various kinds of considerations. They are, 1st, *Executed*, or 2dly, *Executory*; to which may be added, 3dly, *Concurrent*, and 4thly, *Continuing Considerations*.

(*p*) 7 T. R. 350 a.
(*q*) *Id.* 348.
(*r*) 3 T. R. 653; see *id.* 149; 1 M. & Sel. 557; 1 B. & Ald. 681; 16 East, 45; 3 B. & C. 668, 690; 5 D. & R. 512, S. C.
(*s*) *Ante*, 2, 3. But see 4 Bar. & Adol. 433; 1 Nev. & Man. 303, S. C.
(*t*) Ring *v.* Roxbrough, 2 Crom. & Jer. 418; 2 Tyr. 463; King *v.* Sears, 2 Crom. M. & Ros. 48; Cro. Eliz. 148, 848; Cro. Jac. 128; 1 Sid. 38; Bul. N. P. 147.
(*u*) Cro. Eliz. 199; 4 Leon. 3; T. Jones, 24; Com. Dig. Action, Assumpsit, B. 13. As to the distinction of a consideration being *illegal* in *part* at *common law*, or by *statute*, see Hob. 14; 1 Saund. 66, n. 1; 3 Taunt. 244; 5 *Id.* 746; 6 *Id.* 359; 4 M. & Sel. 66; Chit. jun. Contr. 228, 229.
(*x*) See the general rule as to certainty in pleading, *ante*, 267.

(604) See Beach *v.* Lee, 2 Dall. Rep. 256. Buckner *v.* Smyth, 4 Desaus. Cha. Rep. 371.

(605) { Where a son who was of full age, and had ceased to be a member of his father's family, was suddenly taken sick among strangers, and being poor and in distress, was relieved by the plaintiff, and afterwards the father wrote to the plaintiff, promising to pay him the expenses incurred, it was held that such promise would not sustain the action, there being no consideration for it. Mills *v.* Wyman, 3 Pick. Rep. 207. See the limitation of the rule, "that a moral obligation is sufficient to support an express promise," there stated by PARKER, C. J. See also Cooke *v.* Bradley, 7 Conn. Rep. 57. }

IV. ITS PARTS, &c.

5thly. The cause of action.

1. In assumpsit.

2. The consideration.

Statement of *Executed* considerations.

1st. An *executed* consideration consists of something *past* or *done* before the making of the promise. It is said not to be necessary, in stating *executed* considerations, to allege them with the certainty of time and place required in stating executory considerations, nor with the same particularity in other respects as to quantity, quality, value, &c. (*y*); because the allegation of a past consideration is considered to be matter of inducement, and as such, not in itself traversable (*z*). It must, however, be shown, that the executed consideration *arose *at the defendant's request* (*a*) (606), though such request may, in some cases, be *implied* (607) *in evidence*, as when the defendant has derived benefit from the consideration, and has afterwards made an express promise to the plaintiff (608) or has recognized the plaintiff's act; and it is only necessary in cases of *executed consideration* to state that the consideration for the defendant's promise moved at *his request* (*b*), the executed consideration [*324] must, in legal estimation, be of some value, but the performance by the plaintiff of any act he was not legally *bound* to perform would suffice, as the producing or giving to the defendant a certain letter (*c*). There are some cases in which the plaintiff has the option of stating the consideration either as an executed or as an executory consideration, and which will be hereafter noticed (*d*).

Statement of *Executory* considerations.

2dly. In the statement of an *Executory* consideration a greater degree of certainty is required (*e*). The consideration and the promise of the defendant are two distinct things, and in order to show that the plaintiff possesses a right of action, it is in general necessary to aver performance of the consideration on his part, which allegation being material and traversable must be made with proper certainty of time and place &c. (*f*). This obligation of averring

(*y*) See 13 East, 105, 116, 117; Stephen, 2d edit. 364, 415; see as to matter of inducement, *ante*, 318.

(*z*) *Id.*; Bul. N. P. 146; Salk. 22; Hob. 106. *Sed quære*, it is certainly *traversable*, and though it need not be averred on what *precise day* the executed consideration took place, yet it must be shown that it had *previously* occurred as "*before then*," &c.

(*a*) 1 Saund. 264, n. 1; 2 Stra. 933; Dyer, 272; and *per* Parke, B., in King *v.* Sears, 2 Cr. M. & Ros. 53.

(*b*) King *v.* Sears, 2 Cr. M. & R. 48; 1 Saund. 264, note 1, a good instance; it was there stated, that in consideration that the plaintiff *would* forbear to distrain on a third person (without saying at *defendant's request*), defendant undertook to pay, &c., and held sufficient on special demurrer.

(*c*) Wilkinson *v.* Olivera, 1 Bing. N. C. 490.

(*d*) *Post*, 326, note (*t*); 7 Bar. & Cres. 423.

(*e*) 1 Saund. 264, n. 1.

(*f*) Bul. N. P. 146 a; Salk. 22; Ring *v.* Roxbrough, 2 Tyr. 468; 2 Crom. & J. 418. A special traverse of the allegation of performance was not, at least before the pleading rules, H. T. 4 W. 4, usual, in consequence of the latitude heretofore allowed to the general issue in assumpsit. But since those rules the allegation of consideration and performance in a special count need not be proved, unless expressly denied in pleading.

(606) The law relating to past or executed considerations, is fully discussed in the opinion of KENT, J., in Livingston *v.* Rogers, 1 Caines' Rep. 583, where it is held, in conformity to the case of Hayes *v.* Warren, Str. 933, (cited in note e.) that a promise laid to have been made, afterwards, on the same day with the consideration, is a *nudum pactum.* See also Comstock *v.* Smith, 7 Johns. Rep. 87. Hicks *v.* Burhans and others, 10 Johns. Rep. 243. Everts and Allen *v.* Adams, 12 Johns. Rep. 352. Mitchell *v.* Bell, Taylor, 61. Frear *v.* Hardenbergh, 5 Johns. Rep. 272. Robertson *v.* Bethune and Boorman, 3 Johns. Rep. 350. { See also Edwards *v.* Davis, 16 Johns. Rep. 281, and the Reporter's note, 283. But see Clark *v.* Herring, 5 Binn. 33. Greeves *v.* M'Allister, 2 Binn. 591. 6 Mass. 43. }

(607) As, from the beneficial nature of the act performed by the defendant. Hicks *v.* Burhans and others, 10 Johns. Rep. 243. Livingston *v.* Rogers, 1 Caines' Rep. 585, 586. Comstock *v.* Smith, 7 Johns. Rep. 88.

(608) { Greeves *v.* M'Allister, 2 Binn. 591. }

IV. ITS PARTS, &c. — 5thly. The cause of action. 1. In assumpsit. 2. The consideration.

performance imposes upon the plaintiff the necessity of stating the consideration with a greater degree of certainty and minuteness than in the case of executed considerations; for the Court would otherwise be unable to judge whether the performance averred in the declaration were sufficient (*g*). Thus, in an action for wages, agreed to be paid to the plaintiff in consideration that he *would* proceed on a certain voyage, it has been held necessary to state the particular voyage (*h*)(609). But the same degree of certainty is not required in stating any particular part of the consideration, with respect to which the circumstances of the case render it unnecessary to aver performance. Thus, in actions for negligence, &c. against attornies, carriers, and other bailees, who have been employed by the plaintiff for reward, it is not necessary to specify the amount of the remuneration stipulated to be given, but the plaintiff may state that the retainer was "for certain reasonable reward." (*i*) It will be observed, that in [*325] *these cases the payment of the reward does not constitute a condition precedent, and that in point of fact it is the retainer that constitutes the consideration: the reward may or may not become payable according to circumstances. But it is obviously essential in general to aver that the retainer was for reward, otherwise the promise would appear to be *nudum pactum* (*k*).

Statement of *Concurrent* considerations.

3dly. A *Concurrent* consideration occurs in the case of mutual promises, which are a third species of consideration, partaking of the nature of the preceding two. The plaintiff's *promise* is *executed*, but the *thing* which he has engaged to perform is *executory*, as in promises to marry, to submit to an award on wagers, &c. The promises of each party must in general be concurrent or obligatory on *both* at the same time (610), to render the promise of either binding, and must be so stated in pleading (*l*). And in these cases it is not always necessary to aver performance of the thing stipulated to be done (611), the plaintiff's *agreement* to perform being a sufficient consideration (*m*); unless the *performance* of one act be the consideration of the performance of the other, in which case an averment of *performance*, or *readiness* to perform, is in general necessary, even in the case of mutual promises (*n*); as upon mutual promises to marry and bargains to sell and accept goods (*o*) (612).

(*g*) See Com. Dig. Action, Assumpsit, H. 4; Pleader, C.

(*h*) 2 B. & P. 116, 120, 265.

(*i*) See the precedents of declarations in assumpsit against attornies, carriers, &c. for negligence, in the second volume; and see 13 East, 114, note; 2 New Rep. 458; and see 2 Bing. 464; M'Clel. & Y. 205, S. C.

(*k*) See *ante*, 321, 322; 4 B. & C. 345; 6 D. & R. 438, S. C.

(*l*) 3 T. R. 148, 653; Bla. Rep. 706; Peake, C. N. P. 228; Hob. 146; Salk. 112; 5 East, 16.

(*m*) 1 Wils. 88; 5 T. R. 409; 1 Ld. Raym. 664; 1 Salk. 171.

(*n*) 1 Salk. 112, 171; 1 Lord Raym. 665; 6 T. R. 570; 7 *Id.* 125; 1 Moore, 56.

(*o*) 1 East, 203; 2 B. & P. 447; 1 Saund. 320 e, n. 5.

(609) Where the performance of the act to be done on the part of the plaintiff is the consideration of the act to be done by the defendant, the declaration states that if the plaintiff would do a certain act, the defendant promised, and then avers performance; and it is not necessary to allege that the plaintiff promised. 10 Mass. Rep. 230, 237, 235.

(610) Vide Porter *v.* Rose, 12 Johns. Rep. 209.

(611) Vide Lent and another *v.* Pandelford, 10 Mass. Rep. 230.

(612) Vide Livingston *v.* Rogers, 1 Caines' Rep. 583. Tucker *v.* Woods, 12 Johns. Rep. 190. Keep and Hale *v.* Goodrich, Id. 397. Gould *v.* Banks, 8 Wend. R. 562.

4thly. In the case of a *Continuing* consideration, the declaration generally states, that in consideration that the defendant *had become and was* tenant to the plaintiff of certain land, &c. he undertook, during the continuance of the tenancy, *to use the premises, in a tenant-like manner, &c.*; and the declaration then avers the continuance of the tenancy and the breach (*p*); or the declaration states the defendant's character and relative duty, and his promise in consideration thereof to perform his duty. But in either of *these cases* of mere *continuing* consideration, the promise must not be stated to have been more extensive than the law would presume, or, at least, support; and, therefore, a promise that, in consideration that the defendant then was tenant to the plaintiff, he promised *to repair*, &c., the declaration will be demurrable (*q*).

IV. ITS PARTS, &c. — 5thly. The cause of action. 1. In assumpsit. 2. The consideration. Statement of *Continuing* considerations.

In the preceding observations we have considered the necessity of showing that the consideration was legally sufficient, *and the degree of certainty and particularity required in stating it. Another important point to be observed is, that the consideration, if expressly traversed or denied by the plea, (but not otherwise, since the new pleading rules of H. T. 4 W. 4,) must be *proved* as stated; or the plaintiff will fail at the trial on the ground of a *variance* (613), unless permitted to amend under 3 & 4 W. 4, c. 42, s. 23. Instances of variance in stating matter of *inducement* have already been given (*r*). It is proposed now to notice the rules relative to *variances* in the statement of the *consideration*; and the doctrine of *variances* in stating the *promise* or *contract* will be explained in a subsequent part of the work.

2. Of *Variances* in stating the consideration. [*326]

Great accuracy is required in the statement of the *consideration*, which in an action of assumpsit forms the basis of the contract, and if any error appear to have been made in describing it, the consequence will be, that the whole contract is mis-described. Thus, in the instance before noticed, of an action brought for wages, to be paid to the plaintiff, in consideration that he would proceed on a particular voyage, it was held that a variance in the description of the voyage was fatal, though laid under a *videlicet* (*s*). So, it would appear to be a general rule, that if the consideration alleged be executory, and that which is proved be executed, the mis-description is fatal; executory and executed considerations being in their nature materially distinct. But when in a declaration in assumpsit the plaintiff alleged, that in consideration that he, at the request of the defendant, *would consent* to suspend proceedings against A., the defendant promised, &c.; and the evidence was an agreement in these terms, viz. "the plaintiff *having, at my request, consented to suspend proceedings* against A., I do hereby, in consideration thereof, promise to pay £30 on

(*p*) 5 T. R. 373; 4 East, 150; 1 Leon. 102; Cro. Eliz. 94, 715; 2 Leon. 224; 2 Bla. Rep. 842; 1 Marsh. 567; *post*, vol. ii.

(*q*) 1 Marsh. 567; 6 Taunt. 300, S. C.; *post*, vol. ii.

(*r*) *Ante*, 318.

(*s*) 2 B. & P. 116; *ante*, 324.

(613) Where the declaration alleged an undertaking in consideration of a contract, entered into by the plaintiff to *build* a ship, and the evidence was of a contract to *finish* a ship partly built, it was held that the variance was fatal. Smith *v.* Barker, 3 Day's Rep. 312. Where the contract stated in the declaration was on a past consideration for the delivery of goods without mention of the place of delivery, and in the alternative as to the time; and the contract proved was an executory consideration, to deliver goods at a particular time and place mentioned, the variance was held fatal and the verdict set aside. Robertson *v.* Lynch, 18 Johns. Rep. 451.

IV. ITS PARTS, &c. — 5thly. The cause of action. 1. In assumpsit. 2. The consideration.

the 1st day of April," it was held, on motion in arrest of judgment, that the consideration was sufficiently described: the fair construction of the agreement being, that the consideration was that the plaintiff would suspend proceedings against A. until the 1st of April (*t*). So where a count of a declaration in assumpsit against a carrier by water, alleged, that in consideration that the plaintiff, at the request of the defendant, **had caused* to be shipped on board the defendant's vessel a quantity of wheat, to be carried to a certain place, for freight to be therefore paid to the defendant, he undertook to carry the wheat safely, and deliver it for the plaintiff on a given day; but it appeared [*327] that the defendant's undertaking to carry was made *before* the whole of the wheat had been shipped on board his vessel; it was held, that the count might be supported, although it was objected that the consideration for the promise was executory; on the ground, that where an order is given to a carrier, antecedently to the delivery of goods, who assents to deal with them, when delivered, in a particular manner, a duty is imposed on him, on the receipt of the goods, to deal with them according to the order previously given; and the law implies a promise by him to perform such duty (*u*).

In accordance with the rule requiring the consideration to be stated accurately, it is necessary that the *whole* of the consideration should in general be stated; and if any part of an entire consideration, or of a consideration consisting of several things, be omitted, the plaintiff will fail at the trial on the ground of variance (*x*). Thus, where in assumpsit on the warranty of a horse, the declaration stated the transaction as upon a sale of a *single* horse, and upon the evidence it appeared that *two* horses had been sold at an entire price and with a joint warranty, the variance was considered fatal, the purchase of the two horses constituting the consideration for the warranty (*y*). The same rule renders it also imperative that the consideration stated in the declaration should be proved to the extent alleged; and in general when the consideration proved falls short of that which is stated in the declaration, as the foundation for the promise, the variance will be equally fatal as when the proof exceeds the statement. In an action brought by *husband and wife and another party*, the declaration stated, that by an agreement between the *plaintiffs* and the defendant, the *plaintiffs* agreed to let to the defendant certain lands; that the defendant became tenant to the plaintiffs, and stated mutual promises by the plaintiffs and defendant to perform all things contained in the agreement: the agreement given in evidence purported to be made by an agent on behalf [*328] of the *wife* and the *third plaintiff only*, without any mention *of the husband, but it appeared that the husband had *subsequently* received rent from the tenant: the Court held, that in order to support the consideration alleged, it was necessary to prove that the husband was a joint contractor *ab initio;* that the evidence fell short of this proof, since, before the receipt of rent by the husband, he was clearly not bound by the agreement; and that the variance

(*t*) 7 B. & C. 423. Littledale, J., observed in this case that there was a *continuing* consideration; for the plaintiff not only *had* consented to suspend the proceedings, but also that they *should be* suspended until the 1st April, and that therefore this might be alleged in pleading either as an executed or executory consideration, see Com. Dig. Action, Assumpsit, B. 12; Cro. Eliz. 94.

(*u*) 7 Moore, 283; 1 Bing. 34, S. C.

(*x*) 6 East, 568; 8 *Id.* 7; Cro. Eliz. 79; Bul. N. P. 147; 12 East, 1; 13 *Id.* 102.

(*y*) 1 Campb. 361.

IV. ITS PARTS, &c.

5thly. The cause of action.

1. In assumpsit.

2. The consideration.

was therefore fatal (z). So also, where in an action for the breach of warranty of a horse, the declaration stated the consideration of the warranty to be the sale to the plaintiff of the horse for the sum of £55, and it was proved that the plaintiff was to have the horse for that sum, but the defendant had agreed to give £1 back, if the horse did not bring the plaintiff £4 or £5; the variance was held fatal, the declaration importing that the price was £55 absolutely, and the evidence showing that the price agreed for was subject to a contingent reduction (a).

An exception, however, prevails in regard to considerations which are in part good, and in part frivolous and insufficient. We have before noticed cases of this description, and have shown that when a consideration of this nature is stated, the declaration will not be vitiated by the insufficient part, but that the promise will be referred to that part of the consideration which is in law sufficient to support it. The insufficient part is regarded as mere surplusage; in a legal point of view it forms no part whatever of the real consideration for the contract, and consequently it becomes wholly unnecessary either to notice it in the declaration or to prove it if stated (b). A variance, therefore, between the evidence and the declaration as to such part of the consideration stated as is frivolous and insufficient will be of no consequence. Thus, where in an action for rent the declartion stated a demise of "a messuage, land, and premises, with the appurtenances;" and the evidence was of a demise of furniture and utensils, as well as of real property, the variance was held to be immaterial, since in point of law the rent issued out of the real property only, and not out of the furniture (c).

[*329] *When there is no direct contradiction between the allegation and the evidence, it is in general sufficient that they agree in substance. Thus, when the consideration of the retainer and employment of the defendant by the plaintiff is stated to be "certain *reasonable* reward," it seems that it will not amount to a variance if it appear by the evidence that a *specific sum* was agreed upon (d). And where it was stated that the defendant agreed to furnish certain goods "at fair and reasonable prices," the averment was held sufficiently proved by showing a contract to furnish such goods, with a certain latitude as to price, viz. between two specified sums (e). In these cases it was considered that the evidence *substantially* supported the allegations in the declarations, and was not inconsistent with it.

How to take advantage of insufficient statement of consideration by demurrer, &c.

When *no consideration* is stated in the declaration, or when that which is stated is *clearly insufficient or illegal*, the defendant may either demur or move in arrest of judgment, or support a writ of error (f). When the mode in which the consideration is stated is defective, informal, or uncertain, the declaration will be bad upon *special demurrer* (g); but after verdict a defective

(z) 5 B. & C. 909; 8 D. & R. 423, S. C.
(a) 3 Bing. 472; see also 1 T. R. 447.
(b) Ring v. Roxbrough, 2 Cromp. & Jer. 418; 2 Tyr. 468; King v. Sears, 2 Crom. M. & Ros. 48; Cro. Jac. 127; Cro. Eliz. 149; Com. Dig. Action, Assumpsit, B. 13; *ante*, 323, n. (t).
(c) 6 B. & C. 251; 9 D. & R. 245, S. C. The action was *debt*, but it is noticed as illustrative of the principle stated in the text.
(d) 2 N. R. 458.
(e) 6 Taunt. 108.
(f) 7 T. R. 348; 4. B & Cres. 345; 6 D. & R. 438, S. C.
(g) 4 East, 455; 13 *Id.* 102.

IV. ITS PARTS, &c.

5thly The cause of action.

1. In assumpsit.

2. The consideration.

How to take advantage of the *illegality* or *untruth* in consideration.

statement of the consideration will be aided (614), provided, by a reasonable construction of the whole declaration, it sufficiently appears that there was a consideration capable of supporting the promise (*h*).

Where the consideration is *untruly stated*, or a part thereof is omitted, or the whole cannot be proved, the objection can only be taken at the trial as a ground of nonsuit (*i*), and since the new pleading rules Reg. Gen. Hil. Term, 4 W. 4, the defendant must *by plea expressly deny* the consideration, or plead specially the want of adequate consideration; and in actions on bills or notes the plea must be very particular (*k*).

3. Statement of the *Contract*.

1. How the *promise* should be stated, so that the declaration may be good on the face of it.

After showing the consideration, the declaration proceeds to state the defendant's *promise* or *contract*. In treating of the manner in which the contract should be stated, we may consider, 1st, the general rules of *pleading* with respect to the statement of the defendant's promise or contract, so that it may appear to be valid *on the face of the record;* and, 2dly, the doctrine of *variances* between the *statement* and the *evidence*.

1st. A declaration in assumpsit should in all cases show that a *promise* has been made, either by expressly averring in the ancient form that the defendant "undertook and faithfully *promised*," or since Reg. Gen. Trin. T. 1 W. 4, more concisely "*promised*," omitting the other words (*l*), or by other equivalent words. The adoption of the terms *assumpsit super se*, *&c.* has been in some cases considered absolutely necessary, and a declaration which omitted them has been held bad even after judgment (*m*), and is certainly bad on *special* demurrer (*n*). But from other authorities it appears that a declaration in assumpsit, which does not contain the word "*promised*," may nevertheless be

[*330] good, provided it sufficiently appear from the whole declaration that what is equivalent to a promise has taken place (615). Thus, in assumpsit on a bill of exchange, where the declaration showed the defendant's liability on the bill as the drawer, but omitted to add that he promised to pay, the Court refused to arrest the judgment for this omission, and held that the count was, notwithstanding such omission, a count in assumpsit, because the drawing of the bill was a promise (*o*); and the same doctrine has been extended to a promis-

(*h*) 2 B. & P. 265; 1 N. R. 172; 4 East, 464; 2 Bingh. 464; M'Clel. & Y. 205.

(*i*) Cro. Eliz. 79. As to amendment of a declaration on a written instrument at the trial, see *post*, 348, 349.

(*k*) See the rules and requisites of *pleas*, *post*, chap. Graham *v.* Pitman, 5 Nev. & Man. 37; Kinder *v.* Smedley, *Id.* 138; so also *illegality of consideration* must be specially pleaded, Barnett *v.* Glossop, 3 Dowl. 625; 1 Bing. N. C. 633; 1 Hodges, 35. According to Passenger *v.* Brookes, 1 Bing. N. C. 587, the *consideration* stated in special assumpsit must be specially denied by plea, or will be admitted; *sed quære*, *post*.

(*l*) See forms prescribed by Reg. Gen. Trin. T. 1 W. 4, as models, *post*, vol ii.

(*m*) Stra. 793; Lord Raym. 1516; 1 Sid. 246; Com. Dig. Action, Assumpsit, H. 3

(*n*) Harding *v.* Hibel, 4 Tyr. 314.

(*o*) Ld. Raym. 538, S. C.; 1 Salk. 128; Carth. 509.

(614) Shaw *v.* Redmond, 11 Serg. Rawle, 27.

(615) Avery *v.* The Inhabitants of Tyringham, 3 Mass. Rep. 160. But in Cook *v.* Simms, 2 Call, 39, it was held that a declaration reciting a written agreement and alleging a breach, without stating an express *assumpsit*, was ill. { So the plaintiff must charge the promise by the defendant *positively*, and not by way of *recital* only; for if the declaration be defective in this respect, it is a fatal error, and not cured by verdict. Sexton *v.* Holmes, 3 Munf. 566. }

IV. ITS PARTS, &c.

5thly. The cause of action.

1. In assumpsit.

3. The promise or contract.

sory note (*p*) (616). So it has been held on motion in arrest of judgment, that a declaration in assumpsit, which stated an agreement between the plaintiff and defendant, but omitted the mutual promises, was sufficient, and the Court said an agreement was a promise (*q*). And in a recent case where one count in a declaration stated that the plaintiff had delivered certain property to the defendant to be taken care of by the defendant for reward to him, and that in consideration thereof the defendant "*undertook* and *agreed*" to take care of the property and to re-deliver it on request; it was held, on motion in arrest of judgment, that this was a count in assumpsit, and was therefore improperly joined with one in tort (*r*). It should however be observed that in all these cases it was considered that the declaration contained averments which were fully tantamount to the allegation of an express promise, a circumstance which is absolutely necessary in a declaration in assumpsit. No distinction exists in pleading between an implied promise and an express one; it is true that in *evidence* the law in many cases implies, from certain facts, that a promise has been made; but in *pleading*, the supposed promise itself should be alleged (617), and it is at least untechnical merely to state that which is only *evidence* of a promise (*s*).

[*331] *It is essential that the contract should be stated with certainty (*t*); but we have formerly seen that in a declaration a less degree of certainty is required than in a plea; and that what in the ordinary technical phrase is called "certainty to a certain intent in general," will be sufficient (*u*); and therefore a statement in a declaration, "For that *whereas* the defendant on, &c." promised, &c. is good on general demurrer, and perhaps even on special demurrer (*v*).

The declaration should specify the *names of the parties* by and to whom the promise was made, but an omission in this respect will frequently be aided, and especially after verdict; and it is even said that when the name of the party making the promise has been omitted, it may be intended after verdict that the defendant made the promise (*w*). And where the declaration omits to state to whom the promise was made, it will be intended that the promise was made to the party from whom the consideration proceeded (*x*). But after verdict for the plaintiff, the judgment was arrested, because the declaration showed only a consideration from a *third person*, and not from the plaintiff, and only stated a promise to *pay* him without showing a promise *to him* (*y*). It was also necessary that the promise should be averred with certainty of *time* and *place*, and is still so as to *time* (*z*). It

(*p*) 1 Stra. 224; see 1 Taunt. 217, 218.
(*q*) 2 N. R. 62.
(*r*) 6 B. & C. 268; 9 D. & R. 258, S. C.
(*s*) See 1 Lord Raym. 538, 539; 6 Mod. 131; 2 Hen. Bla. 563, n. a; *ante*, 258.
(*t*) Com. Dig. Action, Assumpsit, H. 3.
(*u*) *Ante*, 269, 286; Com. Dig. Action, Assumpsit, A. 4.
(*v*) *Id. ibid.*; Ring *v.* Roxbrough, 2 Tyr. 468; 2 Cromp. & J. 418, S. C.
(*w*) Com. Dig. Action, Assumpsit, H. 3; Lut. 283; but see *contra*, Cro. Eliz. 913; Noy, 50, S. C.
(*x*) Cro. Car. 77; Noy, 83; Com. Dig. Action, Assumpsit, A. 5.
(*y*) Price *v.* Easton, 4 Bar. & Adol. 433; 1 Nev. & Man. 303, S. C.
(*z*) See Ring *v.* Roxbrough, *supra*, n. (*v*).

(616) So, in *assumpsit* by the bearer of a note payable to bearer. Dole *v.* Weeks, 4 Mass. Rep. 451. Vide 2 New Rep. 63, n. a.

(617) In assumpsit on an award, a promise must be alleged; but the defect is cured by verdict. Kingsley *v.* Bill, 9 Mass. Rep. 198. It is a general rule in pleading in *assumpsit*, that it must be stated that the defendant undertook and promised, &c. or something equivalent thereto, or the declaration will be held bad, even *after* verdict and judgment. Candler et al. *v.* Rossiter, 10 Wend. R. 487.

IV. ITS PARTS, &c. — 5thly. The cause of action. 1. In assumpsit. 3. The promise or contract.

seldom occurs that the precise time laid in the declaration is material to be proved, but the promise being a material and traversable allegation, the rules of pleading require, as we have previously seen, that a *time* of making it should be specified (*a*). The statement of the contract should in strictness be positive, and not by way of a recital; but it will be considered sufficient if the averment of the defendant's promise be preceded by "whereas." (*b*) And in setting out an agreement the plaintiff may do so by a "*testatum existit.*" (*c*)

All those parts of the contracts, which are material for the purpose of enabling the Court to form a just idea of what the contract actually was, or which are necessary for the purpose of furnishing the jury with a criterion in the assessment of damages, should be stated with certainty and precision (*d*). In a case where the declaration stated that in consideration that the plaintiff had sold to the defendant a certain horse of the plaintiff, at and for a *certain quantity of oil* to be delivered *within a certain time, which had elapsed* before
[*332] the commencement of the action, the defendant promised *to deliver the *said oil to the plaintiff accordingly*, the Court at first entertained some doubt whether so uncertain a statement of the contract was not bad in arrest of judgment, but finally held that it was sufficient after verdict (*e*). In a subsequent case, where, (after stating a former agreement for the sale of goods by the defendant to the plaintiff, "at a certain rate or price per pound, to be paid in a manner then stipulated between them, the goods to be delivered by the defendants to the plaintiffs at a time which had elapsed before making the promise thereinafter mentioned, but which goods had not been delivered,") and the declaration proceeded to state a new contract, that in consideration that the plaintiff would still receive and pay for the goods "*at the rate or price and in manner aforesaid,*" the defendant promised to deliver the same, "*within such reasonable time as aforesaid;*" this mode of statement was held too general, and bad upon special demurrer (*f*). If, however, the uncertainty of the words of the promise be afterwards supplied and rendered certain by an averment, it will be sufficient; as in the ordinary instance of a promise to pay the plaintiff as much as he should deserve, with a subsequent averment that he deserved so much (*g*).

When the contract is in *writing*, it is not necessary to state that circumstance in a declaration. And even in cases where, by the statute of frauds, the promise is rendered ineffectual, unless there be a memorandum of its terms in writing it is not *necessary* in a *declaration* at law (*h*), or a bill in equity (*i*), to show that the requisitions of the statute have been complied with in this re-

(*a*) See *ante*, 287, 290, 331, note (*x*).

(*b*) Hardr. 1; Com Dig. Assumpsit, H. 3; *ante*, 331, note (*x*).

(*c*) This form of setting out an agreement or deed is considered sufficient in a declaration, although in a plea it might be otherwise, *ante*, 268; 1 Saund, 274, n. 1; 1 Lev. 75.

(*d*) See 2 B. & P. 267; 13 East, 115, 116.

(*e*) 2 B. & P. 265.

(*f*) 13 East, 102; and see 4 B. & Ald. 268.

(*g*) Cro. Eliz. 149; Com. Dig. Assumpsit, H. 3.

(*h*) 1 Saund. 276 a; Bac. Ab. Stat. L. 3; *ante*, 254.

(*i*) 1 Sim. & Stu. 543; and see 6 Bing. 529, as to stating the acceptance of a bill to have been in writing since the stat. 1 & 2 G. 4, c. 78, requiring the acceptance of an inland bill to be in writing.

spect (j)(618). The nature of the promise still remains the same in the eye of the law, which does not admit of any distinction between verbal and written agreements, except where the latter are under seal: and it should seem that the provisions of the statute only affect the rules of *evidence* and not those of *pleading* (k). However, since the Reg. Gen. Hil. T. 4 W. 4, requiring a special plea, it might save time if, when the fact, a declaration on a guarantee stated that the contract was in writing, and set the same out verbatim.

IV. ITS PARTS, &c.

5thly. The cause of action.

1. In assumpsit.

3. The promise or contract.

We shall examine hereafter, in treating of the degree of accuracy required in stating the contracts, how much of the contract it is necessary to set out in the declaration, in order to avoid a variance between the pleadings and the evidence *at the trial (l). It should, however, be here observed that it is sufficient to state those parts of the contract whereof a breach is complained of, or in other words to show so much of the terms beneficial to the plaintiff in a contract, as constitutes the point for the failure of which he sues; and that it is not necessary or proper to set out in the declaration other parts not qualifying or varying in any respect the material parts above mentioned (m). The statement of additional matter would be needless prolixity, which, though it does not vitiate the declaration, is much censured by the Courts when carried to any excess (n). And it has been justly observed that the perfection of pleading consists in combining brevity with the requisite certainty and precision (o). Thus in declaring in covenant upon a lease for non-payment of rent, it is advisable not to set out the premises at length as in the deed, but to state that the plaintiff demised to the defendant, "certain premises particularly mentioned and described in the said indenture except as therein is excepted;" to *hold the* same for a certain term or terms, (showing the extent of it, or that it is *still* unexpired,) yielding the rent payable on, &c.: and then to state the covenant for payment of the rent, the entry of the defendant, and the breach in not paying the rent due. Or if the action be for the breach of any other covenants, the plaintiff should in such case state the parts of the indenture referring to the rent, in the like concise way in which he should state the other parts of the indenture not connected with the rent, in an action for non-payment, of rent, viz. "at a certain rent, payable by the defendant to the plaintiff, as in the said indenture is mentioned," and then set forth only the particular covenants which he alleges to have been broken (p). This mode of declaring, it is obvious, is equally applicable and advisable where the lease is not under seal, but by a written agreement only; and also in other actions upon long written agreements, embracing a variety of provisions (q).

[*333]

It is a general rule, that the contract must be stated correctly, and if the

(j) 1 Saund. 276 a; Bac. Ab. Stat. L. 3; *ante*, 254.

(k) See 7 T. R. 351, note. It has, however, been held, that a *plea* must show that the statute has been satisfied, Lord Raym. 450; but see 2 B. & B. 362; Steph. on Pleading, 367, 418, 419, note, 2d ed.

(l) *Post*, 381, 382.

(m) 4 Taunt. 285; 13 East, 19.

(n) Cowp. 665 to 727; 1 Bl. R. 270, Dougl. 667; see as to surplusage, *ante*, 263, 264.

(o) Stephen on Pleading, 417.

(p) See 1 Wms. Saund. 233, note 2; Cowp. 665; Dougl. 667.

(q) And see 6 East, 563.

(618) Vide Nelson *v.* Dubois, 13 Johns. Rep. 177. Anonymous, 2 Salk. 519. Williams *v.* Leper, Burr. Rep. 1890. 1 Esp. Dig. 168. Miller *v.* Drake, 1 Caines' Rep. 45. Elting and others *v.* Vanderlyn, 4 Johns. Rep. 237.

IV. ITS PARTS, &c.

5thly. The cause of action.

1. In assumpsit.

3. The promise or contract.

2. Of variances between the statement and the evidence.

Contract to be stated according to its legal effect and intent of parties though varying from words.

evidence differ from the statement, the whole foundation of the action fails, because the contract is *entire in its nature, and must be proved as laid (*r*) (619). In this respect there is a material distinction between the statement of *torts* and of contracts, the former being divisible in their nature, and the proof of part of the tort or injury being, in general, sufficient to support the declaration (*s*).

It is laid down as a principle on this subject, that a contract or written instrument should be stated *according to its legal effect* (*t*) (620). This rule is of very extensive operation, and applies not only to the statement of contracts in the action of *assumpsit*, but also to the statement by either party of contracts and obligations of every description, whether verbal, written, or specialty, in any form of action. The party is not *compelled* to follow the precise form of words in which the contract was made; it suffices if he state its true legal effect and operation (*u*): and it has been observed that a deed may be declared on, without using a word which was contained therein, except the names of the parties and the sums (*x*). Indeed, in some cases it has been held proper, and indeed absolutely necessary, to depart from the terms of the contract; and a party has been defeated on the ground of variance, when he has used the precise words of the contract, but mis-stated its legal operation (*y*); and where a written contract stated that a bill should be given for £14 19s. whereas it was really intended to be for £13 19s. and was so described in the declaration, it was held that this was proper and no variance (*z*).

Thus, when a conveyance from a joint-tenant to his companion is pleaded, and the expressions used in the conveyance are, "gives, grants, &c." it has been held improper to follow the terms of the deed: for although it purports to be a grant, yet its legal effect and operation is not that of a grant but a release; and it should therefore be pleaded not that he *granted* but that he *released* (*a*). So, if a tenant for life *grant* his estate to him in reversion, this is in effect a *surrender*, and it has been held that it must be pleaded as such, and not as a *grant* (*b*). So, if a deed be in the words, "gives and grants," and operates as a bargain and sale, it must be pleaded as the latter (*c*). And
[*335] it is said that if on *a promise to A. to pay B. a sum of money, the ac-

(*r*) 1 T. R. 240; 3 *Id.* 646, *per* Buller, J.
(*s*) 2 B. & Ald. 863, see *post*.
(*t*) Com. Dig. Pleader, C. 37; 2 Saund. 97, n. 2; Bac. Ab. Pleas, I. 7; Stephen, 2d edit. 432; and see *per* Tindal, C. J., in Bushell *v.* Beavan, 1 Bing. N. C. 120, S. P.
(*u*) As to setting out a deed on *oyer*, see *post*.
(*x*) 1 Marsh. 216, 217; see instances, *post*.
(*y*) 4 Mod. 150, 151; see 2 Saund. 97 b, n. 2; 2 B. & Ald. 66; 1 Chit. Rep. 66, 67, *per* Bayley, J. and Holroyd, J.; Stephen on Pleading, 2d edit 432.
(*z*) Rose *v.* Sims, 1 Bar. & Adol. 522, n. b.
(*a*) 4 Mod 150; 3 Lev. 291.
(*b*) 4 Mod. 151.
(*c*) Cro. Eliz. 166; 1 Lord Raym. 403, 404; 2 Saund. 97 b, n. 2.

(619) {Obert *v.* Whitehead, 6 Halst. Rep. 294. Wheelwright *v.* Moore, 1 Hall's Rep. 201.} Vide Snell and others *v.* Moses and others, 1 Johns. Rep. 105. Allaire *v.* Ouland, 2 Johns. Cas. 55. Perry *v.* Aaron, 1 Johns. Rep. 133. Ante, 232, and n. 19, ibid. Phillips' Ev. Dunl. Ed. 160, 161, and n. a. ibid. Pool *v.* Court, 4 Taunt. 700. A contract in the alternative must be stated in the declaration according to the terms of it. Thus, to transport 15 or 20 tons of marble from one place to another, if stated as an absolute contract, the variance will be fatal. Stone *v.* Knowlton, 3 Wend. R. 374. So, to allege a consideration for the promise different from the true consideration, not supported by the proof will be cause of nonsuit, *ib.*

(620) Morris *v.* Fort, 2 M'Cord's Rep. 398. Vide Close *v.* Miller, 10 Johns. Rep 90.

tion be brought by the latter, it is proper to state that the promise was made to B. (*d*).

IV. ITS PARTS, &c.

5thly. The cause of action.

1. In assumpsit.

3. The promise or contract.

It frequently becomes an inportant question, when the party is about to set out some *written instrument*, whether it will be advisable to follow the *terms* of the instrument, or to give merely its *substance*. The latter, if given correctly, will be a sufficient compliance with the rule, which only requires the legal effect to be stated (621); but there is this danger, that possibly the party, or the pleader, may mistake the legal effect; while, on the other hand, if he profess to give the terms of the deed, he becomes more liable to misrecitals and literal mistakes. We have already noticed some cases in which it has been held *necessary to depart* from the terms of the instrument; and there are other cases in which it has been laid down that a party must, at his peril, always state an instrument as he intends to use it; and that where a party in pleading sets forth a title by conveyance, in which are the words "give, grant, release, confirm, bargain, sell," &c. he must express for which of them he will use it (*e*). And it was agreed in one case, that setting forth the special matter, which showed that a deed did not operate according to its terms, and leaving the determination of law to the Court, was impertinent and idle. And although three of the judges held in that case that the party having set forth the words of the deed, it was sufficient, the fourth judge differed and held that the party was bound to state the legal effect; and the decision was afterwards reversed upon this ground on a writ of error (*f*). From some later cases, however, it rather appears that the above doctrine should be received with some qualification; and that the true rule in setting out a written *contract* may be, that where the party *professes* to give the legal effect and operation of the deed, and the legal operation is different from that which appears by his statement, a fatal variance will occur, although he adopts the exact expressions contained in the instrument; but that where he does *not profess* to give the substance and legal effect only, but to state *the very words* of the deed, the Court will then construe the deed for him. Thus, when it was stated that A. was entitled to the equity of *redemption, and that, subject thereto, B. was seised in fee, and that they, by lease and release, granted, bargained, &c. the premises, *excepted and always reserved to A.* a right of hunting, &c.; it was held, that as A. had no legal interest, there could be no *exception* or *reservation* to him, and that the statement was therefore bad (*g*). And the Court said that the party had purported to set out the deed according to its legal operation, and had mis-stated such operation; that if he had wished the Court to construe the deed for him, he should have set it out in *hæc verba*, or at least so much as he meant to rely on, and that the Court could form no judgment what operation it might have, unless they saw the very words of the deed (*h*). And in a subsequent case, when it was objected that the legal operation of a deed was different from the statement in the declaration, it was [*336]

(*d*) 1 B & P. 102, *per* Eyre, C J., *ante*, 5. 97 b.

(*e*) See 1 Vent. 109; Co. Lit. 301 b; Carth. 308; 3 Lev. 291; 2 Saund. 97 b.

(*f*) 3 Lev. 241; 4 Mod. 149; 2 Saund.

(*g*) 3 B. & Ald. 66.

(*h*) *Per* Abbott, C. J. and Bayley, J., 3 B. & Ald. 69, 70.

(621) Vide Lent et al. *v.* Padelford, 10 Mass. Rep. 230.

IV. ITS PARTS, &c. — 5thly. The cause of action. 1. In assumpsit. 3. The promise or contract.

held that there could be no variance, since the declaration did not affect to state the legal effect of the deed, but merely stated that by a certain deed "it was witnessed, &c.," following the words of the deed (*i*).

If these cases may be considered as establishing the position, that if, in a doubtful case, a party set out the words of a deed or written instrument, as being those contained in the document itself, the Court will put the proper construction upon it, it seems to be advisable to adopt this course, (namely, to profess to set forth the instrument, and to give its precise words,) when there exists any uncertainty as to the exact legal effect and construction of them; especially, as by the late statutes, which will be particularly noticed hereafter (*k*), certain variances in setting out contracts are amendable at the trial.

Misdescription of the *parties* to the contract.

A misdescription of the contract with regard to the *parties thereto*, and *with whom* it was made, will also in general be fatal as a variance at the trial. Thus, where the plaintiff was a surviving partner, and sued upon a contract made with himself and his deceased partner, but without stating that he was a surviving partner, so that the contract appeared from the declaration to have been made with himself alone, he was nonsuited for the variance; and the Court held the nonsuit right (*l*). Upon the same principle, [*337] *where a contract for the sale of goods was stated to be made with two persons, and it appeared in evidence that it was made with those two *and another*, it was ruled to be a fatal variance, though the declaration stated correctly the quantity of goods which the two were to have (*m*). And where the plaintiff set forth in his declaration a contract for the sale of goods, but mis-stated the party to whom the goods were to be delivered, the variance was considered fatal (*n*). Here we may again allude to the instance of a contract made between A.'s wife and B. of the one part, and C. of the other part, being described as a contract made between A, and his wife, and B. and C. (*o*). But a lease between A. *and his wife* of the one part, and B. of the other part, may be set out as a deed between A. and B. such being its legal effect (*p*). So, if a bond be given to husband and wife administratrix, the husband alone may declare on it, as on a bond made to himself (*q*). If a contract, whether verbal or written, or a bill of exchange, &c. be made *by* two persons, and it be stated that it was made by one only, viz. the defendant, he can only plead in abatement, and cannot treat the omission as a material variance at the trial on the general issue (*r*).

Again, where there are two or more distinct special contracts, it will be a fatal misdescription to blend them together and treat them as one contract; thus, where different lots were sold at an auction for different sums, the contracts were deemed separate both in law and in fact, and the plaintiff having, in assumpsit for refusing to comply with the conditions of sale, consolidated the two contracts, and declared upon them as one agreement, he was nonsuited (*s*). Where, however, an agreement has been made between two parties,

(*i*) 1 B. & C. 358; 2 D. & R. 562, S. C.

(*k*) *Post*, 348 to 352; 9 Geo. 4, c. 15; see 3 & 4 W. 4, c. 42, s. 23, more extensive.

(*l*) 4 B. & Ald. 274. So, a mistake in an avowry, as to the parties of whom plaintiff held as tenant, is fatal, 6 Bing. 104. So is a mis-statement of the condition of a bond, as to the parties by whom the money was to be paid, although the bond was joint and several, &c.; *id.* 110; 3 M. & P. 339, S. C.

(*m*) 5 Esp. 33, 169.

(*n*) 4 T. R. 687.

(*o*) *Ante*, 327.

(*p*) 4 Moore, 66.

(*q*) 4 T. R. 616.

(*r*) 1 B. & Ald. 224; *ante*, 52, 53; see *ante*, 14.

(*s*) 1 Stark. 426; see 2 Taunt. 38.

IV. ITS PARTS, &c.

5thly. The cause of action.

1. In assumpsit.

3. The promise or contract.

and by a subsequent contract between them the terms of the former agreement have been modified and altered, the plaintiff may declare upon the contract as it stands altered by the subsequent arrangement, without noticing the original terms which have been dispensed with (*t*).

Mis-statement of a promise in the *alternative*, &c.

*The plaintiff being bound to state his contract correctly, it follows that a mis-statement of the quality or nature of the defendant's promise, and his consequent liability, will be a fatal error, and will, if the defendant's plea put the fact in issue, subject the plaintiff to a nonsuit. Thus, when a contract is made in the *alternative*, as to deliver one or other of two specified quantities of goods at a particular time, it must be stated in the declaration according to the original terms, and if stated as an absolute contract, it will be a fatal variance, notwithstanding the party who, under the agreement, was to have the option of deciding on the particular quantity may have determined his option; for the mode of executing the contract could not change the original contract itself(*u*)(622). [*338] And on the other hand, when the contract is *absolute*, and it is stated in the declaration as an alternative contract, the variance will be equally serious; thus, where the plaintiff declared on a contract to deliver soil *or* breeze, and the evidence was of a contract to deliver soil only, and soil and breeze appeared to be different things, it was held the plaintiff could not recover (*x*). So where the contract is *conditional*, it will be a fatal mis-description to state it as an absolute one. Thus, when a party accepted a bill of exchange, thereby engaging to pay it as soon as a particular event occurred, and this was stated in the declaration as an absolute acceptance, the variance was held fatal (*y*). And upon the same principle, it should seem that in cases of debts which have been barred by the statute of limitations, if the plaintiff rely on a subsequent promise, to take the case out of the statute, and such promise were qualified or conditional, as to pay when the defendant is able, &c., the plaintiff should declare upon such subsequent promise according to the terms in which it was made, and not upon the original promise (*z*). In actions upon bills of exchange and promissory notes many cases of variances have arisen in consequence of the acceptance or promise being stated to be general and absolute, when in fact it was qualified, the bill or note having been made payable at a particular place. With respect to bills of exchange, an acceptance payable at a particular place is not now a qualified acceptance, unless the payment *be expressly restricted to that place *only* and *not elsewhere* (*a*): [*339] but in cases where it is so restricted, and also in all cases of promissory notes made payable in the *body* of the note at a particular place, it will be a variance to state a qualified contract of this description as an absolute one (*b*). And on the other hand, where the contract is absolute, and is described in the

(*t*) See 1 B. & C. 18; 1 Esp. 53; 1 Stark. R. 336.

(*u*) 2 East, 2; see also 3 T. R. 531; 2 Bos. & Pul. 116; and see *per* Lord Ellenborough, 8 East, 8.

(*x*) 1 B. & P. 351; 5 Esp. 239, S. C.

(*y*) 4 Campb. 176.

(*z*) 6 B. & C. 603, 609; 9 D. & R. 549, S. C.; 1 B. & C. 248; 2 D. & R. 363, S. C.; 7 Bing. 163, *acc.*

(*a*) Stat. 1 & 2 Geo. 4, c. 78, s. 1. If a bill be *drawn* payable at a particular place, and accepted generally, this is not a qualified acceptance, 11 Moore, 511; 3 Bing. 611, S. C.

(*b*) 3 Campb. 247, 463; 4 *Id.* 200; 14 East, 500.

(622) Curley *v.* Dean, 4 Conn. Rep. 265. Per Hosmer, C. J., Stone *v.* Knowlton, 3 Wend. R. 374.

IV. ITS PARTS, &c. — 5thly. The cause of action. 1. In assumpsit. 3. The promise or contract.

declaration as conditional or qualified, the variance will be equally fatal as where in declaring on a promissory note the plaintiff alleged that it was thereby made payable at a particular place, and it appeared, on production of the note, that there was no such restriction contained in the body of the note, but merely in a memorandum at the foot of it, it was held that this was a general and not a qualified promise, and that consequently there was a material mis-description (*c*)(623). If an instrument be so ambiguous in its terms that it may be regarded with reason either as a bill of exchange or a promissory note, the plaintiff has the election to declare upon it either as one or the other of those instruments, at least as against the maker (*d*).

Exceptions or provisos when qualifying liability.

If the defendant's promise or engagement, whether it be verbal, in writing, or under seal, embody or contain, *as part of it*, an *exception* or *proviso* which *qualifies* his liability, or in certain instances renders him altogether irresponsible, so that he was not in law *absolutely* bound, the declaration must notice the exception or proviso, or there will be a fatal mis-statement. Thus, where the declaration stated that the defendant had undertaken to carry and deliver goods safely, and the contract proved was to carry and deliver them safely, *fire and robbery excepted*, it was held that there was a fatal variance (*e*).

And the same will be the case where a like absolute contract is stated, and it is proved to be one of the terms of the contract, that the carrier is not to be liable *to any extent* upon goods above a certain value, unless insured (*f*). Where the plaintiff averred in his declaration generally that the defendant had warrant-
[*340] ed a horse to be sound, and the proof was, that the latter had warranted *the horse to be sound every where *except a kick in the leg*, the Court held this to be a qualified and not a general warranty, and that consequently there was a fatal mistake (*g*) (624). So also, in cases of contracts between landlord and tenant, if the declaration set out a general agreement or covenant to repair, and omit to state an exception as to cases of fire and other casualties, the variance will be fatal (*h*). And where the declaration averred that the defendant had become tenant to the plaintiff, and in consideration thereof had promised to use the land in a husband-like manner, and the evidence was that he had agreed

(*c*) 4 M. & Sel. 505; and see Jelf *v.* Oriel, 4 Car. & P. 22.

(*d*) 6 B. & C. 433; 9 D. & R 492, S. C.

(*e*) 2 B. & C. 20; 3 D. & R. 211, S. C. Instance of variance in action on policy, in not setting out the rules of the society, &c.; 11 Moore, 86; 3 Bing. 315, S. C. Where the regulations of an association of ship-owners combined for the mutual insurance of each other's ships were indorsed on the back of the policy, and declared to form part of the policy to which the ship-owners were subscribers, it was held necessary in an action for a loss under the policy to set out the regulations as well as the policy, 3 Bing. 315.

(*f*) *Per* Abbott, C. J., 3 D. & R. 212; and see 6 East, 569; *post*, 317.

(*g*) Jones *v.* Cowley, 4 B. & C. 446; 6 Dowl. & Ryl. 533; see Heming *v.* Parry, 6 Car. & P. 580; Alderson, B., said, that *that case, although correctly decided, was a disgrace to the English law.*

(*h*) 4 Campb. 20; 2 B. & B. 395; 5 Moore, 161, S. C.

---

(623) The words "value received," in a promissory note, are words of description, and if omitted in the declaration, the variance will be fatal. Saxon *v.* Johnson, 10 Johns. Rep. 418. { Rossiter *v.* Marsh, 4 Conn. Rep. 196 }

(624) If in an action on a promissory note, the plaintiff unnecessarily specifies wherein the *value received* consisted, he must prove it as laid. Jerome *v.* Whitney, 7 Johns. Rep. 321. In an indictment for stopping the mail, a contract with the postmaster general to transport the mail, was alleged, and it was held that the contract must be proved, although the indictment might have been good without such allegation. United States *v.* Porter, 3 Day's Rep. 283. But see Wilson *v.* Codman's Ex'r, 3 Cranch, 209.

to use the land in a husband-like manner, *to be kept constantly in grass*, it was held that the omission of this stipulation was a variance; for though in most cases the keeping of the land in grass might be farming it in a husband-like manner, still there might be some cases in which it would not be so; it was therefore a qualification of the previous stipulation, and ought to have been stated in the declaration as part of the description of the contract (*i*). So, if a lease contain a covenant to repair "except in case of fire," the covenant must not be described as an absolute covenant (*k*). And in covenant on a lease for non-payment of rent, the *reddendum* must not be described as absolute, if it be "yielding, &c. *except as hereinafter is excepted.*" (*l*) Where, however, the proviso in a written instrument is *distinct* from and not even *referred* to by the clause on which the debt is charged, it is considered matter of defeasance, &c. which ought to come from the other side, and then it need not be set forth by the plaintiff (*m*).

5thly. The cause of action.

1. In assumpsit.

3. The promise or contract.

There are a great variety of instances of variances in the statement of some particular *part* or *term* of the contract. Errors of this description are, as we have already observed, in general as fatal to the plaintiff's case, as where he has erred in stating the whole contract, or the parties with whom it was made. It may be useful to enumerate some of the cases which have arisen upon this subject.

Instances of a *mis-statement* of *part* of the contract.

The mis-statement of the *date* of a written instrument is a fatal variance, if the declaration expressly describe it as "bearing date" upon a certain day, instead of stating, that "heretofore, to wit, on, &c." it was made, &c. (*n*).

*In stating a bill of exchange or other instrument, it seems not to be a fatal variance to state that the defendant "subscribed it with his own proper hand," although it was signed by his agent only (*o*). [*341]

Where the plaintiff in a special action of assumpsit against the defendant for refusing to retain the plaintiff in his service according to agreement, stated in his declaration that the defendant had agreed to retain him at a specific sum *per annum*, and it appeared from the evidence that neither a specific sum, nor any specific time had been agreed upon, this was ruled to be variance, notwithstanding the sum mentioned in the declaration was laid under a *videlicet* (*p*). And where in an action against a carrier, the *termini* of the journey on which the goods are to be carried is incorrectly stated, the mistake will be a ground of nonsuit (*q*). In declaring on special agreements relative to goods, mis-descriptions as to quality, quantity, and price, have been held fatal. A declaration on a promise to deliver good *merchantable* wheat has been ruled not to be supported by evidence of an agreement to deliver good *second sort* of wheat (*r*). When the plaintiff stated an agreement to take in a *full cargo*

(*i*) 5 B. & C. 909; 8 D. & R. 643, S. C.

(*k*) 4 Campb. 20, 21; 5 Moore, 164; 2 B. & B. 395, S. C.

(*l*) 6 B. & C. 430; 9 D. & R. 597, S. C.; *ante*, 223.

(*m*) *Ante*, 256.

(*n*) See Chit. Bills, 7th ed 354; 2 Campb. 307; 4 Car. & Pay. 24. It may be shown that the instrument was made on another day, 4 East, 477; see further as to date, 4 B. & C. 908; 7 D. & R. 507, S. C.; 5 B & C. 108; 7 D. & R. 548. Not necessary to state in a declaration that a guarantee within the statute against frauds was in writing, *ante*, 332.

(*o*) See 1 M. & M. 182, and the cases, Chitty on Bills, 7th edit. 357, 359.

(*p*) 1 Stark. 3; 1 M. & P. 735. And see 2 B. & P. 116; *ante*, 296; see *post*, 348, as to the *videlicet*.

(*q*) 2 Stark. 385. See the notes to the precedent, *post*, vol. ii.

(*r*) 1 Ld. Raym. 735.

IV. ITS PARTS, &c.

5thly. The cause of action.

1. In assumpsit.

3. The promise or contract.

of certain goods, and the contract proved was to take in a certain specified quantity, it was ruled to be a variance, notwithstanding such quantity might amount to a full cargo (*s*). And where the contract declared on was, that the defendant should sell and deliver to the plaintiff certain goods "at 4*s.* *per* stone," and the evidence was, that the plaintiff was to give 4*s.* *per* stone, and if he should pay more to any other person for similar goods, that he should then give the same price to the defendant, it was held that the declaration was not supported by the proof (*t*).

Several cases have also occurred in which variances as to the *time* of *performing* the contract declared on have been held fatal. Thus, when the plaintiff
*342] stated a contract to remove *goods within a *reasonable time*, and the agreement proved was to remove in a *month*, it was ruled to be a fatal variance (*u*). Where an usurious contract was set out in the declaration, and the period of forbearance was stated to be from the 21st December, 1774, until the 23d December, 1776, it was held that evidence of a contract on the 23d December, 1774, for two years, would not support the declaration (*x*). And when a similar contract was alleged to be for the forbearance of money until a certain specified day absolutely, but the contract proved was for forbearance until the day named, or a certain other day, at the option of the borrower, it was held that the evidence would not support the statement (*y*).

A great variety of cases are to be found in the books with regard to *literal errors* in setting out deeds, (and in this respect the rule equally applies to all written instruments) (*z*). Thus, in an action on a lease, the following have been deemed fatal variances; namely, "cellar beer" for "allar beer;" (*a*) and "storehouses" for "storehouse;" (*b*) and a mistake of the late tenant's name (625), in setting out the premises demised (*c*). So, an error in stating the local situation to be contrary to that given by the lease, is a material variance (*d*). But the statement of a demise of "lands and premises" is correct, although one piece of ground only was granted (*e*). So is an averment that "a farm and buildings, and certain pieces of land mentioned in the indenture," were demised, although the lease was of "all that farm or land, and buildings," enumerating the parcels; for the declaration sufficiently states the legal effect of the demise (*f*). However these literal variances have now become of less importance, as the late statutes (*g*) give the judge the discretionary power to allow them to be amended at the trial.

(*s*) 2 Esp. Rep. 708.
(*t*) 1 T. R. 447.
(*u*) Peake, N. P. C. 42 (*a*), 2d edit.
(*x*) Cowp. 671. See further as to variances in this respect, *post*, vol. ii. and vol. iii. tit. *Usury*.
(*y*) 3 T. R. 531. See as to alternative contracts, *ante*, 338.
(*z*) As to surplusage in stating irrelevant clauses, &c. *ante*, 262, 263.
(*a*) 9 East, 188.
(*b*) 4 M. & Sel.
(*c*) 1 Campb. 195; 15 East, 161; 1 Stark. 100; but see 2 Marsh. 159; 1 Stark. 47.
(*d*) 3 Campb. 235; 1 *Id.* 195; 6 Taunt. 394; 2 Marsh. 96, S. C.
(*e*) 6 M. & Sel. 115.
(*f*) 1 Y. & J. 2. See 6 B. & C. 252; 9 D. & R. 245, S. C., demise of house and *fixtures*, described as a demise of a house only.
(*g*) 9 Geo 4, c. 15; and 3 & 4 W. 4, c. 42, sect. 23, giving *more extensive powers*, and which *ought* to be acted upon liberally. See observations of Alderson, B., in Heming *v.* Parry, 6 Car. & P. 580, 581; and *post*, 348.

(625) Vide Whitlock *v.* Ramsey's Adm'x, 2 Mun. 510. Moore *v.* Fenwick, Gilm. Rep. 214, and the cases there cited.

*In the cases we have hitherto noticed, an actual mis-statement of some part of the contract had been made, but instances have arisen when the plaintiff has followed the precise terms of the contract, but has nevertheless been defeated on the ground of variance, the statement in the record being by *legal intendment* different from that given in evidence. Thus where the declaration stated a contract to deliver 400 "bushels" of oats, the plaintiff was nonsuited, on proof that the bushels actually contracted for were to be of a particular local measure, and not the ordinary statute measure, which the general description in the declaration was held to import (*h*). And where in declaring upon contracts made in Ireland, relative to the payment of any sum of money of and in the currency of that country, the plaintiff merely followed the terms of the contract, without distinctly showing that the money was to be of Irish currency, it was held to give rise to a fatal variance; the intendment being that when a sum of money is stated generally, English money is meant to be designated (*i*).

IV. ITS PARTS, &c. — 5thly. The cause of action. 1. In assumpsit. 3. The promise or contract.

Although in general a mis-statement of any part of a contract will be fatal, in consequence of the entire nature of the contract, yet many cases may arise in which slight variations between the statement and the proof will be of no importance. We have before noticed the leading and important rule in the statement of contracts, that it will in all cases suffice, if the legal effect of the contract be stated, and that the party is not compelled to follow the exact words of the contract (*k*)(626). We will here notice several cases in which, although the declaration was not literally supported by the proof, it was held that no variance arose, the legal effect and substance of the statement and the evidence being the same. Thus where a demise from a tenant from year to year to another, to hold from year to year, was stated as a demise from year to year during the continuance of the original demise by the superior landlord; and it appeared that in point of fact no such qualification was mentioned in the contract; it was nevertheless held that no variance arose, the legal effect of the demise being according to the statement (*l*). In another case, where a declaration stated that by a certain indenture, made between the plaintiff and the defendant, the plaintiff did demise, &c. "a certain farm and buildings, *and certain pieces or parcels of land particularly mentioned and described in the said indenture;" and then set out the particular covenants and the breaches complained of; and at the trial the terms of the lease appeared to be, "all that farm and buildings herein particularly contained," and then enumerated the particular closes of which the farm consisted; it was objected that there was a variance, the statement in the declaration being more extensive than the proof; but the Court held that a verbatim description was unnecessary, and that the declaration contained a sufficient description of the substance and legal effect of the demise (*m*). So it has been held that a *revoca-* [*344]

(*h*) 4 T. R. 314; 6 *Id.* 338; see also 11 East, 311; *ante*, 251.
(*i*) 1 B. & C. 16; 2 D. & R. 15, S. C.; 2 B. & Ald. 301; *ante*, 251.
(*k*) *Ante*, 334.
(*l*) 9 B. & C. 909.
(*m*) 1 Y. & J. 2.

(626) Vide De Forest *v.* Brainerd, 2 Day's Rep. 528. Beers *v.* Botsford, 3 Day's Rep. 159. Bordman and others *v.* Forman, 8 Johns. Rep. 26. Page *v.* Woods, 9 Johns. Rep. 82. Ferguson *v.* Harwood, 7 Cranch, 413.

IV. ITS PARTS, &c. — 5thly. The cause of action. 1. In assumpsit. 3. The promise or contract.

tion of a submission to arbitration before award made, is in effect a breach of an agreement "to stand to and perform the award;" and that an agreement not to make such revocation, being in legal effect implied in the engagement to stand to the award, the plaintiff may state a promise by the defendant to that effect in the declaration, although no such stipulation in words were contained in the agreement to refer (*n*). Many other instances may be given where the contract declared on has not been literally supported by the evidence, but the statement has been held sufficient, on account of the legal effect of the statement and the proof being identical. Thus when the contract was for the purchase of a certain parcel of hemp, which not being precisely ascertained at the time, was described in the contract as "about eight tons," it was held that it might be declared on under a *videlicet* as a contract for eight tons (*o*)(627). And when the plaintiffs declared that they agreed to sell, and the defendant agreed to buy, certain goods and merchandize, to wit, 328 chests and 30 half chests of oranges and lemons, at and for a certain price, to wit, the price of £623 3*s*., and the contract proved was for 308 chests and 30 half chests of China oranges, and 20 chests of lemons, without specifying any price; the Court held that the particular count of the declaration upon which the question arose, was, in substance, a count for goods bargained and sold; that the precise quantity of goods could not be considered as of the essence of the contract; and that the plaintiffs having shown that in substance they were entitled to recover, they were not, under the particular circumstances of the case, tied down by the statement under [*345] *the *videlicet*, and that therefore the variance was not material (*p*). In a case where the contract upon which the plaintiffs declared, was to deliver stock on the "27th February," and the agreement proved was to deliver it upon "the settling day," which, at the time of the contract, was fixed for the 27th of February, as the parties fully understood; it was held that the contract was substantially and in legal effect for the 27th of February, that the parties might use either one phrase or another to express the same thing, and consequently that there was no variance between the contract proved and that stated in the declaration (*q*). So, where the declaration alleged a loan of lawful money of Great Britain, it was held no variance to show a loan in a foreign country in the coin of that country (*r*). And where the declaration states a contract for the sale of goods at a certain specific sum, which is proved, but it also appears in evidence, as part of the terms of the contract, that the vendor was to receive from the purchaser other goods, in liquidation of a certain specific part of the stipulated purchase-money, it will be no variance; for such a stipulation will only be considered as prescribing a particular mode of payment of part of the purchase-money (*s*).

(*n*) M'Clel. & Y. 464; see 1 M. & P. 239; 2 *Id.* 81.

(*o*) 13 East, 410; and see 1 B. & Ald. 9.

(*p*) 1 Moore, 547; 8 Taunt. 107, S. C. See *post*, 348.

(*q*) 2 B. & Ald. 335; see *contra*, Stra. 74; Bul. N. P. 145, overruled by the case stated in the text.

(*r*) 5 Taunt 228; 1 Marsh. 33, S. C. See *ante*, 343, 251.

(*s*) 9 East, 349; see 3 B. & C. 420; 5 D. & R. 277, S. C.; 1 Hen. Bla. 283; 1 Stark. Rep. 437.

(627) A variance is immaterial when it does not change the nature of the contract, which must receive the same legal construction whether the words be in, or out of the declaration. Ferguson *v.* Harwood, 7 Cranch, 408. { An unnecessary averment of a breach or infringement of a contract declared on, need not be proved, and may be rejected as surplusage. Ferguson *v.* Tucker, 2 Har. & Gill, 183. }

5thly. The cause of action. 1. In assumpsit. 3. The promise or contract. Immaterial omissions, collateral provisions, &c.

We have already seen that the omission of any part of the contract which materially qualifies and alters the legal nature of the promise which is alleged to have been broken, will be fatal; but it is by no means necessary that parts of the contract should be stated which are distinct and collateral provisions, or respect only the liquidation of damages under particular circumstances without extending to absolve the defendant from responsibility (*t*). Thus, where in an action by a sailor against the captain of a ship, the declaration stated a contract for the payment of a certain sum of money to the plaintiff for rum money, and an agreement to this effect was proved, but such agreement contained also an additional stipulation for certain allowance of spirits, it was held no *variance, for the agreement given in evidence corresponded with the declaration as far as the declaration went (*u*). So when the plaintiff declared upon a promise by the defendant to deliver him a horse which should be worth £80, and be a young horse, and the evidence was not only of a promise to the above effect, but also of a warranty that the horse to be delivered by the defendant was sound, and had never been in harness, it was held that there was no variance; and it was laid down by the Court, that if any substantive part of the warranty stated, not qualified by another part omitted, be proved not to be true, it was sufficient to maintain the action; and that it was no more necessary to set out other collateral parts of the contract, whereof no breach was alleged, than it was necessary that in an action of covenant the plaintiff should set out all the covenants contained in the deed, when he did not complain that most of them had been broken (*x*). Upon the same principle, where the plaintiff declared upon a promise by the defendant, that certain bacon which he had purchased of the defendant should be prime bacon, and then averred a breach of this contract, it was held to be no variance that the contract proved was for prime *singed* bacon, for the plaintiff was only bound to state all that related to the point of which he complained, and beyond that it was needless for him to go (*y*). And where, in an action for the non-delivery of goods, the plaintiff stated a contract to deliver goods to be paid for by bill at two months, and the proof was that they were paid for by such bill on invoice or delivery, it was held not to amount to a variance (*z*). So where, in an action for not accepting goods sold, it was averred in the declaration that the defendant bought of the plaintiff a certain quantity of rice, according to certain conditions, and it appeared in evidence that in addition to these conditions the rice was sold *per sample*, it was held not to constitute a variance, the words "per sample" not being any essential part of the description of the contract declared upon, but a mere collateral engagement or warranty that the goods sold should answer the description of a small parcel exhibited at the sale (*a*). An example of such stipulations as do in some measure vary the liability of the defendant, but which only affect the amount of damages to be recovered in particular cases, and do not altogether destroy the plaintiff's right to recover, may arise *in the case of actions against carriers who give notice [*347]

[*346]

(*t*) "There are a great variety of agreements not under seal, containing detailed provisions, regulating prices of labor, rates of hire, times and manner of performance, adjustment of differences, &c. which it may not be necessary to set forth."—*Per* Lord Ellenborough, 6 East, 568; 13 *Id.* 20.

(*u*) 1 B. & P. 7.

(*x*) 8 East, 6.

(*y*) 4 Taunt. 285; see 11 Price, 19.

(*z*) 3 Price, 68.

(*a*) 4 B. & Ald. 387.

IV. ITS PARTS, &c. — 5thly. The cause of action. 1. In assumpsit. 3. The promise or contract.

that they will not be liable in respect of certain goods beyond a particular sum. A stipulation of this description need not be set out in describing the contract, but may be given in evidence by the defendant in reduction of damages (*b*). The result of the cases upon this subject is, that if the carrier only *limit* his responsibility, that need not be noticed in pleading, but if a stipulation be made that under certain circumstances he shall not be liable *at all*, that must be stated (*c*).

Trifling omissions of immaterial forms, not in any way affecting the substance of the contract, will be of no more importance than mis-descriptions of the like nature (*d*). The plaintiff is not bound to state more than the substance and legal effect of the contract he declares on; and except when he renders his allegation of the contract descriptive of a written instrument, he is not bound to support his declaration literally, but substantially. When, therefore, the evidence is precisely the same in substance with the declaration, though some immaterial term may have been omitted in the latter, the plaintiff will not be liable to be nonsuited on the ground of variance. Thus, a declaration on a contract, for not delivering gum Senegal, is supported by evidence of a contract for rough gum Senegal, if it appear that all gum Senegal, on its arrival in this country, is called rough (*e*). So, in an action for not accepting goods, evidence of a contract for the sale of goods to be ready for delivery *from ship or warehouse* before a certain day, will support an averment of a contract for goods to be ready for delivery generally before that day; for the evidence showing that the goods contracted for must be delivered from one or other of the places specified, and the option being with the purchaser, it was tantamount to a contract to deliver generally (*f*). The omission of a term necessarily implied from the statement in the declaration will come under the same principle and be quite immaterial. Thus, where the plaintiff stated a contract relative to the loan of a horse by him to the defendant, and averred that the defendant promised to take care of the horse, and return him in good condition or pay a certain sum of money; and the contract proved was, that in addition to these terms the defendant should find the horse meat for his [*348] work, it was held that the contract was sufficiently *proved according to its legal effect, for the law would imply that the party borrowing a horse was to keep it, unless the contrary appeared (*g*).

In stating the consideration, we have seen that it is in all cases absolutely necessary that *the whole of the entire consideration* for the performance of the act in question should be set forth, and that even where the contract has consisted of several engagements and promises, quite distinct from each other, but founded on one and the same entire consideration, an action cannot be brought for the breach of any one of such engagements or promises, without setting forth in the declaration the *entire* consideration applicable to all the promises collectively (*h*). The rule is different in stating the defendant's *promise* itself: here the plaintiff is only required to set forth with correctness that particular part of the contract which he alleges the defendant to have broken, or, as we have

(*b*) 6 East, 563; and see 2 B. & C. 22; 3 D. & R. 211, S. C.

(*c*) *Per* Abbott, C. J., 2 B. & C. 22; 3 D. & R. 213, S. C.; *ante*, 340.

(*d*) See *ante*, 342.

(*e*) 1 Chit. Rep. 39.

(*f*) 6 Taunt. 581; 2 Marsh. 287, S. C.

(*g*) 2 B. & B. 359; and see 11 Price, 19.

(*h*) *Ante*, 327. See particularly, 11 Moore, 86; 3 Bing. 315, S. C.; 1 Campb. 361.

before observed, to show so much of the terms of the agreement, beneficial to the plaintiff, as constitutes the point for the failure of which he sues (*i*).

IV. ITS PARTS, &c.

5thly. The cause of action.

1. In assumpsit.

3. The promise or contract.

Of scilicets or videlicets.

We may here take occasion to mention a form or phrase which is very frequently used in pleading, and is not altogether unworthy of consideration. The expression alluded to is the *videlicet*, or *scilicet*, ("*to wit*," or "*that is to say*,") which is constantly adopted, not only in mentioning time or place, but also in stating the description or value, &c. of goods, and in other averments in all the forms of action. It is clear that when the matter alleged is *material* and traversable, and must be stated with exactness and certainty, the statement of such matter under a *videlicet* will not avoid the consequences of a variance (628) or repugnancy if the matter be mis-stated, and there would be a fatal variance in the absence of the *videlicet;* and this whether the matter be the consideration or promise in the case of a contract, or be time or place, when material, or relate to other subjects (*k*). Thus, when it is necessary to state the grant of letters of administration to a plaintiff suing as administrator, if the *date* of the grant, though laid under a scilicet, be incorrectly stated to have been on a day *subsequent* to the alleged date of the promise to the intestate, it will be bad on *special demurrer*, although preceded with the words, that after the death of the intestate, to wit, on such *repugnant* day, the letters were granted (*l*). In stating *such* matter, therefore, the *videlicet* is useless to avoid a variance; and although it be used, the averment is considered positive, direct and traversable (*m*).

It is laid down by very great authority (*n*), that "on the other hand the *want* of a *videlicet* will in some cases make an averment material that would not otherwise be so; as if a thing which is not material be positively averred *without a videlicet*, though it were not necessary to be so, yet it is thereby made material and must be proved: therefore where a party does not mean to be concluded by a precise sum or day stated, he ought to plead it under a *videlicet;* for if he do not, he will be bound to prove the exact sum or day laid (629), it being a settled distinction, that where any thing which is not ma-

(*i*) *Ante*, 304; 4 Taunt. 285; 6 East, 564; 8 *Id.* 7; 13 *Id.* 18; 11 Moore, 88, 89.

(*k*) 1 Saund. 170, n. 2; 2 *Id.* 290 a, n. 1; 4 Taunt. 321; 9 B. & C. 215, *per* Bayley, J.; 2 Campb. 231; 1 Stark. 3. As to *scilicets* in general, see 2 Saund. 290 a, n. 1; 5 East, 252; 1 Stark. Crim. Law, 238, 239; 1 Chit. Crim. Law, 226, 227; Steph. Index, *Videlicet.* "Its use is to particularize that which was general before, and to explain that which is indifferent, doubtful, or obscure; but it must be neither contrary to the premises, nor increase nor diminish the precedent matter." Hob. 175; 2 Saund. 291, and 291 a, note.

(*l*) Ring *v.* Roxbrough, 2 Tyr. 468; 2 Cr. m. & J. 418, S. C.

(*m*) 2 Saund. 291 a, note; Stra. 233.

(*n*) Mr. Serjeant Williams, 2 Saund. 291 c, note.

(628) Janson *v.* Ostrander, 1 Cowen's Rep. 676. Attorney General *v.* Jeffreys, 1 M'Clell. & Young's Rep. 277. Where damages are laid subsequent to the commencement of the action on the case for the seduction of a daughter, or previous to the plaintiff having any right of action; in such case, if the matter is laid under a *scilicet*, the court avail themselves of that circumstance to say, that it is not to be intended that the jury took the evidence given into consideration. Stiles *v.* Tilford, 10 Wend. R. 340.

(629) *Times and sums*, if material must be proved, although laid under a *videlicet*. Vail *v.* Lewis and Livingston, 4 Johns. Rep. 450. {Attorney General *v.* Jeffries, 1 M'Clell. & Young's Rep. 270.} Phillips' Ev. 163, n. {"It is true that under a *videlicet*, the plaintiff has stated a time for the receipt of the sums, which is prior to the settlement of either account. But it is a settled rule in pleading, that what comes under a *videlicet* is no averment. It is certain that in this form of pleading the defendant could not have

IV. ITS PARTS, &c.

5thly. The cause of action.

1. In assumpsit.

3. The promise or contract.

terial is laid under a *videlicet*, the party is not concluded by it, but he is where there is no *videlicet*." (630) And there are decisions and *dicta* in support of this doctrine that matter may become material, and must be proved as laid, merely because it is averred without the intervention of the *videlicet* (*o*). But there are also some authorities, though less numerous, which appear to impeach the doctrine, at least as a general rule (*p*). And it seems not to apply even to criminal pleadings (*q*). It is true that the *videlicet* is often considered to be adopted as expressive of the intention of the pleader, not to bind himself to a positive and minute proof of the averment; but still it seems to be a harsh construction that the omission of the phrase shall be held to import that he restricts himself to such limited proof, in cases where in law the matter does not *of itself*, and if averred under a *videlicet*, call for such particular and strict evidence. A *videlicet* will not avoid a variance in an allegation of material matter, neither should the omission of it create the necessity of proving precisely as stated matter which would not otherwise require such precise proof.

(*o*) 3 T. R. 68; 3 M. & Sel. 173; 2 Moore, 114, 93; 8 Taunt. 107, 112; 3 Price, 54; 2 B. & C. 2; 2 D. & R. 226, S. C.; 16 East, 416, 419; 13 East, 410; Peake's Evid. 4th ed. 217; M'Clel. 277, 279.

(*p*) 2 Campb. 307, n. And see 1 Phil. Evid. 4th ed. 227, 228, n., Index, *Videlicet*; 2 Saund. 291 c, *n.* b., *to* 5th edit. See 6 East, 437.

(*q*) 1 Lord Raym. 149; 6 T. R. 265; 3 *Id.* 643; 1 Phil. Evid. 4th edit. 227, 228, note, Index, *Videlicet*; Starkie's and Chitty's Criminal Law; *ante*, 348, note (*k*).

---

traversed the time, although essential to the merits of his defence; he cannot therefore be bound by it." *Per* PARKER, C. J., Paine, Judge, &c. *v.* Fox, 16 Mass. Rep. 133. But in a late case the same judge has said, in reference to this *dictum*, "that it was undoubtedly a mistake; it is only where the allegation so expressed is immaterial, and might have been omitted, that it shall not be traversed, and may be omitted as useless." Hastings *v.* Lovering, 2 Pick. Rep. 223. See what is said as to the decision in Paine *v.* Fox, by SAVAGE, C. J., 7 Cow. Rep. 44. }

(630) As the cases on the subject of variance are very numerous, it may not be improper to collect a few additional ones, whithout, however, stating the point decided in each, and arrange them under distinct heads in order that all which relate to any particular branch of the subject may be presented to the reader at one view.

1. Variance in proof of record. Rodman *v.* Forman, 8 Johns. Rep. 26. Page *v.* Woods, 9 Johns. Rep. 82. Brooks *v.* Remiss, 8 Johns Rep. 455.

2. Of writs, executions, &c. Green *v.* Rennett, 1 Term Rep. 656. Bissell *v.* Kip, 5 Johns. Rep. 89. Byne *v.* Moore, 5 Taunt. 187. Beers *v.* Botsford, 3 Day, 159.

3. Proceedings in Chancery. Thompson *v.* Jameson, 1 Cranch, 283.

4. Grants, leases, bonds, and other instruments under seal. Tempany *v.* Burnaud, 4 Campb. 20. Middleton *v.* Sandford, Id. 34. Phillips v. Rose, 8 Johns. Rep. 392. Franklin *v.* Talmadge, 5 Johns. Rep. 84. Gordon *v.* Brown's Ex'r, 3 Hen. & Mun. 219. Adams *v.* Spear, 1 Hayw. 215. State *v.* Street, Taylor, 128. Evans *v.* Smith, 1 Wash. 172. M'Williams *v.* Willis, Id. 199. Drummond *v.* Crutcher, 2 Wash. 218. James *v.* Walruth, 8 Johns. Rep. 410.

5. Policy of Insurance. Cohen *v.* Hannam, 5 Taunt. 101.

6. Bills of Exchange and Promissory Notes. Roche *v.* Campbell, 3 Campb. 247. Hodge *v.* Fillis, Id. 463. Pense *v.* Morgan, 7 Johns. Rep. 468. Wilmot *v.* Monson, 4 Day, 114. Saxton *v.* Johnston, 10 Johns. Rep. 418. Wood *v.* Bulkley, 13 Johns. Rep. 486. Sheehy *v.* Mandeville, 7 Cranch, 208.

7. Other simple contracts. Crawford *v.* Morrell, 8 Johns. Rep. 253. Smith *v.* Barker, 3 Day, 312. Harrington *v.* Macmorris, 5 Taunt. 228 Baylies *v.* Fettyplace, 7 Mass. Rep. 325. Drake *v.* Watson, 4 Day, 37. Burnham *v.* Webster, 5 Mass. Rep. 270. Alexander *v.* Harris, 4 Cranch. 299.

8. In name of corporation. The People *v.* Runkel, 9 Johns. Rep. 47. Gilbert *v.* Nantucket Bank, 5 Mass. Rep. 98. Medway Cotton Manufactory *v.* Adams, 10 Mass. Rep. 360.

9. In name of place. Phillips' Ev. 165, 166.

10. Other cases of variance. Lewis *v.* Few, 5 Johns. Rep. 1. Southwick *v.* Stevens, 10 Johns. Rep. 443. De Forrest *v.* Brainerd, 2 Day, 528.

IV. ITS PARTS, &c.

5thly. The cause of action.

1. In assumpsit.

3. The promise or contract.

Unless the statement of the contract be denied by the plea, it will not be material, and will be in effect admitted.

One of the most important effects of the new rules of pleading is, that unless there be a plea upon the record denying the *contract* as alleged, it need not be proved; and in actions on bills and notes, those rules exclude the *general issue* non-assumpsit, and require some *special or particular denial;* as that the bill or note was not made, not indorsed, or not accepted, &c. (r); and in other respects those rules very much limit the risk of *variance.* So, if the defendant pay money into Court under a plea of tender, he cannot afterwards avail of a variance in the statement of the contract (s).

Amendment of variance in stating written instruments, at the trial, under 9 G. 4, c. 15.

Moreover by the 9 Geo. 4, c. 15 (t), intituled, "An act to prevent a failure of justice by reason of variances between *records* and *writings*, produced in evidence in support thereof;" after reciting that great expense is often incurred, and delay or failure of justice takes place at trials, by reason of variances between *writings* produced in evidence and the *recital* or *setting forth* thereof upon the record on which the trial is had in *matters not material to the merits of the case*, and such record cannot now in any case be amended at the trial, and in some cases cannot be amended at any time; for remedy thereof it is enacted, "that it shall be lawful for every Court of record holding plea in civil actions, any judge sitting at nisi prius, and any Court of oyer and terminer and general gaol delivery in England, Wales, the town of Berwick-upon-Tweed, and Ireland, *if such Court or judge shall see fit to do so*, to cause the record on which any trial may be pending before any such judge or Court, in any civil action, or in any indictment or information for any misdemeanor, when any variance shall appear between any matter in *writing or in print* produced in evidence, and the *recital* or *setting forth* thereon [*349] *upon the record whereon the trial is pending, to be forthwith amended in such particular by some officer of the Court on payment of such costs (if any) to the other party, as such judge or Court shall think reasonable, and thereupon the trial shall proceed as if no such variance had appeared; and in case such trial shall be had at nisi prius, the order for the amendment shall be indorsed on the postea and returned together with the record; and thereupon the papers, rolls, and other records of the Court from which such record issued shall be amended accordingly."

Upon this statute, in an undefended action upon a bill of exchange, the plaintiff was allowed to amend at the trial, without the payment of any costs, a mistake in stating the *date* of a bill of exchange (u); and in another case, where it was incorrectly stated in assumpsit for not indemnifying the plaintiff, that a judgment was recovered in B. R., whereas it was recovered in C. B., Lord Tenterden, C. J., allowed the error to be amended at the trial (v). But it is reported to have been held by one judge that the statute only applies to cases where some particular written instrument is *professed* to be set out or recited in the pleading (x); and therefore where a common avowry in replevin

(r) Reg. Gen. Hil. T. 4 W. 4.—Pleadings in Particular Actions. I. Assumpsit.

(s) Bulwer v. Horne, 4 Bar. & Adol. 132.

(t) See 2 Chit. Col. Stat. 736, tit. Nisi Prius.

(u) 4 C. & P. 24.

(v) 1 M. & M. 359.

(x) 3 C. & P. 594. If this be law it would be judicious, in declaring upon a written agreement, to profess to set it out, as by averring that "by a certain agreement or instrument in writing, made between," &c. it was agreed, &c. rather than to state it by showing only its substance or effect, without referring to it as a written instrument.

IV. ITS PARTS, &c.

5thly. The cause of action.

1. In assumpsit.

3. The promise or contract.

mis-stated the terms on which the plaintiff held the premises by demise, an amendment at the trial was refused (y).

The subsequent act 3 & 4 W. 4, c. 42, sect. 23, is more extensive, and authorizes a judge pending a trial to amend *every description of variance* when such amendment would not prejudice either party in the *just conduct* of his action or defence *on the merits*. And provided the judges respectively will *in practice* carry into effect the powers with which they have certainly been invested, the law *might* in every case be rescued from its present disgraced state as regards the effects given to *variances* on trivial *points*; but at present the instances of permitting amendments are too limited, and at *all* events, as regards the duties of a pleader, he is not relieved from the task of exerting the utmost care to avoid a variance, which at least occasions considerable risk and great expense (z).

4thly. The necessary *Averments* in assumpsit.

4thly. An *Averment* signifies a positive statement of facts in opposition to argument or inference (a); and when the obligation on the defendant to perform his contract depended on any event which would not otherwise appear from the declaration to have occurred, it is obvious that an averment of such event is essential to a logical statement of the cause of action, and should precede the statement of the defendant's breach. Such averments in a special action of assumpsit usually are, 1st, Of the *performance* or excuse for non-performance of a condition precedent, or of the happening of some event essential to the cause of action; 2dly, That the defendant had *notice* of such performance or of such event; and 3dly, That he was *requested* to perform his contract (b).

1st. Of averments of plaintiff's performance of his part.

When the consideration of the defendant's contract was *executed* (c), or past at the time of making the contract, and his performance was not to depend on any subsequent event, or other circumstance essential to the action, the declaration should proceed at once from the statement of the contract to the breach, without any intermediate averments, as in a count on an *indebitatus assumpsit*, &c. But when the consideration of the defendant's contract was *executory* (d), or his performance was to depend on some act to be done or

[*352] forborne *by the plaintiff, or on some other event, the plaintiff must aver the fulfilment of such condition precedent, whether it were in the affirmative or negative, or to be performed or observed by him or by the defendant, or by

(y) 3 C. & P. 594; Reeves v. Scott, 21st Feb. 1829, at Guildhall, *per* Lord Tenterden. "It is not to be taken that a judge is *bound* to permit an amendment. It is discretionary, and if a party has unnecessarily stated irrelevant matter in which there is a variance, he is not bound to amend." So in Jelf v. Oriel, against drawer of bill, Guildhall, 20th October, 1829, *cor.* Lord Tenterden, where the declaration stated a special acceptance at A. or at B., but the bill produced appeared to be only accepted at A., and the words "at B." were written on the bill, merely as the address of the drawer, which the pleader or attorney mistook for part of the acceptance, Lord Tenterden refused to amend, saying it would only encourage want of care in drawing pleadings, and he was not bound to permit amendments; that the act was meant only to aid *clerical* mistakes, and not such as any man who could read would avoid making; plaintiff obtained a verdict on the account stated. Campbell and Broderick for plaintiff; Denman and Richards for defendant.

(z) See in general the author's observation on the Practice respecting Amendments of Variances Pending a Trial, &c.

(a) Cowp. 683, 684; Bac. Ab. Pleas, B.

(b) See Com. Dig. Pleader, C. 50, &c; Bac. Ab. Pleas; 1 Saund. 235, n. 8.

(c) *Ante*, 323.

(d) *Ante*, 324.

IV. ITS PARTS, &c.

5thly. The cause of action.

1. In assumpsit.

4. Of averments therein.

any other person, or must show some excuse for the non-performance (*d*)(631). And in the case of reciprocal covenants, constituting *mutual conditions* to be performed *at the same time*, the plaintiff must aver performance or a readiness to perform his part of the contract (*e*). Thus, in declaring on a promise to pay a sum of money in consideration that the plaintiff would execute a release, the declaration must aver that such release was executed or tendered and refused (*f*)(632). So, on a promise to pay money in consideration of forbearance by the plaintiff, the declaration must aver such forbearance (*g*); and in actions for not delivering goods sold, the plaintiff must in general aver a readiness on his part to pay the price, &c. (*h*)(633). But upon a lessor's covenant that lessee *paying the rent at the appointed time* should quietly enjoy, it was held that the lessee might sue for a disturbance in possession, although he had not duly paid his rent (*i*). A perusal of the forms of the special counts in assumpsit, which are given in the second volume, will further illustrate this rule. But where an estate or interest passed or vested immediately in the plaintiff, and was to be defeated by a condition *subsequent*, or matter *ex post facto*, whether in the affirmative or negative, or to be performed by the plaintiff or defendant, or by any other person, performance of that matter need not be averred (*k*); as if a grant of an annuity were till the plaintiff should be advanced to a benefice, he need not say that he is not yet advanced (*l*).

As observed by Lord Mansfield, in delivering his judgment in *Kingston* v. *Preston* (*m*), "there are three kinds of covenants: 1st, such as are called *mutual* and *independent*, where either party may recover damages from the other for the injury he may have received by a breach of the covenants in his favor, and where it is no excuse for the defendant to *allege a breach of the [*353] covenants on the part of the plaintiff. 2dly, There are covenants which are *conditions dependent* on each other; in which the performance of one depends on the prior performance of the other, and therefore till this prior condition be performed the other party is not liable to an action on his covenant. 3dly, There is also a third sort of covenants, which are *mutual conditions* to be performed at *the same time*; and in these, if one party was ready, and offered to

(*d*) Ughtred's case, 7 Co. 10 a; Com. Dig. Pleader, C. 51, 52; Dougl. 656; 1 T. R. 638.

(*e*) *Id.*; 1 East, 203; *ante.* 196.

(*f*) 2 Burr. 899; 8 East, 437; 13 *Id.* 117; 2 Saund. 108, note 3.

(*g*) Com. Dig. Pleader, C. 52; *post*, vol. ii. 152, 153.

(*h*) 1 East, 203; *post*, vol. ii. An *offer* need not be alleged, when, 1 Marsh. 412; 7 Taunt. 314; 2 Saund. 352, notes.

(*i*) Dawson *v.* Dyer, 5 Bar. & Adol. 584.

(*k*) 7 Co. 10 a; Willes, 145, 146

(*l*) *Id.*; Plowd. Com. 25 b, 30 a, 32 b; 1 T. R. 645, 646; 2 Hen. Bla. 579.

(*m*) Cited Dougl 690, 691; and see the note in Willes, 157, n. a; 1 Saund. 320, n. 4; 2 *Id* 108, n. 3, 352, n. 1; Platt on Cov. 70; 1 East, 203; Com. Dig. Pleader, C. 50 to C. 68, as to conditions precedent and averments of performance in general.

(631) {Hilt *v.* Campbell, 6 Greenl. Rep. 111.} Vide Dodge *v.* Coddington, 3 Johns. Rep. 146. Jennings *v.* Camp, 13 Johns. Rep. 94. M'Millan *v.* Vandeslip, 12 Johns. Rep. 165. Faxon *v.* Mansfield and Holbrook, 2 Mass. Rep. 147. Ferris *v.* Purdy and Whitney, 10 Johns. Rep. 359. Wright *v.* Tuttle, 4 Day, 323. Wilt and Green *v.* Ogden, 13 Johns. Rep. 57. Thorpe *v.* White and others, 13 Johns. Rep. 53.

(632) Parker *v.* Parmele, 20 Johns. Rep. 130, and the cases there cited. Vide Smith et al., *v.* Woodhouse, 2 New Rep. 233. Miller *v.* Drake, 1 Caines' Rep. 45. Green *v.* Reynolds, 2 Johns. Rep. 207.

(633) Vide Porter *v.* Rose, 12 Johns. Rep. 209. West *v.* Emmons, 5 Johns. Rep. 179.

IV. ITS PARTS, &c. — 5thly. The cause of action. 1. In assumpsit. 4. Of averments therein.

perform his part, and the other neglected or refused to perform his, he who was ready and offered has fulfilled his engagement, and may maintain an action for the default of the other, though it is not certain that either is obliged to do the first act. The dependence or independence of covenants is to be collected from the evident sense and meaning of the parties, and however transposed they may be in the deed, their precedency must depend on the order of time in which the intent of the transaction requires their performance. In the case before the Court it would be the greatest injustice if the plaintiff should prevail: the essence of the agreement was, that the defendant should not trust to the personal security of the plaintiff, but before he delivered up his stock and business should have good security for the payment of the money; the giving such security therefore must necessarily be a condition precedent." (634)

There are no precise technical words in a deed or other contract to make a stipulation a condition precedent or subsequent; neither does it depend on the circumstance whether the clause is placed prior or posterior in the deed, so that it operates as a proviso or covenant; for the same words have been construed to operate as either the one or the other, according to the nature of the transaction (*n*)(635). The contradiction in the determinations has arisen not from a denial, but from a misapplication of this principle in the particular instance (*o*).

The *words* by which conditions precedent are usually created are, *for* (*p*); [*354] in *consideration* of (*q*); *provided*, &c. (*r*); **doing*, &c.; *performing*, &c. (*s*); *upon condition*, &c. (*t*); *having so done*, &c. (*u*); *ita quod* (*x*); *proinde* (*y*); &c. In general, if the agreement be that one party shall do an act, and that *for the doing thereof* the other shall pay a sum of money, the *doing of the act is a condition* precedent to the payment, and the party who is to pay shall not be compelled to part with his money till the thing be performed (636). If there be a condition precedent, however improbable the thing may be, it must be complied with, or the right which was to attach on its being performed does not vest (*z*); as if the condition be that A. shall enfeoff B., and A. do all in his power to perform the condition, and B. will not receive livery of seisin, it is clear that the right which was to depend on the performance of that condition did not arise; and if a person undertake for the act of a stranger, the

(*n*) Per Ashurst, J., 1 T. R. 645; 6 *Id.* 570, 668; 7 *Id.* 130; Platt on Cov. 72, &c. 79.

(*o*) 1 Saund. 320 a; Willes, 157, n. a.

(*p*) Doug. 638; 1 Saund. 320, note 4; Willes, 157, note a; Tidd, 9th edit. 437; 1 Stra. 569; 1 Vent. 177, 218; 2 Saund. 350, S. C.

(*q*) 1 Lord Raym. 665; 2 *Id.* 766; 1 Wils. 88; Willes, 157.

(*r*) 3 Campb. 385; Willes, 498.

(*s*) 2 Bla. Rep. 1313, 1314; Willes, 496, 158, &c.; but see 5 B. & Adol. 584.

(*t*) Co. Lit. 202 b; Willes, 153.

(*u*) 3 M. & Sel. 408.

(*x*) 2 Lord Raym. 766.

(*y*) Dougl. 638; Willes, 149; Platt on Cov. 72.

(*z*) 6 T. R. 710, 722; see 8 *Id.* 373; 1 Saund. 320 d.

(634) Ackley *v.* Elwell, 5 Halst. Rep. 304. Bank of Columbia *v.* Hagner, 1 Peters' S. C. Rep. 464.

(635) Powers *v.* Ware, 2 Pick. Rep. 456, per Putnam, 9. Vide Barnes *v.* Madan, 2 Johns. Rep. 148. Cunningham and another *v.* Morrell, 10 Johns. Rep. 205. Smith et at. *v.* Woodhouse, 2 New Rep. 240.

(636) Vide Dodge *v.* Coddington, 3 Johns. Rep. 146. Cunningham *v.* Morrell, 10 Johns. Rep. 203. Green *v.* Reynolds, 2 Johns. Rep. 207. Jones *v.* Gardner, 10 Johns. Rep. 266.

cases are uniform to show that such act must be performed (*a*). And on this principle, where by the proposals of the Phœnix Insurance Company against fire, it was stipulated that persons insured should, in case of loss by fire, procure a certificate of the minister, &c. of the parish, importing that they knew the character of the assured, and believed that he had really sustained the loss without fraud, it was held that the procuring of such a certificate was a condition precedent to the right of the assured to recover, and that although it was found by verdict that the minister, &c. wrongfully refused to sign the certificate, yet as it was not averred in the declaration that the certificate was actually obtained, the judgment was arrested (*b*).

IV. ITS PARTS, &c. — 5thly. The cause of action. 1. In assumpsit. 4. Of averments therein.

Some rules have been collected, by which to discover the intention of the parties and to ascertain when performance or excuse of performance by the plaintiff is necessary to be averred in the declaration (*c*). *First*, Where a day was appointed for payment by the defendant of money or part of it, or for his doing any other act, and such day was to happen *before* the thing which was the consideration of the defendant's *contract was to be performed, an action may be brought for the money, or for not doing such other act, before performance by the plaintiff (637); for it appears that the defendant relied upon the mere *agreement* to do the act, and upon his remedy if not performed, and did not intend to make the plaintiff's performance (638) a condition precedent (*d*). And so it is where no time is fixed for the performance of that which is the consideration of the money or other act (*e*). 2dly, But when a day was appointed for the performance of the defendant's contract, and such day was to happen *after the* time when the consideration of the defendant's contract was to be performed, in such case in general no action can be supported until the plaintiff has performed his act, and such performance must

[*355]

(*a*) *Per* Lord Kenyon, C. J., and Lawrence, J., 6 T. R. 719, 722.

(*b*) 6 T. R. 710.

(*c*) 1 Saund. 320, note 4; Tidd, 9th edit. 437, 438. Distinction between a *covenant* and a *condition*, Platt, 70, &c.; and see construction in Allen *v.* Cameron, 1 Crom. & M. 833.

(*d*) See the cases referred to in 1 Saund. 320, a, note 4; 1 Wils. 58; 2 New Rep. 433; Platt on Cov. 95.

(*e*) 1 Saund. 320 a.

(637) { See Robb *v.* Montgomery, 20 Johns. Rep. 15. Couch *v.* Ingersoll, 2 Pick. Rep. 292. } Vide Cunningham *v.* Morrell, 10 Johns. Rep. 204. Barruso *v.* Madan, 2 Johns. Rep. 145. 2 Hen. Black. Rep. 392. In Terry *v.* Duntze, 2 Hen. Black. Rep. 389, it was held that if A. agree to finish a piece of work for B. by a certain day, part of which is to be paid by instalments, as the work progressed, and the residue on the completion of it, A may maintain an action for the entire consideration without averring performance; and this rule was adopted by the Supreme Court of the State of New York in Seers *v.* Fowler, 2 Johns. Rep. 272. Havens *v.* Bush, Id. 387. Wilcox *v.* Ten Eyck, 5 Johns. Rep. 78. But these cases were overruled in Cunningham *v.* Morrell, 10 Johns. Rep. 203, where the agreement being to pay the plaintiff a certain sum for completing the whole of the work, to be paid in instalments as the work progressed, it was held that if the plaintiff went for the whole of the consideration money, he must aver performance of the whole work, or if for a ratable part of the money, he must show a ratable performance. Cases of this kind are clearly distinguishable from those in which the day of payment was *fixed before* the performance of the consideration on the part of the defendant; for here either the whole or some part of the work was to be done, before the whole or any part of the price of the sum could be demanded. And if, as in Wilcox *v.* Ten Eyck, *ub. sup.* part is to be paid at *specified times*, and the residue on the delivery of the deed, or other act to be performed by the defendant, and the covenants, as regards the prior payments, are undoubtedly independent, yet it does not therefore follow that the covenant for paying the residue must also be independent. Gould *v.* Banks et al., 8 Wend. R. 562.

(638) Vide Smith et al. *v.* Woodhouse, 2 New Rep. 233. Vide Close *v.* Miller, 10 Johns. Rep. 90. Jones *v.* Gardner, 10 Johns. 266.

IV. ITS PARTS, &c. — 5thly. The cause of action. 1. In assumpsit. 4. Of averments therein.

be averred (*f*). 3dly, That where the plaintiff's covenant or stipulation constituted only a *part* of the consideration of the defendant's contract, and the defendant has actually received a *partial* benefit, and the breach on the part of the plaintiff might be compensated in damages, an action may be supported against the defendant, without averring performance by the plaintiff (*g*)(639); for where a party has received a part of the consideration for his agreement, it would be unjust that because he has not had the whole, he should enjoy that part without paying or doing any thing for it, and therefore the law obliges him to perform the agreement on his part, and leaves him to his remedy to recover any damage he may have sustained in not having received the whole consideration (*h*). In these cases, however, it seems necessary to aver in the declaration performance of at least a part of that which the plaintiff covenanted to be, or to show *that the defendant has otherwise received a partial benefit* (*i*). 4thly, But where the mutual covenants constitute the *whole* consideration on both sides, they are mutual conditions, the one precedent to the other, [*356] *and the plaintiff must aver performance on his part (*j*)(640). 5thly, Where two acts are to be done at *the same time*, as where A. covenants or agrees to convey an estate, or to deliver goods to B. on a named day, or generally, and in consideration thereof B. covenants to pay A. a sum of money on the *same day*, or *generally*; neither can maintain an action without showing performance of, or an offer to perform, or at *least a readiness* to perform his part (641), though it is not certain which of them was obliged to do the first act (642); and this rule particularly applies to contracts of sale (*k*). It is to be observed that several modern cases before the recent pleading rules, show that *under the general*

(*f*) *Id.* 320 b; and *id.* note a, 5th ed.; 8 East, 473; 2 B. & Ald 17; Platt on Cov. 83. There are instances in which the plaintiff having *partly* performed work, &c. may recover *pro tanto*, the defendant receiving the benefit of such part; see *post* as to the common counts for work and labor.

(*g*) 1 Saund. 320 b; Boon *v.* Eyre, 1 Hen. Bla. 273, is a *leading case*; and see 6 T. R. 572; 10 East, 295, 555, 563; 12 *Id.* 389; 3 M. & Sel. 308; 8 Taunt. 576; 2 Moore, 630, S. C.; Platt on Cov. 90.

(*h*) See note (*g*), *ante*.

(*i*) 1 Saund 320 c, d; 10 East, 295; 6 Moore, 114.

(*j*) 1 Saund. 320, note 4; Platt on Cov. 80.

(*k*) 1 Saund. 320 d, note 4; 2 *Id.* 352, note 3; and 108, note 3; 1 East, 203; 8 T. R. 366; 7 T. R. 130; 7 Taunt. 314; 1 Moore, 56, S. C.; 8 Taunt. 62; 1 Moore, 498, S. C.

(639) Acc. Bennet *v.* Executors of Pixley, 7 Johns. Rep. 249. Obermeyer *v.* Nichols, 6 Binn. 159. In the last cited case the jury were allowed to deduct from the sum covenanted to be paid by the defendant to the plaintiff, an equivalent for the injury sustained, by the latter not performing the covenants on h.s part. See 4 Leigh R. 21.

(640) Vide Burruso *v.* Madan, 2 Johns. Rep. 145 Where there are *mutual covenants*, and the defendants have received the principal part of the consideration for the engagements on his part, the covenants of the parties will be construed to be independent, and the plaintiff may maintain an action for the breach of the defendant's covenants, although he has failed in performing in part on his side. Tompkins *v.* Elliot, 5 Wend. R. 496. The case of Dakin *v.* Williams, 11 Wend. R. 70, recognizes the doctrine laid down in the text.

(641) See Dana *v.* King, 2 Pick. R. 156. Where a vendor agreed to sell 100 tons of pressed hay, and to deliver the same within a given period, for which the vendee was to pay at an agreed price, $100 in advance and the residue when the whole quantity should be delivered, and the vendor delivered 50 tons, but omitted to deliver the residue, it was *held*, that the vendor could not recover for the portion delivered. Champlin *v.* Rowley, 13 Wend. R. 258.

(642) Vide Green *v.* Reynolds, 2 Johns. Rep. 207. Porter *v.* Rose, 12 Johns. Rep. 209. So, if it be stated that the defendant gave evidence on the trial of a cause, that is a sufficient averment that he had notice of the pendency of the suit. Barney *v.* Dewey, 10 Johns. Rep. 224.

issue the defendant might have given in evidence non-performance of a condition precedent in *reduction of damages* (*l*). IV. ITS PARTS, &c.

In *point of form*, an *averment* may be in any words amounting to an express allegation that such a fact or facts existed (*m*); as, "the plaintiff *avers*," or "*in fact saith*," or "*although*," or "*because*," or "*with this that*," or "*being*," (*n*) &c. The *simple* and, therefore, *best mode* of averment is, "*and the plaintiff saith that, &c.*" and the words, "*avers, &c.*" or "*in fact saith*," are obviously unnecessary. Where it is necessary to aver the life of a person in pleading, it is often sufficient if it appear by implication that the life continues (*o*); as where one who claims under a rector states that the rector was and *yet is* seised, this is a sufficient averment of his life (*p*). So if it be stated that A. was seised in fee and died, and that the land descended to B. as his son and heir, this is a sufficient averment that A. died seised (*q*). It is not unusual in declarations on mutual promises, and in covenant between landlord and tenant, to aver that the plaintiff hath performed all things on his part to be performed, but this is unnecessary (*r*); though it may after the verdict aid the omission of an averment of plaintiff's performance of a particular act (*s*). 5thly. The cause of action. 1. In assumpsit. 4. Of averments therein.

Where it is necessary on the part of the plaintiff to avèr *performance*, it must be shown to have been according to the *intent* of the contract, for it is not sufficient to pursue the words if the intent be not also performed; as on a promise in consideration that the plaintiff would cause A. to come to be bound to the defendant for £20, it is not sufficient to aver that the plaintiff caused A. to come to be *bound, but it ought to be also alleged that A. was bound (*t*). And an *exact performance* must also be stated; as on a promise in consideration that the plaintiff would procure the loan of £20 for one year, *it is* not sufficient to allege that he procured part at one time and part at another, for he ought to procure the whole for the whole year (*u*). And performance ought to be shown with such certainty, that the Court may judge whether the intent of the covenant has been duly fulfilled, as in consideration that the plaintiff would acquit A. of a debt, it is not sufficient to say that he acquitted him without showing how, viz. by deed (*x*). Where the matter to be performed is a condition precedent, the performance of that matter must be shown, although a third person was to do the act, and he unreasonably refuse his concurrence: and a substituted performance is insufficient; as where a fire policy required that the minister and churchwardens should certify as to the plaintiff's character, &c. it was held that such certificate by those persons was indispensable (*y*). But if the plaintiff show a substantial performance of a matter of a general nature, it is frequently sufficient to state it in general terms, without alleging particularly how he performed; as on a promise to [*357]

(*l*) Allen *v.* Cameron, 1 Crom. & M. 836, and cases there cited; *quære*, the existence or extent of that doctrine since the recent pleading rules as to the practice in actions for torts, see *post*.

(*m*) 1 Saund. 117, note 4; Com. Dig. Pleader, C. 77. As to the manner of making an averment, see Cowp. 683, 684; 1 Saund. 117, note 4; Willes, 134, 427.

(*n*) 2 Burr. 834.

(*o*) 1 Saund. 235, note 8; 2 *Id.* 61, note 9.

(*p*) *Id.*; Dyer, 304 a; Sir T. Jones, 227.

(*q*) 2 Saund. 61 g, note 9.

(*r*) 1 Saund. 234 c, note 6.

(*s*) Lutw. 253; Sir T. Jones, 125; Com. Dig. Pleader, C. 61.

(*t*) Com. Dig. Pleader, C. 58; Yelv. 90. As to *pleas* of performance, see *post*.

(*u*) Com. Dig. Pleader, C. 59; Yelv. 87.

(*x*) Cro. Jac. 503; Com. Dig. Pleader, C. 60; Cro. Eliz. 914; Sir T. Jones, 125.

(*y*) 6 T. R. 710; *ante*, 355.

IV. ITS PARTS, &c. — 5thly. The cause of action. 1. In assumpsit. 4. Of averments therein.

pay so much as the plaintiff should expend for the officers of the army in such a suit, an averment that he spent so much is sufficient, without showing for what officers in particular (z)(643). And there are some instances where the thing agreed to be done by the plaintiff having been substantially performed, though not in the exact manner, nor with all the minute circumstances mentioned, it was considered as a sufficient performance (a); as where the condition was to enfeoff, a conveyance by lease and release was held sufficient (b); so where the condition was to deliver the will of the testator, and the plaintiff delivered letters testamentary (c). So, in a declaration on a contract to pay so much money, if the plaintiff would marry the daughter of the defendant at his request, an allegation that he did marry her, without saying at the defendant's [*358] *request, is sufficiently certain (d). Where the condition precedent was in the disjunctive, the averment of performance must be framed accordingly, and not in the conjunctive (e)(644). Where the defendant's agreement was to pay £45 if the plaintiff would make "a set of sails worth £45," the Court held that an averment that the plaintiff made "the said" sails (not showing their value) was sufficient on demurrer (f).

In averring an *excuse* of performance by the plaintiff, he must state his readiness to perform the act, and the particular circumstances which constitute such excuse; and therefore where the declaration stated that arbitrators *could not* make their award, without showing the special cause which prevented them, it was held insufficient (g).

In stating an excuse for non-performance of a condition precedent, the plaintiff must in general show that the defendant either *prevented* (645) the performance, or rendered it unnecessary to do the prior act, by his neglect, or by his *discharging* the plaintiff from performance (h). The performance of a condition precedent may also be excused by the *absence* of the defendant, if his presence were necessary for the plaintiff's performance; or by his *neglect* to do the first act, if it were incumbent on him to perform it (i). It may also

(z) Com. Dig. Pleader, C. 61.
(a) 6 T. R. 722.
(b) Co. Lit. 207 a.
(c) 1 Rol. Ab. 426, pl. 4.
(d) Cro. Car. 194.
(e) 1 Stra. 594.
(f) *Id.* 88.
(g) 2 Saund. 129, 132.
(h) 1 T. R. 638; Doug. 684, 687, 688; Co. Lit. 206 b; 5 Taunt. 30; 8 *Id.* 70; 8 East, 443; *ante*, 349, 352.
(i) 1 Rol. Abr. 457, 458; 7 T. R. 13.

(643) In a case in Connecticut, where the plaintiff averred generally that he had kept and performed all the covenants in the indenture on his part to be performed, it was held not only sufficient, but the most proper form; and that the distinction was, that where the act involved in it a question of law, viz. whether it was done as the law directed, the *quo modo* must be pointed out; but where it is a mere matter of fact, a general averment of performance is the most proper. Wright *v.* Tuttle, 4 Day, 313. It is not always sufficient to aver performance in the words of a contract; the intent of the contract must be shown to have been performed. The legal import of the contract must be averred to have been done; and where it is necessary, on the part of the plaintiff, to aver performance, it must be set forth with such certainty as to enable the court to see that the contract has been fulfilled. Thomas *v.* Van Ness, 4 Wend. R. 553.

(644) Where several things are to be done by the plaintiff, precedent to the performance of the defendant's part of the agreement, it is necessary for the plaintiff to aver performance of all the things to be done by him; but if the performance of a part be not averred, and it appear by the defendant's plea, that the part in question was performed, the defect in the declaration is cured. Zerger *v.* Sailer, 6 Binn. 24.

(645) { Newcomb *v.* Brackett, 16 Mass. Rep. 161. } A declaration averring that the plaintiff had *performed as nearly as it was possible* without adding that it was accepted as a full performance, would be bad. Stagg *v.* Munro, 8 Wend. R. 399.

IV. ITS PARTS, &c.

5thly. The cause of action.

1. In assumpsit.

4. Of averments therein.

be excused in some cases by the defendant's not giving *notice* to the plaintiff (*k*). We have seen that if a third person was to perform the condition, it is no excuse for the plaintiff that such third person refused to do the act (*l*).

Where the respective acts to be done by the plaintiff and defendant were *mutual*, and were to be performed at the *same time*, the plaintiff should aver his *readiness* to perform *his* part, and either state that the defendant neglected to attend when necessary, or refused to perform his part, or discharged the plaintiff from his performance (*m*)(646). Thus where the defendant stipulated to pay a sum of money on *the plaintiff's assigning to him a certain equity of redemption, and the declaration averred that the plaintiff was ready and willing and offered to assign, and tendered a draft of an assignment to the defendant for his approbation, and offered to execute and deliver and would have executed and delivered such assignment to the defendant, but that he absolutely *discharged* the plaintiff from executing the same or any assignment whatever, and had not paid the money, such declaration was, on demurrer, held sufficient (*n*). So, in an action of assumpsit for not delivering bonds and other securities pursuant to an agreement, where the consideration money was to be paid on the receipt of the securities, it is not necessary to aver an actual tender of the money; an allegation of the plaintiff's readiness to pay is sufficient (*o*). So, in an action for the non-delivery of goods, which the defendant had undertaken to deliver on request at a certain price, it is sufficient for the plaintiff in his declaration, without alleging an actual tender of the price, to aver such request, and that he was ready and willing to receive the goods, and to pay for them according to the terms of the sale, and that the defendant had notice of such readiness, but refused to deliver them (*p*); or if the defendant did not attend at the appointed place, such non-attendance should be stated, which would render an averment of request unnecessary (*q*) (647). And where the acts to be performed by each party are mutual, and to take place at the same time, the plaintiff, it appears, should not only aver his readiness to perform his act, but also a notice of his readiness, or insert some other allegation to dispense with it; thus in an action against a woman for not marrying plaintiff within a reasonable time, an averment of notice of readiness to marry should be stated, though the omission would suffice after verdict (*r*).

[*359]

Consequences of insufficient averments.

The omission of the averment of performance of a condition precedent, or of an excuse for the non-performance, is fatal on demurrer, or in case of judgment by default (*s*); but after verdict the omission may in some cases be

(*k*) 1 Rol. Abr. 457, 458; Co. Lit. 207 a.
(*l*) *Ante*, 354, 357.
(*m*) Dougl. 684; 1 East, 203; 2 Saund. 352, note 3; 7 T. R. 130; 7 Taunt. 314; 1 Moore, 56, S. C.
(*n*) Dougl. 684, 685.
(*o*) 1 Moore, 56; 7 Taunt. 314, S. C.; 7 T. R. 130.
(*p*) 1 East, 203.
(*q*) 7 T. R. 129, 131; 5 East, 107; see 11 Price, 494.
(*r*) 2 D. & R. 55.
(*s*) 2 Burr. 899; 2 Saund. 352, n. 3.

(646) Vide Miller v. Drake, 1 Caines' Rep. 45. Porter v. Rose, 12 Johns. Rep. 209.

(647) Where the power to perform a covenant on the part of the plaintiff depends on an act previously to be done on the part of the defendant, it is unnecessary for the plaintiff to aver a tender and refusal, but an averment of a readiness to perform is sufficient; as, where A. covenants to convey, and B. covenants to execute a bond and mortgage for the land, in an action by B. against A., it is sufficient for the plaintiff to aver his readiness to perform. West v. Emmons, 5 Johns. Rep. 179. Vide Robbins v. Luce, 4 Mass Rep. 474.

IV. ITS PARTS, &c. — 5thly. The cause of action. 1. In assumpsit. 4. Of averments therein.

aided by the common law intendment, that every thing may be presumed to have been proved which was necessary to sustain *the action (648); for a verdict will cure a case defectively stated (*t*). Thus, in actions upon agreements to sell or assign leasehold property, an averment by the plaintiff, the vendor, that he was "*ready* and willing and offered to assign," seems to be sufficient *after verdict*, without alleging that he had a good title (*u*). And, at least, *after verdict*, an averment of *readiness and willingness to assign*, &c. is tantamount to an averment of a tender of an assignment (*x*). But where the non-performance of the condition precedent appears on the face of the pleadings, a verdict will not aid the defect (*y*).

Averment of notice.

It is frequently necessary, particularly in special actions of assumpsit, to aver that the defendant *had notice of* some fact or facts previously stated; and a great variety of the instances where such averment is necessary are collected in the books referred to in the note (*z*). From these it appears, that when the matter alleged in the pleading is to be considered as lying more properly in the knowledge of the plaintiff than of the defendant, then the declaration ought to state that the defendant had notice thereof (649); as where the defendant promised to give the plaintiff as much for a commodity as another person had given, or should give him, for the like; or to pay the plaintiff what damages he had sustained by a battery, or to pay the plaintiff his costs of suit (*a*); and in a declaration against the drawer or indorser of a bill of exchange, it is material to aver notice of non-payment by the acceptor, or some excuse for the neglect (*b*)(650). But where the matter does not lie more properly in the knowledge of the plaintiff than of the defendant, notice need not be averred (*c*)(651). Therefore, if the defendant contracted to do a thing on the performance of an act by a *stranger*, notice need not be averred, for it lies in the defendant's knowledge as much as the plaintiff's, and he ought to take notice at his peril (*d*)(652); *and though it is usual in practice in a [*361]

(*t*) 8 Taunt. 62; 1 Moore, 498, S. C.; 1 East, 209, 210; 2 Saund. 352, n. 3; 2 Burr. 900; Doug. 687, n. (*g*) and (*h*); 1 Saund. 228, n. 1; *sed vide* Doug. 679; Cro. Jac. 503. The rules as to a verdict, &c. curing a defect in pleading, will be considered hereafter.

(*u*) 8 Taunt. 62; 1 Moore, 498, S. C.

(*x*) *Id.*

(*y*) 6 T. R. 710.

(*z*) As to averring *notice*, see Com. Dig. Pleader, C. 73 to 75; Vin. Abr. Notice; Hardr. 42; 5 T. R. 621, 624; 1 Saund. 117, n. 2.

(*a*) 2 Saund. 62 a, n. 4; Cro. Jac. 432; Hardr. 42; Com. Dig. Pleader, C. 73; 5 T. R. 621, 624; 11 Mod. 48.

(*b*) Doug. 679, 680; 2 New Rep. 355; 7 East, 231.

(*c*) 1 Saund. 117, n. 2; 2 *Id.* 62 a, n. 4; Freem. Rep. 285.

(*d*) Com. Dig. Pleader, C. 75.

(648) Vide Rucker *v.* Green, 15 East's Rep. 290, 291. Owens *v.* Morehouse, 1 Johns. Rep. 276, 277. Leffingwell *v.* White, 1 Johns. Cas. 99. Bayard *v.* Malcolm, 2 Johns. Rep. 571.

(649) Vide Lent *v.* Padelford, 10 Mass. Rep. 238.

(650) Vide Slacum *v.* Pomeroy, 6 Cranch, 221.

(651) Vide Lent *v.* Padelford, 10 Mass. Rep. 230, 238. Clough *v.* Hoffman, 5 Wend. R. 500.

(652) So where the defendant has undertaken as a guarantee for A. B., it is unnecessary to aver notice to the defendant of a failure of performance on the part of A. B. Williams *v.* Granger, 4 Day, 444. Lent *v.* Padelford, 10 Mass. Rep. 230, 238. {In an action against a sheriff for a false return to a *ca. sa.* it is not necessary to aver in the declaration, that the sheriff had notice from the plaintiff that the defendant was within his bailiwick, so that he might arrest him. Hereford *v.* Macnamara, 6 Dowl. & Ryl. 953.

IV. ITS PARTS, &c.

5thly. The cause of action.

1. In assumpsit.

4. Of averments therein.

Notice.

declaration of debt upon an award, and in the replication in debt on bond conditioned for the performance of an award, to aver that the defendant had notice of the award, such averment is unnecessary, because the defendant ought to take notice of the award, unless it was expressly provided in the submission that the award should be notified to the parties, when notice must be alleged (*e*). So, if upon a treaty of marriage a promise be made by a third person to pay the feme £100 after the death of the husband, it is not necessary, in an action upon this promise, to aver that the defendant had notice of the death; and in a declaration on a promise to pay a sum of money at the full age of an infant, notice of his attaining that age need not be alleged, because it is as notorious to one as to the other (*f*). On the same principle, if a man be bound to another to indemnify him against the acts of a third person, no notice of those acts is necessary to be alleged (*g*); and in an action on a promissory note by the indorsee against the drawer, notice of the indorsement need not be averred (*h*). If the defendant's promise were to pay on the performance of a certain act, even by the plaintiff himself, to the defendant or a stranger, there are cases in which it has been decided that notice of the act need not be averred, because by the terms of the contract the defendant engaged to take notice of it at his peril; as if the defendant contracted to pay it on the marriage of the obligee with B. (*i*): and in the case of a precedent condition to be performed by the plaintiff to the defendant in person, notice of the plaintiff's performance need not be averred, because it is implied (*k*). But we have before seen (*l*) that where the acts to be performed by each party are mutual, and to take place at the same time, the plaintiff should not only aver a readiness to perform his act, but also a notice of such readiness, or insert some other allegation to dispense with it.

Where notice is necessary, it ought to appear that *the notice was given in due time, and to a proper person* (*m*); but where a special request is averred, notice will sometimes be presumed (*n*). *Where no notice whatever has been given, the absconding of the party, or other circumstances should be stated as an excuse for the want of notice (*o*); but where a notice has been given, but a justifiable *delay* in giving it at the regular time (as in the case of the notice of the dishonor of a bill) has occurred, under the averment that notice was given, sometimes the facts excusing the delay may be proved (*p*). But a careful pleader should consider whether it would not be better to state the facts of the excuse. The omission of an averment of notice when necessary will be fatal on demurrer, or judgment by default (*q*); but may be aided by a verdict (*r*)(653), unless in an action against the drawer of a bill, when the omis- [*362]

(*e*) 2 Saund. 62 a, note 4; Hardr. 42; Com. Dig. Pleader, C. 75; 5 T. R. 621, 624; see 5 B. & Ald. 507.

(*f*) Hardr. 42; 11 Mod. 48.

(*g*) 1 Saund. 116; 11 Price, 494.

(*h*) 1 B. & P. 625.

(*i*) 2 Bulstr. 254; Com. Dig. Pleader, C. 75.

(*k*) Com. Dig. Pleader, C. 75.

(*l*) *Ante*, 353, 355.

(*m*) Com. Dig. Pleader, C. 74.

(*n*) Cro. Jac. 228, 229; 1 B. & P. 626; 3 Bulstr. 326, 327.

(*o*) Chitty on Bills, 7th edit. 362; 1 Salk. 214; Vin. Ab. Notice, A. 2.

(*p*) 8 B. & C. 387; 2 M. & R. 359, S. C.

(*q*) Cro. Jac. 432.

(*r*) 1 Stra. 214; 1 Saund. 228 a; 2 D. & R. 55.

(653) Vide Spencer v. Overton, 1 Day's Rep. 183. { Weigley's Adm. v. Weir, 7 Serg. & Rawle, 309. }

IV. ITS PARTS, &c.

sion of the averment of notice of non-payment of the acceptor is fatal even after verdict (s)(654).

5thly. The cause of action. 1. In assumpsit. 4. Of averments therein. Request.

Whenever it is essential to the cause of action that the plaintiff should have *actually formally requested* the defendant to perform his contract, such *request must be* stated in the declaration and proved (t). It has been observed, that if it had been held that a request were *always* essential to be averred and proved, many vexatious actions might be avoided, but there are a variety of instances in which it is settled that *no request is necessary* anterior to the action, and consequently need not be stated in pleading (u); thus, where the declaration is upon a contract to pay a *precedent* debt (655), as in the case of common counts for goods sold, work and labor, money lent, &c. no request need be stated or proved (x). And in these instances, although the promise has been laid to pay *on request*, the "licet sæpius requisitus" need not be laid or proved (y). And though formerly a distinction was made between a promise to pay a precedent debt, and one to become due on a subsequent event, that distinction appears not to be tenable; thus, where the declaration stated that the defendant, in consideration that the plaintiff *would* make him a set of sails worth £45 promised to pay so much for them on request, it was decided that no request to pay was necessary to be stated, because, on making of the sails the money immediately became due, and the Court said the case differed from those where the payment is to be to a third person, or where an award directs a request (z). [*363] Where the defendant *was to perform the first act (a)(656), or has so acted as to render a previous request of performance useless and unnecessary (b), the statement of a request may be omitted.

But when by the express or implied terms of the contract it was incumbent on the plaintiff, before the commencement of his action, to request the defendant to perform his contract, such request being as it were a condition precedent must be averred (c)(657). Thus, in an action for not delivering a horse, sold by defendant to the plaintiff, or for not finding timber for repairs, the declaration should allege a special request to delivér the same (d). Upon a

(s) Dougl. 679; 7 East, 231.
(t) 7 B. & Cres. 468; 1 M. & R. 394, S. C. As to requests in general, see Com. Dig. Pleader, C. 69 to 73; 1 Saund. 33 a, n. 2; 1 Stra. 88; 2 Ventr. 75; 3 B. & P. 438.
(u) 1 B. & P. 59, 60; Cro. Eliz. 548; *post.*
(x) 1 Saund. 33, and *id.* n. 2; Bul. N. P. 151.
(y) Ring v. Roxbrough, 2 Tyr. 468, 470; 2 Cromp. & J. 418, S. C.
(z) 1 Stra. 88; 2 Ventr. 75; Cro. Jac. 523.
(a) 2 New Rep. 355.
(b) 5 B. & Ald. 712; 1 D. & R. 361, S. C.; 10 East, 359.
(c) Com. Dig. Pleader, C. 69; 2 Hen. Bla. 131; 1 Saund. 32, 33 a, note 2; 5 T. R. 409; 3 Bulstr. 297.
(d) 5 T. R. 409; Sir W. Jones, 56; 1 East, 204; Com. Dig. Pleader, C. 69.

---

(654) { Miles v. O'Hara, 4 Binn. 180. See 7 Serg. & Rawle, 310. } A general averment in a declaration on a bill of exchange, "of all which said premises the defendants afterwards, &c. had notice," is sufficient. Boot v. Franklin, 3 Johns. Rep. 207.

(655) Vide Ernst v. Bartle, 1 Johns. Cas. 319.

(656) Where the promise was to do a certain act, or pay a certain sum of money, and the defendant had not done the act, a special request to pay the money need not be alleged. Lent v. Padelford, 10 Mass. Rep. 230. In an action on a promissory note for a certain sum payable in goods of one description, or of another, at the election of the promisee within eight days after date, it was held unnecessary for the plaintiff to aver an election or notice thereof to the defendant, who became liable immediately on the expiration of the eight days. Townsend v. Wells, 3 Day's Rep. 327.

(657) Vide Ernst v. Bartle, 1 Johns. Cas. 327. Vide 13 Wend. R. 285—7.

IV. ITS PARTS, &c. — 5thly. The cause of action. 1. In assumpsit. 4. Of averments therein. Request.

note payable "one month after demand," a demand must be made (e). So, if the contract were to deliver up a bond to be cancelled "on request;" (f) or to pay money "on request;" (g) or if an award direct the defendant to perform some act "on request;" (h) or if the defendant contracted as surety to pay the debt or rent of a third person "on request;" (i) in these cases the request is parcel of the contract, and must be alleged and proved (k); or there must be some allegation to dispense with it (l). But an action on a bond *conditioned generally for payment* of a specified sum with interest, an action may be supported without alleging or proving a prior demand (m). It should seem, in an action for not marrying *in a reasonable time*, plaintiff should aver a request to marry, or make some other allegation to dispense with it (n). In an action against an agent for not accounting, &c. a request to account and pay over the balance must be stated (o).

[*364] The difference in pleading between a *general* request and a *special* or *express* request.

*In point of *form* there are in *pleading* two descriptions of requests; one termed a *special request*, it alleging by whom and the time when it was made; the other, the *licet sæpius requisitus*, or, "although often requested so to do." When an actual request is essential to the support of the action, a special request must be stated (658), and it must be shown by and to whom the same was made and the time of making it, in order that the Court may judge whether the request were sufficient (p). Since the pleading rules Hil. T. 4 W. 4, requiring venue or place to be stated only in the *margin* and not to be repeated in the *body*, no *place* of request need be stated unless a request at a particular place be material according to the terms of the contract. The statement of a general instead of a special request, when necessary, has been holden bad on a general demurrer (q); and it has even been decided that it would not be aided by verdict (r); but from the principle deducible from other cases and a recent decision, it should seem that a judgment by default or a verdict would aid the defect (s), and that the objection must now be taken by a special de-

(e) 1 R. & M. 388. As to a note payable "upon demand," Christie v. Fonseck, cited in 1 Selw. N. P.; 10 Mod. 38; 13 East, 352; Chitty on Bills, 7th edit. 361, 373.

(f) 3 Bulstr. 297.

(g) 3 Campb. 459. In debt on a single bond, for the payment of money *on demand*, a demand must be made before action. 2 Bar. & Cres. 685; and see 1 Bac. Ab. 671; 6 Mod. 227, 259; 2 Salk. 585, *acc.*; *sed vide* Cro. Eliz. 548, and *id.* 721, case of an annuity payable on request; and in Gibbs v. Southam, 5 Bar. & Adol. 911, it was held that an action on a bond conditioned generally for the payment of a specified sum with interest, may be brought without a demand being made.

(h) 1 Saund. 32.

(i) 6 M. & S. 9; see 11 Price, 494. Even assuming that a surety is in general entitled to a demand on him, yet he cannot be so entitled where there was no express stipulation to that effect, and the money was to be paid at the creditor's house on a named day; 6 M. & Sel. 121, 125.

(k) Cro. Jac. 500; Owen, 109; 1 Saund. 32, 33 a, n. 2; 2 B. & C. 685, S. C; *sed vide* 1 Stra. 88, 89; 4 D. & R. 181.

(l) 10 East, 359, 361; 11 Price, 494.

(m) Gibbs v. Southam, 5 Bar. & Adol. 911.

(n) 2 D. & R. 55.

(o) 1 Taunt. 572.

(p) 1 Stra. 89; Com. Dig. Pleader, C. 69, 70, &c.; 1 Saund. 33; 5 T. R. 409; 14 East, 300, 301.

(q) 5 T. R. 409; *sed vide* 10 East, 359, 365.

(r) 3 Bulstr. 299; Cro. Eliz. 85; Sir W. Jones, 56; 1 Saund. 33 a, note 2; Com. Dig. Pleader, C. 69.

(s) 10 East, 359; see 1 Stra. 89, 214; 1 Wils. 33; 7 T. R. 522; 1 Saund. 228, note 1.

(658) But where a special request is not necessary to impose on the defendant the obligation to pay, nor to render him liable on his covenant, it is not necessary to be averred. Smith v. Emery, 7 Halst. Rep. 53.

IV. ITS PARTS, &c. — 5thly. The cause of action. 1. In assumpsit. 4. Of averments therein. Request.

murrer (*t*) (659). The *licet sæpius requisitus*, or "although often requested so to do," without stating the time of request, though usually inserted in the common breach to the money counts, is of no avail in pleading (*u*), and the omission of it will in no case vitiate the declaration (*x*). And therefore where in a declaration upon a note payable four months after date, it was objected in error, that the request to pay the money in the note was laid in the common breach at the end of the declaration to have been upon the same day and year aforesaid, which was the date of the note, and four months before it became due, it was adjudged upon a writ of error that there was no occasion to lay any request at all, for the bringing the action was a request in law (*y*); and if a special request be unnecessarily stated, it need not be proved (*z*).

[*365] 5thly. The *Breach of Contract.*

*5thly. The *Breach of the contract* being obviously an essential part of the cause of action, must in all cases be stated in the declaration (*a*). When the special count in assumpsit is merely for a *money* demand, and other common counts are subjoined, the usual breach in the conclusion of the declaration will in general suffice; and in declarations on bills of exchange and promissory notes, it has not been usual to state any other breach than that at the end of the common counts (*b*). But when the breach is special, and not merely the non-payment of money, it is usually stated in each special count. The allegation of the breach must obviously be governed by the nature of the stipulation. It should be assigned in the words of the contract, either negatively or affirmatively (660), or in words which are co-extensive with the import and effect of it (*c*)(661); and in many cases this will suffice; thus, in assumpsit on a promise to manage a farm in a good and husband-like manner, and according to the custom of the country, it may suffice to assign a breach in the words of the promise (*d*). Therefore in debt on a bond, conditioned

(*t*) 10 East, 359, 365; Tidd, 9th ed. 439, note (*f*); 2 D. & R. 55, *acc.*

(*u*) Unless as it may be considered as aiding the omission of a special request, on *general* demurrer, or after verdict, &c., see 10 East, 359.

(*x*) 2 Hen. Bla. 131; 1 B. & P. 59, 60; Plowd. 128 b; Hardr. 38, 72; Ring *v.* Roxbrough, 2 Crom. & J. 418; 2 Tyr. 168, 470, S. C.

(*y*) 1 Wils. 33; 1 B. & P. 59, 60.

(*z*) Plowd. 128.

(*a*) Com. Dig. Pleader, C. 44, &c.

(*b*) 1 Wils. 33; 3 M. & Sel. 150; and see the prescribed form of breach in Reg. Gen. Trin. Term, 1 W. 4, *post*, vol. ii.

(*c*) Com. Dig. Pleader, C. 45 to 49; *Id.* 2 V. 2; 2 Saund. 181 a; 1 Price, 109; but see 6 Taunt. 45, 47; and see cases and observations in Earl Falmouth *v.* Thomas, 3 Tyr. 38, 41, 42, 50.

(*d*) Earl Falmouth *v.* Thomas, 1 Crom. & M. 89; 3 Tyr. 38, 41, 50.

(659) In an action against the indorser of a promissory note, the omission of a special demand of payment of the maker in the declaration, is aided by verdict: and the general allegation, although often requested, is then sufficient, admitting that it would be ill on demurrer. Leffingwell *v.* White, 1 Johns. Cas. 100. In a declaration upon a bond conditioned, to pay the taxed costs of a suit, licet sæpius requisitus is good on general demurrer. Bacon et al. *v.* Wilbur, 1 Cowen's Rep. 117.

(660) { M'Geehan *v.* M'Laughlin, 1 Hall's R. 33. Karthans *v.* Owings, 2 Gill & Johns. 541. } But a mere negation of the words of the covenant must necessarily in itself amount to a breach, otherwise it will be insufficient. Jullian *v* Burgott, 11 Johns. Rep. 6. { The exception to the general rule is, that when such general assignment does not necessarily amount to a breach, the breach must be specially assigned, 2 Gill & Johns. 441. } See the cases cited in the next note, as to what is a sufficient assignment.

(661) It is enough that the words of the assignment show, unequivocally, a substantial breach. Fletcher *v.* Peck, 6 Cranch, 127. See further as to assigning breaches, Hughes *v.* Smith, 5 Johns. Rep. 168. Smith *v.* Jansen, 8 Johns. Rep. 111. Sedgwick *v.* Hollenback, 7 Johns. Rep. 376. Craghill *v.* Page, 2 Hen. & Mun. 446. Bender *v.* Fromberger, 4 Dall. 436.

IV. ITS PARTS, &c.

5thly. The cause of action.

1. In assumpsit.

5. The *Breach of Contract.*

for payment of an annual sum to the *wife* of the obligee, a breach assigned in non-payment of the annual sum to the *obligee* is insufficient (*e*). But, though a breach may be assigned in the words of a contract, *it must not be too general;* it must show the subject-matter of complaint (*f*). And therefore it seems that a general averment *quod non performavit*, or that "the defendant did *not perform* the said agreement," is insufficient (*g*); because "did not perform his agreement" might involve a question of law, and also because the object of pleading is to apprize the defendant of the cause of complaint, so that he may prepare his plea and defence and evidence in answer. And yet, as the defendant must know in what respects he has or not performed his contract, any great particularity, it should seem, ought not on principle to be required (*h*). Where the contract was specific, to do or forbear some particular act, it is in general sufficient to assign the breach in the words of the contract; thus, if the contract were to show a sufficient record, it is enough to allege that the defendant "did not show a sufficient record," though issue cannot be joined upon it, because sufficiency of matter of record cannot be tried by a jury; but the defendant, on such breach assigned, may plead that he showed such a record, and upon demurrer the Court will judge whether it be sufficient (*i*). In an action of covenant for revoking an arbitrator's authority, it is sufficient to aver that the defendant by deed revoked, without stating that the defendant gave *notice* of the revocation to the arbitrators (*k*): for without such notice there could be no *revocation* (*l*). So in covenant by an apprentice for not finding victuals and other necessaries, [*366] *a breach in the words of the contract is sufficient (*m*); and a breach in the words of the covenant for not repairing, when not qualified, without enumerating the particular dilapidations, will suffice (*n*). So in assumpsit against a tenant, on his implied contract to manage, use, and cultivate a farm in a good and husband-like manner and according to the custom of the country, it is sufficient, even on special demurrer, to assign as a breach that the defendant did not so manage, use, or cultivate the said farm, but on the contrary managed, used, and cultivated the said farm, lands, and premises in a bad, improper, and unhusband-like manner, and contrary to the custom of the country where the said farm was so situate, without stating any particular acts of bad husbandry, or showing what particular custom of the country had been violated (*o*), and that seems to be the safest course of declaring. And in general, if a breach be assigned in words containing the sense and substance of the contract, though they are not in the precise words of such contract, it is sufficient (*p*)(662); as if the defendant's promise were to *guarantee* the payment of the debt of a third person, a breach that the defendant did *not pay* the

(*e*) 6 Taunt. 140; 1 Marsh. 495.

(*f*) 7 Price, 550.

(*g*) Skin. 344.

(*h*) *Supra*, note (*d*).

(*i*) Yelv. 39, 40; *post*, 369, note (*q*); Com. Dig. Pleader, C, 45; 1 Price, 109; but see 6 Taunt. 45, 47.

(*k*) 5 B. & Ald. 507; 1 D. & R. 106, S. C.; 8 Co. 162. *Sed quære.*

(*l*) See the principle, *ante*, 354, 355.

(*m*) 3 Lev. 170; *sed vide* 2 Cro. 486.

(*n*) Lutw. 329, cited by Lord Lyndhurst, C. B. with approbation in 3 Tyr. 41; 3 T. R. 305, *per* Buller, J.; 1 Saund. 235, note 6.

(*o*) Earl Falmouth *v.* Thomas, 3 Tyr. 26.

(*p*) Com. Dig. Pleader, C. 46; 13 East, 63; see *ante*, 334.

(662) {Camp *v.* Allen, 7 Halst. Rep. 1.} Rickert *v.* Snyder, 9 Wend. R. 41 Potter *v.* Bacon 2 ib. 583.

IV. ITS PARTS, &c. — 5thly. The cause of action. 1. In assumpsit. 5. The *Breach of Contract.*

debt will suffice (*q*); so if a policy insured a ship against the *barratry* of the captain, and the breach assigned was that the ship was lost by the *fraud* of the captain, it was held sufficient (*r*).

If the matter to be performed by the defendant depend on some *other event*, it seems proper not merely to assign the breach in the terms of the contract, but first to aver that such event took place (*s*); as in debt on a bond, conditioned that a collector of poor rates should render an account of monies received, it should be averred that he did receive monies, and then that he did not render an account of such monies (*t*). So in assumpsit against a tenant for not managing a farm according to the custom of the country, although the Court held the declaration sufficient, without showing what the custom was, yet the Court considered it safer to state the custom affirmatively, and then the breach (*u*).

If the contract was in the *disjunctive*, the breach ought to be assigned that the defendant did not do one act or the other; as on a promise to deliver a horse by a particular day, *or* pay a sum of money (*x*); and if a covenant be "that the defendant and his executors and assigns should repair," a breach for not repairing ought not to be in the conjunctive (*y*). But in assigning the breach of a covenant or contract to pay or "*cause to be paid*" a sum of money (*z*), it is sufficient to say that the defendant did not pay, omitting the disjunctive words, for he who causes to pay pays (*a*); and a breach that the defendant did not pay several persons is sufficient, without adding the words, or either of them (*b*). So where there are several defendants, an averment

[*367] that "they have not paid," is sufficient, for payment by one is payment *by all. In *scire facias* on a *recognizance* of bail, conditioned that if J. B. and G. H. be condemned, they shall pay or render; after an allegation that J. B. was condemned, it is not sufficient to aver that J. B. *and* G. H. did not pay or render, without adding "or either of them," for though *payment* by one would be a payment by both, yet a *render* of one is not a render of both, and, consistently with the allegation, B., against whom only judgment was, might have rendered, which would have been sufficient to discharge the recognizance (*c*). A distinction has been taken between a contract to perform a thing *to* a man or his assigns, and *by* a man or his assigns; and that if a thing be to be done *by* a man or his assigns, the breach must be in the disjunctive, that it was done by him or his assigns; but that where a thing is to be done *to* a man or his assigns, it is sufficient to assign for breach that it was done to him (*d*); but there appears to be no foundation for this distinction; and where the action is between the original parties to the contract, as no assignment will be presumed, it will be sufficient to state that the defendant did not perform the act to the plaintiff, without mentioning the assignee or

(*q*) 1 Sid. 178; 2 Rol. 738, l. 15. Indeed a breach in the very words of the contract, stating that the defendant did not guarantee, would be *untechnical* and repugnant.

(*r*) 1 Stra. 581.

(*s*) 6 Taunt. 45, *acc.*; 1 Price, 169, *semb. contra.*

(*t*) *Id. ibid.*

(*u*) Earl Falmouth *v.* Thomas, 1 Crom. & Mees. 110, 111.

(*x*) 1 Sid. 440, 447; Hardr. 320; Com. Dig. Pleader, C.; 1 Stra. 231.

(*y*) Cro. Eliz. 348; 1 Stra. 228.

(*z*) As to the words, "or any part thereof," 7 D. & R. 249.

(*a*) 1 Stra. 231; 1 Saund. 235, n. 6.

(*b*) *Id.*; but see 4 M. & Sel. 33.

(*c*) 4 M. & Sel. 33.

(*d*) 1 Salk. 139; 5 Mod. 133.

5thly. The cause of action.

1. In assumpsit.

5. The *Breach of Contract.*

heir (*e*); but if the action be by or against the assignee, heir, or executor, the breach should then be in the disjunctive (663); and a declaration by husband and wife, or by an administrator, merely stating that the defendant did not pay before the marriage, or that he did not pay since the death, would be bad on demurrer, though aided by verdict (*f*).

If the breach *vary* from the *sense and substance* of the contract, and be either more limited or larger than the covenant, it will be insufficient (*g*) (664): as in covenant to repair a fence, except on the west side thereof, a breach that the defendant did not repair the fence, without showing that the want of repair was in other parts of the fence than on the west, is bad on demurrer, though aided by verdict (*h*). But it is essential, where an exception or proviso is introduced into or referred to by the obligatory clause of an instrument, &c. upon which the defendant is charged (*i*), to negative the exception, &c. restrictive of his liability, in averring *the breach; otherwise the declaration will, it seems, be bad after verdict (*k*). So, if the covenant were for quiet enjoyment, without *lawful* disturbance, a breach merely stating that the plaintiff was disturbed is insufficient, for it should be that he was *legitimo modo* disturbed in the words of the covenant, or otherwise the plaintiff should show by whom he was disturbed, and how (*l*) (665). So, where the declaration is upon a covenant for good title, it should be shown that the person evicting had a lawful title (666) before or at the time of the date of the grant to the plaintiff, and an averment that he had a lawful title without this qualification, is too general and bad after verdict, for it will be intended that the title of the person entering is derived from the plaintiff himself. But it seems that the plaintiff is under no necessity of setting out the title of the person who entered upon him, because he is a stranger to it, it being considered sufficient to allege generally that he had a lawful title before or at the time of the lease or conveyance to the plaintiff (*m*) (667). [*368]

On the other hand it is injudicious unnecessarily to *narrow* the breach. Thus, where the breach of covenant was assigned that the defendant had not used a farm in an husband-like manner, "*but on the contrary* had committed *waste*;" it was held that the plaintiff could not give evidence of the defendant's using the farm in an unhusband-like manner, if such misconduct did not amount to *waste*, though on the former words of the breach such evidence would have been admissible (*n*). The safest course is to state a breach first

(*e*) 1 Stra. 228.

(*f*) 1 Ld. Raym. 284; 1 Vent. 119; 2 Rich. C. P. 293.

(*g*) Sir T. Jones, 125; 4 M. & Sel. 36; but see 3 M. & Sel. 152.

(*h*) Com. Dig. Pleader, C. 47.

(*i*) See *ante*, 255, 339.

(*k*) 1 T. R. 141.

(*l*) 2 Saund. 181 a; Com. Dig. Pleader, C. 47, 49.

(*m*) 2 Saund. 181, n. 10; Com. Dig. Pleader, C. 47, 49. And see *post*, vol. ii. as to actions for not having good title, and how to state the breach, and M'Clel. R. 647.

(*n*) 3 T. R. 307, 637; 5 Taunt. 95, *per* Chambre, J. *Query*, if the breach had been laid under a *videlicet*, 5 Taunt. 95; *ante*, 348; and see Earl Falmouth *v.* Thomas, 1 Crom. & M. 89; 3 Tyr. 38, 41, 50, S. C.

(663) Sed vide Duboise's Ex'rs *v.* Van Orden, 6 Johns. Rep. 105.

(664) { Pomeroy *v.* Bruce, 13 Serg. & Rawle, 186, where the breach stated was broader than the covenant. }

(665) Vide Greenby *v.* Wilcocks, 2 Johns. Rep. 1. { Wait *v.* Maxwell, 4 Pick. Rep. 88. 2 Gill &. Johns. 441. }

(666) Vide Folliard *v.* Wallace, 2 Johns. Rep. 395.

(667) Id. ibid. { Milner *v.* Horton, 1 M'Clell. & Young's Rep. 647. }

IV. ITS PARTS, &c.

5thly. The cause of action.

1. In assumpsit.

5. The *Breach of Contract.*

in the words of the contract, and then to superadd that the defendant disregarding did so and so, showing any particular breaches not narrowing or prejudicing the previous general breach, so that the plaintiff retains the advantage of both; and no inconvenience can result to the plaintiff from laying the breach as extensively as the contract, for the plaintiff may recover though he only prove a part of the breach as laid (*o*). In assigning the breach of a covenant not to release a debt, or not to assign without license, it must be averred that the release or alienation were without license, though the burthen of proof of license would still be affirmatively on the defendant (*p*).

[* 369] *The breach in general should be *certain* and express, and a general statement, "that the defendant *has not performed* (*non performavit*) his agreement or promise, is bad on demurrer, though aided by verdict (*q*) (668). A distinction has been taken with regard to the *degree of requisite certainty* between an action on a bond conditioned for the performance of covenants, and an action of covenant (*r*); however, no such distinction now prevails (*s*). Where to debt on bond conditioned that one B. R. should account for and pay over to the plaintiffs as treasurers of a charity, such voluntary contributions as he should collect for the use of the charity, the defendants pleaded general performance; and the plaintiffs *replied*, that B. R. had received "divers large sums amounting to a large sum, viz. £100, from divers persons for divers voluntary contributions," for the use of the said charity, which he had not accounted for or paid over, &c., it was held on special demurrer that the replication was sufficiently certain (*t*)(669); for it is a general rule in pleading, that where the specification of every particular would tend to great prolixity, a more concise manner of pleading it may be admitted (*u*); and especially where the breach lies more in the defendant's than the plaintiff's knowledge less particularity is required (*x*)(670).

Several Breaches.

Two breaches of the *same* specific stipulation cannot well be assigned in one count (*y*); for this would clearly amount to *duplicity* (671), which, as we have already seen (*z*), is a fault in every stage of pleading. The exception introduced by *statute* as regards *declarations* is confined to debt on bond conditioned for the performance of covenants, &c.: in this case several

(*o*) 5 Taunt. 27; 6 East, 437; 4 M. & Sel. 349; *ante*, 347, 348.

(*p*) Sir T. Jones, 229; Skin. 120; Vin. Ab. Covenant, L. a. 43.

(*q*) *Ante*, 365, note (i); Com. Dig. Pleader, C. 48; Skin. 344; 4 Mod. 185; 3 Lev. 319; 7 Price, 550.

(*r*) 1 Salk. 139; 1 Lev. 94.

(*s*) See 1 B. & P. 642; 1 Crom. & M. 89; 3 Tyr. 38, 41, S. C.

(*t*) 8 T. R. 463; 1 B. & P. 640; 8 East, 85; and see 1 Price, 109; 6 Taunt. 45, 47; 7 B. & C. 812; 1 M. & R. 497, S. C.

(*u*) *Ante*, 270.

(*x*) 8 T. R. 462; 1 Lutw. 421; 8 East, 80; *ante*, 269.

(*y*) Com. Dig. Pleader, C. 33; *ante*, 259; 1 Crom. & M. 89; 3 Tyr. 38, 41.

(*z*) *Ante*, 260.

(668) Vide Smith *v.* Walker, 1 Wash. 135. In Syme *v.* Griffen, 4 Hen. & Mun. 277, it was held that a breach commencing with "whereas," and continuing by way of recital to the end, without any direct averment, was bad on general demurrer.

(669) Vide Hughes *v.* Smith, 5 Johns. Rep. 168. When the breach assigned was that the defendant as under sheriff had collected moneys to the amount of 1000 dollars, which he had refused to account for and pay, and it was held sufficient. Vide Postmaster-General U. S. *v.* Cochran, 2 Johns. Rep. 415, and cases cited ante, p. 365.

(670) Vide Wilcocks *v.* Nichols, 1 Price's Rep. 109.

(671) Vide Taft *v.* Brewster and others, 9 Johns. Rep. 325.

IV. ITS PARTS, &c. — 5thly. The cause of action. 1. In assumpsit. 5. The Breach of Contract.

breaches may be assigned in one count (a) (672). But at common law also, where the defendant's contract was general, and several distinct breaches thereof *can in fact be committed*, as if a tenant agree to observe the due course of husbandry, which is obviously an engagement capable of embracing numerous acts of good husbandry, and extending over the whole tenancy, the declaration *may then state several breaches*, as different violations of the rules of good husbandry (b)(673); and the Reg. Gen. Hil. T. 4 W. 4, though it forbids several counts on the same cause of action, permits *several breaches*.

In point of form it has been usual in *assumpsit* to introduce the statement of the breach, with the allegation that the defendant "contriving and fraudulently intending craftily and *subtly to deceive and defraud the plaintiff, neglected and refused, &c." But this introduction is unnecessary; the gist of the action of assumpsit being the injury sustained by the plaintiff from the breach of promise, without regard to the defendant's intention or fraud (c). And in declarations against a peer the imputation of fraud was always to be omitted (d). And the form of breach prescribed by Trin. T. 1 W. 4, is a sufficient model, and obviously intended that in future pleadings such useless verbiage should be omitted (e). [*370]

The *omission* of a breach cannot be aided or cured even by verdict (f). But the *insufficiency* of the breach will in general be aided by a verdict, by the common law intendment that it is not to be presumed that either the judge would direct the jury to give, or that the jury would have given the verdict without sufficient proof of the breach of contract (g)(674). Therefore, where in an action against husband and wife on the covenont of the wife whilst sole to perform an award, it appeared that the award was made *after* the marriage, which was a legal revocation of the arbitrator's authority, and consequently the breach was improperly assigned in the non-performance of such award, it was decided that the plaintiff was entitled to recover; because it appeared that the feme had broken her covenant by the very act of marriage, which, though a different breach to that assigned, was sufficient after verdict to support the declaration (h). And where in an action on a replevin bond, the breach prominently laid and intended to be charged, but which was defective, was the non-return of the distress, the Court held after verdict that the declaration

(a) *Ante*, 261.

(b) 4 East, 154; *post*, vol. ii.; see the form by a landlord against a tenant, 2 Chitty on Pleading, 6th edit. 191.

(c) 6 East, 443; Gilb. Hist. C. B. 65.

(d) Imp. K. B. 6th edit. 526.

(e) See *post*, vol. ii.

(f) Hob. 198, 233.

(g) Sir T. Jones, 125; 1 Salk. 140; 4 Mod. 189 b; Skin. 344; 5 East, 270, 271; Com. Dig. Pleader, C. 48; 1 Saund. 228, n. 1. Bad breach when not cured by pleading over, 7 Price, 550.

(h) 5 East, 270, 271.

(672) Taft *v.* Brewster, 9 Johns. Rep. 334. *Et Vide* Postmaster-General U. S. *v.* Cochran, 2 Johns. Rep. 415. Munro *v* Allaire, 2 Caines' Rep. 323.

(673) { The following paragraphs immediately follow in the text of the fourth edition —"Where several breaches of the condition of a bond are assigned under the statute, it is usual to allege that they are assigned by virtue or in pursuance of the statute, but this seems unnecessary, the statute being a public law, and the assignment of several breaches a matter of right without the leave of the court." The note to which contains a reference to the following authorities—Com. Dig. title Pleader, 2 V. 2.—1 Hen. Bla 375, 278.—1 Wils. 219.—Cowp. 500, 501.—Andr. 108. 13 East, 3. Mr. Dunlap has added in support of the text a reference to Munro *v.* Allaire, 2 Caines' Rep. 328.

(674) { Weigley's Adm. *v.* Weir, 7 Serg. & Rawle, 310. } Vide Thomas *v.* Roosa, 7 Johns. Rep. 461.

IV. ITS PARTS, &c. — 5thly. The cause of action. 1. In assumpsit. 5. The *Breach of Contract.*

might be upheld in regard to a breach by not prosecuting the replevin suit with effect; which, though not expressly declared upon, was to be collected from the declaration (*i*). We have however seen that in some instances a defective statement of a breach, as of a covenant for quiet enjoyment, will be fatal even after verdict (*k*)(675). And if one of two breaches, or part of a breach, be improperly assigned, leaving a sufficient breach to support the count, the defendant cannot demur to the whole (*l*): although if in such case the defendant plead, and general *damages be given upon the whole declaration, the judgment might be arrested (*m*)(676).

[*371]

A very sensible author has observed that since the Reg. Gen. Hil. T. 2 W. 4, has subjected the unsuccessful party to the costs thereof, it is advisable when there has been a *part payment* or *part performance*, expressly to admit the same on the face of the declaration, and thereby deprive the defendant of all pretence for pleading such part payment or performance (*n*).

6. The Damages.

Whenever there has been a breach of contract, the plaintiff must necessarily be entitled to *some Damages*, and, however difficult it may be to ascertain the amount, the Court must give judgment for such damages, in all personal actions (*o*). The damages, however, must be proximate and not remote or depending upon a contingency, and therefore in an action for not replacing stock (*p*), it will be of no avail to state in the declaration that the plaintiff was prevented from completing an advantageous contract he had entered into (*q*). Such *damages* as may be presumed *necessarily* to result from the breach of contract, need not be stated with any great particularity in the declaration (677). Therefore, in an action for not accepting goods sold to the defendant, damages resulting from a fall of the market price may be recovered under a special count, with a general allegation of loss of profit, without averring that the value of the goods was less at the time the contract was broken than when it was made (*r*). But in other cases it is necessary to state the damage arising from the breach of contract specially and circumstantially in order to apprize the defendant of the facts intended to be proved, or

(*i*) 5 B. & C. 284, 306; 8 D. & R. 72, S. C.

(*k*) 2 Saund. 181, n. 10. And see 1 Sid. 440; 6 Taunt 140; 1 Marsh. 495; *ante*, 366, 368. *Sed quære.*

(*l*) 5 B. & Ald. 712; 1 D. & R. 361, S. C.; see 1 Saund. 285; 3 T. R. 374; 5 B. & Ald. 652; 1 D. & R. 282, S. C.; 6 East, 333; 11 *Id.* 565; 8 B. & C. 70.

(*m*) 6 M. & Sel. 9; 2 Saund. 171 a, note. How corrected, &c. *id.*

(*n*) Bosanquet's Rules, 50, note 48; and *post*, vol. ii., where see forms.

(*o*) 1 Dow's Rep. 207.

(*p*) As to the damages in this action, 3 Taunt 257; 7 *Id.* 14.

(*q*) *Per Cur.* in Parkins and Howard, K. B. Trinity Term, 1817. What are not damages recoverable, see 8 East, 3; 1 Campb. 187; 5 Taunt. 534. In an action for breach of a warranty, plaintiff may recover costs paid by him to a third person to whom he warranted; 2 Marsh. 431; 7 Taunt. 153; and see Holt's N. P. C. 43; 5 Taunt. 247; 3 B. & P. 351.

(*r*) 9 B. & C. 145, 152.

(675) Where it appeared from the plaintiff's own showing, that the breach alleged could not have taken place before the action was brought, it was held bad after verdict. Gordon *v.* Kennedy, 2 Binn. 287.

(676) { As to the proper mode of pleading where some of the breaches of covenant are not well assigned, Wait *v.* Maxwell, 4 Pick. Rep. 87. }

(677) The damages sustained are matter of evidence, and need not be alleged, nor are they scarcely ever stated, but in a general manner. Barruso *v.* Madan, 2 Johns. Rep. 149.

5thly. The cause of action.

1. In assumpsit.

6. The Damages.

the plaintiff will not be permitted to give evidence of such damage on the trial (*s*)(678). And where the plaintiff seeks to recover special damage in regard to the non-completion by third persons of contracts the plaintiff had made with them, the names of such third persons should be stated (*t*). In some cases, where the plaintiff seeks to recover *damages*, he must declare specially, though he might have recovered the principal part of his demand under a common count: thus, in an action against the vendor of an estate, for not making a good title to or conveying the same, only the deposit money *can [*372] be recovered under the count for money had and received, and if the purchaser proceed for interest and expenses, he must declare specially, stating such expenses and the loss arising from the not having the use of the deposit money, &c. (*u*). And where a sum is named as a *penalty* (*x*), the plaintiff may proceed for general damages, and may recover them beyond the amount of the penalty (*y*). The damages should be stated according to the facts of the case and evidence, but no inconvenience will arise from the statement of the damage or injury being larger than the proof (679): thus, in a declaration on a policy of insurance stating a total loss, a partial loss may be recovered (*z*). Where it is positively and expressly averred in the declaration that the plaintiff has sustained damages from a cause *subsequent* to the commencement of the action, or previous to the plaintiff's having any right of action, and the jury give entire damages, judgment would be arrested (680); but where the cause of action is properly laid, and the other matter either comes under a *scilicet*, or is void, insensible, or impossible, and therefore it cannot be intended that the jury ever had it under their consideration, the plaintiff will be entitled to his judgment (*a*)(681). The jury cannot give more damages than are laid at the end of the declaration (*b*). And if they should do so, the surplus should be *remitted* before judgment has been entered. If the plaintiff have merely *incurred liability* to pay costs without having actually *paid* the amount, the declaration should be framed accordingly (*c*), and even noting and postages on a bill must be declared for specially or cannot be recovered (*d*).

(*s*) As to damages in general, see Vin. Ab. Damages, and Sayer's Law of Damages; Chit. jun. Contr. 336, 340, &c.; and see *post* as to the statement of damages in actions for *torts*.

(*t*) See 1 Saund. 243 c, note 5; 11 Price, 19.

(*u*) See 4 Esp. Rep. 223; 1 B. & P. 306; 2 Bla. Rep. 1078; *post*, vol. ii.; 13 East, 98; 2 Bing. 4.

(*x*) As to the distinction between a *penalty* and liquidated damages, see 6 Bing. 141; Chit. jun. Contr. 336.

(*y*) 13 East, 343; 1 Holt, N. P. Rep. 44; 6 B. & C. 224; 9 D. & R. 369, S. C.

(*z*) 2 Burr. 904; 1 Bla. Rep. 198; Marshall on Insurance, 629; Sayer on Damages, 45; Tidd, 9th edit. 871.

(*a*) 2 Saund. 171 b.

(*b*) Tidd, 9th edit. 896.

(*c*) Pritchett *v.* Boevey, 3 Tyr. 949.

(*d*) 2 Crom. & J. 408.

(678) {Dartnall *v.* Howard, 6 Dowl. & Ryl. 442.}

(679) Where the plaintiff claims more damages than on the face of his declaration appear to be due, it will not vitiate, especially after verdict, for the amount of the damages being ascertained by the jury, it is to be presumed they were assessed according to the proof. Executors of Van Rensselaer *v.* Executors of Platner, 2 Johns. Cas. 18.

(680) Vide Gordon *v.* Kennedy, 2 Binn. 287.

(681) Shaw *v.* Wile, 2 Rawle, 280.

IV. ITS PARTS, &c. — 5thly. The cause of action. 1. In assumpsit. The *Common Counts* in Assumpsit.

The *Common* Counts in *Assumpsit* are frequently sufficient without any special count; and even where the declaration contains a special count it is in general advisable to insert one or more of the common counts. Although the pleading rules, Hil. T. 4 W. 4, now prohibit the use of *more than one count on the same cause* of action, excepting that a count upon *an action stated is always admissible* in addition to another count whether special or common, but which still in prudence, as regards costs under Reg. Gen. Hil. Term, 2 W. 4, should never in practice be added, unless there be adequate ground for expecting to prove it. Though it is a rule that when there was an *express* contract the plaintiff cannot resort to an *implied one* (*e*)(682), yet he may in many cases recover on the *common count*, though there was a special agreement, provided it has been executed (683) or completely performed (*f*). A common count used sometimes to save a verdict where the evidence varied from the special count; thus, if the plaintiff declared specially, [*373] *as having built a house according to an agreement, if he failed to prove that he had built it pursuant to agreement, he might still in some cases recover on the common count for the work and labor actually done (*g*)(684). And where a bill of exchange, or promissory note, upon an improper stamp, had been taken in payment of a debt, the plaintiff was at liberty to resort to the common counts appropriate to the original debt (*h*)(685), and which additional counts

(*e*) 2 T. R. 105, 640; 3 East, 80, 85; 6 T. R. 325; 1 Stra. 648; 3 B. & P. 247.

(*f*) See *post*, 381 to 383, and exceptions there stated.

(*g*) See *post*, 382, 383.

(*h*) 1 East, 59; Chit. on Bills, 7th edit. 363 to 366; Phillips on Ev. 5th ed. vol. i. 509.

---

(682) Vide Richardson *v.* Smith, 8 Johns. Rep. 439. Burlingame *v.* Burlingame, 7 Cow. Rep. 93, 94.

(683) *Indebitatus assumpsit* will lie to recover the stipulated price due on a special contract, not under seal, where the contract has been completely executed; and it is not in such case necessary to declare upon a special agreement. Bank of Columbia *v.* Patterson's Adm'r, 7 Cranch, 299. Felton *v.* Dickinson, 10 Mass. Rep. 287. {Sheldon *v.* Cox, 5 Dowl. & Ryl. 277.} 9 Pet. U. S. S. C. R. 541.

(684) Where a party declares on a special contract, seeking to recover thereon, but fails in his right so to do altogether, he may recover on a general count, if the case be such that, supposing there had been no special contract, he might still have recovered for money paid, or for work and labor done. Cooke *v.* Munstone, 1 New Rep. 355. Tuttle *v.* Mayo, 7 Johns. Rep. 132. Linningdale *v.* Livingston, 10 Johns. Rep. 136. Keyes *v.* Stone, 5 Mass. Rep. 391. {Or for use and occupation, (Perrine *v.* Hankinson, 6 Halst. Rep. 181,) or for money had and received, Schillinger *v.* M'Cann, 6 Greenl. Rep. 364.} And although the plaintiff may resort to the general counts without having attempted to prove the special agreement, yet in no case can he recover on the general counts where the special agreement continues in force. Linningdale *v.* Livingston, 10 Johns. Rep. 37. Raymond and others *v.* Bearnard, 12 Johns. Rep. 274. Wilt and Green *v.* Ogden, 13 Johns. Rep. 56. Jennings *v.* Camp, Id. 94. {And where the plaintiff declares specially, he cannot recover on evidence applicable to the general counts only; such evidence being objected to. Davenport *v.* Wheeler, 7 Cow. Rep. 231.} Hollinshead *v.* Mactier, 13 Wend. R. 276. In that case, it was *held*, that if a man contract to work by special contract, so far as the work was done according to the contract, the compensation should be according to the contract; but as to that part where the contract was abandoned, he should recover according to the work done as if no contract had existed. The same rule was adopted by the court in Dubois *v.* The Delaware and Hudson Canal Company, 4 Wend. R. 289.

(685) {So in an action against two defendants upon a promissory note, if the note be void as to *one* of them, the plaintiff may recover against both on the general counts. Wilkins *v.* Reed et al., 6 Greenl. Rep. 220. A promissory note is evidence under the money counts in an action by the *indorsee* against the maker. New Jersey B. Co. *v.* Myers, 7 Halst. Rep. 141.}

IV. ITS PARTS, &c.

5thly. The cause of action.

1. In assumpsit.

Common counts.

is now expressly permitted to be added in an action on a bill or note. He may also ground his claim upon such counts, if applicable to the original consideration, in cases where the bill or note has been dishonored, and the defendant, when necessary, has had due notice (*i*). But where the demand is founded upon a written agreement, which ought to be, but is not, stamped, the plaintiff was not permitted to resort to an implied contract, in order to avoid the production of such express agreement (*k*): and if there were no privity between the parties independently of the special contract, the common counts would be of no avail (*l*). The entering of a *nolle prosequi* to a special count would not bar a recovery upon a common count for the same demand (*m*).

The great variety of common counts.

Common counts in an action of assumpsit are founded on express or implied promises (*n*) to pay *money* in consideration of a *precedent* and *existing* debt. In general the consideration must have been *executed*, not executory, and the plaintiff must have been entitled to payment in *money*, not merely to the delivery of a bill of exchange or of goods, unless the time for payment of such bill has expired (*o*).

When applicable in general.

It has been said that the common counts will not lie in any case in which debt is not sustainable (*p*). This may be true as a general rule, but there are some exceptions. Thus debt on simple contract could not be maintained against an executor, to recover a debt which was due from the testator (*q*), (but which was altered by 3 & 4 W. 4, c. 42, s. 14); nor can debt be brought for the recovery of part of a debt payable by instalments, the whole of which have not [*374] *accrued due (*r*); but assumpsit may be maintained in both these cases. It has also been doubted whether debt lies on a *quantum meruit* count (*s*); but certainly such count was sufficient when framed in assumpsit.

The common counts were of four descriptions. 1st, The *indebitatus* count; 2dly, The *quantum meruit.* 3dly, The *quantum valebant;* and 4thly, The *account stated.*

Indebitatus assumpsit count.

The *indebitatus assumpsit* count (*t*), since the Reg. Gen. Hil. Term, 4 W. 4, states, that "the defendant, on," &c., (a named day before the issuing of the first process in the action (*u*), was *indebted* to the plaintiff in a named sum of money, for, &c. [as for use and occupation, or for real property sold (*x*), or goods sold, or for personal services, or for money lent, paid, or had and received, or for interest, or for some other pre-existing debt on simple contract,

(*i*) See *post*, 381.

(*k*) 2 B. & P. 118; 3 Esp. Rep. 213; 1 N. R. 273; 2 Marsh. 273. If the plaintiff can make out his case without producing a written agreement, or disclosing that there is one, the defendant cannot produce it unless it be stamped, see 6 Bing. 332.

(*l*) 3 M. & Sel. 173; 3 Campb. 101; Chitty on Bills, 7th ed. 364; Phillips on Ev. 5th ed. vol. ii. 109.

(*m*) M. & M. 311.

(*n*) There is not, *in pleading*, any difference between an express and implied promise.

(*o*) *Post*, 380.

(*p*) Salk. 23; 2 Lev. 153; Carth. 276.

(*q*) *Ante*, 128.

(*r*) *Id.*

(*s*) *Ante*, 123, note (*q*).

(*t*) See the form, vol. ii.

(*u*) The exact time is not material in the common counts; but when there is a special count on a bill of exchange, &c. preceding the common counts, it is usual and proper in the first common count to lay the day after the bill was due, or other special cause of action was complete; and in the subsequent counts and in the breach to refer to the *last-mentioned* day; 1 Wils. 33. *Venue* is now to be omitted in the body of the count, but *time* is still to be repeated to every traversable allegation, or the defendant may demur specially.

(*x*) *Sed quære* if it lies for real property sold, &c. See *post*, 376, 377.

IV. ITS PARTS, &c.

incurred at the defendant's *request*;] and that being so *indebted*, the defendant, in consideration thereof, then *promised* the plaintiff to pay him the said sum of money on request."

5thly. The cause of action.

1. In assumpsit.

Common counts.

Quantum meruit count.

The *quantum meruit* count, instead of stating that the defendant was indebted to the plaintiff in a certain sum of money for work, &c., as in the *indebitatus* count, was in this form, "and whereas also, afterwards, to wit, on, &c. in consideration that the plaintiff, at the request of the defendant, had done work, &c. (*stating the subject matter of the debt according to the fact, and usually as in the indebitatus count*), he the defendant promised the plaintiff to pay him so *much money as he therefore *reasonably deserved* to have;" and the count [*375] then averred, "that the plaintiff therefore deserved to have a named sum, whereof the defendant afterwards, to wit, on, &c. aforesaid, had notice."

Quantum valebant count.

The *quantum valebant* count was in general confined to the case of a claim for *goods sold*, and instead of the *quantum meruit*, stated that "the defendant promised to pay so much as the goods were *reasonably worth*;" and concluded with a corresponding averment that they were reasonably worth a named sum, and that the defendant had notice thereof. In other respects this count was similar to the *quantum meruit*. Although Sir William Blackstone mentions the *quantum meruit* and *valebant* as useful, and as then to have been supposed *necessary variations* to avoid the risk of the plaintiff's not being able to prove an agreement to pay a *fixed price*; the opinion of the profession has long been that such *quantum meruit* and *quantum valebant* counts are wholly unnecessary, and that under an *indebitatus count* in assumpsit or debt the plaintiff may recover, although there be no evidence of a fixed price, and Reg. Gen. Trin. T. 1 W. 4, prescribing forms of *indebitatus* counts may be considered as virtually abolishing the *quantum meruit* and *valebant* counts.

Account stated.

The *account stated* still retains its original utility. It alleges, that "the defendant on a named day, month, and year, accounted with the plaintiff of and concerning divers sums of money before then due from the defendant to the plaintiff, and then in arrear and unpaid, and that upon such accounting, the defendant was *then* found to be in arrear to the plaintiff in a named sum, and that being so found in arrear and indebted, the defendant, in consideration thereof, then promised the plaintiff to pay him the same on request."

The *Common Breach* before Reg. Gen. Trin. T. 1 W. 4.

Upon these counts the *Common Breach* was, "Yet the said defendant, not regarding his said promises and undertakings, but contriving and craftily and subtly intending to deceive and defraud the said plaintiff in that respect (y), hath not (although often requested so to do) (z) as yet paid to the said plaintiff the same sums of money or any part thereof, but hath wholly neglected and refused, and still neglects and refuses so to do, to the plaintiff's damage of £—— (a named sum), and thereupon he brings his suit, &c." This breach necessarily varied in actions by and against surviving partners, husband and wife, executors and assignees, &c.(a). The form prescribed by Reg. Gen. Trin. T. 1 W. 4, is even still more concise (a).

(y) *Ante*, 369, 370.

(z) The printed forms generally contain a special request, but this is unnecessary, 1 Wils. 33; *ante*, 364.

(a) See *ante*, 365; *post*, 392; and *post*, vol. ii.

IV. ITS PARTS, &c.

5thly. The cause of action.

1. In assumpsit.

Common counts.

Of the application of these counts in general.

Formerly these general counts for work, goods sold, &c. were not in use; and Lord Holt is stated to have said that he was a bold man who first ventured on them; but they are now much more frequent than the special counts, when the action is for a *Common debt* or for any *money* demand (*b*). It is not sufficient to state merely that the defendant "was indebted to the plaintiff in a certain sum, and promised payment;" it must be shown *what* was the *cause* or *subject-matter* or nature of the debt; as that it was for work done, or for goods sold, &c. (*c*). But it is not necessary to state the particular description of the work done (686), or goods sold, &c.; for the only reason why the plaintiff is bound to show in what respect the defendant is indebted, *is, that it may appear to the Court that it is not a debt of record or specialty (687), recoverable in another form of action, but only on simple contract; and any general words by which that may appear are sufficient (*d*). Unnecessary statements, such as the local situation of the premises, in a count for use and occupation, should be avoided, as a variance might be fatal (*e*). Several distinct debts due in respect of different contracts not under seal, of the same or a different nature, as demands for work, and debts for goods, monies lent, &c. might always be included in one count of this description; and the plaintiff would succeed *pro tanto* though he only prove one of such contracts (*f*)(688). If one of the subject-matters be improperly stated, the defendant should not demur to the whole, but only to the *insufficient part* of the count or declaration (*g*). Under an *indebitatus* count the plaintiff may recover what may be due to him, although no specific price or sum was agreed upon; and therefore it has been observed that the *quantum meruit* and *quantum valebant* counts are in no case necessary, and should in many cases be omitted, to prevent unnecessary prolixity and expense (*h*). It was laid down, that under a *quantum meruit* count the plaintiff could not recover, if the goods were sold, or the work done, &c. at a certain price (*i*).

[*376]

In each of these counts, upon an executed consideration, except that for money had and received, and the account stated, it is necessary to allege that the consideration of the debt was performed at the defendant's *request*, though such request might in some cases be implied in evidence (*k*); and it must also be stated that the defendant promised to pay a specific sum, or so much as the plaintiff reasonably deserved, averring in the latter case what sum is due (*l*). As the common counts are so useful in practice, it may be advisable concisely to consider the *particular applicability of each*.

(*b*) 2 Stra. 933; 1 Saund. 269, n. 2; 2 *Id*. 122, n. 2; 350, n. 2; 374, n. 1; Fitzg. 302; Com. Dig. Assumpsit, H. 3; 13 East, 107.

(*c*) 2 Saund. 350, n. 2; Cro. Jac. 245.

(*d*) Skin. 217, 218; 2 Saund. 350, note 2, 373; 2 Lev. 153; Carth. 276; 2 Wils. 20; 1 Mod. 8; 1 Sid. 425; Bac. Ab. Assumpsit, F.; Ld. Raym. 1429; By special custom even the cause of the debt need not be shown. 2 Stra. 720; 1 Saund. 68, note 2.

(*e*) See *ante*, 307.

(*f*) 2 Saund. 122, note 2; see the form, *post*, vol. ii.

(*g*) 2 Cromp. & Jerv. 418; 2 Tyr. 468.

(*h*) 2 Saund. 122 a, note 2.

(*i*) 1 Stra. 648; but see 6 Taunt. 108.

(*k*) *Post*, 350; 1 Saund. 264, note 1; 5 M. & Sel. 446; 9 B. & C. 543; 4 M. & R. 448, S. C.

(*l*) 2 B. & P. 321.

(686) Lewis, Ex., *v*. Culbertson, Adm. 11 Serg. & Rawle, 49. Vide Edwards *v*. Nicholls, 3 Day's Rep. 16.

(687) 11 Serg. & Rawle, 49.

(688) Acc. Bailey and Bogert *v*. Freeman, 4 Johns. Rep. 280. But a demand *for certain lands sold and conveyed*, is too general, and cannot be joined with the common counts, Nelson *v*. Swan, 13 Johns. Rep. 483.

IV. ITS PARTS, &c. — 5thly. The cause of action. 1. In assumpsit. Common counts as to *Real Property* in particular.

The common counts relating to *Real* Property most frequently occur where the action is brought, either for the recovery of a sum agreed to be paid as the *price* or value of an estate *sold* by the plaintiff to the defendant, or to recover the *rent* of premises holden by the defendant as the plaintiff's tenant.

[*377] *If in the deed by which a freehold or leasehold estate is conveyed, there be an express or even implied *covenant* by the defendant to pay the price, of course assumpsit cannot be maintained (*m*). It has been doubted whether the *indebitatus* counts can be sustained for the price, although the estate has been conveyed, and there be no covenant to pay the money (*n*). But these counts are sometimes adopted in practice (*o*), and may probably be sustained (*p*); although it may be judicious to insert a special count (689). If the objection to the common counts be founded on the notion that the demand *savors of the realty* (*q*), it might be better to declare in debt.

The common count for *use and occupation* is of very frequent occurrence (*r*). It is founded on the statute (*s*), which enacts, "that it shall be lawful for a landlord, where the agreement is not by deed, to recover a reasonable satisfaction for the tenements held or occupied by the defendant, in an action on the case for the use and occupation of the premises;" and if in evidence on the trial, any parol demise or agreement, not by deed, whereon a certain rent is reserved, shall appear, the plaintiff shall not be nonsuited, but may use the same as an evidence of the *quantum* of the damages to be recovered (690).

The object of the statute was the removal of the difficulties experienced by landlords in declaring at common law for rent; the statute remedies this evil but does not entitle a landlord to recover rent in cases in which he had not at common law a right to recover it. It affects only the mode of declaring (*t*).

The effect of the statute is to render the common counts sufficient, although there be a formal written agreement in all cases in which there is not a demise by a lease or instrument [*378] **under seal*. In the latter event covenant or debt is the remedy (*u*). These counts may be supported, if there has been a legal tenancy, although the defendant, to whom the premises were let, did not himself occupy them, but let them to another (*x*); or allowed his servants only to in-

(*m*) *Ante*, 117.

(*n*) *Per* Lord Ellenborough, James *v.* Shore, Sittings at Westminster after Michaelmas Term, 1816; Stirling, attorney for the plaintiff; and see 3 Tyr. 963.

(*o*) See the forms, *post*, vol. ii.

(*p*) See observations in Halles *v.* Rundel, 3 Tyr. 963,

(*q*) See *ante*, 264.

(*r*) See in general Chit. jun. on Contracts, 106; 5 B. & C. 333; 8 D. & R. 67, S. C.; *post*, vol. ii. As to the stamp, if there be a written agreement, 3 Esp. 213; 1 New Rep. 272. Parol agreement to take on terms of a former written agreement, the latter must be stamped, 7 B. & C. 625. In general it suffices if plaintiff can make out his case without disclosing that there was a written agreement. In such case defendant cannot produce it unstamped, 6 Bing. 332.

(*s*) 11 Geo. 2, c. 19.

(*t*) 5 B. & C. 332, 333; 8 D. & R. 67, S. C.

(*u*) *Ante*, 264.

(*x*) 8 T. R. 327.

---

(689) { But see 11 Serg. & Rawle, 50, that the declaration ought to lay the contract strictly. And see Weigley's Adm. *v.* Weir, 7 Serg. & Rawle, 311, and Codman *v.* Jenkins, 14 Mass. Rep. 93. }

(690) In Egler *v.* Marsden, 5 Taunt. 25, which was an action of debt for use and occupation, Gibbs, J., says:—"This is not an action on the statute 11 G. 2. c. 19. The meaning of that act was, you may bring an action upon the case, and although it shall appear that there was a contract under a certain rent reserved, yet you shall recover a reasonable compensation for the use of that which you go for."

habit them (y); or although the premises were destroyed by fire, or otherwise rendered uninhabitable (z) before the rent accrued due. It suffices if there were a constructive legal possession, provided there were a holding or tenancy (a). And it lies against a tenant who holds over after the expiration of a demise by deed, to recover rent accruing due after the end of the term (b). But a husband cannot be sued alone for use and occupation of premises by his wife *dum sola*; as it cannot be said that she occupied at *his* request (c). The mode of describing the premises is pointed out in the second volume (d).

IV. ITS PARTS, &c. 5thly. The cause of action. 1. In assumpsit. Common counts.

The *indebitatus* count may also be brought to recover a remuneration for the use and occupation or enjoyment of a *fishery*, a *water-course* (e), or a pew, and for tolls, &c. (f) or other incorporeal hereditament; although in strictness, as being *incorporeal* matters, there could not have been a sufficient demise or contract otherwise than by instrument under seal (g). So indebitatus assumpsit lies for the antecedent use and occupation of a messuage, together with incorporeal hereditaments, or of the latter alone, although a special count, setting out a contract for letting the same, would be void, because not under seal, and therefore invalid at common law (g).

Goods sold.

The common *indebitatus* count, to recover the price or value of *goods sold* by the plaintiff to the defendant, states, that the defendant was indebted to the plaintiff for goods, chattels, and effects, by the plaintiff *sold* and *delivered* to the defendant "at his request."

It seems that the price or value of *fixtures* and perhaps *crops* sold, may be recovered under the common count, provided there be inserted therein, besides the word *goods*, the terms *fixtures*, *crops*, *chattels*, effects, &c. (h). It is, however, usual to frame the count differently where the price of fixtures (i) or crops (k)(691) is sought to be recovered. If *cattle* were *sold, that word [*379] should be introduced into the count, though the word *chattels*, which includes animate as well as inanimate things, would suffice. Where an agreement between an out-going and incoming tenant was that the latter should buy the hay, &c. of the former upon the farm, allowing the expense of repairing the fences, &c. and that the value of the hay, &c. and of the repairs, should be ascertained by third persons, it was held that the balance settled to be due, that is, the value of the goods, allowing for the repairs, was recoverable upon the count for goods sold (l). Upon one count for goods sold in the common form, the prices of different goods sold at different times may be recovered (m).

(y) 16 East, 33.
(z) 4 Taunt. 45; that is, if the landlord were not bound to render them habitable, see R. & M. 268; 4 C. & P. 65.
(a) 6 Bing. 206.
(b) 4 B. & C. 8; 6 D. & R. 42, S. C.
(c) 1 B. & B. 50.
(d) The situation of the premises need not be shown. As to a variance in stating the parish, *id.* and *ante*, 307.
(e) 4 B. & C. 8; 6 D. & R. 42, S. C.
(f) See the forms and notes, *post*, vol. ii., and *ante*, 114.
(g) Bird *v.* Higginson, 1 Harrison, Rep. 61.
(h) *Post*, vol. ii. See 7 Taunt. 188; 2 Marsh. 495, S. C. The word "*effects*," includes "fixtures," 1 B. & Ald. 206; and see 1 Crom. M. & Ros. 266, as to "*goods*, and *chattels*, *fixtures*, and *effects*," and import of those terms.
(i) *Id.* 43, 187, 185.
(k) *Id.* 44, 185. See 1 B. & P. 397; 3 B. & C. 357, 364; 4 M. & R. 455, S. C.; 9 *Id.* 561; 4 M. & R. 224, S. C.
(l) 12 East, 1.
(m) 2 Saund. 121, 2, note.

(691) See Lewis ex. *v.* Culbertson, Adm. 11 Serg. & Rawle. 48.

IV. ITS PARTS, &c.

5thly. The cause of action.

1. In assumpsit.

Common counts.

In order to maintain a count for goods sold and *delivered*, it is essential that the goods should have been *delivered* to the defendant or his agent, or to a third person, not credited by the plaintiff, at the request of the defendant, or that something equivalent to a delivery should have occurred (*n*), and if *not delivered*, but still on premises of vendor, though packed in boxes furnished by purchaser, plaintiff would be nonsuited, for he should have declared for goods bargained and sold or specially (*o*). Where a contract was made between A. and B., whereby A., having a quantity of apples, agreed to sell his cider to B. at a certain price per hogshead, to be delivered at T. at a future time, the cider to be manufactured by B. on A.'s premises; and A. delivered a quantity of the apples to B.'s servant; but before the time for delivery of the cider it was seised and sold by the excise, in consequence of *B.'s default*; it was held, that as the delivery at T. thus became impossible, B. was liable on a count for goods sold and delivered (*p*). This count may also, it seems, be maintained where goods have been delivered on the terms of sale or return, and have not been returned within the time agreed upon, or within a reasonable time (*q*). But where A. sold beer to B. in casks, giving him notice that unless he returned the casks in a fortnight, he would be considered as the purchaser, it was held by Lord Ellenborough that B. was not liable for the value of the casks retained by him, as for goods sold and delivered, but only upon a special count (*r*). Where a defendant by fraud induced the plaintiff to sell goods to a third person, who was insolvent, and then got the goods into his own possession, it was held that he was liable upon the common count (*s*). But not if by fraud a sale on credit was obtained, and which credit has not expired (*t*).

[*380] *The common counts for goods sold *cannot be maintained*, and it is necessary to declare *specially* in the *following cases*.

1st. If the sale were not to the defendant, but to a third person, and the defendant were only liable collaterally, that is, in case the vendee did not pay (*u*). And in an action against a broker acting under a *del credere* commission, to recover the price of goods sold by the defendant for the plaintiff, the declaration should, it seems, be special (*x*).

2dly. In general, these counts cannot be supported where the plaintiff was to be paid for his goods, not in money, but by the delivery of other goods (*y*). But if the contract by for payment partly in money and partly in goods, and the latter are delivered, and the plaintiff seek to recover the money only, he may declare on the common count for goods sold (*z*). And where the defendant agreed to sell to the plaintiff three unfinished houses, and to finish them within a certain time, and the plaintiff agreed to pay for them by the de-

(*n*) 8 T. R. 328; 2 B. & Ald. 755.
(*o*) Boulter *v.* Arnott, 3 Tyrw. 267.
(*p*) 5 B. & C. 628; 8 D. & R. 403, S. C.
(*q*) Peake, R. 56; see 5 B. & C. 628; 2 Bing. 4.
(*r*) 2 Stark. R. 39.
(*s*) 3 Taunt. 274; 1 B. & C. 101; see 3 Campb. 352, and 4 Taunt. 189, that in general there must be a contract of sale. An executor when liable upon an *implied* contract to pay funeral expenses in burying the testator, 3 Y. & J. 28.
(*t*) Ferguson *v.* Carrington, 9 B. & Cres. 59; Strutt *v.* Smith, 1 Cr. M. & R. 312.
(*u*) 1 Saund. 211 a, b; 2 Campb. 215.
(*x*) 7 Taunt. 558; 1 Moore, 279, S. C. See the special count and note, *post*, vol. ii. An *indebitatus* count by the broker for his *del credere* commission is good, at least after verdict, 8 Taunt. 371; 2 Moore, 420, S. C.
(*y*) 1 Hen. Bla. 287; Holt, C. N. P. 179; 3 Campb. 352.
(*z*) 3 B. & C. 420; 5 D. & R. 277, S. C.

livery of cement at a fixed price, higher than the usual price, and the defendant did not complete the houses within the time, and afterwards said he had sold one of them to a third person, Lord Tenterden, C. J. said, that the common count for cement sold and delivered was sufficient, the defendant having broken the contract and disabled himself from completing it; but he directed the jury to give only the ordinary price of cement (*a*).

IV. ITS PARTS, &c. — 5thly. The cause of action. 1. In assumpsit. Common counts.

3dly. If the goods were to be paid for by a bill of exchange or promissory note, and the defendant has refused to give it, the declaration should be special (*b*): but after the expiration of the credit, or time during which the instrument was to be current, the common count will be sufficient (*c*). And this count is sustainable, although the bill had been given, and the plaintiff had indorsed it away and was not the holder at the time the action was commenced, *provided the defendant dishonored the bill, and the plaintiff had it in his possession at the time of the trial (*d*). If the bill be lost before or after it is due, no action for the price of the goods sold can in general be maintained (*e*). [*381]

4thly. If there have been no delivery of the goods, even the count for goods *bargained and sold* (not showing a delivery) cannot be maintained, unless it appear that there has been a complete sale and the *property* in the goods had become *vested* in the defendant by virtue of such sale, and an actual *acceptance* of the commodity by the defendant (*f*). The property is not vested in the defendant if the goods, being part of a larger quantity, are not separated therefrom, and something remains to be done to distinguish them and ascertain their quantity, or number, or the amount of the price. This rule has been already considered (*g*). Nor is the property in goods vested in the defendant so as to render the common count for goods bargained and sold sufficient, unless the article has been finished, and specifically appropriated and set apart for the purchaser, and he has assented thereto (*h*). In these cases the declaration should be framed specially on the contract for not accepting the goods, or for refusing to complete the bargain (*i*); and in general, where the contract is not substantially for the sale of goods, but is rather for work and materials, the value even of the latter is not recoverable upon a count for goods sold (*k*); and the plaintiff should declare for work and materials. Where the defendant refuses to receive goods which he has agreed to purchase, the special counts are not only necessary, if the property in some identical goods has not become vested in the defendant, but are at all events essential in order to recover any expenses which may have been incurred (*l*) (692). The counts for goods "bargained and sold" should also be

(*a*) Baines *v.* Payne, December, 1828, sittings at Westminster.

(*b*) Strut *v.* Smith, 1 Cr. M. & R. 312.

(*c*) 4 East, 147; 9 *Id.* 498; 13 *Id.* 98; 2 Marsh. 495.

(*d*) 1 M. & P. 223; 4 Bing. 454, S. C.

(*e*) 3 B. & B. 295; 7 B. & C. 90; 9 D. & R. 860, S. C.

(*f*) 5 B. & C. 857, 865; 8 D. & R. 693, S. C.; 6 *Id.* 388; 9 D. & R. 298, S. C.; 8 B. & C. 277; 2 M. & R. 292, S. C.

(*g*) *Ante*, 169.

(*h*) *Id.* and *supra*, n. (*f*); 8 B. & C. 277; 2 M. & R. 292, S. C.; 9 B. & C. 73.

(*i*) Atkinson *v.* Bell, 8 B. & Cres. 277; cited in Laythorp *v.* Bryant, 1 Bing. N. C. 430.

(*k*) 1 Marsh. 581; 6 Taunt. 324, S. C.; 9 B. & C. 73.

(*l*) 6 Taunt. 162; 1 Marsh. 162.

(692) {Outwater *v.* Dodge, 7 Cow. Rep. 85.}

IV. ITS PARTS, &c. added (*m*). *Indebitatus* assumpsit lies to recover "goods and chattels," naming the value, due "for tolls," &c. (*n*).

5thly. The cause of action. 1. In assumpsit. Work and labor and materials.

With respect to debts for *work and labor* or other personal services, and for *materials* used in performing the work, it is a rule that if *preceded* by the defendant's request, then however special the agreement was, *yet if it were not under seal (*o*), and the terms of it have been performed on the plaintiff's part, and the remuneration was to be in money (*p*), it is not necessary to declare specially, and the common *indebitatus* count is sufficient (*q*) (693). Where [*382] the demand is for wages, fees, or work and labor in particular professions, &c. it is usual to insert a count stating concisely the nature of the service (*r*). But the common count for work and labor is in general sufficient, without showing what sort or manner of work was performed (*s*). An attorney, under the count for work and *materials*, may recover a bill for his fees, and for the price or value of parchment vellum (*t*). A farrier, &c. may recover for attendance and medicine, &c. under the common counts for work and *materials* (*u*)(694). And these counts are sufficient though the demand be for building a house (*x*) under a special written agreement and specifications; although as formerly remarked (*y*), it might, in some cases, be advisable to insert a special count. The common count will suffice to support a claim for the services of the plaintiff's apprentice or servant whilst improperly harbored by the defendant (*z*). But under a common count for work and labor and materials done at defendant's request, an outgoing tenant cannot recover the usual remuneration payable to him as outgoing tenant for work and materials on the farm, but must declare *specially* (*a*).

As before observed, where there is an entire contract for work and labor and materials, the value of the latter is not recoverable under a count for goods sold (*b*); nor can the count for work and labor and materials be

(*m*) 1 East, 194. Distinction between this count and the count for goods sold and delivered, 1 Ves. jun. 609. No arrest for goods "bargained and sold," 12 East, 399.

(*n*) 6 B. & C. 385; 9 D. & R. 452, S. C.

(*o*) *Ante*, 117.

(*p*) *Ante*, 380.

(*q*) Fitz. 302; 1 Wils. 117; Bul. N. P. 139; 1 New Rep. 331, 335; 6 East, 569; 2 Marsh. 273; Holt, N. P. Rep. 236; 4 Campb. 186. An *indebitatus* count by a factor to recover a *del credere* commission has been held good after verdict, 2 Moore. 420; 8 Taunt. 371, S. C.; 14 East, 578. Extra freight is recoverable under this count, Holt, C. N. P. 392; and see 1 Stark. 275; 3 Bing. 635.

(*r*) See the forms, *post*, vol. ii. As to contracts for work or services in general, see *id.* 9 B. & C. 92. As to the recovery of wages *pro rata*, see Turner *v.* Robinson, 5 B. & Adol. 789; Fawcett *v.* Cash, *id.* 904.

(*s*) 2 Saund. 350, n. 2.

(*t*) Fisher *v.* Snow, 3 Dowl. 26.

(*u*) 3 Campb. 37; 1 New Rep. 289; 2 Wils. 20.

(*x*) 8 B. & C. 283; 2 M. & R. 390.

(*y*) *Ante*, 372, 373.

(*z*) 3 M. & Sel. 191.

(*a*) Leeds *v.* Burrows, 12 East, 1.

(*b*) *Ante*, 381.

(693) Acc. Felton *v.* Dickinson, 10 Mass. Rep. 287, 289.

(694) To this case the reporter has added the following note:—"I have thought that this decision may be of some use to the profession, although the point was not before thought doubtful among gentlemen at the bar. But in cases of this sort it is not unusual to find at least *ten* counts in the declaration—*two* for work and labor as a farrier, &c.—*two* for work and labor generally—*two* for goods sold and delivered—and the *four money counts*, not omitting *money lent*, which can never be of any use except where there is a specific contract of the lending and borrowing of money.—If a declaration contains *general* and *special* counts for work and labor, the court on motion will order one set to be struck out as superfluous." Meeke *v.* Oxlade, 1 New Rep. 289.

maintained, unless the article agreed for has been finished, and appropriated to the defendant by his consent, and he has acquired a property in the specific chattel (c).

5thly. The cause of action.

1. In assumpsit.

Common counts.

To support this count the plaintiff must in general have *completely performed* the work contracted for (d); and if not, it is necessary to declare specially if the defendant has wrongfully prevented the plaintiff from performing the work; as where a seaman, who was to have wages for his service during an entire voyage, but pending it was left behind on shore, and prevented from serving the whole voyage, a special count was held to be necessary (e). But if a party be hired as a *servant, or clerk, &c. for a specific period, and in part perform the service, and be ready to complete it, but be prevented from so doing by the employer, the wages or salary for the *whole* term may be recovered upon the *indebitatus* count for work done (f). And in some cases, although the original agreement has not been strictly performed by the plaintiff, yet if the defendant avail himself of, and derive a benefit from, the work done, he will be liable upon a common count (g)(695). But where A. undertook for a specific sum to repair and make perfect a given article then in a damaged state, and did repair it in part but did not make it perfect, it was held that he could not recover for the work actually done and materials found, the contract being entire, and the defendant having never been discharged from his obligation to complete it (h). And if a person hired for a period be guilty of misconduct which justifies his employer in discharging him at once, it seems that he cannot recover even for his antecedent services (i).

[*383]

Money lent.

Money lent to the defendant himself on his own credit, may be recovered under the common count for *money lent*, though delivered to another person at his request (j); and sometimes the plaintiff may recover on the common count for money lent, though a special agreement has been entered into and rescinded (k); but the transaction must have been substantially a loan by the *plaintiff* (l). And if money be lent to a third person at the defendant's request, and both be liable to repay the money, the one on the loan, and the other in respect of his collateral engagement, which must be in writing, the count against the latter must be special (m)(696). A declaration against a husband "for money lent to his *wife* at his request" is maintainable (n); *aliter*, if it be alleged that the

(c) *Ante*, 169, 381.

(d) 2 Saund. 350, note 2.

(e) 2 East, 145; 8 *Id.* 300; 6 T. R. 320; see 5 Bing. 135; 2 Chit. R. 320.

(f) 4 Campb. 375; 1 Stark. 198, S. C.; 5 Bing. 132, 135; but see 3 Car. & P. 350.

(g) See Bul. N. P. 139. *Per* Sir J. Mansfield, C. J., 1 New Rep. 355; 4 Taunt. 748. As to *extra* work, where there is a special contract, Peake's Rep. 103; Holt, N. P. Rep. 236; 1 Stark. R. 275; 3 Taunt. 52; 4 *Id.* 745, 748; 3 Bing. 635.

(h) 9 B. & C. 92; 3 Taunt. 52.

(i) 4 C. & P. 208; see 3 Esp. Rep. 235; 2 Stark. Rep. 256; 4 Campb. 375; 6 Car. & P. 15; 1 Chitty's Gen. Prac. 75 to 84.

(j) 8 T. R. 328. As to evidence of loan, see 2 Phil. on Evid. 5th edit. 127; 7 B. & C. 416; 1 M. & R. 125, S. C. When this count lies by the assignee of a bankrupt, *ante*, 28; or an executor, *ante*, 21, 22.

(k) 7 Bing. 266.

(l) 5 Bar. & Ald. 389.

(m) 1 Saund. 211 b; 1 Salk. 23; 3 *Id.* 15; Carth. 446; 2 Wils. 141; 3 *Id.* 388; 2 Bla. R. 872; 2 T. R. 81; 1 Moore, 126.

(n) 3 Wils. 388.

(695) See, however, Stark v. Parker, Moses v. Stevens, 2 Pick. Rep. 267, 332.

(696) See the circumstances under which the plaintiff was held to be entitled to recover as for money lent, under the common count. Perkins' Adm. v. Dunlap, 5 Greenl. Rep 268.

IV. ITS PARTS, &c.

money was lent *to* her at *her* request, or was lent to *both* at their joint solicitation (*o*).

5thly. The cause of action.

1. In assumpsit.

*In general there must have been a *loan* of *money* to support this count; but an advance in foreign coin is sufficient (*p*). The transfer of *stock* into the defendant's name could not, it seems, be regarded as a loan of *money* to him (*q*)(697).

Common counts.

Money paid.

To sustain the common count for *money paid* by the plaintiff for the defendant's use and at his request, it is essential, *first*, that the plaintiff should have *paid money* for the defendant (*r*)(698), and *secondly*, that such payment should have been made at the defendant's *request* express or implied (*s*).

Where the sum which the plaintiff has paid is in the nature of *unliquidated damages or costs*, and cannot be considered as strictly paid in discharge of a *debt* due from the defendant (*t*); or where the plaintiff has not actually made a payment in money, but has merely been obliged to give security (699), or his goods have been sold under a distress for the defendant's debt, the declaration must be special for not indemnifying, &c. (*u*); and where an accommodation acceptor has been obliged to pay *costs* as well as a principal sum, he must, to

(*o*) 4 Price, 48.

(*p*) 1 Marsh. 33; 5 Taunt. 228.

(*q*) 5 Burr. 2589; 1 East, 1; 2 B. & Ald. 51. The exchange of securities, notes, &c. when is not a loan, 8 Taunt. 208.

(*r*) 10 Bar. & Cres. 346; 2 B. & Ald. 51; 3 East, 159; and see 7 Bing. 246; 6 Bar. & Cres. 439; 9 D. & R. 603, S. C.

(*s*) 1 Saund. 264, note 1.

(*t*) 5 Esp. Rep. 3; 4 *Id.* 223; 8 T. Rep. 610; 1 T. R. 269; 7 *Id.* 204, 576; 1 Wils. 188; 4 Campb. 91; Jones *v.* Farney, 1 M'Clel. 25; but see 4 Taunt. 189. Where the plaintiff purchased stock, which the defendant agreed to transfer on a given day, and in consequence of a rise the loss on the sale amounted to £15, which the defendant refused to pay; and the plaintiff afterwards paid that sum to another broker, by whom the transfer was made; it was held, the plaintiff could not recover in an action for money paid, but that he should have declared specially on the contract with the defendant, as his claim was in the nature of unliquidated damages, 2 Moore, 255. A debt paid by a sheriff's officer on an attachment against the sheriff, by defendant's default, is recoverable by the former under the common count, 1 M. & M. 347.

(*u*) 3 East, 169; 11 *Id.* 52; 2 B. & Ald. 51; 2 Esp. 611; see 6 Bing. 229, 305. When parties who have paid money for another should join or sever in suing the latter, *ante*, 8, 9; 7 B. & C. 217.

(697) A note payable in specific articles is admissible in evidence under the money counts, Crandall *v.* Bradley, 7 Wend. R. 311. Smith *v.* Smith, 2 Johns. Rep. 235, and Pierce *v.* Crafts, 12 Johns. Rep. 90.

(698) An accommodation indorser, a *surety*, paid part of a judgment obtained against him and gave his note for the balance which was accepted by the plaintiff in satisfaction of the judgment; *held*, that the cause of action was perfect, and he might recover against his principal as for money paid, and the statute of limitations begins to run. Rodman *v.* Hedden, 10 Wend. R. 498. But as a general rule, a surety cannot recover until he has actually paid the money; and a judgment recovered against, or an imprisonment on the execution are not considered equivalent to payment so as to entitle the surety to call upon his principal for money paid to his use. But where there is an express to indemnify and save harmless, and the surety is sued and charged in execution, the promise to indemnify is broken, and the surety may maintain an action without the debt having been paid; but he can only recover a compensation for the injury. ib. Powell *v.* Smith, 8 Johns. Rep. 249. If the surety give his negotiable note for the debt, which is received in satisfaction, it is equivalent to the payment of money. *ib.* Cumming *v.* Hackley, 8 Johns. Rep. 206. Wetherby *v.* Manns, 11 Johns. Rep. 518. 3 Mass. Rep. 403. If a surety pays money for his principal by virtue of a legal obligation, it gives the surety an immediate cause of action against his principal. Butler *v.* Wright, 20 Johns. Rep. 367. 2 Wend. R. 409.

(699) Acc. Cumming *v.* Hackley, 8 Johns. Rep. 202. Unless that security be a negotiable instrument. Id. 3 Johns. Rep. 206. Barclay *v.* Gooch, 2 Esp. Rep. 571. { Morrison *v.* Berkey, 7 Serg. & Rawle, 246. Kearney *v.* Tanner, 17 Serg. & Rawle, 94. }

IV. ITS PARTS, &c. — 5thly. The cause of action. 1. In assumpsit. Common counts.

recover the former, declare specially (v). Nor is there any ground for supporting the count for money paid unless the payment were made at the express or implied (700) request of the defendant, and the request must be always averred (x). It is clear, however, that if money be paid by a person in consequence of a legal liability to which he is subject, but from which a third person ought to have relieved him by himself paying the amount, a *request* will be *implied*. Thus an executor who has paid the legacy duty may sue the legatee for the amount, as money paid for his use at his request (y).

Money had and received (z).

The form of this count is extremely simple, it merely stating that the defendant is indebted to the plaintiff in a *certain sum "for *money had and received* by the *defendant* to and for the use of the *plaintiff*."

[*385]

It must in general appear that the defendant has received *money* (701), and not merely money's worth, as stock (a)(702), or goods (b); but if the defendant received *foreign* money he would be chargeable upon this count (c). The common count will also suffice against a party who received country bank notes expressly as money (d)(703). Where *goods* or other property improperly received by the defendant are saleable, it may, under circumstances, and after a lapse of time, be *presumed* against him that he has sold the property and received money in return (e)(704), provided there be reasonable evidence that the defendant converted the same into *money* (e), but not otherwise (f). And the assignees of a bankrupt may maintain an action for money had and

(v) Seaver v. Seaver, 6 Car. & P. 673; see form 2 Chitty on Pleading, 5th ed. 316, 6th ed. 197.

(x) 1 T. R. 20; Exall v. Partridge, 8 T. R. 310; 1 Saund. 264, note 1. The *request* must be stated, even in an affidavit to hold to bail for money paid; 9 B. & C. 543. When the request will be *implied*, 1 B. & B. 391; 6 B. & C. 439; 2 B. & B. 59.

(y) Foster v. Ley, 2 Bing. N. C. 269.

(z) See as to this action in general, and the various instances in which it is maintainable, a leading case, Marsh v. Keating, 1 Bing. N. C. 198. It is an action in which the plaintiff should show a just as well as legal right to the money. See 2 Burr. 1012; Dougl. 138; 2 T. R. 370; 6 *Id.* 631; 3 B. & P. 169. It lies for the recovery of money paid under a *mistake of facts*; or obtained by *fraud* or *compulsion*; or *extorted* by unjust and oppressive proceedings; or deposited upon an illegal wager, or an illegal contract, not executed; or paid upon a consideration which has wholly failed, &c. See *id.* But it does not lie to recover back money recovered by a judgment, 7 T. R. 269; 2 Campb. 63; 2 T. R. 645; 4 Campb. 58.

(a) 5 Burr. 2589; 1 East, 1.

(b) 11 East, 52.

(c) 5 Taunt. 228; 1 Marsh. 33, S. C.; but see M'Lachlan v. Evans, 1 Younge & Jerv. 380.

(d) 13 East, 20; 4 Bing. 178.

(e) Dougl. 138; 4 T. R. 687; 3 B. & P. 559; 1 Hen. Bla. 239.

(f) M'Lachlan v. Evans, 1 Younge & Jerv. 380.

---

(700) {See Hassinger v. Solms, 5 Serg. & Rawle, 4. Packard v. Lienow, 12 Mass. Rep. 11. Ott v. Chapline, 3 Harr. & M'Hen. 323. Smith v. Sayward, 5 Greenl. Rep. 504.} Vide Riggs v. Lindsay, 7 Cranch, 500.

(701) {Ralston v. Bell, 2 Dall. 242.} Vide Beardsley v. Root, 11 Johns. Rep. 464. Hantz v. Sealy, 6 Binn. 409. {When the defendant, though he does not receive *money*, receives that for which he engages to pay *money* to a *third* person, such third person may sustain the action. Dearborn v. Parks, 5 Greenl. Rep. 81.}

(702) Morrison v. Berkey, 7 Serg. & Rawle, 246. Nor for the value of foreign securities, unless it appear that the defendant had an opportunity of converting such securities into money. M'Lachlan v. Evans, 1 Younge & Jervis, 380. Nor is evidence that a horse was received by the defendant in exchange for a patent right, admissible either under a count for money paid, laid out and expended, or for money had and received. Dobler v. Fisher, 14 Serg. & Rawle, 179.

(703) Vide etiam Beardsley v. Root, 11 Johns. Rep. 464.

(704) See Witherup v. Hill, 9 Serg. & Rawle, 11. See also Chapman v. Shaw, 5 Greenl. Rep. 59. Hess v. Fox, 10 Wend. R. 436.

IV. ITS PARTS, &c. — 5thly. The cause of action. 1. In assumpsit. Common counts.

received against a party who took the *goods* of the bankrupt in execution after an act of bankruptcy, and then purchased the goods from the sheriff under a bill of sale, although no money actually passed (*g*). So, where an insurance broker received credit in account with an underwriter for a loss upon a policy, it was held that his principal might maintain money *had and received* against him, to recover the amount, although he had not actually received it (*h*).

This count is sustainable in some cases where *money* has been received *tortiously*, or even by the intervention of *forgery* (*i*), without any color of contract (705), or under pretence of a contract not performed by the defendant, although, in general, a party is not at liberty to declare in an action in form *ex contractu*, where there has been no contract express or implied (*k*). Thus, assignees of a bankrupt may declare for money had and received against a creditor who has levied his debt by *fi. fa.* after the act of bankruptcy (*l*); and they may declare in assumpsit for money received from the bankrupt by way [*386] of fraudulent preference anterior to the act of *bankruptcy (*m*). And where the defendant having fraudulently induced the plaintiff to sell goods to A., who could not pay for them, and on the nominal resale of those goods by A., in which the defendant was really concerned, having obtained himself the money paid on such resale, it was held that the plaintiff might, in an action for money had and received, recover of the defendant the value of the goods unpaid for by A. (*n*)(706). And where a landlord refused to allow property-tax and distrained and sold for the whole of the rent, and the tenant did not forego his right to deduct the tax, the tenant recovered the amount of the tax in assumpsit for money had and received (*o*). But this rule is so far qualified, that the Courts will not allow a colorable title to land, &c. to be tried under this form of action, but the plaintiff must declare in tort (*p*), even though the parties agree to waive the objection to the form of action (*q*)(707); and where there was no title, and a tenant having paid rent to A., was ejected at the suit of a third person, who afterwards recovered from him mesne profits for the period in respect of which he had paid rent to A.; it was held, in an action for money had and received, that the tenant might recover back that rent from A., he not

(*g*) 1 Stark. 134.

(*h*) 6 Taunt. 110; 3 Campb. 199.

(*i*) Marsh *v.* Keating, 1 Bing. N. C. 198; held, that a stockholder, whose stock has been sold without his knowledge under a forged power of attorney, may sustain an action for money had and received against the *innocent partners* of the forger, who received the proceeds of the sale.

(*k*) *Ante*, 122, 1 T. R. 36; 1 Taunt. 359.

(*l*) 2 Bla. Rep. 827; 3 Wils. 304; 2 T. R. 144; Bul. N. P. 131; 6 T. R. 695, 683; and see 1 B. & C. 418.

(*m*) 10 East, 378, 418, *ante*, 113, 114. Trover has been thought to be the proper remedy, 4 T. R. 211; 1 Bla. Rep. 194. The defendant's admission that he had received money from the bankrupt, upon his examination before the commissioners, when insufficient to fix him, 7 B. & C. 623; 1 M. & R. 518, S. C.

(*n*) 2 B. & B. 369; 5 Bing. 37.

(*o*) 1 M. & S 609; see 2 B & B. 59.

(*p*) Cowp. 419; 6 T. R. 298; Stra. 915; 2 Hen. Bla. 408.

(*q*) 9 East, 378, 351.

---

(705) Vide Ripley *v.* Gelston, 9 Johns. Rep. 201. Clinton *v.* Strong, Id. 370. Beardslee *v.* Richardson, 11 Wend. R. 25.

(706) To warrant a recovery back of money paid under a special contract, a strict performance must be shown by the plaintiff, unless the contract has been expressly rescinded, or impliedly so. Green *v.* Green, 9 Cowen, 46. Clark *v.* Smith, 14 Johns. Rep. 326.

(707) Baker *v.* Howell, 6 Serg. & Rawle, 481. Sadler *v.* Evans, Stapplefield *v.* Hugh, 4 Burr. 1985, 6. Clark *v.* Smith, 14 Johns. Rep. 326. Jennings *v.* Camp, 13 ib. 94.

having set up any title to the premises on the trial (r). But assumpsit for money had and received does not lie against a sheriff by a landlord, for neglecting to pay a year's rent before the removal of goods of the tenant taken in execution, according to the statute 8 Ann. c. 14, s. 1 (t).

IV. ITS PARTS, &c.

5thly. The cause of action.

1. In assumpsit. Common counts.

It seems that in general under *this count* the plaintiff must substantiate a claim to some particular or specific sum (u); but if he be legally and justly entitled to a certain sum received by the defendant, it is not material that the latter received it in an indirect and circuitous manner; thus, where the holder of a bill of exchange, who held it in trust for the plaintiff, sued the drawer, and pending that suit became bankrupt, and his assignees afterwards brought an action against the drawer in the bankrupt's name, in which action the sheriff having been guilty of an escape on mesne process, the assignees recovered against the sheriff the *amount of the bill as damages, it was held that such amount was recoverable by the plaintiff against the assignees as money had and received for the plaintiff's use (v). [*387]

In order to maintain money had and received, either the *money* or the *goods* for which the plaintiff claims the proceeds must originally, or at the time of the action brought, *have belonged to the plaintiff* (x). Therefore, if the sheriff, after having seized goods under a *fieri facias* at the suit of A., sell them, though irregularly, under another process at the suit and for the benefit of B., an action for money had and received cannot be supported by A. against the sheriff (y). *Mere possession* of the property, for the proceeds of which wrongfully taken by the defendant plaintiff proceeds, is sufficient against a wrongdoer (z); though a mere *seizure* is not sufficient to render the sheriff liable for money had and received (a). But if the *sale* be under the *plaintiff's* process he may maintain the common count against the sheriff (b), even it seems before the return of the process (c); but the action should not be brought until after a demand of the money has been made (d). In the case of bankruptcy, money had and received lies against the sheriff without actual notice (e).

In general, if money be delivered to a *servant* or clerk, or agent, to be paid over to a third person, being his principal, no action for money had and received, to recover it back, can be sustained against the former, although he still have the money in his hands, but the principal only, though insolvent, can be sued, (unless indeed the principal were a lunatic)(f), and there should be a privity of at least implied contract between the plaintiff and the defendant (f). But it lies against an agent of the plaintiff who has received money for a particular purpose, and who by want of due care lost it; and a special count for the negligence is not necessary (g).

(r) 10 Bar. & Cres. 234.
(t) 3 Campb. 260; 2 C. & P. 103, n.
(u) 3 B. & C. 626; 5 D. & R. 500, S. C.
(v) 1 M. & Sel. 714.
(x) *Per* Lord Ellenborough, C. J., 16 East, 274; 3 Bos. & Pul. 465; *post*, 390, n.
(y) 16 East, 254.
(z) 3 B. & Adol. 241.
(a) 16 East, 274.
(b) 3 Campb. 347; 1 B. & B. 370. See further as to this action against the sheriff, 6 B. & C. 739; 9 D. & R. 723, S. C.; 8 B. & C. 16th, 729; 2 M. & R. 68, S. C.; 3 M. & R. 411, S. C.
(c) 8 B. & C. 727; 3 M. & R. 418, S. C.
(d) 3 B. & Ald. 696; 1 B. & B. 380.
(e) 8 Bing. 43.
(f) Stephens v. Badcock, 3 B. & Adol. 354; and Stead v. Thornton, there cited; *infra*, note (k), *sed quære*.
(g) Barry v. Roberts, 1 Harr. & Woll. 242.

IV. ITS PARTS, &c. — 5thly. The cause of action. 1. In assumpsit. Common counts.

In general the *defendant*, or his *agent* or *partner* (*h*), must have received the money for the *plaintiff's use*, and if by mutual consent the money has been paid to a stakeholder in trust for the party entitled, the latter, if liable at all, should be made the defendant (*i*). And if a party receive money for a principal, and be merely the collector or bearer of the money, and *bona fide pay it over before* notice of the claim of the true owner, the action should be brought against the principal, not the servant (*k*). As a *chose in action* is not at law assignable (*l*), if A. receive money for B.'s use, the latter cannot assign the demand to C. so as to enable him in his own name to sue A.: but if in such case A. assent to the transfer, and promise C. to pay him the money, the action may be brought in the name of the latter against A. (*m*). Where [*388] *A. remitted to B. a bank bill, indorsed "pay to the order of B., under provision for my note in favor of C., payable at B.'s house, on, &c.," and B. received the proceeds of the bill, and refused to pay them over to C., it was decided that B. was not liable to C. as for money had and received, as B. had never assented to hold the bill or money to C.'s use (*n*).

This action is frequently brought to recover back a deposit, or money paid upon an agreement, which the defendant omits or refuses to perform. As a general rule, it lies to recover a deposit paid on the purchase of an estate, if the title be defective (*o*); or the vendor be not prepared to show his title on the day fixed for that purpose between the parties by their agreement (*p*); or if neither party be ready, and each make default in performing his part of the agreement (*q*). So money paid on account of the purchase of shares in an undertaking which has been abandoned, may be recovered back in this form of action (*r*). In these cases there is an entire failure of consideration. So where some act is to be done by each party under a special agreement, and the defendant by his neglect prevents the plaintiff from carrying the contract into execution, the latter may recover back money he has paid upon it, as money had and received to his use (*s*)(708). As where the plaintiff bought cordwood of the defendant, to be paid for on a certain day, and it was incumbent on the defendant to cut off the boughs and trunks, and then cord it, and for the plaintiff to re-cord it, but the defendant neglected to cut and cord the whole of it in time, it was held that the plaintiff not having received any part of the wood might recover back the money he had paid (*t*).

Assumpsit for money had and received lies for money paid under an *orig-*

(*h*) 4 M. & Sel. 475; 1 Bing. N. C. 198.
(*i*) 9 East, 378.
(*k*) See the cases, Chitty, jun. Contr. 196; 7 B & C. 101; 9 D. & R. 881, S. C.; 4 Taunt. 198.
(*l*) See *ante*, 16.
(*m*) See *ante*, 54; 3 T. R. 180; 8 B. & C. 395, 855; 14 East, 587, n. a. Effect of order on an agent holding money to pay the plaintiff a debt due to him from the principal, 14 East, 582; 7 Taunt. 339; 1 R. & M. 68; 1 Bing. 150; 7 Moore, 527; 8 *Id.* 10; Chit. jun. Contr. 184; 3 Price, 58; 3 B. & C. 842; 5 D. & R. 735. S. C.; 16 Ves. 443.
(*n*) Crompt. & Jerv. 83; *supra*, note (*m*).
(*o*) 2 Bla. Rep. 1078; 1 Esp. 268; 2 *Id.* 639; 4 *Id.* 221; 1 Stark. R. 65; 2 B. & Ald. 171.
(*p*) 4 Taunt. 334.
(*q*) 1 R. & M. 394.
(*r*) 3 Bar. & Cres. 814; 5 Dowl. & Ryl. 751; 4 Bing. 5.
(*s*) 7 T. R. 181; 2 You. & Jerv. 284.
(*t*) 7 T. R. 181.

(708) { Frost *v.* Clarkson, 7 Cow. Rep. 24. So where *inevitable* accident has prevented a party from fulfilling a contract, he may recover for the part performed, on an implied promise, upon a *quantum meruit* count. Willington *v.* West Boylston, 4 Pick. Rep. 101. }

inal ignorance or a *subsequent forgetfulness* of facts (*u*), but not if paid with knowledge of *fact* or means of knowledge readily accessible, though under an ignorance of *law* (*x*).

IV. ITS PARTS, &c.

5thly. The cause of action.

1. In assumpsit.

Common counts.

But the count for money had and received is not maintainable if a *contract has been in part performed*, and the plaintiff has derived some benefit, and by recovering a verdict the parties cannot be placed in the exact situation in which they originally were when the contract was entered into (*y*). Thus, where A. agreed in consideration of a premium to let a house to B., which A. was to repair and grant a lease of within ten days, but B. was to have immediate possession; and B. paid the premium and *took possession* and retained it after the ten days, although A. omitted to repair and grant the lease; it was held that B. *could not by quitting on account of A.'s default, recover [*389] back the premium in a count for money had and received, but was bound to declare specially for the breach of the agreement (*z*). So where a party sold a patent right, and the vendee paid the money and *used the patent right* and enjoyed some benefit *therefrom*, but it afterwards appeared that the patent was invalid, it was held that money had and received could not be sustained, a partial benefit having been received by the defendant (*a*). And upon the same principle, where the master and part-owner of a vessel agreed to purchase the moiety of his partner, and having paid the purchase-money and *received* the *title-deeds*, which he *deposited* as a security with a third person, and had the *entire possession* of the vessel given up to him, but his partner afterwards refused to execute a bill of sale or refund the money, it was decided that an action for money had and received was not sustainable (*b*). Where a special contract is still *open*, and has not been rescinded *by mutual consent*, it is necessary to declare specially: as if a horse, &c. be sold with a warranty of soundness, although it be unsound, and the purchaser *immediately* offer to return it, he cannot recover back the price on the count for money had and received (709), if the vendor refuse to receive back the horse; for the warranty can only be tried upon a special count (*c*)(710), unless there was an express stipulation to take back, or unless there was actual fraud (*d*); and in such case the count for money had and received is not maintainable, although upon the horse being tendered to the seller he stated that if the horse be unsound he will take it back and return the money; provided he denies the unsoundness, and does not take back the horse (*e*). If, however, either by virtue of an *express* stipulation in the original contract the plaintiff was in a certain event entitled to

(*u*) Lucas *v.* Worswick, 1 Mood. & Rob. 293.

(*x*) *Id. ibid.*; Bilbie *v.* Lumley, 2 East, 469; Milnes *v.* Ducan, 6 Bar. & Cres. 677; 9 D. & R. 735, S. C. *per* Bayley, J.

(*y*) 5 East, 449; 2 You. & Jerv. 278.

(*z*) 5 East, 449.

(*a*) 1 New Rep. 260.

(*b*) 2 You. & Jerv. 278.

(*c*) Doug. 23; 7 East, 274; 2 Campb. 416; 3 M. & Sel. 349, *per* Le Blanc, J. As to an action on a bill given for a horse warranted sound, 2 Taunt. 2; 14 East, 486; 1 Stark. R. 51; 3 *Id.* 175.

(*d*) 1 Crom. & M. 207.

(*e*) 7 East, 274.

(709) Assumpsit lies on a promise to refund the consideration money paid for lands sold, although there be a covenant of warranty, where the grantor expressly engaged to refund, upon being notified of the pendency of ejectment against his grantee; but in such case, the action must be on the special contract. Miller *v.* Watson, 4 Wend. R. 267.

(710) Thornton *v.* Wynn, 12 Wheat. 183. See Ashley *v.* Reeves, 2 M'Cord's Rep. 432.

IV. ITS PARTS, &c. — 5thly. The cause of action. — 1. In assumpsit. — Common counts.

rescind it, or it has been put an end to by the agreement of both parties, the common count may be supported to recover money paid on the contract (*f*)(711).

On a single count for money had and *received in the common form, various sums received at different times may be recovered (*g*).

The count must describe the money to have been received to the use of the person or persons who at the time of receipt of the money by the defendant was legally entitled to it. And in an action by a solvent partner and the assignees of another, if the money was received after the bankruptcy, the count must be for money received to the use of the solvent partner and the assignees as such (*h*); and in an action by an executor, if the money were not received until after the death of the testator, the plaintiff could not recover without a count for money received to his use *as executor* (*i*). Under the count for money had and received, only the sum received for the plaintiff's use is recoverable (712), and if the plaintiff seek to recover *interest* or *expenses incurred* (as in investigating a title to an estate in cases where the claim is for the deposit, &c.), other counts must be inserted accordingly (*j*); unless indeed as to *interest* since the 3 & 4 W. 4, c. 42, sect. 28 (*k*).

Interest.

The *indebitatus* count "for *interest* due upon the forbearance of monies due from the defendant to the plaintiff, and by the latter forborne to the former at his request, &c." is very frequently inserted in a declaration in *assumpsit*, especially in actions on bills of exchange and promissory notes. The rule was, that interest was not recoverable except on those instruments, and a very few other instances (*l*), unless there had been an express agreement to that effect; or unless such agreement could be collected from the usual course of dealing between the parties in former and similar occasions (*m*): even though the debt was due on a written agreement providing an express or contingent period for payment (*n*). Thus, in the absence of an agreement to pay interest, it was not recoverable for goods sold (*o*), work and labor (*p*), money lent (*q*), paid (*r*), had and received (*s*), or upon an account stated (*t*). And it

(*f*) 1 T. R. 133; 7 East, 275, 276; 1 C. & P. 18.

(*g*) 2 Saund. 118, n. 2.

(*h*) 3 Bos. & Pul. 465, *post*, vol. ii.

(*i*) M'Lachlan *v.* Evans, 1 You. & Jerv. 380; and see form in 2 Saund. 207, 208.

(*j*) 1 B. & P. 306; Bla. Rep. 1078; 4 Esp. 223; 2 Campb. 426; see 3 Taunt. 157.

(*k*) *Post.*

(*l*) As bonds, 7 T. R. 124; 15 East, 225; or money awarded to be paid on a named day, if demanded, &c., 3 Campb. 468. See in general Chit. jun. Contr. 195; *post*, vol. ii.

(*m*) 1 Campb. 50; 2 *Id.* 426; 1 B. & P. 307; 2 *Id.* 472; 9 B. & C. 381; 4 M. & R. 308; 1 East, 223; 4 C. & P. 124.

(*n*) 9 B. & C. 378; 4 M. & R. 305, S. C.

(*o*) 6 Esp. 45. Except where a bill was to have been given, 13 East, 98.

(*p*) 1 Hen. Bla. 305; 3 Wils. 205.

(*q*) 9 B. & C. 378; 4 M. & R. 305, S. C.

(*r*) 3 Stark. R. 132.

(*s*) 2 Campb. 426; 1 B. & P. 307. Not even in action against an auctioneer to recover deposit, see 8 Taunt. 45; 6 Bing. 134.

(*t*) 6 Esp. 45.

(711) Vide Gillet *v.* Maynard, 5 Johns. Rep. 85.

(712) Contra Pease *v.* Barber, 3 Caines' Rep. 266. In that case KENT, C. J., delivering the opinion of the court, says:—"The action for money had and received, is an equitable action, and the party must show that he has equity and conscience on his side. The rule in equity is to allow interest in many cases for money had and received. There may be cases in which the defendant ought to refund the principal merely, and there may be other cases in which he ought, *ex æquo et bono*, to refund the principal with interest. Each case will depend upon the justice and equity arising out of its peculiar circumstances, to be disclosed at the trial."

seems to have been a rule, that where the demand was of such a nature that the law did not imply a contract for interest, and none was agreed for, it should not be allowed merely because the debt had been wrongfully withheld after the creditor had repeatedly applied for payment (*u*)(713). This defect in the law encouraged the disposition to delay the payment of just debts and was therefore rectified by 3 & 4 W. 4, c. 42, sect. 28, which enacts, "That upon all debts or sums certain, payable at a certain time or otherwise, the jury on the trial of any issue, or on any inquisition of damages, may, if they shall think fit, *allow interest* to the creditor at a rate not exceeding the current rate of interest from the time when such debts or sums certain were payable, if such debts or sums be payable by virtue of some *written instrument* at a certain time, or if payable otherwise, then from the time when *demand of payment shall have been made in writing, so as such demand shall give notice to the debtor that interest will be claimed from the date of such demand until the term of payment* (*v*); provided that interest shall be payable in all cases in which it is now payable by law."

IV. ITS PARTS, &c.

5thly. The cause of action.

1. In assumpsit. Common counts.

Sect. 29 enacts, "That the jury, on the trial of any issue, or on any inquisition of damages, may, if they shall think fit, give damages in the nature of interest, over and above the value of the goods at the time of the conversion or seizure, in all actions of *trover or trespass de bonis asportatis*, and over and above the money recoverable in all actions on *policies of assurance* made after the passing of this act."

Sect. 30 enacts, "That if any person shall sue out any *writ of error* upon any judgment whatsoever given in any Court in any action personal, and the Court of error shall give judgment for the defendant thereon, then interest *shall be allowed* by the Court of error for such time as execution has been delayed by such writ of error, for the delaying thereof."

In general it was considered that the declaration should be *special* where *damages* for the loss of the use of money are sought to be recovered, and the claim is not *eo nomine* for interest as a debt. Upon a contract for the sale of goods to be paid for by a bill at a certain date, it was holden the price might bear interest from the day when the bill, if it had been given, would have been due, and that *the interest might be recovered as damages on a special count for the non-delivery or non-payment of the bill; and that if in such a case upon a general count for goods sold and delivered, the jury should give the price and interest as damages, the Court would not on that account set aside the verdict (*x*). So where the defendant, who had contracted for goods, was to return them in a year, or otherwise to pay for them *with interest*, and the declaration was only for goods sold, and interest on money forborne, the Court would not set aside the verdict, or reduce the damages, although the jury gave interest, which, in strictness, should have been [*391]

(*u*) 9 B. & C. 380; 4 M. & R. 308, S. C.; *sed vide* 3 Bing. 353; 9 Price, 134.

(*v*) And yet in Pierce *v.* Fothergill, 1 Hodges R. 251, it was held that the issuing a writ of summons is a sufficient demand to entitle the plaintiff to interest from that day.

(*x*) 3 Taunt. 157.

(713) Riley *v.* Seymour, 1 Wend. R. 143. 10 ib. 96.

IV. ITS PARTS, &c.

5thly. The cause of action.

1. In assumpsit.

Common counts.

Account stated.

claimed upon a special count (y). In each of these cases there was a just claim to interest in the shape of *damages* (z). The form of the count for interest will be found in the second volume (a). It may be advisable to insert it where interest may be recoverable; but since the statute 3 & 4 W. 4, c. 42, sect. 28, it may be recoverable in many cases without *expressly* declaring for interest, provided the damages at the conclusion be sufficient to *cover it*.

It is advisable in all declarations in assumpsit for the recovery of a money demand (excepting against an infant, who cannot in law state an account), to insert *a count on an account stated* (b). The acknowledgment by the defendant that a certain sum is due, creates an implied promise to pay the amount, and it is not necessary to set forth the *subject-matter* of the original debt (c)(714); nor is the amount of the sum alleged in the count to be due material (d)(715); nor is it necessary, in order to support this count, that the defendant's admission should relate to more than one item or transaction, or that there should have been cross dealings or accounts between the parties (e). The present rule is, that if a fixed and certain sum is admitted to be due to a plaintiff, for which an action would lie, that will be evidence to support a count upon an account stated (f). But an account stated is not proper to recover a *single sum* under an express contract, but lies only where an account has been stated with reference to *former* transactions (g). An attorney's bill cannot be recovered under this count without due proof of delivery of a signed bill (h). Where arbitrators award a sum of money to be due, it may be recovered under this count, unless the submission was by bond (i). But a party can only recover under this count when a certain and precise sum is admitted to be due (k); and an acknowledgment of a debt, but without naming or referring to a sum certain, does not enable a plaintiff to recover on this count even nominal damages (l): and where a debt is actually in exist-

(y) 2 Bing. 4.

(z) See *Id.* 6; and 12 East, 419.

(a) *Post*, vol. ii.

(b) 2 Mod. 44; 1 T. R. 42. What is evidence of an account stated, see 10 East, 104; 11 *Id.* 118, 124; 13 *Id.* 249; 2 B. & P. 363; 2 M. & Sel. 265; 16 East, 420; 3 Stark. R. 10; 1 R. & M. 239; 7 Bing. 104; Breckon *v.* Smith, 1 Adol. & Ell. 488. Admission of the receipt of money before commissioners of bankrupt on a compulsory examination, 7 B. & C. 623; 1 M. & R. 518, S. C. Not *conclusive* evidence, when, 1 T. R. 42; 4 B. & C. 281, 715; 1 Esp. 159; 6 *Id.* 24. As to stamp, 1 Bing. 134.

(c) 2 Mod. 44; 2 T. R. 480.

(d) 2 Saund. 122, n. 3; 1 Bla. Rep. 65; 1 Burr. 9.

(e) 13 East, 249; 5 M. & Sel. 65; 2 Saund. 122, n. 6, 5th ed.; 3 C. & P. 236.

(f) *Per* Parke, B. and Alderson, B., Porter *v.* Cooper, 4 Tyr. 264, 265; 1 Cr. M. & R. 387.

(g) Clarke *v.* Webb, 2 Dowl. 671; 1 Cr. M. & R. 29; and see Allen *v.* Crop, 2 Dowl. 546; or when it lies, Eicke *v.* Nokes, 3 Car. & P. 170; 1 Mood. & R. 359.

(h) See preceding note.

(i) 1 Esp. 194; Tidd, 9th ed. 834; Peake's C. N. P. 227; 5 T. R. 6; but see 1 Esp. 377.

(k) 4 Moore, 542; 13 East, 249.

(l) Bernasconi *v.* Anderson, Mood. & Malk. 183.

(714) It was held in Cathell *v.* Goodwin, 1 Har. & Gill, 468, that under the counts for money lent, paid, laid out and expended, and an *insimul computassent*, the plaintiff was entitled to recover by evidence of the defendant's dishonored bill, drawn payable to the order of the plaintiff's wife.

(715) { But where the count was on an account stated between the parties, wherein the defendant was found in arrear, &c. to the plaintiff, in the sum of £21 6s. and that the defendant promised to pay it in consideration of forbearance, it was held, that the exact sum must be proved, and the plaintiff having proved a debt due of £20 18s. was nonsuited, though it would have been sufficient if the sum were laid under a *videlicet*. Arnfield *v.* Bate, 3 Mau. & Selw. 173. }

ence (*m*), and a *prior* transaction (*n*). But it may be shown by other evidence than the defendant's admission, *that the sum to which he referred was of a precise and stipulated amount (*o*). An admission by the defendant in a conversation with a *third person* that he was indebted to the plaintiff in a named sum, is not evidence of an account stated, unless the third person was the plaintiff's agent (*p*). In an action by an *executor*, evidence that the defendant, on being applied to for payment of interest, stated he would bring him some on a certain day, is insufficient to support an account stated; there being no acknowledgment of any precise debt of a given character, or any thing to show in what capacity the plaintiff was entitled (*q*). And it seems that the admission should be clear and unqualified (*r*).

5thly. The cause of action. 1. In assumpsit. Common counts.

If an account be stated and agreed of what is due for *growing* crops not previously severed, it is a valid plea that there was no contract *in writing* signed, so as to take the case out of the statute against frauds, 29 Car. 2, c. 3, s. 4, but if the account were stated after the severance, that fact might be replied (*s*).

When a count upon an account stated should or not be added.

In framing the pleading rules of Hil. Term, 4 W. 4, it was considered that in assumpsit and debt on simple contract it is just that the plaintiff should be at liberty to proceed as well for the original debt as also upon an admission that it is due, and therefore the rule expressly *provides*, "that a count for money due on an account stated *may be* joined with any other count for a money demand, though it may not be intended to establish a distinct subject-matter of complaint in respect of each of such counts." But as Reg. Gen. Hil. T. 2 W. 4, subjects a plaintiff to the payment of costs upon every *issue* which he does not establish in evidence, this count should not be added unless there be strong ground for expecting that it will be proved by evidence.

Common counts in actions by and against *persons suing or being sued in particular rights or characters.*

We have seen that in actions by or against executors, where six years have elapsed since the death of the testator, or if it be on any other account material for the plaintiff to avail himself of a promise or acknowledgment by the defendant since the death, it may be necessary to add all or one of the common counts on promises to or by the executor in that character, for otherwise such promise or *acknowledgment* cannot be given in evidence (*t*)(716); and this set of counts usually follows the common breach at the end of the first set of counts (*u*). The same necessity may arise in actions by the *assignees of a bankrupt.* And so in an action against A., B., and C., the husband of B., in order to give in evidence a promise by A. and B. before the marriage of B. and C., to take the case out of the statute, a count on such promise before marriage must be added (*x*). In general, however, where there has been an absolute promise or acknowledgment to the original creditor within six years, so as to take the case out of the statute of limitations, it suffices to declare

(*m*) 5 Moore, 114 to 116; or a moral obligation, 3 Car. & P. 170.

(*n*) 1 Crom. M. & Ros. 29.

(*o*) 5 Moore, 114; 2 C. & P. 109.

(*p*) Breckon v. Smith, 1 Adol. & Ell. 488.

(*q*) 4 B. & C. 235.

(*r*) 1 R. & M. 239.

(*s*) Earl Falmouth v. Thomas, 3 Tyr. 26.

(*t*) *Ante*, 233; 1 Young & Jervis, 380; and see form, 2 Saund. 207, 208.

(*u*) See the forms, *post*, vol. ii., and see an old form, 2 Saund. 207, 208.

(*x*) 1 B. & C. 248; 2 D. & R. 363, S. C.

(716) See Bishop v. Harrison, 2 Leigh's Virg. Rep. 532.

IV. ITS PARTS, &c. — 5thly. The cause of action. 1. In assumpsit.

upon the original contract (y). In declaring at the suit of a surviving partner in *indebitatus*, *every* count should *technically* state the death of the deceased partner; but if the death be averred in the first count it will suffice, and a demurrer in respect of an omission in *a subsequent count* has been considered frivolous (z).

Common counts. The breach of the common counts.

The statement of a *breach* of a *special* contract stated in *assumpsit* has already been considered (a). The Reg. Gen. Trin. Term, 1 W. 4, prescribed a more concise form of stating the *breach* of one or more common *indebitatus* counts than had heretofore been adopted, and which should be pursued as an admirable model (b). Even in assigning this breach by non-payment of the common counts, it is advisable to admit in the aggregate all payments made by the defendant on account, so as to avoid the expense of a plea of payment (c). In an action by assignees in that character, a breach that the defendant did not pay the plaintiffs, without alleging *as* assignees, is sufficient on special demurrer, and indeed proper and preferable (d).

II. IN DEBT.

We have already considered *when* the action of *debt* may be *supported* (e). In *framing* the declaration in this action, the *general* requisites and qualities of all declarations, which have already been pointed out, must be observed (f). The *particular* parts may be considered under the same arrangement as in *assumpsit* (g); and most of the rules to be observed in framing declarations in that form of action equally govern in the action of debt, and therefore it will only be necessary to point out the distinctions.

[*393] Title of Court, term, venue, and commencement.

*The title of the *Court* and the *actual date* of the day of delivering or filing the declaration and the *venue*, have already been considered (h). The *commencement* of the declaration preceding the statement of the cause of action is similar to that in assumpsit (i); except in the description of the form of action, when that is stated, and even that description may be omitted (k). In an action on a specialty, the party should be declared against in the name by which he signed the deed (l). The debt demanded, if unnecessarily stated in the commencement, should regularly be the aggregate of all the sums alleged to be due in the different counts; but a mistake in this respect, whether more or less be stated, will not be a cause of demurrer; nor is it necessary to prove that the debt amounted precisely to the sum alleged to be due (m). In general, the declaration should be in the *debet* and *detinet* (n); but upon the

(y) *Ante*, 338; 7 Bing. 163.
(z) Undershell *v.* Fuller, 5 Tyr. 392; 1 Crom. M. & Ros. 900.
(a) *Ante*, 365.
(b) See form, *post*, vol. ii.
(c) *Ante*, 371; Bosanquet's Rules, 85, 86; and see forms of admission *post*, vol. ii.
(d) Cobbett *v.* Cockrane, 3 Bing. 17.
(e) *Ante*, 123 to 130.
(f) *Ante*, 279 to 291.
(g) *Ante*, 316 to 372.
(h) *Ante*, 291 to 311.
(i) *Ante*, 311 to 316. See the form, *post*, vol. ii.
(k) 11 East, 62; Straughan *v.* Buckle, 1 Harr. & Woll. 519.
(l) *Ante*, 279, 280.
(m) *Ante*, 129, 130. See the form, *post*, vol. ii.; 11 East, 62.
(n) Com. Dig. Pleader, 2 W. 8; Bac. Ab. Debt, F.

principle that a man may complain of only a part of his grievance, and not of the whole, the plaintiff may abridge his demand and declare in the *detinet* only, instead of the *debet* and *detinet* (m). And in an action by and against executors and administrators, the declaration should technically be in the *detinet* only; except in an action upon a judgment recovered against an executor suggesting a *devastavit*, when the *debet* and *detinet* is proper (n); and the defendant cannot in such action plead *plene administravit* (o) (717). But a declaration in the *debet* and *detinet* against an executor is not subject to a special demurrer, as the former will be rejected as surplusage (p). An heir should be sued in the *debet* and *detinet*, but the omission of the *debet* will be aided by verdict (q).

IV. ITS PARTS, &c.

5thly. The cause of action.

2. In debt.

On simple contract.

The mode of stating the *cause of action* varies as in assumpsit, according to the nature of the contract or matter declared on, which, we have seen, may be a simple contract, a specialty, a record, or a statute (r). In debt on *simple contract*, express or implied, to pay money in consideration of a precedent debt or duty, the *subject-matter* of the debt *is to be described precisely as in [*394] the common counts in assumpsit (s); but in point of *form* the *indebitatus* count in debt differs from those in assumpsit; for although the *indebitatus* count states that the defendant, on, &c. "was indebted to the plaintiff" in a named sum of money "for goods sold," precisely as in assumpsit; and it is not necessary to set forth the nature or particulars of the debt with more precision than in that action (t); yet in *this indebitatus* count, no *promise* should be stated as in assumpsit (u); and although it has been usual to conclude each count with the allegation that "by reason of the said sum of money being unpaid, an action had accrued to the plaintiff to demand and have the same from the defendant, being parcel of the money above demanded," yet that allegation is unnecessary, and the usual breach at the end of the declaration will suffice (v); and the distinction is stated to be, that whenever the debt arises merely by the judgment or obligation, &c. and not from any thing *dehors*, a non-performance of the obligation is to be laid, and the conclusion is to be with the breach *ad damnum*; but that where the debt arises, not by the obligation alone, but also by some matter *dehors* stated in the declaration, there the count should conclude *per quod actio accrevit*, &c. as in debt on a lease for rent (x). The *quantum meruit* and *quantum valebant* counts, when formerly adopted, but which always seemed to be unnecessary and injudicious (y), resembled those in assumpsit, except that the words "*agreed* to pay" should be inserted, instead of "*promised* to pay," (z) and that such counts in general conclude with the same allegation *per quod actio accrevit*,

(m) Per Lord Ellenborough, C. J., 4 M. & S. 125.

(n) *Post*, vol. ii.; Rol. Ab. 603; Bac. Ab. Debt, F.; 3 East, 2; Com. Dig. Pleader, 2 W. 8.

(o) 1 Wils. 258.

(p) Gardner v. Bowman, 4 Tyr. 412.

(q) Com. Dig. Pleader, 2 East, 2; 3 East, 2; 2 Saund. 7. n. 4.

(r) *Ante*, 124 to 123.

(s) See the cases, Com. Dig. Pleader, 2 W. 11.

(t) 2 T. R. 28; *post*, vol. ii.

(u) *Id.*; 12 Mod. 511; 3 B. & Ald. 208; 2 Smith Rep. 618; 2 B. & P. 78.

(v) *Post*, vol. ii.; Gilb. Debt, 414.

(x) Gilb. Debt, 415.

(y) *Ante*, 123, note (q).

(z) *Supra*, note (u).

(717) Vide Spotswood v. Price, 3 Hen. & Munf. 123.

IV. ITS PARTS, &c. — 5thly. The cause of action. 2. In debt. On simple contract.

&c. as the *indebitatus* count (*a*). And it has been recently held that the words "*undertook* and agreed to pay," in a *quantum meruit* count, do not necessarily import the form of action to be in assumpsit, but are good in debt (*b*). The Reg. Gen. Trin. T. 1 W. 4, although it does not prescribe any form in *debt*, yet directs that declarations on bills and notes, and for common debts, shall be drawn *as concisely in debt as in assumpsit*, and that no costs for any extra length shall be allowed, and as the same rule impliedly abolishes a *quantum meruit* or *valebant* count in assumpsit, so those forms are impliedly abolished in *debt* (*c*).

The mode of framing a declaration in debt on *legal liabilities*, on *awards*, and for *escapes*, &c. is shown in the second volume (*d*). Debt lies on a special contract to pay *money*, and if such contract be specially declared upon, and be not under seal, so that a consideration is necessary, the declaration
[*395] should show such *consideration, and may in general be framed like a declaration in assumpsit, with this exception, that it must be alleged that the defendant *agreed*, not that he *promised* to pay (*e*)(718).

On specialties.

In debt upon a *Specialty*, the declaration usually proceeds at once to the statement of the specialty, without any inducement or statement of the consideration upon which the contract was founded (*f*); for in general the circumstances under which the deed was made are immaterial, and a consideration is seldom essential (*g*) (719). It is principally in this respect that the declaration on debt or covenant on a specialty differs from that in assumpsit. Thus in debt upon a bond, the declaration states, " that the defendant, on, &c. by his certain writing obligatory, sealed with his seal, and now shown to the Court here, acknowledged himself to be held and firmly bound to the plaintiff in the sum of £——, to be paid to the plaintiff," and then states the breach by the non-payment of that sum. So, in debt, or covenant upon a lease by the *lessor against the lessee*, it is not necessary to set forth the lessor's title to the lands demised; but the declaration merely alleges " that the plaintiff, on, &c. by a certain indenture made between him and the defendant, and under the defendant's seal, and of which the plaintiff makes a profert, demised," &c. (*h*); and in this case, if the title be unnecessarily set forth, an imperfect statement of it may not be fatal on error (*i*) (720).

Inducement when or not necessary.

Inducements however are sometimes necessary, and in the statement of them the preceding rules and observations in the statement of inducements in as-

(*a*) *Post*, vol. ii.; Gilb. Debt, 414.
(*b*) Gardner *v.* Bowman, 4 Tyr. 412, citing Ninfrn *v.* Bland, 3 Smith, 114.
(*c*) See the rule and prescribed form, *post*, vol. ii.; and the forms in debt, *id.*
(*d*) *Post*, vol. ii.; *ante*, 123. See also Com. Dig. Pleader, 2 W. 11.
(*e*) See *ante*, 130; and as to *variances* in stating the consideration and contract, see *ante*, 325 and 334.
(*f*) See the cases, Com. Dig. Pleader, 2 W. 9.
(*g*) Plowd. 308; 7 T. R. 477; 4 East, 200; 1 Fonbl. 347; *post*, 399.
(*h*) Stra. 230, 231; 1 Saund. 233 a, note 2.
(*i*) Stra. 230, 231. *Quære* if *traversed* by defendant, *vide infra*.

(718) { See the second count in Seymour *v.* Harvey, 8 Conn. Rep. 65. }
(719) The want or failure of consideration, is not sufficient at law to avoid a specialty; and a false representation or warranty, whether in writing or by parol, as to the quality of property sold, cannot be pleaded in discharge of a bond given for the consideration. Vrooman *v.* Phelps, 2 Johns. Rep. 177. Dorlan *v.* Sarmnis, Id. 177, n. Dorr *v.* Munsell, 13 Johns. Rep. 430. { See the note vol. 2, p. 963. }
(720) Backus *v.* Taylor, 6 Munf. 488.

IV. ITS PARTS, &c. — 5thly. The cause of action. 2. In debt. On specialties.

sumpsit will be here applicable (*k*). In an action on a lease at the suit of the assignee of the reversion, or of the heir of the lessor, or by an executor of a termor, for rent which became due after the death of the testator, the declaration must state the title of the lessor to the demised premises, in order that it may appear that he had *such* an estate in the reversion as might be legally vested in the plaintiff in the character in *which he sues, and legally entitle him to recover the damages claimed in respect of the breaches of covenant (*l*); and this even where the estate of the plaintiff is derived from the king or a corporation (*m*); and such inducement is specially traversable (*n*). [*396] Even if the omission to state the lessor's title in an action by a reversioner be not aided by verdict (*o*), yet after verdict, in covenant by a devisee in fee, an averment that the testator, the lessor, was *seised* and died *seised*, (not showing of what *particular* estate in the premises), is sufficient (*p*). Such title is usually shown by way of *inducement* preceding the statement of the lease; as when the action is at the suit of an heir, by alleging that the lessor was seised of the premises in his demesne as of fee (*q*); or when the estate demised is copyhold, by showing that fact, and that the lessor was seised at the will of the lord, according to the custom of the manor (*r*); or where the plaintiff claims as assignee of a term, or as executor of the lessor for rent, &c. due since his death, by stating that the lessor, at the time of making the lease, was possessed of the demised premises for the residue of a certain term of years, &c (*s*). As, however, the lessor's title in the action upon the lease by the owner of the reversion is only inducement, it is not necessary to show its *origin* or commencement, although the lessor had not a title in fee-simple; but had only a *particular* estate, that is, an estate less than a seisin in fee-simple, as an estate tail, or for life, or years, &c. Thus, if the lessor held for a term of years, and the plaintiff sue as his executor or assignee of the reversion therein, it is not necessary to deduce the title thereto from the freeholder; it suffices to show the term which the lessor had, and to deduce the title from him (*t*). This is an exception to the general rule that the *commencement* *of particular [*397] estates must be shown in pleading (*u*). In these cases the lessee and his assignee being estopped by the deed from denying the lessor's title *generally*, cannot plead *nil habuit*, or traverse the entire inducement; but admitting by his plea that the lessor had *some* legal interest in the premises, he may show that he was entitled to a *different* estate, and thereby in effect traverse the *derivative* title stated in the declaration (*x*). The form of declaring against an heir is pointed out in the second volume (*y*).

(*k*) *Ante*, 316 to 321.

(*l*) 1 Saund. 233, n. 2; Stra. 230; 7 T. R. 538; Com. Dig. Pleader, C. 36; Gilb. Debt, 410; Dyer, 365 b; 4 Moore, 303; 1 B. & B. 531, S. C.; 1 Dowl. & Ry. N. P. 1; 1 M. & P. 633. See *post*, vol. ii. as to manner of stating inducements.

(*m*) 1 Saund. 187, n. 1.

(*n*) 4 Moore, 303; 1 B. & B. 531, S. C.

(*o*) See 11 Mod. 179; Vin. Ab. Title, D. 16; 1 Show. 71; 1 M. & P. 640, 642.

(*p*) 1 M. & P. 633; 4 Bingh. 616, S. C.

(*q*) 2 Saund. 361, 416.

(*r*) *Post*, vol. ii.

(*s*) *Post*, vol. ii.; 4 Moore, 303; 1 B. & B. 531, S. C.; 7 T. R. 538. See the various modes of stating different titles and the nature of the estate, and how acquired, *post*, vol. ii.

(*t*) See Com. Dig. Pleader, E. 19, C. 43; *post*, vol. ii; Stephen, 2d edit. 364.

(*u*) *Id. ibid.*; Co. Lit. 308 b; 1 Saund. 186 d, n. 1.

(*x*) 7 T. R. 538, 539. See 4 Moore, 303; 1 Dow. & Ry. N. P. C. 1; 2 Bing. 54; 9 Moore, 130; 9 Bar. & Cres. 254; 4 M. & R. 201, S. C.; Seymour *v.* Franco, 7 Law Journal, 18, K. B.; and Whitton *v.* Peacock, in C. P. 3d June, 1835. Shearman, attorney.

(*y*) See *ante*, 59.

IV. ITS PARTS, &c.

5thly. The cause of action.

2. In debt.

On specialties.

Time of making specialty and other requisite allegations.

The *time* of making the contract should be stated as in *assumpsit* and it must appear and be expressly shown, when a specialty is the gist of the action, that such *contract* was by *deed;* except in debt for rent on a demise, which is perhaps almost the only instance where a deed may be adduced in evidence in support of a count not mentioning it (*z*). It must also appear that the contract was under *seal* (721); but there are some technical words, such as *indenture, deed,* or *writing obligatory,* which of themselves import that the instrument was sealed, and which will suffice (*a*) (722); and the omission of the statement that the instrument was under seal will be aided, if the defendant by his plea admit that the writing was sealed (*b*). The *delivery* of the deed, though essential to its validity, need not be stated in pleading (*d*); and though dated on a particular day, a deed may be stated in pleading to have been made on another day (*e*).

Profert of specialty.

It is a general rule that in all pleadings, whether by a plaintiff or defendant, if a *deed* be alleged, and the party *claim* or *justify* under it, and is presumed to have the deed in his possession, he must make a *profert* of the deed, that is, must profess that he brings it into Court to be shown to the Court and his adversary: the import and practical meaning of which is, that the party has the deed itself ready to give the opponent *oyer* thereof (*f*).

[*398] *The *profert in curiam* of the deed, or the excuse for the omission, usually follows the statement of the time of making the deed and of the parties thereto, and precedes the statement of the defendant's contract. Such profert is usually in the following words :—"Which said writing obligatory (or indenture or articles of agreement,) sealed with the seal of the defendant, the plaintiff now *brings here into Court,* the date whereof is the day and year aforesaid." (*g*) The *excuse* for the omission of a profert being traversable must be stated according to the fact; as, either that "the deed has been lost," or "destroyed," "by accident," or "that it is in the possession of the defendant," and that "therefore the plaintiff cannot produce the same to the Court." (*h*)(723) But in declaring upon a bill of exchange or other *simple* contract, no profert is to be made. So, when a conveyance operates under the statute of uses, as a lease and release, or a covenant to stand seised

(*z*) 1 New Rep 104, 109; 1 Saund. 276 a, note 1, 2; 202, 211; 2 *Id.* 297, note 1; see, however, *ante,* 125; 4 B. & C. 962, 963.

(*a*) 1 Saund. 291, note 1, 320, note 3; Com. Dig. Fait; Platt on Cov. 6.

(*b*) *Id.;* Lord Raym. 1536, 1541; Cro. Car. 209.

(*d*) 1 Saund 291, note 1.

(*e*) 4 East, 477; 3 Salk. 120.

(*f*) As to proferts in general, see Com. Dig. Pleader, O. P.; 1 Saund. 9, note 1; 10 Co. 92 b; 4 T. R. 338; *post,* vol. ii.; Stephen, 2d edit. 487; as to *oyer, post,* chap. v. s. 3; and as to compelling a party to give copy of an instrument *not* under seal, Tidd, 9th edit. 590.

(*g*) *Post,* vol. ii.

(*h*) 3 T. R. 151; 2 Hen. Bla. 259; *post,* vol. ii.; 2 Campb. 557; 10 East, 57; as to the deed being in the hands of a third person, Tidd, 9th edit. 587, 487.

(721) Acc. Van Santwood *v.* Sandford 12 Johns. Rep. 197. As to the law respecting seals, vide Warren *v.* Lynch, 5 Johns. Rep. 239. Phillips' Ev. Dunl. Ed. 361. n. a. 5 Johns. Rep. 247. n. b.

(722) Vide Van Santwood *v.* Sandford, 12 Johns. Rep. 198.

(723) Vide Phillips' Ev. 348. Cutts *v.* United States, 1 Gallison's Rep. 69. { Powers *v.* Ware, 2 Pick. Rep. 451. Smith *v.* Emery, 7 Halst. Rep. 53. Rees *v.* Overbaugh, 6 Cow. 748, 749. }

IV. ITS PARTS, &c. — 5thly. The cause of action. 2. In debt. On specialties. Profert.

to uses, it has been considered that a profert is unnecessary (*i*); the reason assigned is that the party in such case obtains his title, not in virtue of the intrinsic effect of the deed itself, but by the operation of the statute, and is said to be *in by the law;* as tenant in dower by elegit, or statute staple, in which case a profert need not be stated (*k*). Nor is a profert necessary where the party, though he relies on a deed, is not, by the form of his pleading, compelled to state or allude to it in his pleading, as in the case of a feoffment; and the statute against frauds, which requires that the livery should be accompanied by some instrument in writing, has not altered the form of pleading (*l*). So when a deed is stated only as inducement (*m*); or where the plaintiff has no right to the possession of it, or of the counterpart (*n*); a profert is *unnecessary; and it has been held that the assignees of a bankrupt obligee need not make a profert of the bond (*o*); and a sealed will, or an award, though under seal, not being a *deed* in the technical sense of the word, need not be pleaded with a profert (*p*)(724). But letters testamentary and letters of administration must be pleaded with a profert, at least when the executor or administrator is a plaintiff (*q*). [*399]

When or not *Oyer* is demandable.

When a profert, or an excuse for the omission, was unnecessary, the statement of it will be considered as surplusage, and will not entitle the other party to oyer (*r*). And oyer of a private act of parliament, or of a record, as of letters-patent enrolled in Chancery, cannot be claimed, though pleaded with a profert (*s*). But where a profert, or an excuse for the want of it is necessary, if the plaintiff make profert of and thereby profess to produce the deed, when he is not prepared to do so, and the defendnat plead *non est factum*, the plaintiff will be nonsuited on the trial, as it will not be sufficient in such case to prove that the deed was lost or destroyed, or in the defendant's possession (*t*)(725). If therefore in such case the plaintiff be not prepared to produce the deed on oyer being claimed, or at the trial, and has inadvertently pleaded the deed with a profert, the declaration must be amended (726), and the circumstances which excuse the omission to make a profert should be stated in the declaration (*u*). However, the omission of a profert, when necessary, can only be taken advantage of by special demurrer (*x*)(727).

(*i*) 9 Moore, 593; Tidd, 9th edit. 587; see 8 T. R. 573; 1 Saund. 9 a, note 1; 1 Ves. 394; 2 B. & P. 357; 2 Hen. Bla. 262; 3 T. R. 156; Carth. 315; Dyer, 277 a; Cro. Jac. 217; Cro. Car. 441; Co. Lit. 35 b, note 6; precedents stating it, 3 Wils. 134; 3 Lev. 229; see 13 Vin. Ab. 76; see, however, *post*, vol. ii.

(*k*) *Id.;* 10 Co. 93; Stephen, 2d edit. 489; 2 Stark. Evid. 483, 1st edit.

(*l*) *Id.;* 3 T. R. 156; 8 *Id.* 573; 1 Saund. 276, n. 1, 2; *post*, vol. ii.

(*m*) 8 T R. 573; Com. Dig. Pleader, O. 15.

(*n*) 1 Saund. 9 and 9 a, note 1; 1 Ves. 394.

(*o*) Cro. Car. 209; Cullen, 417, *sed quære.*

(*p*) 2 Saund. 62 b, note 5.

(*q*) Stephen, 2d edit. 488.

(*r*) 2 Salk. 497.

(*s*) 1 T. R. 149; 1 Saund. 9 b, note 1. It seems that in general profert of letters patent is necessary, see 5 Co. 74 b; 1 Ld. Raym. 299; Doct. Plac. 215; Lutw. 1172; Cro. Jac. 317; see 1 T. R. 149, 150; 1 Lil. Ent. 154; Com. Dig. Pleader, O.

(*t*) 4 East, 585; 1 Esp. Rep. 337.

(*u*) *Id.;* 1 Saund. 9 a, note 1.

(*x*) 4 & 5 Ann. c. 16; Com. Dig. Pleader, S. 17.

(724) Acc. Weed *v.* Ellis, 3 Caines' Rep. 256.
(725) Vide Phillips' Ev. 348.
(726) See Powers *v.* Ware, 2 Pick. Rep. 460.
(727) Bank U. States *v.* Sill, 5 Conn. Rep. 111.

IV. ITS PARTS, &c. — 5thly. The cause of action. 2 In debt. On specialties. Profert. Statement of Consideration in general unnecessary in a count on a specialty.

In general, the declaration in debt upon a *specialty* proceeds immediately from the profert to the statement of the defendant's contract, without disclosing the *consideration* upon which it was founded, because a consideration is not in general essential to the validity of a *deed* (y)(728). But in pleading a conveyance under the statute of uses, it is necessary to state that a *valuable* consideration was paid (z), or that there was a *good* consideration, as in the instance of a covenant *to stand seised to uses made in respect of relationship, &c. (a); in which cases, if the statement of the consideration be omitted, the declaration will be bad on special demurrer (b). Where a consideration is necessary to give validity to the deed, as where it operates in partial restraint of trade, the proper course is to show fully the consideration expressed in the deed; but an allegation in the declaration in setting out the deed, that it is witnessed that the defendant covenanted "for the consideration therein mentioned," is sufficient on *general demurrer* (c). So, when an act to be done by

[*400]

the plaintiff was the consideration of the defendant's covenant, and constituted a condition precedent, it is necessary to show such consideration as well as the performance of it (d). It is sufficient if the consideration or condition be stated according to its legal effect (e), but a variance would be fatal (f); and in stating the consideration, when necessary, the whole of it should be set forth (g). The rules as to the statement of the consideration in an action of assumpsit (h) have equal relevance to the action of debt in those instances in which it is essential in the latter form of action to show the existence of a consideration for the defendant's contract.

The specialty *Contract* itself.

In stating the *Contract* by *deed*, either in debt or covenant, the rules which we have considered in pointing out the mode of framing the declaration in *assumpsit* in general apply. The defendant's contract should in strictness be set forth in positive terms, and not with the *testatum existit*, viz. that "it was and is witnessed" by the deed, &c.; but this will suffice in a declaration, though it may be objectionable in a plea (i).

In considering the mode of setting out a contract in *assumpsit*, we have fully explained the rule that an instrument should be stated according to its *legal operation and effect*; or may, as it seems, be set forth in *hæc verba*, and the expediency of adopting the latter course in some instances has also been

[*401] suggested (k)(729). We have also under the *same head pointed out the mode of pleading contracts or obligations, which are in the *alternative* or *con-*

(y) *Ante*, 395.
(z) *Post*, vol. ii.
(a) *Post*, vol. ii.
(b) 2 Hen. Bla. 259, 261; 2 Saund. 13, note 20; 2 Stra. 1229; 2 Saund. on Uses, 53.
(c) 3 Bingh. 322.
(d) 2 Saund. 352 b; 6 East, 568; 3 T. R. 590; *ante*, 352 to 360.
(e) *Ante*, 334.
(f) 3 Moore, 114; as to variances, *ante*, 326, 334.
(g) *Ante*, 327; 2 B. & Ald. 765; 1 Chitty's Rep. 718, S. C.
(h) *Ante*, 321, 325.
(i) 1 Saund. 274, note 1; 2 *Id.* 312, note 5; *ante*, 268, 331.
(k) *Ante*, 334, 336. A declaration, setting out the *fac simile* of a deed, will be read so as to make it sense, however incorrect and illiteral the deed may be, Smith *v.* Barnard, E. T. 1818, K. B. MS.

(728) Grubb *v.* Willis, 11 Serg. & Rawle, 107.
(729) Contracts must be set forth in the words, or according to their legal effect; but if there are distinct parts of an agreement, in declaring for the breach of a particular part, other parts need not be set forth. Scott *v.* Lieber et al., 2 Wend. R. 479.

ditional, or subject to *exceptions*, *provisoes*, and *qualifications*, and have fully considered the doctrine of *variances* in regard to a mis-statement of the contract or instrument in material or trivial respects (*l*). As these principles and rules equally apply to debt or covenant upon *specialties*, it will be useless here to repeat them. The late statutes, 9 Geo. 4, c. 14, and 3 & 4 W. 4, c. 42, s. 23, permitting clerical mistakes in stating instruments to be amended even pending a trial, has also been alluded to (*m*). The impolicy of setting out unnecessary covenants and clauses (*n*), and the doctrine of surplusage (*o*), have also undergone consideration in a preceding part of this volume.

IV. ITS PARTS, &c. — 5thly. The cause of action. 2. In debt. On specialties.

Averments.

In many cases it is necessary to introduce in the declaration an *Averment of Performance* by the plaintiff of a *condition precedent* or other matter, or to show a legal *excuse* for the omission to perform the act: and in some instances it must be alleged that the defendant had *Notice* of the plaintiff's completion of the matter he was bound to perform, and was *Requested* to fulfil his, the defendant's, covenant. Our observations upon these points in *assumpsit* (*p*) equally apply to actions upon specialties.

Reference to deed. Lessee's entry. Performance of conditions precedent. Statements of *Derivative Title*.

In actions on specialties, after stating the covenants, it is *usual*, though *unnecessary*, to *refer* to the indenture by the words "as by the said indenture fully appears;" and in actions on leases to state the *lessee's entry* on the demised premises (*q*); and when the action is between the original parties to the contract, the declaration then proceeds immediately to the averments of the plaintiff's performance of the conditions precedent, when necessary, and to the breach. But when the declaration is by or against a person who was not a party to the original contract, and particularly in actions upon leases, the statement of the *derivative title* of the plaintiff or the defendant precedes the breach. And in an action on a lease by a party claiming from the lessor, there must be an *inducement* of the *lessor's* title, as before explained (*r*). Thus, when an action is brought *by* the *heir* of the lessor, the title and death of his ancestor, and the *descent to the plaintiff as heir, is shown (*s*); and it [*402] must appear *how* he is heir, viz. whether as son or otherwise (*t*); and if he claim by mediate, not immediate, descent, he must show the pedigree; for example, if he claim as nephew, he must show *how* nephew (*u*). And when the plaintiff claims as assignee of the reversion by lease and release or other conveyance, the nature and operative part of the conveyance must be set forth (*v*). In an action brought *by* the assignee of a term, all the mesne assignments of the term down to himself should be specifically stated; for he being privy to them, shall not be allowed to plead generally "that the estate of the lessee of and in the demised premises came to him by assignment;" but when the action is brought *against* the assignee of a lessee, such general form of pleading is sufficient, because the plaintiff is a stranger to the defendant's title, and it is therefore reasonably supposed he cannot set it out particular-

(*l*) *Ante*, 338, 334.
(*m*) *Ante*, 348.
(*n*) *Ante*, 262.
(*o*) *Ante*, 262.
(*p*) *Ante*, 359 to 364.
(*q*) *Post*, vol. ii.
(*r*) *Ante*, 395.
(*s*) *Post*, vol. ii.
(*t*) 1 Salk. 355; 1 Lev. 190; 1 Ld. Raym. 202.
(*u*) 3 B. & P. 453; 12 Mod. 619; 2 Bla. Rep. 1099.
(*v*) *Post*, vol. ii.; Com. Dig. Pleader, E. 23, 24.

IV. ITS PARTS, &c. — 5thly. The cause of action. 2. In debt. On specialties. Averments.

ly (730). It is not, however, sufficient in the latter case to allege that the *tenements* came to the defendant by assignment; but it must be shown that he is assignee of the *term*, or *estate*, or *interest* therein; for otherwise it might be an assignment of another estate than the term of the lessee. The usual form is, "that *all* the said estate, right, title, and interest of the said E. F. (the lessee) of, in, and to the said demised premises with the appurtenances, afterwards, to wit on, &c. by assignment thereof then duly made, came to and vested in the defendant." (*x*)(731) An heir may be sued either generally as heir, without showing how he became so, or if he has held possession, or exercised acts of ownership over the property, he may be declared against as an assignee, upon a covenant running with the land (*y*). And an executor who has entered, &c. may be sued in the *debet* and *detinet* as assignee for rent which became due after the death of his testator, who was the lessee (*z*). The mode of declaring by and against persons suing or being sued in a *representative or derivative character*, is pointed out in the numerous precedents in the second volume (*a*).

As to setting forth Condition of Bond and assigning breaches in the Declaration (*b*).

Sometimes it is *absolutely necessary* in *declaring* on a *bond*, to set forth the condition and breach, as in an action on a *bail bond* or *replevin bond*, in order to show that the plaintiff is entitled to sue as assignee of the sheriff, or in the case of a bastardy bond, that the succeeding overseers are entitled to sue (*c*). In *other cases* where, under the 8 & 9 W. 3, c. 11, s. 8, it is necessary *before execution* to ascertain in what respect the special condition has been broken, and to assess by a jury what *damages* have thereby been really sustained (*d*); there has been some contradiction in the books as regards the *expediency* of setting out the condition and breaches in the *declaration*, or waiting till the replication or other stage in the cause (*e*).

(*x*) 1 Saund. 112 a, note 1; *post*, vol. ii.

(*y*) 1 Salk. 353; 4 T. R. 75.

(*z*) 1 Salk. 317; 4 T. R. 75.

(*a*) On bonds by or against *particular persons*, *post*, vol. ii.; against an *heir* or *devisee*, *id.*; statements of *various titles*, *id.*

(*b*) See *post*, vol. ii.; 2 Arch. K. B. 609.

(*c*) See 2 New Rep. 362.

(*d*) As to *what* bonds are or not within that statute, see *post*, vol. ii.

(*e*) See 1 Saund. Rep. 58 d; 2 Saund. Rep 107 a, note 2, 187 a; 8 T. R. 255; 2 Chitty Rep. 187; 3 Car. & P. 608; *post*, 618, 5th edit. In some cases, though not absolutely requisite, *it may be advisable to state the condition of the bond and breach in the declaration*, and especially where a plea not leading to an issue, or the breach, as non est factum, or the like, or where a judgment by default is expected, for in the latter case some delay would be avoided, and the plaintiff moreover would not have to prove, nor could the defendant deny the truth of the breach, on the execution of the inquiry, which would otherwise be the case. See 1 Saund. 58 d; Barwise *v.* Russell, 3 Car. & P. 608; and see Hodgkinson *v.* Marsden, 2 Campb. 121. And in Cox and others *v.* Hollingworth, in K. B. Aug. 1835, Alderson, B, on summons, directed the plaintiff to declare on the bond, setting out the condition and breaches; and in Stothert *v.* Goodfellow, 1 Nev. & Man. 202, the declaration set forth the condition, and assigned breaches.

On the other hand, in many cases where it is not absolutely necessary to state the condition and breaches in the declaration, it may be advisable *not to do so*, and especially where a defence, either sham or otherwise, is expected. In such cases it is best to reserve the assignment of the breaches for the replication, (as may be done, 8 T. R. 255; 2 Chit. Rep. 298; 2 Saund. 187 a,) because the defendant in rejoining to the replication, can only present one answer to each breach, whereas in pleading to the declaration and breaches stated therein, he may answer each breach by any number of pleas.

If the condition and breach of a bond within the above statute of William 3, be not stated in the declaration, and the de-

(730) Vide Folliard *v.* Wallace, 2 Johns. Rep. 402. { Norton *v.* Vultee, 1 Hall's Rep. 394, 389. }

(731) Lansing *v.* Alstyne, 2 Wend. R. 561.

IV. ITS PARTS, &c.

5thly. The cause of action.

2. In debt.

On specialties.

Averments.

In *practice* it is now most usual not to state the condition or the breaches in the *declaration*; but there may be cases in which it would be advisable there to state them. The assigning of the breach or breaches is affected by the same rules as those relating to the breach in assumpsit or covenant. If the breach of the condition be well assigned in other respects, it will not be vitiated by the superaddition of immaterial allegations (f). The breach of the condition of a bond, otherwise well assigned, is not vitiated by the superaddition of immaterial allegations (g).

[*403]

On Records.

*We have seen that debt is the proper remedy on *Records*, as recognizances of bail, statutes merchant, recognizances in the nature of a statute staple, and on judgments (h). The validity of these cannot in general *in pleading* be impeached or affected by any supposed defect or illegality in the consideration or transaction on which they were founded; nor can there be any allegation against the validity of a record (732), except by a writ of error (i); and consequently it is not necessary to state the circumstances or consideration on which the record was founded. In debt upon a *recognizance of bail*, it must be stated with certainty, following the description in the entry of the recognizance, and should set forth in what Court, at whose suit, and for what sum or cause the defendant became bail (k): and in pleading a *statute staple*, it should be shown to have been by writing obligatory or under seal (l). Formerly in an action upon a *judgment*, it was usual to set forth in the declaration the whole of the proceedings in the former suit; but this is no longer the practice(m); and it is sufficient to state the judgment concisely, even though it were recovered in an inferior Court not of record; and although it has been supposed to be unnecessary to aver that the defendant became indebted within

fendant plead any plea on which the plaintiff might at common law have taken an issue in his replication without showing a breach, such as a plea of non est factum, or that the bond was obtained by fraud or the like, the plaintiff may still take such issue, and must enter a distinct and separate suggestion of breaches under the statute, but he cannot incorporate such issue and such suggestion in one and the same replication, see 8 T. R. 255; 1 Esp. 277; 5 M. & Sel. 60; 5 J. B. Moore, 198.

If to such a declaration the defendant plead a plea which made it necessary at common law for the plaintiff to assign a breach in the replication, as for instance, a plea of general performance, the plaintiff must still assign the breach in the replication, with this difference, that he may now assign several breaches under the statute, whereas at common law he could only assign one. If only one breach be assigned in the replication, it is not necessary to state it in terms to be "according to the form of the statute," 13 East, 1, otherwise if more than one.

Before the above statute of William 3, the plaintiff could assign in the declaration only one breach of the condition, and if he assigned more, the declaration was demurrable for duplicity, 1 Saund. 58, n. 1, and this is expressly permitted by Reg. Gen. Hil. T. 4 W. 4, reg. 5, although several counts are not permitted. It is not however necessary in a declaration assigning more than one breach to refer to its being according to the statute, 13 East, 1. It suffices to prove part of the breach assigned, *id.*

(f) Stothert *v.* Goodfellow, 1 Nev. & Man. 202, the form of declaration in which will assist as a precedent.

(g) Stothert *v.* Goodfellow and another, 1 Nev. & Man. 202.

(h) *Ante*, 126.

(i) 4 East, 311; 2 Lev. 161; Gilb. on Uses and Trusts, 109; Gilb. Debt, 412; Burr. 1007; 3 East, 258; 3 T. R. 689; 2 Marsh. 392, 393.

(k) 1 Wils. 284; *post*, vol ii.; Com. Dig. Pleader, 2 W. 10. As to variance, see 11 East, 516; 4 Bar. & Cres. 403.

(l) Cro. Car. 363; Com. Dig. Pleader, 2 W. 10.

(m) 1 Wils. 318.

(732) Green *v.* Ovington et al., 16 Johns. Rep. 55. See Cardesa *v.* Humes et al., 5 Serg. & Rawle, 65.

IV. ITS PARTS, &c. — 5thly. The cause of action. 2. In debt. On records.

the jurisdiction of the Court (n) (733); it has been recently held that it must be averred that the *original cause* of action arose within the jurisdiction of the inferior Court (o). It is unquestionably necessary in debt upon a judgment in the Courts at Westminster, to show with certainty the term and parties and the sum recovered. It is said that if the declaration be on a judgment in the Common Pleas, it should be stated before what judges by name it was recovered (p); and that in debt on a judgment in an inferior Court, the names of the suitors who were the judges should be stated; but the omission will at all events be aided by verdict (q).

[*404] Variances.

*Care must be taken that there be no *Variance* in the statement of the judgment, for such variance is in general fatal (r). Thus, if there has been a judgment for £388 0s. 1d. and debt be brought on it as for £388 recovered, omitting the penny, it was a variance(734), and could not be cured by a remittitur of the penny (s). In debt upon a judgment, or other matter of record, unless when it has been stated as inducement, it is necessary, after showing the matter of record, to refer to it by the *prout patet per recordum* (t). But the omission will be aided unless the defendant demur specially (u): and these words do not render certainty of description in the allegation more material than it would otherwise have been (x). It is usual also to allege that the judgment still remains in full force and effect, and that the plaintiff has not obtained execution or satisfaction thereof; but this allegation is unnecessary (y). The late statutes (z), permitting the amendment at the trial of clerical errors and other variances in stating a record, &c. have been fully stated (a).

On Statutes.

In debt on a *Statute* at the suit of a party grieved, or by an informer, where the whole of the penalty is given to him, the *commencement* is the same as in debt on a contract; but where a part of the penalty is given to the informer and the king, or the poor of the parish, &c., the commencement and other parts of the declaration usually state that the plaintiff sues *qui tam*, &c., though this is not necessary unless there has been a contempt of the king (b). In a

(n) 1 Wils. 316; 1 Saund. 92, note 2; *post*, vol. ii.; Com. Dig. Pleader, 2 W. 12; Carth. 85, 86; Thomp. Ent. 118; 8 T. R. 127.

(o) Read *v.* Pope, 1 Cr. M. & R. 302; 4 Tyr. 403; overruling 1 Wm. Saund. 92, note 2.

(p) Com. Dig. Pleader, 2 W. 12, 3 L. 3. But see the usual form, *post*, vol. ii.

(q) *Id.*; Carth. 86. In debt on replevin bond it is not necessary, in averring the holding of the County Court, to state the names of the suitors, 2 B. & C. 2.

(r) *Ante*, 264, 333; 11 East, 516; "The said Court of the Bench" means C. P. 7 Taunt. 271; 1 Moore, 19, S. C. An averment that judgment was recovered on *promises*, whereas it was recovered on one count only, was considered a fatal variance; 5 B. & C. 339. See other instances in the notes, *post*, vol. ii.

(s) 2 Stra. 1171; 9 East, 157; 1 Esp. Rep. 356; 4 Taunt. 13; 11 East, 516; 1 Hen. Bla. 49.

(t) Gilb. Debt, 412; Willes, 127, in which Salk. 565, referred to in Com. Dig. Pleader, 2 W. 12, is corrected.

(u) 4 & 5 Anne, c. 16, s. 1; and see 11 East, 565.

(x) 10 Price, 154.

(y) 1 Saund. 330, note 4; *sed vide* Com. Dig. Pleader, 2 W. 12.

(z) 9 Geo. 4, c. 15; 3 & 4 W. 4, c. 42, s. 23.

(a) *Ante*, 346.

(b) Com. Dig. Action on Statute, E. 1; 7 T. R. 152; 1 Saund. 136, n. 1; 2 Saund. 374, n. 1. As to variance in stating the parish, *ante*, 308; 3 Bing. 449. As to pleadings in general on statutes, see Com. Dig. Pleader, C. 76; Bac. Ab. Statute; 1 Saund. 135, n. 3; 2 Saund. 377 b, n. 12; 1 Chit. Crim. Law, 275, &c.

(733) See Rogers *v.* Davis, 1 Aiken's Vermont Rep. 296.

(734) Vide Bissell *v.* Kip, 5 Johns. Rep. 89.

IV. ITS PARTS, &c. 5thly. The cause of action. 2. In debt. On statutes.

declaration on a public statute, it is not necessary or advisable to state the title or year of the reign when the statute was passed, or to *recite any part of the act: and if it be unnecessarily stated, any material variance will be fatal, particularly if the declaration conclude against the form of the statute *aforesaid* (c); and it would be fatal to describe a statute as made in 2 and 3 years of the reign of W. 4, though if stated to have been made in a *sessions holden* in the 2 and 3 years of the reign, it would have sufficed (d). It is material however in all cases that the offence or act charged to have been committed or omitted by the defendant, appear to have been within the provision of the statute, and all circumstances necessary to support the action must be alleged (735), and the conclusion *contra formam statuti* will not aid the omission (e). If, however, the necessary matter be stated in substance and effect, it will suffice, although the precise words of the statute are not used; and therefore a declaration for *feloniously* setting fire to two stacks of oats is sufficient, though the words of the act are *unlawfully* and *maliciously* (f). The instances in which in declaring upon a statute it is necessary to set out and negative an *exception* or *proviso*, which qualifies or discharges the liability in a certain event, have been already pointed out and explained (g). In a declaration on the game laws it is not necessary to negative the particular qualifications, though it is otherwise in an information (h). When an act of parliament, which has been *recently passed*, enacts that if a party commit an offence after a named day he shall be liable to a penalty, it is usual to aver that the offence was committed after that day; but when the act has been long passed such averment is not necessary (i). It is usual also when the particular statute limits the time within which the action should be brought, to *aver that the offence was* committed within such time; but this also does not seem material (k).

Contra formam statuti.

Where the act or omission, which is the foundation of the suit, was not an offence at common law, it is necessary in all cases *to conclude* "*against the form of the statute*," or *"statutes;" (l) or to show at least that the declaration is founded on the statute, by introducing the words *de placito transgressionis et contemptus contra formam statuti* (m)(736); and this is necessary also in [*406]

(c) *Ante*, 246; Com. Dig. Action on Statute, H. 1; 2 Saund. 374, n. 2; 6 T. R. 776; 2 East, 341; 1 Saund. 135 a, note, 5th edit.

(d) Rex *v.* Biers, 1 Adol. & Ell. 327; and see Com. Dig. Action on Statute, 1 J. B. Moore, 303; Cowp. 474.

(e) 1 Saund. 135, note 3; 1 Salk. 212; Com. Dig. Action, Statute, A. 3; Pleader, C. 76; 1 Taunt. 128, 511; 1 New Rep. 245; 1 Leach, Cro. Law, 4th edit. 493; 2 Marsh. 364, n. c; 13 East, 258.

(f) 3 Wils. 318; 2 Bla. Rep. 842; 5 East, 244; 2 Marsh. 361; but see 1 Leach, Cro. Law, 4th edit. 493.

(g) *Ante*, 255.

(h) 1 T. R. 144, 145; 1 Lev. 26; Com. Dig. Action on Statute; 1 East, 639; 2 Com. Rep. 524.

(i) Gilb. Cases L. & E. 242; 1 Saund. 309, note 5; and see Fitzgib. 136; Bac. Ab. Usury, K. 209.

(k) 2 East, 340, 362.

(l) 2 East, 339; 1 Saund. 134, note 3; 6 East, 140; 7 *Id.* 516; 1 Chitty Crim. Law, 290; 3 B. & C. 186.

(m) 2 East, 341; see 3 B. & C. 189.

(735) { M'Keon *v.* Lane, 1 Hall's Rep. 318. } Vide Burnham *v.* Webster, 5 Mass. Rep. 270. Bigelow *v.* Johnston, 13 Johns. Rep. 428. Hassenfrats *v.* Kelly, 13 Johns. Rep. 468.

(736) { Wells *v.* Iggulden, 5 Dowl. & Ryl. 13, and *quære*, whether the words (*contra formam statuti*) can be supplied by any other words of equivalent import. Barter *v.* Martin, 5 Greenl. Rep. 76. }

IV. ITS PARTS, &c. — 5thly. The cause of action. 2. In debt. On statutes.

an action to recover back money won at play (n)(737). In debt for the recovery of a penalty given by statute for an offence thereby created, the Court arrested the judgment, on the ground that the declaration, after truly describing the offence, contained no averment that the offence was committed "contrary to the statute," although it was alleged "whereby and by force of the statute in such case made and provided the defendant forfeited £100, and thereby and by force of the statute an action hath accrued," &c. (o). The words "whereby and according to the form of the *statute*" will not suffice, when the action is founded on two statutes (p); in this case the conclusion should be "against the form of the statutes." (q)(738) Where, however, a statute refers to a former act, and adopts and continues the provisions of it, the declaration should conclude only against the form of the statute (r). But where a statute has been wholly discontinued and is afterwards revived, there seem to have been some opinions that a prosecution on it ought to conclude against the form of the statutes (s). So where an offence is prohibited by several statutes, if only one is the foundation of the action, and the others are explanatory or restrictive, it is proper to conclude against the form of the statute in the singular number (t). The omission of the words "against the form of the statute," or "statutes," when proper to be inserted, is fatal even after verdict (u). In general, however, there is no difference as to the doctrine of [*407] *amending at common law between penal and other actions (x); and the statute 4 Geo. 2, c. 26, extends the provisions of the statute of jeofails to penal actions (y); and it has before been determined that the 32 Hen. 8, c. 30, extended to penal actions (z).

Per quod actio accrevit. It is usual, in addition to the statement *contra formam statuti*, and of the consequent forfeiture of the penalty, to allege that "by means of the premises, and by force of the statute in such case made and provided, an action hath accrued to the plaintiff to demand and have the said sum, &c.," but this appears unnecessary (a). And even assuming it to be requisite, yet a count for a penalty on the statute 5 Ann. stating the defendant kept a snare to kill game "against the form of the statute in such case made and provided, and by reason thereof and by force of the statute in such case made and provided, an action hath accrued," is sufficient; for the first-mentioned statute refers to the 5 Ann. c. 14, creating the offence and giving the penalty; and the last-

(n) 1 M. & Sel. 500.
(o) 3 B. & C. 186; 5 D. & R. 186, S. C.; *sed vide* 9 Price, 397, in which part of the Court held that an information for a penalty for smuggling was good, although the words "contrary to the statute" were omitted in describing the offence, such offence being laid minutely, so as to bring it within the words of the act, and it being alleged that the forfeiture was "according to the statute." *Sed quære.*
(p) 2 East, 340.
(q) *Id.*; Lutw. 212; 4 Hawk. 71; Com. Dig. Action on Statute, H.
(r) 1 Lutw. 212; 1 Saund. 135, note 3; 2 Saund. 377, note 12; 7 East, 516.
(s) 2 Hawk. c. 25, s. 117; *sed vide* 2 East, P. C. 601, 599; 2 Hale, 173; Cro. Eliz. 750; 2 Leach, 827.
(t) Yelv. 11; 2 Saund. 377, note 12.
(u) 2 East, 333; Willes, 599; 1 M. & Sel. 500; 3 B. & C. 186.
(x) 1 Saund. 250 d; 1 Stra. 137; 2 *Id.* 1227; 1 Wils. 256; 1 Burr. 402.
(y) Willes, 600.
(z) 3 Lev. 375; 1 Stra. 136; 2 *Id.* 1227; Dougl. 115.
(a) See 3 B. & C. 189.

(737) { M'Keon v. M'Caberty, 1 Hall's Rep. 300. }
(738) Vide Haywood v. Sheldon, 13 Johns. Rep. 88.

mentioned statute refers to the 2 Geo. 3, c. 19, by which the whole penalty is given to the common informer, the half only of which had been given to him by an intervening statute (*b*).

IV. ITS PARTS, &c.

5thly. The cause of action.

2. In debt, On statutes.

Statement of the *Breach* in general in *Debt*.

As the action of debt is only sustainable for the recovery of a *debt*, the *Breach* is necessarily confined to a statement of the non-payment of the money previously alleged to be payable; and such breach is nearly similar, whether the action be in debt on simple contract, or upon a specialty, record, or statute, and is usually as follows:—"Yet the defendant, although often requested so to do, hath not as yet paid the sum of £—— (*c*) above demanded, or any part thereof, to the plaintiff (or if *qui tam*, &c. to our said Lord the King, and to the plaintiff, who sues as aforesaid,) but hath hitherto wholly neglected and refused so to do. To the damage of the plaintiff of £—— and thereupon he brings suit, &c." (739). In debt upon a *bond*, whether it be a common money bond, or be a special bond for the performance of covenants, &c. within the statute (*d*) the *penalty* is the debt *at law, and the breach in non-payment thereof is alleged in the above form. If, however, the bond have a condition within the statute, it is essential that there be upon the record an assignment of the breaches of such condition. As these breaches may be assigned in the replication as well as in the declaration, it is proposed that we notice the rules upon this subject when we treat of the replication in debt. [*408]

Damages in general in debt.

The *Damages* in an action for a debt are in general merely nominal, and not, as in *assumpsit*, the principal object of the suit; and therefore a small sum, as £10, is usually inserted. But if the contract declared upon be limited to a particular sum, and the plaintiff proceed for a larger sum for interest or delay of payment, then the sum at the conclusion should be proportionably large, so as to cover the utmost interest or damages for the detention that may be claimable either by contract or damages under 3 & 4 W. 4, c. 42, s. 28 (*e*).

In an action by a common informer, as he is not entitled to damages, no claim for them should be inserted (*f*).

III. IN COVENANT.

As the action of *Covenant* can in general only be supported on a *deed* (*g*), there is less variety in the declarations in that action than in assumpsit or debt, and therefore but few observations will here be necessary, as most of the rules to be observed in framing a declaration in *assumpsit* or debt equally apply in

(*b*) 7 East, 516; see 2 East, 338.

(*c*) This is to be the sum named in the commencement of the delaration, being the aggregate of all the sums stated to be due in the different counts.

(*d*) 8 & 9 Wm. 3, c. 11, s. 8.

(*e*) Watkins *v.* Morgan, 6 Car. & P. 661.

(*f*) 4 Burr. 2021, 2490. *Quære*, whether the statement might not be rejected as surplusage?

(*g*) *Ante*, 131, 135. As to the action of covenant in general, see *ante*, 131 to 137.

(739) It seems that a declaration in debt on bond assigning breaches under the statute, may conclude as in covenant. Gale and Stanley *v.* O'Brian, 12 Johns. Rep. 216. S. C. 13 Johns. Rep. 189.

IV. ITS PARTS, &c.

5thly. The cause of action.

3. In covenant.

framing the declaration in this action. The *Commencement* of the declaration in covenant is now alike in all the superior actions commenced in either of the superior Courts.

The various points which we have already observed upon with regard to the *inducement* or statement of introductory matter in declaring upon a lease, &c. (*h*); the *consideration* of the deed (*i*); the mode of setting out the *deed* (*k*); [*409] the *profert* (*l*); the usual *averments* and statement of title, &c. (*m*); and *the statement of the *breach* (*n*) in an action of *debt*; are equally applicable to the action of *covenant*. If the declaration profess to make profert of the indenture, it suffices for plaintiff to produce and prove the *counterpart* (*o*). The plaintiff may assign in the same count a distinct breach of each separate covenant contained in the deed (*p*). And the general pleading rules, Hil. T. 4 W. 4, reg. 5, although they prohibit several *counts*, expressly permit *several breaches*. It is usual, after stating the breaches of covenant, to *conclude* by alleging "And so the plaintiff in fact saith that the defendant, (although often requested so to do), hath not kept his said covenant, but hath broken the same;" but this is mere form, and unnecessary (*q*). *Damages* being the principal object in this action (*r*), there should be laid as such a sum sufficiently large to cover the utmost demand, and even a claim for interest, when claimable under 3 & 4 W. 4, c. 42, s. 28 (*s*).

IN ACTIONS FOR TORTS.

THE STATEMENT IN ACTIONS EX DELICTO OF THE CAUSE OF ACTION.

Actions in form *ex delicto* are *Case*, *Trover* (*t*), *Replevin*, *Trespass*, and *Ejectment*. The applicability of these forms of action has already been fully considered; and in the second volume will be found a copious collection of the forms of declarations which are usually in requisition, with notes explanatory of the different allegations, &c. (*u*).

In actions for *wrongs*, the declaration should state, 1st, The *matter* or *thing* affected; 2dly, The plaintiff's *right* thereto; 3dly, The *injury*; and, 4thly, The *damage* sustained by the plaintiff. We will consider each of these as regards *general rules*; and then state the *particular rules* relating to declarations for *written* and *verbal Slander*.

1st. Statement of the *matter* or *thing* injured.

In actions brought for *injuries* to *real property* (*v*), the *quality* of the realty,

(*h*) *Ante*, 395.

(*i*) *Ante*, 399.

(*k*) *Ante*, 334, 336, 400. As to *variances*, *ante*, 334, 337. Amendment, 348.

(*l*) *Ante*, 398.

(*m*) *Ante*, 401.

(*n*) *Ante*, 408. And the rules as to assigning a breach in assumpsit may in general be applied to covenant, see *ante*, 365; as to a *general* assignment of breach, *ante*, 368; *post*.

(*o*) Pearce *v.* Morrice, 2 Bar. & Adol. 396.

(*p*) 3 Co. 4 a; 1 Saund. 58 b.

(*q*) 1 Saund. 235 a, note 7; *post*, vol. ii.; see 2 Taunt. 278.

(*r*) 13 East, 343.

(*s*) Watkins *v.* Morgan, 6 Car. & P. 661.

(*t*) As to *detinue* being an action *ex contractu*, see *ante*, 138, 229, note (*b*).

(*u*) The author would suggest to the student the perusal of the forms as the best mode of understanding the general rules here attempted to be explained with regard to the construction of the pleadings. See *post*, vol. ii. *Declaration* in *Detinue*, *Case*, *Trover*, *Replevin*, *Trespass*, and *Ejectment*.

(*v*) As to the rule in a real action for the recovery of realty itself, Stephen, 2d edit. 347, 349; forms, *post*, vol. iii.

IV. 1TH PARTS, &c.

5thly. The cause of action.

as whether it consist of houses, lands, or other *corporeal* hereditaments, should be shown (*x*). If the declaration charge "*the breaking and entering into* the plaintiff's *dwelling house*," the plaintiff will fail, if it appear that the defendant only broke an *external* rail fence, and trespassed on leads forming the *roof* of a counting-house, occupied by A. B. but used only as an easement to the plaintiff's house (*y*).

[*410]

*In trespass to *land*, the term "*close*" is proper, although the ground be not inclosed, as it imports the exclusive right of possession and *interest* in the soil (*z*). In order to avoid the necessity for a new assignment, the pleading rules, Hil. T. 4 W. 4, reg. V. *In Trespass*, expressly require that the *name* of the close, *or* the *abuttals*, or *some other description*, be used in the statement, or that the defendant may demur specially, and *towards* instead of *upon* has been considered an improper description by abuttals (*a*). Where the declaration stated that the defendants, A., B., and C., broke a close of the plaintiff abutting on a close of the *defendant*, in the singular, and it appeared in evidence that the plaintiff's close abutted on a close of the first-named defendant, it was held that this was an *ambiguity*, not a *variance* (*b*).

As trespass (*c*) and ejectment (*d*) do not lie in general for wrongs which relate to incorporeal hereditaments, the word "*tenement*" should be avoided in the *first* description of the premises, though after stating them with sufficient certainty, "*said tenements*," by way of reference to the antecedent description, would not be objectionable. It is not necessary to show the *quantity* of the land (except, perhaps, in replevin) (*e*). A way ought not to be described as a passage."(*f*)

In *prescribing* for, or otherwise stating a right of *common* or *way*, or a right to *tolls*, &c. it is judicious to avoid claiming or stating more than constitutes the subject-matter of the particular dispute, for by this precaution a variance may be avoided (*g*); but in general in actions of tort the plaintiff may succeed although he only prove a part of his complaint (*h*). Where a declaration in *case* alleged that "the plaintiff was possessed of a house, *belonging* to and supporting which there were certain *foundations*, which the plaintiff had enjoyed, and ought to enjoy;" it was held that this was a sufficient description of the plaintiff's right to the enjoyment of the foundations as an *easement* (*i*).

In actions for injuring or taking away *goods or chattels*, it is in general necessary that their *quality*, *quantity*, or *number*, and *value* or price, should be

(*x*) Stephen, 347, 2d ed.
(*y*) 3 C. & P. 331.
(*z*) Dr. & Stud. 30; 7 East, 207; Vin. Ab. Fences; *ante*, 200.
(*a*) Lempriere *v.* Humphrey, 4 Nev. & Man. 638; 1 Harr. & Woll. 171; and see form and notes, *post*, vol. ii.
(*b*) Walford *v.* Anthony and others, 8 Bing. 75.
(*c*) *Ante*, 200.
(*d*) *Ante*, 217.
(*e*) 2 M. & P. 78; as to stating the parish, *ante*, 308.
(*f*) Yelv. 163.
(*g*) 2 Saund. 172, note 1; 1 Taunt. 142; 4 T. R. 160; Bul. N. P. 59; 1 Campb. 315 a; 4 *Id.* 189; 2 Hen. Bla. 234; Vin. Ab. Prescriptions, W.; 1 Esp. Rep. 437; Selw. N. P. Trespass, IV. 7.
(*h*) *Id.*; *post*, 420.
(*i*) 1 Cromp. & Jerv. 20.

IV. ITS PARTS, &c. — 8thly. The cause of action.

stated (k)(740); the assigned reason is, that a former recovery could not otherwise be pleaded in bar of a second action for the same goods, neither could the defendant properly defend himself (l). Therefore, in all the forms of action for a tort to goods, it is in general insufficient, even after judgment by default or verdict, to allege that the defendant injured or took, &c. "divers

[*411] goods and chattels" of the plaintiff, without giving any description *of them (m). And an averment that the defendant took the plaintiff's "fish," not showing their number or nature (n); or "divers, to wit, ten articles of household furniture," not stating their nature or quality (o); is substantially defective. It must be confessed that as the description of goods or land must in general be exceedingly similar, there is but little practical utility in this rule except as regards the description of a close by *abuttals*.

In trover, trespass, and case, less particularity is required than in detinue and replevin, because it is only in the two latter forms of action that the plaintiff can claim or recover the goods themselves (p). In trover, trespass, and case, *damages* only are recoverable, and the specification of quality and quantity in a general way is allowed; as "two *packs* of flax," "two ricks of hay," a "library of books." (q) But in *detinue* the value of the goods, either of each article, or the aggregate value of the whole, should be stated (r).

Perhaps less particularity may be required where the *gravamen* or gist of the action is the breaking and injuring a house, &c. and the injury to goods is laid chiefly as *aggravation;* as trespass for breaking, &c. a house, and taking "several keys" belonging to the doors thereof (s), or *damaging* "the goods and chattels therein," and wrenching open and injuring the "doors thereof."(t)

With regard to the *quality* or *species* of the goods, the plaintiff is perhaps bound to prove the fact as laid (u); but with regard to the *quantity* or *number* and *value* of the goods, he may prove *less* than he charges in his declaration, but he cannot prove *more*, although the statement be under a *videlicet* (x); as if the declaration be "divers, to wit, ten horses," he may show an injury to or conversion of one horse, but not of eleven horses (y). Of course, therefore, it is prudent to lay the quantity to an extent clearly adequate to cover the largest possible amount, but at the same time according to the facts.

9thly. Statement of the plaintiff's right or interest in such matter, &c.(z).

The *plaintiff's right or interest* in or *title* to the matter or thing affected may exist independently of any particular obligation or duty on the part of the de-

(k) See 11 Rep. 25, 26; 1 Saund. 333, n. 7; 2 *Id.* 74, note 1; 4 Burr. 2455; Stephen, 2d edit. 347; M'Clel. R. 277, 278.

(l) M'Clel. R. 278; 11 East, 576.

(m) *Vide* last two notes; and 7 Taunt. 642; 1 Moore, 386, S. C.; 8 *Id.* 379.

(n) 5 Rep. 34 b; see observations 2 Saund. 74, note 1; Stephen, 348.

(o) 8 Moore, 379; see, however, 2 Saund. 74 a, note.

(p) 2 Saund. 74, note 1.

(q) 2 Saund. 74, note 1; Stephen, 349, 350. Cattle may be described with a *videlicet* under the word "chattels," 17 Edw. 3, pl. 41.

(r) 4 B. & Ald. 271; *per Cur.*

(s) Salk. 643; after verdict, 2 Saund. 74 b, n. 1; Stephen, 2d ed. 350.

(t) 3 Wils. 292.

(u) See Stephen, 2d ed. 352.

(x) As to the *videlicet* in general, see *ante*, 348.

(y) See 8 Taunt. 107; M'Clel. Rep. 270; Stephen, 2d edit. 351; Rep. T. Hardw. 121; 2 Saund. 74 b; Gilb. Evid. 229.

(740) Vide The People v. Dunlap, 13 Johns. Rep. 446.

IV. ITS PARTS, &c.

5thly. The cause of action.

fendant; or it may *be a right to insist on the performance by the defendant of some *particular* duty, founded either on contract between the parties, or an implied obligation of law, resulting from the defendant's particular character or situation (z). Where the *law* gives a *general* or *public* right, as for all persons to fish in a public navigable river, it is improper, at least unnecessary, *specially* to state such public right, and it will suffice to show with brevity that there was a public right, as the instance just put, that such a particular place was a public navigable river, and that the defendant prevented the plaintiff from fishing, &c. (a). And whenever the right of the plaintiff is *implied by law*, as the absolute right of personal security, it is unnecessary to state the same in pleading. Thus, in actions for assault and battery, false imprisonment, words or libels, when actionable in themselves, and malicious prosecutions, it is sufficient to allege the injury, without any *inducement of the* plaintiff's right to personal security, &c.; though it is usual in an action for slander to begin the declaration with a statement of the plaintiff's good character (b). But where the law does not imply the right to the matter or thing affected, it must be stated either *generally* or *specially* (c); in other words, some *general* or *special* allegation of a title or right must be made in the declaration. Thus, in a declaration for slander, affecting a person in the way of his trade (741), his carrying on the particular trade must be shown by way of inducement (d). And in an action for an injury to the relative rights of persons, the relation of husband (e), or master (f), in respect of which the plaintiff was injured, must be stated.

It is chiefly in actions for trespasses and torts, committed to and in respect of *personal* and *real* property, that it becomes material to consider to what extent the plaintiff must show his *title or interest*. It is hardly necessary to observe that if *no property or interest* in the subject-matter of the suit be stated in the declaration to have existed, or been vested in the plaintiff, at the time the wrong was committed, the omission will be fatal even after verdict: the objection being the total *omission*, not the *defective statement* *of a title (g). [*413] But the error in the declaration may be cured if the *plea* admit the plaintiff's property (h).

The fundamental rule upon the subject of showing title in actions *ex delicto* is, that as against a mere *wrong-doer*, or person apparently having no color of right, mere *possession* suffices, and a *special* statement of title is unnecessary (i). In personal actions therefore title is mere inducement, at least in a

(z) It seems that unless inducement be traversed by plea it now stands admitted, Dukes v. Gostling, 3 Dowl. 619.

(a) Willes, 268; Vin. Ab. Prescription, U.; Ld. Raym. 1091.

(b) *Post*, vol. ii.

(c) Com. Dig. Pleader, C. 34.

(d) 1 Saund. 242 a, note 3; 2 Saund. 307, n. 1; 2 B. & P. 284; *post*, vol. ii.; as to this *post*, 429, 430.

(e) *Post*, vol. ii.

(f) *Id.*

(g) 2 Saund. 379, n. 13; Com. Dig. Pleader, 3 M. 9.

(h) 1 Sid. 184.

(i) *Ante*, 71, 170, 194, 202; 10 Co. 59 b; Com. Dig. Plead. C. 39, 41; Tidd, 9th ed. 443; Steph. 2d edit. 356; 1 East, 212. For this purpose, and until the defendant has pleaded and shown a superior title, he must be taken to be a mere trespasser, Steph. 357. Even in an action of *ejectment*, where the general rule is *that the* lessor of the plaintiff must recover upon the strength of his own title as proved by him, yet *mere priority* of *possession* will enable a plaintiff to recover against a third person, a trespasser, who intrudes, Doe v. Cook, 7 Bing. 346.

(741) So, in a declaration for slander of an attorney there must be a *colloquium* of his profession. Gilbert v. Field, 3 Caines' Rep. 389.

IV. ITS PARTS, &c.

5thly. The cause of action.

pleading point of view, as regards the declaration; although *in real actions* (*k*), and as we shall hereafter observe in many *pleas* in personal actions, a strict and *particular* statement of *title* is essential. In *personal* actions *damages* are the gist of the suit; in *real* actions *the right* or *title* forms the prominent subject of inquiry (*l*).

It is proposed to defer the consideration of the rules affecting the statement of a *title specially*, and the mode of pleading a derivative title, a right by *custom*, *prescription*, or *grant*, &c. until we examine the structure of *pleas*, in which title is in general to be shown with particularity.

In trespass, trover, detinue, case, or replevin, for an injury to or taking away, &c. goods, the plaintiff's right to or interest in the goods, either as absolute owner, or as having a limited right therein (*m*), is no otherwise described in the declaration than by the averment, that they were the goods "of the plaintiff," or that he was lawfully possessed of them as of his own property." (*n*)(742) When the plaintiff has not a possessory right, and his interest in the chattel is *reversionary*, it must be expressly so described in the declaration, which, as we have before explained, must then be framed in case (*o*).

[*414] Upon the principle just alluded to, in *trespass* for a wrong relating to land, or other *real* property, a *special* or particular *title in the plaintiff need not be shown in the declaration. The averment in describing the trespass, that the close or house, &c. in reference to which it was committed, was the *close*, &c. "of the plaintiff," or other equivalent allegation (*p*), is sufficient (*q*); and under it may be given in evidence any title or interest in *possession*, which is adequate to the support of the form of action under the circumstances of the case.

In *other* personal actions for injuries to *real* property corporeal or incorporeal, it was formerly usual to state the plaintiff's title *specially*, as that he was *seised in his demesne as of fee* of a house, mill, &c. and was entitled by *prescription* or *grant*, &c. to the right of common, way, watercourse, or other right affected (*r*); but it is now fully settled that in a personal action against a *wrong-doer* for the recovery of damages, and not the land itself, it is sufficient at *common law* to state in the *declaration* that the plaintiff, at the time the injury was commi tted, was *possessed* of a house or land, &c., and that *by reason of such possession* he was entitled to the common of pasture, way, or other right, in the exercise of which he has been disturbed (*s*). And though a distinction has been taken between a declaration against a wrong-doer and against the *owner of the soil* (*t*); and it has been considered that in the latter case the

(*k*) Com. Dig. Pleader, 3 I. 5; Bul. N. P. 122; *post*, vol. iii.

(*l*) As to the distinction between actions that *sound in damages* and those that do not, Steph. 2d ed. 138, 474.

(*m*) As to this distinction, and when such parties may sue, see *ante*, 71, 170, 194, 202.

(*n*) See 2 Saund. 279, n. 13; Stephen 2d. ed. 355; *post*, vol. ii. As to the words, "as of his own property," *post*, vol. ii.

(*o*) *Ante*, 169, 170, 174; *post*, vol. ii.

(*p*) Com. Dig. Pleader, 3 M. 9.

(*q*) *Id.*; 2 Bulstr. 288; *post*, vol. ii. Steph. 2d edit. 355, 356.

(*r*) See the cases in Com. Dig. Pleader, C. 34 to C. 38; 2 Saund. 113 a, n. 1; and precedents referred to, 1 Saund. 346, n. 2.

(*s*) Com. Dig. Pleader, C. 39, and Action on the Case for Disturbance, B.; 2 Saund. 113 a, n. 1, 172, n. 1; 3 T. R. 766; Willes, 508, 654; 1 Saund. 346, n. 2; 6 East, 438, n. a; see precedents, *post*, vol. ii. 568 to 574; 10 Co. 59, b.

(*t*) See 4 Mod. 421; 1 Stra. 5; Willes, 619; 1 Burr. 440; 4 T. R. 718; Tidd, 9th edit. 444; 1 T. R. 431.

(742) Good *v.* Harnish, 13 Serg. & Rawle, 93.

IV. ITS PARTS, &c.

5thly. The cause of action.

plaintiff's title by grant, &c. must be specially stated, because it might be qualified by some condition precedent, the performance of which ought to be shown, &c. (u); yet it appears sufficient in both cases to *declare* generally on the plaintiff's possession; though in a *plea* it was, before the statute 2 & 3 W. 4, c. 71, necessary to state the seisin in fee and prescriptive right or grant (x). And in pleading a prescriptive right of common, &c. as a *justification*, the defendant [*415] *must show a seisin in fee of the land in respect of which it is claimed, and prescribe in the *que* estate for the right; and if he claim as tenant of the freeholder, he must prescribe in the *latter*, not in himself (y).

How to declare if right not appurtenant.

If the right of common, way, or watercourse, &c. be *not appurtenant* to the house, land, &c. and the plaintiff be entitled thereto by agreement or license, the allegation in the *declaration* that he was entitled, "*by reason of the possession, &c.*" would be improper (z). And when a *reversioner* sues for an injury to houses, land, &c. in possession of his tenant, his interest must be described accordingly; though it is sufficient to allege generally that the lands were in possession of the third person, "as tenant thereof to the plaintiff," without stating a seisin in fee, &c. (a).

How to declare by a reversioner.

How to declare for obstruction to ancient lights,

In an action on the case for obstructing *ancient* (b) *lights*, the *declaration* usually states that the plaintiff, at the time of committing the grievances complained of, was lawfully possessed of a messuage, situate, &c. wherein there of right were and ought to be certain windows, through which the light and air ought to have entered the messuage, and then states the injury; and this is sufficient without alleging that the windows were ancient (c). So, if the declaration be for diverting a *watercourse* from the plaintiff's mill, his possession of the mill should be concisely stated, and that *by reason thereof* he ought to have had the use and benefit of the watercourse, without stating that it was an ancient mill, or disclosing the particular grounds upon which the right to the water is claimed (d). And in an action for a disturbance of a *right of common* (e), or *way* (f), or of a *seat* or *pew* in a church (g), the *declaration* states the possession of a house, or land, &c. and *that by reason thereof* the plaintiff was entitled to the right, in the exercise of which he had been disturbed. The same mode of *declaring* has long been considered to be sufficient in actions for disturbance of *franchises*, or subtraction [*416] *of *tolls*, (h), *ferries* (i), and *offices* (k). The mode in which an *easement* may be claimed has been already pointed out (l). In case, upon a custom for not grinding at the plaintiff's mill,

or water-courses,

or common or way, or seat in a pew, &c.

Disturbance of franchises.

(u) 1 Burr. 443, 444.

(x) 3 T. R. 766, 768; 2 Saund. 113 a, n. 1, and cases there collected; and see the precedents, Lutw. 119, 120; 1 Barnard. K. B. 432; 6 East, 438, n. a; 1 Rol. Rep. 394; 1 Show. 18, 19; 3 Lev. 266; 4 T. R. 719; 1 Saund. 346, n. 2; *post*, vol. ii.

(y) 3 You. & Jerv. 93.

(z) 4 East, 107; 6 *Id.* 438; *post*, vol. ii. See 15 East, 108; 3 Taunt. 24.

(a) *Post*, vol. ii. When not, see 1 Camp. 320.

(b) As to the word "ancient" in this case, 1 M. & M. 400.

(c) *Post*, vol. ii.; Cro. Car. 325; 1 Show. 17, 18.

(d) *Post*, vol. ii.; 1 Leon. 247; Palm. 290; 3 Lev. 133; 4 East, 107. See 2 B. & C. 910.

(e) See *post*, vol. ii.; 4 Mod. 418; 1 Saund. 346, n. 2; Comb. 370.

(f) *Post*, vol. ii.

(g) *Id.* *Quære*, if the plaintiff claim against the ordinary, Tidd, 9th ed. 444.

(h) 2 Saund. 113 a, 172 o, n. 1; 6 East, 438, n. (a); Willes, 654; Owen, 109; Cro. Jac. 43; *post*, vol. ii.; 1 Cromp. & Jerv. 57.

(i) 6 B. & C. 703; Willes, 508; 2 Saund. 114, 172, n. 1; 2 You. & Jerv. 285; title thereto, *id.*

(k) 10 Co. 59 b; Cro. Eliz. 335; 8 Wentw. Index, 58; Morg. Prec. 345, 347; 4 Mod. 422.

(l) *Ante*, 409.

IV. ITS PARTS, &c. — 6thly. The cause of action.

the plaintiff may declare generally, without showing the amount *of toll or the* consideration for it (*m*). And where a corporation brings an action for any due, it is sufficient to state in a *declaration*, though it is otherwise in a plea, that it is an ancient borough, and that the burgesses thereof are, and for divers years have been, a body politic, in the name of the mayor, &c., without setting out the name of incorporation, or any title to the duty; for the declaration being founded upon their possession, there is no necessity to state a title to the thing (*n*). However, though it is not necessary in these actions for damages to lay a title in the *declaration* by grant or prescription, &c. yet the title or consideration must be *proved* on the trial (*o*). It suffices to aver, that the plaintiff had the title or right when the wrong was committed; and an averment that he *still is* possessed may be rejected as surplusage (*p*).

The common law mode of declaring generally is expressly sanctioned by 2 & 3 W. 4, c. 71, s. 5.

In affirmance of this common law right of declaring generally in these cases, the 2 & 3 W. 4, c. 71, sect. 5, enacts, "that in all actions on the case and other pleadings, wherein the party claiming may now by law allege his right generally, without averring the existence of such right from time immemorial, such general allegation *shall still be deemed sufficient*; and if the same shall be denied, all and every the matters in this act mentioned and provided, which shall be applicable to the case, shall be admissible in evidence to sustain or rebut such allegation."

More general modes of stating rights in pleas, &c. under 2 & 3 W. 4, c. 71, s. 5.

With respect to *pleas and subsequent* pleadings, such a *general mode* of stating a right of common or other easement, &c. in a justification was not permitted (*q*), and every defendant was required in his plea to show a *seisin in fee* of the land in respect of which it was claimed, and to prescribe in the *que estate* for the right, and if he claimed as tenant of a freeholder, he must have prescribed in the latter, not in himself (*r*). But the above statute now authorizes a more general plea, as will be shown when we examine the requisites of pleas (*s*).

Mode of declaring where *defendant* is under any particular obligation or duty.

When the plaintiff's right consists in an *obligation on the defendant to observe some particular duty*, the declaration must state the nature of *such duty*, which we have seen may be founded either on a *contract* between the parties, or on the obligation of law, arising out of the defendant's *particular* character or situation; and the plaintiff must prove such duty as laid, and a variance will, as in actions on contracts, be fatal. When the declaration is for the breach of an express or implied *contract*, and proceeds for *nonfeasance*, the *consideration* of the contract must be stated either in terms or in substance (*t*);
[*417] but when it is for a *misfeasance* or *malfeasance*, no consideration need be stated (*u*); and when *it is founded on the obligation of *law*, unconnected

(*m*) 6 M. & Sel. 69.

(*n*) 1 Saund. 340, n. 2; Owen, 109; Cro. Jac. 43, 123; 2 Ventr. 291; 6 East, 438. What a variance, 1 Campb. 466; 8 East, 487; 6 Taunt. 467; 2 Marsh. 174, S. C.; 7 Taunt. 546; 1 Moore, 267, S. C.

(*o*) 2 Saund. 114 c; 4 Mod. 421, 424; 1 Saund. 346, n. 2.

(*p*) 3 Taunt. 137.

(*q*) *Ante*, note.

(*r*) 3 Young & Jerv. 93; and see forms of pleas, *post*, vol. iii.

(*s*) And see forms, *post*, vol. iii. and Bosanquet's Rules, 117.

(*t*) 5 T. R. 143; 3 Wils. 348; 12 East, 94.

(*u*) 5 T. R. 143; 3 Wils. 348; 3 East, 62; 6 East, 332; 2 Lord Raym. 909; 12 East, 89.

IV. ITS PARTS, &c.

5thly. The cause of action.

with any contract between the parties, it is sufficient to state very concisely the circumstances which gave rise to the defendant's particular duty or liability; as in actions against sheriffs, carriers, innkeepers, &c. (x). Where the defendant *is liable of common right*, as to repair a wall for preventing damage to his neighbor, according to the maxim, *sic utere tuo ut alienum non lædas*, it was always considered sufficient to state that the defendant was *possessed* of a certain close, &c. and that *by reason thereof he* was bound to repair, &c. without showing the particular ground of the defendant's liability (y). But where a *charge* was imposed on another *against common* right, as owner of the soil or terre-tenant, it was formerly thought that the plaintiff ought to disclose the particular grounds on which the defendant's liability is founded (z); as in an action for not repairing a fence, or for not keeping a bull or a boar, &c. (a). But it is now settled that there is no foundation for this distinction; and in the case of *Rider* and *Smith* (b), where an action was brought for the defendant's not repairing a private road leading through his close, it was held sufficient to allege that the defendant *as occupier* of the close ought to have repaired it (743); and Mr. Justice Buller stated the distinction to be between the case where the *plaintiff* in his *declaration* lays a charge on the right of the defendant, and where the *defendant* in his *plea* prescribes in right of his own estate; in the former case the plaintiff is presumed to be ignorant of the defendant's estate, and therefore need not state it, but in the latter the defendant, knowing his own estate in right of which he claims a privilege, must set it forth (c).

In an action on the *case*, founded on an express or implied *contract* (d), as against an attorney, agent, carrier, innkeeper, or other bailee, for negligence, &c. the declaration must *correctly state the contract*, or the particular duty or consideration from which the liability results, and on which it is founded (e); and a variance in the description of a *contract*, though in an action *ex delicto*, may be as fatal as in an action in form ex contractu (f). The declaration in such case usually begins with a statement of the particular profession or situation of the defendant and his retainer, and consequent *duty or liability (g). [*418] The declaration will be defective if it do not show that by express contract, or by implication of law in respect to the defendant's particular character or situation, &c. stated by the plaintiff, the defendant was bound to do or omit the act in reference to which he is charged (h). In an action for a breach of warranty the contract of sale is stated (i); and in a declaration by a landlord against his tenant for not cultivating according to good husbandry, or for not repairing, or for waste, &c. the relation of landlord and tenant is concisely

(x) 5 T. R. 149, 150; 1 Saund. 312 c, n. 2; 12 East, 89.

(y) 6 Mod. 311; 1 Salk. 22, 360; Ld. Raym. 1090; *post*, vol. ii.; 3 T. R. 766.

(z) *Ante*, 414.

(a) 1 Salk. 335, 336; 4 Mod. 241.

(b) 3 T. R. 766; Lutw. 119; 4 T. R. 718, 76, 77; 2 Saund. 414 a, b, c; Steph. 2d ed. 370.

(c) 2 Saund. 113, note 1, 172 a, n. 1; 1 Bar. & Cres. 329; *ante*, 267, 254.

(d) In general, when sustainable in such instances, *ante*, 153.

(e) 12 East, 89; *ante*, 318.

(f) Ireland *v.* Johnson, 1 Bing. N. C. 162; Brotherton *v.* Wood, 6 Moore, 34; 3 Brod. & Bing. 54; 9 Price, 408.

(g) See forms, *post*, vol. ii.

(h) 12 East, 89; *ante*, 179; and 8 B. & C. 114; 6 Bing. 235.

(i) *Post*, vol. ii.

(743) { *Per* PETERS, J., Goshen, &c. Turnp. Co. *v.* Sears, 7 Conn. Rep. 93. }

IV. ITS PARTS, &c.

5thly. The cause of action.

stated (*k*). In a declaration on the case against a surgeon for improper treatment of the plaintiff, whereby he was worse, &c. it is sufficient to aver that the defendant was a surgeon and "was retained and employed as such," (not stating by whom,) "for reward to him," to treat and cure the plaintiff, and that the defendant *entered upon the treatment, &c.* without showing any undertaking by defendant, or averring in words that it "was defendant's duty to act skilfully, &c." (*l*). Care must be taken in declaring in case in actions of this nature that the count be not framed as in assumpsit, laying a promise, &c. (*m*).

Declarations for non-observance of the *general obligation* of law may be either for the consequences of the negligent driving of carriages, &c. (*n*); or navigating ships (*o*); or for not removing a nuisance from the defendant's lands (*p*); or against the late rector or vicar, or his executor or administrator, on the custom of the realm, for dilapidations (*q*); or against the occupier of land, for not repairing a fence or the bank of a river, &c. (*r*); or for not repairing a way over his land (*s*); or against the proprietor of tithes for not taking them away (*t*). In these cases it is sufficient to state concisely the defendant's *possession* of the personal or real property, and *his consequent obligation* or duty, the non-observance of which is complained of (*u*).

Declarations for the breach of *duty*, to which the defendant was subject in respect of his *particular character* or *situation*, are against carriers or innkeepers, for refusing to carry goods or to receive a guest, or for the loss of

[*419] *goods; or against sheriffs and other public officers for escapes on mesne (*x*) or final process (*y*); or for not arresting a debtor when the defendant had an opportunity (*z*); for false returns, &c. to mesne or final process (*a*); for not taking a replevin bond; or for taking insufficient pledges (*b*); or for not assigning a bail bond (*c*). In these cases the particular situation of the defendant from which his duty and liability arise must be concisely stated (*d*).

Variance in stating the plaintiff's right or interest (*e*).

With regard to *variances* in stating the plaintiff's title to or interest in personal or real property in actions *ex delicto*, it is important to bear in mind the general rule that in most actions in that form the plaintiff is not bound to state in his *declaration* a *special* title; it suffices in general that he allege a general title or mere possession; for his title or interest is often regarded for the purposes of pleading in the light of *inducement* only (*f*). But as the inducement in such case relates to material matter, there will be a fatal variance, if, instead of relying on the *general* statement of his title, interest, or right, the plaintiff enter into a more particular and detailed statement thereof, and there be a mis-description. *Mere* surplusage, which can be rejected, will not

(*k*) *Id.*
(*l*) 11 Price, 200.
(*m*) *Ante*, 156, 228.
(*n*) *Post*, vol. ii.
(*o*) *Id.*
(*p*) *Id.*
(*q*) *Id.*
(*r*) *Id.*
(*s*) 3 T. R. 766; Lutw. 119.
(*t*) *Post*, vol. ii.
(*u*) *Post*, vol. ii.; *ante*, 155, 318.
(*x*) *Post*, vol. ii.
(*y*) *Id.*
(*z*) *Id.*
(*a*) *Id.*
(*b*) *Id.*
(*c*) *Id.*
(*d*) 12 East, 89; *ante*, 155, 318; 8 B. & C. 114; 2 M. & R. 35, S. C.
(*e*) As to variances in stating the consideration and the promise in *assumpsit*, *ante*, 328 and 333.
(*f*) *Ante*, 412, 319; and see the instances there.

IV. ITS PARTS, &c.

5thly. The cause of action.

vitiate (g); but where some statement upon the subject is necessary, and it cannot be rejected *in toto*, the variance in the detail is a ground of nonsuit, although such minute description were not essential.

Having fully stated this principle already, and illustrated it by several instances (h), it will be useless here to attempt further explanation. We may however add as an additional instance, the observations of Mr. J. Lawrence, in an action for slander of a physician (i), namely, "Even if it be not necessary in general for the party to show that he has regularly taken his degree, in this case it was necessary, because the plaintiff alleged in his declaration that he had *duly taken the degree* of doctor of physic." And if the unnecessarily *particular detail of title disclose that the plaintiff had no claim, the pleading is defective (k). It is also a rule, that if a necessary inducement of the plaintiff's right, &c. even in actions for torts, relate to and describe and be founded on a matter of *contract*, it is necessary to be strictly correct in stating such contract, it being matter of *description* (l). Thus, even in *case* against a carrier, if the *termini* of the journey which was to be undertaken be mis-stated, the variance will be fatal (m). Here the allegation in the inducement relates to matter of description. As a *prescription* is founded on a supposed grant, and is therefore *entire*, for the subject-matter granted must necessarily be *descriptive* of the grant itself, it follows that *partial* proof of that which is claimed by the prescription is insufficient, although the proof fail only as to part which is not material in the particular case on the trial (n). Therefore if a party, in stating a prescription, allege a prescriptive right to fish "in *four* specified places," but it extend to three of them only, the variance is fatal, although the tort were not committed in the excepted part (o). So, if he lay a prescriptive right of common generally, and the proof be of a *limited, qualified*, or *conditional* right, as "paying 1*d*." (p); or allege it to be for "all commonable cattle," but the proof show that the right relates to certain particular cattle, either in number or species (q), there is a fatal mis-description. These rules apply to the statement of a *prescription* by either party. But although the prescriptive right be general and absolute for all commonable cattle, yet if the tort relate to a particular description of cattle only, it may be simply alleged that the party had the right for such cattle; as if the prescription be laid "for two horses," proof that it *also* extended to "two cows" will not be considered a variance from the allegation; for it does not disprove it, or destroy the identity of the prescription; and the party need only show *so much as applies to his case, provided he do not introduce an allegation *contradicting* the prescription (r).

[*420]

[*421]

(g) *Ante*, 261.

(h) *Ante*, 261 to 267. The same doctrine holds as to inducements in *assumpsit*, *ante*, 318; see 3 Stark. Evid. *Variance*, 1542, on the rule that *descriptive* allegations, though unnecessarily confined, cannot be rejected.

(i) 8 T. R. 308.

(k) Ireland *v.* Johnson, 1 Bingh. N. C. 162; and *ante*, 417, note (f); *ante*, 264; 1 Saund. 346 a, note.

(l) Dougl. 640; 1 B. & B. 538; 1 Esp. Rep. 302; 12 East, 452; 2 Marsh. 485; *ante*, 318, 319, 332; and instances there. Variances in stating contracts, *ante*, 333.

(m) 1 M. & P. 735; 4 Bingh. 706, S. C. The *termini* may be described according to common parlance, "*London* to Blackheath," will include "Charing Cross," or "Saint George's Fields," to "Blackheath;" when, *id.*

(n) 3 Stark. Evid. 1548, *Variance*.

(o) 1 Campb. 309; see Noy, 67; Clay, 19; see Cro. Eliz 593.

(p) Cro. Eliz. 563; 5 Co. 78 b.

(q) Bul. N. P. 59; see 4 B. & C. 161; 6 D. & R. 291, S. C.

(r) Cro. Eliz. 722; Bul. N. P. 29; Hob. 64; 3 Stark. Evid. 1560, *Variance*; see also Phillips on Evid. *Variance* and *Prescription*.

IV. THE PARTS, &c.

5thly. The cause of action.

However, the broad and general distinctions between *contracts* and *torts* in this respect, viz. that the former are *entire* and matter of description, whereas the latter are divisible, and the allegations therein are in general matters of substance, should be here adverted to (*s*). In torts the plaintiff may prove a part of his charge, if the averment be divisible, and there be enough proved to support his case (*s*)(744). Therefore, if in a declaration for slandering the plaintiff in two trades mentioned in the declaration, there be proof of one trade only, the proof will support the declaration if the words apply to the latter trade (*t*). In case for disturbance of a right of common, the plaintiff stated that he was entitled by reason of his possession of a "messuage and land," and it was held sufficient to prove that he was possessed of *land* only (*u*): but Abbott, C. J., said, that if there had been words of connexion, such as "thereunto belonging," or other words of like import, to connect the messuage and land together as one entire tenement, he should have thought the plaintiff was not entitled to recover (*x*).

3dly. Statement of the injury, and of variances in the description thereof.

Injuries ex delicto are either committed with or without *force* (*y*), and are immediate or *consequential* (*z*); they may also arise from malfeasance, misfeasance, or nonfeasance (*a*). In declarations in *trespass*, which lies only for wrongs immediate and committed with force, the injury is stated without any inducement of the defendant's motive or intent, or of the circumstances under which the injury was committed (*b*). The injury in trespass should be stated directly and positively, and not by way of recital; and therefore a declaration

[*422] *charging "for that *whereas*," or "*wherefore*," the defendant committed the trespass, is bad on special demurrer (*c*) (745); and was formerly holden to be so in arrest of judgment; but it was afterwards holden that it might be amended at any time before or after judgment by a right bill, the time of filing which the Court would not inquire into (*d*) (746). In the Common Pleas, when the supposed writ was recited, the mistake was aided, and was not deemed a ground even of special demurrer (*e*). In the statement of the *trespass-*

(*s*) Gilb Evid. 229; Rep. t. Hardw. 121; 2 Saund. 74 b, 207, n. 24; *ante*, 343, 348. There is a distinction between allegations of matter of *substance* and allegations of matter of description; the latter only need be literally proved, 9 East, 160; 3 B. & C. 4; 4 D. & R. 624, S. C.

(*t*) 3 M. & Sel. 369; 1 M. & Sel. 386; *post*, 427.

(*u*) 2 B. & Ald. 360.

(*x*) *Id.* And *semble*, that a *prescription* for a right of common for a messuage and land, with the appurtenances, would not be supported by evidence of a prescriptive right appurtenant to the land only. See *Id.*; Palmer, 269; 7 Co. 5; Freem. 211; Bul. N. P. 59; 3 Stark. Evid. 1549; Selw. N. P. Replevin, VII 6th edit. 1180.

(*y*) *Ante*, 142.

(*z*) *Ante*, 142, 143.

(*a*) *Ante*, 151.

(*b*) See the forms and notes, *post*, vol. ii.

(*c*) 2 Salk. 636; 1 Stra. 621; Andr. 282; Com. Dig. Pleader, C. 86; *post*, vol. ii.

(*d*) 2 Stra. 1151, 1162.

(*e*) 1 Wils. 99; 2 *Id.* 203; Andr. 282; Barnes, 452; Com. Dig. Pleader, C. 86; S. P. ruled in Howard and Ramsbottom, in C. P. Easter Term, 1810. Smith, Attorney MS.

(744) Vide Cheetham v. Tillotson, 5 Johns Rep. 430.

(745) Vide Collier v. Moulton, 7 Johns. Rep. 111. Coffin v. Coffin, 2 Mass. Rep. 364.

(746) In Collier v. Moulton, 7 Johns. Rep. 109, and Coffin v. Coffin, 2 Mass. Rep. 358, it was held that the "*whereas*" might after verdict be rejected as surplusage. But in Hord's Ex'r v. Dishman, 2 Hen. & Mun. 595. Moore's Adm'r v. Dawney and another, 3 Hen. & Mun. 127, it was held that *quod cum* was bad on general demurrer, and was not cured by verdict. Vide 3 Hen. & Mun. 278, note. So, in Domax v. Hord, 3 Hen. & Mun. 271, which was an action on the case for *champerty*, a declaration commencing with *quod cum*, was held bad on general demurrer. Vide Marsteller and others v. M'Clean, 7 Cranch, 158.

IV. ITS PARTS, &c. — 5thly. The cause of action.

as the words "with force and arms," (*vi et armis*) should be adopted (*f*) (747), though the only mode of taking advantage of the omission is by special demurrer (*g*) (748); and in the Common Pleas, when the words appear in the recital of the supposed writ, and not in the count part, it is sufficient (*h*); and in one case Lord Holt said, that these words might be omitted (*i*); and there is an express legislative provision to this effect in regard to indictments (*k*). The conclusion of the declaration in trespass or ejectment for these forcible injuries, should also be "*contra pacem regis*," though they are mere words of form, and not traversable (*l*) (749); the omission of that allegation will however be aided, if not specially demurred to (*m*); and in the Common Pleas, if the words appeared in the recital of the supposed writ, that would suffice (*n*).

In *actions on the case*, when the act or nonfeasance complained of was not *prima facie* actionable, it is usual to state that the act complained of was *wrongfully* done (*o*). In general it is necessary to state not only the *injury* complained of, but also the *motive*, that it was *wrongfully* or *maliciously* committed; as that *the defendant *well knowing* the mischievous propensity of his [*423] dog, or having been *requested* to remove a nuisance erected by another, *maliciously* or fraudulently contriving and *intending*, &c. (stating a bad intent corresponding with the wrongful act complained of,) *committed* or *permitted* the tort (*p*).

In some actions the *scienter* being material must be *alleged* and *proved*; as in the declaration for keeping a dog used to bite mankind or sheep (*q*), or for enticing away a servant or apprentice (*r*), or for falsely representing a third person fit to be trusted, though in the latter case the word "*fraudulently*" might be sufficient (*s*). In an action on the case for a malicious prosecution in an inferior Court having no jurisdiction, a *scienter* in the defendant that the Court had no jurisdiction should it seems be averred (*t*). But in an action for debauching a wife or servant, it is not necessary to allege or prove that the defendant knew that the female was the wife or servant of the plaintiff (*u*).

(*f*) Com. Dig. Pleader, 3 M. 7; 1 Saund. 81, 82, n. 1, 140, n. 4; Jenk. Cent. 186; *per* Parke, B., in Stancliffe *v.* Hardwicke, 3 Dowl. 769.

(*g*) 4 & 5 Anne, c. 16, s. 1; 4 D. & R. 215.

(*h*) Com. Dig. Pleader, 3 M. 7.

(*i*) Lord Raym. 985; Vin. Ab. Trespass, 2. a. 5.

(*k*) 37 Hen. 8, c. 8; Crown Circ. Comp. 9th edit. (1820); 4 Hawk. P. C. 55, 56.

(*l*) Cowp. 174; 2 Bla. Rep. 1058; 2 Salk. 640, 641; Com. Dig. Pleader, 3 M. 8; Vin. Abr. *Contra pacem*, and Trespass, Q. a. 5. Though there is no longer any judgment for the fine, (see 1 Salk. 54; 3 Bl. Com. 118, 119, 398, 399; 2 Sel. Prac. 641; 2 Ld. Raym. 985; Vin. Ab. Trespass, Q. a. 5), yet Lord Holt, in 2 Ld. Raym. 985, said the words must not be omitted; and see the above cases; and yet in some instances *cessante ratione cessat et ipsa lex*, as in the case of pledges, 3 T. R. 157; 2 Hen. Bla. 161.

(*m*) 4 & 5 Anne, c. 16.

(*n*) Com. Dig. Pleader, 3 M. 8.

(*o*) Stancliffe *v.* Hardwicke, 3 Dowl. 769.

(*p*) In *trespass* the injury must be described as having been committed *vi et armis*; in case that the act complained of was *wrongfully* done, *per* Parke, B., in Stancliffe *v.* Hardwicke, 3 Dowl. 769.

(*q*) *Ante*, 94, 147; see *post*, vol. ii.

(*r*) *Post*, vol. ii.

(*s*) *Post*, vol. ii. Willes, 584. The representation must be in writing, 9 Geo. 4, c. 14. *Scienter* not material in case for driving unruly horses, 2 Lev. 172.

(*t*) 2 Wils. 302.

(*u*) *Post*, vol. ii.

(747) Vide 2 Reeve's Hist. E. L. 265.

(748) { 14 Serg. & Rawle, 403. The omission of *vi et armis* is aided by verdict. 4 Dowl. & Ryl. 215. Kerr *v.* Sharp, 14 Serg. & Rawle, 399. }

(749) Vide Gardner *v.* Thomas, 14 Johns. Rep. 134.

IV. ITS PARTS, &c. — 5thly. The cause of action.

And in an action upon an express warranty the *scienter* need not be alleged, nor if stated need it be proved (*x*). In a declaration against the mere continuer of a nuisance, it is advisable to state that he was *requested* to remove it (*y*). In an action against a sheriff for removing goods from a tenant's premises under a *fieri facias*, without paying the landlord's rent in arrear, it is necessary to aver in the declaration that the defendant had notice of the rent being in arrear; but the usual averment in stating the injury, that "the defendant well knowing the premises," did, &c. will cure the want of such an averment after verdict (*z*).

We have already seen how far the defendant's *motive* or *intent* affects the *form* of the action; and that in general when the act occasioning damage is in itself unlawful, without any other extrinsic circumstance, the intent of the wrong-doer is immaterial in point of law, though it may enhance the damages (*a*). As observed by Lord Kenyon, there is a *distinction between answering *civiliter et criminaliter* for acts injurious to others; in the latter case the maxim applies, *actus non facit reum nisi mens sit rea:* but it is otherwise in civil actions, where the intent is in general immaterial, if the act were injurious to another (*b*). Lord Ellenborough's observations in the case of *The King* v. *Phillips* (*c*), in regard to indictments, elucidate this doctrine: "If any particular bad intention accompanying the act be necessary to constitute it a crime, such intention should be laid in the indictment. In many cases the allegation of intent is a merely formal one; being no more than the result and inference which the law draws from the act itself, and which therefore requires no proof but what the act itself supplies. But where the act is indifferent in itself, the intent with which it was done then becomes material, and requires, as any substantive matter of fact does, specific allegation and proof." In declarations for slander, the defendant's malicious intent must be alleged, but it may in evidence be presumed (*d*). In an action for a malicious arrest, *malice* is a question of *fact* for the jury, who are at *liberty* but not absolutely *bound* to infer it from the want of probable cause (*e*). In an action for the consequences of a public nuisance, it is not usual to state any undue intent on the part of the defendant (*f*). So in an action on the case for pirating the plaintiff's copyright in a book, it is sufficient to state that the defendant published and sold the spurious copies, without alleging or proving any intention on the part of the defendant to pirate the copyright or injure the sale of the plaintiff's book (*g*); and in an action on a statute, as on the Black Act against the hundred, it is sufficient to follow the words of the act; and on that particular statute it was held unnecessary to state that the stack of oats and barn were unlaw-

[*424]

(*x*) 2 East, 446.
(*y*) Willes, 583; *post*, vol. ii.
(*z*) 7 Price, 566; *post*, vol. ii.; *ante*, 271, 272; 4 Bing. 66.
(*a*) *Ante*, 147.
(*b*) *Per* Kenyon, C. J., 2 East, 104. The other judges differed from his lordship, but only in the *application* of this principle to the particular case. As to the materiality of a bad intent, see the observations in *The Bailiffs, &c. of* Tewkesbury *v.* Diston, 6 East, 438, and in the King *v.* Phillips, *id.* 464. A servant when liable in trover, &c. though acting *bona fide* for his employer, *ante*, 154.
(*c*) 6 East, 473, 474. And see Crown Circ. Comp. 9th edit. (1820).
(*d*) Moor, 459; Owen, 51, S. C.; 4 Burr. 2423; 3 Taunt. 246.
(*e*) Mitchell *v.* Jenkins, 5 Bar. & Adol. 588.
(*f*) *Post*, vol. ii.
(*g*) 1 Campb. 94, 93; *post*, vol. ii.

fully or wilfully and maliciously set on fire (*h*). If, however, a malicious or wrongful intent be unnecessarily stated, it need not be proved (*i*); and where there is evidence to prove the allegation, it may be *advisable, in aggravation of the damages, to state the defendant's malicious intent (*j*).

IV. ITS PARTS &c. 5thly. The cause of action.

[*425]

In stating the *defendant's intent or motive*, when necessary the language, as in all other parts of pleading, should correspond with the real or probable facts of the particular case. In an action for a malicious arrest for a pretended debt, it is usual to state "that the defendant wrongfully and unjustly contriving and intending to imprison, harass, oppress, and injure the plaintiff, falsely and maliciously *caused the writ to be issued*, the statement of which writ is essential (*k*), and the arrest made, &c." (*l*); and in a declaration for a malicious prosecution of a criminal charge, injurious as well to the character as to the liberty of the plaintiff, the intent to prejudice the character is also stated (*m*). So, in actions for verbal or written slander, the malicious intent to injure the plaintiff in his character, and if the words relate to his trade, in such trade, should be stated (*n*); but where, from the nature of the injury, the defendant could hardly have been actuated by express malice towards the plaintiff, as in an action for debauching a daughter or servant, the imputation may be and often is omitted (*o*). And where the injury is the breach of a contract, express or implied, as for a false warranty, or against a carrier, bailee, &c. the declaration frequently states the deceit or breach of contract, without any allegation of malice (*p*). So, in actions against officers, &c. for the non-observance of a public duty, (unless malice be essential, as in an action against a returning officer of a borough for refusing a vote at an election, &c. (*q*), the breach of duty and intention to deceive or injure the plaintiff are stated, without alleging any other undue intent, as in an action against the sheriff for an escape, &c. (*r*).

When it is material to show an undue motive or intent, it is seldom necessary in a civil action to state it in *terms*, it is sufficient if it be *substantially* shown (750). Thus, in an action against a returning officer for refusing a vote at an election, though a bad intent is necessary to the support of the action, yet the word *wrongfully* intending to deprive the plaintiff, &c., is sufficiently indicative of a *malicious* intent (*s*)(751). So, in a *declaration for slander, though it is usual to state that the defendant *maliciously* published the [*426]

(*h*) 2 Bla. Rep. 842; Crown Circ. Comp. 9th edit. (1820); see also 2 Marsh. 362; but see 1 Leach, C. L. 4th edit. 403; and *ante*, 405.

(*i*) 2 East, 446.

(*j*) On the same principle as stated in 4 Hawk. P. C. 56.

(*k*) Gadd *v.* Bennett, 5 Price, 540.

(*l*) *Post*, vol. ii.

(*m*) *Id.*

(*n*) *Id.*

(*o*) *Id.*

(*p*) *Id.*

(*q*) 1 East, 555, 563, 568, n. a.

(*r*) *Post*, vol. ii.

(*s*) 1 East, 563, 567; see the observations on the words "*malitiose*," and "*sine rationabili or probabili, causa*," Gilb. Cas. Law and Evid. 199, &c.; and as to the word *fraudulently*, see 6 East, 445, &c.

(750) Marshall *v.* Bussard, Gilm. Rep. 9, and the cases cited in the argument, and by the court.

(751) { So in case for malicious prosecution, stating that the defendant *maliciously* caused, &c. the plaintiff to be indicted. Graham *v.* Noble, 13 Serg. & Rawle, 233. }

IV. ITS PARTS, &c. — 5thly. The cause of action.

scandal, yet the word *falsely* alone is sufficient (*t*)(752); so in an action for harboring the plaintiff's wife, though the mere statement of the harboring might be insufficient, because it is lawful in some instances for the wife to leave her husband, yet the words *unlawfully* and *unjustly* harbored, &c. will sufficiently designate the defendant's conduct to have been illegal (*u*).

Statement of the tort itself;— and of variances in so doing.

With regard to the *statement* of the *tortious act* or *injury itself*, it is frequently sufficient to describe it generally (*x*), without setting out the particulars of the defendant's misconduct. Thus in an action on the case for inducing the plaintiff's wife to continue absent, it is sufficient to state that the defendant "unlawfully and unjustly *persuaded*, *procured*, and *enticed* the wife to continue absent," by means of which persuasion she did continue absent, &c. whereby the plaintiff lost her society; without setting forth the means of persuasion used by the defendant (*y*). So, in actions for diverting water from a stream, or for disturbance of a right of common (*z*), way, &c. it is sufficient to allege a diversion or disturbance generally, without showing the particular means adopted (*a*). Care, however, must be observed in an action on the case not to describe the injurious acts as *trespasses*, remediable by actions of trespass, though, if shown to have been committed under color of a warrant or other process prima facie regular, then the acts, otherwise the subject only of an action of trespass, may be properly joined in case (*b*); and an informal count partly in case and partly in trespass may be aided on a motion in arrest of judgment, as in effect an informal count in trover (*b*). It will in general suffice that the tort is correctly laid in substance though the statement be not literally true, provided there be no material mis-statement. Thus, where the declaration charged that the defendant struck the plaintiff's cow, &c. whereof she died, it was held, after verdict, that there was not a fatal variance, although the proof was that the plaintiff was obliged to kill the cow to shorten her misery, in consequence of defendant's violence (*c*). In an action on the case against a master for the negligence of his servant, it has been decided that the negligence may be stated according to its legal effect, namely, as
[*427] that of the master, without *noticing the servant; but as the object of pleading is to apprize the opposite party of the facts, it is more correct to state them truly (*d*). If the plaintiff declare as reversioner for an injury done to his reversionary interest, the declaration must allege it to have been done to the damage of his reversion, or must state an injury of such a permanent nature as to be necessarily injurious to his reversion (*e*).

(*t*) 1 Saund. 242 a, note 2. From the want of probable cause, malice may be, and most usually is, implied, 1 T. R. 545.

(*u*) Willes, 584.

(*x*) But a general and indefinite statement, admitting of almost any proof, is objectionable, *ante*, 232; 11 Price, 235.

(*y*) Willes, 577; 1 B. & P. 180; Ld. Raym. 452; 3 Leon. 13.

(*z*) *Aliter* in case against the lord of the soil for a surcharge, 1 Saund. 346 a; *post*, vol. ii. 570.

(*a*) 3 Leon. 13; Ld. Raym. 452; Com. Dig. Actions on the Case for Disturbance, B.; 1 Saund. 346 a; *post*, vol. ii. 556, 559, 570.

(*b*) Hensworth *v.* Fowkes, 4 Bar. & Adol. 449; 1 Nev. & Man. 321, S. C.; Smith *v.* Goodwin, 4 B. & Adol. 443.

(*c*) 4 D. & R. 202; and *per* Bayley, J., in 4 Bar. & Cress. 255.

(*d*) 6 T. R. 659; 1 East, 110.

(*e*) 1 M. & Sel. 234; in general, *ante*, 63, 140.

(752) { But to sustain the averment of malice, a charge of felony must be *wilfully false*. Cohen *v.* Morgan, 6 Dowl. & Ryl. 8. }

IV. ITS PARTS, &c. — 5thly. The cause of action.

But if the plaintiff, though needlessly, describe the tort, and the means adopted in effecting it, with minuteness and particularity, and the proof substantially vary from the statement, there will be a fatal variance, which will occasion a nonsuit. Thus, in an action for diverting, &c. a water-course, a count for diverting and turning a stream of water will not be supported by proof of penning back and checking it, whereby the water was made to overflow the plaintiff's meadow (*f*); and under a count for causing the water to rush impetuously against the plaintiff's land, he cannot prove that the water was at times prevented from coming thereto (*g*). But where in case for diverting a stream from the plaintiff's mills, the declaration alleged that the defendant placed and raised a certain dam across the stream, and thereby diverted and turned the water, and prevented it from running along its usual course to the mill, and from supplying the same with water for the necessary working thereof, as the same of right ought and otherwise would have done; it was held that such allegation was supported by proof that in consequence of the dam the water was prevented from being *regularly* supplied to the mill, although the stream was not diverted, as the dam was erected above the mill and the water returned to its regular course long before it reached the mill, and there was no waste of water occasioned by the erection of the dam (*h*).

Where the declaration stated that the defendant "wrongfully placed and continued a heap of earth, whereby a water-course was obstructed," it was decided that the allegation was not supported by proof that the heap was not originally placed so as to cause the obstruction, but that in time earth from the heap fell, and by changing its position, occasioned *the injury; the count should have been for suffering the earth to fall down (*i*). [*428]

In an action *ex delicto*, upon proof of *part only of the injury charged*, or of *one* of several injuries laid in the same count, the plaintiff will be entitled to recover *pro tanto*, provided the part which is proved afford *per se* a sufficient cause of action, for torts are, generally speaking, divisible (*k*); and this even in a count for words or libel, for though the jury find that part of alleged libel and innuendo do not relate to plaintiff, but that the rest does, he may recover *pro tanto*, though the defendant will be entitled to costs of the part negatived (*l*). The same rule as to proving part of a breach, applies in general *in assumpsit*, as we have already observed and explained by example (*m*). In case, charging a defendant with "composing and publishing" a libel, he may be found guilty of publishing only (*n*). And in declarations for injuries to land, trees, goods, &c. a tort to *any part* thereof may be proved (*o*).

The rule that a general averment, including several particulars, may be construed *reddendo singula singulis*, may be here noticed. Thus, an averment that lands are occupied by "A. and B." may be supported by showing that each occupies a part (*p*); and an allegation that lands are "in the par-

(*f*) 6 Price, 1.

(*g*) *Id.*; 2 B. & C. 910; 4 D. & R. 583, S. C. In a declaration for preventing a stream from flowing to plaintiff's land, it must be averred that plaintiff was beneficially entitled to use the water, *id.*

(*h*) 7 Moore, 345.

(*i*) 5 Taunt. 534.

(*k*) 2 East, 438; 2 Bla. Rep. 790; 3 T. R. 645; 5 Taunt. 27; 4 M. & Sel. 349.

(*l*) Prudhomme *v.* Fraser, 1 Harr. 5.

(*m*) *Ante*, 385.

(*n*) 3 Stark. Evid. 1536, 1541; 2 Campb. 507. Proving part of words spoken, 2 East, 438; *post*.

(*o*) 3 Stark. Evid. 1538, 1539; *ante*, 410.

(*p*) 3 Stark. Evid. 1541.

IV. ITS PARTS, &c.
5thly. The cause of action.

ishes A. and B." may be sustained by proof that part is situate in each parish (q). So, where a declaration for a false return to a *fi. fa.* against the goods of A. and B. alleged that A. *and* B. had goods within the bailiwick, it was held to be sufficient to prove that either of them had, the averment being severable (r).

Time in stating torts in general.

The statement of the *time* of committing injuries *ex delicto* is seldom material; it may be proved to have been committed either on a day anterior or subsequent to that stated in the declaration (s). And in an action on the case for a malicious prosecution, it is not necessary for the plaintiff to prove the exact day of his acquittal as laid in the declaration, so that it appear to have been before the action brought, and therefore a variance between the day laid and the day of trial mentioned in the record, produced to prove the acquittal, is not material, the day not being laid in the declaration as part of the description of such record of acquittal; but if it had been so laid, or if the plaintiff affect to state the teste or return of process and misdescribe it, the mistake would be fatal (t). Where the injury was capable of being committed on several days, as in trespass to land, &c. it may be described as having been committed on such a day, "and on divers other days and times between that day and the exhibiting of the plaintiff's bill," (753) (or "*now* the commencement of the suit"); and in such case the first day should be laid anterior to the first injurious act, because the plaintiff would not be permitted to give in evidence repeated acts of trespass, unless committed during the space of time laid in his declaration; though he might recover as to a *single* trespass committed anterior to the first day (u) (754). Where a particular space of time is assigned by a *continuando* for the torts, it seems to become matter of *description*, and not a mere formal allegation of time; but the *continuando.* may be waived, and one trespass even before the first day laid may be proved, for a *continuando* ought not to place the plaintiff in a worse situation than if one trespass only were laid (v). But where the act complained of was single in its nature, as an assault, it would be demurrable to state that "*an assault*" was committed "on divers days and times." (x) (755) The defect of a declaration, even in an action of trespass for mesne profits, in not stating any

(q) 4 Taunt. 671, 700; see *ante*, 308, 309.

(r) 4 M. & Sel. 349.

(s) Co. Lit. 283 a; 1 Saund. 24, note 1; 2 Saund. 295, n. 2. Mis-statement as to the priority of two facts in regard to time not in general material; 5 T. R. 496; 1 Campb. 139; Dougl. 497; 3 B. & P. 23; when otherwise, 6 Taunt. 461; when time is material, see 5 Taunt. 2, 15; and when the plaintiff may vary in his replication from the time named in the declaration, Ld. Raym. 120; Lutw. 1415; 1 Selw. 45; *post*, *Departure*; variances in stating time, 3 Stark Evid. 1568, *Variance*.

(t) 9 East, 157; 11 *Id.* 508; 2 Campb. 193.

(u) *Post*, vol. ii. Bul. N. P. 86; Stra. 1095; Salk. 639, 1 Stark. Rep. 351; Skin. 641; Co. Lit. 283. But in 5 Price, 614, it was held that a period thus limited in stating arrears of duties in an inquisition, might be rejected as surplusage; and that a different space of time during which the monies accrued due might be shown.

(v) *Id.*

(x) *Id. ibid.*; 6 East, 395, 391; as to laying that defendant on divers days "*assaulted*," id

(753) Vide Burnham *v.* Webster, 5 Mass Rep 266, 269.

(754) Vide Phillips' Ev. 134. { Sanders *v* Palmer, 1 M'Cord's Rep. 165 }

(755) Contra Burgess *v.* Freelove, 2 Bos. & Pul. 425. Phillips' Ev. 134. The words, "*then* afterwards continuing his said assault," were held not to be within the technical meaning of a *continuando*, and were good at least after verdict. Blurm *v.* Swift, 2 Mass. Rep. 50.

time when the injury was committed, is aided even after a judgment by default (y). IV. ITS PARTS, &c.

5thly. The cause of action.

Place where the injury was committed.

The *place* is only material in *local* actions (z), or where the precise *situation*, or rather *description* of the land, houses, &c. is particularly stated, as in trespass and replevin (756). Before the recent pleading rules, Hil. T. 4 W. 4, reg. 8, it was necessary as well in civil as in criminal proceedings not only to state the county in the margin as venue, but to repeat the allegation throughout, that *every material* and traversable fact there occurred; but that rule orders that *place* should only be stated in the margin and not repeated in the body, except in *trespass quare clausum fregit*, when it is essential that the name of the close or the abuttals or other particular description be given, subject to a special demurrer in case of omission (a). We have seen that it is sufficient, at all events in transitory actions, to state that the tort was committed in the county at large, without naming any parish or place therein (b); and though an action for a nuisance to realty be local, yet a particular local description of the nuisance or lands, &c. affected is unnecessary (c). In trespass to land, and in ejectment, even before the above rule, it was usual to state the parish or place where the premises were situate (d); and in replevin it was considered that the name or abuttals of the close as well as the parish should be stated (e). As a general rule, it is injudicious to give, when not necessary to do so, a particular local description, as a variance will be fatal (f).

Where the *place* of doing an act is precisely alleged, if the description be *wholly immaterial*, the ground of charge or of complaint not being local, the description may perhaps be rejected as surplusage (g); as if in trespass for taking *goods*, the declaration were to allege that they were taken "in a house," it would seem to be sufficient to prove that they were taken elsewhere, unless indeed a local trespass as to the house be laid in the same count (h).

6thly. The statement of the *damages* in general in actions for *torts*.

In *real* actions, the object being the recovery of the *land itself*, *damages* are unimportant and are not to be laid; but in all *personal* and *mixed* actions (i) the declaration should claim *damages* (k). In *personal* and *mixed* actions there is this difference, that in such actions as *sound in damages*, (as is the legal phrase,) as assumpsit, covenant (l), trespass, case, &c. damages are the main object of the suit, and are therefore always laid high enough to

(y) 13 East, 407.

(z) As to the *venue* in general, *ante*, 266.

(a) *Ante*, 311.

(b) *Ante*, 305 to 308.

(c) 2 East, 497; 11 *Id.* 226.

(d) *Ante*, 305, 306; Co. Lit. 125 b, n. 2.

(e) 2 M. & P. 78; *post*, vol. ii.

(f) See as to variance in this respect, *ante*, 308, 309.

(g) 3 Stark. Evid. 1571; *Variance*. Mr. Starkie instances indictments for robbery "*near* a highway," and proof of a robbery *in a* house, &c.

(h) See *id.* and 1 T. R. 475; as to an allegation that slander was spoken in a particular place, Bul. N. P. 5.

(i) As to these distinctions, *ante*, 95. In penal actions and *scire facias*, no damages are laid. See, in general, *post*.

(k) Com. Dig. Pleader, C. 84; 10 Co. Rep. 116 b, 117 a, b; Steph. 2d edit. 474.

(l) As to damages in actions *ex contractu*, *ante*, 371.

(756) If a trespass be committed in a township which before action brought is sub-divided, the trespass may be laid in the original township. Renaudet *v.* Crockery, 1 Caines' Rep. 167.

IV. ITS PARTS, &c. — 5thly. The cause of action.

cover the whole demand; but in actions that do not sound in damages, as debt, detinue, ejectment, &c., damages are not the gist of the action, and it is usual to lay only a nominal sum as damages (m).

Damages are either general or special. *General* damages are such as the law *implies* or presumes to have accrued from the wrong complained of. *Special* damages are such as *really* took place and are *not implied* by law, and are either superadded to general damages arising from an act injurious in itself, as where some particular loss arises from the uttering of slanderous words actionable in themselves; or are such as arise from an act indifferent and not actionable in itself, but injurious only in its consequences, as where words become actionable only by reason of special damage ensuing (n). It has been held that the special damage must be a *legal* and *natural* consequence arising from the tort, and not a mere *wrongful* act of a third person (o); as that in consequence of the slander certain persons threw the plaintiff into a horse-pond, or broke the windows of his house (p); nor a *remote* consequence, as the loss of a lieutenancy by imprisonment (q); and in an action against an insurance company for loss by fire, the plaintiff cannot recover damages for the loss of customers and trade occurring between the fire and the rebuilding the premises, provided they were restored to a proper state in a reasonable time (r). It does not appear necessary to state the formal description of damages in the declaration, because *presumptions of law* are not in general to be pleaded or averred as facts (s). Therefore, though it is usual in an action on the case for calling the plaintiff "a thief," to state that by reason of the speaking of the words the plaintiff's character was injured, yet that statement appears unnecessary, because it is an intendment of law that the plaintiff was injured by the speaking of such words (t). And the observation applies to slander of the plaintiff in his trade; it being unnecessary to allege that he was injured therein, because the law infers that such was the case.

When to be specially stated.

But when the law does *not necessarily imply* that the plaintiff sustained damage by the act complained of, it is essential to the validity of the declaration that the resulting damage should be shown with particularity; as in an action by a master for beating his servant, or by a commoner for surcharging a common; in which the allegations *per quod servitium amisit*, or *per quod proficium communiæ suæ habere non potuit* are material (u)(757). So in an action for words not actionable in themselves, but becoming so only in respect of particular damage (x). And whenever the damages sustained have not

(m) Steph. 2d edit. 474.

(n) See *instances*, 1 Adol. & Ell. 43.

(o) 8 East, 1; 2 B. & P. 289, Salk. 693; 1 Mod. Ent. 242; Kelly *v.* Partington, 5 B. & Adol. 645; 7 Bing. 2.0.

(p) See preceding note; *sed quære.*

(q) 1 Campb. 58, 60; 2 Taunt 314; *ante*, 338; 5 Taunt. 534; 2 Chit. R. 198. In case for not repairing a fence, *per quod* plaintiff's horse escaped and was killed by a haystack falling, it was decided that the damage was too *remote*, 2 Y. & J. 391; *sed quære.*

(r) *In re* Wright and Pole, 1 Adol. & Ell. 621.

(s) *Ante*, 253; and Tidd, 9th edit. 441.

(t) Sir Wm. Jones, 196; 1 Saund. 243 b, n. 5.

(u) 9 Co. 113 a; 1 Saund. 346 a, b, n. 2; 2 East, 154; Bul. N. P. 89.

(x) 1 Saund. 243, note 5; 2 *Id.* 411, n. 4; Sir W. Jones, 196; 1 Stark. R. 172. Loss of the benefits arising from the hospitality of friends, &c. 1 Taunt. 39.

(757) Vide Monell and Weller *v.* Colden, 13 Johns. Rep 403.

IV. ITS PARTS, &c.

5thly. The cause of action.

necessarily accrued from the act complained of, and consequently are not *implied* by law, then in order to prevent the surprise on the defendant which might otherwise ensue on the trial, the plaintiff must in general state the particular damage which he has sustained, or he will not be permitted to give evidence of it (y)(758). Thus in an action of trespass and false imprisonment, where the plaintiff offered to give in evidence that during his imprisonment he was stinted in his allowance of food, he was not permitted to do so, because that fact was not, as it should have been, stated in his declaration (z); and in a similar action it was held that the plaintiff could not give evidence of his health being injured, unless specially stated (a). So in trespass "for taking a horse," nothing can be given in evidence which is not expressed in the declaration (b); and if money was paid over in order to regain possession, such payment should be alleged as special damage (c). So in an action for defamation, whether the words are actionable in themselves or not, yet the plaintiff will not be permitted to give evidence of any *particular* loss or injury, unless it be stated specially in his declaration (d). If an action be brought for words not in themselves actionable, and the plaintiff do not prove the special damage laid in the declaration, he will be nonsuited, because the special damage is in such case the gist of the action; but where the words are of themselves actionable, the jury must find for the plaintiff, though the special damage be not proved (e), and if the plaintiff allege special damage to have ensued from words spoken by the *defendant*, he cannot recover on proof that the damage resulted from a *third* person repeating what the defendant had said (f). Words, though actionable in themselves, and not stated in the declaration, may, we have seen, be given in evidence to show the malice of the defendant, but the jury ought not to give damages for such words (g). So in an action at the suit of a reversioner, it must be specially shown that the injury was such as to affect his *reversionary* interest (h); and in case for deceit, some resulting damage must be alleged and proved (i).

Before the 3 & 4 W. 4, c 42, s. 29, *interest* was recoverable only in a few cases of *contract*, but under that act a jury may give damages, in the nature of interest, over and above the value of the goods at the time of the conversion or seizure in all actions of trover or trespass *de bonis asportatis*, and over and above the money recoverable in all actions on policies of assurance.

Alia enormia.

In trespass the declaration concludes, "*and other wrongs to the plaintiff then did, against the peace, &c.*;" and under this allegation of *alia enormia* damages and matters which naturally arise from the act complained of, or cannot with decency be stated, may be given in evidence in aggravation of dam-

(y) See the rule in assumpsit, *ante*, 371; 8 T. R. 133.
(z) Peake, C. N. P. 46, 3d ed. 64.
(a) Peake, C. N. P. 62; 3d ed. 87.
(b) 1 Sid. 225; Bul N. P. 89; Vin. Ab. Evidence, T. b. 6; Holt, 700; Tidd, 9th ed. 441.
(c) Cowp. 418.
(d) 1 Saund. 243, note 5.
(e) *Id. ibid.*; Bul N. P. 6; Sir W. Jones, 196; 2 B. & P. 284; 7 Bing. 211.
(f) Ward *v.* Weeks, 7 Bing. 211.
(g) 1 Campb. Ni. Pri. 49; Ward *v.* Weeks, 7 Bing. 211; but the defendant may prove *such* words to be true, 2 Stark. R. 417.
(h) 1 M. & Sel. 234.
(i) 2 Marsh. 217.

(758) De Forest *v.* Leete, 16 Johns. Rep. 122. See page 128.

IV. ITS PARTS, &c. — 8thly. The cause of action.

ages, though not specified in any other part of the declaration (*k*). Thus, in trespass for breaking and entering a house, the plaintiff may, in aggravation of damages, give in evidence the debauching of his daughter, or the battery of his servants, under the general allegation *alia enormia*, &c. (*l*) and yet this matter may be stated specially (*m*); but he cannot under the *alia enormia* give in evidence the *loss of service*, or any other matter which would *of itself* bear an action; for if it would, it should be stated specially. Therefore in trespass *quare clausum fregit*, the plaintiff would not, under the above general allegation, be permitted to give evidence of the defendant's taking away a horse, &c. (*n*); and in the other cases the evidence is allowed to be given not as a substantive ground of action, but merely to show the violence of the defendant's conduct (*o*), and give a character to the case. *Trespass* will lie for breaking and entering the plaintiff's house "under a false and unfounded charge and assertion that the plaintiff had stolen property therein, *per quod* he was injured in his credit, &c." and the jury may give damages for the trespass, as it is aggravated by and with reference to such false charge (*p*).

The particular damage in respect of which the plaintiff proceeds must be the *legal* and *natural* consequence of the injury done, and not an *illegal* consequence thereof (*q*). Therefore, in an action for words, it is not sufficient special damage to allege or prove a mere *wrongful* act of a third person induced by the slander; as that the third person dismissed the plaintiff from his employ before the end of the time for which he was hired; or that in consequence of the words spoken, other persons afterwards assembled and seized the plaintiff and beat him; because these tortious acts of others may be compensated in actions brought by the plaintiff against them, and the law supposes that in such actions the plaintiff would receive a full indemnity (*r*). But if the evidence will support the allegation, it may in some cases be stated that the defendant *procured* the third person to commit the injury, though such person might also be liable to an action (*s*). In an action of trespass against a huntsman for riding over lands, he is liable not only for mischief occasioned by himself, but also for a concourse of people following him (*t*). It seems to be a general rule, that *extra* costs occasioned by the defendant's tort are not recoverable as damages (*u*).

Special damage must be stated with particularity, in order that the defendant may be enabled to meet the charge if it be false, and if it be not so stated, it cannot be given in evidence; and, therefore, a declaration by a victualler for calling his wife "a whore," whereby *several* customers left his house, without naming any in particular, is too general, and no evidence of *particular*

(*k*) Bul. N. P. 89; Holt, 699, 700; 1 Stark. C. N. P. 98; Peake, C. N. P. 46, 62; 3d ed. 64, 87.

(*l*) See preceding note; 6 Mod. 127; 1 Stark. Rep. 98; Tidd, 9th ed. 441; *sed vide* Peake, Evid. 87, 3d ed.; 2 Phil. Evid. 134.

(*m*) *Id.*

(*n*) Bul. N. P. 89; Holt, 700; 1 Sid. 225; 2 Salk. 643; 1 Stra. 61.

(*o*) 1 Stark. 98.

(*p*) 2 M. & Sel. 77; see 5 Taunt. 442; 1 Marsh. 139, S. C.

(*q*) 8 East, 3; 2 B. & P. 289; Salk. 693 1 Mod. 242; Kelly *v.* Partington, 5 Bar. & Adol. 645; *ante*, 428, note (*b*).

(*r*) 8 East, 1, 3; 2 B. & P. 289; *ante*, 428, (*b*). *Sed quære.*

(*s*) Fortesc. 211; 1 Mod. 215.

(*t*) 1 Stark. 351.

(*u*) 1 Campb. 151, 152; 4 Taunt. 7; 4 Bing. 160; but see 1 Stark. 306. What recoverable in action for mesne profits, *ante*, 226.

customers leaving the house will be admissible (x). So in a declaration for slander of title to an estate, whereby the plaintiff *lost the sale* of it (y); or for slandering a single woman, by saying "she was with child, and had miscarried," in consequence of which she lost *several* suitors, &c. is insufficient (z). But in an action for consequential damage arising from slander, imputing incontinence to the plaintiff, it is sufficient to state "that he was employed to preach to a dissenting congregation at a certain licensed chapel, situate, &c. and that he derived considerable profit for his preaching there, and that by reason of the scandal, *persons* frequenting the chapel had refused to permit him to preach there, and had discontinued giving him profits which they usually had, and otherwise would have given," without saying who those persons were, or by what authority they excluded him (a). In this case a general allegation is sufficient, in consequence of a minute statement being inconvenient, and tending to prolixity (b). So where a declaration in assumpsit for not permitting the plaintiff to take possession of premises which the defendant had let to him, stated that "thereby the plaintiff sustained loss;" it was held that the plaintiff might prove a particular loss in respect of his wife being a milliner, and having lost a profitable part of the year (c). In stating the damages, care must be taken that no part of it appear to have accrued after the commencement of the action, though if it be laid under a *videlicet* it will be aided by verdict (d).

IV. ITS PARTS, &c. — 5thly. The cause of action.

THE REQUISITES OF DECLARATIONS FOR WRITTEN OR VERBAL SLANDER IN PARTICULAR.

In the Second Volume are given a great variety of forms of declarations for libels and slander, and to those forms there are appended explanatory notes (e); *technical* objections to declarations for causes of action of *this description*, whether for *written* or *verbal* slander, have certainly been admitted to an extent injurious to the mode of administering justice (f). The principal rules which regulate the framing of a *declaration* for this *injury*, may be conveniently considered under the following heads, namely, 1st, The *inducement* or prefatory statement of *introductory* matter; 2dly, The *colloquium*, or statement that the libellous or slanderous imputations have reference to the plaintiff, and sometimes also to the antecedent inducement or introductory matter; 3dly, The *statement* of the *scandal itself*, whether written or verbal, and the publication thereof; 4thly, The *innuendoes*; and, 5thly, The consequent *damage*.

THE PARTICULAR REQUISITES OF DECLARATIONS FOR LIBELS AND VERBAL SLANDER.

(x) Bul. Ni. Pri. 7; 1 Saund. 243 c, n. 5; 1 Rol. Ab. 58.
(y) Sir W. Jones, 196.
(z) 8 T. R. 132; 1 Sid. 396; 1 Vent. 4, S. C.; Cro. Jac. 499.
(a) 8 T. R. 130; 3 M. & Sel. 73.
(b) *Ante*, 269.
(c) 11 Price, 19.
(d) 2 Saund. 169, 171 b; Vin. Ab. Damages, Q. R.

(e) *Post*, vol. ii. See Stark. on Slander, &c 2d edit. Index, *Declaration*; and Phillips and Starkie on Evid.; also, Selw. N. P. Libel and Slander.
(f) MS. per Tenterden, C. J. and Best, C. J., on error from the Exchequer, in Adams v. Meredew, 3 You. & Jer. 219; overruling the judgment 2 You. & Jer. 417; see analysis Harrison's Index, 927.

IV. ITS PARTS, &c.

5thly. The cause of action.

Introduction and *Inducement.*

*1st. *Inducement or prefatory or introductory statement.* An *inference* or presumption of law need not in general be stated in pleading (*g*); and because the law presumes the innocence of a crime or other misconduct, the plaintiff need not in his declaration aver his innocence of the charge or attack upon his character (*h*). It is, however, *usual* to state by way of introduction, the plaintiff's innocence of the imputation; and the defendant could not, even before the Reg. Gen. Hil. T. 4 W. 4, under the general issue, assert the plaintiff's guilt, although the declaration contained such introduction (*i*), and the same rule now continues even in stronger force.

Libels and slander in particular.

Where the libel or slander is *prima facie* or *per se* actionable, a declaration stating the defendant's malicious intent and the defamatory matter, showing that it refers to the plaintiff, is sufficient without any *prefatory inducement* of the circumstances under which the words, &c. were spoken, &c. (*k*) and if unnecessarily an inducement be stated, it is not material to prove it (*l*). But if the libel or words do not *naturally* and *per se* convey the meaning the plaintiff would wish to assign to them, or are ambiguous and equivocal, and require explanation by reference to some *extrinsic matter* to show that they are actionable, it must be expressly shown that such matter existed, and that the slander related thereto (*m*)(759). Thus, if the imputation be that the plaintiff was "*forsworn*," this not being of *itself* actionable, because it does not necessarily impute the offence of *perjury* (*n*), it must be specifically alleged, by way of inducement, that there had been a suit or other judicial proceeding, in which the plaintiff was a witness and gave evidence, and that the defendant, when speaking the words, referred to such matter in using the term "forsworn," (*o*)(760) and intended to impute that the plaintiff had been guilty of the crime of perjury. So if the slander were, "you have *robbed* me of one shilling tan money," as the word "*robbed*" does not *necessarily* impute a felony, an innuendo of that intent, without any inducement or prefatory allegation of the defendant's having used the words in a *felonious* sense, will be defective (*p*). Where what is complained of in the declaration as a libel, does not upon the face of it apply to the plaintiff, and impute a libel, there must be an inducement stating such facts as will support such an *innuendo*, and show the libellous application of the statement to the plaintiff (*q*).

(*g*) *Ante*, 253.
(*h*) *Id.*; 1 Stark. on Slander, 2d ed. 357.
(*i*) See *post*, as to Pleas in Case. And if there be a preferable statement of *general* good character, the defendant cannot traverse it by his plea, Styles, 118; 11 Price, 235.
(*k*) Com. Dig. Action for Defamation, G. 9; 3 Y. & J. 219; 6 B. & C. 154; 9 D. & R. 197, S. C.; same case in error, in 1 M. & P. 402, and 4 Bingh. 409. See 2 M. & P. 32; 5 Bingh. 17, S. C.; and next note.
(*l*) Cox v Thomason, 2 Cr. & J. 361.
(*m*) 8 East, 431; 9 *Id.* 93; 4 M. & S. 164; 13 East, 554; 5 B. & A. 615; 1 D. & R. 230, S. C.
(*n*) 6 T. R. 691; 8 East, 427; 9 *Id.* 93.
(*o*) See *post*, vol. ii.
(*p*) Day v. Robinson, 1 Adol. & Ell. 555.
(*q*) 1 Y. & J. 480.

(759) { See Bloss v. Tobey, 2 Pick. Rep. 320. }
(760) So, to say that the plaintiff has sworn false or taken a false oath, is not actionable; Vaughan v. Havens, 8 Johns. Rep. 109; without a *colloquium* of its being in a cause pending in a court of competent jurisdiction, and on a point material to the issue. Niven v. Munn, 13 Johns. Rep. 48. Hopkins v. Beedle, 1 Caines' Rep. 347. Ward v. Clark, 2 Johns. Rep. 10. M'Claughey v. Wetmore, 6 Johns. Rep. 82. Chapman v. Smith, 13 Johns. Rep. 68. { Crookshank v. Gray *et ux.*, 20 Johns. Rep. 344. Harvey v. Boies, 1 Penns. Rep. 12. }

IV. ITS PARTS, &c.

5thly. The cause of action.

Upon the same ground in declarations upon libels and words, which are only actionable in regard to their having *affected the plaintiff in his *profession, trade, or business* (r), there must be a distinct allegation that the plaintiff was, at the time of the scandal (s), in such profession, or exercised such calling, &c.; otherwise the record will be substantially defective (t). In these cases care should be taken to avoid *unnecessary minuteness* in showing the plaintiff's profession; a simple statement that he exercised it, without alleging that he was "qualified," or had "taken a degree," is all that is necessary or judicious (u). Where an averment of extrinsic matter is material, the allegation that the slander applies to such extrinsic matter is matter of description, and must be in general proved as laid, though unnecessarily minute; thus, in a declaration for slander of an attorney, if after alleging that he was an attorney, it be averred that he had conducted a particular suit, and then state that the slander was published of and concerning his conduct in *that suit*, it is essential to prove the existence of the suit, and that the scandal had reference to the particular occasion stated (x). Since the general pleading rules, Hil. T. 4 W. 4, unless the inducement or prefatory matter be particularly traversed or denied, it will in effect be admitted, and certainly need not be proved by the plaintiff upon a mere plea of not guilty (y).

But where the slanderous matter is actionable of itself, and independently of the plaintiff's profession or trade, it will not be fatal to introduce an averment of the plaintiff's profession, &c. and to state that the matter was published of and concerning him, "*and of and concerning him in his profession,*" *&c.*; for the averment is divisible (z). And on the same ground, if the matter be actionable as it relates to one of two of the plaintiff's trades mentioned in the inducement, the declaration is sufficient, although one trade only be proved (a). Where in a declaration for a libel it was alleged that the plaintiff's carriage and that *of E. F. were in a highway, and that they had come in contact without any furious driving by the plaintiff, and that E. F. was injured, &c. and that the libel was published of and concerning the plaintiff, "and of and concerning the said accident;" the Court held the averments as to the accident were divisible, and did not form entire matter of description thereof, so that it became immaterial that the jury found that the accident was occasioned by the plaintiff's furious driving, (there not being a sufficient plea of justification to protect the defendant as to the whole libel) (b). A declaration alleged [*431]

(r) It need not appear to be a trade in which the plaintiff might become a bankrupt, see 5 B. & C. 160.

(s) It need not, it seems, be expressly averred, that "at the time of the publishing," &c. plaintiff carried on, &c. If it be alleged that he was and is an attorney, &c. and hath for a long time carried on, &c. it will suffice, 2 Roll. Rep. 84; 1 Vin. Ab. 538; Alleyne, 63; Yelv. 159; see Cro. Car. 282; 1 Stark. Slander, 402 to 404.

(t) Com. Dig. Action for Defamation, G. 8; 2 Saund. 307 a, n. 1; 1 Saund. 243, n. 3; *post*, vol. ii.; 1 Stark. on Slander, 400, 2d ed.; 3 B. & C. 135; 4 D. & R. 670, S. C.

(u) 8 T. R. 303, 131; 1 New Rep. 196; 2 Bulst. 230; 11 Price, 235. See *ante*, 319, 320; and *post*, 431.

(x) See 5 Esp. Rep. 339; 1 Chit. Rep. 603; 3 B. & C. 124; 4 D. & R. 680, S. C.; 4 Esp. Rep. 437; and other cases, 1 Stark. Slander, 405, 2d ed.

(y) Duke v. Jostling, 3 Dowl. 618; Chalmers v. Shackle, 6 Car. & P. 475.

(z) 3 B. & C. 138, note (b); 5 T. R. 436; 2 Stark. Rep. 559.

(a) Figgins v. Cogswell, cited and approved by Tindal, C. J., in Chalmers v. Shackle, 6 Car. & P. 477; 3 M. & Sel. 369; *ante*, 421.

(b) 2 B. & Ald. 685. See 1 M. & Sel. 287.

IV. ITS PARTS, &c. — 8thly. The cause of action.

that the plaintiff was vestry clerk of the parish of M., and that whilst he was vestry clerk certain prosecutions were carried on against B. for certain misdemeanors, and that in furtherance of such proceedings, and to bring the same to a successful issue, certain sums of money belonging to the parishioners were applied in discharge of the expenses; and that the defendant, to cause it to be suspected that the plaintiff had fraudulently applied money belonging to the parishioners, falsely and maliciously published of and concerning the plaintiff, and of and concerning his conduct in his office of vestry clerk, *and of and concerning the matters aforesaid*, a certain libel, stating the libellous parts; and it appeared upon the trial, upon the production of the libel, that the imputation was that the plaintiff had applied the parish money in payment of the expenses of the prosecution after it had terminated, it was held that the variance was unimportant; for it was immaterial to the character of the libel whether the money were so applied before or after the termination of the prosecution (*c*). The principle seems to be in declaring upon a libel, that where there are several matters alleged as inducement. each as bearing upon the libel and jointly constituting it, the Court will consider, in construing the subsequent averment, that the libel was published "of and concerning the matters aforesaid," the degree in which each matter bears upon the libel, and is essential to it. If the matter referred to by the averment be material, and affect the charge in such a manner that the omission of it would alter the character of the libel, either in the degree in which it is charged to be injurious, or in the estimate of damages, the court will hold that it must be strictly [*432] proved as it is charged, and the failure of proof, or *the disproof of it, will be a fatal variance. This was the case of *Rex* v. *Horne* (*d*), in which it was held necessary to prove all the matters to which reference was made by the averment "of and concerning the matters aforesaid;" because, first, the libel was alleged to be of and concerning these matters and all the matters jointly: and each in its relative importance constituted the libel (*e*). But where the matters referred to consist of several particulars, some of which are material and others not, the Court will distinguish between such as are material and such as are not (*f*); and if any one particular be disproved to which the libel is alleged to relate, if the charge would remain entire and libellous without such proof, the Court will not consider it to be a variance (761); that was the case of *May* v. *Brown* (*g*), which establishes this position, that the words "of and concerning," incorporate and render necessary to prove such antecedent matter only as make up the entire charge, and are essential to the character of the libel.

Where the *libellous matter* can be collected *from the words themselves*, there need be no averment as to circumstances, to the supposed existence of which the words referred; as the gist of the action appears on the face of the

(*c*) May v. Brown, 3 B. & C. 113; 4 D. & R. 670, S. C.

(*d*) Cowp. 672.

(*e*) See also 1 Chit. Rep. 603; 2 Stark. 510; 4 B. & Ald. 314.

(*f*) 2 Crom. & Jerv. 361.

(*g*) 3 B. & C. 113; 4 D. & R. 670, S. C.; *ante*, 431.

(761) { "The general inducement of good character or innocence of the particular charge is unnecessary, because the law presumes innocence of a crime till the contrary be established. 1 B. & A. 463." 4 Lond. Ed. 342. } See Coleman v. Southwicke, 9 Johns. Rep. 48, 49.

libel, or words, there can be no reason that the plaintiff should resort to any statement of the facts to which the defendant may have alluded. If these facts be true to the extent he represented, it is for the defendant to *plead* their truth. Thus, if the declaration be, "he *perjured* himself," or "he *perjured* himself in the action," it is unnecessary to show in the declaration that there was an action, &c. (*h*). The statement in the libel or slander itself of a particular fact, dispenses with the proof thereof on the part of the plaintiff (*i*).

IV. ITS PARTS, &c. — 5thly. The cause of action.

2dly. The declaration must show by a *colloquium*, or otherwise, that the words were spoken, or the libel was composed and published "*of and concerning the plaintiff.*" And where an inducement of extrinsic matter is necessary, it must not only be shown that the imputation related to the plaintiff's character, but it must also be charged that it had reference to such extrinsic matter; as (in regard to the instances just put) that it was published "of and concerning the plaintiff's *said evidence in the said suit, &c." or "of and concerning him in his said profession, &c." (*k*)(762). [*433]

2. *The colloquium of and concerning the plaintiff, &c.*

Where a declaration stated that the defendant, contriving, &c. published a libel containing the false and scandalous matter following, without alleging that that matter was "of and concerning the plaintiff," and then set out the libel, which on the face of it did *not manifestly appear to* relate to the plaintiff, and there was no *innuendo* to connect it with the plaintiff, it was held, upon a writ of error, that the count was bad (*l*).

Where the actionable words were spoken *to a* plaintiff, "*you* are, &c." it appears to be sufficient to lay a colloquium *with* him, without an express averment that the words were spoken "of and concerning him;" for it cannot but be intended that the words were spoken to *him* with whom the conversation is alleged to have been had (*m*). But where actionable words are spoken in the third person, as "*he* is a thief," though a *colloquium* of the plaintiff be laid, it is necessary to aver that the words were spoken "concerning the plaintiff." (*n*) And it is not, it seems, sufficient, in such case, to connect the words with the plaintiff by means of an *innuendo* (*o*).

But where a *colloquium* is laid, and there is an *innuendo* of the plaintiff, it seems that the want of a direct averment, that the words were spoken "of and concerning the plaintiff," must be pointed out by special demurrer, and that it will be intended after verdict, or upon general demurrer, that the words were spoken of the plaintiff; but where no *colloquium* concerning the plaintiff is laid, the omission of such an averment is fatal to the declaration (*p*)(763).

The neglect to aver that the libellous or slanderous matter was published "of and concerning the plaintiff," is not cured by an allegation that the de-

(*h*) Cro. Car. 337; 8 Mod. 24; 1 Stark. Slander, 2d ed. 392, 397, 85.

(*i*) 11 Price, 235.

(*k*) 1 Saund. 242 b, n. 3; 1 Stark. Slander, 2d ed. 383.

(*l*) Clement *v.* Fisher, 7 B. & C. 459; 1 M. & R. 281, S. C.; 4 Bing. 162.

(*m*) Rol. Abr. 85, pl. 8; 1 Saund. 242 a, n. 3.

(*n*) Rol. Abr. 85, pl. 30; 1 Sid. 62; 1 Com. Dig. Action upon the Case for Defamation, G. 7.

(*o*) Cro. Jac. 126; *post*, 436, 437; see 7 B. & C. 459; 1 M. & R. 281, S. C.

(*p*) Rol. Rep. 244; Skutt *v.* Hawkins, 1 Saund. 242 b, n. 3.

(762) Vide Linsey *v.* Smith, 7 Johns. Rep. 359. Gidney *v.* Blake, 11 Johns. Rep. 54. Thomas *v.* Croswell, 7 ib. 271. Milligan *v.* Thorn, 6 Wend. Rep. 413.

(763) Vide Milligan *v.* Thorn, 6 Wend. Rep. 413.

IV. ITS PARTS, &c.

fendant published the matter with intent to injure the plaintiff, and impute to him the crime after mentioned." (q)

8thly. The cause of action.

[*434] 3. The *slander*, written or verbal, and *publication* complained of.

*3dly. Great care must be taken in setting out *the particular libellous matter or words complained of.* The libel itself, or slanderous words, must be set out in *hæc verba;* and the declaration must *profess* so to set forth the matter; and an averment that the libellous or slanderous matter was "to the *effect* following;" (r) or "*in substance* as follows," (s)(764) setting out the libel or words, would be bad in arrest of judgment, although the words themselves be set out. It is not sufficient to declare generally that the defendant published a libel concerning the plaintiff in his trade, "purporting that his beer was of a bad quality, and sold in deficient measure;" or that the defendant "charged and asserted, and accused the plaintiff, a tradesman, of being insolvent." (t) The libel or slander itself ought to be expressly stated (u)(765). Where a libellous paragraph, as proved, contained two references, by which it appeared to be in fact the language of a third person, speaking of the plaintiff's conduct, and the declaration in setting it out had omitted those references, it was held that these omissions altered the sense of the remainder, and that the variance was fatal (x). And when a declaration alleges that the defendant spoke certain words, it must be taken to mean that the defendant himself used them as his own words, and if he repeated them as the words of another it is a variance (y). The slanderous words should be stated as they were uttered (z)(766); and a proof of words spoken in the third person will not support a count for words spoken in the second, and *vice versa* (a)(767); nor will words spoken by way of interrogation support a charge of words spoken affirmatively (b). So if words are spoken ironically (c), or the slander is to be collected from a question and answer, not from the latter only (d), there must be an express averment accordingly; in the first case, stating the words, and averring they were ironically spoken; in the second, showing the question and

(q) 4 M. & Sel. 464; 1 Stark. Slander, 2d ed. 416. Even, it seems, although there be an *innuendo* applying the matter to the plaintiff, *id.;* see *ante*, 432; and *post*, 436.

(r) 3 Salk. 417; 11 Mod. 78, 849; 5 Vin. Ab. Libel, E.; 3 Mod. 72; 2 Show. 436; 3 M. & Sel. 115; 1 Marsh. 522; 6 Taunt. 169, S. C. To the "*tenor*," or "*tenor and effect*," setting out the scandal in *hæc verba*, seems to be good, *id.;* 1 Stark. Slander, 2d ed 365 b. "*Crimen feloniæ imposuit*," good after verdict, because it can be supported only by proof of a *charge* before a *magistrate*, not by proof of words in conversation, 2 B. & C. 283; 3 D. & R. 519, S. C.

(s) 3 B. & Ald. 503; 3 M. & Sel. 110; 4 Bar. & Cres. 473; 6 D. & R. 528, S. C.

(t) 3 M. & Sel. 110.

(u) 6 Taunt. 169.

(x) 5 B. & Ald. 615; 13 East, 554. As to setting out divided sentences, as if they followed continuously, 1 Stark. Slander, 2d ed. 380.

(y) 10 Bar. & Cres. 274; 13 East, 554.

(z) 3 M. & Sel. 110; 1 M. & Sel. 287.

(a) 4 T. R. 217; Bul. N. P. 5; *post*, vol. ii.

(b) 8 T. R. 150.

(c) 11 Mod. 86.

(d) 4 B. & C. 247; 6 D. & R. 296, S. C.

---

(764) { Contra Kennedy v. Lowry, 1 Binn. 393. }

(765) { In an action for a libel in a review, it is sufficient to set out the contents of an index, (referring to an article in the body of the review,) which is of itself a libel; and no reference need be made to the article itself, if the index contain *per se, prima facie* libellous matter. Buckingham v. Murray, 2 Carr & Payne, 46. }

(766) { And therefore a count in slander, stating merely that the defendant charged the plaintiff with the crime of forgery, is bad. Yundt v. Yundt, 12 Serg. & Rawle, 427. }

(767) Vide Miller v. Miller, 8 Johns. 75. Contra, Tracy v. Harkins, 1 Binn. 395, n. { But see M'Connell v. M'Coy, 7 Serg. & Rawle, 223, overruling Tracy v. Harkins. }

IV. ITS PARTS, &c. — 5thly. The cause of action.

answer, &c. If the words are so laid as to import that they were spoken concerning a thing *then present, and the words proved concerned and imported that they related to a thing not then present, the variance is fatal (e). However, the addition or omission of a word in setting out a libel or slander, will not prejudice unless it alter the sense (f); and the plaintiff need not prove all the words laid, if they do not constitute one entire charge, and the non proof would not alter its meaning; though he must prove such of them as will be sufficient to sustain his action, and it will not suffice to prove *equivalent expressions* (g)(768). Where the words omitted to be proved do not qualify or affect those proved, the omission is immaterial, as where the words were—"Ware hawk, you must take care of yourself—mind what you are about," the variance was immaterial where the plaintiff failed to prove the words "mind what you are about." (h) Where some of the words were not actionable, yet, if spoken at the same time as the actionable words, they may all be stated in one count; but if words not actionable be stated by themselves in a distinct count, and entire damages be given, judgment will be arrested (i)(769); and words not actionable may be given in evidence in aggravation of damages, though not stated in the declaration (k)(770); and it has even been decided that words actionable of themselves, though not stated in the pleadings, may be proved in order to show *quo animo* the words declared upon were stated (l).

The unlawful publication.

The declaration must show a *publication* of the libel or slander; but *any words* that denote a publication are sufficient (m). *After verdict*, an allegation that the defendant "*printed* and *caused* to be printed a libel in a newspaper," was held to be sufficient (n). And an averment that words were spoken "in the *presence* of divers persons," although not stating that they heard or understood them, is sustainable (o): but it is not correct merely to aver that the words were *spoken*, omitting the words, "and *published*." (p)

(e) 2 B. & Ald. 756.

(f) Bul. N. P. 6; 2 M. & Sel. 502; Rep. temp. Hardw. 305, 306; 1 Campb. 353; 13 East, 554; see 1 Stark. Slander, 2d ed. 369 to 383.

(g) 2 East, 438; Gilb. Law and Evid. 229; 2 Saund. 74 b; 1 Salk. 11, in notes; Rep. temp. Hardw. 305, 306; 4 T. R. 217; Bul. N. P. 5; 2 Campb. 134; 1 Stark. Slander, 374; 2 Esp. R. 491; and see 4 Bing. 261.

(h) 4 Bing. 261; 6 Bing. 451.

(i) 10 Co. 131 a; 2 Saund. 307 a, n. 1; 3 Wils. 185; Vin. Ab. Damages, Q.

(k) Peake's C. N. P. 125, 22, 166; Bul. N. P. 7; 3 Esp. 133, 134; 1 Campb. 48; but the defendant may prove the truth of these words, 2 Stark. 417.

(l) *Id.*; 1 Campb. 48, 49.

(m) 1 Saund. 242, n. 1; 1 Stark. Slander, 2d ed. 358, 411.

(n) 2 Bla. Rep. 1037. Published, *or* caused to be published, when aided, 8 Mod. 328; 1 Show. 125; Vin Ab. Libel, E. pl. 4.

(o) Cro. Eliz. 480; Noy, 57; Goulds. 119; Cro. Jac. 39; Cro. Car. 199.

(p) Sty. 70; 1 Stark. Slander, 2d ed. 360.

---

(768) It is sufficient if the plaintiff prove the substance of the words. Phillips' Ev. 154. Ward *v.* Clark, 2 Johns. Rep. 12. If the words laid are, that the plaintiff stole the goods of A., they will not be supported by proof that the defendant said, that he stole the goods of B.; or if it be charged that the defendant said, that the plaintiff conspired with B, C., and D., it will not be sufficient to prove the defendant said, that the plaintiff conspired with B. and C.: these being distinct offences. Johnston *v.* Tate, 6 Binn. 121. Different sets of words, importing the same charge, laid as spoken at the same time, may be included in the same count. Rathbun *v.* Emigh, 6 Wend. R. 407.

(769) Vide Cheetham *v.* Tillotson, 5 Johns. Rep. 430.

(770) Vide Thomas *v.* Croswell, 7 Johns. Rep. 270, 271.

IV. ITS PARTS, &c.

5thly. The cause of action.

In an action for a libel in a *foreign* language, the original must be set out (q); and it seems to be necessary also to give a *translation in English (r); and perhaps, if slanderous *words* be spoken in a *foreign* language, *a translation of* them should be set forth (s); although it has been considered sufficient to aver that the hearers understood such language (t). But provincial expressions in this country may be set forth without express explanation on the record (u).

There should be an averment that the defendant *maliciously* published the matter, but any equivalent expressions, as "wrongfully and falsely," &c. will, it seems, suffice (x); the word *maliciously* appears to import that the words were *falsely* uttered (y); but it is usual and better to state that the matter was "*falsely and maliciously*" published, &c.

We have already adverted to the statute (z), which gives the Court the power to permit amendments of errors in setting out *written* instruments to be made at the trial of the cause (a); and the enactment in 3 & 4 W. 4, c. 42, s. 23, should also be referred to.

4. *The Innuendoes.*

4thly. The *innuendo*, as "he, (*meaning* the plaintiff,) &c." also requires great attention and care (b). It is merely a form or mode of introducing *explanation*:—"It means no more than the words '*id est*,' '*scilicet*,' or '*meaning*,' or '*aforesaid*,' as *explanatory of a subject-matter sufficiently expressed before*; as such a one, meaning the defendant, or such a subject, meaning the subject in question." (c) It is only explanatory of some matter already expressed; it serves to *point out* where there is precedent matter, but never for a new charge; it may *apply* what is *already expressed*, but cannot add to or enlarge, or change the sense of the previous words (d) (771). Thus, where the declaration charged that the slander was "he has *forsworn* himself, (*meaning* that the plaintiff had committed wilful and corrupt perjury,") it was held, that as there was no inducement or previous or other statement, that
[*437] the words related to false swearing in a *judicial proceeding*, the *declaration was bad, for the *innuendo* could not extend their meaning (e). Whenever therefore an inducement, or prefatory statement of the existence of some extrinsic fact, to which the libel or words referred is essential, the omission, as we have seen, is fatal (f), and there must also be an innuendo expressly referring to such inducement.

(q) 6 T. R. 162; 3 M. & Sel. 116.

(r) See 3 B. & B. 201; 10 Price, 88; 1 Saund. 242 a, note b. 5th edit.; 1 Stark. Slander, 2d edit. 368, 369; Bayl. on Bills, 5th edit. 445.

(s) *Id.*: *sed vide* 1 Saund. 242 a, note.

(t) 1 Saund. 242 a, note. *Sed query.*

(u) Com. Dig. Action, Defamation, G. 6; 1 Rol. Ab. 86, pl. 1.

(x) See 1 Saund. 242 a, note 2; 1 Stark. Slander, 2d edit. 433; *ante*, 425; *post*, vol. ii.

(y) 1 T. R. 493; 1 Stark. Slander, 2d ed. 436; *ante*, 425, 426.

(z) 9 Geo. 4, c. 15.

(a) *Ante*, 345.

(b) See 1 Stark. Slander, 418, 2d edit.; Selw. Slander, III.; 1 Saund. 243, n. 4.

(c) *Per* De Grey, C. J., Cowp. 683.

(d) 1 Saund. 243, note 4; see *post*, vol. ii.; 8 East, 430, 431; 9 *Id.* 95.

(e) 6 T. R. 691; Yelv. 27; see *ante*, 429. So, if the declaration be, "he has burnt my barn," an *innuendo*, "a barn *full of* corn" is bad; there being no inducement that the plaintiff had corn in a barn, and that the words related thereto, 4 Coke's Rep. 20.

(f) *Ante*, 429 to 432. The author, however, ventures to assume that if the *essential* matter to be averred appear in *any part* of the declaration, however out of order or clumsily, still if it sufficiently *relate to* and *control* the other parts, it will suffice.

(771) { M'Clurg v. Ross, 5 Binn. 218. } Vide Pelton v. Ward, 3 Caines' Rep. 76. Thomas v. Croswell, 7 Johns. Rep. 271. Van Vechten v. Hopkins, 5 Johns. Rep. 211. Vaughan v. Havens, 8 Johns. Rep. 109.

IV. ITS PARTS, &c.

4thly. The cause of action.

A declaration for libel, after certain introductory matter, which was immaterial, because not properly connected with the libel, set out the following publication "*of and concerning the plaintiff*:"—"Society of Guardians, for the Protection of Trade against Swindlers and Sharpers, &c. I (meaning defendant) am directed to inform you, that A. B. (meaning plaintiff) and C. D. are reported to this society as improper to be proposed to be balloted for as members thereof; (*meaning* that the plaintiff was a swindler and a sharper, and an improper person to be a member of the said society)." After verdict for the plaintiff, it was held, in arrest of judgment, that the *innuendo* was not warranted by the libel, and that the words of the libel, unexplained by *introductory* matter, were not actionable (*g*). The *innuendo* cannot supply the omission of a necessary inducement of matter; and an innuendo introducing new facts or otherwise than by reference to a previous inducement is fatally defective (*h*); and a statement that he is a regular prover under bankruptcies, "meaning that plaintiff was accustomed to prove fictitious debts under commissions," was held ill without a previous averment that the defendant had been accustomed to employ the words in that sense (*i*).

An *innuendo*, though it may in the particular case be unnecessary, will sometimes limit and confine the plaintiff in his proof, to show that the slander had the meaning thereby imputed to it; thus, where the plaintiff alleged that he was treasurer and collector of certain tolls, and that the defendant spoke of him, as such treasurer and collector, certain words, "*thereby meaning* that the plaintiff, *as such treasurer and collector*, had been guilty," &c., it was held that the plaintiff was bound by the *innuendo* to prove that he was treasurer and collector (*k*). If the words imported either fraud *or* felony, but by the innuendo they be *confined* to the latter, the plaintiff must prove they were spoken in the latter sense (*l*). The *innuendo* affixing a particular signification to the slander should therefore never be unnecessarily adopted, as is too frequently the case (*l*). It is not unusual, even after setting out words which clearly *of themselves* import a charge of felony, to add, "thereby then meaning that the plaintiff had feloniously stolen, &c.:" this is unnecessary; and as it is a statement of a mere legal conclusion, is improper, though it may be surplusage (*m*)(772).

[*438] *On the other hand, where *new* matter introduced by an *innuendo*, without any *antecedent colloquium* or statement to which it can refer to support it, it is altogether *unnecessary* to sustain the action, then the *innuendo* may be rejected as surplusage (*n*).

5thly. Statement of Resulting Damages.

5thly. Little explanation need here be given with regard to the statement of the *injury* or *damage* resulting from the *scandal*, because the observations

(*g*) Goldstein *v.* Foss, 6 B. & C. 154. Affirmed in error, 1 M. & P. 402; 4 Bing. 489; and 2 Y. & J. 156, S. C.

(*h*) Day *v.* Robinson, 1 Adol. & El. 554.

(*i*) 7 Bing. 119, and see note (*g*) *supra*.

(*k*) 4 B. & C. 655; 7 D. & R. 121; 3 Campb. 461; 7 Price, 544; and see 3 Bar. & Cres. 128.

(*l*) 3 Campb. 461; Williams *v.* Stott, 1 Cr. & M. 675; 3 Tyr. 688, S. C.

(*m*) See Cowp. 175; 5 East, 463; 1 Stark. Slander, 2d edit. 428. The general rule, *ante*, 244, 253, 258.

(*n*) 9 East, 93; 1 Crom. & M. 11; 2 Cr. & J. 361; 1 Stark. Slander, 2d edit. 426.

(772) Vide Thomas *v.* Croswell, 7 Johns. Rep. 272.

IV. ITS PARTS, &c.

5thly. The cause of action.

which we shall presently make as to the statement of *damages in all actions ex delicto* will equally apply to an action for a libel or slander (o). The general rule is, that where *the law infers damage*, and the words are actionable without special damage, none need be laid in the declaration; but that it is otherwise when the words are only actionable in respect of the *particular injury* resulting from them (773 to 780).

6thly. Of several counts (p).

6thly. Having ascertained the *mode* of stating the *cause of action*, the points relating to *several counts* in the *same* declaration are next to be considered. The rules as to the *joinder* of different *forms* and *causes* of action have already been treated of (q); and it is here only necessary to inquire *when* or to *what extent* the statement of the *same* cause of action in different counts is at present permitted. We will however first consider the practice *before* the *recent* rules, and then state those rules and the advisable course of framing declarations as respects *several counts*.

The practice *antecedent* to the pleading rules of Hil. T. 4 W. 4.

Before the recent pleading rules, Hil. T. 4 W. 4, r. 5,† a declaration might consist of numerous counts, and the jury might assess entire or distinct damages on all the counts (r)(781); and it was usual, particularly in assumpsit and in actions on the case, to set forth the plaintiff's same cause of action *in various shapes* in different counts, so that if he failed in the proof of one count he might succeed on another (s). Such additional counts have been aptly termed *safety valves* (t). The variations, however, must even then have been *substantial*; for if the different counts were so similar that the same evidence would support each, and the variation was of any considerable length and

(o) *Ante*, 428 a to 428 d; *post*, 451 d; 1 Stark. Slander, 2d edit. 439; 1 Saund. 243 c, n. 5.

(p) In general, Stephen, 2d ed. 309; 3d edit. 266, 267 to 277.

(q) *Ante*, 228.

(r) *Per* De Grey, C. J., 3 Wils. 185. In C. P. the Court would compel the plaintiff to elect in the term after the trial on what count he would enter up a verdict taken generally, 2 Taunt. 36.

(s) 3 Bla. Com. 295. In mixed actions, as *quare impedit*, several counts are admissible and often essential, see 1 Adol. & Ell. 394; in indictments the Courts object to there being several counts, when, 2 Stark. Crim. Law, 460; 1 Chit. Crim. Law, 252.

(t) *Per* Vaughan, B., in 2 Dowl. 76; 1 Cromp. & M. 848.

(773) { Shipman v. Burrows, 1 Hall's Rep. 399. }

(774) { Harcourt v. Harrison, 1 Hall's Rep. 474. }

(775) { So in an action for overflowing the plaintiff's land by the erection of a dam on the land of the defendant, in which the nature and extent of the alleged injury are specially described in the declaration, the plaintiff is entitled to a verdict for nominal damages, though he fail to prove the particular injury complained of, or any other actual injury. Pastorius v. Fisher, 1 Rawle, 27. }

(776) { 15 Mass. Rep. 194. Gilm. 227. } A declaration in trespass for entering the plaintiff's house, taking his goods, and terrifying and falsely imprisoning his wife, was held good after verdict, and that the injury to the wife should be taken as matter of aggravation only. Heminway v. Saxton and others, 3 Mass. Rep. 222. { And see Dimmett et al. v. Eskridge, 6 Munf. 308. pl. 4. }

(777) { Nor of an assault and battery upon *himself*. Sampson v. Coy, 15 Mass. Rep. 493. }

(778) { Treat v. Barber, 7 Conn. Rep. 275. }

(779) { Butler v. Kent, 19 Johns. Rep. 223. }

(780) See Butler v. Kent, 19 Johns. Rep. 223.

(781) Vide Neal v. Lewis, 2 Bay, 206.

† See American Editor's Preface.

IV. ITS PARTS, &c. 6thly. Of several counts.

vexatiously inserted (u), the Court would, on application, refer it to the master for examination, and to strike out the redundant counts, and in gross cases direct the costs to be paid by the attorney (v); but under the restriction of avoiding as much as possible any unnecessary increase of the costs, it was advisable, when the case would admit, to state in various counts the facts in different ways, corresponding with the evidence which might probably be adduced, and such counts were in general progressively more brief and concise; and this was particularly necessary in special assumpsits, where there was a doubt either as to the *consideration* or of the terms of the contract or its legal effect, or the mode in which the plaintiff had performed his part, or the defendant had violated his (x). Thus, in a special action of *assumpsit* for a breach of promise of marriage, if the defendant promised to marry upon a particular day, the first count was framed accordingly, but for fear the plaintiff should not be able to prove such particular promise, it was usual when the evidence would probably support the allegation to add a count to marry on request, another to marry in a reasonable time, and another to marry generally (y). So in declaring on a contract to deliver goods, if the stipulation was to deliver within a specified time and at a particular place, the first count was adapted to such facts, and the second to deliver on request or generally, and a third within a reasonable time (z); and it was frequently advisable to declare in different counts, the one on an executory, the other on an executed consideration, the first to admit of evidence of the defendant's stipulation at the time of entering into the contract, the other of subsequent admissions or promises. And we have seen that in an action at the suit of an executor or administrator, it is frequently necessary to add a set of counts on promises to the plaintiff in his representative capacity, in order to admit of evidence of a promise or acknowledgment to the plaintiff, to take the case out of the statute of limitations (a). It was usual also to add such *common* counts as were applicable to any part of the plaintiff's case (b), and after the *indebitatus* count for work and labor, or goods sold, &c. it was usual to add a *quantum meruit* or *valebant* count (c), though the latter we have seen had of late been considered unnecessary (d).

Also in *debt* on simple contracts, legal liabilities, and penal statutes, it was frequently advisable to vary the statement of the cause of action in different counts. But in *debt* on specialties and records, and in *covenant*, as the instrument declared upon could not, if due care were taken, vary from the statement in the declaration, one count would in general suffice. In an action upon a deed, of which a profert, or an excuse for it, might be necessary, if it were doubtful whether the deed could be produced, or whether it were in the possession of the defendant, or be lost or destroyed, it was proper to declare in one count, stating the profert; in another count, stating the deed to be in

(u) 3 Smith, 113.

(v) 1 New Rep. 289; Rep. T. Hardw. 129; see the former practice as to *striking out superfluous counts*, Tidd, 9th edit. 616; and 3 Chitty's Gen. Prac. 638; see 1 D. & R. 171, 508; 1 Chit. R. 709; 2 Bing. 412.

(x) See Stephen, 2d ed. 315.

(y) *Post*, vol. ii.; 1 M. & P. 239.

(z) *Id.* 164, 165.

(a) *Ante*, 392. See the form, *post*, vol. ii.; and see fully the form in Foxwist *v.* Tremaine, 2 Saund. 207, 208.

(b) *Ante*, 372 to 392.

(c) 3 Bla. Com. 295.

(d) *Ante*, 376; 2 Saund. 122 a.

IV. ITS PARTS, &c.

6thly. Of several counts.

the possession of the defendant; and in a third that it was lost, &c. (e); so that the risk of being restricted to making a profert without being able to give oyer, *or of alleging an excuse which could not be established, might be avoided.

In declarations for *torts*, several counts for the same cause of action were also frequently advisable, particularly in actions for *words* which are usually stated in different ways, and sometimes with different *innuendoes*, so as to meet the probable evidence (*f*). In trespass, if there had been two or more assaults, it was proper to insert as many counts as there were assaults, in order to avoid the necessity for a new assignment (*g*); and if there were only one count, and the plaintiff failed in proving one battery, he could not after attempting to do so give in evidence another assault, as he might do if there had been two counts (*h*). So in trespass *quare clausum fregit*, if there have been any asportation of personal property, it was usual to insert two counts, in the first charging an injury to the land and taking the goods there, which is in its nature local and must be proved as laid; and in the second declaring merely for the asportation of the goods, which is transitory, and may be supported though the taking be proved elsewhere (*i*)(782). And where there had been an *asportation* of personal property, (which in the case of roots, earth, or other matter *affixed* to the *freehold*, must be an actual *carrying away* from the land where the same was dug, &c. and not a mere conveyance of it to another part of the premises where the same was dug)(*k*), it was expedient to insert the common asportavit count (*l*). If, however, a declaration in trespass contained two counts, and the defendant pleaded not guilty to the first, and suffered judgment by default as to the other, and on the trial the plaintiff only proved one act of trespass, to which the second count was applicable, he was not entitled to a verdict on the first (*m*). So if a declaration contained two counts in fact on the same bond or instrument, and the defendant pleaded a plea applicable to both the counts, and also a special plea which was an answer to the first count only, and such special plea was substantiated, then the plaintiff could not at the trial abandon the first count and proceed on the second, so as to avoid the effect of the special plea (*n*)(783).

[*448] *In the adoption of several counts care must be taken that there be *no misjoinder* (*o*). The jury may indeed assess entire or distinct damages on each of the counts (784) when separate injuries have been proved (*p*). If *distinct*

(*e*) 4 East, 585; 1 Esp. Rep. 337; *post*, vol. ii.

(*f*) *Post*, vol. ii.; in Replevin, see Vin. Ab. Declaration, Q.

(*g*) 1 Saund. 299, n. 6; 1 T. R. 479; *post*, vol. ii.

(*h*) 1 Campb. 473.

(*i*) *Per* Buller, J., 1 T. R. 479; and see 7 East, 325.

(*k*) Hullock, 76.

(*l*) Hullock, 74 to 84; and see 7 East, 325; and *post*, vol. ii. as to costs.

(*m*) 7 T. R. 727.

(*n*) And see *ante*, 372, 373.

(*o*) As to misjoinder, see *ante*, 228 to 236; 1 Nev. & Man. 321.

(*p*) *Id.*

(782) { Where in trespass for breaking the plaintiff's close, and taking away his chattels, the declaration does not contain a count for only taking the chattels, the plaintiff cannot recover for taking them, unless he proves a breach of the close. Ropps *v.* Barker, 4 Pick. Rep. 239. }

(783) Driggs *v.* Rockwell, 11 Wend. R. 506.

(784) Vide Burnham *v.* Webster, 5 Mass. Rep. 269. And the plaintiff may enter a *nolle prosequi* as to the insufficient count. Livingston *v.* Executors of Livingston, 3 Johns. Rep. 189.

IV. ITS PARTS, &c. — 6thly. Of several counts.

damages be assessed, judgment may be given upon either of the counts; but if the jury find *entire* damages on all the counts, the judgment must be entire, in which case if one of the counts be insufficient judgment will be arrested, or a writ of error be sustainable (q)(785), and the judgment will be arrested *in toto*, and no *venire de novo* awarded (r)(786). In case, therefore, if there be an insufficient count, if the mistake be discovered before verdict, it is expedient to strike it out by leave of the judge, or to enter a *nolle prosequi* as to such count; or at the trial to take a verdict only on the sufficient counts, cautiously avoiding to give evidence in support of the bad count. However, where a general verdict has been taken and evidence given only on the good counts, the Court will permit the verdict to be *amended* by the judge's notes, &c. (787); and if it appear by the judge's notes that the jury calculated the damages on evidence applicable to the good count only, the judge will amend the postea by directing that the verdict be entered on those counts, though evidence was given applicable to the bad count also (s). And where judgment has been given on demurrer or by *nil dicet* in favor of the plaintiff, he may, after entering judgment for himself upon the whole declaration, upon discovering any error in one of the counts, waive his judgment on that count and enter it for the defendant (t)(788). A *nolle prosequi* as to one count does not preclude the plaintiff from proceeding at the trial upon another count, which, although apparently for a different cause of action, is in reality founded on the demand which might have been recovered upon the count which the plaintiff abandoned (u).

Costs of several counts (x).

The *costs* also were always to be considered in adding *several* counts. Before the late rules the law was thus,—where the plaintiff obtained a verdict only upon one of several counts or issues, whether in the King's Bench or Common Pleas, he was only entitled to the costs relating to the trial of such issue; and the defendant was not allowed the costs of the counts found for

(q) Cowp. 276; 3 Wils. 185; 2 Saund. 171 b; Dougl. 722, 730; 3 M. & Sel. 110.
(r) *Id. ibid.*
(s) 2 Saund. 171 b; Dougl. 730; 10 Moore, 446, 452 a; Tidd, 9th ed. 901, 713.
(t) 2 B. & P. 49.
(u) 1 R. & M. 311.
(x) See Tidd, 9th ed. 917, 971.

(785) Vide Backus *v.* Richardson, 5 Johns. Rep. 476. Cheetham *v.* Tillotson, Id. 435. Bayard *v.* Malcom, 2 Johns. Rep. 573. Ex'rs of Van Rensselaer *v.* Ex'rs of Platner, 2 Johns. Cas. 18, 21, 23. Hopkins *v.* Beedle, 1 Caines' Rep. 349. Vaughan *v.* Havens, 8 Johns. Rep. 110. Benson *v.* Swift, 2 Mass. Rep. 53. Contra Neal *v.* Lewis, 2 Bay, 204. Neilson *v.* Emerson, 2 Bay, 439. Where in an action of covenant, several breaches were alleged, and a discharge pleaded as to part, on which the defendant had judgment on demurrer, and issue taken as to the residue, and a general verdict for the plaintiff, it was intended that the verdict was for such breaches only as were not covered by the special plea. Eastman *v.* Chapman, 1 Day, 30.

(786) {See Gordon *v.* Kennedy, 2 Binn. 287.} But in Hopkins *v.* Beedle, 1 Caines' Rep. 347, where judgment was arrested on account of entire damages having been given, some of the counts in the declaration being bad, the court said that the plaintiff, on application, might have been entitled to a *venire de novo*, on payment of costs. And in another case, Lyle *v.* Clayson, 1 Caines' Rep. 581, where judgment went by default, the court held that the plaintiff was entitled to a writ of inquiry *de novo* on payment of costs. *Et vide* Livingston *v.* Rogers, 1 Caines' Rep. 583.

(787) Acc. Union Turnpike Company *v.* Jenkins, 1 Caines' Rep. 381. *Et vide* Stafford *v.* Green, 1 Johns. Rep. 505. Ex'rs of Van Rensselaer *v.* Ex'rs of Platner, 2 Johns. Cas. 17. Roe *v.* Crutchfield, 1 Hen. & Mun. 365.

(788) Contra Backus *v.* Richardson, 5 Johns. Rep. 476. {Unless he obtain leave of the court to do so. Ibid.}

IV. ITS PARTS, &c. — 6thly. Of several counts.

him, though upon supposed causes of action different from that in respect of which the *plaintiff recovered (y); and the same rule prevailed where a defendant succeeded on a demurrer as to part of the plaintiff's demand, and the plaintiff had obtained a verdict as to the residue, in which case no costs were allowed to the defendant in respect of the demurrer (z): but if there were two distinct causes of action in two separate counts, and as to one the defendant suffered judgment by default, and as to the other took issue and obtained a verdict, he was entitled to judgment for his costs on the latter count, notwithstanding the plaintiff was entitled to judgment and costs on the first count (a). It was considered that where the plaintiff in different counts varied the statement of the *same* cause of action for fear of a variance and nonsuit on the trial, and succeeded upon one, it was but reasonable that he should not be punished with the payment of costs in respect of such other of the counts as he might not be able to prove; but that where he unnecessarily and without foundation proceeded in the same declaration in different counts for *distinct* causes of action, requiring the defendant to adduce different or additional evidence to resist them, it might be more reasonable to allow the *defendant* the costs of such *improper counts*, and of the *evidence* which the defendant adduced to negative them (b); but according to the practice the defendant was not in either case entitled to costs (c) (789).

The existing Rule Hil. T. 2 W. 4, c. 74, as to costs of several Issues.

At length however the General Rule, Hil. T. 2 W. 4, r. 74, ordered "that no costs shall be allowed on taxation to a plaintiff upon any counts or issues upon which he has not succeeded; and the costs of all issues found for the defendant shall be deducted from the plaintiff's costs;" and it has been held that the general issue to a declaration containing many counts creates as *many issues* within the meaning of this rule, and the defendant is now entitled to costs upon *every count* on which the plaintiff fails (d), and the rule also applies to *each separate count in ejectment* (e); and it has been held that if the plaintiff do not prove all the words in a count in slander the defendant is entitled to the costs of the pleadings found for him (f). The decisions and practical operations upon this rule have been pointed out in another work, to which the reader is referred (g).

[*450] Form of subsequent counts.

*In framing a second or subsequent count for the same cause of action, care was and still is essential to avoid any *unnecessary* repetition of the *same* matter; and by an inducement in the first count, applying any matter to the following counts, and by conferring concisely in the subsequent counts to

(y) 2 B. & P. 334; 5 East, 261; 2 Marsh. 201; 3 M. & Sel. 323; 16 East, 129. In Tidd, 4th edit. 874, n. 8, and 5 East, 263, the practice of the Common Pleas is stated otherwise, but the case in 2 B. & P. 334, appears to have escaped observation; and see Tidd, 9th ed. 974, 975.

(z) 5 East, 261; Tidd, 9th ed. 972.

(a) 3 T. R. 654; 6 *Id.* 602, 603.

(b) See Lord Eldon's observations in 2 B. & P. 335, and Lord Kenyon's in 6 T. R. 601.

(c) 2 B. & P. 335; 5 East, 261; Tidd, 971, 972; Hopkins v. Barnes, 2 Price, 136; and see Jervis's Rules, Hil. T. 2 W. 4, r. 74, note (x).

(d) Cox v. Thomson, 2 Crom. & Jer. 498.

(e) Doe v. Webber, 1 Har. Rep. 10.

(f) Prudhomme v. Fraser, 1 Har. Rep. 5.

(g) 3 Chitty's Gen. Prac. 476 to 479.

(789) If judgment is arrested for one bad count, the defendant is entitled to his full costs on all the issues, as the party prevailing. Gibson v. Waterhouse, 5 Greenl. 19.

IV. ITS PARTS &c.

such inducement, much unnecessary prolixity may be avoided; and this is usual in actions for words, and proper to be attended to in all cases (*h*). But unless the second count expressly refers to the first no defect therein will be aided by the preceding count; for though both counts are in the same declaration, yet they are for all purposes as distinct as if they were in separate declarations; and consequently they must independently contain all necessary allegations, or the latter count must expressly refer to the former (*i*)(790). The commencement of a second count, "And whereas also," &c. is sufficiently positive (*k*). In order to avoid any objection on the ground of duplicity (*l*), it is advisable to insert in the second count for the same cause of action, the word "other" goods, &c. (*m*), or in ejectment "other" messuages, &c. (*n*); but after verdict the Court will not intend the goods, &c. mentioned in the second count to be the same as those in the first, unless it be expressly so stated (*o*).

6thly. Of several counts.

Pleading *to several* counts for *same* cause of action.

It not unfrequently happens that the defendant attempts to defeat the advantage to be derived from several counts, by alleging in his plea thereto that the supposed causes of action therein mentioned are one and the same cause of action, and then showing matter which is only an answer to one cause of action; as in the instance of two counts for two assaults, the plea often has been, "that the assaults in the different counts are but one and the same;" and then *son assault demesne* to the whole has been pleaded (*p*). This mode of pleading is bad on demurrer (*q*); but if the plaintiff *reply* to the plea instead of demurring, he admits the allegation that there is but one cause of action, and is restricted thereto at the trial (*r*). The plaintiff should therefore in such case demur, if it be material to him to rely upon each separate count, and *not to be limited to proof of one cause of action: or if there be two distinct causes of action, he might, it should seem, traverse and take issue upon the allegation that the torts are one and the same. [*451]

The rule, Hil. T. 4 W. 4, reg. 5, 6, 7, *prohibiting several* counts and decisions thereon.

The common law right to introduce several counts into the same declara-

(*h*) See the observations of Lawrence, J., 7 East, 50, and 2 Hen. Bla. 131, 132; 2 Wils. 114, 115; Cro. Eliz. 240; 2 Bla. Rep. 1038; and precedents, Crown. Circ. Comp. 9th edit. (1820); *post*, vol. ii. In a second count, on a deed or agreement, it is not unusual to commence the count by alleging that "the deed or agreement in the first count mentioned, having been made as therein mentioned," &c. But it would seem to be more correct to aver, that "a certain *other* deed or agreement was made between the parties containing the like terms and stipulations as were and are contained in the deed set forth in the first count:" for, as observed by Mr. Serjeant Stephen, (2d ed. 318, 319,) whether the subjects of several counts be *really* distinct or identical, they must always *purport* to be founded on distinct causes of action, and not to refer to the same matter. This is evidently rendered necessary by the rule against duplicity, (see *ante*, 259,) which, though *evaded* as to the declaration by the use of several counts in the manner here described, is not to be *directly violated*.

(*i*) Bac. Ab. Pleas and Pleading, B. 1.

(*k*) *Post*, vol. ii.

(*l*) See *ante*, 259, 260.

(*m*) 2 Ld. Raym. 842; 7 Mod. 148, S. C.; Com. Dig. Pleader, C. 33; *sed vide* Salk. 213; see *supra*, n. (*h*).

(*n*) 2 Stra. 908.

(*o*) Salk. 213; Bac. Ab. Pleas, B. 1; Vin. Ab. Declaration.

(*p*) See *post*, vol. iii.

(*q*) See Index, "*Quæ sunt eadem.*"

(*r*) 1 R. & M. 118.

(790) Where there is a special demurrer to the whole declaration, a count which is bad cannot be referred to, for the purpose of helping out another count. Nelson *v.* Swan, 13 Johns. Rep. 483.

IV. ITS PARTS, &c.

6thly. Of several counts.

tion, in fact, for the *same subject-matter of complaint*, and varying from the first count only in *statement, description*, or *circumstances*, having been vexatiously abused, and the *necessity* for permitting such variations having been removed by the 3 & 4 W. 4, c. 42,† s. 23, giving the judge power to amend *pending* the trial of an action in almost every case of *variance*, not prejudicing the opponent on the trial of the *merits*, the Reg. Gen. Hil. Term, 4 W. 4, reg. 5,† after reciting that consequence, then limits the use of several counts.

Several counts and pleas not allowed. Reg. 5 orders, that *several counts* shall not be allowed, unless *a distinct subject-matter of complaint is intended to be established in respect of each*; nor shall *several* pleas, or avowries, or cognizances be allowed, unless *a distinct ground of answer or defence* is intended to be established in respect of each.

Instances in declarations. Therefore counts founded on one and the same principal matter of complaint, but varied in statement, description, or circumstances only, are not be allowed.

Contract with condition. *Ex. gr.* Counts founded upon the same contract, described in one as a contract without a condition, and in another as a contract with a condition, are not to be allowed; for they are founded on the same subject-matter of complaint, and are only variations in the statement of one and the same contract.

Non-delivery of bill in payment. So, counts for not giving, or delivering, or accepting a bill of exchange in payment, according to the contract of sale, for goods sold and delivered, and for the price of the same goods to be paid in money, are not to be allowed.

Not accepting and paying for goods. So, counts for not accepting and paying for goods sold, and for the price of the same goods, as goods bargained and sold, are not to be allowed.

Bills and notes. But counts upon a bill of exchange or promissory note, and for the consideration of the bill or note in goods, money, or otherwise, are to be considered as founded on distinct subject-matters of complaint; for the debt and the security are different contracts, and such counts are to be allowed.

Policies. Two counts upon the same policy of insurance are not to be allowed.

Premium. But a count upon a policy of insurance, and a count for money had and received, to recover back the premium upon a contract implied by law, are to be allowed.

Charter-parties. Two counts on the same charter-party are not to be allowed.

Freight pro rata. But a count for freight upon a charter-party, and for freight *pro ratâ itineris*, upon a contract implied by law, are to be allowed.

Demise and use and occupation. Counts upon a demise, and for use and occupation of the same land for the same time, are not to be allowed.

Misfeasance. In actions of tort for misfeasance, several counts for the same injury, varying the description of it, are not to be allowed.

Nonfeasance. In the like actions for nonfeasance, several counts founded on varied statements of the same duty are not to be allowed.

Trespass. Several counts in trespass for acts committed at the same time and place, are not to be allowed.

Indebitatus assumpsit. Where several debts are alleged in *indebitatus assumpsit* to be due in re-

† See American Editor's Preface.

spect of several matters, *ex. gr.*, for wages, work and labor as a hired servant, *work and labor generally*, goods sold and delivered, goods bargained and sold, money lent, money paid, money had and received, and the like, the statement of each debt is to be considered as amounting to a several count within the meaning of the rule which forbids the use of several counts, though one promise to pay only is alleged in consideration of all the debts.

IV. ITS PARTS &c.

6thly. Of several counts.

Provided that a count for money due on an account stated may be joined with any other count for a money demand, though it may not be intended to establish a distinct subject-matter of complaint in respect of each of such counts.

Account stated.

The rule which forbids the use of several counts is not to be considered as precluding the plaintiff from alleging *more breaches* than one of the same contract in the same count.

Several breaches.

Pleas, avowries, and cognizances, founded on one and the same principal matter, but varied in statement, description, or circumstances only, (and pleas in bar in replevin are within the rule), are not to be allowed. The rule then contains directions as to pleas of payment; accord and satisfaction, release; liability of third party; agreement to forbear in consideration of liability of third party; *lib. ten.*, easement, right of way, right of common, common of turbary, and estovers; distress for rent, and damage *feasant*, and avowries for distress for rent.

Instances of pleas and avowries, &c.

The rule then declares that the examples in this and other places specified are given as *instances* only of the application of the rules to which they relate; but the *principles* contained in the rules are not to be considered as restricted by the examples specified.

The cases above mentioned as instances only.

Where more than one count, plea, avowry, or cognizance, shall have been used in apparent violation of the preceding rule, the opposite party shall be at liberty *to apply to a judge* (s), suggesting that two or more of the counts, pleas, avowries, or cognizances are founded on the same subject-matter of complaint or ground of answer or defence, for an order that all the counts, pleas, avowries, or recognizances, introduced in violation of the rule, be struck out at the cost of the party pleading; whereupon the judge shall order accordingly, unless he shall be satisfied, upon cause shown, that *some distinct subject-matter* of complaint is *bona fide* intended to be established in respect of each of such counts, or some distinct ground of answer or defence in respect of each of such pleas, avowries, or cognizances, in which case he shall indorse upon the summons, or state in his order, as the case may be, that he is so satisfied; and shall also specify the counts, pleas, avowries, or cognizances mentioned in such application, which shall be allowed.

Departure from these rules, how taken advantage of.

Upon the trial, where there is more than one count, plea, avowry or cognizance upon the record, and the party pleading fails to establish a distinct subject-matter of complaint in respect of each count, or some distinct ground of

Costs of counts and pleas.

(s) *Semble*, that according to Temple *v.* Melton, Hil. T. 1836, C. P. the application must in first instance be *to a Judge at Chambers*, and it is doubtful whether there can be an appeal to the Court; and see 3 Chitty's Gen. Prac. 35, n. (*u*).

IV. ITS PARTS, &c.

6thly. Of several counts.

answer or defence in respect of each plea, avowry, or cognizance, a verdict and judgment shall pass against him upon each count, plea, avowry, or cognizance, which he shall have so failed to establish, and he shall be liable to the other party for all the costs occasioned by such count, plea, avowry, or cognizance, including those of the evidence as well as those of the pleadings; and further, in all cases in which an application to a judge has been made under the preceding rule, and any count, plea, avowry, or cognizance, allowed as aforesaid, upon the ground that some distinct subject-matter of complaint was *bona fide* intended to be established at the trial in respect of each count, or some distinct ground of answer or defence in respect of each plea, avowry, or cognizance so allowed, if the Court or judge, before whom the trial is had, shall be of opinion that no such distinct subject-matter of complaint was *bona fide* intended to be established in respect of each count so allowed, or no such distinct ground of answer or defence in respect of each plea, avowry or cognizance so allowed, and shall so certify before final judgment, such party so pleading shall not recover any cost upon the issue or issues upon which *he succeeds*, arising out of any count, plea, avowry, or cognizance with respect to which the judge shall so certify."

Meaning of and decisions upon these rules.

The meaning of the terms of the rule, "unless a *distinct subject-matter of complaint* is intended to be established in respect of each," is in some measure explained by the *instances* stated in the rule, and by the instances given of several pleas to be permitted or rejected. But we have seen it is still rather uncertain when a second varying count may be permitted, and the cases are contradictory (*t*). It seems that in an action on the case for an injury to a water-course there may be two counts, one claiming it in right of an ancient building, and another in right of a close (*u*), and that in an action against the sheriff there may be a count for an arrest and escape, and another for not arresting the third person when there was an opportunity (*v*); and in a declaration for treble value in not setting out tithes there may be a second count for tithes as bargained and sold (*x*); and in a declaration for double rent a count for use and occupation may be added (*x*); but in one of the latest cases Parke, B., refused to allow a count to recover four-pence per chaldron for metage on all coals imported into the port of Truro, and another for the same sum claimed to be due as a port duty, saying, that at the trial of such a cause of action he should certainly, if necessary, amend the declaration by altering one statement to the other to meet the proof; and that in all the instances given in the rules in which two counts are to be permitted for the same cause of action, though grounded on the same cause, they were not framed so as to claim exactly the same sum; *ex. gr.* on a bill of exchange, and on the consideration for it, a count on a charter-party and a count *pro rata itineris* (*y*).

(*t*) See 3 Chitty's Gen. Prac. 482, 483.

(*u*) Per Patteson, J., in Frankum *v.* Earl Falmouth, as stated in Bosanquet's Rules, 14; 1 Harr. & Wol. 1; 4 Nev. & Man. 330; 6 Car. & P. 529.

(*v*) Per Patteson, J., in Guest *v.* Everest, 9 Legal Observer, 75; and Bosanquet's Rules, 13, in note.

(*x*) Lawrence *v.* Stevens, 1 Gale, 164; but see 3 Dowl. 777, differently reported. See also Jenkins *v.* Trebar, Legal Examiner, 263; and Thomas *v.* Whitbread, *id.* 305, 306. See cases and observations, 3 Chitty's Gen. Prac. 481 to 489; and practice as to striking out a count, *id.* 638.

(*y*) Jenkins *v.* Trebar, Hil. T. 1836; Legal Examiner, 263, 305 to 307.

The construction of this rule prohibiting the use of more than one count or plea being much connected with the *practice* of the Courts has been fully considered in another work (*x*). As yet the admissibility of several counts seems to be unsettled, and upon the whole, in practice, when, after full consideration, it appears that the proposed several counts are essential for the purpose of just security to the plaintiff, and that they do not contravene the rule, it seems to be advisable to insert such counts in the declaration, and explicitly to state the reasons for so doing to the learned judge in answer to any application to strike out all but one; and then, in case that judge should order them to be erased, to submit to his decision, and not pertinaciously retain the counts objected to, at the risk of losing the costs under the seventh rule; and in which case, should a variance appear on the trial, it is most probable the judge who will try the cause, on proof of such prior proceedings at chambers, will permit an amendment.

IV. ITS PARTS, &c. — 6thly. Of several counts.

After stating the tort or cause of action, and, when necessary, the *special* injury or damage resulting therefrom, the declaration concludes, "*to the damage of the plaintiff of £— &c.*" (*y*).

7thly. The conclusion *ad damnum, &c.*

In *penal actions* at the suit of a common informer, as the plaintiff's right to the penalty did not accrue till the bringing of the action, and he cannot have sustained any damage by a previous detention of the penalty, it is not proper to conclude *ad damnum* (*z*); but the mistake may be amended even after error brought (*a*). In an action by *husband and wife* for a battery, &c. of the wife, or whenever the wife is properly joined in the action, the declaration should conclude *ad damnum ipsorum* (*b*); and when the plaintiff sues *as executor, administrator, or assignee* of a bankrupt, it is usual to state that he was injured *as* such executor, &c. (791). In *debt* the object of the action being to recover a sum of money *eo nomine*, and in *detinue* the main object of the action being the recovery of the goods themselves, the damages are generally nominal (*c*). But in *assumpsit, covenant, case, replevin, trespass*, and other actions really for the recovery of *damages*, the sum in the conclusion of the declaration must be sufficient to cover the real demand (*d*); for in general the plaintiff cannot recover greater damages than he has declared for, and laid in the conclusion of his declaration (*e*); and after a verdict taken the Court will not give leave to increase the damages laid in the declaration, and take judgment for the enlarged damages (*f*). But if the plaintiff will waive the verdict, he may be allowed to amend his declaration by increasing the damages, and will be let in to a new *trial (*g*). If judgment be given for more damages than those laid in the declaration, it is error, and a Court of error [*452]

(*x*) 3 Chitty's Gen. Prac. 475 to 489.

(*y*) Com. Dig. Pleader, C. 84; 10 Co. 116 b, 117 a, b. As to this conclusion see 1 M. & Sel. 236. When *damages* should in general be claimed, *ante*, 428 *b*. In assumpsit, *ante*, 371; in actions *ex delicto*, *ante*, 428 *b*.

(*z*) 4 Burr. 2021, 2490; 1 Marsh. 180.

(*a*) 1 Marsh. 180; *query*, if the claim to damages might not in such case be viewed as mere surplusage.

(*b*) Com. Dig. Pleader, C. 84; *id.* 2 A. 1; 1 Salk. 114; *post*, vol. ii.

(*c*) *Ante*, 129, 130.

(*d*) 2 Lev. 57.

(*e*) 10 Co. 117 a, b; Vin. Ab. Damages, R.; Com. Dig. Pleader, C. 84; 4 M. & Sel. 100.

(*f*) 1 M. & Sel. 675.

(*g*) 7 T. R. 132.

(791) But this is unnecessary. Martin *v.* Smith, 5 Binn. 16, 21.

IV. ITS PARTS, &c. — 7thly. The conclusion.

cannot reduce the sum to the amount stated in the declaration (*h*). But the Court in which the action was brought will allow the plaintiff to enter a remittitur of the surplus damages, and thus aid the error (*i*)(792). If, therefore, the verdict be for more than the damages laid in the declaration, a remittitur should be entered as to the surplus before judgment. The jury, however, may give a verdict for as much as is declared for, and also give *costs separately*, which costs may afterwards be increased by the Court, though such damages and costs might together exceed the damages laid in the declaration (*k*). It is usual in practice to state a sum sufficient to cover the real demand, with interest up to the time of final judgment.

The *forms* of conclusion.

In point of *form* the usual conclusion of a declaration in the *King's Bench* before the recent rules had always been, "to the damage of the plaintiff of £—, and therefore he brings his suit, &c.;" or in a *qui tam* action "and therefore as well for our said lord the king (or 'for the poor of the said parish of ——,') as for himself in this behalf he brings his suit, &c.;" but in the latter case the general conclusion, "and therefore he brings his suit, &c." would suffice (*m*). In the *Common Pleas* the conclusion was, "wherefore the said plaintiff saith that he is injured, and hath sustained damage to the value (or 'amount') of £— and therefore he brings his suit, &c.;" and in the *Exchequer*, the form was, "To the damage of the said plaintiff of £—, whereby he is the less able to satisfy our said lord the king the debt which he owes his said Majesty at his Exchequer, and therefore he brings his suit, &c." The above differences in the form of concluding in each Court are still to be observed in declarations in actions *removed* from an inferior Court, but in *all personal* actions *commenced* in either of the superior Courts, the Reg. Gen.

The present form.

Trin. T. 1 W. 4,† prescribes the following form: "*To the damage of the plaintiff of £—, and thereupon he brings suit, &c.*" (*n*) but which it is implied is to vary when at the suit of husband and wife, executors, administrators, or assignees (*o*).

By the above word *suit* or *secta* (*a sequendo*), was anciently understood the witnesses or followers of the plaintiff, by whom he proposed to prove his case, for in ancient times the law would not put the defendant to the trouble of answering the charge till the plaintiff had professed himself ready to make

[*453] out his case; but the actual production of *the suit, the *secta*, or followers, has long been antiquated, though the form of it still continues (*p*). In actions against *attornies* and other officers of the Court, the declaration used to conclude *unde petit remedium*, instead of bringing suit (*q*); but an inaccurate

(*h*) 4 M. & Sel 94; 1 M & Sel. 675; 5 East, 142

(*i*) 4 M. & Sel. 94.

(*k*) Vin. Ab Damages, R pl. 9, 10, 11; 10 Co. 117 a, b.

(*m*) 10 Mod. 253.

(*n*) See the rule, *post*, vol. ii.

(*o*) See forms, *post*, vol. ii.

(*p*) 3 Bla. Com. 295; Gilb. C. P. 48; Stephen on Pleading, 2d edit. 475. Perhaps in the spirit of conciseness evinced in the modern rules, the concluding words, "*and thereupon he brings suit*," might have been omitted. Those words seem equivalent to "and this the plaintiff is ready to verify."

(*q*) Gilb. C. P. 49.

(792) Vide Burger v. Kortwright, 4 Johns. Rep. 415. } And the amendment has been permitted *after* judgment, and after writ of error brought, and the excess of the judgment assigned as error. Herbert v. Hardenberg, 5 Halst Rep. 222. See the *English* and *American* cases cited by Ch. Justice Ewing —

† See American Editor's Preface.

IV. ITS PARTS, &c.

7thly. The conclusion.

conclusion in that case was no cause of demurrer (r); however, in one case, on a special demurrer, the Court, for the sake of keeping up the old established form of "prays relief, &c." proposed an amendment without payment of costs (s). When the action was by bill against a member of the House of Commons, the *bill* concluded with a prayer of process to be made to the plaintiff, according to the statute, &c. but now in all cases as well against attornies as privileged persons the above-mentioned common conclusion "To the damage of the plaintiff of £—, and thereupon he brings suit, &c." is proper and sufficient (t).

8thly. The Profert.

In an action at the suit of an executor or administrator, immediately after the conclusion, "to the damage," &c. and before the pledges, it was always the course to make a *profert* of the letters testamentary or letters of administration (u)(793); but in *scire facias* the profert might be either in the middle or at the end of the declaration (v); and in an action on a note indorsed to the plaintiff by an administrator no profert is necessary, because the plaintiff is not entitled to the custody of the letters of administration, which however must be proved on the trial (x). The omission of the profert when necessary is now aided unless the defendant demur specially for the defect (y).

Pledges now to be omitted.

At the end of the declaration in the King's Bench by bill, it was usual to add the plaintiff's common *pledges to prosecute*, John Doe and Richard Roe (z). But in proceedings by original, and in the Common Pleas, pledges omitted were supposed to have been found in the first instance before the defendant was summoned, and therefore they were not to be stated at the end of the declaration unless in proceedings against attornies, &c. (a). In an action at the suit of the king, the queen, or an infant, pledges were not at any time necessary (b); and as they have long ceased to be real (c), the statement *of them had long been considered to be unnecessary, and the omission could not be taken advantage of even by special demurrer (794), because *cessante ratione, cessat et ipsa lex* (d); and the recent Reg. Gen. Mich. T. 3 W. 4, reg. 15, *expressly prohibits* the addition of *pledges* in any declaration in a *personal* action. [*454]

(r) Andr. 247; Barnes, 3.
(s) Barnes, 167.
(t) Reg. Gen. Mich. Term, 1 W. 4, reg. 15.
(u) Bac. Ab. Executor, C.; Dougl. 5, in notes. As to the statement of administration, see 1 Rich. C. P. 443.
(v) Carth. 69.
(x) Willes, 560.
(y) 4 & 5 Anne, c. 16, s. 1.
(z) 3 Bla. Com. 295; Co. Lit. 161 a, n. 4; Com. Dig. Pleader, C. 16.
(a) Summary on Pleading, 42; Barnes, 163.
(b) 8 Co. 61; Cro. Car. 161; Co. Lit. 133 a; Sir W. Jones, 177.
(c) 3 Bla. Com. 295; Co. Lit. 161 a, note 4; Fortes. 330; 1 Cromp. Intr. 48.
(d) 3 T. R. 157, 158; Barnes, 163; 2 Hen. Bla. 161; Summary on Pleading, 43. And yet it was enacted by the statute 4 Ann. c. 16, s. 1, that no advantage shall be taken of the omission of pledges, *unless assigned specially as cause of demurrer*, thereby admitting the omission to be then an existing objection: and since that statute leave has been given to amend, see 1 Wils. 226; 2 Wils. 142; Rep. temp. Hard. 315; Fortesc. 330; Barnes, 163; Palm. 518.

(793) In *Connecticut* it is not common to make profert of letters testamentary. Champlin v. Tilley and Tilley, 3 Day's Rep. 305. { And in debt by an administrator upon a judgment recovered by him, he need not declare as administrator. Talmadge v. Chapel, 16 Mass. Rep. 71. Crawford v. Whittal, 1 Doug. 4, n. (1.) }
(794) Acc. Baker v. Phillips, 4 Johns. Rep. 190.

IV. ITS PARTS, &c.

8thly. The profert and pledges.

Defects when aided.

In considering the various parts of a declaration, we have incidentally noticed a great variety of instances, in which a defect may be aided or become unimportant, either by the defendant's omission to demur specially or generally, or by his pleading over (e), or by virtue of the statutes of jeofails, or by the effect of a verdict. It is proposed to consider these rules in a connected point of view, as they have relevance to all parts of pleading, towards the end of this volume, and therefore no further notice need here be taken of the subject (f).

(e) See an instance, Darling v. Gurney, 2 Cr. & M. 226.

(f) See Index, "*Defects.*"

*CHAPTER V.

Of the Claim of Conusance, Appearance and Defence, Oyer, and Imparlances:

Before we consider the differentpleas in personal actions, it may be proper in this chapter to examine a few points relating to, 1st, The claim of *Conusance;* 2dly, *Appearance and Defence;* 3dly, *Oyer;* and 4thly, *Imparlances.* The *first* has long been a proceeding of rare occurrence. The *second,* viz., the statement in pleading of any appearance and defence, has been almost entirely altered by the Reg. Gen. Hil. T. 4 W. 4; and the *fourth,* relating to Imparlances, has as respects *personal actions commenced* in one of the superior Courts been virtually abolished; but still it is advisable for students and practitioners to take a concise view of the ancient practice respecting those three subjects. As regards the third, *Oyer* and pleadings thereupon, there has been but one recent alteration.—We will consider each in the above order.

I. CLAIM OF CONUSANCE.

I. CLAIM OF CONUSANCE.

The claim of *Conusance,* or *Cognizance of a suit* (*a*), is defined to be an intervention by a *third person,* demanding judicature in the cause against the plaintiff, who has chosen to commence his action out of the claimant's Court (*b*). It is in form a question of jurisdiction between the two Courts (*c*), and not between the plaintiff and defendant, as in the case of a plea to the jurisdiction, and therefore it must be demanded by the party entitled to conusance, or by his representative, and by the defendant or his attorney (*d*). A plea to the jurisdiction must be pleaded in person, but a claim of conusance may be made by attorney (*e*). Hence the consideration of this claim might on first view appear to be foreign to a treatise of this nature; but as it was frequently made at the instigation of the defendant, and affects the pleadings, it is proper to be concisely inquired into. This claim, when made against the jurisdiction of the Courts of Westminster, has not been encouraged, and therefore the greatest accuracy must be observed in the time and manner of making it. (*f*). It may be considered with reference, 1*st*, To the several sorts of inferior jurisdiction; 2*dly*, To the actions in which conusance may

(*a*) As to conusance in general, see Gilb. C. P. 192, &c.; 1 Sellon, c. vii.; Tidd, 9th ed. 631; Vin. Ab. Conusance; Com. Dig. Courts, P.; Bac. Ab. Courts, D. 3; 3 Bla. Com. 298. As it is stated that the claim of conusance should be made *before defence,* see 3 Bla. Com. 298, I have considered the nature of such claim anterior to defence and imparlance, oyer, and pleas to the jurisdiction and in abatement.

(*b*) 2 Wils. 409; see the precedents in Rast. Ent. 128; Willes, 233; 2 Wils. 410; 11 East, 543; 12 *Id.* 12.

(*c*) Fortesc. 157; 5 Vin. Ab. 588, 589, S. C.

(*d*) *Id.;* 5 Vin. Ab. Conusance, 588, 593, 596, 600; 12 Mod. 666.

(*e*) 2 Wils. 410; 5 Vin. Ab. 599.

(*f*) See the reason, 2 Wils. 108, 109; Willes, 237, 238.

I. CLAIM OF CONUSANCE. be claimed; 3dly, To the time and manner of claiming it; and 4thly, To the proceedings thereon.

1st. What Courts may claim it. *The privilege of claiming conusance is confined to Courts of record, except in the case of ancient demesne (g). According to the various decisions collected in Viner's Abridgment (h), there are *three* sorts of *inferior* jurisdictions. The *first* is by grant *tenere placita*, which is of the lowest description, and is merely a *concurrent* jurisdiction, and can neither be claimed nor pleaded, and where priority of suit gives one court the preference (i). The *second* is by grant *habere cognitionem placitorum* and gives a *general conusance of pleas*, and this must be limited as to place, and being intended for the benefit of the lord, may be claimed by him, though it cannot be pleaded by the defendant to the jurisdiction. The *third* is by grant *habere cognitionem placitorum, with exclusive words*, as where the king grants to a city that the inhabitants shall be sued within the city, and *not elsewhere*. This may follow the person, and need not be confined to any place, and being an exempt jurisdiction may be either claimed by the lord or pleaded by the defendant to the jurisdiction; but even in the latter case the proceedings in the superior Courts must be objected to in the first instance by claim of conusance, or plea to the jurisdiction (k). Hence it is a general rule that where the defendant is at liberty to plead to the jurisdiction of the Court, the lord of the franchise may claim conusance, but not *vice versa* (l). Where two persons claim conusance, it is to be granted to him who first demanded it, and the right of the parties claiming conusance must be tried in another action between them (m). The principal modern instances of conusance having been claimed and allowed, have been on behalf of the *Universities of Oxford and Cambridge* (n).

2dly. In what actions. The power of claiming conusance is restricted to *local* actions (o); except where the defendant is a member of the University of Oxford or Cambridge (p). It is also confined to *such actions as were *in esse* at the time of the grant (q); and does not extend to those created since by act of parliament, except where a common law action is given against a person by another name as debt against an administrator (r). Neither will this privilege be allowed where the Court claiming conusance cannot give remedy (s), and when there would consequently be a failure of justice (t); as in replevin, because if the plaintiff be nonsuited, a second deliverance should be granted, which the franchise cannot issue (u); nor in *quare impedit*, because the inferior Court can-

[*457]

(g) 2 Gilb. C. P. 191, 192; 2 Inst. 140; Willes, 239; 5 East, 284.

(h) Tit. Conusance, vol. v. 569; see also Com. Dig. Courts, P.; Bac. Ab. Courts, D; Fortesc. 156; Tidd, 9th ed. 631.

(i) *Id.*; 10 Mod. 126; Hardr. 509; Palm. 456; 12 Mod. 643.

(k) *Id.*; Andr. 198; in some cases the jurisdiction of the Courts at Westminster is expressly taken away by different statutes, which create Courts of Requests for the recovery of small debts, and in such cases the objection may be pleaded in bar, or given in evidence under the general issue, &c. 1 East, 352; 6 *Id.* 583; see Tidd, 9th ed. 954 to 962.

(l) Gilb, C. P, 193.

(m) 5 Vin. Ab. 599.

(n) Thornton v. Ford, 15 East, 634; Williams v. Brickenden, 11 East, 543; Perrin v. West, 1 Har. & Woll. 401, for *Oxford*; and Brown v. Renourd, 12 East, 12, for *Cambridge*, and see other cases, Harrison's Index, tit. University, III.

(o) 4 Inst. 213; 1 Sid. 103.

(p) Gilb. C. P. 193; Bac. Ab. 102; 11 East, 543. He must be a *resident* member, 2 Wils. 310.

(q) 14 Hen. 4, 20, B.

(r) *Id.*; 22 Edw. 4, 22.

(s) 2 Ventr. 363.

(t) *Id.*; Hardr. 507.

(u) 2 Inst. 140.

not send a writ to the bishop (x); nor in waste, or where the lord is a party and the plea is to be holden before himself (y); or where the defendant is a stranger who hath nothing within the franchise (z); or where the plaintiff is a privileged person, as an attorney or officer of the Court (a). It also seems that the Court cannot grant conusance in part (b); though upon a plea in abatement the writ may abate as to a part (c). Conusance may, however, be claimed where the defendant is in the actual custody of the marshal (d).

1. CLAIM OF CONUSANCE.

3dly. The time, &c. of claiming it.

With respect to the *time* when conusance should be claimed, it should be after the defendant has appeared, because till then there is no cause in Court, and the defendant might counterplead the conusance (e). It is said that it should be before full defence (f), and according to the entries, it is to be made before any defence, immediately after the statement of the defendant's appearance (g). It is an established rule of law, "that it must be claimed in the first instance, or at the first day," (h) and consequently it *should be made before imparlance (i): though in general when a declaration has been delivered in vacation as of the preceding term, the claim of conusance may be entered on the first day of the following term as of the preceding term (k). Where the writ discloses the particulars of the causes of action, it appears to have been considered as legal notice to the lord, &c. of the invasion of his jurisdiction, so as to make it incumbent on him to claim conusance on the very first day the defendant hath in Court, even upon the return day of the writ; but when the writ does not disclose the precise cause of action, then it is sufficient to make the claim on the first day given upon the declaration (l).

[*458]

The form and mode of claim, &c.

In point of *form* (m) conusance may be claimed by the lord of the franchise, or by his bailiff or attorney (n). It may be claimed by the Vice-Chancellor of Oxford University, the Chancellor being dead, &c. (o). If it be claimed by attorney, the warrant of attorney must be produced in Court and filed (p). The *grant* of conusance must also be produced (q), or an exemplification of it under the great seal (r), and if the grant was before time of memory, an allowance must be shown in the King's Bench, or before justices in eyre, or confirmation by patent (s), and it cannot be claimed by prescription (t).

(x) Bac. Ab. Courts, D. 3.

(y) 8 Hen. 6, 18 to 21; Hob. 87; see the singular argument, 3 Bl Com. 299, n. d.

(z) 1 Rol. Ab. 493, pl. 16, 1, 49; 22 Ass 83.

(a) Willes, 233; 3 Leon. 149; Lit. Rep. 304; Barnes, 346; 5 Vin. Ab. Conusance, 590, S. C.; *id.* 562, *acc.*; Bendl. 233, *contra*; nor where the *defendant* is an attorney, see 5 Vin. Ab. 572; 1 Rol. Ab. 489, *acc*; 5 Vin. Ab. 594, *contra*. Not claimable in the *Court of Exchequer*, Hardr. 188; Tidd, 9th ed. 81, 82.

(b) 5 Vin. Ab. 597; 1 Rol. 495.

(c) 2 Saund. 209 e, 210, *in notis*.

(d) 1 Salk 2; Gilb. C. P. 195; Bro. Ab. Conusance, 50.

(e) Gilb. C. P. 196; Comb. 319; 12 East, 12.

(f) 3 Bla. Com. 298; but see 5 Vin. Ab. 597; 1 Rol. Ab. 495.

(g) Rast. Ent 128; 2 Wils. 416.

(h) 5 Burr. 2823; Rep. temp. Hardw. 241; 2 Wils. 411; Willes, 233.

(i) *Id. ibid.*; 2 Wils. 411; Willes, 233; 3 Bla. Com. 298; 10 Mod. 127; Fortesc. 157.

(k) 2 Wils. 411, 412; 12 East, 18.

(l) 5 Burr. 2823; 2 Wils. 413; 10 Mod. 127.

(m) Com. Dig. Courts, p. 3; Rast. Ent. 128; see the form, 11 East, 543; 12 *Id.* 12.

(n) Bro. Ab. Conusance, 50; 12 Mod. 644, 656; see the entry, Rast. Ent. 128; Willes, 234.

(o) 11 East, 543, 547, note.

(p) See the form, Willes, 233, 234; Palm. 456; 1 Sid. 103; 1 Lev. 89; 2 Wils. 404.

(q) 12 Mod. 944; 1 Bla. Rep. 454.

(r) 5 Burr. 2820.

(s) Keilw. 189, 190; 1 Sid. 103; 1 Salk. 183; 1 Ld. Raym. 427, 428, 475, S. C.; Gilb. C. P. 195; but see Bro. Ab. Conusance, 51.

(t) Com. Dig. Courts, p. 3.

1. CLAIM OF CONUSANCE. Upon a claim made by either of the Universities of Oxford or Cambridge (*u*), there must, in addition to the grant, be an exemplification of the private statute confirming it (*x*), together with an affidavit of the defendant's residence within [*459] the local jurisdiction (*y*). The claim of conusance is usually supported *by affidavits verifying the necessary facts (*z*). The claim itself must be entered upon a roll (*a*). It being a demand of something *quod sibi debetur*, it must be perfectly entered upon record, and must state every thing that is to take away the general jurisdiction of the superior Court, and *the whole ought to be set forth with all the proceedings in the cause in the superior Court* till the instant of making the claim, and after stating the proceedings the entry runs thus: "And the said defendant by E. F. his attorney comes," (*but the defendant says no more, nor makes any defence, and then the entry proceeds as follows:*) "and hereupon comes —— chancellor of the University of Oxford, by G. H. his attorney, to demand, claim, prosecute, and defend his liberties and privileges thereof, that is to say, to have the conusance of the plea aforesaid, because he saith," &c. (*setting out with great precision all the circumstances on which the claim is founded, and concluding thus:*) "and the said chancellor demands his liberties and privileges aforesaid, according to the form and effect of the letters patent aforesaid, and the confirmation aforesaid in this plea, between the parties aforesaid, here in the Court of our said lord the king now depending, to be allowed to him *as heretofore hath been allowed*," (*b*) though the latter words are not necessary where the franchise is given by act of parliament (*c*).

4thly. The proceedings thereon. The claim of conusance, if insufficient in form or substance, may be demurred to, or the facts therein alleged may be traversed by the plaintiff (*d*). If the claim be disallowed on demurrer, the judgment, after the usual entry of *curia advisari vult*, and giving day to hear judgment, as well to the plaintiff and person claiming conusance as to the defendant, is, "that the matter aforesaid, by the party claiming conusance in manner and form aforesaid alleged, is not sufficient in law, therefore it is considered that the said, &c. (the person claiming conusance) have not his aforesaid liberty in his said plea mentioned, and it is commanded by the said Court, as well to the said, &c. (the person claiming conusance) as to the said defendant, that to the writ and count aforesaid, the said defendant to answer, &c. and thereupon the said defendant defends the wrong and injury, when, &c. and prays leave to imparl," &c and the pleadings proceed as usual (*e*).

[*460] *If the claim be allowed, a day is given upon the roll for the lord of the franchise to hold his Court, and the parties are commanded to be there on that day (*f*). But the record still remains in the Court above, and a transcript

(*u*) 10 Mod. 126; 1 Bla. Rep. 454; 12 East, 12.

(*x*) 13 Eliz. c. 29; 2 Wils. 412.

(*y*) 1 Barn. K. B. 49, 65; 2 Stra 810; 2 Wils. 311; 1 Bla. R 454; 5 Burr. 2820; 12 East, 12. But in 15 East, 634, an affidavit of the residence of a common serjeant, called marshal of the University, having local duties to perform, was dispensed with.

(*z*) 12 East, 12.

(*a*) Comb. 319; 1 Barn. K. B. 65; 2 Stra. 810.

(*b*) *Per* Wilmot, C. J., 2 Wils. 409, 410; Rast. 128; Willes, 234; 12 East, 12.

(*c*) *Id.*

(*d*) 2 Wils. 410; Comb. 319; Rast. Ent. 129.

(*e*) Rast. Ent. 128 b.

(*f*) *Id.* 129; 2 Wils. 411; 2 Ld. Raym. 836, 837; 12 Mod. 644; 3 Salk. 79, S. C.

only is sent down to the court below (g), in order that if justice be not done there, as if the defendant be a stranger, and has nothing within the franchise, by which he can be summoned, or if the judge refuse to do justice, the plaintiff may have a *re-summons* upon the record in the Court above (h), the cause assigned in which re-summons may be traversed by the party who originally claimed conusance, and if found for him the cause will be remanded, but if found against him, the parties go on in the superior Court from the period or stage in which the cause was at the allowance of the claim, just as if such claim had never been allowed (i). And if a re-summons issue upon failure of right in a franchise, the lord of the franchise shall never afterwards have conusance of that plea (k).

I. CLAIM OF CONUSANCE.

II. OF APPEARANCE AND DEFENCE, AND FORMS OF STATING THEM.

Before we inquire into the qualities and parts of the various pleas in personal actions, it is advisable to consider the statement of the defendant's *Appearance;* of his *Defence;* and of *Imparlances;* which, when they occur in pleading, usually precede the statement of the subject-matter of the defence. The language of the *plea* and of the *entry on the record* of these allegations *used until recently*† *in all* cases to be thus: "And the said C. D. (*the defendant*) by E. F. his attorney, *comes* and *defends* the *wrong* (*or in trespass*, '*force*') and injury, when, &c. and craves *oyer* of the said writing obligatory, and it is read to him, &c., he also craves *oyer* of the condition of the said writing obligatory, and it is read to him in these words: The condition, &c. (*setting out the condition verbatim*). Which being read and heard, the said C. D. prays leave to *imparl* to the said declaration until —— *next after —— and it is granted to him, and the same day is given to the said A. B. (*the plaintiff*) here, &c. At which day, to wit, on —— next after ——, at Westminster aforesaid, come as well the said A. B. as the said C. D. by their respective attornies aforesaid; and the said C. D. saith that the said A. B. ought not to have or maintain his aforesaid action thereof against him, because he saith that, &c. (*stating the ground of defence*)." (l)

II. OF APPEARANCE AND DEFENCE AND FORMS OF STATING THEM. The old forms and practice.

[*461]

The above "*venit*," was the statement on record of the defendant's *appearance* in Court, and was said to be necessary to make him a party to the suit, because *dicit* without *venit* might be *ore tenus* (m). It has however been decided, that the word *venit* was no part of the *plea*, so that if defence were made without it, it would be good, for the defendant's making defence shows him to be in Court, and makes him a party to the plea, particularly where he appears to be *in custodia* (n). When the defendant pleaded in a *different*

(g) *Id.*; Jenk. 31; 5 Vin. Ab. 599.
(h) 2 Wils. 411; 12 Mod. 644; Hardr. 507. But see 5 Vin. Ab. Conusance, 589; 10 Mod. 127.
(i) 2 Wils. 411; 6 Vin. Ab. 3, 4.
(k) Jenk. 34; 5 Vin. Ab. 576, 588.
(l) See the forms, 3 Bla. Com. Appendix, No. III.; *post*, vol. iii.
(m) Skin. 582; Gilb. C. P. 186; Bac. Ab. Pleas, D.; Com. Dig. Abatement, I. 16; Lutw. 8, 9; Co. Lit. 127 b. See Stephen, 2d edit. 29 to 36, as to appearance.
(n) Salk. 544; Skin. 582; Com. Dig. Abatement, I. 16; Stephen, 2d edit. 480.

† See American Editor's Preface.

II. APPEARANCE AND DEFENCE.

name to that in the writ, whether in abatement or in bar, the statement of his appearance must not have been, "and the *said* C. D. comes, &c." but should be "and C. D. (the real name) against whom the said A. B. hath exhibited his said bill by the name of E. D. by —— his attorney comes and defends," &c. (*o*). In general the appearance might be stated to have been *in person* or by *attorney*, according to the fact (*p*), but in an action against a feme covert sued alone, it was essential to allege that she had appeared *in person* (*q*); and an infant must always have *pleaded by guardian* (795), and not by attorney or *prochein ami* (*r*); and this though he be sued with others in a representative character as administrator (*s*). Nor could common bail be filed for an infant under the statute, even when he was sued jointly with other defendants (*t*). [*462] And in pleas to the jurisdiction, *the appearance must be stated to have been in person (*u*). And though several attornies in partnership may be retained by the defendant, he can only plead by one, and not in the name of *the firm* (*v*), and therefore a plea should be in the name of that one attorney only who appeared (*x*). A defendant may plead in person to an information by the crown (*y*).

DEFENCE.

After the statement of the appearance follows that of the *Defence*, which has been defined to be the *denial* of the truth or validity of the complaint, and does not merely signify a *justification*. It is a *general* assertion that the plaintiff has no ground of action, and which assertion is afterwards extended and maintained in the body of the plea (*z*). This was so essential in pleading, that formerly if no defence were stated in the commencement of the plea, though the plea were in other respects sufficient, judgment was given against the defendant (*a*). In *scire facias*, however, no defence used to be stated (*b*); and it was not necessary in a plea of ancient demesne (*c*), or in a plea to the jurisdiction of an inferior Court having no jurisdiction of the matter, though it was otherwise when the plea related rather to the person than to the subject-matter of the action (*d*). Where, however, an attorney of the Common Pleas was sued in the King's Bench, and pleaded his privilege without any com-

(*o*) 5 T. R. 487; Willes, 41, n. c.; 2 Saund. 209 a, note 1; 5 Taunt. 653.

(*p*) Tidd, 9th edit. 92, 93. Appearance by lunatics, &c. *id.*; 3 Taunt. 261.

(*q*) 2 Saund. 209 b, note.

(*r*) 2 Saund. 117 f, note 1; *id.* 212 a, n. 4, 5.

(*s*) Stra. 784; 1 Moore, 250. The *infant defendant* may avail himself of the objection on writ of error, 2 Saund. 212 a, note; Cro. Jac. 289; but the *plaintiff* cannot, 5 B. & Ald. 418.

(*t*) Tidd, 9th edit. 99.

(*u*) 2 Saund. 209 b, note; but see 2 *Id.* 2 b, n. (*i*).

(*v*) See 4 East, 195, *per* Lord Ellenborough.

(*x*) 2 New Rep. 509.

(*y*) 1 Tyr. 351.

(*z*) 3 Bla. Com. 296; Co. Lit. 127 b; Yelv. 210. This denial is mere matter of form, for it is used, although the plea in the body of it, so far from denying the matters alleged in the declaration, confesses and avoids them. See Stephen, 2d edit. 480. The word "*defends*" in this place means *denies* the supposed *wrong* or *injury*. As to defence in general, see the same references, and Bac. Ab. Pleas, D. and 8 T. R. 631; Steph. 2d ed. 478.

(*a*) Co. Lit. 127 b; 3 Lev. 240; Bac. Ab. Pleas, D.; Willes, 41. But see Skin. 582. See Steph. 2d edit. 482, 483.

(*b*) 3 Lev. 182.

(*c*) *Id.*; Ld. Raym. 117.

(*d*) Bac. Ab. Pleas, D.

(795) Vide Mockey *v.* Grey, 2 Johns. Rep. 192. And if an infant defend by attorney, he may bring a writ of error *coram vobis* to reverse the judgment. Dewitt *v.* Post, 11 Johns. Rep. 460. { See Moore *v.* M'Ewen, 5 Serg. & Rawle, 373. Silver *v.* Shelback, 1 Dall. 165. }

mencement of defence, it was held sufficient (*e*). Defence was of two descriptions, first, *half* defence, which was as follows, "*venit et defendit vim et injuriam et dicet*, &c." or secondly, *full* defence, "*venit et defendit vim et injuriam quando*, &c." (meaning "*quando et ubi curia consideravit*," or when and where it shall behove him), "*et damna et quicquid quod ipse defendere debet et dicit*," &c. (*f*). It was a maxim that the words "*quando*, &c." ought not to be added when only half defence was to be made, and that after the words "*venit et defendit vim* *[*463] *et injuriam*," the subject-matter of the *plea* should immediately be stated (*g*). It had however of late become the practice in all cases whether half or full defence were intended, to state it as follows: "and the said C. D. by —— his attorney, comes and defends the *wrong*) *or in trespass*, '*force*,') and injury, *when, &c.* and saith, that, &c." which would be considered as half defence in cases where such a defence should be made, but as full defence when the latter was necessary (*h*). If *full defence* were made expressly by the words, "when and where it shall behove him," and "the damages and whatever else he ought to defend," the defendant would be precluded to the jurisdiction or in abatement, for by defending *when and where* it shall behove him, the defendant acknowledges the jurisdiction of the Court, and by defending the *damages* he waives all exceptions to the person of the plaintiff (*i*). Want of defence being only matter of form, the omission was aided on a general demurrer (*k*).

II. APPEARANCE AND DEFENCE.

The recent Pleading Rule Hil. T. 4 W. 4, r. 10, and present forms and practice.

The Reg. Gen. Hil. Term, 4 W. 4, reg. 10, orders that *no formal defence shall be required* in a plea, and *it shall* be commenced as follows:—"The said defendant by —— his attorney (or 'in person,' &c.) says that, &c., so that the *venit* or *comes* is to be omitted. And it has been observed that by this clause the distinction between *whole* defence and *half* defence is abolished (*l*), although formerly, and indeed in modern times, that distinction was much insisted upon. It has been observed that although this recent pleading rule orders that every plea *shall commence* in the prescribed form, still that a slight variation, or the adoption of the ancient *full formal defence*, would not be any ground of demurrer, but at most would be the ground of summons or motion to strike out the part objected to as an unnecessary prolixity with costs (*m*).

(*e*) 1 Salk. 30; Bac. Ab. Pleas, D.
(*f*) Co. Lit. 127 b; Bac. Ab. Pleas, D.; Rast. Ent. 652; Willes, 41; Gilb. C. P. 188; 8 T. R. 633. See the forms, 3 Bla. Com. Appendix, No. III.; *post*, vol. iii.
(*g*) Gilb. C. P. 188; 8 T. R. 632; 3 B. & P. 9, n. a.
(*h*) 8 T. R. 633; Willes, 41; 3 B. & P. 9; 2 Saund. 209 b, n. 1; Stephen on Pleading, 2d ed. 481.
(*i*) 2 Saund. 209 c.; 3 Bl. Com. 297, 298; Co. Lit. 127 b; Bac. Ab. Pleas, D.
(*k*) 3 Salk. 271.
(*l*) Bosanquet on Rules of Pleading, 37. It has been considered that this rule extends to pleas in abatement as well as pleas in bar and all other pleas. J. Chitty, jun., Pleas in Abatement, 20, note (*d*).
(*m*) *Id.* 37, note 33.

III. OF OYER.

III. OYER (m). Oyer is a prayer or petition recited or entered in pleading (n), that the party may *hear* read to him the deed, &c. stated in the pleadings of the opposite party, and which deed is by intendment of law in Court when it is pleaded with a profert (o)(796). The statement of the prayer of oyer, and that the deed has been read to the defendant, (setting it out) used to *follow* the *defence*, and precede the entry of the imparlance, if any (p). But now it is to be stated immediately after the statement of the appearance.

[*465] *It is a principle of pleading, that a party relying upon a *deed*, &c. either as the foundation of a cause of action, or as a ground of defence or answer to the pleading of his opponent, shall make a *profert* of the instrument, that is, produce it (nominally) in Court (q). But in alleging the deed the plaintiff need not in his pleading show more of it than answers *his* own immediate purpose; and even that part which he states may be set forth according to its legal purport or in substance. The obtaining oyer therefore becomes frequently important, especially on the part of the defendant, not only to ascertain the authenticity of the instrument, but also for the purpose of rendering available other parts of the deed which may restrict or explain that portion of the instrument which is shown in the adverse pleading. It is demandable by either party, whether plaintiff or defendant, and in every action, whether real, personal, or mixed.

In what cases demandable. If the plaintiff in his declaration, or the defendant in his plea, have *necessarily* made a *profert* of any deed, probate, letters of administration, or other instrument under seal, the other party *may* pray oyer, which cannot in such case be refused by the Court (r). If the deed be lost or destroyed, the party, instead of making a profert thereof, should state the excuse for omitting it; and then the opponent, though he may traverse the truth of the excuse alleged, will be precluded from praying oyer (s). But if a profert be *unnecessarily* made, the defendant must plead without oyer (t); though if it be craved and given, he has a right to make use of it (u). The defendant cannot crave oyer except where profert has been made. Oyer was formerly allowed of

(m) As to demanding oyer and form of demand, see 3 Chitty's, Gen. Prac. 618.

(n) See the form, *ante*, 460, 461. At the present day oyer is demanded before the party pleads, by a note in writing addressed to the attorney of the party on the other side; and it is given by providing the party requiring it with a copy of the deed, &c. at his expense, showing him the original if desired, Tidd, 9th ed. 586; Stephen, 2d ed. 93, 94.

(o) 3 Bla. Com. 299; 3 Salk, 119; 12 Mod. 598; Bac. Ab. Pleas, I. 12, 13; 1 Sid. 308, *acc.*; Lutw. 1644, *contra*. The practice relative to the demand of oyer has been so fully considered in the works referred to in this note, that it will be sufficient here to confine our attention to such points as relate to pleading. Tidd, 9th ed. 586; 1 Sel. 261, 285 to 291; 1 Saund. 9, and notes; Com. Dig. Pleader, P.; Steph. 2d ed. 92.

(p) *Ante*, 460, 461. But see instances of oyer after imparlance, 1 Saund. 3, 289.

(q) See as to the profert, *ante*, 398.

(r) 2 Stra. 1186; 3 T. R. 151; Tidd, 9th ed. 587.

(s) *Ante*, 239, 446.

(t) 2 Salk. 497; 1 T. R. 149, 150; *ante*, 399.

(u) Doug. 476; 1 Saund. 317, note 2; 9 a, note (d).

(796) Where *oyer* of a deed pleaded with *profert*, is not prayed, no part of the deed will be noticed by the Court, but that which the plaintiff has declared on. Bender v. Fromberger, 4 Dall. 131.

the original *writ*, in order to demur or plead in abatement for any insufficiency or variance between the writ and declaration; but that practice was altered by rule of court, and if the defendant demand oyer of the writ, the plaintiff may proceed as if no such demand had been made (*x*). Oyer is not demandable of a record (*y*); nor of a recognizance (*z*); nor of a private act of parliament (*a*); nor of letters patent, though pleaded with a profert (*b*); nor of a writ of re-summons (*c*); nor of the precept or warrant of a justice of the peace (*d*). And oyer cannot be craved of an agreement, a note, or other instrument not under seal (*e*); nor of a demise to a stranger, where the party pleading it was neither party nor privy to it (*f*). As it cannot be granted of any deed, &c. which is not presumed to have been brought into Court (*g*), the defendant cannot, in an action upon a bond conditioned for the performance of covenants in another deed, crave oyer of such deed, but he, and not the plaintiff, must show it or the counterpart with a profert or an excuse for the omission; but it seems that the Court will compel the plaintiff to give the defendant a copy to enable him to plead, by granting the defendant time to plead until the copy be provided, or the defendant making an affidavit that he has no copy (*h*). In *scire facias* on a judgment on a deed, the defendant cannot demand oyer of the deed, for the *scire facias* is founded not on the deed, but on the judgment; if, however, oyer be improperly craved and granted, and the deed be stated upon it, the defect in the plea will be aided on a general demurrer (*i*).

When it should be demanded.

Though a party be entitled to crave oyer, yet he is not in general bound to do so (*k*). But in some cases it *must* be craved. Thus, if the defence be founded upon any objection to the form of the bond, as where a bail bond has been given to the sheriff, but not by his name of office, and the defect do not appear upon the face of the declaration, oyer *must* be craved, and after setting forth the bond, the defendant may demur (*l*)(797). And in an action at the suit of an administrator, the defendant should crave oyer, and set out *the [*466] letters of administration, if he wish to avail himself of any variance in the statement of them in the declaration (*m*). The instances in which oyer should be demanded, if the defendant's contract be not truly stated in the

(*x*) Tidd, 9th ed. 583.
(*y*) 1 Ld. Raym. 250, 347; Doug. 476; 1 T. R. 149. But where a judgment or record of the *same* Court is pleaded, the defendant must give a note in writing of the term and number roll of the record, Tidd, 9th ed. 587; and see Reg. Gen. Hil. T. 4 W. 4, reg. 8.
(*z*) Poph. 202.
(*a*) Dougl. 476, 477; Tidd, 9th ed. 588, but Godb. 186, is *contra*.
(*b*) 1 T. R. 149; Archb. 161.
(*c*) 3 Hen. 6, 56.
(*d*) 21 Hen. 5, 6; Bro. Oyer, 13.
(*e*) Salk. 215. But the Courts or judges, by analogy to the doctrine of oyer, will in most cases order that the party have an inspection and copy of the instrument, see Tidd, 9th ed. 589, &c.
(*f*) 3 Hen. 6, 46.
(*g*) Willes, 200.
(*h*) *Per Cur.* Hilary Term, 21 Geo. 3, K. B. Tidd, 9th ed. 586; 1 Saund. 10, note 1, and 52.
(*i*) 1 Saund. 8 b.
(*k*) 2 Lil. Rep. 221; Archb. 164, 165.
(*l*) Ld. Raym. 1135; 2 Saund. 60, n. 3; 366, n. 1; 2 T. R. 575; Bac. Ab. Pleas, I. 12. So in a plea of nonjoinder of a co-obligor, 1 Saund. 291.
(*m*) 2 Wils. 413.

(797) So, in debt on award, if it be mis-stated in the declaration, the defendant cannot take advantage of the error by pleading no award, but must crave oyer and demur. James *v.* Walruth, 8 Johns. Rep. 410. Ut semble. Sed quære; for an award under seal need not be pleaded with profert, and the insertion of a profert will not entitle to oyer.

III. OYER. declaration, will be hereafter considered (n). In pleading payment or performance of the condition of a bond, if the condition be not set out in the declaration, the defendant must set forth the condition after craving oyer (o)(798). But it is necessary in an action on a bond or deed, conditioned for the performance of covenants in *another* deed, for the defendant, in his plea of performance, to show such deed without craving oyer (p).

Where either the plaintiff or the defendant omits, in pleading a deed, of which a profert is made, to state any part which is material to the case of his opponent, the only way by which the latter can relieve himself is by praying oyer of the deed, and setting it out in *hæc verba;* for he cannot plead that by the said deed "it was further agreed," &c. (q)(799).

Refusing oyer. If oyer be denied when it ought to be granted, the party making the claim should move the court to have the prayer of oyer entered on record, which entry is in the nature of a plea; and the plaintiff may counterplead the right to oyer, or strike out the rest of the pleading following the oyer and demur; upon which the judgment of the Court is, either that the defendant have oyer, or that he answer without it (r). On the latter judgment the defendant may bring a writ of error, for to deny oyer when it ought to be granted is error; but not *à converso* (s).

How given. The oyer of a deed that has been altered by a stranger must be of the deed as originally drawn, and must be so set out in the pleading, or the variance [*467] will be fatal (t). If oyer of a bond *only be craved, the other party is not bound to give oyer of the condition, unless that be craved also (u). But if there be a condition or other matter indorsed on a deed, and which was indorsed before execution, oyer must be granted of the indorsement as well as of the deed (x). And a party craving oyer is entitled to a copy of the attestation and names of the witnesses (y). But, as before observed, on oyer of a bond and condition, the copy of a deed referred to in the condition need not be furnished (z).

What advantage to be taken of oyer, and the manner of taking advantage. Oyer having been granted, the defendant has, it seems, at least in the King's Bench (a), an election whether or not he will set forth the deed in his

(n) *Post*, 467.

(o) Com. Dig. Pleader, 2 V. 4; 2 Saund. 409, n. 2; 1 *Id.* 9 b, n. 1. In Lil. Prac. Reg. Oyer, it is said that the defendant may plead, if he please, without oyer; for he may take upon himself to remember the bond without hearing it; but see Hutt. Rep. 33; 1 Keb. 513; 1 Saund. 317, note 2; Com. Dig. Pleader, 2 W. 33; Vin. Ab. Oyer, D.

(p) See *ante*, 465; 1 Saund. 10, n. 1; Com. Dig. Pleader, 2 W. 33; 6 Mod. 237.

(q) 1 Saund. 317, note 2; 1 Stra. 227.

(r) 1 Saund. 9 c, note 1; 2 *Id.* 46 b, n. 7; Tidd, 9th ed. 588; Stephen, 2d ed. 102, 103, note. A party properly craving oyer cannot be compelled to plead until it is given, 2 Stra. 1186; 1 Wils. 16.

(s) 1 Saund. 9 c, n. 1; Tidd, 9th ed. 583; Bac. Ab. Pleas, I. 12.

(t) 1 Marsh. 217.

(u) 6 Mod. 237; 1 Saund. 9 b, note 1.

(x) *Id.*

(y) Willes, 288; 1 Saund. 9 b, note (e).

(z) *Ante*, 465, 466.

(a) Stra. 1241; 1 Wils. 97; Tidd, 9th ed. 589; Com. Dig. Pleader, P. 1.

(798) And the omission is fatal on a writ of error. United States *v.* Arthur and Patterson, 5 Cranch, 257.

(799) Oyer of a deed of which profert is made in the first count of a declaration, does not make it part of the record so as to apply to the other counts. Hughes *v.* Moore, 7 Cranch, 176.

plea. In that Court it appears that he may plead without noticing that he has craved oyer or stating the deed; and if the plaintiff would avail himself of the deed, he should pray that it be enrolled, and should state it in his replication (*b*). But it is said that in the Common Pleas, if the defendant has had oyer, and omit to set it out in his plea, *the plaintiff might insert* it for him at the head of his plea in making up the issue (*c*). The Reg. Gen. Hil. T. 2 W. 4, reg. 44, expressly provides for a case of this nature, and renders the practice uniform. It orders "that if a defendant, after craving oyer of a deed, omit to insert it at the head of his plea, the plaintiff, in making up the issue or demurrer book, may, if he think fit, *insert it for him;* but the costs of such insertion shall be in the discretion of the taxing officer." (*d*) We have before remarked, that if the party craving oyer desire to avail himself in pleading of the condition of a bond, or a part of a deed not shown by the pleading of the other party, he must show the oyer and instrument on the face of his own pleading (*e*). If no occasion of this sort occur, it is important to consider whether or not the deed be truly described by the opponent; for by setting it out on oyer, and then pleading *non est factum*, an error in such description might be cured. If the deed be set out on oyer, it becomes parcel of the record (800), and the Court will adjudge upon it accordingly, though it were not strictly demandable when granted (*f*). Should the true effect and meaning of the deed be mis-stated in the declaration, the variance is cured and becomes immaterial, if the deed be set out on the plea on oyer, and *non est factum* be pleaded; for *on that issue* the only question at the trial is, whether the deed as *set out in the plea* was executed by the defendant or not, and the jury are not *competent to decide what is the legal effect of the [*468] deed. In such case the defendant had better plead *non est factum* (*g*), without craving oyer; and then the question would be, whether the deed, *as described in the declaration*, was executed by the defendant (*h*).

III. OYER.

The tenor of the deed, as it appears upon oyer, is considered as forming part of the precedent pleading; and, therefore, if the breach laid in the declaration be not supported by the deed, in other words, if the deed thus set out in the plea be found to contain in itself matter of objection or answer to the plaintiff's case as stated in the declaration, the defendant's course (after setting out the deed on oyer) is to *demur*, not to make the objection the subject-matter of a plea (*i*). The *defendant may demur* after setting out the deed on oyer, if in the declaration any part of the deed which qualifies the contract as shown in the declaration, or which renders it dissimilar to that described in the declaration, be omitted or mis-stated by the plaintiff therein (*k*).

(*b*) *Id.*

(*c*) *Id.*; Barnes, 327; Steph. 2d ed. 96, n. (*c*).

(*d*) See Jervis's Rules, 54, note (*t*).

(*e*) *Ante*, 465.

(*f*) 1 Saund. 316, 317; 3 Salk. 119; Doug. 476; Tidd, 9th ed. 589.

(*g*) See the late act, 9 Geo. 4, c. 15, for amending at the trial certain variances in setting out written instruments, *ante*, 348.

(*h*) 4 B. & C. 741; 7 D. & R. 257, S. C.; see 11 East, 633; 5 Taunt. 707. Where the declaration was upon a certain *writing*, it was held that the defendant, by praying oyer *conditiones scripti obligatorii prædicti*, admitted it to be a bond. Lord Raym. 1541; Cro. Car. 209.

(*i*) 4 B. & C. 741, 750; 7 D. & R. 257, S. C.; Dougl. 476; Steph. 2d ed. 97; Tidd, 9th ed. 589.

(*k*) *Id.*; 2 Saund. 366, n. 1.

(800) Vide Cooke *v.* Graham's Adm'r, 3 Cranch, 234. {See 2 Har. & Gill, 86.}

ML. OYER. And if it appear at the trial on *non est factum* that there is a variance between the deed produced and the oyer, it is fatal (*l*). But the defendant cannot demur on account of a variance in an immaterial part between the deed as stated in the declaration, and as set out on oyer (*m*). If it be material for the plaintiff in his replication, &c. to show the indenture, he may pray an enrolment, and so make it part of his replication (*n*).

Before the recent pleading rules, Hil. T. 4 W. 4,† if the oyer were stated, the plea should in strictness be entitled of the same term as the declaration, for in contemplation of law the deed, unless denied, was in Court only during the term of which it was pleaded, and was afterwards in the custody of the party to whom it belonged, and therefore when that practice prevailed, oyer of such deed ought not in pleading to be stated to have been demanded in a *subsequent* term, and consequently not after a general imparlance (*o*). But now by that rule a plea setting out a deed on oyer is, like all others, to be dated
[*469] of the very day it is pleaded. But oyer might have been *craved after a special imparlance to another day in the same term (*p*); and there are precedents where oyer was craved after the statement of an imparlance (*q*); and where the plaintiff declared in vacation before the essoign day of the following term, with analogy to the claim of conusance and pleas in abatement, a plea stating the claim of oyer might have been entitled of a term subsequent to the declaration with a special imparlance, or might have been entitled generally of the preceding term (*r*). But the recent rules put an end to imparlances, and now require that every plea be entitled on the very day it is pleaded (*s*).

If the defendant assumed to set out the whole of the deed or condition of a bond on oyer, the whole should be stated with all recitals *verbatim et literatim*; and if the defendant do not set forth the whole, or state it untruly, the plaintiff may sign judgment as for want of plea (*t*); or may by his replication pray that the deed be enrolled, and set it forth, and then it seems may demur, for by craving oyer the defendant undertakes to set out the whole (*u*), or according to Reg. Gen. Hil. T. 2 W. 4, reg. 44,† he may insert the deed for the defendant. But in pleading to a bond conditioned for the performance of covenants in *another* deed distinct from that set out on oyer, though the party must state the deed referred to in the condition truly, or subject his plea to a demurrer, and the practice is to set forth the whole deed (*x*); it may perhaps suffice to state the substance of the deed and those covenants only which he has engaged to perform, averring that the indenture contains no other cove-

(*l*) 1 Marsh. 214; see *ante*, 341.

(*m*) 1 B. & C. 358; 2 D. & R. 662, S. C.

(*n*) 2 Stra. 1241; 1 Wils. 97; 1 Saund. 9 b, n. 1, *acc.*; Barnes, 327, *contra*.

(*o*) Tidd, 9th ed. 587; Steph. 2d ed. 95; 2 Saund. 2, note 2; Vin. Ab. Oyer, F.; Bac. Ab. Pleas, I. 12. See the form, 3 Bla. Com. Appendix, No. 3, *acc.*; 2 Ld. Raym. 970, *contra*. And see the precedents, 1 Saund. 3, 289.

(*p*) 12 Mod. 99; 2 Show. 10; Tidd, 9th ed. 587.

(*q*) 1 Saund. 3, 289.

(*r*) 2 Wils. 411, 412; 1 T. R. 278; 7 T. R. 447, note (*d*); 2 Saund. 2, n. 2.

(*s*) Reg. Gen. Hil. T. 4 W. 4, reg. 1 and 2.

(*t*) 1 Saund. 9 b, n. 1; 4 T. R. 370; Slater *v.* Horne, Tidd, 9th ed. 565; 5 T. R. 662, 663.

(*u*) Com. Dig. Pleader, P. 1; 4 T. R. 371, note (*b*); 1 Saund. 9 b, note 1. But it is laid down in Tidd, 9th ed. 589, which cites 2 Salk. 602, that the plaintiff cannot demur to the plea for not setting out the whole of the deed on oyer.

(*x*) 1 Saund. 9; 4 East, 344, 345.

† See American Editor's Preface.

nants on his part (y); or perhaps even an allegation that the indenture contains no negative or disjunctive covenants, with an averment of general performance, would be sufficient (z); and the plaintiff might pray an enrolment, and set it forth if untruly stated (a). Certainly it would be desirable to promulgate a rule that it shall be sufficient for either party to set out only such parts of deeds or instruments as may be sufficient to sustain any charge or defence without setting forth useless matters. III. OYER.

When oyer is prayed of a bond and the condition, it is usual in a plea not to set forth the obligatory part of the bond, but to say, "and it is read to him, &c." and then to pray oyer of the *condition, and set it forth in *hæc verba* (801); but the bond ought to be entered at large as well as the condition, if the terms of the obligatory part be material to the defence (b). So, if it be material to the plaintiff that the penal part of the bond be set forth, he may in his replication pray that it may be enrolled, and set it forth (c), or under Reg. Gen. Hil. T. 2 W. 4, reg. 44, † insert the deed in the defendant's plea for him. If no use is intended to be made of the bond there is no need to pray oyer of it at all, or to enter any such prayer, but it is sufficient to pray oyer of the *condition* only (d); for the bond and condition are considered as distinct, the bond being complete without the condition, therefore there may be oyer of one without the other (e). If it appear to the Court that with reference to the deed as set out on oyer the defendant has pleaded a false plea, the Court will give judgment for the plaintiff upon a demurrer to the plea (f). [*470]

IV. IMPARLANCES.

IV. IMPARLANCES.

The ancient practice and forms of.

The term *imparlance*, or *licentia loquendi*, in its most general signification, means time given by the Court to either party to answer the pleading of his opponent, as either to plead, reply, rejoin, &c. and is said to be nothing else but the continuance of the cause till a further day (g). But the more common signification of the term was *time to plead* (h) †. In making up the issue joined between the parties, and in which all the proceedings are necessa-

(y) 1 Saund. 317, note 2.

(z) 4 East, 340, 344, note (f).

(a) 1 Saund. 9 b, note 1; 317, note 2.

(b) Lord Raym. 1135; *ante*, 465, 467.

(c) Carth. 301, 302; 1 Lutw. 680, 686; 1 Saund. 9 b, n. 1.

(d) Lib. Plac. 209, pl. 220; 1 Saund. 9 b, note 1.

(e) 1 Saund. 9 c, n 1; 290, n. 2.

(f) 1 Saund. 9, 317, note 2; 3 Salk. 119.

(g) Bac. Ab. Pleas, G.; see Com Dig. Pleader, D. and *id. ibid.*; 1 Sel. Pr. ch. vii. sect. 3; 2 Saund. 1, note 2; Tidd, 9th ed. 462; Steph. 2d edit. 97; as to the nature of imparlances in general. In Doct. Plac. *Imparlance*, it is thus defined, '*imparlance est quando ipse defendens petit licentiam interloquendi, scilicet, quant le defendant desire le cour de donor a luy temps de pleader al suit ou action que et commence vers luy.*" Before declaration the continuance is by *dies datus prece partium*; after declaration and before issue joined by *imparlance*; after issue joined, and before verdict, *by vicecomes non misit breve*; and after verdict or demurrer, by *curia advisari vult*.

(h) 2 Saund. 1, n. 2; 2 Show. 310; Barnes, 346.

(801) { A small variance between the *oyer* of a bond and the declaration, is not regarded; as where the words were, "or delay," and in the declaration, "or other delay," the variance was held immaterial. Henry v. Brown, 19 Johns. Rep. 49. }

† See American Editor's Preface.

IV. IMPARLANCES. rily stated, an entry of an imparlance between the declaration and plea was formerly frequent and sometimes necessary (i); but it was not usual in framing a plea or replication to state an imparlance separately, unless some *new matter has arisen since the former pleading when it was proper (k), as a mode of introducing and stating at what time the new matter had arisen (k).

Imparlances were of three descriptions: 1st, A *Common* or General Imparlance; 2dly, A *Special* Imparlance; and 3dly, A *General Special* Imparlance (l). The *first* was without saving to the defendant any exception against the writ or jurisdiction, and was always to a subsequent term (m). In making up the issue the entry of such an imparlance might have been necessary, in order to continue the cause in Court (n); but in framing a plea such an entry of imparlance was not necessary unless the matter of defence had arisen after the declaration. In general, pleas in bar were entitled of the term of which they were pleaded, without reference to the title of the declaration; and as a plea of tender might have been pleaded as well after as before an imparlance, even such plea might have been entitled of a term subsequent to the declaration, though it was said to be more correct to entitle it of the same term as the declaration, in order to avoid the inconsistency of first praying an imparlance and then averring that the defendant has been *always ready* to pay (o). After the entry of such a general imparlance, the defendant might plead *in bar* of the action though not in *abatement* (p), or to the *jurisdiction* of the Court; and therefore, when by the practice of the Court the defendant was at liberty to plead in abatement in a term subsequent to the declaration, (as occurred when the process was returnable on the last return of a term, or even before, and the plaintiff had neglected to deliver or file his declaration four days exclusive before the end of the term, or had neglected to declare before the essoign day of that term,) the defendant must have pleaded such plea in abatement either of the same term as the declaration, or of the subsequent term with a special imparlance; and if it were pleaded of the latter without such a special imparlance, the plaintiff might have signed judgment as for want of a plea (q). [*472] But where a bill was filed in *Trinity vacation against an attorney, entitled as of Trinity term, and the defendant pleaded in abatement as of Michaelmas term, without an imparlance, the plea was held good (r).

A *Special Imparlance* was with a *saving* of all exceptions to the writ, bill, or count, and after this imparlance the defendant may plead in abatement (s), but not to the jurisdiction of the Court, unless founded on a *personal* privilege, as that of an attorney, &c. (t). In cases where the defendant was entitled to a special imparlance, it was in the Common Pleas granted of course by the prothonotary upon an application to him within the first four days of the term

(i) 2 Saund. 1, n. 2; 5 Co. 75; Tidd, 9th ed. 720.

(k) See the form in a *plea*, and in a *replication*, vol. iii. 889 to 891. After *issue*, any new matter must have been pleaded *puis darrein continuance*. See the forms, *post*, vol. iii. 1244.

(l) 2 Bla. Rep. 1095, 1096. And as to the different kinds of imparlances, and when and how granted, and what may or may not be done after each, see 2 Saund. 1, n. 2; Tidd, 9th ed. 462.

(m) 6 Mod. 2?; 2 Saund. 2 a.

(n) *Ante*, 470.

(o) 2 Saund. 1, 2, n. 2; 1 *Id.* 33, note 2; Burr. 59; Tidd, 9th ed. 463.

(p) 2 M. & Sel. 484.

(q) 2 Saund. 1, n. 2; 4 T. R. 520; 6 T. R. 369; 7 T. R. 447, note d.

(r) 3 B. & Ald. 259; 1 Chit. Rep. 704, S. C.

(s) 1 Lutw. 6, and Bac. Ab. Pleas, C. 4; 2 Bla. Rep. 1095.

(t) Hardr. 365; Bac. Ab. Pleas, C. 4.

subsequent to that of the declaration; but in the King's Bench, it was said to be granted only by leave of the Court obtained by a side bar rule (*u*). In both Courts the special imparlance must have been stated in a plea in abatement, when it was entitled of a term subsequent to the declaration (*x*).

IV. IMPARLANCES.

The *third* description of imparlance, usually denominated a *General Special* Imparlance, was with a saving of all exceptions whatsoever (*y*), and could only be obtained by an application to the Court on motion within the four first days of the next term after the declaration; and it was in the discretion of the Court, governed by the particular circumstances of the case, to grant it or not; and it would not be granted in order to enable the defendant to plead to the jurisdiction if he had appeared by attorney. The prothonotary had no power to grant this description of imparlance, and a plea under a grant by him would be a nullity, and the plaintiff might sign judgment, or at least a *respondeas ouster* might be awarded (*z*). When this imparlance had been obtained, the defendant might not only plead in abatement of the writ or count, but also personal privilege (*a*). In point of form this imparlance was similar to the last with the exception of the words, "*saving to himself all advantages and exceptions whatsoever*," and sometimes in addition to these words the *following [*473] are added: "*as well to the writ and declaration as to the jurisdiction of this Court;*" (*b*) but the first is the better form.

If the defendant pleaded to the jurisdiction, or to the disability of the plaintiff or defendant to sue or be sued, after a general imparlance, or to the jurisdiction after a special imparlance, the plaintiff might in general either sign judgment or apply to the Court to set aside the plea, or he might demur to it, or allege the imparlance in his replication by way of estoppel: but if the plaintiff, instead of taking any of these advantages, reply to the special matter of the plea, the fault was aided (*c*).

Imparlances in *personal* actions now virtually abolished and *suggestions* in lieu.

As regards *personal* actions *commenced* in either of the superior Courts, after the distinctions between the Terms and Vacations were for many purposes annulled by statute 11 G. 4, and 1 W. 4, c. 70, and 1 W. 4, c. 3, and plaintiffs were, by 2 W. 4, c. 39, sect. 11, enabled to declare and expedite their actions in the vacations, it was finally settled, after some opinions and decisions to the contrary, that *imparlances* in such actions were *virtually abolished* (*d*); and Reg. Gen. Hil. T. 4 W. 4, reg. 2,† expressly orders that no entry of continuances by way of *imparlance* shall be made, but provides for the statement of matters that may have arisen pending the action and since the last pleading, by way of *suggestion* or *allegation*, and the forms of which statements will be found in the commencement of the third volume of this edi-

(*u*) 2 Bla. R. 1094; 2 Saund. 1, 2, note 2; R. E. 5 Ann.; Tidd, 9th ed. 462, 463.

(*x*) 4 T. R. 520, 521; 6 T. R. 369; 7 T. R. 447, in which 1 Bla. Rep. 51; 1 Wils. 261, were overruled. In all cases the imparlance in such case should be stated in the issue, 2 Saund. 1 e, note 2.

(*y*) See the forms, *post*, vol. iii. 889 to 892.

(*z*) 2 Saund. 2 b, note 2.

(*a*) *Id.*; 1 Lev. 54.

(*b*) 2 Bla. R. 1094; 2 Saund. 2 a, note 2.

(*c*) 2 Saund. 2 b, n. 2; Tidd, 9th edit. 463, 464.

(*d*) Nurse *v.* Geeting, 3 Dowl. 157, 158; 1 Crom. M. & Ros. 567; Wigley *v.* Tomlins, 3 Dowl. 7; 3 Chitty's Gen. Prac. 103, 104.

† See American Editor's Preface.

IV. IMPARLANCES. tion (e). In case of the death of one of several plaintiffs or defendants pending a suit, the 8 & 9 W. 3, c. 11, sect 7, directs that if the cause of action survive, the suit shall not abate, provided the death be duly suggested or stated on the record. In the commencement of the third volume there will be found several forms of such suggestions, which should be duly made in the earliest instance, or at least within eight days afterwards (f).

(e) See Bosanquet's Rules 5 and 6 in notes; see form, id. 131.

(f) See Reg. Gen. Hil. T. 4 W. 4, reg. 2; and see form, Bosanquet's Rules, 131; and *post*, vol. iii.

*CHAPTER VI.

Of Pleas to the Jurisdiction, and in Abatement, and the Proceedings thereon.

THE law has prescribed and settled the order of pleading which the defendant is to pursue, and although it has been objected that as regards pleas in abatement the division is more subtle than useful, yet as regulating in some respects the forms of commencements and conclusions of the pleas, and the right to plead another plea in abatement in some cases after judgment against the defendant of respondeas ouster, it is deemed here expedient to adhere to the ancient order, especially as no preferable arrangement has been suggested, *viz.* (*a*) Order of pleading.

- 1st. *To the jurisdiction of the Court.*
- 2dly. *To the disability, &c. of the person.*
  - 1st. *Of the plaintiff.*
  - 2dly. *Of the defendant.*
- 3dly. *To the Count or Declaration.*
- 4thly. *To the Writ.*
  - 1st. *To the form of the writ.*
    - 1st. *Matter apparent on the face of it.*
    - 2dly. *Matter* dehors.
  - 2dly. *To the action of the writ.*
- 5thly. *To the action itself in bar thereof* (*b*)(802).

This, it is said, is the natural order of pleading, because each subsequent plea admits that there is no foundation for the former, and precludes the defendant from afterwards availing himself of the matter, as when the defendant pleads to the person of the plaintiff he admits the jurisdiction of the Court, for it would be nugatory to plead that defence in a court which has no jurisdiction (*c*); and when the defendant pleads to the count he admits that the plaintiff is able to sue him and the defendant to be sued; and when the

(*a*) See Stephens on Pleading, 2d ed. 71, n. (*c*); and see the arrangement of the subject of Abatement, Comyn's Digest and Bacon's Abridgment, tit. Abatement.

(*b*) *Per* Holt, C. J., 2 Ld. Raym. 970; Latch. 178; Co. Lit. 303, 304; Gilb. C. P. 49; Doc. Plac. in Preface; Com. Dig. Abatement, C.; Tidd, 9th ed. 630; and for an account of the various kinds of pleas in *Equity*, and their essential difference, see Beames' Pl. Eq. chap. II.

(*c*) In *inferior* Courts, however, this does not obtain, for if such Court have not jurisdiction over the subject-matter, it will be a ground of nonsuit on the trial, 1 T. R. 151; *ante*, 456; and if there be a total want of jurisdiction in any of the Courts in England, the matter may be pleaded in bar, or given in evidence under the general issue, even in actions in the superior Court at Westminster; 6 East, 583; 1 East, 352; Tidd, 9th ed. 960.

(802) The order of pleading does not appear to have varied much from this scheme, even at the earliest periods of the law. 1 Reeve's Hist. E. L. 451. 2 Reeve's Hist. E. G. 266.

ORDER OF PLEADING. defendant pleads to the form of the writ he admits the form of the count; and after a *plea in bar* to the action the defendant cannot plead in *abatement, unless for new matter arising after the commencement of the suit (*d*)(803).

If this order of pleading be inverted, the defendant will be precluded from pleading any matter prior in point of order (*e*). And this is material, for though it is said that after a judgment of *respondeas ouster* there can be no plea in abatement, because, if it were allowed, there would be no end of such pleas (*f*); yet this must be understood of pleas in abatement in the *same degree* as popish recusancy and outlawry (*g*), which are both to the *person*; for the defendant may plead to the person of the plaintiff, and if that be overruled he might afterwards, if in time, plead to the form of the writ (*h*).

The more general division of *pleas* is, however, 1st, Pleas *Dilatory*; 2dly, Pleas *Peremptory* (*i*). Of the *former* description are pleas to the *jurisdiction*; to the disability of the *person*; to the *count* or *declaration*, and to the *writ*; of the *latter* or peremptory kind, and which lead to an issue which finally settles the dispute, are pleas in *bar* of the action.

I. OF PLEAS TO THE JURISDICTION.

I. PLEAS TO THE JURISDICTION. Pleas of this description though in effect they abate the writ, yet differ from pleas in abatement, principally in three points, viz. that they must be pleaded in person; that at all events before the recent pleading rules, Hil. Term, 4 W. 4, only half defence should be made; and that they should conclude *si curia cognoscere velit*, and not *quod billa cassetur* (*k*). Objections even to the jurisdiction of the superior Courts may in some cases be taken under the general issue, but in general they must be pleaded (804). In all transitory actions, and in local actions arising in England or Wales, if there be no plea [*476] to the jurisdiction, the Courts at Westminster may *in general hold plea thereof (*l*). And therefore it cannot be *pleaded* that the debt is under 40*s*. and ought to have been sued for in the County Court, because the superior Courts have concurrent jurisdiction, and the only course is to apply to the superior Court by motion to stay the proceedings (*m*). The instances in which an action may be brought here, although the cause of action arose in a foreign country, have been already noticed (*n*). Where the Court has *no jurisdiction*

(*d*) Gilb. C. P. 50; Com. Dig. Abatement, C. I. 23, 24.

(*e*) Co. Lit. 303; Com. Dig. Abatement, C.; Doc. Plac. Preface.

(*f*) Bac. Ab. Abatement, O.; Gilb. C. P. 186; 2 Saund. 401; 12 Mod. 230.

(*g*) Hetl. 126.

(*h*) Com. Dig. Abatement, I. 3, 4; Bac. Abr. Pleas, K. 1.

(*i*) See Stephen, 2d edit. 67; and *id.* Appendix, note 19.

(*k*) Bac. Abr. Pleas, E. 2, and Abatement; 5 Mod. 146; 1 Salk. 298; 3 Bla. Com. 301. As to pleas to the jurisdiction in general, see claim of conusance, *ante*, 455; Com. Dig. Abatement, D.; Bac. Ab. Pleas, E. and Courts, D. and Gilb. C. P. 187 to 197; Tidd, 9th edit. 630; in equity, Beames' Pl. Eq. 57, 252.

(*l*) And. 198; 1 Wood, 193; Bac. Ab. Pleas, E. 1.

(*m*) Sandall *v.* Bennett, 2 Adol. & El. 204.

(*n*) *Ante*, 298, 299, 306, 307.

(803) { Palmer *v.* Evertson, 2 Cow. Rep. 417. }

(804) It may be shown under the general issue, that there is no court in the country which has jurisdiction of the cause. Rea *v.* Hayden, 3 Mass. Rep. 124. Anthon *v.* Fisher, Doug. 650, n. 132. *Sed vide* Smith *v.* Elder, 3 Johns. Rep. 113.

at common law, or it has been taken away by act of parliament, such want of jurisdiction may in general be pleaded in *bar*, or given in evidence under the general issue, and is not properly the subject of a plea in abatement (*o*). And it has been recently decided that where a public statute for erecting a Court of inferior jurisdiction enacts *that no action for* any debt not amounting to 40*s*., &c. and recoverable by that act, shall be brought against any person residing within the jurisdiction, &c., such statute is a defence upon the general issue to a party bringing himself within it, who is sued in the superior Courts, unless the statute direct another course of proceeding (*p*). In other cases the statutes relating to the Courts of Requests, and which invest them with exclusive jurisdiction in certain cases, enable the debtor, if sued elsewhere, to *plead* the exemption in bar, or direct that a *suggestion* of the matter shall be entered on the roll. The exact mode of relief pointed out by the respective statutes must be strictly pursued (*q*).

In most of the *inferior* Courts the want of jurisdiction is fatal to the suit, without any plea stating the objection, for the cause of action must be alleged to have arisen within the jurisdiction, or a writ of false judgment may be supported; and if the fact be so alleged but not so proved, the plaintiff ought to be nonsuited on the general issue; and if the inferior Court admit the jurisdiction, a bill of exceptions may be tendered, or a prohibition issued (*r*). In these cases, however, the defendant may plead to the jurisdiction, which seems to be the safer course (*s*).

[*477] *We have already seen that the defendant can only plead to the jurisdiction, where the grant to the inferior Court was *habere cognitionem placitorum*, with *exclusive* words (*t*). In this case the plea cannot be in bar. At common law there was a distinction between a *foreign* plea and a plea to the *jurisdiction*. A foreign plea was where the action was carried out of the county or place where the venue was laid (*u*). Ancient demesne, and all pleas of privilege, are pleas to the jurisdiction, and not foreign pleas (*x*). It was always necessary before the statute of Anne to verify a *foreign* plea by affidavit, but not a plea to the jurisdiction (*y*).

Pleas to the jurisdiction, when the objection cannot be otherwise taken, are either in *local* or *transitory* actions. The defendant may, in *local* actions, plead to the jurisdiction, when the cause of action accrued in a jurisdiction into which *breve domini regis non currit* (*z*). Therefore he might plead that

(*o*) 6 East, 583; 1 East, 352; 4 T. R. 503.

(*p*) 1 East, 352.

(*q*) *Per* Lord Kenyon, 1 East, 354. Several of these statutes are collected, and the mode of proceeding is pointed out in Tidd, 8th edition, 989 to 995; 9th edit. 954 to 962; and see Mr. Tidd Pratt's comprehensive collection of the statutes relating to Courts of Request. In many instances if the debt be manifestly less than 40*s*. and be recoverable in the *County Court*. &c. the superior Courts will stay the proceedings in the action, Tidd, 9th edit. 516; but the objection cannot be *pleaded*, see 2 Adol. & El. 204.

(*r*) Gilb. C. P. 188, 189; Bac. Ab. Pleas, E. 1; Courts, D. 4; 1 Saund. 98, note 1.

(*s*) Bac. Ab. Courts, D. 4; see the precedents of plea and replication, 1 Wentw. 51, 60, 69, 78; and 1 Wentw. Index; Lil. Ent. 475. See forms, *post*, vol. iii.

(*t*) *Ante*, 456.

(*u*) 1 Saund. 98, note 1; Carth. 402; Vin. Ab. Foreign Plea. See the precedent, Lil. Ent. 475.

(*x*) Vin. Ab. Foreign Pleas, A. 11; 5 Mod. 335.

(*y*) 1 Saund. 98, note 1; Carth. 402; Vin. Ab. Foreign Pleas, 5 Mod. 335.

(*z*) Bac. Ab. Courts, D. 3; Gilb. C. P. 191; 1 Wils. 206; 3 East, 128.

I. PLEAS TO THE JURISDICTION.

the lands are ancient demesne, holden of the king's manor (a); and before the late statute (b) he might have pleaded that the cause of action arose in Wales (c); or in a county palatine (d). So he may plead that the cause of action arose in the cinque ports (e), or in London (f), or any other *exclusive* jurisdiction (g); but Ely is not an exempt jurisdiction, though the bishop may demand conusance (h). It has been held that it may be pleaded in a local action that the lands are out of the realm (i); but as this might be pleaded in
[*478] bar, or be given in *evidence under the general issue, it is unnecessary to plead such matter in abatement (k). In *ejectment*, as the real defendant is obliged on appearing to enter into the consent rule, and to plead the general issue, he cannot plead to the jurisdiction without leave of the Court (l).

In all *transitory* actions the Courts at Westminster have jurisdiction, unless taken away by particular act of parliament (m), and with the exception in favor of the Universities of Oxford and Cambridge (n), unless the plaintiff by his declaration shows that the action accrued in an exclusive jurisdiction, no objection to that of the Superior Courts can be taken (o). And if the declaration disclose the fact, still the defendant cannot demur or move in arrest of judgment, but must plead to the jurisdiction (p). It has been said that there are no pleas to the jurisdiction of the Courts at Westminster in transitory actions, unless the plaintiff by his declaration admits that the cause of action accrued in a county palatine (q). It is, however, presumed that those cases were only put as instances, and that if it appeared on the face of the declaration that the cause of action arose in any other exclusive or exempt jurisdiction, a plea to the jurisdiction might be pleaded (r).

Some pleas in abatement arising from *privilege* of *person* may be classed under pleas to the jurisdiction, in respect of their affecting the jurisdiction of the Court, and concluding whether the Court ought to have further conusance of the suit (s); as where an attorney or officer of a particular Court, a tinner, or scholar of the Universities, is sued out of the proper Court (t)(805).

(a) 10 East, 523; Com. Dig. Abatement, D. 1; Ld. Raym. 1418; 1 Salk. 56; see the precedents in Herne, 351; Rast. Ent. 101; Thomp. Ent. 2; Mod. Ent. 249; 3 Inst. C. 8, 9; Hans. 103; 1 Wentw. 51; and see other forms and replications, 1 Wentw. Index.

(b) 1 Wm. 4, c. 70, s. 13.

(c) Com. Dig. Abatement, D. 2; 1 Wils. 193; Dougl. 213. See the precedents, 1 Wentw. 45, 49, 68; 1 Wils. 193.

(d) Com. Dig. Abatement, D. 2. See the precedents, Rast. Ent. 419; Herne, 7; 3 Inst. Cl. 14; 1 Wentw. 49.

(e) Com. Dig. Abatement, D. 3; 4 Inst. 224; Jenk. 190; Keil. 88. See the precedents, Bro. Red. 475, and 1 Wentw. Index.

(f) 3 Leon. 148.

(g) Bro. Ab. Conusance, 52; 1 Bla. Rep. 197. See the precedents, 1 Wentw. Index.

(h) Carth. 109; Salk. 183; 3 East, 128, 138.

(i) Show. 191; 1 Salk. 80; Com. Dig. Abatement, D. 3.

(k) 6 East, 583; 4 T. R. 503; *ante*, 309, 310.

(l) Bla. Rep. 197; 3 Wils. 61; 2 Stra. 1120; 8 T. R. 474.

(m) Bac. Ab. Courts, D. 3; see the different statutes, Tidd, 9th edit. 954 to 962.

(n) Bac. Ab. Courts, D. 3; Gilb. C. P. 191; Wood, Inst. 520; Vin. Ab. University, K.

(o) 4 Inst. 213; 1 Sid. 103; Gilb. C. P. 191; Bac. Ab. Courts, D. 3.

(p) Carth. 11, 354; Bac. Ab. Courts, D. 3; Gilb. C. P. 191; 5 Mod. 144.

(q) 4 Inst. 212, 213, and other authorities, Tidd, 9th ed. 631, note (c).

(r) See 1 Wils. 193. See the precedents in transitory actions, *id.*; 1 Wentw. 45, 49, 68.

(s) See the precedents, 8 T. R. 631; Com. Dig. Abatement, D. 4; Bac. Ab. Abatement, C. Pleas, E. 2; Lutw. 45, 639; 22 Vin. Ab. 9; 3 T. R. 186; 5 Mod. 146; Gilb. C. P. 208, 209, cited 5 Mod. 335; 12 East, 544.

(t) See the precedents, *post*, vol. iii.

(805) Vide King *v.* Coit, 4 Day, 134. An attorney sued jointly with another, cannot avail himself of his privilege. Tiffany *v.* Driggs and Lynch, 13 Johns. Rep. 252.

I. PLEAS TO THE JURISDICTION.

Where a person is wrongfully sued in an *inferior* Court, he must tender his plea to the jurisdiction *in propria persona* **sedente curia*, and make oath of the truth thereof; and if the inferior Court will not accept his plea, he may have a *prohibition* from one of the common law Courts at Westminster, or in vacation from the Court of Chancery (*u*). In the *superior* Courts a plea to the jurisdiction must be pleaded within four days, both the first and last of which are inclusive, after declaration (*x*), and generally before imparlance (*y*). Formerly it must have been entitled of the same term as the declaration (*z*), but Reg. Gen. Hil. T. 4 W. 4, now requires every pleading to be entitled of the day of the month and year when the same is pleaded, and shall bear no other time or date. It must be pleaded in person, and not by attorney, because the latter would admit the jurisdiction of the Court (*a*); and for the same reason, at least before Reg. Gen. Hil. T. 4 W. 4, full defence ought not to be made, but only half defence, though the words "*when, &c.*" would suffice (*b*). A party paying money into Court, admits the jurisdiction of such Court, and cannot plead in abatement to it (*c*). After stating the appearance and defence, the plea may proceed at once to show the defect of jurisdiction, without any preliminary prayer *si curia cognoscere velit*, &c. (*d*).

In all pleas to the jurisdiction of the *superior* Courts, it must be shown that there is another Court in which justice may be effectually administered (806), for if there be no other mode of trial, &c. that alone would give the superior Court jurisdiction (*e*). In transitory actions, it was necessary to aver in a plea that a county palatine Court ought to entertain the suit; either that the defendant dwelt in the county palatine, or that he had sufficient goods and chattels there by which he might be attached, otherwise the plea could not be allowed lest a failure of justice should ensue (*f*). But in a plea to the jurisdiction of an *inferior* Court it was sufficient to allege that the cause of action accrued out of its jurisdiction, without *showing the jurisdiction to [*480] which the plaintiff should have resorted (*g*). These pleas should *conclude* with a prayer, "*si curia cognoscere velit*," or "*respondere non debet*," and not "*quod billa vel breve cassetur*." (*h*) The former was the most usual conclusion when the subject-matter of the plea related to the cause of action, and the

(*u*) 1 Saund. 98, n. 1; 6 Mod. 146; Bac. Ab. Pleas, E.; Courts, D. 4; Pleas, E. 1; *ante*, 458.

(*x*) 8 T. R. 474; Com. Dig. Abatement, D. 9; Tidd, 9th edit. 638, 639. When otherwise, *id.*

(*y*) *Ante*, 471; Com. Dig. Abatement, D. 9; Gilb. C. P. 187; Bac. Ab. Pleas, E. 2.

(*z*) *Ante*, 461 to 463.

(*a*) 2 Saund. 209 b; Gilb. C. P. 187; Bac. Ab. Abatement, A. Pleas, &c. 2; 8 T. R. 631.

(*b*) *Ante*, 463; 2 Saund. 209 b.

(*c*) 5 Esp. Rep. 21, 22.

(*d*) See the forms, Rast. Ent. 101, 419; Herne, 351; 1 Wils. 193, and *ante*, 459. But see the precedent, 8 T. R. 631.

(*e*) 6 East, 598, 600; Cowp. 172; Carth. 355; 3 Leon. 148; 4 T. R. 503; 4 Inst. 213; Bac. Ab. Abatement, A. Courts, D. 3. So the Courts by analogy will not stay the proceedings, although the debt be under 40*s*., if there be no inferior Court which has jurisdiction over it, 3 B. & P. 617; Tidd, 9th ed. 516; and see Sandall *v.* Bennett, 2 Adol. & El. 204.

(*f*) Carth. 355; Tidd, 9th ed. 631. See the precedents, *post*, vol. iii.

(*g*) 6 East, 600, 601; and see the precedents, 1 Wentw. 51, 60, 61, 78; *post*, vol. iii.

(*h*) Bac. Ab. Pleas, E. 2; Latch. 178; 5 Mod. 146; Bro. Jurisdiction, pl. 17; 2 Saund. 209; Rast. Ent. 101, 419; Herne, 351; 1 Wils. 193; Lutw. 45, 639; 2 Rich. C. P. 10; Lil. Ent. 9.

(806) Vide Lawrence *v.* Smith and Russell, 5 Mass. Rep. 362. Rea *v.* Hayden, 3 Mass. Rep. 24.

I. PLEAS TO THE JURISDICTION. *respondere non debet* seems proper where the objection to the jurisdiction is a *personal privilege* (*i*). If the plea were to conclude in bar to the action, the jurisdiction would thereby in general be admitted (*k*).

Affidavit (*l*). In support of a plea to the jurisdiction there must in general be an *affidavit* of the truth of its contents (*m*). And where ancient demesne is pleaded, the affidavit must state that the lands are holden of a manor which is ancient demesne, that there is a Court of ancient demesne regularly holden; and that the lessor of the plaintiff has a freehold interest (*n*).

Replication, &c. To the plea of ancient demesne the plaintiff may *reply* that the land is pleadable at common law, and traverse that the manor is ancient demesne, or he may reply without a traverse (*o*). The replication to a plea to the jurisdiction in general commences with a statement that the writ ought not to be quashed, or that the Court ought not to be ousted of their jurisdiction, because, &c. (*p*); and concludes to the country if the replication merely deny the subject-matter of the plea (*q*). Where the plaintiff demurs to the plea, he states that he is not bound to answer the plea, and that the same is not sufficient to prevent the Court from having conusance of the action (*r*); the language of the joinder in demurrer corresponds with that of the demurrer (*s*).

The judgment in these cases is, that the writ shall abate, or *respondeat ouster* (*t*).

[*481]

*II. OF PLEAS IN ABATEMENT (*u*).

II. OF PLEAS IN ABATEMENT. Whenever the subject-matter of the plea or defence is, that the plaintiff cannot maintain *any* action *at any time* whether present or future in respect of the supposed cause of action, it may, and usually must, be pleaded in *bar*; but matter which merely defeats the *present* proceeding, and does not show that the plaintiff is *forever* concluded, should in general be pleaded in *abatement* (807), (from the French *abatre*) (*x*). The criterion or leading dis-

(*i*) *Id.*; but the plea of an attorney sued by latitat in his own Court may conclude *si curia cognoscere velit*, 12 East, 444; and see the present form, *post*, vol. iii.

(*k*) Vin. Ab. Courts, Jurisdiction, N. *a*.

(*l*) As to the *time* of swearing the affidavit, see 3 Chitty's Gen. Prac. 712.

(*m*) 4 Ann. c. 16, s. 11; Bac. Ab. Courts, D. 4. See *ante*, 459.

(*n*) Burr. 1046.

(*o*) Com Dig. Abatement, D. 1.

(*p*) Thomp. Ent. 2; Rast. Ent. 101; Clift. Ent. 17.

(*q*) *Id.*

(*r*) Rast. Ent 419; 1 Wils. 194.

(*s*) *Id.*

(*t*) Vin. Ab. Courts, Jurisdiction, N. a; Com. Dig. Abatement, I. 14.

(*u*) Although pleas in abatement of the writ in respect of *Variance*, &c. have now been virtually abolished by the modern practice of the Courts not permitting oyer of the *writ* so as to disclose that variance, and although pleas of *misnomer* have been expressly abolished by the 3 & 4 W. 4, c. 42, s. 11, and pleas of *nonjoinder* are much limited, yet there are still many instances in which pleas in abatement may still be usefully pleaded, and students and practitioners should examine the subject; see in general Com. Dig. Abatement, 1 Wentw. and *post*, vol. iii. As to pleas in abatement in Courts of *equity*, see Beames' Pl. Eq. 53, 54, 57, 280, &c.

(*x*) 4 T. R. 227; Bac. Ab. Abatement, N.; Com. Dig. Abatement, B.; 3 Campb. 152.

(807) } A plea in abatement, alleging that there are others liable with the defendant does not admit the existence of any contract whatever, the new parties being condition-

II. PLEAS IN ABATEMENT.

tinction between a plea in *abatement* and a plea in *bar* is, that the former must not only point out the plaintiff's error, but must show him how it may be corrected, and furnish him with materials for avoiding the same mistake in another suit in regard to the same cause of action; or in technical language *must give the plaintiff a better writ* (y). There are, however, some matters which may be pleaded either in abatement or in bar; as in replevin for goods, the defendant may plead property in himself or in a stranger (808), either in abatement or in bar (z). So outlawry (809) for felony, alien enemy (810) at the time of the contract (a), and attainder, by either of which the cause of action was *forfeited*, may be pleaded in abatement or in bar (b); and when the defendant has omitted to plead such matter in abatement in due time, he must plead in bar (c).

Parol demurrer abolished by 1 W. 4, c. 47, sect. 10.

There were instances in which the right of action, and even the present suit, was *suspended* only, and not destroyed, and when the matter could only be pleaded in abatement, and the plea should conclude *si responderi debet quousque*, &c. and when the disability is removed the suit will proceed (d). Of that description was *parol demurrer*; the meaning of which was, that the *pleading* should be *stayed*. That occurred where an *infant* heir was sued on the specialty debt of his ancestor, and pleaded his nonage, not as a bar or defence, but merely in *suspension* of the existing proceedings until he arrived at his full *age (e). A plea of this nature was termed, and was for most pur- [*482] poses a plea in abatement; but in this respect it was dissimilar, that it operated only as a *temporary suspension* of the present suit, and did not, like the generality of pleas in abatement, allege matter, which, although it gave a better and another action, had the effect of destroying altogether the suit in which it is pleaded. The right, however, of parol demurrer was taken away by the stat. 1 W. 4, c. 47, sect. 10, which enacts that where any action, suit, or other proceeding for the payment of debts or any other purpose shall be commenced or prosecuted by or against any infant under the age of 21 years, either alone or together with any other person or persons, the parol shall not demur, but such action, suit, or other proceeding shall be prosecuted and carried on in the same manner and as effectually as any action or suit could be.

(y) See 1 Saund. 274, note 3, 285, note 4; see 1 Chitty on Pleading, 5th ed. 491.

(z) 1 Salk. 5.

(a) 3 Campb. 152, 153.

(b) Bac. Ab. Abatement, N.; Com. Dig. Abatement, K.; Co. Lit. 128 b, 129 b; Ld. Raym. 1249; Bro. Vade Mecum, 252; Gilb. C. P. 200; Tidd, 9th ed. 634. But a defendant cannot plead *his own* attainder. Forst. C. L. 61 to 63. As to pleas of these matters in *equity*, see Beames' Pl. Eq. 100, 109, 112.

(c) Bac. Ab. Pleas, C. 3.

(d) Ld. Raym. 105; 12 Mod. 400; 4 East, 504.

(e) See Com. Dig. Infant, D.; Rast. 360, 362, 379; Bro. Red. 195; 4 T. R. 77; 4 East, 485; Stephen, 2d ed. 68. *Parol*, i. e. *loquela*. *Demur*, is from *demorrer*, "to stay."

ally named, to enable the defendant to connect them with whatever contract may be proved; but it operates no further than to preclude an objection for want of parties a second time, and the plaintiff is bound to prove his case against all who are named, as if there had never been a proceeding to ascertain them. Whitner v. Schlatter, 2 Rawle, 359. }

(808) Vide Ilsley et al. v. Stubbs, 5 Mass. Rep. 285. Harrison v. M'Intosh, 1 Johns. Rep. 380.

(809) { See *post*, 483, note f. }

(810) Vide Bell v. Chapman, 10 Johns. Rep. 183. But whether pleaded in abatement or in bar, it is only a temporary disability. Ibid. { Russel v. Skipwith, 1 Serg. & Rawle, 310. }

II. PLEAS IN ABATEMENT. fore the passing of this act be carried on or prosecuted by or against any infant where according to law the infant did not demur.

Pleas in abatement we have already seen (*f*) are divided into those relating

1st. *To the disability of the person suing or being sued; as,*
 1st. *Of the plaintiff;*
 2dly. *Of the defendant.*
2dly. *To the count or declaration.*
3dly. *To the writ (g).*
 1st. *To the form of the writ.*
  1st. *Matter apparent on the face of it.*
  2dly. *Matter dehors.*
 2dly. *To the action of the writ.*

The subject will be considered in reference to the above division, and will be concluded by some observations on the *form* and *qualities* of a plea in abatement, on the *affidavit* of its truth, and on the *replication* and *other proceedings.*

1 RELATING TO THE PERSON. Pleas to the *ability of the plaintiff* show that he is incapable of commencing or continuing his suit by denying his existence, as that he, or one of the plaintiffs, at the time of the commencement of the suit, was a *fictitious* person (*h*)(811), or by alleging that he is dead (*i*). So, where *a sole plaintiff dies* pending the suit, such death may be pleaded in abatement (*k*); but in the case of several plaintiffs or defendants, the death of one does not abate the suit, if the [*483] *cause of action survive to or against the survivors (*l*). So, the defendant may plead in abatement (812), or, as we have just seen (*m*), in bar, that the plaintiff is an *alien enemy* (*n*), attainted of treason or felony (*o*); or outlawed upon mesne or final process (*p*). So, the defendant may plead in

(*f*) *Ante*, 474; Com. Dig. Abatement, C.; Stephen, 2d ed. 70.

(*g*) Mr. Serjeant Stephen obervės, 2d ed. Pleading, 71, n. c. that these divisions of pleas in abatement to the writ, seem to be more subtle than useful, and do not in modern practice often come under consideration. Still, however, as the ancient forms of commencement and conclusion depended in some measure on the classification of the plea the student may find it useful to keep in view the arrangement. There is always great danger in departing from old forms or even arrangements.

(*h*) Com. Dig. Abatement, E. 16; Bac. Ab. Abatement, F.; 1 Wils. 302; Gilb. C. P. 248; see the precedents, Ast. Ent. 10; 3 Inst. Cl. 89; 1 Wentw. 60; and Index, 11.

(*i*) Ast. Ent. 8; 3 Inst. Cl. 75, &c.; 1 Wentw. Index. 11; Bac. Ab. Abatement, L.; Com. Dig. Abatement, E. 17.

(*k*) Bac. Ab. Abatement, F.; Com. Dig. Abatement, H. 32, 33.

(*l*) 8 & 9 W. 3, c. 11, s. 7, Chitty's Col. Stat. 1, 2.

(*m*) *Ante*, 481.

(*n*) Com. Dig. Abatement, E. 4; Bac. Ab. Abatement, B. 3; 1 Doc. Plac. 8. See the forms, 3 Inst. Cl. 16; 2 Stra. 1081; 2 Ld. Raym. 1243; Lutw. 34; 1 Wentw. Index, 8; Gilb. C. P. 205; see the precedents in bar, *post*, vol. iii.

(*o*) Carth. 137, 138; Com. Dig. Abatement, E. 3. See the form, 1 Wentw. 7; 2 B. & Ald. 258.

(*p*) Gilb. C. P. 196, 197; Com. Dig. Abatement, E. 3; Bac. Ab. Abatement, B. 1; see the form Lutw. 6, 1529; 3 Inst. Cl. 23; 1 Wentw. Index, 7; 1 East, 634.

(811) Dob *v.* Penfield, 19 Johns. Rep. 308.

(812) But the death of the lessor in ejectment does not abate the suit. Frier and Cooper *v.* Jackson, 8 Johns. Rep. 495.

abatement that the plaintiff is under a premunire (q); or excommunicated (r); or that the plaintiff (unless he sue with others as executor) is an infant, and has declared by attorney (s)(813), and this is the proper mode of taking advantage of the objection in the case of plaintiffs (t). The effect of the bankruptcy of the plaintiff pending the suit, has been already noticed (u). When a *feme covert* has no interest whatever in the subject-matter of the action, and consequently ought not to be made a party, and she sues either with or without her husband, the defendant will obtain a nonsuit on a plea in bar of her coverture, or a plea in replevin that she had no property in the goods (x). But where the feme was legally interested before or during her coverture in the subject-matter of the action, and might properly join with the husband, but sues alone, her coverture can only be *pleaded in* abatement, and cannot be given in evidence under the general issue, or pleaded in bar; at least this rule obtains in actions for torts (y). If the plaintiff take husband after suing out the writ, and before the declaration, the defendant *cannot give the coverture* in evidence under the general issue, but must plead it in abatement (z)(814), as matter arising before plea or pending the suit (a)(815).

I. RELATING TO THE PERSON.

[*484] Of the defendant.

*Pleas in abatement to the person of the *defendant* (b) are coverture; and formerly infancy before parol demurrer, now abolished, but a defendant could not avail himself of his own attainder (c). *Coverture* at the time when the supposed contract was entered into must be pleaded *in bar* (816), though before the Reg. Gen. Hil. T. 4 W. 4, it might have been given in evidence under the general issue *non assumpsit* or *non est factum* (d); but where the objection does not go to the *liability* of the feme, but is merely that the husband ought to have been *sued jointly* with her, as where, *since* entering into the contract, or committing the tort, she has married, she must, when sued alone, plead her coverture in abatement, and aver that her husband is living (e). If the defendant marry after the commencement of the suit, such coverture cannot be pleaded even in abatement (f)(817). To the plea of coverture the

(q) Co. Lit. 129 b; Com. Dig. Abatement, E. 7.

(r) Lutw. 17; 3 Inst. Cl. 18; Cro. Jac. 82; Bac. Ab. Abatement, B. 3; 1 Wentw. Index; Gilb. C. P. 202. In equity, Beames' Eq. Pl. 9, 106, &c.

(s) Bro. R. 475, 476; 3 Inst. Cl. 55, 19; Clift, 11; 1 Mod. Ent. 20; 1 Wentw. 58; *id.* Index, 10; see the form, 2 Saund. 209 a.

(t) 2 Saund. 212, n. 5.

(u) *Ante*, 25.

(x) *Ante*, 31 to 37.

(y) *Ante*, 31 to 37, 83 to 86.

(z) 6 T. R. 265.

(a) 4 East, 502.

(b) In *equity*, Beames, Pl. Eq. 129.

(c) *Ante*, 481, n. (b).

(d) 12 Mod 101; 8 T. R. 545.

(e) *Ante*, 82, 105, 106.

(f) Bac. Ab. Abatement, G.; 2 Stra. 814; *et vide* Lofft, 27; 2 Ld. Raym. 1525.

(813) Vide Schermerhorn *v.* Jenkins, 7 Johns. Rep 373.

(814) { If a *feme sole* administratrix marry pending an action commenced by her, the suit abates. Swan, adm., *v.* Wilkinson, 14 Mass. Rep. 295. 5 Greenl. Rep. 181. But if she be one of several administrators, and marry pending an action brought by them all, the action is not thereby abated. Newell et al., adm., *v.* Marcy, 17 Mass. Rep. 341. }

(815) { But *coverture* of the plaintiff, since the bringing of the suit cannot be pleaded after a plea in bar; unless it takes place after the plea in bar, in which case it may be done; but the defendant must not suffer a continuance to intervene between the happening of this new matter, or its coming to his knowledge, and pleading it. Wilson *v.* Hamilton, 4 Serg. & Rawle, 238. }

(816) { Coverture between the parties to the action can only be pleaded in bar, as it is impossible in such a case to give the party a better writ. Steer *v.* Steer, 14 Serg. & Rawle, 379. }

(817) { Crocket *v.* Ross, 5 Greenl. Rep. 445. }

I. RELATING TO THE PERSON. plaintiff may reply any matter which affords him a right to sue the defendant alone, although she be a married woman (g). *Infancy* might formerly be pleaded in abatement in an action upon a specialty, when the defendant was sued as heir on the obligation of his ancestor, in which case the parol was to *demur*, or proceedings be stayed till he comes of age (h); but that privilege did not extend to an infant devisee (i)(818), and was finally altogether abolished by 1 W. 4, c. 47, s. 10 (k).

Privilege of a peer. The uniformity of process act, 2 W. 4, c. 39, subjects *peers* and *members of parliament* to a writ of summons, in the same form as ordinary persons, and therefore there cannot be a plea in abatement as a peer, merely on account of his having been served with that process. A plea of *privilege* by a peer is therefore more limited than heretofore (l). But if *arrested*, a peer may obtain his discharge, or his bail may be discharged on summary application (l). A peer cannot now plead *misnomer* any more than any other subject (m).

II. RELATING TO THE COUNT, &c. Pleas in abatement *to the count* could only be pleaded in actions by original writ. The first act of the parties after appearance and admission of the jurisdiction of the Court over the subject-matter of the cause, and of the ability of the plaintiff to sue and the defendant to be sued, is the declaration or count, after which formerly the defendant might demand oyer of the writ, and then the same being set forth on the roll, if there were any variance between the count and the writ, or between the writ and a record, specialty, &c. mentioned in the count, the defendant might plead such variance in abatement or demur, move in arrest of judgment, or sustain error (n). But as a variance between the writ and count could in no case be pleaded without craving oyer of the writ (o), and the defendant cannot now have such oyer (p), the variance or defect is no longer pleadable [*485] in abatement, and if it be pleaded, the plaintiff may sign judgment, or move the Court to set it aside (q); nor will the Court set aside the proceeding in respect of the variance (r).

III. RELATING TO THE WRIT. Pleas in *abatement to the writ or bill* are so termed rather from their *effect* than from their being strictly such pleas, for as oyer of the writ can no longer be craved, no objection can be taken by plea to matter which is *merely* contained in the *writ* (s). But if the mistake in the writ *be carried also into the declaration*, or rather if the declaration which is *presumed* to correspond with the writ, be incorrect in respect of some *extrinsic* matter, it is then open to

(g) See *ante*, 65 to 68.
(h) *Supra*.
(i) 4 East, 485.
(k) See the enactment, *ante*, 481.
(l) 8 Bing. 54, 174, 416.
(m) 3 & 4 W. 4, c. 42, s. 11 & 12, and *post*.
(n) 2 Wils. 394; Com. Dig. Abatement, G. 8; 3 Inst. Cl. 62; Reg. Pl. 277, 278.
(o) 2 Wils. 394, 395.
(p) See *ante*, 279, 465.
(q) 1 B. & P. 646, 647; 3 *Id.* 395; 7 East, 383; Tidd, 9th edit. 636; Steph. 2d. edit. 70, 73.
(r) 2 Wils. 393; 3 East, 167; *ante*, 265, 279.
(s) *Ante*, 279, 465.

(818) It has been held, in Connecticut, that the privilege of the defendant as a member of the legislature was pleadable in abatement. King v. Coit, 4 Day's Rep. 129.

III. RELATING TO THE WRIT.

the defendant to plead in abatement to the writ (*t*)(819); and there is no plea to the *declaration* alone but in bar (*u*). Pleas in abatement of the writ or bill are to the *form* or to the *action* thereof (*x*): those of the first description were formerly either matter apparent on the face of the writ or bill (*y*), or matter *dehors* (*z*). Formerly a defect in the form of the writ, *apparent* on the face of it; as repugnancy, variance from the record or specialty, want of sufficient time between the teste and return (*a*), or in actions by original, the omission or mistake in the writ of the defendant's addition (*b*), either of estate, degree, mystery, or place of abode (*c*), were pleadable in abatement; *but as ouster of the writ can no longer be had*, an omission of the defendant's addition, which is not necessary to be stated in a *declaration*, can in no case be pleaded in abatement; and if it be, the plaintiff may sign judgment or apply to the Court to set the plea aside (*d*).

To the *form* of the writ. [*486]

Pleas in abatement to the *form* of the writ therefore of late years were, and still are, principally for matter *dehors* (*e*), existing at the time of *suing out the writ or arising afterwards (*f*), such as *misnomer* of the plaintiff or the defendant in his christian or surname. Such pleas of *misnomer* have recently been abolished by 3 & 4 W. 4, c. 42, s. 11, but still it may be advisable concisely to notice the subject.

Misnomer.

What in law amounted to a misnomer has been already pointed out (*g*). It was once doubted if a mistake of the *plaintiff's* christian or surname were not a ground of *nonsuit*, but it is now settled that the mistake must be *pleaded* in abatement even in the case of a corporation (*h*)(820); and this objection could not be *pleaded* unless the misnomer also appeared in the declaration (*i*), for the plaintiff might declare in his right name though the name had been mistaken in the process (821). The misnomer of one of several plaintiffs was pleadable in abatement (*k*). Misnomer of the *defendant* must also have been pleaded in abatement (*l*)(822). But misnomer of *another* defendant could not be pleaded by his companion (*m*)(823); and if the declaration were

(*t*) 1 B. & P. 648; 10 Mod. 210, 211.
(*u*) 10 Mod. 210; 2 Saund. 209 d.
(*x*) Com. Dig. Abatement, H. 1, 17.
(*y*) Com. Dig. Abatement, H. 1.
(*z*) Com. Dig. Abatement, H. 17.
(*a*) 1 Lutw. 25; 3 Inst. Cl. 49, 54, 66, &c.
(*b*) 1 Hen. 5, c. 5; 3 Cl. 92; Lil. Ent. 5; 2 Rich. C. P. 5, 8; 1 Stra. 556; Ld. Raym. 1541; 2 Inst. 668.
(*c*) 3 B. & P. 395.
(*d*) 1 Saund. 318, n. 3; *ante*, 279, 465.
(*e*) Com. Dig. Abatement, H. 17, &c.; Gilb. C. P. 51.
(*f*) Com. Dig. Abatement, H. 17, 32.
(*g*) *Ante*, 279.
(*h*) 1 B. & P. 40; 3 Anstr. 935; 3 Campb. 29; 16 East, 110. The misnomer of the plaintiff is no ground for setting aside proceedings, it must be pleaded in abatement, 2 B. & B. 34. If the mis-statement of a name constitute a variance in setting out a written contract it will be fatal under the general issue, 4 T. R. 611; Chitty on Bills, 7th edit. 353.
(*i*) 1 B. & P. 645. As to moving the Court to set aside the proceedings, see *ante*, 281.
(*k*) 6 M. & Sel. 45.
(*l*) Bac. Ab. Abatement, 9; Misnomer, F.; Com. Dig. Abatement, F. 17, 18; and 2 Bla. Rep. 120. See the forms, *post*, vol. iii.; Lutw. 10; Lil. Ent. 6; 2 Rich. Prac. 4.
(*m*) Lutw. 36.

(819) {Schenck v. Schenck, 5 Halst. Rep. 274. Chirac v. Reinicker, 11 Wheat. Rep. 302. Variance between the writ and declaration is matter of abatement, or special demurrer. Newlin v. Palmer, 11 Serg. & Rawle, 98.}

(820) Vide Medway Cotton Manufactory v. Adams, 10 Mass. 360.

(821) Contra Willard v. Missani, 1 Cow. Rep. 37.

(822) So, a corporation defendant cannot take advantage of a misnomer, in arrest of judgment, but must plead in abatement. Gilbert v. Nantucket Bank, 5 Mass. Rep. 97.

(823) Nor can he plead in abatement any matters applicable to himself alone. De Forest v. Jewett, 1 Hall's Rep. 136.

III. RELATING TO THE WRIT. against the defendant in his right name, though varying from that in the writ, he could not plead in abatement (n)(824). In an action for a *tort*, the misnomer of one defendant could only abate the suit as to him, and not as to his companions (o). The consequences of a *misnomer* of the defendant, and the course he should pursue in order to take advantage of the error have been before explained (p)(825).

Pleas in abatement of *misnomer* were abolished by 3 & 4 W. 4, c. 42, s. 11, and another remedy for mis-statement of names is invented by that act. S. 11 enacts, "that no plea *in abatement* for a misnomer shall be allowed in any personal action, but that in all cases in which a misnomer would but for this act have been by law pleadable in abatement in such actions, the defendant shall be at liberty to cause the declaration to be amended, at the costs of the plaintiff, by inserting the right name, upon a judge's summons founded on an affidavit of the right name; and in case such summons shall be discharged, the costs of such application shall be paid by the party applying, if the judge shall think fit."

Section 12. "That in all actions upon bills of exchange and promissory notes, or other written instruments, any of the parties to which are designated by the initial letter or letters or some contraction of the christian or first name or names, it shall be sufficient in every affidavit to hold to bail, and in the process or declaration, to designate such person by the same initial letter or letters or contraction of the christian or first name or names, instead of stating the christian or first name or names in full."

(n) 1 B. & P. 645; 3 East, 167; *ante*, 246.

(o) 1 M. & P. 26.

(p) *Ante*, 280, 281. Where to an action of assumpsit against the defendant as acceptor of a bill of exchange for £15, he pleaded, after setting out the 51 G. 3, c. 124, that the plaintiff sued out a writ of *capias ad respondendum* against him by the name of "*Joseph*" for £15, on an affidavit of debt made by the plaintiff's clerk, under which the defendant was arrested, and afterwards allowed to go at large by the sheriff; that the writ was afterwards altered by inserting the name of "*Robert*" (the real name of defendant) instead of "*Joseph*," under which he was again arrested under a fresh affidavit of debt, as required by that statute; the plea was held bad on special demurrer, as it did not go to the merits of the action, and as the defendant might either have pleaded in abatement or moved to set aside the proceedings for irregularity, 5 Moore, 168.

(824) A defendant cannot plead in abatement because of an *alias dictus* subjoined to his name. Reid v. Lord, 4 Johns. Rep. 118. Where a name appears to be a foreign one, a variance of a letter which, according to the pronunciation of that language, does not vary the sound, is not a misnomer, as Petris for Petrie. Petrie v. Woodworth, 3 Caines' Rep. 219. As to *idem sonans*, see further the King v. Shakespeare, 10 East's Rep. 83. Dickinson v. Bowes, 16 East's Rep. 110. Ahitbol v. Beneditto, 2 Taunt. 400. An initial letter between the christian and surname of the party, is no part of the name, and the omission of it is not a misnomer or variance. Franklin and others v. Talmadge, 5 Johns. Rep. 84. {But in New Jersey in an action before a Justice of the Peace, the *plaintiff*, if he has a middle letter in his name (J. S. M.) must take care to insert it in his summons, for if he does not, and obtains judgment against the defendant in consequence of his not appearing, the judgment will be reversed, although the state of demand filed contains the plaintiff's true name. Bowen v. Medford, 5 Halst. Rep. 230.} The plaintiff may reply that the defendant is known as well by one name as the other. Petrie v. Woodworth, 3 Caines' Rep. 219. Gould v. Barnes, 3 Taunt. 505. An *administrator* sued as *executor* may plead the intestacy and granting letters of administration, in abatement. Rattoon v. Overcuker, 8 Johns. Rep. 126.

(825) The omission of *junior* to the name of the defendant in a writ of error is no cause for quashing the writ, where there is any other *descriptio personæ* by which the real party can be ascertained. Fleet v. Younge, 11 Wend. R. 522. The addition of junior forms no part of the name. Kincaid v. Howe, 10 Mass. R. 203. Vide 3 Pet. U. S. S. C. R. 1.

III. RELATING TO THE WRIT.

Other pleas of this nature.

*Other pleas to the *form of the writ* are, that the *plaintiffs* or *defendants* suing, or being sued, as husband and wife, are not married (*q*)(826); or that one of *the plaintiffs* or defendants was fictitious or dead at the time of issuing the writ (*r*), or any other plea for want of proper parties (*s*), as a joint contractor (*t*), or another executor (*u*), or administrator (*x*), or other person (*y*), not joined, who ought to have been made a party to the suit. The plea in abatement of *nonjoinder* must always have averred that the party omitted *is still living* (*z*)(827). We have already seen, when considering the parties to the action, that in actions on *contracts* the *nonjoinder* of a party who ought to be made *co-plaintiff* will in general be the ground of nonsuit, and need not, though it *may, be* pleaded in abatement (*a*); but that in the case of executors and others suing *jure representationis*, (except assignees of a bankrupt)(*b*), the omission can only be pleaded in abatement (*c*); and that the *nonjoinder* of a person who ought to be made co-plaintiff in an action in form *ex delicto*, as case, trover, trespass, &c. can only be pleaded in abatement (*d*). And we have seen that with regard to *defendants*, the omission of a joint contractor *must* be pleaded in abatement (*e*); and that in actions for *torts* no advantage whatever can in general be taken of the nonjoinder of the defendant (*f*).

Nonjoinder.

A most important and salutary check on pleas in abatement of nonjoinder was introduced by 3 & 4 W. 4, c. 42, s. 8, which enacts that no plea in abatement for the *nonjoinder* of any person as a *co-defendant* shall be allowed in any Court of common law, unless it shall be stated in such plea that such person is resident within the jurisdiction of the Court, and unless the place of residence of such person shall be stated with convenient certainty in an affidavit verifying such plea.

Pleas by *attornies* heretofore sued in their own Court by improper process, as by latitat in the King's Bench, or by a common capias in the Common Pleas, instead of a *bill* against them as such attornies, may also be classed under pleas in abatement to the form of the writ (*g*). But as the uniformity

(*q*) Com. Dig. Abatement, E. 6; 3 Inst. Cl. 69; 1 Wentw. Index, 12. *Sed quære* if this can be pleaded, see 2 Chit. Rep. 642.

(*r*) 1 Doct. Plac. 12; Bac. Ab. Abatement, L.

(*s*) *Ante*, Chap. I. Parties to the action, *per totum*.

(*t*) Davies *v.* Esam, 6 Car. & P. 619.

(*u*) Com. Dig. Abatement, E. 8, F. 4, &c.; 3 Inst. Cl. 51; Rast. Ent. 325 a; 1 Wentw. 9; Reg. 140; 1 Lev. 161; 1 Sid. 242.

(*x*) 3 Inst. Cl. 53; Rast. Ent. 324.

(*y*) 3 Inst. Cl. 53, 119; 1 Lutw. 696; 1 East, 634; 1 Wentw. 10, 11; Index, 12.

(*z*) 1 Saund. 291 a, note 2.

(*a*) *Ante*, 14.

(*b*) *Ante*, 25, 26; 1 Chit. Rep. 71; 2 Stark. 424.

(*c*) *Ante*, 22; 2 Saund. 291 g; 3 B. & P. 465.

(*d*) *Ante*, 76. And the nonjoinder in *this* case is only ground for *plea in abatement*, although the declaration show that there is another party interested jointly with the plaintiff, 8 T. R. 766.

(*e*) *Ante*, 53, 54.

(*f*) *Ante*, 99.

(*g*) See *post*, vol. iii.; 7 Lutw. 639; 12 East, 544; Davidson *v.* Chilman, 1 Bing. N. C. 297.

(826) { See Coombes *et ux. v.* Williams, 15 Mass. Rep. 243. }

(827) The parties not joined should be particularly set forth and described, so as to enable the plaintiff to make a better writ. Wadsworth *v.* Woodford, 1 Day's Rep. 28. { Where judgment by default has been obtained, if the writ be against *two* of *four* joint and several promissors, and it is shown in the writ that four promised, it is material also to show that the other two are dead, or otherwise incapable of being sued, or the judgment will be reversed. Harwood *v.* Roberts, 5 Greenl. Rep. 441. See Osgood *v.* Spencer's Ex., 2 Har. & Gill, 131. }

III. RELATING TO THE WRIT. of process act, 2 W. 4, c. 39, now subjects attornies to be sued by the same form of writ of summons as other persons, a plea of that description is now [*488] abolished. There are two ways of pleading an **attorney's privilege*; first, with a *profert* of a writ of privilege, or of an exemplification of the record of his admission; upon which the plaintiff must reply *nul tiel record*, and cannot otherwise deny the defendant's being an attorney: secondly, as a mere matter of fact, without a profert; and then a *certiorari* shall be awarded, to certify whether he be an attorney or not (*h*). The *present* form of a plea of privilege to be sued in his own Court will be found in the third volume. The plea of privilege to be sued in his own Court, must be verified by affidavit (*i*). A person sued as an attorney may plead that he is not one, if such be the fact (*k*).

To the *action* of the writ. Pleas in abatement to the *action* of the writ, are, that the action is misconceived, as that it is in case when it ought to have been in trespass (*l*), or that it was *prematurely brought* (*m*): but as these matters are the ground of *demurrer* or *nonsuit*, it is now very unusual to plead them in abatement (*n*). It may also be pleaded that there is *another action depending* for the same trespass (*o*) or other cause of action, in the same or in any other superior Court at Westminster (*p*)(828); but the pendency of another suit in the sheriff's or other inferior Court, it is said cannot be pleaded (*q*)(829). In general the pendency of a former action must be pleaded in abatement; but in a penal action, at the suit of a common informer, the priority of a pending suit for the same penalty in the name of a third person, may be pleaded *in bar*, because the party who first sues is entitled to the penalty (*r*) (830). In the latter case the plea, when the two suits were commenced in the same term, should show the precise

(*h*) Tidd, 9th edit. 635; 9 East, 424.

(*i*) Davidson *v.* Chilman, 1 Bing. N. C. 297, *post*

(*k*) 1 Wentw. 6; Prac. Reg 8.

(*l*) 3 Inst. Cl. 120, &c.; Com. Dig. Abatement, G. 5.

(*m*) Com. Dig Abatement, G. 6. Action, E.; Lutw. 8, 13; 3 Inst. Cl. 56; Fortesc. 334; Clift. Ent. 10, 18, 19; *sed qu* Ld. Raym. 1249.

(*n*) See the instances of misjoinder, *ante*, 228, 229.

(*o*) 1 Campb. 60, 61.

(*p*) Com Dig. Abatement, H. 24; Bac. Ab Abatement, M. See the forms, *post*, vol. iii. In an action by the assignees of a bankrupt, the defendant cannot plead the pendency of an action by the bankrupt, 4 B. & C. 920.

(*q*) 5 Co. 62; 2 Wils. 87; Fitzgib. 313; Bac. Ab Abatement, M.; Com. Dig Abatement, H. 24; 2 Lord Raym. 1102; *sed quære*, if it were alleged that the *inferior* court had jurisdiction, Fitzgib. 314.

(*r*) Sayer's Rep. 216; and *post*, vol. iii.

(828) A writ of error pending may be pleaded in abatement of a suit upon the judgment. Jenkins *v.* Pepoon, 2 Johns Cas. 312. A suit subsequently commenced can never be pleaded in abatement. Renner and Bussard *v.* Marshall, 1 Wheaton, 215. In New Jersey under the statute "concerning obligations, &c." (Revised Laws, 305,) a defendant may plead in abatement, "that another action had been previously commenced by him against the plaintiff, in which the matters mentioned in the plaintiff's declaration might be set off." Schenck *v.* Schenck, 5 Halst. Rep. 276. See Douglass *v.* Hoag, 1 Johns. Rep. 283, and Townsend *v.* Chase, 1 Cow. Rep. 116, as to a similar plea in actions before Justices of the Peace under the statute for the recovery of debts under twenty-five dollars. See also Purdon's Digest, (Laws of Penn.) 453. s. 17. Edit. 1824.

(829) An action pending in a foreign court, or in the court of another of the United States, or in the court of the United States in another circuit and district, cannot be pleaded in abatement. Bowne and Seymour *v.* Joy, 9 Johns. Rep. 221. Walsh and Gallagher *v.* Durkin and others, 12 Johns. Rep. 99. But a foreign attachment pending in another State, at the suit of a third person against the subject-matter of the action, may be pleaded in abatement. Embree *v.* Hanna, 5 Johns. Rep 101. Bowne *v.* Joy, 9 Johns. Rep. 221.

(830) } Engle *v.* Nelson, 1 Penn. Rep. 442. }

day or time when the prior suit was commenced (s) (831). The plaintiff cannot, after a plea in abatement of the pendency *of a prior suit, avoid the effect of the plea by discontinuing the first action which was pending at the time of the plea (t) (832). III. RELATING TO THE WRIT.

The *form of a plea in abatement* before the recent pleading rules of Hil. T. 4 W. 4, was as follows, excepting that the *commencement* and *conclusion* varied when the plea was of privilege to be sued in a particular Court and in some other respects, as will be seen on examination of the forms of pleas in abatement in the commencement of the third volume (u).

Of the Forms and *general qualities* and *requisites* of Pleas in Abatement.

Form of Plea in Abatement.

In the King's Bench, [*or* "C. P." *or* "Exchequer of Pleas.]

On the —— day of ——, 1836.

Commencement.

C. D. ats. A. B. } And the defendant [*or* "C. D."] by Y. Z his attorney, [*or* "in person," *or* 'by E. F. admitted by the said Court here as guardian of the defendant, to defend for him, he being an infant within the age of twenty-one years,"] prays judgment of the said writ and declaration, because he says that [here state the subject matter of the plea in abatement as set forth in the third volume, *post*.]

Body.

And this the defendant is ready to verify, wherfore [or sometimes as in pleas of non-joinder are here inserted "wherefore inasmuch as the said O. P. is not named in the said writ and declaration, together with the defendant,"] he prays judgment of the said writ and declaration and that the same may be quashed, &c.

Conclusion.

John Hulme,
[The signature of the Counsel.]

From a very cursory observation of the above form, it will be seen that pleas in abatement are to be considered with reference to, 1st, The title of the *Court*; 2dly, The title as to *date*; 3dly, The title as to the marginal statement of the parties; 4thly, The *commencement of the plea*, showing whether the defendant appears and *pleads in person*, or by *attorney*, or by *guardian*, and whether the plea is to profess to make any and what *defence*, as whether *full* or *half* defence, and whether there is to be any and what *prayer*

(s) 3 Burr. 1423; 1 Bla. Rep. 437; 2 Lev. 141; 2 Stra. 1169.

(t) 1 Salk. 329; 2 Ld. Raym. 1014, S. C.; Doct. Pla. 11.

(u) *Post*, vol. iii.

---

(831) {Two suits were brought on a promissory note payable to B. who, at the execution of such note, was the wife of A.;—one by A. in his individual capacity, the other by A. as administrator of B. then deceased; both of which suits were served at the same time, returned to the same Court, and were therein pending contemporaneously. The defendant pleaded these matters in abatement of each suit, averring, that the cause of action in both suits was the same. The allegations of the pleas were found to be true, and the pleas were held to be good, and that the pendency of each suit was good ground in abatement of the other. Beach *v.* Norton, 8 Conn. Rep. 71.}

(832) Contra Marston *v.* Lawrence and Dayton, 1 Johns. Rep. 397. In Commonwealth *v.* Churchill, 5 Mass. Rep. 174, it was held that the plaintiff could not reply a nonsuit in the former action. The entries of pleas of this kind generally, but not always, aver the then pendency of the first writ; but such averment is unnecessary; and it is sufficient if the first action was pending when the second writ was purchased. And it was not necessary that the first should be pending when the plea was pleaded; for if by law it was once abateable, the subsequent nonsuit could not make it good. The principle also applies to *qui tam* actions sued by different plaintiffs, or to informations *qui tam* for the benefit of different persons, or to a subsequent indictment to recover the same penalty. The principle is, when the prior action is pending, the subsequent writ is bad *ab initio*. *Ib.*

FORMS AND REQUISITES OF.

of judgment; 5thly, The *body* or substance of the plea with or without any and what certainty as to *time or place*; 6thly, The *conclusion*, with any and what prayer of judgment; 7thly, When the *signature* of counsel is necessary and consequences of an omission; 8thly, When any and what *affidavit of the truth* of the plea is *requisite*.

1st. Title of Pleas in Abatement as to the Court.

1st. *Title of Court*. No statute or rule requires a plea in abatement to be entitled at the top or otherwise of any Court, indeed it would seem that unless there were several actions depending between the same parties in *different* Courts at the same time, no ambiguity about the proper Court can well arise;

2ndly. As to the title of the date.

2ndly, as to the *title of the term*, formerly all pleas, excepting those pleaded *puis darrein continuance*, pleaded at the sittings of nisi prius or at the assizes, must have been entitled in or as of a *term* when the Court were supposed to be sitting; and as pleas to the *jurisdiction* of the Court and in *abatement* ought then to be pleaded before a *general imparlance* (833), and within four days *inclusive* after the delivery or filing, and notice of the declaration (*x*), all such pleas must have been entitled, and in general of the term in which the writ was returnable. But if the declaration were delivered or filed in vacation, or so late in the term that the defendant was not bound to plead to it of that term, the defendant might, within the first four days inclusive of the next term, plead to *the jurisdiction of the Court*, or in abatement (*y*), or a tender (*z*), entitling, however, his plea of the preceding term (*a*); or he might plead to the jurisdiction as of the second term, with a *general special imparlance*, which was we have seen with a saving of all advantages and exceptions whatsoever (*b*), or he might plead in *abatement* in the second term with a *special imparlance*, which is as a saving of all exceptions to the writ, bill or count (*c*). And where a bill was filed in the vacation against an attorney as of the preceding term, *with a special memorandum* showing that the bill was filed in vacation, and the defendant's plea in abatement was entitled of the following term without a special imparlance, it was held regular (*d*). If a plea in abatement was improperly entitled of a subsequent term to the declaration, without the proper special imparlance, the plaintiff might either sign judgment (*e*)(834) or apply to [*490] *the Court by motion to set aside the plea (*f*), or he might demur generally to it (*g*), or might allege the imparlance in his replication by way of estoppel (*h*); but if the plaintiff replied to the plea instead of demurring or alleging the estoppel, the fault was aided (*i*).

(*x*) *Ante*, 470, 479; Tidd, 9th ed 638, 639; 2 M. & Sel. 484. Of the four days, the first and last were always inclusive. If Sunday be the fourth day, the plea might be on the Monday. Tidd, 9th ed 638, 639. See present practice, 3 Chitty's Gen. Prac. 702, 703.

(*y*) *Id.*

(*z*) Reg. Gen. Hil T. 2 W. 4, reg. 45.

(*a*) *Ante*, 471, 472; 7 T. R. 447, note d; 1 Salk. 367; Gilb. K B. 344.

(*b*) *Ante*, 472, 473; Com. Dig. Abatement, I. 19; 2 Saund. 2 a, n. 2. See the form, *post*, vol. iii.

(*c*) *Ante*, 471, 472; Bac. Abr. Abatement, C.; 2 Saund. 2 a, note 2. See the form, *id.*; *post*, vol. iii.; Com. Dig. Abatement, I. 20.

(*d*) 1 Chit. Rep. 704; 3 B. & Ald. 259, S. C.

(*e*) 4 T. R. 529; 7 *Id.* 218, 447, n. d; 2 Saund. 2 b, n. 2.

(*f*) 6 T. R. 373.

(*g*) 2 M. & Sel. 484; 6 T. R. 369; 1 Wils. 261; 2 B. & P. 384; 3 Inst. Cl. 40; 2 Saund. 2 b, n. 2.

(*h*) 2 Saund. 2 b, n. 2. See the form of estoppel, 1 Lutw. 23; 1 Wentw. Index, 13; 3 Inst. Cl. 39; Clift. Ent. 18, pl. 46; 19, pl. 50; 20, pl. 53, 54.

(*i*) 2 Saund. 2 b, n. 2; 1 Vent. 236.

(833) M'Carney *v.* M'Camp, 1 Ashm. Rep. 4.

(834) M'Carney *v.* M'Camp, 1 Ashm. Rep. 4.

According to the present practice, all pleas in abatement must be pleaded *within four days both inclusive* from the day of delivering the declaration (*k*), but in some cases further time may be obtained, as in the instance of non-joinder of a defendant (*l*), or where two actions are depending for the same cause (*m*).

FORM AND QUALITIES. Present practice as *to time* of pleading in abatement and *title* of pleas.

As the pleading Reg. Gen. Hil. T. 4 W. 4, reg. 1, orders, "that every pleading shall be *entitled* of the day of the month and year when the same was pleaded, and shall bear *no other time* or date," and that rule applies to pleas in abatement as well as pleas in bar, it seems now to be settled that every plea in abatement should be entitled on the very day it is pleaded.

3rdly. Names of parties in the *margin*.

Although it is the constant practice in the *margin* of a plea in abatement to state the surnames of the parties, as thus, C. D., ats. A. B., yet no statute or rule expressly requires that form, and if omitted, the plea would no doubt be considered as pleaded in the *proper action*. When *one* of *several* defendants pleads separate, it is usual to state his christian and surname in the margin as sued "*together with others*," and afterwards throughout the plea carefully to limit it to him distinct from the others.

4thly. The commencement.

4thly. *The commencement* should always expressly state whether the defendant appears and pleads in person or by attorney. Pleas to the jurisdiction must be pleaded *in person*, because the appointment of an attorney of the Court admits its jurisdiction (*n*); but pleas in abatement in general may be pleaded by attorney, because the jurisdiction of the Court in the latter case is not disputed (*o*). The principle to be extracted from the cases is stated to be, that a defendant cannot plead by attorney in those cases where the doing so would contradict the import of the warrant of attorney (*p*). It appears advisable to frame pleas of misnomer as if pleaded in person and not by attorney, though there are decisions that the plaintiff cannot demur on account of a mistake in this respect, but should refuse to accept the plea (*q*). Coverture also should be pleaded in person (*r*). Where an infant pleads, it must be by guardian, and not by attorney or *prochein ami* (*s*); and this, though he be sued in a representative character, as administrator, &c. (*t*), and the infant defendant may avail himself of the objection on writ of error, though the plaintiff could not (*u*).

Of defence.

The nature of *defence* has already been stated (*x*). Pleas to the jurisdiction and in abatement must have been pleaded after *half*, [*491] *but *before full* defence (*y*). It was advisable to make the former defence, though it seems questionable whether the plaintiff could demur for the omission, or object oth-

(*k*) See 3 Chitty's Gen. Prac. 702.
(*l*) *Id.* page 703.
(*m*) Sowter *v.* Dunston, 1 Man. & Ryl. 508, 810.
(*n*) *Ante*, 461, 462, 479; 2 Saund. 209 b; Summary Treat. on Pleading, 51; Tidd, 9th ed. 631.
(*o*) *Ante*, 461; 2 Saund. 209 b.
(*p*) Summary Treat. on Pleading, 50, &c.
(*q*) 2 Saund. 209 b; 1 Lord Raym. 509; Summary Treat. on Pleading, 50, 51.
(*r*) 2 Saund. 209 b.
(*s*) *Ante*, 461. See the precedents, *post*, vol. iii.
(*t*) 1 Moore, 250; 7 Taunt. 488, S. C.
(*u*) 2 Saund. 212, n. 4; Cro. Jac. 289. But the plaintiff cannot, 5 B. & Ald. 418.
(*x*) *Ante*, 462.
(*y*) *Ante*, 462, 479.

FORM AND QUALITIES. erwise than by refusing to accept the plea (*x*). But now the Reg. Gen. Hil. T. 4 W. 4, expressly orders that no *formal defence shall be required in a plea, and it shall commence as follows, "the said defendant by —— his attorney* (or 'in person, &c.') *says that*, &c." And that rule seems to extend to every description of plea whether in *abatement* or in *bar*.

5thly. Of the body of the plea; and general requisites. As pleas in abatement do not deny and yet tend to delay the trial of the merits of the action, great accuracy and precision are required in framing them (*c*). They should be certain to every intent (*d*), and be pleaded without any repugnancy (*e*). They must in general, as before explained (*f*), give the plaintiff a better writ (*g*), and if it do not give a better writ but tend to show that the plaintiff can maintain no action at all, a plea pleaded as in abatement is bad (*h*); and therefore a plea of misnomer in the christian name before 3 & 4 W. 4, c. 42, s. 11, (abolishing pleas of misnomer), must have stated what was the real name, and also the defendant's surname, even though the latter had been already truly stated in the declaration (*i*). For the same reason, a plea in abatement of defendant's privilege to be sued as a peer should show how defendant derived his title, and that he is a peer of the united kingdom (*k*). And a plea in abatement of the nonjoinder as a defendant of a co-executor, must show that the latter became liable to be sued as *such, as that he had* administered, &c. (*l*). This rule, as regards all matters peculiarly in the knowledge of the defendant pleading, and which would tend to give a better writ, is obviously well founded on principle, but as applying to matter within the knowledge of the plaintiff ought not to be extended. Where the action is by an administrator, stating a grant of administration from a bishop of a peculiar diocese, a plea of *bona notabilia* should be *in bar* and not in abatement, because it shows that the plaintiff, at least at present, has no right to sue *at all* in the character of administrator (*m*).

Duplicity in a plea of this description is as objectionable as in a plea in bar, thus the defendant cannot plead two outlawries or two excommunications in abatement, for one would be sufficient to abate the writ (*n*): though formerly misnomer of christian and surname might have been pleaded in one plea as essential to give the plaintiff a better writ (*o*). The Court will not permit a defendant to plead at the same time in abatement and in bar to the *same* matter, as *non est factum*, and coverture of the plaintiff since making the [*492] bond (*p*) (835); but in an action against two defendants, each *may plead

(*x*) *Id.*; Com. Dig. Abatement, I. 16; Skinn. 582.
(*c*) 3 T. R. 186; Willes, 42; 2 Bla. Rep. 1096; 2 Saund. 209 a, n. 1; Com. Dig. Abatement, I. 11.
(*d*) As to this, see *ante*, 267.
(*e*) Co. Litt. 303; Cro. Jac. 82; 3 Lev. 67; 3 T. R. 186; Willes, 42.
(*f*) *Ante*, 481.
(*g*) Turtle v. Lady Worsley, Tidd, 689.
(*h*) 4 T. R. 227.
(*i*) 8 T. R. 515, 516; Bac. Ab. Misnomer, F.; 5 Taunt. 653.
(*k*) 4 D. & R. 592; and see 8 Bing. 55, 174, 416; 7 Bar. & Cres. 388; 1 Mood. & R. 110, S. C.; and 1 Crom. & M. 241.
(*l*) See 1 Lev. 161; 1 M. & P. 678.
(*m*) 1 Saund. 274, n. 3; see 5 B. & C. 491.
(*n*) Bac. Ab. Abatement, P.
(*o*) *Id.* Misnomer, F.; Rep. temp. Hardw. 286, 287.
(*p*) Rep. temp. Hardw. 135.

(835) {See Palmer v. Dixon, 5 Dowl. & Ryl. 623.}

distinct matter in abatement of the same suit (*q*), or one may plead in abatement and the other in bar (*r*)(836). FORM AND QUALITIES.

As dilatory pleas rarely affect the merits of the suit, and object mere matter of form, they constitute an exception to the general principle of pleading, that a plea must either traverse or confess and avoid the alleged cause of action.

It was not necessary, even before Reg. Gen. Hil. T. 4 W. 4, reg. 8, in a plea in abatement to lay *any venue* in stating even material facts, because they were to be tried in the county laid in the declaration (*s*); and if it were pleaded that another person who ought to have been sued with the defendant was alive, "to wit, in Spain," the place was surplusage, and the plea would be considered as pleaded without any venue (*t*).

Of pleading in abatement to part, and in bar to the residue.

A writ is divisible and may be abated *in part* and remain good as to the residue; and therefore the defendant may plead in abatement to part, and demur or plead in bar to the residue of the writ or bill. For the rule seems to be, that if the plaintiff in his action, brought either upon a general writ, such as debt, detinue, account, or the like, or on a certain and particular one, as assumpsit, trespass, case, &c., demand two or more things, and it appear from his own showing that he cannot have an action or better writ for one of them, the writ shall not abate in the whole, but stand for so much as is good: but if it appear upon his own showing that he has a cause of action for all the things demanded, but the writ is not proper for one of them, and that he might have another for it in a different form, then the whole writ shall abate (*u*). It is said to be a rule, that if the plaintiff himself acknowledge his writ false in the whole or in part, the *whole* writ shall abate (*x*). But where the plaintiff declared in trespass for injuring a ship, and even showed in his declaration that he was only a part owner, it was held that as the nonjoinder in tort is only a ground for a plea in abatement, the defendant could not in any other shape impugn the declaration, though the defect appeared on the face if it (*y*). And *à fortiori* where the nonjoinder of a party or other matter, even if pleaded in abatement, could not abate the writ, it cannot have that *effect from the mere circumstance of its being disclosed in the declaration; and therefore the position in a book of high authority (*z*), that "if in *trespass* against A. only, the plaintiff declare that the defendant, *together with* B., committed the trespass, the writ shall abate; for by his own showing he has falsified his writ," appears to have been very properly disputed (*a*). Formerly it was the practice to plead in abatement, when upon the face of the plaintiff's declaration it appeared that a part of the plaintiff's cause of action was not well founded, but now it is most usual to demur to the whole declaration if there [*493]

(*q*) Com. Dig. Abatement, I 6. *Aliter*, it seems, where husband and wife are defendants, *id.* Pleader, 2 A. 3; Cro. Jac. 239.

(*r*) Com. Dig. Abatement, I 7.

(*s*) 7 T. R. 243; 1 Saund. 8 a; Bac. Ab. Abatement P.

(*t*) *Id.*

(*u*) 2 Saund. 209 e, and 210, n. 1.

(*x*) *Id.* 210 a, note; 396, n. 1.

(*y*) 6 T. R. 766; 2 Saund. 396, n. 1.

(*z*) 2 Saund. 210 c.

(*a*) *Id.* n. k, 5th ed.

(836) { Nor can a defendant plead in bar the same matter which he has previously pleaded in abatement, and which has been overruled. Coxe *v.* Higbee, 5 Halst. Rep. 395. }

FORM AND QUALITIES. be a misjoinder, or if there be no misjoinder then only to the defective part (*b*). Where the matter goes only to defeat a *part* of the plaintiff's cause of action the plea in abatement should be confined to that part, and if the defendant were to plead to the whole his plea would be defective (*c*). So where there are several defendants in an action of tort, and one of the defendants pleaded a misnomer, which then abated the action as to himself only, the plea was holden defective on general demurrer, if it concluded by praying judgment of the writ (or bill) generally, instead of praying judgment that it might be quashed as against himself only (*d*). Where a declaration in debt contained two counts, and to the first the defendant pleaded *non est factum*, and to the second he pleaded in abatement the nonjoinder of another person, and his plea commenced and concluded with praying judgment "of the said writ," (not stating as it regarded the *second* count,) "and of the said declaration as to the second count thereof," the Court held the plea was good, and that they might abridge the petition of the plea by quashing the writ as well as the declaration as to the matter in the second count (*e*).

6thly. The *conclusion* of pleas in *abatement* as respects verification and prayer of judgment. The general rule which prevails in pleading *in bar*, is, that a mere prayer of judgment, without pointing out *what* judgment, or the appropriate judgment, is sufficient; because the facts being shown, the Court will of course pronounce the proper judgment (*f*). Upon this principle it has been held that if a plea which contains matter in *bar* of an action conclude in **abatement*, it is a plea in bar notwithstanding the wrong conclusion, and final judgment should be given upon it, for if the plaintiff have no cause of action he can have no writ (*g*). The same rule applies, if in a plea containing matter in bar there be a right prayer of judgment in the conclusion, although the commencement be improper (*h*). On the other hand, the commencement and conclusion so far give the character of the plea, that if a plea commencing and concluding in abatement show matter in bar, it is to be considered a plea in abatement and not in bar (*i*); and the converse to this, *viz.* a plea containing matter sufficient only to abate the writ, but with the beginning and conclusion of the plea in bar, has been decided the same way (*k*). The anxiety of the Courts to discourage dilatory pleas probably first induced them to depart in construing *such* pleas, from the relaxed rule which applies to pleas in bar, in respect of the prayer of judgment (*l*); and if a plea which contains

[*494]

(*b*) See the cases, 2 Saund. 210, in notes; 1 M. & Sel. 355, 360; *ante*, 236.

(*c*) 5 T. R. 557.

(*d*) 1 M. & P. 26.

(*e*) 2 B. & P. 420; 2 Saund. 210 b, c, note; *sed quære*, see 1 Harr. & Woll. 426; and *vide post*, 494.

(*f*) 4 East, 502, 509; 10 *Id.* 87; 1 Saund. 97, n. 1; see 3 T. R. 186; 1 B. & Ald. 172; 1 M. & P. 26.

(*g*) 2 Saund. 209 c, note.

(*h*) Fortes. 335; Steph. 2d ed. 446.

(*i*) Ld. Raym. 593; 2 Saund. 209 c, note.

(*k*) Godson *v.* Good, 6 Taunt. 587; 2 Marsh. 299, S. C. This was an action against an administratrix on a contract entered into by the intestate; the plea began and concluded in abatement: the substance of it *was in bar*, *viz.* that the intestate made the contract with others, against whom the action survived. The plaintiff took issue on this; and at the trial it appeared that the contract was in fact joint, but that others besides *those named in the plea* joined in it and were alive. If then the plea was to be considered as one in abatement, such proof was an answer to it, *because the plea failed to give the plaintiff a better writ*, and as the Court held the plea to be a plea in abatement, the defendant failed in his defence.

(*l*) 10 East, 87; 1 B. & Ald. 172.

matter in *abatement* conclude in *bar*, and be found against the defendant, it is a plea in bar (837), and final judgment shall be given upon it, because by praying judgment if the plaintiff shall *maintain his action*, the defendant admits the *writ* to be good (*m*). So a plea which *begins* in *bar*, though it contain matter in *abatement*, and *conclude* in abatement, is nevertheless considered to be a plea in bar, and final judgment shall be given (*n*)(838). FORM AND QUALITIES.

Pleas to the jurisdiction, and of personal privilege to be sued in another Court, usually *commence* without any prayer of judgment, and *conclude*, "and this he the plaintiff is ready to verify; wherefore he prays judgment if the said *Court of our said lord the king here will or ought to take cognizance of the said plea," or "whether he ought to be compelled to answer;" (*o*) but sometimes these pleas commence also with a similar prayer (*p*). [*495]

In pleading to the *person* of the plaintiff or defendant, in respect of *disability* to sue or be sued, and not merely on account of the nonjoinder of another party, the plea should *conclude* with a prayer, "if the plaintiff ought to be answered," or "whether the defendant ought to be compelled to answer (*q*);" and these pleas frequently begin with a similar prayer, as alien enemy, &c. (*r*); and a plea of this description concluding merely to the writ would be bad (*s*); but pleas in abatement of coverture of the plaintiff or defendant, as the objection goes rather to the nonjoinder of the husband than to the disability of the feme, conclude with a prayer of judgment as to the writ (*t*). If the defendant plead that the plaintiff is excommunicated, or any other *temporary* disability, the plea should conclude with praying that the suit may remain without day, until, &c. (*u*); and where the death of the plaintiff since the issuing of the writ is pleaded, it should conclude if the Court will *further* proceed, &c. (*x*).

Where the defendant pleads in abatement to the *writ* for matter *apparent* on the face of it, it is said that he should begin as well as conclude his plea, by "*praying judgment of the writ, and that the same may be quashed.*" (*y*) But where the plea is for matter *dehors*, as misnomer when that matter was plead-

(*m*) 1 East, 636; 2 Saund. 209 d; 2 Ld. Raym. 1018, 1019, 694; 2 Marsh. 303; 6 Taunt. 587, S. C.

(*n*) 2 Saund. 209 c, note; Bac. Ab. Abatement, P.; 1 Lord Raym. 694; 10 East, 87, 88.

(*o*) 2 Saund. 209 d; Com. Dig. Abatement, I. 12; Bac. Ab. Abatement, P.; 12 East, 544; *ante*, 480.

(*p*) See the precedent, 8 T. R. 631.

(*q*) 2 Saund. 9, n. 10; 209 d; Latch. 178; Lil. Ent. 1.

(*r*) Lil. Ent. 1; Lutw. 1601; Ast. Ent. 11.

(*s*) Com. Dig. Abatement, I. 12.

(*t*) *Post*, vol. iii.; Lil. Ent. 1, 123; Ast. Ent. 9; 3 Inst. Cl. 70; 1 Wentw. 47.

(*u*) 12 Mod. 400; 3 Lev. 208; Lutw. 19; 1 Str. 521; 3 Inst. Cl. 18; 2 Saund. 209 e, note. See 10 East, 86.

(*x*) Com. Dig. Abatement, I. 12; 3 Lev. 120; 4 East, 502; 2 Saund. 209 e, note.

(*y*) 2 Saund. 209 a, d, note 1; Com. Dig. Abatement, I. 12; Lutw. 11.

---

(837) Vide Jenkins *v.* Pepoon, 2 Johns. Cas. 312. Executors of Schoonmaker *v.* Elmendorf, 10 Johns. Rep. 49.

(838) { M'Laughlin *v.* De Young, 3 Gill & Johns. Rep. 4. } But if matter which ought to be pleaded in abatement be pleaded in the form of a bar, the plaintiff may treat it as a plea in abatement, by proceeding to judgment for want of a plea, if it be not verified by affidavit. Robinson and Hartshorne *v.* Fisher, 3 Caines' Rep. 99, 100. { See also Engle *v.* Nelson, 1 Penn. Rep. 442 } And if there has been an order for the defendant to plead issuably, such plea is not a compliance with the order, and the plaintiff may treat it as a nullity. Davis *v.* Grainger, 3 Johns Rep. 259. The plaintiff may demur to the plea either in bar or abatement. A plea in abatement cannot be amended. Trinder *v.* Durant, 5 Wend. R. 72.

FORM AND QUALITIES.

able, the plea should only conclude with that prayer (z). The Courts having now established a rule that oyer of the writ cannot be allowed, *a variance between the writ and count, or declaration, can be no longer pleaded* (a), and many of the decisions in the books as to the form of the plea are no longer [*496] *applicable; and now in general a plea in abatement of the writ must be pleaded of the writ *and declaration*, when the latter *continues* and discloses the *objection* to the writ, and it must be so where it is intended to plead in abatement only of *part* of the writ, and the cause of abatement arises only on *one* of the counts in the declaration (b). If the action were by *bill*, the plea must have concluded by praying judgment of the bill, and not of the declaration only, which was only a conclusion in bar (c); and it should not have concluded by praying judgment of the "bill and declaration," (d) and if a plea in abatement to the *writ* were to conclude, "if the defendant ought to answer to the said *bill*," it would be insufficient (e)(839).

Great accuracy is necessary in the form of all pleas in abatement as well in the *commencement* as in the *conclusion*, for it is said "*they make the plea.*" (f) A plea which concluded with praying judgment "if" (instead of "of"), the plaintiff's bill was held bad on demurrer, though the words "and that the same may be quashed," were also added (g). So, in the traverse at the end of the plea, a mis-statement of the name by which the defendant was called in the declaration was considered fatal on demurrer (h). The mode of concluding the plea when pleaded to *part* only of the action, has been already observed upon (i). Upon a plea in abatement of pendency of another action in another Court for the same cause, *concluding* with *a prout patet per recordum*, it is sufficient to satisfy the plea if writ be produced (k).

7thly. Of the affidavit of the truth.

At common law, when the defendant pleaded a *foreign* plea, (the nature of which has already been stated) (l), he was obliged to make oath of the truth of the matter therein alleged, but that was not necessary in the case of a plea to the *jurisdiction*, or any plea in *abatement* (m). But by 4 & 5 Ann. c. 16, s. 11 (840), "*no dilatory* plea shall be received in any Court of *record*, unless the party offering such plea do by affidavit prove the truth thereof, *or show some probable matter to the Court* (n), to induce them to believe that the fact of such dilatory plea is true." This statute extends to criminal as well as civil cases (o); and not only to pleas in abatement, but to *all dilatory*

(z) *Id.*; 10 East, 87.
(a) *Ante*, 485, 486.
(b) 2 Saund. 210 b, c, note.
(c) 2 Saund. 209 d; 1 B. & Ald. 172; 2 M. & Sel. 484; 2 Chit. Rep. 539.
(d) *Id.*; 5 Mod. 144; 2 B. & P. 124, note e; 3 T. R. 185. See, however, Com. Dig. Abatement, I. 12.
(e) See the preceding note; 2 Saund. 209 d; 3 Bla. Com. 303; 10 East, 87.
(f) Latch. 178; 2 Saund. 209 c, d; 2 Ld. Raym. 1019; 10 East, 87; But see the entries referred to in 3 T. R. 186.
(g) 3 T. R. 185; and see 2 Saund. 209 a; 8 T. R. 515; 5 Taunt. 652, 653, note.
(h) 1 Chit. Rep. 705, note.
(i) *Ante*, 492, 493.
(k) Kerby *v.* Siggers, 2 Dowl. 659.
(l) *Ante*, 477; 1 Saund. 98, note 1.
(m) 1 Saund. 98, n. 1; Carth. 402; Sty. 435; 5 Mod. 335.
(n) In case of a plea of bankruptcy *puis darrein continuance*, see 1 M'Clel. & Y. 350.
(o) 3 Burr. 1617.

(839) Vide Isley et al. *v.* Stubbs, 5 Mass. Rep. 280.
(840) { The first thirteen sections and the twentieth and twenty-seventh sections are in force in Pennsylvania, 3 Binn. 625. Roberts' Dig. 43. } Vide Laws of N. Y. sess. 36, c. 56, s. 23. 1 R. L. 524. { 2 Rev. Stat. 352, s. 7. }

AFFIDAVIT OF TRUTH.

*pleas, which, if found untrue, would not determine the action, and are only in delay of it, as aid prayer in a real action (*p*); or a plea in *scire facias* against terre-tenants, that there is another terre-tenant not named; though these pleas are not strictly in abatement (*q*). But such pleas in bar as are usually termed sham pleas, are not dilatory pleas within the meaning of this statute. The statute extends only to such matters as are *dehors* the record, and not to such matters as would appear to the Court on inspection of their own proceedings (*r*), as the want of addition in an original writ, when the matter was pleadable in abatement (*s*); or privilege as an attorney of the *same Court* to be sued by bill (*t*); because in the first instance the defect in the writ was apparent on the face of it; and in the latter, the Court, by examination of their own record, might ascertain the truth of the plea: but where the defendant pleaded after *oyer* of the original that it was not returned, the Court set aside the plea for want of an affidavit (*u*). And where to an action in C. P. the defendant pleaded his privilege as an attorney of K. B. to be sued *there* without making an affidavit of the truth, it was recently held that the plaintiff might sign judgment, because the Court of C. P. could not by examination of their own records know that the defendant was an attorney of another Court (*x*).

Requisites of affidavits.

The *affidavit* required by 4 & 5 Ann. c. 16, s. 11, may be made by the defendant or a *third person* (*y*); and although formerly supposed otherwise (*z*), it has recently been held that it must be sworn after the declaration is delivered, and that if it be sworn *before* the declaration was delivered the plaintiff may treat the plea as a nullity and sign judgment (*a*). It must be properly and exactly entitled in the cause (*b*), and be positive (841) as to the truth of every fact contained in the plea, and should leave nothing to be collected by inference (*c*): it should be stated that the plea is true "in substance and fact," and not merely that the plea is a true plea (*d*); and if there be no affidavit, or it be defective in any particular, the plaintiff may treat the plea as a nullity and sign judgment (*e*), or move the Court to set it aside (*f*)(842).

(*p*) 3 B. & P. 384; 2 Saund. 210.

(*q*) 2 Saund. 210 d, e.

(*r*) 3 B. & P. 397; Pr. Reg. 5; Lord Raym. 1409; Say. Rep. 203.

(*s*) Lord Raym. 1409; Prac. Reg. 5.

(*t*) *Claridge, gent. one, &c. ats. Macdougal*, Trinity Term, 47 Geo. 3, K. B. 3 B. & P. 397. But see 2 Stra. 733, and Com. Dig. Abatement, D. 6. If the plea be untrue, or the defendant has ceased to be an attorney, the plea may be set aside, Prac. Reg. 8.

(*u*) 1 Stra. 639; 2 Ld. Raym. 1409.

(*x*) Davidson *v.* Chilman, 1 Bing. N. C. 297.

(*y*) 1 Barnes, 344; Pr. Reg. 6.

(*z*) 4 East, 346; 4 M. & Sel. 332; 13 East, 170.

(*a*) Bower *v.* Kemp, 1 Cromp. & Jarvis, 287.

(*b*) Bac. Ab. Abatement, O.; 2 Stra. 1161; Barnes, 348.

(*c*) Say. Rep. 293.

(*d*) 2 Stra. 705.

(*e*) 2 Saund. 210 d; 1 T. R. 277, 689; 5 *Id.* 210; 7 *Id.* 298; 2 Moore, 213. The plaintiff cannot sign judgment after a plea in abatement, because the affidavit to verify the plea was sworn before the *defendant's attorney*, 3 M. & Sel. 154.

(*f*) 1 Stra. 638; Say. Rep. 19, 293; 3 Burr. 1617; Tidd, 9th ed. 640; *sed quære*, see 2 Moore, 213; 2 B. & C. 618.

(841) Day *v.* Hamburgh, 1 P. A. Browne's Rep. 75.

(842) Richmond *v.* Talmadge, 16 Johns. Rep. 307. Vide Robinson and Hartshorne *v.* Fisher, 3 Caines' Rep. 99.

*REPLICATION AND OTHER PROCEEDINGS ON A PLEA IN ABATEMENT IN GENERAL.

REPLICATION AND OTHER PROCEEDINGS ON A PLEA IN ABATEMENT IN GENERAL.

Where *misnomer* either of the plaintiff or defendant was *truly* pleaded, the plaintiff might in general *amend* his declaration on payment of costs, or without subjecting himself to the payment of the defendant's costs he might enter a *cassetur billa* or *breve* (*g*). But where the *nonjoinder* of one of several co-contractors was pleaded, the plaintiff could not nor can amend, but must enter a *cassetur*, and commence a fresh action, in order that the other parties may in due course be brought by fresh process into Court. And when the plea is true, and the plaintiff is not at liberty to amend, he should enter his *cassetur* before he commence a fresh action, for otherwise the defendant may plead in abatement the pendency of the first action (*h*). If the plea be untrue in fact, the plaintiff should *reply;* or if it be insufficient in point of law, he may *demur*, and in some cases *sign judgment* as for want of a plea (*i*); though if the plea were merely defective in form, the plaintiff should demur (*k*). And where the defendant had appeared in the name by which he was sued, such appearance might have been replied by way of an *estoppel* (*l*). When the plea consists of matter of fact, which the plaintiff denies, the replication may begin without any allegation that the writ ought not to be quashed (*m*). It must not commence as to a plea in bar (*n*), because that would be a discontinuance, but should conclude to the country; and which was proper where to a plea of misnomer the plaintiff replied that the defendant was known as well by the one name as the other (*o*). There are, however, precedents in which the plaintiff concluded with a formal traverse and verification (*p*). It was laid down by Lord Holt, that if the plaintiff took issue upon a plea in abatement, he ought to pray damages, because if it were found against the
[*499] defendant, the jury must assess the plaintiff's damages, *and final judgment was to be given; but that where the plaintiff confessed the defendant's plea, and avoids it by other new matter, he should not pray damages, but must maintain his writ (*q*). If a replication to a plea in abatement of the *writ* begin "that the said declaration" ought not to be quashed, but conclude properly, it is sufficient; for such words may be rejected as surplusage; and it is not necessary in the *beginning* of the replication to say that the writ ought not to be quashed; for in favor of the plaintiff the Court would give judgment according to the fact, without reference to the prayer of the judgment (*r*). If an *issue in fact* be joined upon the replication, and found for the plaintiff, the

(*g*) 7 T. R. 698; 3 Anstr. 935; 1 B. & P. 40; *ante*, 281. It was the practice not to permit such amendment if the defendant has *previously* made a tender.

(*h*) *Ante*, 488; Bac. Ab. Abatement, M.

(*i*) 3 B. & P 395. If plea be no plea at all, party may move to quash it, 2 B. & C. 618; 4 D. & R. 114, S. C.

(*k*) 3 T. R. 185. The plaintiff cannot move to quash it, 4 D. & R. 114; 2 B. & C. 618, S. C

(*l*) 2 New Rep. 453; *ante*, 479, 480.

(*m*) 1 B. & P. 61.

(*n*) Carth. 187; Com. Dig. Abatement, I. 15; 1 B. & P. 61. *Aliter* if the plea commence or conclude improperly *in bar;* Bac. Ab. Abatement, 8; Com. Dig. Abatement, I. 15.

(*o*) 1 B. & P. 60; 1 East, 542; 2 Wils. 367.

(*p*) Lil. Ent. 1, 2; Co. Ent. 160.

(*q*) 1 Lord Raym. 338, 594; 2 *Id.* 1022; 2 Saund. 211 n. 3; Bac. Ab. Abatement, P.; Com. Dig. Abatement, I. 12; *post;* see the precedents. 1 Wentw. Index,

(*r*) 1 B. & P. 60.

jury should assess the damages, and the judgment is peremptory for the delay *quod recuperet*, and not *quod respondeat* (*s*); and the same rule prevails in indictments for misdemeanors, though in cases of felony in *favorem vitæ* it is otherwise (*t*)(843). ON A PLEA IN ABATEMENT IN GENERAL.

Of demurring to a plea in abatement.

If the plaintiff *demur* (*u*) it is *not necessary to assign any special causes*, for it has been decided on the statute of Elizabeth, (the language of which is similar to that of the statute 4 Ann. c. 16), that the statute only applies to pleas *in bar* (*v*); however it may be most advisable to demur specially where the plea is merely informal (*w*). Where the plea demurred to properly commences and concludes as in abatement, but is insufficient in some other respects, the demurrer should pray judgment that the writ may be adjudged good, and that the defendant may answer further thereto, or merely with the latter words, and should not conclude with a prayer of damages; for the plaintiff ought not to conclude in bar, but only affirm his writ (*x*). So, where the plaintiff *replies* to a plea in abatement, and the defendant demurs to the replication, the plaintiff should not conclude his joinder in demurrer with a prayer of judgment of his debt or damages, but should merely *pray that the defendant may answer over* (*y*). And where the plaintiff demurred to a *plea [*500] in abatement, as in bar, praying judgment and damages, and the defendant joined as in bar, it was held to be a discontinuance, because the demurrer in bar was no answer to the plea in abatement, and a discontinuance of part is a discontinuance of the whole (*z*); the plaintiff, however, may amend, and the mistake would be aided by a verdict (*a*). But where the plea in abatement improperly commences or concludes as a plea in bar, the plaintiff may demur either in bar or abatement; and if he adopt the former, which is most advisable, he may conclude his demurrer as in bar, and with a prayer of damages, and the judgment will be final (*b*). On the argument of a demurrer to a plea in abatement, or to a replication thereto, *the defendant cannot* (as usual on argument after a plea *in bar*) take any objection to the declaration, for nothing but the writ is then in question (*c*), unless where matter has been pleaded in abatement which might also be pleaded in bar (*d*), and the Court will not

(*s*) 1 East, 544; 2 Wils. 368; Com. Dig. Abatement, I. 14, 15; 2 Saund. 211, n. 3.

(*t*) 8 East, 107; 3 Bar. & Cres. 513 to 515; 5 D. & R 433, S. C.

(*u*) See the precedents referred to in 2 Saund. 210 e, note 2; *post*, vol. iii. and joinder thereto, *id.*

(*v*) 2 M & Sel 484, 485; 2 Ld. Raym. 1015; and see 1 Ld. Raym. 337; 1 Salk. 194; Tidd, 9th ed. 638; see Reg. Gen. Hil. Term, 4 W. 4, reg. 2, as to the *causes of demurrer being stated in the margin*, &c., *post*, Appendix.

(*w*) 3 T. R. 186.

(*x*) 2 Saund. 210 e, note.

(*y*) *Id.*; 1 Wils 302.

(*z*) Show. 255; 1 Salk. 218, S. C.; 1 East, 542; 2 Saund. 210 e, f, note.

(*a*) 1 Wils. 302; 1 Salk. 218.

(*b*) Bac. Ab. Abatement, P.; Com. Dig. Abatement, I. 15.

(*c*) Salk. 212; Lutw. 1592; Carth. 172; Willes, 478; Bac. Ab. Abatement, P.; Com. Dig. Abatement, I. 14; 1 Saund. 285, note e, 5th ed.

(*d*) Lutw. 1604; Com. Dig. Abatement, I. 14.

(843) Where an issue of *nul tiel* record on a plea in abatement is found for the plaintiff, the judgment is, *quod respondeat ouster*. Marston *v.* Lawrence and Dayton, 1 Johns. Cas. 397. And so where the trial is by inspection, judgment for the plaintiff is that defendant *respondeat ouster*. Amcots *v.* Amcots, 1 Lev. 163. Com. Dig. Abatement, (I. 14.) But where a defendant pleads in abatement, and the plaintiff takes issue upon the plea, and it is found against the defendant, the judgment is final, and the same jury which pass upon the issue assess the damages. M'Cartee *v.* Chambers, 6 Wend. R. 649.

REPLICATION AND OTHER PROCEEDINGS.

in general give leave to amend a plea in abatement (*e*). But a plaintiff has been allowed to withdraw his demurrer to a plea in abatement and to reply (*f*).

Judgment on pleas in abatement.

If the plaintiff succeed on an issue in *fact*, the judgment, as before observed (*g*), *is final*; but if he succeed on *demurrer* to a plea in abatement, or to a replication thereto, the judgment is in general only interlocutory, *quod respondeat ouster* (*h*). Where, however, a plea containing matter which can only be pleaded in abatement, improperly commences or concludes in bar, the judgment on demurrer *may* be final (*i*); and the same rule prevails where matter in abatement is pleaded after the last continuance (*k*), or since Reg. Gen. Hil. T. 4 W. 4, since the last pleading. After judgment of *respondeat* [*501] *ouster* no other plea in abatement *in the same *degree* (*l*) will be allowed (*m*). The judgment for the *defendant* on a plea in abatement, whether it be on an issue in fact or in law, is, that "the writ be quashed;" (*n*) or if a *temporary* disability or privilege be pleaded, that "the plaint remain without day, *until*, &c." (*o*).

Costs on pleas in abatement.

If the plaintiff succeed on *demurrer* to a plea in abatement, and the judgment be interlocutory, *respondeat ouster*, there is no judgment for *costs*, because the statute of *Gloucester* only gives costs where *damages* are recovered (*p*); but when the defendant's plea is on *issue* found to be untrue, the judgment is final, and the plaintiff will recover costs (*q*). If the plaintiff enter a *cassetur billa* or *breve*, he is not liable to costs (*r*). On an issue found for the defendant he is entitled to costs, but not if he succeed on demurrer (*s*); nor is he entitled to the costs of a judgment of *non pros*, obtained by reason of the plaintiff having omitted to enter the issue on record, aftor issue joined on a demurrer to a plea in abatement (*t*)(844).

IV. OF PLEAS OF NONJOINDER IN PARTICULAR.

OF PLEAS OF NONJOINDER IN PARTICULAR.

Before the 3 & 4 W. 4, c. 42, s. 8, 9, 10, pleas in abatement of the nonjoinder, although in some cases just, in order to compel a plaintiff to sue all

(*e*) Cas. Pr. C. P. 29; Tidd, 9th ed. 638.

(*f*) 2 Chit. Rep. 5.

(*g*) *Ante*, 499; Tidd, 9th ed. 641

(*h*) 2 Saund. 211, note 3; Com. Dig. Abatement, I. 14; 1 East, 544; 2 Wils. 367; see the forms, Tidd's Appendix, 4th edit. 263; 10 Wentw. 61; Tidd, 9th edit. 641; *sed vide* 3 B. & C. 502; 5 D. & R. 422, S. C.

(*i*) 1 East, 636; Lutw. 41; Com. Dig. Abatement, I. 15; Bac. Ab. Abatement, P. As to the prayer of judgment in general, see 10 East, 37; *ante* 494.

(*k*) Com. Dig. Abatement, I. 15.

(*l*) See Tidd, 9th ed. 641; Com. Dig. Abatement, I. 4; *ante*, 474, 475.

(*m*) Bac. Ab. Abatement, O.; Com. Dig. Abatement, I. 3; 2 Saund. 40, 41.

(*n*) Bac Ab. Abatement, P.; Gilb. C. P. 52; 3 M. & Sel. 453. See the precedents, 10 Went. Index, 61.

(*o*) Lutw. 19; Clift. Ent. 3; 2 Saund. 209 e; Tidd, 9th ed. 642.

(*p*) Lord Raym. 992; 1 Salk. 194, S. C.; Tidd, 9th ed. 642; *id.* Appendix.

(*q*) *Id.*; 1 East, 544; 2 Wils. 368.

(*r*) *Id.*; Tidd, 9th edit. 683; Hullock, 145.

(*s*) Lord Raym. 337, 992; 1 Salk. 194, S. C.; Hullock, 145; Tidd, 9th ed. 642.

(*t*) 8 B. & C. 642; 3 M. & R. 91, S. C.

(844) { A party applying to amend a declaration after a special demurrer to it has been filed, must pay costs. Condit *v.* Neighbor, 7 Halst. Rep. 320. }

OF PLEAS OF NONJOINDER IN PARTICULAR.

persons liable to pay jointly, so as to make them liable on the record to pay their proportions of the debt or damages to be recovered, had become the source of vexatious delay, especially as each omitted party might in a second action plead in abatement that still another party who ought to be joined had been omitted, and so on (u); and if an omitted partner were abroad, or not to be found, a plaintiff could not declare against those forthcoming until he had *first* outlawed the absent party, and the delay as well as difficulties in proceeding to outlawry not unfrequently rendered that proceeding abortive. To put an end to these grievances, the 3 & 4 W. 4, c. 42, s. 8, enacted, "that no plea in abatement for the nonjoinder of any person as a co-defendant shall be allowed in any Court of common law, unless it shall be stated in such plea that such person is resident within the jurisdiction of the Court, and unless the place of residence of such person shall be stated with convenient certainty in an affidavit verifying such plea.

S. 9. "That to any plea in abatement in any Court of law of the nonjoinder of another person, the plaintiff may reply that such person has been discharged by bankruptcy and certificate, or under an act for the Relief of Insolvent Debtors.

S. 10. "That in all cases in which after such plea in abatement the plaintiff shall, without having proceeded to trial upon an issue thereon, commence another action against the defendant or defendants in the action in which such plea in abatement shall have been pleaded, and the person or persons named in such plea in abatement as joint contractors, if it shall appear by the pleadings in such subsequent action, or on the evidence at the trial thereof, that all the original defendants are liable, but that one or more of the persons named in such plea in abatement or any subsequent plea in abatement are not liable, as a contracting party or parties, the plaintiff shall nevertheless be entitled to judgment, or to a verdict and judgment, as the case may be, against the other defendant or defendants who shall appear to be liable; and every defendant who is not so liable shall have judgment, and shall be entitled to his costs as against the plaintiff, who shall be allowed the same as costs in the cause against the defendant or defendants who shall have so pleaded in abatement the nonjoinder of such person; provided that any such defendant who shall have so pleaded in abatement shall be at liberty on the trial to adduce evidence of the liability of the defendants named by him in such plea in abatement."

Since this enactment a plea in abatement of *nonjoinder* of a co-defendant must state not only that the omitted party *is still living*, but that *he is* resident within the jurisdiction of the Court, and the affidavit of its truth must state the place of residence with *convenient certainty*, and thus the plea and affidavit, according to the true principle of a plea in abatement, point out to the plaintiff an effectual better writ, and also enable the plaintiff in his second action, commenced in consequence of such plea, effectually to proceed against such defendants as he shall on the trial prove to have been liable. The forms of the thus regulated plea of nonjoinder and of the peculiar affidavit to be now annexed will be found in the third volume (x).

The ninth section we have above seen enables the plaintiff to reply to such

(u) See Govett v. Radnidge, 3 East, 62. (x) See *post*, vol. iii.

OF PLEAS OF NONJOINDER IN PARTICULAR.

a plea the bankruptcy and certificate of the omitted party, or his discharge under an insolvent act.

The Reg. Gen. Hil. T. 4 W. 4, reg, 20, gives the form of commencing a *declaration* in a second action after a plea of nonjoinder in abatement, and which form will be found in the second volume (y). The above sections it will be observed in terms only apply to pleas in abatement of *nonjoinder*, and it would seem that a plea by a feme defendant of her *coverture* and nonjoinder of her husband, though it prays an abatement of the present writ on account of such nonjoinder, is not affected by the statute either as to the *allegation* or affidavit of residence of the omitted party, although such plea of coverture seems to be equally within the mischief intended to be prevented.

The statute of limitations, 9 G. 4, c. 14, s. 2, enacts, that if any defendant or defendants in any action on any simple contract shall plead any matter in abatement, to the effect that any other person or persons ought to be jointly sued, and issue be joined on such plea, and it shall appear at the trial that the action could not by reason of the said recited acts or this act (i. e. the want of a written promise by the omitted party) or either of them be maintained against the other person or persons named in such plea, or any of them, the issue joined on such plea shall be found against the party pleading the same." So that where several parties have originally jointly contracted, but the statute of limitations has barred the remedy against some of them, but the other has signed a written promise or acknowledgment within six years, the action may be properly brought against him only; and if he plead the nonjoinder of the other parties so discharged from liability, the plaintiff may safely take issue on the plea, on the ground that the action was properly brought only against the single party *continuing* liable.

(y) See *post*, vol. ii.

*CHAPTER VII.

Of Pleas in Bar.

PLEAS in *bar* go to the *merits* of the case; and deny that the plaintiff has any cause of action (*a*), and do not, like pleas in abatement, give a better writ (*b*). They either conclude the plaintiff by matter of *estoppel*, (which however rarely occurs in a plea) (*c*), or they show that the plaintiff *never had* any cause of action; or admitting that he once had, insist that it has been determined by *some subsequent matter*. They are also either to the whole or to a part of the declaration; and where there is only a defence to a part it is advisable, on account of costs, to confine the plea to that part (*d*). OF PLEAS IN BAR.

We have seen that pleading is in general a mere statement of *facts* (*e*), and pleas in bar state the various *defences* of which, under the circumstances of each particular case, the defendant is at liberty to avail himself in a Court of *law*. Matter of defence *in equity only* (*f*), or founded solely on *the rules or practice* even of a Court of law, or being mere irregularity, is not in general pleadable (*g*)(845); thus bail cannot plead that the principal is a bankrupt, and that he has obtained his certificate (*h*); for although the Court might on *summary application* relieve the bail, yet the matter of defence constitutes no *pleadable* bar; and *bail* to the sheriff cannot *plead* the giving of time to their principal as a defence to an action on bail bond (*i*). But where the matter of defence depends not merely upon the *established practice* of the Court, but also upon *a general rule of law*, as that bail above shall not be proceeded against until a *capias ad satisfaciendum* has been issued against the principal, such matter *is pleadable (*k*). It would be in vain to attempt to state all the various defences in personal actions; those which most usually occur in practice are given in their natural order, in the following Analytical Table in the action of Assumpsit (*l*); and the mode in which they should be taken advantage of are afterwards more fully stated, and precedents of the appropriate pleas are collected in the Third Volume. At the commencement of each head of Pleas, whether in Debt, Covenant, Detinue, Case, Trover, Replevin, or Trespass, a similar analytical table has been given in the previous editions of this work, but omitted in the present edition in order to afford room for the great increase of new matter. What facts can or not be pleaded in bar. [*503]

(*a*) See the definition, Co. Lit. 503 b; Heath's Maxims, and 6 Co. 7; *ante*; Steph. 2d ed. 75.

(*b*) *Ante*, 481, 591.

(*c*) Bac. Ab. Pleas, I. 11; 5 Hen. 7, c. 14; 1 Leon. 77; Say. 86. As pleading matter of *estoppel* more frequently occurs in *replications* and subsequent proceedings, the points relating to it will be hereafter considered. It should be relied upon and *specially pleaded as such*, see 2 B. & Ald. 662; M'Clel. & Y. 509.

(*d*) 5 East, 261; 7 *Id.* 325. See pleas which were held bad, as they might have been pleaded in abatement, or the proceedings might have been set aside for irregularity, 5 Moore, 168; 1 B. & Ald. 390.

(*e*) *Ante*, 244.

(*f*) 7 East, 153; 8 *Id.* 344; 10 *Id.* 377. *Misconduct* of arbitrators not pleadable, 8 East, 344; 2 M. & P. 345; 5 Bing. 200, S. C.; see 1 Y. & J. 37.

(*g*) 2 East, 442; 7 *Id.* 153; 4 East, 311; 2 Campb. 396; 16 East, 39; 1 Wils. 334; 1 D. & R. 50; 7 B. & C. 800.

(*h*) 2 B. & P. 45; 7 East, 153, 154.

(*i*) 8 Price, 467; 1 Young & Jerv. 437; and see Davey *v.* Prendergrass, 5 B. & Ald. 187.

(*k*) 16 East, 39; but see 7 B. & C. 800.

(*l*) See also Com. Dig. Pleader as to the different defences and pleas in each particular action.

(845) Nichols *v.* Nichols, 9 Wend. R. 264. 10 Pet. S. C. 257.

*ANALYTICAL TABLE

OF THE DEFENCES TO ACTIONS ON CONTRACTS NOT UNDER SEAL.

- 1st. Deny that there ever was cause of action.
  - 1st. Deny that a sufficient contract was ever made.
    - 1st. That no contract was in fact made.
    - 2dly. Incompetency of plaintiff to be contracted with. Plaintiff an alien enemy at time of contract.
    - 3dly. Defendant incapable to contract.
      - 1st. Infancy.
      - 2dly. Lunacy, Drunkenness, &c.
      - 3dly. Coverture.
      - 4thly. Duress.
    - 4thly. Insufficiency of consideration.
      - 1st. Inadequacy of consideration.
      - 2d. Illegality of consideration.
        - 1st. At common law.
        - 2d. By different statutes.
    - 5thly. Contract obtained by *fraud*.
    - 6thly. The act to be done illegal or impossible.
    - 7thly. The form of contract insufficient.
      - 1st. At common law.
      - 2d. By statute. As statute against frauds.
    - 8thly. No sufficient stamp.
  - 2dly. Admit a sufficient contract, but show that *before breach* there was—
    - 1st. A release.
    - 2dly. Parol discharge.
    - 3dly. Alteration in terms of contract by consent.
    - 4thly. Non-performance by plaintiff of a condition precedent, alteration, &c.
    - 5thly. Performance, payment, &c.
    - 6thly. Contract become illegal or impossible to perform.
- 2dly. Admit that there *was* cause of action, but avoid it by showing subsequent or other matter.
  - 1st. Plaintiff no longer entitled to sue.
    - 1st. Alien enemy.
    - 2dly. Attainted.
    - 3dly. Outlaw.
    - 4thly. A bankrupt, insolvent debtor, &c.
  - 2dly. Defendant no longer liable to be sued.
    - 1st. A certificated bankrupt.
    - 2dly. An insolvent debtor.
  - 3dly. Debt recoverable only in a Court of conscience.
  - 4thly. Cause of action discharged.
    - 1st. By payment.
    - 2dly. Accord and satisfaction.
    - 3dly. Foreign attachment.
    - 4thly. Tender.
    - 5thly. Account stated, and a negotiable security taken by plaintiff.
    - 6thly. Arbitrament.
    - 7thly. Former recovery.
    - 8thly. Higher security given.
    - 9thly. A release.
    - 10thly. Statute of limitations.
    - 11thly. Set-off.
  - 5thly. Pleas by executors, &c.

GENERAL OBSERVATIONS.

Observations on such analytical tables.

*From these subdivisions, which are nearly the same in each form of action, we may perceive that pleas in bar, as well in actions on contracts as for torts, are of two descriptions; first, they *deny* that the plaintiff *ever* had the cause of action complained of; or, secondly, they *admit* that he *once had* a cause of action, but insist that it *no longer subsists*.

The former indiscriminate use of a *general* plea as non-assumpsit.

In the *ancient course* of pleading there appear to have been three descriptions of pleas in bar, by one of which the above defences were to be taken advantage of,—1st, The general issue.—2dly, A denial of a *particular* allegation in the declaration.—And, 3dly, A special plea of *new matter not apparent* on the face of the declaration. *General issues*, it is said, were framed in words calculated to deny the *whole of the facts* alleged in the declaration (*a*), and were considered proper and indeed necessary when the defence merely denied the plaintiff's allegations, and referred the matter in dispute to the *jury*, the proper judges whether or not the *fact* complained of was committed (*b*). In *Assumpsit*, before the pleading rules, Hil. T. 4 W. 4, almost every matter *might* be given in evidence under the general issue non-assumpsit, on the ground, as was said, that as the action is founded on the contract, and the *injury* is the *non-performance* of it, evidence which disaffirms the *continuing obligation* of the contract *at the time when the action was commenced*, goes to the gist of the action (*c*). In *Debt* on simple contract also, under the plea of *nil debet*, the defendant was at liberty to prove most matters which showed that there was no *existing debt* (*d*); but in debt or covenant founded on a *deed*, on account of the solemnity of the instrument under seal (*e*), and which in general must be dissolved *eo ligamine quo ligatur*, the plea of *non est factum* merely put in issue the existence of the deed, and the defendant was not at liberty to plead *nil debet*, unless where the deed was mere inducement to the action, and the debt accrued by subsequent enjoyment, &c. (*f*). In *Case* or *Trover*, under the *general issue*, "*not *guilty of the premises*," almost any [*509] matter of defence might be given in evidence; though any plea admitting the plaintiff's property and the act committed, but justifying it, *might* be pleaded (*g*). In *Replevin*, the general issue *non cepit modo et formâ*, merely put in issue the act complained of as stated in the declaration. In *Trespass*, whether to the person, personal property, or real property, the general issue was *not guilty* (*h*). In injuries to the *absolute* rights of persons, this only put in issue the act complained of; but in injuries to the *relative* rights, and to personal and real property, it put in issue the existence of the *right*, as well as the *commission* of the act complained of, though in the two latter cases possession would be sufficient against the defendant, unless he could show a better title.

Of pleas of *partial denial*.

Formerly however it was not unusual, even in actions of assumpsit, for the defendant to deny a *particular allegation in the declaration*, instead of pleading the general issue, which denied the whole (*i*); and it is said that this was

(*a*) Gilb. C. P. 57, 63, 64.
(*b*) *Id.* 63.
(*c*) *Id.* 65; Salk. 279; 2 Str. 733; 1 B. & P. 481; 4 Taunt. 165; *sed vide post.*
(*d*) Gilb. C. P. 58.
(*e*) Plowd. 308.
(*f*) Gilb. C. P. 57, 58, 61, 62.
(*g*) *Id.* 64, 65.
(*h*) *Id.* 57.
(*i*) Gilb. C. P. 60, 61; Doct. Plac. 203.

GENERAL OBSERVATIONS.

permitted, in order to bring a *single* point to issue, and that if the jury gave a corrupt verdict they might be more easily attainted, which was not so readily done on a *general issue*, where the matter was more complicated (*k*). Thus, in assumpsit it was usual to traverse in particular the *consideration* of the contract, &c. or the contract itself, or the *plaintiff's performance* of a condition precedent, &c. but *in assumpsit* this practice had long before the recent pleading rules become obsolete. In debt for rent due by deed, the defendant might plead *non est factum*, or nothing in arrear; or if not by deed, *non dimisit*, or nothing in arrear; though those matters might have been given in evidence under the plea of *nil debet* (*l*).

What matters of defence allowed to be pleaded specially.

From the history of our ancient law, it appears that in all personal actions, the defendant was at *liberty* to show specially to the Court matters of defence, not merely consisting in a *denial* of a material part of the plaintiff's declaration, but introductory of *new matter not apparent therein* (*m*); such as coverture, infancy, &c. which, though they were in effect negations of the plaintiff's declaration, yet being matters of *law*, as to their sufficiency in defence, were considered as properly referable to the *Court* in the first instance (*n*) [*510] *though if traversed, the existence in *fact* of such defence was then properly to be tried by a jury (*o*).

So in general whatever ground of defence rendered the fact complained of *lawful*, being matter of *justification*, was to be shown to the Court, as a license, &c., because the Court are judges what is the law, and how far the fact, if it had occurred or existed, was lawful, and the jury were only to find the existence of the fact. Anciently the general issue was seldom pleaded, except when the party meant wholly to deny the charge alleged against him; and when he meant to distinguish away or palliate the charge, it was usual to set forth the particular facts in a special plea, which was originally intended to apprise the Court and the adverse party of the nature and circumstances of the defence, and to keep the law and the fact distinct. But the legislature in many cases have expressly permitted the general issue to be pleaded, and have allowed special matter to be given in evidence under it at the trial (846).

(*k*) Gilb. C. P. 61, 139, 148; 3 Leon. 66.
(*l*) *Id.* 61, 62.
(*m*) *Id.* 62, 66.
(*n*) *Id.* Lord Raym. 88.
(*o*) *Id.*

(846) In the state of New York, any special matter may be given in evidence under the general issue, if notice of the matter so intended to be given in evidence have accompanied the plea Sess. 36. c. 56. s. 1. 1 R L. 515. {2 Rev. Stat. 352. s. 10. See RULE 20, Sup. Ct, and Rule 23, Circt. Ct. of Pennsylvania.} But in covenant, in which there is no general issue, there can be no notice: {See, however, Bender v. Fromberger, 4 Dall. 439. Webster v. Warren, 2 Wash. C. C. Rep. 456. Whart. Dig. 141, for the practice in Pennsylvania;} and for the same reason, notice of special matter cannot be given in an action on a judgment or recognizance. Service v. Heermance, 1 Johns. Rep. 42. Bullis v. Giddons and Brown, 8 Johns. Rep. 83. Beadle v. Hopkins, 3 Caines' Rep. 150. Such notice forms no part of the record; an admission in it does not excuse the plaintiff from proving the matters charged in his declaration and it will not help a defect in the declaration; Vaughan v. Havens, 8 Johns. Rep. 109. See further Raymond v. Smith, 13 Johns. Rep. 329. Shepherd v. Merrill, 13 Johns. Rep. 475. Lawrence v. Kines, 10 Johns. Rep. 142. Kane v. Sanger, 14 Johns. Rep 89. 4 Pet. S. C. R. 411, where it was *held*, "every thing which disaffirms the contract, every thing which shows it to be void, may be given in evidence under the general issue in an action of assumpsit."

These were originally confined to certain *public officers*, such as *justices of the peace*, constables, overseers, custom-house and excise officers, who in fulfilling their arduous duties were frequently drawn into peril of liability to an action for mistake or informality in the *bona fide* execution of their respective offices. It was observed by Sir Wm. Blackstone, that though it should seem much confusion and uncertainty would follow from so great a relaxation of the strictness anciently observed, yet that experience had shown it to be otherwise, especially with the aid of a new trial, in case either party be unfairly surprised by the other (*p*). That supposition for a long time prevailed, but recently a different policy has prevailed, and which induced the Courts to promulgate the general rules of Hil. T. 4 W. 4. GENERAL OBSERVATIONS.

It may be most convenient to arrange the observations respecting Pleas in Bar under the following divisions: Division of the subject of pleas in bar.

I. Of the several Pleas in Bar in each Action, and when or not the Plea must be Special.

First.—*Before the recent Rules relating to Pleading.*

1. On Contracts.
   - In Assumpsit.
   - In Debt.
   - In Covenant.
   - In Account.
   - In Detinue.
   - In actions by and against executors.
   - In actions by and against heirs or devisees.
2. For Torts.
   - In Case.
   - In Trover.
   - In Replevin.
   - In Trespass.
3. In Ejectment.
4. When or not it *was* advisable to plead specially or only the general issue.
5. Estoppel.
6. All defences to be pleaded.
7. Of suffering judgment by default as to part.
8. Of sham and issuable pleas.
9. Instances where general issue given by statutes.

(*p*) 3 Bla. Com. 305, 306; Boote's Suit at Law, 93, 231; *sed vide* 1 East, 217; Lord Raym. 88, 217, 566; and see 12 Mod. 377; and see the observations on the use of a special plea as opposed to the general issue, 1 vol. Ld. Erskine's Speeches, 275 to 278; Sir Wm. Jones's Speeches of Issues, vol. iv. 4to edit. 94; vol. ix. 8vo. edit. 50; and *post*.

GENERAL OBSERVATIONS.

Secondly.—*Since the recent Statutes and Pleading Rules*, Hil. T. 4 W. 4, &c.

Statement of the enactments and rules and the alterations they have introduced.

II. The Qualities and Requisites of Pleas.
III. The Construction of Pleas.
IV. Of the Forms and Parts of Pleas in Bar.
V. Of several Pleas in Bar.
VI. Of Pleas by several Defendants.
VII. Of Set-off and Mutual Credit.

I. Of the several Pleas in Bar, and when or not to plead specially.

First.—*Before the recent Enactments and Rules relating to Pleading.*

First, Before the recent enactments and rules relating to pleading.

Before we proceed to consider the recent enactments, rules, and decisions which are *now* to be observed in practice, it seems essential to take a view of the previous regulations, and most of which have still extensive influence in practice.

In *Assumpsit.*

Before the recent pleading rules, the most comprehensive plea in an action of *Assumpsit* was *non-assumpsit*, (*i. e.* "that the defendant did not undertake or promise as alleged in the declaration,") and on that account was called the *general issue* although *improperly* so. When the allegations in the declaration, whether indebitatus assumpsit or special assumpsit, are considered, it will be obvious that a plea that the defendant did not undertake or promise, *naturally* and *in terms* only puts in issue the allegation of the *promise*, and not the allegation that the defendant *was indebted* in an *indebitatus count*, (unless, as has been insisted, the previous debt or consideration is parcel of the promise,) (*q*) nor is it any grammatical answer to the inducement, consideration, averments of performance, and a breach or breaches in a special count (*r*), except as to the statement of the *promise*, and yet in modern times, and until the Reg. Gen. Hil. T. 4 W. 4, came into operation in Easter term, 1834, the plea of non-assumpsit was considered not only as putting in issue every allegation in the declaration, as well the promise as the inducement, consideration, and all averments in fact, but also as enabling the defendant to give in evidence every description of defence which showed that the promise was void or voidable, or that it had been performed; so that very frequently the pleadings on the record entirely misled the plaintiff and the Court and jury as to the real point to be tried, and upon the trial the defendant might even show that he or she was *under age* or *covert* at the time of the contract. The inconvenience resulting from this illogical and uncertain state of pleadings led to the improvements introduced by the rules alluded to, and which will here-

(*q*) Passenger *v.* Brooks, 1 Bing. N. C. 587; 1 Hodges, 123.

(*r*) See the form of special count, *ante*, 293.

after be fully stated. But first it will be advisable to show the practice existing before those rules were promulgated. IN ASSUMPSIT.

I. Of the several Pleas.

First.—*Before the recent Rules.*

The *general issue* in an action of *Assumpsit* was "*that the defendant did not undertake or promise in manner and *form as the plaintiff hath complained against him, and of this the defendant puts himself upon the country, &c.*" (s), and if *nil debet* were pleaded, it might be treated as a nullity (t). The allegation "*modo et formâ*," did not put in issue the *form* of the count, but only the *substance* of the promise; for which reason the plaintiff might give in evidence a contract different from that mentioned in the declaration, in regard to *time* or *place when immaterial*, though not a contract different in substance (u). [*511]

Non-assumpsit when formerly requisite or sufficient.

It was always a rule, that when the defendant insisted that *no such contract* as that stated in the declaration had been *in fact* made, he *must* have pleaded the *general issue* (x). Under that plea also he might give in evidence various matters of defence, although they admitted that a contract had in fact been made, but denied that it was in *law* obligatory upon the defendant, as that another person ought to have been made co-plaintiff (y)(848): also the defendant's incapacity to contract; as that at the time the supposed contract was entered into, the defendant was an infant (z)(849), a lunatic (a)(850), or drunk (b)(851), or a *feme covert* (c). But coverture, which had taken place

(s) See the precedents, *post*, vol. iii.; Com. Dig. Pleader, 2 G. 1; 3 D. & R. 621. "*Not guilty*" is bad on demurrer, but would be aided by verdict; Stra. 1022; Cases temp. Hardw. 173; but cannot be treated as a nullity, 1 Dowl. 453 (847).

(t) *Nil debet* pleaded in assumpsit is a nullity, though it has been observed, "that it expressed the sense of the general issue in *assumpsit* better than *non-assumpsit*," *per* Mansfield, C. J., 4 Taunt. 165; see Tidd, 9th edit. 563, 476.

(u) Gilb. C. P. 51; Co. Lit. 282 b; Vin. Abr. *Modo et Forma;* 4 Taunt. 320; *per* Tindal, C. J., 6 Bing. 107; see *ante*, 325, 326, 333, as to variances.

(x) Com. Dig. Pleader, 2 G.

(y) *Ante*, 14.

(z) 1 B. & P. 481, note (a); 1 Salk. 279.

(a) 2 Stra. 1104; 3 Campb. 126; 2 Atk. 412; 2 Bl. Com. 292; 1 Fonbl. 46, 47, n. b; 49, n. 9, *&c.;* 1 Fonbl. 45 to 72; Co. Lit. 2 b, note 12; 247 a, b; Powell on Cont. 20, 23; Bac. Ab. Idiots, F. *contra*. But lunacy is not always a defence to an action upon a contract, see *ante*, 47.

(b) 3 Campb. 33; 1 Stark. 126; 2 Stra. 1104, note 1; Bul. N. P. 172; 3 P. W. 131; 1 Ves. sen. 19; Powell on Cont. 29, 30, *&c.;* Beawes Lex Merc. 6th edit. 554, cites Jenk. 1 Cent. 67, *contra*.

(c) 2 Stra. 1104, n. 1; Bul. Ni. Pri. 172; 12 Mod. 101; 3 Keb. 228.

---

(847) Cavene et al. v. M'Michael, 8 S. & R. 441. Ehrington v. Doshant, 1 Lev. 142.

(848) { Mitchell v. Dall, 2 Har. & Gill, 159. } Vide Baker v. Jewell, 6 Mass. Rep. 460. Converse v. Symmes, 10 Mass. Rep. 377. Or that the contract was made with one of the plaintiffs alone. Wilsford et al. v. Wood, 1 Esp. Rep. 178. Or that it was made by all the defendants against whom the action is brought. Tom v. Goodrich and others, 2 Johns. Rep. 213.

(849) Vide Wailing v. Toll, 9 Johns. Rep. 141. Stansbury v. Marks, 4 Dall. 130. Vasse v. Smith, 6 Cranch, 231. One co-defendant cannot give in evidence the infancy of the other, the plea of infancy being a personal privilege of which the party alone can avail himself. Van Bramer and others v. Cooper and another, 2 Johns. Rep. 279. But infancy of the plaintiff must be pleaded in abatement. Schermerhorn v. Jenkins, 7 Johns. Rep. 373.

(850) Vide 3 Day, 90, 100. Webster v. Woodford, in which it was held that a man might show that he was *non compos mentis* in avoidance of his deed. S. P. per Lord Mansfield, Chamberlain of London v. Evans, App. to Black. Com. Letters to Mr. J. Blackstone, Philadelphia, 1773, p. 149.

(851) But it seems that the intoxication must have arisen by the contrivance of the plaintiff. Johnson v. Medlicott, 3 P. Wms. 130. { See also, 4 Desaus. Cha. Rep. 364.

IN ASSUMPSIT. since the making of the contract always must have been pleaded in abatement (*d*). So under non-assumpsit the defendant might give in evidence that he was under duress (*e*): and the want of a sufficient (*f*) or a legal consideration for the contract, or illegality in the contract itself, might be given in evidence under this plea, as gaming (*g*), usury (*h*)(852), stockjobbing act (*i*), &c.; or that the plaintiff was an alien enemy at the time the contract was made (*k*); or that the contract was void by the statute against frauds (*l*). So a release or parol discharge before breach (*m*); or an alteration in the terms of the contract (*n*); or non-performance by the plaintiff of a condition precedent (853); or that the contract was performed by payment, &c. (*o*); or that it afterwards became illegal, or that it was impossible to perform it; might, when they constituted a sufficient defence, have been given in evidence [*512] under this *plea (*p*). The want of a proper stamp on a bill or other written instrument was a defence under the general issue, because the stamp acts not only render the document void, but also inadmissible in evidence (*q*)(854).

Those defences showed that the plaintiff *never* had any cause of action. Anciently matters in *discharge*, which admitted that *once there was cause of action*, must uniformly have been pleaded specially (*r*); afterwards a distinction was made between express and implied assumpsits: in the former these matters were required to be pleaded, but not in the latter (*s*); at length, however, they were allowed to be given in evidence under the general issue (*t*). Therefore, under the plea of non-assumpsit, the defendant might, before the new rules, give in evidence that the plaintiff was a bankrupt, when that cir-

(*d*) 3 T. R. 631; *ante*, 483

(*e*) 5 Co. 119; 1 Saund. 103 a.

(*f*) Want of consideration was certainly admissible under non assumpsit *before* the late rules, Passenger *v.* Brooks, 1 Hodges, 123; 1 Bing. N. C. 587.

(*g*) 1 Ld. Raym. 87; 1 Salk. 344; Carth. 356; 5 Mod. 170; 12 *Id.* 97; Com. Dig. Pleader, 2 G. 8.

(*h*) 1 Str. 498; Com. Dig. Pleader, 2 G. 7; Fortes. 336.

(*i*) 1 M. & P. 145.

(*k*) Dougl. 649, note 132; 6 T. R. 24; 4 East, 407, 410; 13 Ves. 72; 3 Campb. 152.

(*l*) 29 Car. 2, c. 3. As to *pleading* this, see *post*.

(*m*) Com. Dig. Pleader, 2 G. &c. and Action, Assumpsit, G.; 1 Campb. 249; 2 *Id.* 557; 3 Esp. R. 234.

(*n*) 8 T. R. 280.

(*o*) Lord Raym. 217, 566; 12 Mod. 376; 1 Salk. 394; Com. Dig. Pleader, 2 G. 10-15. When it should be pleaded specially, Holt, C. N. P. 6; 4 B. & Ald. 345.

(*p*) 8 T. R. 263; Co. Lit. 206 a; 1 Hen. Bla. 65.

(*q*) Bosanquet on Rules, 105.

(*r*) 1 Lord Raym. 566; 12 Mod. 376; Tidd, 9th ed. 647.

(*s*) Vin. Ab. Evidence, z, a; 1 Salk. 280; Gilb. C. P. 65.

(*t*) 1 Lord Raym. 217, 566; 12 Mod. 376.

(*u*) 7 T. R. 396; Bul. N. P. 153; Lawes on Assumpsit, 713. But in assumpsit by the provisional assignee of the bankrupt, it was held that the fact of the bankrupt's estate having been assigned by the plaintiff to new assignees between the time of issuing the *latitat* and delivery of the declaration, must be pleaded specially, 4 B. & Ald. 345; see *ante*, 26.

Arnold *v.* Hickman, 6 Munf. 15. Campbell *v.* Ketcham, 1 Bibb's Rep. 406. Curtis *v.* Bell, 1 South Rep. 361. Wigglesworth *v.* Steers, 1 Hen. & Munf. 70. Reynolds *v.* Waller's Heirs, 1 Wash. Rep. 164. Wade *v.* Colvert, 3 Rep. Const. Ct. S. Carolina, 27. King's Ex. *v.* Bryant's Ex., 2 Hayw. Rep. 394. Duncan *v.* M'Cullough, 4 Serg. & Rawle, 438.}

(852) {Vide Cuyler *v.* Robinson, 3 Day, 63. Levy *v.* Gadsby, 3 Cranch, 180. Bird and others *v.* Pierpont, 1 Johns. Rep. 124.

(853) The Manchester Iron Manufacturing Co. *v.* Sweeting, 10 Wend. R. 164. In that case it was *held*, that the neglect of the creditor to prosecute the principal upon the request of the surety may be given in evidence under the general issue.

(854) So, the defendant may show under the general issue that he offered to perform his part of the contract, but was prevented by the plaintiff. Will and Green *v.* Ogden, 13 Johns. Rep. 56.

cumstance would defeat his right of action (u); or where a *feme covert* suing alone had no interest in the contract, her coverture; but not that the plaintiff was *covert*, where she would have a right to join in the action, which in such case must always have been pleaded in abatement (v). IN ASSUMPSIT.

*So also payment, (x) (855), accord and satisfaction (y), a promissory note, or other negotiable security, given for the debt (856), and remaining in the hands of a third person, or otherwise outstanding (z), foreign attachment (a) (857), arbitrament (b), former recovery for the same cause (c) (858), a higher security given (d), and a release (e) (859), might have been given in evidence under the plea of *non assumpsit*, although there were also a special plea, in which the ground of defence might not have been correctly stated (860). [*513]

Hence it may be collected that under the general issue any matter which showed that the plaintiff *never* had cause of action, might be given in evidence; and also that under that plea most matters, even in *discharge* of the action, and which showed that at the time of the commencement of the suit the

(u) See note (u) preceding page.

(v) 4 T. R. 364; 3 T. R. 627; 3 Campb. 393, 394; *ante*, 483.

(x) 1 Lord Raym. 217; unless after action brought, Holt, C. N. P. 6; 5 B. & Ald. 886; 1 D. & R. 546, S. C.; and now *payment* must be plead specially, Fidgett *v.* Denny, 4 Tyr. 650, except that in *reduction of damages*, it may be proved under non-assumpsit, Shirly *v.* Jacob, 2 Bing. N. C. 88, but then the defendant must pay costs, Adlard *v.* Booth, 1 Bing. N. C. 693, and see *post*.

(y) 1 Lord Raym. 566; 12 Mod. 376; 5 East, 230; 4 Esp. C. N. P. 181; Bac. Ab. Accord; Com. Dig. Accord; Cooper *v.* Philips, 1 Cr. M. & Ros. 649; 10 Bar. & Cres. 329.

(z) 5 T. R. 513; Bul. Ni. Pri. 182.

(a) 1 Salk. 280, 291; 1 Saund. 67 a, note; 3 East, 367, 378; 2 Ves. jun. 106; Com. Dig. Attachment, A.; and Pleader, 2 G. 5; 5 Taunt. 558; see form, 2 Hen. Bla. 362.

(b) 1 Lord Raym. 122, 1039; Bac. Ab. Arbitrament, G. When a defence, 1 Y. & J. 19; Cald. on Arb. 223; 9 B. & C. 780; 4 M. & R. 571, S. C.

(c) 2 Stra. 733; 1 Saund. 92, note 2; 2 Bing. 377; 3 East, 345; 11 St. Tr. 261; 3 Wils. 304; *sed vide* 2 B. & Ald. 668. In Smith *v.* Wilton, Guildhall, 23d February, 1830, Lord Tenterden declared that under the plea of general issue, he never would receive evidence of a *judgment recovered* in an action of assumpsit, unless *actual payment or satisfaction* could also be shown. Campbell for plaintiff; Kelly for defendant. In the following term. however, on a new trial being moved for, his lordship disclaimed all recollection of his having so laid it down at Nisi Prius, but admitted that if he did, he was wrong. Where the defence is, that in a prior action the defendant had a verdict upon the merits in his favor, there should be a special plea, by way of *estoppel*, or the jury are not bound to consider the verdict conclusive in the second suit, 2 B. & Ald. 662; 2 Bing. 377; M'Clel. & Y. 509.

(d) 3 East, 258; Com. Dig. Pleader, 2 G. 12; *ante*, 117, 118.

(e) 1 Campb. 249; 2 *Id.* 557; 3 Esp. Rep. 234; Dougl. 106; Gilb. C. P. 64.

(855) Vide Brennan *v.* Egan, 4 Taunt. 165. Although the payments were made after the commencement of the suit if before trial. Bird *v.* Randall, 3 Burr. Rep. 1345. Baylies and another *v.* Fettyplace and another, 7 Mass. Rep. 325.

(856) The acceptance by a creditor of the note of a third person in full satisfaction of the amount due on a previous note given by the debtor will extinguish the original consideration; and such acceptance may be pleaded in bar of the original cause of action, Booth *v.* Smith, 3 Wend. R. 66. It would have been good also by way of accord and satisfaction. Boyd et al. *v.* Hitchcock, 20 Johns. Rep. 76. 6 Cranch, 253. A distinction is taken between the note of a *third person* and that of the debtor himself. Hughes *v.* Wheeler, 8 Cowen, 79.

(857) Vide Bird et al. *v.* Caritat, 2 Johns. Rep. 346.

(858) { Prescott *v.* Hall, 17 Johns. Rep. 284. Taylor *v.* Phelps, 1 Har. & Gill, 492. } 8 Wend. R. 1.

(859) { Offutt's Adm. *v.* Offutt, 2 Har. & Gill, 178. } Vide Young et al. *v.* Black, 7 Cranch, 565.

(860) Vide Brennan *v.* Egan, 4 Taunt. 165. { Dawson *v.* Pinsent et al., 4 Yeates, 249. }

IN ASSUMPSIT.

plaintiff had no subsisting cause of action, might be taken advantage of(861). As the true object of pleading always was to apprise the adverse party of the ground of defence, in order that he might be prepared to contest it, and might not be taken by surprise (*f*), it was singular that under the general issue, which in terms only denies a *promise*, the defendant should be permitted to avail himself of a ground of defence which admitted a valid promise, but insisted that it had been performed, or that there was an excuse for the non-performance, or that it had been discharged; it is, as observed by Lord Holt, a [*514] *practice which had crept in improperly, but was then perhaps too settled to be altered (*g*). It had been attempted to be justified on the ground that the gist of the action was the fraud of the defendant in not performing the contract, and that therefore whatever showed there was no fraud, was properly in issue under the plea of *non assumpsit;* but that reasoning does not appear to accord with the logical precision which usually prevails in pleading (*h*) (862). It is also at variance with the rule (which we shall hereafter consider,) that a matter of defence which *admits* the facts stated in the declaration, but *avoids* them, should be specially pleaded (*i*).

When to plead specially.

There were, however, some defences which, even before the recent rules, either *must* or *should* be pleaded specially. Thus, though we have seen that under the general issue it might formerly have been given in evidence that at the time the contract was made the plaintiff was an *alien enemy* (*k*); yet if the disability accrued by war after the contract was made, the same should be pleaded specially (*l*); and if a neutral become an enemy pending the suit, this should be pleaded in abatement, as it only *suspends* the action (*m*). So in assumpsit by the provisional assignee of the bankrupt, the fact of the bankrupt's estate having been assigned by the plaintiff to new assignees between the time of issuing the latitat and delivering the declaration, must be *pleaded* specially (*n*). So outlawry of the plaintiff must be pleaded in abatement, if

(*f*) *Ante*, 244.

(*g*) 12 Mod. 377; Ld. Raym. 217, 566; see Steph 2d edit. 196; and *post*.

(*h*) Gilb. C. P. 65; 3 Bla. Com. 305, 306; *ante* 508.

(*i*) Perhaps the relaxation which permits the general issue to be pleaded, where the defence is, that the contract *was not binding*, *or was invalid in its origin*, on account of the *defendant's incapacity to contract* or the *illegality* of the consideration or act to be done, is much less objectionable, as the substance or legal effect of such defence is, that there was *no valid contract*.

(*k*) *Ante*, 481; 13 Ves. 71, 72. And the Court would not allow a plea of alien enemy to be pleaded with any other plea, 12 East, 206; 1 B. & P. 222, note.

(*l*) 3 Campb. 152 to 154; 15 East, 260; 8 T. R. 166; 6 T. R. 24; 1 F. & P. 222; 2 *Id.* 72; 2 Bla. Rep. 1326; 4 East, 504, &c.

(*m*) 3 Campb 152, &c.

(*n*) 4 B. & Ald. 245; see *ante*, 26.

(861) {Hilt *v.* Bannister, 8 Cow. Rep. 33.} Vide Wilt and Green *v.* Ogden, 13 Johns Rep. 57 58 bird and others *v.* Pierpont, 1 Johns. Rep. 124. Young et al. *v.* Black, 7 Cranch, 567. {Sill *v.* Rood, 15 Johns. Rep. 230. and the Reporter's note. Heck *v.* Shener. 4 Serg. & Rawle, 249. Kennedy *v.* Ferris, 5 Serg. & Rawle, 394. Taft *v.* Inhabitants of Montague, 14 Mass. Rep. 282. Edson *v.* Weston, 7 Cow. Rep. 278.} Sir J. Mansfield observes, that "it is an extraordinary thing, that *nil debet* expresses the sum of the general issue in assumpsit, much better than *non assumpsit.* For upon *non assumpsit* may be given in evidence a release, or payment, or any thing that shows that there was no cause of action at the time of the action brought; although the form of the issue is, that the defendant did not undertake, whereas the truth may be that he has undertaken and has performed." Brennan *v.* Egan, 4 Taunt. 165. Manchester Iron Co. *v.* Sweeting, 10 Wend. R. 164.

(862) The maker of a note may give in evidence under the general issue proceedings under the *absconding debtor's* act. Clarke *v.* Yale, 12 Wend. R. 470.

the cause of action were not forfeited (*o*); and the defendant can avail himself of his discharge as a certificated bankrupt (*p*), or as an insolvent debtor (*q*), only by a special *plea. A bankrupt's certificate obtained at Newfoundland must also have been pleaded in bar (*r*). So neither a tender (*s*), nor the statute of limitations (*t*)(863), could be given in evidence under the general issue. With regard to a set-off, the mode of rendering that defence available will be fully detailed in a subsequent part of the work (*u*)(864). IN ASSUMPSIT. [*515]

With respect to defences under the Court of Conscience Acts, the mode of taking advantage of them depended on the particular enactment, some must be pleaded; others might either be pleaded, or given in evidence under the general issue; and others could only be taken advantage of by entering a suggestion on the roll, and which suggestion might be traversed or demurred to (*x*).

The defendant was, however, always at *liberty to plead any matter which did not amount to the general issue*, and admitted that *in fact* a contract was made, but insisted that it was void or voidable, either on account of the infancy, lunacy, or coverture of the defendant, or coverture of a third person, whose debt defendant undertook to pay (*y*), or his duress, or that the plaintiff was an alien enemy at the time the contract was made (*z*) or for *want of sufficient consideration*, or on account of *illegality* therein, or in the act to be done, as usury, gaming, &c.; or because the contract was void under the statute against frauds (*a*). So a release before breach (*b*), and performance (*c*), or payment (*d*)(865), might have been pleaded; though we have seen that all these matters *might*, before the recent rules, have been given in evidence under the general issue. So all matters in *discharge* of the action might have been pleaded specially. If the plaintiff's bankruptcy, which we have seen might formerly have been given in evidence under the general issue, be pleaded specially, all the circumstances showing the sufficiency of the proceedings

(*o*) Com. Dig. Pleader, 2 G. 4.

(*p*) 1 Campb. 363; 12 East, 664. See the forms, *post*, vol. iii.; 6 Geo. 4, c. 16, s. 126; *ante*, 60; 4 T. R. 156; 1 P. Wms. 258, 259; 10 Mod. 160, 247; 1 B. & P. 467; 3 *Id.* 171; 6 T. R. 496. When to plead bankruptcy of defendant specially, see 6 East, 413; 2 Smith R. 659, S. P.

(*q*) *Ante*, 63. See the forms, *post*, vol. iii.; where general issue suffices, 3 Moore, 234.

(*r*) 3 Moore, 244, 623; 1 B. & B. 13, 294, S. C.

(*s*) 1 Saund. 33.

(*t*) 1 Saund. 283, note 2; 2 *Id.* 63 b, c; Selw. N. P. Assumpsit, 6.

(*u*) *Post.*

(*x*) Tidd, 9th ed. 960; 3 T. R. 452.

(*y*) Maggs *v.* Ames, 4 Bing. 470; 1 Moore & P. 294, S. C.

(*z*) Dougl. 649.

(*a*) 1 Wils. 305; 4 B. & Ald. 595; 1 M. & P. 294, 303; 4 Bing. 470, S. C. Plea to an action against a surety that there was no undertaking in writing held good in House of Lords, 2 Dow. & Clark R. 21. The replication to a plea of statute against frauds must set forth the written signed contract, 1 Crom. & M. 289; *sed vide* 11 Price, 494.

(*b*) Com. Dig. Pleader, 2 G. 13, 14.

(*c*) Com. Dig. Pleader, 2 G. 15.

(*d*) 1 Salk. 394; Lord Raym. 787; Com. Dig. Pleader, 2 G. 10.

(863) Vide 1 Cranch, Appendix, 465.

(864) In the State of New York, notice of set-off may be given with the general issue in all cases. Sess. 36. c. 56 s. 1. 1 R. L. 515. 2 Rev. Stat. 352, s 15. And it has been said that a set-off could be taken advantage of there in no other manner. Caines *v.* Brisbane and others, 13 Johns. Rep. 23, 24. See Chamberlain *v.* Gorham, 20 Johns. Rep. 746.

(865) In a plea of payment it is sufficient to allege, that the defendant paid the plaintiff the several sums of money in the declaration mentioned, without stating that the plaintiff accepted the money in satisfaction. Chew *v.* Woolley, 7 Johns. Rep. 399.

IN ASSUMPSIT. under the bankruptcy must have been stated in the plea (e)(866). Accord and satisfaction (f), foreign attachment, *release (g), arbitrament (h), or that a negotiable or higher security was given for the debt, were seldom pleaded, except for the purpose of delay (i)(867); but it was usual to plead coverture; and advisable to plead infancy specially, because the plaintiff would thereby be compelled to reply only one of several answers which he might have to the defence, viz. either that the defendant was of age, or that the goods or work done were necessaries, or that he confirmed the contract when he came of age; on either of which the plaintiff at his election might rely at the trial in answer to the defence of infancy, if the general issue alone were pleaded. So it was often more advisable to plead a set-off than to give notice of it, for if pleaded, the plaintiff could not reply double, but must have relied on one answer alone; and in a country cause by pleading it, the trouble and expense of proving the service of the notice was avoided (k)(868). Indeed, the principal use of a special plea was, that it narrowed the evidence to be adduced on the trial (l).

IN DEBT. The action of DEBT, we have seen, might be maintained upon, 1st. *Simple Contracts* and *legal liabilities*; 2dly, *Specialties*; 3dly, *Records*; and 4thly, *Statutes*; and the pleas in such actions naturally are to be arranged in the same order.

1st. On simple contracts. In debt on *simple contract* or legal liabilities, or for an escape, &c. (m), the general issue, before the late rules, was in the *present tense nil debet*, "*that the defendant doth not owe the said sum* (n) *above demanded, or any part thereof, in manner and form as the plaintiff hath above complained against him*;" or

[*517] in the case of executors *or administrators "*doth not detain*;" and if *non assumpsit* were pleaded the plaintiff might sign judgment (o). The language of this plea puts in issue the existence of the debt at the time of pleading; and

(e) 1 Lord Raym. 217, 586; 12 Mod. 376; 1 B. & P. 449; 7 T. R. 396.

(f) 10 Bar. & Cres 329.

(g) Com. Dig. Pleader, 2 G. 14.

(h) Arbitrament, even without showing defendant's performance, is a good plea, where the parties had mutual remedies, Gascoigne v. Edwards, 1 Y. & J. 19; Allen v. Milner, 2 Tyr. 113.

(i) As to *sham* pleas, see the end of this chapter.

(k) But in a town cause, to save the expense of the rule to plead double, and the additional expense of the length of the paper-book, it was better to give a notice.

(l) 1 Ld. Erskine's Speeches, 275 to 278; Sir Wm. Jones's Speeches of Isaeus, vol. iv. quarto edit. 94; vol. ix. octavo edit. 50.

(m) 2 Salk. 565; 1 Saund. 38.

(n) Where to a declaration in debt for a named sum, as £500, and defendant pleaded to the whole he don't owe £100, omitting the words "above demanded," *semble*, plaintiff may sign judgment 3 B. & P. 174; or demur, 1 D & R. 473; 11 East, 62; but if he take issue, the Court would not order the defendant to amend his plea, 1 D. & R. 473; and *semble*, that where the words "*above demanded*" are introduced, the sum specified, if incorrect, may be rejected, *id. ibid.* At all events the plaintiff is not at liberty to sign judgment, *id. ibid.*; 1 M. & P. 276.

(o) 6 East, 549; 4 Taunt. 164; Bac. Ab. Pleas, 1.

(866) A surety may plead that the plaintiff being requested by the defendant to collect the money of the principal, neglected to do so, whereby the debt, as against the principal, was lost Pain v. Packard, 13 Johns. Rep. 174. { But see Cope v. Smith et al., 8 Serg. & Rawle, 110, and the cases cited in the note to Rees v. Berrington, 2 Ves jun. 540, Am. Edit. 1821. }

(867) { See Hughes v. Wheeler, 8 Cow. Rep. 77. }

(868) But a notice of set-off can only be given with the plea of the general issue. If there be any other plea besides the general issue, the set-off must be pleaded. Webber v. Venn, 2 Carr. & Payne, 300.

consequently any matter might be given in evidence under such plea, which showed that nothing was due at that time, as payment, or a release, or other matter in discharge of the debt (*p*)(869). It was even supposed that as the plea *nil debet* was in the present tense, the statute of limitations might be given in evidence under the plea (*q*)(870); but that doctrine was questionable, and the practice was to plead the statute in debt as well as in *assumpsit* (*r*); and a tender must have been pleaded specially, and a set-off must, as in assumpsit, be either pleaded or notice thereof given. Formerly wager of law might be pleaded (*s*), but it was abolished by 3 & 4 W. 4, c. 42, s. 13. In debt for use and occupation *nil habuit in tenementis* was not pleadable (*t*).

IN DEBT. 1st. On simple contracts.

In debt on a *specialty* it has been considered that there is a material distinction between those cases in which the deed is only *inducement* to the action, and *matter of fact is the foundation* of it; and those in which the deed itself is the foundation, and the fact merely inducement. In the former case, as in debt for rent due on an indenture of lease, though the plaintiff had declared setting out the indenture, yet as the fact of the subsequent occupation or holding gave the right to the sum demanded and was the foundation of the action, and the lease was mere inducement, the defendant might plead *nil debet* (*u*)(871). For the same reason that plea was sufficient in debt for an escape (*x*)(872), (except where the defence was a *recaption*) (*y*), or on a *devastavit* against an executor (*z*)(873): the judgment in these actions being merely inducement, and the escape or *devastavit* *the foundation of the action (*a*). The plea of [*518] *nil debet* in these cases, as in the instance of the general issue in *assumpsit*, put the plaintiff on proof of the whole of the allegations in the declaration (874); and under it the defendant might give in evidence an eviction (*b*), payment, or a release, or that the escape was occasioned by the plaintiff's fraud and contrivance, &c. (*c*). But in debt for rent on an indenture of *lease*, the declaration not showing the deed, the defendant could not, under the plea of *nil debet*, give in evidence that the plaintiff had *no estate* in the tenements; because,

2dly. On specialties.

(*p*) Com. Dig. Pleader, 2 W. 16; 1 Ld. Raym. 566, 394; 12 Mod. 376, *acc.*; Gilb. Debt, 434, 443, *semble contra*. Generally speaking the observations which we made on *non assumpsit*, *ante*, 513, equally apply to *nil debet*.

(*q*) 1 Salk. 278; 1 Ld. Raym. 153; 1 Saund. 283, note 2; Com. Dig. Pleader, 2 W. 16; 2 Saund. 63 a.

(*r*) 1 Saund. 283, note 2; 2 *Id.* 63, note 6; Peake Ev. 2d ed. 271. Mr. Justice Lawrence's opinion in 2 East, 336, has been considered as supporting the decision in 1 Lord Raym. 153; but note, his observation applied only to *penal* actions, in which the statute may be given in evidence under the general issue, 2 Saund. 63 b, c, note 6.

(*s*) *Ante*, 147.

(*t*) Curtis *v.* Spitty, 1 Bing. N. C. 15.

(*u*) Gilb. C. P. 62; Ld. Raym. 1500; 1 New Rep. 104; 1 Saund. 276, notes 1, 2; 202, 211; 2 *Id.* 297, n. 1.

(*x*) 2 Salk. 565; 1 Saund. 38, note 3.

(*y*) 8 & 9 Wm. 3, c. 27, s. 6; *post.*

(*z*) 1 Saund. 219; Carth. 2.

(*a*) 1 Saund. 219; Carth. 2; Com. Dig. Pleader, 2 W. 16; 2 Saund. 144. n. 2; 1 Saund. 218, n. 4; 219, n. 7.

(*b*) 1 Saund. 204, note 2.

(*c*) 1 M. & M. 169.

(869) Vide Lindo *v.* Gardner, 1 Cranch, 343. Id. Appendix, 465.

(870) Vide Davis *v.* Shoemaker, 135, semble acc. The statute of limitations is not a bar to an action of *debt* upon *award* under the hands and seals of arbitrators, although the submission be not under seal. Smith *v.* Lockwood, 7 Wend. 241.

(871) Vide Bullis *v.* Giddens, 8 Johns. Rep. 83.

(872) Vide Minton *v.* Woodworth and Ferris, 11 Johns. Rep. 474. Brown *v.* Littlefield, 7 Wend. R. 454.

(873) Vide Bullis *v.* Giddens, 8 Johns. Rep. 83.

(874) Jansen *v.* Ostrander, 1 Cowen's Rep. 670. Brown *v.* Littlefield, 7 Wend. R. 454.

IN DEBT. 2dly. On specialties. if he had pleaded that specially, the plaintiff might have replied the indenture and estopped him (*d*)(875). In debt for rent on a parol lease *non dimisit* might be pleaded (*e*), but not in debt for rent on an indenture, even by an assignee of the lease (*f*). And *rien in arrere* it was said was not a sufficient plea, without concluding *et issint nil debet* (*g*); and it was optional in the defendant either to *plead* an eviction, or to give it in evidence upon *nil debet*, though in covenant he must have pleaded it (*h*).

When the deed was the *foundation* of the action, although extrinsic facts are mixed with it, the defendant, if he deny his execution of the deed set forth in the declaration, should plead *non est factum*, and *nil debet* was not a sufficient plea (*i*) (876); as in debt for a penalty on articles of agreement (*k*), or on a bail bond (*l*), or on a bond setting out the condition and breach (*m*) (877). And if in those cases *nil debet* were pleaded, the plaintiff ought to demur (*n*), for if he did not, he would have to prove every allegation in his declaration, and the defendant would be at liberty to avail himself of any ground of defence which in general might be taken advantage of under [*519] the latter plea (*o*). A *party to a deed* who means to deny it must plead **non est factum*, and cannot in pleading deny its *operation* by averring that "he did not grant," "did not demise," &c., but a *stranger* to the deed need not plead *non est factum*, but may deny the effect (*p*), as by pleading *non feoffavit*, &c. (*q*).

In debt on bond or other *specialty*, when the deed is the foundation of the action, the plea of *non est factum* (*r*) is proper (878), either when the plaintiff's *profert* cannot be proved as stated (*s*); or the deed was not executed (879), or not duly stamped (*t*), or varies from the declaration either by a mis-statement, or by the omission of a covenant or clause, constituting a con-

(*d*) 1 Salk. 277; 8 T. R. 487. From the case in 5 T. R. 4, 2 Wils. 208, 213, it appears that the tenant is estopped from disputing the title though the demise was by parol; and see further as to this, 2 Bing. Rep. 10, 54.

(*e*) Gilb. Debt, 438.

(*f*) *Id.* 436; see the cases and arguments, 2 Taunt. 278, &c.

(*g*) Gilb. 440, cites Bro. Debt, 113; Keilw. 153; Gilb. Debt. 440; but see Cowp. 588, and the forms, *post*, vol. iii.

(*h*) 1 Saund. 204, note 2.

(*i*) 1 Saund. 38, n. 3; 2 *Id.* 187 a, n. 2; 2 Ld. Raym. 1500. The instance of debt for rent seems to be an exception.

(*k*) See preceding note; 2 Ld. Raym. 1500; 2 Stra 778; 1 Barnard, K. B. 15; 8 Mod. 106, 323, 382.

(*l*) *Id.*; Fortesc. 363, 367; 2 Saund. 187 a.

(*m*) 2 Saund. 187 a, note 2.

(*n*) A general demurrer will suffice, 2 Wils. 10.

(*o*) 5 Esp. Rep. 38; 2 Saund. 187 a, note 2; 2 Wils. 10.

(*p*) Doct. Plac. 261; 2 Taunt. 278; Stephen, 2d edit. 237, 238, 239. What the general traverse puts in issue, 1 Cromp. & Jerv. 48; *sed vide* 2 Taunt. 282.

(*q*) 3 Nev. & Man. 50, in note.

(*r*) See the rule in general, 1 Tyrw. 197, 205, 206.

(*s*) 4 East, 585; Com. Dig. Pleader, 2 W. 18.

(*t*) 6 T. R. 317.

(875) See Davis *v.* Shoemaker, 1 Rawle, 135.

(876) Vide Minton *v.* Woodworth and Ferris, 11 Johns. Rep. 476. But the plaintiff must demur, and cannot object to it after verdict. Meyer *v.* M'Lean, 1 Johns. Rep. 509, S. C. 2 Johns. Rep. 183. Bullis *v.* Giddens and Brown, 8 Johns. Rep. 83.

(877) { Allen *v.* Smith, 2 Halst. Rep. 159. }

(878) This plea only puts the deed in issue, and the plaintiff need not prove the other averments in his declaration. Gardner *v.* Gardner, 10 Johns. Rep. 47. In covenant or debt the plea of *non est factum* only puts in issue the giving of the deed, and it is not necessary in such a case for the plaintiff to prove the averments or breaches contained in his declaration; the plea against all material averments. Legg *v.* Robinson, 7 Wend. R. 194.

(879) See Seymour *v.* Harvey, 8 Conn. R. 63.

dition precedent or exception (u). The plea of *non est factum*, where a *variance* is relied upon, should not set out the deed on oyer (x). And the defendant may give in evidence under the plea of *non est factum* that the deed was delivered to a third person as an *escrow*, (though it is more usual to plead the fact) (y); or that it was *void* at commom law *ab initio* (z); *as that it was obtained by fraud* (a)(880); or whilst the party was drunk (b); or made by a married *woman* (c)(881); or a lunatic (d)(882); or a person intoxicated, &c.; or that it became void after it was made, and before the commencement of the action (e), by erasure, alteration, addition, &c. (f). If only *non est factum* be pleaded, and it appear that the obligor could not write, defendant's counsel cannot inquire into circumstances (g). And matter which shows that the deed was merely *voidable* (h) on account of infancy (i)(883) *or *duress*(j); [*520] or that it was *void by act of parliament* (k), in respect of usury (l), usury must be *pleaded*, and cannot be objected to by setting out the deed and de-

IN PART. 2dly. On specialties.

(u) *Ante*, 338, 339; 11 East, 633; 1 Campb. 70; Com. Dig. Pleader, 2 W. 18; 2 Stra. 1104; and see 6 Taunt. 394; 2 Marsh. 96, S. C.; 4 M. & Sel. 470; 5 Moore, 164; 1 Stark. 294; 2 D. & R. 662.

(x) *Ante*, 468.

(y) 4 Esp. Rep. 235; 6 Mod. 217; 1 Sid. 450; 1 Salk. 274; 2 Rol. Ab. 683; Sir T. Raym. 197; Com. Dig. Pleader, 2 W. 18; 4 East, 94; 1 Bar. & Adol. 226.

(z 5 Co. 119; 2 Wils. 341, 347; but see 2 Chit. Rep. 334; 2 Stark. 35, S. C., where it was ruled that the defendant cannot, under the plea of *non est factum* to a declaration upon a bond, go into evidence to show that the consideration was illegal at common law. See 11 Moore, 91; 3 Bingh. 322, S. C.

(a) 2 Campb. 272, 273; quoted and overruled as a general position in Edwards v. Brown, 1 Tyr. Rep 196. Where it was holden that a fraudulent misrepresentation of the *legal effect* of a deed must be pleaded specially. The case in 2 Campb. only proves that *coverture* may be given in evidence under *non est factum*.

(b) *Ante*, 511; 3 Campb. 33.

(c) Com. Dig. Pleader, 2 W. 18; 12 Mod. 101; 3 Keb. 228; 2 Stra. 1104; *ante*, 512.

(d) 3 Campb. 126; 2 Atk. 412; 3 Mod. 310; 2 Stra. 1104; 4 Co. 123; Ld. Raym. 315; 2 Salk. 675; see *ante*, 511.

(e) 5 Co. 119 b, *acc.*; Sav. 71, *semble contra*.

(f) 5 Co. 23, 119 b; Bul. Ni. Pri. 172; Co. Lit. 35 b; notes 6, 7; 225 b; 11 Co. 27, 28; what sufficient, 4 Cruise, 368.

(g) Cranbrook v. Dadd, 5 Car. & P. 402.

(h) 5 Co. 119 a; Gilb. Debt, 437; 2 Salk. 675; 1 Lord Raym 315.

(i) 1 Salk. 279; 3 Burr. 1805, 1794; 2 Inst. 483; 3 Mod. 310; 3 M. & Sel. 478; 2 Stra. 1104, note (i); 1 Tyrw. 207, S. P.

(j) 1 Tyrw. Rep. 207, and so must fraud, *id. ibid.*; 5 Co. 119 a; 2 Inst. 482, 483; Com. Dig. Pleader, 2 W. 19, 20; Bac. Ab. Pleader, G. 3; Duress, D.; Bul. Ni. Pri. 171; 9 Vin. Ab. 322; 2 Saund. 155, note 4.

(k) 5 Co. 119 a; Bul. Ni. Pri. 224; 2 Saund. 155 a, note 4; 9 East, 408, 416; 13 East, 87; 7 East, 529, *acc.*; but see 4 M. & Sel. 338. How to plead illegality of consideration, see 11 Moore, 91; 3 Bing. 322, S. C. Usury must be pleaded to action on a deed; and though apparent on face of same, a *demurrer* would not be sustainable, 3 Nev. & Man. 665; 1 Adol. & El. 576.

(l) 1 Stra. 493; Com. Dig. Pleader, 2 W. 23.

(880) As that a different instrument was substituted instead of the one which the defendant supposed he was executing. Van Valkenburg v. Rouk, 12 Johns. Rep. 337. { Taylor v. King, 6 Munf. 358. } So, the defendant may give in evidence under *non est factum*, that he was made to sign the instrument when so drunk as not to know what he did. Phillips' Ev. 128. Pitt v. Smith, 3 Campb. 33. Dorr v. Munsell, 13 Johns. Rep. 430. In an action at law, on a specialty, it is not competent for the defendant to avoid it, by pleading that it was obtained by fraudulent misrepresentations made by the plaintiff. Wyche v. Macklin, 2 Rand. Rep. 426. Vrooman v. Phelps, 2 Johns. Rep. 177. Franchot v. Leach, 5 Cow. Rep. 506. Aliter in Pennsylvania, where there is no court of equity. Stubbs v. Pyle, 14 Serg. & Rawle, 208. Stoever v. Weir, 10 Serg. & Rawle, 25, and in New Jersey the law is the same as in Pennsylvania. Mason v. Evans, Coxe's A. J. Rep. 182. Barrow v. Bispham, 6 Halst. Rep. 110.

(881) Contra, Marine Ins. Co. of Alexandria v. Hodgson, 6 Cranch, 219, per Livingston, J.

(882) Vide ante, 511.

(883) Vide Marine Ins. Co. of Alexandria v. Hodgson, 6 Cranch, 219.

IN DEBT. — 2dly. On specialties.

murring (m), gaming (n), &c.; or that a bail bond was not made according to the 23 Hen. 6, c. 9; must in general be pleaded. In the case, however, of a bail bond, if it appear upon the face of the declaration that the bond has been made contrary to the provisions of the statute, the defendant may demur, or move in arrest of judgment after verdict upon a plea of *non est factum* (o). And if a bail bond be *dated* and made after the return-day of the writ, the defendant may avoid it under a plea of *non est factum* (p). Defences arising on *statutes* must in general be pleaded specially, and therefore under *non est factum* defendant cannot insist that an annuity bond ought to have been enrolled (q). And the defendant, in an action on a bail bond, cannot plead or show that the affidavit to hold to bail was defective (r), or not filed (s), or perhaps that there was *not any* affidavit (s) under the plea of *non est factum*, or take advantage of the objection, that the action is brought in the wrong Court (t)(884). And a specialty cannot in general be avoided by usury, or other illegality in the consideration appearing merely in evidence, or on the face of the condition, but the fact must be pleaded specially (885), and the defendant cannot demur (u). The defendant must also plead specially payment of a bond, &c. (886) either on or after the day (v); and where no interest has been paid on the bond after the time mentioned in the condition, and there is no other circumstance to negative the presumption of payment on that day, arising from twenty years having elapsed, then the plea may be *solvit ad diem*, but otherwise it should be *solvit post diem* (x). So performance, or any matter in excuse of it, as *non damnificatus* to a bond of indemnity (y)(887); no award to an arbitration bond (z), or to a bail bond no process to arrest the defendant,

(m) Ferguson v. Sprang, 1 Adol. & El. 576; 3 Nev. & Man. 665, S. C.

(n) Com. Dig. Pleader, 2 W. 26; 1 Campb. 291.

(o) 1 Saund. 161, n. 1; 2 T. R. 569; 2 Saund. 60, note 8; 1 Bar. & Adol. 226.

(p) 4 M. & Sel. 338.

(q) Mestayer, v. Biggs, 4 Tyr. 471; 2 Dowl. 695.

(r) Norton v. Danvers, 7 T. R. 375; Hume v. Liversedge, 1 Cr. & M. 332; 1 Dowl. 660.

(s) Knowles v. Stevens, 1 Cr. M. & R. 26; *sed quære* as to plea that no affidavit was *made*, *per* Alderson, B.

(t) 2 Campb 396.

(u) 2 Bla. Rep. 1108; 1 Saund. 295 b; 2 M. & Sel. 377; 2 Chit. Rep. 334; 2 Stark. 35, S. C.

(v) 4 Anne, c. 16; *solvit post diem* is not pleadable to a suit by the crown, 1 Price, 23.

(x) 1 Stra. 652; and see Rep. temp. Hardw. 133, as to these pleas in general.

(y) 1 B. & P. 640, note a; 1 Taunt. 428; quality and form of this plea, *post*.

(z) Misconduct of arbitrator not pleadable, 2 M. & P. 345.

---

(884) And bail in action against them will not be permitted to deny the arrest of the principal. Bean v. Parker, 17 Mass. Rep. 591.

(885) See Cowles v. Woodruff, in Equity, 8 Conn. Rep. 35.

(886) In Pennsylvania, matters that show fraud or want of consideration may be given in evidence under a plea of payment, notice being given to the adverse party. Baring v. Shippen, 2 Binn. 154. {See 8 Serg. & Rawle, 25, 26. Gochenauer et al. v. Cooper et al., 8 Serg. & Rawle, 187.} Upon the plea of payment to debt on bond, it is competent for the defendant to give in evidence, that wheat was delivered to the plaintiff on account of the bond, at a certain price: and that the defendant assigned sundry debts to the plaintiff, part of which were collected by the plaintiff, and part lost by his indulgence or negligence. Buddicum v. Kirk, 3 Cranch, 293.

(887) {Andrus v. Waring. 20 Johns. Rep. 162.} To an action of debt for the penalty of a bond given to a sheriff, as security for the liberties of the gaol, *non damnificatus* is not a good plea. {Camp v. Allen, 7 Halst. Rep. 1.} Woods v. Rowan and Coon, 5 Johns. Rep. 42. But *nil debet* is. Minton v. Woodworth and Ferris, 11 Johns. Rep. 474. Bullis v. Giddens and Brown, 8 Johns. Rep. 82. In Fisher v. Ellis et al., 6 Greenl. R. 455, it was *held*, that in debt on bond taken pursuant to the statute in Maine relating to poor debtors, a plea of performance of all the conditions expressed, or necessarily implied in the bond, was sufficient.

&c. (*a*); and matters in *discharge* *of the action, as a tender, set-off (*b*), accord and satisfaction (*c*)(888), former recovery, release, and foreign attachment (*d*)(889), must be pleaded in this action. The nonjoinder of a co-obligor is immaterial except upon a plea in abatement (*e*). IN DEBT.

3dly. On records.

In debt or *scire facias* on a *record*, when the record was the foundation of the action, and not merely inducement, the plea of *nil debet* was always insufficient and bad on demurrer (*f*). In debt on an Irish or foreign judgment, it would seem that *nil debet* was sufficient, because such judgments did not partake of the technical qualities of a record (*g*). A plea of payment, in an action upon a record, was not good at common law, because such payment was matter *in pais*, and not of record; but as set-off *on simple* contract cannot be pleaded, it is best to apply by motion (*h*). By the statute 4 Ann. c. 16, s. 12, the debtor might plead payment to actions brought on records, but in order to come within that statute, he must have paid all the money due on the record or judgment, so that the whole of such judgment must have been satisfied; and if it did not go to that extent, a plea of actual payment would be bad (*i*). Under this act a plea of accord and satisfaction is insufficient, as the act only authorizes a plea of payment (*k*). *Nul tiel record* was the proper plea, where there is either no record, or where there was a variance in the statement of it (*l*)(890); but as this plea merely puts in issue the existence of the record as stated, any matter in discharge must have been pleaded (891), such as payment, which was given by the 4 Ann. c. 16 (*m*); and accord and satisfaction was not a sufficient plea to a bond conditioned for any other act than the payment of money (*n*). It is a maxim in law, that there can be no averment in pleading against the validity of a record, though there may be against its operation, therefore no matter of defence can be pleaded *which existed ante- [*522]

(*a*) Say. 116.
(*b*) 8 Geo. 2, c. 24, s. 5; Bul. N. P. 172; Willes, 262, 263.
(*c*) This is no plea to debt on a money bond, &c.; see 7 East, 150; Com. Dig. Accord and Satisfaction; 1 Taunt. 428.
(*d*) 1 Saund. 67 a, note 1; Co. Ent. 139 b, 142 a; Lib. Plac. 160, pl. 113; 2 Lib. Intrat. 164; 2 Show. 374; 3 East, 378.
(*e*) *Ante*, 52.
(*f*) *Ante*, 517, 518; 2 Saund. 344; 1 Saund. 21; 1 East, 372; 2 Wils. 10.
(*g*) See *ante*, 120; 4 B. & C. 411; 6 D. & R. 471, S. C.
(*h*) 6 Taunt. 176; 8 Bing. 202; 7 Bing. 29, 61.
(*i*) 4 Moore, 165.
(*k*) *Id.*
(*l*) Com. Dig. Pleader, 2 W. 13, and Record, C.; Stra. 1171; 1 Saund. 92, n. 3; Gilb. Debt, 444; 3 Mod. 41.
(*m*) *Solvit post diem* is not pleadable against the crown, 1 Price, 23.
(*n*) 3 East, 251; 7 *Id.* 150.

(888) {Strange *v.* Holmes, 7 Cow. Rep. 224. But the plea in that case was *non est factum*, and a notice of the special matter.} An assignment of debts and balances of account cannot be pleaded as an accord and satisfaction to an action of debt on a bond. Buddicum *v.* Kirk, 3 Cranch, 293. An accord must be executed. Russell *v.* Lytle, 6 Wend. R. 390. A covenant not to sue the obligor of a bond *for a given time*, cannot be pleaded in bar. Winans *v.* Huston, 6 ib. 471. But a covenant not to sue may be pleaded as a release. Chandler *v.* Herrick, 19 Johns. Rep. 129.
(889) Updegraff *v.* Spring, 11 S. & R. 188.
(890) Vide Bullis *v.* Giddens, 8 Johns. Rep. 83. The plaintiff may treat such plea as a nullity, but if he take issue upon it and go to trial, he cannot object to it on motion in arrest of judgment. Rush *v.* Cobbett, 2 Johns. Cas. 256. Pelter *v.* Mulliner, 2 Johns. Rep. 181.
(891) As to the proper plea in an action on the judgment of a court in another State, vide Phillips' Ev. Dunlap's ed. 254, n. (*a*). Mills *v.* Duryce, 7 Cranch 484

IN DEBT. 3dly. On records. rior to the recovery of the judgment (o) (892); and the original defendant himself, or his bail or sureties, could not plead that the judgment had been obtained against him by fraud (p), though it might be pleaded that a judgment against a third person was so obtained (q). The defendant might have pleaded a release (r), or that the debt was levied by a *fi. fa.* (s), or *elegit* (t), or *ca. sa.* (u). But where to a declaration in *scire facias* on a judgment in replevin, damages £473 13*s.* 4*d.* the defendant pleaded, that before the suing out the *scire facias*, the plaintiff sued out a *fieri facias*, commanding the sheriff to levy £274 13*s.* 4*d.* and which writ was delivered to the sheriff, who before the return thereof seized and took in execution goods of the defendant to the value of £37 13*s.*: it was held that such plea was bad, as it did not state that the sheriff had returned the writ (x). An executor might plead *plene administravit* (y), or to debt on a judgment suggesting a *devastavit*, he might plead not guilty (z); and a discharge under the lords' act was an effectual bar to an action of debt on a judgment (a). The pleadings in debt or *scire facias* on a recognizance of bail, have already been pointed out (b).

4thly. On statutes. In debt upon *statute, nil debet* was the proper plea (893), though not guilty would in some cases suffice (c). The pleading rules Hil. T. 4 W. 4, does not seem to prescribe the form of plea to debt on statute, but only applies to debt on *simple contract*. In a recent case, to a declaration *qui tam*, the plea was, "that defendant never was indebted in the said sum above demanded, or any part thereof, *modo et forma*, &c.," and a learned judge at chambers held it sufficient. The statute of limitations might, in an action by a common informer, be given in evidence under the general issue (d); but a former recovery by another person could not (e).

IN COVENANT. [*523] In COVENANT there never was strictly speaking any plea of *general* issue, for the plea of *non est factum* only put the deed in issue (894), as in debt *on a specialty (f), and not the breach of covenant or any other matter of de-

(o) *Ante*; 2 Marsh. 392.
(p) Moore *v.* Bowmaker, 6 Taunt. 379; 2 Marsh. 392, S. C.
(q) *Id.*
(r) Bac. Ab. Release.
(s) 4 Leon. 194; Sav. 123; Cro. Car. 328; Clift. 675.
(t) Dyer, 299 b; 1 Lev. 92.
(u) Off. Brev. 300; 1 Salk. 271; Lutw. 641.
(x) 4 Moore, 163. It seems also that such plea afforded no answer to the whole declaration, as the sum levied was only sufficient to satisfy part of the judgment, and that it was therefore bad on special demurrer, *id*
(y) 1 Lord Raym. 3; 4 Mod. 296; Salk. 296; Skin. 565; 3 East, 2.
(z) 1 T. R. 462.
(a) 32 Geo. 2, c. 28, s. 20.
(b) Tidd, 9th ed. 1128; *ante*, 127.
(c) 1 T. R. 462; Bac. Ab. Pleas, I.; Com. Dig. Pleader, 2 S. 11, 17.
(d) 2 Saund. 63 b; 2 East, 336.
(e) 1 Stra. 701; Bac. Ab. Action, *qui tam*, D.
(f) *Ante*, 517; 1 Stark. 313. As to what may be proved under this plea, see 5 Moore, 164; 1 Stark. 294.

(892) {Cardesa *v.* Humes, 5 Serg. & Rawle, 65.} The rule is the same, whether the judgment were obtained by confession, or default, or upon plea. M'Farland *v.* Irwin, 8 Johns. Rep. 77.

A plaintiff in a judgment, who has taken a note as *collateral security* for the payment, cannot recover on such notes, if he issues an execution and imprisons the defendant. Wakeman et al. *v.* Lyon et al., 9 Wend. R. 241. Sunderland *v.* Loder et al., 5 ib. 58.

(893) Vide Burnham *v.* Webster, 5 Mass. Rep. 270. Stilson *v.* Tobey, 2 Mass. Rep. 521, 522.

(894) Vide Kane *v.* Sanger, 14 Johns. Rep. 89. Cooper *v.* Watson, 10 Wend. R. 205 Gardner *v.* Gardner, 10 Johns. Rep. 47. Dale *v.* Roosevelt, 9 Cowen, 307.

fence; and a plea of *non infregit conventionem* was bad on demurrer, though it would be aided after verdict (g)(895); and *riens en arrere* was also a bad plea in this action (h), because it impliedly admits that although nothing is now due, yet that the money was not paid on the appointed day (h). The defendant must therefore always have pleaded specially every matter which it would be necessary to plead in debt on a bond or other specialty (i), as that the deed was voidable by infancy (896) or illegality of the consideration. However, under the plea of *non est factum*, the defendant may, on the trial, avail himself of a *variance* in the statement of the deed either in respect of a misstatement, or of the omission of a covenant qualifying the contract (k); and this, although the defendant has agreed to admit on the trial the due execution of the deed (l); and if the plaintiff omit to state a condition precedent, the defendant may crave oyer, and set out the deed and demur (m)(897). In an action of covenant upon a lease for the breach of a covenant running with the land, if the plaintiff claim as heir, devisee, or assignee of the lessor, the defendant may traverse the *derivative title* of the plaintiff (n), or admitting that the lessor had *some* legal estate in the premises at the time of the demise, the defendant may plead that such lessor was seised, &c. of a different estate from that stated in the declaration, and thereby show that the derivative title of the plaintiff does not exist. But the defendant is estopped from pleading or traversing *generally*, that the lessor was seised as stated in the declaration (o)(898); though in an action at the suit of the assignee of a termor, the defendant may deny that the lessor was possessed of the residue of the term in the manner alleged in the declaration (p), when a plea of performance in general terms suffices, unless specially demurred to (q). Where the defendant is a party to a deed, he cannot traverse its operation by pleading that "he did *not grant*, &c." but must plead *non est factum*; but the rule is otherwise

IN COVENANT.

(g) 8 T. R. 278; 1 Lev. 183; 3 *Id.* 19; 1 Sid. 289; Com. Dig. Pleader, 2 V. 5.

(h) Cowp. 588.

(i) Com. Dig. Pleader, 2 V. 4, &c.

(k) 9 East, 188; Stra 1146; 11 East, 639; 4 Camph. 20; 2 Stark. 35; *ante*, 338, 342, as to variances.

(l) 1 Camph. 70.

(m) Com. Dig. Pleader, 2 V. 3, 4; 11 East, 639.

(n) Seymour v. Franco, Law Journal, vol. vii Feb. 1829, K. B. p. 18; and Whitton v. Peacock, in C. P. 3d June, 1835, *ante*, 397.

(o) 8 T. R. 437; 2 Stra. 817; 2 Saund. 206, a. n. 207, 418; 1 New Rep. 160. *Non tenuit* is not pleadable to a cognizance for rent in arrear, under a demise from a receiver in Chancery, 4 Bing. 2.

(p) 4 Moore, 303; Carotik v. Blagrave, 1 Brod. & B. 531.

(q) Varley v. Manton, 9 Bing. 363.

(895) Roosevelt v. Fulton's Heirs, 7 Cow Rep. 71.

(896) Vida Marine Ins. Co. of Alexandria v. Hodgson, 6 Cranch, 219.

(897) Snell v. Snell, 7 Dowl & Ryl. 249.

(898) So where there was a demise by the plaintiff and his wife of the wife's estate, in which the plaintiff had no interest, except in right of his wife, and the *reddendum*, and covenant to pay rent, was to the plaintiff and his wife, *and her heirs*, it was held, that the defendant in covenant by the husband for the rent, might plead, after craving oyer of the lease, that the plaintiff never had any estate in his premises, except in right of his wife, whose estate they were; that she died without issue, leaving an heir, whereupon the estate of the plaintiff ceased; and that the heir threatened to enter and eject the defendant, unless he attorned; and the defendant was thereby compelled to attorn, and become tenant to the heir. Hill v Saunders, 7 Dowl. & Ryl. 17. Where the plaintiff assigns a particular breach, a general plea of performance, in the words of the covenant is bad on general demurrer: as where the covenant was to convey a farm, and the plaintiff assigns for breach, that before executing the conveyance, the defendant removed from the premises a cider-mill which was annexed to the freehold, the defendant must answer particularly the breach assigned. Bradley v. Osterhoudt, 13 Johns. Rep. 404.

IN COVENANT. in the case of a stranger to the deed (r). The defendant must also plead *especially*, performance of the covenant (s); or excuse of performance, as [*524] *eviction (t)(899); or by non-performance (900) by the plaintiff of a condition precedent (u), or by a surrender of the lease, &c. (v): or admitting the breach to have been committed, the defendant must plead specially that he is discharged (w); as by his bankruptcy, if the action be for a money demand due before the act of bankruptcy (x); or by accord and satisfaction *after breach* (y); arbitrament (z), former recovery (a), foreign attachment, set-off (b), release, &c. (c)(901). But a parol accord and satisfaction made before breach cannot be pleaded in bar to an action of covenant (d), nor can a parol agreement for a substituted contract be pleaded (e). A tender may be pleaded in covenant for the payment of money (f).

IN ACCOUNT. In an action of ACCOUNT, there is no general issue. The defendant may plead infancy (g); and when sued as bailiff or receiver in fact, he may plead that he was not bailiff or receiver (h); but when sued as tenant in common under the statute (i), if the declaration be properly framed, a plea that the defendant is not bailiff or receiver would be insufficient (k); and if the defendant mean to deny the plaintiff's claim, he should traverse the tenancy in common. The defendant may also plead that he hath accounted, or a release, arbitrament, bond given in satisfaction, and the statute of limitations (l); but other matters, which admit that the defendant was once chargeable and accountable, cannot in general be pleaded in bar to the action, but must be pleaded before the auditors (m).

[*525] IN DETINUE. *In DETINUE the general issue (although improperly so called) was *non detinet*, which, before the recent rules, put in issue the facts of the plaintiff's property or possession, and the defendant's withholding the chattels; but under this plea the defendant could not show that the goods or other chattels were pledged to him, but must have pleaded that defence specially; he might,

(r) *Ante*, 519.
(s) Com. Dig. Pleader, 2 V. 13; Bul. N. P. 165; 1 B. & P. 640.
(t) 1 Saund. 204, n. 2; 2 *Id.* 176; 2 East, 576.
(u) 8 T. R. 366.
(v) 1 Saund. 235.
(w) Com. Dig. Pleader, 2 V. 8.
(x) 4 T. R. 156; 1 Saund. 241, n. 6.
(y) 1 Taunt. 428; see 8 *Id.* 37; 1 Moore, 460, S. C.; *Id.* 358.
(z) 9 Co. Rep. 79; Com. Dig. Pleader, 2 V. 8, 9.
(a) When should be pleaded as an *estoppel*, 2 B. & Ald. 668; *ante*, 513, n. (c).
(b) See the end of this chapter.
(c) Com. Dig. Pleader, 2 V. 8, &c.; *ante*, 513.
(d) 1 Taunt. 428.
(e) 1 East, 630; 3 T. R. 596.
(f) 7 Taunt. 486; 1 Moore, 200, S. C.; 5 Mod. 18; 1 Ld. Raym. 566; 12 Mod. 376. But see Gilb. C. P. 63.
(g) Bac. Ab. Accompt, E.; Com. Dig. Accompt, E. 5.
(h) *Id.*
(i) 4 & 5 Ann. c. 16, s. 27.
(k) Willes, 208.
(l) Bac. Ab. Accompt, E.; Com. Dig. Account, E. 4 to 6.
(m) *Id.*; 3 Wils. 78.

(899) { To an action brought by a master on the covenants of an indenture of apprenticeship, alleging as a breach, that the apprentice had left his service within the stipulated time, it was held to be a good defence that the plaintiff had neglected to instruct the apprentice in his trade, *and* had, unnecessarily, obliged him to work on Sunday. Warner v. Smith, 8 Conn. Rep. 14. }

(900) { But a defendant cannot plead that the plaintiff *intended* to violate a covenant, as an excuse for his own violation of it. Coffin v. Basset, 2 Pick. Rep. 357. }

(901) { Johnson v. Kerr, 1 Serg. & Rawle, 25. }

however, give in evidence a *gift* from the plaintiff, or any other fact, to prove that the property in the chattel was not in the plaintiff (*n*). A lien must always have been pleaded specially (*o*). The bailment or finding alleged in a declaration in *detinue* is not traversable. IN DETINUE.

In each of these actions, when brought *by an executor or administrator*, the defendant might not only avail himself of either of the before-mentioned defences, but might also in some cases deny the plaintiff's representative character (902). Where letters of administration had been obtained in an inferior diocese, the defendant may plead in bar that there were *bona notabilia* (*p*). The general plea, "that the plaintiff was not nor is administrator of all the goods, &c." is not sufficient, where the defence is, that the letters of administration, which were granted by a bishop, were unfounded, because the intestate resided within another diocese in a different province, where there were *bona notabilia* (*q*). The residence elsewhere, &c. should be specially pleaded. So if the defendant, in an action by an executor, contend that the probate is void, as that the stamp is insufficient, or the seal forged, he should plead *ne unques* executor (*r*)(903). Where the plaintiff necessarily sues in his representative character, the defendant cannot, under the general issue, take advantage of any defect, such as the insufficiency of the stamp in the letters of administration or probate, for profert has been made of them, and the defendant has by his pleading admitted them (*s*). But if it were part of the plaintiff's case to prove his representative character, as where he sued in trover upon his constructive possession, for a conversion in his own time, any defect in the letters of administration or probate, which prevented him from proving such character, would, before the recent rule Hil. T. 4 W. 4, be fatal, although there were no special plea (*t*). BY OR AGAINST EXECUTORS, &c.

*In an action against an executor or administrator (*u*), the defendant may, in addition to any of the before-mentioned defences, plead *ne unques* executor (*x*), or administrator (*y*), or that no assets have come to his hands (*z*)(904); or [*526]

(*n*) Co. Lit. 283 a; 4 Bing. 111, 112. See the several pleas, Com. Dig. Pleader, 2 X. 3.

(*o*) 4 Bing. 106, 111, 112; 1 Gale, 127; *ante*, 141.

(*p*) 1 Saund. 274, note 3. As to pleading specially in actions for rent, see Salk. 317.

(*q*) 5 B. & C. 491; 8 D. & R. 247, S. C.

(*r*) 1 Saund. 275 a, notes.

(*s*) 2 M. & Sel. 553.

(*t*) 3 Taunt. 113; 1 Saund. 275, n. (*a*); 2 *Id.* 47, n. (*x*).

(*u*) See the pleadings in general, Com. Dig. Pleader, 2 D. 3.

(*x*) Com. Dig. Pleader, 2 D. 7. Executor not liable till he has proved or acted, 1 M. & P. 663; 4 Bing. 686, S. C.

(*y*) Com. Dig. Pleader, 2 D. 7, 13; see 7 B. & C. 406.

(*z*) Com. Dig. Pleader, 2 D. 7. Although upon an issue of *plene administravit vel non*, the stamp on the probate of testator's will is admissible in evidence, yet it is not even *prima facie* evidence of assets come to the hands of the executor, Mann *v.* Lang, 5 Nev. & Man. 202.

(902) But unless the plaintiff's right to sue as executor or administrator be put in issue by the defendant's plea, it will be deemed to have been admitted.—M'Kimm et al. *v.* Riddle, 2 Dall. 100. Champlin *v.* Tilley and Tilley, 3 Day's Rep. 303.

(903) In Jewett *v.* Jewett, 5 Mass. Rep. 275, although it was decided that it was a good plea in bar, by the law of Massachusetts, for an administrator, that he had been removed from office since the commencement of the suit against him, yet it was admitted, that by the common law, a determination of his power pending the action did not defeat it.

(904) Shaw *v.* M'Cameron, 11 Serg. & Rawle, 252. Vide Douglas *v.* Satterlee, 11 Johns. Rep. 16.

BY OR AGAINST EXECUTORS, &c. *plene administravit præter* a sum not sufficient to satisfy debts of a higher nature, as bonds outstanding, or judgments recovered against the deceased or the defendant by third persons (*a*); or *plene administravit* except a sum ready to be paid to the plaintiff (*b*); and the defendant cannot avail himself of either of these defences under the general issue (*c*); but under the general plea of *plene administravit*, an executor or administrator may give in evidence a retainer for a debt due to himself, though it is in general advisable to plead it (*d*). Where the executor or administrator has no ground on which to dispute the plaintiff's debt, it is in general advisable not to deny it (*e*). So if he cannot dispute his being executor, he should not plead *ne unques* executor, for if he do, and the plaintiff, on the plea of *plene administravit*, take judgment of assets *quando*, and proceed to trial on the other issues, and they are found for the plaintiff, and no issue which goes to the whole cause of action is found for the defendant, the defendant will be liable to costs (*f*)(905); but not so if the plaintiff do not take judgment of assets *quando*, and on the trial the plea of *plene administravit* is found for the defendant (*g*).

AGAINST AN HEIR OR DEVISEE. In an action against an *heir* or *devisee* (*h*), the defendant may not only plead any matter which might have been pleaded by the ancestor or devisor, but may also either deny the character in which he is sued; or admitting it, may
[* 527] plead that he has *nothing by descent* or by *devise*, either generally (*i*), *or specially, viz. that he has nothing but a reversion after an estate for life or years, or that he has paid debts of an equal or superior degree, to the amount of the assets descended or devised; or that he *retains* the assets to satisfy his own debt, of equal or superior degree, or debts of a superior degree due to third persons (*k*)(906). The *heir*, if an *infant*, might also have prayed that the parol should demur, or be stayed till he had become of full age (*l*); but that delay, so injurious to creditors, was abolished by 1 W. 4, c. 47, s. 10. It was a good plea by a devisee, that the debt did not accrue in the life-time of the devisor (*m*).

IN CASE. The *general issue in* an action on the CASE, is, "*that the defendant is not guilty of the premises*, (*or*, 'grievances,') *above laid to his charge, in manner and form as the plaintiff hath above thereof complained against him, and of this he puts himself upon the country*, &c." In *trespass* it is similar, except

(*a*) 1 Saund. 300 to 386, *in notis*; Com Dig. Pleader, 2 D. 9; 10 East, 313, 315.
(*b*) *Post*, vol. iii.
(*c*) Co. Lit 283 a
(*d*) Co. Lit. 283 a; 1 Saund. 333, note 6.
(*e*) 5 Bla. Rep. 1275. See *post*, when advisable to plead the general issue, or not.
(*f*) 12 East, 232. In such case defendant should move to withdraw the pleas of the general issue, and *ne unques* executor; but see 1 Bar. & Ald. 254; and 8 Taunt. 129; overruling 1 Saund. 336 b.
(*g*) 4 Taunt. 135; 1 B. & Ald. 254; 8 Taunt. 129; Tidd, 9th ed. 979, 980.
(*h*) See the proceedings in general, Com. Dig. Pleader, 2 E.; 2 Saund. 7, and notes.
(*i*) *Id.*; Com. Dig. Pleader, 2 E. 3.
(*k*) Com. Dig. Pleader, 2 E. 3.
(*l*) *Id.*; *ante*, 481.
(*m*) 5 Nev. & Man. 42.

(905) In *debt* or *assumpsit* against an executor, the plea of *non est factum* or *non assumpsit*, is admission of a will of which the defendant is executor; but it is otherwise where the action is for a demand on which the testator was not himself liable; as for a legacy. Hantz *v.* Sealy, 6 Binn. 405.

(906) { Or he may plead in abatement the nonjoinder of the heirs of a deceased heir having lands by descent. St. Mary's Church *v.* Wallace, 5 Halst. Rep. 311. }

IN CASE.

that the word "*force*" is substituted for "*wrong*" in the commencement, and "*trespasses*" for "*premises*" or "*grievances*."

It was observed by Lord Mansfield (*n*), that "there is an essential difference in pleading *between* actions of trespass, and actions on the case; the former are actions *stricti juris*, and therefore a former recovery, release, or satisfaction, cannot be given in evidence, but *must be pleaded;* but an action on the case is founded upon the mere justice and conscience of the plaintiff's case, and in the nature of a bill in equity, and in effect is so (*o*); and therefore a former recovery (*p*), release, or accord and satisfaction (*q*), need not, before the late rules, be pleaded, but might have been given in evidence (907); for whatever would in equity and conscience, according to the existing circumstances, *preclude* the plaintiff from recovering, might, in an *action on the case*, be given in evidence by the defendant under the general issue, because the plaintiff must recover upon the justice and conscience of his case, and on that only." And in an action on the case, under the plea of not guilty, *the [*528] defendant might not only put the plaintiff upon proof of the whole charge contained in the declaration, or show the before-mentioned matters which operated *in discharge* of the cause of action, but might give in evidence any *justification* or *excuse* (*r*). Thus, in an action for a malicious indictment, or arrest in a civil action, the defendant might, under the general issue, show that there was a sufficient or probable cause for the proceeding complained of (*s*); and this had, before the late rules, become usual, though more anciently a special plea was preferred (*t*). So in case for obstructing ancient lights, a custom of London to build on an ancient foundation to any height, might have been given in evidence by the defendant (*u*); and though a license must have been pleaded in trespass, yet it was the practice to admit it in evidence in an action on the case (*x*).

SLANDER. Pleas in actions for slander in particular before the recent rules.

With respect to actions for a *libel*, or slanderous *words*, we will consider, 1st, When it was *sufficient* to plead the *general* issue; 2dly, When there *must* have been a *special* plea of justification, and how it should be framed.

1st. Consistently with the relaxation which had obtained in other actions on the case, the defendant might upon the general issue defend himself, if there had been a release, or accord and satisfaction (*y*). And it was clear that if he *denied* or disproved any of the material facts which essentially constituted

(*n*) 3 Burr. 1353; 1 Bla. Rep. 388, S. C.; 1 Wils. 45; 2 Saund. 155 a, n. 4. No doubt the distinction stated by Lord Mansfield was for a time laid down and prevailed, but without any just reason. There was in assumpsit, and debt on simple contract, the same relaxation and departure from the principle of pleading; that matter which *admits* the facts stated in the declaration, and *avoids* it, should be specially pleaded, see *post*.

(*o*) This relaxed description of the action upon the case would not be tenable at the present day.

(*p*) *Sed vide* 2 B. & A. 668; see *ante*, 513, and *id.* note (*c*). It should be specially pleaded, *id.*

(*q*) 1 Stark. R. 97.

(*r*) 3 Burr. 1353; 1 Bla. Rep. 388, S. C.; 1 Stark. 97; 1 Wils. 45; 2 Saund. 155 a, note 4; 2 Mod. 276; 3 *Id.* 166; Com. Rep. 273; 1 Wils. 44, 175; 2 Saund. 155 a.

(*s*) 3 Mod. 166; Cro. Eliz. 871, 900.

(*t*) 1 Rol. R. 438; Cro. Eliz. 871, 900. But now see 2 Bing. N. C. 114.

(*u*) 1 Com. Rep. 273; 1 Wils. 45, 175; 2 Mod 274. See as to such custom, 3 Car. & P. 615.

(*x*) 8 East, 308; 2 Mod. 6, 7.

(*y*) *Ante*; 1 Stark. Rep. 97.

(907) Vide Jones *v.* Scriven, 8 Johns. Rep. 453.

IN CASE. In actions for slander in particular.

the gist or cause of action, the general issue would suffice; as if he disputed the *publication* of the scandal, or that it concerned the plaintiff, or did not bear the *meaning* which was affixed to it in the declaration, and which the plaintiff had bound himself to establish, so that there was a fatal variance; or, the words not being actionable without the aid of special damage, that no such injury had occurred, &c. (z).

So where the defence was, that the libel or slander was published or spoken, not in the malicious sense imputed in the declaration, but in an *innocent sense*, or upon an *occasion* which warranted the publication, the same might have been given [*529] *in evidence under the general issue, because it proved that the defendant was not guilty of the *malicious* slander as charged in the declaration; as if the words were spoken by the defendant as counsel, and were pertinent to the matter in question (a)(908); or were written or spoken in confidence, and without malice, as when a master honestly and fairly had given the character of a servant to one who asked his character with a view to hire him (b)(909); or if the words were innocently read, as a story out of history (c); or were spoken through concern (d); or in a sense not defamatory (e); for by so showing the manner and occasion of speaking the words, the defendant proved that they were not spoken with malice. But in most of the foregoing instances, the defendant *might have pleaded* those matters specially (f), for a defendant should never be compelled to rely alone on the general issue when he confessed the words and justified them, or confessed the words, and by special matter showed that they were not actionable (g); but recently, before Reg. Gen. Hil. T. 4 W. 4, it had become more usual to give them in evidence under the general issue (h).

So, under the general issue, the defendant might, in an action for a libel

(z) See *post*, as to the qualities of pleas, 1 Stark. Slander, 2d edit. 454, 464, 465.

(a) Cro. Jac. 90; Poph. 96; see Holt, C. N. P. 621; 1 B. & Ald. 233.

(b) Bul. N. P. 8; 1 T. R. 110; 1 B. & P. 523; 8 B. & C. 584; 3 M. & R. 101, S. S. *Aliter* if *express* malice, &c. in the master, *id.*; 3 B. & P. 587.

(c) Cro. Jac. 91.

(d) 1 Lev. 82.

(e) 4 Rep. 12 b; Peake R. 4; 1 Campb. 48; 7 Taunt. 431; 4 Price, 46, S. C.

(f) But Mr. Starkie observes, "that in all cases where the circumstances and occasion of the speaking the words or publishing the libel do not afford an *absolute* bar to the action, without regard to the defendant's motives and intention, but merely throw it on the plaintiff to prove malice *in fact*, the defendant *cannot* plead such occasional circumstances specially, but *must* plead the general issue." Stark. on Sland. 2d edit. 457; see 4 B. & Ald. 605. According to this it could not be specially pleaded that the defendant uttered the words in giving the plaintiff, his servant, a character, &c.

(g) 4 Rep. 14 a.

(h) 1 Saund. 130, note 1 and notes, 5th edit.

(908) {15 Mass. Rep. 50. But it is a libel in England, to publish a correct speech of counsel in a case, though the facts of the case and the law as applicable to them, may be published. Flint *v.* Pike, 6 Dowl. & Ryl. 528. And it is no justification to an action for a libel in a newspaper, that the matter complained of is a true, fair, just and correct account of proceedings, which took place at a public police office in the course of a *preliminary* inquiry, openly and publicly conducted before a justice, upon a criminal charge against the plaintiff, although published with no scandalous, defamatory, unworthy or unlawful motive, but merely as public news. Duncan *v.* Thwaites, 5 Dowl. & Ryl. 447. See, however, as to the right to publish a correct account of judicial proceedings. Commonwealth *v.* Blanding, 3 Pick. Rep. 304. Clark *v.* Binney, 2 Pick. Rep. 117. In an action of slander, for charging the plaintiff with perjury in a judicial proceeding; the defendant on the plea of *not guilty* (though not permitted to prove the *falsity* of the words sworn by the plaintiff) may prove *what those words were*, in mitigation of damages. Grant *v.* Hover, 6 Munf. 13.}

(909) {3 Pick. Rep. 315. Per PARKER, C. J.}

upon the plaintiff in his business of a bookseller, accusing him of publishing immoral works, adduce evidence to show that the supposed libel was a fair stricture upon the general run of the plaintiff's publication (*i*). And it was not *necessary* to plead specially that the defendant acted and spoke in his character of a judge, or juror, or as a party, or witness, in a judicial proceeding, in uttering the supposed slander; or that the publication was procured by *the contrivance of the plaintiff with a view to an action (*k*): and it has been held, in an action on a libel in a hand-bill, offering a reward for the recovery of certain bills, and stating that the plaintiff was suspected of having embezzled them, that the defendant may show under the general issue that the hand-bill was published *bona fide* with a view to the protection of persons liable on the bills, or to the conviction of the offender (*l*). [*530]

IN CASE. — In actions for slander in particular.

It appears to be a doubtful question, whether in an action for a libel or slander, the defendant could be admitted to prove, *in mitigation of damages*, facts showing grounds of *suspicion*, short of actual proof, of the plaintiff's guilt; or that he was a person of *general bad character*; or that there was a *general rumor* that he had committed the act with which he was charged. There are some decisions and *dicta* that such evidence might be received to reduce the damages, on the ground that it was material in estimating the extent of injury the plaintiff had received (*m*). But that doctrine, at least as regarded the admissibility of evidence of the plaintiff's *general bad character and repute*, was denied in the case of Jones *v.* Stephens, in the Court of Exchequer (*n*); which was an action for a libel on the plaintiff in his character of attorney, and containing general reflections on his professional conduct and respectability; the defendant pleaded the general issue, and several pleas of justification, some of which alleged in very general terms, that the plaintiff had conducted himself in an unprofessional and disreputable manner; on the trial the defendant proposed to prove by witnesses, in support of the pleas of justification, and in *contradiction of the *general averment* in the declaration that the plaintiff had carried on the profession and business of an attorney with great credit and reputation, that the plaintiff was of general bad character and repute in his business of an attorney; but the evidence was rejected by the Chief Baron as inadmissible: and on motion afterwards for a new trial, the Court of Exchequer was of opinion, and held, with many forcible observations, that such evidence was not admissible, either in mitigation of damages, or in support of any of the allegations contained in the pleas of justification. But in a subsequent case it was held, that if a justification had been pleaded, though [*531]

(*i*) 1 Campb. 350.

(*k*) 1 Stark. Slander, 2d edit. 456, 460; 2 New Rep. 141; 5 Esp. R. 13; 3 Campb. 323. By an M. P. 1 M. & Sel. 273.

(*l*) 1 M. & M. 461, *coram* Tindal, C. J. His Lordship said, "the defence here is, not that the charge was true, but that the defendant acted *bona fide* in making it."

(*m*) See Peake, Ev. App. xcii. 3d ed. App. xciv. 4th ed. 328; 2 Campb. 251; 1 M. & Sel. 284, 286, n.; Holt, N. P. R. 299, 307; Phil. Ev. 7th edit. See 1 M. & M. 47, cited *post*, 532. This was considered *vexata questio*, in 6 Bing. 223, 224. The subject is well discussed in 2 Stark. on Slander, 2d ed. 87, &c. In Waithman *v.* Weaver, 1 Dow. & Ry. N. P. R. 10, (S. C. in 11 Price, 257, but differently stated) it seems, a distinction was taken between proof of *facts* showing *suspicion*, and proof of *rumors*, viz. that at all events *facts* cannot be proved under the general issue in mitigation of damages. The plaintiff is not permitted upon the general issue to prove the truth of the libel, 2 Stark. R. 93; 2 Selw. N. P. 1197.

(*n*) 11 Price, 235.

IN CASE.

In actions for slander in particular.

the evidence might fall short of satisfying the jury that the strict legal offence was committed by the plaintiff, yet they may take the facts into their consideration in estimating the damages (*o*). It is matter of prudence, depending on the facts of each case, whether or not to plead a justification. If the evidence will either establish the plaintiff's guilt or at least establish his culpable conduct, it seems in general advisable to plead a justification as generally as may be admissible.

In Saunders *v.* Mills (*p*), the Court of Common Pleas held that the defendant, in mitigation of damages, might show that he copied a libellous report of an action from another newspaper into his own, and so was not the inventor of the slander, and consequently had less of malice against the plaintiff; but that he could not prove that it had apppeared concurrently in several other newspapers.

When and how to justify specially.

2dly. *When the defendant must specially justify the libel or slander, and how the plea should be framed.* It is now well settled, that in an action for a libel or slanderous words the defendant cannot, *under the general issue*, give in evidence the *truth* of the matter, or any part of it, *even in mitigation of damages*; but *must* justify *specially* (910), stating the particular facts which evince the truth of the imputation (*q*): and this rule holds whether the imputation upon the plaintiff's character be of a general or specific nature (*r*). But in an action for words *not* actionable in themselves it was held, that evidence of their *truth* might be given in evidence under the *general issue* (*s*). In framing a plea of justification of the truth, care must be taken to observe the following rules: 1st. It is necessary, although the libel contain a *general* imputation upon the plaintiff's character, that the plea should state *specific facts*, showing in what particular instances, and in what exact manner he has
[*532] misconducted himself (*t*); 2dly. The matters *set up by way of justification should be strictly conformable with the slander laid in the declaration, and must be proved as laid, at least in substance (*u*); and, 3dly, If the matter of justification can be extended to the whole of the libel or slander, the plea should not be confined to part only, leaving the rest unjustified (*v*).

It is now decided, that in an action for a *libel* it is not a good plea that the libellous matter was communicated to the defendant by a third person, whose name the defendant disclosed when he published the statement (*x*) (911). And

(*o*) Chalmers *v.* Shackle and others, 6 Car. & P. 475.

(*p*) 6 Bing. 213.

(*q*) See Stra. 1200; Willes, 20, 24; 1 Saund. 130, n. 1, 243, c. n. 1; 11 Price, 235; Selw. N. P. Slander, IV. Libel, II.; 3 C. & P. 512; 1 Stark. Slander, 2d ed. 465.

(*r*) *Id.*; Willes, 24. But if the plaintiff prove other words not stated in his declaration, to show malice, &c. (see *ante*, 438) the defendant may, under the general issue, prove the truth of *such* words, 2 Stark. Rep. 457. The defendant cannot be allowed to prove that the *plaintiff libelled him*, 3 B. & C. 113; 4 D. & R. 670, S. C.; 1 R. & M. 422.

(*s*) 1 M. & M. 1.

(*t*) This rule is considered and illustrated by examples in considering *certainty* as one of the qualities of a plea of justification.

(*u*) Cro. Jac. 676, 578; Cro. Eliz. 683; 13 East, 554; 2 B. & C. 678; 4 D. & R. 230, S. C.; 1 Stark. Slander, 2d ed. 480.

(*v*) See an instance, 1 Stark. Slander, 2d ed. 484; Mountney *v.* Watton, 2 B. & Adol. 673.

(*x*) De Crespigney *v.* Wellesley, 2 M. & P. 695; 5 Bing. 392; 3 Bar. & Cres. 24; 4 D. & R. 695, S. C.

(910) Vide Sheppard *v.* Merrill, 13 Johns. Rep. 475.

(911) { See Jackson *v.* Stetson et ux., 15 Mass. Rep. 48. } It has been held that such plea was not admissible in an action for a libel. Dole *v.* Lyon, 10 Johns. Rep. 447, where the cases of Davis *v.* Lewis, and Maitland *v.* Goldney, were considered, and the ap-

it is extremely probable that the same general doctrine would be applied to *oral* slanders (y). At all events, this defence, if any, should be specially pleaded (z). And it would be necessary to state in the plea, in *hæc verba*, the very words used by the author (a); and to give a cause of action against the latter, by showing that he spoke the words falsely and maliciously; and also to allege that the defendant *believed* what he heard, and repeated the words on a justifiable occasion (b).

IN CASE. — In actions for slander in particular.

It appears to be doubtful whether, if the defendant rely upon the defence that the publication was no more than a true and correct *report* or account of a *judicial proceeding* (912), he *must* plead the matter specially (c). That he *may* plead this matter cannot be doubted, and it is usual and better to adopt that course. It has been decided that in an action for a libel, purporting to be a report of a coroner's inquest, evidence of the correctness of the report is admissible under the general issue in mitigation of damages (d); but that no evidence of the truth or falsehood of the facts stated at the inquest is admissible on either side (e).

Where in an action for a libel, which purported to be a report of a trial, the defendant pleaded that the supposed *libel was *in substance* a true account and report of the trial, it was held, upon demurrer, that the plea was bad; for it should have shown *the facts*, so that it might appear on the record whether the report were true in substance, and should not have stated the mere inference or conclusion which *the defendant* drew from that which transpired at the trial (f). Upon the same ground the following case was decided:—A libel purported to be a speech of counsel at the trial of the plaintiff on a criminal charge; and it stated, after setting out the speech, that a witness was called who proved all that had been stated by counsel, and that the defendant was immediately after that acquitted upon a defect in proving some matter of form. The plea stated that in fact such speech was made, and that the witness called *proved all that had been so stated;* but it *did not set out the evidence,* or justify the truth of the charges made in the counsel's speech: and the Court held that the plea was therefore insufficient (g). Where part of a pub-

[*533]

(y) See *id.;* 10 B. & C. 263.

(z) See 7 T. R. 17; 2 East, 426; 5 *Id.* 463; Holt, N. P. R 533; 1 Stark. Slander, 2d ed. 473.

(a) 2 East, 426.

(b) M'Pherson *v.* Daniels, 10 B. & C. 263; and see further 3 Bar. & Cres. 24; 4 D. & R. 695, S. C.; as to requisites of such a plea.

(c) 1 B. & P. 525; 1 Stark. Slander, 2d ed. 468 to 473; see *ante*, 528.

(d) See *ante*, 530. As to its being no *defence* that the publication was a correct report of a *preliminary* inquiry, see 1 B. & Ald. 379; 3 B. & C. 556; 5 D. & R. 447, S. C.

(e) 2 C. & P. 570; 1 M. & M. 46; S. C. *cor.* Tenterden, C. J. His Lordship is reported in 1 M. & M. Reports, to have said, that proof of the correctness of the report being short of a justification, was, upon the general principle, admissible, as governing the damages; but that he should express no opinion whether, if pleaded, there would have been a defence. See *ante*, 530, note (m).

(f) 4 B. & C. 473; 6 D. & R. 528, S. C.

(g) 4 B. & C. 605; and see 2 B. & Adol. 673.

plication of the rule to written slander was denied, and KENT, C. J., observes, that it may well be questioned whether even this rule as to slanderous words ought not to depend upon the *quo animo* with which the words, with the name of the author, are repeated. In the case of The Earl of Leicester *v.* Walter, 2 Campb. 251, which was an action for a libel, Sir James Mansfield, C. J., allowed general suspicion and report to be given in evidence under the general issue. {See also Kennedy *v.* Gregory, Morris *v.* Duane, 1 Binn. 85, 90. Coleman *v.* Southwick, 9 Johns. Rep. 45.}

(912) {See ante, page 259.}

IN CASE. In actions for slander in particular.

lication consists of a report of judicial proceedings, and the rest of comment, since the separation and discrimination of each part necessary for the purpose of defence, the defendant ought to take upon himself the burthen of making it, in order that the Court may see what part he means to justify; and the plea will be defective if it do not specifically point out the exact parts which it is intended to justify as being a correct report (*h*).

To a declaration for a libel, described as contained in the report in a newspaper of a magisterial inquiry, a plea that the several matters and things in the supposed libels contained were true, is bad; because it is uncertain whether it means that the report in the newspaper was a true report of the proceedings, or that the facts mentioned in it were true; and if the latter were the meaning, then the plea is much too general (*i*). And a plea alleging that the supposed libel is justifiable, because it is a true report of a trial, &c. is defective, if, in setting out, as is necessary, the evidence, &c. which was given, it appear therefrom that the account or report is not warranted by such evidence, or
[*534] *that the libel contains unjustifiable comments and observations by the writer (*k*). It is, however, in general sufficient that the report of the former proceedings was in substance correct and faithful; and although the plea should show the facts and detail the evidence, &c. it need not contain every word uttered at the trial (*l*).

Consistently with the elementary principle of pleading, that pleas of justification, or in avoidance, must *confess* the fact to which they are applied, it is essential that a special plea justifying the publication of slanderous matter should admit the libel or words complained of; and the plea will be bad if it show a publication of words substantially different from those laid in the declaration (*m*).

It is also a rule applicable as well to pleas justifying slander as other special pleas, that they should not be extended to the justification of more than the matter to which in the commencement of his plea the defendant *professes* to plead. This rule will be considered fully hereafter. We may, however, here mention, as an example to the rule, that if the libel be that the plaintiff, a proctor, had been "*thrice* suspended for misconduct," a plea to the whole declaration, showing only *one* suspension, is ill on demurrer (*n*). As, however, such libellous matter is divisible, a plea as to one suspension, justifying the libel *pro tanto*, is sustainable (*o*).

Care should therefore be taken to confine the plea in the introductory part to the exact portions of the libel or slander which can be, and afterwards are, justified. In enumerating such portions it is not unusual to repeat and set out the matter in *hæc verba*; (viz. "as to the following parts of the said suppos-

(*h*) 7 East, 492.

(*i*) 3 B. & C. 556; 5 D. & R. 447, S. C. It has also been decided that the publication of proceedings before a magistrate cannot be justified on the ground of its being a correct report of such proceedings, where the matter brought before him is not so brought in his *judicial* character or in discharge of his magisterial functions, 3 Bar. & Cres. 24; 4 D. & R. 695, S. C.

(*k*) See 3 B. & C. 556; 5 D. & R. 447, S. C.; 3 B. & Ald. 702; 7 Moore, 200, S. C. in error; 6 Bing. 213.

(*l*) See *per* Littledale, J., 4 B. & C. 483; 6 D. & R. 533, S. C.; and see 1 Bing. 403, as an authority for the position, that it is sufficient that the *substance* of the libel be justified and proved.

(*m*) See 10 B. & C. 263; Cro. Eliz. 239, 153; Jones, 307; 1 Saund. 244 c, note. And *per* Tindal, C. J., 6 Bing. 593.

(*n*) 6 Bing. 266.

(*o*) 6 Bing. 587.

ed libel, to wit, &c. the said defendant says, &c."); but a general reference to such parts of the slander as are justified may be sufficient, if the Court can see with certainty what parts are referred to. Thus, if the reference be "to so much of the said supposed libel as imputes to the plaintiff perjury," &c. (as the case may be,) "the defendant saith," &c.; that would be sufficient, without repeating all these *parts again, which would tend to prolixity of pleading, and ought to be avoided (p). And where the libel was that the plaintiff, a proctor, had been "suspended *three times* for extortion, once by Lord S. and twice by Sir J. N." and the plea was, as to so much of the libel as imputed that the plaintiff had been "*once* suspended," showing a suspension by Sir J. N., it was held that the plea sufficiently designated the matter to which it was meant to be applied (q). IN CASE. In actions for slander in particular. [*535]

The plea of justification need not *expressly* deny the *innuendoes* and epithets contained in the declaration; for if the fact be justified, the motive, intention, and manner are immaterial (r).

The reasons which render it expedient or injudicious in certain cases to *justify* specially in an action for slander or a libel, will be pointed out upon a future occasion.

It was always necessary to plead the statute of limitations specially (s).

By the statute 8 & 9 W. 3 (t), no *retaking* on fresh pursuit shall be given in evidence on the trial of any issue in any action of *escape* against the marshal, &c. unless the same shall be specially pleaded, nor shall any special plea be received or allowed, unless oath be first made in writing by the defendant, and filed in the proper office, that the prisoner, for whose escape such action is brought, did escape without his consent, privity or knowledge (u). The plea of recaption must show that the party was retaken before the action for the escape was brought (x). A plea that the prisoner escaped without the gaoler's default, and returned before action brought, should allege a detention, and that it continued to the time of action, or that it has been terminated by legal means (y). Plea of recaption to a declaration in case for an escape.

In general, when the defence consists of matters of *law*, though the defendant was at liberty to give the matter in evidence under the general issue, he *might* always plead it specially (z); and this was frequently advisable when there was no fact disputed, but only a point of law which might be decided upon *demurrer, or on a writ of error; or where the plaintiff, by his replication, would be compelled to admit one or more material facts in the plea, and would not be at liberty to reply *de injuria*, and consequently the defendant's proof rendered less difficult (a). Thus, in trover for a dog the defendant When might have pleaded specially in case. [*536]

(p) See *per* Le Blanc, J., 7 East, 507; and Tindal, C. J., 6 Bing. 593. See, however, *ante*, 533, 534.

(q) 6 Bing. 587.

(r) Burr. 807; 1 Stark. Slander, 2d ed. 476.

(s) 2 Saund. 63 a.

(t) 8 & 9 Will. 3, c. 27, s. 6.

(u) 2 T. R. 126; 3 Salk. 150.

(x) Stra. 873; Selw. N. P. Debt, IX. 6th ed. 630. Form of plea, *post*, vol. iii.

(y) 11 East, 406.

(z) 2 Mod. 274, 276; 3 Mod. 166; Com. Rep. 273; 1 Wils. 44, 175; Doc. Plac. 203; Cro. Eliz. 871, 900; and see in general 4 Bar. & Cres. 552, 553.

(a) 2 Mod. 277; 1 Stra. 5; 1 B. & P. 80; Cro. Eliz. 539; 1 East, 217; 1 P. Wms. 258, 259; see further as to this, *post*.

IN CASE. In actions for slander in particular.

might plead that E. F. was seised in fee and lord of a certain manor, and that he by warrant appointed the defendant gamekeeper, and that such warrant was duly entered with the clerk of the peace, and that a certain person not qualified by law to kill game was using the dog for the destruction of game, wherefore the defendant took him, &c.; to which plea the plaintiff could not reply *de injuria*, generally, because that would put in issue the seisin in fee and the warrant (*b*). So, in case for an injury to a right of common, the defendant may plead as a justification, a right of common by grant to himself, or that he acted as servant to the owner of the soil seised in fee, and thereby materially lessen the evidence which he would otherwise have to adduce on the trial (*c*). The statute of limitations is not guilty within *two* years in an action for *verbal* slander *actionable in itself* (*d*); or within *six* years in any other action on the case (*e*)(913), as for criminal conversation, or debauching a daughter, &c. and the statute must in this action be specially pleaded (*f*).

IN TROVER.

In TROVER, the general issue is *not guilty*; and it is not usual in this action to plead any other plea (914), except the statute of limitations, and a release (*g*). The bankruptcy of the *plaintiff*, when it was a defence, might have been given in evidence under the general issue (*h*). The defendant, however, was at *liberty* to plead specially any thing which admitted the property in the plaintiff, and the conversion, but justified the [*537] *latter (*i*). We shall presently see how extensively the Reg. Gen. Hil. T. 4 W. 4, has required a special plea in trover (*j*). The statute of limitations must be specially pleaded (*k*); and it seems to be judicious to plead specially a former recovery or verdict in a prior action (*l*).

AVOWRIES, &c. IN REPLEVIN.

The plea in *denial* in REPLEVIN is *non cepit modo et formâ*, by which the defendant put in issue, not only the taking, but also the taking in the place mentioned in the declaration (*m*). But the defendant could not have a return of the cattle under that plea, and therefore if he want such a return, he should plead that he took the cattle in some other place, describing it, and traverse

(*b*) 1 Wils. 315; Cro. Eliz. 539; 1 B. & P. 80; 1 East, 217.

(*c*) 2 Mod. 274, 277; Cro. Eliz. 539; Willes, 619, 620; 1 Stra. 5.

(*d*) 1 Sid. 95; Sir W. Jones, 196.

(*e*) 21 Jac. 1, c. 16, s. 3.

(*f*) 1 Lutw. 99; 2 Saund. 63, n. 6.

(*g*) In 2 Campb. 558, it is said to have been considered necessary to plead a release specially in trover. *Sed quære*.

(*h*) 7 T. R. 301; see *ante*, 28.

(*i*) *Ante*, 535; 4 Mod. 424; 1 Stra. 5; Com. Dig. Pleader, E. 14; Cro. Eliz. 539. The case in 2 Ld. Raym. 886, is erroneous as to this point.

(*j*) *Post*.

(*k*) *Ante*, 535; 1 Lutw. 99. Form of the plea, 8 B. & C. 285. The statute runs from the time of the conversion, though the plaintiff was ignorant thereof, until within six years, 5 Bar. & Cres. 149.

(*l*) See *ante*, 513, n. (*c*); 1 Show. 146.

(*m*) 1 Stra. 507; 2 Mod. 199; 1 Saund. 347, note 1; Gilb. Repl. 4th ed. (1823); 2 Wils. 355.

---

(913) { See as to New York, 2 Rev. Stat. p. 295, 296, s. 18, 19. See as to Pennsylvania, the Act of 27th March, 1713, sect. 1, 2. 1 Sm. Laws, 77. }

(914) Vide Kennedy *v.* Strong, 10 Johns. Rep. 291.

the place laid in the declaration; and, in order to have return, should avow or make cognizance (915), stating the cause for which he distrained (n); but if the defendant ever had the cattle in the place stated in the declaration, in leading them to the pound, though he took them elsewhere, he should avow accordingly (o). Where the distress is for poors' rates, the defendant may plead not guilty, and give the cause of taking in evidence (p); and a general plea is given by statute where a distress is taken for sewers' rates (q); and the Bankrupt Act gives the general issue to a defendant sued for any thing done in pursuance thereof (r). But the defendant must avow or make cognizance with more particularity under a distress for rent (s)(916), rent-charge (t), or damage feasant (u). And though the statute (x) gives a general avowry in cases of distresses for rent-service, &c. (y)(917), it is still advisable in some cases to set out the title specially, in order that a traverse of a particular part of it may be taken, and that the parties may proceed to trial upon some particular point in issue (z); and this statute does *not extend to avowries for heriot custom, or for a rent-charge (a). And an avowry for cognizance for rent in arrear must correctly describe the terms of the tenancy (b), though under an avowry for two years' rent, the party will succeed though it appear that rent was due for one year only (c). Although in general it is sufficient to allege a mere possessory title against a wrong-doer, yet in replevin there is an exception; and it is not sufficient to plead merely that the defendant was *possessed* of a close, and because the cattle trespassed, &c., he took them damage feasant. But it may be alleged generally that the close was the close, soil, and freehold (*liberum tenementum*) of the defendant (d). IN REPLEVIN. [*538]

(n) 1 Saund. 347, note 1.
(o) *Post*, vol. iii.
(p) 43 Eliz. c. 2, s. 19. See Co. Lit. 283 a.
(q) 23 Hen. 8, c. 5, s. 19.
(r) 6 Geo. 4, c. 16, s. 44.
(s) 11 Geo. 2, c. 19, s. 22; 2 Saund. 284 d, n. 4; 1 Saund. 347, note 6.
(t) 1 B. & P. 213; 1 New Rep. 56.
(u) 2 B. & P. 359; 2 Saund. 284 d; 1 Saund. 347.
(x) 11 Geo. 2, c. 19, s. 22.
(y) As to distinction between an avowry and a justification in replevin, see Marriot v. Shaw, Com. Rep. 274; Vin. Ab. Disclaimer, 503.
(z) 2 Saund. 284 d.
(a) 2 Wils. 28; 2 Saund. 168 a, b; 1 B. & P. 213.
(b) 4 Taunt. 320. See as to variance, &c. *ante*, 334.
(c) 6 East, 434; 6 T. R. 248; 3 B. & P. 348.
(d) *Post*, vol. iii.; 1 Saund. 346 e, note 2; 2 *Id.* 285, note 3; Stephen, 2d ed. 358, 359.

(915) The plea of property in a stranger, which may be pleaded either in abatement or in bar, entitles the party to a return without an avowry. Harrison v. M'Intosh, 1 Johns. Rep. 380, 384. Bemus v. Beekman, 3 Wend. R. 667. M'Farland v. Barker, 1 Mass. R. 152.

(916) Vide Shepherd v. Boyce, 2 Johns. Rep. 446. {In Pennsylvania, by the 10th sect. of the Act of 21st March, 1772, it is provided, "That it shall and may be lawful for all defendants in replevin, to avow and make conusance generally, that the plaintiff in replevin or other tenant of the lands and tenements whereon such distress was made, enjoyed the same under a grant, or demise, at such a certain rent or service, during the time wherein the rent or service distrained for incurred, which rent or service was then and still remains due, without further setting forth the grant, tenure, demise, or title of such landlord, or landlords, lessor, or lessors," &c. 1 Sm. Laws, 370.}

(917) This statute has not been adopted in the state of New York. Harrison v. M'Intosh, 1 Johns. Rep. 384. The 14th and 15th sections of this statute are in force in Pennsylvania, 3 Binn. 626, Roberts' Dig. 236. {But the above stated provision of the Pennsylvania act has been adopted in the Revised Statutes, vol. ii. 529, s. 41.}

IN TRESPASS. The general rule. In TRESPASS, whether to the *person, personal* or *real property*, the defendant can, under the general issue of not guilty, give in evidence matter which directly controverts the fact of his having committed the acts complained of (*e*), as in trespass for driving the shaft of a gig into the plaintiff's horse, if in fact the plaintiff drove his horse against such shaft, and thereby himself occasioned the injury, or if the injury were accidental, such matter may be properly proved under not guilty (*f*), and in trespass for assault and battery with a tearing of clothes, a plea of not guilty of the assault *modo et forma* was held to operate as a denial of the battery and *laceravit* as well as the assault (*g*), and no person is bound to justify who is not *prima facie* a trespasser (*h*)(918). The plea of not guilty therefore is proper in trespass to *persons* if the defendant committed no assault, battery, or imprisonment; and in trespass to *personal* property, if the defendant were not guilty of the taking, &c. (*i*) In trespass to real property, this plea formerly not only put in issue the fact of the trespass, but also the possessory title or right of the plaintiff: because the declaration, as before shown (*k*), states the plaintiff's title to the close, by the allegation that it was the close "of the plaintiff;" a matter which is plainly denied by the general issue not guilty "of the said trespasses, &c." (*l*) It followed that before the recent rules any title (919), whether freehold or possessory, in the defendant, or a person under whom he claimed, might be given in evidence under "not guilty," (920) if such title showed that the right of possession, which was necessary in order to support trespass, was not in the
[*539] plaintiff, but in the defendant, or *the party under whom he justified (*m*). But where the act would at common law *prima facie* appear to be a trespass, and the *facts* stated in the declaration could not be denied, any matter of justification or excuse, or done by virtue of a warrant or authority, must in general be specially pleaded (*n*)(921). And therefore even where the defendant did the act at the request of the plaintiff (*o*); or where the injury was occasioned by the plaintiff's own default (*p*); those matters of defence must always have been specially pleaded. If a plea of justification consisted of two facts, each of which would, when separately pleaded, amount to a good defence, it would, unless in the case of pleas of prescription, sufficiently support the justification, if one of those facts be found by the jury (*q*). Where the committing the trespasses complained of could not be disputed, but could be justified, it was frequently advisable to plead such justification alone, without the plea of the

(*e*) 3 Bing. 135; 10 Moore, 502, S. C.; Pearcy *v.* Walter, 6 Car. & P. 232, and see in general 2 Saund. 159, note 10.
(*f*) 6 Car. & P. 232.
(*g*) 3 Bing. 135; 10 Moore, 502, S. C.
(*h*) Cowp. 478.
(*i*) *Id.*
(*k*) *Ante*, 413, 414.
(*l*) 8 T. R. 403; 7 T. R. 354; Willes, 222; 1 Bing. 158.
(*m*) *Ante*, 538, note (*l*); *aliter* as to tenancy in common with plaintiff, Gow, 201.
(*n*) 2 Campb. 378, 379, 500; Co. Lit. 282 b, 283 a; Dougl. 611; 2 Rol. Ab. 682; 12 Mod. 120; 1 Saund. 298, n. 1; Com. Dig. Pleader, E. 15, 16, 17; Stephen, 2d edit. 377.
(*o*) 2 Campb. 378, 379.
(*p*) 2 Campb. 500.
(*q*) 1 Taunt. 146; Jenk. 4, Cent. 184.

(918) Rawson *v.* Morse, 4 Pick. Rep. 127.
(919) Vide Hyatt *v.* Wood, 4 Johns. Rep. 152. 1 Phillips' Ev. 129. Monumoi *v.* Rogers, 1 Mass. Rep. 160.
(920) But not property in a stranger by whose order the defendant entered. Philpot *v.* Holmes, Peake's Cas. 67.
(921) Rawson *v.* Morse, Waters *v.* Silley, 4 Pick. Rep. 127, 145. Vide Butterworth *v.* Soper, 13 Johns. Rep. 443. Gelston and Schenck *v.* Hoyt, 13 Johns. Rep. 579.

general issue, for by that means the defendant's counsel might on the trial have the general reply (r)(922). Where the defence was that the defendant obtained a verdict in a former suit upon the same cause of action, the plea should be special by way of estoppel (s). IN TRESPASS. To persons

In trespass to *persons*, *son assault demesne* (t); moderate correction (923) of a servant, &c. (u); *molliter manus imposuit* (924) to preserve the peace, or a justification in defence of the possession of real or personal property (v); or by authority of law without process, as a private individual (x); or under civil process either mesne or final (y), of superior (z), or inferior, or foreign courts, must always have been pleaded specially (a)(925). A plea of justification is to enumerate and cover the whole, or the plaintiff without a special replication or new assignment will be entitled to a verdict for the trespasses proved and not pleaded to (b). For whoever assaults or imprisons another (except in some cases under particular statutes hereafter noticed) (c), must justify himself by showing specially to the Court that the act was lawful (926). And a plea justifying an arrest of the plaintiff upon the *ground [*540] that a felony had been committed, and that there was reasonable ground to suspect and accuse the plaintiff, must distinctly state the specific *reasons* for suspecting the plaintiff (d). These are positive rules of law, in order to prevent surprise on the plaintiff at the trial, by the defendant then assigning various reasons and causes of imprisoning the plaintiff, of which he had no notice, and which consequently he could not be prepared to meet at the trial on the plea of not guilty, on fair and equal terms with respect to the evidence and proof of facts (e). But if a person touched another in conversation or in joke, so that no actionable assault or battery was committed, then no special plea was necessary (f). *Molitur manus imposuit* was a justification of a battery as well as an assault (g)(927). In trespass to personalty.

(r) 3 Campb. 366.
(s) 2 B. & Ald. 662; M'Clel. & Y. 509.
(t) 8 T. R. 299; 1 Saund. 77, 296, n. 1.
(u) 2 B. & P. 224.
(v) 8 T. R. 78, 299; 3 Wils. 71.
(x) 6 T. R. 562. A constable, &c. may plead the general issue, *post*.
(y) 3 Wils. 370; 1 Saund. 298, note 1.
(z) *Id.*
(a) 2 East, 260, 274; Cowp. 18.
(b) Bush *v.* Parker, 1 Bing. N. C. 72.
(c) *Post.*
(d) *Ante*, 271.
(e) Co. Lit. 282 b, 383 a; 3 Wils. 370, 371.
(f) Rep. temp. Hardw. 301; 1 Selw. 33.
(g) Com. Dig. Pleader, 3 M. 16. *Per* Best, C. J., 4 Bing. 206.

(922) { See Davis *v.* Mason, 4 Pick. Rep. 156. Weidman *v.* Kohr, 13 Serg. & Rawle, 17. }

(923) Hannah *v.* Edes, 15 Mass. Rep. 347. But in an action of assault and battery, the improper conduct of the plaintiff in the business of the defendant, before the time of the alleged assault, are not admissible in evidence for the purpose of mitigating damages. Matthews *v* Terry, 15 Conn. R. 455. Whenever in answer to the defendant's plea of *son assault*, he relies upon new matter, he should not reply generally *de injuria*, but should state such new matter specially. Brown *v.* Bennett, 5 Cowen, 181.

(924) { *Molliter manus imposuit* may justify a mere *assault*, but it is no answer to a charge of beating, bruising, wounding, and ill treating the plaintiff. Gates *v.* Lounsbury, 20 Johns. Rep. 427. }

(925) Vide Butterworth *v.* Soper, 13 Johns. Rep. 443.

(926) Where the ground on which it is attempted to make the defendant liable is, his having on delivering process to an officer, directed him to arrest and imprison the plaintiff, he may show under the general issue that the arrest and imprisonment were not a consequence of his instructions to the officer, but in pursuance of a competent and paramount authority: for if the arrest and imprisonment were the effect of any other cause than the instructions he gave the officer, he was emphatically, not guilty, and it was not a case for justification. Herrick *v.* Manly, 1 Caines' Rep. 252.

(927) See Gates *v.* Lounsbury, 20 Johns. Rep. 427.

IN TRESPASS.

To persons.

In trespass to personalty.

*In trespass to *personal* property, a seizure as an heriot service (*h*), or for poor rates (*i*), might before the recent rules be given in evidence under the general issue; but in general, matters which admit the plaintiff's property as well as the seizure, &c. must always have been pleaded (*k*); as a justification for cutting ropes or killing dogs (*l*), or taking guns, &c. (*m*), or even the licence of the plaintiff to do the act complained of (*n*), or that it was occasioned by his own negligence (*o*). A distress for *rent*, when made on the demised premises, might by express enactment be given in evidence under the general issue (*p*), but if made *off* the demised premises, as on a common, or under a fraudulent removal, the defence must be specially pleaded (*q*). A distress or seizure for tolls (*r*), stallage at a fair, &c. (*s*), under a by-law (*t*), or for damage feasant by the occupier (*u*), or a commoner (*v*), or other matter of justification, with or without process, must also be pleaded specially (*x*) (928).

To realty. In trespass to *real property*, we have seen that the defendant might under the general issue dispute the plaintiff's possessory right, by showing that the title and possessory right are vested in himself, or in another under whom he claims, or whose authority he had (*y*). Although the plaintiff prove mere possession, that will suffice, if the defendant cannot show a superior right in himself or another under whom he can justify (*z*).

There are some instances in which, although it was not heretofore essential, yet it might be judicious to plead specially the defendant's *title*, or the title of the party under whom he had *authority* to commit the acts complained of.

If the closes were not described by their abuttals or names in the declaration, and the defendant was doubtful as to the exact extent of the property claimed by the plaintiff, and has any close in the parish mentioned in the declaration, he might, before the recent rules, expressly requiring the name or abuttals or other particular description to be stated, compel the plaintiff to *new assign*, designating and describing specifically what property he claimed, by pleading *liberum tenementum*. The reason of this doctrine, and the rules with regard to new assignments, will be explained under the head of *Replications*.

The plea of *liberum tenementum* (929) states a *general freehold title*, without

(*h*) Cro. Eliz. 32; 2 Saund. 168 a, b.
(*i*) 43 Eliz. c. 2, s 19.
(*k*) Com. Dig. Pleader, 3 M. 25; though connected with a possessory claim to land, *post*, 542.
(*l*) 1 Saund. 84; 2 Lutw. 1494; Com. Dig Pleader, 3 M. 33; 1 Taunt 570; 2 Campb. 511.
(*m*) Com Dig. Pleader, 3 M. 25, &c.
(*n*) 2 Campb. 378, 379.
(*o*) 2 Campb. 500.
(*p*) 11 Geo. 2, c. 19, s 21.
(*q*) 1 Esp. R. 257; 4 Campb. 136.
(*r*) Ld. Raym. 384; 3 Burr. 1402; Lutw. 1519; 8 Went. 124; Carth. 357.
(*s*) 3 Lev. 224, 227.
(*t*) 1 T. R. 118; 4 Mod. 377.
(*u*) 1 Saund. 221; 2 *Id.* 294.
(*v*) 2 Wils. 51; Yelv 104; 3 Wils. 126, 291; 1 Saund. 346; 8 East, 394.
(*x*) 2 Campb. 378, 379, 500.
(*y*) *Ante*, 538.
(*z*) *Ante*, 202, 203. The defendant will prevail if he can show a superior title and right of possession, although he *forcibly* broke into the house, and took possession by actual force, and evicted the plaintiff. see 7 Moore, 574; 1 Bing. 158, S. C.

(928) An officer of the revenue, seizing goods as forfeited, and causing them to be libelled and tried, has but two pleas in justification at the suit of the owner, a condemnation, or an acquittal with certificate of probable cause. Gelston and Schenck *v.* Hoyt, 13 Johns. Rep. 579, 661. Vide 10 Conn. R. 322.

(929) Where the plaintiff alleged several trespasses in several closes, at different times, and the defendant pleaded that the several closes were one and the same close, and that it

defining the exact quality or nature of such title. It states that the *locus in quo* was and is the *close, soil, and freehold* of the defendant, &c. Under that plea *any* estate of *freehold*, as in fee, in tail, or for life, but not a freehold in remainder or reversion, might be given in evidence, and the plea was peculiar, and formed an exception to the general rule, that a party must show a *precise* title (a). This general plea was rarely of any other utility than to compel a *new assignment*, describing the closes where they had not been particularly described in the declaration (430). It might, however, be usefully adopted in all cases where the freehold was laid to be in a third person, and the defendant justified as the servant of the third party; as the plaintiff in his replication could deny one only of the two facts pleaded, viz. the freehold title pleaded, or the authority or command from the alleged freeholder to the defendant, and could not by his replication put *both those matters in issue; and that which is not denied is admitted on the record. *Liberum tenementum* was a good plea to trespass in a several or free fishery, the owner of the soil being *prima facie* owner of the fishery (b). IN TRESPASS. To realty. [*542]

2dly. If the defendant be anxious to compel the plaintiff to state his title *specially* upon the record, or admit some part of the title of the defendant, or the party under whom he justifies, he may also with propriety plead *liberum tenementum*, or adopt a still more special plea of title. Thus, if the defendant be in reality the freeholder, so that the plaintiff cannot with safety deny the plea, he is driven to admit its truth, and to deduce a title from the defendant, as that he demised the close to the plaintiff, &c.

In observing upon the *qualities* of pleas, we shall hereafter see that a special plea in trespass which claims for the defendant a *possessory* right, and yet does not give the plaintiff *express color*, is bad; because it amounts to the general issue, and violates the principle that a plea must *deny*, or must confess and avoid the matter alleged in the declaration. A plea of *liberum tenementum* is free from this objection because it gives *apparent* color; as it is not absolutely and manifestly inconsistent therewith, that the plaintiff had some inferior leasehold or minor title, in respect whereof he might have had a possessory right or title, or at least possession. But a special plea disclosing a *possessory* title in the defendant, as a *leaseholder* or *termor*, is openly at variance with, and directly contradicts, the very gist of the plaintiff's action of trespass. In such case, therefore, an *express color*, that is, a plausible or apparent but fictitious title, must be given to the plaintiff, according to the rules which will hereafter be explained. The object is to compel the plaintiff to state *specifically his* title, or deny that alleged in the special plea, an object which is rarely to be attained *liberum tenementum*, the replication to which may simply traverse the general allegation. In framing the special plea of title, care must be taken to attend to the following general rules, which are ably pointed out

(a) Stephen, 2d edit, 370; 1 Saund. 347 R. 201. d, n. 6. As to tenancy in common, Gow. (b) 18 Edw. 4; 4 Co. Lit. 127 a, notes.

was his freehold, it was held bad, and that the defendant should have justified as to all the closes, or have denied the trespasses as to all the closes, except one, and justified as to that. Nevins v. Keeler, 6 Johns. Rep. 63.

(230) {The plea admits the possession in the plaintiff, and the trespass charged in the plaintiff's pleading. Caruth v. Allen, 2 M'Cord's Rep. 226.}

IN TRESPASS. — To realty.

by Mr. Serjeant Stephen, with regard to the statement of a derivative title:— 1st. The derivation or commencement of an estate *in fee simple* need not be shown, as this would tend to useless prolixity. It suffices in general to deduce the title from the last absolute owner in fee simple, from or through whom [*543] the defendant *claims, although the fee was only conditional, or determinable on a certain event (*c*). 2dly. In the case of *particular estates*, being interests or titles less than a seisin in fee simple, and in the case of copyholds, their commencement must be shown; that is, the derivation of the title from the last seisin in fee must be alleged (*d*). 3dly. A party claiming by *inheritance* or descent, must specially show *how* and in what character he is heir (*e*). 4thly. If the party claim by *conveyance*, each distinct conveyance, and the nature thereof, must be specially set forth (*f*). The different forms of pleading title and conveyances are fully stated in the second volume. 5thly. It is a rule that the conveyance should be pleaded according to its legal import and effect, rather than its form of words (*g*). 6thly. Where the nature of the conveyance is such, that it would at common law be valid without deed or writing, there no deed or writing need be alleged in the pleading, though such document exist, and a statute render it necessary, as in the case of a conveyance with livery of seisin, &c.; but where the nature of the conveyance requires at common law a deed or other writing, such instrument must be alleged, as in the case of a grant of any thing which lies in grant, and cannot be granted without deed (*h*). And if a transfer of property be inoperative, except by statute, and the act require writing, as in the case of a devise of lands, the pleading must show that the will was in writing (*i*).

Although in general *liberum tenementum* may be given in evidence under the general issue, yet if the defendant, in taking possession of his close, &c. has necessarily injured or destroyed or removed *goods, the property of the plaintiff*, it is proper to plead *liberum tenementum*, justifying such acts as to the personalty, and the general issue is not sufficient. As if the defendant justify cutting the *plaintiff's* posts and rails, put on his, the defendant's, land, and the defendant do not claim such posts and rails (*k*)(931). But if the [*544] plaintiff has *affixed any thing to the defendant's freehold, so that it becomes part thereof, as a wall, &c., then the general issue will suffice, and it is not necessary specially to justify the destruction of such fixture, as it became the defendant's property by being annexed to his freehold (*l*).

An *excuse* of the trespass, as on account of a defect of fences which the plaintiff was bound to repair (*m*), or a license from the plaintiff (*n*); and a

(*c*) Stephen, 2d edit. 361; Co. Lit. 303 b; Cro. Car. 571; Doct. Pl. 287.

(*d*) Stephen, 2d edit. 362, 363; *ante*, 379, 380; 1 Saund. 186 d, n. 1. There is an exception where the title is only inducement, *ante*, 413, 414.

(*e*) Stephen, 2d edit. 365; *ante*, 402.

(*f*) *Id.*

(*g*) Stephen, 2d edit. 365; 1 Saund. 235 b, note 9. See *ante*, 334 to 336.

(*h*) Stephen, 2d edit. 366, 367; 1 Saund. 276 a, n. 2; *ante*, 254. A lease for years is, however, always pleaded by *deed*.

(*i*) 1 Saund. 276 a, n. 2; *ante*, 254, 257.

(*k*) 8 East, 394; *ante*, 541.

(*l*) 8 T. R. 403; 7 East, 329.

(*m*) Co. Lit. 283; 2 Saund. 285.

(*n*) *Ante*, 542; 2 Campb. 379; 2 T. R. 168; 7 Taunt. 156; Hob. 175; Gilb. C. P. 63; Vin. Ab. License; Com. Dig. Pleader, 3 M. 35; but see 21 Hen. 7, 28, pl. 5.

(931) The title to the soil does not come in question upon a declaration, only for cutting down and carrying away trees on the plaintiff's ground. Weidham v. Kohr, 13 Serg. & Rawle, 17.

justification under a rent-charge, or in respect of any *easement* or incorporeal right (*o*), as *common* of fishery (*p*), or of pasture (*q*), or of turbary (*r*), and a right of *way*, either public (*s*) or private (*t*), and whether by grant (*u*), will (*x*), prescription (*y*), custom, or necessity (*z*), must be pleaded specially (932). The forms and explanatory notes will be found in the third volume.

IN TRESPASS. — To realty.

In justifying a trespass to *land* under a *right of way*, &c., it was not sufficient for the defendant to plead that he was lawfully *possessed* of another close, and by reason of such possession was entitled to a right of way over the plaintiff's land; but he must set forth some special title to his close and right of way, as for example, that of seisin in fee of the close, and a prescription in a *que* estate (*a*) to the right of way, &c. (*b*). We shall presently see in the next division, stating the *present rules of pleading*, the effect of the recent statute, relieving parties from the necessity of pleading a right of *way* or of *common*, &c. in a *que* estate, and authorizing a more general mode of stating the right.

In pleading a right of common by prescription, the defendant must also have shown a seisin in fee of the land in respect of which he claims, and prescribed in the *que* estate for the right. Where a defendant justified under a right of common of pasture, by showing a demise from a freeholder for *life [*545] of the land in respect of which he claimed, and averred that *he*, the defendant, and all those whose estate he then had, and his landlord, from time, &c. had common of pasture in respect of the demised premises; it was held upon demurrer that the plea was bad (*c*).

An entry by authority of law without process; as that the *locus in quo* was an inn (*d*); or that the defendant entered to demand payment of his debt (*e*) (933); or to prevent murder (*f*); or to abate a nuisance to a water-course (*g*); or by virtue of process (*h*), criminal or civil, of a superior (*i*) or inferior Court (*k*); under mesne process, as a latitat, &c. (*l*), or under final process, as a *fi. fa.* (934), *elegit*, &c.; must be specially pleaded.

In all actions of trespass, whether to the person, personal or real property, matters in *discharge* or in *confession and avoidance* of the action, must be

(*o*) *Per* Lord Loughborough, 1 Hen. Bla. 352; 2 Saund. 402, note 1; Co. Lit. 283; 2 Wils. 173; Com. Dig. Pleader, E. 15.
(*p*) Com. Dig. Piscary.
(*q*) 1 Saund. 25, 340; 2 *Id.* 2.
(*r*) 6 T. R. 748.
(*s*) 1 Hen. Bla. 352; 8 T. R. 606; 2 Saund. 158 c, notes 4 and 6.
(*t*) *Id.*
(*u*) 2 Mod. 274; 3 East, 294.
(*x*) 1 B. & P. 371; 1 Saund. 323, n. 6; *Id.* 151 c.
(*y*) 1 East, 350, 377, 381; 1 B. & P. 371; 1 Saund. 322, n. 6.
(*z*) 1 Saund. 323; 8 T. R. 50; Lutw. 1487.
(*a*) As to this, see 2 Bla. Com. 264; 1 Saund. 346, n. 2; 4 T. R. 718, 719. As to a *declaration* for obstructing common, &c. *ante*, 415. As to variances in stating prescriptions, *ante*, 386.
(*b*) 1 Saund. 346, n. 2; Steph. 2d ed. 359. As to a right of way of *necessity*, see Peake's Addenda, or vol. ii. 152.
(*c*) 3 Young and Jerv. 93.
(*d*) Com. Dig. Pleader, 3 M. 35.
(*e*) *Id.*; Cro. Eliz. 876.
(*f*) 2 B. & P. 260.
(*g*) Raikes *v.* Townsend, 2 Smith's Rep. 9.
(*h*) 1 Saund. 298, n. 1.
(*i*) 3 B. & P. 223.
(*k*) 7 T. R. 665; Lutw. 914.
(*l*) 3 B. & P. 223.

(932) Matter of excuse or justification at common law must be pleaded, and cannot be received in evidence under the general issue. Root *v.* Chandler, 10 Wend. R. 112, 113. Demick *v.* Chapman, 11 Johns. Rep. 132. The reason of the rule is to prevent surprise. 7 Cowen, 35.

(933) { Van Buskirk *v.* Irving, 7 Cow. Rep. 36. }

(934) { Carson *v.* Wilson, 6 Halst. Rep. 43. }

IN TRESPASS. — To realty.

specially pleaded (*m*); as accord and satisfaction (*n*), arbitrament, release (*o*), former recovery (*p*), or to an action for an assault, a magistrate's certificate of acquittal of the assault (*q*), or tender of sufficient amends (*r*). So the statute of limitations, which in trespass to persons is, that the defendant was not guilty within four years, and in trespass to personal or real property within six years (*s*) (935), must be specially pleaded.

When the general issue authorized by statute, as in actions against *justices*, &c. 21 Jac. 1, c. 12.

In an action against *justices of the peace, mayors, constables, and other peace officers, or any others acting in their aid and assistance, or by their command* (*t*), for any thing done by them by virtue or by reason of their offices; or against persons for any thing done in pursuance of the bankrupt act (*u*); the general issue may be pleaded, and the special matter given in evidence. And if the lord chancellor be sued for committing a person to prison he may plead the general issue (*x*). There is a similar provision *in the highway (*y*), turnpike (*z*), militia, and assessed tax acts, building act, and in various other [*546] statutes, in protection of persons acting in the execution of their office, or others in aid of them (*a*)(936). In these cases, as well before as since the pleading rule Hil. T. 4 W. 4, the plea of not guilty suffices, and all the special matters may be given in issue under that plea (*b*). It is also a general rule at common law, that matters in mitigation of damages, &c. which cannot be specially pleaded, may be given in evidence under the general issue (*c*).

IN EJECTMENT.

In Ejectment, a defendant when he appears is compelled to enter into the consent rule and to plead the *general issue;* consequently in that action no special plea can be adopted (937). We have seen, however, that the Courts

(*m*) 3 Burr. 1353; 1 Bla. Rep. 388; 1 Wils. 45; *ante*, 538, 539.

(*n*) 3 Burr. 1353; 4 Taunt. 459.

(*o*) 3 Burr. 1353.

(*p*) *Id*; see *ante*, 513, note (*c*). Former recovery against co-trespasser, *ante*, 101. Form of plea, 3 C. & P. 489, note (*a*).

(*q*) Harding *v.* King, 6 Car. & P. 427.

(*r*) 21 Jac. 1, c. 16; Com. Dig. Pleader, 3 M. 36; Vin. Ab. Trespass, S. a, 542; 3 Lev. 37.

(*s*) 21 Jac. 1, c. 52; 6 East, 390.

(*t*) 21 Jac. 1, c. 12, s. 5; Co. Lit. 283; Vaugh. 111; see 3 Campb. 257; Holt, C. N. P. 478. As to when individual acting in aid must plead specially, see 3 Campb. 257; Holt, C. N. P. 478; 4 Taunt. 34; *ante*, 303.

(*u*) 6 Geo. 4, c. 16, s. 44; but it is more usual to plead this latter defence, 1 Montag. Bank. Law, 410; see pleas, *post*, vol. iii.; 2 M. & Sel. 133.

(*x*) Dicas *v.* Lord Brougham, 6 Car. & P. 249, 268.

(*y*) 13 Geo. 3, c. 78, s. 82; see 16 East, 215.

(*z*) 3 Geo. 4, c. 126, s. 147.

(*a*) See particularly the statutes 43 Eliz. c. 2, s. 19; 7 Jac. 1, c. 5; 11 Geo. 2, c. 19, s. 21; 23 Geo. 3, c. 70, s. 34; 24 Geo. 3, sess. 2, c. 47, s. 35, 39; 28 Geo. 3, c. 37, s. 23; 42 Geo. 2, c. 85, s. 6; and the 43 Geo. 3, c. 99, s. 70; under larceny acts, &c. 7 & 8 Geo. 4, c. 4, s. 155; c. 29, s. 75; c. 30, s. 41; 9 Geo. 4, c. 4, s. 155.

(*b*) Wells *v.* Ody, 2 Crom. M. & Ros. 128. But observe the suggestion of Alderson, B.

(*c*) Co. Lit. 283 a; 2 B. & P. 225.

---

(935) { As to Pennsylvania, see Act of 27th March, 1713, 1 Sm. Laws, 76; and to New York, 2 Rev. Stat. 295, 296, s. 18, 19. }

(936) The party at whose instance process, either civil or criminal, issued, if he voluntarily assisted the officer in executing it, may protect himself under the general issue. Nathan *v.* Cohen, 3 Campb. 237. But if he merely delivered it to the officer and directed him to arrest the plaintiff, he must plead the special matter as in other cases. Henick *v.* Manly, 1 Caines' Rep. 252.

(937) { In Pennsylvania, by the Act of 13th April, 1807, (4 Sm. Laws, 476,) "the plea in Ejectment shall be, "not guilty." }

have in some cases on special application permitted the defendant to plead to the jurisdiction (*d*). IN EJECTMENT.

WHEN IT IS ADVISABLE TO PLEAD SPECIALLY OR ONLY THE GENERAL ISSUE.

The various instances in which the general issue was sufficient, and in which a special plea was necessary before the late rules, have been pointed out, and may be collected from our observations on the pleas peculiar to each form of action. The important rule that a plea in bar must either deny, or must confess and avoid the plaintiff's allegation, and the consequent doctrine that a plea in confession and avoidance must give express or implied color, and that a special plea which amounts to the general issue is bad, will be considered hereafter (*e*). We may collect, that in general it was always essential to plead specially, 1st, where *new* matter was brought forward by way of defence, and the defendant admitted all the plaintiff's allegations, but denied or avoided their operation; subject however to the extensive innovations upon that rule in more modern times in *assumpsit*, debt on simple contract, and in case; 2dly, whenever the defence arises *after* the commencement of the action (*f*).

There are, it will be remembered, many instances in which there was, before the Reg. Gen. Hil. T. 4 W. 4,† the *option* of pleading the matter specially, or *setting it up as a defence under the general issue, it being matter which confessed and avoided the cause of action, or gave the plaintiff implied color (*g*). The pleas of infancy in assumpsit, and *liberum tenementum* in trespass, were of this kind. In cases of this nature it was often expedient to plead specially, in order either to compel the plaintiff in his replication to admit some of the facts stated in the plea, and thereby to narrow the defendant's evidence, or to compel the plaintiff to disclose his title or answer to the defence, and thereby narrow the ground on which he might rest his case on the trial. Thus, in his replication to the plea of infancy, the plaintiff must admit *or* deny the infancy; if he admit it, he must obviate its effect by showing that the debt arose for necessaries supplied, *or* must allege a ratification after the defendant attained his full age. Under the general issue all or any of these answers to the defence might be be set up. So *liberum tenementum* would often compel the plaintiff to new assign, giving an exact description of the *locus in quo*, &c.; or would oblige him to show his specific title, as a demise from the defendant, &c., and thereby admit that the defendant was the freeholder. And sometimes a special plea was proper in order to raise a question of law on the face of the pleadings, and thus obtain the opinion of the Court upon demurrer, without the intervention of a jury. It would be beyond the limits of this treatise to attempt to enumerate all the various instances in which it might be advisable or not to plead specially. [*547]

When advisable to plead only a justification.

In some cases, where a justification was to be pleaded, it was advisable not also to plead the general issue. Thus in trespass *quare clausum fregit*,

(*d*) *Ante*, 291, 477.
(*e*) *Post.*
(*f*) *Ante*, 513; *post.*
(*g*) See *ante*, 515, *post*; 4 B. & C. 547; 1 M. & P. 308.

† See American Editor's Preface.

WHEN TO PLEAD SPECIALLY. if the plaintiff's possession could not be disputed, and the defendant relied upon a right of way, it was better not to plead the general issue, because if only the right of way were pleaded and traversed then the defendant's counsel had a right to begin at the trial, and thereby, in case the plaintiff should examine any witness in chief, the defendant's counsel would have the advantage of the reply (*h*). And this course was sometimes advisedly adopted in actions for a libel, where the publication of the libel as described in the declaration was to be admitted (*i*). And in actions against executors and administrators, upon causes of action which accrued against the deceased, it was often impolitic in reference to costs to plead the general issue, and there- [*548] by drive *the plaintiff to trial to prove the debt, in cases in which there was no reasonable ground to dispute it (*k*).

When advisable not to plead specially. On the other hand, in an action for assault and battery, it was not advisable to plead specially, justifying the battery, if there were the least doubt of establishing the justification, for where a battery is not admitted by the plea the judge must certify to give the plaintiff his full costs, if he obtain a verdict for damages less than 40*s*.; but where the defendant by his plea admits a battery, and it is found against him, no certificate is necessary (*l*). So, in trespass *quare clausum fregit*, if the defendant plead a licence or other justification (which does not make title to the land,) to the whole of the trespasses, and it be found against him, the plaintiff is entitled to full costs without a certificate, though he do not recover 40*s*. damages (*m*)(938); and the special plea should therefore in these cases be confined merely to such trespasses as the defendant can certainly justify. However, in case for slander, though the defendant justify, and it be found against him, yet if the damages be under 40*s*. the plaintiff cannot recover more costs than damages (*n*); in the latter action, therefore, there is no objection to a special plea on the ground of costs, though it is not advisable to justify on the ground that the words are true, unless the plea can be supported by indisputable evidence, because such a justification when ineffectual will in general materially enhance the damages. But there are however some decisions that under the general issue, in case for slanderous matter, the truth cannot be proved even in mitigation of damages (*o*); and therefore a special plea is often necessary with a view to reduce the damages, although the proofs fall short of substantiating the exact truth of all the slander stated. It is also doubtful whether *rumors* or *suspicions* of the plaintiff's guilt can be shown even in mitigation of damages (*p*), which often presents an additional reason for pleading specially to let in such evidence.

MATTER OF ESTOPPEL, WHEN [*549] Matter of *estoppel* should be specially pleaded as such. Thus, if the defendant obtained a verdict against the plaintiff *in a former action upon the

(*h*) 3 Campb. 366, 368.
(*i*) 3 C. & P. 474.
(*k*) See Tidd, 9th edit. 979, 980.
(*l*) 6 T. R. 562; Tidd, 9th edit. 965; see 7 Taunt. 689; 1 Moore, 420, S. C.
(*m*). 7 T. R. 660; 7 East, 325; Tidd, 9th ed. 963; see 9 Price, 314.
(*n*) 4 East, 567; 21 Jac. 1, c. 16, s. 6. As to what actions for slander this statute extends to, see Tidd, 9th edit. 962.
(*o*). *Ante*, 493.
(*p*) *Id. Ibid.*

(938) As to costs in trespass *quare clausum fregit*, see Crane v. Comstock, and Jackson v. Randall, 11 Johns. Rep. 404, 405.

same cause of action as that which forms the subject of the second suit, if the verdict be not pleaded as an *estoppel* the defendant refers the merits to the second jury, and the verdict is merely *argument*, and is not *conclusive* in his favor (*r*). MUST BE SPECIALLY PLEADED AT COMMON LAW (*q*).

Care should be taken to plead in the first instance *every matter of defence* of which the defendant would not be at liberty to avail himself under the general issue. For, though the Court will in general give the defendant leave to add or alter a plea where *the justice of the case requires it*, yet this will be only on payment of the costs incurred by his mistake; and if the defendant be obliged to ask indulgence, as time to plead, he will not afterwards be allowed to plead a plea contrary to the merits or justice of the case; thus to a declaration by an attorney on his bill of costs, a defendant, after obtaining time, was not allowed to plead that the plaintiff had not delivered his signed bill a month before action brought (*s*); and if the cause should proceed to trial and be found against the defendant on account of the omission of one or more grounds of defence, he will in general be precluded for ever from taking advantage thereof, unless in some cases by *audita querela* or error in fact *coram nobis*, &c. (*t*). And as it is a rule of pleading that a departure will not be allowed, the defendant cannot in general rectify the omission of a ground of defence by his rejoinder. In debt on an arbitration bond, if the defendant merely plead no award, and the plaintiff reply setting out an award, the defendant cannot rejoin that he performed it, &c. (*u*)(939). ALL DEFENCES SHOULD BE PLEADED.

There are many cases in which it may be advisable to plead in one plea all the grounds of defence, and in which it may suffice to prove part of the allegations in the plea (*v*). When it will suffice to prove part of the ground of defence.

It is sometimes advisable not to plead either the general issue of a special plea to the *whole* declaration, but to suffer judgment by default to certain parts of the declaration, which the plaintiff can indisputably establish. Thus, where the plaintiff's demand is altogether denied by the pleas, and at the trial the plaintiff obtain a verdict for part of his demand, and the defendant obtain a verdict as to the other part, the plaintiff is entitled to the costs of the issues found for him, which include the general costs of the trial, but do not include the costs of the issues found for the defendant; and on which last-mentioned issues the defendant was not formerly entitled to claim any costs from the plaintiff. But where the defendant suffered judgment by default as to part of the plaintiff's demand, and pleaded only to the other part, and the plaintiff took issue on the pleas, and at the trial *all* the issues were found for the defendant, then the defendant was entitled to the costs of the issues found for him, and the OF SUFFERING JUDGMENT BY DEFAULT AS TO PART.

(*q*) See further as to pleas of estoppel, *post*; and see Index, Estoppel, and Reg. Gen. Hil. T. 4 W. 4, r. 9.

(*r*) 3 B. & Ald. 668; 2 Bing. 377; and see M'Clel. & Y. 509.

(*s*) Neale *v.* M'Kenzie, 1 Crom. M. & Ros. 61; 2 Dowl. 702; 4 Tyr. 670, S. C.; Beck *v.* Mordaunt, 2 Bing. N. C. 140; 3 Dowl. 407.

(*t*) Tidd, 9th edit. 907; *id.* Index, tit. "*Audita querela*;" 2 Saund. 137 g to 150.

(*u*) See *post*, as to departure in pleading.

(*v*) 1 Bing. N. C. 72; 3 Dowl. 483; 1 Adol. & El. 264; 3 Nev. & Man. 259, S. C.; 1 Har. & Woll. 15.

(939) Acc. Barlow *v.* Todd, 3 Johns. Rep. 367. Munro *v.* Allaire, 2 Caines' Rep. 320. And see Fowler *v.* Clark, 3 Day, 231.

WHEN TO PLEAD SPECIALLY.

plaintiff was entitled only to the costs of the judgment *by default, and what he would have been entitled to on executing a writ of inquiry (x).

OF ISSUABLE PLEAS.

In framing a special plea it is also necessary to consider whether the defendant is under terms of pleading *issuably*. An issuable plea is a plea in chief to the merits, upon which the plaintiff may take issue and go to trial (y); or a general demurrer for some defect in substance (z)(940). A plea in abatement is not an issuable plea (a)(941), nor a plea of alien enemy (b), nor an untrue plea of judgment recovered (c); nor can a *special* demurrer be pleaded if the defendant be bound to plead issuably, although the causes assigned be well founded, and, it seems, although they be matter of substance (d). But a true plea that a bail bond was taken for ease and favor (e), and a tender (f), and the statute of limitations (g)(942), are issuable pleas. So, where the defendant in an action on a recognizance of bail under a judge's order to plead issuably, pleaded *nul tiel record*, and that no *ca. sa.* was issued against the principal, the court of C. P. held that such pleas might be considered issuable, and that the plaintiff could not sign judgment as for want of a plea (h). And if a plea be in substance a fair issuable plea to the merits, the mere circumstance of its being informal will not render it a nullity (i). Where the *replication* does not tender a fair issue, but affords reasonable and good cause of demurrer, the defendant, though under terms of pleading issuably, may, it seems, in the Common Pleas, *demur even specially to such replication*; for a reasonable and fair demurrer to the replication, even
[*551] for want of form only, is not in that *Court a contravention of the terms of pleading issuably (k). But it seems that the Court of King's Bench consider that these terms extend to the subsequent pleadings, and forbid a *special demurrer* to the replication (l).

When the defendant, being under the terms of pleading issuably, pleads a sham plea (m); or demurs for want of form, or, at least in the Common Pleas, specially for want of substance; judgment may be signed (n)(943).

(x) Tidd, 9th ed. 973, 974.

(y) 7 T. R. 530; 2 Burr. 782; Tidd, 9th edit. 471. The defendant is usually put upon terms of pleading issuably when he obtains time to plead.

(z) 3 Burr. 1788; 2 B & P. 446; Tidd, 9th edit. 472; 8 Moore, 379; 1 Chit. R. 711. Where the defendant was advised he had a substantial ground of demurrer, the Court set aside the judgment signed for want of a plea, upon terms, 7 T. R. 530; 1 East, 414 a, S. C.

(a) 1 Burr. 59; Barnes, 263.

(b) 8 T. R. 71.

(c) 1 Bla. Rep. 376; 2 Wils. 117; 3 *Id.* 33; 1 Moore, 431; 2 Chit. Rep 292. Nor any other plea which does not go to the *merits*, Tidd, 9th ed. 471, and note (n).

(d) 1 Bing. 379; 8 Moore, 427, S. C.; see 7 T. R. 530; 5 D. & R. 620; *sed vide* 1 Chit. R. 711.

(e) 1 Burr. 605.

(f) 1 Burr. 59; 1 Hen. Bla. 369

(g) 3 T. R 124; 1 B. & P. 228; Tidd, 9th ed. 471.

(h) 1 Moore, 430.

(i) Rep. Temp. Hardw. 179; 5 T. R. 152.

(k) 4 Bing. 267; Betts v. Applegarth, C. P. Trinity Term, 1827; Gude, attorney for the plaintiff; MS.; see further, Gurborne v. Wyatt, 3 Dowl. 505.

(l) 5 D & R 620; *sed vide* Tidd, 9th ed. 472; 2 Stra. 1185, 1186; 3 Burr. 1789; 2 Bla. Rep. 923; 3 Dowl. 505, S. P.

(m) As to sham pleas, see *post.*

(n) Tidd, 9th ed. 472; 1 Bing. 379.

(940) Vide Syme v. Griffin, 4 Hen. & Mun. 277.

(941) So, a plea of another action pending is not an issuable plea. Davis v. Grainger, 3 Johns. Rep. 259.

(942) Tomlin's Adm. v. How's Adm. Gilmer's Rep. 11, Contra.

(943) Sawtell v. Gillard, 5 Dowl. & Ryl. 620.

Where several pleas are pleaded, one of which is not issuable, it will vitiate all the others (*o*), and where the defendant being under an order to plead issuably puts in a sham demurrer to some of the counts, and pleads issuably to the rest, judgment by *nil dicet* as to the whole may be signed (*p*). Where, however, it is doubtful whether the plea be issuable, the safer course in term time is to move the court to set it aside (*q*) ; and where the defendant has been ruled to abide by his plea, it cannot afterwards be treated as a nullity.

OF ISSUABLE PLEAS.

I. OF THE SEVERAL PLEAS.—SECONDLY, SINCE THE RECENT RULES.

HAVING thus endeavored to show the practice as to pleas before the modern improvements, and to which it will continue to be essential frequently to refer, we will now state the principal of such improvements.

Before the 2 & 3 W. 4, c. 71, s. 5, † although plaintiffs were allowed to *declare* generally in actions on the case, stating that by reason of their possession of a messuage or other corporeal tenement, they were entitled to a right of common or of way, &c , without showing the origin of the right or any derivative title (*r*) ; yet in *other pleadings*, particularly in *trespass* and *replevin*, it was essential to justify or claim under some owner *in fee*, and then to state the derivative title, however difficult and prolix (*s*). The above statute enacts, "that in all pleadings to actions of trespass, and in all other pleadings wherein, before the passing of that act, it would have been necessary to allege the right (*scilicet*, of *common* or other profit *a prendre*, or of *way*, or *other easement*, or to the use of *lights*,) to have existed from time immemorial, it shall be sufficient to allege the enjoyment thereof as of right by the occupiers of the tenement in respect whereof the same is claimed for and during such of the periods mentioned in that act as may be applicable to the case, and without claiming in the name or right of the owner in fee, as was before usually done ; and if the other party shall intend to rely on any proviso, exception, incapacity, disability, contract, agreement, or other matter thereinbefore mentioned, or any cause or matter of fact or of law not inconsistent with the simple fact of enjoyment, the same shall be specially alleged and set forth in answer to the allegation of the party claiming, and shall not be received in evidence on any general traverse or denial of such allegation." This enactment has introduced a much more concise mode of claiming rights of this nature (*t*).

Statements of *prescriptive rights* in a plea, &c. under 2 & 3 W. 4, c. 71, s. 5.

But by far the most important modern improvements are those introduced

Reg. Gen. Hil. T. 4 W. 4. Pleadings in particular actions.

(*o*) 3 T. R. 305.
(*p*) 1 East, 411.
(*q*) 1 Burr. 59 ; 2 T. R. 390 ; 7 *Id.* 530 ; Tidd, 9th edit. 472 ; 4 Taunt. 668 ; 1 Chit. Rep. 355 a.
(*r*) *Ante*, 414.
(*s*) *Ante*, 414.
(*t*) See forms in Bosanquet's Rules, 117, 118, 125, 126, and *post*, vol. iii.

† See American Editor's Preface.

I. IN ASSUMPSIT.

by the Reg. Gen. Hil. T. 4 W. 4,† which puts an end to the misapplication and abuse of the *general issue*, and compels a defendant in terms to deny particular parts of the declaration, and to *plead specially* every matter of defence not merely consisting of denial of the allegations in the declaration. The most convenient course will be, to print the rules verbatim in the context, and to state the decisions in notes (*u*).

REG. GEN. HIL. T. 4 W. 4, PLEADINGS IN PARTICULAR ACTIONS (*x*).

I. *Pleas in Assumpsit in Particular.*
II. *In Covenant and Debt.*
III. *In Detinue.*
IV. *In Case.*
V. *In Trespass.*

I. *Assumpsit.*

I. Plea of *non assumpsit* to put in issue only *express* contract or the facts from which contract *implied*. and no', &c.

"1. In all actions of *assumpsit*, (except on bills of exchange and promissory notes,) the plea of *non assumpsit* shall operate *only* as a denial in fact of the *express contract* or *promise* alleged (*y*), or of the *matters of fact* from which the contract or promise alleged may be *implied* by law (*z*).

(*u*) See also the precedents of Pleas and notes in 3 Chitty on Pleading, 6th edit. *per tot.*

(*x*) See further as to the cases when or not the *general issue* is pleadable, 3 Chit. Gen. Prac. 723 to 737, and Mr. Roscoe's Occasional Tracts, No. 1, as to the *General Issue*, a summary written with the perspicuity observable in all the works of that able author.

(*y*) *Non assumpsit.*—This plea naturally puts in issue the *contract or promise* as stated in the declaration, and enables a defendant to insist that he never *in fact* contracted *at all*, and also that he *did not contract in the manner stated* in the declaration, and thus to take advantage of any material variance, Neale v. M'Kenzie, 2 Crom. M. & Ros. 67; also of the nonjoinder of a person who ought to have been a co-plaintiff, which is a ground of nonsuit in respect of the *variance*. So, under non assumpsit, the defendant may show that the contract was conditional, and part not performed by plaintiff, where he had declared on the contract as having been absolute, Alexander v. Gardner 5 Moore & Scott, 281; 1 Bing N. S. 671; 3 Dowl. 146, S. C.

So, although a plea of *non assumpsit* in terms seems merely to deny the *promise*, and not the debt in respect of which the promise to pay was actually made or implied; yet by the terms of the above rule the plea in the case of an indebitatus count puts in issue all the facts essential to establish a *present debt*; although in case of a *special count* it would be otherwise. In the latest case, Cousens v. Patten, 2 Crom. M. & Ros. 547, it was held that under non assumpsit to an indebitatus assumpsit count for *goods sold and delivered*, or for *work and labor done*, the defendant may prove that the goods delivered were not such as were contracted for, or that the work was done in an unworkmanlike manner, although there was a special contract to pay for the goods or work at a certain price, and the plaintiff can then recover only on the *quantum meruit*; and see further as to work done, Cooper v. Whitehouse, 6 Car. & P. 545; Roffey v. Smith, *id.* 547, 662; Tubran v. Warren, 1 Tyr. & Gr. 153.

In Bradley v Milnes, 1 Bing. N. C. 644, to indebitatus assumpsit for work and labor and materials, defendant pleaded specially that there was an agreement that the work and materials should be to the satisfaction of the defendant or his surveyor; and that the building had not been completed to the satisfaction of defendant or his surveyor; and a replication unnecessarily in the conjunctive was proved by evidence that *defendant* was satisfied.

To an indebitatus assumpsit count for goods sold, the defendant may, under non assumpsit, prove that the *agreed credit had not elapsed* at the date of the writ, Taylor v. Hillary, 1 Crom. Mee. & Ros. 741; 1 Gale, 22; 3 Dowl. 461, S. C., overruling Edmunds

(*z*) *Or of the matters of fact from which the contract or promise alleged may be implied by law.*—In the instance of an *indebitatus assumpsit*, where the promise is usually *presumed* from the fact of the defendant being indebted, as previously alleged, this seems to put in issue whatever would *in fact*, and not merely as matter of law, negative the pre-existing debt; which constitutes the premises or consideration from which the alleged promise is to be inferred. Hence, Parke, B., in 3 Dowl. 627, observed there is no longer any *general issue* in assumpsit.

† See American Editor's Preface.

I. IN ASSUMPSIT.

"*Ex. gr.* In an action on a warranty, the plea will operate as a denial of the fact of the warranty having been given upon the alleged *consideration*, but not of the breach; and in an action on a policy of insurance, of the subscription to the alleged policy by the defendant, but not of the interest, of the commencement of the risk, of the loss, or of the alleged compliance with warranties.

In actions against carriers or bailees, not of breach.

"In actions against *carriers and other bailees*, for not delivering or not keeping goods safe, or not returning them on request, and in actions against *agents* for not accounting, the plea will operate as a denial of any express contract to the effect alleged in the declaration, and of such bailment or employment as would raise a promise in law to the effect alleged, *but not of the breach*.

In *indebitatus* for goods sold or money received, *non assumpsit* to put in issue only sale and delivery, and receipt of money to use of plaintiff.

"In an action of *indebitatus assumpsit* for goods sold and delivered, the plea of *non assumpsit* will operate as a denial of the sale and delivery in *point of fact* (*x*); in the like actions for money had and received, it will operate as a denial both of the receipt of the money, and the existence of those facts which make such receipt by the defendant a receipt to the use of the plaintiff.

2. *Non assumpsit* inadmissible in action on bill or note, but defendant must traverse in particular the drawing, making, indorsing, accepting, presenting, or notice of dishonor.

"2. In all actions upon *bills of exchange and promissory notes*, the plea of *non assumpsit shall be inadmissible*. In such actions, therefore, a plea in denial must traverse some matter of fact, *e. g.*, the drawing or making, or indorsing, or accepting, or presenting, or notice of dishonor of the bill or note (*a*).

v. Harris, 4 Nev. & Man. 182; 6 Car. & P. 745. But according to Knapp v. Barden, 1 Gale, 47; 6 Car. & P. 745, S. C. it is *safer to plead specially that the time of credit has not expired*. In Taylor v Hillary, 1 Gale, 23, Parke, B. thought that non assumpsit was sufficient; because if the credit had not expired, the contract declared on, describing the defendant as already *indebted* in præsenti, was not proved.

This rule also in effect puts in issue *the sufficiency of the stamp*, when a *written* contract must be proved, and a stamp is essential; because the 23 G. 3, c. 58, s. 12, not only enacts that the agreement, unless duly stamped, shall be unavailable, but further, that it shall not be admissible *in evidence*; so that the plaintiff cannot prove the allegation that it was made, if it be unstamped. If the question depended on the preceding words, then it might have been necessary to plead specially the want of a stamp as rendering the agreement void in point of law; but the latter words in the stamp acts seem clearly to render the objection available under a plea of non assumpsit, or *non est factum*. or any plea rendering it necessary *to prove* the contract declared upon. However, the defendant may plead specially that the contract was not duly stamped See forms of pleas of the want of a proper stamp, Bosanquet's Rules, 105; Chitty, jun. on Pleading, 258; *post*, vol. iii.

(*x*) See *ante*, 551 *a*, note (*x*); Bosanquet's Rules, 48, note 46. In Edmunds v. Harris, 4 Nev. & Man. 182; 6 Car. & P. 547, it was held that to indebitatus assumpsit for goods sold or work done, defendant must plead specially that the *credit* had not elapsed; but in Taylor v. Hillary, 1 Gale, 23; 3 Dowl. 461; 1 Cromp. M. & Ros. 741, S. C., Mr. Baron Parke said, "doubts have been expressed with regard to the decision in Edmunds v. Harris. If the time of credit has not expired, the plaintiff proves *a different contract* from that stated in the declaration, viz. to pay on request;" and see Knapp v. Harden, 1 Gale, 47; 6 Car. & P. 745, S. C.; and in Gardner v. Alexander, 3 Dowl. 146, the propriety of that decision was also doubted. So it has been supposed that to assumpsit for goods sold or work done, defendant must plead specially that the goods were of *bad quality*, or that the work *was improper*, so as to reduce the claim, Cooper v. Whitehome, 6 Car. & P. 545: Roffey v. Smith, 6 Car. & P. 662; but as the allegation in the declaration *indebitatus assumpsit* affirms that there is already an existing debt for goods sold or work done, whatever shows that there was no such debt, as that the goods or work were insufficient, or the credit not expired, directly negatives such allegation, and should therefore be admissible without a special plea. However the safest course will be to plead specially, as in Knapp v. Harden, 1 Gale, 47; 6 Car. & P. 745, S. C.

(*a*) If it be apprehended that the stamp on the bill was insufficient, there should, at

I. IN ASSUMPSIT.

3 Matters in confession and avoidance, and in discharge, and defences in law, to be pleaded particularly, as infancy, coverture, release, payment, performance, illegality of consideration, &c.

3. In *every species of assumpsit*, all *matters in confession and avoidance* (b), including not only those by way of discharge, but those which show the transaction to be either void or voidable in point of law, on the ground of *fraud* (c) *or otherwise*, shall be specially pleaded (d). *Ex. gr.* Infancy (e), coverture, release, payment (*f*), performance (*g*), want of consideration, ille-

all events, be a plea denying the making of the bill, Bosanquet's Rules, 47, note 45, or a plea that it was not sufficiently stamped. See form, Bosanquet's Rules, 105, for otherwise the sufficiency of the stamp will not be in issue, Bosanquet's Rules, 47, note 45.

(*b*) "*All matters in confession and avoidance, including, &c. shall be specially pleaded.*"—To an indebitatus assumpsit on an account stated, if the defendant wish to rely on a *subsequent account* in *his* favor, he must plead this specially, and cannot give the same in evidence under the general issue, Fidgett *v.* Penny, 1 Crom. M. & Ros. 108; 2 Dowl. 714, S. C.; and see Taylor *v.* Hillary, 1 Gale, 22. So a defendant must plead specially that after the guarantee declared on, he and the plaintiff entered into a different contract of guarantee, and thereby discharged defendant from liability to perform that declared upon, and must aver that such agreement was in writing, Taylor *v.* Hillary, 1 Gale, 22; 3 Dowl. 461; 1 Crom. M. & Ros. 741. Plea to indebitatus assumpsit for goods sold, that defendant accepted a bill which plaintiff indorsed to a holder, &c., Atkinson *v.* Handon, 1 Har. & Woll. 77. So a plea of gaming consideration, where there has been a *renewed bill* or note, must be pleaded to the first bill or note, Boulton *v.* Coghlan, 1 Bing. N. C. 640. So a substituted guarantee or agreement in lieu of first, 1 Gale, 23, 47, 48; 3 Dowl. 641; 5 Bing. 373.

(*c*) "*Void or voidable in point of law on ground of fraud or, &c.*"—Thus to an action on a sale by auction puffing must be pleaded specially, Iceley *v.* Crew, 6 Car. & P. 671. How to plead fraud in obtaining a bill, see 1 Hodges, 66; 1 Bing. N. C. 460; 2 Crom. M. & Ros 59.

(*d*) "*Or otherwise shall be specially pleaded.*"—*Even before* the Reg. Gen. Hil. T. 4 W. 4, defendant *might* plead specially that the contract was not in writing according to the statute against frauds, 29 Car. 2, c. 3, s. 4 and 17; 1 Wils. 305; 4 B. & Ald. 595; 1 Moore & P. 294, 308; 4 Bing. 470, S. C.; but see 11 Price, 494. So a surety might have pleaded that he had signed no undertaking in writing, see a plea held good, 2 Dow. & Clark, 211. And now such defence *must be pleaded*, and see form of plea and replication, Hawes *v.* Armstrong, 1 Bing. N. C. 763; Clancey *v.* Piggott, 1 Harr. & Woll. 20; 4 Nev. & Man. 469, S. C. So in assumpsit for the price of a copyright it must be pleaded specially that the assignment of such copyright was not in writing, Barnett *v.* Glossop, 1 Bing. N. C. 633; 1 Hodges, 94; 3 Dowl. 625, S. C. If a contract be *specially* declared on in assumpsit, Bolland, B. held that under non assumpsit the defendant could not insist that the contract was not in writing and signed, Ross *v.* Humphreys, Easter T. 1835, Exchequer. But if a statute expressly require a fact to be *proved by the plaintiff* as part of *his* case, as the apothecary act, requiring proof of plaintiff's certificate, or that he was in practice before a certain day, then the absence of that evidence need not be pleaded specially to an action by such apothecary for the amount of his bill, Morgan *v.* Ruddock, 1 Harr. & Woll. 505. So it is proper to plead specially that defendant's guarantee was not in writing and signed, Clancey *v.* Piggott, 4 Nev. & Man. 496; 1 Harr. & Woll. 20. It should seem that to such a plea plaintiff should *not merely reply* that there was an agreement in writing, and conclude to the country, but should set out the written agreement in the very words, and conclude with a verification, so that the Court may judge of the sufficiency of the agreement, Lowe *v.* Eldred, 3 Tyr. 234; and see form of plea and replication, Hawes *v.* Armstrong, 1 Bing. N. C. 763. If *defendant* be confident that the written contract is insufficient as a guarantee, he may and should set out the agreement in *his plea*, Clancey *v.* Piggott, 4 Nev. & Man. 496; 1 Harr. & Woll. 20.

A defence that the contract was not to be completely performed within a year, and not in writing, must be specially pleaded, Ross *v.* Humphreys, Exch. Tr. T. 1835; Bosanquet, 183; Charnock's Rules, 147.

To assumpsit by an *attorney* for fees and business done, it has been considered necessary to plead specially that he had not delivered his bill signed a month before action commenced, Moore *v.* Boulcott, 5 Moore & Scott, 122; 1 Bing. N. C. 323; 3 Dowl. 145, S. C. But see Bosanquet's Rules, 51, 52, and case as to an apothecary's evidence, *supra*. So to special assumpsit for non-performance of an agreement for *incorporeal* hereditaments, a plea that the agreement was void because not under seal is good; but the plaintiff recovered under an indebitatus count for bye-gone rent, Bird *v.* Higginson, 1 Harr. & Woll. 61.

(*e*) Before this rule infancy might be given in evidence under non assumpsit, but now by the express terms of that rule it *must* be pleaded, and see the pleas, replications, &c. in Burghart *v.* Angerstein, 6 Car. & P. 690 to 700, and *post*.

(*f*) *Payment* must now be pleaded, Linley *v.* Polden, 3 Dowl. 780; Fidgett *v.* Penny, 1 Crom. M. & Ros. 108; 4 Tyr. 650; unless the particulars of the plaintiff's demand admit all the payments, and limit the claim to the sum unpaid, *per* Parke, B. in

gality of *consideration*, either by statute or common law (*h*), drawing, indorsing, accepting, &c., bills or notes by way of accommodation (*i*), set-off (*k*), 1. IN ASSUMPSIT.

Coats *v.* Stevens, 2 Crom. M. & Ros. 119. It seems, however, that under non assumpsit payments may be given in evidence in reduction of damages, Shirley *v.* Jacobs, 7 Car. & P. 3; 2 Bing. N. C. 88; but then unless the plaintiff's particulars have admitted the payments, the defendant will have to pay the costs, although he paid the money into Court, Adlard *v.* Booth, 1 Bing. N. C. 693; 2 Crom. M. & Ros. 75. Before this recent rule, payment between writ and declaration was admissible in bar under non assumpsit, 1 B. & Adol. 570; 10 B. & Cres. 676. Payment *before* breach may be pleaded without averring acceptance in satisfaction, but when pleaded *after breach*, although before commencement of action, the plea must aver that the payment was made and accepted in satisfaction, and the plea must conclude with a verification, Ansell *v* Smith, 3 Dowl 193. If money be paid into Court pending an action, it must be pleaded in a particular form, as prescribed by 3 & 4 W. 4, c. 42, s. 21, and Reg. Gen. Hil. T. 4 W. 4, reg. 17 to 19; Adlard *v.* Booth, 1 Bing. N. C. 693. Plea of payment in accord and satisfaction and replication held good, Bramah *v.* Barker, 1 Hodges, 39; 1 Bing. N. C. 502, S. C. An averment in the plea that the payment was made and accepted in accord and satisfaction is essential, Ansell *v.* Smith, 3 Dowl. 193. But payments that do not amount to a bar, but merely to reduce the damages, need not be pleaded specially, but may be given in evidence under the general issue, Ledeard *v.* Boucher, 7 Car. & P. 1, *et supra. Sed quære* the rule requiring *payment* to be pleaded specially, was to prevent *surprise* on the plaintiff upon the trial, and to enable him to be prepared to *negative pretended* payments by evidence. It would seem, therefore, the admission of some evidence under the general issue is on principle objectionable.

(*g*) "*Want of consideration*."—The pleading rules, Hil. T. 4 W. 4, are silent as to *pleading* the *want* of consideration. According to Passenger *v.* Brookes, 7 Car & P. 110; 1 Bing. N. C. 587, to a *special* count in assumpsit, the *want* of consideration should be pleaded specially, but to a *common indebitatus count*, the want of consideration for the promise is admissible under the common plea of non assumpsit, and see Chitty, jun. Precedents, 203, 204, 289, 290; see forms of pleas, *id.* And yet according to the instance in reg. 1, viz. that in an action on a warranty, the plea of non assumpsit will operate as a denial of the fact of a warranty *upon the alleged consideration*, seems to import that non assumpsit puts in issue as well the *consideration as the promise*.

To a general plea of no consideration, plaintiff, instead of demurring, *may* reply generally that there was a consideration, 1 Hodges, 66; 1 Bing. N. C. 409; 2 Crom. M. & Ros. 59; as to a plea of gaming consideration, Boulton *v.* Coghlan, 1 Bing. N. C. 640.

(*h*) "*Illegality of consideration, either by statute or common law*."—This rule is very explicit, see a good note in Bosanquet's Rules, 51, note 49. No assignment *in writing* of a copyright must be pleaded. Barnett *v.* Glossop, 1 Bing. N. C. 633; 3 Dowl. 665; 1 Hodges, 94. *Usury* must be pleaded specially, 3 Nev. & Man. 665; 1 Adol. & Ell. 576, S. C. As to illegality of business transacted by an attorney being a defence to an action on his bill, Potts *v.* Sparrow, 1 Bing. N. C. 594; 3 Dowl. 630, S. C.; Barnett *v.* Glossop, 1 Bing. N.C. 633; 3 Dow. 625, S. C.; Triebneer *v.* Duerr, 1 B. N.C. 266, and such a plea was admitted with non assumpsit, *id. ibid.* In the first case it was held that *illegality of consideration* must be pleaded specially as a defence, not only where the express contract in which the plaintiff sues was illegal, but also where illegal services having been performed no contract to pay for them could be inferred. *Usury*, 1 Hodges, Rep. 6.

If a contract be void as entered into on a Sunday, that objection must be pleaded specially, but need not aver that such contract was against the statute, Peate *v.* Dickens, 1 Crom. M. & Ros. 422, 427.

(*i*) A plea of *no consideration generally* for accepting or indorsing, without stating affirmatively *how* there was no consideration, and showing the facts why the defendant ought not to pay, and knowledge of them on the part of the plaintiff, is bad, first, because it amounts to the general issue, the law *implying* a consideration for an acceptance and indorsement, but principally because it does not confess and avoid, or state, as required by the new rules, with particularity, the facts, which probably are more within the knowledge of the defendant than the plaintiff. The plaintiff may therefore demur to such a general plea, as in Law *v.* Chifney, 1 Bing. N. C. 267; 1 Scott, 95; French *v.* Archer, 3 Dowl. 130; Stoughton *v.* Earl Kilmorey, 1 Gale, 91; 3 Dowl 705, S. C.; Easton *v.* Pratchet, 6 Car. & P. 736; 1 Gale, 30; 3 Dowl. 472, S. C.; Mills *v.* Oddy, 3 Dowl. 730; 1 Gale, 92; 3 Car. & P. 728, S. C.; Pearce *v.* Champneys, 3 Dowl. 276; Stein *v.* Yglesias, 3 Dowl. 252; Reynolds *v.* Joemry, 3 Dowl. 453; Bramah *v.* Roberts, 1 Scott, 350; 1 Bing. N. C. 409, such a plea in the terms of the rule must be that the defendant accepted, &c. for the accommodation of a named person, 2 Crom. M. & Ros. 59; 1 Mood. & Rob. 379; 1 Gale, 39; 3 Dowl. 472; plea no consideration for payment bad, 1 Gale, 59; see a good form of plea, Stein *v.* Yglesias, 1 Gale, 98; 1 Bing. N. C. 479, 491. And after de-

I. IN ASSUMPSIT.

mutual credit, unseaworthiness, misrepresentation, concealment, deviation, and various other defences *must* be pleaded.

4. In declaration on policy the interest may be averred to have been in several, and proof of either shall suffice.

"4. In actions on policies of assurance, the interest of the assured may be averred thus:—'That A., B., C., and D., or some or one of them, were or was interested, &c.;' and it may also be averred, 'That the insurance was made for the use and benefit, and on the account of the person or persons so interested.'

II. *In Covenant and Debt.*

1. *Non est factum* to be considered as merely denying the execution of the deed, and all other defences must be specially stated.

"1. In debt on specialty or covenant, the plea of *non est factum* shall operate as a denial of the execution of the deed in point of fact only (*l*); and all other defences shall be specially pleaded, including matters which make the deed absolutely void, as well as those which make it voidable.

2. *Nil debet* abolished.

"2. The plea of '*nil debet*' shall not be allowed in any action.

3. Plea of "never indebted," to be admissible to the like extent as non *assumpsit*, but matters in avoidance to be specially pleaded.

"3. In actions of debt on simple contract, other than on bills of exchange and promissory notes, the defendant may plead that '*he never was indebted in manner and form as in the declaration alleged*;'(*m*) and such plea shall have the same operation as the plea of *non assumpsit* in *indebitatus assumpsit*, and all matters in confession and avoidance shall be pleaded specially, as above directed in actions of *assumpsit*.

4. In other actions of debt the plea to traverse a particular fact, and to state matter in avoidance.

"4. In other actions of debt in which the plea of *nil debet* has been hitherto allowed, including those on bills of exchange and promissory notes, the defendant shall deny specially some particular matter of fact alleged in the declaration or plead specially in confession and avoidance.

murrer to such a plea, *leave to amend has been refused*, without an affidavit of merits, *id. ibid.*; and Stoughton *v.* Kilmorey, 3 Dowl. 706; 1 Gale, 91, S. P. But as an issue on a *general* plea of no consideration found for or against the defendant will be good after verdict, the plaintiff may safely take issue, either *generally* that there was a sufficient consideration, Mills *v.* Oddy, 6 Car. & P. 728; 3 Dowl. 730; 1 Gale, 92, S. C.; Easton *v.* Pratchett, 6 Car. & P. 736; 1 Gale, 30; 3 Dowl. 472; 1 Mood. & Rob. 379; (and *defendant's* counsel is to begin at the trial, Mills *v.* Oddy, 6 Car. & P. 728; Homan *v.* Thompson, *id.* 717, S. P.); or the plaintiff may reply *more specially*, setting out a consideration under a videlicet, and yet concluding to the country, Low *v.* Burrows, 4 Nev. & Man. 366; 1 Har. & Wol. 12.

How to plead specially, and forms of sufficient pleas, or pleas that may be readily made sufficient, see Stein *v.* Yglesias, 1 Gale, 98; Percival *v.* Framplin, 3 Dowl. 748; Heydon *v.* Thompson, 1 Adol. & El. 210; Bosanquet's Rules, 104; Byers *v.* Wylie, 3 Dowl. 525; 1 Gale, 50; 1 Crom. M. & Ros. 686, S. C.; Bramah *v.* Baker, 1 Hodges, 66; 1 Bing. N. C. 169; 3 Dowl. 392, S. C.

(*k*) As to pleading a *set-off* see Bosanquet's Rules, 52, note 50; and see Duncan *v.* Grant, 1 Crom M. & Ros. 283; 2 Dowl. 683; 4 Tyr. 818, S. C.; 5 Bar. & Adol. 866, and *post*.

(*l*) But if a public body be incorporated by a statute, with a special power of executing a deed in a certain form, then *non est factum* puts in issue whether the deed was executed in the legal form.

(*m*) If a plea be that defendant never did *owe*, instead of "never was indebted," the form prescribed by this rule, it is insufficient, but the Court will permit an amendment on an affidavit of merits, Smedley *v.* Joyce, 1 Tyr. & Granger, 84.

III. IN DETINUE.

III. *Detinue.*

"The plea of *non detinet* shall operate as a denial of the detention of the goods by the defendant, but not of the plaintiff's property therein, and no other defence than such denial shall be admissible under that plea (*n*).

Non detinet only to put in issue the fact of detention of the specified goods, and not plaintiff's property therein, or other ground of defence.

IV. *In Case.*

"1. In actions on the case, the plea of *not guilty* shall operate as a denial only of the *breach of duty* or *wrongful act* alleged to have been committed by the defendant (*o*), and not of the facts stated in the *inducement* (*p*); and no other defence than such denial shall be admissible under that plea; all other pleas in denial shall take issue on some particular matter of fact alleged in the declaration. *Ex. gr.* In an action on the case, for a nuisance to the occupation of a house, by carrying on an offensive trade, the plea of 'not guilty' will operate as a denial only that the defendant carried on the alleged trade in such a way as to be a nuisance to the occupation of the house, and will not operate as a denial of the plaintiff's occupation of the house. In an action on the case for obstructing a right of way, such plea will operate as a denial of the obstruction only, and not of the plaintiff's right of way (*r*); and in an action for *converting* the plaintiff's goods, the conversion only, and not the plaintiff's title to the goods (*s*). In an action of *slander* of the plaintiff in his office, profession, or trade, the plea of 'not guilty' will operate to the same extent precisely as at present in denial of the fact of speaking the words, of speaking them maliciously, and in the sense imputed, and with reference to the plaintiff's office, profession, or trade (*t*); but it will not operate as a denial of the fact of the plaintiff holding the office, or being of the profession or

1. Not guilty in case, only to put in issue the alleged wrongful act or omission, and not facts stated as inducement.

Instances in elucidation of this rule.

(*n*) *Semble*, that if a defendant merely refused to deliver up a chattel on the ground of his lien thereon, that would be no conversion, and might at least *in trover* be given in evidence under "not guilty," and *quære* whether if not in detinue under non detinet. See *per* Parke, B. in Stancliffe *v.* Hardwick, 1 Gale, 130, and 2 Crom. M. & Ros. 1, S. C.

(*o*) So in an action for keeping a mischievous animal, plea of "not guilty," denies the *scienter* as well as the injury, Thomas *v.* Morgan, 2 Crom. M. & Ros. 496. In an action for a malicious outlawry, "not guilty" puts in issue as well the original debt, as the existence of reasonable and probable cause for the proceeding, but not the reversal of the outlawry, Drummond *v.* Pigou, 2 Bing. N. C. 114.

(*p*) Dukes *v.* Gostling, 1 Bing. N. C. 588; 3 Dowl. 619, S. C. "Not guilty" does not put in issue the *inducement* as to plaintiff's right, though in some degree part of description of the injury, Frankum *v.* Earl of Falmouth, 1 Harr. & Wol. 1; 4 Nev. & Man. 330; 6 Carr. & P. 529, S. P.

(*r*) Or right to a drain, 1 Gale, 62.

(*s*) See pleas of property in defendant in trespass, Wilton *v.* Edwards, 6 Car. & P. 677; plea that sale to plaintiff was fraudulent, 1 Moo & Rob 400; transfer for value and replication, 1 Hodges, 98; 1 Bing. N. C. 681; seizure under a *fi. fa.* and replication, 1 Bing. N. C. 721; seizure under four warrants, 1 Adol. & El. 264; tenancy in common, or partnership, must be pleaded, Stancliffe *v.* Hardwick, 3 Dowl. 762; 2 Crom. M. & Ros. 1; 1 Gale, 127; Bosanquet's Rules, 57, note 55. But a mere refusal to deliver a chattel on the ground that defendant had a lien may be admissible under "not guilty," *id. ibid.*; *Supra*, n. (*n*).

(*t*) In an action for a libel, "not guilty" suffices, if, upon the whole context, the jury can be induced to find it to be no libel, 1 Gale, 69. When it may be advisable to plead a justification to mitigate damages, Chalmers *v.* Shackle, 6 Car. & P. 475.

IV. IN CASE.

trade alleged. In actions for an *escape*, it will operate as a denial of the neglect or default of the sheriff or his officers, but not of the debt, judgment, or preliminary proceedings. In this form of action against a *carrier*, the plea of 'not guilty' will operate as a denial of the loss or damage, but not of the receipt of the goods by the defendant, as a carrier for hire, or of the purpose for which they were received.

2. All matters in confession and avoidance to be pleaded specially

"2. All matters in confession and avoidance shall be pleaded specially, as in actions of *assumpsit* (u).

V. *In Trespass.*

1. A declaration in trespass to land, &c. must state the name or abuttals, &c., or the defendant may demur.

"1. In actions of trespass *quare clausum fregit*, the close or place in which, &c., must be designated in the declaration by *name* or *abuttals*, or *other description*, in failure whereof the defendant may demur specially.

2. "Not guilty" to be a denial of the defendant's trespasses, but not of plaintiff's possession or right of possession, and which must be specially traversed.

"2. In actions of trespass *quare clausum fregit*, the plea of 'not guilty' shall operate as a denial that the defendant committed the trespass alleged (x) in the place mentioned, but not as a denial of the plaintiff's possession, or right of possession of that place, which, if intended to be denied, must be traversed specially.

3. "Not guilty" to trespass *de bonis asportatis*, to be considered only a denial of taking, or merely damaging the goods, and not of plaintiff's property.

"3. In actions of trespass *de bonis asportatis*, the plea of 'not guilty' shal operate as a denial of the defendant having committed the trespass alleged (x) by taking or damaging the goods mentioned (x), but not of the plaintiff's property therein (y).

4. Plea of right of way with carriages, cattle, and on foot, if traversed, shall be considered distributive, and the proof of either shall, *pro tanto*, entitle the defendant to a verdict, &c.

"4. Where in an action of trespass *quare clausum fregit*, the defendant pleads a right of way with carriages and cattle, and on foot, in the same plea, and issue is taken thereon, the plea shall be taken distributively; and if the right of way with cattle, or on foot only, shall be found by the jury, a verdict shall pass for the defendant in respect of such of the trespasses proved as shall be justified by the right of way so found, and for the plaintiff in respect of such of the trespasses as shall not be so justified.

5. So, in plea of right of common, if defendant do not prove a right for all kinds of cat-

"5. And where in an action of trespass *quare clausum fregit*, the defendant pleads a right of common of pasture for divers kinds of cattle, *ex. gr.* horses, sheep, oxen, and cows, and issue is taken thereon, if a right of common for some particular kind of commonable cattle only be found by the jury, a verdict

(u) Therefore defendant's *partnership* with plaintiff must be pleaded in *trover*, Stancliffe *v.* Hardwick, 3 Dowl. 762. A denial of plaintiff's possession of goods, or assignees' denial of their being assignees of a bankrupt, Best *v.* Thomas, 6 Car. & P. 611. The *truth* of the slander must be pleaded specially, Chalmers *v.* Shackle, 6 Car. & P. 475; and it seems questionable whether it could be given in evidence under "not guilty," even in mitigation of damages, *id. ibid.* 385, 588, 589; 5 Moore & P. 520; 2 Bos. & Pul. 589.

(x) Pearcy *v.* Walter, 6 Car. & P. 232.

(y) Therefore, to trespass for taking goods, the defendant must plead specially that the goods were their property as assignees of a bankrupt, Jones *v.* Brown, 1 Bing. N. C. 484, where see form of plea and replication.

shall pass for the defendant in respect of such of the trespasses proved, as shall be justified by the right of common so found, and for the plaintiff in respect of the trespasses which shall not be so justified. V. IN TRESPASS. tle, he is to have a verdict *pro tanto.*

"6. And in all actions in which such right of way or common as aforesaid, or other similar right, is so pleaded, that the allegations as to the extent of the right are capable of being construed distributively, they shall be taken distributively." 6. In all actions the same rule to prevail as regards rights of way or common.

The 3 & 4 W. 4, c. 42, s. 21, and Reg. Gen. 4 W. 4, give a plea of payment of money into Court by leave of a judge in some actions *for torts* (z); and Reg. Gen. Hil. T. 4 W. 4, reg. 17, prescribes the form of such plea (a) †. Plea of payment of money into Court.

II. OF THE QUALITY OF PLEAS IN BAR.

There are some *general qualities* which affect pleas in bar, and some *rules* which prevail *in the construction* of them, which it is advisable to consider before we inquire into their *form*. The *general qualities* of a plea in bar are,— II. QUALITIES.

1st, That it be adapted to the nature and form of the action, and also be conformable to the count.

2dly, That it answer all which it assumes to answer, and no more.

3dly, That it deny, or admit and avoid the facts; and herein of giving color, and of pleas amounting to the general issue.

4thly, That it be single.

5thly, Certain.

6thly, Direct and positive, and not argumentative.

7thly, Capable of trial.

And, 8thly, True; and herein of *sham* pleas.

[*552] *1st. *Every plea in bar must be adapted to the nature of the action, and conformable to the count* (b). Therefore in an action against husband and wife for words spoken by the wife, a plea that "they" are not guilty, instead of "she is not guilty," appears to be improper (c)(944.) We have already seen what are the appropriate general issues and special pleas in each action. If the defendant plead a plea not adapted to the nature of the actions, as *nil debet* in assumpsit (d); or non-assumpsit in debt (e); or a plea of set-off to 1st. Conformable to the action and count, and to the alleged *breach.*

(z) See form in *trover* and replication, 6 Car. & P. 712.

(a) 3 Chit. Gen. Prac. 684 to 687.

(b) Co. Lit. 303 a, 285 b; Bac. Ab. Pleas, I. *per tot.*; 1 Rol. Rep. 216.

(c) 1 Rol. Rep. 216.

(d) Barnes, 257; Tidd, 9th ed. 563, 476. *Sed vide* Rep. T. Hardw. 179; 4 Taunt. 164. See 1 Chit. Rep. 715, 716, n., and cases there collected as to pleading *not guilty* in *assumpsit*, or *non-assumpsit* in an action for a *tort*. And see Stra. 574, 1022; Lawes on Pl. 527.

(e) 6 East, 549; 14 *Id.* 442; 4 Taunt. 164; 1 Chit. Rep. 716, note; Tidd, 9th ed. 476.

(944) Vide Chew *v.* Woolley, 7 Johns. Rep. 402.

† See American Editor's Preface.

II. QUALITIES.

an action of debt, as if it were an action of assumpsit (*f*); the plaintiff may treat it as a nullity, and sign judgment (*g*). But the plea of "not guilty" in an action of debt on a penal statute, is not such a nullity as will warrant the plaintiff in signing judgment (*h*); nor is the plea of *nil debet* in an action of debt on a judgment (*i*). So, a plea in assumpsit that the defendant "did not undertake, (omitting "or promise,") in manner," &c. concluding to the country, is not a plea which can be treated as a nullity (*k*). Where the plea, though informal, goes to the substance of the action, as *nil debet* to debt on bond, the plaintiff should demur, and not sign judgment (*l*); and in general, where the defendant pleads an improper plea, the safer course is to demur, or move the Court to set it aside (*m*)(945). In debt for £1,800, the defendant pleaded that he did not owe "the said sum of £10 above demanded;" and the Court, after issue joined, would not compel him to amend (*n*). If declaration state breach of condition of bond in non payment of a *principal sum*, a plea of payment of that and of the *interest thereon* is bad (*o*). But the plaintiff *might*, instead of demurring, safely take issue in the words of the plea, so that the unnecessary averment in the plea cannot be treated by the defendant *as surplusage* (*o*).

The plea must not only be *adapted to the nature of the action, but also be conformable to the count* Thus, if an assignee of a bankrupt declare that the defendant was indebted to the bankrupt, and promised the plaintiff, *as assignee*, to pay him, the defendant cannot plead that the [*553] *cause of action did not accrue to the *bankrupt* within six years; because the plea does not answer the promise laid in the declaration, and precludes the plaintiff from proving a promise to himself, and is therefore bad on demurrer (*p*). And in debt *qui tam*, a plea that the defendant doth not owe the money "to the plaintiff" alone, is insufficient, though if it had been *nil debet* generally, it would have sufficed (*q*). So the plea must not, contrary to the legal effect, treat an instrument as a promissory note when it was not so declared on (*r*). So, it is a rule that if to a transitory action, the defendant plead any matter which is itself transitory, he is obliged to lay it at the *place* mentioned in the declaration (*s*); but if the justification be local, the defendant must plead it in the county or parish where the matter arose, and conclude with a traverse of having been guilty elsewhere (*t*); and at common law, the cause must have been tried there, and not in the county where the action was laid, otherwise it was error; though this, as far as regards the trial, no longer obtains, the action being uniformly tried in the county where the venue is laid in the declaration (*u*).

(*f*) 2 M. & Sel. 606.
(*g*) See Tidd, 9th ed 563.
(*h*) 1 T. R. 462; 3 B. & P. 111, 174; Com. Dig. Pleader, 2 S. 11. s. 17.
(*i*) 2 Chit. Rep. 239.
(*k*) 3 D. & R. 621.
(*l*) 5 T. R. 152; 5 Esp. Rep 38; *ante*, 518.
(*m*) 1 Burr. 59; 2 T. R. 390; 7 *Id.* 530; Rep. Temp. Hardw. 179; 5 T. R. 152
(*n*) 1 D. & R. 473. See 1 M. & P. 276. *Sed vide* 3 B. & P. 174; *ante*, 516 note (*n*).
(*o*) Bishton *v.* Evans, 2 Crom. M. & Ros. 14.
(*p*) 2 Stra. 919; 2 Hen. Bla. 561.
(*q*) Hob. 327, 328; Reg. Plac. 302; Bac. Ab. Action, *qui tam*, D. See *ante*, 552.
(*r*) 1 Harr. & Woll. 426.
(*s*) 1 Saund. 247, note 1, 8 a, note 1; 85, note 1; 2 *Id.* 5 b, note 3.
(*t*) *Id.*
(*u*) *Id.* See 1 Saund. 98, n. 1.

(945) But in Falls *v.* Stickney, 3 Johns. Rep. 541, the court say, that if a plea is bad or frivolous, the plaintiff ought either to demur to it, or treat it as a nullity, and enter a default without any application to the court. } See Mawin *v.* Wilkins, 1 Aiken's (Vermont) Rep. 107. }

So, when the time is not material, it is a rule that the plea should follow the day in the declaration, and if it be material to vary from it the plea should conclude with a traverse (x). Where, however, there is no ground to intend the contrary, the plea will be considered as conformable to the count: thus, in assumpsit against an executor, on the promise of his *testator*, the defendant pleaded that *he* did not undertake, and it was objected, that it did not appear by the plea who did not assume, but it was adjudged that it should be intended that the defendant meant to plead that the testator did not promise, as there was no count in the declaration on a promise by the executor (y). II. QUALITIES.

The instances in which a plea may be treated as a sham plea and as a nullity, in consequence of the matter pleaded being inconsistent and impossible, with reference to the declaration, will be hereafter mentioned.

2dly. The defendant must take care in the introductory part of his plea as well as in the body to plead to and answer every part of the causes of action charged in the declaration, for otherwise the plaintiff, after proving the facts under the general issue, will recover for all that has not been justified, and this without new assigning, but not so as to mere matters in aggravation (z). 2dly. Should answer the whole charges, with the exception of matters in aggravation.

3dly. It is a rule that every plea must answer the whole declaration or count, or rather all that it assumes in the *introductory part to answer, and no more (a) (946). If a plea begin only as an answer to part, and is in truth but an answer to part, as if the defendant in trespass for taking two sheep plead that the plaintiff "ought not to have his action as to *one*," because he took that *one* doing damage on his close, &c. and does not in that or any other plea (b) notice the remainder of the declaration, the plaintiff cannot demur to the plea, for it is sufficient as far as it extends, but must take judgment for the part unanswered as by *nil dicit*. If he demur or plead over, without taking such judgment the *whole* action is *discontinued* (c)(947); for in such case the 3dly. Must answer all it assumes to answer, and no more. [*554]

(x) 1 Saund. 14, 81 a, note 3; 2 *Id.* 5 b, note 3; Com. Dig. Pleader, E. 4; See *post*, as to *Quæ est eadem*.

(y) 1 Lev. 184; Latch. 126.

(z) Bush *v.* Parker, 1 Bing. N. C. 72; and see 2 Crom. M. & Ros. 329.

(a) Co. Lit. 303 a; Com. Dig. Pleader, E 1. 36; 1 Saund. 28, n. 3, and notes e, f, g, h, 5th edit.; 2 B. & P. 427; 3 *Id.* 174; Steph. 2d ed. 253; 1 Tyr. & Gr. 85; 5 Tyr. 421; 2 Cr. M. & Ros. 56.

(b) 1 Saund. 28, n. g. 5th edit.; 6 Bing. 595, *per* Bosanquet, J.

(c) Salk. 179; 1 Saund. 28, note 3; 1 Hen. Bla. 645; 1 B. & P. 411; 6 Taunt. 606, 607; 2 Marsh. 304, S. C. However, at any time during the same term, the plaintiff may rectify his mistake by taking judgment, Stra. 303; Lord Raym. 716; 1 Salk. 180. And a discontinuance is cured after verdict by statute 32 Hen. 8, c. 30; 1 Hen. Bla. 644; and after judgment by *nil dicit*, *confession*, or *non sum informatus*, by 4 & 5 Ann. c. 16.

(946) Vide Nevins *v.* Keeler, 6 Johns. Rep. 63. Riggs *v.* Denniston, 3 Johns. Cas. 198. Fletcher *v.* Peck, 6 Cranch, 126. Barnard *v.* Duthy, 5 Taunt. 27. Spencer *v.* Southwick, 11 Johns. Rep. 583, 587. {Van Ness *v.* Hamilton, 19 Johns. Rep. 374. Hallett *v.* Holmes, 18 Johns. Rep. 28.}

(947) {"It appears to me," says Ch. Justice SPENCER, in reference to the text, and to 1 Saund. 28, n. 3, "that the position laid down by Mr. Chitty, and Serjeant Williams, is not law, and the cases they refer to do not bear out the proposition. On the contrary, there are several cases which are directly opposed to it," &c. Sterling *v.* Sherwood, 20 Johns. Rep. 206. In Riggs *v.* Denniston, 3 Johns. Cas. 205. Kent, J., lays down the rule thus: That as the plea did not, either by denying or justifying, meet the whole matter or *gravamen* contained in the count, it was for that reason, *bad*; and he referred to 2 Vent. 193. Cro. Jac. 27. Cro. Eliz. 434. It does not expressly appear by the case, whether the plea professed to answer the whole declaration or not; but I infer that it did not, or else that would have been relied on in the opinion delivered.

III. QUALITIES. plaintiff, by omitting to enforce his claim in respect of the unanswered portion of such claim by taking judgment, or to resign it by entering a *nolle prosequi* thereto, causes a chasm or hiatus in the proceedings (*d*). But where to a declaration in debt demanding £60 and containing six counts for £10 each, the defendant pleaded that he did not owe the said sum of £10, above demanded, and the plaintiff treated the plea as a nullity and signed judgment, the Court set the judgment aside on the ground that the "of £10" might be struck out as surplusage (*e*). If the plea profess to answer only a part, but afterwards answers more, it has been held that the plaintiff should not demur, but should take judgment for the part not mentioned in the beginning of the plea (*f*)(948). But if a plea profess in its commencement to answer the whole cause of action, and afterwards answer only a part, the whole plea is bad (*g*): and in this instance the plea being insufficient, the plaintiff's course is to demur generally or specially, and there will be no discontinuance by so doing, or by replying, instead of taking judgment as to the unanswered part (*h*). As if in covenant for seven quarters' rent, *a plea profess to answer the whole, but only show a surrender
[*555] before the last four of the seven quarters' rent accrued due, it is bad on demurrer, because it does not answer the whole breach, which is not entire, but part of it may be proved (*i*). And where to a declaration for a libel, which charged that the plaintiff had been *three* times suspended for misconduct as a proctor, the defendant pleaded to the *whole* declaration that the plaintiff had been *once* so suspended, it was held on demurrer that the plea was altogether bad: although as the libel was divisible, the plea would have been sufficient had it been confined in the introduction, &c. to the charge of the single suspension (*k*). So, if in trespass the defendant assume in the introductory part of his plea to justify an assault, battery, and *wounding*, and afterwards merely show that by virtue of a writ he *arrested* the plaintiff, but allege nothing to justify the *wounding*, this is bad on demurrer (*l*) (949). But these rules

(*d*) Discontinuance is either of process or of pleading. As to continuances, &c. Tidd, 9th ed. 678; Steph. 2d edit. 33.

(*e*) Risdale *v.* Kelly, 1 Cromp. & Jer. 410.

(*f*) 1 Stra. 303; 1 Saund. 28, note 3, *sec.* But see 2 B. & P. 427, where it was decided that when a plea begins as an answer to part, and contains in the body of it an answer to the whole, the plaintiff may demur; but (as observed in note g. to 1 Saund. 28, 5th ed.) in this case there was a plea of *non assumpsit* to the whole declaration, so that the special plea which was demurred to could not operate as a discontinuance. And see *per* Bosanquet, J. 6 Bing. 595.

(*g*) 1 Saund. 28, n. 3; Willes, 55; 1 Salk. 179; 1 Chit. Rep. 132; 2 B. & C. 477; 3 D. & R. 647, S. C.

(*h*) Crump *v.* Adney, 3 Tyr. 270; 6 Taunt. 646, 647; Steph. 2d edit. 245; 2 B. & C. 477; 3 D. & R. 647, S. C.; 6 Bing. 266.

(*i*) 5 Taunt. 27. See 1 B. & C. 460.

(*k*) 6 Bing. 266, and 587, S. C.

(*l*) 1 Saund. 296, n. 1; 8 T. R. 299; 6 T. R. 562; 7 Taunt. 689; 1 Moore, 420, S. C.

(948) Hallett *v.* Holmes, 18 Johns. Rep. 28. Vide Nevins *v.* Keeler, 6 Johns. Rep. 63. Loder *v.* Phelps, 13 Wend. R. 48. In England, if a plea begins as an answer only to a part of the declaration, and is in truth only an answer to part, the plaintiff must take judgment for the part unanswered as by *nil dicit*. Here, a general demurrer to such a plea is sustained. Etheridge *v.* Osborn, 12 Wend. R. 402. This is a fatal defect. Sterling *v.* Sherwood, 20 Johns. Rep. 204. Hecock *v.* Coates, 2 Wend. R. 419. Slocum *v.* Despard, 8 ib. 615. The court repose themselves upon the opinion of Willis, Ch. J., in Bullythrope *v.* Turner, Willes, 475, 80, and Yelv. 38., Cro. Jac. 27, Cro. Eliz. 434, 2 Ventris, 193, and 3 Johns. Cas. 205. Vide 6 Greenl. R. 476.

(949) See Gates *v.* Lounsbury, 20 Johns. Rep. 427.

should be understood with this qualification, that the part of the declaration which is professed to be, but is not answered by the plea, is material, and the gist of the action; for where any thing is inserted in the declaration merely as matter of *aggravation*, the plea need not answer or justify that, and the answering the matter which is the gist of the action will suffice (*m*).

II. QUALITIES.

A general charge ought to be answered in every part, but it is said to be sufficient to answer a collateral issue in the words of the plaintiff (*n*). Thus, in an action of waste in cutting twenty trees, the defendant ought to plead that he did not cut the said trees, *or either of them*, or the traverse would be too large; though in debt on an obligation that he shall do no waste, if the breach assigned is that he cut twenty oaks, it is sufficient to plead that he did not cut the said twenty oaks *modo et forma* (*o*). A plea in bar to an avowry for rent for £120 that the said £120 were not due, without saying "or any part thereof," is bad on demurrer (*p*). The points on this subject will be more fully stated when we consider the nature of *Traverses*.

[*556]

*The fault of *discontinuance* in pleading may occur in a replication; as where a plea to the whole of an entire and indivisible claim is not answered or noticed *in toto* by the plaintiff (*q*).

4thly. A plea must deny or confess, and avoid: and herein of giving color, and of special pleas, amounting to the general issue.

4thly. A plea in bar, unlike a plea in abatement, offers matter which is a conclusive answer or defence to the action upon the merits. It is obvious that such a plea must contain either, 1st, a *traverse* or denial of the plaintiff's allegations; or, 2dly, an express or implied *admission* that such allegations are true, with a statement of matter which destroys their effect. In other words, a plea in bar must *deny*, or *confess and avoid* the facts stated in the declaration (*r*). Pleas in bar are not therefore susceptible of any other division than, 1st, pleas of *traverse* or *denial*; 2dly, pleas by way of *confession and avoidance*.

Pleas in *denial* are either the general issue in those actions in which so general a traverse is admissible, or they occur in instances in which, there being no general issue, as in covenant, &c., some specific fact is specially disputed. The doctrine of *Traverses* will be discussed in a subsequent part of the work.

The quality of a plea in *confession* and *avoidance* is more peculiar, and demands particular attention. A plea of this description is either in *justification* or *excuse* of the matters alleged in the declaration; as imprisonment under a magistrate's warrant, or *son assault demesne* in trespass; or it is in *discharge* of the cause of action by subsequent matter, as accord and satisfaction, or a release (*s*). It is observable that each of these pleas admits the mere *facts*

(*m*) 1 Hen. Bl. 555; 2 Camph. 175; 1 Saund. 28, note 3; 3 T. R. 297; 3 Wils. 20; 2 Wils. 313, Com. Dig. Pleader, E. 1. *Quære* whether a plea directly and expressly denying the facts alleged in one count and wholly inapplicable to the other cause of action stated in the declaration, but without *any introductory statement professedly limiting its application to the first count*, is to be considered as a plea to that count only, or as an informal answer to the whole declaration, Worley *v.* Harrison, 5 Nev. & Man. 173.

(*n*) Cro. Eliz. 84; 3 B. & P. 348; Com. Dig. Pleader, G. 15.

(*o*) Cro. Eliz. 84; Yelv. 225; see 2 Saund. 5 b, c, d, e, when to traverse the place alleged.

(*p*) 3 B. & P. 348.

(*q*) See 1 B. & C. 460, 465, 466; 2 D. & R. 471, S. C.; and *post*, as to Traverses.

(*r*) See Reg. Pl. 59; 21 H. 6, 19; Tidd, 9th ed. 653; 5 B. & C. 479; 4 B. & C. 457; Steph. on Pleading, 2d ed. 171.

(*s*) See Com. Dig. Pleader, 3 M. 12; Steph. 2d ed. 239, 240.

II. QUALITIES. stated in the declaration, as that the defendant committed the trespasses charged; that the *contract was made or the debt* was incurred, &c. But the matter which they allege by way of defence defeats or avoids the legal effect of those facts, and disproves, if true, the plaintiff's right of action. As a part of this rule that a plea must either traverse or deny, or *confess and avoid*, it was in a late case held that a plea of discharge under an insolvent act, from liability to perform the promises laid in the declaration, must expressly confess such promises to have been made, and this not hypothetically; and that therefore a plea of discharge from the alleged promises, "*if any such were made*," was demurrable (*t*). So, very recently, a plea of the statute of limitations, alleging that the cause of action, "if any such there be," did not accrue, &c., was bad on special demurrer (*u*); and yet it has been the course in various pleas, as in those to the jurisdiction, and in pleas in abatement of nonjoinder, to introduce those words.

The *principles* of pleading, and now as we have just seen the express rules (*x*), require in general that matter in confession and avoidance should be *specially pleaded*, and not be given in evidence under the general issue or [*557] traverse (*y*). The important relaxation of or departure *from this rule, in many instances in assumpsit, debt on simple contract, and case, has been already adverted to; but we have shown that the defendant, even in those actions, always had the *option* of pleading matter in confession and avoidance specially (*z*).

Of giving *Color* (*a*). An important rule of pleading is deducible from the principle that a plea in bar must traverse, or confess and avoid, the matter to which it is applied, namely, that a plea in confession and avoidance must *give Color;* and on this rule chiefly depends the doctrine that a special plea, not pleaded as a general issue, but which is so in effect, will be defective.

It is plain that a plea which shows new matter in *avoidance* or *discharge* of the plaintiff's allegations is double and argumentative (*b*), if it do not admit the apparent truth of those allegations as matter of fact. There can be no occasion to adduce grounds for defeating the operation of disputed facts. The plea in avoidance must therefore give color to the plaintiff, that is, must give him credit for having an apparent or *prima facie* right of action, independently of the matter disclosed in the plea to destroy it.

Of pleas amounting to the general issue. Where the defence consists of matter of *fact*, merely amounting to a *denial* of such allegations in the declaration, as the plaintiff would on the general issue be bound to prove in support of his case, a *special* plea is bad as unnecessary, and amounting to the general issue (950); first, because such spe-

(*t*) Gould *v.* Lasbury, 1 Crom. M. & Ros. 254; 2 Dowl. 707; *sed quære*, this has since been doubted.

(*u*) Margetts *v.* Bays, K. B. 15 Jan. Hil. T. A. D. 1836.

(*x*) *Ante*, 551 *f*.

(*y*) *Ante*, 513, 515; Stephen, 2d ed. 198, 199.

(*z*) *Ante*, 515; 4 B. & C. 547; 1 M. & P. 308; see Steph. 2d ed. 198 to 201.

(*a*) See a recent form of color, 1 Bing. N. C. 484.

(*b*) As to these faults in a plea, see *post;* and *ante*, 259, 271, 272.

(950) { Therefore the plea of *nul tiel corporation* to an action of *assumpsit* against a corporation, is bad on special demurrer, as amounting to the general issue. Bank of Au-

cial plea, if considered as a *traverse*, tends to needless prolixity and expense, and is an argumentative denial and a departure from the prescribed forms of pleading the general issue; and, secondly, if viewed as a plea in *confession and avoidance*, it does not give color or a plausible ground of action to the plaintiff (c).

II. QUALITIES.

Of giving color.

Thus, in assumpsit or debt on simple contract, a plea of matter which shows that no such contract was *in fact* made, is bad; as a plea in an action for the price of a horse, "that the defendant did not buy the horse." (d) So in an action of *assumpsit against a defendant for the use and occupation of a house "by A. his wife, at his request," a plea that A. was not the defendant's wife is bad (e). And in trespass for taking personal property, the defendant cannot plead *property* in a stranger or himself (f); because that goes to contradict the evidence which the plaintiff must adduce on the general issue in support of his case. So in trespass to land, the plaintiff must prove upon the general issue his possession thereof at the time the trespasses were committed (g); therefore a plea that the plaintiff "had no such close," (h) is bad. And if in trespass for breaking and entering the plaintiff's house and taking "*his*" goods, the defendant justify as sheriff under a *fieri facias* against the goods of a *third* person, the plea will be bad if it state that the defendant took the goods *mentioned in the declaration* (i). So, where in a declaration for slander, the words set out imported an unqualified assertion by the defendant that the plaintiff was insolvent, and in a plea of justification, the defendant only admitted that he had uttered words importing that he had mentioned the fact, *on the authority of a third person*, who was the author; the Court held the plea bad, because it did not confess *and avoid the charge* laid in the declaration (k). In trespass for an assault and battery, where the defendant pleaded that he was riding a horse in the highway, and that his horse being frightened ran away with him, and that the plaintiff was desired to go out of the way, and did not, and the horse ran upon the plaintiff against the defendant's will; on demurrer, the plaintiff had judgment, because the defendant had assumed to justify the battery, and yet had not confessed that which amounted to a battery by himself; for if the horse ran away against the will of the rider, it could not be said, with any color of reason, to be a battery in the rider; and it was ob-

[*558]

(c) Com. Dig. Pleader, E. 13; Bac. Ab. Pleas, G. 3; 3 Bla. Com. 309; 1 M. & P. 294, 308; 4 B. & C. 547; Stephen, 2d ed. 4?9. In 1 M. & P. 307, the Court complained of the contradiction in the books as to what plea amounts to the general issue.

(d) Vin. Ab. *Certainty in pleading*, E. 15, cites Bro. Traverse, pl. 275; 22 Edw. 4, 29.

(e) 2 Chit. Rep. 642.

(f) Ld. Raym. 88, 89; 1 Vent. 249; 2 Lev. 92; Cro. Eliz. 329.

(g) *Ante*, 538.

(h) 10 Hen. 6, 16; Stephen, 2d ed. 459. See various other instances put, *id.* 459 to 461.

(i) See the forms, *post*, vol. iii.

(k) 10 B. & C. 263.

burn v. Weed, 19 Johns. Rep. 300.} Vide Kennedy v. Strong, 10 Johns. Rep. 289. {Little v. Bolles, 7 Halst. Rep. 171.} So, in action upon a joint promissory note, a plea that it was the separate note of the defendant, is bad upon special demurrer, as amounting to the general issue. Van Ness v. Forrest, 8 Cranch, 30. See Wheeler v. Curtis, 11 Wend. R. 660. A plea of licence in an action *quare clausum fregit*, from one havingonly a possessory right to the *locus in quo*, without giving color to the plaintiff, is bad, as amounting only to the general issue. Underwood v. Campbell, 13 Wend. R. 78. Collett v. Flinn, 5 Cowen, 466. Under the general issue, the plaintiff must prove his possession, and the plea of licence as there pleaded raised a question of possession only, and was therefore bad. *Ib.*

II. QUALITIES.

served by the Court, that if the plaintiff had pleaded not guilty, this matter might have acquitted him upon evidence (*l*).

Of giving color.

The common allegation in a plea, by way of introduction, that the cause of action laid in one count, and the cause of action laid in another count, are [*559] one and the same, showing *matter in discharge of one cause of action only, seems to render the plea defective, as amounting to the general issue (*m*). The fault in question is no ground of error; and can it seems only be objected to by a *special* demurrer (*n*). It has even been said that the only mode of taking advantage of the defect is to apply to the Court to set aside the plea (*o*)(951); but it is difficult to imagine upon what principle the right of demurrer can be excluded; and there are many instances in which it has been exercised (*p*).

Of implied color.

In the above instances the mere *facts* are denied, and no question of *law* upon their effect is raised. Where the cause of action is avoided by matter *ex post facto*, as payment, accord and satisfaction, &c. it may always be specially pleaded (*q*). So, where the defence consists of matter of *law*, where in other words the mere facts charged in the declaration are admitted, and their *legal* operation is disputed by matter alleged in the plea, the defendant need not plead the general issue, and the plea may be special. In this case, from the nature of the defence, the plaintiff has an *implied color* of action, bad indeed in point of law if the facts pleaded be true, but which is properly referred to the decision of the Court (*r*). Thus, in assumpsit, the defendant may specially plead infancy, lunacy, or coverture, when the contract was made; or illegality of consideration, as usury or gaming; or that the engagement was void, as not being in writing, according to the statute of frauds (*s*). So, a plea in assumpsit for goods sold, that they were sold by A. as the plaintiff's agent, that the agent sold them as his own with the plaintiff's privity, and that the defendant was not aware of the real facts, and showing a debt from the agent as a set-off is good; for this matter operates as a legal extinguish- [*560] ment of a debt not otherwise denied (*t*). So, a plea in *trover, that A. was possessed of and lost the goods, that B. found them, and gave them to the plaintiff, who lost them, and that the defendant found them, and by the command of A. converted them, was held sufficient, because it gave an implied color by confessing the *possession and property* in the plaintiff against all but the lawful owner (*u*).

So, without giving express color, the defendant may plead in trespass or trover that A. was *possessed* of the goods, not alleging they were his own, and

(*l*) Salk. 637; Ld. Raym. 38; 3 Wils. 411.

(*m*) *Ante*, 449; Freem. 367; *vide post*, as to the *Quæ est eadem*.

(*n*) See *post*, as to the consequences of not giving express color when necessary.

(*o*) See Hob. 127; 1 Leon. 178; 2 Rol. Rep. 140; Com. Dig. Pleader, G. 14; Stephen, 2d ed. 463.

(*p*) And see 6 East, 583, 597; 2 Chit. Rep. 642.

(*q*) 1 M. & P. 308; 4 B. & C. 552.

(*r*) Tidd, 9th ed. 653.

(*s*) 1 M. & P. 294, 308; 4 Bing. 470, S. C.; 4 B. & Ald. 595; *sed vide* 11 Price, 494; and as to the replication, &c. see *id.*; *ante*, 515, 547; 1 Crom. & M. 239. At the trial of an action on a guarantee, the plaintiff would be bound to prove a *written* contract, but still it is not stated in the declaration that it was in writing, and this may be considered a defence on matter of *law*.

(*t*) 4 B. & C. 547; 7 D. & R. 42, S. C.

(*u*) Cro. El. 262, 539; 8 Co. 99 b; Com. Dig. Pleader, E. 14, *acc.*; Latch. 185; 1 Leon. 178, *semb. contra*.

(951) Vide Whittlesey v. Wolcott, 2 Day's Rep. 431.

sold them in market overt to the defendant; or that B. took them *de quodam ignoto*, and waived them within the defendant's manor, wherefore he took them: because such plea gives an implied color, and does not deny but that the *property* was in the plaintiff; and the defendant is not bound to show expressly in whom it was (*x*). So, in trespass for taking corn, the defendant may plead that he took them as tithe or as wreck, without giving express color (*y*). The plea of *liberum tenementum* may also be considered as giving implied color (*z*), for it tacitly admits that in point of *fact* the plaintiff may have been in *possession* of the *locus in quo*, (which, as in the case of personal property, *prima facie* entitles the plaintiff to maintain trespass against all the world but the rightful owner (*a*),) but insists that in point of *law* such possession is unlawful (*b*). So, in trespass to lands, if the defendant aver that the plaintiff was seised, and claim under a demise from him, *express color* need not be given (*c*); but a plea of such demise "by virtue whereof the defendant entered and was *possessed*," at the time of the trespasses, appears to be bad, as amounting to the general issue (*d*). The unnecessary addition of color appears to be no ground of demurrer, for the introduction of superfluous words of form will not vitiate (*e*).

II. QUALITIES. — Of giving color.

But where from the nature of the defence, the plaintiff would have no implied color of action, the defendant cannot plead specially any matter which controverts what the plaintiff would on the general issue be bound to prove without *giving *express color* (*f*). Express color is defined to be "a feigned matter pleaded by the defendant in trespass, from which the plaintiff seems to have a good cause of action, whereas he has in truth only an appearance or color of cause." (*g*) Thus, in an action of trespass to land, if the defendant plead a possessory title under a demise from a third person, this plea, showing that the right of possession is in the defendant, would, without giving express color, amount to the general issue (*h*); for it goes to deny that the trespass was, as alleged in the declaration, committed in the *plaintiff's* close, and shows the right of possession in the defendant, although the possessory right and possession of the plaintiff are the very gist of his action. But if the defendant, after stating his own title, allege, as is usual, that the plaintiff entered upon his possession "*under color* of a charter of *demise for life* made to the plaintiff before the demise to the defendant," by the former proprietor of the estate, from whom the defendant derives title, and "that the defendant re-entered, &c.," this creates a question of law for the decision of the Court, and by that means prevents the plea from amounting to the general issue, and being matter of fiction or supposal, is not traversable (*i*). As the plaintiff cannot traverse the colorable title given him, he must in his replication either

Of *express* color. [*561]

(*x*) 10 Co. 90 b.
(*y*) 10 Co. 88 a, &c.; Reg. Pl. 304.
(*z*) 7 T. R. 354; 8 *Id.* 403; see *ante*, 541, 542.
(*a*) Cro. El. 262; 1 East, 244.
(*b*) As to this plea, see 1 Saund. 299 c.
(*c*) 3 Salk. 273; Tidd, 9th ed. 653.
(*d*) Sty. 355; Steph. 2d edit. 460.
(*e*) 1 East, 219; *ante*, 262.
(*f*) 2 Saund. 401 a; 10 Co. 88, &c.; Cro. El. 76; 8 T. R. 406. As to color in pleading in general, see 10 Co. 88, &c.; 1 East, 215; 3 Bla. Com. 309; Reg. Plac. 303; Doc. Plac. Color; Doct. & Stud. lib. 2, c. 53; 3 Salk. 273; Bac. Ab. Pleas, I. 8; Com. Dig. Plead. 3 M. 40. Express color explained, Stephen, 2d ed. 245; see the form and notes, *post*, vol. iii.
(*g*) Bac. Ab. Trespass, I. 4.
(*h*) 2 Saund. 401; 7 T. R. 354; 8 *Id.* 406; 1 East, 215; Com. Dig. Pleader, 3 M. 40, 41.
(*i*) 1 East, 213, 215; 3 Salk. 273.

II. QUALITIES. traverse or avoid the defendant's title as alleged in the plea, or demur if it be insufficient in law. So, in trespass for taking goods, if the defendant plead

Of giving color. that A. was possessed of them *as of his own proper goods*, and sold them in market overt to the defendant, the defendant must give express color, for this plea alleging that A. was possessed of his own property, amounts to a denial that the plaintiff had any property in them, and therefore gives no color of action: and the color usually given in such case is that the defendant bailed the goods to a stranger, who delivered them to the plaintiff, from whom the defendant took them (*k*).

[*562] *The subtle and somewhat intricate doctrine of *express* color is not of very frequent occurrence in pleading, and it seems can only arise at the present day in trespass, and is rarely adopted except in trespass to land. It is obviously founded on the principle that a plea in bar must deny, or admit and avoid the facts charged by the plaintiff. The object of using it is in general either to compel the plaintiff expressly to traverse or avoid the defendant's title. If the plea consists of distinct allegations, showing a lengthened descent from several successive persons or various deeds, &c. constituting the defendant's title, the plaintiff can traverse one only of such allegations or deeds, &c.; and thus he admits the rest, which often presents an adequate reason for giving express color in trespass to land. And where the facts are admitted by both parties, and a legal question only arises on the title, the plea is useful and proper, as the question may thus be put upon record and may be tried upon a demurrer, and the expense of a trial will thus be avoided (*l*).

Form of color. It is impolitic unnecessarily to venture upon new forms of pleading in any case, but especially when the defendant has recourse to fiction, and so technical a doctrine as that under consideration. The plea should give the color just mentioned, namely, a "charter of demise to the plaintiff for life," &c., averring that nothing passed thereby; as it is the form which is always used (*m*). It is a most important rule that the colorable title given must be *plausible* or afford a *supposititious* right;—such as might induce an unlearned person to imagine sufficient; and yet it must be in *legal* strictness inadequate to defeat the defendant's title as shown in the plea (*n*). Thus, the prior charter of demise to the plaintiff for life, might, to a non-professional person, seem to confer a superior title, but there is this legal vice that the charter, though a charter of demise for life, is not pleaded as a *feoffment*, and does not appear to have been accompanied by livery of seisin (*o*). The plea is

*563] bad if the title given be not even specious, and be at the first blush *manifestly insufficient: on the other hand, it is defective if the color given be in legal contemplation and strictness sufficient to invest the plaintiff with the legal right; for in that event, the defendant has no legal title on his own showing (*p*). "The plea ought to have four qualities; *first*, it ought to be a matter of title, doubtful to a jury, as where the defendant pleads that the plaintiff,

(*k*) 10 Co. 90 b; see an instance of a plea in such action, which was held defective, as giving the plaintiff a *real* right, *viz.* by showing a prior deed of *gift* to him from the party from whom defendant claimed, Cro. Jac. 122.

(*l*) See Steph. on Pl. 2d edit. 247.

(*m*) See a form of a deed of feoffment *without livery*, pleaded by way of color, 2 Rich. C. P. 443.

(*n*) Bac. Ab. Pleas, I. 8; Com. Dig. Pleader, 3 M. 41; Keilw. 103 b.

(*o*) Doct. Pl. 73; 10 Co. 89 b; Steph. 2d edit. 249.

(*p*) Doct. Pl. 73; 10 Co. 89 b; Steph. 2d edit. 252.

claiming by color of a deed of feoffment, &c. that is sufficient, for it is a doubt to lay gents, if lands shall pass by deed only without livery (*q*); *secondly*, that color as such ought to have continuance, although it wants effect; as if the defendant give color by color of a deed of demise to the plaintiff for the life 'of J. S.' who it appears by the pleadings was dead before the trespass, this is not sufficient, because the color doth not continue; but the defendant may well deny the effect of it, *viz*. that the plaintiff claims by color of a deed of demise 'to him for his life;' whereas nothing passed thereby: therefore, there is a difference between the continuance of the color and the effect of it; *thirdly*, it ought to be such a color, as if it were of effect would maintain the nature of the action, as in an assize, (where the disseisin of a *freehold* is complained of,) color of a *freehold*, (not of a demise for years,) ought to be given, &c.; *fourthly*, color ought to be given by the *first* conveyance, otherwise all the conveyance before is waived." (*r*). Therefore, where the defendant derived a title to himself by divers mesne conveyances, and gave color to the plaintiff by one who was last named in the conveyance, this was held insufficient, and he should have given color by him who was first named in the conveyance (*s*); and in giving color under a feoffment, the word *charter* or *deed* must not be omitted (*t*). The omission to give express color when necessary will be aided if the plaintiff reply (*u*) instead of demurring (*x*): and it will, as a mere matter of form, be aided upon *general* demurrer (*y*); and the defect is expressly rendered *immaterial after verdict by the statute 32 Hen. 8, c. 30 (*z*). We have before remarked, that as the law allows the fictitious statement of a colorable title for a particular purpose, such allegation is not traversable (*a*): and the giving unnecessary color may be rejected as surplusage (*b*).

II. QUALITIES.

Of giving color.

[*564]

5thly. The fault of *duplicity* in pleading, which we have already considered in examining the structure of, and as it affects a declaration, may equally occur in a plea (*c*). Every plea must in general be *single*; and if it contain two distinct matters, either of which would bar the action, and each of which requires a separate answer, it will in general be subject to a *special* demurrer for duplicity (952). Thus, if *several* outlawries be pleaded in the same plea to the same matter, or if *son assault demesne*, and a release, be relied upon in one plea to the same trespass, as either of these would defeat the action, the plea would be considered double (*d*). But the defendant is not, as before explained, precluded from introducing several facts into one plea, if they be con-

5thly. Must be single.

(*q*) It should be shown affirmatively in the plea that it was a charter of *demise* for life, or a feoffment *without livery*; for it seems that in pleading, the term "feoffment," or "enfeoffed," means and includes the necessary livery of seisin, see *ante*, 253; Co. Lit. 303 b; 2 Saund. 305 a, n. 13; Doct. Pl. 72.

(*r*) 10 Co. 91 b.

(*s*) 2 Rol. Rep. 140.

(*t*) *Id*.

(*u*) Ld. Raym. 551, 552.

(*x*) *Id*.

(*y*) *Ante*, 559; 4 Ann. c. 16, s. 1; 10 East, 363; Cro. Jac. 229.

(*z*) 1 Saund. 228 c.

(*a*) *Ante*, 561; Steph. 2d ed. 250; Tidd, 9th ed. 653, 654.

(*b*) *Ante*, 560.

(*c*) See *ante*, 259, and the authorities cited *id*. 260, note (*y*). See Vivian *v*. Jenkins, 5 Nev. & Man. 14.

(*d*) *Id*.; Co. Lit. 304 a. See instances, Vin. Abr. Double Pleas, A. 23; 1 M. & P. 102, 112.

(952) Vide Kennedy *v*. Strong, 10 Johns. Rep. 259. { 20 Johns. Rep. 405. }

II. QUALITIES. Single.

stituent parts of the same entire defence, and form one connected proposition (953), or be alleged as inducement to, or as a consequence of another fact (e). Thus in detinue at the suit of a feme, the defendant pleaded that after bailment of the goods to him by the plaintiff, she married E. F., and that during such marriage E. F. released to him all actions, it was objected that the plea was double, viz. property in the husband by the intermarriage, and a release by him; but it was resolved not to be double, because he could not plead the release without showing the marriage (f)(954). So it will be no duplicity to set out several matters, as a will or deed, *and* a fine constituting a title; although one of those matters would defeat the action (g). So, to a declaration in slander, stating that the plaintiff had been guilty of fraud or felony, several offences may be stated in a plea of justification, although it would not be necessary to prove the whole. And at common law the defendant may plead to a part of the declaration one ground of defence, and to another part a different ground (i); and one defendant may plead one matter, and the other defendant [*565] *another matter to the same cause of action (k). So, a defendant may plead in abatement to part, and in bar to other part, and may demur to the residue (l). The rule that a plea must be single also precludes the defendant from pleading and demurring to the same part, especially as such duplicity would draw the matter to a different inquiry; the demurrer to be tried by the Court, and the fact by a jury (m). So, a plea confessing and avoiding, and also traversing the same point, is in the nature of a double plea (n). An executor, however, may and ought to plead several judgments, &c. outstanding (o): and in a plea of set-off the defendant may rely on a debt on record, and a debt on simple contract, though one will create an issue of law, and the other an issue of fact (p). The statute of Anne, allowing several pleas (q), and the particular effect of which will hereafter be considered, does not aid a duplicity in one and the same plea, though it allows of different grounds of defence being stated in different pleas. Duplicity can only be objected to by *special* demurrer, and the particular duplicity must

(e) *Ante*, 261. When defendant need not prove all he has alleged, 1 Taunt. 146.

(f) Bac. Ab. Pleas, K. 2; Moor, 25, pl. 85; Dalis. 30, pl. 9; 1 M. & P. 112.

(g) 1 M. & P. 102.

(i) Bac. Ab Pleas, K. 1; Co. Lit. 304 a. See 3 Campb. 366.

(k) Com. Dig. Pleader, E. 2.

(l) *Ante*, 492.

(m) 11 Co 52; Bac. Abr. Pleas, N.

(n) 2 Ventr. 212; 3 Mod. 318; Co. Ent. 504; *ante*, 557.

(o) 1 Saund. 336 c, 337, and notes.

(p) 1 East, 370.

(q) 4 & 5 Ann. c. 16.

(953) Vide Strong v. Smith, 3 Caines' Rep. 162. Cooper v. Heermance, 3 Johns. Rep. 318. Patcher v Sprague, 2 Johns. Rep. 462. Thomas v. Rumsey, 6 Johns. Rep. 33. { Bradner et al. v. Demick, 20 Johns. Rep. 404. }

(954) To a declaration in debt against a sheriff for an escape, the defendant pleaded an involuntary escape, and the return of the prisoner into custody before suit brought, and also that the prisoner was discharged under the act for the relief of debtors, with respect to the imprisonment of their persons; and the plea was held good. The defendant could not have pleaded the involuntary escape, and return before suit brought, without also alleging that the prisoner was at the time of the plea pleaded in his custody. And if he had relied solely on the discharge, then at the trial he might have been surprised, and charged for the escape. So that both facts were necessarily blended in his defence, and went to one point, viz. an escape for which he was not responsible. Currie v. Henry, 2 Johns. Rep. 433. Potter v. Titcomb, 1 Fairf. R. 53.

be distinctly pointed out (*r*) (955); and if the plaintiff do not demur, he must reply to both material parts of the plea (*s*). II. QUALITIES.

6thly. Must be certain.

6thly. A plea in bar must also be *certain* (*t*), or it will be defective upon demurrer (*u*). We have already attempted to define the different degrees of certainty in pleading, and to show the application of each, and we have seen that it is a general rule that the minor degree of certainty, viz. that to a *common intent*, that is, if the matter be clear enough according to the natural sense of the words used (*x*), is sufficient in a plea in bar (*y*). Thus, in debt on bond conditioned to procure A. S. to surrender a copyhold "to the use of the plaintiff," a plea that A. S. surrendered and released the copyhold to the plaintiff in full Court, &c. and the plaintiff accepted it, [*566] *without alleging that the surrender was *to the plaintiff's use*, is sufficient; for this shall be intended (*z*). So, in debt on bond conditioned that the plaintiff shall enjoy certain land, &c. a plea that after the making of the bond until the day of exhibiting the bill the plaintiff did enjoy, is good, though it be not said that *always* after the making until, &c. he enjoyed, for this shall be intended (*a*).

There, however, appear to be some instances in which greater certainty is necessary in a plea than in a declaration. Thus, in a declaration on a promise to pay the debt of another in consideration of forbearance, it is not necessary to show that the promise was in writing, according to the statute of frauds, but it is said to be otherwise in a plea (*b*). So, we have seen that in a declaration claiming a right of way or other easement, it is sufficient to state that the plaintiff by virtue of his possession of a messuage, &c. is entitled to such easement, without setting forth the particulars of the plaintiff's title; but in a plea justifying an entry into land, &c. in respect of such easement, it is necessary to set forth the right by prescription or grant, &c. (*c*). And in trespass, where the defendant justifies under a writ, warrant, precept, or any other authority, he must set it forth particularly in his plea, and it is not sufficient to allege generally that he committed the act complained of by virtue of a certain writ or warrant directed to him, but he must set it forth specially (956), and the defendant ought further to aver in his plea that he has substantially pursued such authority (*d*). And a justification in trespass "as servant" must also state that the act was done "by the command" of the principal (*e*). So, in a declaration on a deed, whether in debt or covenant, it

(*r*) 1 Saund. 337 b, note 3; Doctr. Plac. 147; Bac. Ab. Pleas, K. 1; Com. Dig. Pleader, E. 2; 1 B. & P. 415, 416.

(*s*) 1 Ventr. 272.

(*t*) Com. Dig. Pleader, E. 5. C. 41. E. 7, 8, 9, 10, 11, *per totum*.

(*u*) See *ante*, 271; 3 Bing. 61.

(*x*) *Ante*, 268. See Steph. on Plead. 380; 2d ed. 421, 423.

(*y*) *Id.* And see 1 Saund. 49, n. 1; 346, n. 2; Willes, 52. As to an ungrammatical averment, 13 Price, 172.

(*z*) Cro. Car. 6.

(*a*) Cro. Car. 195.

(*b*) *Ante*, 254, 332. *Sed quære*, and *vide* 2 B. & B. 362. But there the demurrer was general.

(*c*) *Ante*, 414; 3 T. R. 768; 4 *Id.* 719.

(*d*) Co. Lit. 2-3 a, 303 b; 1 Saund. 298, n. 1. When a *return* of the process must be shown, 5 B. & C. 488.

(*e*) Chubb and Mallock, Hil. Term, 52 Geo. 3, K. B.; MS.

(955) Vide Currie *v.* Henry, 2 Johns. Rep. 433.

(956) Vide Stoyell *v.* Westcott, 2 Day's Rep. 418. Cruger *v.* Cropsy, 3 Johns. Rep. 242. A plea by a defendant who had been discharged under the act for the relief of debtors, with respect to the imprisonment of their persons, *that he had been discharged out of custody by due course of law*, is bad. Currie *v.* Henry, 2 Johns. Rep. 433.

II. QUALITIES. Certainty. is sufficient in setting out the deed to allege that "*it was thereby witnessed*" that, &c. (*testatum existit*); but in pleas and avowries the deed must not be stated by way of recital or argument (*f*), but the neglect of this rule can be
[*567] objected to only by a special demurrer (*g*). The rules with regard to *the mode of setting out a deed in its words, or according to its legal import or substance, have already been explained (*h*). Where the defendant states his right only as *inducement* or conveyance, so much certainty is not required (*i*). Thus, it is sufficient to allege in a plea to a declaration in trespass, that the defendant was possessed of a close, from which his cattle escaped into the close of the plaintiff, in consequence of the defect of a fence which the latter ought to have repaired (*k*).

The doctrine of certainty in pleading is open to a very important exception, applicable to pleas as well as other pleadings, namely, that a general mode of pleading shall often be permitted where the matter is of so intricate and complicated a nature, and embraces such a variety and extent of minute circumstances, that a particular statement would cause great prolixity (*l*)(957).

A plea of *performance* of a condition or covenant should in general show specially the time, place, and manner of performance of the specific matters required to be done; and it is not in general sufficient to aver merely that the defendant "performed the matter," or "paid the money," &c. (*m*). Thus, if the condition be to pay £5 to A. and £10 to B. as each attains twenty-one years of age, the plea must show when each came of age, and that each was then paid; not that the defendant paid the sums when they came of age (*n*). So, if a bond be conditioned for the performance of a specific act, as that the defendant should indemnify the plaintiff against a certain liability he was under to a third person, "by paying the latter that sum," the plea will be equivocal and uncertain, and therefore insufficient if it merely state that the defendant "indemnified the plaintiff" without alleging a payment of the money (*o*). Where, however, the thing required to be performed includes matter of the multifarious nature alluded to, there, to prevent inconvenient prolixity, a
[*568] general form of plea shall be allowed. Thus, *in debt on bond to pay over "from time to time all such monies as he should receive, &c." a plea that the

(*f*) 1 Saund. 274, n. 1; Lord Raym. 1539; 1 Leon. 242; Com. Dig. Pleader, E. 3; Bac. Ab. Pleas, I. 5; and see 8 Bing. 256.

(*g*) 1 Saund. and Com. Dig. *ubi supra*.

(*h*) *Ante*, 333, 334.

(*i*) *Ante*, 319.

(*k*) 1 Saund. 346 e, n. 2. See another reason assigned for this instance, Stephen, 358, n. p. 2d edit.

(*l*) *Ante*, 269, 270. The words "*reasonable*" and "*seasonable* times of the year," will often suffice *per se* on this ground, 3 Bing. 61, 65, &c.

(*m*) 1 Lev. 303; Com. Dig. Pleader, E. 25; 2 W. 33; 1 Saund. 116, n. 1; Steph. 2d edit. 382.

(*n*) Cro. Jac. 359.

(*o*) 1 B. & P. 638. See other similar instances, Steph. 2d ed. 406; 1 Saund. 117, n. 1.

(957) Vide Postmaster General U. S. *v*. Cochran, 2 Johns. Rep. 415, 416. Hughes *v*. Smith, 5 Johns. Rep. 168. Frary *v*. Dakin, 7 Johns. Rep. 79. In setting forth the proceedings of an inferior court or magistrate, (for instance, in pleading the discharge of an insolvent debtor,) it is only necessary to set forth so much as was sufficient to give the court or magistrate jurisdiction, and then to state that *taliter processum est*, such proceedings were thereupon had, that a certain judgment was rendered; or that the defendant was discharged from his debts. Service *v*. Heermane, 1 Johns. Rep. 91. Peebles *v*. Kittle, 2 Johns. Rep. 363. Frary *v*. Dakin, 7 Johns. Rep. 75. Cantillon *v*. Graves, 8 Johns. Rep. 472. Cruger *v*. Cropsy, 3 Johns. Rep. 242. {Roosevelt *v*. Kellogg, 20 Johns. Rep. 208.}

defendant paid over all such monies as he received is good, without showing when and of whom he received each particular sum (*p*). II. QUALITIES.

As well in virtue of the rule that less particularity is required in cases where excessive prolixity is thereby avoided, as in consequence of the principle that it is for the *plaintiff* complaining of the breach of the condition of a bond, to show on the record in what instances it has been violated, it is competent to a defendant, in an action on a bond conditioned for the performance of covenants of an *affirmative* nature, contained in another instrument, and not set out in the condition, to plead *generally* "that he hath performed all and singular the said covenants, &c. according to the condition, &c. (*q*) In this case there is no occasion to allege a specific performance of each of the covenants in detail, and it is for the plaintiff to show in his replication a specific breach of such of the covenants as he contends have been broken (*r*). It is plain, however, that if any of the covenants are of a *negative* nature, viz. that the defendant shall not perform an act, or are in the *alternative* or *disjunctive*, a general plea that the defendant has performed such covenants is illogical and argumentative in the first instance, and in the second is ambiguous: and is therefore defective (*s*). In these cases the plea of performance should be more specific, viz. that the defendant "did not," as regards the negative covenant, "commit the act forbidden," and as respects the covenant to perform one thing or another, that he performed *one* of those matters, showing *which* of them was completed (*t*). Mispleading in these instances must be pointed out by a *special* demurrer, and is not otherwise objectionable (*u*). An obligor, who binds himself to perform certain works according to a specification, and other detailed and working drawings to be furnished during the progress of the works, with power for the obligee, by his surveyor, to direct *additions* or omissions, must in a plea of performance, *quoad* such parts in which no orders were *given by the surveyor to *vary* and *deviate* from the original plan, show an authority in the surveyor to give such directions, or aver that the *deviation* or *variation* was an *omission* or *addition* (*x*). The plea of *non damnificatus*, in the general form, applies to cases where the condition is general to indemnify or discharge the plaintiff from any damage by reason of a certain thing, as in the ordinary case of a bastardy bond, &c. (*y*) Certainty. [*569]

In a recent case (*z*), where, in replevin, an avowry was made in respect of a right of common claimed by the corporation of Alnwick, under a grant from the De Vesci; and the plaintiff pleaded that the corporation had been accustomed to appoint a *reasonable* number of herds for, *amongst other things*, superintending the common and cattle thereon, and also to appoint for the pains of each herd a *reasonable* and proper number of stints of each such herd to be depastured upon the common; the Court held that the plea in bar was good after verdict, and Best, C. J., and Burrough, J., appear to have been of opinion that it would not have been bad on demurrer, because the allegation could not

(*p*) 1 Sid. 334; Cro. Eliz. 749.

(*q*) 2 Saund. 403 b; 410, n. 3; 1 Saund. 55, 117, n. 1; 4 East, 340. See the form, *post*, vol. iii.; 2 Steph. 2d ed. 407.

(*r*) *Id.*; 5 Taunt. 386; Cowp. 578.

(*s*) *Id.*; Steph. 2d ed. 409, 410.

(*t*) *Id.*; Cro. Eliz. 233; 8 T. R. 280; 2 Taunt. 278.

(*u*) *Id.*

(*x*) 1 Y. & J. 37.

(*y*) See *post*, vol. iii.; 2 Saund. 84; 1 Saund. 117, n. 1; 1 Hen. Bla. 253.

(*z*) 3 Bing. 61.

II. QUALITIES. Certainty.

have been made with greater certainty, as the reasonableness of the number of herds must vary at times.

Where the covenant is to do some act of record (a), or any matter of law, as to convey, discharge an obligation, ratify or confirm, &c. performance must be pleaded specially; because being a matter of *law* to be performed, it ought to be exhibited to the Court, who are judges of the law, to see if it be well performed, and not to a jury, who are judges only of the fact (b).

General pleading is not allowed in a plea justifying the truth of a libel or slander (c). Therefore where a defendant pleaded "that the plaintiff had been illegally connected with a gang of swindlers, and had been guilty of defrauding divers persons," without stating the particular instances of fraud, and thereby following the terms of the libel, the plea was held bad on demurrer (d)(958). [*570] So, where a libel charged an *attorney with general misconduct, viz. gross negligence, falsehood, prevarication, and excessive bills of costs, in the business he had conducted for the defendant, it was held that a plea in justification, repeating the same general charges, without specifying the particular acts of misconduct, was insufficient on special demurrer; although it was objected that the charge related only to private transactions between the parties themselves, of which it might be presumed the plaintiff was conusant (e). And in a recent case (f), Mr. Baron Wood strongly reprobated general pleas of justification aspersing the plaintiff's general character, without disclosing instances of misconduct, and said it was the duty of the plaintiff to demur to them; and that by so doing the plaintiff did not admit the truth of the matters thus indefinitely justified. Where, however, the charge contained in the slander is in itself specific, the defendant need not further particularize it in his plea: as where the words were, "he stole two sheep of J. S." a plea that the plaintiff "stole the said sheep," is sufficient (g).

So, a general plea of usury, not stating the particulars of the contract, the time of forbearance, or the sum to be forborne, is bad on special demurrer (h). But a general plea that a deed was "obtained by the plaintiff by fraud and misrepresentation," has been holden sufficient, on the ground that fraud usually consists of a multiplicity of circumstances, and therefore it might be inconvenient to require them to be particularly set forth (i). In trespass for an assault and imprisonment, a plea justifying on the ground that a felony had been committed, and that there was reason to suspect the plaintiff, must set forth the facts or reasons which gave rise to and justify the suspicion (k). And in a plea justifying a trespass to the person, every part of the

(a) Co. Lit. 303 b; Bac. Ab. Pleas, I. 3; Show. P. C. 97.

(b) *Id.*

(c) 1 Saund. 244 a, 244 b, note (m); 1 Stark. Slander, 2d ed. 478. See as to general pleas, justifying a libel, as being a correct report of a trial, &c. *ante*, 533.

(d) 1 T. R. 748; 3 B. & P. 284; 11 Price, 235, 273.

(e) 1 Taunt. 543; and see 2 Chit. Rep. 665; 3 B. & C. 566. A plea justifying a libel in respect of the *occasion* on which it was published, must also be specific as to the names of third persons, &c.; 1 M. & Sel. 304.

(f) 11 Price, 235, 255, 277, 278.

(g) Bro. Action sur Cas. 27 H. 8, 22, pl. 3; 1 Rol. Ab. 87.

(h) 2 M. & Sel. 377.

(i) 9 Co. 110. *Per* Lord Ellenborough, 2 M. & Sel. 378; but see 1 Tyrw. & Gr. 87.

(k) *Ante*, 539, 540.

(958) Van Ness *v.* Hamilton, 19 Johns. Rep. 349.

matter which the plea professes to answer must be stated with great precision, as if a wounding or handcuffing be justified under a latitat, &c., an attempt to rescue, or other resistance, must be fully stated (*l*). And if an officer justify breaking an inner door of a house, in order to search *for and arrest a party, it must be alleged that he demanded the key, or that no one was present of whom such demand could be made, and it is not sufficient to say that the door was locked so that without breaking open the same the defendant could not enter, without alleging the particular circumstances which rendered the breaking necessary (*m*). And a plea in trover for taking a ship, that the defendant as captain of a man-of-war seized it "as a prize," without showing how it became such, is demurrable (*n*). So, in pleading matters in excuse, all the circumstances should be shown (*o*) (959).

II. QUALITIES.

[*571]

Necessary circumstances will, however, in general, be intended in a plea, as if a feoffment be pleaded, livery need not be alleged, for it shall be intended, and is included in the word *feoffment* or *enfeoffed* (*p*); and it is not requisite to have so much certainty in pleading a matter which is only conveyance or inducement (*q*), or matter in the negative (*r*). And in a plea, as well as a declaration, less certainty is required in stating a matter which is more properly and peculiarly within the knowledge of the opponent (*s*).

Certainty as to time and place.

With regard to the *certainty* required in a plea in the statement of the *time* and *place* when and where material facts have happened, we shall hereafter see that it was an ancient rule that the time and place mentioned in the declaration should be adhered to, unless it be necessary for the defence to vary therefrom (*t*). Matter of discharge, as a release, &c., must be shown to have taken place after the trespass, &c. (*u*), and at common law in pleading payment of a bond, &c. it was necessary to show that it was made on a named day (*x*). Unless a particular place was material to the defence, it does not appear to have ever been necessary to state *any place* where the facts happened (960); for though a distinction was formerly taken between a plea in abatement and a plea in bar, a venue was afterwards deemed to be unnecessary in both (*y*). The doctrine of venues was clearly and correctly stated by Eyre, C. J. in *Ilderton* v. *Ilderton* (*z*), who said, "that as defendants, with respect to transitory matters, are obliged to lay the venue in their plea in the place *laid in the declaration, and since the statute (*a*) has directed that the jury shall come *de corpore comitatus*, the law of venues will be found to be very substantially altered, and to lie in a narrow compass, and the distinction between laying no venue at all in a plea, and being obliged to lay the same venue as in the declaration, will be a distinction without a difference; and

[*572]

(*l*) 1 Saund. 296, note 1; 8 T. R. 299; 4 B. & C. 596.
(*m*) 3 B. & P. 223. *Sed vide* 3 Lev. 92.
(*n*) Carth. 31.
(*o*) Bac. Ab. Trespass, I.
(*p*) Com Dig. Pleader, E. 9; *ante*, 253.
(*q*) Com. Dig. Pleader, E. 10; 1 Saund. 346, n. 2; *ante*, 319.
(*r*) Com. Dig. Pleader, E. 11.
(*s*) *Ante*, 254, 269, 417.
(*t*) 2 Saund. 5, note 3.
(*u*) Plowd. 46.
(*x*) Plowd. 104; Com. Dig. Pleader, E. 6.
(*y*) 1 Saund. 8 a, note 1.
(*z*) 2 Hen. Bla. 161.
(*a*) 4 Ann. c. 16, s. 6.

(959) Vide The King v. Bridekirk, 11 East's Rep. 304.
(960) Acc. Thomas v. Rumsay, 6 Johns. Rep. 33, 34. Furman v. Haskin, 2 Caines' Rep. 373.

II. QUALITIES. — Certainty. the principle now is, that the place laid in the declaration draws to it the trial of every thing that is transitory, and it should seem that neither forms of pleading, nor ancient rules of pleading established on a different principle ought now to prevail." (*b*) We have seen that the recent pleading rule, Hil. T. 4 W. 4, reg. 8, orders that no venue shall be stated in the body of the declaration, or in any subsequent pleading (*c*), but provides that in cases where local description is now required, such local description shall be given (*d*) †.

A plea need not state facts of which the Court will *ex officio* take notice (*e*).

7thly. Must be direct and positive, and not argumentative.

7thly. We have already seen that pleading is a statement of *facts*, and not a statement of argument; it is therefore a rule that a plea shoud be direct and positive, and advance its position of fact in an absolute form, and not by way of rehearsal (*f*), reasoning, or argument, (961), which would lead the fact to be collected by inference and argument only, and thereby tend to create unnecessary prolixity and expense (*g*). If *scire facias* be brought against a parson for the arrears of an annuity recovered against him, and he plead that before the writ brought he had resigned into the hands of the ordinary, who accepted thereof, this plea is argumentative, for he should have pleaded directly that he was not parson on the day of the writ brought, instead of merely pleading facts from which that conclusion was to be drawn (*h*). A plea in debt for an escape that "*if* the party escaped, he escaped without the defendant's knowledge, and returned, &c." is bad (*i*). So, a surrender by operation of law should be pleaded as a surrender, and not merely circumstantially; thus, if a surrender be by acceptance of a new lease, it is not sufficient to say "that the lessee being possessed under a former lease, the lessor demised to
[*573] him," but the plea *should be that the lessee "surrendered," and then that the lessor demised, or that the lessor entered and demised (*k*). In trespass for taking goods, a plea that the plaintiff "never had any goods" is argumentative, and therefore bad (*l*). And in a late case it was held that a plea to debt on a bail bond that there was no *proper* affidavit of debt made and filed of record before issuing the process against the bail, on the ground that issues tendered in pleading must not be alleged argumentatively, but in terms on which a direct issue can be taken (*m*).

Special pleas which amount to the general issue, without professing to be so, seem to be defective chiefly on account of their being opposed to the rule

(*b*) 1 Saund. 8 a, note 1.

(*c*) But the unnecessary statement of venue in a plea, according to Harper *v.* Champneys, 2 Dowl. 680, would not be ground of demurrer; and see Charnock's Rules, 136, n.

(*d*) *Id. ibid.*

(*e*) *Ante*, 246.

(*f*) The *testatum existit*, in setting out a deed in a plea, seems incorrect on this ground. See Stephen, 2d edit. 431; *ante*, 566.

(*g*) *Ante*, 271, 272; Co. Lit. 303 a, 304 a; Com. Dig. Pleader, E. 3; 6 East, 507; Hob. 295; see Steph. on Pl. 1st edit. 384; 2d edit. 426, where some excellent instances are given relating to this quality of a plea.

(*h*) 2 Anders. 179, 180; Bac. Ab. Pleas, I. 5.

(*i*) 1 B. & P. 413.

(*k*) Com. Dig. Surrender, N.

(*l*) Doct. Pl. 41; Dyer, 43 a.

(*m*) Hume *v.* Liversedge, 3 Tyrw. 287.

(961) Vide Fletcher *v.* Peck, 6 Cranch, 126. Spencer *v.* Southwick, 9 Johns. Rep. 313. 10 Pet. S. C. R. 343.

† See American Editor's Preface.

under consideration (*n*). The general rule that deeds and other matters should be pleaded according to their legal effect and meaning (*o*), seems also to be partly founded on the maxim that pleading should not be circuitous and argumentative. This fault sometimes occurs in a *traverse*, as will be explained when we consider the nature of Traverses. An argumentative plea is aided after verdict, and upon a *general* demurrer (*p*)(962).

II. QUALITIES.

8thly. Every plea should be so pleaded as to be *capable of trial*, and therefore must consist of matter of *fact*, the *existence* of which may be tried by a *jury* on an issue (963), or the *sufficiency* of which as a defence may be determined by the *Court* upon *demurrer* (964); or of matter of *record*, which is triable by the record itself (*q*). And if fact be improperly confounded or mixed in the plea with matter of law, so that it cannot be tried by the Court or jury, the plea is bad; as if the defendant plead that A. *lawfully* enjoyed the goods of felons, it will be bad; for the jury cannot determine whether he *lawfully* enjoyed, nor the Court whether he in *fact* enjoyed, and the plea should have stated the particular facts and title by virtue of which A. did enjoy (*r*). So, if the condition of a bond be that the defendant will show a *sufficient* discharge of an annuity, it seems that it cannot be pleaded merely that he showed a *sufficient* discharge; for the jury cannot try whether it is sufficient, and he ought to show what discharge he gave, in order that the Court may judge whether it was sufficient (*s*). But where the effect of the words presents a matter triable, it is sufficient, though according to the precise words it would not be triable; as in covenant for quiet enjoyment free from arrears of rent, a plea that he delivered money to the plaintiff with *intent* that he should *therewith discharge the arrears will be sufficient, though the intent is not triable, for it is equivalent to the allegation that the defendant delivered the money to pay (*t*). A defect in this respect in a plea may be aided by the plaintiff's taking issue upon a triable point; but if he should take issue upon an immaterial matter, it might be necessary to award a repleader.

8thly. Must be capable of trial.

[*574]

9thly. Every plea should be true and capable of proof, for as it has been quaintly said, "truth is the goodness and virtue of pleading, and certainty is the grace and beauty of it," and if it appear judicially to the Court on the defendant's own showing that he hath pleaded a false plea, this is a good cause of demurrer (*u*). Thus, where the defendant pleaded to an action of debt upon bond condition for performance of covenants contained in an indenture, of which he made a profert that there were no covenants contained in the indenture, and upon oyer by the plaintiff it appeared that the deed did

9thly. Must be true, and must not be too large.

(*n*) See *ante*, 557.
(*o*) *Ante*, 334; 2 Saund. 97 b, note 2; Bac. Ab. Pleas, I. 7; Steph. 2d edit. 432.
(*p*) Com. Dig. Pleader, E. 3; Alleyn, 48; 2 Saund. 319, n. 6.
(*q*) Co. Lit. 303 b; Com. Dig. Pleader, E. 34; 9 Co. 24 b, 25 a; 1 Marsh. 207.
(*r*) 9 Co. 25.
(*s*) 9 Co. 25 a; *ante*, 258, and 244, 245.
(*t*) 4 Mod. 249, as to traversing a local justification; 2 Saund. 5 b, c, d, e.
(*u*) Hob. 295; Bac. Ab. Pleas, G. 4; 1 Campb. 176; 2 Wils. 394; Stephen, 2d ed. 493.

(962) Vide Spencer v. Southwick, 9 Johns. Rep. 313.
(963) { Van Ness v. Hamilton, 19 Johns. Rep. 371. }
(964) Vide Frary v. Dakin, 7 Johns. Rep. 78.

II. QUALITIES. — True, and not too large.

contain divers covenants on the part of the defendant, the plea on demurrer was held insufficient (*x*). The plea must not be too large, and claim more than the defendant is capable of proving to support his defence. Thus, where the defendant pleaded that a close called A. had been separated and inclosed from a waste for twenty years, to support the allegation, it was held necessary to prove that every part of the close has been so long enclosed, and only part of the close having been so enclosed, the defendant failed in the plea (*y*). This subject will be further explained when the doctrine of Traverses comes under consideration.

Of sham pleas (*z*).

Sham pleading, that is the pleading a matter known by the party to be false for the purpose of delay or other unworthy object, has always been considered a very culpable abuse of justice, and has often been censured and set aside with costs (*a*).

It is of course in general the sole province of the jury to decide upon the truth or falsity of a mere matter of *fact* [*575] *pleaded by a defendant. But there are many instances in which a plea may be so palpably and manifestly untrue, that the Court will *assume* that it is so, or will, on an affidavit *that it is false*, permit the plaintiff to sign judgment as for want of a plea, and make the defendant or his attorney pay the costs occasioned by the plea, with the costs of the application (*b*). Although in these cases it is prudent to obtain the prior sanction of the Court, yet it seems that the plaintiff may in general sign judgment without such previous authority (*c*). But unless the plea be manifestly absurd, or probably a sham plea, the plaintiff, in the King's Bench, will not be justified in signing judgment as for want of a plea without a previous application to the Court (*d*), which is also necessary, it is said, after the defendant has been ruled to abide by his plea (*e*). But it has been decided that the plaintiff is not estopped from making the application to the Court by having ruled the defendant to abide by his plea (*f*).

The following are instances in which false pleas have been treated as falling within the description of sham pleas which shall be regarded as a nullity, although the defendant may not be under terms of pleading issuably (*g*).

(*x*) 1 Saund. 316, 317; 1 *Id.* 9 b, n. 1.

(*y*) 2 Taunt. 156, and see 2 B. & C. 918; 7 *Id.* 346. A plea justifying a libel must be true *in toto*. See 2 B. & C. 678; 4 D. & R. 230, S. C.; 1 Bing. 403.

(*z*) See further as to sham pleas, 3 Chit. Gen. Pr. 729. As to whether attorney is liable to pay the costs of a sham plea, 1 Chitty's Rep. 182, 584.

(*a*) Bac. Ab. Pleas, G. 4; 2 Wils. 394; Salk. 515; 2 B. & A. 198.

(*b*) 2 B. & Ald. 197; 1 Chit. R. 182, 564 a; Tidd, 9th ed. 565; and see 1 Moore & P. 643; 4 Bing. 663. And in debt on a judgment the defendant pleaded a *release destroyed by accident*. Upon affidavit that the plea was false, the Court allowed the plaintiff to sign judgment as for want of a plea, Smith *v.* Hardy, 8 Bing. 435; but see 4 Bing. 512; 1 Moore & P. 538, where the Court of C. P. refused leave to sign judgment on an affidavit that a plea of delivery of a pipe of wine in satisfaction was false. As to sham pleas, see further 3 Chitty's Gen. Pr. 729 to 731. And as to plea of *judgment recovered* in particular, *id.* 730.

(*c*) 6 M. & Sel. 134; 3 B. & P. [illegible]; Tidd, 9th edit. 564, 565, 473.

(*d*) 1 Chit. Rep. 525, notes; 6 M. & Sel. 133; Tidd, 9th ed. 564, 565.

(*e*) *Id.*; 1 Chit. Rep. 565, note; 5 M. & Sel. 518, S. C.; see, however, 2 B. & Ald. 197. To support a motion for leave to sign judgment for want of a plea, on the ground that improper pleas have been pleaded, it seems that in the King's Bench there must be an affidavit, not only that they are *untrue*, but also that they are *vexatious*, and calculated to create unnecessary delay and expense, 1 Chit. Rep. 524, 355, 564; 2 B. & Ald. 777; 1 D. & R. 359; 2 B. & C. 81; 3 D. & R. 231; but see 1 B. & C. 286; 3 D. & R. 661, S. C. *contra*.

(*f*) 2 B. & Ald. 197.

(*g*) As to *issuable* pleas, *ante*, 550.

Of sham pleas.

1st. False pleas, calculated to raise issues requiring different modes of trial, as a set-off for money due upon a judgment or recognizance enrolled, (the issue upon which is liable by the record,) and for money due on simple contract, the truth of which is triable by the country (*h*); or a plea of judgment recovered as to some of the counts, and another plea of payment as to the other counts (*i*). But in these cases there must be something to convince the Court that the pleas are untrue; "unless the inference be irresistible, *the plaintiff is not at liberty to take upon himself to pronounce that the plea is a nullity." (*j*) [*576]

2dly. Pleas obviously false on the face of them, and the truth of which is impossible on the defendant's own showing, as a plea of judgment appearing and shown in the plea to have been recovered in the Exchequer in Ireland, (or elsewhere,) before the cause of action accrued (*k*).

3dly. False pleas, which, although they might by possibility be true, yet are in all probability fictitious; as a plea of judgment recovered in the Court of *Pie Poudrie*, in Bartholomew Fair, couched in terms and showing proceedings palpably fictitious or unlikely (*l*). And in *Pierce* v. *Blake* (*m*), Lord Holt said that he remembered a case where judgment having been given against a defendant above forty years of age, he brought a writ of error, and assigned for error, infancy and appearance by attorney, and the Court fined the attorney for assigning those errors which were notoriously false and frivolous.

4thly. False pleas, being subtle and ensnaring, and tending to raise nice and intricate points of law, upon which it would be proper for the plaintiff's attorney to consult counsel, whereby delay and expense are occasioned (*n*). Thus, where to a declaration on a bill of exchange and the money counts, the defendant pleaded that the parties accounted together; that a certain sum was found due; that in satisfaction of part, the defendant indorsed a bill to the plaintiff, which was outstanding in the hands of a third person; and that in satisfaction of the remainder, the defendant assigned to the plaintiff an Irish judgment, which was in force, as appeared by the record; the Court, on an affidavit of the falsity of the plea, allowed the plaintiff to sign judgment, and directed that the defendant's attorney should pay the costs of the application (*o*). And a false plea in assumpsit on a bill, that the plaintiff was indebted on a recognizance of bail, as appears by the record (*p*), is open to objection on the same ground. And where in debt on a bail-bond, the defendant pleaded that the writ was sued out before the *assignment was stamped, and before the cause of action accrued, which he averred and prayed judgment, and that the plaintiff might be directed to cause the writ to be returned and filed of record, and that the record might be inspected, &c., [*577]

(*h*) 5 M. & Sel. 518; 2 M. & Sel. 606; and see 1 Chit. Rep. 564 a.

(*i*) 2 B. & Ald. 197.

(*j*) 6 M. & Sel. 133; see *id.* 136.

(*k*) 6 M. & Sel. 134; see 1 Chit. Rep. 525, 526, notes; 4 Taunt. 668; 1 D. & R. 577.

(*l*) 10 East, 237.

(*m*) 2 Salk. 515; recognized in 2 B. & Ald. 198, *per* Bayley and Holroyd, Justices.

(*n*) See 1 Saund. 327 a, where the Court reproved Saunders for pleading subtly, to trick the Court, and see recital in 36 H. 8, c. 30; 1 Bla. R. 276.

(*o*) 2 B. & Ald. 199; see 1 Taunt. 224, 225.

(*p*) 5 B. & Ald. 750; 2 Chit. R. 335; 1 D. & R. 446, 448, S. C.

II. QUALITIES.

the Court directed that if the defendant did not amend this subtle plea, the plaintiff might sign judgment (*q*).

Of sham pleas.

There are some pleas, which have long been used as sham pleas, for the purposes of procrastination, and which may be pleaded even at the present day with impunity, if the defendant has not subjected himself to the necessity of pleading an issuable plea. Pleas of this kind are simple and concise in their form, and long and inveterate practice has obtained for them this impunity. Pleas of *judgment already recovered for the same cause of action*, and of accord and satisfaction by the creditor's acceptance of goods, were of late years the pleas usually adopted. With regard to the former plea it has been permitted after the defendant had delayed and deluded the plaintiff by promises of payment (*r*), and had taken out a summons to stay proceedings on payment of debt and costs (*s*). With respect to the plea of accord and satisfaction, in a late case in the Court of Common Pleas, in which it was pleaded to a declaration on a bill of exchange, the Court refused to allow the plaintiff to sign judgment upon an affidavit that the plea was utterly false, and intimated that in future such applications would be discharged with costs (*t*). In one case the Court (*u*) set aside a false plea in assumpsit for use and occupation, that the defendant delivered to the plaintiff, and he accepted in satisfaction Riga hemp and Russia tallow. But in a subsequent case (*v*) they declined to interfere where a similar plea was pleaded, although its falsity was sworn to.

An executor, by pleading a plea manifestly untrue, and which he knows to be false, may render himself liable *de bonis propriis* (*x*).

[*578] *As a discouragement to sham pleading, the Court has suffered a plaintiff to amend a defective replication to a false plea without payment of costs (*y*).

Recent rules compelling defendant to *abide by his plea*.

Formerly it was the practice for a defendant to gain time by first pleading a sham plea, and when the plaintiff had replied to the same, then the defendant would abandon such plea, and plead only the general issue; but now Reg. Gen. Hil. T. 2 W. 4, reg. 46,† precludes a defendant from abandoning his first plea without express leave, which cannot be obtained unless when essential for the purposes of justice (*z*). This rule has greatly tended to put an end to the practice of sham pleading.

Reg. Gen. Hil. T. 4 W. 4, reg. 8, as to pleas of *judgment recovered*.

The Prac. Reg. Hil. T. 4 W. 4, reg. 8,† orders that "Where a defendant shall plead a plea of judgment recovered in *another Court*, he shall in the margin of such plea state the date of such judgment; and if such judgment shall be in a Court of record, the number of the roll on which such proceed-

(*q*) 3 Taunt. 339.

(*r*) 1 Bing. 380; 8 Moore, 437, S. C. When this plea is used as a sham plea, it should be alleged that the judgment was recovered in *another* Court, see the reason, *ante*, 465, n. (*y*).

(*s*) Hill *v.* Tybatt, Hil. Term, 1820, K. B.; 1 Archb. Prac. 137, 2d ed.

(*t*) 1 M. & P. 338; 4 Bingh. 512, S. C.

(*u*) 2 D. & R. 661; 1 B. & C. 266, S. C. *coram* Bayley and Holroyd, Justices; see 3 D. & R. 232. In 1 B. & C. it is stated that the Court assigned no reason for making the rule absolute.

(*v*) 2 B. & C. 31; 3 D. & R. 231, S. C. more fully reported.

(*x*) 1 Saund. 336, note 10; 1 Marsh. 312, 313; *ante*, 526.

(*y*) 1 East, 370.

(*z*) See further 3 Chit. Gen. Prac. 722.

† See American Editor's Preface.

ings are entered, if any, and in default of his so doing the plaintiff shall be at liberty to sign judgment as for want of a plea; and in case the same be falsely stated by the defendant, the plaintiff, on producing a certificate from the proper officer or person having the custody of the records or proceedings of the Court where such judgment is alleged to have been recovered, that there is no such record or entry of a judgment as therein stated, shall be at liberty to sign judgment as for want of a plea by leave of the Court *or a judge.*" (*a*) This rule entitles a plaintiff to sign judgment as for want of a plea, unless the defendant, in the margin of his plea of judgment recovered in *another court*, truly states in the margin thereof the particulars by which the judgment may be found on record. The effect of the rule prevents any such plea from gaining time during a vacation until the next term, and has put an end to the utility of a sham plea of judgment recovered in ordinary cases. But that rule does not apply to a plea by an executor or administrator of a judgment recovered against him by another creditor (*b*).

II. QUALITIES.

Of sham pleas.

III. RULES OF CONSTRUCTION, &c.

The rules which prevail in the *construction* and allowance of a plea in bar are,

1st, That it is to be construed most strongly against the defendant; 2dly, That a general plea, if bad in part, is bad for the whole; and 3dly, That surplusage will not in general vitiate.

1st. Construction against the plea.

1st. As it is a natural presumption that the party pleading will state his case as favorably for himself as possible, and that if he do not state it with all its legal circumstances, the case is not in fact favorable to him, it is a rule of construction, that if a plea has on the face of it two intendments, it shall be taken most strongly against the defendant; that is, the most unfavorable meaning shall be put upon the plea (*c*); a rule which we have seen (*d*) obtains also in the case of other pleadings. Therefore in trespass, if the defendant plead a release, without saying at what time it was made, it shall be intended to have been made before the trespass was committed (*e*); and in trespass to land, a plea of *liberum tenementum*, not stating that the close was the defendant's freehold at the *time* of the *trespasses*, is insufficient (*f*). So at common law, if to a bond the defendant plead payment, it shall be intended to have been made after the day appointed for payment, if he do not aver it to be otherwise; and in pleading a promise by a third person to pay the debt of another, it seems to be necessary to aver in the *plea* that the promise was in writing (*g*).

But this rule of construction does not obtain where the unfavorable meaning is inconsistent with another part of the plea (*h*). And there are some cases in which matters are implied in favor of the plea; thus, it is said by

(*a*) See Jervis's Rules, 89, note (*q*).

(*b*) Power *v.* Izod, 1 Bing. N. C. 304; 3 Dowl. 140; 3 M. & Scott, 119, S. C.

(*c*) Com. Dig. Pleader, E. 6; Co. Lit. 303 b; Plowd. 29, 46.

(*d*) *Ante*, 272. Effect of pleading over, *ante*, 273.

(*e*) Plowd. 46.

(*f*) Com. Dig. Pleader, E. 5.

(*g*) *Ante*, 254; 1 Saund. 276 a. *Sed quære*, *ante*, 566, n. (*b*).

(*h*) 10 Co. 59 b; *ante*, 264, 265, 272.

RULES OF CONSTRUCTION, &c.

Lord Coke (*i*), that "all necessary circumstances implied by law need not be expressed, as in the plea of a feoffment of a *manor, livery and attornment are implied (*j*); so where it is pleaded that land was assigned for dower, it is not necessary to say it was by metes and bounds, for it shall be intended a lawful assignment, which is by metes and bounds (*k*); and where a surrender of a lease for years is pleaded, and that it was agreed to by the lessor, it is not necessary to say that he entered, for it shall be intended, and it is not usual to plead a re-entry upon a surrender, any more than it is to plead livery upon a feoffment (*l*); so, where it is pleaded that a sheriff made his warrant, it is unnecessary to say that it was under his seal, for it could not be his warrant if it were not." (*m*) And if a man plead that he is heir to A. he need not say either that A. is dead, or had no son (*n*). Other instances of this rule have been before given (*o*). And we have seen that if an allegation is *capable* of two meanings, that exposition shall be adopted which will support, not that which will destroy the pleading (*p*).

2dly. Bad in part, bad in whole.

2dly. If one entire plea be *bad in part, it is insufficient for the whole*(*q*)(965). We have already in part noticed this doctrine in considering that a plea must contain an answer to all it assumes to answer; and if it fail to do so, it is not an effective bar even as to the part really answered (*r*). In *assumpsit* on several promises in different counts, if the defendant plead the statute of limitations to the whole, and it is a bad plea as to one of the counts, it will also be insufficient as to the residue (*s*)(966); and in an action against an executor or administrator, if the defendant plead several judgments recovered against *himself* in that character, and that he has not sufficient to satisfy them, if the plea be bad, or false, or avoided, as to one of the judgments, it will be bad for the whole; but if the judgments pleaded had been against the *testator*, it would be otherwise (*t*)(967). In one case, however, it was held that if one of the judgments pleaded were
[*580] against the testator and a third person, and the defendant *do not show that the testator survived, without which the executor is not chargeable, the plea is bad for the whole (*u*); but the propriety of this decision was questioned by Lord Vaughan (*x*). So, if several persons join in one plea, if it be bad for one, it will be bad for the others (*y*). The extent of this rule will be considered when we treat of pleas by several defendants (*z*). It seems that if a

(*i*) 8 Co. Rep. 81 b; *ante*, 253.
(*j*) Co. Lit. 303 b, S. P.; Cro. Eliz. 401.
(*k*) Com. Dig. Pleader, E. 9.
(*l*) Cro. Car. 101.
(*m*) Cro. Eliz. 53; Palm. 357, S. P.
(*n*) 2 Saund. 305 a, note 13.
(*o*) *Ante*, 253, 254.
(*p*) *Ante*, 273.
(*q*) Com. Dig. Pleader, E 36, F. 25; 3 T. R. 376; 3 B. & P. 174; 1 Saund. 337, note 1, 28, note 2; 2 B. & C. 216; 6 Bing. 274. The rule explained, &c. Steph. on Plead. 2d ed. 448; and see Tremeere v. Morison, 1 Bing. N. C. 96; and 1 Tyr. & Gr. 85; 3 Dowl 193, 194.
(*r*) *Ante*, 552, 553; 6 Bing. 274.
(*s*) 1 Lev. 48.
(*t*) 1 Saund. 337, and notes; 5 T. R. 80, 307.
(*u*) 2 Saund. 50, 51, note 4; 1 Saund. 337, note 1.
(*x*) Vaugh. R. 104; 1 Saund. 337, note 1.
(*y*) 3 T R. 376, 377; 1 Saund. 28, note 2; 2 Bing. 523, instance of a constable joining in a bad plea in trespass.
(*z*) *Post*.

(965) {Ten Eyck v. Waterbury, 7 Cow. Rep. 51. Briggs v. Cox, 7 Dowl. & Ryl. 410}
(966) Vide Perkins v. Burbank, 2 Mass. Rep. 81.
(967) Acc. Douglas v. Satterlee and others, 11 Johns. Rep. 16. The plaintiff should demur specially to the judgments which are badly pleaded, and traverse the residue. *Ibid.*

special plea amount in part to the general issue, and be to that extent defective, for that reason it is bad *in toto* (a). The statement of several distinct debts in a plea of *set-off* is an exception, because the statement of the debts in such a plea is in the nature of a declaration containing several counts; and therefore if one of such debts be insufficient, the plaintiff must not demur to the whole plea, but only to that part of it which relates to the objectionable ground of set-off (b). In trespass, if a plea of justification consists of two facts, each of which would, when separately pleaded, amount to a good defence, it will sufficiently support the justification if one of these facts be found by the jury (c): the other might be rejected as surplusage. RULES OF CONSTRUCTION, &c.

3dly. Surplusage and repugnancy.

3dly. The rules with regard to surplusage and unnecessary allegations which we have before considered, prevail in general with respect to pleas and every other part of pleading (d): and we have explained that surplusage, or unnecessary matter, *repugnant* and contradictory to what went *before* in any point *not material*, will not vitiate the pleadings, according to the maxim, *utile per inutile non vitiatur;* and such surplusage and redundant or repugnant part shall be rejected, especially after a verdict (e). Various illustrations of the general rule have been given. As an additional instance we may observe that if the defendant in replevin make cognizance as bailiff to A. administrator of B. where A. might have distrained in his own right, the words "administrator of B." shall be rejected as surplusage (f). There is, however, *considerable danger in surplusage in the statement of *material* matter; for [*581] where a party takes upon himself to state in any pleading a substantive matter, or alleges a precise estate, (although not bound to do so,) if it be *material* and bear on the question, he gives the other side the advantage of traversing it (g). Thus in *Leake's case* (h), it was necessary that the plaintiff should show that he had some right to put his cattle into the close, against which the defendant was bound to repair the fence, but a *seisin in fee* was not necessary to give that right; for a term for life or years, or even an estate at will, or right of common, or the owner's license, would have conferred that right (i); the plaintiff, however, thought proper to allege that the right he had arose from a *seisin in fee*, therefore the defendant was at liberty to deny that right as much as any other right which the plaintiff might have had to put his cattle into the close. So, in another case (k), the ground of the plaintiff's action was that the defendant would not permit him to cut down the remaining 200 trees; in order to show that so many trees were left standing in the wood, he stated that at the time of the agreement he had cut down *only* 800 trees, and though it was not necessary for him to have stated that precise number, but having done so, and the number that was left being material to show the damage which the plaintiff had sustained by the defendant's refusal to permit him to cut them down, he gave the defendant an advantage of traversing

(a) See 1 Saund. 27; Com. Dig. Pleader, E. 36; see, however, 3 Lev. 40.
(b) 2 Bla. Rep. 910.
(c) 1 Taunt. 146.
(d) *Ante*, 261 to 266.
(e) *Id.*; Bac. Ab. Pleas, I. 4; Com. Dig. Pleader, E. 12; Co. Lit. 303 b; 2 Saund. 305, 306, note 14; *id.* 291.
(f) Hob. 208.
(g) *Ante*, 266.
(h) Dyer, 365; 2 Saund. 206 a, n. 21, 22; and 207, n. 24.
(i) 1 Saund. 346, n. 2.
(k) Yelv. 195.

RULES OF CONSTRUCTION, &c.

it (*l*). It seems, therefore, that a too precise or particular statement of material matter may be taken advantage of upon the trial of a traverse thereof; but in general not by demurrer, as the objection does not appear upon the record, but depends upon the evidence; except where it is repugnant or contrary to matter precedent (*m*), and though such repugnancy may not in some cases be aided by verdict (*n*), yet if it appear that the verdict was given on another part of the plea the mistake will be aided (*o*).

[*582]

*IV. FORMAL PARTS OF PLEAS IN GENERAL.

In framing *every plea*, whether in abatement or in bar, the pleader must constantly keep in view the following formal parts of the plea, and the rules and decisions respecting them, and the opponent, when endeavoring to discover a defect, should pursue the same course of examination.

The following is the outline of the usual form.

(1) In the King's Bench.

(2) On the 10th day of March, A. D. 1836.

IV. FORM AND PARTS.

(3) Johnson ats. Davis. } (4) The defendant, by E. F. his attorney, [*or* "in his own proper person," (*p*)] says that, (5) &c. [*here follows the ground of defence.*] And of this he the said defendant puts himself upon the country, &c.; (6) [*or if the conclusion be with a* verification, *the form is thus:* "and this he the said defendant is ready to verify, wherefore he prays judgment if the said plaintiff ought [*or* "ought *further*"] to have or maintain his aforesaid action thereof against him, &c.

(7) *John Hulme.*

1st. The title of Court at top.
2dly. The date at top.
3dly. The names of parties in margin.
4thly. The commencement; describing
 1st. Defendant's appearance, whether in person or by attorney, or *prochein ami.*
 2dly. When he is to make full or half defence.
 3dly. Whether there is to be any preliminary suggestion or statement.
 4thly. Whether there is to be any prayer of judgment in the commencement or other *petitio*, or *actionem non.*
 5thly. Whether the plea is to be in abatement to the whole, or to a part only.
 6thly. Whether to be in bar, and whether to the whole or to a part.

(*l*) 2 Saund. 207, note 24; 206, note 22; 2 East, 452.

(*m*) Co. Lit. 303 b.

(*n*) Bac. Ab. Pleas, I. 4.

(*o*) *Id.*

(*p*) *Formerly* the nature of the *defence*, whether *full* or *half*, used to be stated, and then followed the allegation that the plaintiff ought not to have or maintain his action, and then followed the statement of the ground of defence, and which is still retained. The alterations were introduced by the Reg. Gen. Hil. T. 4 W. 4, as will be presently shown. The ancient form was thus:—"*comes* and *defends* the wrong, [*or in trespass*, 'force,'] and injury, *when, &c.* and says that the said plaintiff ought not to have or maintain his aforesaid action thereof against him, because he, &c."

5thly. The body of the plea. IV. FORM AND PARTS.

1st. Statement of time.

2dly. Statement of place.

3dly. Statement of circumstances, and herein of forms of allegations.

6thly. The conclusion (*q*).

7thly. Signature of counsel.

8thly. Affidavit when and what to be annexed.

9thly. The forms of second or subsequent pleas.

We will consider each part separately.

*1. It was always usual at the head of the plea to state *in what Court it* was pleaded, as "In the King's Bench," *or* "In the Common Pleas," *or* "In the Exchequer of Pleas;" and without this title *of the Court*, it might be doubtful, especially if there should happen to be several actions between parties of the same names in different Courts at the same time, to what action or declaration the plea referred. There is not, however, any statute or rule prescribing that a *plea* shall be entitled in any Court. And it is apprehended that the omission of the statement of the Court would not be material, and that the plea would be considered as having reference to the declaration, which must necessarily have been in the same Court as the plea. [*583] 1st. Title of the Court.

2. With respect to the *title*, before the Reg. Gen. Hil. T. 4 W. 4,† all pleas were entitled of a *term*, and pleas to the jurisdiction, or in abatement, were, as we have seen, in general required to be entitled of the same term as the declaration (*r*); but pleas in bar might be, and usually were entitled of the term of which they were pleaded, which was frequently subsequent to that of which the declaration was entitled (*s*), and where matter of defence had arisen after the first day of the term, the plea was properly to be entitled specially of a subsequent day (*t*). But the Reg. Gen. Hil. T. 4 W. 4, reg. 1,† now expressly requires *every pleading* to be entitled of the day of the month and the year when the same was pleaded. But there cannot be a *demurrer* on account of an improper date at the top (*u*). 2dly. Title or *date* of *time*.

3. *The names of the parties in the margin* do not strictly constitute any part of the plea. The surnames only are usually inserted, and that of the defendant precedes the plaintiff's, as "*Johnson* ats. *Davis*." They should correspond with the names in the declaration, or if the defendant plead in abatement or bar by another name to that in the declaration, the difference should be specified in the margin, thus, "*C. D.* sued by the name of *E. D.* ats. *A. B.*" It has been decided that it is sufficient, in a *qui tam* action, to entitle the plea of *nil debet* with the names of the parties as above, without the 3dly. The names of the parties in the margin.

(*q*) Every plea in bar must conclude to the country or with a verification, 2 Dowl. 664; 2 Cr. M. & Ros. 26, S. C.

(*r*) *Ante*, 488.

(*s*) Bac. Ab. Pleas, C. 2; 2 Saund. 1 f, 2 a, b, c, d.

(*t*) *Post*, vol. iii. And see also a suggestion after imparlance, *post*, vol. iii.

(*u*) Neal *v.* Richards, 2 Dowl. 94; and 3 Chitty's Gen. Prac. 716.

† See American Editor's Preface.

IV. FORM AND PARTS. — 3. Names of parties in margin.

addition of *qui tam*, &c. to the plaintiff's name (*v*). After the parties have once been named in the previous pleading by christian and surname, they may in the plea be described as the said defendant and the said plaintiff, without repeating the names (*x*).

4thly. The commencement. Before the recent rules.

4. With respect to the *commencement*, we will first state the practice *before* the recent rules, and then the *present* practice. And *first* the *name* of the defendant; we have seen that when the defendant pleaded misnomer in abatement, a plea commencing with the words, "And the *said* Richard, sued by the name of Robert," or thus, "and *he* against whom the plaintiff hath exhibited his bill by the name of J. S., &c." was insufficient (*y*). A plea in bar commencing in the same manner was also bad on special demurrer (*z*). When the defendant was sued by a wrong name, and wished to defend in his [*564] right name without *pleading in abatement, it was proper to begin his plea thus: "And C. D. against whom the said A. B. hath exhibited his bill by the name of E. D. comes and defends the wrong and injury, when, &c." (*a*) A mis-statement of the defendant's *christian* name in the commencement of his plea in bar, did not entitle the plaintiff to treat it as a nullity, and sign judgment as for want of a plea (*b*).

After the names of the parties in the margin, the defendant's *appearance* and *defence*, (*venit et defendit vim et injuriam*,) were to be stated. Some observations have already been made on these parts of pleading (*c*). The *appearance* might in general be stated to have been either in *person* or by *attorney*, for a defendant was at liberty to appear and defend in person, and this was usual in an action against an attorney or prisoner (*d*). As a feme covert, when sued alone, is incapable of appointing an attorney, she should defend in person (*e*); an idiot should also appear in person, and it is said that any one who can make a better defence, shall be admitted to defend for him; but a lunatic, or one who becomes *non compos mentis*, must appear by guardian, if he be within age, and by attorney if of full age (*f*). An infant must plead by guardian, and not by attorney(968) or *prochein ami* (*g*), and if he, whether in the case of a sole or several defendants, pleaded by attorney (969), it was error (*h*) (970); and therefore the plaintiff was bound in such a case, for his own security, to take out a summons to compel him to appear by guardian, and to alter his plea, or for leave to do it for him (*i*). A plea by a corporation aggregate, which is incapable of a personal appearance, must purport to

(*v*) 7 East, 333.

(*x*) So decided as to a declaration in Meeke *v.* Oxlade, 1 New R. 289, and other cases, 3 Chitty's Gen. Pr. 467, note (*r*).

(*y*) *Ante*, 490, 460.

(*z*) 3 Wils. 412.

(*a*) *Post*, vol. iii.; 3 Wentw. 210.

(*b*) 7 D. & R. 511.

(*c*) *Ante*, 461, 462.

(*d*) Sayer, 217.

(*e*) Co. Lit. 125 b; 2 Inst. 390; F. N. B. 27; 2 Saund. 209 c; *ante*, 461; see the forms, *post*, vol. iii.

(*f*) *Id*; 4 Co. 124 b; 2 Saund. 333, note 4, 335; Bac. Ab. Idiots and Lunatics

(*g*) *Ante*, 461, *post*, vol. iii.

(*h*) *Ante*, 461. But the infant only could bring error, 5 B. & Ald. 418.

(*i*) 2 Wils. 50; 2 Saund. 117 f; 7 Taunt. 418; 1 Moore, 251, S. C.

(968) Vide Morkey *v.* Grey, 2 Johns. Rep. 182. Dewitt *v.* Post, 11 Johns. Rep. 460.

(969) That the plaintiff may enter a *nolle prosequi* as to the infant, vide Hartness *v.* Thompson, 5 Johns. Rep. 160. { Woodward *v.* Newhall, 1 Pick. Rep. 500. 20 Johns. Rep. 160, 161. Or as to a *feme* covert. Beidman *v.* Vanderslice, 2 Rawle, 344. }

(970) Vide Dewitt *v.* Post, 11 Johns. Rep. 460. { Silver *v.* Shelback, 1 Dall. 165. Moore *v.* M'Ewen, 5 Serg. & Rawle, 373. }

be by attorney (*k*). In a plea by husband and wife, it was stated that they appear by their attorney (*l*). The plea should also be in the name of an attorney of the Court in which the action is brought, legally competent to practice therein (*m*). It must also be in the name of the attorney by *whom the defendant appeared, unless there has been an order to change the attorney, or the plaintiff may sign judgment (*n*). Though the appearance has been entered in the name of an agent to a country attorney, the plea may be in the name of the principal attorney (*o*); it ought not, however, where there are several attorneys in partnership, to be in the name of the firm, but only in the name of one of them (*p*).

IV. FORM AND PARTS. — 4thly. The commencement. [*585]

We have already stated the signification of the term *defence*, its nature, and the form of it in a plea in bar (*q*). Before the recent rules every plea in bar must have begun with the defence (*r*); and it should seem that if the defendant plead only to part, and confessed the residue, the defence should be confined to the part intended to be pleaded to, and not cover the whole (*s*).

In a plea of the *general issue*, or other plea in bar to the whole declaration, which *merely denied* what was alleged in the declaration, and did not introduce any *new* matter, it was not usual to insert the allegation, "that the plaintiff ought not to have or maintain his aforesaid action against the defendant;" but after stating the defendant's appearance and his defence, the plea immediately denied the matter stated in the declaration, and concluded to the country (*t*). But special pleas, after stating the appearance and defence, began with this allegation, *actio non habere debet*(*u*); which always alluded to the commencement of the action, and not to the time of the plea (*x*), and payment of the debt without costs, after action brought, was therefore no defence (*y*). No defence which arose after action brought could be given in evidence under the general issue: such defences always were required to be specially pleaded (*z*). In debt on bond, if the defendant by his plea denied the validity of the deed, or if an heir pleaded *rien per descent*, it was more formally correct to say *onerari non debet*, and not *actio non* (*a*); and in that case the plea should describe the deed as a *writing*, or "*supposed* writing obligatory," and should not admit that it was a deed (*b*). In replevin, if the defendant said "he well avows," instead of well *acknowledges* the caption, no objection could be taken (*c*). When the matter of *defence* arose before the commencement of [*586]

(*k*) Bro. Ab. Corporation, 28; Co. Lit. 66 b; Com. Dig. Pleader, 2 B. 2.

(*l*) 2 Saund. 219; Com. Dig. Pleader, 2 A. But the objection would not entitle the plaintiff to treat the plea as a nullity, Hill *v.* Mills, 2 Dowl. 696.

(*m*) Barnes, 259. By an uncertificated attorney, Tidd, 9th ed. 77.

(*n*) 2 New Rep. 609; 6 East, 549; Tidd, 9th ed. 94; *sed vide* 13 Ves. 161, 195, in Chancery.

(*o*) 3 B. & P. 111; Barnes, 239.

(*p*) 4 East, 195.

(*q*) *Ante*, 462. And see further, 3 Lev. 240; Com. Dig. Abatement, I. 16.

(*r*) Com. Dig. Pleader, E. 27; 3 B. & P. 9 a; Co. Lit. 127 b; *ante*, 461, 462.

(*s*) Com Dig. Pleader, E. 27. See, as to qualities of a plea, *ante* 583, 584.

(*t*) Salk. 516; *post*, vol. iii.

(*u*) Salk. 211; *post*, vol. iii.

(*x*) 7 East, 536; 3 East, 316; 4 B. & C. 393.

(*y*) 3 T. R. 186; 4 East, 502; 1 Campb. 558, 559. Payment of debt and costs, in full satisfaction, after action brought, if specially pleaded, was a good plea, Holt's C. N. P. 6; 5 B. & Ald. 886; 1 D. & R. 546, S. C.

(*z*) Holt's C. N. P. 6; 4 B. & Ald. 345; 5 *Id.* 886; 4 B. & C. 390.

(*a*) 1 Saund. 290, n. 3; Lord Raym. 217; 2 Salk. 516.

(*b*) Cro. Eliz. 800; 1 Saund. 290, note 3; 291, note 1; Ld. Raym. 1541; 2 Rol. Rep. 140; Com. Dig. Pleader, E. 27.

(*c*) Cro. Jac. 373; 1 Saund. 347 e, note 4; and see Nicholson *v.* Lightfoot, E. T. 3 May, 1831, K. B.

IV. FORM AND PARTS. — 4thly. The commencement.

the suit, *actio non*, &c. was generally the proper commencement; but matter of defence, arising after action brought, must have been specially pleaded in bar of the *further* maintenance of the suit (*d*). If the matter of defence arose after issue joined, it must have been pleaded *puis darrein continuance* (*e*) (971); and if it arose after trial, an *audita querela* was in general the only remedy (972); although in some instances the Court would afford relief on a summary application. In an action against husband and wife, both must have defended and joined in the plea, or the plaintiff should demur, or there would be a repleader, although the action were merely for the tort of the wife (*f*). Where the plea was only to a part of the declaration, it must not in the commencement profess to cover the whole declaration (*g*); and it must designate specifically the part to which it was to be applied, or the plaintiff might demur (*h*). The mode of pleading in these cases was thus: "And the said defendant, by E. F. his attorney, comes and defends the wrong and injury, when, &c." and "as to the said first count of the said declaration," (or, if in *covenant*, "as to the said supposed breach of covenant first above assigned," or, if in *trespass*, "as to the breaking and entering, &c." enumerating the particular trespasses mentioned in the declaration intended to be justified) (*i*) "the said C. D. says, that the said A. B. ought not to have or maintain his aforesaid action thereof against him, because he says, that, &c."

At common law, before the statute of Anne, which introduced several pleas, [*587] it was usual, particularly in actions of trespass, for the defendant *to plead as to the force and arms, and whatever else was against the peace of the king, not guilty, and as to the residue of the supposed trespasses, a justification (*k*). And the defendant must take care to state in the commencement the whole of the trespasses he intends to justify, and if he omit any material part, the plaintiff will be entitled to recover *pro tanto* (*l*), as where the declaration *inter alia* alleged that the defendant dragged the plaintiff through a pond, and the special plea only covered other trespasses; it was held that the plaintiff was entitled to recover for such dragging through the pond, although it was insisted that he ought to have new assigned (*l*).

In actions of trespass to personal or real property, where the declaration contains several counts, varying the statement of the injury to the *same* personal chattels, or to the *same* closes, it has been usual, in order to save the expense of several distinct pleas to each count, to render the same plea applicable to all the counts (*m*). In this case the trespasses complained of in the

(*d*) 4 East, 502; 6 *Id.* 414; *ante*, 546, 585. As to pleading bankruptcy after action brought and before plea, see 9 East, 82. After issue, 6 B. & C. 105.

(*e*) See *post*, as to these pleas.

(*f*) Com. Dig. Pleader, 2 A. e; Cro. Jac. 288.

(*g*) As to this rule, *ante*, 553, 554.

(*h*) Com. Dig. Pleader, E. 27; 1 Sid. 338; Lutw. 241; 3 B. & P. 174; *ante*, 554, 555.

(*i*) As to the effect of this on the replication in trespass, see 2 Campb. 175.

(*k*) See 1 Saund. 10, 24, 82, 296.

(*l*) Bush *v.* Parker and others, 1 Bing. N. C. 72.

(*m*) See *ante*, 450, 451, and 558, 559; 1 Marsh. 17, 18; 5 Taunt. 198, S. C.; 11 Moore, 43. But where there had been but one trespass, &c. it sufficed to plead specially to one of the counts which contained the fullest description of the injury, and to plead

(971) Vide Cobb *v.* Curtis, 8 Johns. Rep. 470.

(972) It is usual, however, to grant the same relief on motion as the party might have obtained by *audita querela*. Baker *v.* Judges of Ulster, 4 Johns. Rep. 191, and see n. b' 2d edit. ibid.

different counts, and which were intended to be justified, were first enumerated in the introductory part of the plea; and then followed the statement of *actio non*, &c.; and it was then alleged that the close and grass, &c. mentioned in the first count, and the close and grass, &c. mentioned in the last count, at the several times when, &c. were the *same* close and grass, &c. and *not other or different*, and that the seizing and taking, &c. mentioned in the first count, and the seizing and taking, &c. mentioned in the last count, were the *same*, and *not other or different* (n). But, as before observed, these allegations identifying the trespasses were traversable; and this mode of pleading could not in strictness be supported, but was demurrable (o). Where it is certain that the different counts were for the same trespass, and it is expected that the plaintiff would not demur, it was considered advisable, in order to save expense, to risk that concise mode of pleading; but the plaintiff should demur or traverse the allegation if he really contended that several distinct trespasses thus united in the plea were committed (p).

IV. FORM AND PARTS. — 4thly. The commencement.

The Reg. Gen. Hil. T. 4 W. 4, reg. 9, 10, 11,† have introduced material alterations as well respecting the *commencements* as the *conclusions* of pleas, and have put an end to the subtle distinctions respecting *half* and *full defence*. The reg. 9 orders that "In the plea or subsequent pleading intended to be pleaded *in bar* of the *whole action* generally, it shall not be *necessary* to use any allegation of *actionem non*, or to the like effect, or any prayer of judgment; nor shall it be necessary in any replication or subsequent pleading, intended to be pleaded in maintenance of the whole action, to use any allegation of *precludi non*, or to the like effect, or any prayer of judgment; and *all* pleas, replications, and subsequent pleadings, pleaded without such formal parts as aforesaid, *shall be taken*, unless otherwise expressed, as pleaded respectively in bar of the whole action, provided that nothing herein contained shall extend to cases where an estoppel is pleaded."

Forms of *commencement* prescribed by Reg. Gen. Hil. T. 4. W. 4, reg. 9.

Actionem non to be unnecessary.

It will be observed that this rule is expressly confined to pleas *in bar*, and does not therefore extend to pleas in *abatement*, and which according to the antecedent rules of pleading must always be *expressly limited* when the matter in abatement only affects *part* of the alleged cause of action.

It was held that the expression "*whole actions generally*" in this new rule means as well the whole case stated in any *one* count (q) as the *whole declaration* containing several counts, unless the commencement expressly limit the plea to a particular count, or it may be open to a special demurrer (r).

To a declaration containing two counts, first, on a bill of exchange, and

only the general issue to the rest, or generally, in which case the plaintiff could not proceed on the other counts so as to avoid the defence on the special plea, see *ante*, 428 *e*; 318, n. (*f*).

(n) See Plead. Ass. 401; *post*, vol. iii.; 9 Wentw. 47, 57; Sir T. Raym. 449; but see *ante*, 450, and 557, 558.

(o) *Id.*; 5 Taunt. 200; 1 Marsh. 17, 18, S. C. So to a declaration containing two counts, as for two different libels, a plea of justification to the whole declaration, alleging that the libel in each count was one and the same, and that the publications thereof was but one act, and then justifying one libel, was holden bad, 2 Chit. Rep. 291.

(p) *Ante*, 450, 451.

(q) Bird *v.* Higginson, 1 Har. & Wol. 61; 4 Nev. & Man. 505.

(r) Worley *v.* Harrison, 1 Har. & Wol 426; 5 Nev. & Man. 173, S. C.; and see Vere *v.* Goldsborough, 1 Bing. N. C., 353, as to an informal plea to two counts without distinguishing which.

† See American Editor's Preface.

IV. FORM AND PARTS. — 4thly. The commencement. secondly, on an account stated, the defendant without *a rule to plead several* matters pleaded "that he did not accept the bill," and for a further plea that "he did not account," and it was held that the informality of omitting to confine each plea to the count to which it applied did not authorize the plaintiff to sign judgment (*s*). It may here be proper to refer to the recent decision (*t*), that the several statements of debts for goods sold, work and labor, money lent, paid, had and received, and account stated, are for *all pleading* purposes to be considered as separate counts. But still it is necessary and proper that when a plea is pleaded, or when the matter pleaded is properly applicable only to a part of the declaration, that the commencement of the plea should be expressly and in terms limited to that part (*u*).

No formal defence requisite. The Reg. Gen. Hil. T. 4 W. 4, reg. 10,† orders "that no formal *defence* shall be *required* in a plea, and it *shall commence* as follows: 'The said defendant by Y. Z. his attorney (*or*, 'in person,') says that, &c.'"

By leave of Court, &c. not essential in case of several pleas. Reg. 11 orders that "It shall not be *necessary* to state in a second or other plea or avowry that it is pleaded by leave of the Court, or according to the form of the statute, or to that effect."

5thly. The body of the plea. 5. With respect to the *body of the plea*, which states the *substance of the defence*, the allegations depend on the *circumstances of each particular [*568] case. The forms of those pleas which usually occur in practice are given in the Third Volume; and the *qualities* of a plea, as well in respect to certainty of time and place, &c. as in relation to more material matters, have already been considered (*x*). As a *protestando* (*y*), and a *formal traverse* (*z*), more frequently occur in *replications*, we will postpone the particular consideration of them till that part of the work.

Quæ est eadem. In point of form in trespass and other actions, when the plea necessarily states the trespass to have been committed at some other time or place than that laid in the declaration (*a*), it is proper, immediately preceding the conclusion of the plea, to allege that the supposed trespasses mentioned in the plea are the *same* as those whereof the plaintiff hath complained. This allegation is usually termed *quæ est eadem* (973); and when it is adopted in the above case, if the plea *also* conclude with a *traverse* that the defendant was guilty at any other time or place, the plaintiff may demur specially (*b*). But when it

(*s*) Vere *v.* Goldsborough, 1 Bing. N. C. 353.

(*t*) Jourdain *v.* Johnson, 2 Cr. M. & Ros. 564; 5 Tyr 421.

(*u*) Dueer *v.* Triebner, 3 Dowl. 133.

(*x*) See *ante*, 551 *h*.

(*y*) Com. Dig. Pleader, N.

(*z*) Com. Dig. Pleader, G. 1, &c.

(*a*) The plea should follow the *time* and *place* laid in the declaration, unless either be, from the nature of the case, material, and the gist of the dispute, and, by pursuing the declaration, there would be an incongruity in the plea in this respect. See *ante*, 552; 2 Saund. 5 a, note.

(*b*) Com. Dig. Pleader, E. 31; Cro. Jac. 372; 2 Saund. 5, n. 3; Cowp. 162; 1 Saund. 297; Willes, 202. Where the plea varies from the *day* laid in the declaration, *either* the averment of *quæ est eadem*, *or* the *traverse* of the time laid in the declaration is proper, and will suffice; but it is superfluous and improper to have *both* the *quæ est eadem* and the traverse, *id.* And, as remarked by the learned editors of the 5th edit. of Saunders' Rep. vol. ii. 5 e, note (*p*), there seems to be no good reason why the averment of *quæ est eadem* should not be considered a good traverse of the *place* in the declaration, as much as it is of *time*. *Sed vide* Mr. Serjeant Williams' note, *id.*

(973) Vide Nevins *v.* Keeler, 6 Johns. Rep. 63

† See American Editor's Preface.

is unnecessary, and consequently improper, to vary from the time or place laid in the declaration, and the declaration and plea are in these respects conformable with each other, the *quæ est eadem* need not be inserted (*c*), though the insertion will not predjudice: but in that case if a traverse were added, the plea would be informal (*d*). If, however, the traverse were defective, it was holden that it would be rejected as surplusage (*e*); but, in a late case, it was held that an unnecessary traverse after the *quæ est eadem* is bad on special demurrer (*f*).

IV. FORM AND PARTS.

5thly. The body of the plea.

A plea of illegal consideration or contract contrary to any express statute should, like a declaration on a statute for a penalty incurred, in strictness conclude *contrary to the form of the statute*. It has nevertheless been decided that if such conclusion be omitted the plea may be sustained (*g*).

Contra formam statuti, when requisite in a plea.

[*589]

*Every plea in bar must have its proper *Conclusion* (*h*), which is either *to the country*, or *with a verification*; and the latter is either of *fact*, or of matter of *record* (*h*). An avowry or cognizance in replevin, in which the defendant is an actor, is an exception to this rule, and need not have any conclusion (*i*). In an action against husband and wife, both should join in the concluding part of the plea (*j*)(974).

6thly. The Conclusion.

When there is a complete issue between the parties, viz. a direct affirmative and negative; as if the general issue be pleaded (975); or the defendant simply deny some material fact alleged in the declaration (976), as where the plaintiff declares on an award, and the defendant pleads no such award; the plea should conclude to the country (*k*). And such conclusion seems to be proper, although the plea unnecessarily contain a formal traverse (*l*). This rule equally prevails whether the affirmative be first in the pleading, and the negative subsequent, or *vice versa* (*m*); and therefore, though the negative be asserted by the plaintiff, and the affirmative by the defendant, as where the plaintiff in his declaration alleges a breach of non-payment of a sum of money on a particular day, or in not repairing, &c., and the defendant pleads *solvit ad diem*, or that he did repair, the plea should conclude to the country; but in debt on bond, if the declaration be general, and no particular breach be assigned, a plea of performance of the condition must con-

(*c*) Skin. 387; Com. Dig. Pleader, E. 31; Carth. 281; 2 Saund. 5 b, note l.

(*d*) 2 Saund. 5, note 3; Com. Dig. Pleader, E. 31.

(*e*) *Id.*; Salk. 641, 642; 2 Saund. 5, note 3.

(*f*) Henbrow *v.* Bailey and others, 3 Tyr. 152.

(*g*) Peate *v.* Dicken, 1 Crom. M. & Ros. 427.

(*h*) Knowles *v.* Stevens, 2 Dowl. 664; 1 Crom. M. & Ros. 26; Com. Dig. Pleader, E. 28, &c.; Co. Lit. 303 b.

(*i*) 1 Saund. 348, note 7; Co. Lit. 303 a; Plowd. Com. 342, 163 a; Willes, 6.

(*j*) Com. Dig. Pleader, 2 A. 3; Cro. Car. 594.

(*k*) Com Dig. Pleader, E. 32; 2 Saund. 337, n. 1, 196, and 1 Saund. 103, n. 1, 103 a, b. note 3. A plea in bar of *riens en arrere* to an avowry for rent should so conclude, Ld. Raym. 641.

(*l*) 1 Saund. 103 b; Com. Dig. Pleader, E. 33.

(*m*) Carth. 88, 89; Com. Dig. Pleader, E. 32.

(974) In trespass *quare clausum* the defendant pleaded a licence upon which issue was joined; and held that the plaintiff might show that the licence was obtained by fraud without pleading it specially. Anthony *v.* Wilson, 4 Pick. 303.

(975) { Gazley *v.* Price, 16 Johns. Rep. 267. }

(976) Vide Manhattan Company *v.* Miller, 2 Caines' Rep. 60. Snyder and others *v.* Croy, 2 Johns. Rep. 428.

IV. FORM AND PARTS. — 6thly. The Conclusion.

clude with a verification (*n*). So, where a plea puts in issue matter of fact as well as matter of record, it should conclude to the country (977); as if it be alleged in a declaration that the plaintiff procured letters patent, and the defendant plead that the plaintiff did not procure them, the plea should conclude to the country; because the procurement is the principal point in issue; so, if the issuing of a *fieri facias* and a levy under it be put in issue, the matter may be referred to the country by the party traversing those facts (*o*).
[*590] And if a plea conclude with *a special negative to the affirmative in the declaration, it should conclude to the country: as, for instance, in debt on bond, the allegation in the declaration of the making of the bond includes the allegation of the delivery as a deed; and therefore, if the defendant plead that he delivered the deed as an escrow, he may conclude to the country (*p*). But where there is not a direct negative and affirmative the plea need not so conclude; as if in debt on a bond to account, the declaration allege that the defendant received £20 for which he did not account, and the defendant plead that he accounted in manner following, viz. that he was robbed of it, and gave notice to the plaintiff; this plea giving color to the plaintiff, and referring the sufficiency of the mode of accounting to the Court, may conclude with a verification (*q*). And where the declaration is founded on matter of record, which is traversed in the plea, the plea should not in general conclude to the country, but should allege that there is no such record, and usually concludes with a verification, and prayer of judgment, *si actio*, &c. (*r*); but a verification appears to be unnecessary in this case as the plea is in the negative (*s*): and if an action of debt be brought here on a judgment in Ireland, the plea of *nul tiel record* must conclude to the country (*t*).

Conclusion with a verification.

It is an established rule in pleading, that whenever *new matter* is introduced on either side, the pleading must *conclude with a verification or averment*, in order that the other party may have an opportunity of answering it (*u*)(978). The usual verification of a plea containing matter of *fact* runs thus, "and this the said defendant is ready to verify, wherefore he prays judgment if the said plaintiff ought to have or maintain his aforesaid action thereof against him," &c.; and if the word "*certify*" be inserted instead of "*verify*," no advantage can be taken of the mistake (*x*). An avowry, we have seen, does not require any conclusion (*y*). A plea of bankruptcy pleaded under the statute, though introductory of new matter, should pursue the terms of the act,

(*n*) *Id.*

(*o*) 3 Mod. 79; Com. Dig. Pleader, E. 32; Sayer's Rep. 208, 299; Hob. 244; Stra. 522; 1 M. & P. 102; 4 Bing. 428, S. C.; *post*, 591.

(*p*) 1 Salk. 274; 4 Esp. Rep. 255; Com. Dig. Pleader, E. 32; *post*, vol. iii.

(*q*) 2 Lev. 5; Com. Dig. Pleader, E. 32.

(*r*) 2 Wils. 114; Lil. Ent. 182, 404, 473.

(*s*) Fortes. 339; Com. Dig. Pleader, E. 29; Salk. 520.

(*t*) 5 East. 473; 2 Smith R. 25, S. C.; 4 B. & C. 411; 9 Price, 1.

(*u*) 1 Saund. 163 a, n. 3, and cases there cited; Com. Dig. Pleader, E. 33.

(*x*) Willes. 6.

(*y*) *Ante*, 589; 1 Saund. n. 7.

(977) { Allen v. Crofoot, 7 Cow. Rep. 46. } Vide Lytle v. Lee, 5 Johns. Rep. 112. Thomas v. Rumsey, 6 Johns. Rep. 26.

(978) Vide Hord's Ex'r v. Dishman, 2 Hen. & Mun. 660. Smith v. Walker, 1 Wash. 135. Service v. Heermance, 1 Johns. Rep. 91.

and conclude *to the country (z)(979). And where one of several facts in a declaration is denied with a formal traverse, the plea may conclude with a verification, or to the country (a). If matter of *record* be pleaded, as a judgment recovered for the same demand, &c., the plea should conclude with a *prout patet per recordum*, and a verification by the record; and if several records be pleaded, they should be respectively verified (b). But if matter of fact as well as matter of record be jointly put in issue, the trial may be by jury, and the plea may conclude to the country (c). So, if matter of record, as a fine, be pleaded with other matters not of record and constituting one entire defence, although that part of the pleading which states the fine should refer to the record thereof, yet the plea may conclude with the general verification, without verifying by the record (d). To a *scire facias* upon a recognizance against bail in error, if the defendant plead that the judgment is pending and not determined, he need not conclude *prout patet*, &c. the plea being in the negative (e). The usage and practice of the Court is not matter of conclusion to the country, for such usage is not admissible in a plea which puts it in issue (f).

IV. FORM AND PARTS.

8thly. The Conclusion.

Where the plea contained a verification, it generally concluded *with a prayer of judgment* in favor of the defendant, which was termed the *demand or petition* of the plea (g), as "wherefore the defendant prays judgment if the said plaintiff ought to have or maintain his aforesaid action thereof (h) against him, &c." This prayer, before the recent rule, ought properly to have corresponded with, and be founded on, the commencement of the plea, and the effect of the matters contained in the body of it; and therefore it was necessary that a plea of matter of defence arising after the commencement of the suit should be concluded with a prayer as to the *further* maintenance of the suit (i): and a plea in abatement, which contained matters in part abatement of the writ, must be pleaded accordingly (k). But as the Court would *ex officio* give judgment in favor of the defendant according *to the substance of the plea, without reference to its conclusion (980), an error with regard to the prayer of judgment in the concluding part of the plea was not material, except in the case of a plea in *abatement* (l). In an action of *debt* the defendant, in pleading a tender, ought to have concluded his plea by praying judgment if the plaintiff ought to have or maintain his action to recover *any* damages against him; for in that action the debt is the principal, and the damages were only accessary;

Prayer of Judgment.

[*592]

(z) 1 P. Wms. 258, 259; 10 Mod. 190, 247; Fortes. 334; Barnes, 330; 4 T. R. 156; 3 B. & P. 171; 6 Bing. 686. To a special plea of bankruptcy, the plaintiff may reply that the certificate was obtained by fraud, and such replication will be a good answer to the plea, though the enactment to that effect in 5 G. 2, c. 30, s. 7, is not repeated in 6 G. 4, c. 78; Horn v. Ion, 4 B. & Adol. 78.

(a) 1 Saund 103 b, c; Com. Dig. Pleader, E. 33.

(b) Com. Dig. Pleader, E. 29; Willes, 126.

(c) *Ante*, 589.

(d) 1 M. & P. 102; 4 Bing. 428, S. C.

(e) 2 Salk. 520.

(f) 4 Price. 122; see *ante*, 502.

(g) 2 B. & P. 423; 2 Saund. 210 d; 4 East, 502.

(h) See 1 M. & P. 114.

(i) 4 East, 502; *ante*, 586; see Steph. 2d ed. 445.

(k) *Ante*, 492, 494.

(l) *Ante*, 494; 1 M. & P. 124, 125; 4 Bing 428, S. C.

(979) Vide Lytle v. Lee, 5 Johns. Rep. 112. Thomas v. Rumsey, 6 Johns. Rep. 26.

(980) The King v. Taylor, 5 Dowl. & Ryl. 431. Per ABBOTT, C. J.

IV. FORM AND PARTS. — 6thly. The conclusion. but in *assumpsit* the damages are the principal, and therefore in pleading a tender in that action, the defendant ought to have concluded his plea with a prayer of judgment if the plaintiff ought to have or maintain his action, to recover any *more* or *greater* damages than the sum tendered, or any damages by reason of the non-payment thereof (*m*). In pleading matter of *estoppel*, the defendant in the conclusion of his plea should rely upon it (*n*); and that established rule as applied to *estoppel* was expressly continued by Reg. Gen. Hil. T. 4 W. 4, reg. 9.

How and when to object to conclusion of plea. It was enacted by the statute of 4 & 5 Ann. c. 16, s. 1 (981), "that no advantage or exception shall be taken of or for the want of averment of *hoc paratus est verificare*, or *hoc paratus est verificare per recordum*; or of or for not alleging *prout patet per recordum*, or any other matter of like nature, except the same shall be specially and particularly set down, and shown for the cause of demurrer." Since this statute, a wrong or defective conclusion, either to the country or with a verification, &c. can only be objected to by special demurrer (*o*).

When no prayer of judgment is necessary *since* Reg. Gen. Hil. T. 4 W. 4, reg. 9. We have just seen that Reg. Gen. Hil. T. 4 W. 4, reg. 9, orders that "in a plea or subsequent pleading intended to be pleaded *in bar* of the *whole action generally* (*p*), it shall not be necessary to use *any prayer of judgment*, but the case of an estoppel is excepted (*p*)."

Conclusion of traverses. Reg. Gen. Hil. T. 4 W. 4, reg. 13, orders that "all special traverses, or traverses with an inducement of affirmative matter, shall *conclude to the country*, provided that this regulation shall not preclude the opposite party from pleading over to the inducement when the traverse is immaterial."†

No protestation to be made. Reg. 12 orders that "no *protestation* shall hereafter be made in any pleading, but either party shall be entitled to the same advantage in that or other actions as if a protestation had been made."

Consequences of defect in a plea. A defendant has a right to give evidence in support of his plea on which an issue in fact has been taken, however defective such plea may be (*q*).

V. OF SEVERAL PLEAS.

V. OF SEVERAL PLEAS. With respect to the pleading of *several* pleas to the *same declaration*, we will *first* consider the former practice, and, *secondly*, the practice since Reg. Gen. Hil. T. 4 W. 4.†

With respect to the *former* practice we have already fully considered the

(*m*) 2 Salk. 622, 623; 1 Ld. Raym. 254; Willes, 13.

(*n*) Co. Lit. 303 b; Com. Dig. Pleader, E. 31; Estoppel, E.; *vide* also 1 Saund. 325 a, n. 4; Willes, 13; Steph. 2d ed. 443; *ante*, 457, 458; 2 C. & P. 148.

(*o*) 2 Saund. 190, n. 5.

(*p*) See the rule *ante*; see the meaning of those words *ante*, 587.

(*q*) Bowman *v.* Rostrow, 4 Nev. & Man. 551.

(981) {The first *thirteen* sections and the 20th and 27th sections, are in force in Pennsylvania, 3 Binn. 625. Roberts' Dig. 43.} See Laws of N. Y. sess. 11. c. 32. s. 6. 1 R. L. 120. {2 Rev. Stat. 352, s. 4.}

† See American Editor's Preface.

doctrine of *duplicity* in pleading, not only as it affects pleading in general, but also as it more immediately relates to pleas in bar (r). Each plea, taken separately, is still open to objection if it be double, that is, if it contain two or more perfectly distinct and independent answers to the same charge, either of which would defeat it (s). At *common law* a defendant could not plead several distinct pleas to the same *declaration or a part threof (t), which often led to much inartificial and repugnant pleading, as it naturally induced the defendant to endeavor to crowd as many facts and arguments into his plea as he possibly could (u). At length it was provided by the statute 4 & 5 Ann. c. 16, s. 4 & 5. (x)(982), (but which does not extend to actions at the suit of the king (y),) "that it shall be lawful for any *defendant* or tenant in any action or suit, or for any *plaintiff in replevin*, in any Court of *record*, with the *leave of the Court*, to plead as many several matters thereto as he shall think necessary for his defence (z); provided nevertheless that if any such matter shall, upon a demurrer joined, be judged insufficient, costs shall be given at the discretion of the Court; or if a verdict shall be found upon any issue in the said cause for the plaintiff or demandant, costs shall be also given in like manner; unless the judge who tried the said issue shall certify that the defendant or tenant, or plaintiff in replevin, had a probable cause to plead such matter, which upon the issue shall be found against him. Provided also, that nothing in this act shall extend to any writ, declaration, or suit of appeal of felony, &c. or to any writ, bill, action, or information upon *any penal statute*." V. OF SEVERAL PLEAS. [*593]

The liberty to plead several pleas is confined to Courts of *record*; and therefore if in the County Court, and other inferior Courts not of record (a), the defendant plead two or more pleas to the same part of the declaration, the plaintiff may demur for duplicity, or treat the second plea as a nullity, and proceed to trial on the first (b). And in Courts of record the defendant cannot plead non assumpsit (c), or *non est factum* (d), to the whole declaration, and a *tender* as to part (983); for one of these pleas goes to deny that the plaintiff ever had any cause of action, and the other absolutely admits it to the extent of the sum tendered and paid into Court (984). In an action on a deed made beyond seas, the defendant relying in some of his pleas on matters of defence which necessarily imported the execution of the deed, the Court would

(r) *Ante*, 259, 260 and 564.
(s) *Id.*
(t) *Ante*, 563, 564; 5 Bing. 45, 47.
(u) 2 Eunomous, 141; see Boote's Suit at Law, 104; Cowp. Eq. Pl. 227; and Beames Pl. Eq. Index, "*Plea.*"
(x) The construction of, and practice upon, this statute, are stated in Com. Dig. Pleader, E. 2, and Tidd, 9th ed. 654, 657.
(y) Rex v. Cadwell, Forrest. 57.
(z) The statute does not extend to pleas in *abatement*.
(a) See Bac. Ab. Courts.
(b) Chitty v. Dendy, 1 Harr. & Woll. 169.
(c) 4 T. R. 194.
(d) Bla. Rep. 905; 5 T. R. 97; 4 Taunt. 459.

(982) Laws of N. Y. sess. 36. c. 56. s. 10. 1 R. L. 519. { 2 Rev. Stat. 352, s. 9. }
(983) And *non est factum*, and a *tender* to the whole declaration cannot be pleaded together. Orgill v. Kimshead, 4 Taunt. 459. { See Jackson v. Webster, 6 Munf. 462. 1 Har. & Gill, 407. 15 Mass. Rep. 54, 55. } Payment at the day, and payment before the day, cannot be pleaded together. Thayer v. Rogers, 1 Johns. Cas. 152.
(984) { The pleas of general performance and *non est factum*, may be pleaded together, for defendants are not confined to pleas strictly consistent. Union Bank v. Ridgeley, 1 Har. & Gill. 324. }

V. OF SEVERAL PLEAS.

not permit him to plead *non est factum* (*e*); and the defendant will not be allowed to plead *non-assumpsit*, and the stock-jobbing *act (*f*); or non-assumpsit, and alien enemy (*g*). The Court of Common Pleas refused to allow the assignees of a bankrupt to plead in covenant on a lease *non est factum*, and that the premises did not come to them by assignment (*h*). And in the exercise of their discretion, that Court, in *scire facias* on a judgment, would not permit the defendant to plead, 1st, Payment; 2dly, Judgment by fraud; and 3dly, That the judgment was upon a warrant of attorney obtained by fraud (*i*). And where the plaintiff's title to an advowson was traced in *quare impedit* through a period of two centuries, and the defendant's claim arose on the alleged invalidity of a deed of 1672, the Court would not allow him to traverse all the allegations in the declaration, or to plead more pleas than were necessary to contest the deed of 1672 (*k*). Nor can the defendant plead several matters which require different trials, as in dower, *ne unques accouple en loyal matrimonie*, and *ne unques seisie que dower* (*l*)(985); for the first matter is triable by the bishop, and the other by a jury, and if the former be found against the defendant, the judge cannot certify that he had a probable cause for pleading it. Nor is the king bound by this statute; and where he is plaintiff, the defendant cannot plead double without leave of the attorney-general (*m*). Nor does *this statute extend to any action or information upon a penal statute* (*n*); and as the king is not bound by this statute (*o*), the defendant cannot plead double to an information of intrusion (*p*), in *quare impedit*, where the king is a party (*q*); or in *scire facias* for a bond debt to the king (*r*); nor could he plead double till the 32 Geo. 3, c. 58, in an information in nature of a *quo warranto* (*s*). And a defendant will not be permitted to plead the general issue and also a plea of justification, where a statute allows him to give the special matter in evidence under the general issue (*t*).

With the above exceptions the defendant may in general in *different pleas* state as many *substantially different grounds of defence* as may be thought

[*595] necessary, though they may appear to be *contradictory or inconsistent (*u*). Thus, infancy, a release, or the statute of limitations, might be pleaded with *non assumpsit*; and the *statute of gaming or usury might be joined with non*

(*e*) 3 Taunt. 385.

(*f*) 1 B. & P. 222; 1 M. & P. 148.

(*g*) 1 B. & P. 222, n. (*a*); 2 *Id.* 72; 12 East, 206; 10 East, 326.

(*h*) 5 Bing. 12.

(*i*) 2 Bing. 325.

(*k*) 5 Bing. 42; S. C. in 2 M. & P. 105, and 4 Bing. 525.

(*l*) 2 Bla. Rep. 1157, 1207.

(*m*) Willes, 533; Forr. Rep. Exch. 57, A. D. 1801.

(*n*) 2 Stra. 1044; Rep. Temp. Hardw. 262; 4 T. R. 701; 9 East, 469; Tidd, 9th ed. 655.

(*o*) 1 P. Wms. 220; Forr. 57.

(*p*) Parker, 1, 16.

(*q*) Willes, 133; Barnes, 353, S. C.

(*r*) Forrest, 57; Parker, 1.

(*s*) 1 P. Wms. 220; Parker, 10. Decisions on the act, 8 T. R. 467; 9 East, 469; 5 B. & Ald. 774; 1 D. & R. 438, S. C.; 2 Chit. R. 371; Tidd, 9th ed. 656; 6 B. & C. 267.

(*t*) Neale v. Mackenzie, 4 Tyr. 670.

(*u*) See the instances, Com. Dig. Pleader, E. 2; Tidd, 9th ed. 655, 656.

---

(985) So, *nul tiel record*, and *nil debet*, or payment, cannot be pleaded together. Le Conte v. Pendleton, 1 Johns. Cas. 104. S. C. Coleman, 72. Carnes v. Duncan, Coleman, 35. } But in covenant, *non est factum* may be joined with a plea of payment. Mervey v. Gay, 3 Pick. Rep. 388. And see Cutts v. The United States, 1 Gall. Rep. 69, where in an action of debt on bond, *non est factum* and payment were pleaded without objection. See, also, 5 Serg. & Rawle, 411. See also Union Bank v. Ridgely, 1 Har. & Gill 324. }

est factum (x)(986). So, in trespass, not guilty, a justification, and accord and satisfaction; or not guilty, and *son assault demesne;* may be pleaded together (y); and not guilty and *liberum tenementum* may be joined (z). So, *non tenuit*, no rent in arrear, and infancy may be separately pleaded in bar to the same avowry (a).

V. OF SEVERAL PLEAS.

When, however, the various pleas are clearly repugnant, and would create unjust delay, the Court will sometimes rescind the rule to plead double, and compel the defendant to rely on one of his pleas (b). And in the Common Pleas a second perplexing plea containing matter which might be given in evidence under the general issue, is not allowed to be pleaded therewith (c). We have already alluded to the instances in which it is impolitic to plead the general issue (d). As the defendant will not be entitled to the costs of unnecessary pleas, though he succeed on the trial upon one of them, unless the judge certify that he had probable cause for pleading them, care should in general be taken to plead only defences which will probably be sustained (e)(987).

It is hardly necessary to observe, that if a defendant succeed on either of his several pleas, he is entitled to judgment, and will defeat the action, as regards the matters covered by such successful plea, although he may be unable to substantiate his other pleas to the same matters charged in the declaration (f).

Form of pleading a second or subsequent plea *before* Reg. Gen. Hil. T. 4 W. 4, reg. 5.

Before the recent rules, when several pleas were pleaded under the statutes, each second and subsequent pleas should in strictness, in the introductory parts of each, have stated that the same was pleaded "*by leave of the Court first had and obtained*," (988) but the omission, *though untechnical, appears to be no cause of demurrer (g). If, in fact, no leave had been obtained, the proper course was either to sign judgment, or *to apply to the Court to strike out* all but one of the pleas (h): and the latter course should be adopted [*596]

(x) Tidd, 9th edit. 656; see other instances, *id.* 657; *ante*, 593, 594.

(y) 5 Bac. Ab. 448, and other instances, *id.*

(z) Tidd, 9th ed. 656.

(a) 1 Marsh. 74; 5 Taunt. 340, S. C.

(b) 13 East, 255; and see 3 Bing. 635; 1 M. & P. 345; 4 Bing. 525; 5 *Id.* 42; *ante*, 593, 594. And where several pleas in covenant traversing title were pleaded, after defendant had paid prior rent to the plaintiff, the rule to plead double was rescinded, *per* Bayley, J. in Craigh *v.* Struch, 25th Feb. 1830.

(c) 6 Bing. 197. What are pleas of this nature, and as to *sham* pleas, *ante*, 557, 574.

(d) *Ante*, 546.

(e) 4 & 5 Ann. c. 16, s. 5; Tidd, 9th ed. 658; 7 Moore, 351.

(f) The defendant is entitled to the general costs if he succeed on one plea, which is a complete answer to the action, 1 B. & Ald. 254; 8 Taunt. 129.

(g) Andr. 108; 1 Wils. 219; Cowp. 500, 501; *sed vide* 1 Hen. Bla. 275, 278.

(h) *Id.;* Tidd, 9th ed. 658; 1 B. & P. 415.

(986) So, *non est factum*, and a discharge by bankruptcy. Atkinson *v.* Atkinson, Str 871. Phillips *v.* Wood et al., Str. 1000. *Non est factum*, and usury. Lechmere *v.* Rice, 2 Bos. & Pul. 12. The general issue, and the statute of limitations. Da Costa *v.* Cartaret et al., Str. 889. In trespass, a licence and justification. Bac. Ab. Pleas, K. 3. In debt for rent upon a parol demise, *nil habuit in tenementis*, and *non demisit.* Ibid. *Non assumpsit* and infancy. Wilson *v.* Ames, 5 Taunt. 340. *Non demisit*, and no rent in arrear. Van Holten *v.* Lewis et al., 1 M'Cord's Rep. 12. In replevin, *non cepit* and property in the defendant. Shuter *v.* Page, 11 Johns. Rep. 196. So, *non cepit*, property in a stranger, and *liberum tenementum.* Barnes, 364. In debt for rent a tender and eviction. Cary *v.* Jenkins, Str. 496.

987) In the Supreme Court of Massachusetts, a motion for leave to plead double to a writ of error was denied, the court doubting whether the statute allowing double pleading extended to writs of error. Parker *v.* Gilson, 1 Mass. Rep. 230.

(988) { See Richardson *v.* Whitfield, 2 M'Cord's Rep. 150.

V. OF SEVERAL PLEAS.

where several pleas were improperly pleaded on a rule improperly obtained. Where there were several pleas, it was advisable, in order to avoid prolixity and expense, if practicable, to refer, in subsequent pleas, to a statement of the same matter in a preceding plea, the same as in the case of several counts in a declaration (*i*). But one plea could not be taken advantage of to help or vitiate another, for every plea must stand or fall by itself, unless expressly referred to by an appropriate allegation (*k*)(989): and the plaintiff cannot use one plea as evidence of the fact which the defendant disputes in another plea (*l*)(990). So, where there was a demurrer to part only of the pleadings, the Court, in considering what judgment should be pronounced upon the demurrer, could look only to that part of the record upon which the demurrer arose, and not at other collateral parts of the record not connected with it; and therefore upon a demurrer to a defective plea, the defendant could not claim in aid a replication to another plea, by which the plaintiff admitted that he had become a bankrupt and assigned his estate to an assignee, &c. (*m*) Where one plea refers expressly to the exception in another plea, and also contains an averment of performance of covenants in the *said* deed, which deed is set forth in the plea referred to, but not mentioned in the exception to that plea, both pleas may be taken together (*n*).

Rule to plead double.

Where the plaintiff signed judgment for want of a plea, because the rule to plead several matters was erroneously entitled C. and W. instead of C. and W. *and another*, the Court of C. P. set aside the judgment without costs, on an affidavit that the pleas were true, and that the defendant had a good defence (*o*).

2dly. Of several pleas *since* Reg. Gen. Hil. T. 4 W. 4, reg. 5 (*p*).

The liberty to plead *several pleas* having been abused, and the usual excuse for several varying pleas, to avoid the risk of variance, having been in a great measure removed by the power afforded to the judge trying a cause to amend even during the trial, in case of variances, the judges thought it advisable, by a *general* rule, to qualify the liberty of pleading several pleas, given by 4 & 5 Ann. c. 16, and therefore promulgated the rule of Hil. T. 4 W. 4,† which in terms prohibits more than one plea, stating the *same subject-matter of defence*, but varying only *in statement, description*, or circumstances. Formerly, and when the 4 Ann. c. 16, was first enacted, the practice was in all cases for the defendant's counsel actually to move the Court for leave to plead more than one plea, and the Court in each case *actually* exercised its discretion whether or not to allow the several pleas. But it soon became, especially in the Court

(*i*) *Ante*, 450; Willes, 380; 1 Marsh. 33, 35; 5 Taunt. 228, S. C.

(*k*) Willes, 380; 1 Marsh. 33; 5 Taunt. 228, S. C.; 1 M. & P. 147, 175; S. C. in 4 Bing. 435, and 2 Y. & J. 11.

(*l*) 5 Taunt. 228; 1 Marsh. Rep. 33, S. C.

(*m*) 6 B. & C. 216; 9 D. & R. 369, S. C.

(*n*) Macdougall *v.* Robertson, 2 Younge & J. 11.

(*o*) 1 Bing. 187; 7 Moore, 599, S. C.

(*p*) See fully 3 Chitty's Gen. Prac. 731 to 737.

(989) Pleas pleaded under leave of the court must contain, in each of them, sufficient matter in law, to bar the plaintiff's action, and they can not be made to depend on facts stated in other pleas. Currie and Whitney *v.* Henry, 2 Johns. Rep. 437. Sevey *v.* Blacklin and others, 2 Mass. Rep. 543.

(990) { See Alderman *v.* French, 1 Pick. Rep. 1, *contra*. But see Cilley *v.* Tenney, 2 New Hamp. Rep. 19, and Starkie on Evidence, (Am. Ed. 1828,) 295 n. (1). }

† See American Editor's Preface.

of King's Bench, too much as of course for a defendant to plead as many pleas as he might think fit; and it became expedient to repress the practice by the express Reg. Gen. Hil. T. 4 W. 4, reg. 5.† However, *inconsistent* pleas may still be pleaded under the new rules, if intended *bona fide* to support different substantial grounds of defence; for *per* Bosanquet, J. "The word '*inconsistent*' was studiously kept out of the rules, for the subject was discussed, and it was felt that there might be cases in which pleas might be inconsistent with each other, and sustain substantially different defences. The object had in view was to prevent the *same* defence being pleaded in *different forms*." (q)

However, since these pleading rules prohibited several pleas of the *same subject-matter* of defence, a defendant may still plead *as many pleas of different* matters of defence *as may be reasonable* (r).

The Reg. Gen. Hil. T. 4 W. 4, reg. 5,† expressly orders "that several counts shall not be allowed, unless a distinct subject-matter of complaint is intended to be established in respect of each; nor shall *several* pleas, or *avowries*, or *cognizances* be allowed, unless *a distinct ground* of answer or defence is intended to be established in respect of each." The rule then gives several instances when or not a second count shall or not be allowed (s), and proceeds thus as to pleas.

Instances of pleas and avowries, &c.

Pleas, avowries, and cognizances, founded on one and the same principal matter, but varied in statement, description, or circumstances only, (and pleas in bar in replevin are within the rule), are not to be allowed.

Payment.

Ex. gr. Pleas of *solvit ad diem*, and of *solvit post diem*, are both pleas of payment, varied in the circumstances of time only, and are not to be allowed.

Accord and satisfaction—Release.

But pleas of payment, and of accord and satisfaction, or of release, are distinct, and are to be allowed.

Liability of third party.

Pleas of an agreement to accept the security of A. B. in discharge of the plaintiff's demand, and of an agreement to accept the security of C. D. for the like purpose, are also distinct, and to be allowed.

Agreement to forbear in consideration of liability of third party.

But pleas of an agreement to accept the security of a third person in discharge of the plaintiff's demand, and of the same agreement, describing it to be an agreement to forbear for a time, in consideration of the same security, are not distinct; for they are only variations in the statement of one and the same agreement, whether more or less extensive, in consideration of the same security, and not to be allowed.

Lib. ten., easement, right of way, right of common, common of turbary, and estovers.

In trespass *quare clausum fregit*, pleas of soil and freehold of the defendant in the *locus in quo*, and of the defendant's right to an easement there—pleas of right of way, of common of pasture, of common of turbary, and of common of estovers, are distinct, and are to be allowed.

Right of common.

But pleas of right of common at all times of the year, and of such right at particular times, or in a qualified manner, are not to be allowed.

(q) Dueere v. Triebuer, 3 Dowl. 133; 7 Bing. N. C. 266, 267.

(r) Hart v. Bell, 1 Hodges' Rep. 6, 16, 18; 3 Dowl. 133, 135, 415; 1 Bing. N. C. 266, 323, 326, 509.

(s) See *ante*, 451, 451 a; and see the rule at length, *post*, Appendix.

† See American Editor's Preface.

V. OF SEVERAL PLEAS.

So pleas of right of way over the *locus in quo*, varying the *termini* or the purposes, are not to be allowed.

Distress for rent, and damage *feasant*.

Avowries for distress for rent, and for distress for damage *feasant*, are to be allowed.

But avowries for distress for rent, varying the amount of rent reserved, or the time at which the rent is payable, are not to be allowed.

Distress for rent.

The cases above mentioned as instances only.

The examples, in this and other places specified, are given as some instances only of the application of the rules to which they relate; but the principles contained in the rules are not to be considered as restricted by the examples specified.

The 6th and 7th rules then provide the remedy for the violation of this 5th rule, as well in the case of an improper second count as in the case of an improper *second plea* (*t*). The *practice* as to the *permitting* or *refusing* several pleas is stated in the author's work on General Practice (*u*).

A second plea need not state that it is pleaded by leave, &c.

The Reg. Gen. Hil. T. 4 W. 4, reg. 11,† orders, that "it shall not be necessary to state in a second or other plea or avowry that it is pleaded by leave of the Court, or according to the form of the statute, or to that effect." But still Reg. Gen. Hil. T. 2 W. 4, reg. 34, orders. "that if a party plead several pleas, avowries, or cognizances, without a rule for that purpose, the opposite party shall be at liberty to sign judgment." (*x*) But where a rule to plead several matters had in fact been obtained, though by mistake intituled *C.* v. *W.* instead of *C.* v. *W. and another*, the Court of C. P. set aside the judgment without costs, on an affidavit that the pleas were true, and that the defendants had a good defence (*y*), and which decision, although before this recent rule, would still apply in practice.

VI. OF PLEAS BY SEVERAL DEFENDANTS.

VI. OF PLEAS BY SEVERAL DEFENDANTS (*z*).

In general when the defence is in its nature joint, *several defendants* may join in the same plea, or they may sever, without committing the fault of duplicity in pleading (*a*); and one defendant may plead in abatement (*b*); another in bar, and the other may demur (*c*); except in an action against husband and wife, when the husband must join in the plea with his wife (*d*). And by way of defence two may join, although the subject-matter of [*597] *their plea be several, as in an *audita querela* (*e*), or though their different defences may be inconsistent (*f*); and in trespass against two for a battery, they may jointly

(*t*) See the rules, *ante*, 451 *a*, and *post*, Appendix.

(*u*) 3 Chitty's Gen. Prac. 732 to 737.

(*x*) Jervis's Rules, 51, note (*i*); and Hockley *v.* Sutton, 2 Dowl. 700.

(*y*) 1 Bing. 187; 7 Moore, 599, S. C.

(*z*) As to several defendants joining or severing in their pleas, 3 Chitty's Gen. Prac. 737, 738.

(*a*) *Ante*, 260, 564; Stephen, 2d ed. 298.

(*b*) It is said *arguendo* in Hob. 245, that defendants cannot sever in *dilatory* pleas; *sed quære*, see *id.* 250; Stephen, 2d ed. 298, note (*a*). The practice is quite otherwise.

(*c*) 2 Vin. Ab. 75; Action, Joinder, H. D.; Com. Dig. Pleader, E. 35.

(*d*) Com. Dig. Pleader, 2 A. 3; Cro. Jac. 239, 288.

(*e*) Cro. Eliz. 473.

(*f*) 2 Hen. Bla. 396; 2 Mod. 67.

† See American Editor's Preface.

plead that the plaintiff assaulted them, and that they in self-defence beat the plaintiff; or that they may sever (*g*); or they may jointly plead that they were servants of N. and committed the assault in his defence. So, two may jointly justify an arrest under a joint warrant (*h*). And one of several defendants may plead not guilty, and the other a justification as his servant, for one defendant cannot by pleading oust the other of his defence (*i*).

VI. OF PLEAS BY SEVERAL DEFENDANTS.

Joint-tenants and co-parceners must join in an avowry, and a cognizance as their bailiff should be for the entire rent (*j*); but tenants in common must sever (991), and the avowry of each must be *de unâ medietate* of the whole rent, and not of a certain sum which amounts to a moiety (*k*). When the action is against one of several tenants in common, he should avow for his own proportion, and in general he makes cognizance as bailiff of his companion for the residue (*l*); or he may avow only for his undivided share of the rent (*m*). If the action of replevin be against two tenants in common, they should join, one avowing, and the other as his bailiff making cognizance, for an undivided moiety of the rent; and then the one who first made cognizance avowing in his own right, and the other who first avowed making cognizance as his bailiff for the other undivided moiety (*n*). If three tenants in common distrain thirty beasts, it is said they each should avow separately for ten (*o*); and one tenant in common cannot avow alone, for taking cattle damage feasant, but he ought also to make cognizance as bailiff of his companion (*p*). And where two persons are defendants in replevin they cannot, it seems, make several avowries in their own right for distinct matters; thus, if one avow for rent-service, and the other for rent-charge, both the avowries shall abate, for the *Court would be in doubt to which of them return should be awarded (*q*). [*598]
Several persons having several estates cannot join in prescribing, because the prescription of one does not concern the other (*r*); though an exception has been allowed where two persons commit a joint trespass (*s*). So personal defences, as coverture, infancy, &c. should be pleaded separately; and one of several defendants may justify by command of another defendant who suffers judgment by default, for his act shall not take away the ground of defence from his servant (*t*).

A plea which is bad in part is bad *in toto* (*u*); if, therefore, two defendants join in a plea, which is sufficient for one, but not for the other, the plea is bad as to both (992), for the Court cannot sever it and say that one is guilty, and

(*g*) 2 Vin. Ab. 76, pl. 14.
(*h*) *Id.* pl. 15, 16.
(*i*) 2 Mod. 67.
(*j*) Bac. Ab. Joint-tenant, K.; Replevin, K.; 5 T. R. 246; 1 Lev. 109; Sir T. Raym. 80.
(*k*) *Aliter* in *covenant for rent*, 4 B. & C. 157; 6 D. & R. 72, S. C.
(*l*) Bac. Ab. Joint-tenant, K.; Replevin, K.; 5 T. R. 246; 1 Lev. 109; Sir T. Raym. 80; 2 Vin. Ab. 59, pl. 27.
(*m*) 5 T. R. 246; 2 Hen. Bla. 387.
(*n*) Salk. 207; 5 T. R. 247; see the form, *post*, vol. iii.
(*o*) *Id*; Co. Lit. s. 314, 317.
(*p*) 2 Hen. Bla. 386.
(*q*) 5 Co. 19 *b*, 38 b.
(*r*) 2 Vin. Ab. 56, pl. 47; 76, pl. 18.
(*s*) *Id.* 76, pl. 18; see *ante*, 10, 11, *Sed quære*.
(*t*) 2 Mod. 67.
(*u*) *Ante*, 579.

(991) Decker *v.* Livingston, 15 Johns. Rep. 482.
(992) Vide Moore *v.* Parker et al., 3 Mass. Rep. 310, 312. Schermerhorn and others *v.* Tripp, 2 Caines' Rep. 108. Marsteller and others *v.* M'Lean, 7 Cranch, 158. { Bradley *v.* Hunt, 7 Cow. Rep. 330. }

VI. OF PLEAS BY SEVERAL DEFENDANTS.

that the other is not, when they all put themselves on the same terms (x)(993). Thus, it has been held that if an officer plead separately under a writ of *fi. fa.* or other process, he need not state the judgment on which the writ was founded; but if he join in the plea with the plaintiff in the former action, and the judgment be not stated, the plea will be bad as to both the defendants, unless the plaintiff in the former suit justify merely in aid of the officer (y). But this rule does not apply where the objection to the plea is merely on account of surplusage (z); and if several executors join in the same plea of *plene administravit*, each will only be liable to pay the assets found by the jury to be in his own hands, though it is more usual for each executor to plead separately (a) (994). In an action of trespass against several defendants, if it be expected that one of them will be acquitted, and that the others will be found guilty, it is advisable for the former to plead separately, for otherwise he could only obtain 40*s.* costs (b). If several defendants join in the plea, and it is in the singular number, it will be bad on demurrer (c).

[*599] The plaintiff may, in an action in form *ex delicto* against *several defendants, enter a *nolle prosequi* as to one of them (d); but in actions in form *ex contractu*, unless the defence be merely in the *personal* discharge of one of the defendants, a *nolle prosequi* cannot be entered as to one defendant without discharging the others, for the cause of action is entire and indivisible (e)(995). And upon the same principle, in the latter form of action the success of one defendant upon a plea which goes to the merits, will preclude the plaintiff from obtaining any benefit from a judgment by default suffered by another defendant (f). If the defendants plead severally, the plaintiff may demur to one plea, and join issue on the other (g)(996), and may in an action *ex delicto* afterwards enter a *nolle prosequi* on the demurrer, and proceed against the other defendant (h), or if several issues are joined, he may enter a *nolle prosequi* to one before or after judgment (i). If defendants join in a plea, they should not sever in the rejoinder; and they cannot unite in the latter pleading if they did not concur in the plea to the declaration (k).

Defects when aided.

As a defective declaration may be aided at common law by the plea or by the verdict, so *a defective plea may be aided* in some cases by the replication or verdict (997); and the statute of jeofails and the statute for the amendment

(x) 1 Saund. 28, n. 2; 3 T. R. 376, 377; 1 Stra. 509, 994, 1184; 3 Wils. 344; 3 East, 132, 133; 2 East, 263.

(y) *Id.*; 2 East, 263, 270; 3 East, 132, 133, 142; 3 Wils. 376. Constable joining in bad special plea, 2 Bing. 523.

(z) 3 T. R. 377.

(a) 1 Saund. 336, note 10.

(b) 2 M. & Sel. 172; Tidd, 9th ed. 986; 4 B. & Ald. 43, 700.

(c) Lutw. 1531; Com. Dig. Pleader, E. 35.

(d) Salk. 457; 1 Wils. 306; Tidd, 9th ed. 682.

(e) 1 Wils. 89; 3 Esp. Rep. 76; 2 M. & Sel. 23, 444; Tidd, 9th ed. 682; *ante*, 51.

(f) *Ante*, 51.

(g) Cro. Car. 239, 243; Hob. 70; Com. Dig. Pleader, E. 35.

(h) *Id.* When not, see 4 T. R. 360; 1 Saund. 285, note 5; Tidd, 9th ed. 681, 682.

(i) *Id.*

(k) 4 B. & C. 704; 7 D. & R. 187, S. C.; Stephen, 2d. ed. 298, 299.

(993) { Higley *v.* Williams, 16 Johns. Rep. 217. }
(994) { See App *v.* Driesbach, 2 Rawle, 287. }
(995) Beidman *v.* Vanderslice, 2 Rawle, 334.
(996) Vide Lansing *v.* Montgomery, 2 Johns. Rep. 382.
(997) See Gavene *v.* M'Michael, 8 Serg. & Rawle, 441. Rockfeller *v.* Donnelly, 8 Cow. Rep. 655.

of the law, also aid many mistakes after verdict or judgment (*l*). These rules will be fully considered hereafter.

VI. OF PLEAS BY SEVERAL DEFENDANTS.

VII. OF PLEAS OF SET-OFF.

VII. PLEAS OF SET-OFF, AND HEREIN OF MUTUAL CREDIT.

In actions upon *simple contracts* or *specialties*, for the payment of *money*, the defence frequently is a cross demand for a *debt* due from the plaintiff to the defendant. We will therefore now examine the law of *set-off* and *mutual credit* (*m*), but so far only as it is connected with the subject of pleading.

[*600]

*At *common* law, and independently of the statutes of set-off, a defendant is in general entitled to retain, or claim by way of *deduction*, all just allowances or demands accruing to him, or payments made by him, in respect of the *same* transaction or account, which forms the ground of action. But this cannot be termed a *set-off* in the strict legal sense of the word, because it is not in the nature of a *cross* demand, or *mutual* debt, but rather constitutes a *deduction*, rendering the sum to be recovered by the plaintiff so much less (*n*). So, where demands, originally cross, and not arising out of the same transaction, have by subsequent *express agreement* been stipulated to be deducted, or set-off against each other, only the *balance* is the debt and sum recoverable, without any special plea or notice of set-off; though it is *advisable* in most cases, and *necessary* when the action is on a specialty, to plead it (*o*); and since Reg. Gen. Hil. T. 4 W. 4, a special plea claiming such *deduction* would in most cases be requisite. So if an account has been settled, and a balance struck between the parties, it may be given in evidence on the general issue; though it seems a defendant cannot reduce a plaintiff's demand for goods sold, by producing a debtor and creditor account in the hand-writing of the plaintiff's clerk, showing goods to have been sold by the defendant to plaintiff, unless he has pleaded or given a notice of set-off (*p*).

When or not *deductions* may be made under non assumpsit.

In an action for work and labor or goods sold, though the contract was at a certain price, the defendant may, at least after a notice, prove under the general issue, in reduction of the claim, that the work was improperly done (*q*)(998); or that the goods were not so good as warranted (*r*)(999). And where in an

(*l*) 4 & 5 Ann c. 16; Com. Dig. Pleader, E. 37 to 39; Vin. Ab. Replication; 1 Saund. 228 a, note 1.

(*m*) As to the law of set-off in general, see Montague on set-off; Tidd, 9th ed. 662 to 668; 3 Chit. Com. Law, 669; and see Chit. Col. of Statutes, 874, tit. "*Set-off*," a full note; Eden's Bank. Law, 2d edit. 186; Montag. & Gregg. Bank. Law, 242 to 261; Manning's Index, tit. "*Set-off*;" Chitty, jun. on Contr. 327 to 335; Selw. N. P. tit. "*Assumpsit*;" Gibson *v.* Bell. 1 Bing. N. C. 746. Set-off cannot be pleaded to an action for not repairing, Seal *v.* Burrel, 4 Nev. & Man. 200, 201; Auber *v.* Lewis, Man. Dig. 2d ed. 251.

(*n*) 1 Bla. Rep. 651; 4 Burr. 2133, 2221, and other cases in Montague's Law of Set-off, 1 to 3.

(*o*) 5 T. R. 135; 3 T. R. 599; 3 Taunt. 76; 2 Taunt. 170; 1 Bla. Rep. 651; 4 Burr. 2133; Montague's Law of Set-off, 1 to 3, and 28, note (2 *p*).

(*p*) 1 C. & P. 133.

(*q*) 7 East, 479; 1 Campb. 38; 2 *Id.* 63; 3 Stark. Rep. 6; and see *ante*, 513, note (*x*).

(*r*) 1 Campb. 190; 3 Stark. Rep. 32; and see *ante*, 551 *a*, note (*x*).

(998) {See Heck *v.* Shener, 4 Serg. & Rawle, 249.}

(999) {Steigleman *v.* Jeffries, 1 Serg. & Rawle, 477. See Cornell *v.* Green, 10 Serg. & Rawle, 14. Shaw *v.* Badger, 12 Serg. & Rawle, 275. Light *v.* Stoever, 12 Serg. & Rawle, 431. Harper *v.* Kean, 11 Serg. & Rawle, 280.}

VII. PLEAS OF SET-OFF. action for the price of seed sold, and which was warranted to be good new growing seed, it appeared that soon after the sale the buyer was told that it did not correspond with the warranty, but afterwards sowed part, and sold the residue, it was held to be an answer to the action upon the general issue that the seed was *wholly* unproductive and worthless (*s*). But it has been held that negligence in the conduct of a cause, cannot be set up as a defence to an
[*601] action on an attorney's bill; at least unless it was such *negligence as to deprive the defendant of *all possible benefit* from the cause (*t*). And if a consignee of goods accept any benefit from the carriage, he cannot defend himself from the payment of freight, on the ground that the goods have been damaged by the master in carrying them, although the damage exceed the amount of the freight (*u*).

So, in an action by a servant against his master for wages, the latter cannot in general set off or deduct the value of goods lost or damaged by the negligence of the former, unless it can be proved to have been part of the original agreement between them that the servant should pay, out of his wages, for all his master's goods lost through his negligence, in which case the value of the goods lost may, under the general issue, be deducted from the amount of the wages (*x*). Where by the custom of the hat trade, the amount of the injury sustained by the hats in the process of dyeing, is always to be deducted from the charge of dyeing, the defendant is entitled to such deduction, in an action brought by the dyer, without giving any notice of set-off, and although there has not been any previous adjustment of the amount of the damage done (*y*). And it is a clear rule at common law that if a principal permit his factor to assume the apparent ownership of goods, and to sell them in his, the factor's, own name, the vendee, who bought them in ignorance that the factor acted merely as an agent, may, to an action by the principal for the price, set off a debt due to him from the agent (*z*); and this defence may be given in evidence under the general issue, or specially pleaded in bar (*a*).

The statutes 2 G. 2, c. 22, s. 13, and 8 G. 2, c. 24, as to set-off. But before the statutes of set-off, where there were *cross demands unconnected with each other*, a defendant could not in a Court of law defeat the action by establishing that the plaintiff was indebted to him even in a larger sum than that sought to be recovered, and relief could only be obtained in a Court of equity (*b*). To remedy this injustice, it was enacted by the 2 Geo. 2, c. 22,
[*602] s. 13 (*c*), "that where *there are mutual debts between the plaintiff and defendant, or if either party sue or be sued *as executor or administrator*, where there are mutual debts between the testator or intestate and either party, one debt may be set against the other; and such matter may be given in evidence upon the *general issue*, or *pleaded in bar*, as the nature of the case shall re-

(*s*) 9 B. & C. 259; 4 Man. & Ry. 208, S. C.

(*t*) 2 New R. 136; 7 B. & C. 443; 1 M. & R. 241, S. C.; 1 R. & M. 317; 3 Campb. 451; Peake Rep. 59; but see 2 Campb. 63, 64; *ante*, 551 *a*, note (*x*).

(*u*) 6 Taunt. 65; 4 Campb. 119.

(*x*) 4 Campb. 134.

(*y*) 1 Stark. Rep. 343.

(*z*) See the statute 6 Geo. 4, c. 94; 7 T. R. 359, 360, note; 1 M. & Sel. 576; 2 Marsh. 501; Holt, N. P. C. 124; 2 B. & Ald. 137; Chit. Col. of Statutes, 876, note, tit. "*Set-off.*"

(*a*) 4 B. & C. 547; 7 D. & R. 42, S. C.

(*b*) 2 Burr. 820, 1230; 4 *Id.* 2220; Montague, on Set-off, 1 to 3, 15.

(*c*) This is intituled "An Act for the Relief of Debtors with respect to the Relief of their persons." It is singular that the important provisions in this and the following act respecting *set-off* should be introduced in statutes in all other respects relating only to insolvent debtors.

quire, so as at the time of his pleading the general issue, where any such debt of the plaintiff, his testator or intestate, is intended to be insisted on in evidence, *notice* shall be given of the particular sum or debt so intended to be insisted on, and upon what account it became due, or otherwise such matter shall not be allowed in evidence upon such general issue." This clause was made perpetual by 8 Geo. 2, c. 24, s. 4; and it having been doubted whether mutual debts of a *different* nature could be set against each other (*d*), it was by the last-mentioned statute (*e*) further declared, "that by virtue of the said clause *mutual debts* may be set against each other, either by being pleaded in bar or given in evidence under the general issue, in the manner therein mentioned, notwithstanding that such debts are deemed in law to be of a *different nature*, unless in cases where either of the said debts shall accrue by reason of a *penalty* contained in any bond or specialty, and in all cases where either the debts for which the action hath been or shall be brought, or the debt intended to be set against the same hath accrued or shall accrue by reason of any such *penalty*, the debt intended to be set off shall be *pleaded in bar*, in which plea shall be shown how much is truly and justly due on either side; and in case the plaintiff shall recover in any such action or suit, judgment shall be entered for no more than shall appear to be truly and justly due to the plaintiff after one debt being set against the other as aforesaid." VII. PLEAS OF SET-OFF.

These statutes were passed for the benefit of defendants, and they are not imperative, so that a defendant may waive his right to set off, and bring a cross action for the debt due to him from the plaintiff (*f*)(1000); and where he is not prepared at *the time the plaintiff sues him to prove his cross demand, it is most advisable not to plead or give notice of set-off, for in case he should go into evidence upon the trial in support of his cross demand, and fail in the attempt, he cannot afterwards proceed in a cross action for the amount; and a party cannot bring an action for money which he has succeeded in setting off in a former action against him, although, if the set-off were more than sufficient to cover the plaintiff's demand in the former action, the defendant therein may maintain an action for the surplus (*g*). [*603]

The principal rules upon the subject of set-off may perhaps be here concisely alluded to with propriety. The statutes require, 1st, That the debt sued for, and that sought to be set off, should be *mutual* debts, and due to each of the parties respectively in the *same right* or *character* (*h*); so that a joint debt cannot, by virtue of the statutes, and in the absence of an express agreement to that effect, be set off against a separate demand, nor a sepa- The rules respecting set-off.

(*d*) Willes, 262.
(*e*) Sect. 5.
(*f*) 2 Campb. 595; 5 Taunt. 148. But the plaintiff may prevent such cross action by allowing the set-off, and having it indorsed on the *postea*; see 1 Campb. 252; *post*. One party cannot arrest another for the amount of one side of an account without deducting what is due on the other, 3 Bar. & Cres. 139; 4 D. & R. 653, S. C.

(*g*) 3 Esp. Rep. 104.
(*h*) See further upon this rule, Chit. Col. of Statutes, 876, tit. "*Set-off*," note. As to set-off between *principal* and *agent*, *id.*; *policy broker* and *under-writer*, *id.*; 1 M. & P. 502; 4 Bing. 573, S. C. In actions by and against husband and wife, or the husband only, or by or against *executors*, or *administrators*, or *trustees*, &c. see Chit. Col. of Stat. *ubi supra*.

(1000) Carpenter v. Butterfield, 3 Johns. Cas. 146, *aliter* in New Jersey, Schenck v. Schenck, 5 Halst. Rep. 276. Vide Gilliat v. Lynch, 2 Leigh's R. 493.

VII. PLEAS OF SET-OFF.

rate debt against a joint one (i)(1001); but a debt due to a defendant as surviving partner may be set off against a demand on him in his own right, and *vice versa* (k) (1002). Nor can there be any set-off at law or in equity if one of the debts be due to the party in his *private* right, and the other be claimable by his opponent in *autre droit*, that is, as assignee of a bankrupt, executor, &c. (l) (1003). 2dly, With respect to the nature of the demands to be set off against each other, it will be remarked, that the statutes speak only of mutual *debts;* consequently the demand of each party must be in the nature of a *debt*, so that a set-off is excluded in all actions *ex delicto;* and it cannot be admitted even in actions *ex contractu*, if the claim of either
[*604] party be for uncertain or unliquidated *damages*, as *for not delivering goods according to contract, &c. (m). But if the plaintiff declare specially in assumpsit, with the common counts, (as in assumpsit for not accounting, with a count for money had and received,) and he might recover his whole demand, as well upon the common count as upon the special count, the benefit of a set-off may be obtained upon the common count, and the plaintiff shall not be permitted to exclude it by professing to rely upon the special count only (n). It has been held that a debt of *inferior degree* cannot be set off against one of *higher degree*, not even a bond against rent, because the latter is higher than the former (o). And 3dly, The debt attempted to be set off must be *completely due* and in *arrear* at the time the action *was commenced*, not merely at the time of *pleading* (p); and it must, at the former period, have been a legal and *subsisting* debt, and not barred by the statute of limitations (q), or satisfied in law in consequence of the debtor having been taken in execution upon a judgment by which it was recovered (r). But an attorney may set off his bill although it was not delivered a month before the commencement

(i) 5 M. & Sel. 439; 2 Taunt. 173; 4 Bing 217; Montag. 23; Eden, 2d ed. 197; 10 Ves. 106; 11 *Id.* 517; 1 Y. & J. 180. But a claim on a joint and several bond executed by the plaintiff may be set off to an ac ion brought by him, 2 T. R. 32. See further, Chit. Col. of Stat. tit. "*Set-off*," 876, note.

(k) 5 T. R. 493; 6 *Id.* 582; 2 T. R. 476.

(l) *Supra*, note (h); and see 1 Y. & J. 180.

(m) Cowp. 56, 57; 1 Bla. Rep 394; Bul. N. P. 181; M'Clel. 198; 13 Price, 434; 5 B. & Ald. 92; 3 Campb. 329.

In *replevin*, however, though a set-off cannot, in general, be pleaded to an avowry for rent, yet the plaintiff may plead in bar to an avowry or cognizance the payment of ground-rent, (4 T. R. 511; 2 Bing. 54; 9 B. & C. 245; 4 M. & R. 193, S. C.;) or of an annuity charged upon the premises (6 Taunt. 524; 2 Marsh. 22[illegible].) or of land tax, &c. paid for the same, after the rent distrained for had become due, or whilst it was accruing, though any previous payment of land tax, &c. cannot be pleaded to an avowry for rent subsequently due; though it may be sued for, 1 B. & Ald. 123; 3 Moore, 278; 1 B. & B. 37; 3 B. & Ald. 516; 4 Moore, 431; 2 B. & B. 59; 2 Chit. Rep. 531; M'Clel. 622; 4 Bing. 11.

(n) 4 Campb. 385; *ante*, 447, 587.

(o) *Per* Denman, C. J. in Davis *v.* Gyde, 1 Harr. R. 52, citing Gage *v.* Acton, 1 Salk. 326, *sed quære*.

(p) 3 T. R. 186; 1 Bing. 93; 7 Moore, 412; Braithwaite *v.* Coleman, 4 Nev. & Man. 654; and see 8 Bar. & Cres. 11; 2 M. & R. 181, S. C.

(q) Stra. 1271; Bul. N. P. 180; 1 C. & J. 1; 9 Geo. 4, c. 14, s. 4.

(r) 5 M. & Sel. 103; *sed vide* 1 Taunt. 426; 1 M. & Sel. 696; 3 East, 258.

(1001) Francis *v.* Rand, 7 Conn. Rep 221. But see Crist *v.* Brindle, 2 Rawle, 121, and Stewart *v.* Coulter, 12 Serg. & Rawle, 252, 445.

(1002) { Lewis *v.* Culbertson, Adm. 11 Serg. & Rawle, 48. }

(1003) { But an action instituted by L. upon a single bill, payable to "L., executor of B.," is an action in his own right, to which a debt due from him may be pleaded, and proved as a set-off; and he cannot go into evidence of the consideration of the bill, to show that it was for a debt due B., in order to exclude the set-off as due in another right. Turner *v.* Plowden, 2 Gill & Johns. 455. }

of the action; but it ought, if possible, to be delivered time enough to be taxed, and at least should be delivered sufficiently early to prevent the plaintiff from being taken by surprise at the trial (s). The pendency of an action for the debt set off (t), or of a writ of error where the set-off is upon a judgment (u), will not however defeat the right.

VII. PLEAS OF SET-OFF.

The *Bankrupt Act* (x) provides, that where there has been *mutual credit* given by the bankrupt and any other person, *or where there are mutual debts between the bankrupt and any other person, the *commissioners* shall state the account between them, and one debt or demand may be set against another, *notwithstanding any prior act of bankruptcy* committed by such bankrupt before the *credit* given to, or the *debt* contracted by him, and *what shall appear due* on either side on the *balance* of such account, *and no more, shall be claimed* or paid on either side respectively, and every debt or demand hereby made payable against the estate of the bankrupt, may also be set off in manner aforesaid against such estate; provided that the person claiming the benefit of such set-off had not, when such credit was given, notice of an act of bankruptcy by such bankrupt committed.

Set-off, &c. in cases of bankruptcy. [*605]

With respect to the *mode* by which the defendant should avail himself of a strict legal *set-off*, we have seen (y) that when either the debt sued for, or that which is the subject of the set-off, accrued by reason of a *penalty* contained in any bond or specialty, the statute enacts that the debt intended to be set off shall be *pleaded* in bar, and a notice of set-off is not then allowed. The plea in that case must show how much is truly due on either side, and the sum admitted in the plea to be due to the plaintiff is traversable, though laid under a *videlicet* (z); and therefore the plaintiff may, in such case, either take issue on the amount of the debt alleged to be due to himself, or may deny the defendant's set-off (a): and if the plaintiff reply that more was due on the bond than the sum named in the plea, and fail in proving that allegation, he will be nonsuited (b). But in cases where neither the plaintiff's not the defendant's debt accrued by reason of a *penalty*, the defendant has the election to *plead*, or *give notice* of his set-off. It has been said, that if at the time of the action brought, a larger sum is due from the plaintiff to the defendant, it is more proper to *plead* the set-off, but that where *the sum intended to be set off is less than that for which the action is brought, a *notice* of set-off should be given (c); but the statutes of set-off do not seem to warrant this distinction. In general a no-

Mode of setting off.

[*606]

(s) Dougl. 115, 192; 1 Esp. Rep. 449; Montag. 36.

(t) 2 Burr. 1229; Peake Rep. 210; 3 T. R. 186; 4 East, 507.

(u) 3 T. R. 188, notes; Dougl. 112; Montag. 36; *sed vide* 2 Hen. Bla. 372.

(x) 6 Geo. 4, c. 16, s. 50. There are two modes of balancing an account in the case of *bankruptcy*; 1st, Upon an action at law; or, 2dly, By the commissioners, who, by the above act, have jurisdiction to state the account without the assignees. It seems the chancellor will restrain any attempt to re-open the account by bringing an action after the commissioners have adjusted it, see 1 Rose, 395. See in general as to *set-off* and as to *mutual credit*, (which is more comprehensive than the word *debt*, in the statutes of set-off,) in cases of *bankruptcy*, Eden, 2d edit. 186 to 206; Chit. Col. of Stat. 879, n. (c); 9 B. & C. 738; 4 M. & R. 593, S. C. *Mutual credit* must, since Reg. Gen. Hil. T. 4 W. 4, be pleaded specially.

(y) *Ante*, 601, 602.

(z) 3 T. R. 65; 6 *Id*. 460.

(a) Holt, C. N. P. 293. See the forms, *post*, vol. iii.

(b) Holt, C. N. P. 293.

(c) Bul. N. P. 179; Tidd, 9th edit. 667; Montague, 41, *acc*. Lawes on Assumpsit, 538, *contra*; 6 Bing. 734.

VII. PLEAS OF SET-OFF. — Mode of setting off.

tice of set-off is less expensive than a plea; but where the plaintiff in his replication must necessarily admit a part of the defendant's case (*d*), a plea is preferable; and a set-off is usually pleaded in country causes, to save the trouble and expense of proving the service of notice (*e*).

When a set-off is not pursuant to the enactment *pleaded*, the statute (*f*) provides that the defendant's demand may be given in evidence under the *general issue* so as at the time of pleading such plea *notice* shall be given of the particular debt intended to be insisted upon by the defendant, and upon what account it became due. But as there is no general issue in an action on a specialty, and a plea of *non est factum* to an action of covenant on an indenture for non-payment of money only puts in issue the deed, such plea is not a general issue within the meaning of this act, and therefore in an action of covenant or debt on a deed, though no penalty be proceeded for, a set-off should be specially pleaded (*g*). And it seems that the statute confines the right to give a notice of set-off to a case where the general issue is pleaded alone. At all events, such *notice* cannot be given where *several* pleas are pleaded (*h*).

Semble, set-off and mutual credit now to be pleaded.

The Reg. Gen. Hil. T. 4 W. 4,† Pleadings in Assumpsit, reg. 3, orders that "*set-off* and *mutual credit must* be pleaded;" and it has been supposed that this rule abolishes a *notice of set-off* (*i*).

In cases of *bankruptcy* the accounts may be balanced either upon an action at law, or before the commissioners (*k*). And in an action at the suit of assignees, a set-off or mutual credit might formerly be given in evidence under the general issue, without a plea or notice of set-off (*l*). But now since Reg. Gen. Hil. T. 4 W. 4,† each should be pleaded. And to an action by assignee for a debt due to the bankrupt, the defendant might have pleaded a tender as to part, and give evidence of a set-off as to the rest without a plea of set-off (*m*). But it has been observed, that the practice was to plead or give notice

[*607] of set-off *in an action at law in the case of bankruptcy, in the same manner as under the general statutes relating to set-off, and that that practice seems to be just, because it apprises the plaintiff of the intended defence (*n*).

(*d*) Thus, if it be apprehended that the statute of limitations constitutes an answer to the set-off, it may be judicious to plead instead of giving notice of set-off; because the plaintiff must specially reply the statute if he intend to rely thereon. See 1 C. & J. 1. And if the set-off were on a deed executed by plaintiff, the general replication, *nil debet*, might be insufficient, and therefore in his replication the plaintiff would be compelled to admit the deed, or the existence of the debt accruing thereon.

(*e*) Tidd, 9th ed. 667; 6 Esp. Rep. 52.

(*f*) 2 Geo. 2, c. 22, s. 13.

(*g*) 1 Starkie, 311; 5 M. & Sel. 164; 2 Chit. Rep. 388, S. C.; Selw. N. P. 6th edit. 535, *acc.*; but see Bul. N. P. 181; Barnes, 191.

(*h*) R. & M. 413; 2 C. & P. 310, S. C.; 6 Esp. Rep. 50; Duncan *v.* Grant, 1 Cr. M. & Ros. 383, S. P.; 4 Tyr. 318, 818; 2 Dowl. 683, S. C.

(*i*) Bosanquet's Rules 52, note 50; Duncan *v.* Grant, 1 Crom. M. & Ros. 283; 2 Dowl. 683; 4 Tyr. 816, S. C. *Sed quære* the *notice of* set-off was given by *statute*, and Reg. Gen. Hil. T. 4 W. 4, contains no express regulation to take it away.

(*k*) *Ante*, 604; *id.* note (*x*).

(*l*) 1 T. R. 115, 116; 6 *Id.* 58, 59; Montag. 61. To assumpsit by assignees for money had and received to their use as assignees, defendant cannot plead a set-off for money due to him from the *bankrupt*; Groom *v.* Mealey, 2 Bing. N. C. 138.

(*m*) 4 Car. & P. 332.

(*n*) Montag. 61, *in notis*; and see forms, *post*, vol. iii. But where any inconvenience might result from the delivery of the particulars of the set-off, it should seem to be most advisable to plead only the general issue, in actions by assignees.

† See American Editor's Preface.

In point of form, the *plea of set-off* should not only contain all the requisites essential to the validity of other pleas in bar, but must of course show that the debt is of a nature which entitles the defendant to set it off against the plaintiff's claim (*o*); and must describe the debt intended to be set off with the same certainty as in a declaration for the like demand (*p*). With respect to *notices of set-off*, it has been observed, "that they should be almost as certain as declarations;" (*q*) and therefore where the notice of set-off was in these words, "Take notice, you are indebted to me for the use and occupation of a house for a long time held and enjoyed, and now lately elapsed," and the defendant attempted to give in evidence a demand for rent due on a lease under seal, it was held that as the lease was not mentioned in the notice, such evidence was inadmissible (*r*). But where the demand would have been recoverable under the common money counts in a declaration, the amount may be set off under a similar description of the debt, however particular the circumstances may have been (*s*). A plea of set-off so much resembles a declaration, that two parts of a plea of set-off, stating distinct debts, are considered as two counts in a declaration, and if one part be good, a demurrer for the mispleading in the other part must be confined to the defective statement, and a general demurrer to the whole is not sustainable (*t*); though we have seen, that in general if one part of a plea in bar be bad, the whole is insufficient (*u*). So, in a plea of set-off, an imperfect statement of one debt intended to be set off, will not prejudice a sufficient allegation of another ground of set-off. To the plea of set-off the plaintiff may *reply*; or in answer to the notice of set-off *may, at the trial, give in evidence the statute of limitations (*x*); but if [*608] both the demands of the plaintiff and defendant accrued more than six years before the time of pleading, and the plaintiff issued process to prevent the statute of limitations affecting his demand, it will equally prevent the statute from barring the defendant's set-off, although the latter issued no process (*y*). The statute of limitations cannot be relied upon under the usual replication of *nil debet* to the plea of set-off (*z*).

VII. PLEAS OF SET-OFF. — Mode of setting off. The *forms* of plea and *notices of set off.*

When the defendant has a cross demand against the plaintiff, of which he gives notice, but does not offer any evidence on the trial in support of it, the plaintiff may either take a verdict for the whole sum he proves to be due to him, subject to be reduced to the sum really due on a balance of accounts, if the defendant will afterwards enter into a rule not to sue for the debt intended to be set off, or he may take a verdict for the smaller sum, with a special indorsement on the *postea*, as a foundation for the Court to order a stay of proceedings, if another action should be brought for the amount of the set-off (*a*).

Besides these modes of deduction, in cases of connected accounts at common law, and of set-off and mutual credit in cases of bankruptcy, of which

Of setting off judgments and costs against each other on summary application.

(*o*) *Ante*, 602.
(*p*) See the forms of pleas and notices of set-off, *post*, vol. iii.
(*q*) Bul. N. P. 179; Selw. N. P. 4th ed. 148, n. 101.
(*r*) Bul. N. P. 179. See the proper form, *post*, vol. iii.
(*s*) 2 Esp. Rep. 560, 569.
(*t*) 2 Bla. Rep. 910.
(*u*) *Ante*, 579, 598.
(*x*) 2 Stra. 1271; Bul. N. P. 180. See *ante*, 606, note (*d*).
(*y*) 2 Esp. Rep. 569; 6 T. R. 189; 2 Saund. 127 c, d; Montag. 20, 21.
(*z*) 1 C. & J. 1.
(*a*) 1 Campb. 252; 1 Chit. R. 178.

VII. PLEAS OF SET-OFF.

we have seen the defendant may avail himself as a matter of right in defence of the action, opposite demands, as well for debts as for costs, founded on *cross judgments*, may, by the practice of the Court, in many cases, be set off against each other on a summary application to the Court; but this is rather a matter of *practice* than of *pleading*, and therefore it will suffice to refer to the practical works on the subject (b).

(b) Tidd, 9th ed. 991; Montague's Law of Set-off, 5 to 15; 6 Taunt. 176; 1 Chitty's Gen. Prac. 667.

*CHAPTER VIII.

Of Replications.

GENERAL OBSERVATIONS.

Steps to be taken before replying.

BEFORE the plaintiff *replies* or *demurs* to the plea, he should consider whether or not he *may* treat it as a nullity, and sign judgment with or without leave of the Court, as on account of the plea being such a description of *sham plea*, that the Court will not permit to be pleaded (*a*), or as being totally *inappropriate* to the form of action (*b*). If several pleas be pleaded, it will be material to consider whether some of them are not so wholly inconsistent with the rest, that the Court will on application restrain the defendant from pleading all of them (*c*). Sometimes it becomes necessary to apply to the Court to set aside the plea, or one or more of several pleas, as having been pleaded contrary to good faith, &c.; as where the defendant pleads a release, fraudulently given by a *nominal* plaintiff to the prejudice of the real claimant (*d*). And it was frequently important, where a special plea was pleaded in the King's Bench, to *rule* the defendant to *abide by* his plea, in order to prevent him, when not under terms of pleading issuably, from striking out his special plea and subsequent pleadings when the paper-book was delivered to him and returning it with the general issue, a mode of obtaining time formerly very unfairly practised (*e*). But such a rule was rendered unnecessary by Reg. Gen. Hil. T. 2 W. 4,† reg. 46, which orders that a defendant shall not be allowed to waive his plea without leave of a judge for that purpose, and which will not be granted unless justice require (*f*). It is sometimes necessary to apply to the Court of Chancery to prevent the defendant from relying on a plea, as where the statute of limitations is pleaded, and the plaintiff did not sue before in consequence of a bill in equity having been filed and injunction obtained by the defendant (*g*).

Of plaintiff's Discontinuing, and *Nolle prosequi* (*h*).

If the plaintiff perceive that he cannot support his action to any extent, he should either obtain leave to *discontinue* (*i*), *or he may enter a *nolle prosequi* as to the whole or a part of the cause of action (*k*) (1004), unless there has

[*610]

(*a*) *Ante*, 574.

(*b*) As to *nil debet* in assumpsit, &c. see *ante*, 552.

(*c*) *Ante*, 552; 2 M. & P. 19; 5 Bing. 12, S. C.; 2 M. & P. 105; 5 Bing. 42, S. C.; 6 *Id.* 197.

(*d*) 1 B. & P. 447; 7 Moore, 617; 1 Y. & J. 362; 1 Campb 392; 1 Chit Rep. 390, and notes; see further, Tidd, 9th edit. 677; fraudulent release by *one* of several plaintiffs, 1 Y. & J. 362; 1 Chit. Rep. 390.

(*e*) See Tidd, 9th edit. 673; in C. P. the defendant could not waive his plea after the plaintiff has replied, *id.* 674.

(*f*) Jervis's Rules, 54, note (*v*).

(*g*) 1 Vern. 73; 2 Y. & J. 75. But of late application to a Court of equity has been considered of very limited utility.

(*h*) See 3 Chitty's Gen. Prac. 739.

(*i*) Tidd, 9th ed. 678.

(*k*) Tidd, 9th ed. 681; see the form, *post*, vol. iii. A *nolle prosequi* to one count does not bar evidence upon another count for the same demand, *ante*, 448.

(1004) Vide Hughes v. Moore, 7 Cranch, 565. To entitle to have the benefit of the *proviso* of the statute of limitations in favor of infants, &c. the infancy and bringing of the suit within the time limited after disability removed, should be pleaded specially. Hyde v. Stone, 7 Wend. Rep. 354. Palister v. Little, 6 Greenl. Rep. 351, 352.

† See American Editor's Preface.

GENERAL OBSERVATIONS.

been a demurrer for misjoinder (*l*). Where there are several defendants in an action for a *tort*, or if in an action *ex contractu*, the plea of one of the defendants is merely in *his* particular discharge, as bankruptcy, &c. the plaintiff may enter a *nolle prosequi* as to him (*m*). So the plaintiff might enter a *stet processus* or *cassetur billa vel breve* (*n*). The points relating to *discontinuing* the action (*o*) and entering a *nolle prosequi*, &c. (*p*) are fully treated of in the Books of Practice.

What answers to the plea the plaintiff may reply.

As the replication is in general influenced by the plea, and most frequently *denies it*, the pleader has not often much difficulty in deciding what replication he should adopt. If the plea does not profess to answer the *whole* action, and leaves a part unanswered, the plaintiff should sign judgment *pro tanto* (*q*). And if a plea do not cover the whole of alleged trespasses, the plaintiff is entitled on proof of part to a verdict *pro tanto*, and need not new assign.

When the plea properly *concludes to the country*, which we have seen can only be when the allegations in the declaration have merely been traversed or denied, then the plaintiff cannot in general reply otherwise than by adding what is termed the *similiter* (*r*); but when the plea has introduced *new matter* and has therefore *concluded with a verification*, and the plaintiff does not *demur*, the replication must then either, *first*, insist that the defendant could not so plead by showing matter of *estoppel*; or, *secondly*, may *traverse* or *deny* the truth of the matter alleged in the plea *either in whole or in part*; in the first case by a general replication *de injuria*, and in the second by *a denial of a part*, according to the facts of the particular case; or, *thirdly*, the replication may *confess and avoid* the plea; in which case, as will be fully explained when we consider the *qualities* of replications in general, the truth of the matter alleged in the plea must be admitted; or, *fourthly*, in the case of an evasive plea, may *new assign* the cause of action. And though at common law a replication cannot be double, or contain two or more answers to the same plea, and the statute 4 Ann. c. 16, does not extend to replications, (except in the instance of a plea in bar to an avowry in replevin, which is in the nature of a replication,) yet the plaintiff in many cases has an *election* of different replications; thus, if infancy be pleaded in assumpsit, the plaintiff may reply, either that the defendant was of age, or that the goods, &c. were necessaries, [*611] or that the defendant after he came of age ratified and confirmed *the promise; or he may reply as to part of his demand, that it was for necessaries, and to other part, that the defendant was of full age at the time of the contract, and to the residue, that he confirmed it after he came of age. So, if an executor or administrator plead several judgments outstanding and no assets *ultra*, the plaintiff may reply as to one of the judgments, *nul tiel record*, and to another, that it was obtained or kept on foot by fraud (*s*). So, if a set-

(*l*) 1 Hen. Bla. 108; 1 Saund. 285, n. 5; 2 Marsh. 144.

(*m*) *Ante*, 599; Tidd, 9th ed. 682.

(*n*) Tidd, 9th ed. 682, 683; *ante*, 498.

(*o*) *Ante*, 227, 228, 243; Tidd, 9th ed. 678; 2 Saund. 73, n. 1; 3 Chitty's Gen. Prac. 739.

(*p*) Tidd, 9th edit. 681 to 683; 1 Saund. 207, note 2; 2 M. & Sel. 23, 444.

(*q*) Bush *v.* Parker, 1 Bing. N. C. 72.

(*r*) Com Dig. Pleader, R. 1. See observations on the *similiter*, Boote's Suit at Law, 103, note *. If a defendant at the end of his plea concluding to the country, add the, &c. that may supply the want of a formal similiter, 6 Car. & P. 712.

(*s*) 1 Saund. 337 b, note 2; 1 Salk. 298; 1 Lord Raym. 263, S. C.

off on a recognizance or judgment, and also on simple contract, be pleaded, the plaintiff may reply as to the first, *nul tiel record*, and as to the residue of the plea, *nil debet* (*t*). And if a tender be pleaded, the plaintiff may either deny the tender or its sufficiency, or may reply a demand before or after the tender, or that a writ was previously issued (*u*). And in the case of a set-off, the plaintiff may either deny the existence of the debt, or may reply the statute of limitations. And if the statute of limitations be pleaded, the plaintiff may reply either that the defendant did undertake, or that the cause of action did accrue, within six years, in the negative of the words of the plea, or that the accounts were between merchants, or that the writ was issued within six years. In short, in almost every form of action, the plaintiff has frequently the choice of one of several replications, *viz.* either, 1st, to deny the allegations in the plea, or one of them; 2dly, to insist that the defendant was *estopped* or precluded from setting up the defence relied upon in the plea; or, 3dly, admitting the allegation in the plea, the plaintiff may reply setting up new matter, as where the defendant in trespass *quare clausum fregit* pleads *liberum tenementum*, or that the close was his freehold, the replication may state a lease from the defendant to the plaintiff, which entitles him to the present action, and to sue the defendant for the trespass pending such lease.

GENERAL OBSERVATIONS.

When a defendant has pleaded a *special plea* and the plaintiff denies the *whole of the several grounds of defence* stated in such plea, then it is obvious that the most general and comprehensive replication, putting the defendant on the proof of all the material allegations in his plea, is the most advantageous to the plaintiff, because it imposes most difficulty on the defendant. In trespass to persons and personal property, where a special plea of justification or excuse had been pleaded, the plaintiff was allowed to put in issue the *whole plea*, by replying generally that the defendant committed the said alleged trespasses of his own wrong, and without the cause (*i. e.* excuse) alleged in the plea. That comprehensive mode of replying was not anciently adopted in any other form of action; but at length it seems to have been considered that such a replication is admissible *in covenant* or *special assumpsit*, in answer to a special plea in excuse of performance; for instance, a replication that the defendant *committed* the said breach or breaches of covenant, or committed or suffered the said breach of the said promises of his own wrong, and without the cause alleged in the said plea, and concluding to the country (*x*), although according to prior decisions so general a replication was illegal and insufficient (*y*). The pleader should well consider when a common replication traversing the plea will suffice, or when it must state new facts, either by special replication or new assignment; for if the latter when requisite be omitted the plaintiff may fail in toto (*z*). Where the plaintiff, instead of demurring or taking advan-

As to replications merely in *Denial* of the plea, as the replication *de injuria*, and when it is admissible.

(*t*) 1 East, 369. But the plaintiff should not reply *nul tiel record* if the recognizance be not of record, but merely deny the set-off, 1 B. & Ald. 153.

(*u*) 1 Saund. 33.

(*x*) Griffin *v.* Yates and Isaac *v.* Flather, Westminster Hall Chronicle, 382, 383.

(*y*) Noel *v.* Rich, Exchequer, Trin. T. 1835, Legal Observer, 135, 136; Solly *v.* Neish, *id.* 359; 2 Bing. N. C. 359; Crisp *v.* Griffiths, 3 Dowl. 752, 754, 755; 1 Gale, 106; Moore *v.* Boulcott, 3 Dowl. 145; 1 Bing. N. C. 323.

(*z*) Price *v.* Peck, 1 Bing. N. C. 386, 387. But as to when a new assignment is not necessary, see Nevill *v.* Cooper, 2 Crom. & M. 329; Reece *v.* Templar, 1 Harr. & Wol. 15, 16.

GENERAL OBSERVATIONS. tage of matter of estoppel, takes issue on the plea or pleas, he will lose the advantage of such estoppel (*a*).

Subdivisions of subjects relative to replications. We will consider the points relating to replications under the following divisions :—

- I. The several replications which usually occur in practice.
  - 1st. In assumpsit.
  - 2dly. In debt.
  - 3dly. In covenant.
  - 4thly. In detinue.
  - 5thly. In actions against executors and heirs.
  - 6thly. In case.
  - 7thly. In trover.
  - 8thly. Pleas in bar in replevin.
  - 9thly. In trespass.
- II. Their forms and parts.
- III. Their qualities and requisites in general.

[*612]

*I. OF THE SEVERAL REPLICATIONS.

IN ASSUMPSIT. In *assumpsit* as well as in other actions the replication may, if the plea properly conclude to the country, add the similiter, or if the plea conclude with a verification may deny the alleged matter of defence, or may confess and avoid it by replying new matter.

In assumpsit, if the defendant has pleaded *Infancy* in bar, the plaintiff may, if the plea were untrue, reply, denying the fact (*b*), or if true, he may reply, that the goods mentioned in some of the counts of the declaration to have been sold to the defendant were necessaries, which fact will not be intended unless alleged, and that the money mentioned in the count for money paid was paid in the purchase of necessaries for the defendant, and may enter a *nolle prosequi* as to the counts for money lent, had and received, and upon an account stated (*c*); or he may reply to the whole or part, that the defendant ratified and confirmed the promise after he came of age (*d*); and a ratification by defendant of his acceptance of a bill of exchange after he came of age, and before the bill fell due, will support a count on a promise to pay according to the tenor and effect of the bill (*e*). But to a plea in bar of *Coverture* at the time the promises were made, the plaintiff can only deny the fact, or reply some matter which shows that at the time the defendant was competent to contract, as that her husband was then *civiliter mortuus* (1005); and the plaintiff cannot reply that she had a separate maintenance secured to her by deed (*f*), or that the husband was an alien living out of the kingdom (*g*), and

(*a*) 4 Nev. & Man. 276, note (*c*).
(*b*) *Post*, vol. iii.; Cl. Assist. 76.
(*c*) 1 Salk. 223; *post*, vol. iii.; Cro. Jac. 560; 1 T. R. 40; Com. Dig. Pleader, 2 W. 22.
(*d*) *Post*, vol. iii.; 1 T. R. 648. See the proper form, *id.*; 1 M. & Sel. 724, 725; 3 *Id.* 481.
(*e*) Hunt *v.* Massey, 5 Bar. & Adol. 902.
(*f*) 8 T. R. 545.
(*g*) Stretton *v.* Busnach, 1 Bing. N. C. 139.

(1005) Gregory *v.* Paul, 15 Mass. Rep. 31.

therefore there is seldom any answer to this plea. When *Alien Enemy* has been pleaded, the plaintiff may either deny the fact, or if true may reply a license, &c. to reside in this country (*h*). When a discharge under the *Insolvent Act* (*i*), or *Lords' Act* (*k*) is pleaded, the replication may either deny the fact, or allege that the discharge was obtained by fraud, &c. (*l*). If *Gaming*, *Usury*, or any *other Illegality* in the consideration or contract be pleaded, the plaintiff may reply, that the contract was made upon a good and legal consideration, and not upon the supposed unlawful consideration mentioned in the plea (*m*). To a plea of *tender*, the replication might formerly have either denied the tender generally (*n*), or stated that a writ was previously issued (*o*); or a writ with *continuances (*p*); but if the plea stated that the tender was made before the commencement of the suit, instead of exhibiting the bill, then there appeared no necessity to reply the writ, and it would be sufficient to produce it in evidence (*q*); or the plaintiff might reply a prior (*r*) or subsequent (*s*) demand; or admitting the tender, might proceed to trial on the plea of *non assumpsit*, when he was prepared to prove that more was due than the sum tendered (*t*). But as since the uniformity of process act 2 W. 4, c. 39, treats the writ as the commencement of the action, it is not now necessary in any case to reply *specially* the time of issuing the writ. The replication to a plea of *Accord and Satisfaction* may either deny the delivery of the chattel in satisfaction, or protesting against that fact, may deny the acceptance (*u*), or the plaintiff may deny *both* the delivery *and* acceptance in satisfaction (*x*). If an *Award* were pleaded, the plaintiff might either deny the submission or the award, or may set out the whole award, and if bad in point of law, may demur (*y*). If a *Former Recovery* for the same debt, or a plea of SET-OFF on a recognizance of record be pleaded, the replication was to be *nul tiel record* (*z*); and to a plea of judgment recovered, the plaintiff might *New Assign* that his action was for the breach of different promises (*a*)(1006); and if the defendant pleaded a judgment recovered in an inferior Court, not stating that the contract arose within the jurisdiction of that Court, the plaintiff may reply that the cause of action arose out of its jurisdiction (*b*). To a plea of *Release*, he might reply *non est factum* (*c*), or that it was obtained by *duress* or *fraud* (*d*)(1007), and it was then considered to be unnecessary

IN ASSUMPSIT.

[*613]

(*h*) 43 Geo. 3, c. 155.
(*i*) In general, *ante*, 63.
(*k*) *Ante*, 65.
(*l*) 7 Geo. 4, c. 57, s. 61.
(*m*) Com. Dig. Pleader, 2 W. 23; 2 T. R. 439; 1 Saund. 103 b, note 3; *post*, vol. iii.; 3 Wentw. 104, 108, and *id.* Index, v.
(*n*) *Post*, vol. iii.
(*o*) *Post*, vol. iii.
(*p*) *Post*, vol. iii. When it need not be stated, 1 Wils. 167; 5 B. & Ald. 452; 1 D. & R. 27, S. C.
(*q*) 5 B. & Ald. 452; 1 D. & R. 27, S. C.; *post*, vol. iii. notes.
(*r*) *Post*, vol. iii.
(*s*) *Id.*; 1 Campb. 182.
(*t*) *Post*, vol. iii.
(*u*) *Id.*; see 3 Wentw. Index, vi. vii. x.
(*x*) 1 Bing. N. C. 502; 1 Hodges, 39, S. C.
(*y*) *Post*, vol. iii.; 3 Wentw. Index, viii.
(*z*) *Post*, vol. iii.
(*a*) *Post*, vol. iii.
(*b*) 2 Bing. 213.
(*c*) *Post*, vol. iii.
(*d*) *Id.*; 3 Wentw. Index, xii.

(1006) Vide Snider *v.* Croy, 9 Johns. Rep. 327, where it was held that the plaintiff might avoid the effect of the former judgment, by replying that he was prevented by the court from proceeding for one of the causes of action mentioned in his declaration, and which was the subject of the present suit.

(1007) It has been held in the Supreme Court of the State of New York, that to a plea of a release or payment, the plaintiff may reply that, previous to the execution of the release or to the payment, he had assigned the bond to A. B. of which the plaintiff had

IN ASSUMPSIT.

and injudicious to state the particulars of the fraud (*e*); or to a plea of release by a third person, the plaintiff might reply *ne releasa pas* (*f*). To a plea of *Set-Off* on simple contract, the plaintiff might reply *nil debet* (*g*), or the statute of limitations (*h*), or any matter which a defendant in an action might plead; but if the set-off be on a specialty or judgment, or other matter of record, such replication would be insufficient, and the plaintiff should reply *non est factum*, *nul tiel record*, or payment, &c. (*i*)—[*614] *and the statute of limitations could not be relied upon under the general replication of *nil debet*, to a plea of set-off (*k*); but where the defendant pleaded a set-off on a recognizance not of record, and on a simple contract, it was held the plaintiff should merely deny the set-off, and not reply *nul tiel record* (*l*).

Not two replications to *same* ground of defence.

As the statute 4 & 5 Ann. (*m*) does not extend to *replications*, and the statutes which give the plea of set-off do not specify *how* the plaintiff is to reply, it should seem that the plaintiff cannot reply several distinct answers to a plea of set-off. When the *Court of Conscience Act* has been pleaded, the plaintiff may deny the residence of the defendant with the jurisdiction, or may allege that more than 40*s*. &c. was due (*n*).

Replication to statute of limitations.

When the *statute of limitations* had been pleaded, either that the defendant did not undertake, or that the cause of action did not accrue, within six years "before the exhibiting of the plaintiff's bill," and the plaintiff could prove a promise or acknowledgment within that time, the replication might deny the *plea generally*, and conclude to the country (*o*)(1008); but if the time of issuing the first writ in the action were material, it must have been replied specially, as in the case of a tender; and if continued process be stated, the re-

(*e*) 9 Co. 110.
(*f*) 2 Bulstr. 55; 2 Taunt. 278; but see 1 Tyr. & Gran. 87. *Quære non est factum* should be replied if the plea state that the *plaintiff* released, see Steph. 2d ed. 239, 237.
(*g*) *Id.*
(*h*) *Post*, vol iii.
(*i*) 1 East, 369; 3 Wentw. Index, xiv.
(*k*) 1 Cromp. & Jerv. 1.
(*l*) 1 B. & Ald. 153.
(*m*) 4 Anne, c. 16.
(*n*) *Post*, vol. iii.; 3 Wentw. Index, xviii.
(*o*) *Post*, vol. iii. When an acknowledgment is of no avail, see 2 Campb. 160. This is stated by Saunders to be an anomalous case, the plaintiff being bound to do more than fully answer the plea, but see a similar case in 1 Mod. 227. See also, *post*, vol. iii.

notice. Andrews *v.* Bucker, 1 Johns. Cas. 411. Littlefield *v.* Storey, 3 Johns. Rep. 425. Raymond *v.* Squire, 11 Johns. Rep. 47. {Dawson *v.* Coles, 16 Johns. Rep. 51. Prescott *v.* Hull, 17 Johns. Rep. 284.} It is laid down however as a general rule, that matter of defence in equity cannot be pleaded. And the English courts have never gone further than to set aside the plea on an application to their equitable jurisdiction. Legh *v.* Legh, 1 Bos. & Pul. 447. Alner *v.* George, 1 Camp. 393. And they will not permit a bond debt assigned to the defendant by another person, to whom and for whose use it was originally given, to be pleaded by way of set-off. Wake *v.* Tinkler, 16 East's Rep. 36. But it has been frequently held in this country, that a debt may be the subject of a set-off, for which the party could not have maintained an action in his own name. Tuttle *v.* Bebee, 8 Johns. Rep. 152. Winchester *v.* Hackley, 2 Cranch, 342. Adm'rs of Compty *v.* Alken, 2 Bay, 483. Caines *v.* Brisban, 13 Johns. Rep. 9. The case of Winch *v.* Keely, 1 Term Rep. 619, fully supports our practice of permitting an assignment to be replied: that was an action of *assumpsit;* the defendant pleaded the bankruptcy of the plaintiff; the plaintiff replied that before his bankruptcy he assigned the debt to J. S., and averred that the writ was sued out in the name of the plaintiff, for and on the behalf of J. S.: this replication was held good on demurrer. The Supreme Court of the United States, in a late case, fully confirmed the doctrine, that the equitable rights of a third person, not party to the record, might be replied to as legal bar. Welch *v.* Mandeville, 1 Wheaton, 233.

(1008) Bargamin *v.* Poitiax, 4 Leigh's Rep. 419.

turn of the first must have been shown (*p*); but this did not seem necessary when the plea stated "before the commencement of the suit," instead of "exhibiting the bill," (*q*) though a special replication was in general advisable, because it may reduce the proof to be adduced by the plaintiff on the trial (1009). The replication might also be that the plaintiff or the defendant was abroad when the cause of action accrued, and that the action was commenced within six years after his first return (*r*)(1010); and any other circumstance which brought the case within either of the exceptions mentioned in the statute should have been replied (*s*)(1011). As the uniformity of process act 2 W. 4, c. 39, now declares that the issuing of the writ of summons, capias or detainer shall be considered in all cases to be the commencement of the action, the plea of the statute of limitations will always be that the defendant did not promise or that the causes of action did not accrue within six years *next before the commencement of this suit;* and no special replication showing the time of commencing the action can be required. IN ASSUMPSIT.

When the alleged matter of defence is to be denied, it has been usual in the replication to traverse the *most material part*, but there are cases where *all the grounds* of defence may conjunctively be traversed without rendering the replication bad for multifariousness; thus to a plea of delivery of a pipe of wine in satisfaction, the replication may traverse as well the delivery as the acceptance (*t*), and although it has been doubted whether a replication *de injuria* in assumpsit is not too comprehensive (*u*), the most recent decisions seem to establish that it may in some cases be sufficient (*x*). If the plea in effect de-

(*p*) *Post*, vol. iii.
(*q*) 5 B. & Ald. 452; 1 D. & R. 27, S. C. See *post*, vol. iii. note.
(*r*) *Post*, vol. iii.; 4 Bar. & Cres. 625.
(*s*) See the instances, *post*, vol. iii.; 3 Wentw. Index, xx. &c. See as to replying fraud, 2 B. & C. 149.
(*t*) 1 Bing. N. C. 502; 1 Hodges, 32, S. C.
(*u*) 2 Bing. N. C. 359; 3 Dowl. 754, 755; 1 Gale, 106, 227, where see form of replication *de injuria*, in assumpsit.
(*x*) Griffin *v.* Yates, and Isaac *v.* Flather, Westminster Hall Chronicle, 382, 383, and see 1 Crom. & M. 500.

(1009) See Satterlee *v.* Sterling, 8 Cow. Rep. 232. Livingston *v.* Ostrander, 9 Wend. Rep. 306.

(1010) Plummer *v.* Woodburne, 7 Dowl. & Ryl. 25. In an action for a breach of a contract in making a turnpike road, the defendants pleaded the statute of limitations; the plaintiffs replied fraud and deceit in the execution of the work, and that the action was commenced within six years after the discovery of the fraud: the court held that fraud might be replied to a plea of the statute, which did not become a bar until six years after the fraud was discovered, and accordingly that the replication was good. First Massachusetts Turnpike Corporation *v.* Field and others, 3 Mass. Rep. 201.

In suits not affected by the Revised Statutes in respect to the limitation of actions and the bringing of new suits by executors, &c. he may bring a new suit at any time before the expiration of the limitation by statute; but a replication showing the commencement of a new action after two years, subsequent to the abatement of the first, is bad. Huntington *v.* Brinckerhoff, 10 Wend. Rep. 284.

The cases whether open accounts are or are not barred (though they be between merchant and merchant,) where the last item is above five years standing, Chancellor Kent is in favor of the bar in such cases. Carter *v.* Murray, 5 J. C. R. 522 and a like opinion is intimated in 6 Ves. 580. 15 ib. 196. 18 ib. 286. Yet in Foster *v.* Hodgson, 19 ib. 179, 185 the whole matter seems to be again unsettled in England. But in Mandeville *v.* Willson, 5 Cranch, 15, the supreme court was clearly of opinion, that it is *not* necessary that any of the items, in the case of merchants' accounts, should come within the five years. And this also the court of appeals in Virginia considered the reasonable doctrine. Watson *v.* Lyle, 4 Leigh's Rep. 236.

(1011) In an action by joint plaintiffs, a replication to a plea of the statute of limitations, must avoid the effect of the bar as to all the plaintiffs; for it seems to be a settled rule that all must be competent to sue, otherwise the action cannot be supported. Marsteller and others *v.* M'Clean, 7 Cranch, 156.

IN ASSUMPSIT. nied or showed that no valid contract or promise was ever made, or claimed for the defendant an *interest* in the goods stated in the declaration, then a replication *de injuria* or *that defendant broke his promise of his own wrong*, without the cause stated in the plea, would be insufficient, because, in the first case, the plea in effect was that the defendant *never undertook*, and therefore it is illogical to reply that he broke his promise (y); but if the plea merely stated in effect *an excuse* for the breach, then such a general replication would be admissible (z). The Court of Common Pleas and Exchequer have recently so decided in two cases, on the *general principles of pleading*, and not on consideration of the convenience of permitting such a replication (z); but the applicability of that general replication will presently be fully considered.

[*615] IN DEBT. On Simple Contract and on specialties. *In actions of DEBT on *simple* contract, the replications have always been and are to be substantially the same as in the action of assumpsit. If to debt on a *specialty*, fraud or duress be pleaded, the plaintiff may reply that it was duly or fairly obtained (a), or he denies the plea of infancy (b), or to a plea of usury, gaming, &c. traverses the illegality of the contract (c). Replications to a plea of tender resemble those in assumpsit (d); and to a plea of set-off to debt on bond, the replication may either deny the subject-matter of the defendant's set-off or allege that more was due on the bond than the sum mentioned in the plea (e). The only replication to a plea of *solvit ad* or *post diem* is a denial of the payment (f)(1012); and if to debt on an annuity bond or deed, it be pleaded that no memorial was enrolled containing the names of the witnesses, &c. the replication sets out the memorial *verbatim*, and states that it was duly enrolled (g). If to debt on a bail bond by the assignee of the sheriff, the defendant has pleaded ease and favor, the plaintiff should reply, stating that it was duly executed, and deny the ease and favor (h); or if the action be in the name of the sheriff, and the bond is not set forth in the plea, the plaintiff should pray that the bond may be enrolled, and then set it out, and state that he was sheriff, &c. and the arrest of the defendant, and that the bond was made to the plaintiff as sheriff, and traverse the ease and favor (i); and to a plea of release, it is sufficient to deny it in the replication (k).

Replications in actions on *Bonds*. At common law, and independently of the statute 8 & 9 Wm. 3, c. 11, s. 8 (1013), it is frequently necessary in a bond for performance of covenants,

(y) Solly v. Neish, 1 Gale, 227.
(z) Griffin v. Yates, and Isaac v. Flather, Hil. T. 1836, 1 Westminster Chronicle, 382, 383.
(a) Com. Dig. Pleader, 2 W. 19, 20.
(b) *Post*, vol. iii.
(c) *Id.*
(d) *Id.*
(e) 3 T. R. 65; *post*, vol. iii.
(f) *Post*, vol. iii. See 5 Moore, 198; 2 Chit. Rep. 697, S. C.
(g) *Post*, vol. iii.
(h) *Post*, vol. iii.; 1 Saund. 159; Com. Dig. Pleader, 2 W. 25.
(i) 1 Lutw. 680, 685; 2 Saund. 60 a, note 3.
(k) 2 Burr. 944.

(1012) A general replication to the plea of "payment," does not of itself constitute an issue. Nadenbouch v. M'Rea, Gilm. Rep. 228.

(1013) This statute has not been adopted in Massachusetts, Sevey v. Blacklin and others, 2 Mass. Rep. 542. { It is in force in Pennsylvania, 3 Binn. 625. Roberts' Dig. 139. }

where the defendant has pleaded performance, and the plaintiff has not assigned the breach in his declaration (*l*), to deny the effect of the plea, and show a particular breach. The rule is, that in all cases, (except in the case of an award, which stands upon a particular ground), when the defendant pleads matter of excuse, which admits a non-performance, it is sufficient if the plaintiff deny the plea, and he need not assign a breach in his replication, but *it is otherwise where the defendant has pleaded performance, or in other words, where the plea does not put in issue any particular fact or breach (*m*); and in the latter case, to a plea of general performance of the condition of the bond, the replication must state the breach with particularity, and should conclude with a verification, in order that the defendant may have an opportunity of answering it (*n*). And in the case of bonds affected by the 8 & 9 Wm. 3, c. 11, s. 8, the plaintiff should state in his replication, (or suggest, in case of *non est factum*, &c. pleaded,) all the breaches of the bond, &c. on which he means to rely (*o*) (1014). It must necessarily depend on the nature of the case and the plea, as to what will amount to a plea of general performance, or one which in effect puts in issue a particular fact. In debt on a bond, conditioned for the performance of an award, if the defendant has pleaded no award, the replication must state the whole of the award *verbatim*, and also assign a breach (*p*). If to debt on a bastardy or indemnity bond, the defendant plead *non damnificatus*, the plaintiff must reply specially, setting forth how he was damnified (*q*). Upon a bond conditioned that a collector of poor-rates shall render an account of monies received, after general performance pleaded, it is necessary to reply that he received monies to be accounted for (*r*). But where to debt on bond the defendant craved oyer, and after reciting a mortgage deed, which showed the condition to be for payment of a sum of money on a day specified, according to the tenor of a proviso contained in the indenture, and for the performance of the covenants therein pleaded, that there were no negative or disjunctive covenants in the indenture, and that he paid the money mentioned in the condition on the day therein specified according to the effect thereof, and performed all the covenants and provisoes in the indenture on his part to be performed; and the plaintiff in his replication took issue generally on the non-payment of the money, and concluded to the country; on special demurrer, assigning for causes that *it should have concluded with a verification, and that no breach of the condition was assigned according to the 8 & 9 Wm. 3, c. 11, s. 8, it was held that such replication was good, as the only point in issue was the payment of the money, and as the plaintiff had

IN DEBT.

On specialties.

[*616]

[*617]

(*l*) It is now considered best not to assign the breach in the declaration, see *post*.

(*m*) Willes, 12, 13.

(*n*) 2 Burr. 774; 1 Saund. 101, 102; Com. Dig. Pleader, F. 14, 15; *post*, vol. iii.

(*o*) See 1 Saund. 58, n. 1; 2 Saund. 187 a, n. 2; 2 New Rep. 362; 2 Moore, 220; 5 M. & Sel. 60.

(*p*) Willes, 12; 2 Saund. 62 b, n. 5; 1 Saund. 103, n. 1; n. 4, 317. See the mode, 1 Price, 109; 6 Taunt. 45, 47.

(*q*) *Post*, vol. iii.

(*r*) 6 Taunt. 45; 1 Marsh. 441, S. C.; *semble*, over-ruling 1 Price, 109; and see Dougl. 214. Sums received need not be specially mentioned, &c. As to replication, rejoinder, surrejoinder, &c. see 7 B. & C. 809.

(1014) In an action on a bond requiring the assignment of breaches of the condition, the plaintiff, since the *Revised Statutes*, is bound to assign his breaches in the declaration, and can no longer, as was the former practice, assign them in the replication or upon the record. Reed *v.* Drake, 7 Wend. Rep. 345.

IN DEBT. — On specialties.

therein denied the whole substance of the defendant's plea (s). And a plea (to a declaration on a bond conditioned amongst other things for the payment of £3000) that all the sums of money which became due on the bond were paid, may be replied to generally by a general denial of the words of the plea, without assigning any breach (t). The mode of framing the replication will be hereafter considered (u).

Before the passing (x) of the 8 & 9 Wm. 3, c. 11, s. 8, the plaintiff, in an action on a bond, with a condition for the performance of any thing, could only have assigned one breach, and under that assignment was entitled to the full penalty of the bond; but now by the above statute, it is enacted, "that in an action upon a bond, or any penal sum for non-performance of any covenants or agreements in any indenture, deed, or writing contained, the plaintiff *may assign as many breaches* of the covenants and agreements as he shall think fit; and the jury, upon the *trial* of such action or actions, shall and may assess not only such damages and costs of suit as have heretofore been usually done in such cases, but also *damages* for such of the said *breaches* so to be assigned as the plaintiff upon the trial of the issues shall prove to have been broken, and that the like judgment shall be entered on such verdict as heretofore hath been usually done in such like actions." Where the defendant does not plead, the statute provides, "that if judgment shall be given for the plaintiff on *demurrer*, or by *confession* or *nil dicit*, the plaintiff *may suggest* upon the *roll* as many breaches as he shall think fit;" and upon such suggestion, a writ of inquiry is to be executed before the judge at the assizes, or at *nisi prius*, according to the *venue*, to ascertain the *truth of the breaches*, and to assess the plaintiff's *damage* (y). This statute is compulsory on the plaintiff to proceed [*618] *in the method it prescribes (z); and under the act the breaches must be assigned as at common law, not merely in the words of the condition, but specially stating the facts (a). At one time it was considered advisable to state the breaches in the declaration, because it was supposed that if the defendant should plead *non est factum* or any other plea on which the plaintiff might at common law have taken issue in his replication, without assigning a breach, it would be incorrect to assign a breach in a replication to such a plea: but the better opinion now is, *that the breaches should not be stated in the declaration*, but reserved for the replication, because the defendant in rejoining can only present one answer to each breach, whereas in pleading to the declaration he may answer each breach by any number of pleas; and if the defendant plead any plea on which the plaintiff might at common law have taken an issue in his replication, without assigning a breach of the condition of the bond, the plaintiff may still take issue, and enter a distinct and separate suggestion in the nature of an assignment of breaches

Whether to state breach of condition in the *declaration*, or not until replication.

(s) 5 Moore, 198.
(t) 2 Chit. Rep. 697.
(u) See *post*, vol. iii.; 13 East, 1; 1 T. R. 743; 1 Lutw. 421; 2 Saund. 410; 2 Burr. 772; 1 B. & P. 140; 8 T. R. 459.
(x) See the reason explained, *ante*, 260, 261.
(y) There are also provisions that the proceedings shall be stayed on payment of the sum really due, with costs, and that the judgment shall be a security for *future* breaches on a further suggestion being entered, &c.
(z) 1 Saund. 58; 2 *Id.* 107 a, n. 2; 2 Wils. 377; Sayer on Damages, 67, S. C.; Cowp. 357; Tidd's Prac. 9th edit. 584; 13 East, 3, (a). The statute does not bind the crown, 1 Y. & J. 171.
(a) 1 Marsh. 95; 5 Taunt. 358, S. C.

under the statute, though he cannot *incorporate* such issue and such suggestion in one and the same replication (*b*). If the defendant plead any plea which makes it necessary for the plaintiff at common law to assign a breach in the replication, as for instance, general performance, the plaintiff must still assign the breach in the replication, with this difference, that he may now assign several breaches under the statute, whereas at common law he could only assign one. If only one breach be assigned in the replication, it is not necessary to state that it is assigned "according to the form of the statute," and it is doubtful whether that allegation be necessary in any case (*c*). If issue joined on *non est factum* and plea of fraud, and there be no suggestion of breaches, the judge will try the issues, but refuse immediate execution, and leave the plaintiff to suggest breaches, &c. (*d*) The breach of the condition of a bond, otherwise well assigned, is not vitiated by the superaddition of immaterial breaches (*e*).

IN DEBT. On specialties.

Where there is *no plea* to the declaration, and consequently no *issue* to be tried, judgment, either upon demurrer or by default, is to be signed for the penalty, as at common law, and the plaintiff suggests breaches on the roll, *of [*619] which a copy should be given to the defendant, with notice of inquiry for the sittings or assizes, and a writ of inquiry is executed, and upon that there is an award of execution (*f*).

This statute does not extend to a bond conditioned for the payment of a sum certain at a day certain, or to a *post obit* bond (*g*); nor a common money bond (*h*); nor a warrant of attorney payable by instalments (*i*), though a bond be also given (*k*); nor to a bail bond (*l*), nor a petitioning creditor's bond (*m*), nor a replevin bond (*n*). But *bonds for the payment of money by instalments* (*o*), or of annuities, or for the performance of an award, are within the statute (*p*). And although a bond be on the face of it a common money bond, yet if there be a concurrent instrument showing that it is in substance a bond intended to secure the performance of covenants, &c. within the meaning of the statute, it is necessary to suggest or assign breaches in pursuance of the act, although the bond does not refer to the instrument which explains it (*q*).

The 3 & 4 W. 4, c. 42, s. 5, gives a special replication of a written acknowledgement or part payment to a *plea of the statute of limitations* to debt on an *indenture*, specialty, or recognizance, under the third section.

To a plea of *nul tiel record* in debt on a record, the replication must state that there is such record, and conclude *prout patet per recordum*, with a

On records, &c.

(*b*) See 2 Saund. 187 a, &c. and note (*c*) by the editors of the 5th edit.; 5 M. & Sel. 60; 5 Moore, 198; 1 Marsh. 95; 5 Taunt. 386; 8 T. R. 255; 2 Chit. Rep. 278; 2 N. R. 362; 2 Moore, 220; Tidd, 9th ed. 686. See, however, 3 C. & P. 608, why better in declaration.

(*c*) 13 East, 1; 2 Saund. 187 a, &c. 5th edit.

(*d*) D'Aranda *v.* Houston, 6 Car. & P. 512, 514.

(*e*) Stothert *v.* Goodfellow, 1 Nev. & Man. 202.

(*f*) Tidd, 9th edit. 585; see forms, &c. *post*, vol. iii.

(*g*) 2 B. & C. 82, 89; 3 D. & R. 278, S. C.; 2 Campb. 285; 2 Moore, 220.

(*h*) 4 Ann. c. 16, s. 13; 1 Saund. 58, 5th edit.

(*i*) 3 Taunt. 74; 5 *Id.* 264; 16 East, 164; 6 Bing. 335; 5 B. & C. 656.

(*k*) 2 Taunt. 195.

(*l*) 2 B. & P. 446.

(*m*) 3 East, 22; 7 T. R. 300.

(*n*) 3 M. & Sel. 155.

(*o*) D'Aranda *v.* Houston, 6 Car. & P. 511, S. P.

(*p*) See 8 T. R. 126; 6 East, 550, 613; 2 Saund. 187, n. c; Tidd, 9th ed. 584; 3 M. & Sel. 156.

(*q*) 5 B. & C. 650; 8 D. & R. 424, S. C.

IN DEBT. On records, &c. prayer that it may be inspected, &c. (r) (1015). If to debt on a recognizance of bail, the defendant has pleaded no *ca. sa.* against the principal, the replication must state the *ca. sa.* and conclude with a verification (s); and where the defendant has pleaded the death of the principal, before the return of a *ca. sa.*, the writ and return must be replied, and it must be averred that the principal was then living (t). If to debt on a *statute* the defendant plead a prior action depending, or a compromise by rule of Court, &c., the plaintiff may traverse the fact, or reply *per fraudem* (u).

[*620] IN COVENANT. *In COVENANT, as the declaration states the breach, and the plea usually denies it, and concludes to the country, a special replication does not so often occur as in assumpsit and some other actions (x)(1016).

IN ACTIONS AGAINST EXECUTORS, &c. In actions, whether of assumpsit, debt, or covenant, against an EXECUTOR or ADMINISTRATOR, as such, to the plea of *ne unques* executor, or administrator, the plaintiff may re-assert the fact (y). To the plea of *plene administravit*, if untrue, the plaintiff should reply, that at the time of the exhibiting the bill, or the commencement of the suit, the defendant had assets (z); or if assets have come to his hands since the commencement of the suit, and before the plea (a), or if at the time the defendant first had notice of the action he had assets, but unduly administered them afterwards, these facts may be replied specially (b). So, if the plea be *plene administravit*, except a sum not sufficient to satisfy bonds or judgments outstanding, the plaintiff may reply that the defendant had assets *ultra* (c); or that the judgments mentioned in the plea were obtained by fraud and covin (d), or suffered fraudulently for more than was due (e), or that the bond pleaded as an outstanding debt is satisfied, and kept on foot by fraud (f). If the plaintiff cannot deny the plea of *plene administravit* he should pray judgment of assets *quando acciderint*, either generally or specially; as, "which, after satisfying monies due on the outstanding judgments, bonds, &c. mentioned in the defendant's plea, shall come to the defendant's hands as executor, &c. to be administered;" (g) or if *plene administravit præter* a sum acknowledged to be in hand has been pleaded, the plaintiff should pray and take judgment *pro tanto*, and of assets *quando acciderint* as to the residue in case the plea be true. If the defendant has pleaded the general issue, or any other plea denying the debt or cause of action,

(r) Com. Dig. Pleader, 2 W. 13; *post*, vol. iii.
(s) 2 T. R. 576; *post*, vol iii.
(t) *Post*, vol. iii.; see Petersdorff on Bail.
(u) *Post*, vol iii.
(x) See the forms, *post*, vol. iii.; 5 Wentw. Index, cii. to cxliv.
(y) *Post*, vol. iii.
(z) *Id.*
(a) 6 T. R. 10; 3 Wentw. 281.
(b) *Post*, vol. iii.
(c) *Id.*
(d) *Post*, vol. iii.; *ante*, 611.
(e) 5 T. R. 82; *post*, vol. iii.
(f) *Post*, vol. iii.; Com. Dig. Pleader, 2 D. 9.
(g) Com. Dig. Pleader, 2 D. 9; *post*, vol. iii.

(1015) { Share v. Becker, 8 Serg. & Rawle, 239. }
(1016) Morris v. Wadsworth, 11 Wend. Rep. 100.

with the *plea of *plene administravit*, the plaintiff must proceed to trial to establish his debt, and on the prayer of judgment of assets, *quando*, &c. upon the plea of *plene administravit*, there is a stay of judgment till the determination of the issue. But where the debt has not been denied, and the defendant has merely pleaded *plene administravit* generally or specially, and the plaintiff prays judgment of assets *quando acciderint* thereon, there should be an entry of that judgment immediately, and an award of an inquiry to ascertain the amount of the plaintiff's demand, unless the defendant has by *cognovit* confessed the same in order to save the expense of an inquiry (*h*); or unless in reference to the form of action the judgment is final in the first instance, as in debt, &c. On a plea of *plene administravit præter*, the plaintiff is entitled to judgment of assets *in futuro quando* for *costs* as well as for the debt (*i*), and the plaintiff should not take issue on the plea, for if he do, and the plea be found for the defendant, the latter will be entitled to all the costs (*k*). IN ACTIONS AGAINST EXECUTORS, &c.

In debt against an HEIR on the bond of his ancestor, to a plea of parol demurrer, the plaintiff may deny or confess the plea (*l*); and to a plea of *rien per descent* the plaintiff may reply either that the defendant had such assets at the time of the commencement of the suit (*m*), or that he had them between that time and the death of his ancestor (*n*)(1017), or if *rien præter* a reversion be pleaded the plaintiff may take judgment, &c. *cum acciderint* (*o*).

In an ACTION ON THE CASE for a libel or verbal slander, the general replication *de injuriâ suâ propria absque tali causa*, (the nature of which will be hereafter fully considered), is sufficient to a plea of justification when untrue (*p*)(1018); unless the plea allege that the plaintiff committed perjury in a Court of record, when this general replication would be improper, because it would refer the matter of record to be tried by the jury (*q*). So if in an action on the case for slander of title, if the defendant has pleaded that he spoke them in defence of his own title, the replication *de injuria* is incorrect on general demurrer, though good after verdict (*r*). But if the plea be true, the plaintiff must reply some matter in confession and avoidance; as that after the commission of the crime, and before the speaking, &c. he was pardoned, &c. (*s*) IN CASE.

To a plea by a sheriff in an action for *an escape*, that the *escape was negligent, and that the party was taken on fresh suit, the plaintiff may reply that the escape was voluntary, or allege that the party was not, after the retaking, [*622]

(*h*) *Post*, vol. iii.; see *ante*, 526.
(*i*) Cox *v.* Peacock, 2 Scott's Rep. 125.
(*k*) Iggulden *v.* Tenson, 2 Dowl. 277.
(*l*) *Post*, vol. iii; Com. Dig. Pleader, 2 E. 4.
(*m*) *Id.*
(*n*) *Id.*; 5 Mod. 122, 123.
(*o*) Com. Dig. Pleader, E. 4, 5.
(*p*) 1 Saund. 244, note 7; Com. Dig. Pleader, 3 L. 4; *post*, vol. iii.
(*q*) Leon. 81, 102; Com. Dig. Pleader, F. 20.
(*r*) Cro. Jac. 163, 164; *post*.
(*s*) Dan. 163; Moore, 868, 872.

(1017) And the replication in this case may conclude with a verification. Labagh and wife *v.* Cantine and others, 13 Johns. Rep. 272.
(1018) { Allen *v.* Crowfoot, 7 Cow. Rep. 46. }

IN CASE. kept in safe custody (t). If accord and satisfaction, or the statute of limitations be pleaded in case or trover, the replications will resemble those in assumpsit (u).

PLEAS IN BAR IN REPLEVIN. It has been supposed that in *Replevin de injuria* never occurs (x)(1019); but this is not so; and to an avowry under a distress for an arrear of a poor-rate a general plea in bar *de injuria* is sufficient (y); but by the statute (z) he may in general, with leave of the Court, plead several *pleas in bar*. If the defendant has pleaded *cepit in alio loco*, with an avowry or cognizance for a return, the plaintiff cannot traverse any matter in the avowry or cognizance, but must take issue on the traverse of the place or amend his declaration; but if the defendant *had* them in the place mentioned in the declaration, though he *took* them elsewhere, the plaintiff may safely take issue (a); and to any cognizance the plaintiff may traverse that the defendant was bailiff, concluding to the country (b).

To an avowry or cognizance for *rent*, the plaintiff may in one plea in bar deny the demise or tenancy (c), and in another, that any part of the rent was in arrear (d) (1020), concluding each to the country (e); or he may plead payment of rent to a ground landlord, or prior incumbrancer, or of land or property tax in respect of the premises, though he cannot avail himself of any other set-off (f). So a party may plead a former distress and satisfaction

(t) 1 B. & P. 413, 416, 417; 1 Saund. 35, note 1; 2 T. R. 127; 5 East, 293; see 11 East, 406.

(u) *Ante*, 613, 614.

(x) Finch's Law, 396; 1 B. & P. 76; 2 Saund. 284 c, n. 3.

(y) Bardons *v.* Selby, 1 Crom. & Mees, 500, in Exchequer Chamber, and S. C. in K. B. 3 B. & Adol. 2. But *de injuria* is a bad replication to a plea justifying an entry as landlord to distrain, 4 Tyr. 777.

(z) 4 Anne, c. 16.

(a) 1 Saund. 347, note 1; *post*, vol. iii.; Ast. Ent. 475. And as to the pleas in bar connected with the *place*, see 1 Saund. 347, note 1; Com. Dig. Pleader, 3 K. 11 to 29.

(b) *Post*, vol. iii.; Ld. Raym. 641; Com. Dig. Pleader, K. 14.

(c) *Post*, vol. iii.; Com. Dig. Pleader, 3 K. 16, 20 b.

(d) *Post*, vol. iii.; Com. Dig. Pleader, 3 K. 16, 20.

(e) Ld. Raym. 641; 1 Saund. 103 b.

(f) 4 T. R. 511; 6 Taunt. 524; Dougl. 624, 625; 2 Chit. Rep. 531; 2 Bing. 94. And as to pleas of payment of ground rent, see 1 B. & B. 37; 3 Moore, 287, S C.; see 3 B. & Ald. 516; As to property-tax, 1 B. & Ald. 123; *post*, vol. iii.

(1019) Vide Hopkins *v.* Hopkins, 10 Johns. Rep. 369. But if pleaded, it can only be taken advantage of by demurrer. Ibid. Lytle *v.* Lee and Ruggles, 5 Johns. Rep. 112.

(1020) Middleton's Ex. *v.* Quigley, 7 Halst. Rep. 352. A plea of no rent in arrear is an admission of the demise and of the title of the defendant, as laid in the avowry. Alexander *v.* Harris, 4 Cranch, 299. Hill *v.* Wright, 2 Esp. Rep. 669. Hill *v.* Miller, 5 Serg. & Rawle, 255. Hence the advantage of also pleading *non dimisit*. The general principle is, that any thing may be given in evidence under the *general issue*, which shows that no right of action ever existed; and in some cases facts may be shown which prove that no right of action existed at the *commencement of the suit*. In *debt* for rent, the defendant, under the plea of *nil debet*, may show an eviction by the plaintiff. But in *covenant*, an eviction cannot be proved, unless pleaded. *Riens in arrere* is the general issue to an avowry for rent; and under it an eviction may be shown. Lewis et al. *v.* Payn, 4 Wend. Rep. 423. If the lord or lessor disseises or ousts the tenant or lessee of any part, the whole rent is suspended. (9 Coke, 135.) This principle was recognized and adopted in Dyett *v.* Pendleton, 8 Cowen, 728. In that case it was said that such defence could be given in evidence under a plea of eviction only; that, however, was an action of covenant, in which there is no general issue. In the case of Watts *v.* Coffin, 11 Johns. Rep. 499, it was said by Van Ness, Justice, that an eviction to produce an apportionment or a suspension of the rent, must be of part or the whole of the thing demised.

PLEAS IN BAR IN REPLEVIN.

under it (g); eviction is also a good plea in bar (h). But since the statute 11 Geo. 2, c. 19, when the defendant avails *himself of the general avowry, the plaintiff cannot in terms plead *nil habuit in tenementis*; though he may traverse the tenancy, which if the avowant claims under a derivative title and has never received rent, will put such title in issue (i). So where the plaintiff admits the tenancy and that part of the rent was in arrear, he may plead *rien en arrere* as to part, and a tender of the residue (k) (1021).

To an avowry or cognizance by a freeholder, or a copyholder, or his tenant, for a *distress damage feasant*, the plaintiff may deny his title, and conclude to the country; or state his own title specially, and conclude with a traverse; though the former seems preferable (m). So the plaintiff may in his plea in bar state a demise to himself from the defendant (n); or a right of common in the *locus in quo* either as a freeholder or copyholder, or as his tenant (o). In general, a freeholder claims a right of common by *prescription* (p); and a copyholder grounds the right upon a *custom* within the manor, either for all copyholders within the manor, or for the tenant of the defendant's land in particular (q). Where a copyholder claims common or other profit in the soil of a stranger, which is not parcel of the manor, he must prescribe in the name of the *lord*, viz. that the lord of the manor and his ancestors, and all those whose estate he hath, have immemorially had common, &c. in the *locus in quo* for themselves and their customary tenants (r). So the plaintiff may plead in bar a right of way over the *locus in quo* (s); or in excuse for the cattle having been in the *locus in quo*, he may plead defect of fences, which the defendant ought to have repaired (t); so, admitting that the cattle trespassed in the *locus in quo*, the plaintiff may traverse that the distress was made whilst the cattle were *damage feasant* (u); or may *plead a tender before the impounding (x). [*624] It should seem that in the case of a distress *damage feasant*, the plaintiff might plead in bar, that the avowant, after making the distress, *used* the cattle, or otherwise became a trespasser *ab initio* (y) (1022).

(g) 5 Moore, 542; 4 Moore, 409; 1 B. & Ald. 157.

(h) *Post*, vol. iii.

(i) 2 Wils. 208; 5 T. R. 4; 2 Saund. 284 d; 1 New Rep. 56; 4 Moore, 303; 2 Bing. 54, 10; 4 T. R. 511; *ante*, 487. *Non tenuit* is not pleadable to a cognizance for rent in arrear under a demise of a receiver in Chancery, 4 Bing. 2.

(k) *Post*, vol. iii.; Clift. Ent. 646; Com. Dig. Pleader, 3 K. 20.

(m) *Post*, vol. iii.; 2 Saund. 206 a, note 22; 1 Saund. 103 b; 1 Co. 63, 64.

(n) *Post*, vol. iii.

(o) *Id.*; Com. Dig. Pleader, 3 K. 24.

(p) *Post*, vol. iii.; Com. Dig. Pleader, 3 K. 24; 1 Saund. 348, note 10.

(q) *Id.*; 1 Saund. 348, note 8, 11.

(r) 1 Saund 349, note 11; Com. Dig. Pleader, 3 K. 24; see the forms referred to, *post*, vol. iii.

(s) Com. Dig. Pleader, 3 K. 24; *post*, vol. iii.

(t) *Post*, vol. iii.; 2 Saund. 284 c, 285, n. 4, 289, n. 7; 2 Hen. Bla. 527.

(u) 3 Esp. Rep. 95.

(x) *Post*, vol. iii.; Com. Dig. Pleader, 3 K. 23; Bul. N. P. 60; Lutw. 1596; 1 Campb. 285; 1 Taunt. 261, S. C., *et vide* 1 Bing. 341; 8 Moore, 234, S. C.; 4 Bing. 230; 2 Moore, 454, S. C.

(y) Com. Dig. Pleader, 3 K. 20; Bac. Ab. Trespass, B.; 3 Wils. 20; 1 M. & P. 802; *ante*, 158. *Aliter* in the case of a distress for rent, *ante*, 158.

(1021) There can be no such thing as a general issue to an avowry; but some special point must be traversed. Hill *v.* Miller, 5 S. & R. 357.

(1022) Acc. Hopkins *v.* Hopkins, 10 Johns. Rep. 369.

REPLICATIONS IN TRESPASS.

In trespass to persons, if the defendant has pleaded *son assault demesne*, and self defence, or a defence of a father, mother, son, &c., or any other plea merely in excuse (1023) of an injury to the person, (and not a justification under process of a court of record,) the replication or general traverse *de injuriâ*, or *de son tort demesne*, the qualities of which will be explained hereafter, is in general proper if the plea be wholly untrue (z). And this *general replication* will suffice, though title be alleged as inducement; as if to a declaration for an assault and battery, the defendant plead that he was possessed, (or, according to some cases, seized in fee) (a) of a close, and had cut his corn, and that the plaintiff came to take it away, and the defendant, in defence thereof, assaulted the plaintiff, *de son tort* is a good replication (b). But if the plea be true, and the plaintiff did in fact commit what in point of law amounted to the first assault, *but can justify it, he must reply specially*, confessing and avoiding the plea; as if the plaintiff did in fact make the first assault in defence of his father, son, &c. or to turn the defendant out of his house, whereupon the defendant assaulted and beat the plaintiff, *this answer to the plea must be replied specially* (c). So, if the defendant has pleaded *son assault demesne* in defence of the possession of his close, and the plaintiff claim a right of way over it, he must specially reply such right of way, and that he was upon the land in the exercise of such right (d). It is said, that [*625] if the defendant's battery were outrageous, or more than was *necessary for *self-defence, that matter should be so replied* (e). And matter in aggravation, or an excess, must be new assigned (f). So where to assault and battery the defendant pleaded that the plaintiff was his apprentice, and behaved saucily and refused to obey his lawful commands, and that he moderately corrected him, and the plaintiff replied *de injuria*, the full Court of Exchequer held, that under that replication the plaintiff could not insist that the chastisement was immoderate, because that matter should have been specially re-

(z) *Post*, vol. iii.; Com. Dig. Pleader, F. 18; Cro. Jac. 224; Yelv. 157; Willes, 54, 101; 1 B. & P. 80.

(a) *Post*, 594; *sed quære*, see Willes, 100, 101.

(b) Com. Dig. Pleader, F. 21; *id.* 18; 2 Saund. 295 b, n. 1.

(c) *Post*, vol. iii; Carth. 280; 1 Salk. 407; Skin. 387; 7 Moore, 33; 7 Taunt. 156; and see 2 Bla. Rep. 1165, S. P.; and see in general when or not a replication *de injuria* is proper, Price *v.* Peek, 1 Bing. N. C. 386, 7; Hosker *v.* Nize, 1 Crom. M. & Ros. 258. When defendant must prove all the grounds of justification stated in his plea, Rees *v.* Taylor, 1 Harr. 15.

(d) *Post*, vol. iii.

(e) Nevill *v.* Cooper, 2 Crom. & M. 320; Reece *v.* Taylor, 1 Harr. & Wol. 15; Price *v.* Peck, 1 Bing. N. C. 386, 387; 7 Moore, 33; 2 Campb. 176; 3 Wils. 20; 5 B. & A. 220; *semble*, Skin. 387; Willes, 17; 1 Selw. N. P. 29, note 9; *sed quære*, if not sufficient to reply *de injuria;* Gilb. C. P. 154; 5 T. R. 81. And Lord Tenterden, C. J. at Nisi Prius, signified that he was of this latter opinion; and see Reece *v.* Taylor, 1 Harrison, R. 15, 16, *per* Littledale, J.

(f) 2 Campb. 176. 177, 629; 10 East, 73; 7 Moore, 33. As to new assignments, see *post*.

(1023) That the general replication *de injuria* is good only when the defendant pleads matter in excuse, see Lytle *v.* Lee, 5 Johns. Rep. 112. Hyatt *v.* Wood, 4 Johns. Rep. 150. Plumb *v.* M'Crea, 12 Johns. Rep. 491. Strong *v.* Smith, 3 Caines' Rep. 164. {Hannen *v.* Edes, 15 Mass. Rep. 347.} Coffin *v.* Bassett, 2 Pick. Rep. 359. But in New York, where, in an action of trespass, the defendant under the *act for the more easy pleading in certain suits*, (sess. 24. c. 47. s. 2. 1 R. L. 155,) pleads, that the supposed trespass was done by authority of a statute of this State, without expressing any other matter or circumstance contained in such statute, the plaintiff must reply *de injuria*, &c. concluding to the country; and a special replication, concluding with an averment, is bad. Comly *v.* Lockwood, 15 Johns. Rep. 188.}

pled (g). So, if there be only one count in the declaration, and the defendant has pleaded *son assault*, and there have been two distinct assaults, one excusable and the other not, the plaintiff should not reply, but should new assign another assault (h); but if there be several counts in the declaration, equal to the number of assaults, this would be unnecessary and improper (i). The course which the plaintiff should adopt, if the defendant plead that the two assaults mentioned in different counts are one and the same, and then show matter justifying in the same plea one assault only, has already been pointed out (k). Where the justification is under a writ, warrant, or other process of a court of *record*, the plaintiff cannot reply *de injuria* generally, putting the whole of the plea in issue (l); but must, according to the facts of each particular case, either specifically deny the issuing of the writ, or the making of the warrant (m), or protest the writ or warrant, which in effect admits it, and reply *de injuria* as to the *residue* (n). If the parties have been guilty of any illegal conduct, as undue violence, or an imprisonment before the issuing, or after the return of the writ, the plaintiff should reply the facts, or new assign (o); and matter which shows that the defendant, by subsequent misconduct, became a trespasser *ab initio* (p), should be specially replied (q)(1024).

1st. To persons.

In trespass to *personal* property, where the defendant has in his plea merely justified *in his own right*, the *chasing* cattle, or *removing* personal property from a close, &c. whereof he was *possessed*, the plaintiff may reply *de injuria* generally (r); and it appears to have been considered that *this replication would also suffice, where, in a similar plea, it is stated that the defendant was seised in fee (s); and although when the defendant had justified as *servant of another* (t); or under a distress for rent (u); or the *taking* and *impounding*, and not merely the *chasing* of cattle, &c. (x); it has been considered that this general replication will not suffice, that doctrine was doubted, and it has been recently decided that, although the defendant has justified as servant of a third person, *de injuria* may be replied (y). And in cases where this general replication might not be bad on demurrer, it may, nevertheless, be advisable, and in some cases necessary, to reply specially; as if there be two tenants in common, and one bring trespass against the other for taking his cattle, to which the defendant pleads that he took them *damage feasant*; in this

2dly. To personalty.

[*626]

(g) Penn v. Ward, Exchequer, Westminster, 5 June, 1835.

(h) *Post*. vol. iii.; 1 Saund. 299, note 6.

(i) *Id. ibid.*

(k) *Ante*, 450; R. & M. 118.

(l) 6 Co. 67 a; Com. Dig. Pleader, F. 19, 20.

(m) 1 Saund. 299 b.

(n) *Post*, vol. iii.

(o) *Post*, vol. iii.; 1 Saund. 299, n. 6; Lutw. 1436; Skin. 387; Com. Dig. Pleader, 3 M. 16; 2 T. R. 172; 2 Campb. 176, 177; 16 East, 85; 7 Moore, 33; see *post*.

(p) As to which, *ante*, 199.

(q) 5 B. & C. 485, *supra*, n. (o).

(r) 1 East, 212; 1 Crom. & M. 197; *post*, vol. iii.

(s) 1 East, 212; Yelv. 157; Lutw. 221; 1 Brownl. 215; Com. Dig. Pleader, F. 21; 2 Saund. 295 a, n. 1; 7 Price, 679, S. P.; Willes, 52, 202; *sed vide* Willes, 103; 1 B. & P. 80; 12 Mod. 582; and *post*.

(t) Willes, 99; 1 B. & P. 80.

(u) Willes, 52.

(x) Willes, 101, 102; Cro. Jac. 225.

(y) Piggott v. Kemp, 1 Crom. & M. 197; and see in general Bardons v. Selby, in Exchequer Chamber, 1 Crom. & M. 500.

(1024) Curtis v. Carson, 2 New Hamp. Rep. 539. Hannen v. Edes, 15 Mass. Rep. 347.

case, it seems, that the plaintiff ought to reply specially that he was tenant in common with the defendant, and so show that he was not a trespasser (z).

2dly. To personalty.

But if the justification be under a *fieri facias*, or other process, the replication must not be *de injuria* generally, but must state the particular answer to the plea, as in the case of trespass to persons (a). Where the answer to a plea *confesses* and *avoids* it, the replication should be special; thus the plaintiff ought to reply his right of common, or defect of fences, to a plea of a distress *damage feasant* (b); or he may show that the plaintiff converted such distress to his own use or abused it (c).

3dly. To realty.

In trespass to *real property*, the plaintiff might to the plea of *liberum tenementum*, reply, according to the facts, in either of four ways (1025), 1st, If the name or abuttals of the close had been so minutely stated in the declaration that there could be no question what close was alluded to (d), and the plaintiff's title was inconsistent with the defendant's, as if the plaintiff insist that the *locus in quo* is his freehold, or the freehold of another person, then the replication should deny the defendant's title, by replying, that it is the plaintiff's, or the third person's freehold, and not the defendant's, and should conclude to the country; or the replication may merely deny that the close is

[*627] the defendant's *freehold, which latter mode is proper where the plaintiff is not entitled to the freehold (e); or, 2dly, If the plaintiff derive title under the defendant, than he must traverse his plea, but confessing the defendant's title, must reply the lease or some other title under him, concluding with a verification (f); or, 3dly, If the plaintiff has a middle case, and neither derives a title under the defendant, nor has a title inconsistent with the defendant's, he may reply, that before the defendant had any thing in the premises another person was seised, and made a lease for years to a person, under whom the plaintiff claims, stating his derivative title, without either expressly confessing or denying the defendant's plea, and concluding with a verification (g); but, 4thly, If the declaration be general, without naming the *locus in quo* or the abuttals, and there be any reason to apprehend that the defendant has any land in the same parish, the plaintiff must always have new assigned, setting out the *locus in quo* with more particularity (h). The doctrine of *new assignments* will be considered in a subsequent part of the work.

(z) 1 East, 218.

(a) *Ante*, 625, and notes.

(b) *Post*, vol. iii. See 1 M. & P. 783.

(c) 3 Wils. 26; 1 Salk. 221; Cro. Jac. 147; *post*, vol. iii.

(d) It is now *necessary* by Reg. Gen. Hil. T. 4 W. 4, reg. V., *in a declaration* in trespass, to state the abuttals or name, or other description of close, or defendant may demur specially, *ante*, 551 *g*. As to a variance or ambiguity in abuttals, see 8 Bing. 75.

(e) Willes, 225; 1 B. & C. 489; 2 D. & R. 719, S. C.; *post*, vol. iii.

(f) Willes, 225; *post*, vol. iii.

(g) *Id.* 225, 226.

(h) 1 Saund. 299 b, c; Steph. 2d edit. 265; Com. Dig. Pleader, 3 M. 34; 7 T. R. 335; 2 Salk. 453; 6 Mod. 119; Willes, 223; 2 Taunt. 156; 2 B. & C. 918, 409; *post*, vol. iii. *acc.*; Dyer, 23, *contra*. See *post*.

(1025) To a plea of *liberum tenementum* the plaintiff cannot reply de injuria *sua propria*. Hyatt *v.* Wood, 4 Johns. Rep. 150. In trespass *quare clausum fregit*, if the declaration be general, without naming the *locus in quo*, or the abuttals of the close, and the defendant pleads *liberum tenementum*, upon which the plaintiff takes issue, instead of new assigning, the defendant verifies his plea by showing title to any lands in the town where the premises are alleged in the declaration to be situate. Austin *v.* Morse, 8 Wend. 477.

Where in trespass *quare clausum fregit* the defendant in his plea claims an *interest in the land* (as a right to distrain for rent in arrear,) a replication of *de injuria* is bad on general demurrer (*i*). IN TRESPASS.

It was formerly considered that, if the defendant justified as *servant or bailiff of a freeholder or termor*, the plaintiff could not traverse the defendant's authority, because he would leave unanswered the other parts of the plea, and thereby admit that another is entitled to the possession; though if both parties claimed under the same person, the command was always considered as traversable (*k*). But now it is settled that the plaintiff may in all cases take issue upon the fact of the defendant's having been authorised to commit the trespass (*l*). If the defendant in his plea has relied on a possessory title derived from the *seisin in fee* of a stranger, the plaintiff cannot take issue on the matter stated in the plea by way of express color (*m*), but may deny the demise, &c. to the defendant, without showing any title in himself (*n*); or may reply that the defendant, before the *trespasses were committed, demised the close to the plaintiff; or if the plaintiff deny the title of the party under whom the color is given, he should show his own title, and traverse that stated by the defendant (*o*); and if the plaintiff insist that the defendant's tenancy has been determined by a notice to quit, or a surrender, or forfeiture, &c. he should reply that matter specially (*p*). [*628]

To a plea of *license*, the plaintiff may reply generally, that the defendant of his own wrong, and without the supposed license, committed the trespasses, concluding to the country (*q*); or, as it has been considered if the plaintiff did license the defendant to commit some acts, then he should reply a revocation, or new assign that he brought his action for other different trespasses (*r*); but it seems that if the license only extended to some of the trespasses, and that other trespasses were committed at different times, and not covered in evidence by the license, then the general replication *de injuria* will suffice (*s*).

To a plea of *escape of cattle through defect of fences*, which the plaintiff ought to have repaired, it is said, that as the plea contains mere matter of excuse, the plaintiff may reply *de injuria* (*t*), or he may deny in particular the obligation to repair, or the defect of the fences, or the defendant's right to put the cattle in the close adjoining the *locus in quo*, concluding to the country (*u*); but he should reply specially that the defendant turned the cattle into the *locus in quo*, or that they were unruly, and conclude with a verification (*x*).

To a plea claiming a *right of common*, the plaintiff cannot reply *de injuria* (*y*), but must either deny the *seisin in fee* or other title to the estate, as

(*i*) Hooker v. Nye, 1 Crom. M. & Ros. 258; 4 Tyr. 777, where see most of the modern cases cided; and see *ante*, 626, note (*y*).

(*k*) 1 East, 245; Cro. Car. 586; 6 Co. 24, a; Salk. 107; 1 Saund. 347 c, n. 4.

(*l*) 13 East, 65.

(*m*) As to this, see *ante*, 560, 561.

(*n*) 2 Stra. 1238; Fortsc. 378; Poph. 1, 2.

(*o*) Poph. 2; Com. Dig. Pleader, F. 13; 10 East, 189.

(*p*) 7 T. R. 431; 1 Lev. 307; *post*, vol. iii.

(*q*) 11 East, 45; *post*, vol. iii.; 1 Saund. 103 b.

(*r*) 1 Saund. 300 a; 2 *Id.* 5, end of note 3. See replication of a waiver of a forfeiture, 2 Campb. 629.

(*s*) 11 East, 451; see *post*.

(*t*) Willes, 54; Rast. Ent. 621 a; Com. Dig. Pleader, M. 29; *post*, 638 to 640.

(*u*) 1 Saund. 103 b; Com. Dig. Pleader, 3 M. 29; *post*, vol. iii.

(*x*) *Post*, vol. iii.; Lutw. 1358, 1359; Com. Dig. Pleader, 3 M. 29; Rast. Ent. 621 a.

(*y*) 8 Co. 67 a; Willes, 101; 16 East, 350; 7 Price, 670.

IN TRESPASS. — 3dly. To realty. [*629]

appurtenant to which the defendant claims his right, or may deny the right of common as stated in the plea (z)(1026), or that the cattle were the defendant's own commonable cattle, *levant* and *couchant* upon *the premises (a), concluding to the country, and not with a formal traverse (b). But it is said, that in the latter case, where the defendant has turned on his own commonable cattle, as well as other cattle, the plaintiff should new assign, stating that he brought his action for depasturing the common with other cattle, and ought not to traverse the *levancy* and *couchancy* (c). The plaintiff may also reply an approvement (d); or he may reply that the close in which, &c. had been inclosed from the common more than thirty years and enjoyed adversely (e). But it seems to be sufficient in these cases, merely to deny the existence of the common of pasture, &c. stated in the plea, without replying specially, &c. (f)

If a public or private *right of way* be pleaded, the plaintiff may deny the way, and conclude to the country, and he may also new assign (g), or allege that the defendant used the way to another tenement than that alleged in the plea (h): or to a plea of a private way, the defendant's title may be denied (i), and the plaintiff may, under such replication, give in evidence an order of justices under 13 Geo. 3, c. 78, s. 19, and 55 Geo. 3, c. 68, whereby the public or private way has been stopped (k). But where the plaintiff cannot deny the plea, and only insists that the defendant trespassed out of the way, or was guilty of unnecessary damage in removing an obstruction, or actually converted the materials to his own use, in order to save unnecessary expense, the plaintiff should not deny the right of way, but should merely new assign, *extra viam*, &c. *De injuria* generally cannot be replied to a plea justifying under a right of way (l). If the plaintiff merely traverse a non-existing grant of a way, he cannot on the trial give evidence to show that the supposed grantor was not, as alleged in the plea, seised in fee, even for the purpose of rebutting the presumption of the grant (m). And under a general
[*630] traverse of a custom *which is laid in the plea to exist, with a *certain exception*, the plaintiff cannot contend that he is *within the exception* (n).

The replication to pleas justifying a trespass to real property, under *process* of Courts of *record*, are similar to those in trespass to persons, in which we have seen that the plaintiff cannot, in general, put in issue the whole of the matters in the plea, by replying *de injuria* (o).

The replications to pleas in trespass of matters *in discharge* in general, re-

(z) See, however, 2 Y. & J. 79; *post*, 629.
(a) 1 Burr. 320; Willes, 100, note c; Bul. N. P. 93; 8 Co. 67 b.
(b) 1 Saund. 103 b; *post*, vol. iii.
(c) 1 Saund. 346 d.
(d) *Post*, vol. iii.; 7 B. & C. 346.
(e) 2 B. & C. 918; and see 2 Taunt. 156. But if only part of the close wherein the alleged trespass was committed has been so inclosed, the plaintiff should reply so, as it would be incorrect to reply the whole close had been inclosed, *id. ib.*
(f) 7 B. & C. 346.
(g) 1 Saund. 103 b; *post*, vol. iii.
(h) 16 East, 350.
(i) *Post*, vol. iii.
(k) 1 East, 64; Selw. N. P. 1130.
(l) 8 Co. 67; 7 Price, 670; Tidd, 9th ed. 683.
(m) 1 Crompt. & Jerv. 48.
(n) 2 Y. & J. 79.
(o) *Ante*, 625.

(1026) { And a replication to a plea that the *locus in quo* had been enclosed by consent of the lord, must state that after the enclosure there was sufficient common left for the commoners. Rodgers *v.* Wynne, 7 Dowl. & Ryl. 581. }

semble those in assumpsit (*p*). Thus, if a release be pleaded, the replication may be *non est factum*, or that it was obtained by fraud (*q*). To a plea of accord and satisfaction, the plaintiff may deny the accord, or state that it was for another trespass, with a traverse of the acceptance in satisfaction of the trespass complained of, or he may allege, that the defendant was guilty after the accord (*r*); or to a plea of a distress for the same trespass, he may reply that the cattle died in the pound (*s*); or to a plea of tender, that no tender was made, or that it was insufficient (*t*). And to a plea of the statute of limitations, the plaintiff may reply a writ, or any other matter of which he could avail himself in the action of assumpsit (*u*).

IN TRESPASS.

3dly. To realty.

II. OF THE FORMS AND PARTS OF REPLICATIONS.

A replication, before the recent pleading rules, was usually *entitled* in the *Court* and of the *term* of which it was pleaded; and the *names* of the *plaintiff* and *defendant* were stated in the *margin*, thus, "A. B. against C. D." (*x*). Where any new matter was stated in the replication, which occurred *pending the suit*, and after the last pleading, as the death of one of several plaintiffs or defendants between the plea and replication, this was to be *suggested*, and a *special imparlance* was then stated at the head of the replication (*y*).

TITLE, &c.

Since the Reg. Gen. Hil. T. 4 W. 4,† the same practice as to the title of the *Court* still continues, although no advantage could be taken of the *omission*. With respect to the date the Reg. Gen. Hil. 4 W. 4, reg. 1, is express, that every pleading shall be entitled of the day of the month and year when the same was pleaded, unless otherwise specially ordered by the Court, or a judge. The *names of the parties* should be accurately stated in the *margin* as heretofore. Imparlances we have seen have been abolished (*z*), but the statement of recent deaths or other events that have occurred within eight days may still be suggested (*z*).

The Reg. Gen. Hil. T. 4 W. 4, reg. 9, orders, "nor shall it be necessary in any *replication* or subsequent pleading intended to be pleaded in maintenance of the *whole action*, to use any allegation of '*precludi non*,' or to the like effect, or any prayer of judgment; and all pleas, *replications*, and subsequent pleadings, pleaded without such formal parts as aforesaid, shall be taken, unless otherwise expressed, as pleaded respectively in bar of the whole action, or in maintenance of the *whole* action, provided that nothing herein contained shall extend to cases where an estoppel is pleaded." The 19th reg. directs the form of replication to a plea of payment of money into Court. The title of the Court, date, margin, commencements and conclusions may be thus :—

(*p*) As to these, see *ante*, 613.
(*q*) Com. Dig. Pleader, 3 M. 12.
(*r*) *Id.* 3 M. 13. *Sed quære*, if the plaintiff ought not, in such case, to *new assign*, see *post*, vol. iii.
(*s*) 1 Salk. 248.
(*t*) Thomp. Ent. 304; *post*, vol. iii.; Com. Dig. Pleader, 3 M. 36.
(*u*) *Ante*, 614, and notes.
(*x*) See forms, *post*, vol. iii.
(*y*) *Id.*
(*z*) Reg. Gen. Hil. T. 4 W. 4, reg. 2, and *ante*, 473. The observations with respect to the title of a plea will in general here apply, see *ante*, 489, 583.

† See American Editor's Preface.

TITLE, &c. In the King's Bench, [*or* "C. P." *or* "Exchequer of Pleas."]

On the —— day of —— A. D. 1836.

Commencement and conclusion, with similiter.

A. B. agt. C. D. } The plaintiff as to the said first plea of the defendant, and whereof he hath put himself upon the country, doth the like.

The conclusion to a special plea may be to the *country*, as thus, "and this the plaintiff prays may be inquired of by the country, &c." or with a verification thus, "and this the plaintiff is ready to verify." If the replication be to a plea affecting only *a part of the cause of action*, the form usually begins and concludes precludi non, and prayer of judgment, as before the recent rules (*a*).

TO A PLEA CONCLUDING TO THE COUNTRY. [*631] When the plea concludes to the *country*, the replication consists either of the common or special *similiter*. The first *is, "and the plaintiff doth the like;" and the latter is thus, "and the plaintiff, as to the said pleas of the defendant, by him first and secondly above pleaded, and whereof he hath put himself upon the country, doth the like;" and the plaintiff must join issue or demur, and cannot reply any new matter when a plea concludes to the country (*b*). If in the *similiter* there be any mistake in the names, the defendant may demur; but where to an issue tendered by the plaintiff, the defendant has added the *similiter* in the *plaintiff's* name, this defect will be aided after verdict, there being an affirmative and negative before. It was once held that the want of a *similiter* was not aided by or amendable after verdict; and where in the *similiter* the defendant's name was put instead of the plaintiff's, the chief justice dismissed the jury, conceiving he had no commission to try the issue; but in a subsequent case, where a similar mistake was made, the Court, after trial of the issue, refused to arrest the judgment, and at length the *similiter* was allowed to be inserted after verdict, instead of the "&c." upon three grounds; first, that it was an omission of the clerk; secondly, that it was implied in the "&c." added to the last pleading; and, thirdly, that by amending, the Court only made that right which the defendant himself understood to be so, by his going down to trial (*c*). So where, to a rejoinder concluding with a verification, the plaintiff, instead of taking issue and concluding to the country, added the *similiter*, and took down the record to trial, and the defendant obtained a verdict, the Court would not grant a new trial, but amended the record (*d*). And where the parties had gone down to trial upon a plea which had not been traversed, after verdict for the plaintiff, he was permitted to amend by adding a traverse (*e*); and in a *qui tam* action, the Court of King's Bench, after verdict, directed a *similiter* to be entered, though the objection was taken on the trial (*f*). But in the Common Pleas it should

(*a*) See the several forms *post*, vol. iii.

(*b*) Com. Dig. Pleader, R. 1; Co. Lit. 126 a; Hob. 271; 2 M. & Sel. 519.

(*c*) Cowp. 407; 2 Saund. 319, note 6; Com. Dig. Pleader, B. 11, 12, &c.; 1 Stra. 551; 1 Stark. 400; Tidd, 9th ed. 924; 9 Moore, 741; 2 Bing. 384, S. C.; 3 Dowl. 700.

(*d*) 1 New Rep. 28. *As to the similiter*, see fully Seabrook *v.* Cave, 2 Dowl. 691; Rawlinson *v.* Rountre, 6 Car. & P. 551; Clarke *v.* Nicholson, 1 Gale, 21; 3 Dowl. 454; 6 Car. & P. 712, 713; 3 Dow. Rep. 1.

(*e*) 5 Taunt. 164; 3 Dowl. 698.

(*f*) 1 Stark. 400; S. C. in 2 Chit. R. 25; and 6 M. & Sel. 60.

seem otherwise, and the want of a *similiter* is a ground of error (*g*), or for setting aside the verdict (*h*). But the Court will, when the justice of *the case requires, amend the record by the insertion of a *similiter* (*i*)(1027). TO A PLEA CONCLUDING TO THE COUNTRY.

We have seen that a plea of *nul tiel record* concludes with an averment and prayer of judgment *si actio*, &c. except in the case of a judgment in Ireland, &c. (*k*)(1028). If the plea deny a record in the *same Court*, the replication thereto should re-assert the existence of the record, and conclude with a prayer that it may be viewed and inspected by the Court, and a day is given to the parties (*l*)(1029); and when the record of *another* Court is denied, the replication re-asserts it, and a day is given to the plaintiff to bring it in (*m*). When the *defendant* has pleaded a record of the *same* Court, the replication denying it concludes with a verification, and a day is given to the parties to hear judgment (*n*); and where the defendant has pleaded a record of *another* Court, the replication of *nul tiel record* may either conclude by giving the defendant a day to bring it in (*o*), or with an averment and prayer of the debt and damages, &c. (*p*). In the former case the issue is complete upon the replication (*q*); but in the latter, there should be a rejoinder re-asserting the existence of the record (*r*); and therefore the first form, being the most concise, is obviously preferable. Where mattor of *fact*, as well as matter of *record*, is properly put in issue, the replication may conclude to the country (*s*)(1030). TO A PLEA OF NUL TIEL RECORD, OR STATING A RECORD.

The replication to a plea containing *new matter*, and therefore of necessity so framed as to afford the defendant an opportunity of answering it, may be considered with reference, 1st, to the *commencement*; 2dly, the *body*; and, 3dly, its *conclusion*. The *commencement* of the replication in such case professes wholly to deny the effect of the defendant's plea; the *body* shows the ground on which that denial is founded; and the *conclusion* is either to the country or to the record, if it merely deny the plea; but if the replication contain *new matter*, it should *conclude* with a *verification*, and a prayer that judgment may be awarded in the plaintiff's favor (*t*). TO A SPECIAL PLEA, &c. — TO A SPECIAL PLEA CONCLUDING WITH A VERIFICATION. [*633]

(*g*) 2 Moore, 215.
(*h*) 3 B. & B. 1; 6 Moore, 51, S. C.
(*i*) 2 Bing. 384; 9 Moore, 741, S. C.
(*k*) 2 Wils. 114; 5 East, 473; *ante*, 521.
(*l*) *Post*, vol. iii.; 2 Lutw. 1514; Herne, 278; Barnes, 336.
(*m*) *Post*, vol. iii.; 2 Salk. 566; 3 Bla. Com. 330, 331.
(*n*) *Post*, vol. iii. See the practice, Tidd, 9th ed. 742.
(*o*) See *post*, vol. iii.
(*p*) 2 Wils. 113; Barnes, 161.
(*q*) 2 B. & P. 302.
(*r*) Tidd, 9th ed. 743.
(*s*) Sayer, 208, 299; see 1 B. & Ald. 153.
(*t*) 2 New Rep. 363.

(1027) {See Shaw *v.* Redmond, 11 Serg. & Rawle, 32.}
(1028) {Or of the Circuit Court of the United States. Baldwin *v.* Hall, 17 Johns. Rep. 272.}
(1029) {Share *v.* Becker, 8 Serg. & Rawle, 293.}
(1030) {Share *v.* Becker, 8 Serg. & Rawle, 242. Peter *v.* Stafford, Hob. Rep. 244.}

1. THE COMMENCEMENT. 1st. The *Commencement* of the replication, when matter of *Estoppel* is to be replied, after stating the title of the Court and term, or, since Reg. Gen. Hil. T. 4 W. 4, reg. 1,† the day of the month and year, and the names of the parties in the margin, is thus: "And the plaintiff saith, that the defendant ought not to be admitted in his said plea to aver, that, &c." (*stating fully the matter alleged in the plea, which the replication afterwards shows the defendant is estopped from relying on*) "because he saith that, &c." (*stating the matter of estoppel*) (*u*).

The Reg. Gen. Hil. T. 4 W. 4, reg. 9, seems still to require the same formal commencement as regards Estoppel as prevailed heretofore.

Of the form *precludi non*, &c. When the replication *denied* or *confessed and avoided* the plea, it *commenced* with an allegation, technically termed the *precludi non*, and which was as follows: "And A. B. as to the said plea of C. D. by him secondly above pleaded, saith, that he A. B. by reason of any thing by C. D. in that plea alleged, ought not to be barred from having or maintaining his aforesaid action thereof against C. D.; because he says, that, &c." (*x*) When the body of the replication only contained an answer to a *part* of the plea, the *commencement* then was to recite or specify the part intended to be answered; for, should the commencement assume to answer the whole plea, but the body contained an answer to part only, the whole replication was insufficient, and so *vice versa* (*y*). In this case the form ran thus: And A. B. as to so much of the said plea of C. D. by him secondly above pleaded, as relates to the said supposed *recognizance in that plea mentioned*, (according to the fact,) says, that he ought not to be barred from having or maintaining his aforesaid action thereof against him, because he says, that, &c." (*stating the answer to such* [*634] *part of the plea, and with the proper conclusion *thereto.*) The answer to the *other part* of the plea commenced as follows: "And A. B. as to the residue of the said plea, saith, *precludi non*, &c. because," &c. (*z*) On the other hand, when the matter to be replied was equally an answer to several pleas, it was proper, in order to avoid expense, to answer all the pleas in one replication (*a*); and the replication *de injuriis suis propriis, absque tali causa* to two several justifications by different defendants in the same action, was held sufficient (*b*): in these cases the commencement should apply to and profess to answer all the pleas. So, where to a plea by an executor of judgments outstanding, the plaintiff replies that each judgment is fraudulent, &c. he may conclude his replication with one verification, or with a separate verification to the answer to each of the judgments; the former is perhaps the better course (*c*).

(*u*) See the form, *post*, vol. iii.; 3 East, 348; Willes, 10; Carth. 66, 67; 1 Saund. 257, 276, n. 1, 325, n. 1; 6 T. R. 62; *post*, 635.

(*x*) 2 Wils. 42. If the plea be in bar of the *further* maintenance of the suit, the replication should be framed accordingly, 4 East, 502, 503.

(*y*) 1 Saund. 28, n. 3, 377, 378; Com. Dig. Pleader, F. 25; Lutw. 241; 2 B. & P. 427; Summary on Pleading, 72; 4 East, 503, 504. See further as to the qualities of a replication, *post*.

(*z*) 1 Saund. 337, 338; see the forms, *post*, vol. iii.; Lutw. 241; Com. Dig. Pleader, F. 4.

(*a*) See the form, 8 Wentw. 5; 1 Leon. 124; 1 Sid. 39; Yelv. 65; Com. Dig. Pleader, F. 4 and 24; Summary Treat. on Pleading, 71, 72; *sed vide* 1 Leon. 139, as to a demurrer.

(*b*) *Id.*; 1 Leon. 124; Cro. Eliz. 139; 1 Sid. 39.

(*c*) 1 Saund. 338, note 5; 1 Salk. 298, 312.

† See American Editor's Preface.

I. THE COMMENCEMENT.

The above form of *precludi non* is still admissible and sometimes useful; but the Reg. Gen. Hil. T. 4 W. 4,† expressly declares, "nor shall it be *necessary*, in any replication or subsequent pleading intended to be pleaded in maintenance of the whole action, to use any allegation of *precludi non*, or to the like effect, *or any prayer of judgment;* and all pleas, replications, and subsequent pleadings, pleaded without such formal parts as aforesaid, shall be taken, unless otherwise expressed, as pleaded respectively in bar of the whole action; provided that nothing herein contained shall extend to cases where an estoppel is pleaded."

II. THE BODY.

No venue to be stated.

It is first to be observed, that the Reg. Gen. Hil. T. 4 W. 4,† reg. 8, directs that *no venue* shall be stated in the body of the declaration, or *in any subsequent* pleading; but provides, that in cases where *local description* is now required, such local description shall be given.

With respect to the *body* of the replication, we have seen that it contains, either, 1st, matter of *estoppel;* 2dly, a *traverse* or *denial* of the plea; 3dly, a *confession and avoidance* of it; or, 4thly, in the case of an *evasive* plea, a *new assignment*. We will consider each of these in the above order.

1st. Estoppel (*d*).

When the matter which operates as an *estoppel* (*e*) appears on the face of the declaration, the plaintiff may demur to a plea by which the defendant attempts to set up such matter as a defence (*f*). Thus, if in covenant on a lease by the lessor, the defendant plead *nil habuit in tenementis*, that is, in effect, that the lessor had *no title* to or interest in the land, the plea will be defective, because the matter of estoppel, viz. the demise by deed and holding thereby, appears in the declaration (*g*). But where an action upon a lease *is brought by a party who claims derivatively from the lessor, in which case the declaration must show the lessor's title and the derivative title of the plaintiff, it is competent to the defendant to deny that the lessor had the *particular title* alleged in the declaration (*h*). [*635]

If the matter of estoppel do not appear from the anterior pleading, the replication must expressly show such matter and rely thereon, and there must be an appropriate commencement and conclusion to the replication; for by replying an estoppel without relying upon it, the advantage of the *estoppel* as such may often be lost (*i*). As where in debt for rent on a demise by indenture by one who has nothing in the land, (the declaration not showing the

(*d*) See express regulation as to matter of estoppel. Reg. Gen. Hil. T. 4 W. 4, reg. 9.

(*e*) As to estoppel in general, see Co. Lit. 352 a; Com. Dig. Estoppel; Steph. 2d ed. 238, 260. An estoppel arises either, 1st, From matter of *record;* 2dly, By *deed;* or, 3dly, By matter *in pais*, *id.* In a *plea*, *ante*, 502.

(*f*) 1 Saund. 325 a, note 4; 2 Stra. 817; 7 T. R. 537; 8 *Id.* 487; Willes, 13; 2 Taunt. 278.

(*g*) 1 Saund. 325 a, note 4; 2 *Id.* 418, note 1.

(*h*) 1 Saund. 418, n. 1; *ante*, 523; see Steph. 2d ed. 217. In covenant by the assignee of a lessor, if the declaration allege that the lessor was seised in fee, and conveyed by lease and release, the defendant may traverse the seisin in fee. Seymour *v.* Franco, after Trinity Term, 1828, 7 Law Journal, 18, K. B.; and Whitton *v.* Peacock, in C. P., 3d June, 1835, Shearman attorney; *ante*, 397; 4 Bing. 403; 4 Moore, 5.

(*i*) 1 Saund. 325 a, n. 4; and see Jervis, Reg. Gen. Hil. T. 4 W. 4, reg. 9.

† See American Editor's Preface.

II. THE BODY.

1st. Estoppel.

deed (*k*),) the defendant pleads *nil habuit in tenementis*, if the plaintiff reply that he had a sufficient estate to make the demise, he loses the benefit of the estoppel; but if he reply that the lease was made *by indenture*, and conclude *unde petit judicium*, if the defendant shall be admitted to plead the plea against his own acceptance of the lease by indenture, the defendant shall be estopped (*l*). Where the demise is not by deed there can be no *pleading* by way of estoppel, especially as the declaration may by virtue of the statute 11 Geo. 2, c. 19, be in the general form for use and occupation: but it must be remembered that in general, even in such case, the party to whom the premises were let, or his assignee, shall not be permitted to dispute the title of the landlord by whom the former was let into possession, or the title of the assignee of such lessor (*m*)(1031). So, if in a declaration in debt on bond, not showing the condition, it be recited in the condition that a fact exists, and the obligor attempt to dispute such fact, the plaintiff may reply, setting out the
[*636] condition and relying on the estoppel (*n*). Where the matter *in question has been tried upon a particular issue between the same parties in a former suit, and there has been a finding thereon by the jury, such finding operates as an estoppel by matter of *record*, provided it be specially pleaded and relied upon as such (*o*)(1032).

As a species of estoppel it may be proper here to notice, that if in debt on a bond, conditioned for the performance of covenants, the defendant falsely plead that there were no covenants in the indenture on his part, the plaintiff may reply, setting out the indenture containing such covenants, and demur (*p*). A party who has executed a deed is not *estopped* from denying that fact, and may plead *non est factum*; but he cannot, (admitting his deed,) deny its *operation* or effect by a plea of *non concessit*, &c. (1033); as a stranger to the deed is permitted to do (*q*).

Exception in Reg. Gen. Hil. T. 4 W. 4, reg. 9, as to estoppel.

The Reg. Gen. Hil. T. 4 W. 4, reg. 9, expressly provides "that nothing herein contained shall extend to cases where an estoppel is pleaded;" so that the above regulations in pleading estoppel still continue in force.

(*k*) See *ante*, 398.

(*l*) 1 Saund. 325 a, note 4; Ld. Raym. 1051; Salk. 277; 6 T. R. 62.

(*m*) See 5 T. R. 4; 1 B. & Ald. 50; 4 M. & Sel. 347; 2 Taunt 278; 1 Bing. 147; 2 Campb. 11. But the *termination* of the landlord's title after the letting may be shown, when, 2 Saund. 418, n. 1; 4 T. R. 682; 3 M. & Sel. 516; see further 2 Bing. 54; 9 Moore. 130, S. C.; 4 Bing. 348, 356; 9 B. & Cres. 245.

(*n*) 1 Saund. 325 a, note 4, and 215, note 2; 6 T. R. 62; Willes, 9; 5 B. & Ald. 682; 1 B. & C. 704.

(*o*) 3 East, 346; M'Clel. & Y. 509; 2 B. & Ald. 662. And see the precedents in trespass for mesne profits, where to a plea of title the recovery in ejectment was replied, 2 Rich. C. P. 444. Any confession or admission, express or implied, upon the pleadings, operates as an estoppel in a subsequent suit between the same parties as to the matter admitted, Steph. 238. As to the effect of a *protestation* to prevent this, see *post*.

(*p*) 1 Saund. 316, 317, 318, and 319.

(*q*) See Steph. 2d ed. 239, 237; 2 Taunt. 278; 2 Bulstr. 55.

(1031) {In an action of debt for rent reserved by indenture, the plaintiff may state in his declaration the substance of the demise, and is not bound to declare upon the deed; and if the defendant to such a declaration pleads, *nil habuit in tenementis*, *actio non accrevit infra sex annos*, or any plea which is *prima facie* a good plea, no estoppel appearing on the record, the plaintiff may reply, that the demise was by indenture, and such a replication will not be a departure. Davis *v.* Shoemaker, 1 Rawle, 135.}

(1032) Where the tenant in a writ of entry, demanding a freehold, pleaded the general issue, it was held that he had thereby admitted in the record, that he was tenant of the freehold; and was therefore estopped from proving that he was tenant at will only. Kelieran *v.* Brown, 4 Mass. Rep. 443.

(1033) {Stow *v.* Wise, 7 Conn. Rep. 214.}

The *second* description of replication is that which neither concludes the defendant by matter of estoppel, nor confesses and avoids the plea, but *traverses or denies the truth thereof, either in part or in whole* (r). It will be proper to consider the nature of these replications under the following heads :— II. THE BODY. 2dly. Denial of the plea.

- 1st. A denial of the *whole plea*, or *de injuria*, &c. 1st. Of the *whole* plea.
  - 1st. When allowed, or not proper, or not advisable.
  - 2dly. The form of such replication.
- 2dly. A denial of only *part* of the plea.
  - 1st. Of what fact.
  - 2dly. The mode of such special denial.
- 3dly. A denial, and stating a particular breach, &c.

There is no real distinction between *traverses* and *denials*; they are the same in substance (s). Any pleading by which the truth of the opponent's allegation is disputed is termed a pleading by way of traverse or denial. Traverses are of *two kinds, general or special. The *general* traverses or [*637] denials were the general issue (t), and the replication *de injuria sua propria*, and such pleadings as simply deny a *particular fact* pleaded by the adversary; the *special* traverse in its strict legal sense imports the technical and now unusual formal traverse, with an inducement and *absque hoc*, which will be presently explained (u).

It is the first object of pleading to bring the point in dispute between the parties, at as early a stage of the cause as possible, to an *issue* or point which is *not multifarious or complex* (v); and therefore the issue must in general be single (x)(1034). But this *single point* may consist of *several facts* if they be dependent and connected (y)(1035); and therefore where in trespass the defendant justified under a right of common, and the plaintiff in his replication traversed, "that the cattle were the defendant's own cattle, and that they were *levant* and *couchant* upon the premises, and commonable cattle;" the replication was on a special demurrer, assigning for cause that it was multifarious, holden to be good (z). So, according to the first resolution in *Crogate's case*, to a justification under proceedings in the Admiralty Court, Hundred Court, or County Court, or any other Court which is *not of record*, *de injuria sua propria* is good; all being matter of fact and making but one cause or justificaton (a). And in a late case, where in an action for maliciously suing out a commission of bankruptcy against the plaintiff, the defendant pleaded that the plaintiff being a trader, and being indebted to the defendant in

(r) See in general, Com. Dig. Pleader, G.; Saund. Index, "*Traverse*." Summary Treat. on Pleading, 75 to 80; Steph. 2d ed. 185 to 231.

(s) Willes, 224.

(t) But since the Reg. Gen. Hil. T. 4 W. 4, there is no *general* issue, i. e. denying every allegation in a declaration.

(u) 1 Saund. 103, n.; Stephen, 2d ed. 205.

(v) Willes, 204, 54; 1 East, 217; 1 Burr. 320; Summary Treat. on Pleading, 77.

(x) *Id. Ibid.*

(y) 1 Burr. 320; Willes, 100, n. c.; Bul. N. P. 93; 8 Co. 67 b; 2 B. & C. 908.

(z) 1 Burr. 320; Willes, 100, n. c.; Bul. N. P. 93; 8 Co. 67 b; and see 1 Crom. & M. 500.

(a) 8 Co. 67 b; Willes, 101, note a.

(1034) Vide Rogers v. Burk, 10 Johns. Rep. 400.
(1035) Vide Strong v. Smith, 3 Caines' Rep. 160.

II. THE BODY.

2dly. Denial of the plea. 1st Of the *whole* plea.

the sum of £100 became bankrupt, whereupon the defendant sued out the commission; and the plaintiff replied *de injuria sua propria*, on demurrer, assigning for cause that the plaintiff by his replication had attempted to put in issue the distinct facts, the act of bankruptcy, the trading, and the petitioning creditor's debt; it was held that these three facts constituted but one entire proposition, and that the replication was therefore good (*b*). Indeed, in some [*638] cases the traverse or denial *must consist of more than one fact, for it is another rule that in a traverse the plaintiff cannot narrow the title set up by the defendant (*c*). And the reason why the general replication *de injuria*, which will presently be fully explained, cannot in many instances be adopted, is not because it puts two or three things in issue (*d*).

First, *General denial as by de injuria*, when allowed or not proper or advisable.

In actions on contracts and in replevin, the replication usually denies the *material* facts, or *one of the facts* alleged in the plea, with particularity and in express words (*e*). But we have seen that *de injuria* may be proper in assumpsit, case, covenant, or replevin (*f*). If a replication deny the *whole* of a plea, yet proof of so much as in justice entitles plaintiff to recover will suffice (*g*). In *trespass*, and in actions on the case for slander, the replication containing a *general denial of the whole plea* sometimes occurs, and is termed a replication *de injuria sua propria absque tali causa*, or "*de son tort demesne sans tiel cause*;" (*h*) or if a *part* of the plea be admitted, then it is termed *de injuria absqe residuo causa*, thereby denying all but the admitted fact or facts. This replication tenders issue upon and compels the defendant to prove every material allegation in his plea (*i*), and therefore it is frequently advantageous to the plaintiff to adopt it, when by the rules of pleading it is permitted.

As to *de injuria*.

In general, when the defendant's plea in *trespass* or *case* consists merely of matter of *excuse*, and *not of matter of right or interest* inconsistent with or affecting the right, the infringement of which is complained of in the declaration, whether it relate to the person, or to personal or real property, the general replication *de injuria* is sufficient (*k*). And in these cases, when a title is stated merely as *inducement* to the defence, the plaintiff need not answer, or particularly deny it, because it is merely *collateral* to the matter in dispute: but there is a material difference between these cases and the instances in which the plaintiff makes title by his declaration to any thing, and the defendant in his plea denies the title, or claims an *interest*

(*b*) 2 B. & C. 903; 4 D. & R. 579, S. C.; *vide* 4 B. & Cres. 353.

(*c*) 4 T. R. 157; Summary Treat. on Pleading, 78.

(*d*) 1 B. & P. 80; 2 Saund. 295 a, note; 1 Bing. N. C. 644. When a replication traversing the *whole* of a plea is bad, see Moore v. Boulcott, 5 Moore & Scott, 124; 3 Dowl. 145, S. C. *De injuria* to a plea, justifying an expulsion from a house as servant of lawful occupier, is good, 1 Crom. & M. 197; and is good as a plea in bar to an avowry for poor rate, 1 Crom. & M. 500.

(*e*) In replevin, the replication *de injuria*, it was said, never occurs. Finch. Law. 396; 1 B. & P. 76; but see 1 Crom. & M. 197, 500.

(*f*) *Ante*, 614.

(*g*) See late instance in Bradley v. Milnes, 1 Bing. N. C. 664.

(*h*) Com. Dig. Pleader, F. 18; Crogate's case, 8 Co. 67. Most of the points relating to this replication are collected in Crogate's case, 8 Co. 67; Cockrell v. Armstrong, Willes, 99; Doc. Plac. vol. i. 113 to 115; and Com. Dig. Pleader, F. 18. &c.; 1 B. & P. 79, 80, Finch. Law, 395, 396; 2 Saund. 295, n. 1; 1 Saund. 244 c. n. 7; Archb. 238.

(*i*) Com. Dig. Pleader, F. 18 to 24; 8 Co. 67 a; Willes, 100.

(*k*) 8 Co. 67, a; Com. Dig. Pleader, F. 18 &c.; Doc. Pl. 113 to 115; 1 B. & P. 80; 1 East, 212, 214, 218; 2 Saund. 295, n. 1; 7 Price, 670.

II. THE BODY. 2dly. Denial of the plea. 1st. Of the whole plea.

in the subject-matter; for then the plaintiff must reply *specially (*l*). Thus, in an action for an assault, if the defendant plead *son assault demesne*, or that he arrested the plaintiff upon hue and cry levied (*m*); or the plea be moderate correction of a servant for his neglect of service, the general replication *de injuria* is sufficient, if the plea be untrue (*n*). And though such excuse for the personal injury may be stated in the plea to depend on the *possession* of land or personal property; as if the defendant plead that the plaintiff entered upon his possession, and that therefore the defendant *molliter manus imposuit* to remove him (*o*); or if the plea be that the defendant was *seised*, &c. as rector, and that the tithes were severed, and that the plaintiff endeavored to carry them away, and that the defendant, in defence of his tithes, *molliter manus imposuit*, &c ; yet in these cases the general replication is sufficient, and the plaintiff need not answer the defendant's title ; because the plaintiff by his action claims nothing in the soil or corn, but only damages for the battery, which is merely *collateral* to the title, and which is stated merely as inducement (*p*). However, in a recent case, it seems to have been considered that where the *excuse* arises, even in part, out of the *seisin in fee* of another, then *de injuria* is insufficient (*q*). So, in trespass to *personal* property, if the defendant merely justify the chasing cattle or removing goods from land of which he was *possessed*, the general replication will suffice (*r*). And in trespass to *real* property, if the defendant in his plea do not claim any interest therein, or easement over the same, the replication *de injuria* is sufficient; as if in trespass for pulling down a building, the defendant, without claiming any interest therein, plead that he removed it as being a nuisance on his land, this general replication will suffice (*s*). So, if in trespass to land with cattle, the defendant plead that the plaintiff's fences were out of repair, whereby the defendant's cattle escaped into the plaintiff's close, this plea consisting merely *of matter of *excuse*, and claiming no *interest* in the land, may, [*640] it is said, be answered by the general replication (*t*). And though it is stated as a general rule, that where the defence rests upon an authority of law the replication must be special (*u*), yet this, as a general position, is inaccurate (*x*). For if the defendant justify, that he, as a constable, without a warrant, took the plaintiff for a breach of the peace; or as a vagrant or lunatic (*y*); or under a public act of parliament; or under a right for all persons given by the common law (*z*); or if in trespass for false imprisonment, the defendant justify by process out of the Admiralty, Hundred, or County Court, or other court not of record, the general replication is sufficient; all being matter of fact, and making but one cause (*a*). The instance of an entry to view waste

(*l*) Yelv. 157; Cro. Jac. 225; Willes, 102, 103; Com. Dig. Pleader, F. 20, 21.

(*m*) 8 Co 67 a; 1 Saund. 244 a, note 7.

(*n*) Gilb. C. P. 154; Willes, 102.

(*o*) Latch. 128, 221; Com. Dig. Plead., F. 18; 12 Mod. 582; *ante*, 626, n. (*y*).

(*p*) Yelv. 157; Cro. Jac. 224, 225; Com. Dig. Pleader, F. 18; 2 Saund. 295, n. 1; 1 Crom. & M. 200.

(*q*) *Ante*, 638; 1 B. & P. 80; and see Willes, 102, 103; 12 Mod. 582; Cro. Eliz. 539, 540; Cro. Jac. 598; 7 Price, 670.

(*r*) *Ante*, 626, 627.

(*s*) Summary Treat. on Pleading, 81, 82; *ante*, 626, 627.

(*t*) *Ante*, 628; 1 Cr. & M. 500.

(*u*) 8 Co. 67 b.

(*x*) 12 Mod. 582.

(*y*) Com. Dig. Pleader, F. 18; 12 Mod. 532.

(*z*) 12 Mod. 580, 581; 1 B. & P. 77; Summary Treat. on Pleading, 81. *acc.*; Tidd, 9th edit. 684; and 8 Co. 67 b, *contra*.

(*a*) Com. Dig. Pleader, F. 19; 12 Mod. 582; 8 Co. 67 a; Doc. Plac. 114.

II. THE BODY.

proceeds on a special reason (*b*); for suppose the lessor was seised in fee, such seisin would be involved in the issue (*b*).

2dly. Denial of the plea. 1st. Of the *whole* plea. When *de injuria* is not proper, but a qualified replication or denial is required.

If in any case the defendant justified under the *warrant* of a justice of the peace (*c*), or as *servant of another*, or *by his command*, the replication must have been special, and admit or protest the warrant or commandment, and reply *de injuria absque residuo causa*, or take issue simply on the warrant or commandment (*d*). However in a late case it was held that *de injuria* was a good replication to a plea justifying *as servant* of an occupier in turning out the plaintiff from an house (*e*), and *de injuria* is a good plea in bar to an avowry for a poor-rate (*f*). So, "when by the defendant's plea any *authority or power* is mediately or immediately derived from the plaintiff, there, although no interest be claimed, the plaintiff ought to answer it specially, and shall not reply *de injuria* generally;" (*g*) as if he justified by virtue of the leave, or licence, or command of the plaintiff (*h*). So, when the defendant in his plea claims in his own right, or as lessee or servant of another, any right to, or interest in,
[*641] *the person (*i*), personal property (*k*), or real property (*l*), for a supposed injury to which the plaintiff has declared; or any right of way (*m*), common (*n*), or other easement, &c. (*o*); or rent issuing out of the land claimed in the declaration (*p*); or right to enter for a distress for rent (*q*); or if the plea contain matter of record not stated merely as inducement (*r*)(1036), and of which a jury cannot be competent judges, as if the sheriff or his officer justify under process of a Court of record (*s*); or if the defendant justify under the warrant of a justice of the peace (*t*); or under a particular custom of a manor (*u*); or in some cases by authority of law, as to view waste (*x*); in these cases the general replication *de injuria* is improper (*y*). In such instances the plaintiff must either deny the title, easement, warrant, &c. in particular (*z*); or admitting, or in some cases *protesting* (which in effect admits) those mat-

(*b*) 12 Mod. 582.

(*c*) 12 Mod. 582, 583.

(*d*) *Id.*; 8 Co. 67 a, b; Lutw. 1459; Doc. Plac. 113, 114; 1 B. & P. 76; Com. Dig. Pleader, F.; Willes, 100, 101; 2 Saund. 295 b, n. 1; 2 Bro. Ab. *De son tort Demesne*, pl. 13, 15.

(*e*) Piggott *v.* Kemp, 1 Crom. & M. 197; *ante*, 594, n. (y).

(*f*) Bardons *v.* Selby, 1 Crom. & M. 500; 3 Barn. & Adol. 2.

(*g*) 8 Co. 67, 68; 1 B. & P. 80; Com. Dig. Pleader, F. 22; 2 Saund. 295, n. 1; Stephen, 2d ed. 204; Willes, 99.

(*h*) Com. Dig. Pleader, F. 22; Summary Treat. on. Pleading, 83; Bro. Ab. *De son tort*, pl. 30; Ld. Raym. 104, 105. However, to the common plea of *licence* to a declaration in trespass, it is usual to reply that defendant, of *his own* wrong, and without the supposed *licence*, committed, &c. see *post*, vol. iii.; 11 East, 451.

(*i*) Willes, 102.

(*k*) Yelv, 157; Cro. Jac. 225; Cro. Eliz. 539.

(*l*) 8 Co. 67 a; 1 B. & P. 79 c, 80; Willes, 52, 99, 101, 102; Doc. Plac. 114; Com. Dig. Pleader, F. 21, &c.

(*m*) *Id.*; 1 B. & P. 79.

(*n*) *Id.*

(*o*) *Id.*

(*p*) 8 Co. 67 a; 1 B. & P. 76; Willes, 52; Com. Dig. Pleader, F. 21; Hooker *v.* Nye, 1 Crom. M. & Ros. 258; 4 Tyr. 777.

(*q*) 1 Crom. M. & Ros. 258; 4 Tyr. 777; *aliter* as to a distress for poor-rate; 1 Crom. & M. 500; 3 B. & Adol. 2.

(*r*) Willes, 103, note a; Com. Dig. Plead., F. 19, 20; 2 Leon. 81.

(*s*) 8 Co. 67 a; Doc. Plac. 114; Com. Dig. Pleader, F. 20; Hardr. 6; 12 Mod. 580, 581, 582.

(*t*) 12 Mod. 582, 583; Doc. Plac. 113.

(*u*) Com. Dig. Pleader, F. 20; Hob. 76; 3 Lev. 49; 8 Co. 67 a; Willes, 202.

(*x*) Co. 67 b; Com. Dig. Pleader, F. 23; 12 Mod. 582.

(*y*) See all the above cases, and 8 Co. 67; 1 B. & P. 79, 80; Doct. Plac. 114; Com. Dig. Pleader, F. 20, &c.; 4 Bing. 729; 1 M. & P. 723; S. C. 2 Y. & J. 304, 372. See the form, *post*, vol. iii.

(*z*) Lutw. 1459.

(1036) {See Allen *v.* Crofoot, 7 Cow. Rep. 46.} Griswold *v.* Sedgwick, 1 Wend. R. 130. Coburn *v.* Hopkins, 4 Ib. 578.

ters (y), must reply, that the defendant, of his own wrong, and without *the residue* of the cause alleged by the defendant, committed the trespasses; in which case it will not be incumbent on the defendant to prove either of those matters so admitted or protested (z). Where matter of record is denied, the replication should be merely *nul tiel record* (a)(1037).

II. THE BODY. 2dly. Denial of the plea. 1st. Of the *whole* plea.

Thus, where in trespass for taking the plaintiff's servant, the defendant pleaded that the father of the person taken held of the defendant by knight's service and died seized, and that the person taken being under age the defendant seized him as his ward, the general replication *de injuria* was held insufficient, the plea claiming an interest in the *person claimed by the plaintiff in his declaration (b). So, if in trespass for taking goods, trees, &c. the defendant plead that he took them as tithe, or as a distress for rent, or as *damage feasant*, showing title thereto, the general replication will be improper (c). But by the statute of sewers, and in the instance for distresses for poor's-rates, exceptions are introduced; and where in a justification of *taking* cattle damage feasant, the defendant sets out a title and does not rely merely on possession, the replication should be special (d). Other instances have already been sufficiently enumerated. It also seems, that though the plea claim no *interest* in the property mentioned in the plaintiff's declaration, but merely contain matter of *excuse*, yet where such matter of excuse arises in part out of the *seisin in fee* of another, it is not advisable to reply *de injuria*; because that replication is only allowed where in the plea an excuse is offered to *personal* injuries, and not even then if it relate to any *interest* in land, which would make part of the issue (e); there being a distinction in this respect between a plea relying merely on *possession* as inducement, and where an interest is pleaded by way of title (f). [*642]

There are also many cases in which, though the replication *de injuria* might not be objectionable upon demurrer, still it will not be proper to adopt it, and it may be necessary in effect to confess and avoid the plea. Thus, if in trespass for an assault the defendant plead *son assault demesne*, and the plaintiff did in fact commit the first assault, but can justify it as having occurred in defence of his house, &c., it would be improper to use the traverse *de injuria, &c.*, and the plaintiff should reply his possession of the house, and defendant's entry and refusal to quit, &c. (g) And in an action for false imprisonment, where the defendant justifies the commitment as a magistrate for a bailable offence, in consequence of an information upon oath, the plaintiff, under the general replication *de injuria sua propria*, &c. *cannot give in evidence a tender and refusal of bail, but ought to reply that matter specially (h). But where in trespass for breaking and entering the plaintiff's ship, and seizing [*643]

(y) *Post*, 611.
(z) 1 C. & J. 48.
(a) 3 Lev. 243, 244; Lutw. 1459.
(b) Willes, 102; Yelv. 158; 1 Brownl. 215; Com. Dig. Pleader, F. 21.
(c) *Ante*, 626, 627, 639; Cro. Jac. 226; Yelv. 157; Cro. Eliz. 539; Com. Dig. Pleader, F. 21; 1 B. & P. 76; Willes, 52, 99.
(d) *Ante*, 639; 1 Lev. 307; Com. Dig. Pleader.
(e) 1 B. & P. 80; Willes, 102, 103; Cro. Jac. 598; Lord Raym. 649; 12 Mod. 582; Cro. Eliz. 539, 540; Yelv. 157, observed upon in Willes, 101; 2 Saund. 295, n. 1; 7 Price, 670.
(f) Cro. Car. 139; Ld. Raym. 120; Carth. 10.
(g) *Ante*, 624.
(h) 2 Bla. Rep. 1165.

(1037) { See Green et al. v. Overington. 16 Johns. Rep. 55. }

II. THE BODY.

2dly. Denial of the plea.

1st. Of the whole plea.

and converting his goods, the defendants justified under a writ of *fieri facias*, to which the plaintiff replied *de injuria sua propria absque residuo causa*, and new assigned that the defendants entered the ship and took the goods for other purposes than those mentioned in the plea;—it was held, that it was competent to the judge to leave it to the jury to say whether the goods were *bona fide* taken under the writ, or whether the execution was resorted to as a color for taking them to evade payment of freight, to which they would have been liable had the defendants accepted them under the bill of lading, and not to effect a levy by virtue of the writ (*i*). In many cases, where it may not be absolutely necessary to reply specially, it may be advisable so to do in order to narrow the plaintiff's evidence, and to compel the defendant to admit a part of his title (*k*).

Where *de injuria* is improperly replied, the defendant may demur generally, but the defect will be aided after verdict (*l*).

Form of general denial, *de injuria*, &c.

In point of *form*, the general replication *de injuria* or *de son tort demesne* would be defective, unless the words *absque tali causa* be added, though the omission will be aided by verdict (*m*). The usual language of this replication in trespass is "*precludi non*," because he says, that the defendant, at the said times when, &c. *of his own wrong*, and *without the cause* by him in his said second plea alleged, committed the said trespasses in the introductory part of that plea mentioned, *in manner and form* as the plaintiff hath above thereof complained against him, and this he the plaintiff prays may be inquired of by the country, &c. (*n*) which is uniformly the conclusion of such a replication. The word *cause*, which means without the matter of excuse alleged, though in the singular number, puts in issue all the facts in the plea, which constitute but one cause (*o*); and if such a replication be adopted, as we have [*644] seen it may be, *in answer to two or more pleas by different defendants, the *tali causa* will suffice, *reddendo singula singulis* (*p*); and the words *modo et forma* only put in issue material allegations in the plea (*q*).

Secondly, denial of only *part* of the plea.

When the plaintiff is not at liberty to reply *de injuria* to the whole plea, but must deny some *paticular* fact or facts, it is *first* to be considered *what fact* he may deny; and *secondly*, the *form* of such denial (*r*).

1st. What fact or part in particular may be traversed.

1st. A party may traverse or deny any *material* and issuable allegation in his opponent's pleading; and this although the matter be stated with more preciseness or particularity than is necessary (1038); as if in an avowry, it be stated that the defendant was seised in fee, though it would have been suffi-

(*i*) 4 Bing. 729; S. C. affirmed in error, 1 M. & P. 783; 2 Y. & J. 304. See *id.* 79.

(*k*) Willes, 204, 54; 1 East, 217.

(*l*) Com. Dig. Pleader, F. 24; 3 Lev. 65; Hob. 76; Sir T. Raym. 50.

(*m*) Com. Dig Pleader, F. 24; Cro. Jac. 599; Gilb. C. P. 153; 1 Sid. 341; Lutw. 1384.

(*n*) See the form of the replication *de injuria* in assumpsit, *ante*, 614, note (*x*); 2 Bing. N. C. 359; 3 Dowl. 754; Isaac v. Farrer, 1 Westm. Chronicle, 383; and *post*, vol. iii.

(*o*) 8 Co. 67; 11 East, 451, 455.

(*p*) 1 Leon. 124; Cro. Eliz. 139; 1 Sid. 39.

(*q*) *Ante*, 611; Gilb. C. P. 51.

(*r*) As to traverses in general, Com. Dig. Pleader, G.

(1038) { Bradner v. Demick, 20 Johns. Rep. 406. }

cient to have alleged that the close was his freehold, &c., the seisin in fee may be traversed (*s*). And a material fact may be denied, though laid under a *videlicet* (*t*) (1039). II. THE BODY. 2dly. Denial of the plea.

So, whatever is necessarily understood, intended, or *implied* from the plea, is traversable as much as if it were *expressly alleged* (*u*). Thus, the allegation that "A. is seised of a close," imports that he was *sole* seised, and therefore it may be shown that B. was seised of a third part, with a traverse that A. *alone* was seised (*x*). But matter not before stated in the adverse pleading, or necessarily implied, is not traversable though it affect the merits (*y*). In replevin and trespass to *personal* chattels, if the defendant justify as bailiff or by the command of another, his authority might always be traversed; and the same rule now holds in trespass to *real property* (*z*). When a party appears on the face of the pleadings to be estopped from denying a fact, if he were to traverse it his pleading would be demurrable (*a*). *The plaintiff must be extremely careful in traversing one of several facts, that he denies that which is most open to objection, for he admits those which are not expressly denied. In trespass to land, the defendant pleaded that A. was seised in fee, and being so seised granted a right of way by non-existing grant; and the replication traversed *the grant*, and it was held that on these pleadings it was not competent to the plaintiff to prove that A. was not seised in fee, for the purpose of rebutting the presumption of the grant (*b*). 2dly. Of part of the plea. [*645]

If, however, an allegation in the opposite pleading be altogether *immaterial*, it cannot be traversed; otherwise the object of pleading, viz. the bringing the parties to an issue upon a matter or point decisive of the merits, would be defeated (*c*). And upon this ground, mere matter of aggravation, not going to the cause of action, or mere inducement or explanatory matter not in itself essential to or the substance of the case, should not be traversed (*d*).

It is also a most material rule upon this subject, that a traverse should be taken on matter of fact, not mere matter or conclusion of *law*; for to raise an issue upon a legal inference or question would be to submit to the jury that which it is the province of the Court to decide (*e*); thus, where in trespass for fishing in the plaintiff's fishery, the defendant justified that it was an arm of the sea, wherein every one might fish; a replication, traversing that in the said arm of the sea every subject had the privilege of fishing, was held to be de-

(*s*) 2 Saund. 206, 207, notes 21, 22, 24; 1 Saund. 22, note 2; Com. Dig. Pleader, Q.; see 4 Moore, 303; 1 B. & B. 531; as to the danger of unnecessary particularity, see *ante*, 261, 262.

(*t*) 1 Saund. 170, n 2 As to the *videlicet*, see *ante*, 348.

(*u*) 2 Saund. 10, note 14; 11 East, 416; 1 Lord Raym. 39.

(*x*) *Id.*; Salk. 629.

(*y*) 1 Saund. 312, note 4. Instances, Stephen, 2d edit. 235. But the demurrer to such traverse should be special, *id.*

(*z*) 11 East, 65; 1 Saund. 347 c, n. 4; 1 East, 245, n. c; Cro. Car. 586; Willes, 100, note b; *ante*, 627.

(*a*) Stra. 817; 8 T. R. 487; 7 T. R. 557; *ante*, 634.

(*b*) 1 C. & J. 48.

(*c*) See 2 Saund. 207 a; Com. Dig. Pleader, R. 8, G. 10; Bac. Ab. Pleas, H. 5. Instances, Stephen, 2d ed. 283

(*d*) *Id.*; Stephen, 2d ed. 284, 285.

(*e*) Plowd 231 a; 11 Rep. 10 b; 1 Saund. 23, note 5; 2 Hen. Bla. 182. See as to the rule that a plea must be capable of trial, *ante*, 573.

(1039) { Hastings *v.* Lovering, 2 Pick. Rep. 223. Gleason *v.* M'Vikar, 7 Cow. Rep. 42, explaining the *dictum* in Paine, Judge, &c. *v.* Fox, 16 Mass. Rep. 133. }

II. THE BODY. 2dly. Denial of the plea. 2dly. Of part of the plea.

fective, as putting in issue a mere *legal* conclusion (*f*). This erroneous traverse more frequently occurs in cases where the plea alleges certain facts in justification, and then concludes or infers from them "by virtue whereof," (*virtute cujus*,) the party "became seised," or "became liable." In such case the preceding facts, or some or one of them, if any, should be alone traversed; and no traverse should be taken on the mere legal result drawn from them, and alleged, perhaps unnecessarily, in the plea (*g*). But where the allegation, [*646] whether in the *shape of the *virtute cujus*, *prætextu* or *per quod*, be compounded of law and fact, and they be connected together, a traverse may be properly taken thereon (*h*). This subject was clearly explained and settled in a late case (*i*), already referred to, as showing what may be put in issue by *de injuria*, &c. to a plea justifying under a *fieri facias*; the Chief Justice observed (*k*), "it has been argued before us, that motives are not examinable, and that the allegation in pleas of *virtute cujus* is not traversable. If a man do that which he is justified in doing, and no more, the law, in many cases, will not permit his motives to be inquired into, as if he have a right to prosecute for a crime, or to arrest for a debt, there can be no inquiry as to the motives with which these acts were done; but if he do more than as a prosecutor or creditor he have a right to do, he will not be justified, and it becomes proper to inquire whether the prosecution or arrest were not mere pretence. Such an inquiry is material for the purpose of getting at the real nature of the transaction, and enabling a jury to award proper damages. The *virtute cujus* is sometimes a mere inference of law, as to what is the meaning of a writ, or the extent of authority given by it. In such cases a question of law is raised, and there can be no traverse, for that withdraws the consideration of law from the judges, and presents it to the jury. But the *virtute cujus* sometimes raises a mixed question of law and fact, and when this is the case, there may be a traverse, for that is the only mode by which the facts are to be settled on which the law depends. In *Beal* v. *Simpson* (*l*), Mr. Justice Powell says, 'that when a matter of law is only comprised in a *virtute cujus*, then it is not traversable; but matter of fact in the *virtute cujus* is traversable.' Lord Chief Justice Treby differed from Mr. Justice Powell on this point, and said, 'By *virtue of the writ*, means by authority of the writ by an operation of law on the writ, without any ingredient or mixture of matter of fact.' The other judges agreed with Mr. Justice Powell, and said 'that when the *virtute cujus* [*647] is mixed with fact, it may be traversed.' (*l*) *It appears from Williams' Saunders (*m*), that *virtute cujus*, may be traversed, and he refers, in support of this opinion, to Hobart (*n*), and 9 Hen. 6 (*o*). The learned editor, Mr. Serjeant Williams, says, 'that when the words *virtute prætextu per quod*, *&c.*, introduce a consequence from the preceding matter, they are not traversable, but that

(*f*) 2 Hen. Bla. 182; 5 T. R. 367; 2 Saund. 159 a; 161, note 11.

(*g*) 1 Saund. 23, n. 5.

(*h*) 1 Saund. 23, n. 5; Stephen, 2d ed. 233, 234, and instances there, 11 Price, 343. As to traversing the *due* issuing of process, &c., 16 East, 41; 1 B. & Ald. 348; *ante*, 502. An averment that a party was "duly elected," 4 B. & C. 368; or that an assembly was "duly constituted," 4 B. & C. 427, is good.

(*i*) 4 Bing. 729. Affirmed in error, 1 M. & P. 783; 2 Y. & J. 304. Again affirmed in Dom. Proc. 3 Moore & Scott, 627; 10 Bar. & Cres. 157, S. C.; and 1 Crom. & M. 500.

(*k*) 1 M. & P. 803.

(*l*) 1 Ld. Raym. 410.

(*m*) 1 Saund. 23, n. 5.

(*n*) Page 52.

(*o*) Fol. 14, 20.

II. THE BODY. 2dly. Denial of the plea.

matter of law connected with fact, or rather matter of right resulting from facts, is traversable.' In *The Grocers' Company* v. *The Archbishop of Canterbury*, Lord Chief Justice De Grey, in giving the judgment of the Court, says (p), 'law connected with fact is clearly traversable.'"

2dly. Of part of the plea.

Traverse should be of affirmative allegations, and not put in issue a negative allegation.

The traverse should also be on some *affirmative* matter, and not put in issue a negative allegation; thus, if a plea state a request to deliver an abstract, and a refusal, a replication that the plaintiff did *not neglect* and refuse to deliver such abstract, would be insufficient (q).

Traverse must not be too large.

The traverse *must not be too large* (r). Thus, to an avowry for £20 arrears of rent, the plea in bar must be, that "no part of it is in arrear," and if it were merely, that "the said sum of £20" is not in arrear, without saying "or any part thereof," it would be demurrable (s). So, if a defendant show that on a certain day and at a certain place, the plaintiff demised to him the close in question, a traverse that "on the day," or "at the place stated," the plaintiff did not demise, &c. is bad, as involving in the issue the time or place, neither of which is material (t). And where in trespass for entering the plaintiff's house, the defendant pleads that the plaintiff's daughter licensed him to enter, a replication that defendant "did not enter *per licentiam suam*," is bad, as a *negative pregnant*, though good after verdict (u). It is enough to deny the substance and effect of *the averment, without pursuing the words of the party (x). But where to a declaration against a rector for not carrying away tithe, the defendant pleaded that the close was surrounded with ditches, and that the ditches, ways, and passages were so filled with water that the defendant could not carry off his tithes; a replication that the ditches, ways, and passages were not so, was held sufficient on demurrer, though in the conjunctive; because the plea is one entire matter of excuse, and the defendant relies on the whole, and not on each particular part being impassable (y). So, a replication to a plea claiming a right of common, traversing "that the cattle were the defendant's own cattle, and that they were *levant* and *couchant* upon the premises, and commonable cattle," was held sufficient; because, though issue must be taken upon a single point, it is not necessary that such single point should consist only of a single fact, and the point of defence was the cattle in question being entitled to common (z). So, to a plea prescribing for tolls, and also showing a prescriptive right to distrain for the same, the replication may deny both the prescriptions.

Negative pregnant.

[*648]

(p) 3 Wils. 234.
(q) 6 East, 556, 557.
(r) 1 Saund. 268, note 1; 269, note 2; Com. Dig. Pleader, G. 15; Stephen, 2d ed. 286. A traverse may be too large by including quantity, time, place, or other circumstances, which, though forming part of the allegation traversed, are not of the *substance* of the matter, *id.*
(s) 3 B. & P. 348; Com. Dig. Pleader, G. 12, 15; 2 Saund. 207, n. 24; 319, n. 6; 1 Saund. 268; the reason, 269, n. 2.
(t) 2 Saund. 319, note 6; 1 Saund. 268 a, note; Steph. 2d edit. 287, 288.
(u) Cro. Jac. 87; 2 Saund. 319, note 6. A negative pregnant is such a form of negative expression as implies or imports an affirmative. See Steph. 2d edit. 424. In the instances put in the text, the denial that there was a demise "on a particular day," and that the defendant "entered by virtue of the licence," is pregnant with an admission that there was *some* demise, and that there was *some* licence. See further, Ventr. 70.
(x) Salk. 629; 1 Saund. 269, note.
(y) 1 Stra. 245.
(z) 1 Burr. 317; 1 Saund. 346 c.

II. THE BODY. — 2dly. Denial of the plea. 3dly. Of *part* of the plea. What entire allegation is or not divisible, so as to enable a party to recover *pro tanto* on proof of part.

In general a traverse, or denial, or allegation, should be so framed as to be *divisible*, and entitle the party pleading to recover *pro tanto*, if he prove part of the allegation (*a*). And in one case, where the defendant pleaded a right of common over the plaintiff's close, which the plaintiff had wrongfully inclosed, and the plaintiff replied that "the close in which, &c." had been inclosed twenty years, and the jury found that part only of the close had been so inclosed, and that the trespass was committed on that part, that the defendant was entitled to a verdict, on the ground that the plaintiff should have replied that that *part* of the close, and not that the close had been so inclosed (*b*). But in a subsequent action of trespass, where plaintiff declared for entering two closes, and the plea was, that *the said closes*, in which, &c. were from time immemorial parcels of a waste, and that the defendant had a prescriptive right of common in the waste, and entered at the times when, &c. to use his right of common thereon; and because the closes, in which, &c. were wrongfully separated from the residue of the waste, he broke down the gate; and the *replication* was, that the *said closes*, in which, &c. at the said time when, &c. were not wrongfully separated from the residue of the waste, but, continually, for twenty years and more, and before the first time when, &c., had been and were separated, and divided, and inclosed from the residue of the waste, and occupied and enjoyed in severalty; and the *rejoinder* traversed the averment, and issue was joined thereon: it was held that the allegation in the replication was divisible, and the plaintiff entitled to recover on proof that *any part* of the closes had been inclosed for twenty years (*c*). This latter decision establishes that the word *close* in which, &c. is to be taken as divisible into several parts. There are other instances also in which an entire allegation in pleading is to be read as divisible. Thus a replication to a plea of infancy, that the goods mentioned in the declaration were necessaries suitable to the defendant's degree, is a divisible allegation, and may be proved only in part, so as to enable the plaintiff to recover *pro tanto*, if he prove that a part of the goods were necessaries (*d*). But care must be observed not to introduce into the allegation any words that may impose the burthen of proving the *whole*, as, for instance, in the above cases, "that *all* the goods were necessaries," or that *the whole and every part* of the said close had been inclosed for twenty years, &c., for such words may prevent the entire allegation from being treated as divisible (*e*). Where the defendant pleaded to indebitatus assumpsit for work and labor and materials, that there was an agreement that the work should be to the satisfaction of the defendant *or* his surveyor, and that the building had not been completed to the satisfaction of the defendant *or* his surveyor, and the replication unnecessarily was in the conjunctive, yet it was holden to be supported in evidence by proof that the *defendant* was satisfied (*f*).

(*a*) 2 Bar. & Cres. 918; 7 B. & Cres. 346.

(*b*) Hawke *v.* Bacon, 2 Taunt. 159; 2 Bar. & Cres. 918; 7 Bar. & Cres. 346. But overruled, see 5 Bar. & Adol. 395.

(*c*) Tapley *v.* Wainwright, 5 B. & Adol. 395.

(*d*) *Per* Denman, C. J. in Tapley *v.* Wainwright, 5 B. & Adol. 399.

(*e*) *Id. ibid.*; and see 2 Saund. 206, note 21, as to the improper introduction of the word "*only*."

(*f*) Bradley *v.* Milnes, 1 Bing. N. C. 644.

A traverse may be *too extensive*, and therefore defective, by being taken in the *conjunctive* instead of the *disjunctive*, where proof of the allegation in the conjunctive is not essential. Thus, in an action on a policy on ship and tackle, the defendant should not deny that the ship *and* tackle were lost, but that *neither* was lost (*g*).

II. THE BODY. 2dly. Denial of the plea. 2dly. Of *part* of the plea. Must not be too extensive.

*On the other hand the traverse must not be *too narrow*, so as to prejudice the defence (*h*). Thus, if in an action of trespass in a common called A., the defendant pleads that A. the *locus in quo*, and B. are commons which lie open to each other, and then prescribes for a right in *both* the commons, the plaintiff must traverse the entire prescription, and not the prescriptive right in A. only; for the prescription is entire, and it may be important to the defendant to be let in to prove acts in exercise of the right in B. (*i*) But in general a party is not bound to traverse more than one fact material to the matter in dispute (*k*). And in trespass, if the defendant justify under a prescriptive right to a duty, and the like right to distrain for it, a replication traversing the duty without denying the right to distrain, is sufficient (*l*). And where the claim is divisible, and damages *pro tanto* are recoverable, the allegation should not attempt to confine the party to evidence of a *tort* continuing for a specific and named period (*m*).

[*649] Nor *too narrow*.

Replications denying a *particular* fact or facts, are, in point of *form*, of *three* descriptions; *first*, the plaintiff protests some fact or facts, and denies the other, concluding to the country; or, *secondly*, he at once denies the particular fact intended to be put in issue, and concludes to the country; or, *thirdly*, formally traverses a particular fact, and concludes with a verification.

2dly. The modes of *special* denial.

1st. When the pleading of either party contains several matters, and the opposite party is not at liberty to put the whole in issue, he may *protest* against one or more facts, and deny the other. Thus, if in assumpsit the defendant plead an accord and satisfaction, as that he delivered to the plaintiff, and the latter accepted, a pipe of wine in satisfaction of the promises, the plaintiff may *protest* the delivery in satisfaction (*n*), and reply that he did not accept the wine in satisfaction (*o*); or in trespass, where the defendant in his plea has justified an arrest and wounding under a writ and *warrant, the plaintiff may protest the writ and warrant and reply *de injuria sua propria absque residuo causa* (*p*), or may protest one fact, and traverse another (*q*). And if to a plea of performance of several matters in the condition of a bond, the plaintiff mean in that suit to insist on the breach of one only, he may protest the performance of the others (*r*). This is termed a *protestation*, and its only possible use is, that in case the party making it succeeds in the point to be

1st. With a *protestation*.

[*650]

(*g*) 2 Saund. 205; Steph. 2d ed. 288, 289. As to traversing a particular estate, though unnecessarily stated so precisely, *ante*, 262, 263.

(*h*) Com. Dig. Pleader, G. 16; Steph. 2d ed. 291.

(*i*) 4 T. R. 157; 1 Saund. 269, n. 1; Steph. 2d ed. 291, 292. *Sed quære*.

(*k*) 1 Saund. 268, n. 1.

(*l*) 1 Wils. 338.

(*m*) 1 Saund. 267.

(*n*) *Precludi non*, because "*protesting* that the defendant *did not deliver* to him the plaintiff the said pipe of wine as in the said plea alleged," for replication he saith, &c.

(*o*) 3 Wentw. 135; Bac. Ab. Accord, C.

(*p*) 1 Burr. 320; *post*, vol. iii.

(*q*) Poph. 1.

(*r*) Dyer, 184 a.

II. THE BODY.

2dly. Denial of the plea.

2dly. Of part of the plea.

tried, he thereby saves to himself the liberty of disputing in *any other* suit the truth of the allegation which is protested against (*s*) (1040). It is wholly unavailable in the particular suit in which it is adopted, for the allegation protested against is in effect admitted *in that suit*, so that no evidence need be adduced in support of it; for it is a rule that every pleading is taken to confess such traversable matter of *fact* alleged on the other side as it does not traverse (*t*): and it is of no service in any other action, if the issue be found against the party making it, unless it be of matter which could not be pleaded, or on which issue could not be joined, and then the party protesting will not be concluded, though the issue be found against him (*u*). It is said that matter which is the ground of the suit, or upon which issue might be taken, cannot be protested (1041); as that in detinue by the executor of A. the defendant cannot protest that A. did not make the plaintiff his executor, for it is the ground of the suit, and utterly destroys the plaintiff's action (*x*). It is also a rule, that a protestation which is *repugnant* to, or inconsistent with, the plea which it accompanies, is inartificial and improper (*y*). In these cases the replication should either admit the part of the plea which is not disputed, by saying, "true it is, that, &c.;" or should at once deny the matter intended
[*651] to be tried; though the *latter mode, as being the most concise, appears preferable, for whatever is not traversed is in effect admitted. However, a repugnant, or inconsistent, or idle, or superfluous protestation, does not vitiate the plea, though it be shown for cause of demurrer, for the intent of a protestation is, that the party may not be concluded in *another* action, and in the *existing* suit it is surplusage, and may be rejected as such (*z*). Hence it appears that a protestation was, even before the recent rules, in general an unnecessary form (*a*), and the replication might at once deny the fact intended to be put in issue, as in the next description of replications (*b*). Though it is not unusual, when it is doubtful whether a plea is sufficient in *law* to protest the *legal* sufficiency of it in the beginning of the replication (*c*), yet this is unnecessary, for without such protestation the plaintiff would afterwards be at liberty to object to the plea by motion in arrest of judgment, writ of error, &c. The pleading over to certain of the facts, admits, in general, the truth of the rest of the allegations, without recognizing the *legal* sufficiency of either of such allegations. But, as will be more fully explained hereafter, there are some *faults* in pleading which may be cured by *pleading over*, without demurring. In point of form, the proper place in which to introduce a protestation

(*s*) 2 Saund. 103 a, note 1; Com. Dig. Pleader, N.; Doc. Plac. 295; Co. Lit. 124 b; Plowd. 276; Steph. 2d edit. 256.

(*t*) Com. Dig. Pleader, G. 2; Steph. 2d edit. 255, 259; *ante*, 614, 615.

(*u*) 2 Saund. 103 a, note 1; Com. Dig. Pleader, N.; Bro Ab. Protestation; Finch's Law, 359; Plowd. 276; Co. Lit. 124 b.

(*x*) Com. Dig. Pleader, N.; 2 Saund. 103, n. 1; Plowd. 276; Doc. Plac. 296; Moor, 355, 356; Cro. Car. 365; 3 Wils. 109, 116; *sed quære*, see the cases in 2 Saund. 103, note 1, in which there are instances of protestation of matter, upon which issue might have been taken.

(*y*) 2 Saund. 103, n. 1; Bro. Ab. Protestation, 1, 5; Plowd. 276; Steph. 2d ed. 258.

(*z*) Com. Dig. Pleader, N.; 2 Saund. 103 b, n. 1.

(*a*) 3 Lev. 425.

(*b*) See the form, 3 Lev. 105.

(*c*) *Precludi non*, because "*protesting* that the said plea is wholly insufficient in *law*," for replication he saith, that, &c.

(1040) {Briggs v. Dorr, 19 Johns. Rep. 96.}

(1041) Vide Snider v. Croy, 2 Johns. Rep. 227.

in a plea, is immediately after the words *actio non*, &c. (*d*); and in a replication, after the words *precludi non*, &c. (*e*). 3. IN THE BODY.

But Reg. Gen. Hil. T. 4 W. 4, reg. 12,† directs "that *no protestation* shall hereafter be made in any pleading; but either party shall be entitled to the same advantage in that or other actions as if a protestation had been made." Reg. Gen. Hil. T. 4 W. 4, reg. 12, abolishing protestations.

2dly. The next description of replication, *at once denying the particular fact intended to be put in issue, and concluding to the country*, without any preamble, and without a formal traverse, most frequently occurs in practice, and on account of its conciseness should, when admissible, be adopted (1042). Indeed, the Reg. Gen. Hil. T. 4 W. 4, reg. 13, requires a traverse or denial of this description so to conclude to the country (*f*). In *assumpsit* and other actions on contracts, when the plaintiff denies, and does not confess and avoid the plea, this replication is frequent; as that the defendant was not an infant (*g*), or that no tender was made, &c. (*h*) So to a plea of accord and satisfaction, the plaintiff may, without protestation, reply either that the defendant did not *deliver the pipe of wine in satisfaction, or that the plaintiff [*652] did not accept the same in satisfaction (*i*). So in actions in form *ex delicto*, in general, when the plaintiff denies any allegation in the plea, the better and shorter method is directly to deny the fact, without a formal traverse, and to conclude *to the country* (*k*)(1043). Thus, if the defendant has pleaded defect of fences, or a prescriptive right of common or of way, or a licence, instead of alleging in the replication that the defendant of his own wrong committed the trespasses, or other matters complained of, and then adding a formal traverse, and concluding with a verification, (in which case there must be a rejoinder re-asserting the matter of the plea, although there has already been an affirmative and negative), the proper way is to say "*precludi non*, because, &c." and then immediately denying the defect of fences, or the obligation to repair, or the prescriptive right of common or way, or the licence, and concluding to the country (*l*). The replying with a formal traverse and verification is a practice tending to unnecessary repetition and useless expense, and it may be hoped that the observations of the learned editor of Saunder's Reports (*m*) will have the effect of altering the practice; which was reprobated even in the time of William 3 (*n*), and in the reign of George 2, was considered by the Court as an antiquated mode of pleading, tending to unnecessary prolixity, and was said to have been altered of late (*o*). In this description of replication care must be taken not to attempt to put in issue any immaterial matter (*p*). The form of traverse has been already noticed (*q*). 2dly. A direct and simple denial of *one fact*.

(*d*) Plowd. 276; 2 Saund. 103 a. n. 1; see forms Plowd. 276; Com. Dig. Pleader, N.; *post*, vol. iii.
(*e*) See the forms, *post*, vol. iii.; 3 Wentw. 135.
(*f*) *Post*.
(*g*) *Post*, vol. iii.
(*h*) *Id*.
(*i*) *Post*, vol. iii; Lil. Ent. 105, 106; *query* whether both might not be traversed, see *ante*, 637.
(*k*) 1 Saund. 103 b.
(*l*) *Id.*; 4 Burr. 320; see the forms, *post*, vol. iii.
(*m*) 1 Saund. 103 b.
(*n*) 1 Ld. Raym. 641.
(*o*) 1 Burr. 320.
(*p*) *Ante*, 645.
(*q*) *Ante*, 647, 648.

(1042) { Andrus v. Waring, Bradner v. Demick, 20 Johns. Rep. 165, 404. }
(1043) Vide Snider and others v. Croy, 2 Johns. Rep. 428.

† See American Editor's Preface.

III. THE BODY.

2dly. Denial of the plea.

2dly. Of part of the plea.

3dly. A *formal* traverse with a verification

3dly. A *formal* or *special traverse* of the matter alleged in the plea, and concluding with a verification (*r*), is rarely necessary; for we have just seen that when the plaintiff is at liberty, without introducing any new matter, to deny that alleged in the plea, he may, and indeed should concisely deny it, and conclude to the country; but when it is necessary in the replication, or other pleading, to show a title in the plaintiff, *or to introduce *new matter* inconsistent with that stated by the other party (*s*), or where there are two affirmatives which do not impliedly negative each other, or a confession and avoidance by argument only, a traverse was considered to be necessary, for otherwise pleadings would run to infinite prolixity (*t*) (1044). Thus, where the defendant [*653] alleged *seisin* in A. from whom he claimed, the plaintiff could not in his replication allege *seisin* in B. from whom he claims, without either traversing, or confessing and avoiding the seisin alleged by the defendant (*u*). So where in replevin the defendant avowed as for a distress damage feasant, and the plaintiff pleaded in bar a right of common in *six* acres of land, alleging that the *locus in quo* was parcel thereof, and the defendant replied that the plaintiff *formerly had* common in forty acres, whereof the said six acres were and are parcel, and all lying open together, and that the plaintiff before the distress purchased two acres, parcel of the said forty acres, whereby the right of common became extinguished; as this replication did not confess and avoid the plea in bar, it was held bad for not traversing the right of common in six acres only (*x*). So if a custom be pleaded, another custom or prescription repugnant to it cannot be replied without a traverse, but a custom or matter consistent with it, or which only qualifies, may (*y*) (1045). In trespass to land, if the defendant justify under a custom in a manor that each copyholder shall have common of pasture, the plaintiff may, under a traverse of the custom, show another custom defeating the operation of that stated in the plea, as it regards the *locus in quo*, viz. a custom to inclose, &c., without replying such custom specially (*z*). In real actions, and in *quare impedit*, the plaintiff (then called the demandant) must frequently state a title in his replication inconsistent with that of the defendant, in which case a traverse is necessary (*a*). But in personal actions it is not in general necessary to state a title in the replication, when the defendant by his [*654] plea admits the *plaintiff to be in *possession*, which is sufficient against a wrongdoer (*b*). As if in trespass *quare clausum fregit*, the defendant plead that E. F. was seised in fee of the *locus in quo*, and enfeoffed G. H. who thereby be-

(*r*) See in general, Steph. 2d edit. 205, *et seq.* where this now almost disused species of traverse is very ably explained; and see Reg. Gen. Hil. T. 4 W. 4, reg. 13, *post*, 655.

(*s*) When necessary to show a title in a replication, Com. Dig. Pleader, F. 13, G. 3.

(*t*) 1 Wils. 253; 1 Saund. 22, note 2.

(*u*) Cro. Eliz. 30; Cro. Jac. 682; Cro. Eliz. 651; 6 Co. 25 b; Dyer, 312 b; Com. Dig. Pleader, G. 2, 3.

(*x*) 1 Leon. 43, 44; Com. Dig. Pleader, G. 2.

(*y*) 1 Wils. 253; Bac. Ab. Pleas and Pleading, H.; 1 M. & Sel. 680; 1 B. & P. 285; 2 Leon. 209; 2 Hen. Bla. 234.

(*z*) 7 B. & C. 346; 9 *Id.* 671, S. C.

(*a*) Cro. Eliz. 288, 670; Com. Dig. Pleader, F. 13; *Id.* 3 I. 10.

(*b*) *Id. ibid.*; 8 B. & C. 534.

(1044) Vide Bindon *v.* Robinson, 1 Johns. Rep. 516.

(1045) In trespass *quare clausum fregit* the defendant pleaded that the *locus in quo* was part of a public highway, and that the plaintiff had wrongfully incumbered it with a gate; the plaintiff replied a prescription in those whose estate he had, to maintain a gate on the highway; it was held that he need not traverse the highway, or the wrongful incumbering it with a gate. Spear *v.* Bicknell, 5 Mass. Rep. 125.

II. THE BODY.

came seised, and being so seised, enfeoffed the defendant, by which he became seised, until the plaintiff, claiming by color of a prior deed of feoffment made by E. F. by which nothing passed, entered, &c., here the plaintiff may well traverse the feoffment supposed to have been made by E. F. to G. H. without making title; because the defendant admits the plaintiff to be in possession by virtue of what amounts to an estate at will, but if the plaintiff were to traverse the title of E. F. then he must state his own title, and conclude with a traverse (c).

2dly. Denial of the plea.

3dly. Of part of the plea.

Forms of traverse.

When a formal traverse is adopted, it ought to be introduced with a proper title or *inducement*, to show the matter contained in the traverse to be material (d). Where no new matter is stated in the replication, and a formal traverse is adopted (though, as we have seen, unnecessarily), it is usual in trespass, after the words "*precludi non*," &c. to introduce the traverse with the allegation, "that the defendant of his own wrong committed the trespasses complained of, in manner and form as the plaintiff hath complained against the defendant, *without this, that* &c.," denying the right of common or way, &c. as stated in the plea, and concluding with a verification (e). But where *new matter* is to be stated as inducement to the traverse, it must appear to be sufficient in substance to defeat the opposite party's allegation, and if a defective title be shown, the inducement will be bad; though in stating it, so much certainty does not appear to be requisite as in other parts of pleading, because it is seldom traversable (1046), the other party being in general compellable in his rejoinder or other pleading to adhere to his own allegation, which has been traversed (f). The usual words of the *beginning* of a traverse are, "without this, that, &c." (*absque hoc*); but any words amounting to a denial of the allegation of the other party are sufficient, as *et non, &c." (g) The traverse must neither be *too large* nor *too narrow* (h); and though it is in general in the negative of the words of the plea, yet time and place, or other matter when immaterial must not be included (i); but the words *in manner and form* as the defendant hath in his said plea above alleged, may be added, for they only put in issue matter of substance (k). The *conclusion* must before the recent rules in general have been *with a verification*, unless where no new matter was stated by way of inducement, or where the traverse comprised the *whole matter of the plea*, in which case it might be to the country (l). [*655]

No traverse to be after a traverse.

It is a general rule that there cannot be a traverse after a traverse where the first was material, and of matter necessarily alleged (m). As if the plain-

(c) See the case in Poph. 1, 2.

(d) Parker's Rep. 131; Com. Dig. Pleader, G. 20; see 1 M. & Sel. 680; Stephen, 2d ed. 226.

(e) See the forms, Rast Ent. 622, 623; Co. Ent. 656. We have just seen that a formal traverse is not necessary in this case.

(f) Com. Dig. Pleader, G. 20. When not, see *id.* G. 17, 18; 1 Saund. 22, n. 2.

(g) Com. Dig. Pleader, G. 1.

(h) As to this, see 11 East, 407, 410, 411; 1 Ld. Raym. 39; *ante*, 647, 648.

(i) *Id.*; Bac. Ab. Pleas, H. 5.

(k) 2 Leon. 5; Hardr. 39; Com. Dig. Pleader, G. 1; *vide* 3 Bing. 135; 10 Moore, 502, S. C.

(l) 1 Saund. 103 a, b; Dougl. 428, and see Reg. Gen. Hil. T. 4 W. 4, reg. 13, *infra*.

(m) Com. Dig. Pleader, G. 17; Vaugh. 62; 1 Hen. Bla. 376 to 412. And see the reasons, 4 T. R. 439, though the *decision* was reversed in 5 T. R. 367; 2 Hen. Bla. 182.

(1046) Vide Fowler v. Clark, 3 Day, 231. Van Ness v. Hamilton, 19 Johns. Rep. 371.

II. THE BODY.

2dly. Denial of the plea.

3dly. Of part of the plea.

tiff has declared on a seisin in fee in B. who granted, &c. and the defendant shows a seisin *pur autre vie*, and traverses the seisin in fee, the plaintiff cannot waive such traverse, and traverse that he was seised *pur autre vie*, for this would be a departure from and desertion of his prior allegation, and the parties are not to go on *ad infinitum* (n). In some cases however a traverse may be taken after a former *apt* and *pertinent* one. As where in a transitory action there is a special local justification with a traverse of the place laid in the declaration, the plaintiff may either join in the defendant's traverse, or traverse the special justification, for in this case the place laid in the declaration being immaterial the plaintiff is not bound by it (o); and the same rule prevails where time or any other immaterial matter alleged in the declaration, is traversed in the plea (p). And if a traverse be of matter immaterial (q), or of an inference of law (r), or not to the substance and point of the action, the other party may either demur specially or may pass it by and tender another traverse (s).

Reg. Gen. Hil. T. 4 W. 4, reg. 13, as to traverses.

The Reg. Gen. Hil. T. 4 W. 4, reg. 13,† orders that "all special traverses, or traverses with an inducement of affirmative matter, shall conclude to the *country*, provided that this regulation shall not preclude the opposite party from pleading over to the inducement when the traverse is immaterial."

[*656] *The king is allowed to take a traverse after a traverse, where his title appears by *office* or other matter of *record;* though if it do not so appear, such second traverse cannot be taken (t).

A *defect* in a traverse can only be taken advantage of by special demurrer; and therefore it was decided that where the inducement to a traverse confesses and avoids the other party's title, the traverse, though idle and bad on special demurrer, is aided by a general demurrer (u); and an immaterial traverse (x), or the want of a traverse when necessary, is aided upon a general demurrer and by verdict or pleading over (y).

3dly. A denial; and stating a breach.

With respect to a replication *denying the effect of the plea, and showing a particular breach* without confessing and avoiding the plea, it most frequently occurs in debt on a bond conditioned to perform covenants, &c. (z) We have already seen (a) when this replication is necessary, both at common law and under the 8 & 9 Wm. 3, c. 11, s. 8, and therefore no further observations thereon will be here necessary.

3dly. Confession and avoidance of the plea.

The *third* description of replication *admits*, either in words or in effect,

(n) *Id. ibid.*
(o) 1 Saund. 22, n. 2; Com. Dig. Pleader, G. 18; Bac. Ab. Pleas, H. 4; Lutw. 1438; 1 Hen. Bla. 403; 4 T. R. 439, 440, reversed, see 5 *Id.* 367; 2 Hen. Bla. 182.
(p) *Id. ibid.*
(q) *Ante*, 644, 645.
(r) *Ante*, 645.
(s) 2 H. Bla. 186; 1 Saund. 22, n. 2; Com. Dig. Pleader, G. 19; Bac. Ab. Pleas, H. 4; 1 Hen. Bla. 402, 403.
(t) Vaughan 62; Com. Dig. Pleader, G. 17, 19.
(u) 1 Saund. 207, note 5; 22, note 2; Com. Dig. Pleader, G. 22.
(x) 1 Saund. 14, n. 2; 4 Ann. c. 16, s. 1. An *immaterial issue* is not cured by verdict, 2 Saund. 319 a; Tidd, 9th ed. 921. *Aliter* as to an *informal* issue, *id.*
(y) Com. Dig. Pleader, G. 22; 1 Saund. 14, note 2.
(z) Com. Dig. Pleader, F. 14, 15.
(a) *Ante*, 615.

† See American Editor's Preface.

II. THE BODY.

3dly. Confession and avoidance of the plea.

the fact alleged in the plea, and *avoids* the effect of it by stating *new matter*; and this replication frequently occurs in practice. The general rule is, that *a replication must confess and avoid or traverse the matter stated in the plea* (*b*); and in this respect a replication resembles a plea (*c*). Where the plaintiff declares on a fact which at first view is a trespass, and the defendant in his plea acknowledges that fact, but states such new circumstances, as, if true, amount to a justification, if the plaintiff can suggest additional new matter, which shows that the defendant's plea (though true) will not justify the trespass committed, he ought to reply that new matter in a *special replication, that the defendant may demur or take issue upon it. [*657] Thus, to a plea in trespass justifying under a warrant upon an information for treasonable practices, for which offence the plaintiff had been admitted to bail by the Chief Justice of the King's Bench, the plaintiff, instead of traversing the plea, should confess and avoid it by replying a tender and refusal of bail (*d*). So, where to trespass *quare clausum fregit*, the defendant pleaded a custom applicable to all farms within the parish, which were not exempted by special agreement or otherwise, and the plaintiff traversed the custom generally; it was held that it was not competent for the plaintiff to prove that his particular farm was exempted by special agreement or otherwise (*e*); the proper mode of availing himself of such a defence would have been to have confessed the custom, and avoided it by showing that the exception applied to his farm (*f*). If infancy be pleaded, the plaintiff may reply that the goods were necessaries, or that the defendant, after he came of age ratified and confirmed the promise (*g*). And in replevin to an avowry by a freeholder for a distress damage feasant, the plaintiff may plead in bar a demise to him from the defendant (*h*); or in trespass, where the defendant has pleaded *son assault demesne*, the plaintiff admitting that he made the first assault, may reply, showing that it was justifiable (*i*). So, to a plea of *liberum tenementum*, the plaintiff may, as in replevin, reply a demise from the defendant (*k*), or from some person seised of the estate before the defendant had or claimed to have any interest in the *locus in quo* (*l*); or if the defendant has justified under a demise, he may show a notice to quit, or to a justification under a distress *damage feasant*, may reply a subsequent conversion (*m*). We have already seen that in some cases a plea may be *generally* and apparently true, and yet the plaintiff may safely traverse it, and need not bring forward in his replication matter which disproves the plea as applied to the subject in dispute. Thus, in trespass to land, if the defendant justify under a custom for all copyholders to enjoy common of pasture over the *locus in quo*, as part of the waste, the plaintiff, under *a traverse of the custom, may prove another custom for the lord to inclose part of the waste, and that the *locus in quo* was inclosed and became freed from the common of pasture by virtue of such custom (*n*). [*658]

(*b*) Com. Dig. Pleader, G. 2; Cro. El. 754; 4 B. & C. 379, *per* Holroyd, J.
(*c*) See *ante*, 556.
(*d*) *Ante*, 643, 624; 2 Bla. Rep. 1165; and see Carth. 280.
(*e*) 2 You. & Jerv. 79.
(*f*) *Id.*
(*g*) *Post*, vol. iii.
(*h*) *Id.*
(*i*) *Id.*; 2 Campb. 629.
(*k*) *Post*, vol. iii.; Willes, 225; 1 East, 212.
(*l*) *Id.*; Dyer, 171 b.
(*m*) 3 Wilics, 20. *Ante*, 200, 207. And see *ante*, 643, 645, as to replying, &c. to a justification under a *fieri facias*.
(*n*) *Ante*, 629, 653.

II. THE BODY.

3dly. Confession and avoidance of the plea.

In replications of this description it is necessary that the material parts of the defendant's title be *admitted* either in terms or in effect (o). It is indeed a principle applicable to other pleadings as well as a replication, that by not traversing the statement of the adversary, it being material and traversable, its truth is to be taken to be admitted (p). It behoves the plaintiff therefore to be cautious in deciding whether he should deny the allegation in the plea, or, admitting its apparent truth, should obviate or defeat its effect by an assertion of new matter. It is not unusual to admit the material facts alleged in the defendant's plea, in *express* terms, by stating, after the words *precludi non*, "that although true it is that the said demise was made to the defendant, as in his said plea is alleged, yet for replication in this behalf the plaintiff in fact saith, that, &c.:" but where the plaintiff in the subsequent part of his replication claims immediately from the defendant, or states generally, "that before the defendant had any thing in the *locus in quo*, &c." this form appears unnecessary (q); though it may be advisable to adopt it, when the plaintiff claims title from a party alleged to have been seised in fee prior to the party under whom the defendant claimed (r). When the replication completely confesses and avoids the defendant's plea, it should not conclude with a traverse (s); though as it introduces new matter, it must conclude with a verification, in order that the defendant may have an opportunity of answering it (t). A replication of this nature must confess as well as avoid the effect of the defendant's plea, and if
[*659] the *plaintiff rely on some excess as an imprisonment under color of process after a voluntary escape, this matter should be new assigned, and not replied (u). For a *replication* must state matter which entitles the plaintiff to his action for the *same* trespasses as those which are mentioned in and attempted to be justified by the plea; of which description are replications of new matter, showing that the defendant is a trespasser *ab initio* (x); but when the plaintiff relies on trespasses *different* from those pleaded to, he must *new assign* (y).

4thly. Of *New Assignments.*

The fourth description of replication, if it can be so termed, is a *New Assignment* (z). A new assignment is not however, properly speaking, a replication, since it does not profess to *reply* to any thing contained in the defendant's plea, but if so vulgar a term can be tolerated, gives the go-by and throws aside as useless the previous pleading, or rather *re-states, in a more minute and circumstantial manner*, the cause of action, or some part thereof, alleged in the declaration, in consequence of the defendant having, through

(o) Dyer, 171 b; Sir W. Jones, 352. In trespass for taking and driving the plaintiff's cattle, to which there was a justification that the defendant was *lawfully possessed* of a close, and that he took the cattle there damage feasant, the plaintiff may specially reply title in another, as whose servant he entered, and the giving unnecessary color will not vitiate, 1 East, 212.

(p) *Ante*, 554, 559, 645; Steph. 2d edit. 255.

(q) Dyer, 171 b; Sir Wm. Jones, 352; 1 East, 212, 213.

(r) *Id.*

(s) 1 Saund. 22, n. 2; 2 *Id.* 28, n. 2; Com. Dig. Pleader, 2 G. 3. So where a plaintiff sets up matter consistent with, but qualifying the matter alleged on the other side, he should not also traverse, 1 Wils. 253.

(t) 1 Saund. 103, *in notis*.

(u) 2 Wils. 3, 4; 2 T. R. 172; see *ante*, 624, 625, and *post*, 667, 671, as to this.

(x) 1 Saund. 300 a; 3 Wils. 20; 3 T. R. 297, 298; 1 Hen Bla. 560, 561. See as to *replying* excess, &c. *ante*, 624, 625, *post*, 667, 671.

(y) 2 Wils. 4.

(z) See in general Com. Dig. Pleader, 3 M. 34; Bac. Abr. Trespass, I. 42; Vin. Abr. Trespass, U. a, 4, and Novel Assignment; 1 Saund. 299, note 6; Steph. 2d ed. 262; Tidd, 9th ed. 690.

II. THE BODY.

mistake or design, omitted to answer it in his plea (*a*). It is therefore in the nature of a new declaration, or rather it is a more precise and particular *repetition* of the declaration in those cases where the law permitted a *general* form of declaring equally *applicable* to two or more states of facts, but leaving it doubtful in the description *which* was intended. The necessity for, or use of, a new assignment arises from the very general mode of statement sometimes permitted in the declaration, and the latitude allowed in the proof of many of the allegations therein. It is obvious therefore that a new assignment may be admissible in an action of *assumpsit*, as well as in other actions; as if to a declaration in *indebitatus* assumpsit *for goods sold*, the defendant plead a plea applicable to one sale and delivery, but not to that in relation to which the plaintiff's present action was brought, he may *new assign* accordingly that he brought his action for the price of *other* goods sold and delivered (*b*). It is clear that in other cases a new assignment may occur in *assumpsit*, as if to an action for goods sold the defendant plead a *judgment recovered*, the plaintiff may new assign that his present action is for *other and different goods sold* than in the action in which the judgment was recovered (*c*). And there is a recent instance of a new assignment and subsequent pleadings in an action on a bill of exchange (*d*).

4thly. New assignments.

On reference to the preceding parts of this treatise relative to the form of the declaration, it will be seen that the cause of action is sometimes described in very general terms. In actions upon *contracts* the declaration, when special, in most cases, contains a tolerably particular description of the true cause of action; and in actions for *torts*, where the form of declaration is *in case*, the description of the injury is also in general sufficiently certain; accordingly it will be seen that a new assignment *rarely occurs* in those forms of action (*e*). So where the action was in *trespass*, a general mode of declaring in *trespass quare clausum fregit* *was permitted; and, under the ordinary form of declaration, the plaintiff was in general entitled to recover upon proof of *any trespass* of a similar nature to that stated in any close or land in the same parish that had been committed by the defendant before the commencement of the action. Where several trespasses had been committed, some of which the defendant might conceive to be justifiable, it had become highly important for the interests of defendants, and also expedient for the ends of justice, that the true cause of action, in respect of which the plaintiff meant to proceed, should be better ascertained by the record; for otherwise the defendant might be misled by the generality of the declaration, and be met at the trial by the proof of a different injury from that which he came prepared to dispute; and on other accounts it was often very desirable for the defendant to confine and limit in some degree the general description in the declaration. In order to effect that object he was allowed to frame his plea in such a manner as would often render it necessary that the plaintiff should *re-state*, with

Arises from generality of declaration, which entitles defendant to plead an evasive plea.

[*660]

(*a*) 3 Bla. Com. 311; Steph. 2d ed. 266; 1 Saund. 299, note 6.

(*b*) 6 T. R. 607, see also Heydon *v.* Thompson, 1 Adol. & Ell. 210. It was supposed otherwise in assumpsit, Solly *v.* Neish, Trin. T. Exch. 1835, Legal Obs. 134, 135; see *post*, 672, 673.

(*c*) 6 Term R. 607; 3 Wils. 304; 3 Bar. & Cres. 235; 5 D. & R. 87, S. C.; and see forms *post*, vol. iii. Index, New Assignment.

(*d*) Heydon *v.* Thompson, 1 Adol. & Ell. 210.

(*e*) See *post*, 672.

II. THE BODY. — 4thly. New assignments.

greater precision and particularity, the real cause of action intended by his declaration; and such re-statement was termed a *new assignment*. This *repetition* of the real cause of action occasioned evasive and exponsive pleading, and on that account the Reg. Gen. Hil. T. 4 W. 4, reg. V.,† directed that in declarations in trespass *quare clausum fregit*, the name of the close or its abuttals, or other particular description, should be added, by which means the necessity for, and utility of a plea of *liberum tenementum* has in a great measure been avoided.

When a new assignment is necessary in general.

It is a general rule, that where the defendant has committed *several* trespasses either to the person, or the personal or real property of another, some of which were justifiable, and others not, and the action is brought for those trespasses which were not justifiable, but the defendant by his plea answers only those which were so, then the plaintiff should *new assign* (*f*).

In case of trespasses to the person (*g*).

Thus, in an action of trespass for an *assault*, if there have been two assaults, one justifiable, on the ground of it having been committed in self-defence, and the other not, and the declaration contain only one count for an assault, and the defendant plead *son assault demesne*, the plaintiff should new assign the illegal assault (*h*). In a case of this description we have seen that the defendant cannot, with any degree of certainty, collect from the declaration which of the two assaults the plaintiff means to proceed for, and as the plaintiff would be allowed to prove either under the declaration, it becomes a matter of necessity that the defendant should put his justification upon the record, or

[*661] *otherwise the plaintiff might recover at the trial on proof of the very assault which was legally justifiable. The defendant is therefore, by the rules of pleading, allowed to suppose that the action was brought for the latter assault, and he consequently pleads *son assault demesne*. Now, in such a case, the plaintiff cannot safely traverse this plea, for if he were to do so, and the justification were to be proved, the defendant would be entitled to a verdict. The reason of this is, that the general terms of the declaration are confined by the effect of the plea and the replication. The plea admits the fact of an assault having been committed, and then gives a more minute and circumstantial account of it, by showing how it originated, and what circumstances rendered it, as the defendant conceives, justifiable. By traversing the plea the plaintiff is held to admit that the defendant is right as to the particular assault complained of; for if he were allowed to traverse the plea, and afterwards to prove an assault totally unconnected from all circumstances approaching to justification, it would be an act of gross deception towards the defendant. The issue is therefore confined to such an assault as is described in the plea, if any such has actually taken place, viz. an assault committed under some circumstances of provocation, which the defendant asserts amount to a legal excuse, but which assertion the plaintiff denies. In order to avoid this result, and to enable the plaintiff to give evidence of that assault which was wholly destitute of

(*f*) 1 Saund. 299 a, n. 6; 1 Ld. Raym. 465; 2 Wils. 3, 4.

(*g*) The plaintiff must in general *reply* excess, *ante*, 624, 625; 2 Crom. M. & Ros. 338.

(*h*) *Id. Ibid.*; 2 Saund. 5 e, 5th ed.

(1047) {Troup *v.* Smith, 20 Johns. Rep. 43.}
† See American Editor's Preface.

excuse, it is necessary that he should not traverse the defendant's plea, but correct the error, or affected error into which the plaintiff has fallen, by a new assignment, viz. by stating that he brought his action not for the assault alluded to, and answered by the plea, but for *another* and a *different* assault committed on a *different occasion*. The same observations will be applicable to cases where the defendant justifies an assault or other trespass under process, &c., and the plaintiff relies on an assault or trespass committed *before* the issuing of the writ, or after the return of it, or after the plaintiff in the second action was discharged by the plaintiff in the first action, or after a voluntary escape on process in execution (*i*).

II. THE BODY. — 4thly. New assignments.

If *son assault demesne* has been pleaded, and the evidence will establish that the defendant's battery of the plaintiff was *excessive*, and more than was necessary for self-defence, it seems that according to the latest decisions the plaintiff may under *de injuria*, and without a special replication or new assignment give in evidence the excess (*j*). But it has been decided that a plaintiff cannot reply *de injuria*, and *also new assign* that the defendant committed the trespasses with more violence than was necessary, such pleading being demurrable for duplicity, though if not demurred to, plaintiff may proceed on either on the trial (*k*).

Trespasses to personal property.

In like manner in trespass for injuries to *personal* property, where there have been two or more injuries to the *same property, or two takings of similar property, a new assignment will become necessary in cases analogous to those we have noticed with respect to assaults (*l*). Thus, where in an action of trespass for taking away the plaintiff's oaks, the defendant pleaded that the oaks were standing in a certain close, situate in the manor of A. the freehold of B. who felled them, and justified taking them away by the command of B., it was held that the plaintiff might new assign that the oaks were growing in his own close within the manor of W., and were other oaks than those mentioned in the plea (*m*). And in transitory actions of this nature, not only the *place* but the *time* may be made material by the plea, and the plaintiff must then, when it becomes necessary, new assign the trespass at another time (*n*). But if to trespass for removing goods, and casting, flinging, or throwing goods out of a barn the plea only justify the removal, and *except* the casting, flinging, and throwing the goods out of the barn, no new assignment is necessary, and plaintiff may recover for any damage done by the excepted act if proved under the general issue (*o*).

[*662]

Trespasses to real property.

And in trespass for an injury to *real* property where the defendant justifies under a right of way, &c. if the defendant has used the way in a different manner from what he was entitled to do by virtue of the prescription or grant, the plaintiff must new assign (*p*). So, if in an action for trespasses to the plaintiff's land, committed with cattle, the defendant prescribe for commonable cattle *levant* and *couchant*, and allege that the cattle mentioned in the declara-

(*i*) 1 Saund. 299, note 6, and see 2 Campb. 175; 1 Bing. 317; 3 Taunt. 525, 526.

(*j*) *Ante*, 625, n. (*e*); Reece *v.* Taylor, 1 Har. & Wol. Rep. 15.

(*k*) Thomas *v.* Marsh, 5 Car. & P. 596.

(*l*) *Ante*, 660.

(*m*) 1 Saund. 300 a.

(*n*) 1 Saund. 300 a; 2 Ld. Raym. 1015.

(*o*) Neville *v.* Cooper, 2 Crom. & M. 329, and see Bush *v.* Parker, 1 Bing. N. C. 72.

(*p*) 1 T. R. 560, 562.

II. THE BODY. — 4thly. New assignments.

tion were such cattle, and in truth the defendant has put on such cattle, and also other cattle not *levant* and *couchant*, the plaintiff should new assign, stating that he brought his action for depasturing the common with *other* cattle, and should not traverse the *levancy* and *couchancy*; for upon such a traverse it would appear to be sufficient to show any thing which excuses the trespass, and the number mentioned in the declaration would not be material (*q*). And it has been held that if in an action for breaking and entering the plaintiff's house, land, &c. the defendant plead a licence which the plaintiff had revoked before any of the trespasses for which the action was brought were committed, or which was confined to some particular act, and the defendant exceeded, the plaintiff must state the revocation or excess in a new assignment (*r*).

[*663] After plea of *liberum tenementum*.

*In all the preceding instances in which a new assignment may become necessary, it will be observed the very circumstance of the new assignment supposes that two or more trespasses, or acts apparently amounting to trespasses, have taken place. The plaintiff declares in the new assignment that he brought his action, not for the trespass admitted and justified by the plea, but for *another* and different *trespass* committed upon *another* and different *occasion*, and which the defendant has not answered by his plea (*s*). And in general the effect of the new assignment is, to admit that one of the assaults, or apparent trespasses, has been justified; and it operates as an entire waiver or abandonment of that particular trespass (*t*). But it may often occur in trespass to real property that a new assignment will become necessary on a different ground. We have seen that in declaring in trespass for an injury committed by breaking and entering the plaintiff's close, it *was* unnecessary to give either the name or abuttals or any specific description of the close, and that it was sufficient to state the parish or place in which it is situate (*u*). Under that general description it was obvious the plaintiff would be entitled to give evidence of any act of trespass committed by the defendant in any close of the plaintiff within the particular parish or place mentioned in the declaration; and the consequence of this was, that the defendant was under some difficulty in knowing in what part of the particular parish or place the alleged trespass was committed; and unless he could obtain a specific description of the particular close, he would not know what he was to come prepared to dispute at the trial. To remedy that inconvenience, we have seen that the defendant was permitted to plead the plea of *liberum tenementum*, or as it was called the *common bar* (*x*). This plea the plaintiff can seldom safely traverse if the declaration did not describe the close by name or abuttals, for if he did so, and the defendant could prove that at the time of the supposed trespasses he had any land within the particular parish or place laid in the declaration, the

[*664] issue must be found for him (*y*)(1048); and it was *perhaps reasonable that

(*q*) Willes, 638; 2 Saund. 346 e.

(*r*) See 3 Campb. 524; 1 Saund. 300 c, d, 5th ed. But this, it appears, only applies to these cases in which the declaration is confined to a single act of trespass, or in which the defendant confines the general terms of the declaration, by specifying the particular acts to which the license extended in his plea. See *post*, 666; 11 East, 451.

(*s*) See the usual forms, *post*, vol. iii.

(*t*) See 16 East, 82, 86; 1 Saund. 299 a, n. 6; 2 T. R. 176, 177; *per Cur.* 10 East, 80; *post*, 667, 668.

(*u*) See *ante*, 428 a. It seems to have been *sufficient* to name the *county* only, *id.*

(*x*) See *ante*, 511; 11 East, 51.

(*y*) 2 Taunt. 156; *per* Lawrence, J. 7 T. R. 335; 1 Saund. 299 b, c; Com. Dig. Pleader, 3 M. 34; 1 B. & C. 489; 2 D. & R. 719, S C.

(1048) { Ellet *v.* Pullen, 7 Halst. Rep. 357. }

it should be so, for the object of the plea of freehold in such a case being to compel the plaintiff to give a more particular description of the particular close alluded to in his declaration, in the event of his declining to give the required information, he was held to admit that the defendant was right as to the particular place, and the only issue raised by the replication was, whether the defendant could prove that he had any close answering the description contained in his plea. If plaintiff therefore were not able to traverse the plea of *liberum tenementum* with safety, he was driven to a new assignment, in which he stated the place with proper exactness (z). This is usually done by setting forth the name and abuttals of the close, and in case the defendant has given any particular description to the close mentioned in his plea, the description of the plaintiff's close in the new assignment must be such that a plain difference may be perceived between the place so newly assigned and that mentioned in the plea (a)(1049). It may be observed with respect to new assignments after the plea of *liberum tenementum*, that whenever the defendant possesses any close which he describes in his plea, and alleges it to be his soil and freehold, the effect of a new assignment is entirely to exclude the consideration of any trespass committed within such close. The plaintiff in his new assignment avers that the place newly assigned is *another and different place* from that mentioned in the plea, and he thereby waives and abandons any claim in respect of trespasses committed in the latter place. And the same principle supports the position, that where the defendant in his plea specifies a particular trespass, and justifies it, and the plaintiff new assigns in respect of a different trespass, the former trespass is considered to be entirely abandoned (b). And as in the latter case the new assignment supposes two different *trespasses*, so in the former it supposes two different *places*; for, as we shall see more particularly hereafter, whenever the plaintiff and defendant are agreed as to the particular trespass or place, and there appears sufficient upon the record to ascertain *and identify it, a new assignment is unnecessary [*665] and improper (c).

II. THE BODY.

4thly. New assignments.

The cases of new assignment we have hitherto considered are those in which the trespass complained of, or the place in which it was committed, have been *wholly* mistaken or evaded by the defendant in his plea. And in these cases the plaintiff merely new assigns, without taking any other notice of the plea than stating that it was wholly foreign to the true ground of complaint, and that it does not at all meet the declaration. But the same cause, viz. the generality of the declaration, which, as we have seen, often gives rise to a plea entirely foreign to the real cause of action, may sometimes have the effect of producing a plea whereby *some of* the trespasses which the plaintiff complains of are answered, but others are left entirely unnoticed. Thus, where the plaintiff complains in his declaration that the defendant on a cer-

In what cases it is necessary to reply to part, and also to new assign.

(z) 2 Salk. 453; 6 Mod. 117; Willes, 223; 2 Bla. Rep. 1089; 1 Saund. 299 b, note.

(a) Dyer, 264; Cro. Jac. 594; Cro. Eliz. 365, 492; Bro. Tresp. 203; 1 Saund. 299 c, 300 c, 5th ed.; see the form, *post*, vol. iii.

(b) See 15 East, 235; 16 *Id.* 82, 86; 1 Saund. 299 c, 5th edit.

(c) *Post*, 667, 668; 1 Saund. 300 b, note, 5th ed.

(1049) Hollock v. Robinson, 2 Caines' Rep. 233. Ellice v. Boyer, 8 Wend. R. 503.

II. THE BODY. — 4thly. New assignments.

tain day, "and on divers other days and times between that day and the commencement of the action," committed trespasses in the plaintiff's close, the plaintiff will be at liberty under this allegation to prove any number of acts of trespass committed by the defendant within the space of time mentioned, in any part of the close. Now it may happen that the defendant claims a right of way, or common, &c. in the plaintiff's close, and as he has no means of telling from the declaration whether the plaintiff's cause of complaint is confined to acts committed in the exercise of such right of way or common, &c., or whether any other acts of trespass are complained of, he is allowed to assume the former, and may consequently justify under such alleged right. In this case, if the plaintiff dispute the existence and validity of the right of way or common, he will of course traverse the defendant's plea. But the effect of such traverse without any new assignment, will be to confine the issue to the question of the right of way, &c. as pleaded by the defendant; and if this should be found in the defendant's favor, he will be entitled to a verdict (d). If therefore the defendant has committed any acts of trespass, which, supposing him to be entitled to the alleged right of way, &c., would not be justified by it, it will be necessary for the plaintiff not merely to traverse the plea, but also to new assign in respect of such other trespasses, and aver in [*666] *his new assignment that the action was brought *as well* for the trespass or trespasses mentioned in the plea, as for the trespasses newly assigned (e). Thus, where the plaintiff complained in the declaration that the defendant had committed trespasses in his closes, and the defendant pleaded that one of the closes was called Blackacre and the other Whiteacre, and pleaded that they were his freehold, the plaintiff traversed that Blackacre was the defendant's freehold, and new assigned in respect of trespasses in twenty acres other than Whiteacre; upon this it was objected, that by new assigning, the plaintiff had waived the former pleadings as to all, and therefore ought to have omitted the traverse; but the Court disallowed the objection, and held that as the defendant had pleaded in respect of some of the places in which the plaintiff intended to lay the trespass, the plaintiff was at liberty to answer as to that part, and that the defendant was not entitled to waive his plea thereto and plead to all *de novo* (f). So where an action is brought for fishing in a certain river, being the plaintiff's fishery, and the trespass intended by the declaration is for fishing to the extent of two miles and upwards; if the defendant plead that he is seised in fee of ten acres adjoining the river, and prescribes for a free fishery in the river along the side of the ten acres, the plaintiff ought not *merely* to traverse the prescription, and go to issue upon it, because at the trial he would not be permitted to give evidence of any act of fishing by the defendant, either above or below the ten acres, for the question would be confined to the prescription only; but the plaintiff should *also new assign*, and state that the trespass complained of was not only for fishing in the river adjoining the ten acres, but also above and below the same, and then the defendant will be under the necessity of giving

(d) 1 Saund. 300 b, c, 5th ed.; and see 2 Campb. 175, 176.

(e) 1 Saund. 300 b, c; 7 B. & C. 346; 9 D. & R. 897, S. C.; 9 B. & C. 613; 4 M. & R. 290, S. C.

(f) Cro. Eliz. 812, and see 7 B. & C. 346; 9 D. & R. 897, S. C.

some answer to the whole trespass (*g*). In this case it has been observed, that without a new assignment the plaintiff would run a great risk of being tricked; for if the prescription were found for the defendant, he would succeed in the action, though guilty of almost the whole trespass for which the action was brought (*g*). Upon the same principles, in the case before adverted to of a right of way, &c. pleaded by the defendant, where the plaintiff disputes the alleged right, and also affirms that the defendant *has committed trespasses in *other* parts of his land, he should traverse the right of way, and new assign for trespasses *extra viam* (*h*). [*667]

II. THE BODY.

4thly. New assignments.

When a new assignment is unnecessary and improper.

It will be observed to be perfectly clear that the mode of pleading by traverse *and* new assignment, is inapplicable where only a *single act* of trespass is complained of in the declaration; but where the declaration is capable of covering *several trespasses*, and the defendant pleads some matter of justification which only applies to *part*, it seems to be open to the plaintiff both to traverse the justification and to new assign in respect of the trespasses unanswered, in all cases of trespass, whether to the person or to personal or real property. And although where only a single act of trespass is complained of, this mode of pleading would in general be objectionable (*i*), yet where the trespass is of a *continuing* nature, as in the case of imprisonment, or remaining in possession of a house or goods under color of process, the plaintiff may it should seem dispute the writ, &c. and also new assign in respect of a continuation of imprisonment, possession, &c. unauthorized by the process, even supposing it to be valid (*k*).

In the course of the preceding pages it has been more than once incidentally observed, and from the whole tenor of what has been said on the subject of new assignment it will be collected, that it can never be necessary for the plaintiff to new assign where there has been only a *single* act of trespass, except, as we have lately seen, where that act has been of a *continuing* nature, (in which case it may perhaps more properly be said to consist of several acts of trespass,) or except where the plea of *liberum tenementum* has rendered a particular description of the *locus in quo* necessary. And in general, where a new assignment is unnecessary, it will be improper and sometimes fatal to the plaintiff's right to recover. It has been shown, that in general the object of a new assignment is to correct an error or affected error in the defendant's plea, and that (where there is no traverse of the plea) it operates as an entire waiver and abandonment of the particular trespass justified *by the plea (*l*). [*668] And upon this ground, in a case where the plaintiff brought trespass for false imprisonment, and the defendant justified under process, which was in fact irregular, but the plaintiff (instead of traversing the plea as he ought to have done, and relying on the irregularity,) new assigned that the trespass complained of was upon *another* and a different *occasion*, it was held that he was bound to prove a new and substantive trespass wholly unconnected with the

(*g*) 1 Saund. 300 c, 5th edit.

(*h*) 1 Saund. 300 c, 5th edit.; 9 B. & C. 613; 5 Bing. 196; 2 Bing. 26.

(*i*) Thomas *v.* Marsh, 5 Car. & P. 596.

(*k*) 1 Bing. 317; 2 Campb. 175; 3 Taunt. 425. As to replying *de injuria*, and new assigning, in answer to a plea justifying under a *fieri facias*, see 4 Bing. 729; S. C. in Error in 1 M. & P. 783; and 2 Y. & J. 304; *ante*, 643, 646. See further as to *Excess*, *ante*, 624, 625, 659, 660; *post*, 671.

(*l*) *Ante*, 663.

II. THE BODY.

4thly. New assignments.

process, and that as there was only one arrest and imprisonment proved, which would have been authorized by the process had it been regular, it was answered by the plea, and the defendant was therefore entitled to a verdict (m). Upon the same principle, where the defendant described the place in which the trespass was alleged to have been committed in his plea, and justified under a right of common there, and the plaintiff new assigned, setting out the abuttals of the *locus in quo*, and alleged in the usual form that the closes newly assigned were other and different closes than the place mentioned in the plea, and it appeared at the trial that they were the same, it was held the defendants were entitled to a verdict on the new assignment. And the Court observed, that the plea of not guilty to the new assignment put the whole of it in issue, a part of which was that the closes were different from that mentioned in the plea (n).

Such being the effect of a new assignment, where only a single act of trespass has been committed, it is equally plain that where only one such act is charged in the declaration and is justified by the defendant, the plaintiff cannot traverse the defendant's plea and also new assign. In a case where the plaintiff complained of a single act of trespass in each count of the declaration, and the defendant justified each of the trespasses thus charged in his pleas, and the plaintiff traversed the matter alleged in justification, and also new assigned in respect of other acts of trespass; the Court held, on demurrer, that this mode [*669] of pleading was objectionable on the ground of *duplicity*, and that it was an attempt by a new assignment to amplify the cause of *action stated in the declaration; and they observed that the object of a new assignment was to lay out of the question all that the defendant had pleaded, by saying that the trespass stated and justified by the defendant was not that which the plaintiff had complained of in his declaration (o). So, in another case, where the plaintiff alleged a single act of trespass in his declaration, and the defendant pleaded a justification thereto, to which the plaintiff replied *de injuria*, and also new assigned that the defendant committed trespasses at other times, the Court held it to be clear that where a single act only of trespass was laid, and not *diversi vicibus et diebus*, and that act was covered by the plea, there could be no new assignment (p).

Again, as the object of a new assignment is to correct an error in the plea, and to aver that the defendant has omitted to answer the whole or a part of the true ground of complaint, it can never be necessary to new assign where the defendant in his plea justifies or attempts to justify all the trespasses in respect of which the plaintiff proceeds. Thus, where the declaration charged that the defendant assaulted and imprisoned the plaintiff, and during such imprisonment assaulted and struck him, and the defendant justified an arrest and imprisonment under process, and also justified the beating, in consequence of subsequent outrageous and violent conduct on the part of the plaintiff, it was held, that although the defendant proved the first part of his justification, viz.

(m) 16 East, 82. Where the trespass charged is a *single* act, but is committed in a more violent manner than the subject of justification authorized, this should it seems be put on the record in a *replication*, and not as a new assignment of a distinct trespass, 7 Moore, 33; *ante*, 624, 625, 667; *post*, 671.

(n) 15 East, 235.

(o) 10 East, 73, and 81, n.; see also Thomas v. Marsh, 5 Car. & P. 596.

(p) 7 Taunt. 156.

the arrest under process, yet as he failed to show a *sufficient cause* for the battery, the plaintiff was entitled to a verdict without having new assigned (q). II. THE BODY.

4thly. New assignments.

Upon the same principle, apparently, it has been held, in the case of a licence pleaded, that where the declaration alleges the commission of trespasses on *divers days and times*, and the defendant pleads a licence generally, viz. on the several days and times when, &c., without confining the generality of the declaration by specifying any particular trespass or trespasses, he is bound to show a licence co-extensive with the *trespasses* proved; and that therefore the plaintiff having shown a trespass prior to the licence was entitled to a verdict on the general replication *de injuria*, without any new assignment (r).

[*670]

New assignment not necessary when name or abuttals, or description of close is stated in declaration as is now required by Reg. Gen. Hil. T. 4 W. 4, reg. V.

*Another case in which a new assignment is unnecessary, is where in trespass to real property the plaintiff describes the close by its name in the declaration, (as since Reg. Gen. Hil. T. 4 W. 4, reg, V., he must do, subject to a special demurrer if omitted,) and the defendant pleads *liberum tenementum*, without giving any more specific description of the *locus in quo* than the plaintiff had done. We have seen that in all cases where the plaintiff had given no particular designation of the *locus in quo*, the general plea of *liberum tenementum* compelled him to new assign, or otherwise the only question at the trial was, whether the defendant could support his plea by showing that he possessed any land within the parish or place named in the declaration (s). But it has been considered, that wherever the plaintiff ascertains the place in his declaration, the plea of *liberum tenementum* cannot be supported (t). And at all events it is clear that it can be of no avail to the defendant in a case of this description, where he merely follows the name given by the plaintiff in his declaration. Thus, where the declaration stated a trespass in the plaintiff's close called the *Foldyard*, in the parish of A., and the defendant pleaded that the said close in the declaration mentioned was his freehold, which the plaintiff traversed, and upon the trial it appeared that both the plaintiff and the defendant had a close called the *Foldyard*; it was held by the Court that the plaintiff having proved a trespass committed in his close, was entitled to recover, and that there was clearly no necessity for a new assignment; that in order to compel him to new assign, as a name was given to the close in the declaration, the defendant should have given some further description in his plea; and that as the issue stood the question was, whether the close described in the declaration as the plaintiff's was the defendant's freehold or not (u). And in another case, where the plaintiff after the plea of *liberum tenementum*, had newly assigned that the *locus in quo* "abutted on certain closes called A., B., and C., or some or one of them," to which the defendant again pleaded *liberum tenementum*; and it appeared in evidence that the plaintiff had a close abutting on A., and the defendant a close abutting on B. and C., it was held that the plaintiff was entitled to a verdict on the new assignment (x).

*It is of no avail to new assign an *excess* in committing a legal act, if in *law* the *excess* were strictly justifiable, though not necessary in *fact* to the full [*671]

(q) 5 B. & Ald. 220.
(r) 11 East, 451; *ante*, 662, and note (r).
(s) *Ante*, 662.
(t) *Per* Willes, C. J., Willes' R. 222.
(u) 1 B. & C. 489, 490; 2 D. & R. 719, S. C.
(x) 2 Bing. 49.

II. THE BODY. — 4thly. New assignments.

exercise of the defendant's right or claim in the particular case. Thus, a commoner may pull down *all* the fences which are wrongfully erected upon the common, although the destruction of part would have afforded him the full benefit and enjoyment of his right; and therefore if in trespass against him the plaintiff new assign the excess, the defendant will be entitled to a verdict thereon (y). So, the *cutting* or destruction of a gate or other *public* nuisance to an highway, though an excess, not absolutely essential for the enjoyment of the public right, may, it has been supposed, be justified, and if so, it would be of no use to reply or new assign any such excess (z).

When new assignment unnecessary in case of two or more counts.

Lastly, A new assignment will frequently be rendered unnecessary by the use of several counts in the declaration when admissible. Thus where two assaults, &c. have been committed, and the declaration contains as many counts as are equal to the number of assaults, and the defendant pleads a general issue to the whole, and a justification to one of the counts, the plaintiff had better put the justification in issue, and in case the defendant proves it, give evidence of the other assault upon the other counts, than make a new assignment; for if the plaintiff fail in proof of the allegation in the new assignment he cannot afterwards have recourse to the second count, because, by the new assignment, he acknowledges that one of the trespasses is justified, and has therefore abandoned one count, and relied on the trespass mentioned in the new assignment; he cannot therefore avail himself of one and the same act of trespass, both on the new assignment and on the second count; but if he could prove two trespasses besides that which he has waived, he might then have recourse to the second count (a).

Replications in nature of new assignments.

There are some replications which rather partake of the nature of new assignments than are properly and strictly so. As where the defendant has abused an authority or licence which the law gives him, by which he became a trespasser *ab initio* (b). In an action brought for a trespass thus committed, where the defendant pleads the licence or authority, the plaintiff may *reply* the abuse (c). Such a replication it will be observed differs from a new assignment, because it does not operate in any manner as a waiver or abandonment of the trespass attempted to be justified, but states matter in confession and avoidance of the justification.

[*672] Of New Assignments in *other actions besides trespass.*

*The instances we have given upon the law of new assignment have been confined to the action of trespass, because, as we have formerly observed, it rarely becomes necessary to new assign in any other form of action. The following instances will however show that a new assignment may occur in most forms of action. Thus, if in an action in *case* for the publication of a libel, without mentioning the particular person to whom it was published, the

(y) 7 B. & C. 346; 9 D. & R 897; and see 5 Car. & P. 596, 597; 1 Chitty's Gen. Prac. 654.

(z) James *v.* Hayward, Cro. Car. 184; Lodie *v.* Arnold, 2 Salk. 458; 1 Chitty's Gen. Prac. 654.

(a) 2 T. R. 172; *per* Buller, J.; *id.* 177; 6 Mod. 120; 1 Saund. 299, n. 6; *ante*, 625.

(b) See *ante*, 199, 626.

(c) See *ante*, 199, 625; 5 Car. & P. 596, 597; 7 B. & Cres. 809; 1 M. & R. 497, S. C.; 8 Rep. 146; 3 Wils. 20; 3 T. R. 292; 1 Hen. Bla. 555; 5 Taunt. 69, 72; 1 Saund. 300 d, 5th edit.; 4 Bing. 729; 1 M. & P. 783, S. C.

defendant has pleaded that he published it lawfully, as to members of a committee of the house of commons, and the plaintiff proceeds for a publication to other persons not members of the committee, he should reply, or rather new assign, such illegal publication (*d*). So, in an action for an escape, if the defendant plead a negligent escape and voluntary return, the plaintiff should new assign a subsequent escape (*e*); and if in case for disturbance of a right of common, by cutting turves, the defendant plead that he cut the turves as servant of the lord of the manor, the plaintiff may new assign that the defendant cut other turves for sale, and not for the use of the lord (*f*).

IX. THE BODY.

4thly. New assignments.

In the action of *replevin*, as the plaintiff is bound to show the place in certain where the taking was, it is said there can be no new assignment (*g*). In the action of *assumpsit* for goods sold, &c. where the defendant plead a judgment recovered, and the plaintiff has in point of fact obtained a judgment in a former action for goods sold, &c. but for different goods and causes of action, the plaintiff ought not to reply *nul tiel record*, for in such case he would be defeated by the production of the record; but he should reply that the causes of action mentioned in the declaration were not the same identical causes of action for which the former judgment was recovered (*h*)(1050). This replication is in some degree analogous in its object and effect to a new assignment, but it will be observed that it is not strictly a new assignment, inasmuch as it consists of a traverse of a material allegation in the defendant's plea.

[*673] Form of New assignment.

*In point of *form* there are two modes of *introducing* the matter new assigned. If the plaintiff traverse the plea as well as new assign after framing the replication to the plea as in ordinary cases, the form runs thus (*i*), "And the said plaintiff further saith, that he issued his writ against the defendant, and declared thereupon, *not only* for the said several trespasses in the said second plea mentioned, and therein attempted to be justified, *but also* for that the defendant, on, &c." (stating the matter new assigned)(*k*); but if the plaintiff *merely* new assign, then the form is thus, "And as to the said plea of the defendant by him secondly above pleaded, the plaintiff saith, that he, by reason of any thing by the defendant therein alleged, ought not to be barred from having and maintaining his aforesaid action thereof against the defendant, because he saith, that he issued his writ against the defendant, and declared thereupon, *not for* the said supposed trespasses, in the introductory part of the said second plea mentioned, *but for* that the defendant, on, &c." (stating the matter new assigned)(*l*). A new assignment being in the nature of a new declaration, should be equally certain as to *time*, *place*, and other *circumstances* (*m*), and it must not be negatively, that the trespasses mentioned

(*d*) 1 Saund. 133; 2 Campb. 175.
(*e*) 1 B. & P. 413; 11 East, 408.
(*f*) Willes, 619, 620.
(*g*) Freem. 238.
(*h*) 6 T. R. 607; 3 B. & C. 235; 7 Bar. & Cres. 809; 1 M. & R. 497; see the form, *id.* and *post*, vol. iii.; 3 Wentw. 151; *semble*, that the plaintiff might *new assign* that the action is brought for different promises, *post*, vol. iii. and notes.
(*i*) See forms, *post*, vol. iii. *et seq.*; and see a form in trespass, 5 Car. & P. 596.
(*k*) 3 B. & B. 119; 6 Moore, 330, S. C.; 1 Saund. 300.
(*l*) See forms, *post*, vol. iii. *et seq.*; 2 Co. 6 a, 18 b; 1 Saund. 300 a.
(*m*) Com. Dig. Pleader, 3 M. 34; Vin. Ab. Trespass, U. a, 4, pl. 13; Bac. Abr. Trespass, I. 4, 2; Dyer, 264 a.

(1050) Vide Snider and Van Vechten *v.* Croy, 2 Johns. Rep. 227.

II. THE BODY.

4thly. New assignments.

in the plea were not the same as those for which the plaintiff complained, but some other trespasses must be shown (n). If the new assignment be in *another close* or *place*, the plaintiff should give the place a name, or otherwise describe it with some certainty (o), and which, on not guilty thereto, must be proved as stated (p); and if it be in the *same close*, it is said the particular spot should be set forth in such a manner, that a plain difference may be per-
[*674] ceived between the place newly assigned and that mentioned *in the plea (q); but where a right of way is pleaded, it is usual to new assign *extra viam*, without showing in what particular part of the *locus in quo* (r).

When the defendant justifies under a right of common, or way, &c. at particular times of the year, or in particular parts of the close, &c. the plaintiff may new assign that the trespasses were committed, "*at other times, and on other occasions, and for other and different purposes than those mentioned in the plea*;" or that the defendant, "in a *greater* degree, and with *more force* and violence than was *necessary* for removing the supposed obstructions to the said supposed way, &c. cut down the gates, &c." (s). The matter new assigned must be consistent with the declaration, and not varying from or more extensive than the trespasses therein enumerated (t), or those which the defendant has answered in his plea; for a new assignment is merely to avoid the effect of the plea, which can only operate upon the trespasses thereby admitted (u). It should also only be of *material* matter, and therefore, if the plea set up a right of way, or common, &c. at *all times* of the year, the new assignment should not be, that the defendant "at other times, &c." time in that case being immaterial; and in an action of trespass against several, if some of the defendants suffer judgment by default, and the others plead a justification, the new assignment should be as to all the defendants, and not merely to those who have pleaded, for that would be a departure (x).

Conclusion of new assignment.

The *conclusion* of a new assignment must be with a verification, in order that the defendant may have an opportunity of answering it (y). After stating the matter newly assigned, the form usually is thus: "and which said trespasses above newly assigned, are other and different trespasses than the said trespasses in the said second plea mentioned, and therein attempted to be justified; wherefore, inasmuch as the defendant hath not answered the said trespasses above newly assigned, the plaintiff prays judgment, and his dama-
[*675] ges by him sustained, on occasion *of the committing thereof, to be adjudged to him, &c." (z) And though with respect to the latter part of this conclusion, it has been said that it would be more correct if it were to stop at the

(n) 3 Leon. 92; *post*, vol. iii. notes.
(o) Dyer, 264 a. 23 b. pl. 147; 1 Saund. 299 c; Vin. Abr. Novel Assignment, A.; Bro. Abr. Trespass, 203; see the forms, *post*, vol. iii.; 2 Co. 6 a. 18 b; 2 Andr. 103; Benl. & Dal. 177; 2 Bing. 49; 1 B. & C. 489; 2 D & R. 719, S. C.
(p) Com. Dig. Pleader, 3 M. 34; Vin. Ab. Trespass, U. a, 4, pl. 12, &c.; Bul. N. P. 82; 1 T. R. 479.
(q) See note (m), *supra*; Vin. Ab. Trespass, U. a, 4, pl. 3.
(r) *Post*, vol. iii. *Sed vide* Vin. Ab. Trespass, U. a, 4, pl. 3.
(s) See forms, *post*, vol. iii. As to replying this, see *ante*, 624, 625, 668, n. (m).
(t) Vin. Ab. Trespass, U. a, 4, pl. 19; Winch. 65; 4 Leon. 15, 16; 10 East, 79, 81; 7 Taunt. 156; *ante*, 667, 668.
(u) 10 East, 80.
(x) 2 Leon. 199; Com. Dig. Pleader, F. 11; *post*, 682.
(y) Bac. Ab. Trespass, I. 4, 2; Lutw. 1401; 1 Saund. 103.
(z) See the form, 2 Co. 6 a, 18 b; Rast. Ent. 608; *post*, vol. iii. and 9 Wentw. Index, cxxiv.

4thly. New assignments.

words, "*et hoc paratus, est verificare*," without praying judgment against the defendant, for not answering the trespasses newly assigned, when it was impossible he should answer it before it was alleged (*a*); yet it may be observed that matter newly assigned is always considered as having been already stated in the declaration, and consequently the defendant might have answered it if he had thought fit to plead to the injury really intended to be complained of.

Pleas to new assignments.

A new assignment being, as already observed, in the nature of a new declaration, and dismissing the previous pleading from consideration, so far as respects the matter newly assigned, the defendant should plead to it precisely as to a declaration (*b*), either by denying the matter newly assigned, by the plea of not guilty, &c., (*c*)(1051) or by answering it by a special plea of matter of justification (*d*), and he may plead several pleas (*e*). As the plaintiff avers that the trespasses newly assigned are other and different to those mentioned in the plea, he waives or abandons the trespasses which the defendant has justified, and it is not necessary to plead over again to the new assignment any matter of justification necessarily covered by the plea; as if common of pasture at all times of the year be pleaded, and the plaintiff new assigns that the defendant entered at other times, the right of common of pasture cannot be set up in the plea to the new assignment (*f*). So the defendant cannot plead to the new assignment, that the place (*g*) or trespass, &c. mentioned therein, is the same as that mentioned in the plea; and if in truth they are the same, the defendant should plead not guilty, and take advantage of it in evidence, as the plaintiff would be estopped from proving any trespass in the same place, &c. (*h*) For the same reason the defendant *cannot justify at a different place, and traverse the place mentioned in the new assignment (*i*); and when the plaintiff traverses the plea, as well as new assigns, the defendant cannot, as to the matter answered in the plea, plead new matter, but must stand by his plea (*k*). If the new assignment be bad, the defendant should demur, and it may be frequently necessary so to do, if the defendant wish to avail himself of his plea of *liberum tenementum* (*l*). [*676]

Suffering judgment by default to new assignment. Effect as to costs &c.

In an action of trespass *quare clausum fregit*, where the plaintiff new assigns, it often becomes prudent to suffer judgment by default to the new assignment (*m*), or perhaps since the stat. 3 & 4 W. 4, c. 42, sect. 21, permitting a defendant by leave of a judge, in some actions, to pay money into Court,

(*a*) Freem. 238.

(*b*) Gouldsb. 101; Moore, 540; Cro. Eliz. 590, S. C.

(*c*) See the form, *post*, vol. iii.; Bro Ab. Trespass, pl. 359.

(*d*) Bro. Ab. Trespass, pl. 168, 203, 359.

(*e*) Bac. Ab. Trespass I. 4, 2.

(*f*) Gouldsb. 191; Moore, 540; Cro. Eliz 590, S. C.; and see the cases in note (*h*) *infra*.

(*g*) Moore, 460; Jenk. 6th Cent. 265.

(*h*) *Supra*, note (*f*); Vin. Ab. Trespass, U. a, 4, pl. 10; Bac. Ab. Trespass, I. 4, 2; 1 Saund. 299 c, 115; Cro. Eliz. 355, 493; 14 H. 8, 4, pl. 3; Bro. Ab. Trespass, 168; 27 H. 8, 7, pl. 21; Bro. Ab. Trespass, 3.

(*i*) Bro. Ab. Trespass, pl. 168; Vin. Ab. Trespass, U. a, 4, pl. 9, 10, 15.

(*k*) Cro. Eliz. 812; Bac. Ab. Trespass, I. 4, 2.

(*l*) 2 Bing. 49; Dyer, 23 b. pl. 147.

(*m*) See 1 Saund. 300, n. And see the note of the editors of the fifth edition, in which the cases on this subject are all collected, and the result very perspicuously stated. And see Tidd, 9th edit. 966, 973.

(1051) Vide Pratt *v.* Groome, 15 East's Rep. 235.

II. THE BODY. — 4thly. New assignments.

to do so, and plead such payment. This arises from the provisions of the statute 22 & 23 Car. 2, c. 9, s. 136, as to costs. It has been determined, upon the construction of that statute, that a certificate to entitle the plaintiff to full costs, where the damages are under 40*s.*, is unnecessary, whenever it appears from the whole record that the freehold did or did not come in question (*n*). And it has been held in consequence, that when there is a special plea and a new assignment, and the plaintiff recovers upon the new assignment, he will in general be entitled to full costs, whether the special plea be not traversed, or whether it be traversed and found for the defendant (*o*). This often renders it dangerous *to plead* to the new assignment, and particularly so when the defendant has a good case upon his special pleas, since, notwithstanding he may succeed on his pleas, and thus fully answer the whole matter substantially in dispute, the plaintiff will be entitled to the *general costs* of the action, if he can prove any trifling act of excess on the part of the defendant. In cases of this description, it is therefore often expedient to suffer judgment by default to the new assignment, and thus at the trial to confine the matters in dispute to those which are answered by the pleas; for although this mode of proceeding enables the plaintiff to obtain costs, as upon a judgment
[*677] *by default*, if he think *proper, yet if he proceed to trial on the special plea, and fail, the defendant will be entitled to the general costs; for the plaintiff might have entered a *nolle prosequi* as to that plea, and assessed his damages on the new assignment before the sheriff, and consequently need not have proceeded to trial (*p*). The defendant must, however, take care that a plea of not guilty be not left entire upon the record, for as the matters newly assigned are considered as virtually contained in the declaration, it has been held that the effect of a general plea of not guilty to the whole declaration is to prevent the plaintiff from availing himself of the judgment by default to the new assignment, by assessing the damages before the sheriff, and to compel him to go to trial notwithstanding such judgment (*q*). The defendant, therefore, where he has *originally* pleaded the general issue, and is afterwards desirous of suffering judgment by default to a new assignment, should, when he suffers such judgment, enter a *retraxit* of the plea of the general issue, as far as the same relates to the trespasses newly assigned. It is justly observed that there is nothing incongruous in this, since the decisions upon this point have proceeded entirely upon the ground that the trespasses newly assigned are virtually included in the declaration (*r*); And it has accordingly been decided, that where the defendant adopted this course, and afterwards obtained a verdict upon one issue going to the whole cause of action, (exclusive, of course, of the trespasses newly assigned), he was entitled to the costs of the trial (*s*).

(*n*) 2 Hen. Bla. 2; *id.* 341; 7 T. R. 659.

(*o*) 2 Lev. 234; 2 Stra. 1168; 1 East, 350; 3 B. & Ald. 443. The cases in 4 Taunt. 48, and Cockerill *v.* Allanson, Hullock on Costs, 76, seem scarcely reconcilable with the authorities before mentioned.

(*p*) 13 East, 191.

(*q*) 3 B. & B. 117; 5 Bing. 196; 2 M. & P. 359, S. C.; 1 Y. & J. 354; 1 B. & C. 278.

(*r*) 1 Saund. 300 b, n. (*f*), 5th edit.

(*s*) 9 B. & C. 613; and see *per* Best, C. J., 5 Bing. 199. The form of such *retraxit*, as given in 1 Saund. 5th edit. *ut supra*, is as follows, "and the said defendant, relinquishing his said plea by him *first* above pleaded *to the said declaration*, so far as the same plea relates to the said trespasses above newly assigned, says nothing in bar or preclusion of the said trespasses above newly assigned; wherefore, &c."

To the plea or pleas to the new assignment, the plaintiff should *reply* precisely as to pleas to a declaration, and if the plea be such as would require a new assignment, if pleaded to a declaration, the plaintiff should again new assign to such plea (*t*). Replication to a plea to a new assignment.

*The *Conclusion* of replications, in *particular* instances, has already been pointed out (*u*). We have seen that *every* replication must, in point of *form*, conclude either to the *country* or *with a verification* (*x*). We have also shown when or not a *prayer of judgment* is or not essential or advisable (*y*). It may here suffice to observe, that when a replication *denies* the whole of the defendant's plea, containing matter of fact, it should conclude *to the country*, thus: "and this he the plaintiff prays may be inquired of by the country, &c." (*z*) And it is an established rule applicable to every part of pleading, subsequent to the declaration, that when there is an affirmative on one side, and a negative on the other, or *vice versa*, the conclusion should be to the country (1052), although the affirmative and negative be not in express words, but only tantamount thereto (*a*). It may also be laid down as a safe rule, that where a defendant cannot take any new or other issue in his rejoinder than the matter he had before pleaded without a departure from his plea, or where the issue on the rejoinder would be the same in substance as on the plea, the plaintiff should conclude to the country (*b*); and it is not material in this case, whether the replication contain a formal traverse, for where a traverse comprises the *whole* matter of the plea, the replication may still conclude to the country (*c*)(1053). It suffices that there is a good traverse of the substance of the plea (*d*). In debt on bond for not accounting, the defendant pleaded that he did account. Replication that defendant received £2000, for which he did not account. Rejoinder that he received it from particular persons, and that he accounted for the same. It was held that a surrejoinder that the monies mentioned in the replication, and those mentioned in the rejoinder, were different monies, might conclude to the country (*e*). This conclusion is also proper, where a particular fact is selected and denied, without any inducement or formal trraverse (*f*). But the plaintiff is still at liberty, where he only denies one of several facts, and not the whole substance of the plea, to commence his replication with an inducement, and formally to traverse the *particular [*679]

[*678] III. THE CONCLUSION.

(*t*) 1 Saund. 299 c. See the forms referred to, in 9 Wentw. Ind.; 2 Co. 6, and *post*, vol. iii.

(*u*) *Ante*, 630 to 633, and see, as to the conclusion in general, Com. Dig. Pleader, F. 5, E. 32; Co. Lit. 303 a. All *affirmative* pleadings which do not conclude to the country, must conclude with a verification, Steph. 2d ed. 485. Origin of the rule, *id.* 486.

(*x*) *Ante*, 630, 631.

(*y*) *Ante*, 634.

(*z*) 1 Saund. 103; 1 Burr. 316; 2 *Id.* 1022; Dougl. 94, 428; 2 T. R. 442, 443.

(*a*) 1 Saund. 103; 2 New R. 363.

(*b*) 1 Saund. 103 b; and see the reason, 2 *Id.* 189, 190.

(*c*) 1 Salk. 4; 1 Saund. 103 a, b.

(*d*) 2 T. R. 443.

(*e*) 7 B. & C. 809.

(*f*) 2 T. R. 349; 1 Salk. 4; 7 Lord Raym. 641; 1 Saund. 103 a, b; Sayer, 234.

(1052) Vide Labagh v. Cantine, 13 Johns. Rep. 274. Bindon v. Robinson, 1 Johns. Rep. 516.

(1053) Vide Manhattan Company v. Miller, 2 Caines' Rep. 60. Snider v. Croy, 2 Johns. Rep. 428. Patcher v. Sprague, Id. 462. Bindon v. Robinson, 1 Johns. Rep. 516.

III. THE CONCLUSION. fact, and conclude with a verification, though this, as already observed, tends to unnecessary prolixity, delay, and expense (*g*); and when this form is adopted, the conclusion should be with an averment and prayer of damages, or of the debt and damages (*h*).

Must be with a *verification* when new matter is stated. It is a general rule that when *new matter* is alleged in the replication, it should conclude with an averment or verification, in order to give the defendant an opportunity of answering it, and an appropriate prayer of judgment for for debt and damages, or damages only, according to the form of action, and the subject-matter of dispute (*i*), and not merely *unde petit judicium si actione precludi debet* (*j*). But when the defendant would not be at liberty to traverse or answer the new matter without a departure, the replication may notwithstanding the introduction of new matter, conclude to the country; as if to debt on an award the defendant plead no award, and the plaintiff reply an award, and set forth a breach, it is said that he may conclude to the country (*k*), though a conclusion with a verification is most usual (*l*) And in an action of debt on a recognizance of bail in the same Court, where the defendant pleads that no *ca. sa.* issued against the principal, a replication setting out the *ca. sa.* and concluding with a verification by the record, and a prayer that the record may be inspected by the Court is good, though no formal issue be joined (*m*). If the new matter introduced in the replication be of a *negative* nature, *no conclusion* seems to be necessary, though it is usually adopted by using the common *verification*, "and this the plaintiff is ready to verify, &c." (*n*)

Estoppel. Where matter of *estoppel* is replied, the plaintiff should expressly rely on it, or he will lose the benefit of it (*o*)(1054), and it is usual to conclude the replication in that case, with a verification and prayer of judgment, if the defendant ought [*680] *to be admitted or received against his own acknowledgment, &c. to plead his plea (*q*). But in this, and indeed all other replications, it is sufficient, after the proper verification, to pray judgment generally, without pointing out the appropriate judgment (*r*); and where the word "*certify*" was by mistake inserted instead of "*verify*," the Court appeared to consider the replication sufficient (*s*). And unless assigned specially as a cause of demurrer, a defect in the conclusion of a replication is aided (*t*).

Where matter of *record* is relied upon, the plaintiff should conclude his replication with a verification by the record (*u*).

(*g*) *Id*; 2 T. R. 442, 443; 1 Burr. 320, 321; 2 Str. 971; 2 Wils. 173; Dougl 428.
(*h*) *Id.*; Say. 234; 1 Salk. 4; 1 Burr. 319; 2 T. R. 442, 443; 2 Marsh. 354.
(*i*) *Vide* Vivian *v.* Jenkins, 5 Nev. & Man. 14.
(*j*) 2 New Rep. 363, 364; 1 Saund. 103, n. 1; 327, n. 1; 2 *Id.* 63 g; Carth. 337; 1 Lutw. 101; 2 Wils. 66; Dougl. 60; 2 T. R. 576; 4 Mod. 376.
(*k*) 1 Saund. 327, note 1, cites 3 Lev. 165.
(*l*) *Post*, vol. iii.
(*m*) 2 Marsh. 354, *acc.*; 2 T. R. 576, *semble contra.*
(*n*) See Co. Lit. 303 a; 1 Show. 335; Stephen, 2d ed. 487; Willes, 6.
(*o*) 1 Saund. 325, note 4; 1 Co. 52 a; *ante*, 502, 635, 636, note (*o*).
(*q*) *Post*, vol. iii.; Willes, 11. 13.
(*r*) Willes, 13; 1 Saund. 97 a; 4 East, 502, 509; Vivian *v.* Jenkins, 5 Nev. & Man. 14. As to prayer of judgment in a *plea* in abatement or bar, *ante*, 497, 498.
(*s*) Willes, 6, 7.
(*t*) 16 & 17 Car. 2, c. 8; 4 & 5 Ann. c. 16, s. 1; 1 Saund. 99, note 2.
(*u*) See *post*, vol. iii

(1054) See Howard *v.* Mitchell, 14 Mass. R. 241.

The Reg. Gen. Hil. T. 2 W. 4, reg. 107,† orders, "that it shall not be necessary that any pleadings which conclude to the country be signed by counsel." (*x*). — III. THE CONCLUSION. — Signature of Counsel.

III. THE QUALITIES OF A REPLICATION.

The *qualities* of a replication, in a great measure, resemble those of a plea (*y*), and are—*First*, that it must answer so much of the plea as it professes to answer, and that if bad in part it is bad for the whole; *Secondly*, that it must be conformable to, and not depart from the count; *Thirdly*, that it must present matter of *estoppel;* or must *traverse* or *confess and avoid* the plea; *Fourthly*, that, like a plea, it should be certain, direct, and positive, and not argumentative, and also that it be triable; and, *Fifthly*, that it must be single.

1st. We have already pointed out the course which the plaintiff should adopt where the defendant has omitted to plead to a part of the plaintiff's demand, or where one of the defendants has not pleaded at all; and that the plaintiff's omission to adopt the proper course of proceeding thereon will sometimes occasion a *discontinuance* (*z*). Where there are several defendants in an action *ex contractu*, the plaintiff cannot enter a *nolle prosequi* as to one of them, except upon a plea by him, which operates merely in his personal or individual discharge without affecting the validity *of the debt, as bankruptcy or insolvency; but in an action *ex delicto*, a *nolle prosequi* as to one defendant does not in any instance discharge the others (*a*). A replication should also answer so much of the plea as it professes to answer (1055), or it will be a discontinuance (*b*). And it is a rule that an entire replication bad in part is bad for the whole (1056); as if to a plea of the statute of limitations to two counts of a declaration, the plaintiff should reply that the accounts were between the plaintiff and defendant as merchants, if this replication should be bad as to one of the counts it is bad also to the other (*c*). But this rule does not apply where the matter objected to is merely surplusage (*d*); and where a defendant sued as an executor or administrator has pleaded several judgments outstanding it would be a sufficient answer to the whole plea to deny the validity of one of the judgments (*e*). — I. MUST ANSWER THE PLEA. — [*681]

2dly. It is also a settled rule, that the replication must not *depart* from the allegations in the declaration in any *material* matter (*f*). But if the allegation in the *declaration* be immaterial, the replication may vary, and state an- — II. MUST NOT DEPART FROM DECLARATION, &c.

(*x*) Jervis's Rules, 71; Tidd, 672, 673, 693.

(*y*) *Ante*, 556.

(*z*) *Ante*, 554; and see Com. Dig. Pleader, F. 4; W. 1, 2, 3; 1 B. & P. 411.

(*a*) *Ante*, 51, n. (*y*), 598, 599.

(*b*) Com. Dig. Pleader, F. 4, W. 2; 1 Saund. 338. See this rule illustrated, as it applies to a plea, *ante*, 553. The same principles apply to a replication.

(*c*) Com. Dig. Pleader, F. 25; 3 T. R. 376; 1 Saund. 28, n. 3; 2 *Id.* 127.

(*d*) *Id.*; 3 T. R. 374, 377; 1 East, 219.

(*e*) 1 Saund. 337 b, note 2.

(*f*) See the discussion in Gledstane *v.* Hewitt, 1 Tyr. 445.

(1055) Vide Marsteller and others *v.* M'Clean, 7 Cranch, 156.

(1056) Vide Martin and others *v.* Williams, 13 Johns. Rep. 268.

† See American Editor's Preface.

H. MUST NOT DEPART FROM DECLARATION, &c.

other ground: thus, in detinue, if the declaration state a bailment that is in general immaterial, and therefore if the defendant in his plea state a different bailment, the plaintiff may, without traversing that in the plea, show the *detention* was wrongful without being guilty of a departure (*g*). A *departure* in pleading is said to be when a party quits or departs from the case or defence which he has first made, and has recourse to another; it occurs when the replication or rejoinder, &c. contains matter not pursuant to the declaration or plea, &c. and which does not support and fortify it (*h*)(1057). A departure in pleading cannot of course take place until the replication, but it may arise in that or any subsequent pleading (1058). It is not allowed, because the record would, by such means, be spun into endless prolixity, for if it were permitted, he who has departed from and relinquished his first ground or plea, might, in every different stage of the cause, resort to a second, third, or even further case or defence, and thereby pleading would become infinite (*i*); and if parties were permitted to wander from fact to fact, forsaking one to set up another, [*682] no issue *could be joined, nor could there be any termination of the suit (*j*). A departure may be either in the *substance* of the action or defence, or the law on which it is founded (*k*); as if a declaration be founded on the common law, and the replication attempt to maintain it by a special custom, or act of parliament (*l*). So, if in replevin for taking the plaintiff's goods and chattels, to wit, a lime-kiln, the defendant avows under a distress for rent, and the plaintiff pleads in bar that the lime-kiln was affixed to the freehold: this is a departure, the declaration being for goods and chattels, and the plea in bar stating the property to be part of the freehold (*m*) (1059). And where in replevin for taking goods of the plaintiff, the defendant made cognizance of the taking as a distress for rent upon a demise to the plaintiff, and she pleaded in bar that she was a married woman at the time of the demise, and when the rent accrued due it was held that such plea in bar negatived the cause of action, as it was to be presumed the husband was alive, so that the goods could not be the plaintiff's property (*n*). So where in assumpsit by an executor on several promises, which were all laid to have been made *to the testator*, to which the defendant pleaded the statute of limitations, and the plaintiff replied a subsequent promise *to himself*, the replication was held to be a departure, and therefore bad (*o*) (1060). A variety of other instances are collected in the

(*g*) Gledstane *v.* Hewitt, 1 Tyr. 445; 1 Cromp. & Jer. 565.

(*h*) 2 Saund. 84 a, note 1; Co. Lit. 304 a; 2 Wils. 98; Com. Dig. Pleader, F. 7, 11; 16 East, 39; 1 B. & C. 460; Tidd, 9th ed. 688; Stephen, 2d ed. 451.

(*i*) 2 Saund. 84 a, note 1; Stephen, 2d ed. 458.

(*j*) Summary Treatise on Pleading, 92.

(*k*) Co. Lit. 304 a; 2 Saund. 84 a.

(*l*) Co. Lit. 304 a; Com. Dig. Pleader, F. 7, 8; Carth. 306.

(*m*) 4 T. R. 504; 2 Saund. 84 b.

(*n*) 7 Taunt. 72.

(*o*) 2 Saund. 63 g, 84 c; Willes, 29; 1 Salk. 28; 6 Mod. 309; 2 Stra. 890; 3 East, 409.

(1057) { Andrus *v.* Waring, 20 Johns. Rep. 163. Wyman *v.* Mitchell, 1 Cowen's Rep. 319. 14 Mass. Rep. 103. }

(1058) Vide Sterns and others *v.* Patterson and others, 14 Johns. Rep. 132. Munro *v.* Allaire, 2 Caines' Rep. 320. Barlow *v.* Todd, 3 Johns. Rep. 367. Spencer *v.* Southwick, 10 Johns. Rep. 259. { 20 Johns. Rep. 163. 5 Greenl. Rep. 481. }

(1059) See also, Sibley *v.* Brown, 4 Pick. Rep. 137.

(1060) An averment of the value of goods in a plea of *plene administravit præter*, is not material and traversable. A rejoinder averring that the defendant has assets but not more than sufficient to pay and satisfy a judgment of upwards of $1000, was held not a departure from a plea of *plene administravit præter*, averring the goods unadministered to be of the value only of $1.

digests (*p*). But where in detinue on a bailment of a promissory note, to be re-delivered on request, defendant pleaded that the note was deposited by plaintiff as a pledge for the repayment to defendant of a loan of £50, and the replication stated a tender of £50, on special demurrer the replication was held good and no departure (*q*). If a declaration describe a bill or note as having been indorsed to the plaintiff by the payee, and the defendant plead that indorsee was a married woman, it is no *departure* in the replication to state that she indorsed by the authority of her husband (*r*).

II: MUST NOT DEPART FROM DECLARATION, &c.

But a departure more frequently occurs in a rejoinder (*s*). Thus, if in an action of debt on an arbitration bond, the defendant plead that *no award* was made, and the plaintiff in his replication set out an award, and assign a breach, it has been held that the defendant cannot rejoin that an *award was not tendered (1061), or that the defendant hath performed or been ready to perform it (*t*)(1062) If the award be in such case set out by the plaintiff in his replication, and a fatal defect appear on the face of it, the defendant may, it seems, demur (*u*); or, if the plaintiff set it out partially, the defendant may set out the whole, and then demur (*x*). So, where in an action on a bond conditioned for the payment of an annuity, the defendant pleaded *no such memorial* as the statute 17 G. 3 required; and the plaintiff replied that there was a memorial which contained the names of the parties, &c. and the consideration for which the annuity was granted; and the defendant rejoined that the consideration was untruly alleged *in the memorial* to have been paid to both obligors, for that one of them did not receive any part of it; it was held that this rejoinder, stating a new fact, was bad, as being a departure from the plea (*y*). So, if bail plead *no ca. sa.* against the principal, and in their rejoinder allege that the *ca. sa.* stated in the replication did not lie four days in the office, this is a departure (*z*). So, in an action of debt on bond, conditioned for performance of covenants, if the defendant plead *performance*, and the plaintiff reply and assign a breach, the defendant cannot rejoin any matter in *excuse* of performance (*a*). So, where in trespass for impounding the plaintiff's mare, the

[*683]

(*p*) Com. Dig. Pleader, F. 6, 7, 8, 9, &c.; Bac Ab. Pleas, L.; Vin. Ab. Departure; 1 Archb. 247, 253.

(*q*) Gledstane *v.* Hewitt, 1 Cromp. & J. 565; 1 Tyr. 450.

(*r*) Prince *v.* Brunatte, 1 Bing. N. C. 435.

(*s*) See Com. Dig. Pleader, F. 6, 7, 8, 9, &c. for the instances of a defective rejoinder, and 2 Saund. 83, 84, note 1; 188; 1 Saund. 117, note 3; 346 c. In trespass against three for an assault and battery, all pleaded the general issue, and *one* justified in defence of his freehold. Replication unnecessary force by *him*. A rejoinder that *all* the defendants did not use unnecessary force was held bad on demurrer, as not pursuing the prior pleadings, 4 B. & C. 704.

(*t*) 2 Saund. 188; 1 Sid. 10; Stephen, 2d edit. 452. As to rejoining that the award was void on account of some extrinsic fact, see *post*, 685.

(*u*) 1 Salk. 72; 1 Saund 103, note 1; 2 Saund. 62 b, note 5; 11 East, 188.

(*x*) 11 East, 188.

(*y*) 4 T. R. 585; 2 Hen. Bla. 280, S. C.; 16 East, 41; see 11 East, 188. It should be observed that the case in the text did not turn on the 53 Geo. 3, c. 141; but on the 17 Geo 3, c. 26, which requires that the *deed* shall truly state the consideration; and the defendant's rejoinder, therefore, contained an objection which applied more to the *deed* than the *memorial*.

(*z*) 1 Wils. 334; 16 East, 41; 7 B. & C. 800; see *ante*, 502.

(*a*) 2 Saund. 83 c; Co. Lit. 304 a; Com. Dig. Pleader, F. 6, &c.; see instances, Stephen, 2d ed. 453.

(1061) See, however, Allen *v.* Watson, 16 Johns. Rep. 205, recognizing Fisher *v.* Pimbley, 11 East, 183.

(1062) So, he cannot rejoin that the award was not final. Barlow *v.* Todd, 3 Johns. Rep. 363.

II. MUST NOT DEPART FROM DECLARATION, &c.

defendant pleaded that she was doing damage to the king in his forest of Waltham, and the plaintiff replied a right of common in the forest, and the defendant rejoined that the mare was mangy, and doing damage, and that therefore he took and impounded her; this was held to be a departure from the plea, because the plea was, that the mare was doing a *private* trespass to the king in his forest, and that therefore the defendant impounded her, but the
[*684] rejoinder is, that the mare was mangy, which is a *common nuisance (*b*). And where in trespass for impounding the plaintiff's ox, the defendant justified the taking *damage feasant*, and the plaintiff entitled himself to common of pasture for one ox, in the place in which, &c. and the defendant rejoined that the plaintiff had surcharged the common with that ox, it was adjudged that the rejoinder was a departure from the plea, because there is a great difference between damage feasant and a surcharge of common, and the surcharge should have been pleaded at first (*c*). So, in debt on bond conditioned to perform the covenants in a lease, one of which was that at every felling of timber defendant would make a fence, the defendant pleaded that he *had not felled any wood*. Replication that he felled wood but made no fence; and the Court held that a rejoinder that the defendant *did make a fence*, was a departure from the plea (*d*). The *plea* should have been that defendant felled wood and made a fence, and in all these cases, to avoid a departure, the whole matter should be shown at once in the plea (*e*).

But matter which maintains, explains, and fortifies the declaration or plea, is not a departure (*f*). Thus, if bail plead that no *ca. sa.* was *duly* sued out and returned according to the practice of the Court, and the plaintiff reply setting out a *ca. sa.* but directed to the sheriff of a wrong county, the defendant may rejoin that the venue was laid in another county, and that therefore the *ca. sa.* was not *duly* sued out (*g*). So in trespass for taking a horse, if the defendant justify for a *distress damage feasant*, the plaintiff may reply that the defendant afterwards used the horse, which shows that he was a trespasser *ab initio* (*h*)(1063). So if debt on bond to indemnify the plaintiff from tonnage due to A. the defendant plead *non damnificatus*, and the plaintiff reply that A. distrained for the said tonnage, and the defendant rejoin that nothing was due to A. for tonnage, this is not a departure, for if nothing were due there was in law no damage (*i*). And it seems that in debt on bond conditioned to perform an award, the defendant, though he pleaded *no award made*,
[*685] *may, to a replication setting out an award in part, rejoin setting out the whole award *verbatim*, by which it appeared that the award was bad in law, being made as to matters not within the submission (*k*). The Court, on demurrer, considered that there was no departure, as the plea of no award meant no legal and valid award, according to the submission (*k*). And if a declaration on

(*b*) 2 Wils. 96; 2 Saund. 84 b.
(*c*) 1 Salk. 221; Willes, 638; 2 Saund. 84 c.
(*d*) Dyer, 253 b.
(*e*) See Dyer, 253 b; Plowd. 102; Dyer, 102 b, S. C.
(*f*) Com. Dig. Peader, F. 11; 1 B. & C. 466.
(*g*) 16 East, 39.
(*h*) *Id.*; 1 D. & R. 50; 5 *Id.* 615; 1 Salk 221; 3 Wils. 20; Cro. Jac. 148; *ante*, 199, 207; replication, &c. to justification under a *fi. fa.*, *ante*, 643; 1 M. & P. 783.
(*i*) Fortes. 341; Com. Dig. Pleader, F. 11.
(*k*) 11 East, 188; 16 *Id.* 39; *sed vide* 1 Sid. 180; 1 Wils. 122; 4 T. R. 585; 2 Hen. Bla. 280, S. C.

(1063) { Darling v. Chapman, 14 Mass. Rep. 103. }

an apprenticeship deed charge that the defendant would not instruct the apprentice, and compelled him to leave his service, and the defendant plead that the apprentice misconducted and absented himself, it will be no departure to reply that after the misconduct, &c. the apprentice offered to return, &c. but the defendant refused; for this supports, explains, and fortifies the declaration (*l*). And if the plaintiff vary in his replication from this count, or the defendant in his rejoinder from his plea, in *time*, *place*, or other matter, *when immaterial*, it is not a departure. As if in a declaration, a promise be stated to have been made twenty years ago, and when the defendant pleads the statute of limitations the plaintiff replies that the defendant did undertake within six years; this is not a departure, because in this case the statement of the time in the declaration was immaterial (*m*). So, if in trespass for an assault at H., if the defendant plead *molliter manus imposuit* to remove the plaintiff from his close at A., and the plaintiff replies that he had a way over that close, it is not a departure; for in transitory actions the venue in the declaration is immaterial (*n*). In the case of a deed or other instrument, the plaintiff may reply or show in evidence that it was really made on a day different to the day of the date (*o*); and where a bill or note is stated in the declaration to have been made on a day which appears to have been above six years before the commencement of the suit, a subsequent promise or acknowledgment within six years may be shown in evidence under the common replication to the plea of the statute of limitations (*p*). But where time or place, or any *other circumstance, is *material*, the plaintiff cannot, as we have seen, vary from his previous statement of it (*q*); though where matter of defence has arisen *pending* the suit, it may be pleaded *puis darrein continuance*, *relicta verificatione* of the former plea. And if in an action against a person as executor, he plead a retainer for a debt due to himself, and the plaintiff reply that he was only *executor de son tort*, the defendant may, by way of plea *puis darrein continuance*, rejoin that he has since obtained letters of administration (*r*).

IT MUST NOT DEPART FROM DECLARATION, &c.

[*686]

The only mode of taking advantage of a departure is by demurrer, which may be either general (1064) or special (*s*); and if the defendant or the plaintiff, instead of demurring, take issue upon the replication or the rejoinder containing a departure, and it be found against him, the Court will not arrest the judgment (*t*).

(*l*) 1 B. & C 460. And see an instance in which a *surrejoinder* in an action upon a bond for the fidelity of a clerk was held not to be a departure from the replication, 7 *Id.* 809.

(*m*) Com. Dig. Pleader, F. 11; 1 Lev. 110; 10 Mod. 345.

(*n*) Com. Dig Pleader, F. 11; 1 Salk. 222; 1 Lord Raym. 120.

(*o*) 4 East, 477; see *ante*, 287, 288; *sed vide* Tidd, 9th ed. 629; cites 1 Salk. 222; 3 Lev. 348; Stra. 22, 806.

(*p*) See *ante*, 614 and *supra*, note (*n*). The case in 10 Mod. 312, is not law, and what was said in Stra. 22 and 806, as to a promissory note, was extra judicial.

(*q*) *Ante*, 287, 571, 681.

(*r*) 2 Stra. 1106.

(*s*) 2 Saund. 84 d; 2 Wils. 96; *quære* if it ought not to be a special demurrer, Com. Dig. Pleader, F. 10; 1 Saund. 117.

(*t*) Sir T. Raym 86; 2 Saund. 84 d.

(1064) { Dyson *v.* Wood, 5 Dowl. & Ryl. 295 } The Supreme Court of the State of New York has decided, that departure was fatal on general demurrer. Sterns *v.* Patterson, 14 Johns. Rep. 132. Munro *v.* Allaire, 2 Caines' Rep. 320, 329 Spencer *v.* Southwick, 10 Johns. Rep. 259. { Andrus *v.* Waring, 20 Johns. Rep. 160. Keay *v.* Goodwin, 16 Mass. Rep. 1. }

III. MUST CONTAIN MATTER OF ESTOPPEL, OR TRAVERSE, OR CONFESS AND AVOID.

3dly. It is a rule that a replication must either, *first*, present matter of *estoppel* to the plea, or, *secondly*, must *traverse*, or, *thirdly*, *confess and avoid* the matter pleaded by the defendant (*u*). If the plaintiff do not dispute, and cannot avoid the *facts* stated in the plea, but contends that their legal operation is insufficient to defeat the action, he must *demur* to the plea.

IV. THE CERTAINTY, &C. REQUISITE.

4thly. Another quality essential to a replication is *certainty*; and it is said that more is requisite in a replication than a declaration, though certainty to a common intent is in general sufficient (*x*). Where the replication is only to a *part* of the plea, the part alluded to should be ascertained with certainty; as if in assumpsit on several promises the defendant has pleaded infancy, and the plaintiff reply that part of the goods were for necessary food, and part for clothes, it is said to be insufficient if he do not show what part was for the one and what for the other (*y*). In general, also, when material to the action,
[*687] time, place, and other *circumstances must be stated with the same certainty and precision as in the previous pleadings; but where time or place is immaterial it should seem, with analogy to pleas in bar, that as the time and place mentioned in the declaration must when immaterial be adhered to, no repetition of either would be necessary (*z*). We have seen, that where extreme particularity in pleading would tend to great prolixity and inconvenience, a general allegation is allowed; on which principle it is settled, that in debt on a bond to account for all monies, &c. which the defendant or a third person receive in the course of a certain employment, it is sufficient to assign the breach generally, that divers sums of money were received from divers persons, &c., without naming from whom in particular (*a*). There is so much similarity between pleas and replications, in regard to the rule that a replication must not be argumentative, and must offer matter which is triable, that any further observations than those which were made upon the subject in relation to pleas (*b*) will be unnecessary.

V. MUST BE SINGLE.

5thly. The replication must not be *double*, or in other words, contain two answers to the same plea (*c*). For the plaintiff ought not to perplex the Court with two matters, to attempt to inveigle their judgment, and if two issues were permitted to be joined upon two several traverses on the plaintiff's replication, and one should be found for the plaintiff and the other for the defendant, the Court would not know for whom to give judgment, whether for the plaintiff or the defendant (*d*). And the Court will not give leave to *reply* double, under the statute 4 & 5 Ann. c. 16 (*e*); though under that statute the plaintiff *in replevin* may, with leave of the Court, plead several pleas in bar

(*u*) See *ante*, 556, 610; Steph. 2d ed. 82.
(*x*) Com. Dig. Pleader, F. 17; 12 East, 263; as to certainty in a declaration, see *ante*, 286.
(*y*) Lutw. 241; Com. Dig. Pleader, F. 4; *ante*, 534, 535.
(*z*) See 2 Hen. Bla. 161; 1 Saund. 8 a; *ante*, 553.
(*a*) 8 T. R. 463; 1 B. & P. 640; 1 Price, 109; 7 B. & C. 809; *ante*, 269, 270, 428 *b*.
(*b*) *Ante*, 572 and 573. See an instance of an argumentative traverse of a plea of a custom or liberty to dig for coal, &c. 10 East, 189.
(*c*) 10 East, 73; 2 Campb. 176, 177; Com. Dig. Pleader, F. 16; Rep. Temp. Hardw. 289. See in general, *ante*, 260; duplicity in a *plea*, *ante*, 491, 564.
(*d*) 2 Saund. 49, 50.
(*e*) Fortesc. 335; Barnes, 364.

to an avowry or cognizance (*f*)(1065). So a replication or traverse should be in the *disjunctive* and not conjunctive, when if a part of the plea be true the action would not be tenable; as, if to an action by an attorney for fees, the defendant plead that the action was brought for fees at law and in equity, and that plaintiff had not a month before action brought delivered a signed bill; a replication that the bill was not for fees at law *and* in equity is bad, for it should have been in the disjunctive (*g*). But a replication may frequently put in issue several facts, where they amount to only one connected *proposition or answer to the plea (*h*). And, as we have already seen, a replication may contain several distinct answers to different parts of a plea divisible in its nature (*i*); as where infancy has been pleaded to a declaration consisting of several counts, the plaintiff may reply as to part of the demand that it was for necessaries, to other part that the defendant was of full age at the time the contract was made, and to other part that he confirmed it after he came of age (*k*)(1066). So, if an executor or administrator plead several judgments outstanding and no assets *ultra*, the plaintiff may reply as to one of the judgments *nul tiel record*, and to another that it was obtained and kept on foot by fraud (*l*). In trespass *de bonis asportatis* of several articles, a plea justifying the removal *quia damage feasant* enures as a *several* plea in respect of each article, and the plaintiff may reply *severally;* thus he may traverse the justification as to *one* article, and as to another reply excess (*m*). So if a plea justify the removal of goods of a similar description enumerated in different counts, if the identity of the goods in the different counts be not alleged the plaintiff may reply severally in respect of the articles in each count (*n*); and the insufficiency of one of such sectional replications demurred to for duplicity, in putting in issue the whole plea by a traverse *absque tali causa*, where, in respect of matter of title disclosed by the defendant, the plaintiff should have put in issue a portion only of the plea, by traversing *absque residuo causæ*, does not affect the validity of the other replications to

V. MUST BE SINGLE.

[*688]

(*f*) 2 B. & P. 368, 376. As to the costs, see Tidd, 9th ed. 654, 660; 1 Marsh. 234.

(*g*) Moore *v.* Boulcott, 1 Bing. N. C. 323.

(*h*) 1 Burr. 317; Rep. Temp. Hardw. 289; *ante*, 637, 638.

(*i*) *Ante*, 261, 564, 565.

(*k*) *Ante*, 612.

(*l*) 1 Saund. 337 b, note 2; 1 Lord Raym. 263; 1 Salk. 298.

(*m*) Vivian *v.* Jenkins, 5 Nev. & Man. 14.

(*n*) *Id. ibid.*

(1065) The doctrine of duplicity in pleading has been somewhat vague and unsettled. The plaintiff cannot reply two distinct replications to the defendant's plea. This cannot be done at common law; and under the Statute (2 R. S. 356. s. 27) can be done only by leave of court (4 Wend. R. 211). The court, however, permitted the replications to stand, on payment of costs. Frisbie *v.* Riley, 12 Wend. R. 249. The objection to pleading for duplicity is an objection of form, and not of substance, and can only be taken advantage of on special demurrer. If the plaintiff reply that the promise was made by the defendant and a third person, and that a *release* was executed to such third person, denying both the joint promise and the release, is bad for duplicity. Tubbs *v.* Caswell et al., 8 ib. 129.

The rule that on demurrer judgment shall be given against the party who commits the first fault, applies not to a case where the pleading is bad merely in form. There is a class of cases in *tort* where the defendant sets up matter merely by way of excuse, in which the plaintiff may reply that the defendant of his own wrong, and without the cause by him alleged in his plea, committed the injury complained of in the declaration, and by this general traverse, he may put in issue *every material allegation* in the plea; but this manner of replying appears to be confined to cases of tort where the defence is by way of excuse merely, and is not allowed where the defendant by his plea insists upon a full and adequate *right*. ib. Lytle *v.* Lee et al., 5 Johns. Rep. 112. Plumb *v.* M'Crea, 12 ib. 491.

(1066) Vide Sevey *v.* Blacklin and others, 2 Mass. Rep. 542.

V. MUST BE SINGLE. the same plea (n). In an action of debt on bond, conditioned for the performance of covenants, the plaintiff may, and indeed ought, by the statute 8 & 9 W. 3, c. 11, s. 8, to assign as many breaches in his replication as he intends to rely upon at the trial, if such breaches be not assigned in the declaration; and it need not be shown that this is done by virtue of the statute (o). And to a plea of set-off, consisting of several demands upon judgment or recognizance of record, and simple contract, the plaintiff in his replication should give several answers, *viz.* as to the judgment or recognizance *nul tiel record*, and as to the simple contract, that he was not indebted (p); or he may reply as to a part, the statute of limitations (q). Duplicity in a replication is aided, unless the defendant demur specially, pointing out the particular defect (r)(1067).

(n) *Id. ibid.*

(o) 13 East, 1, 2, 3; *post*, vol. iii.; see *ante*, 617.

(p) 1 East, 369; see the form, *post*, vol. iii.; and *ante*, 613, 614.

(q) *Post*, vol. iii.; *ante*, 613, 614.

(r) 27 Eliz. c. 5; 4 & 5 Anne, c. 16, s. 1; 1 Saund. 337 b, n. 3; Doc. Pl. 147; 10 East, 73.

(1067) If the replication contains two distinct matters in avoidance of the plea, the defendant is not bound to demur for duplicity or to answer *both* matters, but may take issue upon either of the matters set up in avoidance. If such issue be found for the defendant, the plaintiff will be entitled to judgment *non obstante veredicto*; the other matters set forth in the replication being admitted as they were not answered. Gould *v.* Ray, 13 Wend. R. 633.

*CHAPTER IX.

Of Rejoinders and the subsequent Pleadings; of Issues, Repleaders, Judgments non obstante veredicto, and Pleas puis darrein continuance, or of Matter pending Action; and of Demurrers and Joinders in Demurrer.

A REJOINDER is the defendant's answer to the replication (*a*), and is in general governed by the same rules as those which affect pleas (*b*); with this additional quality, that it must *support* and not *depart* from the plea (*c*). If there be several defendants, and they *joined* in the plea, they cannot sever in the rejoinder (*d*). It must also be *single*; and the Court cannot give leave to the defendant to rejoin several matters, for the statute of Anne does not extend to rejoinders (*e*). Hence it may suffice to refer to the preceding pages, and to the forms which are given in the third volume, without taking further notice of the rejoinder with regard to its general construction and qualities (1068). OF REJOINDERS.

When a replication, or a plea in bar in replevin, concludes *to the country*, the defendant can only demur; or add the common *similiter*, which is, "And the defendant doth the like." And it is material that the defendant should take care that the *similiter* be added, for otherwise he cannot move for judgment as in case of a nonsuit (*f*). And where there are several replications, particularly when some conclude to the country, and others with a verification, it may be, "And the defendant as to the said replications of the plaintiff, to the said second and third pleas of him the defendant, and which the plaintiff hath prayed may be inquired of by the country, doth the like." (*g*) In the King's Bench, if the replication conclude to the country, the plaintiff is at liberty to add the *similiter* for the defendant, it being a rule in that Court that in all special pleadings, when the plaintiff takes issues upon the defendant's pleading, or traverses the same, or demurs, so that the defendant is not at liberty to allege any new matter, the plaintiff may add the *similiter* or joinder in demurrer, and make up the paper-book without giving a *rule to rejoin (*h*); but otherwise a rule must be given, unless the defendant be bound by a judge's order to rejoin *gratis*. In the Common Pleas, where the replication concludes to the country, it is usual for the plaintiff to add the *similiter*, and make up and deliver the FORM AND REQUISITES OF. [*690]

(*a*) Com. Dig. Pleader, H.
(*b*) *Ante*, 551, 578; Co. Lit. 303 b.
(*c*) See *ante*, 681; 2 Saund. 189, 190; Com. Dig. Pleader, F. 6 to F. 11.
(*d*) 4 B. & C. 704.
(*e*) Stra. 908; see *ante*, 260, 564, 687.
(*f*) Seabrook *v.* Cave, 2 Dowl. 691.
(*g*) See forms, *post*, vol. iii.
(*h*) Rule, Trin. 1 Geo. 2, n. a; Tidd, 9th edit. 717, 718.

(1068) { See, however, Nadenbousch *v.* M'Rea, Gilm. Rep. 228. }
Where several facts constituting but one defence are pleaded by a party, each fact cannot be traversed by the other side; the latter is confined to a denial of the facts alleged, if such denial, verified by proof, will bar the claim or defeat the defence. Tuttle *v.* Smith, 10 Wend. R. 388. Gould's Pl. 407.

FORM AND REQUISITES OF.

issue with notice of trial; but unless under terms of rejoining *gratis*, it seems that in the latter Court the defendant may insist upon having a rule to rejoin; and that if the plaintiff add the *similiter*, the defendant may strike it out, and demur to the replication, which is the usual course when the defendant has no merits, and wishes to obtain time (*i*). The consequences of a defect in or omission of a *similiter*, have already been considered (*k*).

When the replication concludes with a *verification*, the rejoinder usually denies it, and concludes to the country, "and of this he the defendant puts himself upon the country, &c." But when the rejoinder introduces any *new matter*, it must, as in the case of a plea or replication, conclude with a *verification*, in order that the plaintiff may have an opportunity of answering it (*l*). If the defendant deny several matters alleged in the replication, the rejoinder may conclude to the country, without putting the matters in issue severally and distinctly; thus, if to a plea of infancy, the plaintiff has replied that a part of the goods was necessary clothing, and the residue necessary food, a general denial in the rejoinder concluding to the country will suffice (*m*).

SURREJOINDERS, &c.

Surrejoinders, *rebutters*, and *surrebutters*, seldom occur in pleading (*n*). It may suffice to observe that they are governed by the same rules as those to which the previous pleading of the party adopting them is subject, and the forms which most frequently occur in practice are given in the third volume (*o*).

[*691]

OF ISSUES.

*From the preceding observations on the different parts of pleading, particularly those relating to traverses (*p*), we may collect what points may in general be put in *issue*. As, however, the parties respectively may be disinclined to demur, or otherwise to object to their opponent's pleading, it may be advisable to consider on what *issue* the parties may venture to proceed to trial, so as to obtain the judgment of the Court, and to avoid the necessity of a *repleader*, on account of the issue having been upon *immaterial matter*.

An *issue* is defined to be a single, certain, and material point, issuing out of the allegations or pleadings of the plaintiff and defendant (*q*); though, in common acceptation, it signifies the *entry* of the pleadings themselves (*r*). An

(*i*) Tidd, 9th edit. 718, 719; Imp. C. P. 358; 1 Sel. Prac. Chap. ix. s. 1.

(*k*) *Ante*, 631.

(*l*) *Ante*, 678, 679; 1 Saund. 103, note 1; see the forms *post*, vol. iii.

(*m*) Lutw. 241; Com. Dig. Pleader, H.

(*n*) See these heads in Com. Dig. Pleader, I. K. L. There is no technical name for any pleading subsequent to a surrebutter. It is very rarely, if ever, that the pleadings go beyond the surrebutter. It is hardly necessary to observe that the surrejoinder and surrebutter are the plaintiff's pleadings, and that the rebutter is the defendant's pleading.

(*o*) See *post*, vol. iii.

(*p*) *Ante*, 644 to 656.

(*q*) Co Lit. 126 a. As to *issues* in general, see Com. Dig. Pleader, R.; Bac. Ab. Pleas, M.; Tidd, 9th ed. 717.

(*r*) As to the form of such entry, see Tidd, 9th edit. 719, 733; and Tidd's App. c. 30, s. 1, &c. Issues in *fact* are not to be noticed in the *Demurrer* Book in K. B. 7 B. & C. 642. As to the language of this entry, it is said that the acts of a Court ought to be in the *present* tense, as "*præceptum est*," not "*preceptum fuit*," but the acts of the party may be in the preterperfect tense, as "*venit et protulit hic in curia quondam querelam suam*," and the continuances are in the preterperfect tense, as "*venerunt*," not "*veniunt*," 1 Mod. 81; 2 Saund. 393, note 1; 1 Stra. 608; but see 1 T. R. 320.

issue is either in *law*, upon a demurrer; or in *fact*, when the matter is triable by the court upon *nul tiel record*, or by a jury upon pleadings concluding to the country. Both these descriptions of issues may occur in the same cause as to distinct parts of the declaration. The term "issue" is proper where only one plea has been pleaded, though it be applied to several counts, and issue is joined upon such plea (*s*). An issue should in general be upon *an affirmative and a negative*, and not upon two affirmatives; as if the defendant plead that A. is living, and the plaintiff reply that he is dead, it is more formal, though not absolutely necessary, also to deny that he is living (*t*). Nor should the issue be on two negatives (*u*). Thus, if the defendant plead that he requested the plaintiff to deliver an abstract of his title, but that the plaintiff did not, when so requested, deliver such abstract, but neglected and refused so to do; the plaintiff cannot reply "that he did not neglect and refuse *to deliver such abstract," but should reply, either denying the request, or affirmatively, that he did deliver the abstract (*x*). But it is not necessary that the negative and affirmative should be in precise words (*y*); and it will suffice though there be two affirmatives, if the second is so contrary to the first that it cannot in any degree be true. Thus, if *duress* of imprisonment be pleaded to a bond, it is a good replication that the defendant was at large at his own disposal, and executed the bond of his own free will, and not for fear of imprisonment (*z*). An issue should also be upon a *single and a certain point* (*a*); but it is not necessary that such point should consist of a single fact; and therefore if the defendant in trespass justify under a right of common, and the replication traverses that the cattle were the defendant's own, and *levant* and *couchant*, and commonable cattle, it is not multifarious, for all these circumstances are requisite to the point of defence (*b*). The issue also should not be on a negative pregnant (*c*); but it may sometimes be upon a disjunctive averment (*d*). In some cases the plaintiff may incorporate in the traverse or issue more than was alleged in the plea (*e*). OF ISSUES. [*692]

The principal quality of an issue is, that it must be upon a *material* point (*f*). An *informal* issue is, where a *material* allegation is traversed in an *improper or artificial manner* (*g*)(1069); and this mistake is aided by verdict by the 32 Hen. 8, c. 30 (*h*)(1070). But a verdict does not help an *immaterial* issue (*i*)(1071), which is, where a material allegation in the pleadings is not traversed, but an issue is taken on some other point (1072), which, though

(*s*) Peake's C. N. P. 37.
(*t*) Com. Dig. Pleader, R. 3.
(*u*) *Id.*; 8 T. R. 280; Bac. Ab. Pleas, I. 3.
(*x*) 6 East, 557.
(*y*) Co. Lit. 126 a.
(*z*) 2 Stra. 1177; 1 Wils. 6.
(*a*) Com. Dig. Pleader, R. 4.
(*b*) 1 Burr. 316. Other instances, *ante*, 637, 651, 652, 653.
(*c*) See as to this, *ante*, 647, note (*u*); Com. Dig. Pleader, R. 5, 6; Bac. Ab. Pleas, I. 6. It must be objected to by demurrer, *id.*; 2 Saund. 319, n. 6.
(*d*) Com. Dig. Pleader, R. 7; see *ante*, 648.
(*e*) 11 East, 410; *ante*, 644.
(*f*) Com. Dig. Pleader, R. 8.
(*g*) Cro. Eliz. 227; 1 Lev. 32; Carth. 371; 2 Mod. 137.
(*h*) Gilb. C. P. 147; 2 Saund. 319, note 6.
(*i*) 2 Saund. 319 a, note 6.

(1069) Vide Winstanly *v.* Head 3 Taunt. 237.
(1070) Vide Cobb *v.* Bryan, 3 Bos. & Pul. 348, 352.
(1071) Vide Cobb *v.* Bryan, 3 Bos. & Pul. 352.
(1072) Vide Strong and Udall *v.* Smith, 3 Caines' Rep. 163.

OF ISSUES. found by verdict, will not determine the merits of the cause, and would leave the Court at a loss for which of the parties to give judgment (*k*). Therefore, where in debt on bond, conditioned for the payment of £60 on the 25th of June, the defendant pleaded payment on the 20th of June, according to the form and effect of the condition, and issue was joined, and the verdict found [*693] that he did not pay *£60 on the 20th, it was held that the plaintiff should not have judgment; for the issue was out of the matter of the condition, and therefore void, and the money might have been paid on the 25th, though it was not paid on the 20th, so that it did not appear that the condition was broken, and it is not aided by the before mentioned statute (*l*). So where in an action of assumpsit against an administratrix, on promises of the intestate, she pleaded that *she* (instead of the intestate) did not promise, after verdict a repleader was awarded (*m*). And where in an action of *debt* against a lessee for years, the defendant pleaded that before the rent became due, he assigned the term to a third person, of which the plaintiff had notice, and issue was joined on the averment of notice, a repleader was awarded; it being perfectly immaterial whether or not the plaintiff had notice of the assignment, if it were executed (*n*).

Of the modern regulations respecting issues.

Reg. Gen. Hil. T. 2 W. 4, orders, "that if a defendant, after craving oyer of a deed, omit to insert it at the *head* of his plea, the plaintiff, on making up the issue or demurrer book, may, if he think fit, insert it for him, but the costs of such insertion shall be in the discretion of the taxing officer (*o*).

The Reg. Gen. Hil. T. 4 W. 4, sec. 1 & 2, orders that every declaration and other pleading shall be dated of the day and month when pleaded, and shall be entered on the record made up for trial, and on the judgment-roll under the date of the day of the month and year when the same respectively took place, and without reference to any other time or date unless otherwise specially ordered by the Court or a judge; and no entry of continuances by way of imparlance, *curia advisari vult, vicecomes non misit breve*, or *otherwise, shall be made* upon any record or roll whatever, or in the pleadings, except the *jurata ponitur in respectu*, which is to be retained. Provided, that such regulation shall not alter or affect any existing rules of practice as to the times of proceeding in the cause. Provided also, that in all cases in which a plea *puis darrein continuance* is now by law pleadable in Banc, or at Nisi Prius, the same defence may be pleaded with an allegation that the matter arose after the last pleading, or the issuing of the jury process, as the case may be. Provided also that no such plea shall be allowed, unless accompanied by an affidavit that the matter thereof arose within eight days next before the pleading of such pleas, or unless the Court or a judge shall otherwise order. And in the conclusion of these rules the forms of an issue, and Nisi Prius record, and judgment, and other forms are given (*p*).

(*k*) *Id.*; Gilb. C. P. 147; 1 Lev. 32. See the instances, *id.* and Com. Dig. Pleader, R. 18; 3 Bar. & Cres. 449.

(*l*) Cro. Jac. 434; Stra. 994; 2 Saund. 319 b, note 6.

(*m*) 3 Ventr. 96.

(*n*) 1 Lev. 32.

(*o*) Jervis's Rules, 54, note (*t*).

(*p*) See forms of issue with notes, 3 Chitty's Gen. Prac. 766.

When the issue is *immaterial*, the Court will award a *repleader*, if it will be the means of effecting substantial justice between the parties, but not otherwise (*q*)(1073). As where in debt on bond, the defendant pleaded performance generally, and the plaintiff replied denying the general performance, and concluding to the country, and stated breaches, by way of *suggestion* instead of *replying* them, after verdict for the plaintiff a repleader was awarded, such issue being insufficient (*r*). In trespass for taking the plaintiff's cattle, the defendant justified taking them upon land demised by him to one W. for rent in arrear. Replication that they were not *levant* and *couchant*. The defendant took issue upon that, and after it was found for the plaintiff, he moved for a repleader, which was refused, because the issue might be material; and a repleader is never granted unless the issue *must* be immaterial (*s*). The following rules as to repleaders were laid down in the case of *Staple* v. *Hayden* (*t*): *first*, *that at common law, a repleader was allowed before trial, because a verdict did not cure an immaterial (*u*) issue, but now a repleader ought not to be allowed till after trial, in any case where the fault of the issue might be helped after verdict by the statute of jeofails (*x*). *Secondly*, that if a repleader be denied where it should be granted, or *vice versa*, it is error. *Thirdly*, that the Cout will not award a repleader excepting where complete justice cannot be answered without it (*y*). *Fourthly*, that the judgment of repleader is general, *quod partes replacitent*, and the parties must begin again at the first fault which occasioned the immaterial issue (*z*): thus, if the declaration be insufficient, and the bar and replication are also bad, the parties must begin *de novo* (1074); but if the bar be good, and the replication ill, at the replication (*a*)(1075). *Fifthly*, no costs are allowed on either side (*b*). *Sixthly*,

OF REPLEADERS.

[*694]

(*q*) 2 Saund. 319 b, note 6; 2 Salk. 579; 6 Mod. 1; 2 Ld. Raym. 922; 3 Salk 121, S. C.; Cowp. 489. See Chitty on the Game Laws, 1st edit. 965, cites Raym. 458; see *post*.

(*r*) 5 Taunt. 386; 1 Marsh. 95, S. C; see *ante*, 61^q.

(*s*) Ld. Raym. 167; 5 B. & C. 645.

(*t*) 2 Salk. 579; and 6 Mod. 1; 2 Lord Raym. 922; 3 Salk. 121, S. C.; as to a *repleader* in general, see Com. Dig. Pleader, R. 18; Bac. Ab. Pleas, M.; Doc. Plac. Repleader; Stephen, 2d ed. 130; Tidd, 9th edit. 921; see the forms there referred to, and 2 Saund. 20; and 319 b, n. 6.

(*u*) In the 5th edition of Saunders' Rep. (vol. ii. 319 b, note 6,) it is observed that "the word *immaterial* is in the report of this case, but it should seem to be a mistake; for the reason given, if that word alone be used, is wholly unsatisfactory, inasmuch as a verdict does not cure an immaterial issue at this day. It should seem that the reason of the distinction between the practice before and since the statute of jeofails is this; that before the statute a verdict did not cure either an *immaterial* or an *informal* issue, and therefore a repleader was awarded before a trial, because the trial could not have any effect upon the issue, and therefore the Court will not interfere until the result of a trial is seen, which may render a motion for a repleader unnecessary."

(*x*) Bac Ab. Pleas, M.; Com. Dig. Pleader, R. 18; 3 B. & P. 352; 2 Saund. 319 b. But where the point in issue is *altogether* immaterial and could not be *modified* by the verdict, because collateral to the merits, it would be otherwise. See further 9 Bing. 532.

(*y*) Goodtwine v. Bowman, 9 Bing. 532.

(*z*) 1 Ld. Raym. 169.

(*a*) 3 Keb. 664.

(*b*) 2 Vent. 196; 6 T. R. 131; Barnes, 125; 2 B. & P. 376.

(1073) Vide Stafford v. Corporation of Albany, 6 Johns. Rep. 1. Also, Terrel v. Page's Adm'r, 3 Hen. & Mun. 118. Taylor v. Huston, Id. 161. Cobb v. Bryan, 3 Bos. & Pul. 353. Havens v. Bush, 2 Johns. Rep. 388, 389. Bac. Abr. Pleas, (M. I.) { Macomb v. Wiber, 11 Johns. Rep. 230. }

(1074) Sed vide Smith v. Walker, 1 Wash. 135, 136, where the court says, "When we are seeking for a good foundation upon which to erect future pleadings, and find all defective, including the declaration itself, the uncertainty cannot be cured:" and therefore the court of appeals in giving the judgment, that ought to have been given in the court below, ordered the suit to be dismissed.

(1075) Vide Stevens v. Taliaferro, 1 Wash. 155.

WHEN NECESSARY, &c.

that a repleader cannot be awarded after a default at *nisi prius*. To which may be added, that in general a repleader cannot be awarded after a demurrer or writ of error, without the consent of the parties, but only after issue joined (*c*). Where, however, there is a bad bar, and a bad replication, it is said that a repleader may be awarded upon a demurrer (*d*)(1076). A repleader also will not be awarded, where the Court can give judgment on the whole record (*e*); and it is not grantable in favor of the person who made the first fault in pleading (*f*)(1077).

[*695] Distinction between a repleader and judgment *non obstante veredicto*.

*Where a plea confesses the action, and does not sufficiently avoid it, judgment shall be given upon the confession without regard to a verdict for the defendant, which is called a judgment *non obstante veredicto*; and in such case a writ of inquiry shall issue (*g*). The distinction between a repleader and a judgment *non obstante veredicto* is this: that where the plea is good in form, though not in fact, or in other words, if it contain a defective title, or ground of defence by which it is apparent to the Court, upon the defendant's own showing, that in *any* way of putting it, he can have *no merits*, and the issue joined thereon be found for him, there, as the awarding of a repleader could not mend the case, the Court, for the sake of the plaintiff, will at once give judgment *non obstante veredicto* (1078); but where the defect is not so much *in the title* as in the *manner of stating it*, and the issue joined thereon is immaterial, so that the Court know not for whom to give judgment, whether for the plaintiff or the defendant, then for the more satisfactory administration of justice they will award a repleader. A judgment therefore *non obstante veredicto* is always upon the *merits*, and never granted but in a very clear case; a repleader is upon the *form* and manner of pleading (*h*). If a plea be defective, and the defendant succeed at the trial thereon, the question, whether the plaintiff can have judgment *non obstante veredicto*, or whether there ought to be a repleader, depends upon the question, whether the plea does or does not contain a confession of a cause of action; if a cause of action be confessed by the plea, and the matter pleaded in avoidance be insufficient, the plaintiff is entitled to judgment notwithstanding the verdict. If the plea do not confess a cause of action, there must be a repleader (*i*).

OF PLEAS OF MATTERS OF DEFENCE THAT HAVE ARISEN PENDING THE ACTION(*j*).

Before the uniformity of process act, 2 W. 4, c. 39, it was decided that a payment to assignees of a bankrupt plaintiff, after a latitat had issued, and

(*c*) 3 Salk. 306.

(*d*) *Semble* Cro. Eliz. 318; 1 And. 167. *Sed quære.*

(*e*) Willes, 532, 533.

(*f*) 1 Ld. Raym. 170; Dougl. 396, 747; Tidd, 9th edit. 921; 2 Saund. 5th ed. 319 c; *sed vide* 2 Stra. 994. See further 9 Bing. 532.

(*g*) Tidd, 9th edit. 920; and cases cited, *id.* note g.

(*h*) Tidd, 9th edit. 922; Bac. Ab. Pleas, M.; Com. Dig. Pleader, R. 18; 5 Taunt. 386; 1 Marsh. 95, S. C.; 3 Taunt. 237.

(*i*) Ld. Raym. 390. *Per* Abbott, C. J. 4 B. & C. 152; 6 D. & R. 199; see the instances, *id.*

(*j*) As to these pleas in general, see Bac. Ab. Pleas, Q.; Com. Dig. Abatement, I. 24, 34; Doct. Plac. 297; Bul. N. P. 309; Gilb. C. P. 101; Tidd, 9th edit. 847; and see the forms, *post*, vol. iii.; and see Reg. Gen. Hil. T. 4 W. 4, reg. 2, Bosanquet's Rules, 130 to 134.

(1076) Vide Perkins *v.* Burbank, 2 Mass. Rep. 81.
(1077) Vide Kitley *v.* Deck, 3 Hen. & Mun. 388.
(1078) Lambert *v.* Taylor, 6 Dowl. & Ryl. 188.

before declaration, might be given in defence under the general issue (*k*). When matter of defence had arisen after the commencement of the suit, it could not be pleaded in bar of the action **generally*, but must, when it had arisen *before plea* or continuance, be pleaded as to the *further* maintenance of the suit (*l*)(1079); and when it had arisen after plea pleaded, and before replication, or *after issue joined*, then *puis darrein continuance* (1080). The instances of a defendant having obtained his certificate as a bankrupt pending the suit, *and before plea* (*m*), and of an executor pleading judgments obtained against him after the issuing of the writ, and before plea, were exceptions (*n*). WHEN NECESSARY, &c. [*696]

If any matter of defence has arisen after an *issue in fact* has been joined, or after a joinder in demurrer (*o*), it may be pleaded by the defendant; as that the plaintiff has given him a release (*p*); or that the plaintiff is a bankrupt (*q*), or has *been outlawed or excommunicated (*r*); or that there has been an award made on a reference after issue joined (*s*). And if the defendant became bankrupt, and obtain his certificate after issue joined, he should plead this defence *puis darrein continuance* (1081); and if he neglect [*697]

(*k*) 1 B. & Adol. 568; and 10 Bar. & Cres. 676.

(*l*) 4 East, 507; *ante*, 585; Lut. 1178; Com. Dig. Abatement, I. 24; plaintiff become an alien enemy, 3 Campb. 152.

(*m*) 9 East, 82.

(*n*) 4 East, 507, 8; 9 *Id.* 84; 1 Marsh. 70, 280; 5 Taunt. 333; and an executor may plead *puis darrein continuance*, a judgment purposely confessed by him for a *bona fide* debt, though such judgment be in *debt* on a simple contract; 5 Taunt. 665; 1 Marsh. 230, S. C.; 3 B. & C. 317; 5 D. & R. 175.

(*o*) Hob. 81; Com. Dig. Abatement, I. 24, *acc;* Ld. Raym. 266; Stra. 493, *contra;* see Com. Dig. Abatement, I. 24.

(*p*) Bul. N. P. 309; see the form, *post*, vol. iii. But in ejectment the defendant is not allowed to plead a release by the lessor of the plaintiff, 4 M. & S. 300; 2 Chit. Rep. 323, S. C.; and see 7 Taunt. 9. And where a landlord, with the permission of his bailiff, who had made a distress for rent, commenced an action in the bailiff's name against the sheriff for taking insufficient pledges, and the bailiff afterwards, without the landlord's privity, released to the sheriff, who pleaded it *puis darrein continuance*, the Court of C. P. set aside the plea, and ordered the release to be delivered up to be cancelled. 7 Taunt. 48; Tidd, 9th edit. 677, 848; so where husband and wife lived separate under a deed, by which he stipulated that his wife should enjoy as her separate property all effects, &c. which she might acquire, and that he would not do any act to impede the operation of that deed, but would ratify proceedings in their names for recovering such property; and the wife having, as executrix of N. R., commenced an action on a promissory note against defendants, in the names of her husband and herself, and the husband released the debt, which release was pleaded *puis darrein continuance;* the Court, on application, ordered the plea to be taken off the record, and the release to be given up to be cancelled, 4 B. & A. 419. So a plea *puis darrein continuance* of a release by one of several plaintiffs, was set aside by the Court of K. B. without costs, on the terms of indemnifying the plaintiffs, who had released the action, against the costs of it, although their consent had not been obtained before action brought; it appearing that no consideration had been given for the release, and that the plaintiffs sued as trustees of an insolvent person, 1 Chit. Rep. 390. But unless a very strong case of fraud be made out, the Court of C. P. will not control the legal power of a co-plaintiff to execute a release, 7 Taunt. 421; Tidd, 9th edit. 678, 848; 4 Moore, 192; 7 *Id.* 356; *ante*, 502.

(*q*) Tidd, 9th edit. 847; 15 East, 622; 4 B. & C. 920; 7 D. & R. 409, S. C.; as to the effect of the *plaintiff's* bankruptcy, see *ante*, 25.

(*r*) *Supra*, n. (*p*).

(*s*) 2 Esp. Rep. 504.

(1079) {Cowell *v.* Weston et al., 20 Johns. Rep. 414. Lee *v.* Levy, 6 Dowl. & Ryl. 475.}

(1080) Such matter cannot be given in evidence at the trial. Jackson d. Colden *v.* Rich, 7 Johns. Rep. 194.

(1081) Accord and satisfaction may be pleaded *puis darrein continuance*. Watkinson *v.* Inglesby and Stokes, 5 Johns. Rep. 392. When two actions are brought for the same cause, satisfaction of the judgment in one suit may be pleaded *puis darrein continuance* to the other suit. Bourne *v.* Joy, 9 Johns. Rep. 221. 5 Peters, 232. Gould's Pl. vi. 124.

WHEN NECESSARY, &c.

to do so he cannot plead his certificate to an action upon such judgment (*t*). So it may be pleaded in abatement that a feme sole plaintiff has married (*u*); or in an action by an administrator that the plaintiff's letters of administration have been revoked, *puis darrein continuance* (*x*). So a defendant sued as executor *de son tort* may plead that he has since obtained letters of administration, so as to support a previous plea of retainer in the character of executor (*y*).

Pleas of this kind are either in abatement or in bar (*z*). If any thing happen pending the suit, which would in effect abate it, this might have been pleaded *puis darrein continuance*, though there has been a plea in bar; because the latter plea only waives such matters in abatement as existed at the time of pleading, and not matter which arose afterwards; but if matter in abatement be pleaded *puis darrein continuance*, the judgment, if against the defendant, will be peremptory, as well on demurrer as on trial (*a*)(1082). A plea *puis darrein continuance* is not a departure from, but is a waiver of the [*698] first *plea, and no advantage can afterwards be taken of it, nor can even the *plaintiff* afterwards proceed thereon (*b*).

TIME OF PLEADING THEM (*c*) BEFORE THE RECENT RULE.

With respect to the *time* when matter of this description is to be pleaded, if the ground of defence arose after plea, or after issue joined, and before the return of the *venire facias*, it should be pleaded in *bank* (*d*); but matter arising after the return of the *venire facias*, or last continuance, may be pleaded at *nisi prius*, although there was an opportunity of pleading it previously in *bank* (*e*)(1083). And where the defendant, after pleading, obtained his certificate as a bankrupt, and then pleaded it in *bank*, as a matter which had arisen after the last continuance, but in fact another continuance had intervened between the certificate and plea, the Court permitted him to plead it *nunc pro tunc*, on payment of costs (*f*)(1084); but matters which have

(*t*) 6 B. & C. 105; 9 D. & R. 171, S. C. It would seem to be advisable, and perhaps necessary in such case, to plead the bankruptcy *specially*, and not in the general form prescribed by the stat. 6 Geo. 4, c. 16, s. 126; see *id.*; 6 East, 413; 2 Smith's Rep. 659; 1 M'Clel. & Y. 350; Mr. Justice Ashhurst's Paper Books, vol. xxiv. 154; Tidd, 9th ed. 847, note (*d*); 3 Taunt. 46; 3 B. & C. 23; *post*, vol. iii.; but see 2 Hen. Bla. 553; 9 East, 82; Tidd, 9th edit. 647, 8; see 1 M. & M. 122.

(*u*) Bro. Abr. Continuance, pl. 57; Bul. N. P. 310.

(*x*) Bul. N. P. 309; Com. Dig. Abatement, I. 24.

(*y*) 2 Stra. 1106; 1 Saund. 265, note 2.

(*z*) Com. Dig. Abatement, I. 24; Tidd, 9th ed. 849; see Form, *id.* Appendix, c. 37, s. 4.

(*a*) Gilb. C. P. 105; Alleyn, 66; Freem. 252; 2 Stra. 1105, 1106.

(*b*) 1 Salk. 168; 2 Stra. 1105; Hob. 81; 1 Marsh. 70, 280; 5 Taunt. 333; Tidd, 9th ed. 849.

(*c*) See Tidd, 9th edit. 847, 848; 3 B. & Ald. 577; 1 D. & R. 521; 5 B. & Ald. 858, S. C.; 4 B. & Ald. 249; 3 B. & Cres. 317.

(*d*) See Com. Dig. Abatement, I. 24; 2 Smith's Rep. 396; see the form, *post*, vol. iii.

(*e*) 5 Taunt. 333 and 665; S. C. in 1 Marsh. 70, and 280.

(*f*) 2 Smith's Rep. 396; Tidd, 9th ed. 848. See a plea, in vol. xxiv. 154, Mr. Justice Ashhurst's Paper Books, MS.

(1082) Acc. Renner and Bussard v. Marshall, 1 Wheaton, 215.

(1083) Lyttleton v. Cross, 5 Dowl. & Ryl. 175. Broome v. Beardsley, 3 Caines' Rep. 173.

(1084) Vide Morgan v. Dyer, 9 Johns. Rep. 255. Merchants' Bank v. Moore, 2 Johns. Rep. 294. It is in the discretion of the court to receive the plea or not, even after more than one continuance has intervened, and this discretion will be governed by circumstances extrinsic, and which cannot appear on the face of the plea. Morgan v. Dyer, 10 Johns. Rep. 161. { Wilson v. Hamilton, Lyons v. Miller et al., 4 Serg. & Rawle, 239, 281. The King v. Taylor, 5 Dowl. & Ryl. 521. }

arisen after the trial, and before the day in *bank*, cannot be so pleaded (*g*); and though such a plea may be pleaded after the jury have gone from the bar, yet it cannot after they have given their verdict (*h*)(1085). A plea of bankruptcy in the defendant after the last continuance, was set aside as having been pleaded after the proceedings had been stayed in an action upon the bail bond (*i*). But a plea *puis darrein continuance* of new matter may be pleaded although the defendant were under terms of rejoining issuably and taking short notice of trial (*k*). TIME OF PLEADING THEM.

The Reg. Gen. Hil. T. 4 W. 4, reg. 2,† puts an end to the entry of continuances, except the *jurator ponitur in respectu*, which is to be retained. But the same rule provides "that in all cases in which a plea *puis darrein continuance* is now by law pleadable *in bank*, or at *nisi prius*, the same defence may be pleaded *with an allegation that the matter arose after the last pleading, or the issuing of the jury process, as* the case may be." Provided "that no such plea shall be allowed unless *accompanied by an affidavit that the matter thereof arose within eight days next before the pleading of such pleas, or unless the Court or a judge shall otherwise order.*" Since the Reg. Gen. Hil. T. 4 W. 4, reg. 2.

Great certainty was always required in pleas of this description (*l*); and it was not sufficient to say generally that "after the last continuance" such a thing happened, but the *day* of the continuance must have [*699] been alleged where the matter of defence arose (*m*). The present forms of such pleas, whether pleaded in *bank* (1086) or at the assizes, are given in the third volume (*n*). The plea, when it contains matter in abatement, concludes by praying judgment of the writ, and that the same may be quashed (*o*); or if the writ would be abated *de facto*, by praying judgment if the Court will further proceed (*p*). In *bar* the conclusion of the plea is, that the plaintiff ought not *further to* maintain his action, and not that the former inquest should not be taken, because it is a substantive bar of itself, in lieu of the former, and consequently must be pleaded to the action (*q*). Form of these pleas.

(*g*) Tidd, 9th ed. 848, 849.

(*h*) Doctr. Plac. 177; Bul. Ni. Pri. 310; 9 East, 321; Com. Dig. Abatement, I. 34; see further, 3 B. & Ald. 577; 1 D. & R. 521; 5 B. & Ald. 852, S. C.; 4 B. & Ald. 249; Tidd, 9th ed. 849.

(*i*) 4 B. & Ald. 249; 6 B. & Cres. 145.

(*k*) 2 M. & P. 760; 5 Bing. 414, S. C.

(*l*) Doc. Plac. 297; Yelv. 141; Cro. Jac. 261; Freem. 112; 2 Lutw. 1143; 2 Salk. 519; 2 Wils. 139; Co. Ent. 517 b; Rast. Ent. 549.

(*m*) *Id. ibid.*; Bul. N. P. 309.

(*n*) *Post*, vol. iii.; and see Bul. N. P. 310; Co. Ent. 517; Rast. Ent. 549; Tidd, 9th ed. 850.

(*o*) Gilb. C. P. 105; 2 Lutw. 1143; in general, *ante*, 493.

(*p*) 3 Lev. 120; Bul. N. P. 311.

(*q*) Cro. Eliz. 49; 2 Lutw. 1143; Bul. N. P. 310.

(1085) But an insolvent has been allowed to plead his discharge even after verdict. Mechanics' Bank *v.* Hazard, 9 Johns. Rep. 392.

(1086) { In covenant against executors the defendants pleaded at *nisi prius*, as a plea *puis darrein continuance*, a judgment recovered upon a bond of the testator after the last continuance, to wit: on the 2d day of August, as to the preceding Trinity Term, and the plaintiff having pleaded over.—*Held*, that the plea was an answer to the action, although by fiction of law the judgment was obtained before the last continuance. Where the purposes of justice require that the true time when a judgment is recovered, or a writ tested, shall be shown, it is competent to a party to avail himself of the fact by averment in pleading. Lyttleton *v.* Cross, 5 Dowl. & Ryl. 175. }

† See American Editor's Preface.

TIME OF PLEADING THEM. — How pleaded, and proceedings thereon.

Pleas after the last continuance must, even before Reg. Gen. Hil. T. 4 W. 4. reg. 2, have been verified *on oath* before they could be allowed, whether pleaded in *bank* or at *nisi prius* (r); but the affidavit need not have been entitled in the cause when annexed to the plea (s). The Reg. Gen. Hil. T. 4 W. 4, reg. 2,† we have just seen, also requires that the affidavit state that the matter of defence arose *within eight days* next before the pleading such plea, or that the Court or a judge has otherwise ordered (t). These pleas, it is said, cannot be amended after the assizes are over (u)(1087); nor can there be more than one plea *puis darrein continuance* (x), and such a plea cannot, it is said, be pleaded after a demurrer (y). But if a plea *puis darrein continuance* be filed and verified on oath, the Court cannot set it aside on motion, but are bound to receive it (z), provided it be pleaded in proper time (a). When a plea *puis darrein continuance* is put in at the assizes, the plaintiff is not to reply to it there, for the judge has no power to accept of a replication, nor to try it (1088); but ought to return the plea as parcel of the record of *nisi prius*; and if the plaintiff demur, it cannot be argued there (b). Where the plea
[*700] *puis darrien continuance* is *certified on the back of the postea, and the plaintiff demurs, if the defendant, on the expiration of a rule given for him to join in demurrer, neglect to do so, the plaintiff may sign judgment (c).

The Courts will sometimes set aside a plea *puis darrein continuance* when it is manifestly fraudulent, and against the justice of the case. But where an action was brought by two out of four executors, and those who were not joined in the action released to the defendant, and who pleaded such release *puis darrein continuance*, the Court refused to set aside such plea, the plaintiff having failed to establish a case of fraud; and as a general rule a plea of that nature is not to be set aside unless in a case of gross fraud (d).

(r) Freem. 252; 1 Stra. 493; 2 Smith's Rep. 396. Form of affidavit of plea of bankruptcy, M'Clel. & Y. 350. As to pleas in abatement, *ante*, 496. When pleaded at the assizes, the affidavit should be sworn before one of the judges, not before a commissioner, 3 C. & P. 408.

(s) 1 Marsh. 70; 5 Taunt. 333, S. C.; *sed vide* 3 Price, 200.

(t) *Ante*, 698.

(u) Bac. Ab. Pleas, Q.; Yelv. 181; Freem. 252; Bul. N. P. 309. But see 2 Smith's Rep. 659, where such a plea was amended upon terms; and vol. xxiv. of Mr. Justice Ashhurst's Paper Books, 154, *see*.

(x) Bro. Abr. Continuance, pl. 5, 41; Jenk. 160; Gilb. C. P. 105.

(y) 1 Stra. 493, cites Moore, 871; and see 1 Ld. Raym. 266; 6 Mod. 9; but see Hob. 81, *contra*; Com. Dig. Abatement, I. 24.

(z) 2 Wils. 157; 3 T. R. 544; 1 Marsh. 70, 280; 5 Taunt. 333; 1 Stark. 62.

(a) When or not set aside, 3 Chitty's Gen. Prac. 120; 2 Cr. & M. 384; 3 B. & Cres. 612.

(b) Com. Dig. Abatement, I. 24. If pleaded by one of several defendants, the plaintiff cannot at the trial confess the plea, &c. 3 C. & P. 372.

(c) Bac. Ab. Pleas, Q.; Bul. N. P. 311; 1 Stark. 62. As to *costs*, see 4 B. & C. 117; 6 D. & R. 81, S. C.; 1 M. & P. 138.

(d) Herbert *v.* Piggott, 2 Crom. & M. 384; but see Smith *v.* Newman, 4 B. & Ald. 419; 7 Taunt. 421; 1 Chitty's Rep. 390.

(1087) { See Sharpe *v.* Witham, 2 M'Clell. & Younge, 350. }

(1088) When pleaded at *nisi prius*, a copy of it need not then be served. Jackson *v.* Clow, 13 Johns. Rep. 157.

† See American Editor's Preface.

OF DEMURRERS (*e*).

OF DEMURRERS WHEN PROPER.

When the declaration, plea, or replication, &c. appears on the *face of it*, and without reference to *extrinsic* matter, to be defective, either in substance or form, the opposite party may in general *demur* (*f*). A demurrer has been defined to be a declaration that the party demurring will "go no farther," because the other has not shown sufficient matter against him that he is bound to answer (*g*). Where the pleading is defective in *substance* it is adviseable in general to demur, because the party succeeding thereon is entitled to costs; but where the judgment is reversed on a writ of error, &c. (*h*) no costs are recoverable.

It should, however, be remembered that a demurrer admits the *facts* pleaded (*i*), and merely refers the question of their *legal* sufficiency to the decision of the Court (1089). If, therefore, there be reason to deny the facts, it is better not to demur, but to plead thereto, especially if the defect in the opposite pleading be of so substantial a nature that even after a verdict on the issue the judgment might be arrested, or a writ of error could be sustained (*k*). But the common doctrine that a demurrer admits the facts stated in the pleading, demurred to, must be understood with this qualification, that it is so only upon the argument, for it has been held that the statements in a special plea which has been holden bad on demurrer are *not evidence* for the plaintiff on the general issue, although the jury are to assess damages as well as to try the case on the general issue (*l*).

*When the objection is a defect in matter of *form*, a *special* demurrer is still permitted; for, as observed by Lord Hobart, "the statute of Elizabeth requiring a special demurrer, does not utterly reject *form*, for that would be destructive of the law as a science, but it only requires that the defect in form be discovered, and not used as a secret snare to entrap." (*m*) And it was observed by Eyre, Chief Justice, that "infinite mischief has been produced by the facility of the Courts in overlooking errors in form; it encourages carelessness, and places ignorance too much upon a footing with knowledge amongst those [*701]

(*e*) As to demurrers in general, see Bac. Ab. Pleas, N.; Com. Dig. Pleader, Q.; Saund. Rep. Index to notes, "*Demurrer*;" Tidd, 9th edit. 694; Stephen, 2d ed. Index, "*Demurrer*." As to the *practice* respecting demurrers, see 3 Chit. Gen. Pr. 752 to 763; Reg. Gen. Hil. T. 4 W. 4, reg. 4, orders that no demurrer nor pleading subsequent to the declaration shall in any case be *filed* with any officer of the Court, but shall always be delivered between the parties; and see Jervis's Rules, 86, 87.

(*f*) Moore, 551. *Surplusage* not demurrable, 11 East, 65; Plead. Ass. 292; *ante*, 263.

(*g*) 5 Mod. 132; Co. Lit. 71 b.

(*h*) 1 Stra. 617; Tidd, 9th ed. 1181. As to costs where the judgment is *arrested*, see Cowp. 407; Tidd, 9th ed. 985. On a new trial, *id.* 916; and where a venire *de novo* is awarded, *id.* 923. It seems, that although an objection appear on the record, and might be taken advantage of by motion in arrest of judgment, or writ of error, yet if it be of such a nature that the action clearly cannot be maintained, the judge at nisi prius will nonsuit the plaintiff, 1 Campb. 256; Cowp. 407.

(*i*) That is, when well pleaded, Com. Dig. Pleader, Q. 6; 1 Saund. 337 b, n. 3; Steph. 2d ed. 175; 11 Price, 235; *ante*, 568; but see note *infra*.

(*k*) 4 Co. Rep. 14 a. As to the expediency of demurring or pleading, in general, see Steph. 2d ed. 182. What defects are cured by pleading over, and by verdict, &c. *post*.

(*l*) Montgomery v. Richardson, 5 Car. & P. 247; Firmin v. Crucifix, *id.* 247.

(*m*) Hob. 232; 1 Saund. 337, note 3.

(1089) Weems v. Willard, 2 Harr. & Gill, 143. Vide Pease v. Phelps, 10 Conn. R. 62.

WHEN PROPER.

who practice the drawing of pleadings." (n) Where, however, there are merits to be tried, it is in practice more liberal not to demur for a mere mistake in form. But it sometimes becomes material to demur, although the objection be of a mere technical description, if the adverse party will not alter his pleading: as in instances in which the defective pleading imposes upon the opponent the necessity of adducing more evidence than would have been requisite, had the pleading been properly framed; as if *nil debet* be pleaded to a declaration on a deed, or *de injuria* generally be replied where the replication should traverse one only of the several matters alleged in the plea.

To what objections the opponent cannot demur.

There are some well-founded objections to pleadings, but which cannot be the ground of demurrer; such are principally the non-compliance with some rule of *practice* not affecting the *substance of pleading* (o). Thus if, contrary to Reg. Gen. Hil. T. 4 W. 4, reg. 8, venue be repeated in the body of a declaration, the defendant cannot on that account demur, but if taken advantage of at all, should obtain a summons and judge's order to strike out the objectionable venue (p). So in general an inaccuracy in the form of *commencing* a declaration is not ground of demurrer (q).

WHEN GENERAL OR SPECIAL.

Demurrers are either *general* or *special*; *general*, when no particular cause is alleged; *special*, when the particular imperfection is pointed out, and insisted upon, as the ground of demurrer; the former will suffice when the pleading is defective in *substance*, and the latter is requisite where the objection is only to the *form* of pleading (r)(1090). At common law a special demurrer was not necessary, except in the case of duplicity (s), and the party was at liberty on a general demurrer to take advantage of any objection, however trifling (t). To remedy this the 27 Eliz. c. 5, after *reciting* "that excessive charges and expenses, and great delay and hindrance of justice, have grown in actions and suits between the subjects of this realm, by reason that upon some small mistaking, or want of form in pleading, judgments are often reversed by writs of error, and oftentimes upon demurrers in law given otherwise than the matter in law, and the very right of the cause doth require, whereby the parties are constrained either utterly to lose their right, or else [*702] *after long time and great trouble and expenses, to renew again their suits," *enacted*, "that from thenceforth, after demurrer joined and entered in any action or suit in any Court of *record* within this realm, the judges shall proceed and give judgment according as the very right of the cause and matter in law shall appear unto them, without regarding *any imperfection, defect, or want of form, in any writ, return, plaint, declaration, or other pleading*, process, or course of proceeding whatsoever, except those only which the party demurring shall *specially* and particularly set down and express, together with his demurrer; and that no judgment to be given shall be reversed by any writ of error for any

(n) 1 B. & P. 59.

(o) 1 Bing. N. C. 353, 354, 4 M. & Scott, 417; 3 Dowl. 2; 2 Dowl. 236.

(p) Farmer v. Champneys, 1 Crom. M. & Ros. 369; 2 Dowl. 690, S. C.; Fisher v. Snow, 3 Dowl. 27; Townsend v. Gurney, Id. 29; but see 3 Dowl. 2.

(q) 4 Moore & Scott, 417; Stranchan v. Buckle, 1 Harr. & Wol. 519; Turner v. Denman, 4 Tyr. 313; and see 3 Chit. Gen. Prac. 468.

(r) Bac. Ab. Pleas, N. 5; Co. Lit. 72 a.

(s) 11 East, 565.

(t) 3 Salk. 122.

(1090) Vide Snyder v. Crey, 2 Johns. Rep. 428.

such imperfection, defect, or want of form, as is aforesaid, except such only as is before excepted." WHEN GENERAL OR SPECIAL.

The chief difficulty that arose in the construction of this statute, was the distinguishing between what was the matter of form and matter of substance; and many defects which are *now* deemed mere form, were holden not to be aided by this statute, such as the omission of the words *vi et armis, contra pacem, &c.* (*u*). To remedy this the 4 & 5 Ann. c. 16, directs, "that where any demurrer shall be joined and entered in any action or suit in any *Court of record* within this realm the judges shall proceed and give judgment according as the very right of the cause and matter in law shall appear unto them, without regarding *any imperfection, omission, or defect*, in any writ, return, plaint, *declaration, and other pleading*, process, or cause of proceedings whatsoever, *except those only which the party demurring shall specially and particularly set down and express, together with his demurrer, as causes of the same*, notwithstanding that such imperfection, omission, or defect might have heretofore been taken to be *matter of substance, and not aided by the abovementioned statute*, so as sufficient matter appear in the said pleadings, upon which the Court may give judgment according to the very right of the cause." And it is then so provided, "that no advantage or exception shall be taken of or for an im material traverse, or of or for the default of entering pledges upon any bill or declaration, or of or for the default of alleging the bringing into Court any bond, bill, indenture, or other deed whatsoever, mentioned in the declaration or other pleadings, or of or for the default of *alleging of the bringing into [*703] Court letters testamentary, or letters of administration, or of or for the omission of *vi et armis, et contra pacem*, or either of them, or of or for the want of averment of *hoc paratus est verificare*, or *hoc paratus est verificare per recordum*; or of or for not alleging *prout patet per recordum*; but the Court shall give judgment according to the very right of the cause as aforesaid, without regarding any such imperfections, omissions, and defects, *or any other matter of like nature* (*x*), except the same shall be *specially* and particularly set down and *shown for cause of demurrer*." It was provided by the seventh section that the act should not extend to proceedings upon any *penal statute*; but this was altered by the 4 Geo. 2, c. 26, s. 4 (*y*).

Since these statutes, the party on a *general demurrer* can only take advantage of defects in *substance* (1091); and therefore, if the defect objected to be not clearly of that nature, it is safest to demur specially, in which case the party may not only take advantage of those particularly pointed out, but also of any substantial defect, though not specified (*z*)(1092). The effect produced on the right to demur generally or specially, by the circumstance of the defendant being under terms of pleading issuably, has already been considered (*a*). The plaintiff need never demur specially to a plea in abatement (*b*).

(*u*) Com. Dig. Pleader, 3 M. 7; Bac. Ab. Pleas, N. 6; 1 Saund. 81, note 1; Hob. 233; Sav. 88.

(*x*) See observations as to extent of these words, 2 Hen. Bla. 262; 10 East, 359.

(*y*) Willes, 601.

(*z*) 1 Saund. 337 b, note 3; Tidd, 9th ed. 695; 2 Wils. 10.

(*a*) *Ante*, 550, 551.

(*b*) 2 M. & Sel. 485.

(1091) {5 Greenl. Rep. 415.} Vide Hord's Executors *v.* Dishman, 2 Hen. & Mun. 600.

(1092) Vide Burnet *v.* Bisco, 4 Johns. Rep. 235.

WHEN ONLY TO A PART.

Where only to a part of the pleading.

A demurrer is either to *the whole*, or *to a part only* of a *declaration*. If in covenant there be several distinct assignments of breaches of covenant, some of which are sufficient, and the others not, or if a declaration contain several counts, and only one be bad; the defendant should only demur to the defective assignment of breach, or the insufficient count; for if he were to demur to the whole declaration, the Court would give judgment against him (c)(1093). This rule equally applies to one count, part of which is sufficient, and the residue is not, provided the matters alleged are *divisible* in their nature; as if a plaintiff declare in tort for taking his money, and also certain goods, without showing that the goods were his property, the count will be good as to the money, and if the defendant demur generally to the whole count, the [*704] *plaintiff will have judgment (d) (1094). So where the plaintiff declared in *scire facias*, upon a judgment in K. B. with a *prout patet per recordum*, and also on affirmance of that judgment in error in the Exchequer Chamber, without a *prout patet, &c.* and the defendant demurred to the whole, the Court held the demurrer too large, as the plaintiff's demand was divisible, and judgment was given for the plaintiff (e). So, if part of a breach be good, it is no cause of demurrer to the whole, that special damage is laid which is not recoverable (f); but where there is a misjoinder either of parties or causes of action or breaches, the demurrer must be to the whole (g). And if a *plea, avowry*, or *replication*, each of which, we have seen, is in its nature entire, be bad in part, it is bad for the whole (h); and in that case the demurrer should be to the whole plea or replication (i), or it will be a discontinuance (k). There is an exception in the

(c) Ferguson *v.* Mitchell, 2 Crom. M. & Ros. 687; and see Spyer *v.* Thelwell, *id.* 692; 5 B. & Ald. 712, 715; 11 East, 565; Com. Dig. Plead. Q. 3, 5; 1 Saund. 286; and *id.* note 9; 2 *Id.* 379, 380, note 14; 1 Wils. 284; 1 New Rep. 43; Bac. Ab. Pleas, B. 6; Steph. 2d ed. 450.

(d) 2 Saund. 379, 374, note 1; 5 Rep. 34 b; 1 Salk. 218; 2 Saund. 171 a, n. 1; 1 Mod. 271; Com. Dig. Pleader, C. 82; see the form, 1 Saund. 108, 109. In 8 Moore, 379, the plaintiff declared in trespass for breaking and entering his close, and also his house, and seizing and taking his goods, "to wit, one hundred articles of furniture," without describing their nature or quality. The defendant, though under terms of pleading issuably, demurred generally to the *whole* declaration. The Court held that the plaintiff could not sign judgment as for want of a plea; for the declaration was substantially defective as regarded the *goods*. *Semble* (notwithstanding Mr. Justice Burrough's observations,) that the case cannot be considered an authority that the *whole* of the declaration should have been demurred to. The rule in the text would not apply to a count in *assumpsit* upon a contract, the whole of which is considered entire.

(e) 11 East, 565.

(f) 5 B. & Ald. 712; 1 D. & R. 361, S. C.; 3 T. R. 374.

(g) 1 M. & Sel. 355; 4 T. R. 547; *ante*, 236; 2 Saund. 210, and 210 a.

(h) *Ante*, 579, 598, 681; 1 Saund. 28; and *id.* n. 2, 286; 337, n. 7; 2 *Id.* 124; 1 Salk. 312; 1 T. R. 40; 3 *Id.* 374. Effect of one plea referring to another, 1 M. & P. 147; 2 Y. & J. 11, S. C.

(i) See an exception in an avowry, 1 Saund. 286.

(k) Com. Dig. Pleader, Q. 3.

(1093) { Belton *v.* Gibbon, 7 Halst. Rep. 76. Wolf *v.* Luyster, 1 Hall's Rep. 146.} Vide Seddon *v.* Senate, 13 East's Rep. 76, 77. Ward *v.* Sackrider, 3 Caines' Rep. 265. Roe *v.* Crutchfield, 1 Hen. & Mun. 361. Whitney *v.* Crosby, 3 Caines' Rep. 89. Backus *v.* Richardson, 5 Johns. Rep. 476. Kingsley *v.* Bill and another, 9 Mass. Rep. 199, 200. Martin and others *v.* Williams, 13 Johns. Rep. 264. Monell & Weller *v.* Colden, 13 Johns. Rep. 402. Adams *v.* Willoughby, 1 Johns. Rep. 65. So, if the defendant plead several pleas, all of which are demurred to, if one be good, judgment must be given for the defendant. Sevey *v.* Blacklin and others, 2 Mass. Rep. 541. Harrison *v.* M'Intosh, 1 Johns. Rep. 385. Cuyler *v.* Trustees of Rochester, 12 Wend. R. 169.

(1094) So in a plea of outstanding judgment by an executor or administrator, where some of the judgments are well, and the others badly pleaded, the plaintiff should demur only to those which are insufficiently pleaded, and traverse the residue. Douglas *v.* Satterlee, 11 Johns. Rep. 16. { But it is error to demur and reply to the *same* plea. Lang *v.* Lewis's Administrator, 1 Rand. Rep. 277. }

case of a plea of *set-off* which contains a statement that distinct debts are due from the plaintiff, for such averments are considered to be similar to separate counts in a declaration; and if one part be good, a general demurrer to the whole will be bad (*l*)(1095). WHEN ONLY TO A PART.

In general a party cannot demur, unless the objection appear on the *face of the preceding pleadings* (*m*); but in some *cases, where the plaintiff in the declaration partially states a deed which is defective, or contains matter qualifying the part stated, the defendant may crave oyer of the deed, and set forth [*705] the whole, thereby making it part of the declaration, and then demur either in respect of the defect in the deed, or the improper manner in which the plaintiff has stated it; and this is the proper course, when upon oyer it would appear that a bail bond is defective (*n*). So, a deed untruly stated in a plea, being set out upon oyer by the plaintiff, becomes part of the plea, and if it thereby appear that the plea is false, the plaintiff need not show any matter in his replication to maintain his action, but may demur (*o*); for it is a general rule, that an indenture set out upon oyer becomes part of the preceding plea (*p*). We have seen that Reg. Gen. Hil. T. 2 W. 4, reg. 44, orders "that if a defendant, after *craving oyer* of a deed, omit to insert it at the head of his plea, the plaintiff, on making up the *issue* or *demurrer book*, may, if he think fit, insert it for him; but the costs of such insertion shall be in the discretion of the taxing officer." (*q*)

As to setting out a deed on oyer, and demurring.

In point of *form*, no precise words are necessary in a demurrer, and a plea which is in substance a demurrer, though very informal, will be considered as such (*r*); and it is a general rule that there cannot be a demurrer to a demurrer (*s*). The usual form of a *general* demurrer to a *declaration*, after stating the title of the Court and term, and the names of the parties in the margin, and the defence, as in the commencement of a plea (*t*), alleges that the declaration and the matters therein contained, as therein stated, are not sufficient in law to enable the plaintiff to support his action, and concludes with a verification and an appropriate prayer of judgment, though a verification is unnecessary (*u*); or if the demurrer be to a particular count or breach, it is qualified accordingly (*x*). A general demurrer to a *plea in abatement*, *states that it [*706]

Forms of demurrer.

(*l*) 2 Bla. Rep. 910; *ante*, 579.

(*m*) Moore, 551. See the forms and notes, 2 Saund. 364 to 367; Com. Dig. Pleader, 3; Wils. 119.

(*n*) 2 Saund. 60, *in notis*. See the exceptions, and when the facts must be pleaded, *ante*, 519, 520, 465; and 1 Saund. 295 b. But if the deed be described in the declaration, and on the defendant's setting it out on oyer, and demurring, it appear that as to some part of the deed immaterial to the action, there is a variance between the deed as described and as set out on oyer, this will not support the demurrer, not even if the variance be such as would be available on a plea of *non est factum*, 1 B. & C. 358; 2 D. & R. 662, S. C.; *ante*, 468.

(*o*) 1 Saund. 316, 317.

(*p*) 1 Saund. 317; *ante*, 467.

(*q*) Jervis's Rules, 54, note (*t*).

(*r*) 5 Mod. 131; 3 Lev. 222; 2 Saund. 129, note 6; Plowd. 400. As to the form in general, see Com. Dig. Pleader, Q. 3.

(*s*) Bac. Ab. Pleas, N. 2; Salk. 219; Stephen, 2d edit. 281.

(*t*) As *ante*, 583; and see the form, *post*, vol. iii.

(*u*) *Id.*; Co. Lit. 71 b; 1 Leon. 24.

(*x*) *Post*, vol. iii.

(1095) And where breaches are assigned in the replication, if one be bad, it does not vitiate the others. Martin and others *v.* Williams, 13 Johns. Rep. 264. Cuyler *v.* The Trustees of Rochester, 12 Wend. R. 169.

FORMS OF DEMURRER.

is not sufficient to quash the bill or writ, and prays judgment that the defendant may answer over or further to the declaration (y). To a plea in bar the demurrer is, that the plea and the matters, &c. are not sufficient in law to bar the plaintiff, &c. wherefore for want of a sufficient plea he prays judgment and his damages, &c. (according to the nature of the action.) (z) If the demurrer be to a *replication, rejoinder, &c.* after stating that the same, and the matters therein contained, are not sufficient in law, it concludes with a prayer of judgment either against or for the plaintiff, according to the situation of the party demurring (a). If the demurrer be *special*, the assignment of the *causes of demurrer* were usually introduced at the end of the general demurrer in the following words:— "And the said ——, according to the form of the statute in such case made and provided (b), states and shows to the Court here the following causes of demurrer to the said declaration, [*or*, 'to the said *first count* of the said declaration,' *or*, 'to the said *breach of covenant* first above assigned,' *or*, 'to the said *plea*, &c.'] (c) And it was usual, after stating the causes of demurrer, to conclude, "and also for that the said declaration, [or, '*first count*,' or '*plea*' or '*replication*,'] is in other respects uncertain, informal, and insufficient;" but these latter words are wholly unavailable, for when it is necessary to demur *specially* it is not sufficient to aver that the pleading "wants form," but it must be shown specially in what point in particular the form is defective, and as it has been said, the statutes oblige the party demurring to lay his finger upon the very point (d). Therefore a demurrer for duplicity, *that it is double and wants form*, is not sufficient, and it should show in what the duplicity consists (e); and after the passing of the statute of Elizabeth a rule was made, "that upon demurrers the causes shall be specially assigned, and not involved with general unapplied expressions of 'double,' 'negative pregnant,' 'uncertainty,' 'wanting form,' *and the like*; but shall show [*707] specially wherein, in order that the other party may as the cause *shall require, either join in demurrer or amend, or discontinue his action." (f) If the plaintiff demur to a plea in abatement, as if it had been a plea in bar, it will be a discontinuance (g); and a demurrer to such plea should conclude with praying judgment that the writ or bill may be adjudged good, and that the defendant may answer further or over thereto (h).

Form of demurrer as prescribed by Reg Gen. Hil. T. 4 W. 4.

The Reg. Gen. Hil. T. 4 W. 4, reg. 14,† thus orders: "The form of a demurrer shall be as follows,—'The said defendant by —— his attorney, [*or* 'in person, &c.,' *or* 'plaintiff,'] says, that the declaration [*or* 'plea, &c.'] is not sufficient in law,' showing the special causes of demurrer, if any."

Form of joinder in demurrer as prescribed by Reg. Gen Hil. T. 4 W. 4.

And that the form of a *joinder* in demurrer shall be as follows,—"The said plaintiff [*or* 'defendant'] says that the declaration [*or* 'plea, &c.'] is

(y) *Post*, vol. iii.
(z) Co. Lit. 71 b; *post*, vol. iii.
(a) *Post*, vol. iii.
(b) 4 & 5 Anne, c. 16.
(c) *Post*, vol. iii.
(d) Com. Dig. Pleader, Q. 9; Hob. 232; *per* Holt, C. J., 1 Salk. 219; 1 Saund. 10, n. 1; 337, n. 3.
(e) 10 East, 79; 1 Wils. 219; 1 Salk. 219; 1 Saund. 160, n. 1; 337 b, n. 3; Willes, 220; Doc. Pl. 147; 1 M. & P. 102; 4 Bing. 428, S. C.
(f) Rule, Michaelmas Term, A. D. 1654, sect. 17; Willes, 220; 1 Saund. 160, note 1; 337 b, note 1.
(g) 1 Salk. 218; *ante*, 497, 498.
(h) 2 Saund. 210 g, note 9; *ante*, 499.

† See American Editor's Preface.

sufficient in law." Perhaps these are two of the best instances of what *conciseness* may suffice in pleading.

FORMS OF DEMURRER.

The Reg. Gen. Hil. T. 4 W. 4, reg. 2,† contains a further excellent regulation requiring an explicit statement in the margin of the demurrer of *at least one prima facie* well founded objection. It orders that "In the margin *of every demurrer*, before it is signed by counsel, *some matter of law* intended to be argued shall be stated, and if any demurrer shall be delivered without such statement, or with a *frivolous statement*, it may be set aside as irregular by the Court or a judge, and leave may be given to sign judgment as for want of a plea. Provided that the party demurring may at the time of the argument insist upon *any further* matters of law, of which notice shall have been given to the Court in the usual way." (*i*)

Reg. Gen. Hil. T. 4 W. 4, reg. 2, requires one *well founded objection* to be stated in *margin*.

A party should not demur unless he be certain that his own previous pleading is substantially correct, for it is an established rule that upon the argument of a demurrer, the Court will, notwithstanding the defect of the pleading demurred to, give judgment against the party whose pleading was first defective in *substance* (1096); as if the plea which is demurred to be bad, the

When the Court will give judgment against the first defective pleading.

(*i*) Jervis's Rules, 87, note b; Reg. Gen. Hil. T. 4 W. 4, reg. 3, orders that "No rule for joinder in demurrer shall be required, but the party demurring may demand a joinder in demurrer, and the opposite party shall be bound within four days after such demand to deliver the same, otherwise judgment.

Reg. 4. "To a joinder in demurrer no signature of a serjeant or other counsel shall be necessary, nor any fee allowed in respect thereof.

Reg. 5. "The issue or demurrer book shall on all occasions be made up by the suitor, his attorney or agent, as the case may be, and not as heretofore by any officer of the Court.

Reg. 6. "No motion or rule for a *concilium* shall be required; but demurrers, as well as all special cases and special verdicts, shall be set down for argument, at the request of either party, with the clerk of the rules in the King's Bench and Exchequer, and a secondary in the Common Pleas, upon payment of a fee of one shilling, and notice thereof shall be given forthwith by such party to the opposite party.

Reg. 7. "Four clear days before the day appointed for argument, the plaintiff shall deliver copies of the demurrer book, special case, or special verdict, to the lord chief justice of the King's Bench or Common Pleas, or lord chief baron, as the case may be, and the senior judge of the Court in which the action is brought; and the defendant shall deliver copies to the other two judges of the Court next in seniority; and in default thereof by either party, the other party may on the day following deliver such copies as ought to have been so delivered by the party making default: and the party making default shall not be heard until he shall have paid for such copies, or deposited with the clerk of the rules in the King's Bench and Exchequer, or the secondary in the Common Pleas, as the case may be, a sufficient sum to pay for such copies."

(1096) { Murdock v. Winter's Adm'r, 1 Harr. & Gill, 471. Allen v. Crofoot, 7 Cow. Rep. 46. } Vide Hord's Executors v. Dishman, 2 Hen. & Mun. 652. Smith v. Walker, 1 Wash. 135. Stephens v. Taliaferro, 1 Wash. 155. Patcher v. Sprague, 2 Johns. Rep. 465. Bennet v. Irwin, 3 Johns. Rep. 366. United States v. Arthen, 5 Cranch, 257. Smith v. Wilson, 8 East's R. 442. Barruso v. Madan, 2 Johns. Rep. 149. Gelston v. Burr, 11 Johns. Rep. 482. Spencer v. Southwick, Id. 583, 587. { Hallett v. Holmes, 18 Johns. Rep. 30. Wyman v. Mitchell, 1 Cowen's Rep. 316. See, however, Keay v. Goodwin, 16 Mass. Rep. 3. } If the declaration contain two counts, one good and one bad, and the defendant plead a plea which goes to the whole cause of action, to which the plaintiff demurs, the latter is, notwithstanding his having committed the first fault in pleading, entitled to judgment on the count which is good. Ward v. Sackrider, 3 Caines' Rep. 263. Tubbs v. Caswell et al., 8 Wend. R 129. Spring v. The Bank of Mount Pleasant, 10 Pet., S. C. 257, where it was held, that although the pleading demurred to may be defective, the court will give judgment against the party whose pleading was first defective in matter of substance.

† See American Editor's Preface.

WHEN THE COURT WILL GIVE JUDGMENT &c.

defendant may avail himself of a substantial defect in the declaration (*k*)(1097), unless such defect has been aided by pleading over (*l*); and if the first fault would constitute *error* the Court will decide upon it though it be not noticed in margin of demurrer book (*m*); for on demurrer the Court will consider the *whole* record, and give judgment for the party who thereon appears to be entitled to it (*n*)(1098). But the rule that the Court will view the *whole* record on demurrer does not enable either party to call in aid *other* parts of the pleadings in the cause, which are expressly withdrawn from the consideration of the Court upon demurrer, and have become the subject of an issue in *fact* between the parties. If, therefore, the Court consider the pleading of a party is defective, they will give judgment against him, although it appear from, and is admitted upon *other* parts of the pleadings on the record, not demurred to, that his opponent has become a bankrupt, and that his assignees have the right, &c.: for the Court can, in giving judgment upon demurrer, look only to that part of the record upon which the demurrer arises, and not to other collateral parts of the record not connected with it (*o*). And although on the whole record the right may appear to be with the plaintiff, the Court will not adjudge in favor of such right, unless the plaintiff have himself put his action upon that ground. Thus, where on a covenant to perform an award, and not [*708] to prevent the arbitrators from making *an award, the plaintiff declared in covenant, and assigned as a breach that the defendant would not pay the sum awarded, and the defendant pleaded that before the award made, he revoked by deed the authority of the arbitrators, to which the plaintiff demurred; the Court held the plea good, as being a sufficient answer to *the breach alleged* and therefore gave judgment for the defendant; although they also were of opinion that the matter stated in the plea would have entitled the plaintiff to maintain his action, if he had alleged by way of breach that the defendant prevented the arbitrators from making their award (*p*). And the rule that the Court will decide upon demurrer against the party who has committed the first fault in pleading, does not apply where the objection to the preceding pleading is merely a defect *in form*, and such as would be aided, on a *general* demurrer, by the statute of Elizabeth or Anne, or at common law (*q*). By pleading over, many defects in form are aided (*r*); and we have seen, that upon a demurrer to a plea in *abatement*, no objection can be taken to the form of the declaration (*s*).

Joinder in demurrer.

If the plaintiff or the defendant *join in demurrer*, the joinder concisely contradicts the demurrer, by stating that the declaration, (or the plea, &c.) "and the matters therein contained, in manner and form as stated, are sufficient in

(*k*) 1 Saund. 119, note 7; 285, n. 5; Hob. 56; Willes, 476; 2 Wils. 150; 4 East, 502.
(*l*) Darling *v.* Gurney, 2 Cr. & M. 226; 2 Dowl. 101; *post*, 710.
(*m*) 2 Dowl. 104, 105.
(*n*) See n. (*k*) *supra*; Steph. 2d ed. 176.
(*o*) 6 B. & C. 216.
(*p*) Marsh *v.* Bulteel, 5 B. & Ald. 507.
(*q*) 2 Vent. 222; Stephen, 2d edit. 177.
(*r*) *Post*, 710; 1 Ld. Raym. 369, 370; 3 Wils. 297; Willes, 476; 5 Burr. 2568; Cro. Eliz. 825; Com. Dig. Pleader, E. 37.
(*s*) Lutw. 1592, 1667, 1604; Salk. 212; Steph. 2d. edit. 176.

(1097) The rule is the same whether the demurrer be general or special. Cooke *v.* Graham's Administrators, 3 Cranch, 235.
(1098) Inglehart *v.* The State, &c., 2 Gill & Johns. Rep. 236.

law to bar the action," if the demurrer be to a declaration, or "to quash the bill" or "writ," if in abatement, or "to preclude the plaintiff from maintaining his action," if to a plea in bar; and usually offers to verify the declaration or plea, and concludes with a prayer of judgment, though the latter seems unnecessary (*t*). A joinder in demurrer to a replication to a plea in abatement, should not conclude with praying judgment for debt and damages, for to conclude in chief in such case would be a discontinuance, and the plaintiff should pray judgment that the defendant may answer over (*u*); but if the defendant has demurred to a declaration, and concluded his demurrer as in abatement, the plaintiff may *join in bar, and shall have judgment accordingly (*x*). The points relating to *amendments* have already been partially considered, and are so fully treated of in the books of practice (*y*) that any further observations upon them in this treatise are unnecessary. JOINDER IN DEMURRER. [*709]

The 3 & 4 W. 4, c. 42, sect. 34, enacts, that where judgment shall be given either for or against a plaintiff or demandant, or for or against a defendant or tenant, upon any demurrer joined in any action whatever, the party in whose favor such judgment shall be given shall also have judgment to recover his costs in that behalf (*z*). But in a new case it is sometimes the practice to direct that the costs shall abide the event of the action (*a*). Costs on demurrer under 3 & 4 W. 4, c. 42, sect. 34.

(*t*) Co. Lit. 71 b; 2 Wils. 74. See forms, *post*, vol. iii.

(*u*) 2 Saund. 210 g.

(*x*) 3 Lev. 23.

(*y*) Tidd, 9th ed. 696. Amendment at the trial of variances in setting out written instruments, *ante*, 348.

(*z*) See the use and operation of this enactment, Jarvis's Rules, 207, note (*x*).

(*a*) 2 Dowl. 681; 1 Crom. M. & Ros. 369.

*CHAPTER X.

Defects in pleading, when and how aided.

DEFECTS WHEN AIDED. THERE are several different methods by which defects in pleading are aided or cured, without any actual *amendment*, viz. 1st, By *pleading over*; 2dly, By *intendment or presumption after verdict*; and 3dly, By the *Statutes of Jeofails* (*a*).

1st. By pleading over (*b*). A defect in pleading is *aided*, if the adverse party *plead over* to, or answer the defective pleading in such a manner that an omission or informality therein is *expressly* or *impliedly* supplied, or rendered formal or intelligible (*c*)(1099). The following are a few instances of an *express* aider. In an action of debt on a bond, where the declaration specified no place at which the bond was made, it was held that a plea of duress "*apud B.*" supplied the omission in the declaration; as such a plea contained a distinct admission that the bond was made at the place where the alleged duress was (*d*). In an action for slander, where the declaration averred that the plaintiff was *forsworn*, without showing how, it was determined that this defect was aided by a plea of justification, which alleged that the plaintiff, who was stated in the declaration to be a constable, had taken a *false oath at the sessions* (*e*). And again in an action of trespass for taking a hook, where the plaintiff omitted to state that it was *his* hook, or that it was in his possession; and the defendant, in his plea, justified the taking the hook *out of the plaintiff's hand*, the Court held, on motion in arrest of judgment, that the omission in the declaration was supplied by the plea (*f*).

[*711] *Many instances are to be found in the older reports and writers, of certain defects being aided by an *implied* admission in the subsequent pleading of the adverse party. Thus, where in an action by an administrator *durante minore ætate*, it was not averred that the executor was within the age of sev-

(*a*) It is unnecessary to refer to the law of *amendment* as it is fully noticed in the books of practice. See Tidd, 9th edit. Index "*Amendment*;" and 1 Petersdorff's Abridgment, "*Amendment.*" See, as to amendment *at the trial* in case of *variances* in setting out written instruments, *ante*, 348; and amendments *during* a trial, see 3 & 4 W. 4, c. 42, sec. 23, 24. As to the distinction between the doctrine of amendment and the doctrine of defects being aided or cured by the above means, without amendment, see *post*, 711, 712, 725; Chit. Coll. Stat. 14, note (*a*). Tidd, 9th edit. 928.

(*b*) See recent instances, Darling *v.* Gurney, 2 Cr. & Mees. 226, 230; 2 Dowl. 236, S. C.; Peacock *v.* Day, 3 Dowl. 291.

(*c*) Com. Dig. Pleader, C. 85, E. 37; Co. Lit. 303 b; 1 B. & C. 29; 3 *Id.* 192; Steph. 2d edit. 178.

(*d*) Dyer, 15 a; Com. Dig. Pleader, C. 85; 2 Ld. Raym. 1039; 3 T. R. 387; *ante*, 310. Omission of venue in transitory action cured by judgment by default, &c. *ante*, 310.

(*e*) Cro. Car. 288; Com. Dig. *ut. sup.*

(*f*) Sid. 184; Bac. Ab. Trespass, 603; see another instance, *post*, 719.

(1099) A writ of inquiry of damages may be tested and made returnable after the second week in term; for it is not a process within the meaning of the statute. Cook *v.* Tuttle, 2 Wend. R. 289.

enteen years, it was held that by pleading to the merits of the action, the defect was aided, since the defendant thereby admitted that the plaintiff had authority to sue (*g*). There are many cases in which it has been held that where a particular fact has been informally alleged, and the opposite party, *in pleading over*, admits the particular fact, either by pleading to some other matter alleged in the defective pleading (*h*); or by pleading in confession and avoidance of the matter so informally alleged (*i*); the defect will be aided by the admission resulting and to be collected from such subsequent pleading. If in debt on bond to make an estate *to A.*, the defendant plead that he enfeoffed another to the use of A., (without showing that A. was a party, or had the deed), yet if the plaintiff reply that "the defendant *did not enfeoff*," this aids the plea (*k*). So, if the defendant plead an award, without sufficient certainty, and the plaintiff's replication import that the award was made, the uncertainty of the plea in stating that the award was made is aided (*l*).

DEFECTS WHEN AIDED.

1st. By pleading over.

It is, however, unnecessary to make any further mention of those cases which have been decided with reference to the aider of mere *formal* defects *by pleading over*; for we have already seen, that, at the present day, by virtue of the statutes relative to demurrer, in all cases where any pleading is defective, and the adverse party demurs *generally*, he will be entirely precluded from availing himself afterwards of any *formal* defects in such previous pleading, by the mere effect of his having *omitted to point out such defects upon a special demurrer* (*m*). And we shall see hereafter, in treating of the effect of the statutes of jeofails, that according to the construction now put upon these enactments, after verdict or judgment by default, all *formal* defects are entirely aided (*n*).

[*712] *With regard to a defect *in substance*, it seems that it cannot be *impliedly* cured by the mere effect of pleading over thereto (*o*). Therefore, if the defendant plead accord, and do not show satisfaction (*p*), and the replication merely deny the *agreement*, this traverse cannot cure the fault in the plea, namely, the omission to show a *satisfaction* to the plaintiff in regard to the cause of action (*q*). If, however, the adverse pleading *expressly admit* the fact which ought to have been stated in the defective pleading, and which is substantially incorrect in omitting it, the error becomes, it seems, immaterial; as in the instance before put of a declaration in trespass for taking goods, omitting to show any title to or possession of the goods, and the plea admitting the defendant's possession (*r*). And we have seen that if a *declaration* incorrectly set forth a deed, the variance is aided if the defendant set out the deed on oyer, and plead *non est factum* (*s*).

The second mode by which defects in pleading may be, in some cases, aided, is by *intendment after verdict*. The doctrine upon this subject is found-

2dly. By intendment after verdict.

(*g*) Com. Dig. Pleader, C. 85; Lutw. 632.
(*h*) Cro. Jac. 369, 370; 2 Saund. 324, 328; 3 Lev. 393; Com. Dig. Pleader, 87, E. 37.
(*i*) Cro. Jac. 125, 663, 682; Com. Dig. Pleader, E. 37; Cro. Car. 209.
(*k*) Cro. Eliz. 825; *post*, 719.
(*l*) Com. Dig. Pleader, E. 37.
(*m*) See *ante*, 710, *et. seq.*
(*n*) *Post*, 713, 723 to 725.
(*o*) 8 Rep. 120 b; Cro. Eliz. 416; 7 Rep. 25 a; Cro. Jac. 87; Com. Dig. Pleader, C. 85; E. 37; 2 Wils. 150.
(*p*) See *ante*, 513.
(*q*) Com. Dig. Pleader, E. 37.
(*r*) *Ante*, 710.
(*s*) *Ante*, 467, 468.

DEFECTS WHEN AIDED. ed on the *common law*, and is independent of any statutory enactments (*t*). The general principle upon which it depends, appears to be that where there is any defect, imperfection or omission, in any pleading, whether in substance or *form*, which would have been a fatal objection upon demurrer; yet, if the issue joined be such as necessarily required, on the trial, proof of the facts so defectively or imperfectly stated or omitted, and without which it is not to be presumed that either the judge would direct the jury to give, or the jury would have given, the verdict, such defect, imperfection, or omission, is *cured by the verdict* (*u*)(1100).

2dly. By intendment after verdict.

The expression *cured by verdict* signifies that the Court will, after a verdict, presume or intend that the particular thing which appears to be defectively or imperfectly stated or omitted in the pleadings, was duly proved at the trial. And such intendment must arise, not merely from the verdict, but from the united effect of the verdict and the issue [*713] *upon which such verdict was given. On the one hand the particular thing which is presumed to have been proved must always be such as can be implied *from the allegations on the record, by fair and reasonable intendment* (*x*). And, on the other hand, a verdict for the party in whose favor such intendment is made, is indispensably necessary, for it is in consequence of such verdict, and in order to support it, that the Court is induced to put a liberal construction upon the allegations on the record.

Thus, if to a declaration on a bill of exchange the plea improperly state that there was no consideration, without stating the circumstances with particularity, yet if the plaintiff reply, after verdict the defect in the plea will be aided (*y*). So, the decision in *Humphreys v. Pratt*, in House of Lords, turned on the ground that the verdict aided the defect (*z*).

It is obvious that the doctrine now under consideration does not apply to the case of a judgment *by default*. Such a judgment affords no ground for raising any intendment in favor of the plaintiff; it admits such facts only as are actually alleged (*a*), and there is no necessity for the plaintiff proving any thing further. Where an intendment is made in favor of a party, it is always a presumption relative to matter of fact, viz. that such a particular circumstance was duly proved at the trial; but it is impossible to raise a presumption of this description, when no trial has taken place. In the case, therefore, of a judgment by default, the Court cannot, upon a motion in arrest of judgment, or writ of error, intend any thing in favor of the plaintiff: the only question they will have to consider is, whether the alleged defect is or is not cured by the effect of any express legislative enactment. And as it appears from the more modern cases that the different statutes of jeofails, (the operation of which was extended to judgments by default by the statute for the amendment of the law) (*b*), cure such defects only as are now considered matters of form,

(*t*) See 1 Saund. 228, n. 1.

(*u*) *Id.* and see the authorities there cited; Dougl. 679; and see *per* Ld. Ellenborough, 1 M. & Sel. 237; Steph. 2d ed. 179, 180. Tidd, 9th edit. 919.

(*x*) See *per* Lord Ellenborough, 1 M. & Sel. 237; *per* Buller, J. 1 T. R. 145, 146; Tidd, 8th ed. 919, and cases there cited; see *post*, 723, 724.

(*y*) Easton v. Pratchett, 4 Tyr. 472.

(*z*) 2 Dow. & Clark, Rep. 288.

(*a*) 1 Saund. 228, n. 1.

(*b*) 4 & 5 Ann. c. 16; *post*, 723, 724.

(1100) { See Vandersmith v. Washmein's Adm'r, 1 Harr. & Gill, 43.

it follows that any objection to the declaration, made after judgment by default, will be considered precisely in the same manner as if it had arisen upon general demurrer; and that if the defect be matter of form it will be aided, but if matter of substance it will be fatal (*c*).

DEFECTS WHEN AIDED.

2dly. By intendment after verdict.

It is therefore often very material to attend to the distinction between the doctrine of intendment, and the effect of the statutes of jeofails, in aiding defects in pleading. The statutes of jeofails operate not by way of intendment, *but by positive enactment (*d*); and as they do not extend to cure defects [*714] which are clearly matters of substance, there are necessarily many defects of this nature which may be aided by a verdict, but which are not reached by those statutes, and are consequently still fatal after a judgment by default (*e*).

Having thus explained the general nature of the doctrine of *intendment*, and shown that it is confined to those cases only in which a *verdict* has been given in favor of the party for whom the intendment is required to be made, we shall now proceed to notice some of the cases which have arisen upon the subject, in order to show under what particular circumstances the Court will or will not make an intendment in support of the verdict, and what is the nature of the intendment they will make. Before we notice these cases, it may, however, be proper to remark that it is unnecessary at the present day to have recourse to the doctrine of intendment with respect to defects which are not matters of substance; for we have already observed, and shall hereafter see more particularly, that defects which are mere matters of *form* are aided after verdict by the effect of the statutes of jeofails, without there being any necessity to have recourse to the doctrine of intendment (*f*).

The authorities in the books are very numerous on the subject of defects being aided after verdict, but those we shall select to illustrate the doctrine will be chiefly from the modern reports. It is quite unnecessary to detail a great number of the older cases on the subject, the great majority of them having arisen upon matters which would now be considered mere form. And it would be a task of some difficulty to reconcile all the decisions upon the subject, partly because the Courts have in later times become much more liberal than they were formerly in discriminating between form and substance, and partly because the distinction we have before adverted to, between the doctrine of intendment at common law and the statutes of jeofails, is very often but little attended to in many of the older reports and treatises (*g*).

Instances (*h*).

In an action of *assumpsit* the declaration stated that the defendant had sold to the plaintiff a quantity of furze then *growing upon certain land, to be [*715] taken away by the plaintiff before a certain day; and that in consideration thereof the defendant promised that he would permit the plaintiff peaceably to enjoy and take away the furze without disturbance; and then alleged that the defendant did not permit him to enjoy it, but disturbed him from taking a quantity away. After a verdict for the plaintiff, it was objected upon a writ of er-

(*c*) 2 Burr. 899; 10 East, 359, 363; 13 *Id.* 407; Stephen on Pleading, 181, 2d edit.; 1 Saund. 228, n. b; *ante*, 291.

(*d*) See 1 Saund. 5th ed. 28 a, note (*k*).

(*e*) *Id.* 228, n. 1; 1 Stra. 78; 2 Burr. 899.

(*f*) *Supra*; *post*, 725.

(*g*) See the observations of Mr. Serjeant Williams, 1 Saund. 228 b, c, n. 1.

(*h*) See a further instance in 2 Dow. & Clarke, 295, 296, and cases there quoted.

DEFECTS WHEN AIDED.

2dly. By intendment after verdict. Instances.

ror that no time was shown when the disturbance took place, and that unless it were shown to be before the stipulated day there could be no good ground of action; but the Court held that after the verdict it would be intended within the given time; for otherwise there could have been no proof of any cause to have damages (*i*). This case very clearly illustrates the principles we have above laid down: the plaintiff had not *expressly* made the allegation which was contended to be necessary, but had merely averred that the defendant had committed a breach of his promise by the alleged disturbance: the particular part of the averment in the declaration which related to the disturbance was ambiguous, since it might mean either a disturbance before or a disturbance after the particular day by which the furze was to be taken away; but from the whole declaration it was evident that nothing but proof of a disturbance before the particular day would amount to a breach of the contract set out, so as to entitle the plaintiff to recover; and as in point of fact he had recovered, the Court were in reason and justice bound to presume that such proof had been given. So also in an action of assumpsit brought by an off-going tenant against his landlord to recover compensation, according to the custom of the country, for tilling, fallowing, and manuring *arable* land, where the plaintiff, after setting out the custom, averred that he had tilled, fallowed, and manured, and had sown with wheat and seeds certain *lands* forming part of his farm, but without expressly averring that such lands were *arable*, it was held, on motion in arrest of judgment, after a verdict for the plaintiff, that as the declaration showed that the plaintiff could not be entitled to recover without proving that the lands were arable, it must be intended that he had given such evidence at the trial; and that therefore the *defect or ambiguity, if any, in the declaration was helped by the verdict (*k*). The following cases will also further elucidate this doctrine:—In an action of assumpsit against the executors of the maker of a promissory note, the plaintiff after setting out the note, alleged that the testator at the time of his death was indebted to the payee for the amount of the principal sum secured by the note and interest thereon; and then averred that after the payee's death, it was found upon inquest, by the oaths of honest and lawful men, (but without showing how many), that the payee was *felo de se*, whereby the note and the money due thereon became forfeited to the crown, and the plaintiff then set out a grant to him under the king's sign manual. After a verdict for the plaintiff, it was objected in arrest of judgment, 1st, that a promissory note was only assignable by indorsement, and that though the crown could assign a debt, yet it was not alleged that this was the case of a debt, nor did the plaintiff sue as the assignee of a debt, but only of a promissory note; and, 2dly, that it was not averred in the declaration that the inquisition had been taken by twelve men, which it was contended was necessary. But the Court held that the allegation that the maker, at the time of his death, was indebted to the payee in the principal sum secured by the note and interest thereon, was a sufficient averment that the note was a security for a debt; and also, that supposing it to be necessary that the coroner's inquest should be taken by twelve men

[*716]

(*i*) Cro. Jac. 497. It was also held in this case that it was not material to allege the time of the disturbance, for it was collateral to the promise.

(*k*) 1 B. & B. 224; 3 Moore, R. 536, S. C.

to vest chattels in the crown, it must be intended after verdict that the inquisition in question had been so found (*l*). And where in assumpsit the plaintiff stated in his declaration that he had, at the request of certain persons therein mentioned, sold and delivered to them goods of a certain value, whereof the defendant had notice, and that in consideration thereof, and also in consideration that the plaintiff, at the defendant's request, would forbear and give day of payment of the said sum of money (but without saying to whom), the defendant promised to pay the same at a particular time, and then averred that the plaintiff did forbear and give day of payment of the said money; after a verdict for the plaintiff, the Court held that by necessary intendment the vendees of the goods must have been the persons to whom the plaintiff forbore; and that, though not specifically alleged, it appeared to be so *with a sufficient degree of certainty, but that at all events the defect, if any, was cured by the verdict (*m*). We have formerly seen, in treating of the mode in which contracts should be stated, and the degree of certainty required in pleading (*n*), that in general uncertainty is only matter of form, and that it will consequently be aided either on general demurrer, or after verdict or judgment by default, by the statutes of jeofails. In a case in which the declaration in assumpsit stated that the plaintiff had sold to the defendant a *certain horse*, at and for a *certain quantity of certain oil*, to be delivered within a *certain time*, which had elapsed before the commencement of the suit, it was contended that the judgment ought to be arrested, since the plaintiff had professed to declare on a special contract, but had not specified in any manner what the terms of the contract were; but it was answered on the other side, that though the objection might hold on demurrer, yet after a verdict it must be intended that the jury had ascertained those circumstances; and after some hesitation the Court finally decided that after verdict the declaration was sufficient (*o*). In another case of an action in assumpsit, the declaration stated that the plaintiff had retained the defendant (who was not an attorney) to lay out £700 in the purchase of an annuity, and that defendant promised to lay it out securely, that the plaintiff *delivered the money* to the defendant accordingly, but that the defendant laid it out on a bad and insufficient security. After verdict it was objected on a writ of error, that no consideration appeared in the declaration; that it was not averred that the promise was in consideration of the retainer, nor that the retainer was for reward; but the Court held that it was absolutely necessary under the declaration that the plaintiff should have proved at the trial that he had actually delivered the money to the defendant, and that the latter had engaged to lay it out; that the delivery of the money for this purpose was a sufficient consideration to support the promise, and that although it was not expressly alleged in the declaration that the delivery of the money was in fact the consideration or the promise, the Court would intend after verdict that such was the consideration (*p*).

DEFECTS WHEN AIDED. — 2dly. By intendment after verdict. Instances.

[*717]

*In all these cases the form of action was *assumpsit*. We shall proceed to give a few more instances of intendments made after verdict in different forms of action; but whatever may be the form of action, or the particular pleading [*718]

(*l*) 4 B. & C. 138.
(*m*) 1 New Rep. 172.
(*n*) *Ante*, 271, 290.
(*o*) 3 B. & P. 265.
(*p*) 2 Bing. 464; 1 M'Clel. & Younge, 205, S. C.

DEFECTS WHEN AIDED. — 2dly. By intendment after verdict. Instances.

which is alleged to be defective, the principles which govern the decision of the Court must of course be always the same. In an action of *debt*, in which the plaintiff sought to recover penalties for money lost in gaming, he alleged in his declaration that he sued as well for himself as for the poor of the parish of St. Paul, Coveut Garden, but did not afterwards show that the money had been lost in that parish, but merely "at Westminster aforesaid." After a verdict finding that the defendant did owe part of the money to the plaintiff and the poor of the said parish, it was held, on a writ of error, that it must have been proved on the trial that the money was lost in the particular parish, or the jury could not have found their verdict, and that consequently the defect was cured; for wheresoever it may be presumed that any thing must of necessity have been given in evidence, the want of mentioning it on record will not vitiate it after a verdict (*q*). So in an action of debt upon a bond given by a bailiff to a sheriff for the due discharge of his office in returning warrants, &c. the defendant in his plea craved oyer of the condition, which recited that the bailiff had been appointed for a particular hundred only, and pleaded performance; the plaintiff assigned as a breach, that a particular warrant had been directed to him which had not been duly returned. It was objected in arrest of judgment after a verdict for the plaintiff, that he had not shown that the warrant was to be executed in the particular hundred, and that consequently it did not appear that it was a warrant which the bailiff was bound to return, but the Court held that this objection could not prevail after verdict; for, independently of the necessity of intending that the warrant was proved to be such a one as the bailiff must return, the defendant had in fact admitted that it was by traversing the breach assigned, and that it would in fact be raising an intendment against the verdict, and against the defendant's own admission to hold that the objection should prevail (*r*). Again, in an action
[*719] upon the *case* for refusing to comply with a *subpœna duces tecum*, by *producing the required document, in consequence whereof the plaintiff had been nonsuited, where the plaintiff did not in express terms allege that the defendant had the particular instrument in his possession, but only that he could and might have produced it, and that he had no lawful and reasonable excuse or impediment to the contrary, it was held after verdict, upon motion in arrest of judgment, that the plain import of these words was, that the defendant had the instrument in his possession, and consequently that it was to be intended that this had been proved at the trial; and not that the judge had suffered the allegations to be proved in a strained and unnatural sense, as by showing that the defendant might have acquired the means of producing the instrument by applying to others who might have it in their custody (*s*).

Many other cases might be cited in support of the proposition, that in all cases where the general allegations in the declaration or other pleading, are such as to require proof of any particular fact which is not expressly stated, in order to entitle the plaintiff to a verdict, it will be intended, after a verdict for him, that such fact was duly proved, and the defect in the particular plead-

(*q*) 4 Burr. 2018, 2020; and see Sir T. Raym. 487; Hob. 78; Carth. 304. See as to this objection upon demurrer, Aleyn, 10.

(*r*) 3 Burr. 1725; see *ante*, 710, 711.

(*s*) 9 East, 473.

DEFECTS WHEN AIDED.

2dly By intendment after verdict. Instances.

ing will be aided (*t*). Thus, a plea of prescription for common in a *que estate* is good after verdict, though it be not alleged *expressly* that the owners of the estate have used it immemorially; for unless a prescriptive right had been proved, the party pleading it could not have recovered a verdict (*u*). So, where the grant of a reversion, a rent-charge, advowson, or other incorporeal hereditament, which lies in grant, and can only be conveyed by deed, is not alleged in pleading to have been *by deed*, yet if the grant be put in issue and found by a jury, the imperfection in pleading is cured by the verdict at common law (*x*). And we have seen that an imperfect averment of the performance by the plaintiff of a *condition precedent*, or matter to be performed by him (*y*), or that he gave a proper *notice* to the defendant (*z*), or *requested* *the defendant to perform his promise (*a*), will sometimes be cured by verdict; and that after verdict, an averment in a declaration for a libel, that the defendant "*printed*, and caused to be printed the libel in a *newspaper*," not expressly showing a publication, may be sufficient (*b*). [*720]

It will be observed that in all the cases we have given upon this subject, although the particular matter was not stated in *express terms*, the declaration or other pleading in each case, contained terms sufficiently general to comprehend it in fair and reasonable intendment (*c*). The allegations on the record, taken by themselves, might have been ambiguous, and have been capable of bearing two different constructions, but when they were coupled with the verdict, it became clear that they might and ought to be interpreted in that sense alone, which was absolutely necessary in order to account for and to support the verdict. Some cases, however, have arisen which it is not very easy to bring within the operation of the rule as thus restricted, but in which the Courts, in their anxiety to support verdicts, have held particular defects to be aided. Thus, in an action on the case for a malicious prosecution, it is necessary to allege in the declaration that the prosecution is at an end (*d*); or that the commission or fiat has been superseded (*e*); but it has been held that the want of this averment is cured by verdict (*f*). It is said, that it will be then presumed that proof of the fact of the determination of the prosecution has been given at the trial: but although such a fact may be a reasonable inference from the verdict alone, yet it appears difficult to say how it is comprehended, even by fair and reasonable intendment, in the allegations in the declaration, for there is nothing on the rocord which in any manner appears to imply that the prosecution has been determined. So the omission to al-

(*t*) See 7 T. R. 518, 522; Cro. Jac. 44; 2 Wils. 5; Rep. temp. Hard. 116; 1 Mod. 292; 1 Ventr. 109; 1 Sid. 365; 2 Lord Raym. 1060; 3 Wils. 275; 7 B. & C. 555.

(*u*) 3 T. R. 147.

(*x*) Hutt. 54; 1 Saund. 228, note 1; Steph. 2d ed. 179, 180.

(*y*) *Ante*, 359; see *ante*, 353; and *post*, 722.

(*z*) *Ante*, 361. But the omission of an averment of notice of non-payment, in an action against the drawer of a bill, is fatal after verdict, *id.*; *post*, 722.

(*a*) *Ante*, 364.

(*b*) *Ante*, 435. Statement that damages accrued after action when cured, *ante*, 428 *e*.

(*c*) See *per* Lord Ellenborough, 1 M. & Sel. 236; *per* Buller, J. 1 T. R. 145.

(*d*) 10 Mod. 209; Dougl. 215; 2 T. R. 225; *ante*, 151; 1 Mood. & R. 398.

(*e*) Whitworth *v.* Hall, 2 B. & Adol. 695; when not proved, 1 Mood. & Rob. 398.

(*f*) 1 Saund. 228 a; 1 Sid. 15; 2 Selw. N. P. 6th edit. 1055, n. 7; 1 B. & B. 224; 9 East, 473; 5 B. & Ald. 634; in which it was held, that a count for maliciously indicting the plaintiff for perjury, without setting out the indictment, is good after verdict; but this, it should seem, is by the statutes of jeofails.

DEFECTS WHEN AIDED. — 2dly. By intendment after verdict. Instances.

lege a notice or demand of rent in an action against the sheriff for not paying a year's rent pursuant to 8 Anne, c. 14, is aided by verdict (*g*). Again, in another case of an action to recover an amerciament in an inferior Court, where the declaration omitted a necessary allegation, viz. that the defendant was a resiant, it appears to have been considered that the fact of residence must be intended to *have been proved at the trial, as otherwise the jury [*721] could not have found that there had been any debt due (*h*). But the doctrine which this case would appear to establish, that matters extrinsic of the record are to be *intended* after a verdict, by inference drawn from the verdict *alone*, has been denied by Mr. Justice Buller in a subsequent case (*i*); and appears to be in some degree inconsistent with many other decisions. However one of the most recent cases establishes that, although the declaration do not contain the requisite averment, still the defendant must, if the plaintiff do *not prove* the essential fact the same as if it had been averred, insist on the plaintiff being nonsuited, or have a verdict against him, for otherwise the verdict for the plaintiff will aid as well the defects in the declaration as in the evidence (*k*).

It is at all events clear that the Courts will never, in order to support a verdict, make an intendment which is *inconsistent* with the allegations on the record. Thus, in an action of assumpsit, the declaration stated that a certain person had become bankrupt, and that at his last examination under the commission, in consideration that his assignees and the commissioners, at the request of the defendant, would forbear to examine the bankrupt touching certain monies which the bankrupt had received, and for which he had not accounted, the defendant undertook to pay the assignees all sums received by the bankrupt, and not accounted for by him. After a verdict for the plaintiff it was held on a writ of error, that this contract was void, as being against the policy of the bankrupt laws, and calculated to deprive the creditors of the advantages they might derive from an examination of the bankrupt. And although it was contended that after verdict the Court would intend that the sum which the verdict found to be due to the plaintiff had been ascertained to be the full amount of all monies received and not accounted for by the bankrupt, and so no injury could arise to the creditors; it was held that no such intendment could be made, since it was expressly averred in the declaration that the amount had not been ascertained at the time the contract was made, and it appeared, that by entering into the contract, the assignees had deprived themselves of the opportunity of ascertaining the amount. And the Court appears to have considered that it would be equally improper to intend after verdict, that the contract had been entered into with the consent of the creditors, since there was nothing in the allegations on the record to warrant such an intendment (*l*). So, if a declaration expressly show that a condition precedent was *not* performed by the plaintiff, and state matter which is no excuse for the non-performance, *the declaration will be bad after verdict (*m*). [*722] And in another case, it was laid down by the Court that nothing could be in-

(*g*) 1 Stra. 212; 7 Price, 566.
(*h*) Rep. temp. Hardw. 116.
(*i*) 1 T. R. 141, 145, 146.
(*k*) Whitworth *v.* Hall, 2 B. & Adol. 695.
(*l*) 3 T. R. 17, 25, 26.
(*m*) 6 T. R. 710; *ante*, 353, 359.

tended after verdict but what was expressly stated in the record, or necessarily implied from those facts which were stated (n). DEFECTS WHEN AIDED.

2dly By intendment after verdict. Instances.

The main rule on the subject of intendment is, that a verdict will aid a *defective statement* of title, but will never assist a statement of a *defective title*, or cause of action (o). Instances in illustration of the former part of this rule have already been given; and we have also seen that there can be no presumption to support the verdict, if presumption be negatived by, and be *inconsistent* and at variance with, a material statement in the record (p). We may here add some cases in explanation of the rule that if the plaintiff *totally omit* to state his title or cause of action, it need not be proved at the trial, and therefore there is no room for presumption to maintain the verdict (q). If, therefore, in an action upon a bill of exchange, the plaintiff omit to aver presentment to, and a refusal by the drawee (r); or that the defendant had notice of non-payment (s); when such averments are necessary, the declaration will be bad even after verdict. So, in case for a libel or slander, if the matter as charged be not in itself a libel, and the declaration do not contain any introductory matter, or other averment rendering it so, and connecting the plaintiff with the libellous imputation, and giving it an actionable meaning, as applied to the plaintiff, the declaration will not be aided by verdict, although there be an *innuendo* that the defendant meant to charge that the plaintiff was guilty of a specified offence (t). And a verdict will not cure a statement in a declaration that the defendant published a libel, "in *substance* as follows;" or spoke slanderous words, "to the *tenor* following;" although the matter be set out in *hæc verba* (u). So, where the plaintiff brought an action of trespass on the case, as being entitled to the reversion of a certain yard and wall, to which the declaration stated a certain injury to have been committed, but omitted to allege that the reversion was, in fact, *prejudiced, or to show any grievance which, in its nature, would necessarily prejudice the reversion; the Court arrested the judgment, after a verdict had been given in favor of the plaintiff, and held the fault to be one which the verdict could not cure (x). And where a declaration in debt, for not setting out tithes, on the statute 2 & 3 Edw. 6, c. 13, s. 1, omitted to state that the tithes had been yielded and paid, and of right ought to have been paid, within forty years next before the passing of the act; the Court held that it was defective, even after verdict, and the judgment was arrested (y). [*723]

When a count in part defective is aided by verdict.

Where several causes of action have been stated in one count, one of which is sustainable, but the others not, if there be a verdict for the plaintiff with general damages upon the whole count, such verdict will be sustained by the intendment and presumption that the judge duly directed the jury not to find

(n) 1 T. R. 141; see Tidd, 9th ed. 919.
(o) Salk. 365; Lord Raym. 1225, S. C.; 1 Saund. 228, n. 1; 4 T. R. 470; 4 B. & C. 555.
(p) *Ante*, 411 to 422.
(q) Tidd, 9th ed. 919.
(r) Dougl. 679; 7 B. & C. 468; 1 M. & R. 394, 403, S. C.
(s) *Ante*, 362.
(t) *Ante*, 437.
(u) *Ante*, 434.
(x) 1 M. & Sel. 234.
(y) 4 B. & Ald. 655; and see 1 Taunt. 128; 4 B. & C. 345; 6 D. & R. 438, S. C.; 4 B. & C. 555; 7 D. & R. 56, S. C.; 6 B. & C. 154, 164; 10 Moore, 446.

DEFECTS WHEN AIDED. damages upon the defective allegations (z). But if a declaration contain several counts, any of which is wholly defective, and general damages upon the whole declaration be given, the judgment would be arrested or reversed on error (a).

3dly. Defects aided by the statute of Jeofails.

3dly. Mistakes and omissions in the *declaration*, and other subsequent *pleadings*, are oftentimes cured by the statutes of jeofails, which declare (b), that "judgment, *after verdict* (c), shall not be stayed or reversed by reason of any *mispleading*, lack of color, *insufficient pleading* or *jeofail*, or other default or negligence of the parties, their counsellors or attornies (d); *want of form* in any count, declaration, plaint, bill, suit, or demand (e); lack of averment of any life, so as the person be proved to be alive (f); want of any *profert* or the omission of *vi et armis*, or *contra pacem*, mistaking the christian name or surname of either party (g), sums, day, month, or year, in any bill, declaration, or pleading, being right in any writ, plaint, roll, or record preceding, or in the same roll or record wherein the same is committed, to which the *plaintiff*," (or more properly the *defendant*) "might have demurred, and shown the same for cause; want of the averment of *hoc paratus est verificare*, or *hoc paratus est verificare per recordum*, or for not alleging *prout patet per recordum*, or the want of a right venue, so as the cause were tried by a jury of the proper county where the action is laid (h); *or any other matters of like* [*724] *nature, not being against* *the *right of the matter of the suit, nor whereby the issue or trial is altered*" (i).

The statutes of jeofails are extended by the statute for the amendment of the law (k) to judgments entered upon *confession*, *nihil dicit*, or *non sum informatus* (l), in any Court of record; and it is thereby enacted, that "no such judgment shall be reversed; nor any judgment upon any writ of inquiry of damages executed thereon be stayed or reversed, for or by reason of any imperfection, omission, defect, matter, or thing whatsoever, which would have been aided and cured by any of the said statutes of *jeofails*, in case a verdict

(z) 2 Tyr. 648.

(a) *Id.*; *ante*, 447, 448, where see the course of proceeding.

(b) See Tidd, 9th edit. 923; Chitty's Coll. of Stat. "*Amendments and Jeofails.*"

(c) Distinction between the common law effect of a verdict, and its operation under the statutes 1 Saund. 227, n. 1.; *ante*, 713. An *informal issue* is cured by this statute, but a verdict will not cure an *immaterial issue*, *ante*, 692. *Immaterial traverse*, *ante*, 656.

(d) 32 Hen. 8, c. 30.

(e) 18 Eliz. c. 14.

(f) 21 Jac 1, c. 13.

(g) 3 Wils. 40.

(h) The Statute 16 & 17 Car. 2, c. 8, which cures the want of a right venue, so as the cause be tried by a jury of the proper county where the action is laid, seems to extend, not only to cases where there is a wrong venue in a right county, but also to those where the cause has been improperly tried in a wrong county, 7 T. R. 583; and see 1 Lord Raym. 330; Carth. 448, S. C.; Willes, 431; 2 East, 580; 1 Saund. 248, (3); 2 *Id.* 5, (3), 5th edit. But where in *ejectment* for lands in Cardiganshire the *venire* was awarded out of Shropshire, upon the suggestion of its being the next English county, the Court, after verdict for the plaintiff, arrested the judgment on the ground of a mistrial, Herefordshire being the next adjoining English county to South Wales; although it appeared that Shropshire was in fact nearer to the lands in question, and the cause might have been more conveniently tried there than in Herefordshire; 2 M. & Sel. 270.

(i) 16 & 17 Car. 2, c. 8. These latter words should be construed literally; see observations of Lord Ellenborough, 4 & 5 Anne, c. 16, s. 2, in 10 East, 363, 364.

(k) 4 & 5 Ann. c. 16, s. 2.

(l) But this statute does not seem to apply to judgments on *nul tiel record*; Tidd, 9th edit. 927, note (d).

DEFECTS WHEN AIDED. — 3dly. By the statutes of Jeofails.

of twelve men had been given in the said action or suit, so as there be an original writ or bill, and warrants of attorney duly filed according to law." (*m*) A motion in arrest of judgment, after judgment *by default* is to be considered exactly the same as if the question had arisen on a general demurrer (*n*): and on *demurrer*, we may remember, that by the statute 4 & 5 Ann. c. 16, the Court are required to give judgment according to the very right of the cause, without regarding any such imperfections, omissions, and defects, as are particularly mentioned in the act, or any other matter of like nature, except the same shall be specially set down and [*725] *shown for cause of demurrer, notwithstanding the same might have heretofore been taken to be matter of substance, and not aided by the statute of Queen Elizabeth, so as sufficient matter appear in the pleadings upon which the Court may give judgment, according to the very right of the cause (*o*). As there cannot however be the same intendment in support of a judgment by default as after a verdict, it has been holden that the statutes of jeofails do not protect judgments *by default* against objections that are cured by a *verdict at common law*, but such only as are remedied after a verdict by the statutes (*p*).

It has been determined that the statute 32 Hen. 8, c. 30, extends to *penal* actions (*q*). And by the statute 4 Geo. 2, c. 26, which provides that all legal proceedings shall be in the *English* language, "all statutes for the reformation and amending of the delays arising from any *jeofails*, shall and may extend to all and every form and forms, and to all proceedings in Courts of justice (except in *criminal* cases), when the forms and proceedings are in *English*; and all errors and mistakes are amendable and remedied thereby, in like manner as if the proceedings had been in *Latin*." And though by the 16 & 17 Car. 2, c. 8, the several omissions, variances, and defects therein mentioned are required to be *amended* by the judges of the Court where the judgment is given, or the record removed by writ of error, yet an actual amendment is never made on this statute; but the Court will allow the benefit of the act to be attained by overlooking the exception (*r*).

(*m*) By a subsequent act, 9 Ann. c. 20, s. 7, this and all the statutes of jeofails are extended to writs of *mandamus*, and informations in nature of a *quo warranto*. But pleadings on writs of *extent* are not considered as proceedings for the recovery of the king's debt within the meaning of the statute 4 & 5 Ann. c. 16, s. 24; 5 Price, 621.

(*n*) 2 Burr. 899.

(*o*) *Ante*, 701 to 703; and see 10 East, 359.

(*p*) 2 Str. 933; and see 1 Saund. 228, (1); 13 East, 407; Tidd, 9th edit. 927; *ante*, 714.

(*q*) 3 Lev. 375; 1 Str. 136; 2 *Id*. 1227; Doug. 115; *ante*, 703.

(*r*) 2 Str. 1011; Cas. Temp. Hardw. 314, 315; Tidd, 9th edit. 928; Chitty's Col. Stat. vol. i. 14, n. (*a*).

APPENDIX.

THE PRINCIPAL STATUTES AND RULES

AFFECTING

PLEADING IN GENERAL.

[See the Statutes of Amendments and Jeofails collected, Chitty Col. Stat. tit. Amendments and Jeofails.]

4 ANNE, CAP. XVI.

An Act for the better Amendment of the Law, and the better Advancement of Justice. [1705.]

By 9 Anne, c. 20, sect. 7, this statute is extended to writs of mandamus and informations in nature of quo warranto.

Judges shall give judgment on demurrer, &c. without regarding any defect in writ, declaration, or other pleading, unless there be a special demurrer showing the defect.

27 Eliz. cap. 5.

FOR the amendment of the law in several particulars, and for the easier, speedier, and better advancement of justice, be it enacted by the Queen's most excellent Majesty, by and with the advice and consent of the lords spiritual and temporal, and commons, in this present parliament assembled, and by the authority of the same, that from and after the first day of Trinity term which shall be in the year of our Lord one thousand seven hundred and six, where any demurrer shall be joined, and entered in any action or suit in any court of record within this realm, the judges shall proceed and give judgment according as the very right of the cause and matter in law shall appear unto them, without regarding any imperfection, omission, or defect in any writ, return, plaint, declaration, or other pleading, process, or course of proceeding whatsoever, except those only which the party demurring shall specially and particularly set down and express, together with his demurrer, as causes of the same, notwithstanding that such imperfection, omission, or defect might have heretofore been taken to be matter of substance, and not aided by the statute made in the twenty-seventh year of Queen Elizabeth, intituled, "An Act for the Furtherance of Justice in case of Demurrer and Pleadings," so as sufficient matter appear in the said pleadings, upon which the Court may give judgment according to the very right of the cause; and therefore from and after the said first day of Trinity Term, no advantage or exception shall be taken of or for an immaterial traverse; or of or for the default of entering pledges upon any bill or declaration; or of or for the default of alleging the bringing into Court any bond, bill, indenture, or other deed whatsoever mentioned in the declaration or other pleading; or of or for the default of alleging of the bringing into Court letters testamentary, or letters of administration; or of or for the omission of *vi et armis et contra pacem*, or either of them; or of or for the want of averment of *hoc paratus est verificare*, or, *hoc paratus est verificare per recordum*; or of or for not alleging *prout patet per recordum*; but the Court shall give judgment according to the very right of the cause as aforesaid, without regarding any such imperfections, omissions, and defects, or any other matter of like nature, except the same shall be specially and particularly set down and shown for cause of demurrer.

4 Anne, c. 16. Statutes of jeofails extended to judgments on nihil dicit, &c.

*II. And be it further enacted by the authority aforesaid, that from and after the said first day of Trinity term, all the statutes of jeofails shall be extended to judgments which shall at any time afterwards be entered upon confession, *nihil dicit*, or *non sum informatus*, in any Court of record; and no such judgment shall be reversed, nor any judgment upon any writ of inquiry of damages executed thereon be staid or reversed, for or by reason of any imperfection, omission, defect, matter, or thing whatsoever, which would have been aided and cured by any of the said statutes of jeofails in case a verdict of twelve men had been given in the said action or suit, so as there be an original writ or bill, and warrants of attorney duly filed according to the law as is now used.

When warrants of attorney shall be filed.

III. Provided always, and be it enacted by the authority aforesaid, that the attorney for the plaintiff, or demandant in any action or suit, shall file his warrant of attorney with the proper officer of the Court where the cause is depending the same term he declares; and the attorney for the defendant or tenant shall file his warrant of attorney as aforesaid, the same term he appears, under the penalties inflicted upon attornies by any former law for default of filing their warrants of attorney.

Defendant, &c. may plead several matters. Not extend to qui tam actions.

IV. And be it further enacted by the authority aforesaid, that from and after the said first day of Trinity term it shall and may be lawful for any defendant or tenant in any action or suit, or for any plaintiff in replevin, in any Court of record, with the leave of the same Court, to plead as many several matters thereto, as he shall think necessary for his defence.

No dilatory plea unless on affidavit.

XI. And be it further enacted by the authority aforesaid, that from and after the said first day of Trinity term, no dilatory plea shall be received in any Court of record, unless the party offering such plea, do, by affidavit, prove the truth thereof, or show some probable matter to the Court to induce them to believe that the fact of such dilatory plea is true.

Action of debt brought on single bill or judgment, after money paid, such payment may be pleaded in bar.

XII. And be it further enacted by the authority aforesaid, that from and after the said first day of Trinity term, where any action of debt shall be brought upon any single bill, or where action of debt, or *scire facias*, shall be brought upon any judgment, if the defendant hath paid the money due upon such bill or judgment, such payment shall and may be pleaded in bar of such action or suit, and where an action of debt is brought upon any bond which hath a condition or defeazance to make void the same upon payment of a lesser sum at a day or place certain, if the obligor, his heirs, executors, or administrators, have, before the action brought, paid to the obligee, his executors, or administrators, the principal and interest due by the defeazance or condition of such bond, though such payment was not made strictly according to the condition or defeazance; yet it shall and may nevertheless be pleaded in bar of such action, and shall be as effectual a bar thereof, as if the money had been paid at the day and place according to the condition or defeazance, and had been so pleaded.

The like on bonds.

Principal and interest on bonds paid in Court, &c.

XIII. And be it further enacted by the authority aforesaid, that if at any time, pending an action upon any such bond with a penalty, the defendant shall bring into the Court where the action shall be depending, all the principal money, and interest due on such bond, and also all such costs as have been expended in any suit or suits in law or equity upon such bond, the said money so brought in shall be deemed and taken to be in full satisfaction and discharge of the said bond, and the Court shall and may give judgment to discharge every such defendant of and from the same accordingly.

---

9 Geo. IV. Cap. 14.

9 G. 4, c. 14.

An Act for rendering a written Memorandum necessary to the Validity of certain Promises and Engagements. [9th May, 1828.]

English Act, 21 Jac. 1, c. 16.

Whereas by an Act passed in England in the twenty-first year of the reign of King James the First, it was, among other things, enacted, that all actions of account and upon the case, other than such accounts as concern the trade *of merchandize between merchant and merchant, their factors or servants, all actions of debt grounded upon any lending or contract without specialty, and all actions of debt for arrearages of rent, should be commenced within three years after the end of the then present session of parliament, or within six years next after the cause of such actions or suit, and not after: And whereas a similar enactment is contained in an Act passed in Ireland in the tenth year of the reign of King Charles the First: And whereas various questions have arisen in actions founded on simple contract, as to the proof and effect of acknowledgments and promises offered in evidence for the purpose of taking cases out of the operation of the said enactments; and it is expedient to prevent such questions, and to make provision for giving effect to the said enactments and to the intention thereof: be it therefore enacted by the King's most excellent Majesty, by and with the advice and consent of the lords spiritual and temporal, and commons, in this present parliament assembled, and by the authority of the same, that in actions of debt or upon the case grounded upon any simple contract, no acknowledgment or promise by words only shall be deemed sufficient evidence of a new or continuing contract, whereby to take any case out of the operation of the said enactments, or either of them, or to deprive any party of the benefit thereof, unless such acknowledgment or promise shall be made or contained by or in some writing to be signed by the party chargeable thereby; and that where there shall be two or more joint contractors, or executors or administrators of any contractor, no such joint contractor, executor or administrator, shall lose the benefit of the said enactments, or either of them, so as to be chargeable in respect or by reason only of any written acknowledgment or promise made and signed by any other or others of them: Provided always, that nothing herein contained shall alter or take away or lessen the effect of any payment of any principal or interest made by any person whatsoever: Provided also, that in actions to be commenced against two or more such joint contractors, or executors or administrators, if it shall appear at the trial or otherwise that the plaintiff, though barred by either of the said recited Acts or this Act, as to one or more of such joint contractors, or executors or administrators, shall nevertheless be entitled to recover against any other or others of the defendants, by virtue of a new acknowledgment or promise, or otherwise, judgment may be given and costs allowed for the plaintiff as to such defendant or defendants against whom he shall recover, and for the other defendant or defendants against the plaintiff.

9 G. 4, c. 14

Irish Act, 10 Car. 1, sess. 2, c. 6.

In actions of debt or upon the case, no acknowledgment shall be deemed sufficient unless it be in writing or by part payment.

Joint contractors.

Proviso for the case of joint contractors.

II. And be it further enacted, that if any defendant or defendants in any action on any simple contract shall plead any matter in abatement, to the effect that any other person or persons ought to be jointly sued, and issue be joined on such plea, and it shall appear at the trial that the action could not, by reason of the said recited Acts or this Act, or of either of them, be maintained against the other person or persons named in such plea, or any of them, the issue joined on such plea shall be found against the party pleading the same.

Pleas in abatement.

III. And be it further enacted, that no indorsement or memorandum of any payment written or made after the time appointed for this act to take effect, upon any promissory note, bill of exchange, or other writing, by or on the behalf of the party to whom such payment shall be made, shall be deemed sufficient proof of such payment, so as to take the case out of the operation of either of the said statutes.

Indorsements of payment.

IV. And be it further enacted, that the said recited Acts and this Act shall be deemed and taken to apply to the case of any debt on simple contract alleged by way of set-off on the part of any defendant, either by plea, notice, or otherwise.

Simple contract debts alleged by way of set off.

V. And be it further enacted, that no action shall be maintained whereby to charge any person upon any promise made after full age to pay any debt contracted during infancy, or upon any ratification after full age of any promise or simple contract made during infancy, unless such promise or ratification shall be made by some writing signed by the party to be charged therewith.

Confirmation of promises made by infants.

*9 Geo. IV. Cap. 15.

9 G. 4, c. 15. *An act to prevent a Failure of Justice by reason of Variances between Records and Writings produced in Evidence in support thereof.* [9th May, 1828.]

WHEREAS great expense is often incurred, and delay or failure of justice takes place at trials, by reason of variances between writings produced in evidence, and the recital or setting forth thereof upon the record on which the trial is had, in matters not material to the merits of the case; and such record cannot now in any case be amended at the trial, and in some cases cannot be amended at any time; for remedy thereof, be it enacted, that it shall and may be lawful for every Court of record holding plea in civil actions, any judge sitting at *nisi prius*, and any Court of oyer and terminer and general gaol delivery in England, Wales, the town of Berwick-upon-Tweed, and Ireland, if such Court or judge shall see fit so to do, to cause the record on which any trial may be pending before any such judge or Court in any civil action, or in any indictment or information for any misdemeanor, when any variance shall appear between any matter in writing or in print produced in evidence, and the recital or setting forth thereof upon record whereon the trial is pending, to be forthwith amended in such particular by some officer of the Court, on payment of such costs (if any) to the other party as such judge or Court shall think reasonable; and thereupon the trial shall proceed as if no such variance had appeared; and in case such trial shall be had at *nisi prius*, *the order* for the amendment shall be indorsed on the *postea*, and returned together with the record; and thereupon the papers, rolls, and other records of the Court from which such record issued, shall be amended accordingly.

In cases where a variance shall appear between written or printed evidence and the record, the Court may order the record to be amended on payment of costs.

2 Will. IV. Cap. 39.

2 W. 4, c. 39. *An Act for Uniformity of Process in Personal Actions in His Majesty's Courts of Law at Westminster.* [23 May, 1832.]

WHEREAS the process for the commencement of personal actions in his Majesty's superior Courts of Law at Westminster, is, by reason of its great variety and multiplicity, very inconvenient in practice; for remedy thereof be it enacted by the King's most excellent Majesty, by and with the advice and consent of the lords spiritual and temporal, and commons, in this present parliament assembled, and by the authority of the same, that the process in all such actions commenced in either of the said Courts, in cases where it is not intended to hold the defendant to special bail, or to proceed against a member of parliament, according to the provisions contained in the statute passed in the sixth year of the reign of his late Majesty King George the Fourth, intituled "An Act to amend the Laws relating to Bankrupts," shall, whether the action be brought by or against any person entitled to the privilege of peerage, or of parliament, or of the Court wherein such action shall be brought, or of any other Court, or to any other privilege, or by or against any other person, be according to the form contained in the Schedule to this Act annexed, marked No. 1, and which process may issue from either of the said Courts, and shall be called a writ of summons; and in every such writ, and copy thereof, the place and county of the residence or supposed residence of the party defendant, or wherein the defendant shall be, or shall be supposed to be, shall be mentioned; and such writ shall be issued by the officer of the said Courts respectively by whom process serviceable in the county therein mentioned hath been heretofore issued from such Court; and every such writ may be served in the manner heretofore used in the county therein mentioned, or within two hundred yards of the border thereof, and [*705] *not elsewhere, and the person serving the same shall and is hereby required to indorse on the writ the day of the month and week of the service thereof.

Serviceable process for the commencement of personal actions.

6 G. 4, c. 16.

Writs may be served within two hundred yards of the border of the county.

The day of service to be indorsed on writ.

II. And be it further enacted, that the mode of appearance to every such writ, or under the authority of this Act, shall be by delivering a memorandum in writing according to the form contained in the said Schedule, and marked

Mode of appearance to serviceable process.

No. 2, such memorandum to be delivered to such officer or person as the Court out of which the process issued shall direct, and to be dated on the day of the delivery thereof. 2 W. 4, c. 39.

III. And be it further enacted, that in case it shall be made appear by affidavit, to the satisfaction of the Court out of which the process issued, or, in vacation, of any judge of either of the said Courts, that any defendant has not been personally served with any such writ of summons as hereinbefore mentioned, and has not, according to the exigency thereof, appeared to the action, and cannot be compelled so to do without some more efficacious process, then and in any such case it shall be lawful for such Court or judge to order a writ of distringas to be issued, directed to the sheriff of the county wherein the dwelling-house or place of abode of such defendant shall be situate, or to the sheriff of any other county, or to any other officer to be named by such Court or judge, in order to compel the appearance of such defendant; which writ of distringas shall be in the form, and with the notice subscribed thereto, mentioned in the Schedule to this Act, marked No. 3; which writ of distringas and notice, or a copy thereof, shall be served on such defendant, if he can be met with, or, if not, shall be left at the place where such distringas shall be executed; and a true copy of every such writ and notice shall be delivered together therewith to the sheriff or other officer to whom such writ shall be directed; and every such writ shall be made returnable on some day in term, not being less than fifteen days after the teste thereof, and shall bear *teste* on the day of the issuing thereof, whether in term or in vacation; and if such writ of distringas shall be returned *non est inventus* and *nulla bona*, and the party suing out such writ shall not intend to proceed to outlawry or waiver, according to the authority hereinafter given, and any defendant against whom such writ of distringas issued shall not appear at or within eight days inclusive after the return thereof, and it shall be made appear by affidavit to the satisfaction of the Court out of which such writ of distringas issued, or, in vacation, of any judge of either of the said Courts, that due and proper means were taken and used to serve and execute such writ of distringas, it shall be lawful for such Court or judge to authorize the party suing out such writ to enter an appearance for such defendant, and to proceed thereon to judgment and execution.

Appearance may be enforced by writ of distringas in case a defendant cannot be served with the writ of summons.

IV. And be it further enacted, that in all such actions wherein it shall be intended to arrest and hold any person to special bail who may not be in the custody of the marshal of the Marshalsea of the Court of King's Bench or of the warden of the Fleet prison, the process shall be by writ of capias, according to the form contained in the said Schedule, and marked No. 4; and so many copies of such process, together with every memorandum or notice subscribed thereto, and all indorsements thereon, as there may be persons intended to be arrested thereon or served therewith, shall be delivered therewith to the sheriff or other officer or person to whom the same may be directed, or who may have the execution and return thereof, and who shall, upon or forthwith after the execution of such process, cause one such copy to be delivered to every person upon whom such process shall be executed by him, whether by service or arrest, and shall indorse on such writ the true day of the execution thereof, whether by service or arrest; and if any defendant be taken or charged in custody upon any such process, and imprisoned for want of sureties for his appearance thereto, the plaintiff in such process may, before the end of the next term after the detainer or arrest of such defendant, declare against such defendant, and proceed thereon in the manner, and according to the directions contained in a certain act of parliament made in the fourth and fifth years of the reign of King William and Queen Mary, intituled, "An Act for delivering Declarations against Prisoners:" *provided always, that it shall be lawful for the plaintiff or his attorney to order the sheriff, or other officer or person to whom such writ shall be directed, to arrest one or more only of the defendants therein named, and to serve a copy thereof on one or more of the others, which order shall be duly obeyed by such sheriff or other officer or

Bailable process for the commencement of personal actions.

4 & 5 W. & M. c. 21.

[*706]

2 W. 4, c. 39. person; and such service shall be of the same force and effect as the service of the writ of summons hereinbefore mentioned, and no other.

Proceedings to outlawry. V. And be it further enacted, that upon the return of *non est inventus* as to any defendant against whom such writ of capias shall have been issued, and also upon the return of *non est inventus* and *nulla bona* as to any defendant against whom such writ of distringas as hereinbefore mentioned shall have issued, whether such writ of capias or distringas shall have issued against such defendant only, or against such defendant and any other person or persons, it shall be lawful, until otherwise provided for, to proceed to outlaw or waive such defendant by writs of *exigi facias* and proclamation, and otherwise, in such and the same manner as may now be lawfully done upon the return of *non est inventus* to a *pluries* writ of *capias ad respondendum* issued after an original writ: provided always, that every such writ of *exigent* proclamation, and other writ subsequent to the writ of capias or distringas, shall be made returnable on a day certain in term; and every such first writ of *exigent* and proclamation shall bear *teste* on the day of the return of the writ of capias or distringas, whether such writ be returned in term or in vacation; and every subsequent writ of *exigent* and proclamation shall bear *teste* on the day of the return of the next preceding writ; and no such writ of capias or distringas shall be sufficient for the purpose of outlawry or waiver, if the same be returned within less than fifteen days after the delivery thereof to the sheriff or other officer to whom the same shall be directed.

Proceedings to outlawry may be had after judgment given under the authority of this act. VI. And be it further enacted, that after judgment given in any action commenced by writ of summons or capias under the authority of this Act, proceedings to outlawry or waiver may be had and taken, and judgment of outlawry or waiver given, in such manner and in such cases as may now be lawfully done after judgment in an action commenced by original writ: provided always, that every outlawry or waiver had under the authority of this Act shall and may be vacated or set aside by writ of error or motion, in like manner as outlawry or waiver founded on an original writ may now be vacated or set aside.

Filazer to be appointed in the Court of Exchequer. VII. And be it further enacted, that for the purpose of proceeding to outlawry and waiver upon such writs of capias or distringas returnable in the Court of Exchequer, it shall and may be lawful for the lord chief baron of the said Court, and he is hereby required to appoint, from time to time, a fit person holding some other office in the said Court, to execute the duties of a filazer, exigentur, and clerk of the outlawries in the same Court.

Mode of detaining a prisoner in the custody of the marshal or of the warden of the Fleet. VIII. And be it further enacted, that when it shall be intended to detain in any such action any person being in the custody of the marshal of the Marshalsea of the Court of King's Bench, or of the warden of the Fleet prison, the process of detainer shall be according to the form of the writ of detainer contained in the said Schedule, and marked No. 5; and a copy of such process, and of all indorsements thereon, shall be delivered together with such process to the said marshal or warden to whom the same shall be directed, and who shall forthwith serve such copy upon the defendant personally, or leave the same at his room, lodging, or other place of abode; and such process may issue from either of the said Courts, and the declaration thereupon shall and may allege the prisoner to be in the custody of the said marshal or warden, as the fact may be, and the proceedings shall be as against prisoners in the custody of the sheriff, unless otherwise ordered by some rule to be made by the judges of the said Courts.

Mode of proceeding against a member of parliament to enforce the stat. 6 G. 4, c. 16, s. 10. IX. And be it further enacted, that in all such actions wherein it shall be intended to proceed against a member of parliament according to the provisions of the said statute made in the sixth year of the reign of his late Majesty King George the Fourth, the process shall be according to the form contained *in the said Schedule marked No. 6, and which process, and a copy thereof, shall be in lieu of the summons, or original bill and summons, and [*707] copy thereof, mentioned in the said statute.

X. And be it further enacted, that no writ issued by authority of this Act shall be in force for more than four calendar months from the day of the date thereof, including the day of such date, but every writ of summons and capias may be continued by *alias* and *pluries*, as the case may require, if any defendant therein named may not have been arrested thereon or served therewith: provided always, that no first writ shall be available to prevent the operation of any statute whereby the time for the commencement of the action may be limited, unless the defendant shall be arrested thereon or served therewith, or proceedings to or toward outlawry shall be had thereupon, or unless such writ, and every writ (if any) issued in continuation of a preceding writ, shall be returned *non est inventus* and entered of record within one calendar month next after the expiration thereof, including the day of such expiration, and unless every writ issued in continuation of a preceding writ shall be issued within one such calendar month after the expiration of the preceding writ, and shall contain a memorandum indorsed thereon or subscribed thereto, specifying the day of the date of the first writ; and return to be made in bailable process by the sheriff or other officer to whom the writ shall be directed, or his successor in office, and in process not bailable, by the plaintiff or his attorney suing out the same, as the case may be. 2 W. 4, c. 39. Duration of writs. Proviso as to statute of limitations.

XI. And whereas, according to the present practice, in certain cases no proceedings can be effectually had on any writ returnable within four days of the end of any term, until the beginning of the ensuing term, whereby an unnecessary delay is sometimes created; for remedy thereof be it enacted, that if any writ of summons, capias, or detainer issued by authority of this Act shall be served or executed on any day, whether in term or vacation, all necessary proceedings to judgment and execution may, except as hereinafter provided, be had thereon, without delay, at the expiration of eight days from the service or execution thereof, on whatever day the last of such eight days may happen to fall, whether in term or vacation: provided always, that if the last of such eight days shall in any case happen to fall on a Sunday, Christmas-day, or any day appointed for a public fast or thanksgiving, in either of such cases the following day shall be considered as the last of such eight days; and if the last of such eight days shall happen to fall on any day between the Thursday before and the Wednesday after Easter-day, then in every such case the Wednesday after Easter-day shall be considered as the last of such eight days: provided also, that if such writ shall be served or executed on any day between the tenth day of August and the twenty-fourth day of October in any year, special bail may be put in by the defendant in bailable process, or appearance entered, either by the defendant or the plaintiff, on process not bailable, at the expiration of such eight days: provided also, that no declaration, or pleading after declaration, shall be filed or delivered between the said tenth day of August and twenty-fourth day of October. Proceedings on writs served or executed at certain times. Proviso for Sunday, &c.

XII. And be it further enacted, that every writ issued by authority of this Act shall bear date on the day on which the same shall be issued, and shall be tested in the name of the Lord Chief Justice or the Lord Chief Baron of the Court from which the same shall issue, or in case of a vacancy of such office, then in the name of a senior puisne judge of the said Court, and shall be indorsed with the name and place of abode of the attorney actually suing out the same, and in case such attorney shall not be an attorney of the Court in which the same is sued out, then also with the name and place of abode of the attorney of such Court in whose name such writ shall be taken out; but in case no attorney shall be employed for that purpose, then with a memorandum expressing that the same has been sued out by the plaintiff in person, mentioning the city, town, or parish, and also the name of the hamlet, street, and number of the house of such plaintiff's residence, if any such there be. Date and teste of writs. Indorsement of the name of the attorney or party suing.

[*708] *XIII. And be it further enacted, that every such writ of summons issued against a corporation aggregate may be served on the mayor or other head officer, or on the town clerk, clerk, treasurer, or secretary of such corpora- Service of writs of summons on corporations

2 W. 4, c. 39.

and on inhabitants of hundreds and towns.

tion; and every such writ issued against the inhabitants of a hundred or other like district may be served on the high constable thereof, or any one of the high constables thereof; and every such writ issued against the inhabitants of any county of any city or town, or the inhabitants of any franchise, liberty, city, town, or place not being part of a hundred or other like district, on some peace officer thereof.

General rules to be made by the judges.

XIV. And be it further enacted, that it shall and may be lawful to and for the judges of the said Courts, and they are required from time to time to make all such general rules and orders for the effectual execution of this Act, and of the intention and object hereof, and for fixing the costs to be allowed for and in respect of the matters herein contained, and the performance thereof, as in their judgment shall be deemed necessary or proper, and for that purpose to meet as soon as conveniently may be after the passing hereof.

Rules and orders may be made for the return of writs.

XV. And be it further enacted, that it shall be lawful in term time, for the Court out of which any writ issued by authority of this Act, or any writ of *capias ad satisfaciendum*, *fieri facias*, or *elegit*, shall have issued, to make rules, and also for any judge of either of the said Courts, in vacation, to make orders, for the return of any such writ; and every such order shall be of the same force and effect as a rule of Court made for the like purpose; provided always, that no attachment shall issue for disobedience thereof until the same shall have been made a rule of Court.

Proceedings in default of appearance or special bail.

XVI. And be it further enacted, that all such proceedings as are mentioned in any writ, notice, or warning issued under this Act, shall and may be had and taken in default of a defendant's appearance or putting in special bail, as the case may be.

Attorney to declare whether writ issued by his authority; and to declare name and place of abode of his client, if ordered.

XVII. And be it further enacted, that every attorney whose name shall be indorsed on any writ issued by authority of this Act shall, on demand in writing made by or on behalf of any defendant, declare forthwith whether such writ has been issued by him, or with his authority or privity; and if he shall answer in the affirmative, then he shall also, in case the Court or any judge of the same or of any other Court shall so order and direct, declare in writing, within a time to be allowed by such Court or judge, the profession, occupation, or quality, and place of abode of the plaintiff, on pain of being guilty of a contempt of the Court from which such writ shall have appeared to have been issued; and if such attorney shall declare that the writ was not issued by him, or with his authority or privity, the said Court, or any judge of either of the said Courts, shall and may, if it shall appear reasonable so to do, make an order for the immediate discharge of any defendant or defendants who may have been arrested on any such writ, on entering a common appearance.

If writ not issued by authority of the attornies the defendant may be discharged.

Rules to be made by the Courts for the government of their ministers and officers.

XVIII. And be it further enacted, that it shall and may be lawful to and for the judges of each of the said Courts from time to time to make such rules and orders for the government and conduct of the ministers and officers of their respective Courts, in and relating to the distribution and performance of the duties and business to be done and performed in the execution of this Act, as such judges may think fit and reasonable; provided always, that no additional charge be thereby imposed on the suitors.

Proviso for persons privileged from arrest, &c.

XIX. Provided always, and be it further enacted, that nothing in this Act contained shall subject any person to arrest, outlawry, or waiver, who, by reason of any privilege, usage, or otherwise, may now by law be exempt therefrom, or shall extend to any cause removed into either of the said Courts by writ of *pone*, *certiorari*, *recordari facias loquelam*, *habeas corpus*, or otherwise.

Places, parcel of one county and situate in another, to be deemed part of each.

XX. And whereas there are in divers parts of England certain districts and places, parcel of some one county, but wholly situate within and surrounded by some other county, which is productive of inconvenience and *delay in the service and execution of the process of the said Courts; for remedy thereof be it enacted, that every such district and place shall and

[*709]

may, for the purpose of the service and execution of every writ and process, whether mesne or judicial, issued out of either of the said Courts, be deemed and taken to be part as well of the county wherein such district or place is so situate as aforesaid as of the county whereof the same is parcel: and every such writ and process may be directed accordingly, and executed in either of such counties. 2 W. 4, c. 39.

XXI. And be it further enacted, that from the time when this Act shall commence and take effect, the writs hereinbefore authorized shall be the only writs for the commencement of personal actions in any of the Courts aforesaid, in the cases to which such writs are applicable; and the costs to be allowed and charged for such writs shall be the same as for writs of latitat: provided always, that nothing in this Act contained shall abridge, alter, or affect the franchises and jurisdictions of either of the counties palatine of Lancaster or Durham, or of any officer or minister thereof. Writs hereinbefore authorized to to be the only writs for commencement of personal actions.

XXII. And be it further enacted, that this Act shall commence and take effect on the first day of Michaelmas Term next after the passing hereof. Commencement of act.

XXIII. And be it further enacted, that this Act may be amended, altered, or repealed during the present session of parliament. Act may be altered this session.

SCHEDULE to which this Act refers.

No. 1.

Writ of Summons.

WILLIAM the Fourth, &c.

To *C. D.* of, &c., in the County of greeting:

We command you, [*or* as before *or* often we have commanded you,] that within eight days after the service of this writ on you, inclusive of the day of such service, you do cause an appearance to be entered for you in our Court of , in an action on promises [*or as the case may be*], at the suit of *A. B.* And take notice, that, in default of your so doing, the said *A. B.* may cause an appearance to be entered for you, and proceed therein to judgment and execution.

Witness at Westminster, the day of

Memorandum to be subscribed on the Writ.

N. B. This writ is to be served within four calendar months from the date thereof, including the day of such date, and not afterwards.

Indorsement to be made on the Writ before Service thereof.

This writ was issued by *E. F.* of attorney for the said *A. B.*

Or,

This writ was issued in person by *A. B.* who resides at [*mention the city, town, or parish, and also the name of the hamlet, street, and the number of the house of the plaintiff's residence, if any such.*]

Indorsement to be made on the Writ after Service thereof.

This writ was served by me *X. Y.* on the day 18 .

X. Y.

---

*No. 2. [*710]

Forms of entering an Appearance.

A. plaintiff, against *C. D.* *or,* against *C. D.* and another, *or,* against *C. D.* and others.	The defendant *C. D.* appears in person. *E. F.* attorney for *C. D.* appears for him. *G. H.*, attorney for the plaintiff, appears for the defendant *C. D.* according to the statute.

Entered the day of 18 .

2 W. 4, c. 39.

No. 3.

Writ of Distringas.

WILLIAM the Fourth, &c.

To the sheriff of greeting:

We command you, that you omit not by reason of any liberty in your bailiwick, but that you enter the same, and distrain upon the goods and chattels of *C. D.* for the sum of forty shillings, in order to compel his appearance in our Court of to answer *A. B.* in a plea of trespass on the case [*or* debt, *or as the case may be*]; and how you shall execute this our writ you make known to us in our said Court on the day of now next ensuing.

Witness at Westminster the day of in the year of our reign.

Notice to be subscribed to the foregoing Writ.

In the Court of

Between { *A. B.* plaintiff, and *C. D.* defendant.

Mr. *C. D.*

Take notice, that I have this day distrained upon your goods and chattels in the sum of forty shillings, in consequence of your not having appeared in the said Court to answer to the said *A. B.* according to the exigency of a writ of summons bearing teste on the day of ; and that in default of your appearance to the present writ within eight days inclusive after the return hereof, the said *A. B.* will cause an appearance to be entered for you, and proceed thereon to judgment and execution, [*or if the defendant be subject to outlawry*, will cause proceedings to be taken to outlaw you.]

No. 4.

Writ of Capias.

WILLIAM the Fourth, &c.

To the sheriff of

or,

To the constable of Dover Castle,

or,

To the mayor and bailiffs of Berwick-upon-Tweed,

or,

[*as the case may be,*] greeting:

We command you, [*or*, as before, *or*, often, we have commanded you,] that you omit not by reason of any liberty in your bailiwick, but that you enter the same, and take *C. D.* of if he shall be found in your bailiwick, and him safely keep until he shall have given you bail or made [*711] *deposit with you according to law in an action on promises [*or*, of debt, &c.], at the suit of *A. B.*, or until the said *C. D.* shall by other lawful means be discharged from your custody. And we do further command you, that on execution hereof you do deliver a copy hereof to the said *C. D.* And we hereby require the said *C. D.* to take notice, that within eight days after execution hereof on him, inclusive of the day of such execution, he should cause special bail to be put in for him in our Court of to the said action, and that in default of his so doing such proceedings may be had and taken as are mentioned in the warning hereunder written or indorsed hereon. And we do further command you the said sheriff, that immediately after the execution hereof you do return this writ to our said Court, together with the manner in which you shall have executed the same, and the day of the execution hereof; or that if the same shall remain unexecuted, then that you do so return the same at the expiration of four calendar months from the date hereof, or sooner if you shall be thereto required by order of the said Court or by any judge thereof. 3 W. 4, c. 39.

Witness at Westminster, the day of

Memoranda to be subscribed to the Writ.

N. B. This writ is to be executed within four calendar months from the date thereof, including the day of such date, and not afterwards.

A Warning to the Defendant.

1. If a defendant, being in custody, shall be detained on this writ, or if a defendant, being arrested thereon, shall go to prison for want of bail, the plaintiff may declare against any such defendant before the end of the term next after such detainer or arrest, and proceed thereon to judgment and execution.

2. If a defendant, being arrested on this writ, shall have made a deposit of money according to the stat. 7 & 8 Geo. 4, c. 71, and shall omit to enter a common appearance to the action, the plaintiff will be at liberty to enter a common appearance for the defendant, and proceed thereon to judgment and execution.

3. If a defendant, having given bail on the arrest, shall omit to put in special bail as required, the plaintiff may proceed against the sheriff or on the bail-bond.

4. If a defendant, having been served only with this writ, and not arrested thereon, shall not enter a common appearance within eight days after such service, the plaintiff may enter a common appearance for such defendant, and proceed thereon to judgment and execution.

Indorsements to be made on the Writ of Capias.

Bail for £ by affidavit.

or,

Bail for £ by order of [*naming the judge making the order*], dated the day of .

This writ was issued by *E. F.* of attorney for the plaintiff [*or* plaintiffs] within named.

Or,

This writ was issued in person by the plaintiff within named, who resides at [*mention the city, town, or parish, and also the name of the hamlet, street, and number of the house of the plaintiff's residence, if any such there be.*]

No. 5.

Writ of Detainer.

WILLIAM the Fourth, *&c.*

To the Marshal of the Marshalsea of Our Court before Us [*or*, To the Warden of Our Prison of the Fleet.]

We command you, that you detain *C. D.* if he shall be found in your *custody at the delivery hereof to you, and him safely keep in an action on promises [*or*, of debt, *&c.*, *as the case may be*], at the suit of *A. B.*, until he shall be lawfully discharged from your custody. And we do further command you, that on receipt hereof you do warn the said *C. D.*, by serving a copy hereof on him, that within eight days after service of such copy, inclusive of the day of such service, he do cause special bail to be put in for him in our Court of to the said action; and that in default of his so doing the said *A. B.* may declare against him before the end of the term next after his detainer, and proceed thereon to judgment and execution. And we do further command you the said [Marshal or Warden, *as the case may be*], that immedi- [*712]

3 W. 4, c. 39. ately after the service hereof you do return this our writ, or a copy hereof, to our said Court, together with the day of the service hereof.

Witness at Westminster, the day of .

N. B. *This Writ is to be indorsed in the same manner as the Writ of Capias, but not to contain the Warning on that Writ.*

No. 6.

Writ of Summons to be served on a Member of Parliament in order to enforce the Provisions of the Statute 6 *Geo.* 4, *c.* 16, *s.* 10.

William the Fourth, *&c.*

To *C. D.* of, *&c.* Esquire, having Privilege of Parliament, greeting:

We command you, that, within one calendar month next after personal service hereof on you, you do cause an appearance to be entered for you in our Court of in an action [on promises, debt, &c. *as the case may be*], at the suit of *A. B.*; and you are hereby informed, that an affidavit of debt for the sum of hath been filed in the proper office, according to the provisions of a certain act of parliament made and passed in the sixth year of the reign of his late Majesty King George the Fourth, intituled "An Act to amend the Laws relating to Bankrupts," and that unless you pay, secure, or compound for the debt sought to be recovered in this action, or enter into such bond as by the said Act is provided, and cause an appearance to be entered for you, within one calendar month next after such service hereof, you will be deemed to have committed an act of bankruptcy from the time of the service hereof.

Witness at Westminster, the day of .

N. B. *This Writ is to be served within Four calendar Months from the Date thereof, including the Day of such Date, and not afterwards.*

Direction.—*This Summons is to be indorsed with the name of the plaintiff or his Attorney in like manner as the Writ of Capias.*

2 & 3 Will. IV. Cap. 71.

2 & 3 W. 4, c. 71. *An Act for shortening the Time of Prescription in certain Cases.*

[1st August, 1832.]

Whereas the expression "time immemorial, or time whereof the memory of man runneth not to the contrary," is now by the law of England in many cases considered to include and denote the whole period of time from the reign of King Richard the First, whereby the title to matters that have been long enjoyed is sometimes defeated by showing the commencement of such enjoyment, which is in many cases productive of inconvenience and injustice; for remedy thereof, be it enacted, by the King's most excellent Majesty, by and with the advice and consent of the lords spiritual and temporal, and commons, in this present parliament assembled, and by the authority of the [*713] *same, that no claim which may be lawfully made at the common law, by custom, prescription, or grant, to any right of common or other profit or benefit to be taken and enjoyed from or upon any land of our Sovereign Lord the King, his heirs or successors, or any land being parcel of the Duchy of Lancaster, or of the Duchy of Cornwall, or of any ecclesiastical or lay person or body corporate, except such matters and things as are herein specially provided for, and except tithes, rent, and services, shall, where such right, profit, or benefit shall have been actually taken and enjoyed by any person claiming right thereto, without interruption for the full period of thirty years, be defeated or destroyed by showing only that such right, profit, or benefit was first taken or enjoyed at any time prior to such period of thirty years, but nevertheless such claim may be defeated in any other way by which the same

Claims to right of common and other profits à prendre, not to be defeated after thirty years' enjoyment by showing the commencement;

is now liable to be defeated; and when such right, profit, or benefit shall have been so taken and enjoyed as aforesaid for the full period of sixty years, the right thereto shall be deemed absolute and indefeasible, unless it shall appear that the same was taken and enjoyed by some consent or agreement expressly made or given for that purpose by deed or writing.

2 & 3 W. 4, c. 71.

After sixty years' enjoyment the right to be absolute, unless had by consent or agreement.

II. And be it further enacted, that no claim which may be lawfully made at the common law, by custom, prescription, or grant, to any way or other easement, or to any watercourse, or the use of any water, to be enjoyed or derived upon, over, or from any land or water of our said Lord the King, his heirs or successors, or being parcel of the Duchy of Lancaster or of the Duchy of Cornwall, or being the property of any ecclesiastical or lay person, or body corporate, when such way or other matter as herein last before mentioned shall have been actually enjoyed by any person claiming right thereto without interruption for the full period of twenty years, shall be defeated or destroyed by showing only that such way or other matter was first enjoyed at any time prior to such period of twenty years, but nevertheless such claim may be defeated in any other way by which the same is now liable to be defeated; and where such way or other matter, as herein last before mentioned, shall have been so enjoyed as aforesaid for the full period of forty years, the right thereto shall be deemed absolute and indefeasible, unless it shall appear that the same was enjoyed by some consent or agreement expressly given or made for that purpose by deed or writing.

In claims of right of way or other easements, the periods to be twenty years and forty years.

III. And be it further enacted, that when the access and use of light to and for any dwelling-house, workshop, or other building, shall have been actually enjoyed therewith for the full period of twenty years without interruption, the right thereto shall be deemed absolute and indefeasible, any local usage or custom to the contrary notwithstanding, unless it shall appear that the same was enjoyed by some consent or agreement expressly made or given for that purpose by deed or writing.

Claim to the use of light enjoyed for twenty years indefeasible, unless shown to have been by consent.

IV. And be it further enacted, that each of the respective periods of years hereinbefore mentioned shall be deemed and taken to be the period next before some suit or action wherein the claim or matter to which such period may relate shall have been or shall be brought into question, and that no act or other matter shall be deemed to be an interruption, within the meaning of this statute, unless the same shall have been or shall be submitted to or acquiesced in for one year after the party interrupted shall have had or shall have notice thereof, and of the person making or authorizing the same to be made.

Before mentioned periods to be deemed those next before suits for claims to which such periods relate.

V. And be it further enacted, that, in all actions upon the case and other pleadings, wherein the party claiming may now by law allege his right generally, without averring the existence of such right from time immemorial, such general allegation shall still be deemed sufficient, and, if the same shall be denied, all and every the matters in this act mentioned and provided, which shall be applicable to the case, shall be admissible in evidence to sustain or rebut such allegation: and that in all pleadings to actions of trespass, and in all other pleadings wherein before the passing of this act it would have been necessary to allege the right to have existed from time *immemorial, it shall be sufficient to allege the enjoyment thereof as of right by the occupiers of the tenement in respect whereof the same is claimed for and during such of the periods mentioned in this act as may be applicable to the case, and without claiming in the name or right of the owner of the fee, as is now usually done: and if the other party shall intend to rely on any proviso, exception, incapacity, disability, contract, agreement, or other matter hereinbefore mentioned, or on any cause or matter of fact or of law, not inconsistent with the simple fact of enjoyment, the same shall be specially alleged and set forth in answer to the allegation of the party claiming, and shall not be received in evidence on any general traverse or denial of such allegation.

In actions on the case the claimant may allege his right generally, as at present.

In pleas to trespass and other pleadings, where party used to allege his claim from time immemorial, the period mentioned in this act may be alleged; and exceptions or other matters to be replied specially.

[*714]

VI. And be it further enacted, that, in the several cases mentioned in and provided for by this act, no presumption shall be allowed or made in favor or

Restricting the presumption to be allowed in

3 & 3 W. 4, c. 71

Support of claims herein provided for. support of any claim, upon proof of the exercise or enjoyment of the right or matter claimed for any less period of time or number of years than for such period or number mentioned in this act, as may be applicable to the case and to the nature of the claim.

Proviso for infants, &c. VII. Provided also, that the time during which any person otherwise capable of resisting any claim to any of the matters before mentioned shall have been or shall be an infant, idiot, non compos mentis, feme covert, or tenant for life, or during which any action or suit shall have been pending, and which shall have been diligently prosecuted until abated by the death of any party or parties thereto, shall be excluded in the computation of the periods hereinbefore mentioned, except only in cases where the right or claim is hereby declared to be absolute and indefeasible.

What time to be excluded in computing the term of forty years appointed by this act. VIII. Provided always, and be it further enacted, that when any land or water, upon, over, or from which any such way or other convenient watercourse or use of water shall have been or shall be enjoyed or derived, hath been or shall be held under or by virtue of any term of life, or any term of years exceeding three years from the granting thereof, the time of the enjoyment of any such way or other matter as herein last before mentioned, during the continuance of such term, shall be excluded in the computation of the said period of forty years, in case the claim shall within three years next after the end or sooner determination of such term be resisted by any person entitled to any reversion expectant on the determination thereof.

Not to extend to Scotland or Ireland. IX. And be it further enacted, that this act shall not extend to Scotland or Ireland.

Commencement of act. X. And be it further enacted, that this act shall commence and take effect on the first day of Michaelmas term now next ensuing.

Act may be amended. XI. And be it further enacted, that this act may be amended, altered, or repealed, during this present session of parliament.

---

3 & 4 Will. IV. Cap. 42.

3 & 4 W. 4, c. 42. *An Act for the further Amendment of the Law, and the better Advancement of Justice.* [14th August, 1833.]

Whereas it would greatly contribute to the diminishing of expense in suits in the superior Courts of common law at Westminster if the pleadings therein were in some respects altered, and the questions to be tried by the jury left less at large than they now are according to the course and practice of pleading in several forms of action; but this cannot be conveniently done otherwise than by rules or orders of the judges of the said Courts from time to time to be made, and doubts may arise as to the power of the said judges to make such alterations without the authority of parliament: be it therefore enacted by the King's most excellent Majesty, by and with the advice and consent of the lords spiritual and temporal, and commons, in this present parliament assembled, and by the authority of the same, that the judges of the said superior Courts, or any eight or more of them, of whom the chiefs of each of the said Courts shall be three, shall and may, by any rule or order

Judges to have power to make alterations in the mode of pleading in the superior Courts, &c. [*715] *to be from time to time by them made, in term or vacation, at any time within five years from the time when this Act shall take effect, make such alterations in the mode of pledging in the said Courts, and in the mode of entering and transcribing pleadings, judgments, and other proceedings in actions at law, and such regulations as to the payment of costs, and otherwise for carrying into effect the said alterations, as to them may seem expedient; and all such rules, orders, or regulations shall be laid before both houses of parliament, if parliament be then sitting, immediately upon the making of the same, or if parliament be not sitting, then within five days after the next meeting thereof, and no such rule, order, or regulation shall have effect until six weeks after the same shall have been so laid before both houses of parliament; and any rule or order so made shall, from and after such time aforesaid, be binding and obligatory on the said Courts, and all other Courts of common law, and on all Courts of error into which the judgments of the said Courts or any of them shall be carried by any writ of error, and be of the like force and effect as if the provisions contained therein had been expressly enacted by parliament: provided always, that no such rule or order shall have the effect of depriving any person of the power of pleading the general issue, and giving the special matter in evidence, in any case wherein he is now or hereafter shall be entitled to do so by virtue of any act of parliament now or hereafter to be in force.

3 & 4 W. 4, c. 42.

Not to deprive any person of the power of pleading the general issue.

II. And whereas there is no remedy provided by law for injuries to the real estate of any person deceased, committed in his lifetime, nor for certain wrongs done by a person deceased in his lifetime to another in respect of his property, real or personal; for remedy thereof be it enacted, that an action of trespass, or trespass on the case, as the case may be, may be maintained by the executors or administrators of any person deceased for any injury to the real estate of such person, committed in his lifetime, for which an action might have been maintained by such person, so as such injury shall have been committed within six calendar months before the death of such deceased person, and provided such action shall be brought within one year after the death of such person; and the damages, when recovered, shall be part of the personal estate of such person; and further that an action of trespass, or trespass on the case, as the case may be, may be maintained against the executors or administrators of any person deceased for any wrong committed by him in his lifetime to another in respect of his property, real or personal, so as such injury shall have been committed within six calendar months before such person's death, and so as such action shall be brought within six calendar months after such executors or administrators shall have taken upon themselves the administration of the estate and effects of such person; and the damages to be recovered in such action shall be payable in like order of administration as the simple contract debts of such person.

Executors may bring actions for injuries to the real estates of the deceased; and actions may be brought against executors for an injury to property, real or personal, by their testator.

III. And be it further enacted, that all actions of debt for rent upon an indenture of demise, all actions of covenant or debt upon any bond or other specialty, and all actions of debt or *scire facias* upon any recognizance, and also all actions of debt upon any award where the submission is not by specialty, or for any fine due in respect of any copyhold estates, or for an escape, or for money levied on any *fieri facias*, and all actions for penalties, or damages, or sums of money given to the party grieved, by any statute now or hereafter to be in force, that shall be sued or brought at any time after the end of the present session of parliament, shall be commenced and sued within the time and limitation hereinafter expressed, and not after; that is to say, the said actions of debt for rent upon an indenture of demise, or covenant of debt upon any bond or other specialty, actions of debt or *scire facias* upon recognizance, within ten years after the end of this present session, or within twenty years after the cause of such actions or suits, but not after; the said actions by the party grieved, one year after the end of this present session, or within two years after the cause of such actions or suits, but not after; and the said other actions within three years after the end of the present session, or within six years after the cause of such actions *or suits, but not after; provided that nothing herein contained shall extend to any action given by any statute where the time for bringing such action is or shall be by any statute specially limited.

Limitation of action of debt on specialties, &c.

[*716]

IV. And be it further enacted, that if any person or persons that is or are or shall be entitled to any such action or suit, or to such *scire facias*, is or are or shall be, at the time of any such cause of action accrued, within the age of twenty-one years, *feme covert*, *non compos mentis*, or beyond the seas, then such person or persons shall be at liberty to bring the same actions, so as they commence the same within such times after their coming to or being of full age, discovert, of sound memory, or returned from beyond the seas, as other persons having no such impediment should, according to the provisions of this

Infants, femes covert, &c.

3 & 4 W. 4, c. 42.

Absence of defendants beyond seas provided for.

Act, have done; and that if any person or persons against whom there shall be any such cause of action is or are, or shall be at the time such cause of action accrued, beyond the seas, then the person or persons entitled to any such cause of action shall be at liberty to bring the same against such person or persons within such times as are before limited after the return of such person or persons from beyond the seas.

Proviso in case of acknowledgment in writing, or by part payment.

V. Provided always, that if any acknowledgment shall have been made either by writing signed by the party liable by virtue of such indenture, specialty, or recognizance, or his agent, or by part payment or part satisfaction on account of any principal or interest being then due thereon, it shall and may be lawful for the person or persons entitled to such actions to bring his or their action for the money remaining unpaid and so acknowledged to be due within twenty years after such acknowledgment by writing or part payment or part satisfaction as aforesaid, or in case the person or persons entitled to such action shall at the time of such acknowledgment be under such disability as aforesaid, or the party making such acknowledgment be, at the time of making the same, beyond the seas, then within twenty years after such disability shall have ceased as aforesaid, or the party shall have returned from beyond seas, as the case may be; and the plaintiff or plaintiffs in any such action, or any indenture, specialty, or recognizance, may, by way of replication, state such acknowledgment, and that such action was brought within the time aforesaid, in answer to a plea of this statute.

The limitation after judgment or outlawry reversed.

VI. And nevertheless be it enacted, that if in any of the said actions judgment be given for the plaintiff, and the same be reversed by error, or a verdict pass for the plaintiff, and upon matter alleged in arrest of judgment the judgment be given against the plaintiff, that he take nothing by his plaint, writ, or bill, or if in any of the said actions the defendant shall be outlawed, and shall after reverse the outlawry, that in all such cases the party plaintiff, his executors or administrators, as the case shall require, may commence a new action or suit from time to time within a year after such judgment reversed, or such judgment given against the plaintiff, or outlawry reversed, and not after.

No part of the united kingdom, &c. to be deemed beyond the seas within the meaning of this act.

VII. And be it further enacted, that no part of the united kingdom of Great Britain and Ireland, nor the islands of Man, Guernsey, Jersey, Alderney, and Sark, nor any islands adjacent to any of them, being part of the dominions of his Majesty, shall be deemed to be beyond the seas within the meaning of this Act, or of the Act passed in the twenty-first year of the reign of King James the First, intituled "An Act for Limitation of Actions, and for avoiding of Suits in law."

Restriction as to plea in abatement for nonjoinder of a co-defendant.

VIII. And be it further enacted, that no plea in abatement for the non-joinder of any person as a co-defendant shall be allowed in any Court of common law, unless it shall be stated in such plea that such person is resident within the jurisdiction of the Court, and unless the place of residence of such person shall be stated with convenient certainty in an affidavit verifying such plea.

Reply of plaintiff to plea in abatement of nonjoinder.

IX. And be it further enacted, that to any plea in abatement in any Court of law of the nonjoinder of another person, the plaintiff may reply that such person has been discharged by bankruptcy and certificate, or under an Act for the Relief of Insolvent Debtors.

[*717]

Provision in the case of subsequent proceedings against the persons named in a plea in abatement

*X. And be it further enacted, that in all cases in which after such plea in abatement the plaintiff shall, without having proceeded to trial upon an issue thereon, commence another action against the defendant or defendants in the action in which such plea in abatement shall have been pleaded, and the person or persons named in such plea in abatement as joint contractors, if it shall appear by the pleadings in such subsequent action, or on the evidence at the trial thereof, that all the original defendants are liable, but that one or more of the persons named in such plea in abatement or any subsequent plea in abatement are not liable, as a contracting party or parties, the plaintiff shall nevertheless be entitled to judgment, or to a verdict and judgment, as the case may be, against the other defendant or defendants who shall appear to

be liable; and every defendant who is not so liable shall have judgment, and shall be entitled to his costs as against the plaintiff who shall be allowed the same as costs in the cause against the defendant or defendants who shall have so pleaded in abatement the nonjoinder of such person; provided that any such defendant who shall have so pleaded in abatement shall be at liberty on the trial to adduce evidence of the liability of the defendants named by him in such plea in abatement.

3 & 4 W. 4, c. 42.

XI. And be it further enacted, that no plea in abatement for a misnomer shall be allowed in any personal action, but that in all cases in which a misnomer would but for this Act have been by law pleadable in abatement in such actions, the defendant shall be at liberty to cause the declaration to be amended, at the costs of the plaintiff, by inserting the right name, upon a judge's summons founded on an affidavit of the right name: and in case such summons shall be discharged, the cost of such application shall be paid by the party applying, if the judge shall think fit.

Misnomer not to be pleaded in abatement.

XII. And be it further enacted, that in all actions upon bills of exchange or promissory notes, or other written instruments, any of the parties to which are designated by the initial letter or letters or some contraction of the christian or first name or names, it shall be sufficient in every affidavit to hold to bail, and in the process or declaration, to designate such person by the same initial letter or letters or contraction of the christian or first name or names instead of stating the christian or first name or names in full.

Initials of names may be used in some cases.

XIII. And be it further enacted, that no wager of law shall be hereafter allowed.

Wager of law to be abolished.

XIV. And be it further enacted, that an action of debt on simple contract shall be maintainable in any Court of common law against any executor or administrator.

Action of debt on simple contract.

XV. And whereas it is expedient to lessen the expense of the proof of written or printed documents, or copies thereof, on the trial of causes; be it further enacted, that it shall and may be lawful for the said judges, or any such eight or more of them as aforesaid, at any time within five years after this Act shall take effect, to make regulations by general rules or orders, from time to time, in term or in vacation, touching the voluntary admission, upon an application for that purpose at a reasonable time before the trial, of one party to the other of all such written or printed documents, or copies of documents, as are intended to be offered in evidence on the said trial by the party requiring such admission, and touching the inspection thereof before such admission is made, and touching the costs which may be incurred by the proof of such documents or copies on the trial of the cause, in case of the omitting to apply for such admission, or the not producing of such document or copies for the purpose of obtaining admission thereof, or of the refusal to make such admission, as the case may be, and as to the said judges shall seem meet; and all such rules and orders shall be binding and obligatory in all Courts of common law, and of the like force as if the provisions therein contained had been expressly enacted by parliament.

Power to the judges to make regulations as to the admission of written documents:

XVI. And whereas it would also lessen the expense of trials and prevent delay if such writs of inquiry as hereinafter mentioned were executed, and such issues as hereinafter mentioned were tried, before the sheriff of the county where the venue is laid; be it therefore enacted, that all writs issued *under and by virtue of the statute passed in the session of parliament held in the eighth and ninth years of the reign of King William the Third, intituled "An Act for the better preventing frivolous and vexatious Suits," shall, unless the Court where such action is pending, or a judge of one of the said superior Courts, shall otherwise order, direct the sheriff of the county where the action shall be brought to summon a jury to appear before such sheriff, instead of the justices or justice of assize or nisi prius of that county, to inquire of the truth of the breaches suggested, and assess the damages that the plaintiff shall have sustained thereby, and shall command the said sheriff to make re-

Writs of inquiry under the statute 8 & 9 Will. 3, c. 11, to be executed before the sheriff, unless otherwise ordered.

[*718]

3 & 4 W. 4, c. 42. turn thereof to the Court from whence the same shall issue at a day certain, in term or in vacation, in such writ to be mentioned; and such proceedings shall be had after the return of such writ as are in the said statutes in that behalf mentioned, in like manner as if such writ had been executed before a justice of assize or nisi prius.

Power to direct issues joined in certain actions to be tried before the sheriff or any judge.

XVII. And be it further enacted, that in any action depending in any of the said superior Courts for any debt or demand in which the sum sought to be recovered, and indorsed on the writ of summons, shall not exceed twenty pounds, it shall be lawful for the Court in which such suit shall be depending, or any judge of any of the said Courts, if such court or judge shall be satisfied that the trial will not involve any difficult question of fact or law, and such Court or judge shall think fit so to do, to order and direct that the issue or issues joined shall be tried before the sheriff of the county where the action is brought, or any judge of any Court of record for the recovery of debt in such county, and for that purpose a writ shall issue directed to such sheriff, commanding him to try such issue or issues, by a jury to be summoned by him, and to return such writ, with the finding of the jury thereon indorsed, at a day certain, in term or in vacation, to be named in such writ; and thereupon such sheriff or judge shall summon a jury, and shall proceed to try such issue or issues.

Upon the return of a writ of inquiry or a trial of issues, judgment to be signed, unless, &c.

XVIII. And be it further enacted, that at the return of any such writ of inquiry, or writ for the trial of such issue or issues as aforesaid, costs shall be taxed, judgment signed, and execution issued forthwith, unless the sheriff or his deputy before whom such writ of inquiry may be executed, or such sheriff, deputy, or judge, before whom such trial shall be had, shall certify under his hand upon such writ that judgment ought not to be signed until the defendant shall have had an opportunity to apply to the Court for a new inquiry or trial, or a judge of any of the said Courts shall think fit to order that judgment or execution shall be stayed till a day to be named in such order; and the verdict of such jury on the trial of such issue or issues shall be as valid and of the like force as a verdict of a jury at nisi prius; and the sheriff or his deputy, or judge, presiding at the trial of such issue or issues, shall have the like powers with respect to amendment on such trial as are hereinafter given to judges at nisi prius.

Sheriff, as to such issues, to have the like powers as judges at nisi prius.

Provisions of 1 W. 4, c. 7, to extend to such writs of inquiry and issues.

XIX. Provided also, that all and every the provisions contained in the statute made and passed in the first year of the reign of his present Majesty, intituled "An Act for the more speedy Judgment and Execution in Actions brought in his Majesty's Courts of Law at Westminster, and in the Court of Common Pleas of the County Palatine of Lancaster, and for amending the Law as to Judgment on a *Cognovit Actionem* in Cases of Bankruptcy," shall, so far as the same are applicable thereto, be extended and applied to judgments and executions upon such writs of inquiry and writs for the trials of issues, in like manner as if the same were expressly re-enacted herein.

Sheriffs to name deputies to be resident in London.

XX. And be it further enacted, that from and after the first day of June, one thousand eight hundred and thirty-three, the sheriff of each county in England and Wales shall severally name a sufficient deputy, who shall be resident or have an office within one mile from the Inner Temple Hall, for the receipt of writs, granting warrants thereon, making returns thereto, and accepting of all rules and orders to be made on or touching the execution of any process or writ to be directed to such sheriff.

[*719]

Defendant to be allowed to pay money into Court in certain actions by judge's order.

*XXI. And be it further enacted, that it shall be lawful for the defendant in all personal actions, (except actions for assault and battery, false imprisonment, libel, slander, malicious arrest or prosecution, criminal conversation, or debauching of the plaintiff's daughter or servant,) by leave of any of the said superior Courts where such action is pending, or a judge of any of the said superior Courts, to pay into Court a sum of money by way of compensation or amends, in such manner and under such regulations as to the payment of costs and the form of pleading as the said judges, or such eight or more of them as aforesaid, shall, by any rules or orders by them to be from time to time made, order and direct. 3 & 4 W. 4, c. 42.

XXII. And whereas unnecessary delay and expense is sometimes occasioned by the trial of local actions in the county where the cause of action has arisen; be it therefore enacted, that in any action depending in any of the said superior Courts, the venue in which is by law local, the Court in which such action shall be depending, or any judge of any of the said Courts, may, on the application of either party, order the issue to be tried, or writ of inquiry to be executed, in any other county or place than that in which the venue is laid; and for that purpose any such Court or judge may order a suggestion to be entered on the record, that the trial may be more conveniently had, or writ of inquiry executed, in the county or place where the same is ordered to take place.

Power to direct local actions to be tried in any county.

XXIII. And whereas great expense is often incurred, and delay or failure of justice takes place, at trials, by reason of variances as to some particular or particulars between the proof and the record, or setting forth on the record or document on which the trial is had, of contracts, customs, prescriptions, names, and other matters or circumstances not material to the merits of the case, and by the mis-statement of which the opposite party cannot have been prejudiced, and the same cannot in any case be amended at the trial, except where the variance is between any matter in writing or in print produced in evidence and the record: and whereas it is expedient to allow such amendments as hereinafter mentioned to be made on the trial of the cause; be it therefore enacted, that it shall be lawful for any Court of Record, holding plea in civil actions, and any judge sitting at nisi prius, if such Court or judge shall see fit so to do, to cause the record, writ or document on which any trial may be pending before any such Court or judge, in any civil action, or in any information in the nature of a *quo warranto*, or proceedings on a *mandamus*, when any variance shall appear between the proof and the recital or setting forth on the record, writ, or document on which the trial is proceeding, of any contract, custom, prescription, name, or other matter, in any particular or particulars in the judgment of such Court or judge not material to the merits of the case, and by which the opposite party cannot have been prejudiced in the conduct of his action, prosecution, or defence, to be forthwith amended by some officer of the Court or otherwise, both in the part of the pleadings where such variance occurs, and in every other part of the pleadings which it may become necessary to amend, on such terms as to payment of costs to the other party, or postponing the trial to be had before the same or another jury, or both payment of costs and postponement, as such Court or judge shall think reasonable; and in case such variance shall be in some particular or particulars in the judgment of such Court or judge not material to the merits of the case, but such as that the opposite party may have been prejudiced thereby in the conduct of his action, prosecution or defence, then such Court or judge shall have power to cause the same to be amended, upon payment of costs to the other party, and withdrawing the record or postponing the trial as aforesaid, as such Court or judge shall think reasonable; and after any such amendment the trial shall proceed, in case the same shall be proceeded with, in the same manner in all respects, both with respect to the liability of witnesses to be indicted for perjury, and otherwise, as if no such variance had appeared; and in case such trial shall be had at nisi prius or by virtue of such writ as aforesaid, the order for the amendment shall be indorsed on the postea or the writ, *as the case may be, and returned together with the record or writ, and thereupon such papers, rolls, and other records of the Court from which such record or writ issued, as it may be necessary to amend, shall be amended accordingly; and in case the trial shall be had in any Court of Record, then the order for amendment shall be entered on the roll or other document upon which the trial shall be had; provided that it shall be lawful for any party who is dissatisfied with the decision of such judge at nisi prius, sheriff, or other officer, respecting his allow- [*720]

Allowing amendments to be made on the record in certain cases.

3 & 4 W. 4, c. 42.

ance of any such amendment, to apply to the Court from which such record or writ issued for a new trial upon that ground, and in case any such Court shall think such amendment improper, a new trial shall be granted accordingly, on such terms as the Court shall think fit, or the Court shall make such other order as to them may seem meet.

Power for the Court or judge to direct the facts to be found specially.

XXIV. And be it further enacted, that the said Court or judge shall and may, if they or he think fit, in all such cases of variance, instead of causing the record or document to be amended as aforesaid, direct the jury to find the fact or facts according to the evidence, and thereupon such finding shall be stated on such record or document, and, notwithstanding the finding on the issue joined, the said Court or the Court from which the record has issued shall, if they shall think the said variance immaterial to the merits of the case, and the mis-statement such as could not have prejudiced the opposite party in the conduct of the action or defence, give judgment according to the very right and justice of the case.

Power to state a special case without proceeding to trial.

XXV. And be it further enacted, that it shall be lawful for the parties in any action or information, after issue joined, by consent and by order of any of the judges of the said superior Courts, to state the facts of the case, in the form of a special case, for the opinion of the Court, and to agree that a judgment shall be entered for the plaintiff or defendant, by confession or of *nolle prosequi*, immediately after the decision of the case, or otherwise as the Court may think fit; and judgment shall be entered accordingly.

Witnesses interested solely on account of the verdict to be admissible.

XXVI. And in order to render the rejection of witnesses on the ground of interest less frequent, be it further enacted, that if any witness shall be objected to as incompetent on the ground that the verdict or judgment in the action on which it shall be proposed to examine him would be admissible in evidence for or against him, such witness shall nevertheless be examined, but in that case a verdict or judgment in that action in favor of the party on whose behalf he shall have been examined shall not be admissible in evidence for him or any one claiming under him, nor shall a verdict or judgment against the party on whose behalf he shall have been examined be admissible in evidence against him or any one claiming under him.

Direction to indorse the name of the witness on the record.

XXVII. And be it further enacted, that the name of every witness objected to as incompetent on the ground that such verdict or judgment would be admissible in evidence for or against him, shall at the trial be indorsed on the record or document on which the trial shall be had, together with the name of the party on whose behalf he was examined, by some officer of the Court, at the request of either party, and shall be afterwards entered on the record of the judgment; and such indorsement or entry shall be sufficient evidence that such witness was examined in any subsequent proceeding in which the verdict or judgment shall be offered in evidence.

Jury empowered to allow interest upon debts.

XXVIII. And be it further enacted, that upon all debts or sums certain, payable at a certain time or otherwise, the jury on the trial of any issue, or on any inquisition of damages, may, if they shall think fit, allow interest to the creditor at a rate not exceeding the current rate of interest from the time when such debts or sums certain were payable, if such debts or sums be payable by virtue of some written instrument at a certain time, or if payable otherwise, then from the time when demand of payment shall have been made in writing, so as such demand shall give notice to the debtor that interest will be claimed from the date of such demand until the term of payment; provided that interest shall be payable in all cases in which it is now payable by law.

[*721]

In certain actions the jury may give damages in the nature of interest.

*XXIX. And be it further enacted, that the jury on the trial of any issue, or on any inquisition of damages, may, if they shall think fit, give damages in the nature of interest, over and above the value of the goods at the time of the conversion or seizure, in all actions of trover or trespass *de bonis asportatis*, and over and above the money recoverable in all actions on policies of assurance made after the passing of this Act.

Interest to be allowed on

XXX. And be it further enacted, that if any person shall sue out any writ of error upon any judgment whatsoever given in any Court in any action personal, and the Court of error shall give judgment for the defendant thereon, then interest shall be allowed by the Court of error for such time as execution has been delayed by such writ of error, for the delaying thereof.

3 & 4 W. 4, c. 42.

all writs of error for the time that execution has been delayed.

XXXI. And be it further enacted, that in every action brought by any executor or administrator in right of the testator or intestate, such executor or administrator shall, unless the Court in which such action is brought, or a judge of any of the said superior Courts shall otherwise order, be liable to pay costs to the defendant in case of being nonsuited or a verdict passing against the plaintiff, and in all other cases in which he would be liable if such plaintiff were suing in his own right upon a cause of action accruing to himself; and the defendant shall have judgment for such costs, and they shall be recovered in like manner.

Executors suing in right of the testator to pay costs.

XXXII. And be it further enacted, that where several persons shall be made defendants in any personal action, and any one or more of them shall have a *nolle prosequi* entered as to him or them, or upon the trial of such action shall have a verdict pass for him or them, every such person shall have judgment for and recover his reasonable costs, unless, in the case of a trial, the judge before whom such cause shall be tried shall certify upon the record, under his hand, that there was a reasonable cause for making such person a defendant in such action.

One or more of several defendants in any action having a *nolle prosequi* or a verdict shall have costs.

XXXIII. And be it further enacted, that where any *nolle prosequi* shall have been entered upon any count, or as to part of any declaration, the defendant shall be entitled to, and have judgment for, and recover his reasonable costs in that behalf.

Where *nolle prosequi* entered upon any count, &c.

XXXIV. And be it further enacted, that in all writs of *scire facias* the plaintiff obtaining judgment or an award of execution shall recover his costs of suit upon a judgment by default as well as upon a judgment after plea pleaded or demurrer joined; and that where judgment shall be given either for or against a plaintiff or demandant, or for or against a defendant or tenant, upon any demurrer joined in any action whatever, the party in whose favor such judgment shall be given shall also have judgment to recover his costs in that behalf.

Plaintiff in *scire facias*, and plaintiff or defendant on demurrer, to have costs.

XXXV. And whereas it is provided in and by a statute passed in the sixth year of the reign of his late Majesty, intituled "An Act for consolidating and amending the Law relative to Jurors and Juries," that the person or party who shall apply for a special jury shall pay the fees for striking such jury, and all the expenses occasioned by the trial of the cause by the same, and shall not have any further or other allowance for the same, upon taxation of costs, than such person or party would be entitled unto in case the cause had been tried by a common jury, unless the judge before whom the cause is tried shall, immediately after the verdict, certify under his hand, upon the back of the record, that the same was a cause proper to be tried by a special jury: and whereas the said provision does not apply to cases in which the plaintiff has been nonsuited, and it is expedient that the judge should have such power of certifying as well when a plaintiff is nonsuited as when he has a verdict against him; be it therefore enacted, that the said provisions of the said last-mentioned act of parliament, and every thing therein contained, shall apply to cases in which the plaintiff shall be nonsuited as well as to cases in which a verdict shall pass against him.

Costs of special juries in case of a nonsuit.

6 G. 4, c. 50.

XXXVI. And whereas it would tend to the better dispatch of business, and would be more convenient, and better assimilate the practice and promote uniformity in the allowance of costs, if the officers on the plea side of *the Courts of King's Bench and Exchequer, and the officers of the Court of Common Pleas at Westminster, who now perform the duties of taxing costs, were to be empowered to tax costs which have arisen or may arise in each of the said Courts indiscriminately; be it therefore enacted, that it shall be lawful for the judges of the said Courts, or such eight or more of them as afore-

Power to make regulations as to the officers of each Court at Westminster taxing costs.

[*722]

3 & 4 W. 4, c. 42.

said, by any rule or order to be from time to time made, in term or vacation, to make such regulations for the taxation of costs by any of the said officers of the said Courts indiscriminately as to them may seem expedient, although such costs may not have arisen in respect of business done in the Court to which such officer belongs, and to appoint some convenient place in which the business of taxation shall be transacted for all the said Courts, and to alter the same when and as it may seem to them expedient.

Executors of lessor may distrain for arrears in his lifetime.

XXXVII. And be it further enacted, that it shall be lawful for the executors or administrators of any lessor or landlord to distrain upon the lands demised for any term, or at will, for the arrearages of rent due to such lessor or landlord in his lifetime, in like manner as such lessor or landlord might have done in his lifetime.

Arrears may be distrained for within six months after determination of term.

XXXVIII. And be it further enacted, that such arrearages may be distrained for after the end or determination of such term or lease at will, in the same manner as if such term or lease had not been ended or determined; provided that such distress be made within the space of six calendar months after the determination of such term or lease, and during the continuance of the possession of the tenant from whom such arrears became due: provided also, that all and every the powers and provisions in the several statutes made relating to distresses for rent shall be applicable to the distresses so made as aforesaid.

Submission to arbitration by rule of Court, &c. not to be revocable without leave of the Court.

XXXIX. And whereas it is expedient to render references to arbitration more effectual; be it further enacted, that the power and authority of any arbitrator or umpire appointed by or in pursuance of any rule of Court, or judge's order, or order of nisi prius, in any action now brought or which shall be hereafter brought, or by or in pursuance of any submission to reference containing an agreement that such submission shall be made a rule of any of his Majesty's Courts of Record, shall not be revocable by any party to such reference without the leave of the Court by which such rule or order shall be made, or which shall be mentioned in such submission, or by leave of a judge; and the arbitrator or umpire shall and may and is hereby required to proceed with the reference notwithstanding any such revocation, and to make such award, although the person making such revocation shall not afterwards attend the reference; and that the Court or any judge thereof may from time to time enlarge the term for any such arbitrator making his award.

Power to compel the attendance of witnesses.

XL. And be it further enacted, that when any reference shall have been made by any such rule or order as aforesaid, or by any submission contained in such agreement as aforesaid, it shall be lawful for the Court by which such rule or order shall be made, or which shall be mentioned in such agreement, or for any judge, by rule or order to be made for that purpose, to command the attendance and examination of any person to be named, or the production of any documents to be mentioned in such rule or order; and the disobedience to any such rule or order shall be deemed a contempt of Court, if, in addition to the service of such rule or order, an appointment of the time and place of attendance in obedience thereto, signed by one at least of the arbitrators, or by the umpire, before whom the attendance is required, shall also be served either together with or after the service of such rule or order: provided always, that every person whose attendance shall be so required shall be entitled to the like conduct-money, and payment of expenses and for loss of time, as for and upon attendance at any trial: provided also, that the application made to such Court or judge for such rule or order shall set forth the county where such witness is residing at the time, or satisfy such Court or judge that such person cannot be found: provided also, that no person shall be compelled to produce, under any such rule or order, any writing or other document that he would not be compelled to produce *at a trial, or to attend at more than two consecutive days, to be named in such order.

[*723]

Power for the arbitrators under a

XLI. And be it further enacted, that when in any rule or order of reference, or in any submission to arbitration containing an agreement that the submission shall be made a rule of Court, it shall be ordered or agreed that the witnesses upon such reference shall be examined upon oath, it shall be lawful for the arbitrator or umpire, or any one arbitrator, and he or they are hereby authorized and required, to administer an oath to such witnesses, or to take their affirmation in cases where affirmation is allowed by law instead of oath; and if upon such oath or affirmation any person making the same shall wilfully and corruptly give any false evidence, every person so offending shall be deemed and taken to be guilty of perjury, and shall be prosecuted and punished accordingly.

3 & 4 W. 4, c. 42

rule of Court to administer an oath.

XLII. And whereas it would be convenient if the power of the superior Courts of common law and equity at Westminster to grant commissions for taking affidavits to be used in the said Courts respectively should be extended: be it further enacted by the authority aforesaid, that the lord high chancellor, lord keeper or lords commissioners of the great seal, the said Courts of law, and the several judges of the same, shall have such and the same powers for granting commissions for taking and receiving affidavits in Scotland and Ireland, to be used and read in the said Courts respectively, as they now have in all and every the shires and counties within the kingdom of England, and dominion of Wales, and town of Berwick-upon-Tweed, and in the Isle of Man, by virtue of the statutes now in force; and that all and every person and persons wilfully swearing or affirming falsely in any affidavit to be made before any person or persons who shall be so empowered to take affidavits under the authority aforesaid shall be deemed guilty of perjury, and shall incur and be liable to the same pains and penalties as if such person had wilfully sworn or affirmed falsely in the open Court in which such affidavit shall be entitled, and be liable to be prosecuted for such perjury in any Court of competent jurisdiction in that part of the United Kingdom in which such offence shall have been committed, or in that part of the United Kingdom in which such person shall be apprehended on such a charge.

Power of granting commissions to take affidavits to extend to Scotland and Ireland.

XLIII. And whereas the observance of holidays in the said Courts of common law during term time, and in the offices belonging to the same, on the several days on which holidays are now kept, is very inconvenient, and tends to delay in the administration of justice; be it therefore enacted by the authority aforesaid, that none of the several days mentioned in the statute passed in the sessions of parliament holden in the fifth and sixth years of the reign of King Edward the Sixth, intituled "An Act for keeping Holidays and Fasting Days," shall be observed or kept in the said Courts, or in the several offices belonging thereto, except Sundays, the day of the Nativity of our Lord and the three following days, and Monday and Tuesday in Easter week.

For the abolition of certain holidays.

5 & 6 Edw. 6, c. 3.

XLIV. And be it further enacted, that this statute shall commence and take effect on the first day of June one thousand eight hundred and thirty-three.

Commencement of act

XLV. And be it further enacted, that nothing in this Act shall extend to that part of the United Kingdom called Ireland, or that part of the United Kingdom called Scotland, except in the cases hereinbefore specially mentioned.

Not to extend to Ireland or Scotland.

REGULÆ GENERALES.

OF RULES OF COURT.

TRINITY TERM. 1 WILLIAM IV. 1831.

Reg. Gen. Trin. T. 1 W. 4.

WHEREAS declarations in actions upon bills of exchange, promissory notes, and the counts usually called the common counts, occasion unnecessary expense to parties by reason of their length, and the same may be drawn in a more concise form: Now for the prevention of such expense, it is ordered, *that if any declaration in *assumpsit* hereafter filed or delivered, and to which the plaintiff shall not be entitled to a plea as of this term, being for any of the demands mentioned in the schedule of forms and directions annexed to this

Forms of declarations.

In *assumpsit*.

[*724]

Reg. Gen. Trin. T 1 W. 4

order, or demands of a like nature, shall exceed in length such of the said forms set forth or directed in the said schedule as may be applicable to the case; or, if any declaration in *debt* to be so filed or delivered for similar causes of action, and for which the action of assumpsit would lie, shall exceed such length, no costs of the excess shall be allowed to the plaintiff if he succeeds in the cause; and such costs of the excess as have been incurred by the defendant shall be taxed and allowed to the defendant, and be deducted from the costs allowed to the plaintiff. And it is further ordered, that on the taxation of costs as between attorney and client, no costs shall be allowed to the attorney in respect of any such excess of length; and in case any costs shall be payable by the plaintiff to the defendant on account of such excess, the amount thereof shall be deducted from the amount of the attorney's bill.

In *debt*.

TENTERDEN.	J. VAUGHAN.
N. C. TINDAL.	J PARKE.
LYNDHURST.	W. BOLLAND.
J. BAYLEY.	J. B. BOSANQUET.
J. A. PARK.	W. E. TAUNTON.
J. LITTLEDALE.	E. H. ALDERSON.
S. GASELEE.	J. PATTESON.

SCHEDULE OF FORMS AND DIRECTIONS.

Count on a promissory note against the maker, by payee or indorsee, as the case may be.

For that whereas the defendant, on the —— day of ——, in the year of our Lord ——, at London [*or* in the county of ——] made his promissory note in writing, and delivered the same to the plaintiff, and thereby promised to pay to the plaintiff £——, —— days [weeks *or* months] after the date thereof [*or as the fact may be*], which period has now elapsed; [*or if the note be payable to A. B.*] and then and there delivered the same to *A. B.*, and thereby promised to pay to the said *A. B.* or order £——, —— days [weeks *or* months] after the date thereof [*or as the fact may be*], which period has now elapsed; and the said *A. B.* then and there indorsed the same to the plaintiff, whereof the defendant then and there had notice, and then and there, in consideration of the premises, promised to pay the amount of the said note to the plaintiff, according to the tenor and effect thereof.

Count on a promissory note against payee by indorsee.

Whereas one *C. D.* on the —— day of ——, in the year of our Lord ——, at London [*or* in the county of ——], made his promissory note in writing, and thereby promised to pay the defendant or order £——, —— days [weeks *or* months] after the date thereof, [*or as the fact may be*] which period has now elapsed; and the defendant then and there indorsed the same to the plaintiff, [*or*, and the defendant then and there indorsed the same to *X. Y.*, and the said *X. Y.* then and there indorsed the same to the plaintiff;] and the said *C. D.* did not pay the amount thereof, although the same was there presented to him on the day when it became due; of all which the defendant then and there had due notice.

Count on a promissory note against indorser by indorsee.

Whereas one *C. D.* on ——, at London [*or* in the county of ——], made his promissory note in writing, and thereby promised to pay to *X. Y.* or order £——, —— days [weeks *or* months] after the date thereof, [*or as the fact may be*,] which period has now elapsed; and then and there delivered the said note to the said *X. Y.*, and the said *X. Y.* then and there indorsed the same to the defendant, and the defendant then and there indorsed the same to the plaintiff; [*or*, and the defendant then and there indorsed the same to *Q. R.*, and the said *Q. R.* then and there indorsed the same to the plaintiff;] and the said *C. D.* did not pay the amount thereof although the same was there presented to him on the day when it became due; of all which the defendant then and there had due notice.

[*725]

Count on an inland bill of exchange against the acceptor by

*Whereas the plaintiff on ——, at London [*or* in the county of ——], made his bill of exchange in writing and directed the same to the defendant, and thereby required the defendant to pay to the plaintiff £——, —— days [weeks *or* months] after the date [*or* sight] thereof, which period has now elapsed; and the defendant then and there accepted the said bill, and promised the plaintiff to pay the same, according to the tenor and effect thereof and of his said acceptance thereof, but did not pay the same when due. Reg. Gen. Trin. T. 1 W. 4. the drawer, being also payee.

Whereas the plaintiff on ——, at London [or in the county of ——], made his bill of exchange in writing and directed the same to the defendant, and thereby required the defendant to pay to *O. P.* or order £——, —— days [weeks *or* months] after the date [*or* sight] thereof, which period has now elapsed; and then and there delivered the same to the said *O P.*, and the said defendant then and there accepted the same, and promised the plaintiff to pay the same according to the tenor and effect thereof, and of his acceptance thereof; yet he did not pay the amount thereof, although the said bill was there presented to him on the day when it became due, and thereupon the same was then and there returned to the plaintiff; of all which the defendant then and there had notice. Count on an inland bill of exchange against the acceptor by the drawer, not being the payee.

Whereas one *E. F.* on ——, at London [*or* in the county of ——], made his bill of exchange in writing and directed the same to the defendant, and thereby required the defendant to pay to the said *E. F.* [*or* to *H. G.*] or order £ ——, —— days [weeks *or* months] after date [*or* sight] thereof, which period has now elapsed, and the defendant then and there accepted the said bill, and the said *E. F.* [*or* the said *H. G.*] then and there indorsed the same to the plaintiff; [*or* and the said *E. F.*, *or*, the said *H. G.* then and there indorsed the same to *K. J.*, and the said *K. J.* then and there indorsed the same to the plaintiff;] of all which the defendant then and there had due notice, and then and there promised the plaintiff to pay the amount thereof according to the tenor and effect thereof, and of his acceptance thereof. Count on an inland bill of exchange against the acceptor by indorsee.

Whereas one *E. F.* on ——, at London [*or* in the county of ——], made his bill of exchange in writing and directed the same to the defendant, and thereby required the defendant to pay to the plaintiff £——, —— days [weeks *or* months] after the sight [*or* date] thereof which period has now elapsed, and the defendant then and there accepted the same, and promised the plaintiff to pay the same according to the tenor and effect thereof, and of his acceptance thereof. Count on an inland bill of exchange against the acceptor by the payee.

Whereas the defendant on ——, at London [*or* in the county of ——,] made his bill of exchange in writing and directed the same to *J. K.*, and thereby required the said *J. K.* to pay to the plaintiff £——, —— days [weeks *or* months] after the date [*or* sight] thereof, and then and there delivered the same to the said plaintiff, and the same was then and there presented to the said *J. K.* for acceptance, and the said *J. K.* then and there refused to accept the same; of all which the defendant then and there had due notice. Count on an inland bill of exchange against the drawer by payee on non-acceptance.

Whereas the defendant on ——, at London [*or* in the county of ——], made his bill of exchange in writing and directed the same to *J. K.*, and thereby required the said *J. K.* to pay to the order of the said defendant £——, —— days [weeks *or* months] after the sight [*or* date] thereof, and the said defendant then and there indorsed the same to the plaintiff, [*or*, and the said defendant then and there indorsed the same to *L. M.* and the said *L. M.* then and there indorsed the same to the plaintiff;] and the same was then and there presented to the said *J. K.* for acceptance, and the said *J. K.* then and there refused to accept the same; of all which the defendant then and there had due notice. Count on an inland bill of exchange against drawer by indorsee on non acceptance.

And whereas one *N. O.* on ——, at London [*or* in the county of ——], made his bill of exchange in writing and directed the same to *P. Q.*, and thereby required the said *P. Q.* to pay to his order £——, —— days [weeks *or* months] after the date [*or* sight] therefore, and the said *N. O.* then and there indorsed the said bill to the defendant [*or* to *R. S.* and the said *R. S.* *then and there indorsed the same to the defendant,] and the defendant then and there indorsed the same to the plaintiff; and the same was then and there presented to the said *P. Q.* for acceptance, and the said *P. Q.* then and there refused to accept the same; of all which the defendant then and there had due notice. Count on an inland bill of exchange against indorser by indorsee on non-acceptance. [*726]

Reg. Gen. Trin. T. 1 W. 4.

Count on an inland bill of exchange against payee by indorsee on non-acceptance.

Whereas one *N. O.* on ——, at London [*or* in the county of ——], made his bill of exchange in writing and directed the same to *P. Q.*, and thereby required the said *P. Q.* to pay to the defendant or order £——, —— days [weeks *or* months] after the date [*or* sight] thereof, and then and there delivered the same to the defendant, and the defendant then and there indorsed the said bill to the plaintiff, [*or* to *R. S.*, and the said *R. S* then and there indorsed the same to the plaintiff,] and the same was then and there presented to the said *P. Q.* for acceptance, and the said *P. Q.* then and there refused to accept the same; of all which the defendant then and there had due notice.

Direction for declaration on bills where action brought after time of payment expired.

1st. On bills payable after date.

If the declaration be against any party to the bill except the drawee or acceptor, and the bill be payable at any time after date, and the action not brought till the time is expired, it will be necessary to insert, as in declarations on promissory notes, immediately after the words denoting the time appointed for payment, the following words, viz.: *which period has now elapsed*, and, instead of averring that the bill was presented to the drawee for *acceptance*, and that he refused to *accept* the same, to allege that the drawee [*naming him*] *did not pay the said bill, although the same was there presented to him on the day when it became due.*

2d. On bills payable after sight.

And if the declaration be against any party except the drawee or acceptor, and the bill be payable at any time after sight, it will be necessary to insert, after the words denoting the time appointed for payment, the following words, viz.: *and the said drawee* [*naming him*] *then and there saw and accepted the same, and the said period has now elapsed*, and instead of alleging that the bill was presented for acceptance and refused, to allege that the drawee [*naming him*] *did not pay the said bill, although the same was presented to him on the day when it became due.*

Directions for declarations on bills or notes payable at sight.

If a *Note or Bill* be payable *at sight*, the form of the declaration must be varied so as to suit the case, which may be easily done.

On foreign bills.

Declaration on foreign bills may be drawn according to the principle of these forms, with the necessary variations.

Common Counts.

Goods bargained and sold, or sold and delivered.

Whereas the defendant on ——, at London [*or* in the county of ——], was indebted to the plaintiff in £——, for the price and value of goods then and there bargained [*or* sold] and sold [*or* delivered] by the plaintiff to the defendant, at his request:

Work and materials.

And in £——, for the price and value of work then and there done, and materials for the same provided by the plaintiff for the defendant, at his request:

Money lent.

And in £——, for money then and there lent by the plaintiff to the defendant at his request:

Money paid.

And in £——, for money then and there paid by the plaintiff for the use of the defendant, at his request:

Money received.

And in £——, for money then and there received by the defendant for the use of the plaintiff:

Account stated.

And in £——, for money found to be due from the defendant to the plaintiff, on an account then and there stated between them.

General conclusion.

And whereas the defendant afterwards, on, &c. in consideration of the premises respectively, then and there promised to pay the said several monies respectively to the plaintiff, on request: Yet he hath disregarded his promises, and hath not paid any of the said monies or any part thereof; to the plaintiff's damage of £——, and thereupon he brings suit, &c.

[*727] Direction as to the general conclusion.

*If the declaration contains one or more counts against the maker of a note or acceptor of a bill of exchange, it will be proper to place them first in the declaration, and then in the general conclusion to say, promised to pay the said *last-mentioned several monies respectively.*

REGULÆ GENERALES.

TRINITY TERM. 1 WILLIAM IV. 1831.

Reg. Gen. Trin. T. 1 W. 4.

Justifying at time of putting in bail.

IT IS ORDERED, That a defendant may justify bail at the same time at which they are put in, upon giving four days' notice for that purpose, before eleven o'clock in the morning, and exclusive of Sunday. That if the plaintiff is desirous of time to inquire after the bail, and shall give one day's notice thereof, as aforesaid, to the defendant, his attorney or agent, as the case may be, before the time appointed for justification, stating therein what further time is required, such time not to exceed three days in the case of town bail, and six days in the case of country bail, then (unless the Court or a judge shall otherwise order) the time for putting in and justifying bail shall be postponed accordingly, and all proceedings shall be stayed in the mean time.

Form of notice of bail.

2. And it is further ordered, that every notice of bail shall, in addition to the descriptions of the bail, mention the street or place, and number (if any), where each of the bail resides, and all the streets or places, and numbers (if any), in which each of them has been resident at any time within the last six months, and whether he is a housekeeper or freeholder.

Affidavit of justification by bail.

3. And it is further ordered, that if the notice of bail shall be accompanied by an affidavit of each of the bail according to the form hereto subjoined, and if the plaintiff afterwards except to such bail, he shall, if such bail are allowed, pay the costs of justification, and if such bail are rejected, the defendants shall pay the costs of opposition, unless the Court or a judge thereof shall otherwise order.

Notice of exception.

4. And it is further ordered, that if the plaintiff shall not give one day's notice of exception to the bail, by whom such affidavit shall have been made, the recognizance of such bail may be taken out of Court without other justification than such affidavit..

Bail not to be changed without leave of Court or judge.

5. And it is further ordered, that the bail of whom notice shall be given, shall not be changed without leave of the Court or a judge.

Particulars of plaintiff's demand.

6. And it is further ordered, that with every declaration, if delivered, or with the notice of declaration, if filed, containing counts in *Indebitatus Assumpsit*, or debt on simple contract, the plaintiff shall deliver full particulars of his demand under those counts, where such particulars can be comprised within three folios; and where the same cannot be comprised within three folios, he shall deliver such a statement of the nature of his claim, and the amount of the sum or balance which he claims to be due, as may be comprised within that number of folios. And to secure the delivery of particulars in all such cases, it is further ordered, that if any declaration or notice shall be delivered without such particulars, or such statement as aforesaid, and a judge shall afterwards order a delivery of particulars, the plaintiff shall not be allowed any costs in respect of any summons for the purpose of obtaining such order, or of the particulars he may afterwards deliver. And that a copy of the particulars of the demand, and also particulars (if any) of the defendant's set-off, shall be annexed by the plaintiff's attorney to every record at the time it is entered with the judge's marshal.

Consequence of not delivering.

Copy of particulars of demand, and of set-off, to be annexed to record.

Time for pleading.

7. And it is further ordered, that upon every declaration, delivered or filed on or before the last day of any term, the defendant, whether in or out of any prison, shall be compellable to plead as of such term without being entitled to any imparlance.

Judgment of non pros for not declaring, &c. when signable.

8. And it is further ordered, that no judgment of non pros shall be signed for want of a declaration, replication, or other subsequent pleading, until four *days next after a demand thereof shall have been made in writing, upon the plaintiff, his attorney or agent, as the case may be.

[*728]

Two summonses only to be necessary for attendance before judge.

9. And it is further ordered, that hereafter it shall not be necessary to issue more than two summonses for attendance before a judge upon the same matter; and the party taking out such summonses shall be entitled to an order on the return of the second summons, unless cause is shown to the contrary.

Reg. Gen. Trin. T. 1 W. 4.

Delivery of declaration de bene esse. 10. And it is further ordered, that no declaration *de bene esse* shall be delivered until the expiration of six days from the service of the process in the case of process which is not bailable, or until the expiration of six days from the time of the arrest in case of bailable process; and such six days shall be reckoned inclusive of the day of such service or arrest.

Service of declarations in ejectment. 11. And it is further ordered, that declarations in *ejectment* may be served before the first day of any term, and thereupon the plaintiff shall be entitled to judgment against the casual ejector, in like manner as upon declarations served before the essoign or first general return-day.

Notice of taxation of costs. 12. And it is further ordered, that before taxation of costs, one day's notice shall be given to the opposite party.

Pleading several matters by judge's order. 13. And it is further ordered, that no rule to show cause, or motion shall be required, in order to obtain a rule to plead several matters, or to make several avowries or cognizances; but that such rules shall be drawn up upon a judge's order, to be made upon a summons, accompanied by a short abstract or statement of the intended pleas, avowries or cognizances. Provided, that no summons or order shall be necessary in the following cases, that is to say, where the plea of non-assumpsit, or nil debet, or non detinet, with or without a plea of tender as to part, a plea of the statute of limitations, set-off, bankruptcy of the defendant, discharge under an insolvent act, plene administravit, plene administravit præter, infancy, and coverture, or any two or more of such pleas shall be pleaded together; but in all such cases a rule shall be drawn up by the proper officer, upon the production of the engrossment of the pleas, or a draft or copy thereof.

In what cases judge's order unnecessary.

Commencement of rules. 14. And it is further ordered, that these rules shall take effect on the first day of next Michaelmas term, except the rule as to the service of declarations in ejectment, which shall take effect from the 25th day of October next.

TENTERDEN.	J. VAUGHAN.
N. C. TINDAL.	J. PARKE.
LYNDHURST.	W. BOLLAND.
J. BAILEY.	J. B. BOSANQUET.
J. A. PARK.	W. E. TAUNTON.
J. LITTLEDALE.	E. H. ALDERSON.
S. GASELEE.	J. PATTESON.

FORM OF AFFIDAVIT.

In the

Between, &c.

Affidavit of justification by bail. *A. B.*, one of the bail for the above-named defendant, maketh oath and saith, that he is a housekeeper [*or* freeholder, *as the case may be*], residing at [*describing particularly the street or place, and number, if any,*] that he is possessed of property to the amount of £—— [*the amount required by the practice of the Courts,*] over and above all his just debts; [*if bail in any other action, add* "and every other sum for which he is now bail;"] that he is not bail for any defendant except in this action, [*or if bail in any other action or actions add* "except for *C. D.* at the suit of *E. F.* in the Court of ——, in the sum of £——; for *G. H.*, at the suit of *I. K.* in the Court of —— in the sum of £——;" *specifying the several actions with the Courts in which they are brought, and the sums in which the deponent is bail;*] that the deponent's property, to the amount of the said sum of £——, [*and if bail in any other action or actions* "of all other sums for which he is now bail as aforesaid,"] consists of [*here specify the nature and value of the property, in* [*729] *respect of which the bail proposes to justify as follows;*—stock in trade, in his business of ——, carried on by him at ——, of the value of £——; of good book debts owing to him to the amount of £——; of furniture in his house, at ——, of the value of £——; of a freehold or leasehold farm, of the value of £——, situate at ——, occupied by ——; or of a dwelling-house of the value of £——, situate at ——, occupied by ——; *or of other property, particularizing each description of property, with the value thereof;*] and that the deponent hath for the last six months resided at ——, [*describing the place or places of such residence.*]

Reg. Gen. Trin. T. 1 W. 4.

Sworn, &c.

MICHAELMAS TERM. 3 WILLIAM IV. 1832

I.

Reg. Gen. Mich. T. 3 W. 4.

Writ to contain the name of all the defendants in the action.

It is ordered, that every writ of summons, *capias*, and detainer, shall contain the names of all the defendants if more than one in the action, and shall not contain the name or names of any defendant or defendants in more actions than one.

Fees.

2. It is further ordered, That the following fees shall be taken —

	£	s.	d.
For signing all writs for compelling an appearance, whether of summons, *distringas*, *capias*, or detainer, whether the same shall be the first writ, or an *alias* or *pluries* writ, and whether the same shall issue into the same county as the preceding writ, or into a different county	0	2	6
For sealing the same	0	0	7
For entering an appearance for every defendant	0	1	0
Unless an appearance shall be entered for more than one defendant by the same attorney, and, in that case for every additional defendant	0	0	4

Day of service to be indorsed on writ.

3. It is further ordered, that the person serving a writ of summons shall within three days at least, after such service, indorse on such writ the day of the week and month of such service; otherwise the plaintiff shall not be at liberty to enter an appearance for the defendant according to the statute; and every affidavit upon which such an appearance shall be entered, shall mention the day on which such indorsement was made.

Day of execution to be indorsed on *capias*.

4. It is further ordered, that the sheriff, or other officer or person to whom any writ of *capias* shall be directed, or who shall have the execution and return thereof, shall, within six days, at the latest, after the execution thereof, whether by service or arrest, indorse on such writ the true day of the execution thereof; and, in default thereof, shall be liable, in a summary way, to make such compensation for any damage which may result from his neglect as the Court or a Judge shall direct.

Rule II., H. T. 1832, applicable to new writs.

5. It is further ordered, that Rule II. of H. T., 1832, shall be applicable to all writs of summons, *distringas*, *capias*, and detainer, issued under the authority of the said act, and to the copy of every such writ.

Alias and *pluries* writs may be directed into other counties.

Form of.

6. It is further ordered, that any *alias* or *pluries* writ of summons, if the plaintiff shall think it desirable, be issued into another county and any *alias* or *pluries* writ of *capias* may be directed to the sheriff of any other county; the plaintiff, in such case upon the *alias* or *pluries* writ of summons describing the defendant as late of the place of which he was described in the first writ of summons, and upon the *alias* or *pluries* writ of *capias* referring to the preceding writ or writs as directed to the sheriff to whom they were in fact directed.

Alias or *pluries* summons.

7. It is further ordered, that the *alias* or *pluries* writ of summons into another county shall be in the following form:

William the Fourth, &c.

To C. D, of ——, in the county of ——, late of ——, in the county of [*original county.*]

WE command you, as before [*or* often] we have commanded you, &c. [*as in the writ of summons No.* 1, *in the schedule of the said act.*]

*And that the *alias* and *pluries* writ of *capias* shall be in the following form: [*730]

William the Fourth, &c.

Alias or *pluries capias*.

To the Sheriff of ——.

WE command you, as heretofore we have commanded the Sheriff of ——,

Reg. Gen. Mich. T. 3 W. 4.

that you omit not, &c. [*as in the writ of capias, No. 4, in the schedule of the said act.*]

Non omittas clause in *distringas* without fee.

8. It is further ordered, that in every writ of *distringas capias* issued under the authority of the said act, a *non omittas* clause may be introduced by the plaintiff, without the payment of any additional fee on that account.

Name of attorney in the country to be indorsed on writ as well as name of agent.

9. It is further ordered, that, when the attorney actually suing out any writ shall sue out the same as agent for an attorney in the country, the name and place of abode of such attorney in the country shall also be indorsed upon the said writ.

Writ irregular but not void for want of indorsements.

10. It is further ordered, that if the plaintiff or his attorney shall omit to insert in, or indorse on, any writ or copy thereof, any of the matters required by the said act to be by him inserted therein or indorsed thereon, such writ, or copy thereof, shall not on that account be held void, but it may be set aside as irregular, upon application to be made to the Court out of which the same shall issue, or to any judge.

Declaring *de bene esse* where defendant not in actual custody on *capias*.

Where one arrested and others served.

11. It is further ordered, that upon all writs of *capias*, where the defendant shall not be in actual custody, the plaintiff, at the expiration of eight days after the execution of the writ, inclusive of the day of such execution, shall be at liberty to declare *de bene esse* in case special bail shall not have been perfected. And if there be several defendants, and one or more of them shall have been served only, and not arrested, and the defendant or defendants so served shall not have entered a common appearance, the plaintiff shall be at liberty to enter a common appearance for him or them, and declare against him or them in chief, and *de bene esse* against the defendant or defendants who shall have been arrested, and shall not have perfected special bail.

Where time to plead, &c. expires after 10th August, the same time is to be reckoned from 24th Oct. as if the declaration, &c., had then been delivered. No further rule to plead.

12. It is further ordered, that, in case the time for pleading to any declaration, or for answering any pleadings, shall not have expired before the 10th day of *August* in any year, the party called upon to plead, reply, &c., shall have the same number of days for that purpose, after the 24th day of *October*, as if the declaration or preceding pleading had been delivered or filed on the 24th of *October*; but, in such cases, it shall not be necessary to have a second rule to plead, reply, &c.

If order to return writ in vacation be made a rule of Court, next term an attachment may issue without service of that rule.

13. It is further ordered, that in case a judge shall have made an order in the vacation, for the return of any writ issued by authority of the said act, or any writ of *ca. sa.*, *fi. fa.*, or *elegit*, on any day in the vacation, and such order as shall have been duly served, but obedience shall not have been paid thereto, and the same shall have been made a rule of Court in the term then next following, it shall not be necessary to serve such rule of Court, or to make any fresh demand of performance thereon, but an attachment shall issue forthwith for disobedience of such order, whether the thing required by such order shall or shall not have been done in the mean time.

Writs issued without authority of attorney whose name is indorsed to be stayed.

14. It is further ordered, that if any attorney shall, as required by the said act, declare that any writ of summons, or writ of *capias*, upon which his name is indorsed, was not issued by him, or with his authority or privity, all proceedings upon the same shall be stayed until further notice.

Title of declaration.

15. It is further ordered, that every declaration shall, in future, be intituled in the proper Court, and of the day of the month and year on which it is filed or delivered, and shall commence as follows:—

Declaration after Summons.

Commencement of summons.

[*Venue.*]—*A. B.*, by *E. F.* his attorney, [*or*, in his own proper person], complains of *C. D.*, who has been summoned to answer the said *A. B.*, &c.

[*731]

**Declaration after Arrest where the Party is not in Custody.*

Commencement of declaration in *capias* where defendant is not in custody.

[*Venue*]—*A. B.*, by *E. F.*, his attorney, [*or*, in his own proper person], complains of *C. D.*, who has been arrested at the suit of the said *A. B.*, &c.

Declaration where the Party is in Custody.

[*Venue.*]—*A. B.*, by *E. F.* his attorney, [*or*, in his own proper person], complains of *C. D.* being detained at the suit of *A. B.*, in the custody of the Sheriff, [*or*, the Marshal of the *Marshalsea* of the Court of *King's Bench*, or the Warden of the *Fleet*.]

Reg. Gen. Mich. T. 3 W. 4.

Commencement of declaration in *capias* where defendant is in custody.

Declaration after the Arrest of one or more Defendant or Defendants, and where one or more other Defendant or Defendants shall have been served only, and not arrested.

[*Venue.*]—*A. B.*, by *E. F.*, his attorney, [*or*, in his own proper person], complains of *C. D.*, who has been arrested at the suit of the said *A. B.*, [*or*, being detained at the suit of the said *A. B.*, *&c. as before*], and of *G. H.*, who has been served with a writ of *capias* to answer the said *A. B.*, &c.

Commencement of declaration against several defendants, some of whom have been arrested and the others served.

And that the entry of pledges to prosecute at the conclusion of the declaration shall in future be discontinued.

Pledges discontinued.

II.

It is ordered, that the writ of *capias* and *distringas*, which shall hereafter be issued out of the superior Courts of Law at *Westminster* into the counties palatine of *Lancaster* or *Durham*, shall be directed to the Chancellor of the county palatine of *Lancaster* or his deputy there, or to the Bishop of *Durham* or his Chancellor there, and shall be in the following form:—

Writ of Distringas.

William the Fourth, &c.

To the Chancellor of our county palatine of *Lancaster* or his deputy there: [*or*, To the Rev. Father in God ——, by Divine Providence Lord Bishop of *Durham*, or to his Chancellor there,] Greeting:—We command you, that, by our writ under the seal of our said county palatine, to be duly made and directed to the Sheriff of our said county palatine, you command the said Sheriff [*or if in Durham*, that, by our writ under the seal of your bishopric, to be duly made and directed to the Sheriff of the county of *Durham*, you cause the said Sheriff to be commanded] that he omit not by reason of any liberty in his bailiwick, but that he enter the same and distrain upon the goods and chattels of *C. D.* for the sum of 40*s.*, in order to compel his appearance in our Court of ——, to answer *A. B.* in a plea of trespass on the case [*or*, debt, *or as the case may be*], and how he shall execute that our writ he make known to us in our said Court, on the —— day of —— now next ensuing.

Witness ——, at *Westminster*, the —— day of ——, in the —— year of our reign.

Notice to be subscribed to the foregoing Writ.

In the Court of ———.

Between *A. B.* Plaintiff,
and
C. D. Defendant.

Mr. *C. D.*

Take notice, that I have this day distrained on your goods and chattels in the sum of 40*s.*, in consequence of your not having appeared in the said Court, to answer to the said *A. B.* according to the exigency of a writ of summons, bearing teste on the —— day of ——, and that, in default of your appearance to the present writ within eight days inclusive after the return hereof, the said *A. B.* will cause an appearance to be entered for you, and proceed thereon to judgment and execution, [*or* (*if the defendant be subject to outlawry*) will cause proceedings to be taken to outlaw you.]

**Writ of Capias.* [*732]

William the Fourth, &c.

To the Chancellor of our county palatine of *Lancaster*, or his deputy there: [*or*, To the Rev. Father in God ——, by Divine Providence Lord Bishop of *Durham*, or to his chancellor there], Greeting:—We command you, that, by our writ under the seal of our said county palatine, to be duly made and directed to the Sheriff of our said county palatine, you command the said Sheriff [*or*, *if in Durham*, that, by our writ under the seal of your

Reg. Gen. Mich. T. 3 W. 4. bishopric, to be duly made and directed to the Sheriff of the county of *Durham*, you cause the said Sheriff to be commanded] that he omit not by reason of any liberty in his bailiwick, but that he enter the same, and take *C. D.* of ———, if he shall be found in his bailiwick, and him safely keep until he shall have given him bail or make deposit with him according to law in an action on promises, [*or*, of debt, &c.] at the suit of *A. B.*, or until the said *C. D.* shall by other lawful means be discharged from his custody: and that he further command him, that, in execution thereof, he do deliver a copy thereof to the said *C. D.* And that the said writ do require the said *C. D.* to take notice that within eight days after execution thereof on him, inclusive of the day of such execution, he should cause special bail to be put in for him in our Court of ——— to the said action; and that in default of his so doing, such proceedings may be had and taken as are mentioned in the warning thereunder written, or indorsed thereon; and that he further command the said Sheriff, that, immediately after the execution thereof, he do return that writ to our said Court, together with the manner in which he shall have executed the same, and the day of the execution thereof; or that, if the same shall remain unexecuted, then that he do so return the same at the expiration of four calendar months from the date thereof, or sooner if he shall be thereto required by order of the said Court, or by any judge thereof.

Witness ——, at *Westminster*, the —— day of ——.

Memorandum to be subscribed to the Writ.

N. B. This writ is to be executed within four calendar months from the date hereof, including the day of such date, and not afterwards.

Warning to the Defendant.

1. If a defendant being in custody, shall be detained on this writ, or if a defendant, being arrested thereon, shall go to prison for want of bail, the plaintiff may declare against such defendant before the end of the term next after such detainer or arrest, and proceed thereon to judgment and execution.

2. If a defendant being arrested on this writ, shall have made a deposit of money according to the stat 7 & 8 Geo. 4, c. 71, and shall omit to enter a common appearance to the action, the plaintiff will be at liberty to enter a common appearance for the defendant, and proceed thereon to judgment and execution.

3. If a defendant, having given bail on the arrest, shall omit to put in special bail as required, the plaintiff may proceed against the Sheriff, or on the bail bond.

4. If a defendant having been served only with this writ, and not arrested thereon, shall not enter a common appearance within eight days after such service, the plaintiff may enter a common appearance for such defendant, and proceed thereon to judgment and execution.

Indorsements to be made on a Writ of Capias.

Bail for £——, by affidavit.

Or,

Bail for £——, by order of [*naming the judge making the order*], dated the —— day of ——.

[*733] *This writ was issued by *E. F.* of ——, attorney for the plaintiff [*or plaintiffs*] within named.

Or,

This writ was issued in person by the plaintiff within named [*mention the city or parish, and also the name of the hamlet, street, and also the number of the house of the plaintiff's residence, if any such there be.*]

Hilary Term, 3 W. 4.

It is ordered, that in case a rule of Court or judge's order for returning a bailable writ of *capias* shall expire in vacation, and the sheriff or other officer having the return of such writ, shall return *cepi corpus* thereon, a judge's order may thereupon issue, requiring the sheriff or other officer, within the like number of days after the service of such order, as by the practice of the Court is prescribed with respect to rules to bring in the body issued in Term, to bring the defendant into Court, by forthwith putting in and perfecting bail above to the action; and if the sheriff or other officer shall not duly obey such order, and the same shall have been made a rule of Court in the Term next following, it shall not be necessary to serve such rule of Court, or to make any fresh demand thereon, but an attachment shall issue forthwith for disobedience of such order, whether the bail shall or shall not have been put in and perfected in the mean time.

Reg. Gen. Hil. T. 3 W. 4.

Rules on sheriff to bring in the body of defendant in vacation.

Trinity Term, 3 W. 4.

Reg. Gen. Trin. T. 3 W. 4.

1. It is declared and ordered, that, in all cases in which a defendant shall have been or shall be detained in prison on any writ of *capias* or detainer under the statute 2 W. 4, c. 39, or being arrested thereon, shall go to prison for want of bail, and in all cases in which he shall have been or shall be rendered to prison before declaration on any such process, the plaintiff in such process shall declare against such defendant before the end of the next term after such arrest or detainer, or render, and notice thereof, otherwise such defendant shall be entitled to be discharged from such arrest or detainer, upon entering an appearance according to the form set forth in the aforesaid statute, 2 W. 4, c. 39, schedule No. 2; unless further time to declare shall have been given to such plaintiff by rule of Court, or order of a judge.

Declaring against prisoners.

2. It is ordered, that, from the present day in all actions against prisoners in the custody of the Marshal of the *Marshalsea*, or of the Warden of the *Fleet*, or of the Sheriff, the defendant shall plead to the declaration at the same time, in the same manner, and under the same rules, as in actions against defendants who are not in custody.

Pleas by prisoners.

3. It is ordered, that, from and after the 10th day of July next, where the plaintiff proceeds by action of debt on the recognizance of bail in any of the Courts at Westminster, the bail shall be at liberty to render their principal at any time within the space of fourteen days next after the service of the process upon them, but not at any later period; and that upon such render being duly made, and notice thereof given, the proceedings shall be stayed upon payment of the costs of the writ and service thereof only.

Render after proceedings against bail.

Hilary Term, 4 W. 4.

Reg. Gen. Hil. T. 4 W. 4.

It is ordered, that from and after the first day of Easter term next inclusive, the following rules shall be in force in the Courts of King's Bench, Common Pleas, and Exchequer of Pleas, and Courts of Error in the Exchequer Chamber.

1. No demurrer, nor any pleading subsequent to the declaration, shall in any case be filed with any officer of the Court, but the same shall always be delivered between the parties.

Demurrer to be delivered, not filed.

*2. In the margin of every demurrer, before it is signed by counsel, some matter of law intended to be argued shall be stated, and if any demurrer shall be delivered without such statement, or with a frivolous statement, it may be set aside as irregular by the Court or a judge, and leave may be given to sign judgment as for want of a plea. [*734]

Points to be stated before demurrer signed.

Provided, that the party demurring may, at the time of the argument, insist upon any further matters of law, of which notice shall have been given to the Court in the usual way.

Other points not stated may be argued.

3. No rule for joinder in demurrer shall be required, but the party demur-

No rule to join in demurrer.

Reg. Gen. Hil. T. 4 W. 4.

ring may demand a joinder in demurrer, and the opposite party shall be bound, within four days after such demand, to deliver the same, otherwise judgment.

Joinder in demurrer need not be signed.

4. To a joinder in demurrer no signature of a serjeant, or other counsel, shall be necessary, nor any fee allowed in respect thereof.

Making up issue and demurrer.

5. The issue, or demurrer book, shall, on all occasions, be made up by the suitor, his attorney, or agent, as the case may be, and not, as heretofore, by any officer of the Court.

Setting down special case and demurrer.

6. No motion, or rule for a concilium, shall be required, but demurrers, as well as all special cases, and special verdicts, shall be set down for argument, at the request of either party, with the clerk of the rules in the King's Bench and Exchequer, and a secondary in the Common Pleas, upon payment of a fee of one shilling, and notice thereof shall be given forthwith by such party to the opposite party.

Delivery of paper books.

7. Four clear days, before the day appointed for argument, the plaintiff shall deliver copies of the demurrer book, special case, or special verdict, to the Lord Chief Justice of the King's Bench, or Common Pleas, or Lord Chief Baron, as the case may be, and the senior judge of the Court in which the action is brought, and the defendant shall deliver copies to the other two judges of the Court next in seniority; and, in default thereof, by either party, the other party may, on the day following, deliver such copies as ought to have been so delivered by the party making default; and the party making default shall not be heard until he shall have paid for such copies, or deposited with the clerk of the rules in the King's Bench and Exchequer, or the secondary in the Common Pleas, as the case may be, a sufficient sum to pay for such copies.

Judgment recovered.—In a plea of judgment recovered, the number of roll must be stated in the margin.

8. Where a defendant shall plead a plea of judgment recovered in another Court, he shall, in the margin of such plea, state the date of such judgment, and if such judgment shall be in a Court of record, the number of the roll on which such proceedings are entered, if any; and in default of his so doing, the plaintiff shall be at liberty to sign judgment as for want of a plea; and in case the same be falsely stated by the defendant, the plaintiff, on producing a certificate from the proper officer, or person having the custody of the records or proceedings of the Court where such judgment is alleged to be recovered, that there is no such record or entry of a judgment as therein stated, shall be at liberty to sign judgment as for want of a plea, by leave of the Court or a judge.

Error.-Writ of error not supersedeas till service with points to be argued.

9. No writ of error shall be a supersedeas of execution, until service of the notice of the allowance thereof, containing a statement of some particular ground of error intended to be argued.

Execution if point frivolous.

Provided, that if the error stated in such notice shall appear to be frivolous, the Court, or a judge upon summons, may order execution to issue.

No rule to certify and transcribe.

10. No rule to certify or transcribe the record shall be necessary, but the plaintiff in error shall, within twenty days after the allowance of the writ of error, get the transcript prepared and examined with the clerk of the errors of the Court in which the judgment is given, and pay the transcript money to him; in default whereof, the defendant in error, his executors or administrators, shall be at liberty to sign judgment of *non pros.* The clerk of the errors shall, after payment of the transcript money, deliver the writ of error, when returnable, with the transcript annexed, to the clerk of the errors of the Court of Error.

[*735]

Diminution, assignment of errors, *sci fa. quare execut.*

*11. No rule to allege diminution, nor rule to assign errors, nor *scire facias quare executionem non*, shall be necessary in order to compel an assignment of errors, but within eight days after the writ of error, with the transcript annexed, shall have been delivered to the clerk of the errors of the Court of Error, or to the signer of the writs in the King's Bench, in cases of error to that Court, or within twenty days after the allowance of the writ of error, in cases of error, *coram nobis coram vobis*, the plaintiff in error shall assign errors;

and on failure to assign errors, the defendant in error, his executors or administrators, shall be entitled to sign judgment of *non pros.* Reg. Gen. Hil. T. 4 W. 4.

12. The assignment of errors, and subsequent pleadings thereon, shall be delivered to the attorney of the opposite party, and not filed with any officer of the Court. Delivery of proceedings in error.

13. No *scire facias ad audiendum errores* shall be necessary (unless in case of a change of parties); but the plaintiff in error may demand a joinder in error, or plea to the assignment of errors, and the defendant in error, his executors or administrators, shall be bound, within twenty days after such demand, to deliver a joinder or plea, or to demur, otherwise the judgment shall be reversed. No *sci. fac. ad audiendum errores.* Joinder in error within twenty days.

Provided, that if in any case the time allowed, as hereinbefore mentioned, for getting the transcript prepared and examined, for assigning errors, or for delivering a joinder in error, or plea, or demurrer, shall not have expired before the 10th day of August in any year, the party entitled to such time shall have the like time, for the same purpose, after the 24th day of October, without reckoning any of the days before the 10th of August. Where twenty days expire after 10th August.

Provided also, that in all cases such time may be extended by a judge's order. Further time may be allowed.

Provided also, that in all cases of writs of error to reverse fines and common recoveries, a *scire facias* to the terre-tenants shall issue, as heretofore. Not to apply to errors in fines, &c.

14. When issue in law is joined, either party may set down the case for argument with the clerk of the errors of the Court of Error, or the clerk of the rules in the King's Bench, (as the case may require), and forthwith give notice in writing thereof to the other party, and proceed to argument in like manner as on a demurrer, without any rule or motion for a concilium. Setting down case for argument.

15. Four clear days before the day appointed for argument, the plaintiff in error shall deliver copies of the judgment of the Court below, and of the assignment of errors, and of the pleadings thereon, to the judges of the King's Bench, on writs of error from the Common Pleas or Exchequer, and to the judges of the common Pleas, on writs of error from the King's Bench; and the defendant in error shall deliver copies thereof to the other judges of the Court of Exchequer Chamber before whom the case is to be heard; and in default by either party, the other party may deliver such books as ought to have been delivered by the party making default, and the party making default shall not be heard until he shall have paid for such copies, or deposited with the clerk of the errors or the clerk of the rules in the King's Bench, (as the case may be,) a sufficient sum to pay for such copies. Delivery of error books.

16. No entry on record of the proceedings in error shall be necessary before setting down the case for argument, but after judgment shall have been given in the Court of Error in the Exchequer Chamber, either party shall be at liberty to enter the proceedings in error on the judgment roll remaining in the Court below, on a certificate of a clerk of the errors of the Exchequer Chamber of the judgment given, for which a fee of three shillings and four pence, and no more, shall be charged. Proceedings in error need not be entered before argument.

17. Notice of taxing costs shall not be necessary in any case where the defendant has not appeared in person, or by his attorney or guardian, notwithstanding the general rule of Trinity Term, 1 W. 4, s. 12. Notice of taxation.

18. It shall not be necessary to repass any *nisi prius* record which shall have been once passed, and upon which the fees of passing shall have been paid; and if it shall be necessary to amend the day of the *teste* and return of the *distringas* or *habeas corpora*, or of the clause of *nisi prius*, the same may be done by the order of a judge obtained on an application ex parte. Repassing record.

[*736]

*19. Writs of trial shall be sealed only, and not signed. Writs of trial.

20. Either party, after plea pleaded, and a *reasonable* time before trial, may give notice to the other, either in town or country, in the form hereto annexed, marked A., or to the like effect, of his intention to adduce in evidence certain written or printed documents; and unless the adverse party shall consent Proof of documents.

Reg. Gen. Hil. T. 4 W. 4. by indorsement on such notice, *within forty-eight hours*, to make the admission specified, the party requiring such admission may call on the party required by summons to show cause before a judge why he should not consent to such admission, or, in case of refusal be subject to pay costs of proof; and unless the party required shall expressly consent to make such admission, the judge shall, if he think the application reasonable, make an order, that the costs of proving any document specified in the notice, which shall be proved at the trial to the satisfaction of the judge or other presiding officer, certified by his indorsement thereon, shall be paid by the party so required, whatever may be the result of the cause.

Provided, that if the judge shall think the application unreasonable, he shall indorse the summons accordingly.

Provided also, that the judge may give such time for inquiry or examination of the documents intended to be offered in evidence, and give such directions for inspection and examination, and impose such terms upon the party requiring the admission, as he shall think fit.

If the party required shall consent to the admission, the judge shall order the same to be made.

No costs of proving any written or printed document shall be allowed to any party who shall have adduced the same in evidence on any trial, unless he shall have given such notice as aforesaid, and the adverse party shall have refused or neglected to make such admission, or the judge shall have indorsed upon the summons that he does not think it reasonable to require it.

A judge may make such order as he may think fit respecting the costs of the application, and the costs of the production and inspection, and in the absence of a special order the same shall be costs in the cause.

FORM OF NOTICE REFERRED TO.

A.

In the K. B. [" C. P." *or* " Exchequer."]

A. B.
v.
C. D.

Take notice, that the plaintiff [*or* "defendant"] in this cause proposes to adduce in evidence the several documents hereunder specified and that the same may be inspected by the defendant [*or* " plaintiff"], his attorney or agent, at , on , between the hours of , and that the defendant [*or* " plaintiff"] will be required to admit that such of the said documents as are specified to be originals, were respectively written, signed, or executed, as they purport respectively to have been; that such as are specified as copies are true copies; and such documents as are stated to have been served, sent, or delivered, were so served, sent, or delivered respectively, saving all just exceptions to the admissibility of all such documents as evidence in this cause. Dated, &c.

G. H. attorney for plaintiff [*or* " defendant"].

To *E. F.* attorney or agent for
defendant [*or* " plaintiff"].

[*Here describe the documents, the manner of doing which may be as follows:*]

Reg. Gen. Hil. T. 4 W. 4.

*ORIGINALS.

Description of the Documents.	Date.
Deed of Covenant betwen *A. B.* and *C. D.* first part, and *E. F.* second part	1st January, 1828.
Indenture of Lease from *A. B.* to *C. D.*	1st February, 1828.
Indenture of Release between *A. B.*, *C. D.* first part, &c.	2d February, 1828.
Letter—Defendant to Plaintiff	1st March, 1828.
Policy of Insurance on Goods by Ship Isabella, on voyage from Oporto to London	3d December, 1827.
Memorandum of Agreement between *C. D.*, Captain of said Ship, and *E. F.*	1st January, 1828.
Bill of Exchange for £100, at three months, drawn by *A. B.* on and accepted by *C. D.*, indorsed by *E. F.* and *G. H.*	1st May, 1829.

COPIES.

Description of Documents.	Date.	Original or Duplicate, served, sent, or delivered, when, how, and by whom.
Register of Baptism of *A. B.*, in the parish of *X.*	1st Jan. 1808.	
Letter—Plaintiff to Defendant . .	1st Feb. 1828.	Sent by General Post, 2d Feb. 1828.
Notice to produce Papers . . .	1st March, 1828.	Served 2d March, 1828, on defendant's attorney, by *E. F.* of
Record of a Judgment of the Court of King's Bench, in an action, *J. S.* v. *J. N.* . . .	Trinity Term, 10th Geo. IV.	
Letters Patent of King Charles II. in the Rolls Chapel	1st Jan. 1680.	

[*738]

Reg. Gen. Hil. T. 4 W. 4.

Recital of stat. 3 & 4 Will. 4, c. 42, s. 1.

*HILARY TERM, 4 WILL. 4.

WHEREAS it is provided by the stat. 3 & 4 Will. 4, c. 42, s. 1, that the judges of the superior Courts of Common Law at *Westminster*, or any eight or more of them, of whom the Chiefs of each of the said Courts should be three, should and might, by any rule or order to be from time to time by them made, in term or vacation, at any time within five years from the time when the said act should take effect, *make such alterations in the mode of pleading* in the said Courts, and in the mode of *entering and transcribing pleadings, judgments, and other proceedings* in actions at law, and such regulations as to the *payment of costs*, and otherwise, for carrying into effect the said alterations, as to them might seem expedient; which rules, orders, and regulations were to be laid before both Houses of Parliament as therein mentioned, and were not to have effect until six weeks after the same should have been so laid before both Houses of Parliament, but after that time should be binding and obligatory on the said Courts, and all other Courts of common law, and be of the like

Reg. Gen. Hil. T. 4 W. 4. force and effect as if the provisions contained therein had been expressly enacted by parliament;

Provided that no such rule or order should have the effect of depriving any person of the power of pleading the general issue, and of giving the special matter in evidence, in any case wherein he then was or thereafter should be entitled so to do, by virtue of an act of parliament then or thereafter to be in force;—

It is therefore ordered, that, from and after the first day of *Easter* Term next inclusive, unless parliament shall in the mean time otherwise enact, the following rules and regulations, made pursuant to the said statute, shall be in force.

First, General Rules and Regulations.

All pleadings are to be intitled of the day and year when pleaded, and to be so entered of record.

1. Every pleading, as well as the declaration, shall be intitled of the day of the month and year when the same was pleaded, and shall bear no other time or date, and every declaration and other pleading shall also be entered on the record made up for trial and on the judgment-roll, under the date of the day of the month and year when the same respectively took place, and without reference to any other time or date, unless otherwise specially ordered by the Court or a judge.

No continuances to be entered.

2. No entry of continuances by way of imparlance, *curia advisari vult, vicecomes non misit breve*, or otherwise, *shall be made*, upon any record or roll whatever, or in the pleadings, except the *juratur ponitur in respectu*, which is to be retained.

Not to affect the times of proceeding.

Provided that such regulation shall not alter or affect any existing rules of practice as to the times of proceeding in the cause.

Plea, *puis darrein continuance.*

Provided also, that in all cases in which a plea *puis darrein continuance* is now by law pleadable in banc, or at nisi prius, the same defence may be pleaded, with an allegation that the matter arose after the last pleading, or the issuing of the jury process, as the case may be.

Affidavit to verify.

Provided also, that no such plea shall be allowed, unless accompanied by an affidavit that the matter thereof arose within eight days next before the pleading of such pleas, or unless the Court or a judge shall otherwise order.

Judgment to be entered of the day when signed.

3. All judgments, whether interlocutory or final, shall be entered of record of the day of the month and year, whether in term or vacation, when signed, and shall not have relation to any other day.

Nunc pro tunc.

Provided, that it shall be competent for the Court or a judge to order a judgment to be entered *nunc pro tunc*.

[*739]

Warrants of attorney to be entered.

*4. No entry shall be made on record of any warrants of attorney to sue or defend.

5. And whereas, by the mode of pleading hereinafter prescribed, the several disputed facts material to the merits of the case will, before the trial, be brought to the notice of the respective parties more distinctly than heretofore; and by the said act of the 3d & 4th Will. 4, c. 42, s. 23, the powers of amendment at the trial, in cases of variance in particulars not material to the merits of the case, are greatly enlarged:

Several counts and pleas not allowed.

Several counts shall not be allowed, unless a distinct subject-matter of complaint is intended to be established in respect of each; nor shall *several* pleas, or avowries, or cognizances be allowed, unless a distinct ground of answer or defence is intended to be established in respect of each.

Instances in declarations.

Therefore, counts founded on one and the same principal mattter of complaint, but varied in statement, description, or circumstances only, are not to be allowed.

Contract with condition.

Ex. gr. Counts founded upon the same contract, described in one as contract without a condition, and in another as a contract with a condition, are not to be allowed; for they are founded on the same subject-matter of complaint, and are only variations in the statement of one and the same contract.

Non delivery of bill in payment.

So, counts for not giving, or delivering, or accepting a bill of exchange in payment, according to the contract of sale, for goods sold and delivered, and for the price of the same goods to be paid in money, are not to be allowed.

So, counts for not accepting and paying for goods sold; and for the price of the same goods, as goods bargained and sold, are not to be allowed. Reg. Gen. Hil. T. 4 W. 4.

But counts upon a bill of exchange or promissory note, and for the consideration of the bill or note in goods, money, or otherwise, are to be considered as founded on distinct subject-matters of complaint; for the debt and the security are different contracts, and such counts are not to be allowed. Not accepting and paying for goods. Bills and notes.

Two counts upon the same policy of insurance are not to be allowed. Policies.

But, a count upon a policy of insurance, and a count for money had and received, to recover back the premium upon a contract implied by law, are to be allowed. Premium.

Two counts on the same charter-party are not to be allowed. Charter-parties.

But, a count for freight upon a charter-party, and for freight *pro ratâ itineris*, upon a contract implied by law, are to be allowed. Freight.

Counts upon a demise, and for use and occupation of the same land for the same time, are not to be allowed. Demise and use and occupation.

In actions of tort for misfeazance, several counts for the same injury, varying the description of it, are not to be allowed. Misfeazance.

In the like actions for nonfeazance, several counts founded on varied statements of the same duty are not to be allowed. Nonfeazance.

Several counts in trespass, for acts committed at the same time and place, are not to be allowed. Trespass.

Where several debts are alleged in *indebitatus assumpsit* to be due in respect of several matters, *ex. gr.*, for wages, work, and labor as a hired servant, *work and labor generally*, goods sold and delivered, goods bargained and sold, money lent, money paid, money had and received, and the like, the statement of each debt is to be considered as amounting to a several count within the meaning of the rule which forbids the use of several counts, though one promise to pay only is alleged in consideration of all the debts. *Indebitatus assumpsit.*

Provided, that a count for money due on an account stated may be joined with any other count for a money demand, though it may not be intended to establish a distinct subject-matter of complaint in respect of each of such counts. Account stated.

The rule which forbids the use of several counts is not to be considered as precluding the plaintiff from alleging *more breaches* than one of the same contract in the same count. Several breaches.

*Pleas, avowries, and cognizances, founded on one and the same principal matter, but varied in statement, description, or circumstances only, (and pleas in bar in replevin are within the rule), are not to be allowed. [*740] Instances of pleas and avowries, &c.

Ex. gr. Pleas of *solvit ad diem*, and of *solvit post diem*, are both pleas of payment, varied in the circumstance of time only, and are not to be allowed. Payment.

But pleas of payment, and of accord and satisfaction, or of release, are distinct, and are to be allowed. Accord and satisfaction —Release.

Pleas of an agreement to accept the security of *A. B.*, in discharge of the plaintiff's demand, and of an agreement to accept the security of *C. D.* for the like purpose, are also distinct, and to be allowed. Liability of third party.

But pleas of an agreement to accept the security of a third person, in discharge of the plaintiff's demand, and of the same agreement, describing it to be an agreement to forbear for a time, in consideration of the same security, are not distinct; for they are only variations in the statement of one and the same agreement, whether more or less extensive, in consideration of the same security, and not to be allowed. Agreement to forbear in consideration of liability of third party.

In trespass *quare clausum fregit*, pleas of soil and freehold of the defendant in the *locus in quo*, and of the defendant's right to an easement there—pleas of right of way, of common of pasture, of common of turbary, and of common of estovers, are distinct, and are to be allowed. *Lib. ten.*, easement, right of way, right of common, common of turbary, and estovers.

But pleas of right of common at all times of the year, and of such right at particular times, or in a qualified manner, are not to be allowed. Right of common.

Reg. Gen. Hil. T. 4 W. 4. Right of way. So pleas of a right of way over the *locus in quo*, varying the *termini* or the purposes, are not to be allowed.

Distress for rent, and damage *feasant*. Avowries for distress for rent, and for distress for damage *feasant*, are to be allowed.

Distress for rent. But avowries for distress for rent, varying the amount of rent reserved, or the times at which the rent is payable, are not to be allowed.

The cases above mentioned as instances only. The examples, in this and other places specified, are given as some instances only of the application of the rules to which they relate; but the principles contained in the rules are not to be considered as restricted by the examples specified.

Departure from these rules, how taken advantage of. 6. Where more than one count, plea, avowry, or cognizance, shall have been used in apparent violation of the preceding rule, the opposite party shall be at liberty to apply to a judge, suggesting that two or more of the counts, pleas, avowries, or cognizances are founded on the same subject matter of complaint, or ground of answer or defence, for an order that all the counts, pleas, avowries, or cognizances, introduced in violation of the rule, be struck out at the cost of the party pleading; whereupon the judge shall order accordingly, unless he shall be satisfied, upon cause shown, that *some distinct subject matter* of complaint is *bona fide* intended to be established in respect of each of such counts, or some distinct ground of answer or defence in respect of each of such pleas, avowries, or cognizances, in which case he shall indorse upon the summons, or state in his order, as the case may be, that he is so satisfied; and shall also specify the counts, pleas, avowries, or cognizances mentioned in such application, which shall be allowed.

Costs of counts and pleas. 7. Upon the trial, where there is more than one count, plea, avowry, or cognizance upon the record, and the party pleading fails to establish a distinct subject matter of complaint in respect of each count, or some distinct ground of answer or defence in respect of each plea, avowry, or cognizance, a verdict and judgment shall pass against him upon each count, plea, avowry, or cognizance, which he shall have so failed to establish, and he shall be liable to the other party for all the costs occasioned by such count, plea, avowry, or cognizance, including those of the evidence as well as those of the pleadings; and further, in all cases in which an application to a judge has been made under the preceding rule, and any count, plea, avowry, or cognizance, allowed as aforesaid, upon the ground that some distinct subject matter of [*741] complaint was *bona fide* intended to be established at the *trial in respect of each count, or some distinct ground of answer or defence in respect of each plea, avowry, or cognizance so allowed, if the Court or judge, before whom the trial is had, shall be of opinion that no such distinct subject matter of complaint was *bona fide* intended to be established in respect of each count so allowed, or no such distinct ground of answer or defence in respect of each plea, avowry, or cognizance so allowed, and shall so certify before final judgment, such party so pleading shall not recover any costs upon the issue or issues upon which *he succeeds*, arising out of any count, plea, avowry, or cognizance with respect to which the judge shall so certify.

Special venue. 8. The name of a county shall in all cases be stated in the margin of a declaration, and shall be taken to be the venue intended by the plaintiff, and no venue shall be stated in the *body* of the declaration, or in any subsequent pleading.

Local description. Provided, that, in cases where local description is now required, such local description shall be given.

Commencement and conclusion of pleas, &c. 9. In a plea or subsequent pleading, intended to be pleaded in bar of the whole action generally, it shall not be necessary to use any allegation of *actionem non*, or to the like effect, or any prayer of judgment; nor shall it be necessary in any replication, or subsequent pleading intended to be pleaded in maintenance of the whole action, to use any allegation of "*precludi non*," or to the like effect, or any prayer of judgment; and all pleas, replications, and subsequent pleadings, pleaded without such formal parts as aforesaid, shall be taken, unless otherwise expressed, as pleaded respectively in bar of the whole action, or in the maintenance of the whole action; provided, that nothing herein contained shall extend to cases where an estoppel is pleaded. Reg. Gen. Hil. T. 4 W. 4.

10. No formal defence shall be required in a plea, and it shall commence as follows :—" The said defendant, by ——, his attorney, [*or*, in person, *&c.*], says that —— Commencement of plea

11. It shall not be necessary to state in a second or other plea or avowry, that it is pleaded by leave of the Court, or according to the form of the statute, or to that effect. Second plea

12. No protestation shall hereafter be made in any pleading; but either party shall be entitled to the same advantage in that or other actions, as if a protestation had been made. Protestation

13. All special traverses, or traverses with an inducement of affirmative matter, shall conclude to the country. Traverses.

Provided, that this regulation shall not preclude the opposite party from pleading over to the inducement when the traverse is immaterial. Opposite party may plead over.

14. The form of a demurrer shall be as follows :—" The said defendant, by ——, his attorney, [*or*, in person, *&c.*, *or* plaintiff], says that the declaration [*or* plea, *&c.*] is not sufficient in law," *showing the special causes of demurrer if any.* Form of demurrer.

The form of a joinder in demurrer shall be as follows :—" The said plaintiff [*or* defendant] says that the declaration [*or* plea, *&c.*] is sufficient in law." Joinder in demurrer.

15. *The entry* of proceedings on the record for trial, or on the judgment-roll, (according to the nature of the case), shall be taken to be, and shall be in fact, the first entry of the proceedings in the cause, or of any part thereof, upon record; and no fees shall be payable in respect of any prior entry made or supposed to be made on any roll or record whatever. Entry of proceedings on record.

16. No fees shall be charged in respect of more than *one issue* by any of the officers of the Court, or of any judge at the assizes, or any other officer, in any action of *assumpsit*, or in any action of *debt* on simple contract, or in any action on *the case*. Charge for issue.

*17. when money is paid into Court, such payment shall be pleaded in all cases, and, as near as may be, in the following form, *mutatis mutandis* :— [*742] Payment of money into Court.

" *C. D.* ats. *A. B.* } The —— day of ——.

The defendant, by ——, his attorney, [*or*, in person, *&c.*] says, that the plaintiff ought not further to maintain his action, because the defendant now brings into Court the sum of £——, ready to be paid to the plaintiff; and the defendant further says, that the plaintiff has not sustained damages [*or*, *in actions of debt*, that he is not indebted to the plaintiff] to a greater amount than the said sum, &c., in respect of the cause of action in the declaration mentioned, and this he is ready to verify; wherefore he prays judgment if the plaintiff ought further to maintain his action."

18 No rule or judge's order to pay money into Court shall be necessary, except under the 3 & 4 Will. 4, c. 42, s. 21; but the money shall be paid to the proper officer of each Court, who shall give a receipt for the amount in the margin of the plea; and the said sum shall be paid out to the plaintiff on demand. No order to pay money into Court except in certain cases.

19. The plaintiff, after the delivery of a plea of payment of money into Court, shall be at liberty to reply to the same, by accepting the sum so paid into Court in full satisfaction and discharge of the cause of action in respect of which it has been paid in; and he shall be at liberty in that case to tax his costs of suit, and, in case of non-payment thereof within forty-eight hours, to sign judgment for his costs of suit so taxed; or the plaintiff may reply, " that he has sustained damages [*or*, that the defendant is indebted to him, *as the case may be*,] to a greater amount than the said sum ;" and, in the event of an issue thereon being found for the defendant, the defendant shall be entitled to judgment and his costs of suit. Proceeding by plaintiff after payment of money into Court.

20. In all cases under the 3 & 4 Will. 4, c. 42, s. 10, in which, after a Commencement of dec-

Reg. Gen. Hil. T. 4 W. 4. plea in abatement of the nonjoinder of another person, the plaintiff shall, without having proceeded to trial on an issue thereon, commence another action

Declaration after plea of nonjoinder. against the defendant or defendants in the action, in which such plea in abatement shall have been pleaded, and the person or persons named in such plea in abatement as joint contractors, the commencement of the declaration shall be in the following form :—

" *Venue.*]—*A. B.*, by *E. F.*, his attorney, [*or*, in his own proper person, *&c.*], complains of *C. D.* and *G. H.*, who have been summoned to answer the said *A. B.*, and which said *C. D.* has heretofore pleaded in abatement the nonjoinder of the said *G. H.*, &c." (*The same form to be used* mutatis mutandis *in cases of arrest or detainer.*

Character of assignees, &c. to be taken as admitted, unless specially denied. 21. In all actions by and against assignees of a bankrupt or insolvent, or executors or administrators, or persons authorized by act of parliament to sue or be sued as nominal parties, the character in which the plaintiff or defendant is stated on the record to sue or be sued shall not in any case be considered as in issue, unless specially denied.

PLEADINGS IN PARTICULAR ACTIONS.

I.—*Assumpsit.*

Effect of non assumpsit. 1. In all actions of assumpsit, except on bills of exchange and promissory notes, the plea of *non assumpsit* shall operate only as a denial in fact of the express contract or promise alleged, or of the matters of fact from which the contract or promise alleged may be implied by law.

Instances: Warranty. *Ex. gr.* In an action on a warranty, the plea will operate as a denial of the fact of the warranty having been given upon the alleged consideration,

Policy. but not of the breach; and, in an action on a policy of insurance, of the

[*743] *subscription to the alleged policy by the defendant, but not of the interest, of the commencement of the risk, of the loss, or of the alleged compliance with warranties.

Carriers and bailees. In actions against carriers and other bailees, for not delivering or not keeping goods safe, or not returning them on request, and in actions against agents

Agents. for not accounting, the plea will operate as a denial of any express contract to the effect alleged in the declaration, and of such bailment or employment as would raise a promise in law to the effect alleged, but not of the breach.

Goods sold. In an action of *indebitatus assumpsit*, for goods sold and delivered, the plea of *non assumpsit* will operate as a denial of the sale and delivery in point of

Money had. fact; in the like action for money had and received, it will operate as a denial both of the receipt of the money and the existence of those facts which make such receipt by the defendant a receipt to the use of the plaintiff.

Bills and notes no general issue. 2. In all actions upon bills of exchange and promissory notes, the plea of *non assumpsit* shall be inadmissible. In such actions, therefore, a plea in denial must traverse some matter of fact; *ex. gr.* the drawing, or making, or indorsing, or accepting, or presenting, or notice of dishonor of the bill or note.

In every action of assumpsit matters in confession and avoidance to be pleaded specially. 3. In every species of *assumpsit*, all matters in confession and avoidance, including not only those by way of discharge, but those which show the transaction to be either void or voidable in point of law, on the ground of fraud or otherwise, shall be specially pleaded; *ex. gr*, infancy, coverture, release, payment, performance, illegality of consideration either by statute or common law, drawing, indorsing, accepting, &c., bills or notes by way of accommodation, set-off, mutual credit, unseaworthiness, misrepresentation, concealment, deviation, and various other defences, must be pleaded.

Statement of interest of assured. 4. In actions on policies of assurance the interest of the assured may be averred thus :—" That *A.*, *B.*, *C.*, and *D.*, [*or* some or one of them,] were or was interested," *&c.* And it may also be averred, "that the insurance was made for the use and benefit, and on the account, of the person or persons so interested."

II.—*In Covenant and Debt.*

Reg. Gen. Hil. T. 4 W. 4.

1. In debt on specialty or covenant, the plea of *non est factum* shall operate as a denial of the execution of the deed in point of fact only, and all other defences shall be specially pleaded, including matters which make the deed absolutely void, as well as those which make it voidable. *Non est factum.*

2. The plea of "*nil debet*" shall not be allowed in any action. *Nil debet.*

3. In actions of debt on simple contract, other than on bills of exchange and promissory notes, the defendant may plead that "he never was indebted in manner and form as in the declaration alleged," and such plea shall have the same operation as the plea of *non assumpsit* in *indebitatus assumpsit;* and all matters in confession and avoidance shall be pleaded specially as above directed in actions of *assumpsit.* General issue in debt. Matters in confession and avoidance to be pleaded specially.

4. In other actions of debt, in which the plea of *nil debet* has been hitherto allowed, including those on bills of exchange and promissory notes, the defendant shall deny specifically some particular matter of fact alleged in the declaration, or plead specially in confession and avoidance. Pleas in other cases.

III.—*Detinue.*

The plea of *non detinet* shall operate as a denial of the detention of the goods by the defendant, but not of the plaintiff's property therein, and no other defence than such denial shall be admissible under that plea. *Non detinet.*

*IV.—*In Case.* [*744]

1. In actions on the case, the plea of not guilty shall operate as a denial only of the breach of duty or wrongful act alleged to have been committed by the defendant, and not of the facts stated in the inducement, and no other defence than such denial shall be admissible under that plea: all other pleas in denial shall take issue on some particular matter of fact alleged in the declaration. Effect of not guilty. Other pleas.

Ex. gr. In an action on the case for a nuisance to the occupation of a house by carrying on an offensive trade, the plea of not guilty will operate as a denial only that the defendant carried on the alleged trade in such a way as to be a nuisance to the occupation of the house, and will not operate as a denial of the plaintiff's occupation of the house. *Instances:* Nuisance.

In an action on the case, for obstructing a right of way, such plea will operate as a denial of the obstruction only, and not of the plaintiff's right of way; and in an action for converting the plaintiff's goods, the conversion only, and not the plaintiff's title to the goods. Right of way. Trover.

In an action of slander of the plaintiff in his office, profession, or trade, the plea of not guilty will operate to the same extent precisely as at present in denial of speaking the words, of speaking them maliciously, and in the sense imputed, and with reference to the plaintiff's office, profession, or trade, but it will not operate as a denial of the fact of the plaintiff holding the office or being of the profession or trade alleged. Slander.

In actions for an escape, it will operate as a denial of the neglect or default of the sheriff or his officers, but not of the debt, judgment, or preliminary proceedings. Escape.

In this form of action against a carrier the plea of not guilty will operate as a denial of the loss or damage, but not of the receipt of the goods by the defendant as a carrier for hire, or of the purpose for which they were received. Carriers.

2. All matters in confession and avoidance shall be pleaded specially, as in actions of *assumpsit.* Matters in confession and avoidance to be pleaded specially.

V.—*In Trespass.*

1. In actions of trespass *quare clausum fregit*, the close or place in which, &c. must be designated in the declaration by name or abuttals, or other description, in failure whereof the defendant may demur specially. Abuttals in declaration.

2. In actions of trespass *quare clausum fregit*, the plea of not guilty shall operate as a denial that the defendant committed the trespass alleged in the Effect of not guilty in trespass *qu. cl. fr.*

Reg. Gen. Hil. T. 4 W. 4. place mentioned, but not as a denial of the plaintiff's possession, or right of possession of that place, which, if intended to be denied, must be traversed specially.

In trespass de bon. asp. 3. In actions of trespass *de bonis asportatis*, the plea of not guilty shall operate as a denial of the defendant having committed the trespass alleged by taking or damaging the goods mentioned, but not of the plaintiff's property therein.

Right of way. 4. Where, in an action of trespass *quare clausum fregit*, the defendant pleads a right of way with carriages and cattle and on foot in the same plea, and issue is taken thereon, the plea shall be taken distributively; and if a right of way with cattle, or on foot only, shall be found by the jury, a verdict shall pass for the defendant in respect of such of the trespasses proved as shall be justified by the right of way so found; and for the plaintiff in respect of such of the trespasses as shall not be so justified.

Common of pasture. 5. And where, in an action of trespass *quare clausum fregit*, the defendant pleads a right of common of pasture for divers kinds of cattle, *ex. gr.*, horses, sheep, oxen, and cows, and issue is taken thereon, if a right of common for some particular kind of commonable cattle only be found by the jury, a verdict [*745] shall pass for the defendant in respect of such of the *trespasses proved as shall be justified by the right of common so found; and for the plaintiff in respect of the trespasses which shall not be so justified.

Similar pleas. 6. And in all actions in which such right of way or common as aforesaid, or other similar right, is so pleaded that the allegations as to the extent of the right are capable of being construed distributively, they shall be taken distributively.

Commencement of the rules. Provided nevertheless, that nothing contained in the 5th, 6th, or 7th of the above-mentioned General Rules and Regulations, or in any of the above-mentioned Rules or Regulations relating to pleading in particular actions, shall apply to any case in which the declaration shall bear date before the first day of *Easter* Term next.

Issues, Judgment, and other Proceedings in Actions commenced by process under 2 Will. 4, c. 39, shall be in the several Forms in the Schedule hereunto annexed, or to the like effect, mutatis mutandis: *Provided, that, in case of Non-compliance, the Court or a Judge may give leave to amend.*

No. I.

Form of an issue in the King's Bench, Common Pleas, or Exchequer.

In the King's Bench; *or,*
In the Common Pleas; *or,*
In the Exchequer.

The [*date of declaration*] day of ——, in the —— year of our Lord, 18—.

[*Venue*].—*A. B.*, by *E. F.*, his attorney, [*or*, in his own proper person, *or*, by *E. F.*, who is admitted by the Court here to prosecute for the said *A. B.*, who is an infant within the age of twenty-one years, as the next friend of the said *A. B.*, *as the case may be*], complains of *C. D.*, who has been summoned to answer the said *A. B.* [*or*, arrested *or* detained in custody] by virtue [*or*, served with a copy, *as the case may be*] of a writ issued on [*date of first writ*] the —— day of —— in the year of our Lord 18—, out of the Court of our Lord the King, before the King himself at Westminster, [*or*, out of the Court of our Lord the King, before his Justices at Westminster, *or*, out of the Court of our Lord the King, before the Barons of his Exchequer at Westminster, *as the case may be*]; For that

[*Copy the declaration from these words to the end, and the plea and subsequent pleadings to the joinder of issue.*]

Thereupon the Sheriff is commanded that he cause to come here, on the —— day of ——, twelve, &c., by whom, &c., and who neither, &c., to recognize, &c., because as well, &c. Reg. Gen. Hil. T. 4 W. 4.

No. 2

Form of Nisi Prius Record in the King's Bench, Common Pleas, or Exchequer.

[*The placita are to be omitted.—Copy the issue to the end of the award of the venire, and proceed as follows:*]

Afterwards, on the [*teste of distringas or habeas corpora*] day of ——, in the year ——, the jury between the parties aforesaid is respited here until the [*return day of distringas or habeas corpora*] day of ——, unless —— shall first come on the [*first day of sittings or commission day of assizes*] day of ——, at ——, according to the form of the statute in such case made and provided for default of the jurors, because none of them did appear; therefore let the sheriff have the bodies of the said jurors accordingly.

[*The postea is to be in the usual form.*]

*No. 3. [*746]

Form of Judgment for the Plaintiff in Assumpsit.

[*Copy the issue to the end of the award of the venire, and proceed as follows:*]

Afterwards, the jury between the parties is respited until the [*return of distringas or habeas corpora*] day of ——, unless —— shall first come on the [*day of Sittings or Nisi Prius*] day of ——, at ——, according to the form of the statute in that case made and provided for default of the jurors, because none of them did appear.

Afterwards, on the [*day of signing final judgment*] day of —— come the parties aforesaid, by their respective attornies aforesaid, [*or as the case may be*]; and ——, before whom the said issue was tried, hath sent hither his record, had before him, in these words:

[*Copy postea.*]

Therefore, it is considered that the said *A. B.* do recover, against the said *C. D.*, his said damages, costs, and charges, by the jurors aforesaid, in form aforesaid, assessed; and also —— for his costs and charges, by the Court here adjudged of increase to the said *A. B.* with his assent, which said damages, costs, and charges, in the whole amount to ——, and the said *C. D.* in mercy, &c.

No. 4.

Form of the Issue when it is directed to be tried by the Sheriff.

[*After the joinder of issue proceed as follows:*]

And forasmuch as the sum sought to be recovered in this suit, and indorsed on the said writ of summons, does not exceed £20, hereupon on the [*teste of writ of trial*] day of ——, in the year ——, pursuant to the statute in that case made and provided, the sheriff [*or*, the judge of ——, being a Court of Record for the recovery of debt in the said county, *as the case may be*,] is commanded that he summon twelve, &c., who neither, &c., who shall be sworn truly to try the issue above joined between the parties aforesaid, and that he proceed to try such issue accordingly; and when the same shall have been tried, that he make known to the Court here what shall have been done by virtue of the writ of our Lord the King to him in that behalf directed, with the finding of the jury thereon indorsed, on the —— day of ——, &c.

No. 5.

Form of Writ of Trial.

William the Fourth, by, &c., to the Sheriff of our County of ——, [*or*, to

Reg. Gen. Hil. T. 4 W. 4. the judge of ——, being a Court of Record for the Recovery of Debt, in our County of ——, *as the case may be.*]

Whereas *A. B.*, in our Court before us at Westminster, [*or*, in our Court before our justices at Westminster, *or*, in our Court before the barons of our Exchequer at Westminster, *as the case may be*], on the [*date of first writ of summons*] day of —— last, impleaded *C. D.* in an action on promises [*or, as the case may be*]; for that whereas one, &c. [*here recite the declaration as in a writ of inquiry*], and thereupon he brought suit. And whereas the defendant, on the —— day of —— last, by ——, his attorney, [*or as the case may be*], came into our said Court and said [*here recite the pleas and pleadings to the joinder of issue*], and the plaintiff did the like. And whereas the sum sought to be recovered in the said action, and indorsed on the writ of summons therein, does not exceed £20; and it is fitting that the issue above joined should be tried before you the said sheriff of ——, [*or*, judge, *as the case may be*]: we therefore, pursuant to the statute in such case made and provided, command you that you do summon twelve free and lawful men of your county, duly qualified according to law, who are in nowise akin to the plaintiff or to the defendant, who shall be sworn
[*747] *truly to try the said issue joined between the parties aforesaid, and that you proceed to try such issue accordingly; and when the same shall have been tried in manner aforesaid, we command you that you make known to us at Westminster [*or* to our justices at Westminster, *or*, to the barons of our said Exchequer, *as the case may be*,] what shall have been done by virtue of this writ, with the finding of the jury hereon indorsed, on the —— day of —— next.

Witness, ——, at Westminster, the —— day of ——, in the —— year of our reign.

No. 6.

Form of Indorsement thereon of the Verdict.

Afterwards, on the [*day of trial*] day of ——, in the year ——, before me, sheriff of the county of —— [*or*, judge of the Court of ——], came as well the within-named plaintiff as the within-named defendant, by their respective attornies within-named [*or, as the case may be*], and the jurors of the jury by me duly summoned, as within commanded, also came, and, being duly sworn to try the said issue within mentioned on their oath, said, that ——.

No. 7.

Form of Indorsement thereon, in case a Nonsuit takes place.

[*After the words* "duly sworn to try the issue within mentioned" *proceed as follows*:]

And were ready to give their verdict in that behalf; but the said *A. B.* being solemnly called came not, nor did he further prosecute his said suit against the said *C. D.*

No. 8.

Form of Judgment for the Plaintiff after Trial by the Sheriff.

[*Copy the issue, and then proceed as follows*:]

Afterwards, on the [*day of signing judgment*] day of ——, in the year ——, came the parties aforesaid, by their respective attornies aforesaid, [*or, as the case may be*,] and the said sheriff [*or*, judge, *as the case may be*], before whom the said issue came on to be tried, hath sent hither the said last-mentioned writ, with an indorsement thereon, which said indorsement is in these words; to wit:—

[*Copy the Indorsement.*]

Therefore it is considered, &c., [*in the same form as before.*]

INDEX.

END OF VOLUME ONE.